AMERICAN INDIAN TRIBAL LAW

ASPEN ELECTIVE SERIES

AMERICAN INDIAN TRIBAL LAW

Matthew L.M. Fletcher
Associate Professor of Law
Director of the Indigenous Law and Policy Center
Michigan State University College of Law

Wolters Kluwer
Law & Business

AUSTIN   BOSTON   CHICAGO   NEW YORK   THE NETHERLANDS

Aspen Publishers
Attn: Permissions Department
76 Ninth Avenue, 7th Floor
New York, NY 10011-5201

To contact Customer Care, e-mail customer.care@aspenpublishers.com, call 1-800-234-1660, fax 1-800-901-9075, or mail correspondence to:

Aspen Publishers
Attn: Order Department
PO Box 990
Frederick, MD 21705

Printed in the United States of America.

1 2 3 4 5 6 7 8 9 0

ISBN 978-0-7355-9975-8

Library of Congress Cataloging-in-Publication Data

Fletcher, Matthew L. M.
    American indian tribal law / Mathew L.M. Fletcher.
        p. cm. — (Aspen elective series)
    ISBN 978-0-7355-9975-8 (perfectbound : alk. paper)
    1. Indians of North America — Legal status, laws, etc. 2. Indians of North America — Government relations. 3. Indian courts — United States. 4. Tribal government — United States. 5. Self-determination, National — United States. I. Title.

KF8205.F54 2011
342.7308'72 — dc22

2010053739

This book contains paper from well-managed forests to SFI standards.

About Wolters Kluwer Law & Business

Wolters Kluwer Law & Business is a leading provider of research information and workflow solutions in key specialty areas. The strengths of the individual brands of Aspen Publishers, CCH, Kluwer Law International and Loislaw are aligned within Wolters Kluwer Law & Business to provide comprehensive, in-depth solutions and expert-authored content for the legal, professional and education markets.

CCH was founded in 1913 and has served more than four generations of business professionals and their clients. The CCH products in the Wolters Kluwer Law & Business group are highly regarded electronic and print resources for legal, securities, antitrust and trade regulation, government contracting, banking, pension, payroll, employment and labor, and healthcare reimbursement and compliance professionals.

Aspen Publishers is a leading information provider for attorneys, business professionals and law students. Written by preeminent authorities, Aspen products offer analytical and practical information in a range of specialty practice areas from securities law and intellectual property to mergers and acquisitions and pension/benefits. Aspen's trusted legal education resources provide professors and students with high-quality, up-to-date and effective resources for successful instruction and study in all areas of the law.

Kluwer Law International supplies the global business community with comprehensive English-language international legal information. Legal practitioners, corporate counsel and business executives around the world rely on the Kluwer Law International journals, loose-leafs, books and electronic products for authoritative information in many areas of international legal practice.

Loislaw is a premier provider of digitized legal content to small law firm practitioners of various specializations. Loislaw provides attorneys with the ability to quickly and efficiently find the necessary legal information they need, when and where they need it, by facilitating access to primary law as well as state-specific law, records, forms and treatises.

Wolters Kluwer Law & Business, a unit of Wolters Kluwer, is headquartered in New York and Riverwoods, Illinois. Wolters Kluwer is a leading multinational publisher and information services company.

SUMMARY OF CONTENTS

TABLE OF CONTENTS

PREFACE

There are 565 federally recognized Indian tribes in the United States as of this writing. Each Indian nation has the authority, often expressed in an organic document such as a tribal constitution or a treaty with the United States, to legislate for the general welfare of the tribe, its people, and its land. Tribal ordinances and resolutions often are codified into tribal codes and published in book form and on the Internet, *e.g.*, GRAND TRAVERSE BAND CODE; HOOPA VALLEY TRIBAL CODE; NAVAJO NATION TRIBAL CODE. Other tribes not only publish their laws but make readily available any proposed legislation; the best example is the *Odawa Register*, a circular published by the Little Traverse Bay Bands of Odawa Indians that parallels the *Federal Register*.

There are more than 300 American Indian tribal courts currently in operation, and there will likely be another 100 to 200 in the next few decades. American Indian tribal courts decide thousands of cases daily, with misdemeanor criminal cases, child welfare, and tribal administrative law cases constituting the large portion of tribal court dockets. Some tribal courts, such as those of the Navajo Nation, handle more than 100,000 cases each year, while other tribal courts handle only a very few cases. Many tribal courts span the full panoply of subject areas, from criminal to civil to probate to divorce to environmental law; others handle only a select few subject areas, such as tribal conservation courts, which adjudicate disputes involving tribal treaty fishing and hunting rights. The variety of tribal court disputes is endless.

"Tribal law" is to be distinguished from "federal Indian law." Loosely speaking, federal Indian law is the law covering the relationships between the federal, state, and tribal governments. The key feature of federal Indian law is the exclusion of federal and state laws from the internal governance of Indian tribes. In short, every Indian nation is free to adopt its own laws and be ruled by them, to paraphrase the United States Supreme Court. *Williams v. Lee*, 358 U.S. 217 (1959).

This casebook delves exclusively into the laws of American Indian tribes and the cases decided by tribal courts. Most professors and students will find that a course in Federal Indian Law or a similar topic area will be helpful in engaging the materials in this book. *E.g.*, DAVID H. GETCHES, CHARLES F. WILKINSON, ROBERT A. WILLIAMS & MATTHEW L. M. FLETCHER, CASES AND MATERIALS ON FEDERAL INDIAN LAW (6th ed. 2011). "Federal Indian law" and "tribal law" are linked to some extent, but there are significant differences.

Indian country is ready for a comprehensive set of materials on what some academics and practitioners have called the "real Indian law"—the law of Indian nations and tribal courts. It is a new field, and scholarship on the subject has taken off only in the past few years.

These materials are intended to assist students in navigating tribal courts and other indigenous dispute resolution forums, and how to otherwise practice law in Indian country. Students need to learn that nearly all tribal jurisdictions can and do apply their own laws, not the laws of the United States or state law.

This book will rely heavily on the standard cases and notes format of most law school casebooks, and will offer in-depth legal commentary and background on the history of tribal law and justice systems.

The inspiration for this law school text comes in part from two works commissioned for the Turtle Mountain Band of Chippewa Indians' Project Peacemaker. The first, authored by Justin Richland and Sarah Deer, is *Introduction to Tribal Legal Studies*, published in 2004 and in a second edition in 2009 by AltaMira Press. The second, authored by Carrie E. Garrow and Sarah Deer, is *Tribal Criminal Law and Procedure*, also published by AltaMira Press, in 2004. These materials were designed for tribal community college and undergraduate students, and likely are the first comprehensive American Indian tribal law textbooks. An additional source of inspiration is Frank Pommersheim's *Broken Ground and Flowing Waters: An Introductory Text with Materials on Rosebud Sioux Tribal Government*, published by the Sinte Gleska College in 1977.

One additional note: part of the reason American Indian tribal law materials for law students have been slow in coming is that the law of Indian nations is relatively difficult to find. This is changing, rapidly, as tribes develop their own Internet presence and publish their laws online. Moreover, hundreds of tribal laws and ordinances, as well as tribal constitutions, are posted on the website of the Native American Rights Fund's National Indian Law Library, the University of Oklahoma Law School website, and others. The same is true for tribal court decisions. Many tribal courts post their decisions online, or in self-commissioned reporters, such as the Navajo Reporter and the Muscogee (Creek) Nation Reporter. Other tribes create intertribal court systems as a means of pooling their limited resources, such as the Northwest Indian Tribal Court System (which publishes the NICS Tribal Court Appellate Opinions, or "NICS App."), the Southwest Intertribal Court System (which publishes the SWITCA Reporter), and the Northern Plains Intertribal Court System. The first tribal court reporter was the Tribal Law Reporter, which came and went in the 1970s. Since 1980, the American Indian Law Reporter has published selected tribal court decisions. Another significant reporter is the Oklahoma Tribal Court Reports. In recent years, VersusLaw, Westlaw (American Tribal Reports), and Lexis-Nexis have posted selected tribal court decisions. Finally, many tribal court decisions are available at the Tribal Court Clearinghouse website.

Structure of the Materials

Chapter 1 is a survey of the history of American Indian tribal governments. Indian nations predate the United States and possessed their own forms of government, often radically different from the tribal governments that now exist. Interestingly, a traditional tribal government functioned as a kind of court, deciding disputes among people. The second half of the chapter is a survey of how tribal governments have adapted to the interventions and negligence of the American government.

Chapter 2 is an introduction to tribal justice systems, that is, tribal courts. The first tribal courts were not indigenous institutions; they were imposed upon tribal communities in the nineteenthth century as a means of breaking down tribal cultures. But tribes have now taken over these courts and developed their own justice systems. Chapter 2 also includes an important theoretical discussion about the use and utility of customary and traditional law in modern litigation, as well as a discussion of the role of tribal judges.

Chapter 3 is a survey of modern tribal constitutional law. Nearly all tribes discussed in this casebook are constitutional republics, with some remarkable exceptions. Chapter 3, like the first two chapters, relies heavily on secondary sources, but moves directly into tribal court doctrine by sampling the rich history of tribal constitutional adjudication, where some of the greatest crises of modern tribal governments have occurred.

Chapter 4 concerns tribal citizenship, one of the most important subject areas in tribal law: Who is an Indian? Beginning with this chapter, the large majority of the key materials included in the casebook are tribal court cases.

Chapter 5 concerns tribal elections. Virtually every major tribe has its own version of *Bush v Gore*, and this chapter covers those disputes, as well as cases about the qualifications of voters and candidates.

Chapter 6 covers civil rights claims in tribal courts. While the United States Constitution does not apply to Indian nations, Congress has attempted to impose most of the federal constitutional rights on tribal governments in the Indian Civil Rights Act. The United States Supreme Court has held that tribal courts, and not federal courts, are the sole place to enforce those rights. This chapter surveys several key due process and equal protection cases, but also focuses on important flashpoints in tribal law, including the Cherokee Freemen, tribal banishment, and same-sex marriage.

Chapter 7 surveys tribal criminal law and procedure. This is a microcosm of the field, given that a whole casebook could be dedicated to this subject area. This chapter offers some of the more famous tribal law cases, including the Navajo Nation's prosecution of Russell Means. The chapter also offers a brief history of the tribal police, tribal criminal jurisdiction (which is limited to Indians only), and how tribal legislatures and courts effectively enforce laws against non-Indians.

Chapter 8 deals with domestic relations, including marriage and divorce law, probate law, and the law of children. For many tribal courts, the overwhelming majority of their dockets fall into these areas, but there are relatively few published tribal court decisions.

Chapter 9 involves the very rich tapestry of tribal property. It begins with a long excerpt from an important scholarly article on various traditional tribal property structures, before delving into cases about tribal lands, tribal public trust property, and jurisdiction.

Chapter 10 covers contract law. Contract law in tribal courts generally does not deviate in large measure from the law applied in state and federal courts, but this chapter helps students focus on the practical application of contract law to the unique factual disputes that arise in Indian country. Of note, this chapter involves cases dealing with suits against tribal governments and tribal businesses, the probable clients of students who move on to practice in Indian country.

Chapter 11 — on torts — is also more practical than doctrinal, although a rich history of traditional tribal tort law has survived the assimilation of tribal governments into the American polity. Moreover, many United States Supreme Court cases involving the jurisdiction of Indian tribes begin as tribal court tort actions.

Chapter 12 is on civil procedure but focuses more on the operation and authority of tribal courts than on rote doctrine. This chapter encompasses a wide variety of key practical areas, such as tribal court contempt power, judicial recusal, professional responsibility, and jurisdiction.

Chapter 13 may cover the least obvious tribal law–related subject area — tribal regulatory and administrative law — but may well be the most important chapter. As tribal nations have entered the complex world of shared governance between federal, state, and tribal authorities, tribal government bureaucracies have grown exponentially. This chapter offers a brief survey of tribal administrative law, organized by subject area such as employment, housing, land use, and tribal trust funds, but it also goes into great detail in discussing the wide variety of tribal bureaucratic structures that have arisen just in recent decades. Concomitant with this topic is the underlying authority of tribes to regulate lands and peoples within Indian country.

Chapter 14 covers tribal economic development, a subject area (like tribal criminal law and procedure) that could be a book of its own. This chapter is one of the most theoretical chapters, though it includes several cases. Key cases involve tribal gaming, taxation, and the intervention of federal law into tribal economic development operations.

Miigwetch!

I wish to acknowledge many of the leaders in the field, those who are tribal law academics and tribal court practitioners, and jurists who have assisted me over the years in learning about tribal law and in the development of these materials.

The two people who have taught me the most, by far, about American Indian law are Wenona T. Singel and John Petoskey. Wenona is an appellate justice for the Little Traverse Bay Bands of Odawa Indians and chief appellate justice for the Grand Traverse Band of Ottawa and Chippewa Indians, and she is my colleague on the Michigan State University College of Law and at the Indigenous Law and Policy Center, as well as my lovely spouse. John, the longtime general counsel of the Grand Traverse Band, is one of the great pragmatic Indian law thinkers of his time and a great mentor.

I also wish to thank Zeke Fletcher and Judge Michael Petoskey, two others who have influenced me from the beginnings of my legal career. Judge Petoskey, along with his cousin John, has been most responsible for the development of the law of the Grand Traverse Band. Judge Petoskey has served as a jurist for every tribe in the Lower Peninsula of Michigan, and has served as the initial chief judge of the Grand Traverse Band, the Little Traverse Bay Bands, the Pokagon Band of Potawatomi Indians, the Nottawaseppi Huron Band of Potawatomi Indians, and the Match-E-Bash-She-Wish Band of Pottawatomi Indians (Gun Lake Band). Zeke, my brother, is a brilliant young Indian lawyer, a cutting-edge transactional attorney and litigator who is always willing to talk through all the interesting details of tribal law.

I also say *miigwetch* to the Indian nations that have asked me to serve as an appellate judge. Those tribes include the Hoopa Valley Tribe, the Little River Band of Ottawa Indians, the Nottawaseppi Huron Band of Potawatomi Indians, the Poarch Band of Creek Indians, the Pokagon Band, and Turtle Mountain Band of Chippewa Indians. My colleagues on those courts who have fundamentally influenced and inspired me include Huma Ahsan, Bob Anderson, Karrie Azure, Lisa Brodoff, Trent Crable, Clint Daughtrey, Jerilyn Decoteau, Michelle Demmert, Ron Douglas, Keith Harper, Eric Nielson, Dave Peterson, Brenda Toineeta Pipestem, Brenda Jones Quick, Holly Thompson, Jill Tompkins, Suzanne Ojibwe Townsend, Monique Vondall-Rieke, and John Waubunsee. I especially wish to thank former Seneca Nation of Indians Court of Appeals Judge Irma Cooper, for whom I served as an advisor for several years, and who taught me an enormous amount about Haudenosaunee people and the realities of tribal jurisprudence and tribal court practice.

Other tribal jurists and tribal law practitioners and thinkers who have helped me to develop my ideas about these materials over the years—and who have highlighted important tribal court decisions for me—include Andrew Adams, Ray Austin, Bill Brooks, Bill Brott, Kirsten Carlson, Kristen Carpenter, Bob Clinton, Jo Anne Coleman, Steve Cornell, Brad Dakota, Sarah Deer, Sam Deloria, Angelique EagleWoman, Anita Fineday, Kate Fort, Phil Frickey, Carrie Garrow, JoAnne Gasco, David Getches, David Giampetroni, Carole Goldberg, Francine Hatch, Bob Hershey, Mary Jo Hunter, Myriam Jaïdi, B.J. Jones, Joe Kalt, Riyaz Kanji, Beth Kronk, Del Laverdure, Stacy Leeds, Matt Lesky, Brian Lewis, Kevin Maillard, Allie Maldonado, Matthew Martin, Mike McBride, Kyme McGaw, Robert Medina, Bob Miller, Bryan Newland, Mike Oeser, Rob Porter, Frank Pommersheim, Venus McGhee Prince, Brian Quint, Bill Rastetter, Justin Richland, Bill Rice, Angela Riley, Mary Roberts, Laura Sagolla, Pat Sekaquaptewa, Alex Skibine, Kaighn Smith, Paul Spruhan, Kathryn Tierney, Ann Tweedy, Fred Urbina, Brian Upton, Korey Wahwassuck, Quinton Walker, Kevin Washburn, Jenn Weddle, Charles Wilkinson, Rob Williams, and Christine Zuni Cruz. Special thanks to Ruth Chippewa, Liz Cook, Debra Coon, Tami Hostler, Deb Miller, Sue Nelson, Keesha O'Barr, Steve Rambeaux, Mike Rossotto, Mary Shomin, Terri Walrod, and Karrie Wichtman—all extraordinary legal professionals with whom I have had the pleasure of working. Rhonda Schwartz at the University of North Dakota

School of Law library also deserves special mention for helping me locate tribal law materials years ago. And the law librarians at Michigan State University College of Law — especially Barbara Bean, Robin Doutre, Jane Edwards, Hildur Hanna, Janet Hedin, Lara Leaf, and Kathy Prince — have tirelessly and patiently found for me obscure and sometimes insanely hard-to-get tribal law materials since 2006. I also thank several former students who waded into American Indian tribal law on my behalf, especially Linus Banghart-Linn, Melissa Burkland, Alicia Ivory, Peter Vicaire, and Nova Wilson. Finally, I thank June Mamagona Fletcher and Eva Petoskey, two non-lawyers who have taught me as much about the law as anyone.

Finally, there is no way to know all of American Indian tribal law, and any important omissions and errors in this text are my own.

Matthew L.M. Fletcher

January 2011

ACKNOWLEDGMENTS

I wish to express my appreciation to the following authors, periodicals, and publishers for their permission to reproduce materials from their publications.

Bobroff, Kenneth H. Retelling Allotment: Indian Property Rights and the Myth of Common Ownership. 54 Vanderbilt Law Review 1559 (2001). Reprinted by permission of the Vanderbilt Law Review.

Bushyhead, Julie. The Coquille Indian Tribe, Same-Sex Marriage, and Spousal Benefits: A Practical Guide. 26 Arizona Journal of International and Comparative Law 509 (2009). Reprinted by permission.

Carpenter, Kristen A. Considering Individual Religious Freedoms under Tribal Constitutional Law. 14 Kansas Journal of Law and Public Policy 561 (2005). Reprinted by permission of the Kansas Journal of Law and Public Policy.

Deloria, Jr., Vine, and Clifford M. Lytle. American Indians, American Justice. University of Texas Press, 1983. Reprinted by permission of the University of Texas Press.

EagleWoman, Angelique A. (Wambdi A. Wastewin). Tribal Nation Economies: Rebuilding Commercial Prosperity in Spite of U.S. Trade Restraints — Recommendations for Economic Revitalization in Indian Country. 44 Tulsa Law Review 383 (2008). Reprinted by permission of the Tulsa Law Review.

Gover, Kirsty. Genealogy as Continuity: Explaining the Growing Tribal Preference for Descent Rules in Membership Governance in the United States. 33 American Indian Law Review 243 (2008-2009). Reprinted by permission of the American Indian Law Review.

Harvard Project on American Indian Economic Development. Mississippi Band of Choctaw Indians, Choctaw Tribal Court System. Harvard Project on American Indian Economic Development Honoring Nations 2005 Honoree. Reprinted by permission of the Harvard Project on American Indian Economic Development.

Harvard Project on American Indian Economic Development. Northwest Intertribal Court System. Harvard Project on American Indian Economic Development Honoring Nations 2003 Honoree. Reprinted by permission of the Harvard Project on American Indian Economic Development.

Harvard Project on American Indian Economic Development. Organized Village of Kake, Kake Circle Peacemaking. Harvard Project on American Indian Economic Development Honoring Nations 2003 Honoree. Reprinted by permission of the Harvard Project on American Indian Economic Development.

"The History of the Tribal Police" from *Tribal Policing* by Eileen Luna-Firebaugh. © 2007 The Arizona Board of Regents. Reprinted by permission of the University of Arizona Press.

Kunesh, Patrice. Banishment as Cultural Justice in Contemporary Tribal Legal Systems. 37 New Mexico Law Review 85 (2007). Reprinted by permission of the author.

Leeds, Stacy L. Cross-Jurisdictional Recognition and Enforcement of Judgments: A Tribal Court Perspective. 76 North Dakota Law Review 311 (2000). Reprinted by permission of the North Dakota Law Review.

Lemont, Eric. Overcoming the Politics of Reform: The Story of the Cherokee Nation of Oklahoma Constitutional Convention. 28 American Indian Law Review 1 (2003-2004). Reprinted by permission of the American Indian Law Review.

Ludwick, Brendan. The Scope of Federal Government Authority over Tribal Membership Disputes and the Problem of Disenrollment. 51 Federal Lawyer, October 2004. Reprinted by permission of the author.

Martin, J. Matthew. The Nature and Extent of the Exercise of Criminal Jurisdiction by the Cherokee Supreme Court: 1823-1835. 32 North Carolina Central Law Review 27 (2009). Reprinted by permission of the author.

Mouser, Denette A. A Nation in Crisis: The Government of the Cherokee Nation Struggles to Survive. 23 American Indian Law Review 359 (1998-1999). Reprinted by permission of the American Indian Law Review.

Nash, Douglas R., and Cecelia E. Burke. The Changing Landscape of Indian Estate Planning and Probate: The American Indian Probate Reform Act. 5 Seattle Journal of Social Justice 121 (2006). Reprinted by permission of the Seattle Journal of Social Justice.

Pommersheim, Frank. Tribal Court Jurisprudence: A Snapshot from the Field. 21 Vermont Law Review 8 (1996). Reprinted by permission of the Vermont Law Review.

Pommersheim, Frank. Coyote Paradox: Some Indian Law Reflections from the Edge of the Prairie. 31 Arizona State Law Journal 439 (1999). Reprinted by permission of the author.

Pommersheim, Frank. Looking Forward and Looking Back: The Promise and Potential of a Sioux Nation Judicial Support Center and Sioux Nation Supreme Court. 34 Arizona State Law Journal 269 (2000). Reprinted by permission of the author.

Porter, Robert. Decolonizing Indigenous Governance: Observations on Restoring Greater Faith and Legitimacy in the Government of the Seneca Nation. 8 Kansas Journal of Law and Public Policy 97 (1997). Reprinted by permission of the Kansas Journal of Law and Public Policy.

Porter, Robert B. Strengthening Tribal Sovereignty through Government Reform: What Are the Issues? 7 Kansas Journal of Law and Public Policy 72 (1997). Reprinted by permission of the Kansas Journal of Law and Public Policy.

Savagian, John C. The Tribal Reorganization of the Stockbridge-Munsee: Essential Conditions in the Re-creation of a Native American Community. 77:1 Wisconsin Magazine of History 39 (1993). Reprinted by permission of the Wisconsin Historical Society.

Sekaquaptewa, Pat. Key Concepts in the Finding, Definition, and Consideration of Custom Law in Tribal Lawmaking. 33 American Indian Law Review 319 (2007-2008). Reprinted by permission of the American Indian Law Review.

Singel, Wenona T. Cultural Sovereignty and Transplanted Law: Tensions in Indigenous Self-Rule. 15 Kansas Journal of Law and Public Policy 357 (Winter 2006). Reprinted by permission of the Kansas Journal of Law and Public Policy.

Singel, Wenona T. The Institutional Economics of Tribal Labor Relations. 2008 Michigan State Law Review 487 (2008). Reprinted by permission of the Michigan State Law Review.

Smith, Jr., Kaighn. Ethical "Obligations" and Affirmative Tribal Sovereignty. 2006. Reprinted by permission of the author.

Spruhan, Paul. A Legal History of Blood Quantum in Federal Indian Law to 1935. 51 South Dakota Law Review 1 (2006). Reprinted by permission of the South Dakota Law Review.

Tribal Self-Government and the Indian Reorganization Act of 1934. 70 Michigan Law Review 955 (1972). Reprinted by permission of the Michigan Law Review.

"Two Approaches to the Development of Native Nations: One Works, the Other Doesn't" from *Rebuilding Native Nations* by Miriam Jorgensen. © 2008 The Arizona Board of Regents. Reprinted by permission of the University of Arizona Press.

CHAPTER 1

TRIBAL GOVERNMENT

American Indian tribal government is a bit of a misnomer in significant ways. Indian nations, now commonly referred to as Indian tribes, are much better described as nations, or what Chief Justice Marshall called "distinct, independent political communities." *Worcester v. Georgia*, 31 U.S. 515, 559 (1832). Marshall recognized Indian nations as timeless entities—"undisputed possessors of the soil, from time immemorial." *Id.* American Indian nations predate the United States, having been in existence since what historians call pre-history. American Indian nations as political entities do not necessarily subscribe to the same political philosophy the American people as a whole follow. Indian nations are not bound to the United States Constitution, many federal laws and regulations, and most state and local laws. Indian nations are left to "to make their own laws and be ruled by them." *Williams v. Lee*, 358 U.S. 217, 220 (1959). It is the purpose of this chapter to survey the characteristics of these political entities.

We begin this chapter with the origins of modern American Indian tribal government. We will survey American Indian nationhood as it existed prior to European and American interference, move on to the transition period in which Indian people fought for their own and their nations' survival, and finish with the modern period, where American Indian nations have slowly begun to thrive.

A. A BRIEF HISTORY OF CUSTOMARY AND TRADITIONAL AMERICAN INDIAN GOVERNANCE

1. AMERICAN INDIAN "TRIBALISM"

Well into the period of European and American domination, American Indian government was absolutely nothing like the nations that formed in the Western Hemisphere starting in 1492. It is not an overgeneralization to state that most Indian nations did not view government as a process of coercion of the masses by an enlightened few, as is suggested to be the case for early European government and law in works such as Hobbes's *Leviathan*. Indian nations appear to have governed by consent, often unanimous consent.

1

Many, if not the vast majority of, American Indian nations did not form a "government" as the term is commonly understood by Euro-American political thinkers:

> Given the absence of formally structured institutions within the Indian tribes they encountered, it appeared to the earliest settlers that the tribes existed without any forms of government. The Indians were generally viewed as living almost in a state of anarchy and some early political writers, seeking to conceive a "state of nature" upon which they could build a philosophical framework for their natural law–social contract theories of government, frequently referred to Indians as "children of nature" and applauded their apparent ability to live without the confining and complex rules that had been devised within the European systems of government. Tribal governments of enormous complexity did exist but they differed so radically from the forms used by Europeans that few non-Indian observers could understand them.

VINE DELORIA, JR. & CLIFFORD M. LYTLE, AMERICAN INDIANS, AMERICAN JUSTICE 81 (1983). American Indian nations have long been labeled "tribes," and this label is the standard in that the United States Constitution expressly acknowledges the presence and the sovereignty of "Indian tribes." U.S. CONST. art. I, §8, cl. 3. However, this is an inaccurate characterization for many reasons:

> Tribe is most appropriately a cultural concept. Except for some eastern woodland confederacies, few Indians had tribal organizations that governed their activities. Some, like the Comanches, Apaches, and Navajos, were nomadic families with little in the way of larger organization. Similarly, the Pueblos of New Mexico lived in settled villages rarely, if ever, in contact with each other. Even among the more organized nomadic groups of the Northern Plains, such as the Cheyennes, Sioux, and Blackfeet, the tribes assembled only occasionally, while daily affairs were left to smaller bands. Participation in tribal religious ceremonies or annual buffalo hunts reinforced a sense of larger community, but did not alter the fact that an individual's life focused mainly on the family and clan.

GRAHAM D. TAYLOR, THE NEW DEAL AND AMERICAN INDIAN TRIBALISM: THE ADMINISTRATION OF THE INDIAN REORGANIZATION ACT, 1934-45, at 2 (1980). That said, we must recognize that American Indian "tribalism" is alive and well, and uniquely linked to "sovereignty." Modern American Indian nations view as sacrosanct the legal and political notion, borrowed in large part from Anglo-American political theory, of "sovereignty." Former Principal Chief of the Cherokee Nation of Oklahoma Wilma Mankiller has referred to American Indian sovereignty as a "sacred trust," borrowing the term from her mentors. Wilma Mankiller, *"Tribal Sovereignty is a Sacred Trust": An Open Letter to the Conference*, 23 AM. INDIAN L. REV. 479, 479 (1998-1999). American Indian notions of "sovereignty," however, tend to be completely different from European and American notions.

The key difference is the way American Indian nations are structured. The idea of a formalized, hierarchical government was anathema to many American Indian communities, which typically abhorred government based on coercion rather than consent:

> The primacy of [American Indian] individual conscience dictates a very pure form of democracy characterized by its lack of central authority, and in which

any collective action requires the consent of everyone affected — or at least the consensus of all their families. . . .

Leaders are inherently powerless to deprive any family of its means of subsistence. As long as each family stays within its ancestral lands and retains its economic autonomy, the right to dissent is a practical reality. The evil of modern states is their power to decide who eats. . . .

Representative, majoritarian democracy was an improvement on European feudal monarchies, but from an indigenous perspective it seems authoritarian. For them, the emergence of coercive power in government signifies the failure of authority. Indeed . . . imposing a "republic" on tribal peoples forces them into a second-best form of democracy based on trade-offs they themselves chose not to make. The powerlessness of Native American governments was considered and deliberate, reflecting a sophisticated awareness that an external authority which creates its own legal authority is a challenge to culture itself. . . .

Russel Lawrence Barsh, *The Nature and Spirit of North American Political Systems*, 10 AM. INDIAN Q. 181, 186-87 (1986) (quotations and citations omitted). "[F]ew tribes attempted to form a large encompassing form of government. Indeed, tribes in the plains, like New England townspeople of the seventeenth century, would have abhorred the idea of governing more than a few hundred people." DELORIA & LYTLE, AMERICAN INDIANS, AMERICAN JUSTICE, *supra*, at 97.

Some Indian community governments operated only in terms of what might be called an external and an internal government. Internal government refers to the daily activities of the people, regulated only by the legal structures created locally, while external government deals with the larger political questions that may arise in connection with other communities or nations. The Diné (Navajo people), for example, may have taken up political issues "only when external affairs dictated the need for a political position." AUBREY W. WILLIAMS, JR., NAVAJO POLITICAL PROCESS 5 (Smithsonian Institution Press 1970). Diné government, like so many other Indian governments, was based not on a monopoly of violence but on consent, unanimity, and respect:

> The people of an area assembled to choose a local headman and, while the choice was nearly always unanimous, a close vote would prompt the people to request speeches from the various candidates. In addition, men and women were allowed to speak in favor of a candidate. The speechmaking and voting frequently took several days; a unanimous vote for one candidate was the objective, as great value was placed on community solidarity and harmony. . . .
>
> The local political leaders, the *natani*, operated within a social control system that respected the individual, and uniform collective behavior was achieved not by authoritarian directive imposed from above, but rather by creating a favorable public opinion within the local group. Speeches, debate, and discussion, sometimes all but endless, were consequently the normal means used to create unanimity. . . . The reputation of a local headman depended upon his good judgment and his rhetorical ability to persuade members of his group to lead peaceful, useful, and harmonious lives.

Id. at 6-7.

Similarly, the Lakota people of the northern plains followed a government more akin to a pure democratic model of government decision making:

> In this type of government, there is majority rule by chosen leaders but there is also the opportunity for any member of the tribe to be heard on any particular issue. It has always been considered ill mannered and not in accordance with the Lakota ideal of good citizenship to be unwilling to listen to the opinion of a fellow tribal member regardless of the issue being discussed or the opinion held. . . .
>
> This form of tribal government—democratic as it was—was not always easy for non-Indians to understand. Given the problems of language and the fact that it was so difficult for non-Indians to identify the different *Wicasa Itancan* [chiefs or true leaders] and who they had authority over, there were many misunderstandings about who spoke for whom and how binding their words or actions could or would be on others. Also, the fact that there might be different leaders at different times for different purposes further complicated relations with non-Indians.

FRANK POMMERSHEIM, BROKEN GROUND AND FLOWING WATERS: AN INTRODUCTORY TEXT WITH MATERIALS ON ROSEBUD SIOUX TRIBAL GOVERNMENT 11-12 (1977).

The Cherokee Nation, prior to its establishment of the first American Indian constitutional government since the Haudenosaunee Confederacy, had a national government structure in place, but that structure rarely operated with "a strong sense of centralized political nationalism." DUANE CHAMPAGNE, AMERICAN INDIAN SOCIETIES: STRATEGIES AND CONDITIONS OF POLITICAL AND CULTURAL SURVIVAL 39 (1989).

The paradigmatic differences between European and later American political theory and most American Indian nations' political theories contributed to the sort of confusion Professor Pommersheim mentioned in relation to the Lakota communities. In the eighteenth century, prior to the establishment of the United States, colonial leaders sought to reorganize the Delaware Indians' governance structure, with almost amusing results:

> Between 1718 and 1748 Sassoonan, a leader of a major band, was regarded by colonial officials as "King of the Delaware." Although the officials transacted business through Sassoonan and supported him by giving him authority to distribute material resources, he received only nominal recognition from the Delaware.

CHAMPAGNE, AMERICAN INDIAN SOCIETIES, *supra*, at 17. The same was true with the Carolina colonists and the Cherokees: "Between 1718 and 1752 Carolina officials proclaimed various Cherokee leaders as 'emperor' and declined to recognize the authority of any other leaders who would not work through their designated intermediary." *Id.* at 41. Accounts of European colonists identifying a "king" or "emperor" and calling the female children of these leaders "princesses" are pervasive—and very frequently inaccurate.

American Indian nations developed legal structures, though many of them could be construed as a form of libertarian socialism, to borrow an idea from Bertrand Russell. BERTRAND RUSSELL, PROPOSED ROADS TO FREEDOM 111-38 (1919). These American Indian governments, numbering in the hundreds over the entire continent, incorporated many similar elements, but were characterized by incredible variety and complexity.

In contrast, other communities adopted a rigid political structure based on war and peace, as in the case of the Creek Confederacy. The main political unit of the Creek Confederacy, like so many other Indian communities, was the village. The Creeks would dedicate whole villages to a particular task:

> It is estimated that the Creek Confederacy had between fifty and eighty separate towns in the century before white contact. . . . They divided the towns into red and white towns, red for war and white for peace. The white towns had all the councils, performed the adoption ceremonies, enacted the laws and regulations of the nation, and regulated the internal affairs of the confederation, including intertown relationships. No blood was supposed to be shed in the white towns and it was regarded as a serious offense to do so.
>
> The red towns declared and conducted wars on behalf of the confederacy. They planned the military expeditions and conducted foreign relations on behalf of the nation. To prevent intraconfederacy disputes from fragmenting the tenuous alliance, ball games of some degree of ferocity were initiated matching towns against each other. Traditionally, red towns competed against white towns.

DELORIA & LYTLE, AMERICAN INDIANS, AMERICAN JUSTICE, *supra*, at 85.

During the transition from American Indian treaty-making to the time of tribal reorganization in 1934, Indian communities engaged in a wide variety of experimentation in regards to governance. Some communities, feeling the threat and the effects of American encroachment on their lands and resources, "tightened their traditional forms of government considerably. . . ." DELORIA & LYTLE, AMERICAN INDIANS, AMERICAN JUSTICE, *supra*, at 90.

2. QUASI-JUDICIAL CHARACTER OF TRADITIONAL AMERICAN INDIAN GOVERNANCE

CASE 4. CRIES YIA EYA BANISHED FOR THE MURDER OF CHIEF EAGLE

Karl N. Llewellyn and E. Adamson Hoebel, The Cheyenne Way:
Conflict and Case Law in Primitive Jurisprudence 12-13 (1941)

Cries Yia Eya had been gone from the camp for three years because he had killed Chief Eagle in a whiskey brawl. The chiefs had ordered him away for his murder, so we did not see anything of him for that time. Then one day he came back, leading a horse packed with bundles of old-time tobacco. He stopped outside the camp and sent a messenger in with the horse and tobacco who was to say to the chiefs for him, "I am begging to come home."

The chiefs all got together for a meeting, and the soldier societies were told to convene, for there was an important matter to be considered. The tobacco was divided up and chiefs' messengers were sent out to invite the soldier chiefs to come to the lodge of the tribal council, for the big chiefs wanted to talk to them. "Here is the tobacco that that man sent in," they told the soldier chiefs. "Now we want you soldiers to decide if you think we should accept his request. If you decide that we should let him return, then it is up to you to convince his family that it is all right." (The relatives of Chief Eagle had told everybody that they would kill Cries Yia Eya on sight if they ever found him. "If we set eyes on him, he'll never make another track," they had vowed.) The soldier chiefs took the tobacco and went out to gather their troops. Each society met in its own separate lodge to talk amongst themselves, but the society servants kept passing back and forth between their different lodges to report on the trend of the discussion in the different companies.

At last one man said, "I think it is all right. I believe the stink has blown from him. Let him return!" This view was passed around, and this is the view that won out among the soldiers. Then the father of Chief Eagle was sent for and asked whether he would accept the decision. "Soldiers," he replied, "I shall listen to you. Let him return! But if that man comes back, I want never to hear his voice raised against another person. If he does, we come together. As far as that stuff of his is concerned, I want nothing that belonged to him. Take this share you have set aside for me and give it to someone else."

Cries Yia Eya had always been a mean man, disliked by everyone, but he had been a fierce fighter against the enemies. After he came back to the camp, however, he was always good to the people.

CASE 96. REFUSAL OF DIVORCE BY COURT ORDER

Watson Smith and John M. Roberts, Zuni Law: A Field of Values 98 (1954)

(ca. 1949) A husband wanted to marry another woman. So the wife brought suit before the Council, told them that she could not support her children and did not want a divorce. The husband said at the hearing that he wanted the children and would support them.

The Council decided, however, that the husband should return to his wife and keep the home for the children. There was no fine or penalty imposed.

The husband accepted this decision and returned to his wife.

CASE 31. SLANDER

Watson Smith and John M. Roberts, Zuni Law: A Field of Values 56 (1954)

(Date unknown) The owner of a horse accused another of killing it and demanded payment. The accused denied the charge, and the owner asked the Council for a trial.

After the complainant had stated his case in court, the defendant demanded that if he had any evidence from witnesses or footprints, he should produce it. The parties argued nearly all night, and the Council could not determine which one was telling the truth. Finally, around dawn the plaintiff demanded payment of a similar horse. The judge asked the parties four times if they wanted the Council to decide the matter, each answered affirmatively four times. The judge then decided in favor of the defendant, because the plaintiff had not sufficient evidence to warrant a suit. He added that since the plaintiff had embarrassed the defendant by accusing him falsely, he must pay $30 in damages. Because the suit had caused unnecessary trouble to the councilmen, a fine of $25 was also assessed, payable to the councilmen personally.

The plaintiff attempted to argue further, but the judge "shut him up" and he paid.

A year later the plaintiff brought suit again, and presented the same story without additional evidence. Since the case had already been decided and no new evidence was adduced, the judge found for the defendant again. The plaintiff was fined $80, which was paid the councilmen for their trouble. But no additional damages were ordered because the defendant asked none.

CASE 92. Hωnimiidω v. Dohωωtwe

Jane Richardson, Law and Status among the Kiowa Indians 129 (1966)

(Date unknown) Hωnimiidω and Dohωωtwe, brothers of very high rank, had accumulated a large herd of horses through lucrative raiding. They had always presented their spoils to their mother. Thus the mother owned the whole herd of horses. When she died Hωnimiidω came and took the whole herd of horses without consulting his brother. Dohωωtwe did not object. They didn't have "close relations" after that. But they didn't have an open quarrel "because they were brothers. It would have been a disgrace if such a thing got out. High status especially keeps differences quiet."

CASE 21. Mωkin v. Toyop

Jane Richardson, Law and Status among the Kiowa Indians 54-55 (1966)

(1888)

H — Mωkin, a Mexican captive and the Taime-keeper's assistant; he had an extraordinarily responsible position for a captive: having learned the ritual, he was for years in charge of the sundance for three owners who did not know it as well as he; also had owl power.

W — wife of Mωkin.

C — Toyop, a captive's son, apparently fairly well off kindred.

HBs — Mωkin's foster brothers, very good family.

. . . After the Oak Tree sundance the tribe moved up to Eagle Heart Spring and camped there. The weather was fine. During the warm evenings C made himself conspicuous by mounting his horse and prancing around the camp very enthusiastically. He was happy because he had W as sweetheart. He was planning to abscond with her. While the people were camped here, C decided to go up to the mountains and fast for four days. C returned in two days but in the meantime H had taken his wife and daughter to informant's father's camp to build a sweathouse for his own medicine. While H was occupied with his sweatlodge, W would leave her tipi every night and go to C. A short time later when they were in Anadarko, C tried to elope with W but failed somehow. Later when H went away to fulfill some religious duty, C, W and W's little daughter ran off. C's mother cried when she heard the news because she was afraid of H's power. H sent for his three foster brothers and they all went to C's place to take horses from C or his brothers. Each of the HBs took a horse, including C's best one. H went along but took no horses. Then the HBs and H went into the Cheyenne country to look for C and W, but they couldn't find a trace of them. H went up into the mountains to fast and to use his Taime sorcery.

Later the couple returned with H's daughter. The little girl had become blind. It was said that H's sorcery was being paid for. The couple took sick and had to be cured by Quanah Parker, a Comanche Chief. H's daughter died. Then H dropped the whole affair. No one gave him a peace pipe because HBs had gotten horses and the matter was considered settled. Informant was especially struck by H's despair and suffering. He "had never seen anything like it. It made an old man of H."

Jacob Williams and Tuscarora Nation v. Six Nations Iroquois Council

John A. Noon, Law and Government of the Grand River Iroquois 163 (1949)

(May 11, 1886)

Facts of the Case. The plaintiffs' petition Council to ratify the decision of the Wolf clan and the Tuscarora nation to grant retirement to Chief Jacob Williams.

Chief Williams, due to advanced age and being hard of hearing, has sought and been granted the right to retire by the women of the Wolf clan. The women have already nominated Joseph Green to succeed him. The chiefs of the Tuscarora nation, having ratified the action taken by the women of the Wolf clan, bring the matter to Council for final decision.

Point of Law Involved. The question of law raised by this case is the power of Council over the retirement of chiefs.

Decision. "With reference to Jacob Williams who wishes to resign his chieftainship . . . the Council declines to accept his proposal of resignation but hope that he may continue to act with his brother chiefs as long as he lives."

Catharine Hill v. Alex R. Jamieson

John A. Noon, Law and Government of the Grand River Iroquois 152 (1949)

(May 6, 1884)

Facts of the Case. The plaintiff seeks to recover possession of the north half of Lot 6, in 5th Concession of the township of Tuscarora. Some years ago the plaintiff and her husband, the late John Hill, planning to leave the reservation and reside in the state of Kansas, sold the property in dispute to two Indians from St. Regis, Messrs. Mitchel Muskatoe (Wi-sh-sa-kon-on-ta) and Angus Garo (Evo-nias-ka-e-un-to-toe). These Indians later conveyed their rights to the property to Alex R. Jamieson, a member of the Six Nations for the sum of $400. The plaintiff, having returned to the reservation to live, brings suit to compel the return of the property, claiming that the transaction between herself and husband and Messrs. Muskatoe and Garo, and subsequent transaction between the latter parties and Jamieson, was illegal and hence null and void.

The plaintiff raises the question of the validity of a sale of land on the reservation to non–Six Nations Indians and the resale of the property by the same Indians to a Six Nations Indian. It would appear that the two transactions are inextricably related and hence both must either be legal or illegal. Neither sale was submitted to the Council for confirmation. If such a course had been followed, the present situation would not have arisen because the Council would have refused to confirm the sale. Since both parties are here equally reprehensible, the point cannot be used against either.

Point of Law Involved. Is the sale of property located on the reservation legal when both parties are not Six Nations Indians?

Decision. "The Council . . . decided that the sale between John Hill and his wife to Mitchel Muskatoe and Angus Garo and also the sale between Messrs. Muskatoe and Garo and Alex R. Jamieson shall be respected and on no account allow reconsideration."

NOTES

1. One of the key features of traditional American Indian government was their focus: resolve disputes as they arose, rather than to legislate and enforce. "[T]he primary thrust of traditional government was more judicial than legislative in nature." DELORIA & LYTLE, AMERICAN INDIANS, AMERICAN JUSTICE, *supra*, at 89.

    For example, the Zuni dispute resolution system consisted of leaders of the community, including both secular and religious, who would convene as a "court":

    > When the Council sits as a court it acts in the capacity of both judge and jury. Since there are no verbalized limits to its judicial authority, its powers in this field have been built up by accretion and precedent to the point where it may consider and determine almost any controversy of daily life among the people.

    WATSON SMITH & JOHN M. ROBERTS, ZUNI LAW: A FIELD OF VALUES 36 (1954). Smith and Watson further reported:

    > [M]eetings of the Great Council were formerly held for the purpose of providing a public hearing of cases of extraordinary interest. . . . [S]uch meetings could be convened by the Tribal Council on its own authority or at the request of an individual. They were announced by the crier four days in advance and were held in the plaza. As many as 400 to 500 people might attend.

    SMITH & ROBERTS, ZUNI LAW, *supra*, at 114. But these public hearings ceased sometime in the 1930s. This excerpt demonstrates how a government focused on the reactionary business of resolving disputes as they arise can slowly, over time, become more of a policymaking body, preventing future disputes by establishing the ground rules before arguments arise.

2. The Zuni people of New Mexico constructed a complicated web of secular and religious government structures over centuries. Their particular government structure was not democratic at all. As a nineteenth-century anthropologist observed, perhaps making too broad a generalization,

    > We find, then, that the democracy, or republic, of popular tradition, in its reference to the sedentary Indians of New Mexico and Arizona, is, like most other popular traditions regarding these comparatively unknown peoples, erroneous; that in reality their political fabric is set and woven by an elaborate priesthood, the only semblance of democracy reposing in the power of the

> council—itself composed of all adults of good standing in the nation—to reject a political head chief as thus chosen, while the power of choosing a substitute remains in the hands of the martial priests, and that of confirming him in the four priests of the temple.

F. H. Cushing, *The Zuñi Social, Mythic, and Religious Systems*, 21:2 POPULAR SCI. MONTHLY 186, 187-88 (1882), *quoted in* SMITH & ROBERTS, ZUNI LAW, *supra*, at 31.

3. Non-Indian scholars took to examining the "cases" decided by American Indian councils as if they were case law analogous to Anglo-American common law. Most famously, Karl N. Llewellyn and E. Adamson Hoebel published *The Cheyenne Way: Conflict and Case Law in Primitive Jurisprudence* in 1941, a deeply influential work of legal anthropology involving the reduction of Cheyenne dispute resolution outcomes to writing. Other legal anthropologists followed this methodology of reporting "case law."

Professor Llewellyn, a prominent and influential commercial law professor, supposedly applied his experiences studying the Cheyenne Indians as the Reporter of Article 2 (Sales) of the Uniform Commercial Code. David Ray Papke, *How the Cheyenne Indians Wrote Article 2 of the Uniform Commercial Code*, 47 BUFF. L. REV. 1457 (1999). Papke argues that the Cheyenne Indians' ways of law persuaded Llewellyn to draft Article 2 to remove many of the formalistic aspects of contract, such as sealed instruments, "realiz[ing] that commercial parties formed contracts quickly in various ways. These parties did not want to worry about traditional contracts doctrine, assume they even knew it in the first place." *Id.* at 1472.

Another commentator, drawing heavily on Papke's work, added:

> By incorporating into the Code concepts like usage of trade, Llewellyn also set in motion a particular form of legal evolution. In many contexts, rapid changes in the commercial environment have quickly rendered a body of law inadequate or obsolete. In copyright law, for example, judges and lawyers are now struggling to figure out how to treat computerized databases, which were barely envisioned in 1976 when the current law was drafted. By making commercial law derivative of commercial culture rather than vice-versa, Llewellyn sought to immunize the UCC against such problems. His theory was that as the marketplace evolved, the law would, too, automatically and without the need for formal intervention. This self-amending feature of the UCC is also strongly evocative of Cheyenne law-ways, with their seemingly infinite capacity to adapt informally to changing cultural circumstances.

John M. Conley, *Of Contract, Culture, and the Code: Judge Easterbrook and the Cheyenne Indians*, 16 TOURO L. REV. 1053, 1056 (2000).

B. THE APPLICATION AND UNDERSTANDING OF UNWRITTEN LAW: THE THREE FIRES CONFEDERACY OF ANISHINAABEK

American Indian tribal nations—the Indian nations located within the geographic borders of what is now the United States—have always governed themselves in accordance with their own ways. They did not always memorialize their laws in writing, but sometimes did so as part of their tradition of stories, ancestry, and lifeways.

The first forms of law and order appeared long before the arrival of the Europeans, and usually involved the resolution of disputes involving hunting, fishing, and gathering rights, privileges, and territories. There also was a sophisticated system for dealing with criminal acts, as well as negligent acts.

The unwritten laws of the Anishinaabek—the people of the Three Fires Confederacy of Odawa, Bodewadomi, and Ojibwe—offer a reasonable cross-section of American Indian unwritten law.

The Anishinaabek often taught each other general rules of behavior for all people by relating stories linked to the landscape. The story of the Pukwud-jinni, or little people, at the Picture Rocks in the Upper Peninsula of Michigan is a good example. Gregory E. Dowd, *The Meaning of Article 13 of the Treaty of Washington, March 28, 1836*, Expert Report prepared for the Chippewa Ottawa Resource Authority, at 113-14; *United States v. Michigan*, No. 2:73 CV 26 (W.D. Mich., Oct. 11, 2004) (quoting and citing Ojibwa Narratives of Charles and Charlotte Kawbawgam and Jaques LePique, 1893-1895, at 71-72, 168 (Arthur P. Bourgeois ed., 1994), and Basil Johnston, Ojibway Heritage (1976)).

It is the stories, which are easily remembered and can be told again and again down through generations, that created the structure of American Indian traditional and customary law. Unlike so many tribes that had been removed by the federal government in the west, Great Lakes Indian nations retain many of the stories that provide the backdrop for law and justice in Indian country. These stories are based on the Anishinaabemowin language and upon the geographic characteristics of the Anishinaabek.

Disputes involving hunting and fishing territories often were disputes between families. Given the seasonal character of Anishinaabek existence—shifting from small inland winter hunting camps to larger spring sugar camps, and to still larger summer villages along the coast—different disputes would be resolved by different individuals depending upon where the dispute originated. For example, a conflict—say, over trespassing—concerning the winter hunting and trapping territory of a family would be resolved through discussion between the heads of households of the two families, with threats of violence perhaps, but rarely any physical conflict. A dispute over sugaring grounds, with larger groups of extended family units coming together, would be resolved by the heads of household meeting and talking together. A dispute between villages would have to be resolved by the *ogemuk* (leaders or headmen) of each village. A dispute between regional confederacies would be resolved by the *ogemuk* of each band. But a dispute between tribes (for example, the Odawa and the Ojibwe, or the Seneca and the Huron) would have to be resolved by treaty—or warfare.

On the most fundamental level, family property rights were the basic form of property rights. *See generally* Charles A. Bishop, *The Emergence of Hunting Territories among the Northern Ojibwa*, 9 Ethnology 1 (1971); John M. Cooper, *Is the Algonquian Family Hunting Ground System Pre-Columbian?*, 41 Am. Anthropologist 66 (1939); Frank G. Speck, *The Family Hunting Band as the Basis of Algonkian Social Organization*, 17 Am. Anthropologist 289 (1915). Individuals had little import in the property rights algebra, except for *ogemuk*, who represented a family unit, a village, or a band, and were described as "owning" the property right. These family property rights made little sense to the individualistic Europeans, who often chided Odawa hunters for giving away all the meat they harvested. Alexander Henry, a British fur trader who participated in the 1763 battle at Fort Michilimackinac, described Ottawa hunting rights as follows:

> Arrived here [at a sugar grove near Lake Michigan], we turned our attention to sugar-making, the management of which . . . belongs to the women, the men cutting wood for the fires, and hunting and fishing. In this midst of this, we were joined by several lodges of Indians, most of whom were of the family to which I belonged, and had wintered near us. The lands belonged to this family, and it had therefore the exclusive right to hunt on them. This is according to the custom of the people; for each family has its own lands.

ALEXANDER HENRY, TRAVELS AND ADVENTURES 149 (University of Michigan Press 1968). Johann Kohl, another of the Europeans who interacted with the Great Lakes Anishinaabek, wrote:

> The beaver dams—so persons conversant with the subject assured me—all have owners among the Indians, and are handed down from father to son. The sugar camps . . . have all an owner, and no Indian family would think of making sugar at a place where it had no right. Even the cranberry patches, or places in the swamp and bush where that berry is plucked, are family property; and the same with many other things.

JOHANN KOHL, KITCHI GAMI: LIFE AMONG THE LAKE SUPERIOR OJIBWAY 421 (Minnesota Historical Society Press 1985).

Ruth Landes argued that territorial disputes—or even territories themselves—did not arise unless there was a shortage of some resource, or if there was an outside actor creating a large market for the resource. *See* Ruth Landes, *Ojibwa of Canada, in* COOPERATION AND COMPETITION AMONG PRIMITIVE PEOPLES, at 87 (Margaret Mead ed., 1937). It is possible that there was no need to delineate hunting and fishing territories prior to the arrival of the Europeans, but there is no way to determine this from the printed record. Moreover, trade routes "could be used only by the family who pioneered them and who maintained a gift-exchange and kinship ties which assured safe passage for traders and a supply of goods when they reached their destination." James M. McClurken, *The Ottawa, in* PEOPLE OF THE THREE FIRES: THE OTTAWA, POTAWATOMI, AND OJIBWAY OF MICHIGAN 1, 11 (1986). Even family members used a trade route only with the permission of the *ogema*. Trespassers could be fined, charged some sort of toll, or even executed.

This treatment of property rights was a form of survival. Resources in the region were sufficient for the Michigan Anishinaabek, but the fabric of property rights ensured that the Anishinaabek utilized the correct amount of resources, and at the proper time of the year, so as to preserve the resources for the future. The Anishinaabe calendar system of marking the months by describing the actions to be taken during that time, such as harvesting berries or fishing for sucker, demonstrates how this operated.

As for individual rights, James McClurken wrote that "[t]he first rule in Ottawa society was respect for the individual. No one person could determine the fate of another." McClurken, *The Ottawa, supra*, at 5. But all members of the community shared their wealth, labor, and food. A person acquired prestige, respect, and even wealth by the act of gifting:

> The value of trading and gift giving was not only in acquiring goods for oneself, but in the social act of giving. By giving, individuals and families gained prestige and respect. A rich person did not have any more goods than his kinsmen; he simply gave more of what he had. The exchange of gifts was governed by a set of rules which bound giver and receiver. Each gift required some form of return and extended obligations of reciprocity across family lines to other tribes as well. The emphasis on sharing was so strong in Ottawa society that almost no interaction could be carried on without it.

Id.

An act of violence by one person against another, as well as an act of stealing or even hoarding important resources, posed an enormous danger to the small Ottawa communities. Every person had an important role to play in the day-to-day activities of the community, such as producing food or shelter, and the loss of one person or one person's production capacity could be devastating. Ottawa communities would exile, or even execute, a person who violated the trust of the people through the act of murder or another crime. Attempting to acquire too much personal or family power could also result in exile, which often was voluntary.

Anishinaabe people dealt with acts of violence, especially if they were accidental, not through retaliation but through remediation. One incident involving the accidental death of a small child through the misuse of a firearm by another child in 1846 is instructive. Peter Dougherty, an early nineteenth-century missionary who was instrumental in providing the history of the Grand Traverse Band of Ottawa and Chippewa Indians in Michigan, wrote that the family of the deceased child received a large gift of "guns and traps and blankets" from the other family. Dowd, Expert Report, *supra*, at 359-60 (quoting Peter Dougherty to William A. Richmond (Sept. 26, 1846)). This also demonstrates the importance of hunting and trapping to the Anishinaabek.

Anishinaabe customs and traditions involving domestic rules of marriage and divorce in some ways differ from the norms of today. One Anishinaabek practice exemplifies the relative autonomy that Anishinaabekwewag (Anishinaabe women) enjoyed during this period. About 70 percent of all the food consumed in Anishinaabe villages was produced by women, a fact that gave women individual authority. According to James McClurken, "Because of the work that Odawa women did in their traditional society was so important, they were afforded a great deal of personal freedom. . . . A woman could divorce a man simply by placing his belongings outside the door of the house." JAMES M. MCCLURKEN, GAH-BAEH-JHAGWAH-BUK: THE WAY IT HAPPENED, A VISUAL CULTURE HISTORY OF THE LITTLE TRAVERSE BAY BANDS OF ODAWA INDIANS 46 (1991). The ease of ending intimate relationships may have led outsiders to infer that the Anishinaabek practiced polygamy. In fact, polygamy was not typical for the Michigan Anishinaabek. Certain respected and wealthy *ogemuk* acquired political power within a local tribal community by taking additional wives. *See* McClurken, Gah-Baeh-Jhagwah-Buk, *supra*, at 73 (citing Paul Radin, *Ottawa-Ojibwe No. 5b*, notebook at 105 (American Philosophical Society) (noting information obtained from Joe Shomin of Cross Village, Michigan, in 1926 or 1927)). These *ogemuk* could do so only if they had the economic power to take care of all of these families, and it was this economic power that demonstrated the political power of the *ogemuk*, not to mention the sheer number of supporters one could acquire by taking care of additional families.

Tribal leadership in a particular village involved four different individuals (*ogemuk*), according to James McClurken:

> In the traditional Odawa village, there were four *Ogemuk*, each with a special job to fulfill. *Meaosad*, or head chief, was the most respected man in the village. *Meaosad* was traditionally a middle-aged man with two or three wives and many children and grandchildren. As the head of a prominent family, he could call on his kinspeople to provide food and gifts for feasts as well as to support his opinions in council. Sometimes, *Meaosad* had distinguished himself in war and could call on his fellow warriors to support him.
>
> The *Wendikawad Ogema*, or deputy chief, was a younger man than *Meaosad* who showed promise as a leader. Often, the *Wendikawad Ogema* was a son or son-in-law of *Meaosad*. When *Meaosad* could no longer lead, the *Wendikawad Ogema* filled his position. Then there was *Dewewege*, the leader who beat the drum, who was responsible for opening ceremonies, and *Mejinowe*, the official voice of the village, who was so skilled in oration that when a formal council was held, either between Odawa villages or with non-Anishinaabe people, *Mejinowe* spoke the words of the *Ogemuk* and thus represented the people.

McClurken, Gah-Baeh-Jhagwah-Buk, *supra*, at 73 (citing Radin, *Ottawa-Ojibwe No. 5b*, *supra*, at 105 (noting information obtained from Joe Shomin of Cross Village, Michigan in 1926 or 1927)). Others besides the *ogemuk* had important roles within the Anishinaabe communities: "[T]he *mishinaway* (data collector), the *kekedowenine* (mediator and conflict resolver), and the *oskabewis* (speaker and messenger) were almost as important to group decision making as the *ogima* (head chief) and the *anikeogima* (second or subchief)." Janet E. Chute, *Shingwaukonse: A Nineteenth-Century Innovative Ojibwa Leader*, 45 Ethnohistory 65, 68 (1998).

Leadership in Anishinaabe communities was similar in some respects to non-Indian leadership, in that most of the leaders were male. But as Anton Treuer notes, "[a]lthough the authority to become a civil chief was considered hereditary, influence was not." Anton Steven Treuer, The Assassination of Hole in the Day at 34 (Sept. 1997) (unpublished Ph.D. dissertation, University of Minnesota). Possessing leadership lineage made it easier and more likely for an Anishinaabe-inini (male) to rise to a leadership position, but "clan, military prowess, religious knowledge, political savvy and personal charisma all played a part in determining who had political power in the nineteenth century." *Id.* at 34-35. Moreover, collecting or hoarding or even possessing wealth was mutually exclusive to serving as a leader: "As long as a man has anything, according to the moral law of the [Anishinaabek], he must share it with those who want; and no one can attain any degree of respect among them who does not do so most liberally." *Id.* at 36 (quoting Kohl, Kitchi Gami, *supra*, at 66).

And while men served as leaders, some women ascended to leadership roles, and generally women played a terrifically important behind-the-scenes role in major decision making. *See id.* at 37-38.

The authority and responsibility of the family *ogema* is captured in the story of how one Grand Traverse region family's traps intruded on the trapping territories of another family, recounted by Henry Schoolcraft, former federal Indian Agent for the Great Lakes region:

> Some years ago, a Chippewa hunter of Grand Traverse Bay, Lake Michigan, found that an Indian of a separate band had been found trespassing on his hunting grounds by trapping furred animals. He determined to visit him, but found on reaching his lodge the family absent, and the lodge door carefully closed and tied. In one corner of the lodge he found two small packs of furs, these he seized. He then took his hatchet and blazed a large tree. With a pencil made of a burned end of a stick, he then drew on this surface the figure of a man holding a gun, pointing at another man having traps in his hands. The two packs of furs were placed between them. By these figures he told the tale of the trespass, the seizure of the furs, and the threat of shooting him if he persevered in his trespass.

Dowd, Expert Report, *supra*, at 92 (quoting HENRY ROWE SCHOOLCRAFT, PERSONAL MEMOIRS OF A RESIDENCE OF THIRTY YEARS WITH THE INDIAN TRIBES OF THE AMERICAN FRONTIERS 695 (1851) (AMS 1978)). This ended the dispute.

Ogemuk had a variety of tools at their disposal to enforce territorial rights and obligations. Penalties could range from confiscation to violence. For example, Peter Dougherty stated that the penalty for trespassing on another band's hunting territories could be severe:

> Each family has a certain hunting ground and trespass was in former times considered to be a sufficient cause for retaliation on the life of the trespasser. Now the one against whom the trespass is committed has the right to go to the lodge of the offender and take from him property to satisfy himself. In case of trespass by one tribe on the hunting ground of another tribe, the injured party sends a message to the other, and if satisfaction is not rendered it becomes a just cause of war.

Dowd, Expert Report, *supra*, at 90 (quoting Peter Dougherty to War Department, Office of Indian Affairs, Grand Traverse Bay (Jan. 21, 1848)). *Ogemuk* even enforced Anishinaabe community rights against non-Indians: "When the American, Samual Ashman, started fishing commercially in Goulais Bay, Shingwaukonse [a Sault Ste. Marie *ogema*] had Ashman's property seized and the fish distributed to the Indians to whom they of right belonged." Robert Doherty, *Old-Time Origins of Modern Sovereignty: State-Building among the Keweenaw Bay Ojibway, 1832-1854*, 31 AM. INDIAN Q. 165, 170 (2007) (quotation and citation omitted).

Francis Assikinack, an Odawa Indian from Drummond Island and who lived at L'Arbre Croche at a young age, asserted that tribal sovereignty originates in these territorial boundary questions:

> Each of these tribes had to maintain a small sovereignty of its own and for its own use. The members of the neighboring tribes had no right to go beyond the

limits of their respective districts on their hunting excursions, and encroach upon that belonging to others. Any hunter that was caught trespassing upon the rights of other tribes, or taking beaver in the rivers running through their lands, was in danger of forfeiting his life on the spot for his rashness.

Francis Assikinack, *Legends and Traditions of the Odawah Indians*, 3 CAN. J. INDUSTRY, SCI. & ARTS 115, 117 (1858).

NOTES

1. The traditional form of governance of the Anishinaabek of Michigan demonstrates a few key principles, some of which apply in general terms to nearly all Indian nations.

First, American Indian *nationhood* developed as a response to changing geopolitical circumstances caused by the arrival and interference of European and American nations. Primary Anishinaabe governance centered on villages, and even to some extent on regions, but not on nations. Related to this, the notion of an Indian "tribe" is not an Indian construction, but a label attached to Indian nations by non-Indian governments as a means of denigrating them.

Second, Indian governance largely involved what Deloria and Lytle called "quasi-judicial" functions, and also the maintenance of family-based territorial property structures.

Third, Indian governance was unlike the modern conception of government theorized to involve coercion, or a monopoly of violence.

2. Anishinaabe scholar Benjamin Ramirez-shkwegnaabi analyzed the leadership patterns of Anishinaabe treaty negotiators, concluding:

> Anishinaabeg ogimaag (leaders) were men and women who excelled in areas such as warfare, medicine, hunting, or singing. They did not lead by force or authority (in the European sense), but rather secured their power through service to their communities. There were two main categories of ogimaag: war chiefs and civil leaders. War chiefs were typically young warriors, of lower rank than civil chiefs, who had proved their leadership in war. Ideally they supported the civil ogimaag and asserted their authority only in times of conflict. Civil leaders (by the nineteenth century this was often a hereditary rank) had a responsibility to provide for the welfare of their people, much as parents had responsibility for their children. "He was a father to his people; they looked on him as children do to a parent; and his lightest wish was immediately performed," said a principal warrior of Curly Head, a Mississippi Ojibwe civil chief whose relationship with his people was based on ensuring their well-being: "His lodge was ever full of meat, to which the hungry and destitute were ever welcome. The traders vied with one another [over] who should treat him best, and the presents which he received at their hands he always distributed to his people without reserve. When he had plenty, his people wanted not."

Benjamin Ramirez-shkwegnaabi, *The Dynamics of American Indian Diplomacy in the Great Lakes Region*, 27(4) AM. INDIAN CULTURE & RES. J. 53, 56 (2003) (quoting WILLIAM W. WARREN, THE HISTORY OF THE OJIBWAY 348 (1984)).

C. THE ORIGINS AND DEVELOPMENT OF MODERN AMERICAN INDIAN TRIBAL GOVERNMENTS

The federal government forced the establishment and the development of many western American Indian nations' tribal governments. From the point of view of the Indian people, such artificial tribal governments did not necessarily take the place of what we could call a more localized, indigenous government.

1. EARLY TRIBAL CONSTITUTIONS

The earliest significant known writing establishing a formal government structure among Indian nations is the *Gayanashagowa*, or the Great Law of Peace, established by the five Haudenosaunee nations' confederacy sometime between 1000 and 1525 A.D. *See* DAVID E. WILKINS, DOCUMENTS OF NATIVE AMERICAN POLITICAL DEVELOPMENT 14-15 (2009); *see also* ARTHUR C. PARKER, THE CONSTITUTION OF THE FIVE NATIONS OR THE IROQUOIS BOOK OF THE GREAT LAW (1916) (Iroquois Reprints 1984); ROBERT A. WILLIAMS, JR., LINKING ARMS TOGETHER: AMERICAN INDIAN TREATY VISIONS OF LAW AND PEACE, 1600-1800 (1997). The Great Law of Peace includes a "detailed description of the political and moral principles of the confederacy's structural arrangement." WILKINS, DOCUMENTS OF NATIVE AMERICAN POLITICAL DEVELOPMENT, *supra*, at 14.

GAYANASHAGOWA OR THE GREAT LAW OF PEACE

(C.16th C.)

1. I am Dekanawidah and with the Five Nations' Confederate Lords I plant the Tree of Great Peace. I plant it in your territory, Adodarhoh, and the Onondaga Nation, in the territory of you who are Firekeepers. . . .

We place you upon those seats, spread soft with the feathery down of the globe thistle, there beneath the shade of the spreading branches of the Tree of Peace. There shall you sit and watch the Council Fire of the Confederacy of the Five Nations, and all the affairs of the Five Nations shall be transacted at this place before you, Adodarhoh, and your cousin Lords, by the Confederate Lords of the Five Nations. . . .

3. To you Adodarhoh, the Onondaga cousin Lords, I and the other Confederate Lords have entrusted the caretaking and the watching of the Five Nations Council Fire.

When there is any business to be transacted and the Confederate Council is not in session, a messenger shall be dispatched either to Adodarhoh, Hononwirehtonh or Skanawatih, Fire Keepers, or to their War Chiefs with a full statement of the case desired to be considered. Then shall Adodarhoh call his cousin (associate) Lords together and consider whether or not the case is of sufficient importance to demand the attention of the Confederate Council. If so, Adodarhoh shall dispatch messengers to summon all the Confederate Lords to assemble beneath the Tree of the Long Leaves. . . .

5. The Council of the Mohawk shall be divided into three parties as follows: Tekarihoken, Ayonhwhathah and Shadekariwade are the first party;

Sharenhowaneh, Deyoenhegwenh and Oghrenghrehgowah are the second party, and Dehennakrineh, Aghstawenserenthah and Shoskoharowaneh are the third party. The third party is to listen only to the discussion of the first and second parties and if an error is made or the proceeding is irregular they are to call attention to it, and when the case is right and properly decided by the two parties they shall confirm the decision of the two parties and refer the case to the Seneca Lords for their decision. When the Seneca Lords have decided in accord with the Mohawk Lords, the case or question shall be referred to the Cayuga and Oneida Lords on the opposite side of the house.

6. I, Dekanawidah, appoint the Mohawk Lords the heads and the leaders of the Five Nations Confederacy. The Mohawk Lords are the foundation of the Great Peace and it shall, therefore, be against the Great Binding Law to pass measures in the Confederate Council after the Mohawk Lords have protested against them.

No council of the Confederate Lords shall be legal unless all the Mohawk Lords are present. . . .

8. The Firekeepers shall formally open and close all councils of the Confederate Lords, and they shall pass upon all matters deliberated upon by the two sides and render their decision.

Every Onondaga Lord (or his deputy) must be present at every Confederate Council and must agree with the majority without unwarrantable dissent, so that a unanimous decision may be rendered. . . .

9. All the business of the Five Nations Confederate Council shall be conducted by the two combined bodies of Confederate Lords. First the question shall be passed upon by the Mohawk and Seneca Lords, then it shall be discussed and passed by the Oneida and Cayuga Lords. Their decisions shall then be referred to the Onondaga Lords, (Fire Keepers) for final judgment.

The same process shall obtain when a question is brought before the council by an individual or a War Chief.

10. In all cases the procedure must be as follows: when the Mohawk and Seneca Lords have unanimously agreed upon a question, they shall report their decision to the Cayuga and Oneida Lords, who shall deliberate upon the question and report a unanimous decision to the Mohawk Lords. The Mohawk Lords will then report the standing of the case to the Fire Keepers, who shall render a decision as they see fit in case of a disagreement by the two bodies, or confirm the decisions of the two bodies if they are identical. The Fire Keepers shall then report their decision to the Mohawk Lords who shall announce it to the open council.

11. If through any misunderstanding or obstinacy on the part of the Fire Keepers, they render a decision at variance with that of the Two Sides, the Two Sides shall reconsider the matter and if their decisions are jointly the same as before they shall report to the Fire Keepers who are then compelled to confirm their joint decision.

12. When a case comes before the Onondaga Lords (Fire Keepers) for discussion and decision, Adodarho shall introduce the matter to his comrade Lords, who shall then discuss it in their two bodies. Every Onondaga Lord except Hononwiretonh shall deliberate and he shall listen only. When a unanimous decision shall have been reached by the two bodies of Fire Keepers,

Adodarho shall notify Hononwiretonh of the fact when he shall confirm it. He shall refuse to confirm a decision if it is not unanimously agreed upon by both sides of the Fire Keepers. . . .

16. If the conditions which shall arise at any future time call for an addition to or change of this law, the case shall be carefully considered and if a new beam seems necessary or beneficial, the proposed change shall be voted upon and if adopted it shall be called, "Added to the Rafters."

Rights, Duties and Qualifications of Lords

17. A bunch of a certain number of shell (wampum) strings each two spans in length shall be given to each of the female families in which the Lordship titles are vested. The right of bestowing the title shall be hereditary in the family of the females legally possessing the bunch of shell strings and the strings shall be the token that the females of the family have the proprietary right to the Lordship title for all time to come, subject to certain restrictions hereinafter mentioned.

18. If any Confederate Lord neglects or refuses to attend the Confederate Council, the other Lords of the Nation of which he is a member shall require their War Chief to request the female sponsors of the Lord so guilty of defection to demand his attendance of the Council. If he refuses, the women holding the title shall immediately select another candidate for the title. . . .

19. If at any time it shall be manifest that a Confederate Lord has not in mind the welfare of the people or disobeys the rules of this Great Law, the men or women of the Confederacy, or both jointly, shall come to the Council and upbraid the erring Lord through his War Chief. If the complaint of the people through the War Chief is not heeded the first time it shall be uttered again and then if no attention is given a third complaint and warning shall be given. If the Lord is contumacious the matter shall go to the council of War Chiefs.

The War Chiefs shall then divest the erring Lord of his title by order of the women in whom the titleship is vested. When the Lord is deposed the women shall notify the Confederate Lords through their War Chief, and the Confederate Lords shall sanction the act. The women will then select another of their sons as a candidate and the Lords shall elect him. Then shall the chosen one be installed by the Installation Ceremony.

When a Lord is to be deposed, his War Chief shall address him as follows:

"So you, _____, disregard and set at naught the warnings of your women relatives. So you fling the warnings over your shoulder to cast them behind you.

"Behold the brightness of the Sun and in the brightness of the Sun's light I depose you of your title and remove the sacred emblem of your Lordship title. I remove from your brow the deer's antlers, which was the emblem of your position and token of your nobility. I now depose you and return the antlers to the women whose heritage they are."

The War Chief shall now address the women of the deposed Lord and say:

"Mothers, as I have now deposed your Lord, I now return to you the emblem and the title of Lordship, therefore repossess them." . . .

20. If a Lord of the Confederacy of the Five Nations should commit murder the other Lords of the Nation shall assemble at the place where the corpse lies

and prepare to depose the criminal Lord. If it is impossible to meet at the scene of the crime the Lords shall discuss the matter at the next Council of their Nation and request their War Chief to depose the Lord guilty of crime, to "bury" his women relatives and to transfer the Lordship title to a sister family. . . .

23. Any Lord of the Five Nations Confederacy may construct shell strings (or wampum belts) of any size or length as pledges or records of matters of national or international importance. . . .

Any of the people of the Five Nations may use shells (or wampum) as the record of a pledge, contract or an agreement entered into and the same shall be binding as soon as shell strings shall have been exchanged by both parties. . . .

Names, Duties and Rights of War Chiefs

. . .

37. There shall be one War Chief for each Nation and their duties shall be to carry messages for their Lords and to take up the arms of war in case of emergency. They shall not participate in the proceedings of the Confederate Council but shall watch its progress and in case of an erroneous action by a Lord they shall receive the complaints of the people and convey the warnings of the women to him. The people who wish to convey messages to the Lords in the Confederate Council shall do so through the War Chief of their Nation. It shall ever be his duty to lay the cases, questions and propositions of the people before the Confederate Council. . . .

39. If a War Chief acts contrary to instructions or against the provisions of the Laws of the Great Peace, doing so in the capacity of his office, he shall be deposed by his women relatives and by his men relatives. Either the women or the men alone or jointly may act in such a case. The women title holders shall then choose another candidate. . . .

Clans and Consanguinity

42. Among the Five Nations and their posterity there shall be the following original clans: Great Name Bearer, Ancient Name Bearer, Great Bear, Ancient Bear, Turtle, Painted Turtle, Standing Rock, Large Plover, Deer, Pigeon Hawk, Eel, Ball, Opposite-Side-of-the-Hand, and Wild Potatoes. These clans distributed through their respective Nations, shall be the sole owners and holders of the soil of the country and in them is it vested as a birthright.

43. People of the Five Nations members of a certain clan shall recognize every other member of that clan, irrespective of the Nation, as relatives. Men and women, therefore, members of the same clan are forbidden to marry.

44. The lineal descent of the people of the Five Nations shall run in the female line. Women shall be considered the progenitors of the Nation. They shall own the land and the soil. Men and women shall follow the status of the mother.

45. The women heirs of the Confederated Lordship titles shall be called Royaneh (Noble) for all time to come. . . .

52. The Royaneh women, heirs of the Lordship titles, shall, should it be necessary, correct and admonish the holders of their titles. Those only who attend the Council may do this and those who do not shall not object to what has been said nor strive to undo the action.

53. When the Royaneh women, holders of a Lordship title, select one of their sons as a candidate, they shall select one who is trustworthy, of good character, of honest disposition, one who manages his own affairs, supports his own family, if any, and who has proven a faithful man to his Nation.

54. When a Lordship title becomes vacant through death or other cause, the Royaneh women of the clan in which the title is hereditary shall hold a council and shall choose one from among their sons to fill the office made vacant. . . .

Laws of Adoption

. . .

68. Should any member of the Five Nations, a family or person belonging to a foreign nation submit a proposal for adoption into a clan of one of the Five Nations, he or they shall furnish a string of shells, a span in length, as a pledge to the clan into which he or they wish to be adopted. The Lords of the nation shall then consider the proposal and submit a decision.

69. Any member of the Five Nations who through esteem or other feeling wishes to adopt an individual, a family or number of families may offer adoption to him or them and if accepted the matter shall be brought to the attention of the Lords for confirmation and the Lords must confirm adoption.

70. When the adoption of anyone shall have been confirmed by the Lords of the Nation, the Lords shall address the people of their nation and say: "Now you of our nation, be informed that such a person, such a family or such families have ceased forever to bear their birth nation's name and have buried it in the depths of the earth. Henceforth let no one of our nation ever mention the original name or nation of their birth. To do so will be to hasten the end of our peace." . . .

NOTES

1. The Great Law of Peace established a formal government structure for the five (later six) Haudenosaunee nations, guaranteeing an external political alliance for hundreds of years. The structure merged informal diplomatic ceremony and the laws of the nations into a workable document for these very different nations. Despite the creation of this complicated and venerated international political structure, the confederacy did not often inspire cooperation between the five nations when they were engaging outsiders: "Between 1600 and 1692 the Iroquois appear to have rarely acted in political unison." CHAMPAGNE, AMERICAN INDIAN SOCIETIES, *supra*, at 26; *see also id*. ("Although the Iroquois through the confederacy had formed institutions of social and ceremonial integration, Iroquois kinship and political institutions were not differentiated, and religious mythology dictated the structure of the Iroquois polity, including the kin-based political organization. Primary political alliances remained tied to lineage and clan and regional groupings.") In other words, the Great Law of Peace prevented Haudenosaunee-on-Haudenosaunee bloodshed, but did not always lead to a concrete, unified nationality.

2. In 1848 the Seneca Nation of Indians became one the first Indian nations to promulgate an Anglo-American style form of constitutional government. The constitution adopted that year has remained substantially the same to this day. WILKINS, DOCUMENTS OF NATIVE AMERICAN POLITICAL DEVELOPMENT, *supra*, at 75-81.

2. THE IMPACT OF THE TREATY RELATIONSHIP ON AMERICAN INDIAN GOVERNANCE

In contrast to the obvious example of the Haudenosaunee Confederacy, most Indian nations did not appear to have a governmental structure resembling that of the European explorers. However, the European nations still turned to diplomacy and negotiation—and entered into numerous treaties with those apparently anarchic Indian nations. The treaty relationship developed between Indian nations and England, France, Spain, and other nations carried over into relations with the United States, leading in 1777 to the first treaty between the nascent American Republic and an Indian nation.

The establishment of this treaty relationship perfected the recognition by European nations that American Indian nations existed with a legitimacy comparable to their own. These international agreements held the key to power over much of the continent. For example, the series of treaties and agreements between Great Britain and the Haudenosaunee Confederacy, known as the "Covenant Chain," served as an important linchpin between the competing colonial nations of Great Britain and France:

> English colonial officials universally regarded the Iroquois Covenant Chain as the single most important indigenous political, military, and economic institution on the continent. Through it, as the English clearly recognized, the Five Nations of the Iroquois confederacy maintained an effective capability of tipping the balance of power in North America. Only the Iroquois "empire" stood between England's weakly defended colonies on the Atlantic seaboard and France's desires to assert its hegemony over the North American continent.

WILLIAMS, LINKING ARMS TOGETHER, *supra*, at 117.

The treaty relationship allowed American Indian tribal governments some room to prosper—and served the all-important purpose of explicitly designating Indian nations as sovereigns capable of and eligible for engagement in formal international relations with recognized nations such as the United States. In effect, Indian treaties served as formal recognitions of American Indian nation sovereignty.

TREATY WITH THE OTTAWA AND CHIPPEWA

11 Stat. 621

(July 31, 1855)

Article V

The tribal organization of said Ottawa and Chippewa Indians, except so far as may be necessary for the purpose of carrying into effect the provisions of this agreement, is hereby dissolved; and if at any time hereafter, further negotiations with the United States, in reference to any matters contained herein, should become necessary, no general convention of the Indians shall be called; but such as reside in the vicinity of any usual place of payment, or those only who are immediately interested in the questions involved, may arrange all matters between themselves and the United States, without the concurrence of other portions of their people, and as fully and conclusively, and with the same effect in every respect, as if all were represented. . . .

NOTES

1. Treaty making often served to impose an artificial governing authority on an Indian community that otherwise would not have recognized such an entity. One example is the negotiation of the 1836 Treaty of Washington involving the Anishinaabek of Michigan's northern Lower Peninsula and eastern Upper Peninsula. The 1836 treaty, from the point of view of the Lower Peninsula Anishinaabek, was intended to address their interests alone, with land sales to be limited, even minuscule. It was Henry Schoolcraft and Lewis Cass, the United States treaty commissioner and Indian Affairs Commissioner, who envisioned a much larger treaty cession that would involve half of the Upper Peninsula as well. Gregory Dowd reports that the 1836 treaty delegation consisted primarily of Lower Peninsula Ottawas and Chippewas. The Upper Peninsula Chippewas were only sparsely represented, and by individuals with dubious authority at best. Schoolcraft, as the lead American treaty negotiator, used the very presence of the Upper Peninsula Chippewas as leverage against the Lower Peninsula Anishinaabek and Chippewas. At any moment, all parties knew, if the Ottawas objected to a large land cession or any other treaty term, Schoolcraft could easily acquire the signatures of the Upper Peninsula Chippewa contingent, regardless of their authority to sign away lands that they did not own.

   To enable the federal government to take advantage of this situation, the American treaty commissioners incorporated into the treaty the establishment of an entity called "the Chippewa and Ottawa nations," which existed for the purpose of executing the treaty and binding all the nations assembled. Treaty of Washington, art. I, 6 Stat. 491 (1836). The Anishinaabek did not view themselves as a unified entity. There were two key negotiators, one from the Lower Peninsula and one from the Upper Peninsula. And those speakers had no authority to bind the most important political entities—local villages—without the express consent of those communities. The treaty signature page, divided by region and village, demonstrated this reality more so than the fictional designation "Chippewa and Ottawa nations."

   From the U.S. government's point of view, a signature was a signature. No one in Washington, DC, would question the signatories' authority. Once the United States created this legal fiction, Schoolcraft exploited it to incredible advantage:

   > When the parties reassembled in the Masonic Hall on March 18, the formalities of the calumet ceremony preceded the discussions. Then the "chief

speaker" arose to reject Schoolcraft's offer [to extinguish Indian title to the Anishinaabek lands, amounting to one-third of the land base of the current state of Michigan]. It is not clear from the record who this is, and after his objections no individual is referred to in [the treaty journal] as the "chief speaker." Probably it was Aishquagonabee, the first name listed on the treaty, a "Chippewa Chief of Grand Traverse." . . . It was obvious that the Indians simply did not wish to sell their rights to most of their lands.

Dowd, Expert Report, *supra*, at 204. Schoolcraft, the American treaty commissioner, responded with a play of dirty pool and an effective trump card against the Lower Peninsula Anishinaabek:

Schoolcraft then threatened to treat separately with the Chippewas of the Upper Peninsula unless the Ottawas and Chippewas of the Lower Peninsula changed their minds before the following Tuesday. Since Upper Peninsular peoples had even less to fear from white settlement than did Ottawas, and since the dubiously representative Chippewa delegation from the Sault Ste. Marie region had been practically handpicked by the agent (and was related by marriage to him), it is not surprising that the Chippewas present were more willing to make a deal.

At that point, Augustin Hamelin [spelled Emlin in the treaty journal], Jr., intervened. He declared in English that the Ottawas had spoken, not from their hearts, but after having been, he claimed, manipulated by "white men who wanted [private] reservations." Hamelin reassured the commissioner that "if the Indians were left alone they would sell, with some Reservations for themselves, he was confident it was their wish to dispose of their lands and derive present benefit." Schoolcraft arranged for a private room in which the Indians could counsel among themselves, and that no one else be allowed to "disturb them." . . .

By the eve of the resumption of formal discussions, it was clear that most of the treating Indians would mark the agreement. Mary Holiday wrote that, while the preceding Friday "most of the Ottawas refused to sell," they had since "called on Mr. Schoolcraft, telling him they would sell, if they would be allowed to make large, permanent reservations for themselves."

Dowd, Expert Report, *supra*, at 205.

The 1836 treaty did not solve the problems of the Michigan Anishinaabek, so the Indian nations and the United States entered into negotiations for another treaty in 1855. Once again, the Anishinaabek came to the table as disparate entities, and the United States worked from the fictional "unified bands" notion. The Anishinaabek objected to this characterization, and so upon the conclusion of the treaty the United States included a section eliminating the "Chippewa and Ottawa nations." Treaty of Detroit, art. V, 11 Stat. 621, 624 (1855). But the federal government used the fictional entity anyway, attempting to bind bands, such as the Burt Lake Band of Ottawa and Chippewa Indians, that refused to execute the treaty.

A second, more insidious outcome arose out of Article V of the 1855 Treaty: administrative termination of Michigan Indian nations:

Henry Schoolcraft, who negotiated the 1836 Treaty of Washington on behalf of the United States, combined the Ottawa and Chippewa nations into a joint political unit solely for purposes of facilitating the negotiation of that treaty.

In the years that followed, the Ottawas and Chippewas vociferously complained about being joined together as a single political unit. To address their complaints, the 1855 Treaty of Detroit contained language dissolving the artificial joinder of the two tribes. This language, however, was not intended to terminate federal recognition of either tribe, but to permit the United States to deal with the Ottawas and the Chippewas as separate political entities. Ignoring the historical context of the treaty language, Secretary Delano interpreted the 1855 treaty as providing for the dissolution of the tribes once the annuity payments it called for were completed in the spring of 1872, and hence decreed that upon finalization of those payments "tribal relations will be terminated." *Letter from Secretary of the Interior Delano to Commission of Indian Affairs* at 3 (Mar. 27, 1872). Beginning in that year, the Department of the Interior, believing that the federal government no longer had any trust obligations to the tribes, ceased to recognize the tribes either jointly or separately.

Grand Traverse Band of Ottawa and Chippewa Indians v. Office of the United States Attorney for the Western District of Michigan, 369 F.3d 960, 96162 n. 2 (6th Cir. 2004).

2. One example involves the Indian nations of the Puget Sound area, in which "tribes" and tribal "leaders" came into being when the American treaty commissioner, Issac I. Stevens, named and appointed groupings of Indians as nations and identified leaders among them:

No formal political structure had been created by the Indians living in the Puget Sound area at the time of initial contact with the United States Government. Governor Stevens, acting upon instructions from his superiors and recommendations of his subordinates, deliberately created political entities for purposes of delegating responsibilities and negotiating treaties. In creating these entities Governor Stevens named many chiefs and sub-chiefs.

United States v. Washington, 384 F. Supp. 312, 355 (W.D. Wash. 1974).

3. THE BEGINNINGS OF AMERICAN INDIAN CONSTITUTIONAL GOVERNMENT

In the nineteenth century, American Indian policy compelled American Indian nations to retool their traditional governance structures from primarily judicial entities to primarily legislative and executive authorities. DELORIA & LYTLE, AMERICAN INDIANS, AMERICAN JUSTICE, *supra*, at 96 ("[T]he transition from a wholly traditional tribal government, which basically performed a quasi-judicial function, to the modern tribal council, which performs predominantly executive and legislative functions, varied from tribe to tribe.").

The Cherokee Nation of the southeastern United States was among the very first American Indian nations to take dramatic steps to replicate the structure and philosophy of American governments, largely as an attempt to pre-empt efforts to remove them to the west, and to end blood revenge against Americans and against each other. CHAMPAGNE, AMERICAN INDIAN SOCIETIES, *supra*, at 44. In 1809, the Cherokee nation was born when the "Cherokee council announced that the nation had been united. . . ." *Id.* at 45. In 1810, "[t]he clans agreed to delegate their judicial authority to the national council. With the legitimate use of force now granted solely to the national government, the Cherokee polity became even more centralized. A police force called the light-house acted as police, judge, and executioner." *Id*.

After failing to prevent certain village leaders from signing a removal treaty with the United States, the national council signed another significant treaty in 1819 guaranteeing their lands. Then the nation further centralized, utilizing governmental districts controlled by the national government, and adding a national judiciary and regulatory structure. *See* CHAMPAGNE, AMERICAN INDIAN SOCI-ETIES, *supra*, at 47.

In 1828, the Nation finalized its constitutional system of government, complete with a written constitution, legal code, judiciary, and even a written, dual-language newspaper:

> In late 1826, the Cherokee national council agreed to hold elections for dele-gates to a constitutional convention, which was held in July 1827. The Cherokee constitution was ratified by the national council in 1828 and the first elections were held in October of that year. The new constitution was modeled after the US Constitution: it provided separation of powers among the executive, judiciary, and legislative branches, and a legal code that regu-lated criminal and economic concerns.

CHAMPAGNE, AMERICAN INDIAN SOCIETIES, *supra*, at 47. It also incorporated the American constitutional infirmities of "disenfranchisement of African Amer-icans and women." WILKINS, DOCUMENTS OF NATIVE AMERICAN POLITICAL DEVELOPMENT, *supra*, at 57. "Yet it also contains specific provisions (e.g., communal land ownership) that sustained a measure of traditional Cherokee values and prop-erty notions." *Id*.

CHEROKEE CONSTITUTION OF 1827

We the Representatives of the people of the Cherokee Nation in Conven-tion assembled in order to establish justice, ensure tranquility, promote our common welfare, and secure to ourselves and our posterity the blessings of liberty; acknowledging with humility and gratitude the goodness of the sovereign Ruler of the Universe in offering us an opportunity so favorable to the design and imploring his aid and direction in its accomplishments do ordain and establish this Constitution for the Government of the Cherokee Nation. . . .

Article II

The powers of this Government shall be divided with three distinct depart-ments, the Legislative, Executive, and Judicial.

Section 2. No person or persons belonging to one of these departments shall exercise any of the powers properly belonging to either of the others; except in cases herein after expressly directed or permitted.

Article III

The Legislative power shall be vested in two distinct branches; a Commit-tee, and a Council; each to have a negative on the other, and both to be styled,

[on] the General Council of the Cherokee Nation, and the style of their acts and laws shall be "Resolved by the Committee and Council in General Council convened." . . .

Section 4. No person shall be eligible to a seat in the General Council, but a free Cherokee male citizen, who shall have attained to the age of twenty-five years. The descendants of Cherokee men by all free women, except the African race, whose parents may have been living together as man and wife, according to the customs and laws of this Nation, shall be entitled to all the rights and privileges of this Nation, as well as the posterity of Cherokee women by all free men. No person who is of negro or mulatto parentage, either by the father or mother side, shall be eligible to hold any office of profit, honor or trust under this Government. . . .

Section 7. All free Male citizens (excepting negroes and descendants of white and Indian men by Negro women who may have been set free) who shall have attained to the age of 18 years shall be equally entitled to vote at all public elections. . . .

Section 15. The General Council Shall have power to make, all laws and regulations, which they shall deem necessary and proper, for the good of the nation, which shall not be contrary to his Constitution.

Section 16. It shall be the duty of the General Council to pass such laws, as may be necessary and proper, to decide differences, by Arbitrators to be appointed by the parties, who may choose that summary mode of adjustment.

Section 17. No power of suspending the laws of this nation Shall be exercised, unless by the Legislature or its authority.

Section 18. That no retrospective law, nor any law, impairing the obligation of contracts shall be passed.

Section 19. The Legislature shall have power to make laws for laying and collecting taxes for the purpose of raising a revenue. . . .

Article IV

Section 1. The supreme executive power of this nation, shall be vested in a principal chief who shall be chosen by the General Council and shall hold his office four years. . . .

Section 10. He shall take care that the law be faithfully executed. . . .

Section 14. Every bill which shall have passed both Houses of the General Council shall, before it becomes a law, be presented to the Principal Chief of the Cherokee Nation. If he approves it, he shall sign it, but if not, he shall return it, with his objections, to that house in which it shall have originated, who shall enter the objections at large on their journals, and proceed to reconsider it. If after such reconsideration, two thirds of that house shall agree to pass the Bill, it shall be sent together with the objection to the other House by which it shall likewise be reconsidered and, if approved of by two thirds of that house, it shall become a law. . . .

Article V

Section 1. The Judicial powers shall be vested in a Supreme Court, and such Circuit and inferior Courts, as the General Council may, from time to time, ordain and establish. . . .

Section 14. In all continual prosecutions, the accused shall have the right of being heard, of demanding the nature and cause, of the accusation against him, of meeting the witness face to face, of having compulsory process for obtaining witnesses in his favor, and in prosecutions by indictments or information, a speedy public trial by an impartial Jury of the vicinage, nor shall he be compelled to give evidence against himself.

Section 15. That the people shall be secure in their persons, houses, papers, and possessions from unreasonable seizures and searches, and that no warrant to search any place or to seize any person or things shall issue without describing them as nearly as may be, nor without good excuse, supported by Oath or affirmation. — All prisoners shall be bailable, by sufficient securities, unless for capital offences, where the proof is evident or presumption great.

Article VI

. . .

Section 3. The free exercise of religious worship and serving God without distinction, shall forever be allowed within this nation: Provided that this liberty of conscience shall not be so construed as to excuse acts of licentiousness, or justify practices inconsistent with the peace of safety of this nation. . . .

Section 8. No person shall for the same offence be twice put in jeopardy of life, or limb, nor shall any person's property be taken or applied to public use without his consent; Provided, That nothing shall be so construed in this clause as to impair the right and power of the General Council to lay and collect taxes. That all Courts shall be open, and every person for an injury done him in his property, person, or reputation, shall have remedy by due course of law.

Section 9. The right of trial by Jury shall remain inviolate.

Section 10. Religion, morality, and knowledge being necessary to good government and the preservation of liberty, and the happiness of Mankind, Schools and the means of education, shall forever, be encouraged in this nation.

Section 11. The appointment of all officers not otherwise directed by this constitution, shall be vested in the legislature. . . .

Section 13. The General Council may at any time propose such amendments to this Constitution as two thirds of each House shall deem expedient; and the Principal Chief shall issue a proclamation directing all the Civil officers of the several Districts to promulgate the same as extensively as possible within their respective Districts, at least nine Months previous to the next general election, and if at the first session of the General Council after such general election, two thirds of each House shall by yeas and nays, ratify such proposed amendments they shall be valid to all intents and purposes as parts of this Constitution; Provided, That such proposed amendments shall be read on three several days in each house as will when the same are proposed as when they are finally ratified.

Done in Convention at New Town Echota this 24th day of July 1827.

NOTES

1. The State of Georgia declared a legal and political war on the Cherokee Nation of Oklahoma around this time:

> A crisis came, in 1828, when the Cherokees held a convention and adopted a Constitution for a permanent government, displaying their intention to remain on their lands. The Legislature of Georgia responded by passing, in 1829, a series of laws of the most cruel and stringent nature, invalidating all laws and ordinances adopted by the Indians, and providing for a division of their lands. As these laws were clearly in violation of the treaty with the United States, Congress was forced now to take cognizance of the situation, but its action was feeble; and the new President, Andrew Jackson, was in entire sympathy with the State of Georgia in its claim of right to legislate over all persons within its territory, regardless of the Federal treaty. To an application made by the Cherokees for protection by Federal troops against the efforts made by Georgia to remove the Indians by force, Jackson replied "that the President of the United States has no power to protect them against the laws of Georgia." . . .
>
> The form of action decided upon was an original bill in equity, to be filed in the Supreme Court by the Cherokee Nation as an independent state, against the State of Georgia, seeking an injunction to restrain it from executing the laws claimed to be illegal and unconstitutional. Before this suit was begun, however, another case arose in the State of Georgia which presented the same issues. A Cherokee named Corn Tassel had murdered another Indian within the territory occupied by the tribe. He was arrested by the State authorities under one of the recent State laws, tried and sentenced to be hanged. Application was at once made to the United States Supreme Court for a writ of error to the State trial court, on the ground of the illegality of the State laws. The writ, which was issued on December 22, was treated by the Governor of Georgia, Gilmer, with utter disdain. . . . [O]n December 24, 1830, Tassel was executed.

1 CHARLES WARREN, THE SUPREME COURT IN UNITED STATES HISTORY 731-34 (1926).

The Supreme Court dismissed the first Cherokee case, *Cherokee Nation v. Georgia*, 30 U.S. 1 (1831), with a strongly divided Court ruling that the Cherokee Nation could not bring a claim against Georgia under the Supreme Court's original jurisdiction.

The next year, however, another test case reached the Court: *Worcester v. Georgia*, 31 U.S. 515 (1832). The Marshall Court voted 5-1 to declare unconstitutional the laws of Georgia purporting to invalidate the entire Cherokee Nation in *Worcester*, "one of the most powerful [Chief Justice John Marshall] ever delivered." JEAN EDWARD SMITH, JOHN MARSHALL: DEFINER OF A NATION 518 (1996).

2. The Cherokee experiment of establishing a constitutional form of government encouraged other American Indian nations to do the same. The Keweenaw Bay Indian Community of Ojibwe in Michigan, fearing removal to the west, exemplifies this trend:

> In October 1842, shortly after they heard about the removal treaty signed earlier that month, the Keweenaw Methodists reorganized their community. They wrote a code of laws by which to govern themselves. Unfortunately, the

code has been lost. . . . We do, however, have some clues as to its likely contents.

. . . [Peter] Jones wrote a code of laws for the Village of Credit, which may well have provided a model for the one enacted at Keweenaw Bay. Jones's code provided that Credit was to be governed by a head chief, two second chiefs, and a general council. Elected for life, the chiefs had executive and judicial functions. They had wide coercive power, including banishment. The general council, which included all resident householders, acted as a legislature and controlled public property, including all lands, timber, and the fishery.

Peter Jones admired the Cherokees and believed they had set a course for other Indians to follow: Become Christians; develop a modern economy; protect land and resources; restructure tribal government as a sovereign state; defend tribal rights. The actions of Jones at Credit and the Keweenaw leaders at L'Anse parallel these Cherokee initiatives. Jones encouraged his people to hold on to their lands and resources while selectively adapting to "white" culture. He worried about white aggressiveness, especially as he learned of the pressures leading up to Cherokee removal, so he urged Indians of the region to establish an Ojibway state in which they could perpetuate their sovereignty.

Robert Doherty, *Old-Time Origins of Modern Sovereignty: State-Building among the Keweenaw Bay Ojibway, 1832-1854*, 31 AM. INDIAN Q. 165, 173 (2007) (footnotes omitted).

SENECA NATION OF INDIANS CONSTITUTION OF 1848

We, the people of the Seneca Nation of Indians, by virtue of the right inherent in every people, trusting in the justice and necessity of our undertaking, and humbly invoking the blessing of the God of Nations upon our efforts to improve our civil condition, and to secure to our nation the administration of equitable and wholesome laws, do hereby abolish, abrogate, and annul our form of Government by chiefs, because it has failed to answer the purposes for which all governments should be created.

It affords no security in the enjoyment of property, — it provides no laws regulating the institution of marriage, but tolerates polygamy.

It makes no provision for the poor, but leaves the destitute to perish.

It leaves the people dependent on foreign aid for the means of education.

It has no judiciary, nor executive departments. It is an irresponsible, self-constituted aristocracy.

Its powers are absolute and unlimited in assigning away the people's rights, but indefinite and not exercised, in making municipal regulations for their benefit or protection.

We cannot enumerate the evils growing out of a system so defective, not calculate its overpowering weight on the progress of improvement.

But to remedy these defects, we proclaim and establish the following Constitution or Charter, and implore the Governments of the United States and the State of New York to aid in providing us with laws under which progress shall be possible.

Section 1. Our Government shall have a legislature, Executive and Judiciary departments.

Section 2. The Legislative power shall be vested in a council of Eighteen members who shall be termed the Councillors of the Seneca Nation, and who shall be elected annually on the first Tuesday of May in each year; and who shall be apportioned to each Reservation according to its population, two-thirds of whom assembled in regular session and duly organized shall constitute a quorum, and be competent for the transaction of business; but to all bills for the appropriation of public moneys the assent of two-thirds of the members elected shall be necessary in order that the bill should become a law.

Section 3. The executive power shall be vested in a President, whose duty it shall be to preside at all meetings of the council, having only a casting vote therein. . . .

Section 4. The judiciary power shall be vested in three Peace Makers on each Reservation: any two of whom shall have power to hold courts, subject to an appeal to the council, and to such courts of the State of New York as the Legislature thereof shall permit. The jurisdiction['s] forms of process and proceeding in the Peace Makers' Courts shall be the same as in courts of the justices of the Peace of the State of New York, except in the proof of wills, and the settlement of deceased person's estates, in which cases the Peace Makers shall have such power as shall be conferred by law. . . .

Section 6. The power of making Treaties shall be vested in the Council, but no treaty shall be binding upon the Nation until the same shall be submitted to the people, and approved by three-fourths of all the legal voters and also by three-fourths of all the mothers in the Nation. . . .

Section 14. The council shall have power to make any laws not inconsistent with the Constitution of the United States or of the State of New York.

Section 15. All offenses which shall not be punishable by the laws of the United States or of the State of New York, shall be tried and punished in the Peace Makers' Court, or before the council as shall be prescribed by law.

Section 16. The rights of any member of the ancient Confederacy of the Iroquois to the occupancy of our lands and other privileges shall be respected as heretofore; and the council shall pass laws regulating for the admission of any Indian of other tribes and nations to citizenship and adoption into the Seneca Nation of Indians by his or her application for his or herself or family.

Section 17. This Charter may be altered or amended by a council of the people convened for that purpose on three months previous notice, by a vote of two-thirds of the legal voters present at such convention. . . .

Done in a general council of the people held at the Council House on the Cattaraugus Reservation on the 4th of December, A.D. 1848.

NOTES

1. Seneca scholar, professor, and attorney Robert Odawi Porter (now President of the Seneca Nation of Indians) described the circumstances compelling the Seneca people to create a constitutional form of government and annulling the authority of the traditional government:

   The efforts to displace the traditional government of the Seneca Nation were spawned primarily by the perception that the traditional leadership had betrayed the Seneca People. One of the main issues of contention related to whether the treaty annuities received from the federal and state governments should be distributed to the heads of households or kept by the leadership for governmental purposes. It was widely believed, however, that the chiefs were appropriating the annuities for themselves. The second major issue was the acceptance of bribes by the chiefs and their consequent agreement to sell all remaining Seneca lands and to remove all Senecas in New York to Kansas under the 1838 Treaty of Buffalo Creek.

In 1842, the so-called "Compromise Treaty" restored Seneca ownership to the Allegany and Cattaraugus Reservations by agreeing to relinquish claim to the Tonawanda and Buffalo Creek Reservations. Three years later, however, the state of New York, urged on by those Senecas disgusted with the traditional leadership, passed a law that fundamentally altered the Seneca government. The statute provided for new officers of the Seneca government — a clerk, a treasurer, six peacemakers, and two marshals — to be selected from the traditional chiefs. Furthermore, it defined the duties of the existing chiefs and the new officers. Not surprisingly, two factions of chiefs emerged — those in favor of the "Law" and those who were "Anti-Law" — split along the lines of who had been put in power under the "Law." By 1847, a compromise between the factions had emerged that called for no changes to be made to the 1845 Law. Nonetheless, the State acted unilaterally to amend this law and provide for the popular election of the positions of clerk, treasurer, marshal, and peacemaker that had been earlier provided.

Robert B. Porter, *Decolonizing Indigenous Governance: Observations on Restoring Greater Faith and Legitimacy in the Government of the Seneca Nation*, 8 KAN. J.L. & PUB. POL'Y 97, 108 (Winter 1997).

2. Professor Porter also notes that the 1848 constitution eliminated by implication the important governance authorities provided by the Great Law of Peace, altering gender politics in the Nation for decades:

> The 1848 Constitution made no provision for women to vote or hold office. In part, this prohibition was consistent with the Gayanashagowa, in which only men served in the official governing positions. But fundamentally, the elimination of women from the process of selecting the Nation's officials was a radical departure from the practice that had been in place for hundreds of years.
>
> One logical explanation for this transformation was the fact that women were politically non-existent in American society generally. The drafter of the Nation's constitution — a white lawyer named Chester Howe who was the Nation's attorney — undoubtedly introduced contemporary white customs into the text. [Non-Indians] had little sympathy for such Seneca traditions as preserving a strong role for women in the governmental process.
>
> Despite the lack of a formal role, however, it is most likely that women continued to have some kind of influence upon the Nation's political affairs. . . . Nonetheless, women were formally excluded from the Nation's governing process and remained so for over 100 years.

Porter, *Decolonizing Indigenous Governance*, *supra*, at 110-11.

3. Professor Porter also noted how the informal process by which Seneca leaders talked through a problem in private before reaching a public decision survived the adoption of the 1848 constitution for over 100 years:

> Under the 1848 Constitution, the structure of the decision-making process changed dramatically in two important ways. First, the traditional

decision-making model, the "multicameral" structure of disparate political units each having a participatory role in making societal decisions, was replaced with a unicameral decision-making model — the Council. Second, the decision-making principle that unanimity was necessary before formal action could be taken was abandoned.

Despite this change in structure, until recently, there did not appear to be a significant impact on the decision-making process. Through the 1970s, the sixteen members of the Nation Council had an extraordinary record of voting unanimously or near unanimously during roll call votes. The reason for this most likely was due to the continued adherence to the values of consensus politics underlying the Gayanashagowa.

While not required under the Constitution, the Council appears to have conducted almost all of its important work outside of its formal sessions. Pre-meeting caucuses amongst the councillors and discussions between them with political supporters and community members were common for most of the Nation's political history. This suggests that most of the decision-making process occurred outside of Council meetings and inevitably resulted in the actual Council meetings serving as more of a recording process for what had already been decided, rather than as a genuine forum for debate and discussion. In this way, the actual decision-making process within the Nation more closely tracked the procedures under the Gayanashagowa in which various constituencies were consulted with and involved in the process before a decision was rendered.

The fact that the Nation Council voted unanimously or near unanimously for almost 130 years is also evidence that the process established under the Gayanashagowa continued after the adoption of the Constitution.

Porter, *Decolonizing Indigenous Governance, supra*, at 114.

4. New York Indian nations also must confront the assertion of political authority over them by the State of New York, under its so-called Indian Law. In the case of the Seneca Nation, the state legislature enacted the following statute in 1847:

> The government of the Seneca nation by chiefs is abolished. Each nation shall have as officers a clerk and a treasurer. The Tonawanda nation shall have a marshal and three peacemakers. The Seneca nation shall have a marshal, three peacemakers, and eight councilors for each of its reservations, and a president. Each officer of each nation now in office shall continue in office until the expiration of the term for which he was chosen and until his successor shall be chosen.

N.Y. INDIAN LAW §41 (1847) (McKinney 2000). Professor Porter asserts, justifiably so, that laws like this statute are "invalid on their face." Robert B. Porter, *Legalizing, Decolonizing, and Modernizing New York State's Indian Law*, 63 ALB. L. REV. 125, 167 (1999). He added:

> Not only did State officials in the nineteenth century believe that they had authority to establish Haudenosaunee governments, they also believed that they had the authority to direct Haudenosaunee governments — including those that it didn't "create" — to take action. . . . [State] laws focused more on the States' self-interest, such as those laws "authorizing" tribal governments to lease tribal land to individual Indians and non-Indians and to sell tribal natural resources such as timber, oil, natural gas, and stone. A few of

these laws "authorize" tribal government to take action to protect tribal interests, such as granting permission to tribal leaders to sue in State court to protect tribal lands, to regulate residency and trespass by Indians of other tribes and non-Indians, and to establish fire corporations. . . .

There is a logical explanation why laws such as these were enacted. The State has had a long history of colonizing the Haudenosaunee. The enactment of laws such as these in the nineteenth century are classic demonstrations of the State's historic efforts to obtain control over the Haudenosaunee. . . . Thus, for example, "helping" to transform Seneca governance upon the request of a few disgruntled Senecas was a rare opportunity for the State to seize greater influence and control over the Seneca Nation that could potentially lead to future land cessions.

Porter, *Legalizing, Decolonizing, and Modernizing New York State's Indian Law*, *supra*, at 167-69.

5. Early in 1848, before the ratification of the Seneca constitution, a New York court refused to take jurisdiction over private property matters relating to Seneca Indians, and even appeared to adopt a form of comity toward tribal judgments:

We have never applied our doctrines of descent or distribution to their property, nor subjected them to our laws relating to wills, intestacy or administration; nor are they applicable to their state of society. . . .

If our laws have no jurisdiction over their property, our surrogates have no power to grant letters of administration upon it. . . . I am of the opinion that the private property of the Seneca indians is not within the jurisdiction of our laws respecting administration; and that the letters of administration granted by the surrogate to the plaintiff are void. I am also of the opinion that the distribution of indian property according to their customs passes a good title, which our courts will not disturb; and therefore that the defendant has a good title to the horse in question, and must have judgment on the special verdict.

Dole v. Irish, 2 Barb. 638 (N.Y. Sup. Ct. 1848). *See also* Deborah A. Rosen, *Colonization through Law: The Judicial Defense of State Indian Legislation, 1790-1880*, 36 Am. J. Leg. Hist. 26, 49 n. 42 (2004) (collecting similar cases).

PIMA CONSTITUTION OF 1901

We the Indians of the Santan Reservation, in order to promote the general welfare of our Indians do ordain and establish this Constitution and By-laws for the Government of the Santan Reservation:

1. The executive power of the Reservation shall be vested in a Chief who shall be elected by the People; such election shall be subject to approval by the U.S. Indian Agent at Sacaton, Arizona. . . .

2. The legislative power of the said Reservation shall be vested in the Chief and the Council, the latter to consist of eight Councilmen, two Assistant Chiefs, and the Head Chief. . . .

Head Chief

1. The Head Chief shall have power to enforce the Constitution and By-laws. . . .

Council

1. It shall be the duty of the Council of the Santan Reservation to discuss and decide all general questions relating to the Reservation.

2. They shall try all cases or suits referred to them from the Head Chief.

President of the Canal

1. The President of the Canal of the Santan Reservation shall be elected by the people of the said Reservation for a term of four years.

2. It shall be his duty to have the entire control of the Canal, the same to include Dam water distribution and all general contracts thereof. . . .

Constitution

1. The Head Chief shall be empowered to enforce this Constitution and By-law, and he in turn shall be subject to the Council.

2. It shall be the duty of the Head Chief to take all cases unable to be settled by the Council before the U.S. Indian Agent at Sacaton, Arizona.

3. He shall try all cases with the exception of liquor and murder, said cases to be tried by the U.S. Court.

4. Every bill shall before it becomes a law be presented to the U.S. Indian Agent, who, if approving it, shall attach thereto his signature. If the same does not meet with his approval he shall return it to the Chief stating objections to the same.

NOTES

The Pima Indian community of the Gila and Salt River regions — known as the Akimel O'odham — adopted this written constitution in October 1901 authored by a community member educated at the Carlisle Indian School. The constitution is an excellent example of the transition period that many Indian governments encountered in moving from a quasi-judicial government to a policymaking government complete with checks and balances and separation of powers. *See* Frank Russell, *A Pima Constitution*, 16 J. AM. FOLKLORE 222, 222 (1903); WILKINS, DOCUMENTS OF NATIVE AMERICAN POLITICAL DEVELOPMENT, *supra*, at 281.

This constitution had it all, which helped to condemn it to an early political grave. The complicated separation–of–powers structure provided for the "executive power of the Reservation" to be vested with an elected Chief, with the election to be subject to the approval of the United States Indian Agent for Arizona. The constitution vested the "legislative power of the said Reservation" in the Chief *and* the Council, which would consist of eight council members, the head chief, and two assistant chiefs. The Council also served as a court, with the jurisdiction of this "court" subject to the Head Chief's discretion: "[The Council] shall try all cases or suits referred to them by the Head Chief." To confuse the issue further, the constitution provides much later in the document that the Head Chief "shall try all cases with the exception of liquor and murder, said cases to the tried by the U.S. Court." The constitution also provided for what amounts on paper to a completely separate branch of the government — the "President of the Canal," who would have "the entire control of the Canal, the same to include Dam water distribution and all general contracts thereof." The document proved unworkable, largely as a result of conflict between previous leaders and the newly elected leaders, and the federal Indian agent vetoed the constitution. Russell, *A Pima Constitution, supra*, at 226-27.

Ottawa Laws (1850)

Stealing to Kill

1. If any person shall steal and kill an animal, upon conviction thereof the price of said animal shall be by him paid to the owner; and half the price he shall pay into the treasury.

Theft

2. If any person shall steal an article of property, when it is known the stolen article must be taken. If the owner, upon seeing it, shall discover that it has not been injured, he must take it back. If it be injured, the thief shall pay one price and a half of the article. The full price must be paid to the owner, and the half price into the treasury.

Using without Permission

3. If any person shall, without permission, be seen riding another's horse, for every mile he shall pay 25 cents. The price of horse hire shall be paid to the owner, and the balance into the treasury. If oxen shall be thus stolen, twice the price of ox hired shall be paid — one price of the hire shall belong to the owner, and the balance shall be deposited in the treasury.

Indian Horses

4. If an Indian horse shall come into the Ottawa country no attention shall be paid to him. If any person shall, regardlessly, use him, the same that is paid for an Ottawa horse per mile shall be paid for him. All of it shall be deposited in the treasury.

White Person's Beast

5. If a White person's domestic animal shall come into the Ottawa country, he may be caught, to be taken care of. No person shall be permitted to take him far off, nor to work him. The person, on taking up such an animal, shall write descriptions of him, which must be taken to Westport and to Wolftown to be nailed to the doors, in order that the owner may know it, who must bring proof before he can take him, and sign his name to a written receipt. If the owner shall not come, he may be kept for one year, and then sold. For each month three dollars shall be charged for keeping him if in the winter, and in the summer two dollars. For every dollar 25 cents shall go to the treasury. Half a dollar shall be charged for advertising. . . .

Stock Destroying Crops

7.If either pigs, hog, cattle or horses, get through a good fence, and damage the crop, the owner of the said animals shall pay for it. But if the fence be not good, and animals get in, and damage the crop, the owner of the field shall lose [sic] it and shall neither injure nor kill the said animals.

Debts

8.If any person shall owe his fellow Ottawa, having named a time to pay, and does not pay at that time, the creditor may ask him to set another time to pay, who must then name a time, not far off, but within two months. If he shall not then pay, the creditor may do as he shall think best. If he shall wish to take any articles of property; or animals, he may take them.

Revenge

9.If any person, having his property lawfully taken shall become angry, or threaten to take revenge, or shall injure the other's property, he shall see more trouble. Whatever the lawmen shall decide on, so it shall be.

House Breaking

10.If any person sees a house that is locked, he must not open it, unless he has permission from the owner. If he does regardlessly open it, he shall, on conviction, pay two dollars. One half shall belong to the owner of the house, and the other half shall be deposited in the treasury.

Searching

11.If any person shall miss any thing of his property, he may send the lawmen to search in any suspected house — the owner of which shall submit. If he shall refuse he must stand convicted.

Re-Exchanging

12.If any person swops [sic] away his horse, and wishes to re-call his bargain, he can do so by paying $5.00 in cash. All other articles exchanged may be re-exchanged by paying 25 cents on every dollar.

Bad Stud

13.If any person shall own a bad stud which shall a kill a horse or colt, he must pay to the owner the value of that which is killed.

Slander

14.If any person shall injure another by slander, he shall pay to him the amount of injury done to him.

Burning

15.If any person shall set fire to the prairie, and burn another's property, he shall pay for what is burnt.

Whiskey

16. Whiskey on the Ottawa land cannot come. If any person shall send for it, or bring it into the Ottawa country, he who sends, or he who brings shall pay five dollars, and the whiskey shall be destroyed. Any one sending or bringing the second time, shall forfeit all of his annuity money. For the third offence, he shall be delivered over to the United States officers, to try the severity of the White men's laws.

Gambling

17. If any person on the Ottawa land shall be seen at moccasin playing he shall pay two dollars and a half.

Borrowing

18. If any person shall borrow or hire a horse, ox or wagon, the time shall be named for returning them, although he may be done using them the daily price of hire shall continue to be paid. If however sickness, or a severe rain storm should prevent, he may be excused. And also, all other articles borrowed must be returned at the time appointed. If they are not returned at the time, regular pay must then commence. — For every day the borrower must pay 12½ cents.

Residents

19. Whoever shall live on the Ottawa land must be dealt with if he shall violate any of these laws. He shall also be permitted to prosecute others if he shall be in any way wronged.

Law Men

20. When any one shall be elected to be a lawman he must not refuse to serve, unless he shall pay five dollars in order that he may be excused. . . .

Cancelling Debts

22. The Ottawas, known that much evil has hitherto resulted from their running in debt, now resolve to act differently. Those who, from this time forward, shall go in debt, shall be compelled to cancel all such debts at each annuity payment. If any one shall not, at that time, pay his debts in full, any creditor whose claims have not been cancelled, let him come from whereso-ever he may, can then act according to his own wish. He can require the law-men to seize any property whatsoever belonging to the said debtor which he may wish. If he, the creditor, shall not want said property, the lawmen must sell it, and make payment. The debtor must also pay over to the law ten cents for every dollar thus collected, which must be deposited in the treasury. January, 1850.

Taxing

23. For every acre of land cultivated in the Ottawa country ten cents shall be paid. — For older cattle, ten cents per head shall be paid. For horses the same amounts shall be paid which are to be paid for cattle. The above amounts are to

be paid once every year, and to be deposited in the treasury. The time for collecting these payments shall be in the month of September. If any one shall fail to pay at that time, and shall not have paid at the annuity payment, his money shall then be taken. January, 1850.

Poor Tax

24. Every man living on the Ottawa land shall pay annually 12½ cents. This amount is also to be paid in the month called September, and is to be given for the benefit of the poor. — To be deposited in the treasury. January, 1850.

Widows and Orphans

25. On the Ottawa land if a married man shall die, having children, the said children shall own all of his fields, domestic animals, and houses; and the widow shall own every thing else of his personal estate. If the said man shall die without children the woman shall own all. If another person shall take any part of it by force, as a thief is dealt with by the law, so shall that person be dealt with who shall rob the widow and children of what belongs to them. January, 1850.

NOTES

1. The Ottawa Indians of southeastern Michigan and northern Ohio experienced the injustice of removal to Kansas and later to Oklahoma in the mid-nineteenth century. The "Ottawa laws" came in direct response to their changed circumstances:

   > The laws appear to be an attempt to create a bridge between the tribal customs and traditions under which the Ottawas lived in their traditional homelands and their new surroundings in the Great Plains. One law, "Burning," provides, "If any person shall set fire to the prairie, and burn another's property, he shall pay for what is burnt." Another is "Revenge," which states, "If any person, having his property lawfully taken, shall become angry, or threaten to take revenge, or shall injure another's property, he shall see more trouble. Whatever the lawmen shall decide on, so it shall be." According to commentary on the Ottawa laws, the laws of the Ottawas in 1850 were "primarily customary law," but were "evolving in the direction of statute law made in the tribal council . . . as distinguished from laws simply passed on in an oral manner from generation to generation."

   Matthew L. M. Fletcher, *Rethinking Customary Law in Tribal Court Jurisprudence*, 13 MICH. J. RACE & L. 57, 58-59 (2007).

2. The Ohio Ottawas once exerted a great deal of influence in the major trading and military center of Detroit, and they became known as formidable fighters as well as powerful traders. This was part of Pontiac's legacy. But by 1795, after suffering a critical military setback at the Battle of Fallen Timbers (along with several other tribes), the Ohio Ottawas had lost much of this influence and power. They agreed to the Treaty of Greenville that year, which ceded much of Ohio, Indiana, and Illinois to the Americans. For the next several years, the remaining Ohio Ottawas fought against forced

removal, but in 1837, 1838, and 1839 the United States military forced additional removals. In all, about half of the population fled to Canada, to Manitoulin and Walpole, and about half of those attempting the trek to Kansas died along the way. Just a few hundred Ottawas populated the Ottawa reservation in Kansas.

Kansas was an unmitigated disaster for the Ottawas. Prior to removal to Kansas, the economy and lifeways of the Ohio Ottawas revolved around water, fur trade, travel, and sustenance. Kansas had no such abundance of water, forcing the removed Ottawas to adjust to a prairie-based economy. Upon the Ottawas' arrival, unscrupulous whites tricked them into spending their remaining capital on a university for Ottawa Indian children. Sadly, this became known as the Ottawa University fraud. Worse, the reservation lands truly were desolate and virtually useless for purposes of agriculture and livestock. *See* WILLIAM E. UNRAU & H. CRAIG MINER, TRIBAL DISPOSSESSION AND THE OTTAWA INDIAN UNIVERSITY FRAUD (1985).

4. REMOVAL, ALLOTMENT, AND ASSIMILATION: THE DESTABILIZATION OF NASCENT AMERICAN INDIAN GOVERNANCE

The federal government and a host of non-Indians and others influenced the history of most of the Indian nations between the period of time when the Indian nation entered into a treaty relationship and the enactment of the Indian Reorganization Act in 1934, through three main categories of action: (1) removal, (2) allotment, and (3) assimilation. The government did not remove all Indian nations, nor did it allot all Indian nation property, but those pressures existed in every Indian nation at some point. The third category impacted every Indian nation.

In short, prior to 1934 (and generally after), traditional and more modern Indian governments faced enormous pressure to capitulate and cease their functioning. Many Indian nation governments did, for a time, cease to exist in a viable way.

While the following materials demonstrate how Indian governments declined in dramatic ways, Vine Deloria, Jr. reported that the decades leading up the Indian Reorganization Act were the "time of traditional governments":

> Beginning in Oklahoma in the 1890s and then spreading across the country to most of the larger tribes was the movement to get admitted to a federal district court, or even better, the Court of Claims, to press suits for violations of treaties. Traditional councils and chiefs quickly understood the necessity of using the judicial system, and each Congress saw an increasing number of white lawyers lobbying to get bills passed "that would allow the tribes to sue the United States. After 1900 this movement became a deluge as lawyers saw an opportunity to garner large fees for successful prosecution of these cases. Of importance in this movement is that the traditional councils that did not, as a rule, have formal constitutions and by-laws authorized the cases. We can call this period, 1890-1930, the time of traditional governments.

VINE DELORIA, JR., THE INDIAN REORGANIZATION ACT: CONGRESSES AND BILLS ix (2002).

a. Removal

"Removal" involved the physical relocation of Indian nations away from their homelands, usually to an area west of the Mississippi River for eastern nations. The establishment of American Indian tribal governments had begun in order to help Indian nations resist federal government pressure to cede lands via treaty:

> The "civilization" of a portion of these tribes [in the American southeast] embarrassed United States policy in more ways than one. Long-term contact between the southeastern tribes and white traders, missionaries, and government officials created and trained numerous half-breeds. The half-breed men acted as intermediaries between the less sophisticated Indians and the white Americans. Acquiring direct or indirect control of tribal politics, they often determined the outcome of treaty negotiations. . . . Particularly among the Cherokees and Choctaws, they took pride in their achievements and those of their people in assimilating the trappings of civilization. As "founding Fathers," they prized the political and territorial integrity of the newly organized Indian "nations." These interests and convictions gave birth to a fixed determination, embodied in tribal laws and intertribal agreements, that no more cessions of land should be made.

Mary E. Young, *Indian Removal and Land Allotment: The Civilized Tribes and Jacksonian Justice*, 64:1 AM. HIST. REV. 31, 33-34 (1958). Similarly, intermarriage — or simply straight-up education of American Indians — generated more bargaining power in treaty negotiations for Indian nations in other regions as well. *E.g.*, James M. McClurken, *Ottawa Adaptive Strategies to Indian Removal*, 12 MICH. HIST. REV. 29 (1986); James M. McClurken, *Augustin Hamlin, Jr.: Ottawa Identity and the Politics of Persistence*, in BEING AND BECOMING INDIAN: BIOGRAPHICAL STUDIES OF NORTH AMERICAN FRONTIERS 82 (James A. Clifton ed., 1989).

As a result, President Andrew Jackson pushed through the Indian Removal Act in 1930.

> Congress's enactment of the Indian Removal Act of 1830 was the statutory culmination of a concerted effort by many American politicians, particularly from the South and West, to move the eastern Indian tribes west beyond the Mississippi River. Several factors motivated the federal policy, including an emerging pessimism about the ability of Indians to assimilate into the general population, but the most important factor was the desire for Indian lands. In particular, southerners desired Indian lands to farm cotton.
>
> The removal bill authorized the president to negotiate land cession treaties with Indian tribes in which the United States would offer lands west of the Mississippi River in exchange for all of a tribe's territory in the East. The law also authorized the president to guarantee the Indians' title to their new lands in the West, to protect those lands from trespasses or attacks, to pay for improvements that Natives had built on lands they were surrendering, and to pay for the Indians' costs of relocation. Naively, Congress appropriated only $500,000 for the expected expenses of the removal policy.

Matthew L. M. Fletcher, 1 ENCYCLOPEDIA OF UNITED STATES INDIAN LAW AND POLICY 424, 424 (Paul Finkelman & Tim Alan Garrison eds., 2009). Federal removal of Indian tribes to the west created horrific splits in tribal leadership systems:

> [In 1835 after] the Supreme Court decided *Worcester v. Georgia*, . . . two competing [Cherokee] delegations arrived in Washington, D.C. — one headed by Principal Chief John Ross, who was refusing to accept a removal treaty, and the other by dissident leader John Ridge, who wanted the Cherokees to emigrate. In December the Jackson administration signed the Treaty of New Echota with Ridge's group, which represented a small minority of the overall Cherokee population. Despite a vigorous debate as to the validity of the negotiations, the Senate ratified the treaty by one vote in March 1836. Over sixteen thousand of the remaining Cherokees petitioned Congress to stop the removal, but Congress refused. In 1838 President Martin Van Buren sent the U.S. Army to Cherokee territory and directed it to place the Cherokees into internment camps and prepare them for removal. Over the fall and winter of 1838-1839, the Cherokees marched what became known as the Trail of Tears to the northeastern portion of the Indian Territory. Scholars estimate that at least four thousand Cherokees died as a consequence of their roundup and removal.

Id. at 425. Federal Indian removal policy in the northeast and old northwest followed a different pattern. The tribes in the north were more diffuse and land settlement patterns more haphazard than in the south. Tribes in the Great Lakes region often were able to resist removal to the west for the most part, although the partial success of the federal policy split tribes such as the Oneidas, Ottawas, and Potawatomis and caused many Indians to flee to Canada to avoid removal. In general, the tribes that moved west to Kansas, Oklahoma, and elsewhere often found themselves on land that was ill suited to their way of life. Some tribal communities were able to avoid removal, especially those that lived in areas that were unsuited to American-style farming, such as the Florida, Minnesota, and Wisconsin wetlands and the lands north of the freeze line in Michigan.

b. Allotment

The second federal policy — allotment — involved the transformation of Indian nation property holdings into "allotments," for the express purpose of breaking down tribal governments and assimilating American Indian people into the American nation. Allotment, which has political origins in the seventeenth century, came into prominence in 1853 when Commissioner of Indian Affairs George Manypenny announced that the Department of Interior's policy in relation to further Indian treaties was to negotiate for the allotment of Indian lands. Congress adopted this as express national policy in the 1887 General Allotment Act.

Generally speaking, since there are always exceptions, "allotment" consists first of either a treaty or an act of Congress authorizing the allotment of an Indian nation's land base. Next, the Secretary of Interior promulgates a plan to divide the land base, often a reservation, into "allotted" lands and "surplus" lands. Federal agents identify a chunk of the land base and inform Indian heads of household to select 80, 160, or some other number of acres, depending on the plan. Once the heads of household select their allotment, the land agent delivers to them a certificate stating that the Indian may possess the land for farming or grazing purposes for a certain period of years, often 25 — a trust period in which the land remains in federal government ownership, may not be taxed by local governments, and may not be sold or alienated by the Indian certificate holder. Once the trust period expires, the land agent issues a fee patent, and the Indian owns the land in fee simple. The Indian may then sell the land, and the state and local governments may tax it.

The land agent labels the remainder of the land base as "surplus," announces a public sale of the land in accordance with federal homesteading or other statutes, and divides the proceeds among the Indians, after assessing a healthy administrative fee.

The experience of the Stockbridge-Munsee Indian community during its debate over allotment in the 1830s demonstrates how American Indian communities could disintegrate over the question, even before the community was allotted:

> During the 1830's the Stockbridge-Munsee were beset by an internal conflict that would in time mirror the national debate over the Indian question; namely, would Indians seek a separate existence from white American society or would they opt for assimilation with the prevailing culture? By and large, federal efforts to promote assimilation involved the Indians' removal from their tribal setting through individual allotments of land to the heads of each Indian family. Supporters of allotment assumed that if Native Americans would accept private ownership of the land as the white man had, and adopt all the attendant legalities and cultural notions it implied (such as title and deed, wealth and status), they would be well on the road to civilization. . . .
>
> The debate within the Stockbridge-Munsee tribe split the tribe into two camps: the Citizen Party, which sought U.S. citizenship and supported individual allotment of lands; and the Indian Party, which desired to retain both communal ownership of land and federal annuities. To openly display their philosophies, Citizen Party members sought to dress like their white neighbors while Indian Party members continued to cloak themselves in the traditional blanket.
>
> This split proved far more damaging than simply a difference over the tribe's style of clothing. Buoyed by the desires of the Citizen Party, Congress in 1843 ordered the allotment of all Stockbridge-Munsee lands and offered citizenship to the entire tribe. The Citizen Party eagerly accepted these terms and was promised individual tracts of Stockbridge-Munsee land. The Indian Party, led by John W. Quinney, rejected the terms, forcing Congress to repeal it and order a new enrollment to partition lands to better represent the two factions. To foster a solution, Congress passed an amendment to the treaty in 1849 that offered the Indian Party lands west of the Mississippi River and a one-time payment of $25,000 for resettlement and improvement of those lands if the tribe would leave the newly created state of Wisconsin. Unfortunately, no land was forthcoming, although some Stockbridge delegates were sent west to scout for it. As the Stockbridge-Munsee Community tells the story: "Thus matters continued, government neglecting to provide us with lands; and the Stockbridge nation having, on the faith of the treaty, surrendered title to some of the most valuable lands in Wisconsin at a moderate compensation, were unable to move away, simply because they knew not whither to go."

John C. Savagian, *The Tribal Reorganization of the Stockbridge-Munsee: Essential Conditions in the Re-Creation of a Native American Community*, 77:1 Wis. Mag. Hist. 39, 42-43 (1993).

Angelique EagleWoman offers more details about the allotment process as envisioned by the 1887 statute:

> Under the Dawes Act, the federal policy focused on breaking up the tribal land base from community property and territories to individual allotments as a means to assimilate tribal members to the lifestyle of Euro-American farmers. Specifically, the Allotment Act provided for 160 acres to be apportioned to each head of household and any other lands after this apportionment within the control of the Tribes was regarded as "surplus" which the federal government sold to homesteaders.
>
>   Additionally, the Allotment Act held that the individual allotments were in a federal trust status for twenty-five years preventing the sale of the lands. The stated purpose for the trust period was to familiarize tribal members with the European concept of land ownership. The subsequent amendments by the Burke Act of 1906 allowed for allottees to be declared "competent" by area BIA officials for the alienation of lands formerly held in trust status. A second wave of dispossession occurred as a result of the 1906 Burke Act passed by Congress providing for competency hearings to determine an Indian fit for the purpose of selling lands to an interested buyer.

Angelique A. EagleWoman, *The Philosophy of Colonization Underlying Taxation Imposed upon Tribal Nations within the United States*, 43 Tulsa L. Rev. 43, 51 (2007). "Under the Burke Act of 1906, Indians whom the Secretary of Interior deemed were 'competent' could obtain patents in fee for their allotments. Competency commissions roamed Indian Country between 1909 and 1920, declaring individuals competent and eliminating the trust protections on their allotments." Barbara Leibhardt, *Allotment Policy in an Incongruous Legal System: The Yakima Indian Nation as a Case Study, 1887-1934*, 65:4 Agric. Hist. 78, 99 (1991).

Justice Blackmun noted the most obvious impact of allotment on Indian country:

> The 138 million acres held exclusively by Indians in 1887 when the General Allotment Act was passed had been reduced to 52 million acres by 1934. *See* 2 F. Prucha, The Great Father 896 (1984). John Collier testified before Congress that nearly half of the lands remaining in Indian hands were desert or semidesert, and that 100,000 Indians were "totally landless as a result of allotment." *Hearings on H.R. 7902 before the House Committee on Indian Affairs*, 73d Cong., 2d Sess., 17 (1934); *see also* D. Otis, The Dawes Act and the Allotment of Indian Lands 124-155 (Prucha ed. 1973) (discussing results of the allotments by 1900).

Hagen v. Utah, 510 U.S. 399, 425 n. 5 (1994) (Blackmun, J., dissenting). Quoting Felix S. Cohen's *Handbook of Federal Indian Law* (1942), he added:

> "The theory of assimilation was used to justify the [allotment] legislation as beneficial to Indians. Proponents of assimilation policies maintained that if Indians adopted the habits of civilized life they would need less land, and the surplus would be available for white settlers. The taking of these lands was justified as necessary for the progress of civilization as a whole." Cohen 128.

Id. at 425 n. 4 (Blackmun, J., dissenting). Another commentator noted that the allotment policy worked merely to redistribute wealth from Indian people to non-Indian people:

> Thus the world created by federal allotment laws, beginning with the Dawes Act, was not one peopled by agrarian, or even economically self- sufficient Indian peoples. The Dawes Act and its progeny existed in a legal system that consistently channeled resources toward those who would develop them for individual, and therefore positing the market's benevolent "invisible hand" public good. Here, political power and economic capital were what mattered, and Indian peoples collectively had little of either. To Indians, as the Yakima example shows, the system was doubly unfair because it robbed them of their lands and resources despite the guarantees they believed had been written into their treaties with the United States. "No person should be prohibited from his food by law," Louis Mann wrote in 1916. To Yakima, allotment laws in particular, and U.S. law in general, were white people's laws, not the laws of a civilized people.

Leibhardt, *Allotment Policy in an Incongruous Legal System, supra,* at 103.

The impact on American Indian governance was more insidious, but no less destabilizing. Charles Wilkinson wrote:

> Just as the proprietary side of tribes was hamstrung by allotment, so too was the governmental capacity of tribes. Traditional governance came naturally in reasonably tight-knit cohesive societies. Evolution into more elaborate forms of government would have occurred most smoothly on reservations composed solely of tribal Indians and tribal land. When the reservations were opened, true traditional governments were essentially doomed in most tribes, and the authority of any form of tribal rule was undermined.

CHARLES F. WILKINSON, AMERICAN INDIANS, TIME, AND THE LAW 20-21 (1987).

The changed demographics of Indian country, as well as the dramatic reduction in American Indian land ownership, created a virtual void in Indian country governance:

> The great influx of non-Indian settlers, coupled with the loss of communal lands and the attendant yoke of federal support of these policies, simply erad- icated much of the tribes' ability to govern. In the resulting void, the Bureau of Indian Affairs and Christian missionaries became the true power brokers and the de facto governing forces.

FRANK POMMERSHEIM, BRAID OF FEATHERS 21 (1995).

American Indian governance suffered further with the dramatic changes to Indian cultures resulting from allotment:

> The blow was less economic than psychological and even spiritual. A way of life had been smashed; a value system destroyed. Indian poverty, ignorance and ill health were the results. The admired order and the sense of community often observed in early Indian communities were replaced by the easily caricatured features of rootless, shiftless, drunken outcasts, so familiar to the reader of early twentieth-century newspapers.

WILCOMB E. WASHBURN, RED MAN'S LAND—WHITE MAN'S LAW 75-76 (1971).

c. Assimilation

Allotment contributed greatly to a process already in full swing: the policy of assimilation.

Assimilation has taken a multitude of forms in federal and state official policy and law, but its purpose has been virtually singular; in the words of the most (in)famous director of an American Indian boarding school, Capt. Richard Pratt: "To kill the Indians to save the man."

A key component of assimilation policies was the militarization of American Indian boarding schools under the administration of President Grant:

> The first efforts by non-Indians to formally educate American Indians — by the Jesuits in Florida during the 16th century — attempted to " 'Christianize' and 'civilize' the heathen." . . . President Washington articulated a policy favoring the acculturation or assimilation of American Indians, cheaper than declaring war on them. . . . Over 150 Indian treaties included provisions relating to Indian education. *See* COHEN'S HANDBOOK OF FEDERAL INDIAN LAW §22.03[1][a], at 1356 (2005 ed.). In 1819, Congress established a fund — later known as the "civilization fund" — usually distributed to missionary societies for the purpose of transforming American Indians from "hunters to agriculturalists." . . .
>
> Tribal treaty negotiators who hoped to provide for their children a means to learn English as a second language or to learn a trade did not realize that they had inadvertently negotiated for the kidnapping of their children by American government and military officials, the abuse of their children by educators and missionaries, and the ruinous undermining of their cultures and religions. Captain Richard H. Pratt, superintendent of the famed Carlisle Indian School from 1879 to 1904, is best known for his infamous statement that embodies American Indian education policy in the late 19th century: "A great general has said that the only good Indian is a dead one. . . . In a sense, I agree with the sentiment, but only in this: that all the Indian there is in the race should be dead. *Kill the Indian in him, to save the man.*" Richard H. Pratt, *The Advantages of Mingling Indians with Whites* (1892). . . . Meanwhile, "[i]n 1892 and 1904, federal regulations outlawed the practice of tribal religions entirely, and punished Indian practitioners by either confinement in agency prisons or by withholding rations." . . .
>
> American policymakers harshly criticized the lifestyles of tribal Indians in the late 19th century and sought to eliminate any trace of Indian culture and religion in Indian children. In 1889, General Thomas J. Morgan, Commissioner of Indian Affairs, recommended that Indian children being educated in grammar schools should be structured in such as a way as to eliminate "the irregularities of camp life, which is the type of all tribal life, [to force Indian youth to] give way to the methodical regularity of daily routine." Thomas J. Morgan, *Supplemental Report on Indian Education* (1889). . . . Morgan also recommended that the United States withhold rations, use Indian police, and send United States soldiers to compel Indian children to attend school, . . . a recommendation endorsed by Congress explicitly in 1893 [25 U.S.C. §283].

Brief of *Amicus Curiae* American Indian Studies Professors Dr. Suzanne L. Cross and Dr. K. Tsianina Lomawaima at 1-7, *A.A. ex rel. Betenbaugh v. Needville Indep. Sch. Dist.*, 611 F.3d 248 (5th Cir.) (No. 09-20091).[*]

---

[*]*Disclosure:* The author of this book participated in this case as the lead author of the brief.

The assimilative programming of American Indian children over generations undermined the retention of tribal culture and traditions, not to mention Indian languages, where so much of the tribal law originated.

Federal statutes dating back to at least 1883 have been directly tied to the assimilation of not just Indian people, but tribal governments themselves, into mainstream American policy:

> The Major Crimes Act was one of the first major intrusions of federal law into Indian country. Passed by Congress in 1885, the Major Crimes Act served as the first suggestions that the federal government would exercise authority over crimes that happened in Indian country. . . . The practical impact of the Major Crimes Act, however, is that fewer tribes pursue prosecution of crimes such as murder and rape. Instead of a rape case being handled within the community using the laws, beliefs, and traditions of indigenous people, rape cases have become the domain of the federal government.
>
> Passed in 1953, P.L. 280 served to transfer criminal jurisdiction in certain states from the federal government to the state government. Neither the states nor the tribes, however, consented to this arrangement and states were not provided with any additional resources with which to enforce crimes in Indian country. Instead, this national legislation resulted in what Carole Goldberg at UCLA has called a sense of "lawlessness" in some local communities. . . . For all practical purposes, though, the tribal governments in P.L. 280 states have historically been at a distinct disadvantage when it comes to crime control.

Sarah Deer, *Sovereignty of the Soul: Exploring the Intersection of Rape Law Reform and Federal Indian Law*, 38 SUFFOLK U. L. REV. 455, 460-61 (2005).

5. THE INDIAN REORGANIZATION ACT AS THE ORGANIC DOCUMENT OF MODERN TRIBAL GOVERNANCE

The experience of other Indian nations did not include indigenous, organic political and legal development, but instead involved federal government intervention, which took various forms. A large number, if not the majority, of modern American Indian tribal governments tie their functional origins to the Indian Reorganization Act (IRA), passed by Congress in 1934. The IRA instructed the Secretary of Interior to hold what would become known as Secretarial elections in which the adult citizenry of a given Indian nation would vote upon whether to "reorganize" under the terms of the act—to create a constitutional form of republican government. For the first time, Congress gave Indian nations a say in whether a federal statute would apply to them, as opposed to dictating federal mandates to Indian nations.

TRIBAL SELF-GOVERNMENT AND THE
INDIAN REORGANIZATION ACT OF **1934**

70 Mich. L. Rev. 955, 960-68, 970-72 (1972)

During the period preceding the enactment of the IRA there was some recognition that Indians were living in grinding poverty, that Indian health and education were in an abominable state, and that government policies were not working. As early as 1881 books like Helen Hunt Jackson's crusading

A Century of Dishonor had exposed these conditions to public view and made people aware of broken treaties and other unfulfilled promises. But it was not until publication of the Meriam Report that a movement toward change began.

The Report is an extremely detailed document, describing and analyzing the entire spectrum of Indian life and the problems of governmental administration of Indian affairs. It brought these problems into sharp focus, and in so doing presaged more than any other work the enactment of the IRA six years later.

The basic position taken by the Meriam staff was that

[t]he object of work with or for the Indians is to fit them either to merge into the social and economic life of the prevailing civilization as developed by the whites or to live in the presence of that civilization at least in accordance with a minimum standard of health and decency.

If this goal were accomplished, as the staff saw it, there would be no need for further governmental supervision. This position did not imply automatic cultural assimilation, however. The authors of the Report recognized explicitly that many Indians wished to maintain a separate cultural identity, although they also admitted this would be difficult in so far as the economic underpinnings of the old culture had been destroyed. . . .

II. The Indian Reorganization Act of 1934

A. A Brief Legislative History

The Wheeler-Howard Bill, as the originally proposed legislation was known, was entitled an act "[t]o grant to Indians living under Federal tutelage the freedom to organize for purposes of local self-government and economic enterprise." The bill represented a significant change in the approach to Indian legislation. . . .

B. The Act's Objectives: An Analytical Look behind the Scenes

The thrust of the IRA can be gathered from its operative provisions. Every section in some way affects tribal self-government, although obviously not all are equally relevant to this discussion.

Section 1 of the IRA ended the policy of allotment: "No land of any Indian reservation . . . shall be allotted in severalty to any Indian." This provision, while not going directly to self-government, was a key factor in making it possible; it alone assures the Act's historical significance.

Section 4 related to alienation. In general, it prohibited any transfer of Indian land or shares in the assets of tribal corporations otherwise than to the tribe, except that the Secretary could authorize voluntary exchanges of such lands or interests of equal value when it would be "expedient and beneficial for or compatible with the proper consolidation of Indian lands." This provision has had the desirable effect of further strengthening the tribal land base and tribal control over it.

Section 10 set up a revolving fund from which the Secretary of Interior could make loans to chartered corporations for purposes of economic development. This reversed an earlier policy by which loans were made to individual

Indians and under which there had been problems in repayment. Under the IRA, loans are made only to the tribes, with individual loans being arranged between the tribe and the individual. Also, section 11 appropriated a small amount of funds to be used for loans to Indians for tuition payment and other expenses in "recognized vocational and trade schools" and in high schools and colleges.

Section 18 provided that the Act would not apply to any reservation wherein a majority of the adult Indians voted against its application at a special election to be held within one year after the Act's approval. This section marked a significant change in approach to Indian legislation. Formerly, legislation had been either special, applying by its terms to only one tribe or group of tribes, or general, applying to all Indians without consideration of tribal differences.

Through section 18, the IRA became a type of enabling act, giving each tribe the opportunity to determine for itself whether it wanted to come under the Act. There was, however, a major flaw in the approach: a tribe could hold the election only once. If it voted against application, it did not have the option of later reconsideration.

The essence of the IRA lay in those provisions relating directly to tribal organization, viz., sections 16 and 17. The former provided:

> Any Indian tribe, or tribes, residing on the same reservation, shall have the right to organize for its common welfare, and may adopt an appropriate constitution and by-laws. . . . [Procedure is then established for ratification by members and approval by the Secretary of Interior].
>
> In addition to all powers vested in any tribe or tribal council by existing law, the constitution adopted by said tribe shall also vest in such tribe or its tribal council the following rights and powers: To employ legal counsel, the choice of counsel and fixing of fees to be subject to the approval of the Secretary of the Interior; to prevent the sale, disposition, lease, or encumbrance of tribal lands, interests in lands, or other tribal assets without the consent of the tribe; and to negotiate with the Federal, State, and local governments. . . .

Section 17 first provided for issuance of a charter of incorporation to a tribe and established procedures for petition and ratification. It continued:

> Such charter may convey to the incorporated tribe the power to purchase, take by gift, or bequest, or otherwise, own, hold, manage, operate, and dispose of property of every description, real and personal, including the power to purchase restricted Indian lands and to issue in exchange therefor interests in corporate property, and such further powers as may be incidental to the conduct of corporate business, not inconsistent with law; but no authority shall be granted to sell, mortgage, or lease for a period exceeding ten years any of the land included in the limits of the reservation. Any charter so issued shall not be revoked or surrendered except by Act of Congress.

The purpose of adopting a charter is different than that of adopting a constitution, the charter being oriented more toward business than toward governmental organization.

Perhaps the prime objective of the IRA, which was crucial to any effective establishment of self-government, was elimination of the "absolutist" executive discretion previously exercised by the Interior Department and the Office of Indian Affairs. During the hearings, Commissioner of Indian Affairs John Collier presented to the House Committee examples which revealed the vastness of this discretionary power. Not only had administrative power grown beyond control, but its exercise and the effects of its exercise also changed from year to year, depending on the attitude or whim of a given commissioner. Further, this discretionary power was also exercised by local agency superintendents, a situation that led Senator Wheeler to refer to the local agent as "a czar." So all-encompassing was this power that "the Department [had] absolute discretionary powers over all organized expressions of the Indians. . . . [T]ribal councils exist[ed] by [the Department's] sufferance and [had] no authority except as . . . granted by the Department." Consequently, the IRA sought to eliminate this boundless discretion or at least place a damper on its exercise. "This bill . . . seeks to get away from the bureaucratic control of the Indian Department, and it seeks further to give the Indians the control of their own affairs. . . ."

It was not entirely clear, however, precisely what changes were to be made. Commissioner Collier was the moving force behind the new administrative approach. Of course, as Commissioner, he already possessed broad powers to move the Indian Office in the desired direction. Apparently, however, he was one of that rare breed of administrators who seek actively to undermine their own powers through legislation. To be sure, the Office would not become powerless under the Act. Subsequent developments have shown that it can and will exercise much power, often to the detriment of its constituency. . . .

It is, of course, not essential that a tribe or any group of people have a written constitution before they can govern themselves. The right to self-government exists as well in tribes whose organizational structure may have been based on ancient custom or tradition. Certainly all the tribes were not politically developed to the same degree, and therefore some were less able than others to put into practice their inherent governmental powers. Nonetheless, these powers existed in all the tribes.

Indian tribes seem also to have been regarded as corporate bodies for some purposes prior to enactment of the IRA. In at least one instance there had been specific incorporation by legislative act. Further, if the term "corporation" is used in the broader sense of designating an identifiable group of people to whom a legal personality is affixed, then it becomes dear that tribes have often been assigned a corporate status. For example, there were federal statutes authorizing suits by injured persons against tribes whose members had committed various depredations. Under these statutes liability was tribal only; no liability was imposed on individual members. The distinction between the tribe and its members had also been emphasized in cases involving property rights and other common-law legal rights.

The question of tribal capacity to sue and be sued, in the absence of statutory authority, also appeared occasionally. Where a tribe was recognized as a distinct political community or even as a political subdivision, it was immune from suit unless it had consented thereto, following the general rule of sovereign immunity. Moreover, when the tribe was immune, it was held that tribal officers could not be sued on tribal obligations.

Whether a tribe could bring suit without statutory authorization was a more difficult question, although probably answered in the affirmative. Cases in which tribes were parties to the suit have been entertained by the courts, apparently without any question of standing or capacity being raised. In any case, the objectives of such a suit could have been obtained through a representative suit brought by individual tribal members.

Thus, the powers and capacities "granted" to Indian tribes by the IRA had, in large part, previously existed. This fact has been recognized by those who have closely examined the Act. Commentators have said, for example, that "the constitutions [adopted pursuant to the IRA] add to, but do not detract, from, the powers of an Indian tribe. . . ." But precisely what was added? The answer is that the IRA apparently added nothing in terms of specific substantive powers. From this, however, it does not follow that the IRA accomplished nothing. As previously noted, the mere fact that Congress was willing, with the blessing of the Interior Department and the Indian Office, to enact such a statute signified an abrupt change in policy. Because of this policy change the tribes were able, at least temporarily, to coordinate effectively their organizational efforts and to use these powers for their benefit.

Furthermore, the IRA can be said to have had a stabilizing effect on tribal powers. This effect is more significant in light of the erosion of these powers that had taken place during the previous century. The IRA reaffirmed the principles of tribal self-government. Better organizational machinery could now be worked out through proper definition or limitation of tribal powers in the constitutions and charters. Finally, the mere act of organizing to write an organic instrument in the form of a constitution may have been a stimulus for more effective government, especially if the tribes could be assured that their efforts would not be undermined by arbitrary administrative action.

NOTES

1. After enactment of the IRA, some senators sought an opinion on the meaning of Section 16's provision that Indian tribal government authority includes whatever is incorporated into a tribal constitution and bylaws, and "all powers vested in any Indian tribes or tribal council by existing law." Nathan Margold, the Solicitor of the Department of Interior, signed the resulting document, "The Powers of Indian Tribes," which likely was written by Felix S. Cohen. Here is the conclusion of the memorandum:

> I conclude that under Section 16 of the Wheeler-Howard Act (48 Stat. 984) the "powers vested in any Indian tribe or tribal council by existing law," are those powers of local self-government which have never been terminated by law or waived by treaty, and that chief among these powers are the following:
>
> 1. The power to adopt a form of government, to create various offices and to prescribe the duties thereof, to provide for the manner of election and removal of tribal officers, to prescribe the procedure of the tribal council and subordinate committees or councils, to provide for the salaries or expenses of tribal officers and other expenses of public business, and, in general, to prescribe the forms through which the will of the tribe is to be executed.

2. To define the conditions of membership within the tribe, to prescribe rules for adoption, to classify the members of the tribe, and to grant or withhold the right of suffrage in all matters save those as to which voting qualifications are specifically defined by the Wheeler-Howard Act (that is, the referendum on the act, and votes on acceptance, modification, or revocation of constitution, bylaws, or charter), and to make all other necessary rules and regulations governing the membership of the tribe so far as may be consistent with existing acts of Congress governing the enrollment and property rights of members.

3. To regulate the domestic relations of its members by prescribing rules and regulations concerning marriage, divorce, legitimacy, adoption, the care of dependents, and the punishment of offenses against the marriage relationship, to appoint guardians for minors and mental incompetents, and to issue marriage licenses and decrees of divorce, adopting such State laws as seem advisable or establishing separate tribal laws.

4. To prescribe rules of inheritance with respect to all personal property and all interests in real property other than regular allotments of land.

5. To levy dues, fees, or taxes upon the members of the tribe and upon nonmembers residing or doing any business of any sort within the reservation, so far as may be consistent with the power of the Commissioner of Indian Affairs over licensed traders.

6. To remove or to exclude from the limits of the reservation nonmembers of the tribe, excepting authorized Government officials and other persons now occupying reservation lands under lawful authority, and to prescribe appropriate rules and regulations governing such removal and exclusion, and governing the conditions under which nonmembers of the tribe may come upon tribal land or have dealings with tribal members, providing such acts are consistent with Federal laws governing trade with the Indian tribes.

7. To regulate the use and disposition of all property within the jurisdiction of the tribe and to make public expenditures for the benefit of the tribe out of tribal funds where legal title to such funds lies in the tribe.

8. To administer justice with respect to all disputes and offenses of or among the members of the tribe, other than the ten major crimes reserved to the Federal courts.

9. To prescribe the duties and to regulate the conduct of Federal employees, but only insofar as such powers of supervision may be expressly delegated by the Interior Department.

It must be noted that these conclusions are advanced on the basis of general legislation and judicial decisions of general import and are subject to modification with respect to particular tribes in the light of particular powers granted, or particular restrictions imposed, by special treaties or by special legislation. With this qualification the conclusions advanced are intended to apply to all Indian tribes recognized now or hereafter by the legislative or the executive branch of the Federal Government.

The Powers of Indian Tribes, 1 U.S. DEPARTMENT OF THE INTERIOR, OPINIONS OF THE SOLICITOR OF THE DEPARTMENT OF THE INTERIOR RELATING TO INDIAN AFFAIRS, 1917-1974, at 445, 476-77 (Oct. 25, 1934) (1979).

2. John Collier, the Indian Commissioner who was the primary visionary and promoter of the Wheeler-Howard Act, declared soon after the introduction of the bill in February 1934 that he would host

congresses in various locations in the West to consult with Indian tribes on his legislative proposals. Beginning in early March in Rapid City, South Dakota, with a large meeting of the Northern Plains tribes, the bureau then moved to Chemawa and then to New Mexico, Arizona, and California conducting Collier's meetings, encountering increasing Indian opposition as the consultations continued. In late March Collier held three meetings in Oklahoma, where opposition was very strong against his ideas because dissident groups of Indians had interpreted his proposals as advocating communism and segregation. . . .

The congresses reveal that most Indians had adjusted to the allotment act, and the selfishness that Senator Henry Dawes believed an essential part of civilized life had taken hold in many tribes so that they were reluctant to pool their resources and lands and try to revive the old tribal ways. Many Indian spokesmen made clear to Collier that while they wanted education for their children and better medical care, they were not prepared to welcome mixed bloods back into the tribal community in those instances in which they had sold their lands and tried to adjust to life away from the reservation.

DELORIA, THE INDIAN REORGANIZATION ACT, *supra*, at vii-viii.

Deloria's study of the IRA congresses elucidates several key ideas. First, American Indian views are hardly uniform. Some American Indian nations, particularly those that became subject to allotment prior to the 1887 General Allotment Act, had embraced private land ownership in the context of allotment. Second, Indian people generally mistrusted the reform concepts introduced by Collier and the Bureau of Indian Affairs, none of which had any input from Indian people.

6. ADMINISTRATIVE ASSAULTS ON TRIBAL GOVERNANCE DURING THE TERMINATION ERA

The result of the Red Scare politics of the late 1940s and early 1950s in Indian affairs was House Concurrent Resolution 108, which stated that the policy of Congress was to terminate the relationship between Indian nations and the federal government wherever feasible.

"Termination" consisted of congressional identification, with assistance by federal bureaucrats and by constituents with a financial stake in opposing tribal sovereignty, of Indian nations whose fortunes had improved under the IRA sufficiently for Congress to assert that they were no longer in need of federal assistance. The Secretary prepared a plan, most of which involved auctioning off property owned by American Indian nations to the highest bidder, and eliminating the tribal government altogether. The Secretary then would distribute the proceeds, after taking a healthy cut for administrative costs, per capita to the tribal citizenry.

Congress's "termination" of hundreds of Indian nations had a devastating impact on the American Indian nations affected directly by termination:

Although devastating to the tribes that were actually terminated, the policies of termination affected all Indian tribes in a number of ways. . . . Many educational programs and services were transferred from the federal government to the states. Indian health responsibility was transferred from the BIA to the

Department of Health, Education and Welfare. The federal government implemented relocation programs to encourage Indian migration from their reservations to the cities, with the hope that Indian people would simply disappear. In fact, many eventually returned to their homeland. Of those that stayed in the cities, many lived in cultural isolation and poverty, their identity taken. . . .

The government's attempts to ostensibly "free" Indian people from the bondage of federal supervision via termination policies did not go unopposed. Indians organized against the legislative termination of tribalism, most visibly in the June 1961 American Indian Chicago Conference. Moreover, state governments realized the difficulty of assuming many of the responsibilities of the federal government in Indian country.

By 1958, termination without tribal consent, as it had been practiced, was viewed unfavorably. Under the Kennedy administration, the termination policy was "abandon[ed] in practice." Even so, many elder tribal leaders today still remember the days of termination, and the policy has left an indelible mark on the psyche of Indian people.

John Fredericks III, *America's First Nations: The Origins, History and Future of American Indian Sovereignty*, 7 J.L. & Pol'y 347, 377-79 (1999).

Even without express congressional termination, federal bureaucrats tossed out the progressive policies of the 1930s and early 1940s, and instituted oppressive administrative policies toward Indian communities.

THE EROSION OF INDIAN RIGHTS, 1950-1953: A CASE STUDY IN BUREAUCRACY

Felix S. Cohen, 62 Yale L.J. 348, 353-56, 360-61, 367-71, 380 (1953)

From 1930 to 1950, the Bureau respected the right of Indians to hold their own elections and to select their own representatives and attorneys. Two or three slips from this standard may be found in this 20 year period, but the whole direction of Indian administration was towards increasing freedom. . . .

Freedom of Elections

. . .

Use of federal funds. A notable instance of the use of federal funds to influence local Indian elections occurred on the Blackfeet Reservation during the June, 1950, tribal election. Thirty-six pages of mimeographed materials attacking certain candidates for local tribal office, charging them with various "criminal" and "illegal" acts (none of which were ever prosecuted and most of which were later shown never to have occurred) were prepared by Government employees at Government expense on Government paper and Government mimeograph machines. Hundreds of copies of this campaign literature were circulated by Government employees on the reservation during the two weeks before the election. . . .

Such use of federal funds to influence local Indian elections quickly became accepted Departmental practice after June, 1950. In the Blackfeet referendum election of May, 1952, and the Choctaw referendum election of July, 1952, letters from Interior officials on the merits of referendum issues (as seen by the Indian Bureau) were distributed at Government expense with a view to influencing voters. . . .

Direct interference. Similarly, direct interference with local elections for local offices has increased in frequency during the past three years. When the Blackfeet Tribe held a referendum election on May 9, 1952, on a proposed amendment to the tribal constitution, the Interior Department ran a rival election, managed by Indian Bureau employees; called out its special Bureau police force; closed down one or more tribal polling places; seized tribal funds, without tribal consent, to pay some of the expenses of the Bureau election (notwithstanding Secretary Chapman's assurance that no such action was contemplated); and, in order to validate its own election results, tried to strike more than 1,000 Blackfeet names from the list of eligible voters. This last move was eventually held by the Solicitor of the Interior Department to be illegal, and so the Bureau's election results were declared invalid. But the Bureau continues to insist that it has the right to run future tribal elections even where, as in the Blackfeet case, the tribal constitution provides that all local elections are to be supervised by the Indians themselves.

At San Ildefonso Pueblo, in New Mexico, the Indian Bureau seized control of valuable lands and proceeded to dispose of the resources of the Pueblo without statutory authority, on the pretext that the Pueblo had failed to elect a Governor. In fact, the elected Governor of the Pueblo is recognized by all the other Pueblos, by the public, and by all of the members of the Pueblo except for a few beneficiaries of the Bureau's illegal acts. . . .

Freedom of Speech

The right to speak one's mind freely is so widely taken for granted in American life that it is inconceivable to most of us that anybody could have his bank accounts impounded as a penalty for criticizing the operations of a government bureau. Yet when the Oglala Sioux Tribe on September 28, 1950, petitioned Congress to cut wasteful expenditures of the Indian Bureau in its so-called "extension service" in South Dakota, the Indians were advised that $140,000 of credit funds allocated to the tribe several months earlier would be "frozen" until the tribe withdrew its criticisms. Of course, there was no legal authority for any such action, any more than there would be for the freezing of the bank account of a non-Indian. But the Indian funds were in the possession of federal officials, and possession is at least nine points of the law. Even a non-Indian confronted by his banker with a "freeze order" from the Federal Reserve Board based upon a report by the Post Office Department and the Federal Bureau of Investigation that the depositor was engaged in subversive activities might have a hard time fighting his case through the courts with the world's largest law office on the other side of the case. Indians who are unable to employ counsel of their own choosing face even tougher odds in such a situation. . . .

Freedom in Personal Life

The extent to which the Bureau of Indian Affairs now seems prepared to supervise the intimate details of an Indian's personal life is indicated by an incident reported to the Senate Appropriations Committee on May 7, 1952:

> Last week a tribal policeman on the Blackfeet Reservation reported that the local superintendent had called him in to see that the Indian men and women at Heart Butte stopped playing the stick games (a sort of aboriginal canasta) not later than six o'clock in the evening.
>
> Now of course the Blackfeet Agent and the tribal policeman have no more right to tell adult Indians when to stop playing games and when to go to bed than they have to tell me when I should stop playing poker or chess. Conceding that the Blackfeet Superintendent's intentions are highly moral, is there any reason in the world why the Federal taxpayers should pay for that kind of nonsense?
>
> Back in 1923, the Indian Bureau had a lot of regulations like that, providing that Indian dances could only be held once a month 'in the daylight hours of one day in the midweek' and not in March, April, June, July or August, and 'That none take part in the dances or be present who are under 50 years of age.' Many of us thought that we had outgrown this sort of paternalism when Indians became full-fledged citizens in 1924, but if the Indian Bureau is allowed to proceed unchecked there are no limits to what they will spend Federal funds for.

Telling Indians when to go to bed and when to get up is not just a whimsical bit of paternalism. It has deep roots in a long tradition under which Indians for many decades were subjected to arrest and even death if they did not behave as white officials wanted them to behave. Thus when the Bureau issues an official report telling the Rio Grande Pueblos that their custom of annual elections is causing "much trouble" in the handling of farm machinery; that their communal use of grazing lands is lowering their grazing income; that their individual partitioning of farming lands is lowering their agricultural income; and that their religious customs are causing them to put "too much labor" on their corn fields, these official denunciations have a disastrous effect upon Pueblo life quite similar to the probable effect on a non-Indian of a warning cast in similar terms and bearing the imprint of the F.B.I.

From 1930 to 1950 it looked as though we had definitely put an end to such unauthorized authoritarianism on Indian reservations. It now appears that this view was illusory. . . .

Tribal Income

For many years the Interior Department backed the concept that Indian tribes should be allowed to spend their own earnings without let or hindrance from federal officials. Under Commissioner Myer's administration every bill introduced in Congress for this purpose has been opposed by the Interior Department, on the ground that Indians are "not yet ready" to spend their own money. In some instances, Bureau officials have gone even further. Thus the Blackfeet Tribal Council, which had a limited jurisdiction over some of its own earnings and had done its banking at the First National Bank of Browning, Montana, was peremptorily ordered on June 6, 1950, to deposit all funds in excess of $5,000 with the Agency Superintendent. When the Tribal Council stood its ground and refused to obey this legally unauthorized order, the Indian Bureau backed down.

Why Bureau employees want to keep a stranglehold on Indian income is not difficult to understand. So long as they retain this control they can insist that such Indian funds be used to pay any Bureau employee removed from the federal payroll. They can prevent the use of such funds for carfare in investigating or protesting government frauds and irregularities. This restriction has been placed on the funds of the Fort Belknap Indians in Montana, the Pyramid Lake Indians in Nevada, the Jicarilla Apache Indians in New Mexico, and many other tribes which have been earning substantial incomes for themselves through the management of tribal cattle herds, tribal stores, or other commercial enterprises. . . .

Tribal Cattle

During the drought years in the 1930's, the Government, as a measure of relief to distressed farmers, purchased drought cattle at an average price of about $12 a head. Most of these cattle were given away free to relief clients. Under Commissioner Myer's administration, Indian tribes which received such drought cattle have been charged up to $140 or more a head for what started out as a gift and was a gift to everybody who wasn't an Indian. The practice of making gifts to Indians and then charging the Indians for the gift was not invented by Commissioner Myer — it runs back many decades in our Indian history — but charging Indians $140 or more for a gift that cost the giver only $12 is a new wrinkle on an old game.

The Blackfeet Indians wouldn't have minded being charged for the wobbly, drought-stricken cows they received as a gift. They had no objection to paying retroactive interest on these gifts. In effect, for many of these cattle, the Indian Bureau charged interest at the rate of 70% per annum. But repaying cattle loans, even at 70% interest, was worthwhile, the Blackfeet felt, since only in this way would they achieve final and complete ownership of their own cattle. What shocked the Blackfeet, however, was that in June, 1950, after they had paid back the Indian Bureau many times over for the last cow they had received, they were suddenly advised by the Indian Bureau that title to the cattle was still vested in the Bureau and that the Bureau would arrange for the disposition of the cattle as it thought best. Bitter protests at this breach of faith were completely futile. The Chairman of the House Interior Appropriations Subcommittee, Representative Michael Kirwan, declared that he "will not believe" that "this Government, your Government, and my Government" would do any such thing. But when the Indian Bureau itself supplied facts and figures confirming the charge, the House Committee quickly dropped the subject. . . .

Tribal Claims

. . . First, a number of Indian tribes found themselves excluded from court because Commissioner Myer would not approve the only lawyers they knew and trusted. Second, Commissioner Myer played a large part in blocking enactment of a bill to give Indians additional time to employ lawyers and file their claims. Third, since May, 1950, the Indian Bureau has steadfastly refused to give Indian tribes information in Interior Department files which they need in order to present their cases properly, offering the lame excuse that such Indian requests for information amount to asking the Bureau to do research work for Indian tribes, and alleging that it is illegal for Government employees to "aid or assist" (even by telling the truth) "in the prosecution or support of claims against the United States." In the fourth place, the Indian Bureau has apparently been spying on the activities of tribal attorneys as they go through public files in the Interior Department Building and then advising opposing counsel concerning such activities in order that Indian claims may be more easily defeated. Of course, the Commissioner can always reply that disclosing information concerning the research activities of tribal attorneys helps to achieve truth, but he has made no move so far to acquaint Indian tribes, his alleged "wards," with the facts concerning similar research activities of their legal opponents in the Justice Department." . . .

The attitude of the Department's Solicitor to Indian Bureau decisions was fully expressed in his opinion of July 2, 1951, upholding the Indian Bureau's rejection of the Pyramid Lake Paiute Tribe's attorney contract:

> Perhaps I may venture the suggestion that, in passing upon the policy question in connection with each point, it is necessary to act in the light of two important principles. On one hand, there is the principle that the Department should foster local self-government among organized Indian tribes and, in dealing with such tribes in the exercise of the Department's power over them, should impose requirements on a tribe only when it seems necessary to do so in order to protect some important interest of the tribe or of the Government. On the other hand, there is the principle that, from the standpoint of stability of the administrative process, the head of a Department who has delegated authority and responsibility concerning a particular matter to a subordinate official ought not to overrule such official unless the latter has exceeded his authority, or has failed to conform to instructions issued by the head of the Department, or has made a grave error in judgment which is apt to have serious consequences. If the responsibility for deciding the present case rested upon me I believe that I should give the greater weight to the second of the two principles and affirm the Commissioner's action.

D. SELF-DETERMINATION AND THE FUTURE OF AMERICAN INDIAN TRIBAL GOVERNANCE

STRENGTHENING TRIBAL SOVEREIGNTY THROUGH GOVERNMENT REFORM: WHAT ARE THE ISSUES?

Robert B. Porter, 7 Kan. J.L. & Pub. Pol'y 72, 74-76, 93-98 (Winter 1997)

II. What Is the Current State of Tribal Governance?

To start with, it is first necessary to explore the current state of tribal governance. . . .

Given the raw numbers of different indigenous nations, it should not be surprising that there is a tremendous degree of diversity amongst them.

Land, language, culture, and politics are all factors contributing to our differences. Despite this, however, there are common factors associated with all indigenous communities. Specifically for our purposes, each has some form of government in place that purports to manage and address their internal and external affairs. While any complete assessment of the state of tribal governance would analyze the government of each of these Indian nations in detail, for purposes of this essay, I will discuss these tribal governments within the context of three broad categories which I refer to as: (1) traditional governments, (2) autonomous constitutional governments, and (3) dependent constitutional or corporate governments.

A. Traditional Governments

Traditional governments are those in which the method of governance has not formally changed since the colonization of the American continent. As a general matter, traditional government structure and procedure is unwritten. The governing law is passed down orally and is communicated in the language of the Indian people involved, although there may be cultural mnemonic devices — such as wampum belts or sand paintings — to assist in conveying information. As a result of this nexus between law and culture, traditional government may include social and spiritual elements associated with carrying out what might otherwise be secular governmental activities.

Having a traditional form, however, is not to suggest that governance under such systems has not changed since colonization began. . . . Despite these changes, I will refer to traditional governments simply as those which have their origins within the Indian community itself and which remain fundamentally unchanged in their structure and operations. . . . Examples of these types of governments include the Onondaga Nation and the various Pueblo communities.

B. Autonomous Constitutional Governments

Autonomous constitutional governments are those that have evolved from their aboriginal foundations to a written form of government. Tribal governments of this type, while they may yet be based upon traditional governing principles, no longer function in accordance with the form of the traditional government. Moreover, they have changed not as the result of some forced colonial influence, but rather as the result of deliberate internal effort to transform the method of government organization. . . .

In short, these governments evolved in the absence of direct efforts by the federal government to transform the traditional method of governance. Like the traditional governments, autonomous constitutional governments are not subject to any overriding authority in the exercise of their governing powers. Examples of this type of government include the Cherokee Nation and the Seneca Nation of Indians.

C. Dependent Constitutional or Corporate Governments

Dependent constitutional or corporate governments are those that have been established pursuant to the direct influence of the United States. While tribal governments of this sort are inherently sovereign and thus may establish their own forms of government, they are dependent because they are founded upon non-tribal law as the basis for their governing structure and may even require approval of one of these foreign governments to take official action.

The most significant of the federal laws establishing dependent tribal governments is the Indian Reorganization Act of 1934 (IRA). Approximately 200 tribal governments are organized pursuant the IRA's provisions. Unlike the traditional and autonomous constitutional governments, dependent constitutional or corporate governments are subject to the direct governing authority of the United States. Thus, IRA constitutions generally require that all tribal laws enacted by the tribal council be approved by the United States before they become effective. In addition, federal courts exercise jurisdiction over a wide variety of internal political affairs, including election disputes and membership determinations.

The most significant recent federal legislation establishing tribal governments is the Alaska Native Claims Settlement Act of 1971 (ANCSA). Under ANCSA, traditional governance through the village structure was undermined by the establishment of a system of corporate federalism established pursuant to federal and state law. . . .

Having identified these three categories of tribal governments, it is important to point out that these descriptions may be imprecise to the extent that tribal governance is always in a state of flux and, in many cases, truly unique. For example, several tribal governments organized under the IRA have eliminated the need for Secretarial approval for tribal laws to be effective. Thus, even though some governments are still organized under the IRA, they are clearly more like autonomous constitutional governments. Also, the largest indigenous nation in the United States, the Navajo Nation, does not even have a constitution but is otherwise governed by a well-developed written legal tradition. It may not be a constitutional government, but it also certainly is not a traditional one either. . . .

VI. Can Tribal Governance Dysfunction Be Remedied Through Reform?

. . . The actual process for how tribal government reform might take place will be unique for every indigenous nation. Nonetheless, I believe there are a few basic concepts that should be considered before any Indian nation attempts to take up such an effort.

A. Step 1 — Redefine the Role of Tribal Government

The key to any successful government reform process is for the entire tribe to focus on what they believe to be the central purpose of tribal government authority in their lives. This should be an idealistic process, one driven by notions of what the ideal government could do to help people's lives, not what the old government could do to make things even worse. This is likely to provoke a wide range of responses, but it is necessary to include as many definitions of government as possible. Only when every member of the community has had the opportunity to share his or her view, can the process of consensus building begin. These views should be distilled so as to begin defining a new governmental framework. Once a general framework is established, the parameters for shaping more specific textual provisions will be set.

B. Step 2 — Research Historical Political Behavior and the Historic Function of Tribal Government

When engaging in any new drafting effort — especially if you have lawyers involved — the instinct is to want to look and see what others have done before. This can be especially dangerous when dealing with tribal governmental reform. In too many indigenous nations, the most obvious and well-known governing tradition is not the tribal one, but the American one. Simply borrowing the form and structure of the American constitution is a recipe for self-colonization. The American constitution was based upon a variety of governmental theories that were brought together for the unique purpose of governing a large and immigrant-populated republic. It is unreasonable to think that such a governmental form would be well-suited for the often small, more homogenous indigenous societies.

While the increasing diversity of our nations may mean that many governing principles underlying American government ultimately may be useful to us, if we are to preserve our distinct existence, we should begin with our own traditions, rather than theirs. Where there remains a significant population of elders to share an understanding of earlier times, those elders must be consulted. Even the old dog politicos that have haunted tribal government for years will have important stores of unwritten knowledge about how tribal politics is conducted. All of this information must be identified and recorded.

Moreover, if any ancient texts about tribal life can be obtained, they too must be utilized. This includes some of the old anthropological reports written in terms suggesting that our forefathers were some kind of zoo animals. Regardless of how offensive you might find some of this work, some of this work is quite good and we should be sophisticated enough to be able to sift through the garbage of some of these anthropological conclusions about how our ancestors lived.

In short, the starting point for any governmental precedent should be the unique governing traditions of the indigenous nation itself. If this yields little information, the next best alternative is to look at the governing traditions of related Indian people. If that process too yields little information, the next source of information should be indigenous communities that share many of the same size and demographic characteristics. Only as a last resort, should the governing tradition of the United States be relied upon.

C. Step 3 — Assess the Degree to Which Historical Notions of Governance Still Apply

Once the historical review is complete, there should be a determination of which of the historic governing traditions continue to be relied upon by the People. This includes both the oral and written traditions. If any particular governing traditions within a tribe can be identified as surviving American colonization to the present day, then these practices undoubtedly must be the core of the political belief system. Especially in those tribes that have undergone some form of constitutional development, the identification of political practices that have been carried on under both the traditional and constitutional forms of government is tapping into the mother lode of that tribe's governing traditions.

D. Step 4—Evaluate Historical Norms for Continued Viability

As part of the historical review process, there should be a deliberate effort to evaluate which of the traditional governing practices should be continued and/or revitalized. This may be the most difficult step because it requires a two-pronged approach.

At one level, historical governing provisions must be viewed from the perspective of their literally being continued and/or revitalized. For example, a requirement under traditional governance that no action shall be taken until there is consensus could mean that the tribal council should not be able to act unless there is a unanimous vote. Thus, part of the inquiry should include whether any of the actual traditional governing practices should be continued.

At another level, however, there should be an assessment as to whether any of the values underlying a specific traditional governing provision should be continued and/or revitalized. Thus, to continue with the example above, the value underlying the requirement that no action shall be taken until "all of the people are in agreement" is simply that there should be widespread agreement as to the course of action. As a practical matter, this might be satisfied in a number of different ways other than by unanimous council votes. Council could only have to obtain a three-quarters or two-thirds majority, or council could have to vote twice, at least one week apart, and so on.

Focusing on traditional governing values rather than on literal requirements, is tremendously important for the entire governmental reform process. It may be extremely difficult for some traditional people to relinquish time honored procedures for doing things. Focusing on the fact that the underlying values and teachings of those time honored procedures could be continued and expanded, albeit in a modern form, may be the key to gaining their support for any ultimate changes in governmental form. Similarly, many of the progressives might support traditional governing principles that they otherwise might reject if they are conveyed in a form that they can comprehend. In short, if the focus is on substance, and not exclusively on form, the seeds of compromise can be sown. This will be important when it comes time to address the difficult issue of how much, if any, of the new government structure should be memorialized in writing.

E. Step 5—Be Creative When Drafting

Because of the many changes that have occurred within our nations, it seems inevitable that some important aspects of any governmental reform effort must be reduced to writing. If there are still communities that can sustain a wholly unwritten governing tradition, then obviously few, if any, changes will need to be made. But in all of the others, drafting will take on a special role in the reform process.

Basing tribal governmental reform on historic notions of governance will have little impact unless drafting takes place with an eye towards creativity. Mindlessly borrowing language from federal, state, or even tribal constitutions will wholly undermine the historical research just engaged in and will ensure that the reform process will have little positive long-term effect. If writing is to be done, it must be with original prose and devoid of legalese. Indeed, it may be the case that with some issues, no writing should be done at all. Cutting and pasting is simply too crude of a process for what needs to be done here in redesigning tribal governance. Only when a conscious decision has been made about adopting certain practices from American government should some of the "terms of art" under American law be adopted in the tribal constitutional text (e.g. "due process," "equal protection," etc.).

F. Step 6 — Work Deliberately and Openly

For any governmental reform effort to be successful, the People must understand and support what is happening. The only way I think that this can occur is if the reform process is approached like an educational process. If the tribal members are teaching each other about the governing traditions and working together to develop modern ways to perpetuate those traditions, then, when it comes time to put such changes into place, resistance should be minimal.

Sharing information about the reform process is critical to gaining acceptance. Often in tribal government there is a tendency to keep things close to the vest to minimize the opportunity for the opposition — whoever that might be at any given time — to undermine your efforts. Unless the process is one open to all, the reality, or merely the perception, that something fishy is going on will condemn any possibility that honest reform can be achieved. If the ideas are worth doing, they will be sustained by the people. Good ideas will rise like cream; bad ideas will sink like stones. Allowing an open process will ensure that this natural process will occur.

G. Step 7 — Convince the Conservatives that Good Government Is Good Politics

There is likely to be considerable resistance to governmental reform from conservatives within the tribal community. These conservatives may either be traditional people concerned that any change will undermine their position in the tribe, or old-dog politicos who are fearful that the light of day may shine and expose their long-running con games. If there is one thing in most Indian communities that people can agree on, it is that they do not like what the tribal government is doing. The process of governmental reform is one that the People in any Indian nation will support. Conservatives within the community, who do have the ability to halt change, must be convinced that reform is politically in their self-interest.

H. Step 8 — Exercise Great Patience and Listen to the People

My working theory for dealing with change is based on the axiom that "people usually do not know what they want, but they usually know what they do not want." I think this is especially true when working with Indian people because we have developed such a good defense mechanism against colonization over the years. In many ways, working with Indians is like working with a giant tortoise. At the slightest sign of danger, the head and legs retract to allow the protective shell to do its work. There is no movement and no progress, only the hope that the big shell will keep the threat away.

Well, the threat that we have been dealing with for all these years — American colonization — has been both a poison in our food and an acid eating through our shell. We either have to have some faith that we can change our traditional eating patterns in the face of this danger, get a new shell, or do both. Unfortunately, this kind of change is difficult for many to accept, either because they do not perceive the problem, or because they are simply resistant to change. I think that the time for simply sitting with our head and legs tucked in is over. As things are going, our destruction will come from our failure to act.

There is already some evidence that the People already know that governmental reform must happen if their lives are to improve. One of the best examples of this process of change that I have heard about involves the Comanche Tribe. In the early 1990s, many Comanches had concluded, after an extremely divisive election, that their IRA constitutional "system of governance was a major source of conflict and disharmony among them." They concluded that the process of electing just a handful of leaders contrasted too greatly with the traditional value of consensus-building and thus allowed too many people to feel left out of the decisionmaking process. The resulting "bad feeling" produced considerable anger that intensified the disharmony. In response, the Comanches developed a long term response that would allow the tribe to return to traditional values but within a contemporary, culturally specific process. This lengthy process involved many meetings that allowed all Comanches to have a say, but which focused discussion on critical issues that allowed for a new constitutional scheme to be developed. The changes have yet to be incorporated into a new constitution, but the process appears to have maximized the chances of success.

Another example of a tribe initiating constitutional reform is the San Carlos Apache, who recently are revising their constitution to end "corruption and infighting" by removing the requirement of BIA approval, expanding the size of the tribal council, and establishing independent branches of government. The Mohawks at Akwesasne, the Eastern Band of Cherokee, and the Northern Cheyennes are others who have participated in government reform efforts.

I have had my own experience with constitutional and administrative reform when I served as Attorney General of my own Nation. In 1992, my first major project was to work on proposed constitutional amendments to change the Nation's court system. These proposed changes included expanding the jurisdiction of the Nation's court system, creating an intermediate court of appeals, and staggering and extending the judicial terms of office. While the amendments were eventually approved by our People in a referendum, I learned much about the process of how long-term change can occur. I also learned how easy it is to aim low when engaging in constitutional reform. In retrospect, while I think the changes were an improvement over the old system, they did little to address some of the fundamental problems in how our Nation administers justice.

I was also involved in a year-long effort to restructure the administrative operations of the Seneca government. The project was ambitious, and was designed to give the People greater voice in the government, empower the Council, redefine and strengthen the leadership role of the President, and otherwise develop a systematic method for ensuring accountability among the 800 member tribal workforce. Eventually, the restructuring occurred. Unfortunately, it was implemented less than a year before the next general election. The so-called Government Law became a political issue. In significant part, it was attacked by conservatives on the Council and within the workforce who were opposed to abandoning the old, inefficient regime and being held accountable. After the election, the law was opposed by the new President because it actually required that he act in concert with the Council, and not as a dictator. Eventually, the Government Law was nullified.

What this experience taught me is that many of the most important changes that must be made within Indian nations are outside of the government's power. The administrative reform effort I was involved in tried to do too much in too short a time frame. Many of our deepest governmental problems should have been taken directly to the People and effectuated through constitutional change, not simply through Council actions. Simply put, the merits of proposed changes mean little if the process by which they come about is not accepted. Many of the former opponents of that reform effort who are now in office now admit that much of it was a good thing since they have now seen some of the government's problems as insiders. With time, I am confident that all people can learn these lessons without simply having to rely on their own method of trial-and-error. When we do so, we will have gone a long way toward unleashing the power of our People and preparing ourselves to addressing the challenges to our sovereignty in the future.

NOTES

Richard Loudbear wrote that many American Indian people are searching for ways to make radical changes in tribal governments. Numerous American Indian nations have faced forms of nonviolent (and occasionally violent) revolution. He writes, in a primer about how to effectuate a "nonviolent seizure of political power":

> Are some Indian nations going through civil war? With that in mind, how do systems of government collapse, evolve, and improve? Perhaps revolutionary Indian politics is one form of growing into a better form of government? One useful definition of revolution is found in the Oxford English Dictionary: "A complete overthrow of the established government in any country or state by those who were previously subject to it; a forcible substitution of a new ruler or form of government." Therefore, how does one evolve or revolutionize an ailing political system? If the people mourn when the wicked rule, what is their recourse? When democracy and its methods of elections, petitions, recalls, and letters fail, change is required outside the usual governmental paradigm.

Richard Loudbear, *Indian Country Politics: Theories of Operation and a Strategy for the Nonviolent Seizure of Political Power*, 31:1 AM. INDIAN Q. 66, 66-67, 69-72 (2007).

CHAPTER 2

TRIBAL JUSTICE SYSTEMS

Formal tribal justice systems, and especially tribal courts, are relatively new phenomena in Indian country. Indian people have always dealt with antisocial, criminal behavior in accordance with the needs of their communities, and the imposition—and adaptation—of formal tribal courts has all but supplanted customary and traditional justice.

This chapter examines the origins and development of tribal justice systems. It is fair to say that formal justice systems in Indian country are not, for the most part, indigenous to Indian communities. Beginning in the late nineteenth century, the United States federalized criminal law enforcement in Indian territories, and has systematically enforced American-style laws upon Indian people and Indian tribes from that time until the present day.

Nevertheless, modern tribal justice systems—coming under more and more control by Indian tribes—have begun to incorporate customary and traditional jurisprudence.

A. A HISTORY OF TRIBAL JUSTICE SYSTEMS IN INDIAN COUNTRY

1. THE ORIGINS AND DEVELOPMENT OF TRIBAL COURTS

INDIAN COURTS IN HISTORY AND LAW

National American Indian Court Judges Association, Indian Courts and the Future
7-13 (David H. Getches ed., 1978)

A Brief History

With the exception of a few tribes, reservation judicial systems as they exist today are unable to trace their roots to traditional Indian forums for dispute resolution. Instead, they are descended from an externally imposed Anglo system for keeping "order" among the Indians. Nevertheless, many tribes have been able to influence the character of their courts by utilizing some traditional concepts. If Indian courts have not been terribly destructive of Indian culture, it can be attributed to two facts: (1) most judges historically have been Indians, and (2) federal funding has been so lean that courts have had little influence, destructive or otherwise. Factors such as removal, war, and confinement on reservations were far more powerful.

Until late in the nineteenth century, Indian reservations were controlled by the military, as the Bureau of Indian Affairs was part of the Department of War. Crude forms of control — principally force — led many persons in and out of government to press for civilian controls of Indian affairs. The civilian bureaucracy, with support from organized religion, prevailed. There was a feel that inculcation of what the non-Indians understood as law and order was a necessary ingredient of the civilizing process which they saw as their mission. In order to Christianize, educate, and eventually assimilate the Indians, the institution of a legal system — not just martial law — was necessary. Some of the traditional power of the chiefs among the Indians remained, and this posed a threat to the dominant authority of the government's Indian agents. Consequently, destruction of the remaining authority of the traditional leaders and the systems they represented became essential to the "civilizing" process.

A system of Indian police and courts controlled by the Indian agent on each reservation was started. In 1883 the Commissioner of Indian Affairs authorized creation of Courts of Indian Offenses to operate under a set of rules and procedures created by the Bureau of Indian Affairs. Previously, the Indian agents summarily sentenced those they believed to be guilty. By 1890 agents on most reservations were appointing Indians to serve as police and judges. As purveyors of favors and patronage, Indian agents were able effectively to control police forces by paying virtually nothing to hand-picked Indians. Thus, the military was supplanted on the reservations. Although courts had functioned on some reservations for several years, no funds were appropriated by Congress for judges until . . . 1888.

One federal court described the early Indian courts as "mere educational and disciplinary instrumentalities, by which the government of the United States is endeavoring to improve and elevate the condition of these dependent tribes to whom it sustains the relation of guardian." Judges would often take account of Indian custom when Indians came before the Indian courts. But this did not translate into leniency — it more likely meant a tougher penalty or subjection to traditional sanctions for a uniquely Indian offense. Nevertheless, several important Indian customs and religious practices such as the sun dance, medicine men, and distribution of property owned by a person on his death were outlawed, and violations were punished by the Indian courts. The Indian courts, however, were not destined to fulfill their promise of assimilation, but they appeared to maintain order relatively well. Another important role of Indian courts was the regulation of the activities of avaricious non-Indians (e.g., trespass, grazing on Indian lands). For them, the Washington originated law applied by the courts was as respectable as any on the frontier.

Indians on many reservations continued to solve serious disputes among themselves outside the Courts of Indian Offenses. Such traditional sanctions as restitution, banishment, payment to a victim or his heirs, and vengeance were common. But, as the famous case of *Ex parte Crow Dog* [109 U.S. 556 (1883)] illustrates, federal authorities attempted to arrest and punish Indians under federal law when the Indian remedies seemed inadequate. Crow Dog's traditional punishment — payment to relatives — was seen as inappropriate and not fitting with the "civilizing" plan by many neighboring whites. . . .

After the turn of the century, while the Courts of Indian Offenses continued to function under the control of the Indian agents, the primary thrust of law enforcement became liquor suppression. Ripe opportunities for bootleggers, degeneration of tribalism and social structure, and demoralized individuals on the reservation combined to make alcohol abuse a major problem on all reservations. More money was provided for police, but by 1925 appropriations for Indian courts had decreased to . . . almost one-half of the 1892 level. . . . The number of Indian judges declined similarly. Indian courts waned in importance and were little more than tools of the Indian agents who had to approve of all court decisions.

No specific statutory authority ever has existed for Courts of Indian Offenses. In 1921, however, the Snyder Act [25 U.S.C. §13] empowered the Commissioner of Indian Affairs to expend money for a variety of services to Indians, including "the employment of . . . Indian police, Indian judges. . . ." But Congress was inhospitable to later attempts to validate the courts and clarify their jurisdiction. More recently, courts have found that authority for establishing Indian courts exists under the general statutory powers of the Commissioner of Indian Affairs. [25 U.S.C. §2; *Colliflower v. Garland*, 342 F.2d 369 (9th Cir. 1965).]

The New Deal brought the first thoughtful consideration of Indian self-government, including courts. . . . The administration was concerned not only with the lack of tribal influence on the Courts of Indian Offenses, but also the courts' rather blatant disregard for fair procedures and individual rights. The Indian Reorganization Act (IRA) was passed to allow tribes to reestablish and assert their governing powers, and to redress other adverse effects of earlier policies.

Under the IRA, tribes were to draft their own constitutions and laws and set up their own court systems. Most tribes only had a shaky recollection of their traditional systems and were most familiar with the Bureau's regulations and procedures. Consequently, the abrupt reinstitution of traditional law on reservations was not realized. Most tribes either remained under the old system or adopted codes modeled closely after the BIA code[,] revised in 1935. Courts adopting their own codes became known as "tribal courts." A clear trend since the IRA has been for tribes to develop codes and thereby convert from Courts of Indian Offenses or "CFR Courts" as they are commonly known (rules concerning them are found in 25 C.F.R. pt. 11) to tribal courts which function under the residual sovereignty of the tribes, rather than as agencies of the federal government. But progress has been slow. Antiquated provisions, traceable to the old BIA regulations, including selection of judges by the BIA Commissioner subject to tribal council ratification, remain in a number of cases. Very few tribes — principally, the New Mexico Pueblos — retain judicial systems based on Indian custom. . . .

[The Indian Civil Rights Act] of 1968 was passed. The Act had sweeping provisions dealing with Indian rights. Some were clearly supportive of such self-determining concepts as the requirement that any future state assumptions of jurisdiction over Indians be only with Indian consent. Others restricted self-government. Until the Act, tribes were not subject to the federal Constitution. Concern over some tribes' abuses led to imposition of most Bill of Rights requirements on all tribes. Clearly, this was a limitation on the latitude of self-government which tribes had enjoyed previously. Many tribes questioned the extension of Bill of Rights protections to individual Indians vis-á-vis tribes because of the inherent clash with Indian custom and traditional values. The Act also limited the penalties which Indian courts could impose to $500 and six months in jail.

At a time when policy favored maximum self-government, it would seem inconsistent for tribes to have external limits placed on their functions. The Act not only limited Indian courts in their disposition of cases, but it imposed requirements of due process upon them. And the provision in the Indian Civil Rights Act (ICRA) for federal court habeas corpus review of tribal orders [25 U.S.C. §1303] created a specter of reviews of Indian court procedures by the exacting standards of the well-developed Anglo legal system. Nevertheless, the current policy has enabled Indian courts to flourish more than ever before. The ICRA necessarily has drawn greater attention to the Indian court system, and the policy of federal support for Indian self-government has included strengthening Indian court. It has not been until the last few years, however, that this has been reflected significantly in BIA programs and funding. . . .

Overall, Indian courts have been retarded by their history. They originally were vehicles of an outside force. Later, their intended growth as integral parts of an Indian government was stunted by a lack of effective programs or funding, as well as policy vacillations. . . .

THE DEVELOPMENT OF THE INDIAN COURT SYSTEM

Vine Deloria, Jr. & Clifford M. Lytle, American Indians,
American Justice 111-16 (1983)

The Traditional Courts

. . . [O]ne of the most important powers exercised by tribal governments involved the resolution of disputes among tribal members. The mechanism charged with performing this was not always a body of appointed or elected judges as we use today; rather, it often fell within the authority of the tribal chief, the council of elders or chiefs, the council of warrior society leaders, or the religious leaders. Whatever the mechanism used by the tribe, the adjudicatory function was somewhat different from that to which we are most accustomed. The primary goal was simply to mediate the case to everyone's satisfaction. It was not to ascertain guilt and then bestow punishment upon the offender. Under Anglo-American notions of criminal jurisprudence, the objectives are to establish fault or guilt and then to punish. The sentencing goals of retribution, revenge, and deterrence and isolation of the offender are extremely important. . . . Under the traditional Indian system the major objective was more to ensure restitution and compensation than retribution. The idea, therefore, that tribal laws involved some Old Testament eye-for-an-eye mechanism that worked independently of human personality stems mere from inadequate observations of what really occurred in tribal societies. In most instances the system attempted to compensate the victim and his or her family and to solve the problem in such a manner that all could forgive and forget and continue to live within the tribal society in harmony with one another.

Under the traditional tribal system of justice, the ultimate decision was seldom made by a judge. Rather, the job of the mediator or reconciling chief was to create an atmosphere for participant decision-making. The two conflicting parties would call upon a chief, elder, medicine man, or religious leader more for his assistance in keeping the situation within the bounds of tribal customs than for his decision as to who was "right" and who was "wrong" in a given situation. The role of this tribal figure was to help the parties discuss the problem until a satisfactory compromise or solution could be agreed upon. Each of the parties recognized that a proper settlement required some restitution to the injured party, but restitution that permitted the offending party to continue to live within the tribal community. Banishment was extremely rare in most tribes and represented a very serious breach of fundamental folkways that bound the tribe together. . . .

Courts of Indian Offenses

. . . Courts of Indian Offenses most probably began with the appeal by disputing chiefs to the agent as arbiter of problems that could not be resolved in the traditional manner. . . . [A]gents handled some of the political problems that reservation life entailed and . . . their conception of their job, predicated upon the need to keep an orderly community and to prevent intrusions by the whites, gave a quasi-judicial aspect to early reservation institutions. On some reservations the early councils were both judicial and legislative and exercised, after the influence of the chiefs had declined, executive powers also. Courts of Indian Offenses mark the first evolution away from one body holding all three political powers in its hands to the tripartite arrangement we see on many reservations today.

The development of the Indian police also played a critical role in this movement toward independent institutions. Unable to rely upon the traditional chiefs to carry out their instructions, many of which were anathema to the old people, the agents early began to enroll Indians as agency policemen. This new group enabled the agent to control the Indians without having to rely upon the presences of federal troops, which in many cases might have created an unpleasant incident or war. Although the rise of Courts of Indian Offenses certainly indicated the increasing application of the white laws over the Indians, they were not wholly without respect among the Indians. Manuelito, one of the most respected and beloved of the Navajo war chiefs, served for a time as an Indian policeman and performed duties in a Court of Indian Offenses.

The allotment policy considerably increased the need for Courts of Indian Offenses. In order to break up the traditional family groupings on many reservations, allotments were deliberately mixed so that family members might have their lands scattered all over the reservations. The idea behind this bureaucratic hodgepodge was to encourage the younger generation to move away from the elders and to begin farming on their own. The result of the application of the idea was that it became difficult if not impossible for communities that were dependent on tribal customs to conduct some of their ceremonies because the clan or family was so dispersed. The Courts of Indian Offenses then served to provide them with some forum in which a modicum of justice could be realized. Subsequent sale of allotments and the settling of white purchasers within the reservation borders made it virtually impossible to do anything except rely upon these courts for redress.

In 1883 the Courts of Indian Offenses were made a regular part of the Bureau of Indian Affairs activities on the reservations. . . .

These courts have become known as CFR courts since they operated under the written guidelines as set down in the Code of Federal Regulations. But . . . it is difficult to determine whether they were really courts in the traditional jurisprudential sense of either the Indian or the Anglo-American culture or whether they were not simply instruments of cultural oppression since some of the offenses that were tried in these courts had more to do with suppressing religious dances and certain kinds of ceremonials than with keeping law and order. The sacred Sioux ceremony of "keeping the soul," . . . which was basically a condolence rite, was banned by these courts on the Dakota reservations to the consternation of the people.

Although the CFR courts were staffed by Indian judges, they served at the pleasure of the agent, not the community. The Indian agent appointed his judges as a patronage exercise, which rewarded the Indians who seemed to be assimilating while depriving the traditional people of the opportunity to participate in this vital function of the community. Even though the judges invested a good deal of energy and prestige in serving on these courts, too frequently the ultimate decision rested with the Indian agent, who often acted as though the people had no right to understand the reasoning behind his arbitrary decisions. . . . At its zenith, the CFR court system was operating on about two-thirds of all reservations. With the authorization of the IRA corporate form of tribal government, all but a few tribes assumed judicial functions as a manifestation of tribal government and rid themselves of this hated institution. Since these courts did not have the sanction of the whole tribal community, even the most beneficial parts of their operations have been eyed with suspicion by Indians and historians alike.

Modern Tribal Courts

As with tribal governments, the Indian Reorganization Act of 1934 heralded the beginning of the modern tribal court system. . . . This opportunity afforded the Indians a chance to abandon the already disintegrating CFR court system and replace it with a legal system more responsive to tribal needs and under tribal control. More important, it provided an opportunity to resurrect the traditions and customs that had been so important to Indian culture before being dissipated by the bureaucratic controls from Washington.

The years of assimilation that Washington had thrust upon Indian Country, however, had taken their toll. Most tribes were not in a position to re-create the old traditional courts of justice that had functioned prior to the CFR era. Instead, tribal governments established legal systems closely fashioned after a BIA model. A few tribes simply retained their CFR court system slightly modified to eliminate the objectionable features that had hampered it and made it seem like a foreign institution.

NOTES

1. Federal courts affixed their stamp of approval on the reservation justice systems established by the Bureau of Indian Affairs. One important case, *United States v. Clapox*, 35 F. 575 (D. Or. 1888), rejected claims that the government had no authority to create these courts and police by federal regulation:

> These "courts of Indian offenses" are not the constitutional courts provided for in section 1, art. 3, Const., which congress only has the power to "ordain and establish," but mere educational and disciplinary instrumentalities, by which the government of the United States is endeavoring to improve and elevate the condition of these dependent tribes to whom it sustains the relation of guardian. In fact, the reservation itself is in the nature of a school, and the Indians are gathered there, under the charge of an agent, for the purpose of acquiring the habits, ideas, and aspirations which distinguish the civilized from the uncivilized man. . . .
>
> There is no doubt of the power of the United States to make these rules, nor that the president is authorized by congress to exercise the same. . . .
>
> But, pleasantry aside, and in conclusion, the act with which these defendants are charged is in flagrant opposition to the authority of the United States on this reservation, and directly subversive of this laudable effort to accustom and educate these Indians in the habit and knowledge of self-government. It is therefore appropriate and needful that the power and name of the government of the United States should be invoked to restrain and punish them. The case falls within the letter of the statute (section 5401, Rev. St.) providing for the punishment of persons who are guilty of rescuing any one committed for an offense against the United States, and I see no reason why it should be construed out of it, or the statute held inapplicable to it. . . .

   Clapox, 35 F. at 577-78.

2. In *Iron Crow v. Oglala Sioux Tribe*, 231 F.2d 89 (8th Cir. 1956), Indians challenged the authority of the tribal court at Pine Ridge. The Eighth Circuit held that the Oglala Sioux Tribe had established its tribal court using its residual sovereignty:

> We accordingly are of the opinion that the plaintiffs cannot prevail on their second point. We hold that Indian tribes, such as the defendant Oglala Sioux Tribe of the Pine Ridge Reservation, South Dakota, still possess their inherent sovereignty excepting only where it has been specifically taken from them, either by treaty or by Congressional Act. . . .
>
> Originally, and until 1885, all offenses committed by Indians against Indians within the confines of Indian country were under the jurisdiction of the Tribal Courts. In 1885 Congress passed what is sometimes referred to as the "Seven Major Crimes Act." Therein, . . . Congress brought under federal jurisdiction the crimes of murder, manslaughter, rape, assault with intent to kill, arson, burglary and larceny. Subsequently three additional crimes were included, to-wit: incest, assault with a dangerous weapon and robbery. The clear inference is that Congress left to the Indian Tribal Courts jurisdiction over all crimes not taken by the federal government itself. . . . We

accordingly hold that not only do the Indian Tribal Courts have inherent jurisdiction over all matters not taken over by the federal government, but that federal legislative action and rules promulgated thereunder support the authority of the Tribal Courts.

Id. at 94, 96.

3. In *Colliflower v. Garland*, 342 F.3d 368 (9th Cir. 1965), the court held that an Indian convicted under the criminal code of the Fort Belknap Indian community, which had adopted the federal Indian law and order code in 25 C.F.R. Part 11, could petition for a writ of habeas corpus in federal court on grounds that "it is pure fiction to say that the Indian courts functioning in the Fort Belknap Indian community are not in part, at least, arms of the federal government. Originally they were created by the federal executive and imposed upon the Indian community, and to this day the federal government still maintains a partial control over them." *Id.* at 378. However, the court added:

> It does not follow from our decision that the tribal court must comply with every constitutional restriction that is applicable to federal or state courts. Nor does it follow that the Fourteenth Amendment applies to tribal courts at all; some of the cases cited above indicate that it does not. And the vestige of "sovereignty" that the tribe retains and exercises through its Tribal Council and Tribal Courts may call for application of [different] principles.

Id. at 379.

In 1968, Congress codified a federal right to petition for a writ of habeas corpus from a tribal court conviction. 25 U.S.C. §1303.

4. As this brief survey history of tribal courts indicates, Indian people long have had a complicated relationship with tribal justice systems. Tribal courts often have to work very hard to develop legitimacy in Indian communities.

Law professor and tribal judge Frank Pommersheim is a leader in advocating that tribal courts behave actively in promoting tribal court legitimacy. He offered a blueprint for developing tribal court legitimacy:

> The structure and quality of relationships within tribal court systems—especially those between tribal appellate courts and tribal trial courts, and between tribal courts and litigants, the practicing tribal bar, and the rest of tribal government—are critical coordinates in establishing and measuring the health and vitality of tribal judiciaries.
>
> The relationship between tribal appellate courts and tribal trial courts is of particular importance and significance. Because this relationship is relatively new in most tribal court systems, the need for a good working atmosphere, characterized by integrity and mutual respect, is especially acute. . . .
>
> On the personal level, it is advisable, if not absolutely necessary, that appellate judges have some basic acquaintance with the tribal bench, and vice versa, in order to create a link between their respective efforts. . . . There is no room, inside or outside the court, for personal rancor. The occasion for reversal is a judicial fact of life, but both the content and acceptance of such reversal must accord with the highest canons of professional integrity and cultural respect. Tribal judiciaries—despite rapid growth and development—are still often institutionally fragile and must not be put at risk by needless conflict or confrontation within the court itself.

There is also a need to maximize personal respect, though not descending to fawning or favoritism, in order to ensure that trial and appellate judges avoid the pitfalls of having their decisions held up to claims that they are personally motivated or politically driven. Again, professionalism and cultural integrity control. The conduct of hearings, the language and style of decisions, and personal relationships inside and outside the court must all hew to standards that place the trial and appellate bench beyond reproach to each other and the general tribal and non-Indian public. . . .

. . . Tribal appellate courts will, therefore, often be making and articulating "new" law. Much of this law will identify the legal contours of the relationship between the appellate and trial courts in such areas as standards of review, breadth of habeas relief, and interlocutory appeals. In these areas, it is particularly important—because of the structural implications—that such decisions be especially well-crafted not only in matters of legal and cultural principles, but in public policy as well, in order to make the most compelling and comprehensive case for any particular principle or ruling.

. . . In many tribal traditions, such as the Lakota's at Rosebud and at Cheyenne River, harmony and respect are critical. Tribal judiciaries must recognize these traditions in their working relationships. Without such harmony and respect, the requisite equilibrium and unity of purpose are unlikely to be achieved. . . .

Tribal court litigants are the direct recipients of the "services" and decision-making of tribal courts. Their perceptions of the process and results form the foundation on which reputations are established. Because lawsuits tend to have losing as well as winning sides, they are likely to produce some unhappy parties. This possibility is exacerbated when the results are perceived (correctly or incorrectly) as contrary to traditional cultural expectations or as "inferior" to what might result in state and federal courts. Positive public perception and steady institution-building are often at risk.

Therefore, it is incumbent on tribal courts, at both the trial and appellate levels, to ensure that litigants are treated with dignity and respect. This is especially true at the trial level, where many individuals will not be represented by counsel—particularly in civil matters related to custody, child support, and small claims actions. Explanations by tribal court personnel about completion of forms, the schedule of court hearings, and preparation for hearings are critical to assure individuals that they are being treated fairly. . . .

At the appellate level, the same solicitude is also important because of the unique conduct of appellate hearings where as a general rule neither evidence nor direct testimony is received. . . . Decisions of tribal courts, more so than those of state and federal courts, often have currency and reverberation within the community-at-large beyond the narrow self-interest of the parties. This is especially true, for example, in such areas as jurisdiction and the application of tradition and custom.

All of this connects to the larger issue of legitimacy. What can tribal courts do to ensure their legitimacy in the eyes of the public they serve, and what are they presently doing toward that end? . . . At Rosebud, for example, Chief Tribal Trial Judge Sherman Marshall regularly schedules tribal court "open houses." Members of the public are invited to visit tribal courts for tours, food, and presentations (including the opportunity to ask questions) about the business and mission of the tribal court. These sessions have been quite successful in establishing a better understanding of the tribal court system.

In addition, Judge Marshall and other members of his staff attend community meetings (as far as a hundred miles away from the tribal courthouse) to make presentations about, and answer questions concerning, tribal court activities.

. . . History and conventional civics have given an imprimatur of propriety, even rectitude, to the dominant legal system, while ignoring, if not actually demeaning, tribal courts. This uneven playing ground must be leveled and overcome for tribal courts to obtain parity and take their rightful place within the national (even international) system of justice. Hard work, cultural pride, and the desire for an enduring justice are the central coordinates of this movement.

Many attorneys, particularly non-Indian attorneys, may not know initially what is expected of them and may even have negative stereotypes about tribal courts. Such ambivalence or even negativity must be readily addressed, implicitly and explicitly, from the outset. For example, in a case before the Rosebud Sioux Tribal Court of Appeals, an attorney telephoned the clerk of courts on the day of oral argument and informed the clerk that, because of a conflict with a hearing in state court, he would not be able to make the hearing. He filed no motion for a continuance, but apparently assumed that his "excuse" would be accepted. It was not. The case was heard without his presence. He was cited for contempt and suspended from practice before the tribal court for three months. The attorney never "missed" another court date.

In addition, tribal court advocates who are not law-trained must be held to the same standards as an attorney and must not be permitted to claim that absence of a law degree entitles them to lax standards. To permit such laxity would imperil the quality of both individual representation and institutional development. This is occasionally a problem at the appellate level, where the requirement of written briefs and tight, focused, oral argument may be beyond the training and capability of some tribal advocates. As a result, very few tribal advocates practice at the appellate level at either Rosebud or at Cheyenne River.

These observations, in turn, raise questions in a second key area: the applicable standards for both tribal advocates and law-trained attorneys who practice before tribal trial and appellate courts. To date, the practice has been to admit law-trained attorneys based on their admission to practice before some state or federal court. Tribal advocates usually are admitted based on tribal membership and rather minimal educational requirements, though neither Rosebud nor Cheyenne River have specific requirements in this regard. Increasingly, tribes are revising these esoteric standards for attorneys and the minimal internal standards for tribal advocates. For example, the Rosebud Sioux Tribe recently completed preparation of the Rosebud Sioux tribal bar examination, which was administered for the first time in the summer of 1995. The function of the examination is to ensure basic competence and understanding of the principles of tribal and federal Indian Law.

The Rosebud Sioux Tribe has also formally inaugurated the establishment of the Sicangu Oyate Bar Association. In addition to regulating admission to practice, this bar association oversees the election of officers and tribal bar commissioners and directly regulates such issues as continuing legal education programs, judicial qualifications, screening, investigating and adjudicating complaints against individual members of the tribal bar, and, more generally, strives to develop a sense of élan and rapport among the members of the practicing tribal bar. . . .

Some decisions of tribal courts inevitably rule against other branches or parts of tribal government and may include injunctive or habeas relief ordering cessation or commencement of specific governmental activities. Obviously, such situations are fraught with possibilities for confrontation and governmental crisis. In such situations, certain practical, structural, political, and cultural concerns arise. Decisions implicating other parts of the tribal government, therefore, need to contain both compelling legal analysis and cultural referents to demonstrate that the decisions comport with both applicable law and cultural standards. In addition, tribal court opinions must reflect respect for, and parity with, the coordinate branches of tribal government. Moreover, to avoid the possibility of misunderstanding, or of circumvention of the court's intent, the orders themselves must be precisely drafted to provide absolute clarity about what is required.

On the structural level, a separation of powers, de jure or even de facto, obviously minimizes potential clashes. Separation of powers is not, however, a solution that can be imposed from the top down. Rather, it needs to work its way up from the grassroots with cultural support, percolating locally from the inside-out rather than being imposed from the outside. It is also worth noting that the separation of powers doctrine is not necessarily an immediate panacea. Without an underlying commitment to the separation of powers doctrine, a structural separation of powers can be breached because this lack of commitment is what makes for constitutional crisis in the first place. Additionally, the separation of powers doctrine may clearly contravene the current tradition and governmental structure of some tribes. Moreover, the fact that separation of powers is a vaunted piece of dominant constitutionalism does not give it intrinsic merit in tribal systems.

Finally, there should be the political and legal wisdom to recognize that tribal court decisions and ordered relief are not the first, but rather the last, line of resolution to difficult tribal intra-governmental issues. Nevertheless, such decisions must inevitably be made. Accepting this political reality, the presence of respect, compelling legal analysis, sensitivity to culture, and commitment to incremental change will all play central roles in achieving a good working relationship between the tribal judiciary and the other branches of tribal government. Without such local and intra-governmental legitimacy, many of its benefits could not and would not have been realized. In the absence of strong foundational and institutional roots, enduring tribal jurisprudential growth is quite unlikely to occur. . . .

Frank Pommersheim, *Tribal Court Jurisprudence: A Snapshot from the Field*, 21 VT. L. REV. 7, 8-16 (1996).

2. A MICROCOSM SURVEY OF FIVE MODERN TRIBAL JUSTICE SYSTEMS

GRAND TRAVERSE BAND OF OTTAWA AND CHIPPEWA INDIANS[*]

The Grand Traverse Band tribal court began operations in the late 1980s, with Michael D. Petoskey serving as the court's first chief judge. The tribal

---

[*]Much of the material in this section appears in slightly different form in Matthew L.M. Fletcher, The Return of the Eagle: A Legal History of the Grand Traverse Band of Ottawa and Chippewa Indians (forthcoming 2011, Michigan State University Press).

court was the first tribal court in Michigan to be included in the tribal constitution as a separate and independent branch of government, much like the federal judiciary. *See* Michael D. Petoskey, *Tribal Courts*, 66 MICH. B.J. 366, 367-69 (1988). During the early decades of the tribal court, the court has heard and decided numerous complex and important issues on behalf of the Band, including questions of tribal sovereign immunity, tribal membership, political corruption, tribal election disputes, and many, many other questions. The tribal court also has a robust criminal docket, and an award-winning Peacemaker Court.

A significant part of the Grand Traverse Band's history is captured in cases decided by the tribal court since 1990, when the court's docket began to increase steadily. In 2001, former Chairwoman Ardith (Dodie) Chambers testified before the United States Senate Committee on Indian Affairs to demonstrate the independence, authority, integrity, and competence of the tribal judiciary. *See* Indian Tribal Good Governance Practices as They Relate to Economic Development, Hearing before the Senate Committee on Indian Affairs, 107th Cong., 1st Sess. at 23-25, 55-95 (July 18, 2001) (Testimony and Prepared Statement of Ardith (Dodie) Chambers, Councilwoman, Grand Traverse Band of Ottawa and Chippewa Indians). She highlighted two tribal court cases, *In re McSauby*, No. 97-02-001-CV-JR, 1997 WL 34691849 (Grand Traverse Tribal Judiciary, July 29, 1997), and *DeVerney v. Grand Traverse Band of Ottawa and Chippewa Indians*, No. 96-10-201 CV, 2000 WL 35749822 (Grand Traverse Band Appellate Court, Nov. 15, 2000), showing that the tribal court had ruled against the tribal government in some key cases. The first case, *In re McSauby*, involved the referral of John McSauby, an elected official of the tribal council, to the tribal court for removal for ethics violations. Over the objection of the tribal government, the tribal court first held that McSauby's attorney was entitled to attorney fees, paid for by the tribal government, on the grounds that the question of how and when a tribal council member could be removed was so important and complex that a defending council member should be entitled to adequate legal representation. On the merits, the tribal court agreed to order the removal of Mr. McSauby, on the grounds that he had admitted to using his authority as a tribal council member to push through the sale of his personally owned land to the Band, a violation of provisions in the tribal constitution prohibiting misconduct and self-dealing.

The second case, *DeVerney*, involved a challenge to a decision by the Band's tribal membership department. The case involved a complicated mix of sovereign immunity, due process, administrative law, and tribal constitutional interpretation. The issue involved the administrative disenrollment of several members of the Band in 1996 when the tribal membership office learned that the members were also enrolled members of the Sault Ste. Marie Tribe of Chippewa Indians, a violation of the dual enrollment prohibition in the tribal constitution. The question was whether the membership office could unilaterally terminate a tribal member's membership or whether the tribe had to hold a hearing first. The tribal court and then the tribal appellate court held that the tribe first had to provide due process to the members before they were disenrolled.

Councilwoman Chambers also testified to Congress about the Band's Peacemaker Court, which won an award in 1999 from the Harvard Project on American Indian Economic Development at the John F. Kennedy School of Government. The Peacemaker Court — Mnaweejeendwin — incorporates nonadversarial and traditional dispute resolution techniques, rather than Western-style, adversarial courtroom procedures and rules. The Mnaweejeendwin is designed to help juvenile offenders avoid jail and to learn and understand the consequences of their actions, to help victims of crime reach an agreement where offenders make amends to them. Peacemaking involves talking and reaching consensus on how these goals might be achieved. Western-style justice is all but rejected. According to former Chief Judge Petoskey:

> There is an Indian saying, that the watch is the white man's handcuff. . . . Peacemaking is not time limited. If it takes time, it takes time. Everyone has an opportunity to say what they want to say. They take whatever time necessary to develop a consensus.
>
> The way we typically do things in an adversarial court is really counterproductive. . . . We are saying all the negative things about people instead of working together toward common ground. Things people say about each other can be very hurtful and lasting.

Nancy A. Costello, *Walking Together in a Good Way: Indian Peacemaker Courts in Michigan*, 76 U. Det. Mercy L. Rev. 875, 876, 878 (1999).

The Mnaweejeendwin avoids those problems. Instead of a judge looking down at the parties to a dispute, issuing orders and punishments that may or may not reflect the wishes of the parties, the Mnaweejeendwin forces the parties — with the help of their families and other community members — to face and discuss the fundamental causes of the dispute.

Litigation before the Grand Traverse Band tribal court is very similar in process, rules, and statutes to litigation before state and federal courts — with a key difference. Former Chief Judge of the tribal court JoAnne Cook-Gasco speaks about how the written pleadings of a case between tribal members usually is merely the tip of the iceberg of the dispute. *See* JoAnne Cook-Gasco, Address before the Michigan State University College of Law Indigenous Law and Policy Center, East Lansing, Michigan (Feb. 17, 2009). The tribal court judges will ask the parties to go all the way back to the beginning, maybe as far back as generations, to ascertain and understand the origins of the dispute. Conversely, a state or federal court will do nothing more than look at the pleadings and the arguments made in court. Parties to a state or federal court case know going in that the findings of fact made by the judge or jury will not be a terribly close approximation of the truth, and even the winners walk away with a bad taste in their mouths. Tribal court parties might feel the same way, but tribal court judges at Grand Traverse Band are taught to look beyond the pleadings in order to better craft remedies suitable to the parties.

HOPI TRIBE

The Hopi Tribal Courts are one of the relatively few courts that have incorporated significant tribal custom and tradition into their jurisprudence. Many of the issues that arise in these tribal courts involve the governance disputes between the traditional villages and the national Hopi government, as well as unique property rights questions involving tribal members.

Pat Sekaquaptewa summarizes the history of the tribal court:

> The Hopi Tribal Courts were established by the Tribal Council in 1972. The courts do not have a separate constitutional dedication of powers from Tribal Council at this time. The trial court is housed in a modern courthouse/police headquarters complex on the Hopi reservation near Keams Canyon, Arizona. The trial court is comprised of three associate lay judges and an attorney who serves as the Chief Judge. All the trial court judges are Hopi.
>
> The trial court has general authority, guided by the Indian Civil Rights Act, to decide nearly every type of case, subject to the limitations of the Hopi Constitution, By-laws, and tribal ordinances. The trial court handles civil matters concerning such issues as marital disputes, commercial contracts, torts, employment rights, property disputes and probate matters. The Tribe has also established a Hopi Children's Court with limited jurisdiction over minors who are shown to be dependent, minors who are in need of emergency care, and minors who are shown to be delinquent. . . .
>
> The Hopi Appellate Court was also established by Ordinance 21 in 1972. The Appellate Court is comprised of a three-judge panel of attorneys, which meets to hear oral arguments and deliberates two to three times per year at the Hopi court facility near Keams Canyon, Arizona. . . .
>
> The Hopi Appellate Court's jurisdiction and mandate extend to the review of final trial court civil decisions, including the review of the trial court certification of decisions made by the nine, constitutionally recognized Hopi villages. The Appellate Court also has jurisdiction to review trial court criminal orders exceeding fifty dollars in fines or thirty days in jail. Finally, the Appellate Court is authorized to issue advisory opinions given certified questions of law from tribal agencies or departments or other judicial forums (including village forums).

Pat Sekaquaptewa, *Evolving the Hopi Common Law*, 9 KAN. J.L. & PUB. POL'Y 761, 766-67 (2000).

MISSISSIPPI BAND OF CHOCTAW INDIANS

Harvard Project on American Indian Economic Development
Honoring Nations 2005 Honoree

Choctaw Tribal Court System

. . . The Mississippi Band of Choctaw's economic track record is widely viewed as the standard of excellence against which other Native nations measure their success. Over the last thirty years, the Band has deliberately engaged in business development — through partnerships, tribal enterprise, and entrepreneurship — that has transformed the community. In 1994, the already-thriving economy was given a further boost when the Band government entered the gaming market; today the Mississippi Choctaw own two casino-resorts in addition to their many other joint ventures and enterprises.

With this dramatic increase in economic activity, growing pains were inevitable. In particular, increased interactions between the tribal government, on-

and off-reservation businesses, consumers, the Band's several thousand employees, and its 10,000 citizens heightened the demand for robust and capable tribal institutions for dispute resolution. The Mississippi Band of Choctaw has long had a tribal court, but by 1997 it became apparent that changes were needed if the court system was to be able to efficiently and effectively manage its ever-growing caseload (including disputes which ranged from minor traffic infractions to complex commercial litigation). Strain on the system threatened to compromise the integrity of the Band's judicial system and its commitment to Choctaw principles of justice. As a result, tribal leaders decided that the tribal court system needed to grow — but to do so in a way that was consistent with self-determination.

Critically, these changes were initiated from a position of strength. Shortly after the Mississippi Band of Choctaw organized under a constitution in 1974, the tribal council passed a statute establishing the court, creating balanced oversight by both constitutional branches of government (the executive and legislative branches). Specifically, tribal judges must meet the qualifications laid out in the Choctaw Tribal Code. The Band's Chief has authority to nominate candidates for the bench, but the Tribal Council Committee on Judicial Affairs and Law Enforcement approves them, and the entire council must confirm a candidate with a two-thirds vote. Both tribal judges and court personnel are further bound by statutory Rules of Ethics and Conduct. Together, these provisions help ensure the tribal court's independence and make it possible for the court to serve the justice and related economic and social development needs of the nation.

Building on this base, opportunities were identified for improvement across all components of the court system. The goal was to become a full-service court system capable of handling a wide variety of cases effectively, to deepen the system's grounding in Choctaw practices and law, and to grow the pool of prospective court personnel, so that the supply of Choctaw court services could keep pace with rising demand. Specifically, they created a four-branch court system (civil, criminal, peacemaker, and youth divisions), initiated a video history project focusing on Choctaw law, and began a summer internship program.

Prior to the 1997 court reform, the Mississippi Band of Choctaw Tribal Court had three divisions, youth (handling juvenile offender and child welfare issues), civil, and criminal. The heavy caseload, particularly of misdemeanor, youth, and family-related disputes, slowed the process of justice. By creating a new division and adding diversion programs, the Peacemaker Court can streamline operations, better match court personnel and programs from other departments (like Behavioral Health and Victims Services) to case types, and apply Choctaw law in a culturally relevant way for the parties appearing before the court. The Peacemaker Court is available to parties who agree to handle their dispute through a traditional process in accordance with the traditional Choctaw values of cohesion, cooperation, and peace as opposed to the more Western and adversarial process available in the tribe's civil and criminal courts. Teen Court makes it possible for many of the less complicated juvenile offenses and disputes that would normally be heard in formal Youth Court to be heard by a panel of the defendant's peers, further spreading the caseload and training youth in the practice of Choctaw law.

The Teen Court is a particularly notable aspect of the Choctaw court system, as it not only facilitates smoother Youth Court operations but also results in peer-to-peer community building. For this upcoming generation of tribal citizens (and especially for prior offenders who complete their sentences and join the Teen Court), interactions with peers through court service generates a set of common experiences and a shared sense of accomplishment. In the words of court personnel, having teens that might not otherwise interact come together to decide on appropriate sentencing helps break down walls between youth with different backgrounds, goals, and experiences, heading off divisions that might otherwise persist through adulthood. Youth community building also occurs through mentoring. As new youth join the Teen Court, the more senior members mentor them, stressing the idea that Teen Court proceedings can genuinely affect the lives of the youth offenders (who are also their peers).

Other measures initiated by the Choctaw court system include the Indigenous Law Library and the Summer Internship Program. The library project compiles video-taped interviews with the nation's elders, generating and archiving records of traditional values. The tapes are referenced by the Court and content is applied for judicial direction. In 2003 the internship program provided the opportunity for citizens who are currently enrolled in law school to shadow clerks. In 2004, intern work expanded to all departments, including the judicial branch. The internship program included Teen Court participants in 2005.

Evidence that this multi-part court system is working comes from many quarters. Critically, Choctaw citizens are pleased with their better-functioning court, stressing that the structure leads to the timely adjudication of cases. While it does not speak directly to the rapidity at which cases pass through the system, data on the number of cases heard suggest that Mississippi Band of Choctaw Tribal Court is operating at a very high level: from September 2003 to October 2004, the court (with a staff of 25) heard over 9,400 cases (4,077 criminal cases, 2,831 civil cases, 2,201 juvenile cases, 306 peacemaker resolutions, and 14 Supreme Court cases). The decisions of non-tribal courts provide impressive additional evidence. In 2002 the United States Court of Appeals ruled in favor of tribal jurisdiction in the case *Choctaw Tribe v. Bank One.* More recently, the local county court system referred a proceeding to the Band's Peacemaker Court. Both decisions implicitly acknowledge the Choctaw Tribal Court's capacity and quality. But perhaps most striking is the evidence provided by ongoing economic development. As shown in research conducted by the Harvard Project on American Indian Economic Development and others, a fair, effective, and independent dispute resolution system is critical to economic growth: Mississippi Choctaw's continued economic boom would not be possible without a well-functioning tribal court. . . .

Northwest Intertribal Court System

Harvard Project on American Indian Economic Development
Honoring Nations 2003 Honoree

Confederated Tribes of the Chehalis Reservation, Jamestown S'Klallam Tribe, Muckleshoot Tribe, Port Gamble S'Klallam Tribe, Sauk-Suiattle Tribe, Shoalwater Bay Tribe, Skokomish Tribe, Stillaguamish Tribe, Tulalip Tribes

. . . In 1979, a consortium of thirteen western Washington tribes created the Northwest Intertribal Court System (NICS), an organization that supports tribes in establishing tribal courts. NICS is an innovative, non-profit organization that relies on federal and tribal funding, (72 percent and 28 percent, respectively) and is overseen by a governing board comprised of representatives from each of its seven member tribes. In addition to its member tribes, NICS also serves two affiliate tribes and a handful of tribes that contract NICS' services. Although NICS was established in response to the Boldt decision, it now supports tribal courts in their handling of a full array of civil and criminal matters, including major crimes, misdemeanors, civil suits, infractions, and a host of legal issues related to hunting and fishing offenses, child dependencies, guardianships, adoptions, gambling, zoning and land use, environmental protection, and tribal employment.

NICS is divided into several units that meet these tribal needs. One group of such units serves to provide operational support to their members. For example, the Judicial Unit hires full-time, part-time, and contract judges to preside over tribal courts (currently three staff judges and two contract judges). The NICS Appellate Unit, established in 1987, recruits and trains a roster of appellate judges (currently thirty) who are impaneled on three-member appellate benches that hear roughly thirty cases a year. The Appellate Unit also publishes a compilation of its decisions in the biennial Appellate Reporter. The NICS Prosecutorial Unit consists of prosecutors, paralegals, and assistants who work closely with tribal law enforcement leaders. These services facilitate tribal courts' effective adjudication of tribal law.

Another group of NICS' units provides assistance in the development of tribal law and codes. Its Code Development Unit consists of a code developer, a full-time legal assistant, a law clerk, and several contract code writers. This unit works closely with tribal committees to draft codes and regulations for each member tribe that reflect the unique culture, values, and traditions of the people to whom the law will apply. Without customized codes, courts could not adjudicate tribal policies justly. The Technology Unit has supported the code-developing mandate of NICS since 2001 by converting tribal codes and court forms into electronic documents that are easily accessible to member tribes' judges, prosecutors, attorneys, and staff. This electronic information also helps member tribes' courts work as efficiently as their state and federal counterparts.

Since 1979, NICS member tribes have experienced great success in reclaiming jurisdiction over civil and criminal matters affecting their communities. The Prosecutorial Unit is currently handling 1,910 cases that might otherwise be in state courts. Through NICS support, the Tulalip Tribes have undertaken a retrocession of PL 280 criminal jurisdiction from Washington. Since retrocession, the number of criminal complaints filed in Tulalip's tribal court has risen dramatically from 56 in 2001 to 262 in 2002. Without the support of NICS, this major reassertion of tribal sovereignty would not have been possible: the Tribes would simply not have had the capacity to take up this new caseload. Other member tribes are experiencing similar empowerment. In the past year, the caseload for some tribes has increased 100 percent as they have assumed responsibility for increasingly numerous and complex legal issues. . . .

Legitimate concerns have been expressed over the whether a tribe—particularly a small tribe—can pool its talents and resources with others without forfeiting a measure of control. NICS' member tribes' experiences, however, suggests that creating a shared system for their courts is an important, and bold, exercise of their sovereignty. They contend that their decision to pool resources is, in itself, a sovereign choice and, further, that pooling of resources allows them to sustain courts that they would not otherwise have. The administration of justice has a steep learning curve and requires substantial investments in recording precedents, codes, and processes. NICS member tribes share the knowledge, funds, and, most importantly, the human capital necessary to administer justice effectively and efficiently. . . .

Finally, the tribes' experience within the Northwest Intertribal Court System demonstrates that effective tribal courts may emerge out of the consortium form. Several of NICS past member tribes—the Lummi, Suquamish, Nisqually, and Squaxin Island tribes—now have entirely autonomous tribal courts. This independence is consistent with the NICS mission of assisting tribes in the exercise of their sovereignty. So, too, however, is the continuing cooperative pooling of resources that empowers its current member tribes. Choosing to establish a tribal court—autonomous or shared—is a vital step toward enhanced tribal sovereignty.

ORGANIZED VILLAGE OF KAKE

Harvard Project on American Indian Economic Development Honoring Nations
2003 Honoree

Kake Circle Peacemaking

. . . The Organized Village of Kake had long recognized the devastating toll of rampant alcoholism. Unfortunately, one of the means of combating the problem — the justice system — appeared unavailable to Kake's Native citizens. The Alaska State justice system had not successfully addressed these issues in Alaska Native communities for decades. A primary problem was that its resources were stretched thin. The juvenile probation officer assigned to Kake lived on another island that was accessible only by ferryboat or plane. Responding to felony offenses consumed most of his time; therefore, he could pay only limited attention to the seemingly less serious misdemeanors of Kake's youth. Unfortunately, without the consequences that good probation monitoring could provide, the minor infractions of village youth tended to grow into entrenched adult behavior.

By the late 1990s, Kake residents realized that without breaking this cycle, the Village's future looked bleak. Despite the confined jurisdictional space in which they operated (the state of Alaska has authority over most aspects of criminal justice in Native Alaska), they also realized that they could craft a solution that relied on local human and cultural resources. Looking to the philosophy of peacemaking and the process of circle sentencing, Kake village volunteers organized the Healing Heart Council and Circle Peacemaking in 1999. This reconciliation and sentencing process is embedded in Tlingit tradition and works in conjunction with the Alaska State court system.

Circle Peacemaking begins when a Kake juvenile enters a guilty plea with the state court. Then, the state judge, with the concurrence of the prosecutor, the public defender, and the offender, may turn the juvenile's case over to the Healing Heart Council for sentencing. The Council initiates Circle Peacemaking by bringing together a group of village volunteers to formally sentence the young offender(s). Through the close attention, encouragement, and admonishment of this circle of volunteer justices, the juvenile's misdemeanors have a lower probability of leading to more serious adult substance abuse and crime. Circle Peacemaking heals the offender by addressing the underlying causes of the offending behavior and restores the rupture in community life by repairing the relationship between the offender and victim.

More specifically, Circle Peacemaking involves the participation of individuals and groups who rarely come together under Western systems of justice — the offender, the victim, families, friends, church representatives, police, substance abuse counselors, and concerned or affected community members. Participants, who may number from six to sixty, sit in a circle while a Keeper of the Circle facilitates the discussion. Discussions always begin and end with a prayer, and negative comments are strictly forbidden. Circle discussions are kept entirely confidential, and the Keeper encourages participants to speak from their hearts. The meetings typically last two to four hours, but they can only end when forgiveness and healing are apparent and consensus is reached about the offender's sentence. This sentence then becomes public.

But Circle Peacemaking does not conclude with sentencing. The circle participants are themselves responsible for ensuring that offenders adhere to their sentences. A typical sentence for underage alcohol consumption might include a curfew, community service, or a formal apology. It might also require that the offender meet with elders or others who have worked through comparable experiences. Frequently, a sentence requires the offender's participation in other support circles. Importantly, the circle participants play a key role in assessing whether the offender's compliance is satisfactory. It is not uncommon for them to call for additional circles. Non-compliant offenders must return to the Alaska State court for sentencing.

Since its inception, the dedication of volunteers and judicious use of its minimal annual budget — a few thousand dollars in most years — have enabled Circle Peacemaking to expand its jurisdiction from underage alcohol consumption cases to include broader community needs. Today, the Healing Heart Council offers not only sentencing circles for juvenile offenders, but also sentencing circles for adult offenders who request Circle Peacemaking, healing circles for victims, intervention circles for individuals who seem to be losing control of their lives, celebration circles for offenders who have completed their sentencing requirements, and critical incident circles for individuals involved in an accident or crime who require immediate counseling. Additionally, the Healing Heart Council offers annual Circle Peacemaking Workshops that attract an average of 24 participants from Kake and other villages who are interested in learning how the Alaska State court system and Circle Peacemaking complement each other.

This interest is itself evidence of Circle Peacemaking's success in Kake. Only two offenders out of the eighty sentenced during the program's first four years rejected a circle's outcome and returned to state court for sentencing. All of the twenty-four juveniles who were assigned to circle sentencing for underage drinking successfully completed the terms of their sentences. Circle Peacemaking also reports very low levels of recidivism. Sixty-eight adults participated in circles without repeating their offenses or violating other laws during their probation periods. At the time of writing, approximately thirty village residents are enrolled in substance abuse recovery programs. Circle Peacemaking veterans are moving on with their lives in other ways as well. Several have gone on to trade schools to complete their education; several are enrolled in universities. One adult veteran of a circle is now a juvenile justice associate and working on an alcohol abuse counseling certificate. These successes are reflected in a positive trend in the circles themselves. Over four years, the number of mandated sentencing circles decreased and the number of volunteer support circles increased — initiated by individuals who have not yet committed offenses and are determined to avoid doing so. Unsurprisingly, Kake now sponsors well-attended sobriety marches, and Village residents have begun to comment on the perceptible difference in their community. It is a community in which the intergenerational pattern of substance abuse is being broken, and where youth and adults alike face brighter, healthier futures.

Significantly, Kake Circle Peacemaking's successes are occurring where the Alaska State court system repeatedly failed. Over four years, Circle Peacemaking has experienced a 97.5 percent success rate in sentences fulfillment compared to the Alaskan court system's 22 percent success rate. . . .

This has, of course, been especially significant considering the neglect and even outright hostility that the Alaska state government so frequently displays toward Alaskan tribes. It should be noted, in conclusion, that notwithstanding targeted state efforts to reduce tribal decision-making power, Kake has instituted a system of justice that increases tribal sovereignty. It has done so in a manner that commands the respect of the state judicial system while honoring its own community traditions. Although peacemaking courts are spreading throughout Indian Country, their influence in Alaska has been limited. Other than Kake, the Metlakatla Tribe is the only tribe in Alaska that takes on criminal cases beyond its Indian Child Welfare load. In Alaska, the barriers to constructing tribal courts capable of entering into full faith and comity agreements with the state courts or of raising sentencing controversies to the level of federal court review, as tribal peacemaker courts have done elsewhere, are significant. Still, Kake Circle Peacemaking has, to the great benefit of its village, expertly assumed a state court function that was otherwise executed ineffectively. The Organized Village of Kake intends to make Circle

Peacemaking a permanent fixture of self-governance by enshrining it in their constitution. Circle Peacemaking's success and the village's determination to ensure its perpetuation stand as significant triumphs in the development of a robust tribal judicial system. These are remarkable and desperately needed achievements in Alaska.

B. CHOICE OF LAW: CUSTOMARY, TRADITIONAL, AMERICAN, OR INTERTRIBAL?[*]

1. THE ROLE OF CUSTOM IN MODERN JURISPRUDENCE

Consider the following hypothetical, based in part on *Malaterre v. Estate of St. Claire*, No. 05-007 (Turtle Mountain Band Ct. App. 2006).[†]

A newly married couple move into a new home on the Lake Matchimanitou Indian Reservation in Michigan. They live on trust land and both are citizens of the Lake Matchimanitou Band of Ottawa Indians. They have two children in the first three years of marriage. The husband's parents, who also live on the reservation but in an older home, become ill. One has a stroke and the other has diabetes. Both are unable to walk and require wheelchairs. Their home is not handicap-accessible, but the newlyweds' home is handicap-accessible. The husband and wife discuss the matter and offer to "trade" homes with his parents until they are able to return to their own home. His parents agree. They "trade" homes, but no contract, lease, or other document is executed memorializing the agreement. The wife is never happy with the new arrangement. The newlyweds' relationship degenerates and the husband moves out, leaving the wife and their two children in the old house. The husband's parents, still living in the newlyweds' home, file suit in Lake Matchimanitou tribal court seeking the wife's eviction from the old home, while maintaining they will not move out of the new home. At trial, the wife alleges that she was coerced into agreeing to the "trade" due to the husband's threat of violence.

The hypothetical presents a difficult but typical choice of law problem. In the absence of tribal statutory or common law, should customary law apply? How do the parties and the tribal court find the customary law? Should they follow the Ottawa First Book, assuming any of its provisions apply?

Customary law still appears in many of the decisions of American state and federal courts. Customary law, part and parcel of the English common law adopted and adapted by the Founders of the United States, appears as the basis of decision less often given that statutory and administrative law dominate the field.

In contrast, the importance of customary law in American Indian tribal courts cannot be understated. Indian tribes now take every measure conceivable to preserve indigenous cultures and restore lost cultural knowledge and

---

[*] *Author note:*—Much of the material in this part is derived from Matthew L. M. Fletcher, *Rethinking Customary Law in Tribal Court Jurisprudence*, 13 Mich. J. Race & L. 57 (2007).

[†] *Disclosure:* The author of this book participated in the case as a sitting appellate judge, and wrote the opinion.

practices. Tribal court litigation, especially litigation involving tribal members and issues arising out of tribal law, often turns on the ancient customs and traditions of the people.

2. THE LEGAL FRAMEWORK FOR THE USE OF CUSTOM IN TRIBAL COURT DECISION MAKING: RULES OF RECOGNITION AND CHANGE

Many tribal constitutions, tribal court codes and ordinances, and tribal court rules require the use of customary law in tribal court decision making. And there are tribal courts that are not required to use customary law or are even precluded from using customary law in certain circumstances. The various statutes and rules offer varying ways and means for the use of customary law.

a. Tribal Constitutional Provisions

The constitution of the Passamaquoddy Tribe in Maine offers one example of a constitutional mandate for using customary law. The relevant provision reads:

> Civil disputes which are within the jurisdiction of the Passamaquoddy Tribal Court shall, to the extent consistent with applicable tribal laws, ordinances, customs, and usages, as well as applicable provisions of federal Indian law, be resolved by the Tribal Court in accordance with any corresponding provisions of the applicable civil laws and remedies of the State of Maine, and such laws and remedies shall to that extent be deemed adopted as the law of the Pleasant Point Reservation of the Passamaquoddy Tribe.

CONST. OF THE SIPAYIK MEMBERS OF THE PASSAMAQUODDY TRIBE art. VIII, §1. This provision allows the tribal court to apply tribal customary law on par with tribal statutes and applicable federal and state law. The provision allows for the tribal court to declare the existence and applicability of customary law as the law of the tribe.

In contrast, the Constitution of the Grand Traverse Band of Ottawa and Chippewa Indians is silent as to customary law. The constitution provides, "This Constitution, ordinances, resolutions, regulations, and judicial decisions of the Band shall govern all people subject to the Grand Traverse Band's jurisdiction." CONST. OF THE GRAND TRAVERSE BAND OF OTTAWA AND CHIPPEWA INDIANS art. VI. Silence does not preclude the Grand Traverse Band tribal courts from applying customary law in its decisions, but it does limit the persuasive character and applicability of customary law.

b. Tribal Statutes

DINÉ CHOICE–OF–LAW STATUTE

7 Navajo Nation Code §204

A. In all cases the courts of the Navajo Nation shall first apply applicable Navajo Nation statutory laws and regulations to resolve matters in dispute before the courts. The Courts shall utilize Diné bi beenahaz'áanii (Navajo

Traditional, Customary, Natural or Common Law) to guide the interpretation of Navajo Nation statutory laws and regulations. The courts shall also utilize Diné bi beenahaz'áanii whenever Navajo Nation statutes or regulations are silent on matters in dispute before the courts.

B. To determine the appropriate utilization and interpretation of Diné bi beenahaz'áanii, the court shall request, as it deems necessary, advice from Navajo individuals widely recognized as being knowledgeable about Diné bi beenahaz'áanii.

C. The courts of the Navajo Nation shall apply federal laws or regulations as may be applicable.

D. Any matters not addressed by Navajo Nation statutory laws and regulations, Diné bi beenahaz'áanii or by applicable federal laws and regulations, may be decided according to comity with reference to the laws of the state in which the matter in dispute may have arisen.

NOTES

1. Former long-time Associate Justice of the Navajo Nation Supreme Court Raymond D. Austin's book *Navajo Courts and Navajo Common Law: A Tradition of Tribal Self-Governance* (2009) delves into far greater detail about the sources and interpretation of Navajo common law. *See id.* at 37-51. In 2002, the Navajo legislature adopted Resolution No. CN-69-02, recognizing the Fundamental Laws of the Diné. *See* 2 Navajo Nation Code §§201-206.

   Justice Austin notes that "Navajo Nation courts do not need statutory authorization to use Navajo common law," but that there has been a choice-of-law statute in the Navajo code books authorizing the use of common law since 1959. *See id.* at 44.

2. On February 23, 2010, the Navajo Nation tribal council attempted to bar the Nation's judiciary from using Fundamental Law, leaving tribal customs and traditions to be resolved by the Nation's peacemaker courts exclusively. *See Navajo Council Overrides Veto of Fundamental Law Bill*, Indianz.com, Feb. 24, 2010, *available at* http://64.38.12.138/News/2010/018533.asp. However, Dr. Austin argued that the Fundamental Law could be applied by the Navajo judiciary without statutory authorization, and so it would seem the Navajo courts could continue to utilize the Fundamental Law. *See* Austin, *supra*, at 44-45. In fact, it appears the Navajo Supreme Court has repeatedly utilized the Fundamental Law in recent decisions. *E.g., In re Seanez*, No. SC—CV-58-10, slip op. at 4 (Navajo Nation S. Ct., Oct. 22, 2010) (noting that Frank seanez "claimed attorney-client privilege when asked if he ever advised his client about ways in which the branches may communicate according to the Diné fundamental principle of *k'é*, which we have described in our holdings as vital in the way our leaders are to approach each other").

3. Tribal legislatures provide many different hierarchies and procedures in their choice-of-law provisions. The White Earth Band of Chippewa Indians Judicial Code, for example, requires the tribal court to "[reduce] to writing with a historical justification therefor" any tribal "tradition and custom" it chooses to follow. White Earth Band of Chippewa Indians Judicial Code ch. VII,

§6(a). The decisions of the tribal court "shall become a precedential guide for the unwritten tradition, customs or laws so as to allow future Judges and litigants to be guided on the traditional law and custom." *Id.* Customary law is ranked on par with "other laws" in the choice-of-law hierarchy. §6(b). The tribal court may, if doubt arises, "request the advice and assistance of the panel of elders." *Id.* This statute provides clearer guidance to the White Earth Band tribal court than many other tribal choice-of-law provisions. The code provides that the tribal court may announce customary law and is not required, unless it chooses, to consult with tribal elders on customary law. Moreover, the code mandates that the tribal court follow any customary law that it announces. Finally, the code requires that the tribal court reduce to writing unwritten customary law that it announces so that it may be used as precedent.

4. The Oglala Sioux Tribe Law and Order Code authorizes the tribal code to use customary law, but only if the custom does not conflict with tribal statutes and federal law. The statute provides, "[T]he Oglala Sioux Tribal Court shall give binding effect to . . . any applicable custom or usage of the Oglala Sioux Tribe not in conflict with any of the Tribe or United States." OGLALA SIOUX TRIBE LAW AND ORDER CODE ch. II, §20.27(c). As with the White Earth Band statute, "[w]here doubt arises as to such customs and usages, the Court may request the testimony, as witnesses of the Court, of personal [sic] familiar with such customs and usages." *Id.* The Oglala Sioux legislature made clear that customary law is not on par with tribal law or even federal law. Of course, it is a distinct possibility that the legislature did not or could not act without interference from federal officials, as is often the case where the tribal constitution requires the approval of the Secretary of Interior in the enactment of tribal codes. CONST. AND BY-LAWS OF THE OGLALA SIOUX TRIBE OF THE PINE RIDGE INDIAN RESERVATION OF SOUTH DAKOTA art. XI ("[N]o amendment shall become effective until it shall have been approved by the Secretary of the Interior.").

5. The Stockbridge-Munsee Community of Mohican Indians' tribal court code is similar in some respect to the White Earth Band's code, but applies only to the rules of procedure for the tribal court. The code provides:

> [The Tribal Court Code] is exempted from the rule of strict construction. It shall be read and understood in a manner that gives full effect to the purposes for which it is enacted. Whenever there is uncertainty or a question as to the interpretation of certain provisions of this code, tribal law or custom shall be controlling and where appropriate may be based on the written or oral testimony of a qualified tribal elder, historian or other representative.

STOCKBRIDGE-MUNSEE TRIBAL LAW TRIBAL COURT CODE ch. I, §1.3(B).

As with other tribal court codes, the Stockbridge-Munsee tribal court can and should seek the advice of a tribal person with relevant knowledge. This particular statute is different in that the tribal legislature has mandated that customary law be used not as substantive law but as a device to be used to interpret the tribal court code.

6. The Bay Mills Indian Community's tribal court code puts customary law on par with tribal statutes and applicable federal law, so long as the custom does not conflict with federal law:

> In all civil actions, the Tribal Court shall apply the applicable laws of the United States, any authorized regulations of the Department of Interior which may be applicable, any ordinance of the Bay Mills Indian Community, and any custom of the Chippewa Tribe not prohibited by the laws of the United States.

BAY MILLS INDIAN CMTY. TRIBAL CODE ch. IV, Law Applicable to Civil Actions, §A. The Bay Mills tribal court, however, must "request the advice of persons familiar with these customs and usage's [sic]." §B.

7. Other tribal statutes emphasize the use of customary law in certain types of disputes. The Little River Band of Ottawa Indians' Children's Code provides "because of the vital interest of the Tribe in its children and those children who may become members of the Tribe, this Code, other ordinances, regulations, public policies, recognized customs and common law of the Tribe shall control in any proceeding involving a child who is a member of the Tribe." LITTLE RIVER BAND OF OTTAWA INDIANS CODE ch. 900, §3.08(a). The code adds:

> The substantive law and procedures for the state courts shall not be binding upon the Children's Court except where specifically provided for in this Code. In the absence of promulgated rules of procedure, procedural rules of the State of Michigan shall be utilized as a guide. Michigan case law may serve as a guide for the Court but shall not be binding. Any matters not covered by the substantive laws, regulations, customs or common law of the Little River Band of Ottawa, or by applicable federal laws or regulations, may be decided by the Children's Court according to the laws of the State of Michigan.

§3.08(c).

8. Many court codes simply note the existence of possible customary law, but do not regulate its application. For example, the Kenaitze Indian Tribe's code is nonspecific on how customary law can be used:

> The purpose of this Code is to honor and acknowledge our prior Customs, History, Traditions, and Experience for the purpose of preserving, strengthening, and continuing the Tribal Court into the future. To ensure the efficient and fair administration of justice, the Tribal Court shall continue to resolve conflicts and disputes and enforce Tribal Laws through the application of Cultural Traditions, Customary and Traditional Values, Written Law, Codes, and Ordinances.

1 KENAITZE TRIBAL CODE §3(b). And:

> Issues of Tribal Law, Custom or Procedure on Appeal: If the petition to appeal alleges that the Tribal Court has made an error in applying or interpreting Tribal Law, Custom or Procedure, the Court shall review the applicable law, custom and/or procedure to determine whether the Tribal Court has correctly applied or interpreted the law. If the Appellate Court finds that an

error was made, it can direct the Tribal Court to review its ruling or it can overturn its ruling.

1 KENAITZE TRIBAL CODE §10(d)(ii).

c. Tribal Court Rules

HOOPA VALLEY TRIBE, TRADITIONAL TRIBAL LAW

Hoopa Valley Tribal Code §2.1.04

The traditional law of the Hoopa Valley Tribe is the common law of the Tribe tantamount to the written law of the Tribe and will be applied in all situations where it is relevant to the issues raised in an action before the Court. The Court will first look to the laws adopted by the Tribe and to the Constitution and Bylaws of the Hoopa Valley Tribe. If no written Tribal law applies to a cause of action or the issues involved in an action, the Court will look to the Tribe's traditional law and if it finds the traditional law to be applicable in settling the dispute, will base its decision on traditional Tribal law.

(a) The Tribal Court may be used to facilitate a traditional form of dispute resolution, akin to a mediated settlement. The parties may identify a [go-between], to mediate between the parties until a stipulated agreement is reached. The Court will then issue an order containing the stipulated agreement.

(b) Where the parties choose to follow the civil procedures of Title 2, in any dispute, claim, or action, in which a party asserts that traditional Tribal law governs the outcome, the Court must first determine what the traditional law is. If the traditional Tribal law has been acknowledged by a legal writing of the Tribe the Court will apply the written law.

(1) Evidence that a traditional law is written includes written reference to a traditional law, right, or custom in a Tribal resolution, motion, order, ordinance or other document acted upon by the Tribal Council. Anthropological writings or publications, and personal writings are not evidence that the traditional law is written, but may be presented as persuasive or supporting evidence that the traditional law or custom exists.

(c) In any dispute, claim, or action, in which a party asserts that traditional Tribal law governs the outcome, and the Court finds that the traditional law is unwritten, the Court will hold a hearing to determine what the traditional law is.

(1) The parties may stipulate to what the traditional law to be applied is. If the parties stipulate to the traditional Tribal law, the Court will then hold an evidentiary hearing to determine the facts of the case.

(2) If the parties do not stipulate to the traditional Tribal law, the parties may stipulate to a list of neutral Tribal members to act as expert witnesses, whose testimony will be relied upon to determine the traditional Tribal law.

(A) If the parties do not stipulate to such a list, each party shall be allowed to call their own expert witnesses. The Court will determine how many expert witnesses each party may call to testify except that each party shall be allowed to call the same number of expert witnesses.

(B) Each party shall submit a list of Tribal elders' names that they wish to call as expert witnesses. The opposing party will have the right to Voir Dire the witnesses to determine if they are, in fact, knowledgeable of traditional Tribal law.

(C) Each party shall also submit to the Court a list of Tribal members' names that the party believes to be neutral and impartial, and knowledgeable of traditional Tribal law. The Court shall select from the submitted list names of individuals to act as expert witnesses for the Court.

(3) The Court may, but is not required to, accept recommendations of the parties before determining the neutral and impartial expert witnesses that will testify before the Court. The Court will determine how many neutral and impartial witnesses may testify except that the number will not exceed the number of witnesses that each party will be allowed to call as expert witnesses. The parties will have the right to Voir Dire the witnesses to determine if they are, in fact, knowledgeable of traditional Tribal law.

(d) After the expert witnesses have been determined, the parties will submit to each other and the Court a list of questions to be asked of each of the witnesses. A party may object to any question submitted by an opposing party. The Court will then determine which questions will be asked of each of the expert witnesses. The Court shall have the discretion to ask its own questions of the expert witnesses.

(e) After hearing the expert witnesses' testimony the Court will issue a Conclusion of Law in which the Court will state what it has found to be the traditional Tribal law. If either of the partyies object to the Court's conclusion, the Court will meet in closed session with all of the expert witnesses. The Court will then call for a discussion of the Conclusion of Law by the expert witnesses. Following this discussion, the Court may re-issue or amend and re-issue the Conclusion of Law, or repeat the process as defined herein, selecting different neutral and impartial witnesses and/or a different set of questions to be asked of the expert witnesses.

(f) Once the Court has determined what the traditional law to be applied is, the Court will set a date for a conference hearing pursuant to Title 3, Rule 12 (b).

NOTES

1. The most detailed, complicated, ambitious, and (possibly) unworkable tribal rule relating to customary law is Section 2.1.04 of the Hoopa Valley Tribal Code. (Despite being labeled a "code," this portion of the Hoopa tribal code actually was first promulgated by the tribal court as court rules.) First,

the code provides that customary law must be used by the tribal court where tribal statute is silent. §2.1.04. Second, the code provides a detailed procedure for determining what the tribal customs are. §2.1.04(b). The first step in the procedure is to determine if the tribal custom was written: "If the traditional Tribal law has been acknowledged by a legal writing of the Tribe the Court will apply the written law." *Id.* Tribal custom is "written" if the Hoopa tribal council has taken action that amounts to a ratification of the custom. §2.1.04(b)(1).

So, in the case of the Hoopa tribe, the tribal council may announce customary law to the exclusion of the tribal court, but the code still authorizes the tribal court to announce customary law after following a complex procedure that includes the selection of expert witnesses similar to the way litigants sometimes select arbitrators and a hearing (or series of hearings) in which the tribal court may issue a "Conclusion of Law" declaring the customary law of the tribe. §2.1.04(c).

The Hoopa rule is a serious attempt to deal with many of the potential problems relating to discovering, recovering, and applying customary law. Reasonable minds can differ as to the meaning or validity of tribal customs and traditions, and the rule attempts to create a procedure that alleviates these concerns. But the rule's adopting of an arbitration-style hearing involving a battle of tribal elders as expert witnesses probably has, in the experience of the author as former staff attorney and current appellate judge for the Tribe, prevented the application of any customary law in Hoopa courts.

2. The Winnebago Tribe of Nebraska's court rule is similar to the Oglala Sioux statute noted above. The rule mandates that the tribal court "apply traditional Tribal customs and usages, which shall be called the common law," but only if no tribal statute answers the legal question. WINNEBAGO TRIBAL COURT CODE tit. 1, art. 1, §1-109. The rule also provides that "[w]hen in doubt as to the Tribal common law, the Court may request the advice of counselors and Tribal elders familiar with it." *Id.* Winnebago civil court rules further provide:

> 1. In all civil cases, the tribal court shall apply:
>
> > A. The constitution, statutes, and common law of the Tribe not prohibited by applicable federal law, and, if none, then
> > B. The federal law including federal common law, and, if none, then
> > C. The laws of any state or other jurisdiction which the Court finds to be compatible with the public policy and needs of the Tribe.
>
> 2. No federal or state law shall be applied to a civil action pursuant to paragraphs (B) and (C) of subsection (1) of this section if such law is inconsistent with the laws of the Tribe or the public policy of the Tribe.
>
> 3. Where any doubt arises as to the customs and usages of the Tribe, the Court, either on its own motion or the motion of any party, may subpoena and request the advice of elders and counselors familiar with those customs and usages.

WINNEBAGO TRIBAL COURT CODE tit. 2, art. 1, §2-111.

3. THE USE OF CUSTOM IN TRIBAL COURT OPINIONS: APPLICATIONS OF THE RULES OF ADJUDICATION

Tribal courts vary in the ways that they find, analyze, and apply tribal customary law. Most tribal courts cannot rely upon customary law for various reasons. They are unaware of it; or, if they are aware of it, no customary law they are aware of applies to the fact pattern at issue. It is important to discuss instances of tribal courts applying customary law to locate methods of finding, analyzing, and applying customary law in order to discern the strengths and weaknesses of their methods. Tribal courts that cannot or do not apply much custom in their analysis can learn from these courts.

NAVAJO NATION v. RODRIGUEZ

Navajo Nation Supreme Court No. SC-CR-03-04, 8 Navajo Rep. 604, 5 Am. Tribal L. 473, 2004.NANN.0000014 (December 16, 2004)

Before FERGUSON, Acting Chief Justice, and HOLGATE, Associate Justice (by designation). . . .

I.

The relevant facts are undisputed. The Navajo Nation police arrested Appellant Rafael Rodriguez ("Rodriguez") following a shooting at a trailer park in Kayenta. While in custody, Investigator Kirk Snyder ("Investigator Snyder") of the Kayenta Police District interviewed Rodriguez. Investigator Snyder began the interview by stating to Rodriguez that his alleged actions could put in him in federal prison for up to sixty years and could result in a fine of a million and a half dollars. Investigator Snyder then produced an "advice of rights" form, a document laying out several purported rights, apparently based on the United States Supreme Court's ruling in *Miranda v. Arizona*, 384 U.S. 436 (1966). The form was in English, and there is no evidence that Investigator Snyder explained each of those rights in English or Navajo. Rodriguez signed a waiver on the bottom of the form, and then proceeded to write out a lengthy confession (Confession) implicating himself as the shooter.

. . . The Navajo Nation submitted the advice of rights form and the Confession during the testimony of Investigator Snyder. After hearing objections from Rodriguez, [the Kayenta District Court] admitted both into evidence. After hearing the witnesses and reviewing the evidence the Kayenta District Court found Rodriguez guilty [of aggravated assault], and sentenced him to one year in jail. Rodriguez then filed this appeal. . . .

II.

The issues in this case are . . . (2) whether a coerced confession may be used in a criminal proceeding to establish the truth of the allegations in the criminal complaint; and (3) whether the provision of an English language form informing a person in custody of his or her rights, and a signed waiver by that person on the form, without more, is sufficient for a confession to be voluntary. . . .

IV.

Rodriguez argues that the District Court wrongly allowed the Confession into evidence for the truth of the allegations in the criminal complaint. He contends that Investigator Snyder coerced the statement through threats and other pressure. He also contends that, even if there was no coercion, the "advice of rights form" itself is insufficient, as applied to him, as a waiver of his right not to give a statement to the police. At oral argument the Navajo Nation conceded that there was a "degree of coercion" by Investigator Snyder, but that the confession was nonetheless valid because Rodriguez signed the advice of rights form, thereby waiving his right not to make the statement. . . .

A.

Section 8 of our Navajo Bill of Rights protects criminal defendants from being "compelled . . . to be a witness against themselves." 1 N.N.C. §8, This provision is almost identical in language to the equivalent section of the Indian Civil Rights Act, 25 U.S.C. §1302(4) (Indian tribe cannot "compel any person in a criminal case to be a witness against himself"), and the Fifth Amendment to the United States Constitution (no person can be "compelled in any criminal case to be a witness against himself"). In *Navajo Nation v. McDonald*, we recognized that the right against self-incrimination under our Bill of Rights is fundamental. 7 Nav. R. 1, 13 (Nav. Sup. Ct. 1992). A person cannot give information for his or her own punishment unless there is a "knowing and voluntary decision to do so." *Id.* We interpreted the English words in our Bill of Rights in light of the Navajo principle rejecting coercion. *Id.* We said that "others may 'talk' about a Navajo, but that does not mean coercion can be used to make that person admit guilt or the facts leading to a conclusion of guilt." *Id.*

We reiterate these principles today. Our Navajo Bill of Rights, as informed by the Navajo value of individual freedom, prohibits coerced confessions. We expand upon *McDonald* by applying these principles to a person in police custody. The police department is an arm of the Navajo government, and as such must recognize a person's rights in much the same ways, and to the same extent, as must our courts. Therefore, in this case, the right against coerced self-incrimination attached not when Rodriguez first appeared before the district court, but when he was placed in police custody and was interviewed by Investigator Snyder.

Based on the Navajo Nation's concession that the police coerced Rodriguez, we have no choice but to conclude that coercion occurred. The Navajo Nation did not dispute that the investigator threatened Rodriguez by indicating to him the possibility of sixty years of federal jail time and a fine of one and a half million dollars before Rodriguez reviewed and signed the advice of rights form. Though the Navajo Nation referred to a "degree of coercion" without defining "degree," we do not see how coercion can be measured by degrees. Either the police coerced Rodriguez or it did not. The parties agree that Rodriguez was coerced, and we find that any degree of coercion is in violation of the Navajo Bill of Rights.

B.

The coercion itself may be enough to vacate Rodriguez's conviction; however we also consider the Navajo Nation's argument that his waiver on the advice of rights form was enough for his confession to be admissible. As discussed above, the right against self-incrimination in the Navajo Nation includes the requirement that a confession be "knowing." *McDonald*, 7 Nav. R. at 13. Even if no coercion occurred, we must decide what rights Rodriguez had when he signed the waiver. The main question is whether the protections recognized in the United States Supreme Court's decision in *Miranda* apply on the Navajo Nation, or whether this Court should apply some other approach.

In giving meaning to the right against self-incrimination, this Court does not have to directly apply federal interpretations of the Bill of Rights. In interpreting the Navajo Bill of Rights and the Indian Civil Rights Act, as with other statutes that contain ambiguous language, we first and foremost make sure that such interpretation is consistent with the Fundamental Laws of the Diné. Navajo Nation Council Resolution No. CN-69-02 (November 1, 2002). That the Navajo Nation Council explicitly adopts language from outside sources, or that a statute contains similar language, does not, without more, mean the Council intended us to ignore fundamental Diné principles in giving meaning to such provisions. *Cf. Fort Defiance Housing Corp. v. Lowe*, No. SCCV-32-03, slip op. at 6 (Nav. Sup. Ct. April 12, 2004) (statute adopted from outside source is not illegitimate, but must be carefully interpreted consistent with Navajo values). Indeed, Navajo understanding of the English words adopted in statutes may differ from the accepted Anglo understanding. . . .

While we are not required to apply federal interpretations, we nonetheless consider them in our analysis. We consider all ways of thinking and possible approaches to a problem, including federal law approaches, and we weigh their underlying values and effects to decide what is best for our people. We have applied federal interpretations, but have augmented them with Navajo values, often providing broader rights than that provided in the equivalent federal provision. *See, e.g., Duncan v. Shiprock District Court*, No. SC-CV-51-04, slip op. at 8, n. 5 (Nav. Sup. Ct. October 28, 2004) (applying federal definition of "equitable proceeding" but declining to apply Seventh Amendment historical test on right to jury trial); *Lowe*, No. SC-CV-32-03, slip op. at 4-5 (recognizing that Navajo Due Process protects a greater scope of "property" than federal due process). Our consideration of outside interpretations is especially important for issues involving our modern Navajo government, which includes institutions such as police, jails, and courts that track state and federal government structures not present in traditional Navajo society. *See, e.g., Mitchell v. Davis*, No. SC-CV-52-03, slip op. at 3-4 (Nav. Sup. Ct. August 16, 2004) (using federal interpretations of civil procedure rules as part of analysis for interpreting Navajo court rules adapted from federal rules).

We hereby interpret the right against self-incrimination to require, at a minimum, clear notice by the police in a custodial situation that the person in custody (1) has the right to remain silent and may request the presence of legal counsel during questioning, (2) that any statements can be used against him or her, (3) the right to an attorney, and (4) the right to have an attorney appointed if he or she cannot afford an attorney. These are the rights already recognized by the Kayenta Police District in their advice of rights form, and we confirm here that they apply across the Navajo Nation. Essentially, we adopt the minimum requirements from Miranda as consistent with our Navajo values. We have previously suggested, without explicitly holding, that this is appropriate *See In re A.W.*, 6 Nav. R. 38 (Nav. Sup. Ct. 1989) (referring to "Miranda rights" required to be given in Navajo Children's Code); *Navajo Nation v. McCabe*, 1 Nav. R. 63, 64-65 (Ct. App. 1971) (indicating Miranda rights not necessary without explicitly adopting standard).

However, we add the following: The mere giving of a standardized "advice of rights" form to a person in custody is not enough The relationship between the Navajo Nation government and its individual citizens requires the same level of respect as the relationship between one person to another. In our Navajo way of thinking we must communicate clearly and concisely to each other so that we may understand the meaning of our words and the effect of our actions based on those words. The responsibility of the government is even stronger when a fundamental right, such as the right against self-incrimination, is involved.

In *Miranda*, the U.S. Supreme Court recounted the source of the constitutional protection against self-incrimination. *Miranda*, at 442-443 (quoting *Brown v. Walker*, 161 U.S. 591 (1896). Reminiscing about the English criminal procedure, the Court stated that

> if an accused person be asked to explain his apparent connection with a crime under investigation, the ease with which the questions put to him may assume an inquisitorial character, the temptation to press the witness unduly, to brow-beat him if he be timid or reluctant, to push him into a corner, and to entrap him into fatal contradictions . . . made the system so odious as to give rise to a demand for its total abolition.

Id. With such inequities impressed upon the minds of American colonists, "a denial of the right to question an accused person became clothed in this country with the impregnability of a constitutional enactment." *Id.*

We are not guided in our own criminal jurisprudence by a legacy of internal oppression. Nevertheless, the U.S. Supreme Court's discussion reminds us of our Navajo principle of *hazho'ogo*. *Hazho'ogo* is not a man-made law, but rather a fundamental tenet informing us how we must approach each other as individuals. When discussions become heated, whether in a family setting, in a community meeting or between any people, it's not uncommon for an elderly person to stand and say "*hazhó'ógo, hazho'ogo sha'alchini.*"[3] The intent is to remind those involved that they are *Nohookaa Diné'é*,[4] dealing with another *Nohookaa Diné'é*, and that therefore patience and respect are due. When faced with important matters, it is inappropriate to rush to conclusion or to push a decision without explanation and consideration to those involved. *Aaddd na'nile'dii el dooda.*[5] This is *hazhó'ógo*, and we see that this is an underlying principle in everyday dealings with relatives and other individuals, as well as an underlying principle in our governmental institutions. Modern court

---

3. "hazhó'ógo, hazhó'ógo my children."
4. Earth-surface-people (human beings).
5. Delicate matters and things of importance must not be approached recklessly, carelessly, or with indifference to consequences.

procedures and our other adopted ways are all intended to be conducted with *hazhó'ógo* in mind.

Considering the means by which Rodriguez's confession was obtained and the use of the advice of rights form, we now stand and say *"hazhó'ógo."* The transaction between Rodriguez and Investigator Snyder, and the way that the advice of rights form was presented to Rodriguez does not conform with the ways that people should interact. We must never forget that the accused is still *Nohookaa Diné'é*, and that he or she is entitled to truthful explanation and respectful relations regardless of the nature of the crime that is alleged. Likewise, a police badge cannot eliminate an officer's duty to act toward others in compliance with the principles of *hazhó'ógo*.

We therefore hold that the police, and other law enforcement entities and agencies, must provide a form for the person in custody to show their voluntary waiver. They must also explain the rights on the form sufficiently for the person in custody to understand them. Merely providing a written English language form is not enough. The sufficiency of the explanation in a Navajo setting means, at a minimum that the rights be explained in Navajo if the police officer or other interviewer has reason to know the person speaks or understands Navajo. If the person does not speak or understand Navajo, the rights should be explained in English so that the person has a minimum understanding of the impact of any waiver. Only then will a signature on a waiver form allow admission of any subsequent statement into evidence.

In this case, there is insufficient evidence that the Navajo Nation police explained each of the rights on the form to Rodriguez. Consequently, even if there was no preceding coercion, there was not a "voluntary" waiver of his rights.

V.

The remaining question is the effect of the improper admission of the confession on the conviction. We questioned both sides at oral argument whether, despite the inadmissibility of the confession, there still was sufficient evidence to maintain the conviction. In reviewing the order of the District Court, we conclude that the confession was a significant part of the evidence used by the court to reach its ruling. To parse out the confession from the rest of the evidence at this level and speculate on what the District Court would have done if the confession was never admitted at trial would be improper. Given the importance of the fundamental right of the defendant against self-incrimination, and the difficulty, if not impossibility of retroactively reviewing a case as if that evidence never entered into the court's decision, the vacating of the conviction and release of the defendant was proper.

We did not come to this decision lightly. The crime which Rodriguez was accused of committing is a serious one. However, the seriousness of the crime does not excuse the conceded violation of the defendant's rights. Therefore, though we had significant reservations, we decided the only proper remedy was to vacate the conviction and release the defendant.

VI.

Based on the above, we vacated the conviction and released Rodriguez.

NOTES

1. In *Rodriguez*, the Navajo Nation Supreme Court determined that the Nation's law enforcement officers must give the Miranda warnings to every suspect in custody. The Court was not making new law in the case, as "these are the rights already recognized by the Kayenta Police District in their advice of rights form, and we confirm here that they apply across the Navajo Nation." The United States Constitution did not require this result because the Constitution does not apply to Indian tribes. The Navajo Nation does not have a written constitution, but the Navajo legislature has enacted a Navajo Bill of Rights. Section 8 of the Navajo Bill of Rights protects suspects from being "compelled . . . to be a witness against themselves." NAVAJO NATION CODE tit. 1, §8. The Court recognized that the Navajo statute tracked the Indian Civil Rights Act and the Fifth Amendment. Navajo statutory law requires that the Navajo courts take the "Fundamental Laws of the Diné" into consideration when interpreting statutory language such as the Navajo Bill of Rights. As such, the Court held that the "[Navajo] Bill of Rights, as informed by the Navajo value of individual freedom, prohibits coerced confessions."

2. The *Rodriguez* decision's result was to extend criminal procedure rights of suspects in the custody of the Navajo Nation's law enforcement officers beyond that which is required by federal or state law. This is not unusual for the Navajo Nation's courts.

   More interesting is the reasoning for applying the Miranda warnings in the first instance. The *Miranda* Court focused on the police practices of the day, emphasizing their psychological impacts on the suspect. But the Court had little choice but to acknowledge that law enforcement nationwide had long engaged in physical abuse and coercion to elicit confessions. Aside from physical abuse, the Court noted that law enforcement used psychological coercion on suspects, relying upon police interrogation manuals of the time. The Court concluded that warnings were necessary, in part because of the need to protect "human dignity," but more so because "no statement obtained from the defendant can truly be the product of his free choice." In other words, a more critical purpose for the use of Miranda warnings by state and federal officers is to ensure that confessions will be truthful.

   The *Rodriguez* Court was more concerned not with whether the confessions or statements taken by Kayenta District law enforcement were truthful, but with the relationships between members of the Navajo community. While the Court reached a conclusion that the Miranda warnings applied to suspects held in tribal law enforcement custody, the Court expanded those rights to require that officers treat suspects like relatives, with respect and dignity. As the Court wrote, "[A] police badge cannot eliminate an officer's duty to act toward others in compliance with the principles of *hazhóʼógo*."

   The *Rodriguez* Court incorporated tribal customary law by relying on the language of the Navajo people as a source of custom and tradition. Unlike many tribal court judges, Navajo judges must be fluent in the language of the people. NAVAJO NATION CODE tit. 7, §354(E) (2005) ("Each [judge] must be able to speak both Navajo and English, and have some knowledge of Navajo culture and tradition."). *Rodriguez* is an example where the Court drew upon its understanding of the language to derive important rules of conduct for tribal police officers. For the Navajo people, it is the Navajo language that is the source of the community's customs and traditions.

3. In *Crow Tribe of Indians v. Big Man*, 2000 Crow 7, 2000.NACT.0000007 (Crow Ct. App. 2000), the court held that "criminal defendants are entitled to *Miranda* [sic] protections when they are prosecuted in the Crow Tribal Court." *Id.* at ¶33. The *Big Man* Court recognized that Miranda does not apply in tribal courts as a matter of American constitutional law, *see id.* at ¶19 (citing *United States v. Wheeler*, 435 U.S. 313 (1978); *Talton v. Mayes*, 163 U.S. 376, 384 (1896)), but it also recognized that the Indian Civil Rights Act might serve to extend Anglo-American criminal procedure protections to tribal court defendants. *See id.*; 25 U.S.C. §§1302(4) ("due process"), (8) ("equal protection"). The Court dipped into the legislative history of the Act and found — like the U.S. Supreme Court did — that interpretation of the Act "will frequently depend on question[s] of tribal tradition and custom. . . ." *Id.* at ¶23 (quoting *Santa Clara Pueblo v. Martinez*, 436 U.S. 49, 71 (1978)).

But the *Big Man* Court noted that the Crow legislature had adopted a rule of criminal procedure "that appears to parallel the requirement under current federal constitutional law[, i.e., *Miranda*]." *Id.* at ¶27. The Court noted that the Miranda warnings are "not grounded in Tribal custom or tradition — nor is the rest of the adversarial criminal prosecution process set out in the Crow Rules of Criminal Procedure." *Id.* The Court, constricted by the tribal legislature's decision to adopt the *Miranda* rule, applied federal precedent to decide the case. *See id.* at ¶¶37-50.

4. CHOICE OF LAW

Hopi Indian Credit Association v. Thomas

Hopi Tribe Appellate Court No. 98AC000005, 1 Am. Tribal L. 353, 1998.NAHT.0000013 (November 23, 1998)

Before Sekaquaptewa, Chief Justice and Lomayesva and Abbey, Justices.

I. Factual and Procedural Background

This Court has previously set forth the facts of this case in *Hopi Indian Credit Association v. Thomas*, AP-001-84, (hereinafter *Hopi Indian Credit Association I*) and will do so again only briefly here. This case originally involved a secured chattel mortgage executed on the Hopi Reservation on April 25, 1969, by the Hopi Indian Credit Association, an association organized according to the laws of the Hopi Tribe, to Lee S. Thomas and Mary Inez Thomas, both Hopi citizens, in the amount of $9,600.00. . . . Mr. and Ms. Thomas defaulted on the loan in 1974 leaving an unpaid loan balance of $2,900.17. . . . Nearly ten years after the default, Hopi Indian Credit Association sued Mr. Thomas and Ms. Thomas in tribal court to recover the amount owed on the contract. On July 7, 1984, the trial court granted summary judgment in favor of Mr. and Ms. Thomas based on its determination that the claim was barred by the six-year federal statute of limitations.

On July 30, 1984, Hopi Indian Credit Association noticed an appeal to this Court on the ground that the trial court erred by applying federal law before Hopi custom and tradition. This Court held that Resolution H-12-76 required the trial court to consider Hopi custom, tradition and culture before it applied foreign law and remanded the case to the trial court for further consideration. . . .

On remand, Mr. and Mrs. Thomas once again moved for summary judgment based on the statute of limitations. They argued that an analysis of Hopi custom was not necessary because the mortgage contained a choice of law clause expressly selecting foreign law. The trial court found that the parties' contractual choice of foreign law required the application of a foreign statute of limitations and therefore rendered an inquiry into Hopi custom unnecessary. Interpreting the contract, it found the action was barred by Arizona's six-year statute of limitations and granted summary judgment in favor of Mr. and Ms. Thomas. Hopi Indian Credit Association appeals from this final judgment. . . .

III. Discussion

A. The Parties Choice of Law

We begin our analysis with the observation that while, as a general matter, parties are free to choose foreign law to govern their contracts, this freedom is not without limit. . . .

[A] claim is governed by the statute of limitations of the forum in which it is brought notwithstanding a contrary choice by the parties. . . .

A statute of limitation is a declaration of public policy intended to promote judicial economy and to protect citizens from state claims. . . . Therefore, a jurisdiction has a strong interest in applying its own statute to claims brought in its courts. This rationale is even more compelling where, as here, the contract involves overwhelmingly local contacts. The plaintiff in this case is a Hopi association organized according to Hopi law, the defendants are Hopi citizens, and the contract was executed at Hopi.

We hold that this jurisdiction follows the majority rule that a contractual choice of law provision does not apply to the statute of limitations and that an action on a contract brought in the Hopi jurisdiction is governed by the Hopi statute of limitations, if any. Accordingly, we hold that the trial court erred in applying a foreign statute of limitations rather than the applicable Hopi limitations period.

B. Proof of Hopi Custom, Tradition, and Culture

In determining what, if any, limitations period applies under Hopi law, the trial court is instructed to follow the procedure required by H-12-76 section 2 (a), which provides that:

> The courts of the Hopi Tribe, in deciding matters of both substance and procedure, in case otherwise properly before the Courts of the Hopi Tribe, shall look to, and give weight as precedent to, the following:
> (1)   The Hopi Constitution and Bylaws;
> (2)   Ordinances of the Hopi Tribal Council;
> (3)   Resolutions of the Hopi Tribal Council;
> (4)   Customs, traditions and culture of the Hopi Tribe;

(5) Law, rules, and regulations of the Federal Government and cases interpreting such. Such laws, rules and regulations may, in circumstances
dictated by the Supremacy Clause of the U. S. Constitution, be required
to take a higher order or precedence.

(6) The laws and rules, and cases interpreting such laws and rules, of the
State of Arizona. This provision shall not be deemed to be an adoption
of such laws or rules as the law of the Hopi Tribe nor as a grant or
cession of any right, power or authority by the Hopi Tribe to the
State of Arizona.

(7) The Common Law.

In *Hopi Tribe v. Mahkewa* we held that the first four authorities in this list are
mandatory and the last three are persuasive. Under H-12-76, the trial court
should first determine as a matter of law whether any mandatory authority
exists relevant to the statute of limitations issue. If the trial court finds that
there is no relevant Hopi Constitutional provision, ordinance or resolution, it
must consider whether there is a relevant Hopi custom or tradition. *Hopi Indian
Credit Association I* at 4 ("[T]he customs, traditions and culture of the Hopi Tribe
must take precedence in the court's decision of what law to apply before a court
reaches the use of any foreign law, including federal or Arizona state law. . . .").

In *Hopi Indian Credit Association I*, we observed that "Hopi customs, traditions and culture are often unwritten, and this fact can make them more difficult to define or apply." *Id.* at 4. In this respect, the use of Hopi custom,
tradition, and culture presents problems of notice and proof similar to those
raised where a party asserts a claim based on foreign law. Traditionally, a party
that wishes to apply foreign law must plead and prove its existence and substance. Similarly, this Court has held that where a party intends to raise an
issue of unwritten custom, tradition or culture, it must plead and present clear
proof of the existence and relevance of the custom, tradition or culture. *Hopi
Indian Credit Association I* at 5-6.

We find the federal rule governing the application of foreign law to be
instructive. Federal Rule of Civil Procedure 44.1 provides that the courts
may consider any relevant material or source, including testimony, whether
or not submitted by a party or admissible under the rules of evidence. Thus,
federal courts have considered as relevant evidence local custom . . . , expert
testimony . . . , affidavits by practitioners of the foreign law . . . , scholarly
articles . . . , affidavits by law professors . . . , and briefing by the attorneys. . . .

Accordingly, we hold that when a relevant Hopi custom, tradition, or
culture is asserted, its existence and substance must be proved with clear
evidence and decided by the court as a matter of law. Therefore, on either
the trial court's own motion or on the noticed motion of a party, the court
shall hold a hearing at which the parties may present any relevant testimony or
evidence.

IV. Order of the Court

This case is REMANDED to the trial court with instructions to hold a pre-trial
hearing in order to determine whether there is any Hopi custom, tradition, or
culture revenant to the statute of limitations consistent with this Opinion and
H-12-76.

NOTES

1. In a previous case, *Hopi Indian Credit Assoc. v. Thomas I*, No. AP-001-84, 1996.NAHT.0000007 (Hopi Ct. App. 1996), the Court held that Hopi law, either customary or statutory, must apply before any "foreign law," that is, federal or state law. The Hopi Indian Credit Court explained in great detail the procedure later Hopi courts must follow in applying Hopi customary law:

> The primary issue raised in this appeal concerns the application of Hopi Resolution H-12-76, which was discussed in *Hopi Tribe v. Mahkewa*, . . . (1995) (AP-002-92). In *Mahkewa*, we said that federal law, Arizona state law and the common law are only "persuasive." *Id.*, opinion at 4. The customs, traditions and culture of the Hopi Tribe, however, are one of the authorities considered "mandatory." *Ibid*. The only recognized exception to this precedence is when the U.S. Constitution's Supremacy Clause applies. *See* Hopi Res. H-12-76, §§2(a)(5) & 2(b); U.S. Const., art. IV, §2. This case does not involve the Supremacy Clause as it does not involve issues inconsistent with federal law.
>
> The trial court did not explicitly say that federal law should be given precedence over Hopi custom, tradition or culture, but it noted that when the Hopi Constitution, Ordinances or Rules did not speak on a given issue, then "we should refer to the federal rules as well as to Arizona rules and then common law and [Hopi] custom and tradition as a means to aid the Court. . . ." . . . In effect, the trial court would look to authorities listed in H-12-76, section 2(a), in descending order until it reached the resolutions of the Hopi Tribal Council, then it suggested it should skip over customs, traditions and culture of the Hopi Tribe and apply federal and state law. Customs and traditions would be considered last in aiding a court: alongside the common law. This interpretation is incorrect.
>
> The customs, traditions and culture of the Hopi Tribe deserve great respect in tribal courts, for even as the Hopi Tribal Council has merged laws and regulations into a form familiar to American legal scholars, the essence of our Hopi law, as practiced, remains distinctly Hopi. The Hopi Tribe has a constitution, ordinances and resolutions, but those Western forms of law codify the customs, traditions and culture of the Hopi Tribe, which are the essential sources of our jurisprudence.
>
> Therefore, as we held in *Mahkewa*, the customs, traditions and culture of the Hopi Tribe must take precedence in a court's decision of what law to apply before a court reaches the use of any foreign law, including federal or Arizona state law, with the exceptions as noted above. The trial court erred by applying foreign law before it considered the relevancy of Hopi custom. . . .
>
> Although Hopi customs, traditions and culture are to be considered by a trial court before it considers foreign laws, it is not enough just to say that they are "mandatory" to use as if they could be quickly or easily applied. Hopi customs, traditions and culture are often unwritten, and this fact can make them more difficult to define or apply. While they can and should be used in a court of law, it is much easier to use codified foreign laws. That ease of use may convince a trial court to forego the difficulty and time needed to properly apply our own unwritten customs, traditions and culture. However, the trial court must apply this important source of law when it is relevant.
>
> To make it more likely that parties will plead our own customs, and more likely that courts will properly use them, the following discussion is provided

to guide future trial courts, as related to the present case. The Tribal Council has empowered this court to rule authoritatively on Hopi custom, tradition, and culture. Hopi Ord. 21, §1.2.8. When the legal interpretation of a Hopi custom, tradition or culture is necessary to the resolution of a conflict at the trial court, however, that court shall first resolve the issue at its level. Any decision made by the trial court as to definition or use of custom, culture or tradition may be reviewed by the Court of Appeals de novo on appeal (as if raised for the first time). . . . In all other cases requiring a legal interpretation of a Hopi custom, culture or tradition, the certification shall be made directly to this court.

A party who intends to raise an issue of unwritten custom, tradition or culture shall give notice to the other party and the court through its pleading or other reasonable written notice. The intent of this notice is to prevent unfair surprise, which is consistent with Hopi custom and tradition of fairness.

The proponent of Hopi customs, traditions and culture must then (1) plead them to the court with sufficient evidence so as to establish the existence of such a custom, tradition or culture, and then (2) show that the recognized custom, tradition, or culture is relevant to the issue before the court. . . . The relevancy of Hopi custom, tradition or culture as to any legal matter should not be presumed.

A court may dispense with proof of the existence of a Hopi custom, tradition or culture if it finds the custom, tradition or culture to be generally known and accepted within the Hopi Tribe. In such a case, the judge may take judicial notice of the custom or tradition. This does not dispense with a showing of relevancy.

Just as a trial court must apply Hopi constitutional law when it is applicable, even if neither party pled the Hopi Constitution, so too must a trial court take judicial notice of and then apply Hopi custom, tradition or culture when it is applicable. This requirement is essential for Hopi courts to apply the most authoritative law applicable to the issues, as directed by the Hopi Tribal Council. *See Mahkewa*, Opinion at 5-6. This requirement also ensures Hopi courts will best serve the community properly through the spirit of the law intended.

Hopi Indian Credit Ass'n I, at ¶¶22-25, 28-33.

2. In *Rave v. Reynolds*, 23 Indian L. Rep. 6150 (Winnebago Tribe of Neb. Sup. Ct. 1996), the Winnebago Supreme Court held (among many other things) that tribal members and a tribal member organization have standing to challenge the constitutionality of the rules for tribal elections under tribal law. In *Rave*, the tribal government defendants argued that "voters, tribal members, and organizations composed of interested tribal voters . . . lacked the necessary personal stake or interest in the controversy. . . ." *Id.* at 6156. The Court noted that the defendants cited "only federal cases brought under article III of the United States Constitution. . . ." *Id.*

The *Rave* Court's analysis often relied upon customary law as the Court understood it, but it sometimes relied on federal law as well. The Court first found, however, that the tribal court rules mandated that "[i]n all civil actions the tribal court shall apply . . . [t]he constitution, statutes, and common law of the tribe. . . ." *Id.* at 6156 (quoting WINNEBAGO (NEB.) CODE OF CIVIL PROCEDURE §2-111(1)(A)). The Court interpreted this provision to mean that "the Winnebago tribal courts prefer tribal law as a rule of decision to any rule afforded by federal and state law. Resort to federal or state law therefore is appropriate to inform the tribal courts of a rule of decision only if tribal law is completely silent on the question." *Id.* The Court further interpreted "common law of the tribe" to mean two different types of law:

> First, the term common law may reference the western style common law derived from English legal roots, i.e., the judge-made law articulated in decided cases through written opinions often reflecting the judicial understanding of the customs and practices of a people in a particular sector of endeavor. Such common law may include both already existing decisions and any new rule of law announced by a tribal court in a case before it.
>
> Second, . . . section 2-111 contemplates that tribal customs and usages, both traditional and evolving, will constitute tribal common law.

Rave, 23 Indian L. Rep. at 6157. The Court found that no tribal constitutional or statutory provision applied in the standing analysis. *See id.* ("Neither party cited and this court is unaware of any express provisions in the tribal constitution or statutes that deal with standing or of any decided cases of the Winnebago tribal courts that have previously addressed the issue.").

The *Rave* Court then announced the tribal customary law as it applied to the standing analysis. The Court held that the strict federal standing requirements do not apply in their fullest extent to tribal court litigants, holding that it would rely upon

> the healing approach traditionally taken to resolve tribal disputes. The traditions of most Indian tribes in the United States, including the Ho-Chunk people, part of whom compose the Winnebago Tribe of Nebraska, encouraged participatory and consensual resolution of disputes, maximizing the opportunity for airing grievances (i.e., hearing), participation, and resolution in the interest of healing the participants and preventing friction within the tribal community.

Id.

The *Rave* Court buttressed its announcement of tribal customary law with candid pragmatism through an announcement of public policy:

> In small, close-knit tribal communities, like the Winnebago tribe of Nebraska, denying an opportunity to air and heal grievances in a neutral forum otherwise possessed of jurisdiction, such as the tribal courts, could have disruptive effects by sowing dissention, hostility and distrust that otherwise could be ameliorated by airing and resolving the dispute. Accordingly, adopting the narrow standing rules employed in federal courts could have a disruptive impact on tribal communities and, accordingly, would not constitute sound public policy.

Rave, 23 Indian L. Rep. at 6158.

The tribal government's attorneys represented to the Court (without citing to any authority) during oral argument that "whatever participatory mechanism might have existed then subsequently devolved participatory dispute resolution traditions on the tribal council, but not the Winnebago courts."

Id. at 6157. This argument appeared to be a weak claim that the tribal courts had no jurisdiction over the case at all. The Court rejected that argument and held that "whatever tribal traditions previously controlled tribal council, clan or family dispute resolution in the mid-nineteenth century must, in the absence of express tribal positive law on standing, affect this court's resolution of the standing issue." *Id.*

5. THE PROBLEMS IN FINDING AND APPLYING TRIBAL CUSTOMARY LAW

KEY CONCEPTS IN THE FINDING, DEFINITION, AND CONSIDERATION OF CUSTOM LAW IN TRIBAL LAWMAKING

Pat Sekaquaptewa, 32 Am. Indian L. Rev. 319, 375-85 (2007-2008)

. . .

X. Debates about Working with Custom Nationwide

A. Debates over the Use of Custom

A review of the legal literature reveals two general positions concerning the use of custom. The first position argues that custom must be considered as a fundamental part of self-determination and the second argues that the consideration of custom is at best impractical and at worst simply a form of resistance to all that Western legal culture represents. From a tribal government perspective, compelling arguments are made for the use of custom. [Christine] Zuni, for example, asks us to recall "the heavy hand of the federal government" in the development of our current tribal court systems, which should prompt a critical examination of the present state of our justice systems and the pursuit of future developments by design and not by default. She also reminds us that our inherited systems are embedded in English history, law, and values, including the concepts of private land ownership and patriarchy. Finally, she argues that there is a great danger in the use of exclusively non-Indian approaches, as they will create a gulf between Native people and their law where such law reinforces views that are contrary to accepted local values. [Robert Odawi] Porter echoes Zuni's concerns but goes farther, arguing that the use of the Western adversarial process itself tends to break down relationships and community, thus compromising both persisting traditional ways and tribal sovereignty.

The persuasive arguments against the use of custom, as opposed to those arguing that "it is simply too hard to use," come from both within and without tribal communities. Some traditional people argue that custom cannot change and should not be manipulated, and certainly should not be written down. Some argue that custom no longer exists, or that even if it does, times have changed and not everyone will agree to its interpretation and application. . . .

B. The Argument That We Should Not Mess with Custom

Older members can often be heard to insist that we leave the custom alone, particularly that we not try to write it down. The problem is that custom is being tinkered with all the time in a multitude of ways that we are not noticing. If one thinks of custom and tradition as a smooth sandy beach and tribal codes and resolutions as footprints, it is possible to imagine the smooth outlay of custom and tradition being stamped out or disturbed with the passage of each new law, be it intentional or not. The question then becomes, do we want to alter it blindly or consciously with purpose?

Another important point is that there may be things about our tribal governments that don't fit quite right or that don't seem just or fair as they are based upon imported institutions and laws. For example, does it make any sense to treat a child as abandoned and to involve the court and social services simply because he is living with his grandma? In many ways grandma is traditionally a third parent and the tribal children's (dependency) code should reflect that fact. If we can't document and explore our custom, how can we undertake the task of reform with due care and how can we build any tribal institutional history? This is a conversation that we will need to have with our leaders and elders, especially given that our children will have to live with the institutions that we leave them.

C. The Argument That We Will Never Agree on the Definition, Interpretation, and Application of Custom

Of course we will never all agree on what must be the applicable custom. People the world over argue about the definition and meaning of law to further their own interests or politics or simply given diverse viewpoints. Why would defining custom law be any different? Further, just because not everyone agrees with the definition and application of federal and state laws[, it] does not make them inapplicable. If custom law is applicable, it is applicable. As tribal members we can control the content of our laws through our political systems, by voicing our positions in the legislative process, or by electing or removing leaders consistent with our priorities or views. While it is true that there will be times when we do not trust our leaders, and perhaps when we cannot remove them, these are problems of politics or problems with the distribution of power within our governments and are not necessarily problems specific to our custom. There may even be times when abusive leaders may justify their positions based upon certain customs. But this argues in favor of discussing and clarifying what custom is.

. . .

XI. Problems & Solutions for Documenting Custom in General

Problems with the accessibility of custom can be overcome by establishing and adequately funding permanent bodies mandated to document it. Other societies generate self-studies in the form of historical accounts, sociological and anthropological studies, and critical law reviews. They also compile legal encyclopedias condensing — topic by topic — the legal principles applied by their authorities over time (legal treatises). Such accounts, studies, compilations, reviews, and treatises, while they are not enforceable legal provisions like tribal codes or rules, provide a big picture backdrop for the making and application of written laws. They also generate debate about the deeper meaning of legal principles important to historical and contemporary issues and spur innovation to solve current problems. Many tribes situate the responsibility for the documentation of custom with the tribal legislature, which then may further delegate it to a body of elders and/or culture-bearers. This may happen informally or it may be implemented through code provisions or rules that establish such a body, give it a mandate, and authorize the tribal court to work in tandem with it.

A. Custom Documenting Bodies

It is beyond the scope of this article to undertake a comprehensive review of tribal codes, resolutions, and case law establishing custom documenting bodies. However, there are some generally known tribal provisions that I will analyze here by way of example. [*See, e.g.*, White Mountain Apache Judicial Code §2.3 (1998). Compare *id.* with Hoopa Valley Tribal Code §2.1.03 (2005).] Provisions establishing such bodies tend to be found in tribal judicial codes. These bodies are often given a dual mandate. First, they are mandated to document custom in topical areas designated by the tribal legislature. [*See, e.g.*, Native Village of Barrow Judicial Code §3-7(E) ("The Elders Council shall engage in ongoing documentation of custom in the following areas and in any other areas deemed necessary and funded by Tribal Council: 1. How boys and girls are raised; 2. How property is distributed, transferred, and inherited; and 3. Roles and duties in marriage. . . ."); *see also* White Mountain Apache Judicial Code §2.3(A) ("In order that the ancient wisdom, teachings and ways of the White Mountain Apache people may live on and continue to guide the people in their daily lives, there shall be established an Apache Custom Advisory Panel, whose functions it shall be: (1) To meet at the call of, and under the direction of, the Tribal Council to discuss and record in a Journal their knowledge of the custom of the White Mountain Apache people.").] The preferred form of documentation may take the form of a simple written "journal," or the high-tech "searchable video archive." Alternatives in between might include audio and video tapes and written transcripts. Second, these bodies are mandated to work with tribal courts, either in a general advising capacity, or as a decisional body given questions of custom where the parties either agree to submit questions or where a tribal judge certifies a question on her own.

Tribal legislatures vary in the weight and precedential effect they give to custom found by such a body. In some cases, where the parties agree, the body is empowered to decide the whole case, questions of custom and disputed fact included. But in other cases, it appears that the body is empowered only to find and/or decide specific questions concerning custom, which will then be applied as law, if deemed relevant, by the tribal judge in tribal court. Some tribal legislatures have limited the precedential effect of the custom law decisions of such bodies. Others rely on the precedential effect of the tribal court opinions where they incorporate such body's decision or recommendations concerning custom. In the latter case, the judge is likely to modify or even "spin" the characterization or application of custom somewhat to be consistent with the limited powers and remedies of the court. This is a policymaking activity. . . .

B. Problems and Solutions for Working with Outside Experts and Studies

This is one of those areas where it may be helpful to borrow from, and modify, Western law, particularly rules of evidence. A number of tribes authorize their courts to consider outside expert testimony and studies in identifying applicable custom law, sometimes giving the same or greater weight to these sources than to customs found by elders or culture-bearers. . . .

A good starting point would be to look at the Federal Rules of Evidence provisions governing professional expert witnesses and expert publications (most state evidence rules are based on the federal rules). . . .

C. Problems and Solutions for the Pleading and Proving of Custom

. . . Over the years there has been a good deal of finger pointing between tribal judges, attorneys, advocates, parties, and even elders and culture-bearers over who is ultimately responsible for researching (or knowing) and formally raising questions of custom in tribal court. Tribal judges in the early days argued that they could only address the issues raised by the parties in their written pleadings or in their oral arguments before the court. If a party hired a nonmember attorney or advocate to speak for them in court and that person did not know or understand the local ways, the party was simply out of luck because the tribal judge was not going to notice custom for them. To be fair to the judges, in the early days, many of them were nonmembers who could not be expected to know or understand local customs.

Today, with the advent of revised codes, rules and further developed case law, many tribes now require the judge to notice relevant, generally known custom. Additionally, a growing number of tribes have provisions or rules setting out attorney and advocate responsibilities for the pleading and proving the applicability of custom. Nevertheless there remain some significant concerns. Primarily, who will pay the attorney or advocate to do the extra work? In the Western system the parties pay. This is troubling, as it has been my experience that it is usually the more traditional parties, particularly elders, that need or want to assert the relevance of custom. They are usually the parties least likely to be able to afford attorneys fees. The problem is a structural one. Our tribal governments by default have put the financial burden on our elders to find and plead custom. Where are our institutionally mandated self-studies? Where are our custom law treatises or archives? Where are our tribal bar study materials and exams requiring attorneys and advocates to have some basic knowledge of our custom law? Tribal leaders, and particularly tribal legislatures, need to give serious attention to shifting the financial burden off of our more traditional and elder parties and onto government where it belongs.

D. Problems and Solutions and Tribal Court Hearings to Find Custom

Assuming that custom is pled by a party and can't be noticed by a tribal judge, there needs to be special rules for holding hearings to find it. Three aspects of Western court process are likely to undermine custom law finding goals. First, the evidence rules governing expert witness testimony are designed for scientific expert testimony and will need to be modified to recognize the expertise of local culture-bearers and elders, except in those cases where it is being applied to outside experts. Second, in the Western adversarial process, parties and their attorneys generally select their own witnesses and the attorneys pose the questions to those witnesses. In a purely adversarial process attorneys prioritize winning their case over accurately identifying and applying custom. They are likely to select traditional experts who will favor their client's positions. Consequently witness selection and the questions to be asked of them will require more judicial supervision if there is a commitment to accurately characterizing relevant custom. Third, court rules of civil and criminal procedure permit aggressive questioning by attorneys of expert witnesses. This discourages traditional experts from participating in the custom law-finding hearings. There is a need to modify the rules for questioning expert witness to balance encouraging knowledgeable testimony on relevant customs with the right of the parties to challenge the reliability of the testimony and applicability of the custom.

Some tribes follow a Western approach and allow for party selected witness, subject to preliminary questioning and challenge for lack of knowledge by the other party. Other tribes require judicial approval of the witnesses selected by the parties. In both situations, there are concerns with hearing from traditional experts who will focus on defining relevant customs and not testifying on the facts of the case. At least two tribes actively seek "neutral" experts. With respect to the questions, some tribes allow the parties to initially frame the questions to be asked but authorize the judge to approve the final list of questions to be asked. Other tribes give more control to the judge by authorizing him to draft initial lists of questions, get party feedback, and then to approve the final list of questions.

Finally, considerations of fairness to the parties will require the holding of multiple hearings, typically three or more including: (1) the initial hearing on the disputed facts; (2) the custom finding hearing(s) where the judge hears from the traditional experts and the outside experts; and (3) the fact-finding hearing where the judge applies the custom law to the facts in dispute. The last hearing is critical to ensuring a fair process as it gives the parties a chance to make arguments and present evidence after they know what the applicable custom law standard will be.

Again, this is an expensive process for the parties. Clearly members would benefit greatly from having the option to avoid litigation and to use traditional or alternative dispute resolution processes such as peacemaking. However, it is important to stress here that larger tribes are likely to require both adjudicative and relationship-righting processes. Modern life has changed member needs and expectations, causing them to forum shop—to seek a decision in whatever process that will let them win. Many of us have witnessed what happens in tribes where there is no tribal court or where the only available dispute resolution forum is traditional or alternative. Tribal members will run to state and federal courts to have their matters handled. Zuni's admonition applies here. Do we want to have some control over the way our people's disputes are handled and the laws, principles, and values that will be applied to them or are we content to sit back and let change happen to us? If we seek to control the direction of our future we will need to adopt or amend court rules and rules of evidence accordingly. . . .

NOTES

1. Tribal choice-of-law provisions that require or encourage the application of tribal custom and tradition tend not to provide a procedure or any guidance at all as to how a tribal court should go about finding, understanding, and applying tribal customary law. Some tribal courts that do make a serious effort to apply customary law are hampered by the lack of guidance. Others assert expansive authority to declare customary law. What tribal choice-of-law provisions should include — or what tribal courts can include in their court rules — is a road map for finding, understanding, and applying customary law.

   For tribal judges who are not experts in the culture and traditions of the communities for which they are judges, including those who do not understand the traditional language of the community or those who are not even members of the community, finding customary law is difficult. For judges who do understand their tribal language and do have a strong connection to the communities for which they are judges, the task is made much easier, but it is not obvious.

2. Not every source of customary law is comprehensive or legitimate. Vine Deloria and others have long criticized the work of non-Indian anthropologists and other researchers and scientists. *E.g.*, Vine Deloria, Jr., *Anthropologists and Other Friends*, in CUSTER DIED FOR YOUR SINS 83 (1969). There is a very significant bias by Indian people against the work of these academics. This bias, whether reasonable or not, will be a formidable obstacle to any tribal court judge using written academic literature as a basis for finding and understanding the customary law of a tribal community. The legitimacy of a tribal court opinion declaring customary law based on the findings of an academic would be doubted much of the time.

   But the fact of the matter remains that, for many tribal communities, the work of non-Indian academics is the only source for tribal histories, legends, political science, religious practices, and even customary laws. For these communities, it could be foolish to ignore this work. The work might be 100 years old or very recent. It might contain commentary that offends every Indian person within 1,000 miles of its unveiling, but tribal judges might be able to see through the academic jargon and bias to learn something significant. Or not.

   Another problem — one that this author is very sensitive and careful in discussing — is the legitimacy of the representations made by tribal community "experts." Reasonable minds may differ on customs and traditions. Classic examples include the differences between practitioners of the Native American Church and the Navajo traditional religion, and the differences between the Midewiwin and other Anishinaabe traditional religions. But there may be fundamental differences in the understanding of the culture and traditions of a community on family or political lines. Of course, such differences occur also among law professors outside tribal communities as they try to understand Anglo-American law. Tribal courts, as in the procedure for identifying Hoopa customary law, would be in the unenviable position of choosing between competing understandings of customary law—and this would be a choice that tribal courts might not have the institutional capacity to make. *Cf.* Kristen A. Carpenter, *Considering Individual Religious Freedoms under Tribal Constitutions*, 14 KAN. J.L. & PUB. POL'Y 561, 562-64 (2004) (discussing the difficulty of analyzing tribal religious practices as a scholar).

3. The question of institutional capacity for tribal courts and tribal judges in announcing or declaring tribal customary law is complicated and very important. While many tribal courts are modeled on American common law courts, tribal judges should not have the same notion that they can declare tribal common law. Justice Thomas can rely upon English common law decisions issued around the time of the American Revolution as a source of authority for the origins of many American common law doctrines; however, tribal judges do not have the same sources of authority upon which to rely.

   Tribal customary law as applied by tribal courts now follows (or is moving in the direction of) a pattern similar to the theory of *opinio necessitatus*, or the theory that "individuals purposely follow a certain rule simply because they believe it be a rule of law." Alan Watson, *An Approach to Customary Law*, 1984 U. ILL. L. REV. 561, 563. "Under this view, custom becomes law when it is known to be law, is accepted as law, and is practiced as law by persons who share the same legal system." *Id.* So, tribal courts' adoption or announcement of tribal customary law is an acknowledgment that a certain custom or tradition remains viable within the community. However, "suppose that once the custom is known to be law and is accepted as law, the practice changes. Does the old law cease to be law, and the new practice become law?" *Id.*

   Another issue—again, a very sensitive subject—is whether tribal judges who are not members of the community should be announcing tribal customary law as the law of the tribe. The question is one that each tribal community should face, ask itself, and answer in an official and comprehensive manner.

   In *In re D.H.*, No. 2009-1236-CV-CW, 2009 WL 1619635 (Grand Traverse Band Tribal Court, Feb. 2, 2009), the tribal judge was not a tribal citizen, and demonstrated careful reluctance to adopt a rule based on customary law as asserted by one of the parties:

> Respondent further argues that fundamental due process rights guaranteed by the Constitution of the Grand Traverse Band of Ottawa and Chippewa Indians, and the United States Constitution dictate that Respondent should be entitled to a jury trial in this matter; While the Court agrees that Respondent is entitled to fundamental due process in this proceeding, the Court is not persuaded that a jury trial is a component of that due process requirement in this type of proceeding. Nor is the Court persuaded that a judge cannot adequately protect Respondent's due process rights or reach a determination while also recognizing and acknowledging tribal customs and traditions of the Grand Traverse Band regarding child rearing as required under the Children's Code.
>
> The Court agrees with Respondent that Tribal Council could adopt a provision in the Children's Code providing for a right to a jury trial, and

that the Tribal Court could adopt a court rule providing for the right to a jury trial in this type of proceeding. However, neither has done so to date. 10 GTBC §107(a) states that "[t]he procedures in the Children's Court shall be governed by the rules of procedure for the Tribal Court, not in conflict with this Code. In the absence of Tribal Court promulgated rules of procedure, the Michigan Rules of Civil Procedure shall be utilized as a guide." This Court reads this provision to provide that the Court will look to Michigan law for guidance, but the use of Michigan procedure (including the right to a jury trial) is discretionary, not mandatory. Again, the Court is not persuaded that a jury trial was intended by the Tribal Council in adopting the Children's Code, nor that the Tribal Judiciary has intended to provide for a jury trial in Children's Code proceedings.

In re D.H., 2009 WL 1619635, at * 2.

One somewhat more cynical commentator argued that it is difficult to demonstrate that customary law as identified by tribal judges is sufficiently "Indian":

When a tribal judge does claim to find applicable custom, is it enough—as some opinions suggest—that the custom is generally "Indian"? In a typical case, *In re C.D.C. and C.M.H.*, the tribal judge for the Delaware Tribe of Western Oklahoma based a child custody decision on the following custom: "[I]t is common knowledge in Indian country that both the maternal and paternal grandmothers traditionally play a very significant role in the Indian family." [No. PG-87-A50, 1 Okla. Trib. 200, 205 (Oct. 13, 1988).] This invocation of custom suggests that "Indian" here is meant to be a contrast to non-Indian, or Western values: a rather indeterminate category. Surely the many Indian tribes of North America, originally distributed over a vast geographic range, differ to some extent in their cultural practices. Yet the use of "custom" at this general level can be found in many instances. "Indian" traditions in these decisions represent a number of broad values—community, family, reconciliation, healing, and harmony—which suggest as much a nostalgia for "small-town" norms as they do for Indian ones.

Elizabeth E. Joh, *Custom, Tribal Court Practice, and Popular Justice*, 25 Am. Indian L. Rev. 117 121 (2000-2001).

4. Professor Alexander Tallchief Skibine adds:

One of the most basic interferences with tribal culture that has also had an impact on the evolution of tribal law was the systematic effort to eradicate Native languages. If I remember correctly, when I first visited the Osage reservation as a child in the 1950s, in order to publicly speak at official or social functions such as funerals and weddings, one had to speak in the Osage language. When I came back to the reservation as an adult, this custom had already vanished. Unfortunately for some tribes, the United States' effort to eradicate Indian languages has mostly been successful. This loss has an important impact on tribal court decisions because as some of the decisions of the Navajo Supreme Court remind us, some native concepts of justice can only be expressed in their native tongue. The Navajo Supreme Court has done a great job in not replacing Navajo words with English ones in the text of their opinions. Instead the Court has kept the native words and takes great care to fully explain what they mean.

Other concessions made to the western ways of thinking include the reliance on the written word at the expense of oral tradition. This does pose a problem for those tribes whose laws are related to their religion and the religion requires some aspects of it to remain secret. A second major cultural interference with tribal justice systems was the attempt to eradicate native religions. . . . Justice Austin of the Navajo Supreme Court . . . explained that one could not separate Navajo customary law or what we would call common law, from some of the Navajo's fundamental religious beliefs because these beliefs formed the foundation and were an integral part of the Navajo customary law.

Alex Tallchief Skibine, *Troublesome Aspects of Western Influences on Tribal Justice Systems and Laws*, 1 TRIBAL L.J. 2 (2000).

5. When tribal courts in written opinions do cite to custom, they often do so in a superficial manner, without reference to specific precedents. Far more often than not, tribal court citation to custom amounts to nothing more than a citation to a broad, vague notion to tribal values. And often these tribal values are pan-tribal values — values that the tribal courts recognize as inherent to many or even most tribes.

Only in extremely rare occasions in tribal court opinions available in the public domain does a tribal court judge apply tribal customary law as the basis of decision, with the important exceptions of the Navajo and Hopi tribal courts. Tribal customary law serves as the controlling law in tribal court cases only where the parties consent to its application or where all of the parties are members of the tribe and understand the law as applied.

Professor Justin Richland's description of one such case out of the Hopi tribal court is instructive. *See* Justin B. Richland, *"What Are You Going to Do with the Village's Knowledge?" Talking Tradition, Talking Law in Hopi Tribal Court*, 39 LAW & SOC'Y REV. 235 (June 2005). Richland analyzed one hearing in detail, *James v. Smith*, most of which was conducted in the Hopi language.

The dispute of particular interest here emanated from a conflict between three sisters (petitioners) and their aunt (respondent) over their competing claims to an orchard worked by the petitioners' grandfather (also the respondent's father). The petitioners, who still live in the village where the land is located, claimed to have inherited the property from their mother upon her death, because she was the primary caregiver for their grandfather at the time of his death. According to them, Hopi custom and tradition dictate that property left intestate by a decedent should go to the person in the family who showed the most commitment to its maintenance and to the support of its late owner. They claim that this person was their mother, the respondent's younger sister, and that upon their mother's death (also following custom), this property — like all Hopi women's property — should go to them, her daughters.

The respondent, however, claimed that in 1954 she and her husband, an Apache man (and not a Hopi tribal member), were taken by her father to the field in question and told that she was to inherit the property upon his death. The respondent claimed that because this land is an orchard, traditionally worked by the husband, it does not constitute the kind of clan lands that are inherited through the mother. Consequently, she contended that tradition requires that her father's intent to pass the land to her should prevail. The petitioners countered this, arguing that regardless of the father's prior statements, tradition holds that the respondent had lost her claim to this land when she failed to return to show any commitment to its maintenance and when she married a non-Hopi man and left the reservation to live with him.

Id. at 250-51.

Given that these cases are not litigated in English or with a written opinion, it is very difficult to study them universally. Many of these cases are decided informally, without the burden of imposing formal legal rules. That does not mean that there are very few of these cases — likely, there are many hundreds or even thousands a year — but they are not available for easy analysis. Nevertheless, these are the cases in wich tribal courts understand and apply traditional law in a manner most reflective of the tribe's customs and traditions. The sole limitation of this way of applying tribal customary law is subject matter. Unlike many tribes that have faced more assimilation or have been subject to more importation of non-Indian people and culture, custom and tradition remains more important in insular tribal communities. The Hopi property disputes, for example, are closely related to the property ownership structure that the Hopi people have used since time immemorial. The property dispute discussed at the beginning of this section arising out of the Turtle Mountain Band reservation has little similarity to the kinds of disputes that Ojibwe and Cree customary law was developed to resolve.

Relatively few tribes or tribal judges have the understanding to apply traditional law in this manner. And relatively few subject matters tackled by tribal courts that appear in the available materials can be decided by resort to customary law. Tribal judges must resort to alternative methods.

6. A still infrequent but more common use of tribal customary law is to apply a custom or tradition as a means to modify an Anglo-American legal rule or an intertribal common law rule. In these instances, the tribal court identifies a rule that does not derive from the tribe's customary law with which to use in deciding the case. However, an aspect of the rule may conflict with an understanding of customary law. The tribal court will often still apply the foreign rule, but modify it as much as possible in order to make it conform to understandings of customary law. Much of the very best applications of intertribal common law follow this pattern.

The application of tribal customary law in this context often has advantages, but is still fraught with peril. The advantages include the potential to discover new applications of customary rules. As Vine Deloria and Clifford Lytle suggested decades ago, tribal courts cannot hope to rely only on customary law, noting that cultures and legal regimes change over time, and that tribal law must also develop to meet the needs of modern tribal societies. An additional advantage is that tribal courts will be more likely to take the time to discover customary law, or require that litigants help them discover it. Tribal court judges that take seriously the charge to discover and apply customary law have an excellent opportunity to develop and harmonize tribal customs and traditions with the modern needs of Indian people.

The peril includes the careless invocation of intertribal common law or, worse, the invocation of pan-Indian customs. Non-Indian and nonmember Indian tribal judges (and scholars) have a limited means of accessing or understanding the customs and traditions of the tribe for which they work. One trap is to research and apply the customs and traditions of other Indian tribes, such as the Navajo Nation, in particular.

7. Another common use of tribal customary law in tribal court opinions is as a "gut check" or, worse, "sugar coating." This occurs when a tribal court judge has decided to apply an Anglo-American legal rule from a state or federal court case or an intertribal common law rule as the basis of decision. The judge then compares these rules that will form the basis of decision to an articulation of the judge's understanding of tribal customary law. If the foreign rule is consistent or does not otherwise conflict with the tribal custom or tradition, then the court is satisfied that the application of the foreign rule is acceptable. No modification of the foreign rule is made. The application of customary law as gut check does little to advance the importance, relevance, and understanding of tribal custom and tradition.

There are some explanations as to why this method of applying tribal customary law is so prevalent. For example, the subject matter of the dispute in question simply may have no antecedent in the tribe's customs and traditions. Or perhaps the foreign rule to be applied actually is consistent with the tribe's customs and traditions. Nevertheless, there should be fewer (and hopefully one day, no) cases in which a tribal judge required to apply customary law should ever resort to using the gut check method.

8. Former long-time tribal judge Steven Aycock noted that in at least one major area of law—the so-called Miranda criminal procedure rules—tribal custom may be overcome by dependence on the easy rules of American law.

> Many Tribes have adopted *Miranda v. Arizona*, 384 U.S. 436 (1966). Again, this is not necessarily wrong but should be done after a process of thinking about what it is we do when adopting it.
>
> When you read Miranda and the cases it cites, you get to cases where the Court has to deal with physical beatings, coercive measures and other methods of interrogations that we cannot and do not condone today. . . . For how many Tribes is that their history? Does a particular Tribe that has adopted Miranda have a history of Tribal police brutality? Is this a problem that needs this solution?
>
> A Tribe could certainly decide that their police department operates much like an American police force. It may be that the police force applies foreign legal concepts on members. Police and the concept of police itself may be foreign to the Tribe's history. Brutality may in fact be a part of the Tribal history. All of this may go into deciding that Miranda ought to apply at the Tribe.
>
> On the other hand, there may be no history of brutality. The Tribe may have always "policed" themselves. A Tribe may decide that the solution of suppression runs counter to a value that honors accountability for wrong doing on the part of defendants. These and other factors may weigh into a decision not to adopt Miranda.

> This process of evaluating the reasons for adopting Miranda, not just sim-
> ply adopting it, is what I believe is called for. Miranda or a rule of law that says
> that evidence gathered by the police in a certain manner will be suppressed
> may fit nicely with a Tribes values. But it should be a Tribe by Tribe decision
> and should be a thoughtful, deliberative one.

Hon. Steve Aycock, Thoughts on Creating a Truly Tribal Jurisprudence,
Materials prepared for the Second Annual Indigenous Law Conference,
Indigenous Law and Policy Center, Michigan State University College of
Law, March 17-18, 2006.

6. A NOTE ON INTRATRIBAL COMMON LAW[*]

Intratribal common law is the common law applied by tribal courts in cases
arising out of an indigenous legal construct. Intratribal common law is tribal
custom and traditional law and norms. Intratribal common law also may be
the "law" that traditional or non-adversarial tribal courts, such as peacemaker
courts, use to resolve disputes. In a practical sense, however, many tribes have
not yet recovered their customs and traditions in a manner that is useful to
tribal court judges. Regardless, cases resolved using intratribal common law
tend to involve tribal members to the exclusion of all others, with the exception of nonmember Indians and nonmembers who consent to the application
of intratribal common law.

An indigenous legal construct, in contrast to an Anglo-American legal
construct, is a legal construct that originates within the tribal community.
The form of government that a tribal community chooses may be indigenous
in origin, such as the so-called theocratic government of many of the Pueblos
in the desert Southwest. *See* Angela R. Riley, *(Tribal) Sovereignty and Illiberalism*,
95 CAL. L. REV. 799, 844-47 (2007). The canoe ownership traditions of the
Pacific Northwest tribes, handed down from generation to generation, originated from within the community. The inheritance rules of a community,
whether they are matrilineal, patrilineal, or neither, tend to originate from
within the community. Any legal construct not imposed or imported from
the non-Indian political communities should be classified as an indigenous
legal construct.

As noted by some, e.g., KEITH BASSO, WISDOM SITS IN PLACES: LANDSCAPE AND
LANGUAGE AMONG THE WESTERN APACHE 40 (1996), the customs and traditions of
Indian people often are buried within the peoples' language, stories, and even
the geographic terrain of their homelands. One method of teasing out a tribe's
primary rules may be to focus on important and fundamental rules articulated
in the tribe's language.

The method, in a nutshell, involves this process: First, the tribal court
identifies an important and fundamental value signified by a word or phrase
in the tribal language. In the case of the Navajo Nation courts, the judges often

---

[*]*Author note:* Much of the material here and in the next section is derived from Matthew L. M.
Fletcher, *Toward a Theory of Intertribal and Intratribal Common Law*, 43 HOUSTON L. REV. 701 (2006).

identify the word *hazhó'ógo*. As the court noted in *Rodriguez*, "*Hazhó'ógo* is not a man-made law, but rather a fundamental tenet informing us how we must approach each other as individuals." *Navajo Nation v. Rodriguez*, No. SC-CR-03-04, at 10 (Navajo 2004). *Hazhó'ógo* is, for lack of a better term, a primary rule. *Rodriguez* involved the application of an Anglo-American legal construct to tribal criminal prosecutions (the Miranda rule), a secondary rule, to borrow once again from Professor Hart. The application of the tribal primary rule to the Anglo-American or intertribal secondary rule is necessary to harmonize these outside rules with the tribe's customs and traditions. In the words of the *Rodriguez* Court, "Modern court procedures and our other adopted ways are all intended to be conducted with *hazhó'ógo* in mind." *Id.* As a result, the Navajo court stiffened the Miranda rule far more than the Supreme Court would require state or federal courts to in similar circumstances.

This method may be transferable to other tribal courts as well. For example, many Anishinaabe people from the Great Lakes region are taught how to live in *ni-noo'-do-da-di-win'*, or harmony. *See Edward Benton-Banai, The Mishomis Book: The Voice of the Ojibway* 113 (1988). These Indian people should live in what some refer to as the Good Life, or *bimaadiziwin. Id.* at 12. A Leech Lake Ojibwe elder defined *bimaadiziwin* as follows:

> Every day you will learn something different, every day a new piece of knowledge. That's the way you live your life [*Mii i'w akeyaa bimaadiziyan*]. Then you approach those things a little more to hear them, to see them. And the Spirit shares. That's how you search for the good things. Nothing bad will come of it.

Hartley White, *This Is a Good Way of Life* [*Onizhishin o'ow Bimaadiziwin*], in Living Our Language: Ojibwe Tales & Oral Histories, 216, 219 (Anton Treuer ed., 2001).

"Although the Anishinaabe themselves are loath[e] to establish a limited, set definition of [*bimaadiziwin*], some of the parameters of the Good Life include humility, generosity, and kindness." Lawrence W. Gross, *Cultural Sovereignty and Native American Hermeneutics in the Interpretation of the Sacred Stories of the Anishinaabe*, 18 Wicazo Sa Rev. 127, 128 (2003). These could be identified by Anishinaabe tribal judges as the primary rules of the Anishinaabe people. They provide the ground rules for behavior in Anishinaabe communities and provide interpretative parameters for Anishinaabe tribal judges. The adjudicative work of tribal judges would follow from these understandings in much the same way as the Navajo judges perform their work.

There may be concerns that many Anishinaabe tribal judges are unqualified to interpret *bimaadiziwin* in the context of a modern dispute that turns into complex litigation. More likely than not, these judges will not speak or read Anishinaabemowin, the language of the Anishinaabe people, but that should not preclude the attempt to apply these primary rules.

Identifying primary rules as the method of identifying customary law offers the advantage of allowing tribal courts to bring customary law into the modern era without creating much additional confusion as to its application. The primary rule of *bimaadiziwin* may serve to affect, perhaps, the application of state and federal law analogs in a tribal election dispute or a tribal personnel dispute.

NOTES

1. Intratribal common law is the heart of the intersection of tribal law and culture. As noted by Professor Christine Zuni Cruz, tribal courts that do not apply custom and tradition in this context, relying instead on federal and state law, "participate . . . in their own ethnocide." Here is where Indian tribes and Indian people reach back into the past to relearn the old stories, to learn what it means to be Indian, and to learn how Indian people resolve these kinds of internal disputes. For example, although federal Indian law and policy has depleted much of Indian country, a great deal remains undisturbed. Intratribal common law is strongest in these places. Here is where Indian people, Indian tribes, and tribal courts take what they can from custom and tradition and apply it to the disputes of today, to the extent that they differ from the disputes of the past. Here, then, is the other part of tribal common law, a part that exists parallel to intertribal common law and that tribal courts apply in specific and relevant contexts — contexts not including nonmembers.

2. The classic example of the use of intratribal common law is when a dispute arises between two members involving tribal lands, a dispute tinged with questions relating to what Dean Nell Jessup Newton calls "spiritual significance to the group." In some Indian communities, the location of the land may not be disclosed, nor may the law that would decide the dispute. These disputes touch members to the exclusion of all nonmembers by definition. But most disputes arising out of indigenous legal constructs may be discussed in some manner, although published tribal court opinions relating to the disputes may be difficult to locate.

   Part of the theory of intratribal common law is discovering the relevant customs and traditions of an Indian community. While many scholars have located and published the customs and traditions of several tribal communities, most tribes have not had the benefit of this kind of scholarship. The relevant stories are yet to be discovered.

3. Tribal courts decide family law cases involving members (and even nonmembers who consent) using intratribal common law. *Polingyouma v. Laban*, 25 Indian L. Rep. 6227, 6228 (Hopi Tribe App. Ct. Mar. 28, 1997), is a case that recites customary and traditional law before applying that law to modern Hopi life. The case involved an appeal of a child custody decision reached at the trial court level whereby the trial court decided to award equal periods of physical custody to both parents. The appellate court took judicial notice of "three aspects of Hopi custom concerning children. Under traditional Hopi practice, a child is born into her mother's clan, lives with the mother's household and receives ceremonial training from the mother's household." *Id.* at 6228. The court then "tested" the custom "for relevancy . . . in the context of modern Hopi life." *Id.* Hopi custom seemed to imply that the mother should have retained full custody. To uphold the trial court's order, however, the court relied upon the fact that the parents

wanted the child to remain in Hopi Day School at Hopi and the represen-tation by the father that he would relocate to Hopi to avoid disrupting the child's education. Anglo-American courts would not have considered custom and tradition at all, let alone this particular Hopi custom. *Polin-gyouma* was a case involving members engaged in a family dispute. The tribal court should and did apply intratribal common law to resolve the dispute.

4. Disputes between members over rights to tribal lands are another type of case best decided in accordance with intratribal common law. *Ross v. Sulu*, No. CIV-023-88 (Hopi Tribe App. Ct. July 5, 1991), was a case arising out of a dispute over claims to land within the Hopi reservation by different clans at the First Mesa. The Hopi Constitution provided that the local village there, the Village of First Mesa, had "the power to assign farming land." *Id.* at 4-5. The Hopi intratribal common law provided that each village had the dis-cretion to adopt modern, or Anglo-American, governmental structures, but unless they did so, "they [were] considered as being under the traditional Hopi organization." *Id.* at 5-6. "The Village of First Mesa [had] not adopted a village constitution . . . [and] therefore, remain[ed] under the traditional, [intratribal, law]. . . ." *Id.* at 6. The Hopi appellate court ruled that the lower court could not have exercised jurisdiction in the dispute at issue in Sulu. *See id.* (explaining that the tribal court lacked jurisdiction over an "intravillage dispute between clans over a matter reserved for village decision"). Hopi law allows for traditional villages to resolve certain disputes over land exclusive of tribal court jurisdiction. *See id.* at 6-7. *Sulu* exemplifies a case involving disputes between tribal members to the exclusion of all others. Under Hopi law, it was appropriate to resolve the dispute utilizing intratribal law. In that instance, the relevant intratribal law even precluded the tribal court from exercising jurisdiction over the matter.

5. Tribal government disputes and constitutional law questions are another area where tribal courts can and should apply intratribal common law. Here, tribal courts are confronted with tribal governments that are Anglo-American legal constructs — that is, the federal government more often than not imposed a form of government on the tribe based on outside models, such as municipal or federal government structures. The form a tribal government takes is a decision that originates from within, in theory, but most tribal governments mirror Anglo-American governmental struc-tures in important respects. In these cases, tribal courts adapt intertribal common law and apply the modified laws as intratribal common law. Again, because these cases are wholly tribal, nonmember rights are not implicated.

In re: Certified Question II: Navajo Nation v. MacDonald, 16 Indian L. Rep. 6086 (Navajo Sup. Ct. Apr. 13, 1989), exemplifies this adaptation of inter-tribal common law in a tribal governmental dispute. The key question presented was whether the Navajo Tribal Council had authority to place the tribal chairman on administrative leave pending an investigation into alleged criminal activity. The Nation has no written constitution. The court relied upon the fact that the chairman's authority was derived in all respects from acts and delegations of the tribal council. The court implied from that reality that the tribal council also retained the authority to "withdraw, limit, or supervise the exercise of powers it has bestowed on the offices of Chairman." From that holding, the Court concluded the tribal council could place the chairman on administrative leave. The Navajo court began its analysis with the secretarial regulations creating the Navajo government structures, which are, of course, Anglo-American structures. But the court stayed away from blind reliance upon federal and state law common law precedents. It was, after all, an internal matter to be decided, as much as possible, by intratribal common law.

The practice of applying intratribal common law establishes that there can be a clear line delineating the boundaries between the laws that may be used to resolve disputes between members and tribal entities, and those disputes whose subject matters arise out of indigenous legal constructs. Nonmembers, unless they consent and the community consents, are not affected by intratribal law.

The amazing story of Peter MacDonald is captured here:

> During early February 1989, a United States Senate Select Subcommittee held a series of highly publicized hearings in which various witnesses testified under oath that the then Navajo Tribal Council Chairman, Peter MacDonald, Sr., solicited and received bribes and kickbacks from contractors doing business with the Navajo Nation and had engaged in other asserted illegal actions. On February 17, 1989, the Navajo Tribal Council adopted a resolution placing the chairman on administrative leave with pay, accompanied by a finding that "a state of emergency exists in the management of the Navajo Tribal Council caused by the unique circumstances and events relating to the office of the chairman and the serious allegations raised personally against Peter MacDonald, Sr." The Navajo Nation has never adopted a written constitution. Previous Council resolutions spelled out procedures for *removing* a chairman, but prior to the MacDonald allegations, the Council had not enacted any law governing the placing of a chairman on *leave*. In this case, MacDonald challenged the authority of the Council to relieve him and the Vice–Chairman, who had also been implicated in the scandal, of their executive and legislative authority by placing them on leave. . . .
>
> MacDonald was convicted on 41 counts of bribery, conspiracy, and violating tribal ethics standards in Navajo District Court in October 1990 and sentenced to six years in prison. Subsequently, the Nation revamped its governmental organization, creating separate executive, legislative, and judicial branches of government. The executive powers of the Navajo Nation are exercised under a president chosen through direct election.

DAVID H. GETCHES, CHARLES F. WILKINSON & ROBERT A. WILLIAMS, JR., CASES AND MATERIALS ON FEDERAL INDIAN LAW 428, 431 (5th ed. 2005).

7. THE RISE OF INTERTRIBAL COMMON LAW?

Tribal courts are not organic or indigenous, but Indian tribes have made great strides in taking cultural and legal ownership of them. Indian tribes in the modern era of self-determination and self-governance have adapted tribal courts, once tools of assimilating, "civiliz[ing]," and "educat[ing]" reservation Indians, *United States v. Clapox*, 35 F. 575, 577 (D. Or. 1888), to suit their own purposes and needs—and the purposes and needs of nonmembers. Tribal courts are now tools of adaptation, not assimilation. More than 250 Indian tribes—and perhaps as many as 300—have adopted tribal courts, and the rest have adopted one or more mechanisms of dispute resolution. And many tribal court systems include more than one type of court. Some courts mirror state and federal courts, while more traditional courts are more informal and rely upon traditional and customary procedure and practice. Some of these traditional courts operate under a system that rejects much of the adversarial system of adjudicating disputes.

Though much has been written about tribal courts and tribal law, little is known about them. Scholars and commentators writing about tribal courts can differentiate without difficulty the procedures and infrastructure of tribal courts that mirror federal and state courts, and those tribal courts that are based on customary and traditional methods of dispute resolution. But in the area of tribal law, scholars and commentators either ignore or do not differentiate between the substantive common law applied by the different courts. Discussion of the differences between these two categories of tribal common law, in fact, is necessary to preserve tribal cultures.

This section provides a rough theoretical framework for distinguishing between two very different categories of substantive tribal law as applied by tribal courts. Such work is necessary for the preservation of tribal law and culture. As Anishinaabe and Canadian legal scholar John Borrows wrote,

> [tribal] legal traditions are strong and dynamic and can be interpreted flexibly to deal with the real issues in contemporary . . . law concerning [Indian] communities. Tradition dies without such transmission and reception. Laying claim to a tradition requires work and imagination, as particular individuals interpret it, integrate it into their own experiences, and make it their own. In fact, tradition is altered by the very fact of trying to understand it. It is time that this effort to learn and communicate tradition be facilitated, both within [Indian tribes] and between [Indian tribes] and [other] courts.

JOHN BORROWS, RECOVERING CANADA: THE RESURGENCE OF INDIGENOUS LAW 27 (2002).

Borrows's statement serves as a template for the broader argument in favor of tribal sovereignty. Tribal sovereignty is not a claim to power and authority for its own sake, but a tool to preserve the culture and traditions of Indian people. Tribal sovereignty shields Indian people and Indian tribes from the assimilative effects of non-Indian society imposed through non-Indian governmental control. It follows that tribal law, as the manifestation of internal tribal sovereignty, should operate to reflect and preserve tribal culture and traditions.

But tribal law serves more than one purpose. Tribal law also must allow Indian tribes to interact and survive in a political and legal world dominated by the United States and the various individual states. Tribal law can reduce the distance between Indian tribes and the American economic, legal, and political arenas. Substantive tribal common law reflects those two interests.

RAVE v. REYNOLDS

Winnebago Tribe of Nebraska Supreme Court, No. SC 96-01, 23 Indian L. Rep. 6150 (July 9, 1996)

Before CLINTON, Chief Justice, BOTSFORD and HUNTER, Associate Justices. CLINTON, Chief Justice.

. . .

This matter comes before the court on cross-appeals in a case contending certain aspects of the tribal election conducted October 4, 1994 in which defendants John Blackhawk, Arthur Reynolds, and Delmar Free were certified as elected and thereafter seated as members of the Winnebago tribal Council for their current terms. . . .

Facts

Under the amended provisions of article III of the Constitution of the Winnebago Tribe of Nebraska, the governing body of the tribe is a nine-member tribal council elected at large with staggered terms of three years which expire in a fashion such that three members of the tribal council are elected every year. . . . Article V further provides in relevant part:

> Section 2. All elections held under and by virtue of this Constitution shall be held under the supervision of the Tribal Council, who shall provide all necessary equipment, appoint election officials, and furnish police protection and all other necessary things that pertain to an election.
>
> . . .

In order to establish orderly procedures for and regularize the conduct of tribal elections, the Winnebago Tribal Council passed on September 19, 1972 Ordinance Nos. 4 and 5 which have governed the conduct of tribal council elections since that date. The provisions of Ordinance 5 are central to the resolution of this dispute. They provide for a nomination system for tribal council vacancies based on caucuses. Under this system all candidates appearing on the ballot must be nominated by a caucus. . . . The following provision of section 1(E) of Ordinance 5 created most of the dispute in this case, "No person shall attend or vote in more than one Caucus." While Ordinance 5 provides no express sanctions for violation of this so called "one person, one caucus" rule, the record reflects that the long-standing, well known, and evenhandedly applied custom of the tribal Council of the Winnebago Tribe of Nebraska had been to disqualify all candidates nominated from any and all caucuses attended by any caucus participant whose name also appeared on the caucus list from another caucus for the same election. . . .

Pursuant to the announced election schedule, on September 14, 1994, twenty-six tribal members conducted an election caucus at House 146 in Winnebago, Nebraska. The minutes of this reflect that Katherine LaRose was among the twenty-six participants. This September 14, 1994 caucus nominated David Beaver, plaintiff Russell St. Cyr, and Virgil Free as candidates for tribal council.

Also pursuant to the election schedule, another caucus was conducted at the Anna Bess LaRose residence on September 23, 1994. The minutes reflect the attendance of four tribal members at this caucus, including Kathy LaRose [the same person as Katherine LaRose]. This September 23, 1994 caucus nominated James Louis LaRose . . . as a candidate for tribal council. . . .

Pursuant to the election schedule, the tribal council, pursuant to prior notice published in the *Winnebago Indian News*, conducted an open, public meeting on September 24, 1994 with seven members of the tribal council, more than the requisite quorum, present in order to certify candidates whose names would appear on the ballot for the 1994 election for tribal council. . . . [The tribal council excluded the candidates nominated in the September 14 and September 23 caucuses for violation of the "one person, one caucus" rule.] . . .

On January 30, 1995, almost four months after the 1994 tribal elections, the plaintiffs filed their complaint in this action contesting the seating of [the election winners]. . . .

Defendants later filed a motion to dismiss asserting, among other things, tribal sovereign immunity. . . .

Discussion

. . .

A. Jurisdiction and Justiciability

. . .

3. Sovereign Immunity

In their appeal, defendants reassert their defense of sovereign immunity previous[ly] advanced unsuccessfully before the Special Tribal Court. . . .

This court has already joined the virtually unanimous view of tribal, federal, and state courts on tribal sovereign immunity, finding that the Winnebago Tribe of Nebraska, like all Indian tribes, is immune from suit without its consent or an express waiver of sovereign immunity by either the tribal council or the Congress. *Investment Finance Management, Inc. v. Winnebago Tribe of Nebraska*, No. App. 87-01 (Winn. Sup. Ct. 1991), *see also GNS, Inc. v. Winnebago Tribe of Nebraska*, 21 Indian L. Rep. 6104 (Winn. Tr. Ct. 1994); *see generally* Felix S. Cohen's *Handbook of Federal Indian Law* 324-28 (Rennard Strickland ed., 1982); Robert N. Clinton, Nell Jessup Newton, and Monroe E. Price, *American Indian Law: Cases and Materials* 327-43 (1992). Tribal sovereign immunity therefore constitutes a well established principle of law affecting Indian tribes. This court notes that notions of governmental immunity, such as tribal sovereign immunity, while adopted as tribal law as most tribal governments moved to western style forms of organization, nevertheless constitute distinctly Anglo-American legal doctrines, having no parallels in traditional Indian life where most positions of leadership were the result of earned respect of lineage and leaders ruled by example, wisdom, and respect, rather than coercion. *Moses v. Joseph*, 2 Tribal Court Rptr. A-51, A-53 (Sauk-Suiattle Tr. Ct. 1980). . . . [T]he plaintiffs named as party defendants only certain members of the tribal council including the three elected in disputed 1994 election. This case therefore requires this court to squarely address the *scope* of tribal sovereign immunity defenses applied to tribal officials.

In addressing the scope of tribal sovereign immunity, this court must first decide whether the question is governed by tribal or federal law. Federal common law clearly protects tribal sovereign immunity and governs the scope of that immunity in federal and state courts. . . . In tribal courts, however, the sovereign immunity of the governing tribe is governed primarily by tribal law and, only secondarily, by federal common law. *E.g., Thompson v. Cheyenne River Sioux Tribe Board of Police Commissioners*, 23 Indian L. Re. 6045 (Chy. Riv. Sx. Ct. App. 1996); *see generally* Johnson and Madden, *Sovereign Immunity in Indian Tribal Law*, 12 Am. Ind. L. Rev. 153 (1984). . . .

Federal law . . . classically draws a relatively bright line between suits against governments or governmental agencies, which generally are barred by sovereign immunity, and suits against officials, which, if controlled by any immunity at all, usually involve official, rather than sovereign, immunity. The decisions of other tribes on this matter under tribal law, however, sometimes have been less clear on this point. Indian tribes generally are found immune from suit without their consent or an express waiver under tribal law. *E.g., Colville Confederated Tribes of the Colville Reservation v. Stock West*, 21 Indian L. Rep. 6075 (Colv. Tr. Ct. 1994). While tribal agencies are generally held immune from suit under tribal sovereign immunity, at least one tribal court recently ruled as a matter of tribal law that tribal sovereign immunity did not extend to injunctive and declaratory relief actions filed against a tribal agency and involving tribal land, property or contractual obligations. *Thompson v. Cheyenne River Sioux Tribe Board of Police Commissioners*, 23 Indian L. Re. 6045 (Chy. Riv. Sx. Ct. App. 1996). The tribal courts, however, appear more divided on the scope of tribal sovereign immunity, if any, for suits brought against tribal officials.

Most of the recent tribal court decisions considering the application of tribal sovereign immunity to suits against tribal officials, including members of a tribal council, have determined that tribal officials cannot assert tribal sovereign immunity as an absolute jurisdictional defense to suit. For example, following the principles of federal immunity law, the Confederated Salish & Kootenai Tribes Court of Appeals ruled in *Moran v. Council of the Confederated Salish & Kootenai Tribes*, 22 Indian L. Rep. 6149 (C.S. & K. T. Ct. App. 1995) that tribal sovereign immunity did not bar suits against members of the tribal council even where those members were acting in their official capacity and *within* their lawful authority. The *Moran* court noted that federal law does not extend tribal sovereign immunity to tribal officials, even when acting within the lawful scope of their authority, and it declined to extend tribal doctrines of sovereign immunity any further. Other tribal courts have taken a similar tack, ruling that tribal sovereign immunity does not extend to injunctive and declaratory relief actions even when taken within the lawful delegated authority of the tribal official. *E.g., Thompson v. Cheyenne River Sioux Tribe Board of Police Commissioners*, 23 Indian L. Re. 6045 (Chy. Riv. Sx. Ct. App. 1996); *Clement v. LeCompte*, 22 Indian L. Rep. 6111 (Chy. Riv. Sx. Tr. Ct. 1994); *LeCompte v. Jewett*, 12 Indian L. Rep. 6025 (Chy. Riv. Sx. Tr. Ct. App. 1985); *Bordeaux v. Wilkinson*, 21 Indian L. Rep. 6131 (Ft. Berth. Tr. Ct. 1993). By contrast, some tribal courts hold that tribal sovereign immunity reaches tribal officials, at least where acting within the scope of their authority. *E.g.,*

Francis v. Wilkinson, 20 Indian L. Rep. 6015 (N. Plns. Intertr. Ct. App. 1993); *Whitetail v. Chaske*, 20 Indian L. Rep. 6056 (N. Plns. Intertr. Ct. App. 1992); *Hicks v. Harold*, 20 Indian L. Rep. 6091 (Fallon Tr. Ct. 1993); *Satiacum v. Sterud*, 10 Indian L. Rep. 3015 (Puy. Tr. Ct. 1982). Such cases often focus on determining whether a tribe has waived [its] sovereign immunity in its tribal constitution or statutes. Additionally, such courts consider whether the affected official acted outside of his or her official capacity or otherwise in violation of the tribal constitution and therefore not within the scope of his or her legal authority. Either approach is thought by such courts to lift the shield of sovereign immunity. One unfortunate consequence of this approach is that it frequently forces tribal courts to find waivers of sovereign immunity, which ultimately could adversely affect the tribe in unintended ways albeit not in the pending case, merely to adjudicate legitimate claims against misguided tribal officials who seriously harm persons while acting within the scope of their authority. Clearly demarcating and separating the legal question of tribal sovereign immunity from the issue of tribal official immunity avoids this unfortunate consequence. . . .

. . . Two provisions of the Tribal Code appear to this court plainly relevant. Section 1-919 dealing specifically with and entitled "Sovereign immunity" provides:

> Except as required by federal law or by the Winnebago Tribal Constitution and By-Laws or as specifically waived by resolution adopted by the Winnebago Tribe of Nebraska specifically referring to such, the tribe shall be immune from any civil actions, *and its officers and employees shall be immune from suit for any liability arising from the performance of their official duties.*

Emphasis supplied. Section 1-916 of the Tribal Code entitled "Judicial review of legislative and executive actions" expressly provides in relevant part:

> The tribal courts shall have authority to review any act by the tribal council, or any tribal officer, agent, or employee to determine whether that action, and the procedure or manner of taking that action, is constitutional under the tribal constitution, authorized by tribal law, and not prohibited by the Indian Civil Rights Act.
>
> . . .

The only obvious way to reconcile these two provisions involves recognizing that section 1-919, while entitled "Sovereign immunity," really addresses two separate types of immunity — the sovereign immunity of the tribe and the official immunity of the tribal officials and employees. . . . Since section 1-916 clearly authorizes the Winnebago tribal courts to review the actions of tribal officials, agencies, and the tribal council through injunctive, declaratory, and other noncompensatory forms of relief, the only way to harmonize that section with the official immunity portion of section 1-919 is to interpret the references in that section to "suit for any liability" to include only liability for damage or other monetary forms of relief. So limited, it is clear that section 1-919 really describes two entirely separate forms of immunity that parallel the federal law distinctions between sovereign immunity and official immunity. The tribe therefore possesses absolute immunity from suit for any type of relief under section 1-919 unless the adjudication is "required by federal law or by the Winnebago Tribal Constitution and By-Laws or as specifically waived by [a tribal] resolution . . . specifically referring to such [immunity]." By contrast, most tribal officers and employees, including members of the tribal council, only have a qualified immunity from damage and other forms of monetary relief under section 1-919.

. . . Consequently, it is clear that section 1-919, as construed by this court, adopts the emerging consensus of tribal court decisions that tribal sovereign immunity does not extend to suits against tribal officers and employees. . . . Insofar as tribal officials have any immunity under section 1-919, that immunity is an *official* immunity not a derivative sovereign immunity. . . .

As a result of the foregoing discussion, this action clearly is not barred by sovereign immunity, as claimed by the defendants. . . .

NOTES

1. The *Rave* Court surveyed a series of tribal court decisions from other tribes and reached the conclusion that there was a "consensus of tribal court decisions" supporting its view on tribal official immunity. This is intertribal common law.

   Intertribal common law is the substantive common law applied by tribal courts in cases arising out of an Anglo-American legal construct. It is likely that the vast majority of tribal court cases arise out of an Anglo-American legal construct. Intertribal common law includes the common law decisions of other tribal courts and may include a tribal court's importation of federal and state court common law. Tribal courts create intertribal common law, for example, when litigants ask the court to interpret a statute such as the Indian Civil Rights Act or a tribal secured transactions code. Tribal courts create intertribal common law when they adopt a common law rule of another tribal court or a federal or state court, such as the doctrine of sovereign immunity.

   An Anglo-American legal construct is any legal construct or relationship that has been imported into Indian country, modeled upon a non-Indigenous legal construct. A legal construct is a legal concept or model. It may include, without limitation, a statute, a doctrine of common law, and legal or political infrastructure, such as a court, a governing body, or an executive agency. Tribal courts modeled on state and federal courts are Anglo-American legal constructs. Tribal constitutions adopted during the period following the Indian Reorganization Act are Anglo-American legal constructs. Tribal housing leases; tribal employment contracts; tribal casino financing deals; tribal sovereign immunity; and common law tort, contract, and property law causes of action and defenses are all Anglo-American legal constructs. Indian tribes imported some of these constructs by choice, but outsiders imposed many others. As a function of coexisting within non-Indian American society, some Indian tribes have taken these nonindigenous constructs and made them, as much as possible, more consistent with tribal culture, while other communities have adopted them in haste or without detailed consideration as need arises. At this point in history, in which Indian tribes have begun to see success in their long struggle to preserve their cultures, economies, and even lives using the legal constructs available to them, it is not possible or even desirable to expel all Anglo-American legal constructs from Indian country.

Despite the dearth of theorization behind the use of intertribal common law, the wide majority of tribal courts apply intertribal common law in almost every decision involving nonmembers. As the theory of intertribal common law suggests, tribal courts apply intertribal common law in a wide variety of tribal court cases, including drug-related civil forfeiture cases, contracts with nonmember businesses, and tort claims. In *Muscogee (Creek) Nation v. One Thousand Four Hundred Sixty Three Dollars and 14/100*, 32 Indian L. Rep. 6133, 6134 (Muscogee (Creek) Nation Sup. Ct. Apr. 29, 2005), for example, the Muscogee (Creek) Nation Supreme Court upheld the authority of the tribal government to "regulate public safety through civil laws that restrict the possession, use or distribution of illegal drugs." *Id.* at 6135. The statutes applied to the matter — the tribal legislature's codification of laws that prohibit the possession and use of certain drugs and the confiscation of property related to the possession and use of illegal drugs — were Anglo-American legal constructs. The federal common law that established the tribal government's exclusive jurisdiction over the casino parking lot where the tribal police found the drugs; the federal common law that established the Nation's authority to regulate the nonmembers' on-reservation actions; and the federal treaty reserving to the tribal government certain rights as against state and federal intrusion, are all Anglo-American legal constructs. Even the tribal police's actions were modeled upon American law enforcement tactics. There is nothing wrong with the Nation's choices in this case — the drug ("crystal meth") came from outside the community, brought by nonmembers to the tribal casino, and so it is reasonable for the Nation to employ an outside legal construct in response.

2. Tribal courts also decide tort and contract claims brought against Indian tribes, tribal government officials, and tribal entities using intertribal common law. *Sullivan v. Mashantucket Pequot Gaming Enterprises*, 32 Indian L. Rep. 6128 (Mashantucket Pequot Tribal Ct. May 31, 2005), demonstrates how tribal courts have developed in the last three decades. The tribal court relied upon its own precedent in most instances, citing to Connecticut law or American legal treatises where its own common law was silent. As tribal courts hear more and more cases, they will be more capable of relying upon their own precedents, rather than importing federal, state, and other tribal court decisions. This exemplifies the ongoing process of tribal courts adapting Anglo-American common law in cases involving nonmembers. The oldest tribal courts of record adopted and imported Anglo-American precedents for use in cases involving nonmembers. The next generation does the same, but also relies upon the precedents of older generations of tribal courts. The process suggests that importation and adaptation of Anglo-American common law is useful for tribal courts when resolving disputes involving nonmembers — and that this process will continue.

3. Intertribal common law is a mixture of tribal common law, as well as the common law decisions of other tribal courts, federal courts, and state courts. While there is a definite mixture of authorities, it is unusual to find a tribal

court decision that would depart in a radical manner from the way a state or federal court would decide the case.

Taking the doctrine of due process, one of the more subjective legal doctrines in the law, as an example is useful. *See* Nell Jessup Newton, *Tribal Court Praxis: One Year in the Life of Twenty Indian Tribal Courts*, 22 AM. INDIAN L. REV. 285, 344 & n.238 (1998). State and federal courts tend to apply a balancing test, reaching results that differ from other courts in often dramatic ways. In California, where the notion of "substantive due process" is incorporated into the state's constitutional law, a resident and citizen of that state might be subject to a United States Supreme Court still cringing from its own substantive due process jurisprudence. Due process as envisioned by the framers of the Constitution might be nothing like the due process the Court now applies. *See generally* STEPHEN BREYER, ACTIVE LIBERTY 15-38 (2005) (describing the Constitution as a "continuing instrument" of government that will apply to changing subject matter). While the Rosebud Sioux tribal court might not apply due process the same way as the Little River Band of Ottawa Indians tribal court, they might apply the doctrine the same as Idaho, South Dakota, or Michigan courts. Due process jurisprudence has built-in expectations of variation.

As tribal courts decide more cases, they will have more opportunity to rethink these common law choices, just as federal and state courts rethink their own common law choices. Every Indian tribe is a laboratory for innovation. Every court may live by Justice Holmes's dictum:

> It is revolting to have no better reason for a rule of law than that so it was laid down in the time of Henry IV. It is still more revolting if the grounds upon which it was laid down have vanished long since, and the rule simply persists from blind imitation of the past.

OLIVER WENDELL HOLMES, *The Path of the Law*, in COLLECTED LEGAL PAPERS 167, 187 (1920).

Over time, tribal courts may incorporate the necessary custom and tradition of the tribal community into its own common law. This incorporation must be gradual, but it is a must if the tribal common law is to have value for the community.

C. TRIBAL JUDGES

1. JUDICIAL INDEPENDENCE

LITTLE TRAVERSE BAY BANDS OF ODAWA INDIANS CONSTITUTION

Article IX, Section H

1. Independent Branch of Government. The Judicial Branch shall be independent from the Legislative and Executive branches of the Tribal government and no person exercising the powers of any of the other two (2) branches of government shall exercise powers properly belonging to the Judicial Branch of Tribal government.

2. Funding mandate. The Judicial Branch shall prepare and present an annual budget directly to the Tribal Council for funding. The proposed budget may include funding for representation of indigent defendants. Funding for the Judiciary shall be based on its need and status as a branch of government.

3. Court administration. The Tribal Judiciary shall employ an administrator of the courts and other assistants as may be necessary to aid in the administration of the courts of the Little Traverse Bay Bands of Odawa Indians. The administrator shall perform administrative duties assigned by the Judiciary.

NOTES

1. Judge Fred Gabourie wrote the following in discussing the modern difficulties of tribes without a clear separation-of-powers rule:

> Most tribes are governed by a tribal council, which is comprised of tribal members. As the legislative body of the tribe, it is their duty to enact a law and order code, including the establishment of the judiciary. This procedure may well be a weak link. Instead of "separation of powers" there are tribal councilpersons of the opinion that the tribal council has the power and authority to oversee tribal courts and the judges.
>
> . . .
>
> Not all Tribes have an effective procedure to evaluate applicants for judicial positions. However, there are tribes that require the judge to be a licensed attorney in good standing. And, there are tribes that have no such requirement. A successful applicant just may be chosen because he or she may have the reputation as a "good guy," or, be an ex-cop, a recent law school graduate, or one who dresses and looks like a judge. This caliber of tribal court judge may well have the feeling that his or her job depends upon keeping the tribal council happy and satisfied. On the other hand, there are some tribal courts judges who are not attorneys but have taken the initiative and desire to be good judges. They attend judges training programs, study and work very hard to become proficient and effective tribal court judges.
>
> The majority of tribes recognize the fact that for a strong judiciary, judges must be free from political pressures, and therefore have enacted sections in their Constitution and Law and Order Code clearly defining judicial independence, therefore, separating the judicial branch from the executive and legislative branches of tribal government. Judges in the state system are either political appointees or elected and states wrestle with the issue of judicial independence, aware that it is necessary their judges be free from political pressures.

Hon. Fred W. Gabourie, *Judicial Independence of Tribal Courts*, 44 Advocate (State Bar of Idaho), October 2001, at 24.

2. Samuel Brackel's 1978 study of tribal courts asserted that a lack of tribal judicial independence was a serious roadblock to the development of tribal court legitimacy. Samuel J. Brackel, American Indian Tribal Courts: The Costs of Separate Justice 108-09 (1978). William Vetter noted that the perception that tribal politics influences tribal courts is enough to prejudice tribal interests:

The separation of the judicial and political branches is a fundamental feature of legal ideology in the United States. Obviously, some degree of political influence on the Judicial branch does exist in the federal and state governments. The appointment of federal judges is a political process (as amply demonstrated by recent Supreme Court Justice appointment debates), but after appointment those judges are effectively free from political control. Similarly, state judges are usually elected, also a political process, but the other branches of state government normally become involved only when a vacancy exists and they cannot, for political reasons, remove a judge. Despite actual independence of tribal judges and regardless of actual noninterference by other tribal government branches, so long as the potential for political manipulation exists, tribal courts will be perceived as subservient and, therefore, inadequate to protect individual rights. It takes only a few bad examples to establish a perception of general inadequacy.

William V. Vetter, *A New Corridor for the Maze: Tribal Criminal Jurisdiction and Nonmember Indians*, 17 AM. INDIAN L. REV. 349, 455 (1992). Vetter cited to two federal court cases as the "bad examples": *Shortbull v. Looking Elk*, 677 F.2d 645 (8th Cir. 1982); *Little Horn State Bank v. Crow Tribal Court*, 690 F. Supp. 919 (D. Mont. 1988), *vacated on stipulation*, 704 F. Supp. 1561 (D. Mont. 1989).

3. More recent commentators, such as Kirke Kickingbird, note improvement on this front but caution that more work needs to be done:

[The last c]enturies witnessed long periods of the suppression and negation of independent tribal courts, and even today such courts have neither the independence nor self-sufficiency that most Native Americans would prefer. That said, in the last several decades sophisticated tribal justice mechanisms and judiciaries have once again arisen and are expanding. Only in these decades has the development of tribal legal expertise begun to flourish and be applied in a more widespread manner that serves the needs of Indian communities. Nonetheless, tribal judiciaries are still limited in their jurisdiction and decision making, and a fair and impartial tribal judiciary remains largely unrecognized even as we begin the twenty-first century. . . .

What has become clear to tribal government is that development of governmental infrastructure and economic projects requires Indian law expertise because of the complex issues that arise in applying its many doctrines. Concerns expressed by tribal members; by non-Indians visiting Indian Country; and by businessmen, corporations, and lenders who want to do business in Indian Country center around assurances that tribal authority is enforceable. Likewise, tribal governments need an appropriate forum to address the conflicts affecting tribal members, whether the issue is a domestic matter such as child welfare or a dispute involving major business operations and related financing. Yet, the authority of tribal governments has become more controversial as tribes have engaged in more extensive use of their authority.

Kirke Kickingbird, *Striving for the Independence of Native American Tribal Courts*, 36 HUM. RTS., Winter 2009, at 16, 19-20.

4. In one instance demonstrating that at least some tribal judges have no concerns over judicial independence, a judge for the Lac Vieux Desert Band of Lake Superior Chippewa Indians ordered the jailing of the entire

tribal council for failure to comply with a court order in a tribal election dispute. *See Lac Vieux Desert Band of Lake Superior Chippewa Indians Tribal Council v. Lac Vieux Desert Band Tribal Police*, Order Granting Ex Parte Petition for Habeas Corpus (Lac Vieux Desert Band of Lake Superior Chippewa Indians Court of Appeals, Sept. 9, 2010), available at http://turtletalk.files.wordpress.com/2010/09/order-granting-habeas-corpus.pdf.

2. JUDICIAL CODES

ONEIDA TRIBE OF INDIANS OF WISCONSIN

Judicial Code of Conduct, Judicial Code, Chapter 5

. . .

Article III Who is Bound by this Code

3-1 This Code applies to all Judicial Officers, Pro-Tempore and Former Judicial Officers.

3-2 The Code of Ethics shall be as set out below; recognizing that the concept of ethical conduct shall encompass action as well as inaction, and represents an area of self regulation. Provided further, that it is the policy of the Oneida Tribal Judicial System to demonstrate the highest standards of personal integrity, truthfulness, honesty, and fortitude in all public activities in order to inspire public confidence and trust in the officials of the Oneida Tribal Judicial System.

Article IV Honesty and Independence

4-1 An independent and honest judicial system is the mainstay of trust. This goal should be kept in mind at all times, especially if the Oneida Tribal Judicial System intends to earn the proper respect in the community. The Judicial Officers shall always acknowledge and exhibit a good behavior as part of their role in the Oneida traditional system of justice. Serving on the Oneida Tribal Judicial System should be regarded as highly honored and a respected position of the judicial system of the Oneida Nation. The Judicial Officers should establish and maintain a respectful standing in the community and their lifestyle, and shall observe stringent standards of conduct at all times.

4-2 The Oneida people expect that those who make decisions about their lives and future will be wise and completely independent, and the Judicial Officers will decide without regard to improper influences. Influences that may arise: family, personal, or business relationships; a personal interest in a case before the Oneida Tribal Judicial System; giving in to or fearing political influence; or any consideration other than the equality of the parties and merits of the case. To that end, all Judicial Officers must remain personally impartial and independent, and act to promote and protect the independence of the Oneida Tribal Judicial System.

4-3 Judicial Officers shall adhere to the laws of the tribe.

4-4 Judicial Officers shall be patient, dignified and courteous to constituents, other officials, and others with whom the Judicial Officer deals in any official capacity, and require similar conduct of others in official proceedings and those persons subject to the Oneida Tribal Judicial System's jurisdiction and control.

a. Judicial Officers shall give to every person and party of interest in action time to be heard.

b. Judicial Officers shall not talk to one party without the presence of the other party (ex parte communication).

c. Judicial Officers shall protect the privileged information to which they have access in the course of their duties. Further, they shall not use confidential information for any personal gain.

Article V Impropriety and the Appearance of Impropriety

5-1 Judicial Officers should respect and comply with the laws of Oneida and should at all times act in a manner that promotes public confidence in the integrity and impartiality of the Oneida Tribal Judicial System.

5-2. Judicial Officers should not allow family, social or other personal relationships to influence their judicial conduct. Judicial Officers should not attempt to use the prestige of their position to advance the private interests of themselves, nor convey the impression that anyone has special influence on them.

5-3 A Judicial Officer shall not lobby or advocate any position before a legislative or executive branch for personal gain.

5-4 Once elected to the Oneida Tribal Judicial System, Judicial Officers shall not serve as an Advocate for any party before any hearing body within the jurisdiction of Oneida Tribe of Indians of Wisconsin.

Article VI Disqualification/Recusal

6-1 Judicial Officers shall disqualify themselves in a proceeding in which their impartiality might reasonably be questioned, including instances where:

a. A Judicial Officer has a personal bias or prejudice concerning a party or personal knowledge of disputed evidentiary facts.

b. A Judicial Officer has served as a lawyer, advocate or personal representative in the matter before the Appeals Commission.

c. A Judicial Officer's spouse, and any reasonably close family member in the Judicial Officer or spouse's family:

1. Is a party to the proceeding or officer, director, or trustee of a party; or

2. Is acting as a lawyer or advocate in the proceeding; or

3. Is known by the Judicial Officer to have an interest that could be substantially affected by the outcome of the proceeding; or

4. Is to the Judicial Officers' knowledge likely to be a material witness in a proceeding before the Oneida Tribal Judicial System.

6-2 Judicial Officers shall recuse themselves in cases where some conflict of interest exists, potentially exists, or may be perceived to exist.

. . .

Article VIII Adjudicative Responsibilities

8-1 The duties of the Judicial Officer include all official functions of the Oneida Tribal Judicial System as the judiciary of the Oneida Government. In the performance of these duties, the following standards apply:

a. Judicial Officers should not be swayed by partisan interests, public clamor, political pressure, or fear of criticism and should resist influences on the Oneida Tribal Judicial System by administrators or governmental officials or any others attempting to improperly influence the Judicial Officers in their decisions.

b. Judicial Officers should give to every person holding a legal interest in a proceeding, or his/her representative, a full right to be heard. Judicial Officers should avoid all communication with officials, agents, or others concerning a pending proceeding unless all parties to the proceeding are present or represented. Judicial Officers may, however, consult a disinterested expert on federal, state, or tribal law, and traditions. Judicial Officers may review any source of law applicable to a proceeding in the case they have been assigned.

c. Judicial Officers shall maintain order when conducting a hearing.

. . .

Article X Extra Judicial Activities

10-1 Judicial Officers may engage in activities that do not cast doubt on their capability to decide impartially an issue that may come before the Oneida Tribal Judicial System.

10-2 A Judicial Officer may speak, write, lecture, teach and participate in other activities concerning the legal system of the Oneida Nation.

10-3 A Judicial Officer may appear at a public hearing before the executive, legislative bodies or other officials, but only in matters concerning the general administration of justice.

10-4 A Judicial Officer may serve as a member, officer, or director of an organization or governmental agency outside the Oneida Nation devoted to the improvement of law or the administration of justice. A Judicial Officer may assist such an organization in raising funds and may participate in the management and investment. The Oneida Tribal System may make recommendations to public and private fund granting agencies on projects and programs concerning Oneida law, its legal system and the administration of justice.

10-5   A Judicial Officer may not cross over the bounds separating the powers of government to serve as a member of the executive or legislative branches of the Oneida Government.

10-6   Judicial Officers may engage in social and recreational activities, if these activities do not interfere with the performance of the Oneida Tribal Judicial System responsibilities.

10-7   Judicial Officers may participate in civic, charitable and other activities that do not reflect upon his/her impartiality or interfere with the performance of his/her judicial duties.

10-8   Judicial Officers may participate in ceremonies that are educational, connected with traditional, cultural activities or other religious activities.

10-9   Judicial Officers shall not participate in an organization if it is likely that the organization will be involved in proceedings which would ordinarily come before the Oneida Tribal Judicial System.

10-10   In the event that a Judicial Officer is selected or recommended to serve as a member of a governmental organization or agency, other than the Oneida Nation, devoted to the improvement of law or the administration of justice, the Oneida Tribal Judicial System must approve of the appointment prior to the Judicial Officer commencing his/her position or duties for the new position.

10-11   Judicial Officers may accept appointments to external boards, committees, and commissions outside the jurisdiction of the Oneida Nation that are not judicial in nature and whose activities are not likely to come before the Oneida Tribal Judicial System. However, Judicial Officers must disclose all appointments within thirty (30) days of acceptance or commencement of duties for the position.

Article XI Extra Appeals Commission Appointments

11-1   A Judicial Officer shall not accept appointment to any Oneida governmental entity or other position whose interest is contrary to the Oneida Tribal Judicial System.

Article XII Financial Activities

12-1   Judicial Officers should avoid financial and business dealings that tend to reflect adversely on his/her impartiality, interfere with the performance of his/her judicial duties, exploit his/her judicial position.

12-2   Except as allowed by customs or tradition of the Oneida, a Judicial Officer shall not accept a gift, bequest, favor, or loan from anyone which would affect or appear to affect his/her impartiality in judicial proceedings or in the Oneida Tribal Judicial System's appearance of fairness.

Article XIII Political Activities

13-1   Judicial Officers shall not engage in any political activity except measures to improve the law or enhance the Oneida Judiciary.

13-2 A candidate, including an incumbent Judicial Officer seeking re-election, who is seeking to fill a vacant position on the Oneida Tribal Judicial System by election of the Oneida Nation shall:

> a. Affirm and display the respectful integrity of a person qualified to hold a position on the Oneida Tribal Judicial System, and should refrain from any political activity which might interfere with the performance of his/her duties. Furthermore, a candidate should encourage members of his/her family to adhere to the same standards of political conduct that apply to him/her.
>
> b. Not make pledges or promises of conduct as a Judicial Officer other than the faithful and impartial performance of duties as a Judicial Officer, nor announce his/her views on any disputed legal or political issue.

NOTES

1. Indian nations often are very insular communities in which tribal judges face significant risks of political influence, personal bias, and conflicts of interest. One commentator argues, however, that judicial codes seeking to limit those risks creates the wrong incentives:

> The tribal character of American Indian communities has been eroded, but not altogether obliterated by government assimilation projects, electronic mass media, and integration into the market economy. It is popular to blame advertising and consumerism, but I do not think that people succumb to self-indulgent materialism unless they have already lost a great deal of their attachment to their families, and no longer enjoy much satisfaction from social and spiritual life. . . .
>
> This fragmentation is accompanied by growing contradictions between individuality and group loyalty, and is reflected in the difficulties tribal courts are experiencing in managing conflicts of interest involving councilmen, judges, lawyers and jurors. Tribal courts recognize that everyone in the community is related but try to set arbitrary boundaries on the permissible closeness of relationships, or deny that kinship influences decision-making. In the past, tribal societies recognized that kinship does affect decision-making, and they developed kinship systems that contained the requisite checks and balances. Now that kinship systems are fragmenting, personal bias is potentially more of a problem. The presumption of family bias is tending to undermine the legitimacy of all decisions made by members of the community. Tribal judges aspire to the neutrality of clowns, critics and healers, but such roles depend for their autonomy on an underlying balance of power among families. The easy way out of this dilemma, unfortunately, is to fill judicial posts with outsiders ignorant of local values and traditions.

Russel Lawrence Barsh, *Putting the Tribe in Tribal Courts: Possible? Desirable?*, 8 KAN. J.L. & PUB. POL'Y, Winter 1997, at 74, 76-77.

2. The Wisconsin Oneida judicial code is geared toward tribal judges who will be elected to their positions. Not all tribal judges are elected. Many are appointed by the tribal council; for example, the White Earth Ojibwe:

> All Judges of the Tribal Court shall be selected by appointment by a majority vote of the White Earth Tribal Council.

WHITE EARTH BAND OF CHIPPEWA INDIANS JUDICIAL CODE, title 1, chapter 3, §2.

Others are appointed using a nomination-and-confirmation process involving a tribal executive and a tribal legislature:

> 1. Appointment to the Tribal Court. The Judges of the Tribal Court and such lower courts as established under Section (A) of this Article shall be appointed by an affirmative vote of six (6) of the nine (9) members of the Tribal Council. Initial appointments shall take place within one hundred twenty (120) days of the swearing in of the first Tribal Council elected under this Constitution.
>
> 2. Appointment to the Tribal Appellate Court. Each justice of the Tribal Appellate Court shall be appointed by an affirmative vote of six (6) of the nine (9) members of the Tribal Council.

CONST. OF THE LITTLE TRAVERSE BAY BANDS OF ODAWA INDIANS art. IX (D).

3. THEORIES OF TRIBAL JUDGING

COYOTE PARADOX: SOME INDIAN LAW REFLECTIONS
FROM THE EDGE OF THE PRAIRIE

Frank Pommersheim, 31 Ariz. St. L.J. 439, 455-59 (2002)

. . .

VI. A Model of Tribal Court Jurisprudence

Given the varied challenges that the two "faces" of Indian law as community and resistance pose to tribal institutions, especially tribal courts, it is worthwhile to consider the contours of a workable model of tribal court jurisprudence with which to respond. Such a model suggests idealized aspiration, not an absolute necessity attainable in every case. It also provides a practical checklist of possibilities for tribal court judges who face the exigency of real, often staggering, caseloads, limited legal resources, and usually no law clerks at all. For these reasons tribal court jurisprudence constitutes a pragmatic yet complex art. This model or paradigm (there may well be others) contains the following parts:

(A) Tribal court jurisprudence as craft;
(B) Tribal court jurisprudence as culture;
(C) Tribal court jurisprudence as narrative;
(D) Tribal court jurisprudence as literacy primer;
(E) Tribal court jurisprudence as "the extended hand";
(F) Tribal court jurisprudence as guide to the standards of review.

Ultimately, these pieces will be stitched together in their unique (tribal) patterns by the hearts and minds of real tribal judges doing their jobs day in and day out with their characteristic hard work and enviable commitment to render justice and fair play to the litigants that come before them.

A. Craft

The field of law invokes certain sets of practices and ways of thinking and speaking that make it a craft. It also constitutes a unique way of identifying and resolving legal disputes. The end product of such dialogue and "translation" is usually a judicial decision that summarizes, weighs, and resolves the competing arguments or claims. The expectation is that the judicial decision will speak at least in part through the language or craft of law. In order to be credible to the law community both on and off the reservation and the larger society in general, tribal court decision making must be convincingly rendered in the craft and analytical practices of legal reasoning. This does not mean that this requirement is preemptive or exclusive of other concerns but only that it is necessary in a fundamental way. It is the yeast for the bread of legal conversation and discourse.

B. Culture

The risk of craft standing alone in tribal court jurisprudence is that it will be seen to represent a kind of (dominant) mimicry and it will be perceived as inauthentic and merely imitative. The counterweight to an unhinged craft is the door of culture. Tribal culture provides a context for legal craft to be persuasive because it takes into account tribal history and tradition in the process of legal decision making. Too often legal decision making and the legal system as a whole are seen as a purely formal system of rules and procedures that bear little relationship to the day to day life of people living on the reservation (or elsewhere for that matter). Sensitivity and awareness of (tribal) culture helps to insure that tribal court decision making will not only be analytically sound, but also culturally informed. In many ways, craft and culture are the cornerstones for building a sturdy and enduring tribal court jurisprudence.

C. Narrative

Tribal court decisions both individually and collectively tell a story about law, values, and culture. It is therefore critical for tribal court judges to be aware of the developing narrative or story their jurisprudence tells. How does it, for example, relate to the ongoing struggle to realize sovereignty and to vindicate particular values in unique human circumstances? Attention to narrative allows one to perceive more fully the meaning of tribal court jurisprudence not simply as the interplay of craft and culture but as something that reveals and explains a people to themselves and others. If law is a field of endeavor primarily for the mind and intellect, narrative is a way to the heart. Narrative is critical to tribal self understanding not only in a cultural but in a legal sense as well. This element of narrative in tribal court jurisprudence also connects pointedly with the "story telling" tradition that is central to many tribal traditions.

D. Literacy Primer

Tribal court jurisprudence needs also to function, where it can, as a basic Indian law literacy primer in several different ways. First, since tribal court decisions often generate significant local tribal interest and discourse, it is helpful if such opinions contain background discussion about the nature of basic principles of Indian law and tribal sovereignty. Such descriptions at their best aid local understanding of important legal and cultural matters in the many cases that generate local interest. Since law—for better or worse—plays such an outsized role in reservation life, any background understanding is particularly advantageous to developing an informed and literate citizenry.

Second, most recent United States Supreme Court jurisprudence in Indian law relative to tribal courts reaches back no further than *Montana v. United States*. As a result, current Supreme Court decisions in Indian law are remarkably truncated with little sense of the roots of tribal sovereignty and the sweep of Indian Law history from the colonial era onward. Again, tribal court jurisprudence can provide a valuable corrective to this pernicious historical and doctrinal amnesia. While there is no guarantee that reviewing federal courts—including the United States Supreme Court—will pay attention or even notice, any opportunity to educate and create dialogue needs to be seized.

Third, tribal courts do not have the luxury of assuming that other judges who read and review their decisions are adequately informed about tribal judicial descriptions of tribal law itself. Tribal courts, wherever possible, have to go that extra mile to explain basic tribal law and values. Without such efforts, it becomes all too easy for federal courts to avoid a genuine engagement with tribal court decisions.

Fourth, in a related but somewhat different vein, tribal court jurisprudence provides the opportunity for tribal courts to explain why some decisions of the Supreme Court and Circuit Courts are wrongly decided from the perspective of the federal courts' own precedents and/or from the tribal court's understanding of its own law. None of this is meant to sound arrogant or presumptuous, yet the Supreme Court does seem to be further and further out of touch with its own historical precedents and its understanding of the law and capabilities of tribal courts. Tribal courts, where they can, need to assist the educable within the federal judiciary. . . .

NOTES

1. Tribal justice system legitimacy is an ongoing concern for Indian nations and the parties that appear in tribal courts. Many tribal courts have the respect of the surrounding jurisdictions; for example, the Mashantucket Pequot tribal courts' judgments are routinely recognized in neighboring state courts. *E.g., Mashantucket Pequot Gaming v. Yau*, No. 11789/2009 (N.Y. Sup. Ct., Feb. 17, 2010), available at http://turtletalk.files.wordpress.com/2010/02/mashantucket-pequot-v-yau.pdf. But many other tribal courts are underfunded and do not have the necessary support of the tribal government to develop institutional capacity.

    In another article, Professor Pommersheim offered several suggestions:

    > A primary element in the making of quality legal decisions at both the trial and appellate levels is the capacity to perform the necessary legal research with which to resolve the issues raised by the case. . . .

As a result of these shortcomings, and consonant with the most conventional wisdom, tribal courts need consistent access to the legal research available through the LexisNexis and Westlaw electronic databases. Yet, even here, there are unique Indian law problems because the critical resource of tribal court opinions is not yet consistently available online. . . . It is also true, however, that many other tribal law resources, such as treaties, constitutions, and codes, are not available online and thus, print libraries also must be maintained.

. . . Technology generates the raw material of meaningful research, but it takes a law clerk, a person with some sense of craft, to refine these raw materials into a more usable and malleable form for judges to actually use.

In a related vein, technology and computer programming are necessary ingredients to develop consistently coherent case files and case management systems. . . . Court clerks and administrative personnel are vital cogs in the wheels of justice and meeting their needs is key to enhancing the functioning of this often overlooked and under-appreciated sector of tribal courts. . . .

. . . Given the relative youth of many tribal courts, a considerable number of their decisions involve cases of first impression. The decisions of other tribal courts in similar matters therefore become a crucial ingredient and adjunct in the making of many tribal court decisions.

Currently, much of this jurisprudential base is not available to tribal courts. . . .

The establishment of an effective [tribal court] reporter — both print and electronic — would have the collateral benefits of making such decisions available to others nationally and outside the region. In addition to advancing the legitimacy of the overall program, because of its delivery of important services in a timely and regular manner — just like similar activities in the state and federal judicial systems. Since there is often a paucity of available precedent, such publication efforts will fill a significant void. . . . Such a reporter would also be an invaluable resource to attorneys preparing to appear before these courts. . . .

As discussed above, improved legal research is not the product of a simple technological fix; it requires a law-trained individual not only to assist in doing the research, but also to organize, describe, and synthesize the research for the applicable judge or panel of judges. . . .

Legal research is more than the generation of information. It requires interaction of a trained human with legal intelligence to put that information in a useful and usable context. Regardless of potential cost, the need for law clerks is critical. . . .

. . . [A]ccess to a law clerk to do research is a twofold gift. It is likely to enhance the quality of justice rendered in a particular case and to improve the quality of justice across the entire system because of the greater efficiency that law clerks would create in the administration of justice. . . .

Training is an absolute necessity in order to continue to advance the development of tribal courts. Training is required in all sectors: judges, clerks/administrators, prosecutors/public defenders, and members of the private and tribal bar. . . .

There is also the need for training to assist tribal judges — at both the trial and appellate level — to improve and enhance their ability to write thoughtful and cogent legal opinions to explain and justify their decisions. Such efforts, for example, might reduce the likelihood of appeal in that a fair number of current tribal court appeals are filed simply because there is no adequate explanation of the trial court's decision. This training also knits together with the availability of law clerks to establish a research base from which tribal judges can craft well-written decisions. . . .

Training of clerks and court administrators is no less essential to the well-being and advancement of tribal courts. . . .

Again, the obvious: any person serving as prosecutor or public defender has a tremendous responsibility in the pursuit of justice within the tribal criminal justice system. . . .

Given the raw fact that personal liberty is at stake in criminal proceedings and that the right to counsel guarantee in the Indian Civil Rights Act of 1968 is not mandatory on the tribes, the utmost in training in this area needs to be made a priority and preference. Prosecution and defense work is labor-intensive; therefore training, both procedural and substantive, as well as case management assistance are central to maintaining due process and respect for individual liberty. . . .

As noted in many areas throughout this article, the practice of Indian law, especially in tribal courts, is both unique and subject to rapid change. This fact points to the necessity of training based on the CLE model in state and federal settings for practitioners who practice regularly in tribal court. . . .

The delivery of these programs is best administered through tribal bar associations, where they exist, but in their absence (which is the norm), they must be provided by the tribal courts themselves. . . .

. . . In complementary fashion, it is worth noting that salary levels are generally low in all tribal court sectors, particularly at the clerk and administrator level. As a result, there needs to be attention focused on salary (and benefits) concerns as critical dimensions relative to improving staffing stability and continuity.

Frank Pommersheim, *Looking Forward and Looking Back: The Promise and Potential of a Sioux Nation Judicial Support Center and Sioux Nation Supreme Court*, 34 Ariz. St. L.J. 269, 273-79 (2002)

2. Professor Pommersheim is one of the most influential and experienced tribal court judges in the United States. His recommendations for the development of tribal courts are not entirely new, however, as organizations such as the National American Indian Court Judges Association have been advocating for similar reforms and improvements. *E.g.*, National American Indian Court Judges Association, Indian Courts and the Future: Report of the NAICJA Long Range Planning Project 146-96 (David H. Getches ed., 1978). But these are terribly important recommendations that should be recognized and repeated until they finally come to fruition.

3

TRIBAL CONSTITUTIONS

Most Indian nations had no written or formal constitution prior to the enactment of the Indian Reorganization Act in 1934, according to which Congress encouraged Indian nations to "reorganize" as constitutional democracies. 25 U.S.C. §476. As such, Indian nations have a relatively new tradition of constitutionalism, and some tribes — most notably the Navajo Nation — still have no written constitution. This chapter details the origins, the development, and the jurisprudence of tribal constitutions.

A. MODERN TRIBAL CONSTITUTIONS

1. A BRIEF HISTORY OF TRIBAL CONSTITUTIONS AFTER THE INDIAN REORGANIZATION ACT

The following excerpts focus on Felix S. Cohen, the leading figure in the development of tribal constitutions after the enactment of the Indian Reorganization Act in 1934. Cohen was the primary drafter of the bill that would become the Act, and a leading proponent of encouraging Indian tribes to adopt *tribally generated, indigenous* constitutions. *See generally* DALIA TSUK MITCHELL, ARCHITECT OF JUSTICE: FELIX S. COHEN AND THE FOUNDING OF AMERICAN LEGAL PLURALISM 103-17 (2007).

HOW LONG WILL INDIAN CONSTITUTIONS LAST?

Felix S. Cohen, Indians at Work (Dept. of Interior 1939), Reprinted in
The Legal Conscience 222, 222-28 (Lucy Kramer Cohen ed., 1960)

Between October 28, 1935, and January 15, 1939, ninety-seven Indian tribes framed constitutions for self-government, which were approved under the Act of June 18, 1934 [the Indian Reorganization Act].

How long are these Indian constitutions likely to last? . . .

[One] basic fact that stands out in a survey of the life span of Indian constitutions is that the Indians themselves cease to want a constitution when their constituted government no longer satisfies important wants. When this happens, a tribal government, like any other government, either dissolves into chaos or yields place to some other governing agency that commands greater power or promises to satisfy in great measure the significant wants of the governed. . . .

I

The most fundamental of the goods which a tribe may bring to its members is economic security. Few things bind men so closely as a common interest in the means of their livelihood. No tribe will dissolve so long as there are lands or resources that belong to the tribe or economic enterprises in which all members of the tribe may participate. The young man who in the plastic years of adolescence goes to his tribal government to obtain employment in a tribal lumber mill, cooperative store, hotel, mine, farm, or factory, or who applies to a committee of his tribal council for a chance to build up his herds, or to build a home and garden upon tribal lands assigned to his occupancy, cannot ignore this tribal government.

Government is an affair of human loyalties. These loyalties Indian tribes cannot command if, in the important economic decisions of their lives, the members of the tribe must look elsewhere for opportunity and guidance. . . .

The roots of any tribal constitution are likely to be as deep as the tribe's actual control over economic resources.

II

Less tangible than the possession of common property, but perhaps equally important in the continuity of a social group, is the existence of common enjoyments. In community life, as in marriage, community of interest in the useful and enjoyable things of life makes for stability and loyalty. . . .

In this field, much will depend on the attitude of Indian Service officials, and particularly upon the attitude of teachers, social workers, and extension agents. It will be hard for them to surrender the large measure of control that they now exercise over the recreation and social life of the reservations, but unless they are willing to yield control in this field to the tribal government, that government may find itself barred from the hearts of its people.

III

Outside of Indian reservations, local government finds its chief justification in the performance of municipal services, and particularly the maintenance of law and order, the management of public education, the distribution of water, gas, and electricity, the maintenance of health and sanitation, the relief of the needy, and activities designed to afford citizens protection against fire and other natural calamities. On most Indian reservations all of these functions, if performed at all, are performed not by the tribal councils but by employees of the Indian Service. Thus the usual reason for maintenance of local government is lacking.

The cure for this situation is, obviously, the progressive transfer of municipal functions to the organized tribe. Already some progress has been made in this direction in the field of law and order. Codes of municipal ordinances have been adopted by several organized tribes; judges are removable, in some cases, by the Indians to whom they are responsible; and the former absolute powers of the Superintendent in this field have been substantially abolished. . . .

. . . The shift of control from a Federal bureau to the local community is likely to come not through gifts of delegated authority from the Federal bureau, but rather as a result of insistent demands from the local community that it be entrusted with increasing control over its own municipal affairs.

IV

A fourth source of vitality in any tribal constitution is the community of consciousness which it reflects. Where many people think and feel as one, there is some ground to expect a stable political organization. Where, on the other hand, such unity is threatened either by factionalism within the tribe or by constant assimilation into a surrounding population, continuity of tribal organization cannot be expected.

This is a factor which shows every possible variation. At one extreme of social solidarity are those pueblos that voted unanimously to accept the Wheeler-Howard Act and for centuries have regularly cast unanimous votes for their officers. At the other extreme are those areas of the Northwest where today, as in the days before Columbus, every family is a faction and the "tribe" is only a statistical concept. . . .

V

A fifth source of potential strength for any tribal organization lies in the role which it may assume as protector of the rights of its members. . . .

In this field of activity, tribal governments can achieve significant results. A council, for instance, that employs an attorney to enjoin the enforcement of an unconstitutional statute depriving Indians of the right to vote is likely to secure a first lien on the respect of its constituency and materially increase the life expectancy of the tribal constitution. . . . A rubber stamp council that simply takes what the Indian Office gives it is not likely to establish permanent foundations for tribal autonomy. Rubber is a peculiarly perishable material, and it gives off a bad smell when it decays. . . .

COHEN ON TRIBAL CONSTITUTIONS

David E. Wilkins, *Introduction*, Felix S. Cohen, On the Drafting of Tribal Constitutions xxi, xxi-xxiii, xxviii (David E. Wilkins ed., 2006)

Cohen and his colleagues were convinced, especially at the beginning of the process, that tribal organization via written constitutions, charters, and bylaws was the most appropriate means for Native nations to protect and exercise their basic right of political and economic self-determination. . . .

Shortly before the IRA became law, but well before the major thrust of constitutional development had taken place, some sixty tribes had preexisting constitutions, or "documents in the nature of constitutions," that were already on file with the Department of Interior. It is not known precisely how many of these were early versions of IRA-type constitutions, but it seems fairly certain that at least forty of them well predate the New Deal period. . . .

. . . [A] close review of [Cohen's] archived papers reveals that in the early drafts of the IRA his understanding of, and vision for, tribal constitutional development was heavily influenced, not by preexisting or other indigenous forms of governance, but by the regulations of the municipal governments that dot the American landscape.

In Cohen's view, tribal constitutional governments "were to be like town governments, except that they would have federal protection and their special rights." . . .

After the IRA was adopted in the summer of 1934, 181 tribes adopted the act, with some 77 choosing to reject it. Although tribes that voted to accept the measure were not required to adopt constitutions, many tribes expressed interest in doing so, and Cohen intensified his efforts to learn more about tribal governance, to dig deeper into the prior constitutional history of Indian nations.

The process of modern tribal constitutional development has long been fraught with uncertainty and ambiguity. Many commentators have maintained that Western-styled constitutions were forced on reluctant tribes, thereby eclipsing extant traditional systems that, they argue, had survived the previous century of coercive assimilation. These authors also typically assert that the BIA developed a "model" constitution that it sent out to newly organizing tribes to structure the style and content of their organic documents, forcing a constitutional uniformity that denies the diverse nature of tribal nations.

Contrarily, Elmer Rusco declared in his excellent 2000 study of the IRA, *A Fateful Time*, that the allegation that a coercive and uniform "model" tribal constitution had been sent out was in "error." While acknowledging that the idea had been "considered," Rusco says that this approach was ultimately rejected by the bureau. . . .

My analysis of Cohen's relevant papers and a review of his "Basic Memorandum" on tribal constitutions generally supports Rusco's interpretation of events, although there is incontrovertible evidence that some tribes did, in fact, receive a copy of a "model" constitution . . . or in some cases an "outline" of what a constitution should contain. . . .

. . . Cohen . . . traveled into Indian Country to listen to Indians and to learn more about how they might structure tribal organization. It was during this period of study that Cohen learned of the status and utility of preexisting Indian constitutions and of the residual traditional governing systems that were still active in many places. Nevertheless, we still see evidence of the inherent ideological and policy tension that Cohen and his colleagues faced as federal employees. On one hand, they wanted to facilitate and encourage a degree of Indian self-rule; on the other hand, they were operating under certain cultural and political presuppositions that elevated their own values and governing systems over those of indigenous nations. This produced a set of sometimes conflicting questions, policies, and views that led to contradictory constitutional results throughout Indian Country. . . .

Finally, to add further ambiguity to the question of whether tribes were presented with "model" constitutions, we have a Cohen memo dated December 14, 1935, titled "Criticisms of Wisconsin Oneida Constitution." In the opening paragraph he notes that "except for four short provisions . . . this constitution is identical with the 'Short Form Model Constitution' which *has been presented to and adopted by various other tribes*" [emphasis added]. In fact, is was apparent, said Cohen, that the Oneida had not given "any constructive thought on self-government in this constitution," meaning that it had probably been offered to them and that they had not had an opportunity to express their own views on the document, much less have had a role in its development. . . .

NOTES

1. Frank Pommersheim's important work on tribal law, *Braid of Feathers*, included a harsh assessment of many tribal constitutions adopted during the years following the enactment of the IRA:

   > These BIA constitutions did not provide for any separation of powers, and did not specifically create any court system. Most constitutions, rather facilely, it seems, recognized a power in the tribal council—the elected legislative body—to "promulgate and enforce ordinances providing for the administration of justice by establishing a reservation court and defining its duties and powers." Most tribal legislation also required the approval of the Bureau of Indian Affairs. In recent years a number of tribes have amended their constitutions to remove the Bureau of Indian Affairs approval power.

   FRANK POMMERSHEIM, BRAID OF FEATHERS: AMERICAN INDIAN LAW AND CONTEMPORARY LIFE 65 (1995).

2. Despite Cohen's intentions and efforts, many tribal constitutions adopted in the years following the passage of the IRA were barely organic documents of Indian origin. As an appellate judge, Professor Pommersheim participated in *Snowden v. Saginaw Chippewa Indian Tribe of Michigan*, 32 Indian L. Rep. 6047 (Saginaw Chippewa Indian Tribe Appellate Court, Jan. 7, 2005), a case involving the highly controversial efforts of the then–tribal council to disenroll deceased members of the tribe:

   > This case is not just about the meaning of the Saginaw Chippewa Tribal Constitution of 1986, but it is also a story about a People and a Tribe enmeshed in the coils of an unknowing and meddlesome Bureau of Indian Affairs and Federal Government. This destabilizing federal force is amply demonstrated in the history leading up to the adoption of the first Saginaw Chippewa Tribal Constitution in 1937. The Saginaw Chippewa Tribe of Michigan came into specific *legal* existence as a result of the Indian Reorganization Act (IRA) of 1934. . . .
   >
   > Many local tribal leaders and people were interested in the possibilities offered by the IRA. In fact, even before the referendum on the IRA itself, a Business Committee headed by Elijah Elk was established to meet with various tribal communities and to begin drafting a tribal constitution. The work of this committee resulted in a (draft) constitution that was sent to Secretary of Interior Harold Ickes on Nov. 27, 1934 for his approval.
   >
   > The draft constitution is noteworthy in several respects that are directly pertinent to this litigation. The proposed constitution's preamble began, "We, the members of the Saginaw, Swan Creek, and Black River Bands of

Chippewa Indians. . . ." The proposed Tribal Council represented four districts — three of which were outside the boundaries of the Isabella Reservation — three representatives from Mt. Pleasant (i.e., Isabella Reservation), three from Bay City, one from Caro, and three from Hubbard Lake.

Action on this proposed Constitution was slowed as a result of BIA Commissioner John Collier's direction to Elijah Elk that no action could be taken until the formal referendum to accept the IRA took place. As a result, energy shifted away from the draft constitution toward developing a list of eligible voters to vote in the IRA referendum. The list that was compiled by tribal individuals and BIA special agent George Blakeslee contained the names of many tribal people living outside the boundaries of the Isabella Reservation. The referendum was held on June 17, 1935 and included at least two off reservation voting places. The referendum passed.

With the successful referendum accomplished, attention returned to the Constitution itself. The Tribe's desire to include all of its communities — even those communities outside the Isabella Reservation — met strong resistance from Assistant Commissioner of Indian Affairs, William Zimmerman. Commissioner Zimmerman took the position that a tribe could only organize under the IRA if it had a reservation and its only members could be tribal people residing on the reservation.

With this dubious interpretation at the forefront of his review of the proposed Constitution, he changed the preamble to read, "We, the Indians residing on the Isabella Reservation in the State of Michigan. . . ." In addition, he changed the proposed Tribal Council representation to require all council members be elected from within the Reservation, and required that all tribal members *reside* on the Reservation. Commissioner Zimmerman further advised the Tribe that subsequent to the referendum to accept the constitution the Tribe could "adopt" those individuals living off the reservation. In fact, this "adoption" language appears in Sec. 2 of Art. III — Membership of the 1937 Constitution.

All these "recommendations" were accepted by the Business Committee and incorporated into the proposed Tribal Constitution that was voted on and accepted by tribal members on March 27, 1937. Unfortunately, the 1937 Constitution — whatever its intent — sowed the seeds of membership confusion and discontent that yielded the bitter harvest at the core of this most challenging, even heart wrenching, litigation about the cultural and legal aspects of tribal belonging.

Id. at 6048-49.

3. Even decades later, the Bureau of Indian Affairs would interfere in the adoption of tribal constitutions for newly recognized tribes.[*] The Grand Traverse Band of Ottawa and Chippewa Indians, the first Indian tribe to be administratively recognized by the Branch of Acknowledgement and Research, was an early victim of notorious Department of Interior Secretary James Watt's government-shrinking, anti-Indian policies. After recognition in 1980, the Bureau of Indian Affairs informed the Grand Traverse Band that it "[would] not be eligible to organize and adopt a constitution under the Indian Reorganization Act until a reservation ha[d] been set aside for it." In a classic pincer maneuver that placed the Band's feet to the fire, the Bureau

---

[*]Much of the material in this note appears in different form in Matthew L. M. Fletcher, *The Insidious Colonialism of the Conqueror: The Federal Government in Modern Tribal Affairs*, 19 Wash. U. J.L. & Pol'y 273, 279-83 (2005).

strongly implied that it would not declare the Grand Traverse Band a reservation until the Band agreed to amend its proposed constitution to exclude more than 80 percent of its proposed membership.

> While we admit it is well established that Indian tribes have authority to determine their own members, there is an equally fundamental principle that membership in an Indian tribe is a bilateral, political relationship which derives its legal significance from, and is dependent upon, an interaction between the individual and the tribal community. The existence of such a relationship was one of the criteria considered in the acknowledgement process. During that process it was determined that the group of 297 individuals met this criterion and their acknowledgement as a tribe was based upon that determination.

Letter from Deputy Assistant Sec'y, Indian Affairs (Operations), to Joseph C. Raphael, Chairman Grand Traverse Band of Ottawa and Chippewa Indians (Nov. 4, 1983).

The Bureau told the Band that its federal acknowledgment depended completely on the Bureau's interpretation of the relationship between individual Michigan Ottawas and the Band. As the Band sought to expand its definition of membership, the Bureau responded with threats, saying that it would refuse to distribute Indian Claims Commission judgment funds; refuse to declare a reservation; cut off federal program funds; refuse to take additional land into trust; refuse to issue treaty fishing cards; and, most incredibly, reconsider federal recognition of the Band (which it had no authority whatsoever to do on its own).

Once the Bureau realized that it could extort the Grand Traverse Band in this manner, it extended its extortion to other newly recognized Indian tribes. The Bureau, in reviewing the Jamestown Klallam tribe's proposed constitution, "made some rather significant changes to the membership provisions." The Bureau based its apparent authority to impose these changes on the "precedent" it created by forcing the Grand Traverse Band to amend its membership criteria. The Bureau took the stance that the Jamestown Klallam's members must "have a 'significant community relationship' with the Jamestown Klallam Tribe." This "significant community relationship" requirement has no basis in statutory or case law.

2. SECRETARIAL APPROVAL OF DRAFT TRIBAL CONSTITUTIONS

Coyote Valley Band of Pomo Indians v. United States

United States District Court for the Eastern District of California,
639 F. Supp. 165 (1986)

Milton L. Schwartz, District Judge. . . .

I. Background

Plaintiffs are an individual Native American, Wanda Carrillo, and three Native American tribes, Coyote Valley Band of Pomo Indians, Hopland Band of Pomo Indians, and Karuk Tribe of California. All three tribes are federally recognized tribal entities which have a government-to-government relationship with the United States and are eligible for programs administered by the Bureau of Indian Affairs ("BIA"). . . .

[Plaintiffs alleged that the BIA acted illegally] by (1) unreasonably delaying the calling of secretarial elections on their draft constitutions under the Indian Reorganization Act of 1934 ("IRA"), 25 U.S.C. §461 et seq.; (2) establishing an unwritten policy requiring BIA review and approval of IRA draft constitutions prior to authorizing elections; (3) failing to adopt uniform standards for reviewing and approving IRA constitutions; and (4) refusing to provide BIA benefits and services to plaintiffs until after the calling of IRA elections.

. . . At the heart of this controversy is the proper interpretation of 25 U.S.C. §476 which authorizes any recognized Indian tribe to organize for its common welfare and to adopt an appropriate constitution by a majority vote of the adult members of the tribe. Tribal ratification of a draft constitution in such a manner cannot be accomplished until the Secretary of the Interior authorizes a special election. Plaintiffs challenge the Secretary's practice of withholding authorization of special elections until after the completion of a lengthy process for the review and modification of proposed tribal constitutions by the BIA. They contend that the Secretary has delayed authorization of elections for several years from the time of the tribes' initial request for elections because the tribes did not willingly incorporate the BIA's suggested modifications into their draft constitutions.[2]

Plaintiffs maintain that, in order to be consistent with the statutory policy in favor of tribal self-government, section 476 of the IRA must be interpreted to impose upon the Secretary a mandatory, nondiscretionary duty to authorize elections within a reasonable time after a final request from an eligible tribe. It is their view that, while defendants may offer recommendations for the modification of draft constitutional provisions prior to elections, the Secretary has the discretion to approve or disapprove the constitution only *after* an election has been held and the constitution officially ratified by the majority vote of tribal members. Plaintiffs therefore assert that the Secretary's failure to call elections at this stage of the process violates defendants' trust responsibility to them. . . .

V. Secretary's Duty to Call Elections

The source of the Secretary's duty to call elections on IRA draft constitutions is 25 U.S.C. §476. It provides in relevant part:

> Any Indian tribe, or tribes, residing on the same reservation, shall have the right to organize for its common welfare, and may adopt an appropriate constitution and bylaws, which shall become effective when ratified by a majority vote of the adult members of the tribe, or the adult Indians residing on such reservation, as the case may be, at a special election authorized and called by

---

2. The Coyote Valley Band of Pomo Indians submitted its draft IRA constitution to the BIA on February 22, 1980. . . . They transmitted their first request for a secretarial election to the Central California Agency of the BIA on October 31, 1980. . . . The Hopland Band of Pomo Indians initially requested approval of its proposed constitution on November 7, 1980. . . . The Karuk Tribe made its first request for a secretarial election on November 15, 1979. . . . It made a subsequent request on March 19, 1981 after modifying its draft constitution as recommended by the BIA. . . .

the Secretary of the Interior under such rules and regulations as he may pre-scribe. Such constitution and bylaws, when ratified as aforesaid and approved by the Secretary of the Interior, shall be revocable by an election open to the same voters and conducted in the same manner as hereinabove provided.

Since the court is interpreting a statute in a case of first impression, it must look to the traditional signposts of statutory construction: first, the language of the statute itself; second, its legislative history; and third, the interpretation given to it by its administering agency. . . .

In light of the special trust relationship between the United States and Indian tribes, this court must also be mindful of well-established canons of statutory construction which have been developed to construe federal statutes affecting Indian affairs. *See generally* F. Cohen, Handbook of Federal Indian Law, 220-28 (1982 ed.). . . .

A. Statutory Language

Defendants contend that there are three clauses in 25 U.S.C. §476 which suggest that the Secretary has broad discretion to approve a draft constitution before he calls elections. The court will examine each of these clauses in turn.

Clause (1): "Any Indian tribe . . . may adopt an appropriate constitution and bylaws which shall become effective when ratified. . . ."

"Appropriate" is the word in clause (1) focused upon by defendants. They claim that the Secretary must have discretion to determine what is "appropri-ate" because he cannot call a federal election on a document which "violates" federal law. Following this line of reasoning, defendants assert that a document which the Secretary deems violative of federal law is *a priori* "inappropriate."

The court is not persuaded that the word "appropriate" necessarily confers pre-election discretion upon the Secretary to approve draft constitutions. One of the primary objectives of the IRA was to "encourage Indians to revitalize their self-government" and to participate more directly in developing the laws which intimately affect their lives. . . . Keeping in mind the underlying purpose of the IRA, as well as canons of statutory construction favoring the Indians, an equally plausible interpretation would be that the constitution must be a document "appropriate" to the needs of the tribe as determined by the tribal members themselves. Nothing in the statute suggests that the Secretary must determine the appropriateness of the tribe's governing docu-ment before the tribal members themselves have had an opportunity to review and ratify it.

Clause (2): "[The constitution shall become effective when ratified] at a special election authorized and called by the Secretary of the Interior under such rules and regulations as he may prescribe."

[T]he court finds that clause (2) refers to the procedural steps which must be followed by defendants in calling and administering secretarial elections. *See* 25 C.F.R. §81 et seq. There are no rules and regulations, however, mandat-ing pre-election secretarial approval of the substantive provisions of the tribes' governing documents. . . .

Clause (3): "Such Constitution and bylaws, when ratified as aforesaid and approved by the Secretary of the Interior. . . ."

Clause (3) is the only portion of the statute which makes any mention of secretarial approval. It is not entirely clear, however, that the clause requires secretarial approval of draft constitutions prior to authorization of elections.

. . . If Congress had intended that the Secretary should exercise his discretion to approve or disapprove draft constitutions prior to ratification, it could very easily have juxtaposed the order of the words to read "when approved by the Secretary of the Interior and ratified as aforesaid. . . ." Given the existing language of the statute, however, the court can only conclude that ratification procedures precede secretarial approval and that no element of secretarial discretion exists at the pre-election stage.

Finally, the court must take note of the rule of statutory construction which commands it to avoid construing statutes in a manner which would lead to unjust or absurd consequences. . . . Defendants are concerned that if the Secretary is not allowed to have discretionary authority over draft constitutions prior to the calling of elections, tribes organizing under the IRA will request elections on constitutions which contain objectionable provisions and which are certain to be disapproved by the Secretary after ratification. Defendants maintain that because of the costliness of elections, it makes more sense to conduct elections only on those constitutions which have received prior approval.

Defendants' concerns are overstated. It is unlikely that a tribe would go to the trouble of requesting a secretarial election on a constitution which it knows is destined for disapproval — unless it firmly believes that the provisions found objectionable by the Secretary are valid and lawful. Perhaps a more constructive way for defendants to address any potential problems with hasty or impulsive election requests by tribal leaders would be to set up a more definitive timetable for the BIA's review of draft constitutions. . . .

Under the current challenged procedure, defendants can delay the tribal reorganization process indefinitely simply by holding the draft constitution hostage and requiring modifications to be made prior to releasing it for elections. Such an approach may operate to stultify the initiative shown by tribal leaders in moving toward reorganization and to discourage all of those who have inevitably expended much time and effort in the preparation of the tribe's governing document. It would be an understatement to say that defendants' current procedure is antithetical both to the spirit of the IRA and to traditional notions of meaningful self-government. Thus, it is defendants' interpretation of the statute which would lead to "unjust or absurd" consequences.

The court turns next to the legislative history of the IRA to determine whether it contradicts the court's interpretation of the statute.

B. Legislative History

A careful review of the legislative history of the IRA indicates that the issue of whether the Secretary has a mandatory, as opposed to a discretionary, duty to call elections was never specifically addressed. Nevertheless, an examination of the legislative materials reveals nothing contrary to this court's interpretation of the statute. . . .

The IRA reflects an ambivalent and sometimes precarious balance of federal guardianship principles with ideals of cultural, economic, and political self-determination. While the IRA did not contemplate a complete cessation of secretarial supervision over various aspects of Indian life, one of the major objectives of the legislation was to curb administrative absolutism. . . . In a memorandum of explanation submitted to members of the Senate and House Committees on Indian Affairs, John Collier, former Commissioner of Indian Affairs, stated:

> The first section of the bill states the fundamental purpose of the bill, *i.e.*, to promote Indian self-government, gradually to turn over to organized Indian communities the various functions and powers of supervision which the Interior Department now exercises, and to offer to Indians the opportunities of training and financial assistance which will be needed to carry out this program. It will be seen that the bill looks toward the elimination of the Office of Indian Affairs in its present capacity as a nonrepresentative governing authority over the lives and property of Indians. It contemplates that the Office of Indian Affairs will ultimately exist as a purely advisory and special service body, offering the same type of service to the Indians of the Nation that the Department of Agriculture offers to American farmers. . . .

Id. at 22.

This court's interpretation of section 476 is consistent with the spirit of the IRA. The BIA may provide advice and guidance to aid a tribe in drafting its constitution, but the constitution is subject to secretarial approval only after the tribe has had an opportunity to ratify it. There is no direct evidence in the legislative history to indicate that Congress intended that the Secretary use elections as a *quid pro quo* for concessions on the substantive provisions of the tribe's governing document.

C. The Secretary's Administrative Regulations

The interpretation given a statute by the agency charged with its administration is entitled to great deference. . . . Furthermore, the agency's interpretation of an administrative regulation is controlling unless "plainly erroneous or inconsistent with the regulation." . . . Pursuant to the authority delegated to him by 25 U.S.C. §476, the Secretary has promulgated regulations prescribing the manner in which IRA elections will be called and conducted. *See* 25 C.F.R. §81.1 et seq. The court finds that defendants' argument regarding the existence of pre-election secretarial discretion is belied by the Secretary's own administrative regulations.

For example, 25 C.F.R. §81.4 provides that BIA officials "will cooperate with and offer advice and assistance (including the proposing of amendments), to any tribe in drafting a constitution." The BIA's ability to offer "advice" at the drafting stage does not translate into a power to withhold elections on the proposed constitution once a tribe has decided that it is not within its interest to adopt the BIA's suggested modifications.

The regulation governing requests to call elections is 25 C.F.R. §81.5(a), the meaning of which can hardly be disputed:

> The Secretary *shall* authorize the calling of an election to adopt a constitution and bylaws or to revoke a constitution and bylaws, *upon a request from the tribal government.*

(Emphasis added.) Section 81.5(a)'s use of the word "shall" imposes a nondiscretionary duty on the Secretary to call elections and comports with this court's interpretation of the language in 25 U.S.C. §476. To further bolster plaintiffs' contention that ratification precedes the exercise of secretarial discretion, 25 C.F.R. §81.24(a) provides:

> Action to approve or disapprove constitutional actions will be taken promptly by the authorizing officer *following receipt of the original text of the material voted upon* and the original of the Certificate of Results of Election from the officer in charge.

(Emphasis added.)

In addition, the court notes with interest that as early as 1947, in a pamphlet issued by the federal government, Theodore H. Haas, Chief Counsel for the United States Indian Service, provided a detailed description of the process by which a tribe could organize for self-government under the IRA:

> When a tribe is ready to draft its constitution, a constitutional committee of representative tribal members is chosen. It is the duty of this committee to draw up a constitution which will fit the needs of the tribe. The Department offers its assistance in the preparation of such documents, but only to the extent that such assistance is required. Scrupulous care is exercised to see that the document as drafted represents the wishes of the Indians.
>
> When the constitutional committee has completed its draft and is ready to present the constitution to the tribal members for a vote, an election is requested by the constitutional committee or by a petition signed by one-third of the adult members of the tribe. The calling of this election is mandatory upon the Secretary of the Interior when the request is made in the manner prescribed by law. Thus a tribe may vote repeatedly upon the question of adopting a constitution, in those cases where such elections have failed to carry. *It is not within the Secretary's discretion to determine whether or not the election shall be called.*

T. H. HAAS, UNITED STATES INDIAN SERVICE, TEN YEARS OF TRIBAL GOVERNMENT UNDER I.R.A., p. 2 (1947) (emphasis added). Thus, just 13 years after the passage of the IRA, the agency charged with its administration made it clear that the Secretary's duty to call elections is a mandatory one.

VI. Conclusion

The court finds that defendants' failure to call elections within a reasonable time after plaintiffs' final requests for elections is unlawful under 5 U.S.C. §706(2)(A) of the APA. Defendants' conduct contravenes the procedures described in 25 U.S.C. §476 and the accompanying administrative regulation, 25 C.F.R. §81.5(a). The language of section 476, the policies underlying the statute, and defendants' own administrative regulations all support the conclusion that the Secretary has a mandatory duty to call elections upon a request from an eligible tribe.

Since the court has decided that defendants' current practice of requiring secretarial approval of draft constitutions prior to elections is contrary to law, it is not necessary to address plaintiffs' additional contention that defendants violated the APA by failing to publish that invalid procedure. . . .

NOTES

1. After *Coyote Valley*, Congress amended 25 U.S.C. §476, but some commentators noted that the Department of Interior succeeded in muting the change:

    > Procedurally, Congress adopted suggestions made by the *Coyote Valley* court that a timetable be established for the calling of a constitutional referendum and that the timetable include a process by which the BIA could "suggest possible modifications to objectionable constitutional provisions." As to the substantive terms of the amendment, the new §476 provides that the Secretary "shall approve the constitution and bylaws or amendments thereto within forty-five days after the election unless the Secretary finds that the proposed constitution and bylaws or any amendments are contrary to applicable laws."
    >
    > Congress [defined] "applicable laws" [as such]:

    > > "Applicable laws" means any treaty, Executive order or Act of Congress or any final decision of the Federal courts which are applicable to the tribe, and any other laws which are applicable to the tribe pursuant to an Act of Congress or by any final decision of the Federal courts.

    > Thus, the 1988 amendments set a substantive standard which limits the Secretary's discretion to disapprove constitutional amendments.
    >
    > The 1988 amendments' limitations on secretarial discretion represent a positive shift in the right direction despite the fact that secretarial authority to disapprove amendments is still an infringement on tribal self-determination. The Department of the Interio[r noted, however]:

    > > Secretarial involvement in the calling of elections and approval of constitutions and bylaws, and amendments to them, is not consistent with the policy and goal of tribal self-determination. . . . Any challenges to tribal elections of tribal governing documents should be resolved through a tribal process in the tribal forums.

    > Ironically, after recommending that secretarial involvement be completely removed, the Secretary proceeded to ask Congress to expand the definition of "applicable laws" in order to give the Secretary more latitude to disapprove amendments.

    Timothy W. Joranko & Mark C. Van Norman, *Indian Self-Determination at Bay: Secretarial Authority to Disapprove Tribal Constitutional Amendments*, 29 GONZAGA L. REV. 81, 96-99 (1993-1994).

2. The Constitution and Bylaws of the Hannahville Indian Community contain, to this day, extensive Secretarial approval provisions, and even a detailed process for procuring Secretarial approval:

    Article III — Membership
    . . .
    3. The members of this Community may by a majority vote adopt as a member of the Community any person of Indian blood related by marriage or descent to the members of the Community who will assist the Community, in the fulfillment of its purposes and also any other person whose adoption is approved by the Secretary of the Interior. . . .

Article V — Powers of the Council

. . .

SEC. 5. Manner of Review. — Any action of the Council which by the terms of this Constitution is subject to review by the Secretary of the Interior, shall be presented to the Superintendent of the jurisdiction, who shall within ten (10) days thereafter, approve or disapprove the same. If the Superintendent shall approve such action, it shall thereupon become effective, but the Superintendent shall transmit a copy of the same, bearing his endorsement, to the Secretary of the Interior, who may within ninety (90) days from the date the Council decided action, disapprove such action, for any cause, by notifying the Council of such decision. If the Superintendent shall refuse to approve any action submitted to him, within ten (10) days after the Council made its decision, he shall advise the Council of his reasons therefor. If these reasons appear to the Council insufficient, it may, by a majority vote, refer the action to the Secretary of the Interior, who may, within ninety (90) days from the date the Council made its decision, approve the same in writing, whereupon the action of the Council shall become effective. . . .

Article VI — Assignments of Land

. . .

SEC. 5. The Council shall make all further necessary rules governing assignments, which shall be subject to review by the Secretary of the Interior.

Article VII — Amendments

This Constitution and bylaws may be amended or revoked by a majority vote of the qualified voters of the Hannahville Indian Community voting in an election called for that purpose by the Secretary of the Interior, provided that at least thirty (30) percent of those entitled to vote, shall vote in such election but no amendment shall become effective until it shall have been approved by the Secretary of the Interior. It shall be the duty of the Secretary of the Interior to call an election on any proposed amendment at the request of the Council.

CONST. AND BYLAWS OF THE HANNAHVILLE INDIAN COMMUNITY, MICHIGAN (July 23, 1936).

3. While it has been rare in recent decades for the Secretary to question tribal ordinances in which the tribal constitution requires secretarial approval, some tribal ordinances face scrutiny and possible disapproval from the Secretary. Consider the Moapa Band of Paiute Indians' ordinance permitting houses of prostitution on their reservation. *See Moapa Band of Paiute Indians v. United States Dept. of Interior*, 747 F.2d 563, 564 (9th Cir. 1984). The Ninth Circuit affirmed the Secretary's decision to disapprove the ordinance:

> Under powers granted to it by the tribal constitution and bylaws, the Moapa Business Council enacted an ordinance permitting the licensing and operation of houses of prostitution on the Reservation. The tribal constitution requires the Business Council to submit licensing ordinances to the Department of the Interior for approval, which the Department can deny for "any cause." MOAPA CONSTITUTION, art. V, §4. . . .
>
> The Area Director offered two reasons for rescinding the ordinance: (1) non-Indian patrons would be subject to arrest under Nevada laws relating to prostitution despite the Band's licensing ordinance, and (2) Indians and non-

Indians both would be subject to arrest under the Assimilative Crimes Act, 18 U.S.C. §13 (1976), which makes punishable as a federal crime any act committed on federal land which would be a state crime if committed in the state surrounding that land. The Director also observed that although the federal government encourages the economic development of Indian reservations, the commerce generated by prostitution was "not the kind of economic development envisioned by federal policy" and the likelihood of substantial revenues was slim.

On appeal, the Assistant Secretary for Indian Affairs, acting for the Secretary of the Interior, agreed with the Area Director's reasons, and added his concern that brothels would actually retard the Band's overall economic development. Furthermore, he articulated two additional public policy reasons for rescinding the ordinance: (1) licensing and operation of brothels on the Moapa Reservation would bring about a political reaction adverse to Moapa and other Indian tribes, and (2) prostitution is an activity frowned upon by federal policy. . . .

[W]e interpret the tribal constitution to require the Secretary to approve tribal ordinances unless he finds "cause" to rescind them. Under this interpretation, we review the Secretary's public policy findings of "cause" under the same "arbitrary and capricious" standard that applies to the Secretary's other actions. *See* 5 U.S.C. §706(2)(a) (1976). . . .

While attitudes towards prostitution may have changed somewhat since 1912, there is no indication that Congress has altered its position so as to condone the operation of bordellos. Moapa argues, however, that there is a conflicting federal policy favoring Indian self-determination. . . . Moapa contends that even if federal policy disfavors prostitution, the activity is legal in Nevada and apparently is a profitable economic enterprise for non-Indians. The Secretary's decision denies Moapa an economic opportunity which the Moapa Business Council has determined will benefit the tribe, and which is available to non-Indians nearby albeit not in Clark County.

Our standard of review is determinative of this issue. We cannot say that the Secretary's decision, after weighing the competing federal policies, is arbitrary or capricious. We therefore must affirm the recission on the ground that the operation of houses of prostitution is contrary to federal public policy.

Id. at 565-68.

4. Overhauling tribal constitutions requires the federal government to step back from its traditional and historical role as paternalistic partner of Indian nations, as Eric Lemont writes:

In many ways, the IRA helped revitalize and provide formal federal recognition to tribal governments at a time of their great fragility. But for the many tribes with histories and cultures of decentralized, consensus-oriented, and deliberative methods of decision making, IRA constitutions' centralization of power in small tribal councils acting by divisive majority votes with few checks or balances has been a difficult transition. In addition to their substantive drawbacks, IRA constitutions have been criticized for the way in which they were imposed "top-down" upon tribal memberships that did not fully understand their contents and purposes. . . .

Significantly, the United States Government's impact on the organization of tribal government extends beyond the sheer numbers of IRA governments. Over the course of the last century, numerous non-IRA tribes have adopted provisions from IRA constitutions, including the requirement that the U.S. Government approve constitutional amendments. Others, such as the Navajo Nation, have governed through tribal councils that also were originally created by officials from the Department of the Interior and that share characteristics, such as centralized and unitary government, mirroring those of IRA governments. . . .

American Indian leaders' efforts to revise or replace IRA constitutions have been reinforced and accelerated by the commencement of the U.S. Government's self-determination policy in the 1970s.

On a practical level, the increased governmental responsibilities assumed by tribal governments over the past twenty-five years require stronger and more responsive government institutions. By contracting and compacting with federal agencies of the U.S. Government, numerous American Indian nations have taken over responsibility for managing and delivering a wide range of government programs and services in areas as diverse as health, education, gaming, economic development, housing, and the environment.

Eric Lemont, *Developing Effective Processes of American Indian Constitutional and Governmental Reform*, 26 AM. INDIAN L. REV. 147, 153-56 (2001-2002).

3. CHEROKEE NATION OF OKLAHOMA — A CASE STUDY

OVERCOMING THE POLITICS OF REFORM: THE STORY OF THE CHEROKEE NATION OF OKLAHOMA CONSTITUTIONAL CONVENTION

Eric Lemont, 28 Am. Indian L. Rev. 1, 19-32 (2003-2004)

. . .

III. Major Areas of Reform Debated at Constitution Convention

Topics dominating discussion . . . fell into two broad categories. The first set consisted of concrete proposals for strengthening the accountability and effectiveness of the Nation's government. . . . During the Commission's public hearings, citizens called for procedures allowing for the recall of elected officials, the holding of mandatory community meetings by Council members in their respective districts, open financial records of the Nation's government, publication of the Nation's laws, the creation of an independent election commission, and better publicized notices of open Council meetings.

A number of these concerns subsequently were addressed at the Convention, with delegates voting to create a permanent record of the Nation's laws, remove language requiring their approval by the Bureau of Indian Affairs, stagger terms and implement term limits for Council members, create an independent election commission, and remove the Deputy Principal Chief from service as President of the Council.

A second set of reform proposals stemmed from the growing disconnect between the constitution's corporate model of government and the Nation's phenomenal growth in population, diversity and assumption of governmental responsibilities over the past three decades. Between 1970 and 1999, the Nation's population had grown from 40,000 to over 200,000. The government had contracted or compacted with the U.S. Government in a host of different areas, including housing, health, economic development, elderly programs, education, and environmental management. As a result, the Nation's budget had ballooned from $10,000 to $192 million. This change in the size of the Nation's government matched an equally dramatic change in the Nation's demographics. The absence of a blood quantum requirement in the constitution and the passing of a generation had combined to lower the average blood quantum of the Nation's citizenry by the time of the Convention. And the Nation's citizens, once concentrated in Oklahoma, were increasingly living in places as far-flung as Texas and California. . . .

A. Bicameralism

One of the first major convention debates involved whether the Nation should return to the bicameral form of government of the Nation's 1827 and 1839 constitutions. Across Indian Country, the overwhelming majority of tribal governments concentrate legislative power in unicameral tribal councils. During the nineteenth century, the U.S. Government—frustrated at tribes' slow, consensus-oriented method of political decision making—began pressuring tribes to form small tribal bodies capable of quickly approving treaties and agreements. . . .

[T]he motivation for unicameral councils was to facilitate the receipt and disbursement of federal funds through a corporate structure. . . . Relative to other branches of government, most tribal councils have vast and relatively unchecked powers. . . .

On the second day of the convention, John Keen introduced a motion for the Convention to consider a return to bicameralism. Keen argued that the Nation's current unicameral form of government had allowed nine persons—the Principal Chief and eight Council members—to control the Nation's entire government and only six boycotting Councilors to bring the Nation's government to a halt. Keen's motion called for a lower house (tribal council) apportioned by district population and an upper house (senate) apportioned by one delegate per district. The move to two houses of government would increase the total number of legislators from fifteen to thirty-three and reduce the ratio of legislators to citizens from 1:12,000 to 1:5,500.

Quoting James Madison's Federalist No. 51, Keen argued that a bicameral legislature's dual legislative track structure and form of election as well as its increased size would prevent a small bloc of united Council members from controlling the levers of the Nation's government. A supporter of the motion said the lower house could address local concerns while the upper house would provide "balance" and "stability" by ensuring that the legislature did not get bogged down in debates over local issues. Another argument raised in favor of Keen's bicameral proposal was its consistency with the Nation's bicameral system of government in the 1827 and 1839 constitutions.

In response, several delegates proffered a series of counterarguments against the adoption of a bicameral legislature. Some feared that two houses of government would double the potential for stonewalling and make it more difficult for the Nation to reach consensus. Another delegate argued that, unlike the Founding Fathers of the U.S. Government, who wanted to develop a mechanism for distributing power among states of unequal population, the

Nation did not have a problem with regard to unequal power among its districts. Several members of the Convention Commission reported that bicameralism had been raised during public hearings but felt that such a change would present too many practical difficulties. Commission members said they were "stymied" in their attempt to figure out a way to implement a bicameral legislature without affecting other constitutional provisions. The Nation's Chief Justice quickly and forcefully denounced the Commission's concerns, describing it as "mindboggling" that the leaders at the Convention couldn't figure out how to form a bicameral legislature.

Surprisingly, the argument that appeared to seal victory for opponents of a bicameral legislature was the simple one of cost. Numerous delegates felt that the Nation's annual budget should be spent on delivering services to Cherokee citizens rather than creating a bigger government. Although several delegates said the issue was important enough to justify a fuller examination of structure, powers, and cost, the delegation ultimately voted down the proposal.

B. Judiciary

Much focus at the Convention was spent on restructuring the Nation's judiciary. . . . The [1976] constitution vested the Nation's three-member Judicial Appeal Tribunal with powers only "to hear and resolve any disagreements arising under any provisions of this Constitution or any enactment of the Council." In addition to strengthening the judiciary's powers, the delegates were concerned about its political independence. Great concern was placed on preventing a reoccurrence of the impeachments, standoffs, lockouts, dual court systems and other problems between the judiciary and the other two branches. . . .

To strengthen the powers of the judiciary, the delegates agreed to a two-tiered court system consisting of a Supreme Court (formerly the Judicial Appeals Tribunal) and lower district courts. The proposed constitution vests the Nation's district courts with original jurisdiction to hear and resolve disputes arising under the laws or constitution of the Nation, whether criminal or civil in nature. It vests the Supreme Court with powers of original jurisdiction over all cases involving the Nation or its officials named as a defendant and with exclusive appellate jurisdiction over all district court cases. To improve the scope and depth of decision making of the Supreme Court, the proposed constitution raises the number of justices from three to five.

The delegates also took a series of steps to strengthen the judiciary's independence while providing checks on the exercise of its powers. To protect the Judiciary's independence from various interest groups, delegates voted to have judges and justices appointed by the Principal Chief rather than elected. Under the proposed constitution, judges and justices also serve longer terms (ten years for Supreme Court justices) and cannot have their salaries diminished during their terms. To prevent court-stacking, the proposed constitution staggers the terms of the judges and justices so they do not overlap with the terms of the Principal Chief more than twice in any five year period.

At the same time, the proposed constitution contains several checks. First, it keeps judges and justices subject to removal by the Council for specified causes. The most innovative check, however, is the proposed constitution's

Court on the Judiciary. After suffering through the recent impeachment of the entire judiciary by the Principal Chief and Council, the delegates wanted to preserve the judiciary's integrity without allowing it to police itself entirely. [T]he Court on the Judiciary is a seven-member panel vested with powers of suspension, sanction, discipline and recommendation of removal of judges and justices. Borrowed from a similar body in the Oklahoma Constitution, the Court is composed of two appointees from each of the Nation's three branches of government, who collectively appoint a seventh. . . .

C. Representation on Tribal Council for Off-Reservation Residents

Mandatory federal relocation programs, forced removals, a lack of well-paying jobs on many reservation lands, and routine migration has left many American Indian nations with high numbers of off-reservation citizens. The situation is especially pronounced for American Indian nations lacking a sufficient number of well-paying reservation-based jobs. With approximately forty percent of its 200,000 citizens living off-reservation, the Cherokee Nation is at the forefront of this trend of dispersed Indian citizenry.

The . . . 1976 Constitution does not provide for specific representation on the Tribal Council for off-reservation residents. Instead, off-reservation residents select a district or precinct within the Nation's historical boundaries for purposes of registration and voting. Off-reservation residents claim this has led many candidates to solicit their votes before elections and ignore them afterwards.

Gaining representation on the Council proved to be the foremost priority of the fourteen Convention delegates residing off-reservation. Julia Coates Foster, a Cherokee citizen living in New Mexico, organized a meeting of all fourteen off-reservation delegates on the night before the Convention's first day to develop a strategy for gaining representation. . . .

On the Convention's second day, Foster introduced a motion requesting representation for off-reservation residents. Foster's motion called for twenty percent of Council seats to be reserved for representation of the Nation's off-reservation residents. If off-reservation Cherokees were included as delegates to the Convention, she asked, why shouldn't they have a seat at the legislative table? Foster argued that representation would provide off-reservation residents with the information necessary to advocate for Cherokee issues against outside public and private interests. She also pointed to the need for stronger bonds among Cherokee's diverse citizenry. "Our land base is minimal . . . but in some sense our Nation exists from coast to coast and border to border because our Nation exists in our people, our citizens and our citizens are everywhere."

Opposition by delegates residing within the reservation's boundaries was swift. Delegate David Cornsilk reminded delegates that off-reservation citizens were adequately represented in the Nation. Contrasting Foster's view of the Nation being made up of its citizens, wherever they were, Cornsilk countered that the "Cherokee Nation is a real place, that it is here. That it is within the exterior boundaries of the Cherokee Nation as described in our treaties, and that the focus of the people who live outside the Cherokee Nation should be to strengthen the Nation, the place here." Other delegates argued that the Nation's current system of having off-reservation residents choose a district within which to register and vote was sufficient. Couldn't a group of off-reservation residents simply form an organization and agree to register in the same district as a bloc?

The tide turned when a well-respected current Council member, Barbara Starr-Scott, unexpectedly stood up in support of off-reservation representation with the simple declaration that "[w]hen everybody represents you, nobody represents you." The motion then became renamed the Starr-Scott proposal. Eventually, the two sides reached a compromise calling for the Council to be expanded from fifteen to seventeen members, with the additional two at-large seats reserved specifically for representation of off-reservation residents.

D. Blood Quantum Requirements for Candidates for Principal Chief

. . . At the time of the Convention, approximately ninety percent of the Nation was one-quarter Indian blood or less, with the most common degree of blood quantum being one-sixteenth or one-thirty-second.

The tension between full-blooded and lower-blooded Cherokees manifested itself on the Convention's fifth and sixth day, when delegates introduced motions to establish a minimum blood quantum requirement for candidates for Principal Chief. The first motion was for candidates to be citizens by one-sixteenth of greater blood quantum and be bilingual in Cherokee and English. The motion was immediately and strongly opposed by several delegates. One, referring to the low blood quanta of the Nation's citizenry argued:

> If we put this kind of limitation on ourselves, we are simply saying that we don't trust ourselves to lead our own Nation. We're trying to say that the people, our own children, our own grandchildren, at some point are not capable of leading this Nation, simply because they have some federally imposed degree of Indian blood.

A second delegate opposed the motion with a warning for the future:

> We're saying that we are going to put a time and date on the existence of the Cherokee Nation. If we put a grade of Indian blood on it . . . we're saying that in a hundred years or two hundred years, that we will cease to exist as a people, at least with a leader.

The motion was quickly voted down. The next day, however, the issue was raised again, this time through a motion presented on behalf of a bloc of nondelegates calling for a one-quarter blood quantum for candidates for Principal Chief. The sponsor based the motion on the "pride of not one day seeing a blond-haired, blue-eyed Chief representing me." Supporters of the motion associated low blood quantum Cherokees with dominating the Convention by talking in fast "legalese" that they couldn't understand. One grounded his desire for a blood quantum requirement as a way to maintain the "integrity of the Cherokee Nation." Another felt that a blood quantum requirement for Chief would serve as an important symbol for Cherokee children: ". . . I would like for our Cherokee children, our dark-skinned Cherokee children to able to look at their Chief and see someone like them. I think that's essential for their self-esteem."

In opposition, delegates argued along several lines: the blood quantum requirement could not stand up against the test of time and the Nation's ever decreasing native bloodlines; citizens' opportunities to run for office should not be limited by their blood; those favoring higher blood quantum could express their desire for such a candidate at the ballot box; blood quantum is a nontraditional value introduced by the federal government and not an appropriate criterion for determining the Nation's Chief; the Dawes Commission made mistakes in its original blood quantum determinations, therefore making it inherently inaccurate; and blood quantum is not a perfect match for "Indianness." A final argument was that such a change would never be approved by Cherokee voters at a referendum.

In the end, the delegates voted to reject a minimum blood quantum requirement for candidates for Principal Chief.

IV. Ratification

Notwithstanding the scope of the Convention's work, there was no guarantee that the Cherokee people would vote to ratify the proposed new constitution. Indeed, the sweeping nature of the changes in the proposed constitution posed a significant obstacle to ratification. . . .

. . . David Mullon, former general counsel for the Nation, worried that the Commission's introduction of a replacement constitution would present a "big target" for opposition, where individual opposition to a single proposed provision might lead to a vote against the constitution as a whole. . . .

Notwithstanding these points of disagreement, reform leaders on both sides of the aisle affirmed the legitimacy of the Nation's constitutional revision process and the substance of the proposed constitution. Even [Ross] Swimmer, the primary author of the current constitution, agreed at the time that "the constitution convention and the product they developed seems to be pretty well accepted by most people."

In fact, the most significant obstacle to ratification did not result from internal debates within the Nation. Rather, a referendum vote to approve the Convention's proposed constitution was delayed for over four years because of the Nation's interactions with the Bureau of Indian Affairs. The delay stemmed from Article XV, Section 10 of the 1976 Constitution, which included language requiring that any amendment or new constitution be approved by the "President of the United States or his authorized representative." Because the Cherokee Nation did not organize its government pursuant to the Indian Reorganization Act, it was not required by U.S. law to obtain federal approval for new and amended constitutions. Swimmer said he included the language as a defensive measure to ensure the recognition of the Nation's 1976 constitution by the U.S. Government.

Following the constitution's self-imposed requirement, the Commission sought BIA approval of the proposed constitution adopted by delegates to the Convention. After not hearing from the Bureau for several months, the Commission began to lobby the Bureau with calls and letters from September through December 1999. After nine months of review by two separate field offices, the Solicitor's office, and several internal levels in the Bureau's Washington central office, the Bureau finally decided on December 14, 1999, not to approve the Convention's proposed constitution. In a lengthy disapproval letter to the Nation, the Bureau delivered a series of mandated and recommended changes to specific articles of the proposed constitution. . . .

Finally, in April 2002, after a change in administration at the Bureau and much behind-the-scenes discussions, the Department of Interior approved the Council's proposed amendment removing the need for approval of constitutional amendments by the U.S. Government. With the legal path clear, Cherokee citizens voted on May 24, 2003, to strike the 1976 Constitution's requirement of U.S. Governmental approval of all constitutional amendments. A final referendum on the constitution adopted by Convention delegates in 1999 was scheduled for July 26, 2003.

In preparation for the final vote, the Commission conducted a public education initiative unprecedented in Indian Country. The Commission inserted 100,000 copies of a fourteen page Constitution Education Tabloid into the tribal newspaper and mailed an additional 26,000 copies to all Cherokee registered voters. The Commission also conducted forty-one Constitution Education forums throughout the Nation and the United States, including Texas, California and Kansas, where there were high concentrations of Cherokee citizens. The schedule for the education forums were advertised by 500 posters printed and posted throughout the Cherokee Nation, direct mailings of 26,000 oversized "post cards" to registered voters, and press releases to over forty newspapers. The Commission also made ample use of the Nation's website to disseminate critical information regarding the referendum.

Finally, on July 26, 2003, more than four years after the conclusion of the Convention, the Cherokee citizens voted to approve a new constitution replacing the Nation's current 1976 constitution. . . .

NOTES

1. Several other Indian nations have embarked on a full-fledged tribal constitutional convention, with notable successes and with heartrending failures. *E.g.*, CROW TRIBAL CONSTITUTION (new constitution ratified and adopted in 2001-2002), available at http://www.tribalresourcecenter.org/ccfolder/crow_const.htm; TURTLE MOUNTAIN BAND OF CHIPPEWA CONSTITUTION CONVENTION AND REVISION PROCESS 2001-2002 (Jerilyn DeCoteau ed., 2003) (history of the failed Turtle Mountain Band constitutional convention). The Blackfeet Tribe has been engaged in a constitutional reform discussion for some time. *See* Blackfeet Constitutional Reform website, available at http://www.blackfeetvoice.org. For more discussion on tribal constitutional reform, see AMERICAN INDIAN CONSTITUTIONAL REFORM AND THE REBUILDING OF NATIVE NATIONS (Eric D. Lemont ed., 2006).

2. The White Mountain Band of Chippewa Indians currently is engaged in a process of reviewing a new constitution drafted in part by Gerald Vizenor, a tribal member who is an esteemed novelist and indigenous literary critic. Chapter 2, Article 4 of the draft constitution reads:

   > No person or government has the privilege or power to diminish the sovereignty of the White Earth Nation.

   What are the possible reasons for including this provision? What tribal government actions might be affected by such a provision?

B. TRIBAL CONSTITUTIONAL STRUCTURE

Tribal constitutions often borrow heavily from the United States Constitution — for example, some form of separation of powers. Many tribal constitutions, however, tend to read more like a municipal charter than a constitution, a likely result of the original constitution-drafting process initiated by the Bureau of Indian Affairs in the 1930s. This section will deal with some key features of many tribal constitutions, and with how the tribal courts have interpreted those features.

1. JUDICIAL REVIEW

DOMENCICH V. ONEIDA TRIBAL ENROLLMENT & TRUST DEPARTMENT

Oneida Appeals Commission, No. 95-CVL-0005 (November 30, 1995),
1995.NAOW.0000029

This case has come before the Oneida Appeals Commission. Commissioners Carole Liggins, Kirby Metoxen, Dorothy Skenandore, Mark N. Powless, and Wanda Webster, presiding.

The appellant in this case, Mr. Lee F. Domencich, has had disenrollment proceedings initiated against him by the Oneida Tribal Enrollment and Trust Department (Enrollment Dept.). [T]he appellant is seeking a declaratory ruling as to the appellate jurisdiction over enrollment matters in the Tribe. . . .

Appellate Jurisdiction

This membership matter calls for an interpretation of the Oneida Tribe's membership ordinance which is codified in Resolution 6-2-84-A. Article V Section C of this ordinance sets forth the procedures to be followed when a person is denied enrollment. Implicitly, such procedures should be followed when a person is disenrolled. This ordinance empowers the Enrollment Dept. to hold hearings on membership matters. V.C.2.g. states that a final appeal can be made to the Oneida Business Committee. The appellant seeks a declaratory judgment from this Commission as to the validity of this part of the membership ordinance.

The Oneida Appeals Commission was created pursuant to Resolution 8-19-91-A of the General Tribal Council. It was granted appellate jurisdiction over contested cases that arose within the tribe. The Appeals Commission has appellate review powers over lower hearings held by agencies of the Tribe.

At the time of the Membership Ordinance's passage, the Oneida Appeals Commission did not exist. Nor did the Oneida Administrative Procedures Act which sets forth general procedures for contested cases and their appellate review. Currently, with the passage of the OAPA, there exists a separation of powers within the Oneida Tribe. The role of the Appeals Commission is that of judicial review. The role of the Business Committee is that of a legislative body. It is no longer appropriate for the Business Committee to function as an appellate body in membership matters. This is now the role that the Appeals Commission is empowered to play. It is therefore held by this Commission that Article V Section C 2 (g) of the Oneida Membership Ordinance which states, "(f)inal appeals may be made to the Oneida Business Committee only after they have been processed by the Oneida Trust Committee with a recommendation," shall no longer be valid. The Oneida Appeals Commission shall have final appellate review over the membership determinations of the Oneida Tribal Enrollment and Trust Department. All other sections of the membership ordinance shall remain in effect.

Therefore, the Enrollment Dept. is hereby ordered to stay its proceedings on the disenrollment of Lee F. Domencich until such time as his search for his biological parents is complete. . . . In addition the Enrollment Dept. is put on notice that appellate jurisdiction over the hearings it conducts now resides with the Appeals Commission.

NOTES

1. Like the United States Constitution, many tribal constitutions do not include a specific provision authorizing the tribal judiciary to engage in judicial review of tribal legislative or executive branch acts. Most tribal courts not expressly authorized to engage in judicial review, like the United States Supreme Court in *Marbury v. Madison*, 5 U.S. 137 (1803), simply assume the authority.

2. Other tribal courts, notably the Navajo Nation Supreme Court, asserted the right of judicial review deriving not from the tribe's constitution — as there is none — but from Navajo common law and the Indian Civil Rights Act:

> There is no question in our minds about the existence of such authority. When the Navajo Tribal Council adopted Title 7, Section 133 of the Tribal Code, it did not exclude review of Council actions from its broad grant of power to the courts.
>
> Indeed, in our opinion, Title 25, Section 1302 of the United States Code precludes such an exclusion of judicial review of legislative actions because that law is a mandate for Indian governments which necessarily assumes and requires judicial review of any allegedly illegal action by a tribal government.
>
> In particular, 25 U.S.C. 1302 (8) prohibits the denial of equal protection of the laws and deprivation of liberty or property without due process of law. We cannot imagine how any legislative body accused of violating these primary rights could be the judge of its own actions and at the same time comply with the federal law. Of course, this is not possible.
>
> Judicial review must, therefore, necessarily follow. If the courts established by Indian tribes cannot exercise this power, then the only alternative is review in every case by federal courts.
>
> It is inconceivable to us that the Navajo Tribal Council would prefer review of its actions by far-away federal courts unfamiliar with Navajo customs and laws to review by Navajo courts. We know that this is not the case because the Council has not limited the power of Navajo courts in this respect and has never indicated a willingness to do so.
>
> The courts of the Navajo Nation, including this Court, have frequently reviewed and interpreted legislation passed by the Council and executive actions of the Chairman of the Council. *See Dennison v. Tucson Gas and Electric* (Navajo Court of Appeals, December 23, 1974).

Our right to pass upon the legality or meaning of these actions has been questioned in certain places but never by the Council or its Chairman. That is because they have a traditional and abiding respect for the impartial adjudicatory process. When all have been heard and the decision is made, it is respected. This has been the Navajo way since before the time of the present judicial system. The Navajo People did not learn this principle from the white man. They have carried it with them through history.

The style and the form of problem-solving and dispensing justice has changed over the years but not the principle. Those appointed by the People to resolve their disputes were and are unquestioned in their power to do so. Whereas once the clan was the primary forum (and still is a powerful and respected instrument of justice), now the People through their Council have delegated the ultimate responsibility for this to their courts. That is why 7 N.T.C. 133 is so broadly written.

In any case, judicial review by tribal courts of Council resolutions is mandated by the Indian Civil Rights Act, 25 U.S.C. 1302.

Halona v. McDonald, 1 Navajo Rep. 189, 203-06 (Navajo Nation Court of Appeals 1978). *See also* Bethany R. Berger, *Justice and the Outsider: Jurisdiction over Nonmembers in Tribal Legal Systems*, 37 Ariz. St. L.J. 1047, 1118 (2005).

3. Some tribal councils restrict judicial review in certain circumstances. Consider this statute from the Mashantucket Pequot Nation:

If the Mashantucket Pequot Tribal Council resolves that a matter is private, the courts of the Mashantucket Pequot Tribe must recognize the matter as privileged. Communications made during an announced executive session of the Mashantucket Pequot Tribal Council are privileged.

Mashantucket Pequot Rules of Evidence §508(a).

2. SEPARATION OF POWERS

Wilson v. Business Committee

Cheyenne-Arapaho Tribes Supreme Court, No. CAN-SC-02-02, 8 Oklahoma Tribal Court Rep. 109, 2003 WL 24313610, March 18, 2003, reh'g denied, May 7, 2003

Justice Arrow delivered the Opinion and Order of the Court, in which Chief Justice Rivas and Justice Black join.

I.

Prior to January 8, 2002, Appellant Wilson was the validly-elected representative of Cheyenne District 3 to the Business Committee of the Cheyenne-Arapaho Tribes. On that date, he was provided notice that a recall petition alleging misconduct had been filed against him, and that a removal hearing was scheduled for January 23, 2002, at 11:00 a.m.

On January 14, 2002, then-Business Committee Chairman James Pedro attempted to rescind the notice letter of January 8. On January 17, an emergency hearing was held before the District Court of the Cheyenne-Arapaho Tribes in *Business Committee v. Pedro*, No. CNA-CIV-02-08, 7 Okla. Trib. 391 [, 2002 WL 32099760] (Chey.-Arap. D. Ct. 2002), in which the Court ordered then-Chairman Pedro to proceed with the scheduled January 23 meeting. On

January 23, at 9:00 a.m., then-Chairman Pedro submitted a letter of resignation as Chairman to himself, despite Article VIII, Section 3 of the Cheyenne-Arapaho Constitution, which provides that "[t]he term of office for each committeeman elected after the first election shall be for a period of four (4) years, *or until his successor is duly elected and installed in office.*" *Id.* (emphasis added). Six members of the Business Committee did, however, meet at 11:00 a.m. on January 23, 2002 (including Appellant), but no meeting was convened. Later on the afternoon of the 23rd, the District Court sua sponte ordered the convening a meeting [sic] of the Business Committee at 3:00 p.m. on January 25. *See Pedro*, 7 Okla. Trib. at 394.

At the appointed time on January 25, a quorum was assembled and a Business Committee meeting was convened, with Vice-Chairman Bill Blind (according to one rendition) apparently refusing to formally chair the meeting even though then-Chairman Pedro had again ignored the District Court's Order by failing to appear. Appellant did not attend, though he had notice of the meeting. The petition to remove Appellant from his Business Committee position was discussed, and a removal motion was adopted by a vote of five to one. Appellant was thereupon removed from his C-3 Business Committee seat. . . .

II.

The Cheyenne-Arapaho Constitution establishes two procedures for removal of members of the tribal Business Committee. First, any member of the Business Committee may charge another member, in writing, with misconduct or neglect of duty. The constitutional provision applicable in such an eventuality provides, in whole, as follows:

> Any member of the business committee charged, in writing, with misconduct or neglect of duty by a fellow committeeman may be removed from the business committee or from an office of the business committee, provided at least five (5) of the members vote in favor of removal. A special meeting of the committee shall be called to consider any removal action; and the accused shall be provided with a minimum of fifteen (15) days notice of said hearing and be provided the opportunity to attend and testify in his own behalf. The decision of the committee shall be final.

CHEY.-ARAP. CONST. art. IX, §1 (emphasis added). . . .

IV.

A.

. . . Appellant first argues that the District Court lacked power to have ordered the Chairman to call, convene, attend, and preside over the January 23 Business Committee meeting, and to have ordered the attendance at that meeting of the other Business Committee members. Appellant also challenges the District Court's power to have ordered the convening of the meeting of January 25, and/or the District Court's decision to actually preside at that meeting (if that is in fact the proper characterization of the January 25 events).

Business Committee members are paid in large measure for attending Business Committee meetings and conducting important tribal business therein.

See generally CHEY.-ARAP. CONST. art. IV, §5 (tying compensation of Business Committee members in substantial measure to meeting attendance). Tribal welfare as a general matter, the best interests of individual tribal members, and tribal constitutional law all demand that Business Committee meetings be held regularly, *see, e.g.,* CHEY.-ARAP. CONST. art. XVI, §1 ("Regular monthly meetings of the business committee shall be held on the first Saturday of each month at the tribal headquarters. . . ."), and that tribal business be transacted professionally and efficaciously at such meetings, *see, e.g., id.* art. IV, §4 ("All action taken by the . . . business committee shall be pursuant to duly adopted ordinances or resolutions, and shall be certified by the presiding officer."). Nevertheless, this Court takes judicial notice of the fact that more than one Chairman has refused to convene regular (or otherwise-constitutionally-required) Business Committee meetings over the years, apparently on the assumption that the Chairman has the power to prevent the Business Committee from meeting—apparently forever (or at least until the Chairman's term expires)—by simply refusing to call, convene, attend, or preside over such meetings. That assumption is false.

. . . Article XIV, Section 1 assigns the following five functions (*i.e.,* non-discretionary duties or discretionary powers) to the Chairman of the Cheyenne-Arapaho Tribes:

1. "[P]resid[ing] over all meetings of the [Business C]ommittee";
2. "[P]erform[ing] all the duties of a chairman;
3. "[E]xercis[ing] any authority delegated to him by the [Business C]ommittee";
4. "[V]oting in case of a tie [Business Committee vote]"; and
5. "[P]residing at all meetings of the tribal council, unless a different presiding officer is selected by the tribal council. . . ."

CHEY.-ARAP. CONST. art XIV, §1. In addition, Article XVI, Section 2 assigns the Chairman a sixth function (in this instance, a power): it authorizes the Chairman to call special Business Committee meetings within his own discretion. A seventh function (in this instance, a non-discretionary duty) is established by Article XVI, Section 2 and Article IX, Section 1, which require the Chairman to convene special Business Committee meetings under the circumstances described in those provisions. And Article IV, Section 4 establishes an eighth function (a contingent duty), by requiring the "presiding officer" of the Business Committee or Tribal Council (who will often but not necessarily be the Chairman) to certify duty-adopted ordinances or resolutions. No other functions are assigned to the Chairman of the Cheyenne-Arapaho Tribes by the Cheyenne-Arapaho Constitution, and as noted above, not all of the eight above-described functions are discretionary powers. For ease of identification, the functions described above will be referred to as the Chairman's "eight functions."

It is obvious to this Court (and Appellant's briefs do not dispute) that were the Chairman of the Cheyenne-Arapaho Tribes to enjoy the power to prevent the Cheyenne-Arapaho Business Committee from meeting indefinitely, that power could only be derived from the first of the eight functions described above. [T]he power of a Chairman to prevent the Business Committee from meeting stems either from the "first function" or it does not exist at all. As we shall see, it does not exist at all.

As defined by Article XIV, Section 1 of the Cheyenne-Arapaho Constitution, the Chairman's "first function"—presiding over Business Committee meetings—is a nondiscretionary *duty*, not a discretionary power. Article XIV, Section 1 states that "[t]he chairman of the business committee *shall* preside over all meetings of the committee," *id.* (emphasis added), and the Constitution elsewhere provides:

> As used in this constitution and by-laws, the word *shall* is deemed to mean *imperative or mandatory and to exclude the exercise of discretion*. The word may is deemed to mean permission or liberty and to include the exercise of discretion.

CHEY.-ARAP. CONST. art. I, §9 (second emphasis added). . . . Cheyenne-Arapaho constitutional law leaves the Chairman with no discretion whatsoever to refuse to call, convene, attend, and preside over regular monthly meetings, and such special meetings as are required by Articles IX and XVI of the Cheyenne-Arapaho Constitution.

The residual question then becomes simply a question of judicial remedy for situations in which the Chairman has breached his or her nondiscretionary duty. Unlike the Constitution of the United States of America, the separation-of-powers structure of the Cheyenne-Arapaho Constitution establishes a "legislative-executive branch"—the Business Committee—that both exercises legislative power and (through, among other things, the selection of the Business Manager) indirectly supervises the executive operations of the Tribes. The Business Committee—composed of only eight members, CHEY.-ARAP. CONST. art. I, §3—is an enormously powerful branch of the Cheyenne-Arapaho government. The judicial branch, which is constitutionally necessary to insure the enforcement of tribal members' rights, *see, e.g.*, CHEY.-ARAP. CONST. art. III, enforce tribal law generally, and adjudicate disputes (such as the present one) that arise under the tribal Constitution, is by comparison relatively weak. The judicial branch enjoys no power to run the Cheyenne-Arapaho government even if it wanted to—which it does not. That is the province of the Cheyenne-Arapaho Business Committee. . . .

On the basis of the premise that the Cheyenne-Arapaho Business Committee must run the Cheyenne-Arapaho Tribes (because no other institution can do so), and the inextricably intertwined premise that to run the Cheyenne-Arapaho government, the Business Committee must meet, there can be no conclusions other than the ones we announce today. For purposes of resolving the Business-Committee-meeting issue, we hold:

1. That each member of the Cheyenne-Arapaho Business Committee has the NON-DISCRETIONARY DUTY to assemble "on the first Saturday of each month at the tribal headquarters, unless it falls on a legal holiday; and in such event, [the meeting] will be held on the following Saturday." CHEY.-ARAP. CONST. art. XVI, §1;

2. That the Chairman of the Cheyenne-Arapaho Tribes has the NON-DISCRETIONARY DUTY to call, convene, attend, and preside over regular monthly meetings of the Business Committee, and such special meetings as

are required by Article IX, Section 1, and Article XVI, Section 2 of the Cheyenne-Arapaho Constitution;

3. That if the Chairman of the Cheyenne-Arapaho Tribes fails to perform the NON-DISCRETIONARY DUTY described in the preceding numbered item, the other members of the Cheyenne-Arapaho Business Committee shall have the NON-DISCRETIONARY DUTY to convene the constitutionally-required meeting themselves. In such an event, the meeting shall be chaired by the highest-ranking officer present, in the following order: Vice-Chairman, Secretary, Treasurer; and

4. That because every member of the Cheyenne-Arapaho Tribes is injured by the failure of the tribal Business Committee to meet regularly as required by the tribal Constitution, in the event that the Chairman of the Cheyenne-Arapaho Tribes fails to perform the NON-DISCRETIONARY DUTY described above, or in the event that a quorum cannot be mustered for a regular or constitutionally-required special meeting of the Business Committee for any other reason, any Cheyenne-Arapaho citizen (including but not limited to any Business Committee member) shall have standing to bring an action before the District Court of the Cheyenne-Arapaho Tribes to enforce the provisions of the Cheyenne-Arapaho Constitution and this Order. In securing the attendance of Business Committee members at regular and constitutionally-required special meetings of the Business Committee, the District Court shall enjoy the normal, broad, inherent remedial power of courts of equity in enforcing the above-discussed provisions of the Cheyenne-Arapaho Constitution and this Order. This power shall include but not be limited to the power to actually convene a Business Committee meeting—with attendance compelled by the Court's contempt power—where other remedial options reasonably available to it have proved to be unavailing.

Pursuant to the above reasoning and constitutional authority, it follows that the District Court had the power to: (1) order the Chairman of the Cheyenne-Arapaho Tribes to call, convene, attend, and preside over the January 23rd meeting, which was required by Article IX, Section 1 of the Cheyenne-Arapaho Constitution; (2) order the other members of the Cheyenne-Arapaho Business Committee to present themselves at the January 23 meeting; (3) do the same with respect to the January 25 meeting when the January 23 meeting failed to materialize; and (4) actually convene and preside over the January 25 meeting (if he in fact did so) to secure the transaction of constitutionally-required tribal business at that meeting. . . .

D.

Fourth, Appellant relies on Article XIV, Section 1 of the tribal Constitution, which provides in relevant part that "[t]he chairman of the business committee shall . . . have the privilege of voting in case of a tie." Reasoning (in this respect, correctly) that under the well-known maxim *inclusio unius est exclusio alterius* ["the inclusion of one thing is the exclusion of others"], and on the basis of tribal constitutional structure, the Chairman of the Business Committee may vote in Business Committee meetings only "in case of a tie," Appellant contends that Vice-Chairman Blind (who on his theory—at least for purposes of this argument—was the "acting chairman" of the January 25 meeting) should not have been allowed to vote at the meeting. Without Vice-Chairman Blind's vote to remove him from office, Appellant (again, correctly) points out that there would have been only four votes to remove—less than the five required for his removal by Article IX, Section 1. Appellant's argument, however, fails for either of two individually-dispositive reasons.

First, the Chairman's inability to vote in Business Committee meetings (except "in case of a tie") is a *personal* disability that follows the *incumbent of the Chairman's office* whether or not he or she is present at a particular meeting. *See* CHEY.-ARAP. CONST. art. XIV, §1 ("The *chairman of the business committee* shall . . . have the privilege of voting in case of a tie." (emphasis added)). Thus, Vice-Chairman Blind (or for that matter, any other Business Committee member who finds himself or herself presiding over a Business Committee meeting for whatever reason) is unencumbered by the voting restrictions imposed on the Chairman by Article XIV, Section 1.

Second, while Article XIV, Section 1 establishes as a general matter that the Chairman of the Business Committee may not vote in Business Committee meetings unless there would otherwise be a tie, Article IX, Section 1—which applies *only to proceedings to remove a Business Committee member*—appears to create an exception to the general rule, stating that under the circumstances described earlier in that provision, "a fellow committeeman may be removed . . . provided at least five . . . *of the members* vote in favor of removal." CHEY.-ARAP. CONST. art. IX, §1 (emphasis added). Nothing about Chairman–disqualification from voting is provided by Article IX, Section 1, and its text would appear to authorize any member of the Business Committee—the Chairman included—to cast a vote on the ouster of a fellow Business Committee member.

For either of the above-described reasons, Appellant's fourth theory also fails. . . .

V.

For the reasons described above, the decision of the District Court of the Cheyenne-Arapaho Tribes in Case No. CNA-CIV-02-20 is AFFIRMED. Kent Stonecalf, who prevailed in the special election to replace Appellant as Cheyenne District 3 representative to the Business Committee, is declared to be the rightful occupant of that position.

NOTES

1. Tribal election disputes provide some of the most difficult areas for tribal courts to adjudicate. They are wrought with political questions and implied limitations on judicial authority. Tribal judges deciding these cases face the wrath of the losers and their close supporters, some of whom will invariably be elected to power at a later date, ostensibly with the power to reappoint the judges who once adjudicated their rights.
2. Robert McCarthy described the separation-of-powers conundrum as follows:

> [P]ublished cases would seem to indicate that tribal courts generally prevail in clashes with tribal councils over interpretation and enforcement of the

ICRA and tribal law. For example, the Duck Valley Tribal Court reinstated a chief judge, holding that the Tribal Council may remove a judge only after the Council conducts a hearing complying with tribal law and due process under the ICRA. [*McKinney v. Business Council*, 20 Indian L. Rep. 6020, 6020 (Duck Valley Tr. Ct. 1993).] . . .

[T]he Ute Tribal Court ruled that the Tribal Business Committee lacked authority to withdraw jurisdiction from the court and vest jurisdiction in the Business Committee itself where the Business Committee was a party to the litigation. [*Chapoose v. Ute Indian Tribe*, 13 Indian L. Rep. 6023, 6023 (Ute Tr. Ct. 1986).] . . .

The Southern Ute Tribal Court ruled that it had jurisdiction to hear a claim that the tribal election board violated the ICRA and tribal law although the tribal constitution, without any reference to the tribal court, made the election board the final authority on election disputes. [*Committee for Better Tribal Gov't v. Southern Ute Election Bd.*, 17 Indian L. Rep. 6095, 6095-96 (S. Ute Tr. Ct. 1990).] The court held that, although courts have no inherent authority to hear election disputes, tribal courts are the proper forum to present ICRA claims. The ICRA's guaranty of equal protection makes it impermissible for tribes to intentionally interfere with a member's right to vote as granted by the tribe. Judicial review of actions by tribal agencies and boards is necessary to provide a remedy for an injured party. . . .

Robert J. McCarthy, *Civil Rights in Tribal Courts: The Indian Bill of Rights at Thirty Years*, 34 IDAHO L. REV. 465, 492-94 (1998).

3. In *Little River Band of Ottawa Indians Tribal Council v. Little River Bands of Ottawa Indians Tribal Ogema*, 8 Am. Tribal Law 287 (Little River Band of Ottawa Indians Tribal Court 2009), the court held that the tribal executive branch leader (the tribal *ogema*) had authority to terminate the employment contract of the legislative branch attorney over the objections of the tribal legislature:

> This matter involves the attorney contract of Joseph Martin, Chief Legislative Counsel; specifically, does the Ogema have the authority to terminate the contract. The contract was signed on September 10, 2007, by Joseph Martin, and Ogema Romanelli, and was ratified by the Council. . . .
>
> The Ogema, issued a Notice of Termination of the contract to Mr. Martin for the reasons that upon information and belief, Mr. Martin's license to practice law in the State of Illinois lapsed and that Mr. Martin had not obtained his license to practice law in the State of Michigan within the time frame as provided in the contract, six months, which is a breach of the contract. Council has admitted that the license in Illinois did lapse, but was corrected, and the Mr. Martin does not have a license to practice law in the State of Michigan. . . .
>
> Council argues that they are the intended beneficiary of the contract, and that because the contract states that Mr. Martin would be under the control and supervision of the Council, it is the only one who can terminate the contract.
>
> The Constitution states at Article IV, Section 7(e) as follows:
>
>> Powers of the Tribal Council. The legislative powers of the Little River Band of Ottawa Indians shall be vested in the Tribal Council, subject to any express limitations contained in this Constitution.

> The Tribal Council shall have the power, including by way of illustration, but not be limitation:
>
> . . .
>
> (e) To employ legal counsel, subject to the approval of the secretary of the Interior so long as such approval is required by federal law.

Council argues that the above-cited provision vests Council with the sole and exclusive authority to hire legal counsel, and that the fact that the Ogema signed this contract was an anomaly. . . . In fact, the language simply reflects the fact that at one time, all attorney contracts entered into by Indian Tribes were required to be submitted to the Secretary of Interior pursuant to 25 U.S.C. 81 and the Secretary of Interior always required those submissions to be supported by resolutions from the applicable Tribe's Council. This section, which was no doubt adapted from "boilerplate" language found in many Tribes' Constitutions, simply reflects this prior requirement under federal law. The Court does not believe that contracts with legal counsel should be treated any differently from any other contract the Tribe may enter into. The Constitution vests the Ogema with the authority to execute contracts on behalf of the Tribe subject to ratification by the Council.

. . . [T]he Council (or Mr. Martin, who is after all, an attorney), could have requested that the form of the contract with Mr. Martin be counter-signed by the Council Speaker and could have included terms that gave the Council the sole authority to terminate that contract. . . .

Little River Band Tribal Council, 8 Am. Tribal Law at 287-89.

3. CONSTITUTIONAL AMENDMENT PROCEDURES

MASHANTUCKET PEQUOT TRIBAL NATION v. McKEON

Mashantucket Pequot Tribal Court, No. MPTC-CV-GC-2008-127, 5 Mash. Rep. 94, 2008 WL 2746707, 2008.NAMP.0000015 (July 9, 2008)

The opinion of the court was delivered by: THOMAS J. LONDREGAN, Judge.

I. Facts and Procedural History

This is a declaratory judgment action brought by the Mashantucket Pequot Tribal Nation ("MPTN" or "Tribe") . . . , to determine the validity of a referendum petition ("Petition") presented by a group of un-sponsored Mashantucket Pequot tribal members ("Petitioners"), under Article VIII, §1 of the Mashantucket (Western) Pequot Constitution.

This Court has authority to determine the validity of the Petition by an express grant of jurisdiction from the Mashantucket Pequot Tribal Council ("Tribal Council" or "Council"):

> The Tribal Court shall have jurisdiction to hear and decide, through a declaratory judgment action, matters pertaining to the legal sufficiency or validity of a petition presented pursuant to Article VIII Section 1 of the Mashantucket (Western) Pequot Constitution, and sovereign immunity of the Tribe is hereby waived for the limited purposed of such a declaratory judgment action in Tribal court provided such action is commenced within 20 days from the time the Tribal Council does not accept the validity or sufficiency of the petition.

12 M.P.T.L. ch. 1 §1(b).

Jurisdiction to hear declaratory judgment actions to determine the validity of a petition presented pursuant to Article VIII Section 1 of the Constitution was granted in 2002 by the Mashantucket Pequot Tribal Council via Resolution TCR122602-01. . . .

On or about February 7, 2008, a group of Mashantucket Pequot tribal members began circulating a petition in response to rumors that Tribal Council was planning to eliminate 40 million dollars from the Mashantucket Pequot governmental operating budget. Between February 7, 2008 and March 11, 2008, these petitioners collected signatures, and submitted the Petition to the Tribal Clerk's Office on March 11, 2008. Upon receiving the Petition, the Tribal Clerk counted the signatures, and verified that a sufficient number of signatures had been obtained to meet the 1/3 requirement of Article VIII, §1 of the Constitution. The Tribal Clerk then forwarded the Petition on to the Mashantucket Pequot Office of Legal Counsel ("OLC"), for a determination of the legal validity of the Petition. On March 24, 2008 the OLC submitted a memorandum to Tribal Council recommending that Council declare the Petition invalid on procedural and substantive grounds. On May 1, 2008, . . . Tribal Council determined that the Petition had a sufficient degree of irregularities to forward the matter to Tribal Court for a determination of the Petition's legal status. On May 2, 2008, MPTN initiated a declaratory judgment action in Tribal Court. . . .

The Petition is entitled, "Petition for special meeting of membership regarding government reductions," and its text states in entirety:

> The members of the Mashantucket Pequot Tribal Nation petition to mandate our Tribal council to report any and all information related, directly or indirectly, to the current consideration of tribal government reductions, to the entire Mashantucket Pequot Tribal Membership in a mandatory Special Meeting of the membership under Article VIII of the Constitution. The Mashantucket Pequot Tribal Council shall not make a decision as to how the government budget will [be] reduced by the forty million dollars ($40,000,000) until membership has developed a process to determine what programs and services are necessary to remain and still meet the said reduction target. The members of the Mashantucket Pequot Tribal Nation mandate the Mandatory Special Meeting of the Membership shall be held within fourteen (14) days from the submission of this petition. During the above-mentioned, mandatory special meeting, the membership, by way of vote of general membership, shall then decide the process for membership involvement and timeframe for the implementation of the process.

. . . On the substantive question, the Court must determine if the Petition — as actually drafted by the Petitioners — can constitute a proper subject for referendum under Article VIII, and whether the Court has authority to grant the relief requested by the Petitioners. . . .

III. Discussion

. . .

B. The Powers Present in the Mashantucket (Western) Pequot Constitution

Before beginning its analysis of the Petition's alleged procedural or substantive defects, the Court finds it helpful to first review the text of the

Constitution to determine which powers have and have not been preserved for exercise by the tribal membership.

Traditionally, state and municipal governments have recognized five different kinds of political powers by which an electorate interacts with its representative officials: (1) Initiative; (2) Referendum; (3) Referral; (4) Recall; and (5) Amendment. . . . Initiative generally refers to the power of the people to propose bills and laws, and to enact or reject them at the polls, independent of legislative assembly. . . . Referendum, on the other hand, is a right constitutionally reserved to the people of a state, or local subdivision thereof, to have submitted for their approval or rejection, under prescribed conditions, any law [or] part of law passed by a lawmaking body. . . . Referral is the ability of a governmental legislative body to seek approval from the people before adopting a particular piece of legislation. . . . Recall is a right or procedure by which a public official may be removed from office before the end of his or her term by a vote of the people to be taken on the filing of a petition signed by a required number of qualified voters. . . . Most jurisdictions also provide the people with the power of changing the governing principles for that jurisdiction — most frequently framed in the form of an amendment to the Constitution. . . .

The Mashantucket (Western) Pequot Constitution reserves to the tribal membership only the powers of referendum, recall, and amendment. It does not, however, provide the people with the power of initiative. It does provide Tribal Council — but not the membership — with the prerogative of Referral.

Article VIII of the Mashantucket (Western) Pequot Constitution ("Constitution"), is entitled "Referendum," and comprises two sections. Section 1 is entitled "Petition" and states in its entirety:

> Upon a petition of at least one-third (1/3) of the eligible voters of the Mashantucket (Western) Pequot Tribe, any enacted or proposed law, resolution or other regulative act of the Tribal Council shall be submitted to a referendum of the qualified voters of the Mashantucket (Western) Pequot Tribe.

Article VIII, §1 of the Mashantucket (Western) Pequot Constitution.

Section 2 is entitled "Resolution" and comprises seven sections which together describe how a valid referendum petition would be presented to the tribal membership.

A fair reading of the Petition leads the Court to conclude that Petitioners are seeking neither a recall nor an amendment to the Constitution in this action. Additionally, the Constitution does not provide tribal membership with the initiative power, and the referral power may be exercised only by Tribal Council. Therefore, the Court need not evaluate the Petition under the principles governing initiative, referral, recall, or amendment mechanisms, and need only address whether the Petition suffices as a proper subject for a referendum.

C. Referendum Power

. . .

C2. Substantive Defects

The Tribe next argues that the Petition is insufficient and invalid because it does not form a proper subject matter for a referendum. Specifically, the

Petition does not reference "any enacted or proposed law, resolution or other regulative act of the Tribal Council," as required by Article VIII, §1 of the Constitution. The Tribe maintains that at the time the Petition was circulated and presented to Tribal council, there were no specific proposals or resolutions pending and that Council was simply engaged in policy discussions about the need for budget reductions.

Furthermore, the Tribe argues that a referendum petition must "be in a form which can be reasonably capable of being understood and placed on [a] ballot," and suggests that because the Petition combines two or more thoughts or forms of relief, it is incapable of being presented in a question calling for a single "yes or no" answer on a ballot, and is therefore legally insufficient on a substantive basis.

At oral argument on the Petition, Petitioners summarized the substance of the relief requested in the Petition [as] follows:

1. That the Tribal Council report any and all information related to the current consideration of tribal government reductions;
2. That Tribal membership get access to all financials, including the fiscal 2008 government and departmental budgets;
3. That the requested information be reported to the Mashantucket Pequot membership in a special meeting to be called by Tribal Council to give the membership this information;
4. That the Tribal Council be enjoined from making a decision as to how the governmental budget would be reduced until the membership had an opportunity to participate in the decision-making process;
5. That the membership be included in the decision-making process;
6. That a special meeting of membership be held to determine how membership can work with Council to create a process that can be followed to ensure a fair and equitable process, and timeframe for implementing any cuts to the municipal budget.

A "referendum" is typically the power of the people to accept or reject at the poll any legislation that has been adopted. . . . In Mashantucket, the Constitution has expanded the target of referendum power to include "any enacted or *proposed* law, resolution or other regulative act of the Tribal Council." Article VIII, §1 of Constitution (emphasis added). The right of referendum therefore is not limited just to legislation that has already been adopted. Rather, proposed legislation, resolutions, or any regulative act may also be petitioned to referendum in the Mashantucket system.

The Petition does not request the repeal of any specifically enacted or proposed statute, law, or regulative act of the Council. When the petition was being circulated and filed, Council had not yet even begun to take specific action; on the contrary, Council was still considering what — if any — specific action to take. Apparently, a goal of 40 million dollars was discussed as a budget reduction target, but no discrete proposal had yet been made to identify specific programs or services that would be cut. The Court must therefore decide whether Petitioners' requests for relief can be properly categorized as "proposed legislation, resolutions, or any regulative act" under Article VIII, §1.

Additionally, the Court must be concerned about judicial intrusion into the political process. . . . The Petitioners are asking for reports, for access to financial information, and for a chance to participate in the decision-making process. Petitioners also seek to enjoin Tribal Council from making decisions. This case demonstrates the strained relationship that develops between the power of the people to legislate directly through the process of referendum and the mandate requiring elected officials to discharge their duties in accordance with law. Petitioners seek to advise the Council and to participate in the decision-making process; at the same time, Tribal Council, elected by the voters of the Tribe, seeks to perform its duties which include the adoption or modification of a governmental budget. A referendum question, by definition, must state the specific subject of the proposed action and ask the voters to be "for the statute, regulation or regulative act" or "against the statute, regulation or regulative act." Since, at the time the Petition was circulated, Council had not yet enacted a specific proposal, the Court cannot fashion the required form of referendum question from the relief Petitioners request.[4]

Even if Council had promulgated a discrete proposal or resolution, preparing a budget for a government directly implicates the primary function and authority of a legislative body, such as the Tribal Council. The formulation of the budgetary process is best left to Tribal Council. It is not the province of this court to determine what information, reports, or participation, if any, the Petitioners should have in the formulation of a budget. The electorate's satisfaction with the Tribal Council in matters such as disclosure of reports and information and listening to the Tribal voters is best left to the ballot box and not the courtroom. *See for example, Citizens for a Responsible Government v. Easton*, 04-CBR-0126 (March 24, 2004), where plaintiff Citizens' request for an injunction to stop the construction of an elementary school because the information and financial data provided by the town was incomplete, not accurate, and failed to provide the citizens with sufficient information, was denied because there was no case law that required a certain degree of information to be provided to the voters. The Court can find no authority to place on a ballot the request made by the Petitioners in the Petition which is before this Court.

Once the Council identifies proposed cuts in the budget and a petition is drafted that clearly states what specific services are to be eliminated, then a question, such as, "Shall the [proposed] decision of the Council to eliminate

---

4. Furthermore, even if Council had implemented a particular proposal or resolution that had been discretely identified by the Petition, the Court might still have to address the question of whether the proposal or resolution would be categorized as a legislative, executive, or administrative action. Generally, the power of referendum does not extend to acts that are purely administrative in nature, and some jurisdictions specifically do not permit the power of referendum to be exercised in response to appropriation decisions made by the executive branch of government or one of its administrative agencies. 42 Am. Jur. 2d Initiative and Referendum §6-§14 *et seq.* Since the Court here has decided that the form of the Petition did not precisely address a particular proposal or resolution and that, in fact, no discrete proposal or resolution had been promulgated when the Petition was being created, the Court does not need to reach the classification question here, and saves this analysis for another day.

XYZ services from the government's budget be rescinded [or repealed]," can be submitted to referendum before the voting membership of the Tribe. . . .

Therefore, the Court finds that Tribal Council need not submit this Petition to a referendum of the qualified voters of the Mashantucket (Western) Pequot Tribe.

NOTES

1. In *In re: Status and Implementation of the 1999 Constitution of the Cherokee Nation*, 9 Okla. Trib. 394, 6 Am. Tribal Law 63 (Cherokee 2006), a split Cherokee Nation Judicial Appeals Tribunal held that the proposed constitutional amendments to the 1975 Cherokee Constitution, which had passed by the electorate in 2003, were effective after that election, despite the failure of the Secretary of Interior to ratify the election (then–assistant secretary Neal McCaleb had refused to act on the new constitution due to ongoing litigation involving the Cherokee Freedmen). The majority disregarded Article XV, Section 10 of the 1975 Cherokee Constitution, which provided:

   > [N]o amendment or new constitution shall become effective without the approval of the President of the United States or his authorized representative.

   Justice Dowty wrote in a special concurrence that the three-year period between the election and the Secretary's inaction was especially disturbing:

   > I agree that the requirement of federal approval was self-imposed and that the same provision can be, and was, effectively removed from the 1975 Constitution by the vote of the Citizens on may 24, 2003. The actions of Mr. McCaleb by letter in his official capacity as representative of the federal government, and by his subsequent affidavit coupled with the federal inaction and non-appearance in this litigation is sufficient for this writer to find that the 1999 Constitution has been in effect from and since its approval by the voters on July 26, 2003.

   6 Am. Tribal Law at 67.

   Justice Leeds dissented, noting that "the Cherokee people made it clear that the 1975 Constitution could *never* be amended or superseded by a new constitution without the approval of the federal government. There are no exceptions." 6 Am. Tribal Law at 67 (emphasis in original). Justice Leeds quoted from an earlier opinion of the court rejecting the application of a different constitutional amendment. There, the Court wrote:

   > The Cherokee Constitution is the organic document of the Cherokee government. It must not be trifled with. Any and all amendments to the Cherokee Constitution must be made following the strict, long-established procedure.

   McLain v. Cherokee Nation Election Commission, 6 Okla. Trib. 582, 588 (Cherokee 1998).

C. CONSTITUTIONAL LAW AND TRIBAL GOVERNMENT

1. SOURCES OF TRIBAL GOVERNMENTAL AUTHORITY

IN THE MATTER OF VILLAGE AUTHORITY TO REMOVE TRIBAL COUNCIL
REPRESENTATIVES (BACAVI CERTIFIED QUESTION)

Hopi Appellate Court, No. 2008-AP-0001 (February 11, 2010)

Before Chief Justice ANNA M. ATENCIO and Associate Justices PAUL S. BERMAN
and ROBERT N. CLINTON. . . .

Certified Question of Law

[3] Do Villages, regardless of their form of government, have the authority
to remove or decertify their duly-certified Tribal Council Representatives?

Answer

. . .

[5] This Court unanimously finds that, under both the Constitution and
Hopi custom and tradition, the Hopi and Tewa Villages, regardless of their
form of government, have authority to remove, recall or decertify their duly
certified Tribal Council Representatives during their term of office by whatever
process the Village selects and that Article IV, section 4 of the Constitution
governs both selection and removal, recall, or decertification of Tribal Council
Representatives.

Discussion

. . .

Village Authority to Remove or Decertify Tribal Council Representatives

A. Constitutional Background

[8] Prior to the initial drafting and adoption of the Hopi Constitution in
1936 there was no central Hopi government. Rather, the people comprising
the Hopi Tribe lived in 12 self-governing Villages, each of which retained its
own aboriginal sovereignty. Each was an autonomous, sovereign city-state.
The historical letters and records filed with this Court as part of the record
in this case demonstrate that the creation of a central Hopi government and
the drafting of the Constitution, significantly promoted by the federal government through Oliver La Farge, was highly controversial, a fact well understood
by Mr. La Farge. Accordingly, unlike many of the tribal constitutions drafted
pursuant to section 16 of the Indian Reorganization Act of 1934 (IRA), codified
as amended at 25 U.S.C. §476, the Hopi Constitution avoided boilerplate legal
clauses and was carefully drafted to preserve the Hopi way of life. In particular,
the Hopi Constitution advances a very different theory of the source of power
of the Hopi Tribe than most of the tribal constitutions drafted during this
period. While most of the tribal constitutions drafted at the same time suggest
the source of power of the central tribal government rests with delegation from

the people of the affected tribe, the Hopi Constitution expressly rejects that approach. Instead, the Preamble to the Hopi Constitution states:

> This Constitution, to be known as the Constitution and By-Laws of the Hopi Tribe, *is adopted by the self-governing Hopi and Tewa Villages of Arizona* to provide a way of working together for peace and agreement between the villages, and of preserving the good things of Hopi life, and to provide a way of organizing to deal with modern problems, with the United States Government and with the outside world generally.

(Emphasis supplied.)

[9] Furthermore, the entire structure of the Hopi Constitution indicates that the authority of the central government of the Hopi Tribe rests on the bedrock of the aboriginal sovereignty of the Hopi and Tewa Villages. The Villages delegated limited powers to the central Hopi government. Under Article II, section 4 of the Constitution the Villages determine Village membership. As already noted, the Constitution expressly reserves certain powers of dispute resolution to the Villages in Article III, section 2. The only officials in the current government of the Hopi Tribe selected by all members of the Hopi Tribe are the Chairman and Vice Chairman, who, pursuant to Article IV, section 7 of the Constitution are elected in at-large elections. All members of the Tribal Council Representatives, according to the express language of the Constitution, constitute "representatives from the various villages." Const. Art. IV, sec. 1. The Tribal Council Representatives are apportioned among the Villages, not the population generally, under a formula set forth in Article IV, section 1 of the Constitution. Under Article IV, section 3, each Tribal Council representative "must be a member of the Village he represents." And, of course, Article IV, section 4, the most critical provision for purposes of resolving this certified question of law, provides:

> Each village shall decide for itself how it chooses its representatives, subject to the provisions of SECTION 5. Representatives shall be recognized by the Tribal Council only if they are certified by the Kikmongwi of their respective villages, Certifications may be in writing or in person.

[10] Thus, unlike most tribal governments adopted under section 16 of the Indian Reorganization Act of 1934, which, according to the express language of their constitutions, owe their authority to powers delegated by their people, the authority of the central government of the Hopi Tribe, according the express provisions in the Preamble of the Constitution, derives exclusively from power delegated to it by the Hopi and Tewa Villages. In this respect, as early noted by Oliver La Farge, the legal theory of the Hopi Constitution is far closer to the Articles of Confederation employed by the federal government from 1781 until 1789 than the current legal theory of the United States Constitution. The bedrock constitutional authority upon which the tribal sovereignty of the Hopi Tribe therefore rests is the inherent aboriginal sovereignty of the Hopi and Tewa Villages that comprise the Hopi Tribe. As in the Articles of Confederation, the Hopi Villages retain all aspects of their inherent aboriginal sovereignty not exclusively delegated by the Constitution to the central government of the Hopi Tribe.

[11] The basic structure of the Hopi government reflects this relatively unique tribal constitutional theory and structure. As already noted, under the express terms of the Constitution, Tribal Council Representatives are selected by and represent the Villages from which they came and they must be members of their respective Villages. Certification of their selection occurs through the Kikmongwi of their Village. Article III, Section 4 authorizes Villages that lack a traditional Hopi form of governance or which seek to make a change or add to it to adopt a written Constitution and By-Laws. In so doing any Village "shall clearly say how the Council representatives and other village officials are chosen. . . ." Thus, the Hopi Constitution, therefore leaves both the selection and the manner of selection of the Tribal Council Representatives entirely to the unfettered discretion of the Hopi and Tewa Villages. Unlike virtually all other tribal constitutions adopted under the Indian Reorganization Act of 1934, the Hopi Constitution does not expressly provide the mechanism for selection of Tribal Council Representatives, leaving both the selection and the manner of selection, instead, to processes determined separately and entirely by each Village. . . .

D. Village Powers to Remove, Recall or Decertify Tribal Council Representatives

[14] Prior to adoption of the Hopi Constitution there was no central Hopi government and therefore each of the Hopi and Tewa Villages unquestionably possessed inherent aboriginal powers of self-government. *In re Komaquaptewa*, No. 01-AP-00013 (Hopi Ct. App. 8/16/2002); see also Frank Waters, The Book of the Hopi 316 (1977); Ragsdale, The Institutions, Laws and Values of the Hopi Indians: A Stable State Society, 55 U.M.K.C. L. Rev. 335, 376 (1987); L. Thompson and A. Joseph, The Hopi Way of Law 48 (1944). Those inherent aboriginal powers logically must have included the power to select, remove, recall or decertify spokespersons to negotiate or otherwise deal with other Villages and the outside world because without such powers the Villages would have lacked the authority to create the Hopi Constitution and By-Laws. Thus, selection, removal, recall or decertification of political spokespersons constitutes part of the inherent aboriginal sovereignty of each of the Hopi and Tewa Village.

[15] The problem posed by the certified question of law in this matter involves the question of whether the adoption of the Hopi Constitution operated to deprive the Hopi and Tewa Villages of their pre-existing sovereign right to select, remove, recall or decertify political representatives. The Hopi Tribal Council objects to this formulation of the issue, which was supported by most of the Villages, including the Village of Bacavi, noting that "because prior to 1936, the Hopi Villages had not established a central tribal government and the Villages existed as "autonomous city-states," "the removal of Tribal Council Representatives was not an inherent power of the Villages prior to the adoption of the Hopi Constitution in 1936. . . ." [sic] . . . Nevertheless, the Villages did have pre-existing sovereign authority to select, remove, recall or decertify political spokespersons generally, including the spokespersons who dealt with Oliver La Farge in the drafting of the Hopi Constitution. Clearly, the manner of selection of Tribal Council Representatives set forth in Article IV, section 4 of the Constitution expressly reaffirms the pre-existing

sovereign right of the Hopi and Tewa Villages to select their Tribal Council Representatives in whatever manner they choose. It constitutes a reaffirmation of preexisting sovereign power, not a delegation of new authority to the Villages. Thus, this Court rejects the excessively narrow formulation of the preexisting aboriginal sovereign rights of the Hopi and Tewa Villages advanced by the Tribal Council in its Brief and finds that the Villages did have pre-existing inherent aboriginal sovereign rights to select, remove, recall, or decertify their political spokespersons and representatives.

[16] Clearly, no express provision of the Constitution purports to remove the powers of removal, recall or decertification of political representatives from the Hopi and Tewa Villages. Thus, if any limitation on this pre-existing sovereign power of the Hopi and Tewa Villages is to be found in the Constitution, the argument must derive from implied constitutional limitations on Village authority derived from the structure or clauses in the Constitution. The only obvious source for such an implied limitation on Village authority would be found in the combined effect of the two year term for Tribal Council Representatives set forth in Article IV, section 2 of the Constitution and the grant of a removal for cause authority to the Tribal Council in Article V, section 2. In its postargument submission the Tribal Council took the position that the delegated removal power for officers and representatives set forth in Article V, section 2 vested the exclusive authority over removal of representatives in the Tribal Council. Neither expressly purport to limit pre-existing Village authority and there are good reasons to believe that the granting of removal authority to the Tribal Council was not meant to preclude retention of removal, recall and decertification authority in the Hopi and Tewa Villages. The Constitution established a new central government for the Hopi Tribe and its powers needed to be and were expressly delegated by the Hopi and Tewa Villages in the Constitution. Thus, if the Tribal Council was to exercise any authority to remove officials and Village representatives for cause, such powers needed to be expressly delegated in the Constitution and they were in Article V, section 2. By contrast, the Villages possessed pre-existing aboriginal sovereignty over the selection, removal, recall and decertification of political spokespersons. No express delegation was required to reaffirm that sovereignty since they already possessed it. Article IV, section 2 simply reaffirms that view for purposes of the selection of the Tribal Council Representatives but is otherwise silent on the question of removal, recall, and decertification. The existence of the automatic removal provisions for conviction of described offenses set forth in Article V, section 1 of the Constitution further suggests that the powers of the Tribal Council over removals for cause are not exclusive. Since nothing in the Constitution suggests that the pre-existing sovereign power of the Hopi and Tewa Villages to remove, recall, or decertify their representatives was removed from them or exclusively delegated to the Tribal Council by Article V, section 2 of the Constitution, this Court finds that the Villages continue to retain that authority under the Hopi Constitution.

[17] Numerous other considerations further support this conclusion. First, as many of the Villages reminded this Court, this question needs to be resolved consistently with Hopi custom and tradition. The Preamble to the Constitution itself indicates that one of its main purposes is "preserving the good things

of Hopi life." The history surrounding the drafting and adoption of the Constitution suggests that the Hopi drafters and Oliver La Farge sought to model the Hopi Constitution in accordance with the way Hopi was actually governed, albeit, adding in the process a new central governing authority that Hopi previously lacked. Roads in the Sky: The Hopi Indians in a Century of Change 151-52; Robert A. Hecht, Oliver La Farge and the American Indian: A Biography 102 (1991). According to his own words, La Farge sought to have the Hopi government "listen to the true voice of each village," which he conceived as being part of the Hopi way of doing things. In a letter dated March 7, 1940, just four years after he assisted the Hopi in drafting the original Hopi Constitution, Oliver La Farge wrote, "the villages keep a whole way of running things, which they have inherited and which they know works." He notes that "[t]be Hopi way is to deal with local problems by villages" and indicates that this bedrock principle "must be remembered in studying any part of the Constitution." . . . In addition, this Court is charged by Hopi Resolution H-12-76 with taking account of Hopi customs and traditions in its decision making. *Hopi Indian Credit Association v. Thomas*, No. 98AC000005 (Hopi Ct. App. 11/13/1998). This focus on leaving all local matters primarily to Village decisions, presumably including the selection, removal, recall, or decertification of Village spokespersons including Tribal Council Representatives, constitutes a central part of the Hopi way that the Hopi and Oliver La Farge sought to preserve in the Hopi Constitution.

[18] At oral argument, this Court was repeatedly reminded that an essential part of the Hopi way is the right to decline to participate, i.e. to abstain, in decisions or actions with which one disagrees. As this Court understands the matter, the right of abstention constitutes an important political part of Hopi customs and traditions. It permits Hopi, whether individual Hopi members or whole Villages, to preserve harmony and consensus by not outright disruptively casting dissenting votes, while still politely manifesting their disagreement by declining to participate. It provides a way of preserving political civility while providing an outlet for political dissent — a tradition and custom from which the United States government could learn much. While this Court need not, and on the record before us cannot, trace the cultural origins of the right of abstention, it is sufficient to say that it clearly constitutes an essential part of the Hopi Way that is far older than the Constitution itself. Indeed, a considerable part of the early controversy over the legitimacy of the adoption of the Hopi Constitution turned on how few of the eligible Hopi members voted in the Indian Reorganization Act election that approved the Constitution and the refusal of the Department of the Interior to recognize the abstentions as effective negative votes on the adoption of the document. Peter Whitely, Bacavi Journey to Reed Springs 124 (1988); Frank Waters, The Book of the Hopi 316 (1963). While this Court has no authority to and cannot revisit that debate, it also has no wish to repeat the same mistake again. It recognizes that the right of abstention constitutes an essential part of Hopi custom and tradition. Not only did the Hopi seek to exercise it in the original adoption of the Constitution, but it has consistently been exercised since the adoption of that document. After the Hopi Constitution was adopted and the Tribal Council began to function, three Second Mesa villages withdrew their

representatives in 1937, objecting, among other things, to the boilerplate Law and Order Code the Secretary of the Interior was promoting for the Tribe, which they believed violated both traditional and constitutional rights. The combination of Village abstention and the refusal of the Tribal Council to enforce livestock reduction measures sought by the Secretary of the Interior led to the suspension of the Tribal Council functioning between 1943 and 1955 (with just a brief session in 1951 to submit claims under the Indian Claims Commission Act). Some villages have always refused to send representatives to the Tribal Council. This Court is informed that currently Old Oraibi, Lower Meoncopi and Shongopavi continue to exercise their right of abstention by declining to participate in the central Hopi government. Whatever else this history suggests, it plainly demonstrates that the right of political abstention constitutes a pre-existing and enduring part of the Hopi Way. Accepting the view that the removal for cause power established by Article V, section 2 constitutes the exclusive manner in which Tribal Council representatives can be removed or recalled during their term of office, would deny the Hopi and Tewa Villages and each member of those villages their longstanding right of abstention and force them to participate in the central Hopi government after they had concluded either that their Tribal Council Representatives no longer were serving their interests or positions or that they no longer wished to participate in the central government. Since this Court is charged both by the Preamble to the Constitution and by Hopi law with preserving Hopi customs and traditions, it therefore cannot agree with the Tribal Council and find that Article V, section 2 constitutes the exclusive means by which Tribal Council Representatives can be removed, recalled or decertified during their term of office. To do so would violate both the purposes for which the Constitution was established and Hopi customs and traditions. It would, in short, deny the Hopi and Tewa Villages their inherent aboriginal right of abstention. Since nothing in the Constitution indicates that the Villages gave up or were denied their sovereign right of abstention by that document and since the Hopi custom and tradition both before and since the adoption of the Constitution suggests the right of abstention persists, this Court must find, consistent with the Hopi Way, that the Villages retain their sovereign aboriginal right to select, remove, recall, or decertify their political spokespersons, including their Tribal Council Representatives, by whatever means they select. *Compare, In re Komaquaptewa*, No. -1- AP-00013 (Hopi Ct. App. 8/16/2002) ("Such a result seems at odds with the Constitution that sees the Hopi Tribe as composed of a group of self-governing villages".).

[19] The Tribal Council primarily argues that recognizing a Village power of removal, recall, or decertification of Tribal Council Representatives would imperil the functioning and stability of the Hopi Tribal Council and therefore the functioning [of] the Hopi central government. . . . In making their argument, the Tribe draws close analogies to the United States Constitution. This Court cannot accept either the analogy nor the Tribal Council's argument. As already noted, the form of government adopted by the Hopi Constitution is, in the views of Oliver La Farge, one of its principal drafters, far closer to the Article of Confederation than the United States Constitution. Thus, the analogy offered by the Tribe appears to miss the mark. More importantly, while this

Court recognizes that the extensive exercise of this right may rarely threaten the efficiency and the stability of the Hopi central government, as indeed it apparently did between 1943 and 1955, this result nevertheless appears to be the result compelled by the Hopi Constitution and the Hopi Way which, by its Preamble, the Constitution was meant to preserve. The Court first notes that the Tribe's stability concerns, as voiced in its Brief, appear at odds with and, as argued by the Tribal Council, denies the Hopi right of political abstention discussed above. The fact that Village exercise of this power of removal, recall, or decertification has not threatened the stability of the Hopi Tribal Council since 1955 indicates that the Villages have used this power responsibly and with restraint. It also suggests that the stability concerns strongly voiced by the Tribe may prove to be over-stated. Like many matters involving predictions of the future, however, only time and experience can resolve that question.

[20] The conclusion that the Hopi and Tewa Villages, regardless of their form of government, retain the aboriginal sovereign power to remove, recall, or decertify their Tribal Council Representatives during their constitutional term of office is also bolstered by the prior precedents both of this Court and of the actions of the Villages themselves. This Court has been advised in both written and oral submissions, without contradiction, that the power of removal, recall or decertification of Tribal Council Representatives during their term of office has been consistently, albeit infrequently, exercised by the Villages and until the past few years had always been recognized and honored by the Tribal Council. At least one precedent from this Court appears to confirm that history. In *Youvella v. Dallas*, No. 99-AP-000008 (Hopi Ct. App. 11/06/ 2000), two Tribal Council Representatives from [First] Mesa Consolidated Villages had been decertified by the Kikmongwi. Based on the facts, the Tribal Council clearly recognized the decertification since the Tribal Treasurer ceased to pay them. The two had petitioned the Tribal Council for reinstatement after they were decertified and, at least in that instance, the Tribal Council recognized the power of the Villages to decertify Tribal Council Representatives during their term of office and informed the two former Tribal Council Representatives that the matter was a local one they must take up with their Villages. They sued, claiming that the Treasurer was acting ultra vires (beyond his power) in declining to pay them. Neither the deposed Tribal Council Representatives nor the Tribal government contested the power of the Villages, through the Kikmongwi, to decertify these Tribal Council Representatives during their term of office. The *Youvella* case therefore confirms the historical claims of the Villages that they have long exercised the power of removal, recall, or decertification of their Tribal Council Representatives and have done so, until recently, without contest or objection from the Tribal Council. This case also suggests that until recently, the Tribal Council has long recognized the constitutional conclusion that once removed, recalled, or decertified by a Village a Tribal Council Representative can only be reinstated by the Village, not the Tribal Council. In short, it is a local Village political decision. The Tribal Council therefore lacks authority to reseat or recognize a Tribal Council Representative removed, recalled or decertified by a Village unless and until the Village itself informs the Tribal Council, through its Kikmongwi

or otherwise, that it has under its own processes reselected the previously removed Tribal Council Representative. . . .

[22] In some cases, the Villages will be in a superior position to the Tribal Council in knowing whether any particular Tribal Council Representative is fully performing his or her job. As noted above, the role of the Tribal Council Representative involves bilateral communication—representing the Village interests to the Tribal Council and informing and explaining to the Village the issues before and actions of the Tribal Council. Certainly, the Tribal Council will be fully aware of any failure of a Tribal Council Representative to perform the first duty and, as Article V, section 2, recognizes will be authorized to remove any Representative for "serious neglect of duty." By contrast, the Villages, not the Tribal Council, will be aware of failures by any Tribal Council Representative to inform and explain to the Village the issues before and actions taken by the Tribal Council. Failure to do so may never come to the attention of the full Tribal Council. Thus, the Villages need the continuing ability to remove, recall or decertify Tribal Council Representatives who fail to perform this role or who fail in their actions and votes on the Tribal Council to fully and fairly represent the views and interests of their Village.

[23] For all of these reasons, this Court unanimously concludes that the removal power of the Tribal Council contained in Article V, section 2 is not exclusive and that the Hopi and Tewa Villages, regardless of their form of government, have authority to remove, recall, or decertify their duly certified Tribal Council Representatives during their term of office by whatever process the Village selects. . . .

NOTE

In 2010, the Navajo Supreme Court decided several cases relating to the governing authority of the Nation. *E.g.*, *Nelson v. Initiative Committee to Reduce Navajo Nation Council*, 8 Am. Tribal Law 407 (Navajo Nation Supreme Court 2010); *Todacheenie v. Shirley*, 2010 WL 2834401 (Navajo Nation Supreme Court, July 9, 2010). In *Office of Navajo Nation President and Vice-President v. Navajo Nation Council*, 2010 WL 2834409 (Navajo Nation Supreme Court, July 16 2010), the court enjoined an effort by the tribal legislature to place the Navajo chief executive on "administrative leave." The court rejected the claim of the legislature that all tribal authority derived from the tribal council:

> Passage of CJA-08-10 by the Council [purporting the place the President on leave] underscored Appellants' . . . position that separation of powers does not exist on the Navajo Nation by purporting to restrict the type of law the courts may use to Council-enacted statutes. By stating that "Navajo common law cannot supply a rule of decision about how to allocate lawmaking power between the Council and the courts," Appellants emphasized the competing views of the government on the use of Fundamental Law in judicial decision-making. . . . By asserting that "the Council is the absolute source of governance for the Navajo People," Appellants necessarily involved the Court in sorting out the source of Navajo Nation governmental responsibility and power.

Id., 2010 WL 2834409, at *2. Instead, the court held that the source of governmental authority was the people of the Navajo Nation:

> We have affirmed the power of the people to choose their government by singling out egalitarianism as the fundamental principle of Navajo participatory democracy and explaining its meaning as the ability of the People as a whole to determine the laws by which they will be governed. . . . Most importantly, we have held that "the power over the structure of the Navajo government 'is ultimately in the hands of the People and [the Council] will look to the People to guide it.' " *In re Two Initiative Petitions Filed by President Joe Shirley, Jr.*, No. SC-CV-41-08, slip op. at 9 (Nav. Sup. Ct. July 18, 2008). We have elaborated that the power of the people to participate in their democracy and determine their form of government is a reserved, inherent and fundamental right expressed in Title 1 of our Dine Fundamental Law and the Navajo Bill of Rights. *In re Navajo Nation Election Administration's Determination of Insufficiency Regarding Two Initiative Petitions Filed by Shirley*, SC-CV-24-09, slip op. at 6, fn 2 (Nav. Sup. Ct. June 22, 2009). This "reserved" right cannot be denied or disparaged except by a vote of the People. *Id.* Additionally, CD-68-89 provided the statutory foundation for principles of checks and balances, separation of powers, accountability to the People, acknowledgement of the People as the source of Navajo Nation governmental authority, and service of the anti-corruption principle. The Council may not amend any portion of the Navajo Nation Code in a manner that disturbs and undermines the above stated principles. The Council may not change, modify, override or amend provisions in which the People have expressed a decision through vote or other trustworthy and publicly accepted mechanism, such as Chapter resolutions, recorded and written comments provided to the Government Reform Project, and signed petitions. In other words, once the people have spoken, their proposition becomes law unless the people have acquiesced otherwise with full information and understanding.

Id. at *4.

2. TRIBAL CONSTITUTIONAL CRISES

HOLDER v. BYRD

Cherokee Nation Judicial Appeals Tribunal, No. JAT-97-14, 6 Oklahoma Tribal
Court Rep. 349, 1997 WL 33477675 (April 24, 1997)

Justice BIRDWELL delivered the Opinion of the Court, in which Chief Justice KEEN and Justice VILES join.

I. Facts

On April 15, 1997, approximately 40 individual Cherokee citizens and Council members ["Plaintiffs"] filed a document styled "Complaint and Application for Emergency Temporary Restraining Order" ["Complaint"].

In that Complaint, the Plaintiffs alleged that the Defendants, Joe Byrd, Principal Chief; James "Garland" Eagle, Deputy Chief; and [several] Council members ["Defendants"], participated in an illegally constituted session of the Tribal Council on April 15, 1997. In the meeting, the Defendants voted, among other things, to request the Bureau of Indian Affairs to assume law enforcement duties within the Cherokee Nation. At its conclusion, a recess was voted upon and approved, with the meeting to reconvene on April 28, 1997. James Fields, Area Director of the Bureau of Indian Affairs, was [also] named as a Defendant.

The Plaintiffs assert that the meeting of April 15, 1997, was illegal because it violated the Cherokee Constitution. The bases for the argument that the meeting was illegal were that because only nine members of the 15-member Council were present for the session, a quorum was not present, and that a 10-day notice was not given calling the session. At the hearing on April 21, 1997, the Court was informed that the absent Council members received no notice whatsoever of the April 15, 1997 meeting.

The Plaintiffs . . . ask this Court for a declaratory judgment finding that the session was an illegal meeting, void and without legal effect, and that any matters flowing out of the meeting are of no effect. . . .

On April 21, 1997, the Judicial Appeals Tribunal conducted a hearing on this matter. . . .

Neither the Defendants nor their counsel appeared at the hearing. They instead filed two substantially identical documents styled "Special Appearance Contesting Jurisdiction of the Court." . . .

II. Discussion

A. *Jurisdiction*

This Court is dismayed with the Defendants' argument that the Judicial Appeals Tribunal does not have jurisdiction over them in their official capacities or duties. We are more than dismayed with their legal counsel, who failed to provide the Court with any authority whatsoever in support of the position taken by their clients in the special appearances. This may be an admission that no such legal or equitable authority exists which would support the arguments of the Defendants. Regardless, this Court has no choice but to disregard these unusual pleadings. In the future, lawyers filing motions or other pleadings with this Court that contain unique arguments are urged to file briefs and provide references to legal authorities that support their positions. Under the Federal Rules of Civil Procedure [FRCP] adopted by this Court, there is no such pleading as a special appearance.

The Cherokee Nation Constitution is the highest legal authority within the Cherokee Nation. Article VII of the Constitution provides for the Judicial Appeals Tribunal. It states in part:

> The purpose of this Tribunal shall be to hear and *resolve any disagreements* arising under any provisions of this Constitution or any enactment of the Council.

CHEROKEE CONST. art. VII (emphasis added).

Clearly, pursuant to the Cherokee Nation Constitution, this Court has the jurisdiction to determine this controversy, and also has jurisdiction over the Principal Chief, Deputy Chief, and Council members in order to bring about a resolution of such dispute.

THEREFORE, THIS COURT FINDS that it has jurisdiction in this matter and jurisdiction over the Principal Chief, Deputy Chief and the Council members pursuant to the Cherokee Constitution, especially when the subject of the matters includes resolving "any disagreements under the Constitution" or "any enactment of the Council."

It would defy all logic, common sense and reality to argue that the framers of the Constitution, and the Cherokee citizens who approved it, would have intended the highest Court in the Cherokee Nation to not have jurisdiction over controversies arising out of the conduct of the Principal Chief, Deputy Chief, and Council members while acting in their official capacities. . . .

B. *Preliminary Injunction*

The Plaintiffs have requested a preliminary injunction enjoining the Defendants from taking any action as a result of the purported Council meeting of April 15, 1997. Before the request for a preliminary injunction is considered, the relevant provisions of the Cherokee Constitution relating to regular, special, and extraordinary Council meetings must be analyzed.

As to regular Council meetings, Article V, Section 4 provides in part:

> No business shall be conducted by the Council unless at least two-thirds (2/3) of the members thereof regularly elected and qualified shall be in attendance, *which number shall constitute a quorum.*

CHEROKEE CONST. art. V, §4 (emphasis added). This provision is clear and unambiguous. It means exactly what it says: no business can be conducted by the Council unless two-thirds, or 10 members are present of the total 15-member Council. In essence, a quorum is defined as the presence of at least 10 Council members.

Special Council meetings are authorized by Article V, Section 5, as follows:

> Special meetings of the Council may be called: (A) by the Principal Chief, (B) by the Deputy Principal Chief when he has the full powers of the Principal Chief as elsewhere defined, (C) upon written request of fifty-one percent (51%) of the members of the Council, or (D) upon the written request of ten percent (10%) of the registered voters of the Cherokee Nation. *The purpose of said meeting shall be stated in a notice published not less than ten (10) days prior to the meeting and the Council may not consider any other subject not within such purposes. No special meetings may convene until thirty (30) days have elapsed after the adjournment of a prior session or meeting unless called pursuant to (A) and (B) above.*

CHEROKEE CONST. art. V, §5 (emphasis added).

This section is also unambiguous. It prohibits any special Council meeting unless notice and an agenda are published at least 10 days prior to the special meeting. It is important to note that in Article V, Section 5, the Council may only convene a special meeting when 30 days have elapsed after the adjournment of a prior session or meeting. However, the same restriction does not apply to the Principal Chief or Deputy Chief, when acting as Principal Chief. A special meeting may be called by those officers when only 10 days have elapsed after the adjournment of the last meeting. The 10 day requirement is due to the constitutional mandate of publishing notice of the meeting, and the purposes (agenda) therefor. Naturally, without an agenda, no meeting of the Council or any committee thereof may occur. Moreover, only matters on the agenda can be considered, unless new or additional items brought before such Council or committee meeting are insignificant and have no substantial impact on the business of the Cherokee Nation. Article VI, Section 8, states:

> The Principal Chief may on extraordinary occasions convene the Council at the seat of government pursuant to Article V, Section 5, and such notice and other laws as may be prescribed by the Council. The purpose of said meetings must be stated and the Council may consider only such matters as are specified in the call of the extraordinary meetings. *Before the extraordinary meetings may be legally sufficient to conduct business, a quorum of the Council must be present.*

CHEROKEE CONST. art. VI, §8 (emphasis added).

Obviously, this section is a further definition of the circumstances under which the Principal Chief or Deputy Chief may call meetings as provided for in Article V, Section 5. It can only be read and applied as an *extension* of Article V, Section 5, and cannot be interpreted as a separate grant of power or as a broader grant of power than already provided. In other words, the Principal Chief or Deputy Chief may call meetings under special or extraordinary circumstances, but the requirements of Article V, Section 5 must be satisfied, and a quorum of the Council must be present before any business can be conducted. Article VI, Section 8 cannot, under any circumstances, be construed as standing alone so as to permit a special or extraordinary meeting until at least 10 days have passed since the adjournment of the last meeting. Moreover, notice of the meeting and the purposes (agenda) must be published at least 10 days prior thereto, and a quorum must be present to address the business at hand.

At this point, the question must be answered as to what constitutes a quorum for special or extraordinary meetings. Article V, Section 4, of the Cherokee Constitution defines a quorum as the presence of at least two-thirds (10) members of the 15-member Council. While this constitutional Article and Section deals with regular meetings, it is obvious, for definition purposes, that the Cherokees who drafted and ratified the Constitution intended for the word "quorum" to mean, for all purposes, the presence of at least 10 Council members. Therefore, no Council meeting, whether regular, special or extraordinary, may take votes unless 10 of the 15 Council members are present.

It has been suggested that inasmuch as 19 C.N.C.A. §35 permits the use of *Robert's Rules of Order*, then it is not required that 10 members of the Council be present at special or extraordinary meetings. Under certain limited, specified circumstances, *Robert's Rules of Order* provide that a simple majority of those present may act. It is important to note that 19 C.N.C.A. §35 further provides that the use of *Robert's Rules of Order* is prohibited when such use would violate or conflict with the Cherokee Constitution. Here, the conflict is obvious, because the Constitution requires the presence of 10 members, rather than a simple majority, to constitute a quorum. Therefore, the use of *Robert's Rules of Order* is inapplicable in this or in any other situation where such use would violate the Cherokee Constitution. *See Cornsilk v. Cherokee Nation Tribal Council*, Case No. JAT-96-15[, 5 Okla. Trib. 185, 190-91 (Cherokee 1996)].

Inasmuch as the required 10 day notice was not published for the Council meeting of April 15, 1997, and having further determined that a quorum was not present, THIS COURT HAS, AT THIS TIME, NO CHOICE BUT TO FIND

THAT ALL DECISIONS RENDERED AT SUCH MEETING ARE VOID AND ILLEGAL, INCLUDING THE CALL FOR A MEETING ON APRIL 28, 1997. Moreover, since the meeting of April 15, 1997 was recessed and not adjourned, THIS COURT FURTHER FINDS THAT NO OTHER SPECIAL OR EXTRAORDINARY COUNCIL MEETING CAN BE CONVENED FOR A PERIOD OF AT LEAST 10 DAYS FROM AND AFTER April 28, 1997. This is the earliest date the illegal meeting of April 15, 1997, would have been officially adjourned had the meeting of April 28, 1997, occurred. Consequently, the earliest date any future special or extraordinary meetings can legally occur is May 8, 1997.

The requirements for the issuance of a preliminary injunction include the following:

1. likelihood of prevailing on the merits;
2. immediate harm;
3. no adequate remedy at law;
4. irreparable harm; and
5. balancing of interests, including that of the public.

. . .

A threshold question in issuing a preliminary injunction includes: Is there a likelihood that the claimant will prevail on the merits? All that is required is a showing of a reasonable chance of success on the merits.

The Plaintiffs, in presenting their arguments pursuant to the Cherokee Nation Constitution and Cherokee Nation and United States Supreme Court case law, have shown this Court that they have an almost assured likelihood of prevailing on the merits. Therefore, the first requirement is satisfied.

The next requirement is whether there [is] an immediate threat of injury or harm. Have the Plaintiffs shown some evidence that a right is about to be violated? An injunction is never granted based upon mere apprehension of injury, nor where the injury is nominal or speculative. Immediate is the operative word.

The Plaintiffs as Cherokee citizens (and some of whom are Council members) do have a serious threat of injury. The meeting of April 15, 1997 was in fact illegal, and the business conducted at that meeting is void. Any person acting upon the business of that meeting could damage the individual members of the Cherokee Nation, as well as the Nation as a whole. The Defendants, acting pursuant to the business conducted in that meeting, would bring immediate harm.

The requirements that the Plaintiffs make a showing of no adequate remedy at law and show irreparable harm will be discussed together. These requirements are generally proved by a showing that an injury or right violated is of such a nature that it cannot be adequately compensated by damages. Furthermore, if the injury is such that it is continuing or permanent, and cannot be remedied any other way, it is ripe for injunction.

The circumstances of the instant case most definitely warrant injunctive relief. The issue is not money, but whether elected officials who, by oath, have sworn to uphold the Constitution and laws of the Cherokee Nation, can conduct business without the required notice and the constitutionally-mandated quorum. If the purported meeting was illegal, then anyone acting upon the business conducted at such meeting would injure the tribal members of the Cherokee Nation in a way that money damages would not remedy.

THEREFORE, THIS COURT DETERMINES that there is no adequate remedy at law, and that irreparable harm will occur to the Plaintiffs if injunctive relief is not granted.

The last requirement is to balance the interests of the parties along with a recognition of possible harm, if any, to the public's interest.

The hardships in this matter clearly favor the Plaintiffs. These Defendants, elected officials, have violated the Constitution by meeting and conducting business illegally, and the tribal members individually stand to lose. Moreover, the public interest of the Cherokee Nation is paramount to any other. Indeed, since the Council has met illegally, the public interest of the Cherokee Nation has and will suffer greatly.

Therefore, all requisites of issuing a preliminary injunction being met, and the Defendants having due and proper notice of this proceeding, THIS COURT HEREBY FINDS the situation being grave to the citizens of the Cherokee Nation, and ISSUES A PRELIMINARY INJUNCTION.

The Defendants in this action . . . ; ARE HEREBY ENJOINED FROM ACTING UPON ANY AND ALL BUSINESS THAT WAS VOTED ON, DISCUSSED OR OTHERWISE BEFORE THE COUNCIL AT THE APRIL 15, 1997, COUNCIL MEETING. DEFENDANTS ARE FURTHER ENJOINED FROM CONDUCTING ANY SPECIAL OR EXTRAORDINARY MEETINGS PRIOR TO MAY 8, 1997, FOR THE REASONS SET FORTH ABOVE. . . .

NOTES

1. *Holder v. Byrd* was the first in a series of cases arising out of the Cherokee Nation's constitutional crisis of the late 1990s. *See generally* Denette A. Mouser, *A Nation in Crisis: The Government of the Cherokee Nation Struggles to Survive*, 23 Am. Indian L. Rev. 359, 359-66 (1998-1999). Later tribal court cases included the efforts of a Cherokee District Court judge to set up a "rogue 'tribal court'" in support of Cherokee Principal Chief Joe Byrd. *In re Removal and Suspension of Jordan*, 6 Okla. Trib. 366 (Cherokee 1997). Principal Chief Byrd also authorized "security forces" to seize the Cherokee Nation's Courthouse, the building where the Cherokee Nation's Judicial Appeals Tribunal conducted business. *In the Matter of Access to the Cherokee Nation Courthouse*, 6 Okla. Trib. 375 (Cherokee 1997). In 1997, the Cherokee Nation commissioned a report of independent experts to analyze the Nation's constitutional law — the "Massad Commission." Anthony M. Massad, Robert A. Layden & Daniel G. Gibbons, *The Massad Commission Report to the Tribal Council of the Cherokee Nation*, 23 Am. Indian L. Rev. 375 (1998-1999).

   Mouser summarized the extraordinary events of the Cherokee constitutional crisis:

   > Indications of an impending crisis began as early as the summer of 1996. Director of the Cherokee Nation Marshal Service, Pat Ragsdale, pursued several apparently unrelated investigations. These investigations, primarily

criminal in nature, included . . . complaints lodged against Joel Thompson, Director of the Cherokee Nation Housing Authority and close associate of Principal Chief Joe Byrd. Byrd pressured Ragsdale to squelch his investigation of Thompson, and Ragsdale complied until he received evidence which strongly implicated Thompson in wrongdoing.

The allegations against Thompson ranged from criminal libel to misappropriation of funds. One allegation centered on a supposed "hidden bank account" that financed Byrd's summit at a local State Park lodge, paid $5000 for a car rental, and the use of Housing Authority money to prepare and mail Byrd's campaign materials. Byrd, in an apparent violation of tribal law, then ordered Ragsdale to cease his investigation of Thompson. . . .

At that same time, council members of the Cherokee Nation Tribal Council made repeated requests to Byrd for documents related to financial records of tribal business. Among the documents requested were those showing payments to a Tulsa law firm in which Byrd's brother-in-law was a partner, and records related to a manufacturing deal in India. . . . Byrd refused to force compliance with the requests, and Council members petitioned the Cherokee Nation Judicial Appeals Tribunal (the Tribunal) for a ruling on the disclosure of the contracts. In August of that same year, the Tribunal ruled that the documents were indeed a matter of public record and should be provided to the Council. Byrd and his administrators continued their refusal to provide the documents. . . .

Months passed with tension between Byrd and other tribal officials escalating. Then, in late February 1997, Tribal Prosecutor A. Diane Blalock alleged that Byrd had misused tribal funds and requested that Chief Justice Ralph Keen issue a search warrant of Byrd's office based upon Ragsdale's sworn affidavit. The Tribunal issued the warrant, which was served by tribal marshals on February 25, 1997.

Cherokee marshals made copies of the subject financial records constituting five boxes of documents, but left the originals with Byrd. Outraged at the search of his office, Byrd fired Ragsdale and Lt. Sherry Wright, who were immediately reinstated by Justice Dwight Birdwell. Birdwell also warned that anyone who interfered with the Tribunal's orders or the investigations conducted by the Marshal Service would face charges of contempt.

. . . In response, the FBI instituted its own investigation into tribal activities which may have violated United States federal laws, including illegal wiretaps of some tribal officials. Byrd, refusing to recognize the "reinstated" Ragsdale and fourteen other tribal marshals, hired his own armed security force. . . .

Just four days later, on April 15, 1997, Byrd conducted a Council meeting attended by only eight of the fifteen Council members, and a vote to begin impeachment of the entire Judicial Appeals Tribunal was passed. . . .

By April 24, the Tribunal had ruled that the April 15 Council meeting was illegal due to lack of a quorum, and a contempt citation was issued against Byrd. . . .

Relentless in their determination to gain control of tribal business and tribal government, the eight Byrd-loyalist Council members announced a plan to amend the Cherokee Constitution so that a simple majority of Council members would be all that was required to legally conduct business. More disturbingly, the eight member Council conducted a "court of removal" and carried through with their vote to impeach the entire Tribunal. Byrd's administration confidently announced that he would not recognize the actions of the impeached court, and he remained free from the warrant issued for his arrest. In response to their "illegal" impeachment, and operating despite a lack of funds, members of the Tribunal continued to carry out their functions in the Cherokee Courthouse. . . .

Then, on June 20, 1997, Byrd ordered his security force to conduct an armed takeover of the Courthouse. The takeover, conducted in a pre-dawn raid, left vacant the 1880s-era building which housed not only the Cherokee Nation's judicial branch of government but also the Cherokee Marshal Service. . . . Angry tribe members attempted to storm the building later that morning but were turned back by Byrd's armed security force.

The impeached justices and fired marshals were literally locked out of their offices. . . .

With no Tribunal and a locked Courthouse, the citizens of the Cherokee Nation had no access to an independent judiciary, and no method for handling child custody and other disputes. One Council member called for an end to "this long, long national nightmare" and others expressed a desire for orderliness and restoration of the Tribunal. On August 10, 1997, the "impeached" Tribunal ordered Ragsdale and the "fired" marshals to take back the Cherokee Courthouse on August 13 at noon.

On August 12, 1997, the full membership of the Cherokee Nation Council met to decide whether to reinstate the impeached tribunal. Just after midnight on the 13th, Deputy Chief Garland Eagle broke a 7-7 deadlock in a decision which upheld the impeachment of the tribe's highest court. . . .

Later that day, an unarmed Ragsdale served the Tribunal's eviction notice, requiring Byrd's security forces to vacate the Courthouse. Byrd's forces refused to step aside, and a melee resulted in which non-Indian police forces from five Oklahoma counties, officers from the Oklahoma Highway Patrol, and the Bureau of Indian Affairs police removed impassioned citizens and Ragsdale's team. Hundreds of Marshal Service supporters participated in the fracas, and six people suffered injuries. Among those injured was noted Cherokee artist Lisa Tiger, who alleged she was grabbed by the hair and thrown to the concrete steps of the Courthouse. . . .

The Cherokee Nation's internal turmoil and external physical conflicts captured the attention of U.S. Interior Secretary Bruce Babbitt who, along with U.S. Attorney General Janet Reno, called leaders of the tribe to Washington, D.C. The unprecedented intervention of the United States government occurred against a backdrop of possible federal remedies including: (1) President Clinton's authority to remove Byrd from office; (2) Congressional action to cease federal funding for the tribe; (3) removal of various federal programs; and (4) reinstatement of the BIA as trustee for the tribe, ending Cherokee Nation self-government.

On August 22, 1997, . . . Babbitt proposed a temporary moratorium on all legal action, the reopening of the tribal courthouse, and an outside review of whether the Judicial Appeals Tribunal should be recognized.

. . . Byrd balked at the provision which would have provided for the recognition of the ousted Judicial Appeals Tribunal, and returned to Tahlequah. Claiming fatigue as his reason for leaving the marathon session on Friday, Byrd stated, "I think everything I did was according to the constitution." . . . Upon Byrd's departure, Babbitt warned that Congress may intervene in the crisis if the disputes were not resolved. With the summit apparently ended, Babbitt left the nation's capitol and went on vacation. . . .

> Following a weekend of uncertainty and apprehension, reports broke that Byrd had returned to Washington, D.C. on Monday, August 25. . . . Later that day, word came that an accord had been reached and that Byrd had signed an agreement he termed a "peace settlement." The agreement . . . required Byrd to accept the opinion of an independent commission's investigation into the constitutionality of the impeachment of the Judicial Appeals Tribunal, the reopening the Cherokee courthouse, and a moratorium on any legal action related to the dispute. . . .

Mouser, *supra*, at 359-66.

The constitutional crisis precipitated the Cherokee constitutional convention of 1999, discussed *supra*. *See generally* D. Jay Hannah, *The 1999 Constitutional Convention of the Cherokee Nation*, 35 ARIZ. ST. L.J. 1 (2003).

3. LEGISLATIVE PROCEDURES

HALL v. TRIBAL BUSINESS COUNCIL

Three Affiliated Tribes of the Fort Berthold Reservation Tribal District Court, No. 95C000069, 23 Indian Law Rep. 6039 (January 5, 1996)

Before POMMERSHEIM, Special Judge . . .

I. Introduction

The plaintiffs in this action filed a complaint against the defendants on June 6, 1995. The gravamen of their complaint focused on the actions and procedures employed by the tribal business council in awarding unit grazing leases in early 1995 for the five year period to run from 1995-2000. . . .

C. Due Process

Analysis of the issue of due process proves a more complicated undertaking. The task of parsing this question raises a series of intricate sub-issues and parts. These include:

. . .

2. Whether any procedural due process is, in fact, due under these circumstances and if so,
   A) Whether it has been provided, and
   B) Whether if it was provided, was it adequate. . . .

2. Procedural Due Process

[T]here remains the issue of whether plaintiffs are entitled to any procedural due process and if so, whether it was afforded to them. Due process in its procedural context — whether under the fifth or fourteenth amendments to the U.S. Constitution or the Indian Civil Rights Act at 25 U.S.C. §1302(8) — generally guarantees that an individual shall be accorded a certain "process" if they are deprived of life, liberty, or property. When the power of government — including tribal government — is used against an individual, there is a right to a fair procedure to determine the basis for, and legality of, such action."

The threshold question here is whether plaintiffs have been deprived of "life, liberty or property." The focus is whether plaintiffs have any property right — cognizable under the Indian Civil Rights Act of 1968 — relative to the tribal review and award (in conjunction with the Bureau of Indian Affairs) of tribal grazing unit leases. There is no doubt that the award of a unit grazing lease constitutes "property" for purposes of the due process guarantee as set out in the Indian Civil Rights Act of 1968. A leasehold interest is clearly a property right under any definition of the term. Admittedly, that is not quite the case we have here. Plaintiffs claim a property interest, not based on the actual award (and subsequent impairment) of unit grazing leases, but on the failure to provide due process for those applicants who were not awarded unit grazing leases in the first instance.

In this regard, most courts have focused on the notion of "entitlement." That is, are plaintiffs "entitled" to the government benefits — as defined by local law — as long as they comply with the appropriate requirements? Again, this is an easy question when the "entitlement" has been awarded (not the case here), but more difficult when the plaintiff is simply an applicant for, rather than a recipient of, the government entitlement. Such interests are sometimes referred to as mere "expectancies" without the necessary "present enjoyment."

In the context of Indian land — specifically the tribal and individual trust land that make up range units — such land is clearly a critical tribal resource. As such, tribal member applicants for grazing units leases have more than a mere "expectancy" in potential awards. They do not, obviously, have an ultimate "entitlement" to a unit lease, but they do have the right, *vis-á-vis* the precious tribal resource, to be treated culturally and legally with dignity and appropriate fairness. Plaintiffs, as tribal members, are entitled to due process. Such a view comports not only with the lineaments of due process under the Indian Civil Rights Act of 1968, but also the traditions of dignity and fairness that are central to the history of the Three Affiliated Tribes.

Having decided that due process applies to the procedure utilized in the allocation of grazing unit leases, the question becomes what due process, if any, was provided and lastly, if any was provided, is it sufficient as a matter of law? Plaintiffs claim none was provided despite the specific promises and representations of the defendants to the contrary, while defendants claim that nothing was specifically promised in this situation, but that a "traditional" (tribal) form of due process was available and plaintiffs simply never availed themselves of the procedure to freely place themselves on the agenda for any tribal council meeting to make their concerns known. The parties agree and the relevant testimony supports a conclusion that the tribal business council did not provide any kind of a *special* meeting to hear concerns of plaintiffs or others who were denied range units.[16] Regardless of the promise of any *individual* defendant or tribal business council representative relevant to

---

16. *See, e.g.*, the minutes of the Regular Tribal Business Council Meeting of February 9, 1995 . . . in which Mr. [Austin] Gilette refers to a "memo which he sent out from the Natural Resources Committee, wherein he states that a Special Council Meeting will be held specifically to address the grazing issue in regards to all the discrepancies that the Fort Berthold Livestock Association is concerned with." However, the minutes do not indicate that any proposal for a

a special meeting, such a promise or representation without more has no status as the law or policy of The Three Affiliated Tribes.[17] There is no evidence in the record (at least at this point) that demonstrates that the tribal council ever considered such action, much less authorized it.

Due process, particularly in the civil (as opposed to the criminal) context, contains two broad constitutive elements: notice and the opportunity to be heard. It is also significant to note in this regard that the courts have generally held that due process (and equal protection) clauses of the Indian Civil Rights Act of 1968 need not mirror the exact same substantive content of these clauses under the fifth and fourteenth amendments to the U.S. Constitution. Nevertheless, it is generally required that (procedural) due process be grounded in some *factual* dispute. This requirement is clearly met in the case at bar. For example plaintiffs allege that some defendants did *not* meet the requirements relative to permissive debt loads and/or processing sufficient numbers of cattle called for by the tribal grazing resolution.[20]

The guarantee of due process, while recognizing different situations may call for different procedures, has consistently required fair and impartial means. One element of fairness and impartiality has been the standard that decision makers have no pecuniary interest or otherwise be competitors of the aggrieved party. The potential problem here is therefore apparent. May the tribal council in its capacity as the actual decision makers in hearing claims of a denial of due process fairly discharge its responsibility when some of its members *may* have a direct pecuniary or competitive interest vis-á-vis an individual (aggrieved) claimant for the very same lease unit awarded to a member of the council? Of course, it is well to note that tribal approaches to this problem face significant technical and fiscal constraints not otherwise apparent in the federal context and there are, likely, other ways of avoiding the potential problem. Although this issue is not directly raised in the motion to dismiss, it nevertheless is one that is likely to be confronted in any future proceeding.

The element of notice that inheres in the concept and guarantee of due process is not subject to precise definition. Rather it varies with circumstance. As noted by the Supreme Court, "An elementary and fundamental requirement of due process in a proceeding which is to be accorded finality is notice reasonably calculated, under all the circumstances, to apprise interested parties of the pendency of the action and afford them an opportunity to present their objections." Relevant here, of course, is likely to be the level of general and actual awareness of the alleged tribally sanctioned "traditional"

---

special meeting was actually voted on. *See also* the minutes of Regular Tribal Business Council Meeting of March 9, 1995 . . . at which some aggrieved applicants . . . were heard. Needless to say, the picture that emerges is less than pristine in its clarity.

17. *See, e.g.,* art. III, §2 of the Three Affiliated Tribe's Constitution and Bylaws which states: "Special meetings may be called by the Chairman or by any three Councilmen who shall notify all members of the council at least twenty-four (24) hours before the time of convening such meeting unless a majority of the Council approves a shorter call in an emergency."

20. *See* Resolution 94-40-DSB which states, for example, in relevant part, that "Qualified applicants can secure an allocation of grazing privileges; provided the application owns 40% of the livestock to be grazed on the unit with an approved plan to reach 80% ownership of carrying capacity within three (3) years."

due process that is not (apparently) envisioned to require the tribal government to provide anyone with specific, individual notice.

In the area of deprivation of governmental benefits, the Supreme Court has most often used a balancing test to determine whether the individual interest merits a specific procedure in view of its cost to the government and society in general. This balancing test is particularly appropriate in the tribal context which, as noted above, is subject to unique constraints of fiscal resources and institutional development. In addition, it is important to insure that the tribal sovereign has the opportunity to *fully* articulate why the process (if any) that it provides comports favorably with the kind of balancing test suggested here. That is, a kind of balancing subtle to nuance and local adaptation and not the broad replicative strokes of federal standards. Also, a balancing that recognizes that the process due to an aggrieved *applicant* as compared to an aggrieved range unit *permittee* or *lease holder* may well be different.

By way of summary, tribal applicants for range unit leases are entitled to due process under the Indian Civil Rights Act of 1968. The lineaments of such due process include the basic elements of fairness, notice, and an appropriate balancing of individual and (tribal) government interests to determine the adequacy of the procedure provided. The facts pertinent to these elements are barely discernible at this stage of the litigation and shall be appropriately developed at a trial on the merits.

Two other matters bear mention at this time. This action is not (and the parties have not argued to the contrary) barred by the doctrine of sovereign immunity. The Three Affiliated Tribal Constitution contains an express — albeit limited — waiver of sovereign immunity. At art. VI §3(b), the constitution states:

> The people of the Three Affiliated Tribes, in order to achieve a responsible and wise administration of this sovereignty delegated by this Constitution to the Tribal Business Council, hereby specifically grant to the Tribal Court the authority to enforce the provisions of the Indian Civil Rights Act, 25 U.S.C. §1301, et seq., including the award of injunctive relief only against the Tribal Business Council if it is determined through a adjudication that the Tribal Business Council has in a specific instance violated that Act.

Note, however, that this waiver also explicitly limits potential remedies to *injunctive* relief only. Therefore the plaintiffs, if they prevail on the merits, will be entitled only to said relief and the court will be so limited in this regard.

In addition, it is noted that Bureau of Indian Affairs is not a named party in this lawsuit and whatever relief, if any, administrative or otherwise, that might be available, here (or elsewhere) against it is not currently before this court and the Bureau of Indian Affairs is not — at least at this point in the litigation — considered an indispensable party. . . .

[T]he court specifically orders the implementation of the following to comply with the . . . opinion and order.

1. That the Tribal Business Council of the Three Affiliated Tribes will meet in a special session to consider the appeals, written or otherwise, of each

plaintiff, in regard to each range unit for which any plaintiff submitted a written application to the tribal business council

... and which was not allocated as an entire unit to an individual plaintiff. ...

2. That the plaintiffs through their counsel will be provided at least ten (10) days written notice of the special meeting.

3. That any council member who has applied for any range unit for which one or more of the plaintiffs applied, or who has an "immediate family member" who applied for any range unit in which one or more of the plaintiffs applied, will not participate in any way concerning the decision of the tribal business council on the appeal of that plaintiff or plaintiffs. ... The phrase "immediate family member" includes mother, father, son, daughter, brother and in-laws of the same degree; and

4. That the tribal business council will use the following procedure when conducting the appeal for each contested range unit:

> (a) Each plaintiff will be allowed sufficient time to present relevant information, in the form of written documents and/or oral testimony, with or without an attorney, about their application and the reasons why his or her application should be reconsidered as improperly denied.
>
> (b) Regarding each appeal, the tribal business council will consider only such information that was available at the time of the initial consideration of the range unit applications.
>
> (c) The tribal business council may, either during or after the presentation ..., request from, or consider relevant information presented to it by the individual or individuals to whom the range unit was initially allocated. Such information shall be limited in scope as specified in subparagraph (b), above.

NOTE

In *In re Certified Question from U.S. District Court for the District of Arizona*, 3 Am. Tribal Law 497, 8 Navajo Rep. 132 (Navajo Nation Supreme Court 2001), acting Chief Justice Raymond Austin held that a tribal council resolution ordering Navajo agencies to take certain action was not legislation and could not be retroactive:

> Our concern is that under 2 N.N.C. §164(D)(1) (April 22, 1997), the authorities who are required to review proposed resolutions, and most particularly the Attorney General and the Legislative Counsel, must "Determine whether each proposed resolution is legally sufficient." The precise question posed to us by the United States District Court for the District of Arizona is whether or not the Council's resolution retroactively applies to Jolene Nez and her cause of action. We hold that it does not, because there would have been significant issues implicating her rights under the Navajo Nation Bill of Rights which would have to have been considered to make such a resolution "legally sufficient." ...
>
> While the Navajo Nation Council "recognizes" existing state and Navajo Nation statutory law as the exclusive remedy for worker injuries, Resolution

No. CJA-18-00, Resolved Cl. No. 2, there is no reference to any title in the Navajo Nation Code or any provision of the Navajo Nation Workers' Compensation Act, and the language is not underscored, indicating "new language" for a "new law." 2 N.N.C. §165. The word "recognize" is precatory ("should") policy language, while the word "declare" would have been the kind of language we would expect to find in a statute.

Finally, the Navajo Nation President has the power to "[v]eto legislation passed by the Navajo Nation Council" and no evidence was presented to this Court that the president reviewed Resolution No. CJA-18-00 pursuant to 2 N.N.C. §1005(C)(10) (1995 ed.) (this section gives the president veto power). That also tells us that this resolution is not legislation, so it does not have the weight of statutory law.

8 Navajo Rep. at 140.

4. REMOVAL OF TRIBAL JUDGES

TURTLE MOUNTAIN JUDICIAL BOARD v. TURTLE MOUNTAIN BAND OF CHIPPEWA INDIANS

Turtle Mountain Band of Chippewa Indians Court of Appeals,
No. 04-007 (June 15, 2005)

Before: Justices JERILYN DECOTEAU, MATTHEW L. M. FLETCHER[*] and MONIQUE VONDALL.

By Justice FLETCHER for a unanimous Court.

I. Facts and Procedural History

On May 13, 2004, the Duly Elected and Certified Judicial Board of the Turtle Mountain Band of Chippewa Indians (hereinafter "Judicial Board") "immediately suspend[ed] Tribal Court Administrator/Special Tribal Judge Shirley Cain with pay during the impeachment investigation and impeachment proceedings beginning on May 17, 2004." Duly Elected and Certified Judicial Board of the Turtle Mountain Band of Chippewa Indians Resolution #04-05-101-JB at 1 (May 14, 2004) (hereinafter "Judicial Board Resolution"). The Judicial Board Resolution provided that Judge Cain would be provided with a "Summons and Complaint as her written notice." *Id*. This "Complaint" would "enumerate the impeachment charges against . . . Judge . . . Cain. . . ." *Id*. The Judicial Board Resolution noted that Judge Cain "shall have twenty (20) days to provide the Judicial Board with her Answer." *Id*. In the record, there is no copy of a "Complaint" as contemplated by the Judicial Board Resolution and it appears likely that no such "Complaint" ever existed.

Instead of a "Complaint," the Judicial Board served the Judicial Board Resolution onto Judge Cain on May 17, 2004 at 4:31 p.m. . . . The Judicial Board Resolution itself, however, states that Judge Cain "is hereby notified that she is to cease and desist from attending work and the Turtle Mountain Tribal Court

---

[*] *Disclosure:* The author of this book participated in the case as a sitting appellate judge, and wrote the opinion.

in any capacity." . . . The Judicial Board Resolution further noted that the Judicial Board would hold Judge Cain in contempt if she "failed to obey." . . .

It appears that the Judicial Board anticipated that the twenty days allowed for Judge Cain to file her "Answer" would begin to run on May 17, 2004. Before the expiration of those twenty days, however, the Turtle Mountain Band of Chippewa Indians (hereinafter "Band") initiated this proceeding in Tribal Court on June 4, 2004.

The Band in its Complaint for Injunctive Relief . . . sought an injunction that would prohibit the Board from "the suspension of Tribal Court judges in violation of Judicial Board rules" and vacate the Judicial Board Resolution. . . .

After a June 23, 2004 hearing, Associate Special Judge El Marie Conklin issued a Memorandum Decision and Order on June 29, 2004 . . . substantially granting the relief requested by the Band. . . .

On or about July 1, 2004, the Judicial Board filed a request to appeal with this Court, along with a request for a stay of execution, and a brief in support. . . .

. . . The Judicial Board had represented to this Court that Mr. Eugene L. DeLorme was a primary drafter of Article XIV and much of the tribal code. The Judicial Board also represented to this Court that it would ask Mr. DeLorme to file an Amicus Brief in this matter on the intent of the drafters of Article XIV. On or about May 10, 2005, the Judicial Board filed its Brief on Appeal and Mr. DeLorme filed an Amicus Brief. . . .

III. The Validity of the Judicial Board's Actions

A. Standard of Reviewing the Issuance of Injunctive Relief

This Court must first determine the appropriate standard of review in this matter. Since the Band sought and received an injunction from the tribal court, we must review whether the tribal court's issuance of injunctive relief was appropriate. The issuance of injunctive relief is a question of law. *Cf. Youvella v. Dallas*, No. 99AP000008, 2000.NAHT.0000004, at ¶20 (Hopi Ct. App., Nov. 6, 2000) (holding that the issuance of a writ of mandamus is a question of law). Tribal appellate courts generally review a tribal court's conclusions of law under a *de novo* standard. *See LaFountaine-Gladue v. Ojibwe Indian School*, No. 94-003, at 3 (Turtle Mountain Band Ct. App., Aug. 1996) ("This Court reviews the grant of summary judgment *de novo*. . . ."); *Rose v. Adams*, No. CIV-APP 95-27, 2000.NACT.0000005, at ¶14 (Crow Ct. App., Jan. 11, 2000). The *Rose* Court conducts an "independent review" of questions of law. *Id.* We concur with these conclusions. As such, this Court holds that it will conduct an independent review of the tribal court's issuance of injunctive relief under a *de novo* standard, granting no special deference to the tribal court's conclusions of law.

B. The Judicial Board's Actions Are Unconstitutional

We hold today that the Judicial Board's actions in attempting to summarily suspend Judge Cain are not on sound constitutional footing. We therefore affirm the ruling of the tribal court that the Judicial Board could not suspend Judge Cain without first providing her adequate notice and a meaningful opportunity to be heard.

1. Due Process Rights of Sitting Tribal Court Judges

The purpose of the enactment of Article XIV by the People of the Turtle Mountain Band community was "[t]o provide for a separate branch of government free from political interference and conflicts of interest for the development and enhancement of the fair administration of justice." TURTLE MOUNTAIN BAND CONST. art. XIV, §1. The Judicial Branch of the Turtle Mountain Band government consists of "the Turtle Mountain Appellate Court, the Tribal Court, the Judicial Board and the elected officials, appointees and employees of said courts." TURTLE MOUNTAIN BAND CONST. art. XIV, §2. Given that the Turtle Mountain Band Constitution did not contain an enumerated listing of individual rights, it appears that one of the purposes of amending the Constitution to include Article XIV was to expressly incorporate notions of due process, equal protection, and other individual rights exemplified by the Indian Civil Rights Act (25 U.S.C. §1302). *See* TURTLE MOUNTAIN BAND CONST. art. XIV, §3(a) ("The Judicial Branch of government . . . shall have jurisdiction . . . to ensure due process, equal protection, and protection of rights arising under the Indian Civil Rights Act of 1968. . . ."); *see also* [Letter from Gene DeLorme to Paul W. Picotte, BIA, at 2 (May 17, 1995)[7] (hereinafter "DeLorme Letter")] at 2 (noting that the intent of Article XIV was to incorporate the individual rights protections of the Indian Civil Rights Act into the Constitution).

Given this Court's mandate under Article XIV, we have repeatedly held inviolate the notion that individuals are entitled to due process prior to the taking of their liberty or property by the Turtle Mountain Band government. *E.g., Monette v. Schlenvogt,* No. TMAC 04-2021, at 3-4 (Turtle Mountain Band Ct. App., March 31, 2005) (holding that an individual is entitled to notice of court proceedings prior to being evicted from her home); *St. Germain v. PKG Contracting, Inc.,* No. TMAC 03-005, at 3 (Turtle Mountain Band Ct. App., [2003]) (holding that a notice of appeal must be dismissed for violation of procedural due process if the notice is not served on the opposing party); *Mathiason v. Gate City Bank,* No. TMAC 04-2002, at 10-12 (Turtle Mountain Band Ct. App., Feb. 1, 2005) (holding that the tribal court is obligated to provide "notice and an opportunity to be heard" before issuing a judgment against a party); *Lenoir v. Monette,* No. CIV-02-0039, at 9-10 (Turtle Mountain Band Ct. App., July 2, 2002) (holding that elected officials of the Turtle Mountain Band are entitled to due process prior to being removed for cause); *Monette v. Lenoir,* No. [TMAC docket no. not available], at 4 (Turtle Mountain Band Ct. App., May 22, 2002) (same); *Parisien v. Turtle Mountain Judicial Board,* No. TMAC-96-025, at 4 (Turtle Mountain Band Ct. App., Oct. 1996) (holding that the Judicial Board may not suspend a tribal judge without providing due process).

---

7. We are mindful of the interpretation of the "actual cases and controversies" language given by Eugene L. DeLorme, our Amicus Curiae, on Amendment XI to the Turtle Mountain Band Constitution, approved on November 3, 1992 and codified as Article XIV in the mid-1990s. *See* DECOTEAU, *supra,* at 116 (reprinting the amendment). Mr. DeLorme wrote this letter after the amendment had already been approved and, as such, we do not and cannot consider his interpretation to be the definitive legislative history of Article XIV, but this Court gives his opinion some deference as persuasive authority.

Following this line of authority, this Court has already made a clear statement that the Judicial Board must provide due process to sitting tribal court judges before taking action to suspend those judges. *See Parisien, supra*, at 4. This Court has held, "[T]he Judicial Board has the constitutional authority to suspend tribal judges *provided due process of law is provided." Id.* (emphasis added). Other tribal courts faced with the question of whether tribal judges should be afforded due process prior to being suspended agree. *E.g., In re Matter of CLB 0201*, No. 02-01, 2002.NACT.0000004, at ¶¶67-68 (Crow Ct. App., March 5, 2002).

We hold that the process due a tribal court judge facing suspension or any other disciplinary action, including impeachment, must be extensive and comprehensive and must be strictly complied with by the prosecuting authority. As one other tribal court noted, "It is axiomatic that as the consequences of harm increase, the burden of *strict compliance* with procedural and substantive form likewise increases." *Chitimacha Housing Authority v. Martin*, No. CV-93-0006, 1994.NACH.0000002, at ¶18 (Chitimacha Ct. App., Sept. 1, 1994) (emphasis added). The protection of the Turtle Mountain Band's Judicial Branch from the political machinations of the tribal government, be it Tribal Chairman, Tribal Council, Judicial Board, or whatever, is paramount. As Article XIV expressly states, the primary purpose of Article XIV is "[t]o provide for a separate branch of government *free from political interference.* . . . " Turtle Mountain Band Const. art. XIV, §1 (emphasis added). *Cf.* DeLorme Letter, *supra*, at 2 (discussing Article XIV, §3(b), which authorizes the Judicial Branch to develop an independent operating budget, and opining that "[t]he purpose of this section and the associated intent was to truly establish a [sic] independent tribal court. This section was adamantly added by the tribal council in that they recognized that if they controlled the purse strings, you would never have a *truly independent judicial branch of government.*") (emphasis added). And, although we recognize that the Judicial Board—and only the Judicial Board—is empowered by the Turtle Mountain Band Constitution to oversee the tribal and appellate courts, we must also acknowledge that the Judicial Board is an elected, political body. *See* Turtle Mountain Band Const. art. XIV, §6(c). In order to give meaning to both Section 1, which demands that the Judicial Branch remain free from political interference, and to Section 6, which authorizes an elected body to oversee the tribal and appellate courts, we will therefore require that the Judicial Board strictly comply with its own procedures *and* with the Constitution's procedural due process requirements. . . .

3. The Process Provided to Judge Cain upon Her Suspension Was Insufficient to Meet Constitutional Requirements

The Judicial Board Resolution purporting to suspend Judge Cain failed to meet the due process required under the Turtle Mountain Band Constitution and must be declared invalid insofar as it purports to operate as a summary suspension of Judge Cain. As this Court has continuously reaffirmed, "The basic tenants of due process of law are notice and an opportunity to be heard." *Mathiason, supra*, at 10 (citing *Smith v. Belcourt School District #7*, No. 02-10155, at 2 (Turtle Mountain Band Ct. App., Nov. 30, 2004)). We have held that the notice must be "adequate or reasonable," sufficient "to apprise interested parties of the pendency of the action. . . ." *Monette v. Schlenvogt, supra*, at 3 (citation and quotation marks omitted); *see Chitimacha Housing Authority, supra*, at ¶¶99-105. Moreover, "[r]easonable notice must be given at each new step in the proceedings." *Monette v. Schlenvogt, supra*, at 3 (citation omitted). The Judicial Board Rules on notice, contained in Rule 5(b) (notice of preliminary investigation); Rule 7 (notice of institution of formal proceedings); and Rule 9 (notice of setting of time and place for hearing), meet these constitutional requirements on their face. For example, Rule 5(a) requires the Judicial Board to provide notice to the judge "of the investigation, the nature of the charge, and the name of the [accuser]"; and Rule 7 requires the Judicial Board to provide a notice "specify[ing] in ordinary and concise language the charges against the judge . . . and the alleged facts upon which those charges are based. . . ." If the Judicial Board complies with these Rules, then the judge likely will be given adequate due process.

In this matter, however, we hold that the Judicial Board did not comply with these constitutional requirements. Initially, we hold that the Judicial Board's Resolution suspending Judge Cain does not meet the constitutional requirements for reasonable notice articulated in our *Monette v. Schlenvogt* opinion. The Judicial Board Resolution merely states that Judge Cain is "immediately suspend[ed]" and offers nothing to show why. . . . Moreover, the resolution promises that a "Summons and Complaint" that "will enumerate the impeachment charges" would follow. *See id.* No such "Summons and Complaint" is to be found in the record. As such, the Judicial Board did not provide adequate or reasonable notice to Judge Cain of the charges against her.

Moreover, the Judicial Board did not follow its own Rules, further supporting our finding that the Judicial Board violated Judge Cain's due process rights. An agency's violation of its own procedural rules is presumptive evidence that the agency has violated the due process rights of an accused. *See Chitimacha Housing Authority, supra*, at ¶94 ("At a minimum, due process . . . requires the [tribal agency] to follow its own rules and regulations."). Judicial Board Rule 5(a) requires the Judicial Board to provide notice to the judge "of the investigation, the nature of the charge, and the name of the [accuser]." None of this information is present in the Judicial Board Resolution or any other document served on Judge Cain. As such, we find that the Judicial Board's actions violated Judge Cain's right to due process.

4. Judicial Board Rule 22 Is Unconstitutional

We reach one other question that neither party has explicitly addressed — whether the Judicial Board acted in compliance with Judicial Board Rule 22 and, if so, whether Rule 22 is constitutionally sound. We grant the benefit of the doubt to the Judicial Board where it apparently assumed that it had authority to suspend Judge Cain "immediately." . . . Judicial Board Rule 22 appears to operate as an attempt by the Judicial Board to exert the authority to suspend a judge "while an investigation and/or disciplinary action is pending" if the Judicial Board "deems there is probable cause to believe that it is in the best interests of the Tribe. . . ."

We hold that Judicial Board Rule 22 is facially invalid under the Turtle Mountain Band's constitutional law. This Court has already ruled in *Parisien* that, *prior* to suspending a tribal court judge, the Judicial Board must provide due process of law. After proper notice is given, we have made clear in this context that, at a bare minimum, a judge should be provided with "ample opportunity to call witnesses and cross-examine the Board's witnesses. . . ." *Parisien, supra,* at 4; *see also Hoopa Valley Indian Housing Authority v. Gerstner,* 22 Indian L. Rptr. 6002, 6005 (Hoopa Valley Ct. App., Sept. 27, 1992) (holding that a meaningful opportunity to be heard includes four minimum rights: "(1) adequate notice; (2) a hearing decision by [an] independent arbiter; (3) an initial burden of proof imposed on the [accuser]; and (4) the right to confront and cross-examine those witnesses used against the [accused]"). Even assuming the Judicial Board complied with the terms of Judicial Board Rule 22, which is doubtful given that no valid investigation had begun in accordance with Judicial Band Rule 5 when the Judicial Board suspended Judge Cain, we find that Rule 22 does not provide "ample" opportunity to call witnesses and cross-examine the Judicial Board's witnesses. In fact, it provides no opportunity to respond at all prior to being suspended.

Moreover, we find that the Judicial Board has no constitutional authority to summarily suspend tribal court judges. We have previously so held in *Parisien, supra,* at 4, but we reiterate our holding to emphasize certain constitutional limitations on the Judicial Board. We note first that there is nothing in Article XIV that grants the Judicial Board the authority to suspend sitting judges.[9] As such, the authority that the Judicial Board exerts in this area is authority that is implied from the Constitution. *See Parisien, supra,* at 4 (finding that the authority of the Judicial Board to "implement" the Judicial Board Rules is sufficient to authorize the Judicial Board to suspend tribal judges) (citing TURTLE MOUNTAIN BAND CONST. art. XIV, §6(b)). We note further that the Judicial Board is not authorized to "regulate the day-to-day activities of the court . . . or to interfere with the administration of justice." TURTLE MOUNTAIN BAND CONST. art. XIV, §6(b). And, because we must interpret the Constitution in light of the express purpose of Article XIV — to protect the judicial branch from "political interference" — we hold that Judicial Board Rule 22 is an unconstitutional exercise of authority by the Judicial Board. The Constitution does not empower the Judicial Board to summarily suspend tribal court judges. . . .

---

9. In fact, our Amicus expressly repudiated in very strong language the notion that the Judicial Board would have the authority to suspend judges under Article XIV, §6:

> [T]here was also no intended grant of authority by this constitutional amendment to grant the judicial board the ability to suspend judges. *The power to suspend interferes with the day to day operation of the tribal court and creates the opportunity to have judges rendered ineffective for political purposes.* This constitutional amendment was intended to grant the judges tremendous authority and autonomy. At the same time, this amendment provided a safety valve in the people by allowing impeachment. *Impeachment, however, was the only intended vehicle for the removal of judges. Again, I must point out that the intent of Article 14 was to remove political influence from the judicial system.* In order to accomplish this, the judges were intended to be granted independence. The impeachment process was intended to be difficult by requiring a formal hearing process with an enhanced burden of proof.

DeLorme Letter, *supra,* at 4 (emphasis added).

This Court strongly suspects that the actual intent of the Turtle Mountain Band community was to deny the Judicial Board the power to suspend tribal judges for the reasons our Amicus suggests, but no party has asked us to revisit our holding in *Parisien,* where we upheld the authority of the Judicial Board to suspend judges upon due process. As such, we make no ruling on that question at this time.

V. Conclusion

We note that this is a matter of fundamental constitutional importance to the Turtle Mountain Band, as the parties and our Amicus have thoroughly demonstrated. We urge the parties, as other tribal courts have done in such critical matters, to "place themselves in the heart of Native American jurisprudence by 'healing, restoring balance and harmony, accomplishing reconciliation, and making social relations whole again.'" *Snowden, supra*, at 12-13 (quoting *Chamberlain v. Peters*, 27 Indian L. Rptr. 6085, 6097 (Saginaw Chippewa Indian Tribe Ct. App., Jan. 5, 2000)). It appears that this dispute is a symptom of a basic lack of communication and understanding between the parties that could easily have been resolved before reaching this forum. We sincerely hope in the future that the parties attempt to resolve their disputes in a non-adversarial forum and manner.

NOTES

1. The Turtle Mountain Band had established a form of judicial independence from the politics of the legislative and executive branches of the tribal government by creating a Judicial Board with significant authority to oversee the tribal courts.
2. Prior to the *Turtle Mountain Band Judicial Board* decision, the Turtle Mountain Band established a formal constitutional convention on July 20, 2001. *See* JERILYN DECOTEAU, TURTLE MOUNTAIN BAND OF CHIPPEWA CONSTITUTION CONVENTION AND REVISION PROCESS, 2001-2002, at 24 (Turtle Mountain Community College Project Peacemaker (2005)). The convention proposed two amended constitutions, both of which were voted down by the tribal electorate. *See id.* at v.

5. REMOVAL OF TRIBAL LEGISLATIVE OR EXECUTIVE OFFICIALS

IN RE MCSAUBY

Grand Traverse Band of Ottawa and Chippewa Indians Tribal Judiciary, No. 97-02-001-CV-JR, 1997 WL 34691849 (July 29, 1997)

MICHAEL PETOSKEY, Chief Judge.

This matter comes before the Tribal Judiciary, sitting en banc, to consider two (2) issues. The first is whether Tribal Councilor, John McSauby, is entitled to court-appointed counsel and, if so, who should pay for the representation. The second issue is whether Tribal Councilor, John McSauby should be removed from office for misconduct. The Judiciary addresses these two (2) issues in that order and enters unanimous decisions on both issues.

I. Court-Appointed Counsel and Attorney Fees:

Preliminary Trial Court Determinations:

The trial court made a preliminary determination that Councilor McSauby should be represented by legal counsel for the following reasons:

(1) Councilor McSauby was confused about how to defend against this removal action because there is another civil proceeding pending against him to rescind the land sale that is at the heart of the current controversy. For one untrained in the law and its processes, it is difficult to separate the two. There is a commonality of facts because the two legal actions arise from the same incident. However, the legal issues are different because the nature of the two actions are completely different. It was clear that Mr. McSauby's lack of understanding and familiarity with the law and judicial process would result with an inability to focus cleanly on the issues as the Court would need to deal with them. The result would have been that the Court itself would have been forced by necessity to be pro-actively involved with guiding the case through the judicial process and, undoubtedly, guiding the defense if unrepresented to ensure fairness, due process, and to just get the appropriate legal arguments before the Court. Surely, that would have appeared to some as the Court being biased. More importantly, the Court itself was uneasy about the prospect of guiding, as its role of being decision-maker requires impartiality. Thus, without the appointment of counsel, the necessity of clearly focused proceedings would have resulted in the decision-maker's role being compromised and the helping hand to move the proceedings being viewed by some as biased. In a case of this importance to the tribal community neither of those consequences are acceptable.

(2) This is a matter of utmost importance to the Tribe. This is the first removal action. How the Tribal Judiciary handles this matter will be legal precedence for future removal actions. Thus, fundamental fairness is viewed not only important to the instant matter but for future matters as well. That being the case, fully-developed facts and legal arguments are important to the Court.

It is clear for the above-mentioned reasons Councilor McSauby would not be able to present either to the Court. This entire matter is an unfortunate happening. The last thing the tribal community needs is for bad law to develop on top of it. Good law results from the parties presenting their cases and arguments well. Otherwise, courts are basing decisions on partial facts and incomplete arguments.

Arguments Against Appointment:

Legal counsel for the Tribal Council presents the Judiciary with the following arguments why Mr. McSauby should not be appointed counsel paid by the Tribe:

(1) Indigent status is a prerequisite for court-appointed counsel;
(2) Tribal court should adopt the so-called "American rule";
(3) There is no constitutional or legislative authorization to pay court-appointed counsel;
(4) It results in adding insult to injury; and
(5) There is no budget authorization to pay court-appointed counsel.

En Banc Determinations Regarding Appointment:

The Tribal Judiciary expressly adopts the reasons cited by the trial court for appointing counsel to represent Mr. McSauby. In addition, there are at least two (2) more reasons for ensuring that Mr. McSauby is represented by legal counsel:

(1) This is an important matter to tribal voters. Councilor McSauby was elected to office. To deprive them of their elected voice is a very serious undertaking. Those who elected him to office are entitled to have their chosen representative be represented by legal counsel.

(2) Tribal Councilors with minority opinions should have protections in a system of checks and balances from a tyranny by Council majority. Checks and balances in government serve to ensure good government. One of checks and balances for Councilor removal is the referral to the Tribal Judiciary, but the check and balance would be incomplete without legal representation because the deck is stacked in favor of the majority. It will be represented by the tribal attorney staff. Tribal attorneys work for the Tribal Council using tribal resources, so tribal resources should also be used to "balance" the "check" against majority reprisals against minority office holders.

The Tribal Judiciary by reasoning as above rejects all five (5) arguments made by counsel for the Tribal Council. All five (5) rejections are based on the reasoning above and respectively follow:

(1) Given that this matter is of the utmost importance to the tribal community as a whole for the reasons cited above, indigent status is not required. If Mr. McSauby has unduly profited, there are other remedies available for tribal redress.

(2) The "American rule" adopted by state and federal courts is rejected in its application to this case. If we are to be just like them, with wholesale adoption of their rules and laws, why do we continue to argue that Indian people have very different perspectives than those of the society that surround us and thus, exercise self-government to incorporate our own values? The Tribal Judiciary's sense of what is fair and why can be different than those of other courts and is, as expressed above, in this case.

(3) The Tribal Court is a court of general jurisdiction. *See* TRIBAL CONSTITUTION, Article V, Sec. 1. As such, it has the inherent power to do whatever is reasonably necessary to fairly resolve any matter that is appropriately before it. This is a constitutional power. Thus, the Tribal Constitution gives the Court the power to do what is reasonably necessary. The Tribal Council's authorization is not necessary.

(4) There was no way of knowing whether insult would be added to injury prior to these matters being heard by the Judiciary. Even at the point of releasing this Opinion, much fact-finding must occur to fairly resolve the civil suit between the Tribe and Mr. McSauby. To this point, the stipulated facts and offers of proof presented to the Judiciary are only the tip of the iceberg.

(5) That there is no budget authorization is a woefully inadequate reason to deny representation by counsel in a matter of this importance to the Band. It seems that the Tribal Council can find resources to do many other things that are not expressly included in prior appropriations.

In this time of relative resource-rich ability to do many things for the community benefit and in light of the reasoning expressed above clearly pointing out the numerous benefits to the community as a whole, the Tribal Council must pay Defendant McSauby's attorney fees and court costs.

FOR ALL OF THE FOREGOING REASONS, reasonable attorney fees and costs are awarded to Councilor McSauby's attorney. A detailed invoice must be submitted to the Tribal Court for its review and approval prior to submission to the Tribal Council for payment.

II. Referral for Removal

The referral to the Tribal Judiciary of the removal from office of Tribal Councilor John McSauby was premised on the suspicion that he might have engaged in misconduct. The En Banc Hearing before the Tribal Judiciary on June 18, 1997 only involved the suspicion of misconduct that implicates violations of the Tribal Constitution and tribal law.

It is both unfortunate and surprising that the conflict-of-interest aspects of this matter went unnoticed by those involved until tribal members brought them to the attention of the Tribal Council. "Red flags" should have been jumping up all over and flapping like crazy. It is also clear that this matter would not have gotten this far if Tribal Council would have: (1) worked more closely with legal staff in order to ensure that Council has the legal guidance it needs; and (2) refrained from using polling forms to conduct business and posted the proposed action for public notice. Legal counsel for the Tribal Council acknowledged that mistakes were made but argued that such should not excuse Councilor McSauby. We agree.

Constitutional Interpretation

The pertinent language upon which the decision of the Tribal Judiciary rests in deciding this matter is: "In carrying out the duties of tribal office, no tribal official . . . shall make **or** participate in making decisions . . .". GTB TRIBAL CONSTITUTION, Article XII, Sec. 1 (bold added for emphasis). The question that must be answered is whether Councilor McSauby either made or participated in making the decision to purchase the land from himself.

The Judiciary expressly gives its definitive interpretation of that language as follows:

(1) ". . . make . . ." means affirmatively voting on the issue; and
(2) ". . . participate in making . . ." means engaging in any activity directed toward any decision-maker to influence, directly or indirectly, a decision which involves a personal financial interest.

The Tribal Judiciary rejects the prevailing interpretation of the conflict-of-interest provision that was argued by both counsel during oral argument at the Hearing on June 18, 1997. The pertinent portion involved in that dominant interpretation is ". . . which require balancing a personal financial interest, other than interests held in common by all tribal members, against the best interests of the Band." GTB TRIBAL CONSTITUTION, Article XII, Section 1. The arguments centered upon whether the personal interest of Councilor McSauby was outweighed by the benefit to the Band. This interpretation is fostered by the word "balancing" which leads some to think that a balancing test is required to ascertain whether there is in fact a conflict-of-interest. We think not. The mere fact a personal financial interest is involved is sufficient to create a conflict-of-interest. The benefit to the Band is irrelevant. The word "balancing" simply means that the benefit to the individual must be weighed against the benefit to the Band. The outcome of the balancing is not determinative of a conflict-of-interest. The conflict-of-interest arises because a balancing of Councilor McSauby's personal financial interest against the interest of the Band must occur. Who does the balancing or at what juncture is irrelevant. The promoter of a personal financial interest would not push for action or decision if he/she had not balanced the interests in his/her mind in order to develop the justification to sell the promotion to others. That kind of balancing is inherent in promotion of any personal interest.

Offers of Proof Applied to Constitutional Interpretation:

The Stipulation of Facts and Offers of Proof do not implicate Councilor McSauby in actually casting a vote for the land purchase. However, there is much to show that he actively engaged in promotion of the land purchase to the other members of the Tribal Council, that he pushed the process to make the ultimate decision, and that he influenced the decision. Councilor McSauby's offer of proof is very telling. He offers to prove that he:

(1) discussed the project with individual Tribal Councils [sic] members, the Tribal Chairman and aggregates of Tribal Council members;

(2) subsequently met Tribal Council members to present proposed plans, an itemization of costs and benefits, the engineering site plans, marketing analysis, and discussed the status of the project through several conversation [sic];

(3) took a proposed polling voting form that he prepared to the Tribal Chairman's office;

(4) presented the polling form to a Tribal Council member at a subsequent Gaming Commission Meeting for that Council member's vote;

(5) met with another Council member, who was about to leave town, in order to get her vote;

(6) asked a third Council member to vote;

(7) personally submitted the polling form to the Gaming Commission Accounting Department for the preparation of a check request;

(8) on a later date, December 4, 1996, personally took the signed check request form to the Tribal Chairman's office for his signature, at the request of the Gaming Commission Accounting Department;

(9) returned the signed check request form to the Gaming Commission Accounting Department;

(10) signed the check issued by the Gaming Commission Accounting Department to Leelanau Title Company to purchase the land; and

(11) delivered the signed check to the Leelanau Title Company closing officer.

All of the above are conflict-of-interest activities. (1) through (6) are misconduct in violation of the constitutional prohibition of participating in the making of a decision. (7) through (10) are activities that demonstrate Councilor McSauby's personal financial interest in seeing the deal through. Normally, the (7) through (10) activities are ones which would be handled administratively which points out that this entire matter was handled outside of procedural norms. Councilor McSauby's land sale to the Band was not placed on any Tribal Council agenda for presentation, discussion, consideration, public input, or Tribal Council decision. Those who serve the Tribe can be reasonably expected by its membership to operate within commonly accepted government and administrative procedures. The Judiciary understands that the Tribal Council has taken steps to ensure procedural safeguards for the future by the adoption of the "Tribal Council Meetings Ordinance". It is a good step in the right direction. The Tribal Constitution is clear about open meetings, public notice of meetings, a reasonable opportunity to be heard, and that the Tribal Council shall act only by ordinance, resolution, or motion.

The tribal community has every right to expect that tribal officials and employees will avoid conflicts-of-interest. Tribal members have a right to loyal service and fulfillment of confidence placed in officials and employees. Tribal officials have a fiduciary responsibility to tribal membership. Good government will require that even the appearance of a conflict-of-interest be avoided. In that regard, the Tribal Council is urged to seriously consider the adoption of a code of ethics for tribal official and employee conduct to provide additional guidance beyond that offered in this Opinion.

Removal Authority

Councilor McSauby was referred to the Tribal Judiciary for removal because it was suspected that he might have engaged in misconduct. Having found that there was indeed misconduct, the Tribal Judiciary finds grounds for removal. Having found that grounds for removal exist, the Judiciary must remove Councilor McSauby from office. The removal is mandated under Article VIII, Sec. 2(f) of the Tribal Constitution.

FOR ALL OF THE FOREGOING REASONS, IT IS THE FURTHER ORDER OF THE TRIBAL JUDICIARY that Councilor John McSauby be removed from office. . . .

NOTES

1. In *Coalition for Fair Government II v. Lowe*, 1 Am. Tribal Law 145 (Ho-Chunk Nation Trial Court 1997), the court enjoined a special election called to replace removed tribal council members on grounds that the entity serving notices of removal of council members had no such authority:

    First and foremost, the Notices were deficient because they were prepared and served by people without any authority to prepare and serve such notices. The General Council has never given the authority to issue charges of malfeasance to the GCPC. . . . The Notices were apparently prepared by the General Council Planning Committee [GCPC], on April 23, 1996 although the conscious absence of the GCPC makes it impossible to determine this with certainty.

The GCPC is a committee of Tribal members who serve in a capacity to assist the operation of the General Council by among other things, securing the site, arranging for meals, ceremonial openings and payments of costs associated with holding the General Council and setting a proposed agenda. The GCPC exists through a delegation of authority from the HCN Legislature and has no independent authority that has not been delegated to it from either the Legislature or a General Council itself. . . . No minutes or official actions of any General Council were ever produced showing a delegation of authority to the GCPC or to the server of the Notices, Sanford Decorah, despite the self serving announcement of that fact by the drafters of the Notice itself.

Id. at 163.

2. In *Youvella v. Dallas*, 2 Am. Tribal Law 369 (Hopi Appellate Court 2000), the court held that a suit brought by removed tribal council members against the tribal treasurer seeking payment due the council members was not barred by sovereign immunity:

Respondents would have us believe that a voice vote on a motion whose meaning, on its face, is ambiguous, could be converted into "direction" to the Secretary and Treasurer to stop payment to Appellants. . . .

Official action of such magnitude often has serious consequences for all parties involved and, therefore, ought to be accompanied by a greater degree of procedural formality than the voice vote to ensure the parties understand precisely what action has been taken. In this case, the Council could easily have formalized their decision about Appellants' status, but failed to do so. Subsequent actions of the Council, while indicative that Council no longer considered Appellants to be members of the Council, do little to cure the lack of formality with which they made their initial decision. We are not prepared to instruct the Council as to the exact standard, but we find that on these facts that Council's actions were insufficiently formal and insufficiently clear to constitute direction to the Secretary and Treasurer to stop payments to Appellants.

Id. at 372-73.

D. TRIBAL SOVEREIGN IMMUNITY

Deckrow v. Little Traverse Bay Bands of Odawa Indians

Little Traverse Bay Bands of Odawa Indians, No. C-006-0398, 1999 WL 35000425
(September 30, 1999)

Michael Petoskey, Chief Judge. . . .

Defendants raise several affirmative defenses in their Answer to Plaintiff's Complaint[, which seeks to disallow results of tribal election]. Those defenses are that: . . .

(2) the claims are barred by the sovereign immunity of the Defendant; . . .

The Court will address these defenses one-by-one: . . .

(2) The claims are barred by sovereign immunity — Defendant argues that it is immune from suit because it is a federally-recognized Indian tribe. Indian tribes enjoy sovereign immunity under federal law unless the immunity has been expressly waived by the U.S. Congress or by the tribe itself. The issue that must be addressed by courts is whether there has been an express waiver either by Congress or the Tribe.

Sovereign immunity is an English-law doctrine that "the king can do no wrong." One cannot sue the king. This ancient doctrine came to this country with the adoption of English law as the legal foundation for the development of law in the new United States. A new country was superimposed over numerous indigenous Native communities. Each with their own political structure and tribal law. Since that earlier time, many non-Native governments have waived their immunity in various areas to provide redress for government negligence and wrongdoing. Reasons for the various waivers might be generalized to say that the people of a representative democracy realize that "the king" can do wrong and does make mistakes. After all, government is a human institution and the maxim "to err is human" is undisputed. Fundamental fairness requires that there be an opportunity for redress, surely in everyone's book. However on the other hand, governmental immunity ensures that no one can "break the bank" by a bank-breaking award of tribal assets. No one wants to see the government bankrupted. It seems reasonable to expect the Tribal Council to look at these various considerations and develop well-reasoned positions on immunity as it relates to this tribal community. After all, this is not England. We do give a lot of lip service to the fact that Indian communities are different [than] those of dominant society. We point out that our judicial and legal systems need not be mirror-images of those of dominant society. If that is truly the case, why should tribal government adopt the Anglo-American concept of sovereign immunity?

Rather, why shouldn't tribal sovereign immunity mirror tribal culture? It is difficult to imagine that an outdated ancient English doctrine fits this tribe's needs. Importantly, the Court recognizes that these policy questions are political questions that can only be addressed by the Tribe's political body. Thus, the Court respectfully suggests that Tribal Council duly deliberate on these issues, rather than relying on the Tribal Court to simply dismiss everything based upon arguments of sovereign immunity.

ARTICLE VIII of the Tribe's Interim Constitution entitled "Bill of Rights" expressly provides that members have ". . . the right to petition for action or the redress of grievances. . . ." This is the supreme law of Tribe because the Tribal Constitution is the supreme law. It is the peoples' expression of its delegation of power to the government. The right to petition for action or redress would be rendered meaningless if sovereign immunity is deemed to be a bar. If the provision is meaningless, why the expression of a right? Why bother? The expression must have a purpose, otherwise the language would not be included. Thus, the Court construes the cited constitutional provision to be an express waiver of sovereign immunity by the Tribe. Whether the "Bill of Rights" provision of the Interim Tribal Constitution is construed a reservation of the power in the people or a waiver of immunity by those who drafted its provisions is not significant for the purposes of deciding the instant matter. It is still an express waiver. For all of the foregoing, sovereign immunity is not a bar to this action. . . .

FOR ALL OF THE FOREGOING, this Honorable Court rejects all of the Defendant's arguments and denies the Defendant's Motion to Dismiss. This Court will schedule this matter for a hearing on the merits.

NOTES[*]

1. In an earlier opinion in the same case, Judge Petoskey pondered the dilemma posed to tribal courts about sovereign immunity under Tribal law and suggested that the Tribal government must deliberate carefully on its application. *Deckrow v. Little Traverse Bay Bands of Odawa Indians*, No. C-006-0398, slip op. at 4-5 (Little Traverse Bay Bands Tribal Ct., Feb. 22, 1999).

    The *Deckrow* decisions came down under an "Interim" tribal constitution that the Little Traverse community replaced in 2002 with a permanent constitution. Article XVIII of that document governs the sovereign immunity of tribe:

    > **A. Tribal Immunity from Suit**
    > The Little Traverse Bay Bands of Odawa Indians, including all subordinate entities, shall be immune from suit except to the extent that the Tribal Council clearly and expressly waives its sovereign immunity, and officials and employees of the Tribe acting within the scope of their duties or authority shall be immune from suit.

    > **B. Suit against Officials and Employees**
    > Officials and employees of the Little Traverse Bay Bands of Odawa Indians who act beyond the scope of their duties and authority shall be subject to suit in Tribal Court for purposes of enforcing rights and duties established by this Constitution or other applicable laws.

    CONSTITUTION OF THE LITTLE TRAVERSE BAY BANDS OF ODAWA INDIANS art. XVIII (2002).

2. As a matter of both tribal and federal law, Indian Tribes possess sovereign immunity. *Santa Clara Pueblo v. Martinez*, 436 U.S. 49 (1978). *E.g., Martin v. Hopi Tribe*, 25 Indian L. Rep. 6185, 6187 (Hopi Tribe Ct. App. 1996); *McCormick v. Election Committee of the Sac & Fox Tribe*, 1980 WL 128844 (Court of Indian Offenses for Sac & Fox Tribe 1980). "When a tribe or its agencies are sued in tribal court, the scope, protection, and meaning of tribal sovereign immunity are governed primarily by tribal, rather than federal or state, law, although other bodies of doctrine may be looked to for guidance by analogy." *Thompson v. Cheyenne River Sioux Tribe Board of Police Commissioners*, 23 Indian L. Rep. 6045, 6046 (Cheyenne River Sioux Ct. App. 1996).

    Sovereign immunity is an important element to the efficient development of Tribal government and is "necessary to promote 'tribal self-determination,

---

[*]*Author's Note:* Some of the material in the notes appears in Matthew L. M. Fletcher, *Tribal Court Conundrum*, 38 U. MICH. J. L. REFORM 273 (2005).

economic development, and cultural autonomy.'" *Martin v. Hopi Tribe*, 25 Indian L. Rptr. 6185, 6187 (Hopi Tribe Ct. App. Mar. 29, 1996). As one Tribal Court wrote, "[S]overeign immunity [is] an essential attribute of Indian tribes and [is] to be highly supported unless clearly waived. It serves to avoid interruption of tribal government and agents in improper law suits and to protect public funds from improper distribution under the Tribal Constitution." *DeVerney v. Grand Traverse Band of Ottawa & Chippewa Indians*, 2000 WL 35749822, at *2 (Grand Traverse Band Court of Appeals 2000). *See also Sturgeon Electric Co. v. AHA MACA Power Service*, 26 Indian L. Rptr. 6026, 6027-28 (Fort Mojave Indian Reservation Court of Appeals 1998) ("Immunity is a fundamental aspect of sovereignty which protects a government from suit to avoid undue intrusion on governmental functions or depletion of the government's assets without the government's consent."). Sovereign immunity prevents depletion of valuable common resources and protects against litigation interfering with the operation of the Tribe. *See Guardipee v. Confederated Tribes of Grand Ronde Cmty. of Or.*, 19 Indian L. Rptr. 6111 (Confederated Tribes of Grand Ronde Cmty. of Or. Tribal Court 1992) ("Moreover, it has been held that tribal sovereign immunity is necessary to preserve and protect tribal assets from claims and judgments that would soon deplete tribal resources.") The influential Navajo Nation Supreme Court agreed:

> The Navajo people are entitled to a representative and accountable Navajo tribal government. For this reason, important decisions having direct consequences on the Navajo tribal treasury should be made by the elected representatives of the Navajo people. If we hold that the ICRA has waived the sovereign immunity of the Navajo Nation in Navajo courts, we will be sanctioning an attack on the tribal treasury. Such decisions are best made by elected Navajo representatives after consultation with their constituents.
>
> In addition, the funds of the Navajo Nation are not unlimited. Each year the funds maintained by the Navajo Nation for the operation of the Navajo tribal government are exceeded by the people's demand for more governmental services. ICRA suits which result in money damages against the Navajo Nation will only divert funds allocated for essential governmental services.

Johnson v. Navajo Nation, 14 Indian L. Rptr. 6037 (Navajo Nation Supreme Court 1987). See also *Gonzales v. Allen*, 17 Indian L. Rptr. 6121, 6122 (Shoshone-Bannock Tribal Court 1990) ("The legislative and executive branches of government have the responsibility for determining the purposes and the extent to which government funds will be utilized. Absent explicit waiver of such authority the courts do not usually have the authority to spend such funds. Nor do the courts have authority to waive sovereign immunity on behalf of the government.").

Tribal courts generally hold that the concept of sovereign immunity "does not defy Native American traditions. . . ." *Novak Construction Co. v. Grand Traverse Band of Ottawa & Chippewa Indians*, 2001 WL 36194389, at *2 (Grand Traverse Band Court of Appeals 2001). *See also Sulcer v. Barrett*, 17 Indian L. Rptr. 6138, 6139-40 (Citizen Band Potawatomi Indians of Okla. Supreme Court 1990) (Rice, J., concurring) ("While the doctrine of sovereign immunity is admittedly of European origin, it is entirely consistent with the tribal constitution and common law. . . .").

Some tribal courts have explicitly rejected tribal sovereign immunity. *E.g., O'Brien v. Fort Mojave Tribal Ct.,* 11 Indian L. Rptr. 6001, 6002 (Fort Mojave Tribal Ct. Dec. 8, 1983).

3. One prominent Indian law practitioner and commentator argued that some aspects of tribal immunity can hurt Indian communities:

> Tribal sovereignty can be exercised affirmatively or defensively. Affirmative sovereignty is the positive assertion of tribal authority, including the enactment of tribal law, to govern matters within the jurisdiction of a given tribe. Defensive tribal sovereignty involves the use of sovereign immunity to shield tribes, tribal enterprises, and tribal officials from lawsuits or the invocation of legal doctrines to shield tribes, their reservation affairs, and their reservation enterprises from the imposition of state or federal authority. Defensive tribal sovereignty draws, by far, the most media attention, and when tribes, tribal enterprises, or tribal officials appear to avoid liability or accountability, that attention is often negative.
>
> The exercise of affirmative tribal sovereignty can offset the negative perception of defensive tribal sovereignty. Consider, for example, an Indian tribe with a tribal law providing employees with enforceable tribal court remedies for workplace sexual harassment. Such an "affirmative tribe" will be far less vulnerable to media attack when it, or one of its enterprises, prevails in dismissing a federal court action by an employee under Title VII of the Civil Rights Act; for it can point to fair and enforceable tribal law protections for the employee. Similarly, the EEOC or the Department of Labor will be less inclined to push for the imposition of federal employment remedies upon tribes and their enterprises if employees can pursue remedies in tribal court, under tribal law, that are on a par with federal law remedies.
>
> Thus, it can be argued that to stave off negative perceptions of defensive tribal sovereignty, tribes should enact laws, consistent with the values of the tribal community, that protect the health, safety, and welfare of Indians and non-Indians within their jurisdiction; and to do so as well as any state or federal authority would do it if the latter had jurisdiction. . . .
>
> Affirmative sovereignty may also mean taking a long range view of whether to litigate a defensive tribal sovereignty position in the federal courts. Again, considering the adage that bad facts make bad law, this could mean careful consideration of the risks of creating bad precedent for the field of federal Indian law, not just the consequences for the particular case. Is there any "ethical" obligation for a tribal attorney to take into account how a particular case for a particular tribal client might affect federal court precedent in the field of federal Indian law? Surely there is no equivalent obligation in most other fields of law. But federal Indian law is unique. . . .

Kaighn Smith, Jr., *Ethical "Obligations" and Affirmative Tribal Sovereignty: Some Considerations for Tribal Attorneys* at 532, 533-35, *in* 31st Annual Federal Bar Association Indian Law Conference — Active Sovereignty in the 21st Century: Course Materials (April 6-7, 2006).

CHAPTER 4

TRIBAL MEMBERSHIP

The law of tribal membership (the terms "citizenship" and "membership" will be used interchangeably in this book) is the most fundamental to Indian nations. The law of tribal citizenship determines who is an Indian for purposes of eligibility for tribal government and for services and benefits such as housing, health, education, and employment. In recent years, as some Indian nations have chosen to distribute gaming wealth to tribal members, tribal membership has acquired an economic value, sometimes making tribal members incredibly wealthy. This value may have encouraged some Indian nations to pursue the thinning of their membership ranks through disenrollment proceedings. In no short order, tribal citizenship disputes are among the most "bitter" and "heartwrenching" cases, to quote Frank Pommersheim. In other words, such disputes create a civil war of sorts.

Extended family relationships used to form the backbone of traditional American Indian governments—for example, the Anishinaabe family governance—with membership in a community being based on family relationships almost exclusively. The key rules regulating the relationships of these communities, which were very small in number of members, often derived from a clan system. For example, one could not marry into one's own clan, which provided some assurance that one was not marrying a close relative. This meant, for example, that innumerable Anishinaabek would marry outside of their small communities, creating complicated family relationships that extended beyond villages. In this way, to a great extent—since so many Michigan Ottawas from Grand Traverse Bay married Chippewas from Sault Ste. Marie, for example—the family relationships cemented political relationships between the bands. However, residence determined final membership in a community, so that an Anishinaabekwe (Anishinaabe woman) who moved in with her spouse's family in another village became a member of that community, and vice versa.

The classic Anishinaabe example is the story of Leopold Pokagon. Leopold, born into an Ottawa or Ojibwe community in the late eighteenth century in northern lower Michigan, married a Potawatomi woman from the St. Joseph River basin. He moved south to live with her family, which was one of the most prominent families in the region. Leopold developed influence and authority over time, was adopted by the local tribal community, and eventually represented his community in the fateful 1833 treaty council. That treaty resulted in the forced removal of all the Michigan and northern Indiana Potawatomis to Kansas and later Oklahoma—except for Leopold's band, which the United States allowed to remain in Michigan due to his negotiating tactics and skills. And so the federally recognized Indian tribe known as the Pokagon Band of Potawatomi Indians is named after someone who started his life as an Ottawa or Ojibwe Indian.

This traditional form of family and village membership often survived in many Indian nations until the early part of the twentieth century, when the United States began to interject blood quantum requirements into federal-tribal relations. The government accomplished this feat in different ways. First, the United States incorporated blood quantum requirements into treaties. Much treaty language appears to assume that most Indians subject to the treaties were full-blood Indians, but the treaty had provisions for half-blood Indians, likely at the request of the tribal treaty negotiators. From the point of view of Indian leaders, these half-blood Indians were family members. From the point of view of the federal government, these half-blood Indians were problems. They were not true Indians, and might not even be Indians anymore. And they were not white, either. This mixed racial status, combined with requests from the tribal leadership to include them in the benefits of the treaty, appears to have confused U.S. government officials. Moreover, especially during a later treaty council, many of these half-blood Indians participated in the treaty negotiations as English-speaking, educated Indians, making more trouble for the U.S. government treaty commissioners.

Second, the federal government continued to informally recognize many Indian tribes as half-blood Indian communities. Statutes in 1921 and 1924 formalized the duty of the Department of Interior to provide services to all half-blood Indians, and the 1934 Indian Reorganization Act continued this requirement.

Third, after tribal communities would sue the United States for an accounting of treaty annuities promised under various treaties or other claims, the federal government often ordered the creation of a judgment roll for the purpose of paying out the judgment on a per capita basis. These rolls often served to create two classes of individuals: full-bloods and half bloods.

Fourth, and more generally, the federal government conditioned some federal programs on blood quantum.

But the recognition of blood quantum in these areas—and others—has helped to create crises regarding Indian citizenship that undermined the family orientation of Indian tribes and forced the creation of an American-style citizenship regime based on blood quantum, as opposed to tribal membership based on family relationships.

Federal Indian law principles leave tribal membership up to Indian nations. In *Santa Clara Pueblo v. Martinez*, 436 U.S. 49, 72 n.32 (1978), Justice Marshall wrote: "A tribe's right to define its own membership for tribal purposes has long been recognized as central to its existence as an independent political community." But as much of the material in this chapter demonstrates, tribal control over its own membership criteria often is illusory.

A. TRIBAL MEMBERSHIP CRITERIA

GENEALOGY AS CONTINUITY: EXPLAINING THE GROWING
TRIBAL PREFERENCE FOR DESCENT RULES IN MEMBERSHIP
GOVERNANCE IN THE UNITED STATES

Kirsty Gover, 33 Am. Indian L. Rev. 243, 262-73 (2008-2009)

. . .

III. The Federal Concept of Blood Quantum and Its Enduring Influence on Tribes

A. The Indispensability of Indianness in the Federal Conception of Tribes

Notwithstanding the formal autonomy of tribes in membership governance and the rarity of congressional interventions, the federal concepts of Indianness and tribalism have an enduring influence on tribes. It is important, then, to consider the logic underpinning these concepts in federal policy. This helps to show the way tribes have adopted, adapted, and resisted federal preferences in the design of membership rules.

Since the 1930s, federal policy on tribal membership has been organized around the principle that persons should be enrolled in a tribe only if they can be expected to "participate in tribal relations and affairs." . . . In addition to insisting that the relation between members and tribes be political, the federal government also believes that tribes should be comprised of persons who are Indian. When reviewing tribal constitutions, the Department of the Interior has historically acted to "prevent . . . the admission to tribal membership of a large number of applicants of small degree of Indian blood" and has further attempted to limit discretionary adoptions to "person[s] of Indian descent related by marriage or descent to the members of the tribe." Hence the view expressed by the Department's solicitor in 1969 that "[m]embership of non-Indians in the past as 'naturalized citizens' of Indian tribes . . . reflects the political nature of Indian tribes; however, recognition given Indians and Indian tribes by the United States Government is in essence a recognition of race."

Therefore, federal ideology on tribalism has long been dependant on the idea that tribes are politically organized, racially-Indian communities. However, the federal emphasis on Indian blood quantum is a relatively more recent phenomenon. It is commonly assumed that Indian blood quantum was the federal government's preferred membership rule in the IRA era and that it was imposed on the tribes during that period through the Department's drafting and approval of constitutions. In fact, constitutional membership regimes enacted during the IRA era were not heavily reliant on Indian blood quantum. Less than half used a blood-quantum rule, compared to seventy percent today. Instead, blood-quantum rules were only to be deployed as a stand-in where a two-parent enrollment rule or a residency rule could not be used[.] . . . Indian blood rules are more frequently used in tribal constitutions after 1960, where there has been a break in continuity between the recognition of a tribe for IRA purposes and the drafting of a formal constitution.

B. Indian Blood Quantum and the Sovereign Status of Tribes

The federal concept of tribes as politically-organized racially-Indian communities has important normative consequences. From the standpoint of federal policy, if these elements of tribalism are missing or attenuated, the sovereign status of the tribe is jeopardized. . . . According to this logic, a tribe's sovereign status could be withdrawn by an act of Congress or federal court on the grounds that the community is no longer sufficiently tribe-like to exercise tribal sovereignty. The Department's view is revealed in its advice to the Lac Courte Oreilles Band of Lake Superior Chippewa Indians in 1992:

> We share your concern about eliminating the blood quantum in favor of mere descendancy. . . . If there ceases to exist a demonstrable bilateral, political relationship between a tribe and its members, the courts or Congress may well decide that a tribe has so diluted the relationship between a tribal government and its members that it has "self-determined" its sovereignty away.

. . . In the landmark Supreme Court case of *Morton v. Mancari*, [417 U.S. 535 (1974),] legislation directed to "Indians" was found to be shielded from strict scrutiny. . . . The regulation in question (the BIA's hiring preference for Indians) was limited to tribal members of a specified blood quantum, and on this basis, the Court found that it was "not directed towards a 'racial' group consisting of 'Indians'; instead, it applied only to members of 'federally recognized' tribes." Because it operated to "exclude many individuals who are racially to be classified as 'Indians' . . . the preference [was] political rather than racial in nature."

Extrapolating from this finding, the Department asserts that it is the political relationship between tribes and their members that saves special measures for Indians from the category of constitutionally impermissible racial classifications. If the political relationship is lost, so too is the protection of the federal-Indian trust relationship. The tribe becomes a racial association, and all special measures applying to it are rendered suspect. . . . Importantly, the Department considers blood quantum to be a measure of a person's political relationship to the tribe.

Because it constructs blood quantum as evidence of political relations, federal policy contains the prior notion that intra- and inter-tribal endogamy is a display of political affiliation. By implication, exogamous marriage (marriage to a person who is not the descendant of a tribal member) is equated to "out-marriage." In this model, the tribal spouse and his or her children assimilate into a non-Indian community and the non-tribal spouse is not integrated into the tribe. The result is a particular understanding of blood-quantum rules as tied intrinsically to the idea of a tribe as a political entity. . . .

[W]hile the Department has never formally refused to approve an IRA constitution or constitutional amendment on the basis of its over-inclusivity, its position is as follows: "If an amendment to a tribal constitution would change the requirements for membership from those which would evidence some continuing relationship with the tribe or other tribal members to requirements which could evidence only descendancy, the Secretary could in his discretion disprove it." This could occur, for instance, where a tribe seeks to amend its constitution to remove a blood quantum requirement and operate instead with an unqualified lineal descent rule, as was the case in the

Department's 1983 dispute with the Citizen Band of Potawatomi Indians. In this instance, the Department eventually dropped its opposition to the amendment, on the basis that the blood-quantum rule "had been inserted by the BIA in the first place." Two other contentious instances involved newly recognized tribes — the Grand Traverse Band of Ottawa and Chippewa Indians and the Narragansett Tribe of Rhode Island, both of which sought to expand their membership provisions beyond the list of descendants provided to the Department during the acknowledgment process.

The documentary record of the Grand Traverse Band dispute illustrates the anatomy of a dispute involving the assertion of federal policy on tribal membership as a condition of federal acknowledgment. It reveals the federal government's interest in controlling the composition of tribal base rolls, notwithstanding the tribe's formal sovereign authority to admit any person as a member. The Band was the first tribe to be recognized through the regulatory acknowledgments process, and therefore, the negotiations were the first in which competing conceptions of tribal membership had to be formally addressed.

After it was formally acknowledged in 1980, the Band proposed membership criteria for inclusion in its constitution that would have increased the number of persons on the base roll from around 600 to more than 2400. In its negotiations with the Band, the Department urged the adoption of membership rules that would "maintain the integrity of the acknowledgement decision" by ensuring that members were "descended from individuals of the historical Grand Traverse bands" and "have maintained political and community ties to the modern-day tribal entity." The Department provided replacement criteria that limited base enrollment to persons who were on the original petition roll and others of one-fourth Ottawa or Chippewa blood who were lineal descendants of members of the historic Grand Traverse Bands and had "political and community ties to the Band." Correspondence with the Band also shows the Department's insistence that other federal discretions concerning the Band's property were dependant on its adoption of acceptable membership criteria. These included the Department's decision to designate land held in trust as the Band's reservation and the assignment of the band's share of a multi-tribal judgment award. The Band initiated litigation against the Department for its refusal to approve the constitution, but ultimately agreed to modify its proposed base roll in line with the Department's proposals. According to the Department, membership rules were so closely tied to the legitimacy of the acknowledgment decision itself, that if the Band had refused to amend its constitution, the Department would have taken steps to reverse its determination. . . .

IV. Changes in Tribal Membership Governance: The Genealogic Shift

. . .

A. Constitutional Amendments and Membership Path-Dependency

As noted above, there are two epochs of tribal constitutional activity evident in the study: the IRA era (1934-1950) and the early self-determination era (1970-1980), separated by a period of inactivity during the termination-policy era (1950-1970). More than seventy-five percent of tribes in the study adopted a constitution in one of these two periods. The frequency of adoption of new constitutions is at its highest in the 1930s and rises sharply again in the first decade of the self-determination era, beginning in 1970. There is a comparable rise in the frequency of tribal constitutional amendments beginning in the mid-seventies and extending through the mid-eighties.

Just over a third of the current constitutions in the study are second or third iteration constitutions, amended versions of the original document. The distinction between first and second iteration constitutions is an analytically important one. The membership regimes in the post-1970 "new constitutions" and the "second iteration" constitutions do not share the same characteristics. This is because tribes do not generally alter the fundamental structure of their membership regimes when they revise their constitutions. Accordingly, since most of the second-iteration constitutions in the study belong to tribes who first drafted a constitution in the IRA era, the vast majority continue to use the parental-enrollment rules that characterize constitutions drafted in that period. They do not jettison parental-enrollment rules in favor of the lineal descent rules preferred by tribes writing constitutions for the first time after 1970. Instead they tend to keep the parental-enrollment rules and add or subtract additional criteria. Most commonly, they remove a residency rule or require future members to demonstrate tribal or Indian blood in addition to parental enrollment. One explanation for the reluctance to amend parental-enrollment rules is that these establish an unbroken, documented intergenerational link between applicants and base enrollees. Unless other corrective mechanisms are used, switching to lineal descent from a parental-enrollment regime could have two destabilizing effects. First, the status of non-descendant members would be called into question. This class would include persons incorporated into the tribe, such as spouses and adopted children. Second, the descendants of all base-enrollees could become retrospectively eligible for enrollment, whether or not there is a generational break in enrollment. This could require the admittance of an indeterminate and potentially very large class of persons. Tribes consequently tend to favor the addition of tribal blood to a parental-enrollment regime, likely because this approach introduces a tribally-specific descent rule for future members without calling into question the status of existing members. Importantly the number of tribes adding tribal blood rules is more than twice that of tribes imposing Indian blood rules. When tribes choose a blood rule to supplement parental enrollment, they overwhelmingly opt for measures of tribe-specific ancestry.

B. Changes in Membership Governance: Genealogy, Flexibility, and Insularity

The membership rules used by tribes as a class of actors have changed over time. These changes are revealed by observing the distribution of rules amongst constitutions in force within each decade since 1930. The number of tribes with constitutions has more than doubled over the period covered by the study, from 102 to 245. This increase is because new tribes have been recognized since the 1930s and because recognized tribes are increasingly likely to draft and publish written constitutions. The changes are of three basic kinds. First, there are changes in the substantive content of mandatory rules; those criteria that determine the class of persons eligible for membership "as of right." Second, there are changes in the frequency and scope of discretionary rules, allowing the incorporation of persons not qualifying under the mandatory rules; through tribal adoptions and honorary membership. Third, the study shows changes in the frequency of provisions prohibiting multiple membership.

1. Genealogy: Changes in Mandatory Regimes

The most striking change evident in tribal constitutions is the increasingly genealogic quality of tribal membership rules over time. This is revealed in the transition from the use of parental enrollment and residency rules, to lineal descent and blood rules. First, the proportion of tribal constitutions using a lineal descent rule has increased significantly from fifteen percent of tribal constitutions in force before 1941 to forty-four percent of constitutions in force today. In pre-1941 constitutions, the vast majority of tribes use parental-enrollment rules.

Second, the use of blood-quantum rules has increased from forty-four percent of pre-1941 constitutions to seventy-one percent today. The rise in the frequency of tribal blood rules is especially striking. These specify that applicants must show requisite blood quantum derived from persons affiliated with the accepting tribe. They appeared very rarely in constitutions in operation prior to 1941 but are now used by just over one-third of tribes in the study. Third, the use of parental residency rules in tribal membership regimes has dropped sharply. Only one-in-five tribes requires parental residency as a condition of eligibility today, compared with over half of tribes with constitutions operative before 1950. Significantly, while the frequency of both lineal descent and tribal blood rules has increased, blood-quantum rules are more likely to be added to parental-enrollment regimes by tribes amending older constitutions, while descent rules are more often used by tribes adopting constitutions for the first time. The rise in lineal descent trunk rules therefore is primarily a function of the strong preference for lineal descent shown by tribes adopting constitutions for the first time after 1970. The rise in blood rules, on the other hand, is partly the result of constitutional amendment. Overall, there is a marked shift from the "parental enrollment plus parental residence" configuration, to the "lineal descent plus blood quantum" configuration.

2. Flexibility: Changes in Discretionary Regimes

The proportion of tribal constitutions making reference to tribal adoptions has dropped from ninety-two percent in the pre-1941 era to seventy-four percent of current constitutions. An increasing number of tribes, however, omit a constitutional requirement for secretarial review of adoptions. The decrease in the frequency of explicitly permissive adoption rules is largely due to the decision of tribes to exclude these rules from their first iteration constitutions, not the removal of these rules by constitutional amendment.

3. Insularity: Changes to Multiple Membership Rules

The third striking set of changes demonstrated in the data is the increased use of provisions expressly prohibiting multiple membership. Today more than half of tribes in the study prohibit multiple membership, whereas such provisions were rarely used in the IRA era.

Multiple membership prohibition rules are among those most likely to be added to existing regimes as part of tribal constitutional reform. Just under half of the tribes that amended their membership rules did so by adding a multiple membership prohibition. The uptake of multiple membership rules increases sharply after 1960. . . .

NOTES

1. Consider the following tribal constitutional provision dealing with tribal membership, this one imposing a one-quarter blood quantum on tribal members:

> Section 1. The membership of the Ely Shoshone Tribe shall consist of the following:
>
> > (a) All persons of at least one-quarter (1/4) degree Shoshone Indian blood whose names appear on the census roll of the Ely Colony dated April 1, 1930, revised April 19, 1983; Provided, That the Ely Shoshone Tribal Council shall have the authority to make any necessary corrections in the above specified roll.
> > (b) All persons of at least one-quarter (1/4) degree Shoshone Indian blood who are descendants of members.
>
> Section 2. The Ely Shoshone Tribal Council shall have the power to enact ordinances governing enrollment procedures including the loss of membership and the adoption of new members.
> Section 3. No persons enrolled with another Indian tribe or group, whether Federally recognized or not, shall be a member of the Ely Shoshone Tribe.
> Section 4. Written applications must be filed on behalf of all applicants applying for enrollment with the Ely Shoshone Tribe. Any person refused membership or who is subject to loss of membership by the Ely Shoshone Tribal Council shall have the right to appeal in accordance with tribal ordinances.

ELY SHOSHONE TRIBE CONSTITUTION AND BYLAWS art. II (May 8, 1990).

2. The following constitutional provision establishes lineal descendancy as the rule for tribal membership:

> Section 1. The following persons shall be entitled to membership in the Sault Ste. Marie Tribe of Chippewa Indians, provided that such persons possess Indian blood and are not currently enrolled with any other tribe or band of North American Indians, and provided further that such persons are citizens of the United States of America:
>
> > (a) All persons descended from the six historical bands (Grand Island, Point Iroquois, Sault Ste. Marie, Garden River, Sugar Island, and Drummond Island Bands) of the Sault Ste. Marie Chippewa Indians whose names appear on any historical roll, census or record made by officials of the Department of the Interior or Bureau of Indian Affairs.

(b) All persons enrolled on the membership roll of the organization, known as the Original Bands of the Sault Ste. Marie Chippewa Indians who are alive on the date of approval of this constitution and who are descendants of the original bands.

(c) All persons who may hereafter be adopted into the tribe in accordance with any ordinance enacted for that purpose by the board of directors;

(d) All lineal descendants of such persons as are described in (a), (b) or (c) above.

Section 2. The board of directors shall have the power to enact ordinances consistent with this article to govern future membership, loss of membership and adoption.

CONSTITUTION AND BYLAWS OF THE SAULT STE. MARIE TRIBE OF CHIPPEWA INDIANS art. III (November 13, 1975).

3. The following provision allows for membership into the community through the process of adoption:

SECTION 1. Membership of the Saginaw Chippewa Indian Tribe shall consist of: . . .

d.) Any person of at least one-quarter degree Indian blood who is an adopted child of any member of the Saginaw Chippewa Indian Tribe of Michigan or is married to any member may become an adopted member of the Tribe pursuant to any adoption ordinance which the Tribal Council may enact. Every person adopted pursuant to this section shall be deemed to be a member of the Tribe for all intents and purposes, EXCEPT that no person so adopted into the Tribe shall be eligible to hold the office of Chief, Subchief, Tribal Secretary, Tribal Treasurer or Tribal Council member. . . .

SECTION 3. Any adopted member of the Saginaw Chippewa Indian Tribe of Michigan may be subject to disenrollment in the Tribe for the following reasons:

a.) The individual became an adopted member of the Tribe by reason of marriage to a member of the Tribe and such marriage has been terminated by annulment or divorce and such adopted member has neither maintained a principal residence on the Isabella or Saganing Reservation nor remarried to another member of the Tribe for a period of twelve or more consecutive months preceding Tribal disenrollment action; or

b.) The individual became an adopted member of the Tribe by being an adopted child of member of the Tribe, upon reaching the age of 18 or older, elects to abandon Tribal relations with the Saginaw Chippewa Indian Tribe of Michigan in favor of re-establishing Tribal relations with the Tribe from which they are descendants by blood.

c.) Individuals so disenrolled shall thereafter not be entitled to share any subsequent rights of membership. . . .

SAGINAW CHIPPEWA INDIAN TRIBE OF MICHIGAN CONSTITUTION art. III (November 4, 1986).

4. Paul Spruhan's excellent study of the legal history of blood quantum in federal Indian law concludes with the following:

> The legal history of blood quantum to 1935 is more striking for its lack of use than its application. Rules defining the status of mixed-ancestry persons by blood and descent existed from at least 1705 in Anglo-American law, but the federal government only applied blood quantum to Indians on a large scale in the early twentieth century. Though early federal officials knew of blood quantum, and used it to describe individuals of mixed ancestry, they generally avoided its application. . . .
>
> . . . The muddled array of individual uses of the legal term Indian that developed to 1935, some requiring a threshold blood quantum (without a consistent quantum) and some requiring tribal membership, reflects that the United States failed to resolve these inherent contradictions in its Indian law. Instead, individual statutes, regulations, and court rulings emphasized different aspects of Indian status, with no cohesive explanation for the varied definitions.
>
> . . . In 1846 the Supreme Court extended federal criminal jurisdiction over white tribal members by interpreting the statutory term Indian to refer to a race of Indians. Further, federal law barred Indians from American citizenship, explained by some officials as due to the alleged incapacity of the Indian race. . . .
>
> However, nineteenth-century federal officials also treated tribes as autonomous political entities, and "Indian" as a political citizen of a tribe. The federal government negotiated treaties with tribes for various purposes, and mostly did not interfere with internal membership. Early treaty provisions included references to half-breeds or quarter-bloods, and a few treaties defined eligibility for specific benefits by blood, but no treaty stated that mixed-bloods were not tribal members or were not Indian. Indeed, some later treaties explicitly recognized mixed-bloods and even intermarried whites and black freedmen as tribal members. Bureau of Indian Affairs administrative practice generally made no distinction between mixed-bloods and other Indians for distribution of benefits, and generally left the decision up to tribal officials whether to recognize mixed-bloods as members. Even when the Attorney General and federal judges suggested a distinction between Indians and white citizens, defined by the amount of Indian blood, they declined to apply it. Instead, the branches of the federal government preferred rules of matrilineal or patrilineal descent or tribal membership to classify mixed-bloods.
>
> While the federal government viewed Indians as members of political entities, it also exerted supervision and control over Indian property as the guardian of Indian wards. The government barred Indians from making contracts, from selling land, and from other activities associated with "competent" citizens of the United States under the notion of guardianship. Federal officials selectively extended their guardianship authority to protect mixed-bloods as Indians by supervising their transactions.
>
> By the 1870s the federal government increasingly asserted its guardianship authority and de-emphasized the concept of Indians as citizens of autonomous tribes. . . .
>
> However, the political conception of Indian identity never completely went away. When the federal government distributed allotments, all three branches eventually applied tribal membership to define eligibility. Officials

recognized intermarried white men as empowered to vote on land cession agreements, and these white men shared in the distribution of property at certain times as tribal members. Even when Congress in 1888 barred newly intermarried white men from sharing in tribal property, it still recognized the authority of tribes to recognize them as members.

In the early twentieth century the federal government asserted virtually absolute control over Indian lands and applied the pre-existing concept of blood quantum directly. . . . Both Congress and the Bureau of Indian Affairs used blood quantum as one of the defining elements of competency to release whole classes of Indians, while retaining restrictions on others. Congress then conditioned funding and, for certain tribes, membership itself, based on blood quantum, limiting its responsibilities to a subset of biological wards. . . .

To add to the confusion, the [1934 Indian Reorganization Act] combined the various conceptions of Indian identity in one piece of legislation. With the exception of adopted non-Indian tribal members, both political and biological Indians were beneficiaries of the act. Tribal membership continued to be important, as the IRA included all tribal members of "Indian descent." However, Congress also included on-reservation descendants of members and Indians of one-half or more Indian blood not affiliated with any tribe. . . . The IRA set up a process for tribes to organize constitutional governments and corporate entities, and subsequent BIA interpretation left membership to the tribes themselves. However, the increase of the blood quantum threshold from one-quarter to one-half perpetuated the notion of Indian as biological ward. . . .

. . . The resulting muddle will continue as long as the United States applies blood quantum and tribal membership inconsistently, frustrating future generations of Indian people, as well as those who practice federal Indian law, by perpetuating the inconsistencies of Indian legal identity.

Paul Spruhan, *A Legal History of Blood Quantum in Federal Indian Law to 1935*, 51 S.D. L. REV. 1, 47-50 (2006).

5. Tribal membership criteria do create seeming inequities in application. People who are undoubtedly Indians may nevertheless be ineligible for membership. The classic case is the child of Indians who have worked for the Bureau of Indian Affairs or the child of urban Indians who intermarry with Indians of other tribes. These children may be full-blood Indians, but without the requisite blood quantum to meet membership eligibility criteria in any one tribe. Nicole Laughlin examines the inequities of blood quantum, and the underlying reasons for the use of blood quantum in the first place:

The goal of most tribes today is to have "enrollment reflect some sort of valid cultural affiliation." To achieve this objective, modern tribes flipped the ideology of early Euro-Americans, electing to favor membership to those who possess greater amounts of Indian blood. This is based in part on the theory that the more Indian blood a person possesses, the more likely they will be to adhere to cultural standards. This reasoning, however, is inherently flawed, because a higher fraction of Indian blood does not guarantee that a member will adhere to traditional customs or acclimate to the tribal community.

Additionally, this method precludes individuals with legitimate cultural ties from membership simply because they cannot meet the blood quantum threshold. . . . [T]his policy directly conflicts with the goal of gaining culturally affiliated members, and the result is a diminishing number of Indians eligible for membership[.] . . .

This very scenario is illustrated . . . through the story of Robert Upham. Robert is considered a mixed blood because he has ancestors from the Assiniboine, Kootenai, Nakota, and Salish tribes. However, Robert was brought up on the reservation of the Gros Ventre Indians in Montana. Although four generations of his mother's family lived on the reservation and are buried there, Robert is not eligible for membership within the Gros Ventre because his blood lines have become too thin. Even though Robert is "entirely Indian by heritage" because he is not able to meet the blood quantum threshold for any tribe he is foreclosed from membership and any of the accompanying benefits.

Nicole J. Laughlin, *Identity Crisis: An Examination of Federal Infringement on Tribal Autonomy to Determine Membership*, 30 HAMLINE L. REV. 97, 111-13 (2006).

6. Many tribal membership rules are based on a federally generated annuity roll often dating back to the nineteenth or early twentieth century. As Carole Goldberg points out, such reliance may create legal and political problems:

> The phenomenon of federally-devised lists or "rolls" of citizens is not confined to the termination/restoration process. Beginning in the late nineteenth century, various federal laws compelled the Department of the Interior to compile such lists for purposes of distributing Indian allotments and land claims judgments. In other words, these lists attended the dismantling of tribal land bases. Professor John Lavelle has powerfully pierced the misconception that these laws imposed blood quantum requirements. Nevertheless, these laws did exert a force on tribal governing documents, offering a convenient starting point for citizenship criteria that turn on lineal descendance. Unfortunately, these federally-mandated lists are sometimes inadequate and incomplete, excluding some people with deep and continuous tribal connections, whose ancestors failed to show up for the sign-ups because their traditional beliefs counseled nonparticipation or for other culturally-based reasons. Dean Rennard Strickland relates the poignant story of a Seminole woman who could not qualify for an Indian scholarship program because she could not document her Indian ancestry based on federally-compiled rolls. Her Seminole grandmother, who barely spoke English, had resisted enrollment and hidden from the enrollment parties because she did not believe that the tribal land base should be broken up. As Strickland points out, "[h]er granddaughter could not qualify to enroll in law school under the Native American Scholarship program because the tribal rolls were closed to her despite her historic Indianness." The impact of such omissions becomes magnified with each generation. Once a roll is established as the basis for citizenship, it becomes politically difficult to expand citizenship beyond its confines.

Carole Goldberg, *Members Only? Designing Citizenship Requirements for Indian Nations*, 40 U. KAN. L. REV. 437, 457-58 (2002).

B. JUDICIAL REVIEW OF TRIBAL MEMBERSHIP DETERMINATIONS

Much litigation in tribal courts involves challenges to decisions by tribal election determination entities that have decided membership or citizenship questions. On occasion, the administrative decision of the election board is final, and on other occasions, the tribal court is the body entrusted to hear these questions in the first instance. And there are other variations as well, such as tribes that entrust final election decisions to a panel of elders, who can and occasionally do reverse election results.

1. TRIBAL COURT AUTHORITY TO REVIEW TRIBAL MEMBERSHIP DETERMINATIONS

MALTOS V. SAUK-SUIATTLE TRIBE

Sauk-Suiattle Tribal Court of Appeals, No. SAU-CIV-5-3/01/001,
6 NICS App. 132 (November 24, 2003),
Reconsideration Denied (February 27, 2004)

WOODROW, J.:

Procedural History

[Plaintiff brought suit against the Tribe after the Tribal Council revoked the Plaintiff's citizenship.]

The Tribe asserted sovereign immunity. On February 11, 2002 the Honorable Chief Judge Martin Bohl of the Sauk-Suiattle Tribal Court issued an order granting the Plaintiff's motion to dismiss on sovereign immunity grounds and directing notice of rehearing for Respondent.

The Appellant Tribe appeals the trial court's order. The appellant appeals (1) the trial court's conclusion that it has jurisdiction to order a rehearing upon a finding of denial of due process, and (2) the trial court's order for a rehearing.

Jurisdiction

This Court having reviewed the record and listened to the arguments of counsel, agrees that the trial court does have jurisdiction to order a rehearing. We reached this opinion by deciding that sovereign immunity[2] does not apply. The rehearing is an administrative remedy and as such does not constitute a suit against the Tribe.

---

2. The principal that tribes enjoy the sovereign's common law immunity from suit is well established. *Santa Clara Pueblo v. Martinez*, 436 U.S. 49, 58 (1978). The immunity extends to agencies of the tribes. *Weeks Construction, Inc. v. Oglala Sioux Housing Authority*, 797 F.2d 668 (8th Cir. 1986). It applies in both state and federal court. *See Pan American Co. v. Sycuan Band of Mission Indians*, 84 F.2d 416 (9th Cir. 1989) Tribal immunity extends to claims for declaratory and injunctive relief, not merely damages, and it is not defeated by a claim that the tribe acted beyond its power. *Imperial Granite Co. v. Pala Band of Mission Indians*, 940 F.2d 1269 (9th Cir. 1991).

Rehearing

The trial court did not conduct a trial on any issue of fact. The trial court held, however, that the Respondent was denied due process which pierced the sovereign immunity of the tribe for the limited purposes of allowing a rehearing. There is no factual record before this Court that would allow it to determine if this conclusion of law is supported by substantial evidence. On remand the trial court is to conduct a finding of fact and determine after the Respondent loss his membership in the Sauk-Suiattle Tribe if he was afforded or given notice of his right to appeal. The trial court shall also determine if the Respondent was given notice of his right to appeal and if he waived this right by not filing an appeal or pursuing his administrative remedies. The trial court shall also determine if Respondent was given notice of his right to appeal and if he understood that he could appeal his loss of membership in the tribe because of the ambiguous nature of the Enrollment Ordinance.[4]

Enrollment Ordinance of the Sauk-Suiattle Indian Tribe

The enrollment ordinance is ambiguous. It is unclear if a member may appeal a disenrollment or a relinquishment of membership in the tribe. This court holds that a member may appeal a loss of membership in which privileges of membership are revoked by the Tribal council or the Enrollment Committee. There is no distinction that this court can find between a loss of membership and a denial of membership. This conclusion is based upon the following facts: (1) the tribal membership is a valuable property right and all member must be afforded due process when that right is taken by the tribe; (2) tribal members should have the same appeal rights as other Indians seeking to become tribal members; (3) the Enrollment Ordinance is ambiguous regarding appeals rights and this ambiguity should be resolved in favor of the tribal members; (4) there does not appear to be any appeal process or right to re-apply for membership if a member is disenrolled or relinquishes membership

---

4. For example:

Section 11 Loss of Membership or Enrollment: The Tribal Council may, upon its own motion or the recommendation of the Enrollment Committee, remove person from the Tribal Roll and revoke the privileges of membership under any of the following conditions: a. (Degree of Blood is incorrect). b. The member in question is enrolled in another tribe or band or community in violation of Article II of the Sauk-Suiattle Constitution, unless dual enrollment is the result of a mistake and is corrected as soon as possible. . . . d. The member in question request dis-enrollment or relinquishment of membership. e. (Convictions) f. (Membership affects the cultural integrity of the tribe).

Section 12 Appeals: In those cases where enrollment is denied, the applicant shall also be informed in the same notice that he or she has thirty (30) days from receipt of the notice of denial to petition the Tribal Council in writing for a re-hearing or to request additional time. . . . a. Upon request for such a rehearing, the Enrollment Clerk shall set a specific date. . . . The notice of hearing shall again inform the applicant of the applicant's right to submit evidence and to appear with or without representation or assistance at their own expenses. . . . c. After final denial by the Tribal Council, an applicant denied enrollment shall have such further appeal to the Sauk-Suiattle Tribal Court. Its decision shall be final. d. Any applicant denied membership may file a new application along with proper documentation as outlined in this ordinance.

The above is curious because non-member Indians are given a right to appeal their rejection, are given a right to present evidence, a right to counsel, a right to file again for membership and a right to appeal to Tribal Court. Member Indians that are dis-enrolled have no such rights.

brought by the motion of the Tribal Council or the Enrollment Committee. There should always be a remedy for mistake or error.

Conclusion

The court concludes that tribal sovereignty was never at issue in this case. The trial court must hold a hearing to determine if the Respondent was given notice of his right to appeal, and if the Respondent understood that he had the right to appeal a disenrollment or relinquishment or if the Respondent was given his notice to appeal and waive that right by inaction and a failure to exhaust his administrative remedies.

Dissenting Opinion

ELDEMAR, J.: . . .

B. Sovereign Immunity

The Council acted pursuant to its constitutional authority when it enacted the Enrollment Ordinance and directed that it (the Council) could revoke privileges of enrollment. The Council did not create a procedure for appeal of revocation. This must be done expressly because all matters heard in review of Council action must arise from an express waiver of immunity or from application of the . . . *Accardi* doctrine.[*] Absent a waiver of sovereign immunity, this Court lacks the personal jurisdiction in any dispute against the Council. *Santa Clara Pueblo*, 436 U.S. [49,] 58 [(1978)]. A waiver of sovereign immunity "cannot be implied but must be unequivocally expressed." *Id.* Only by clear, express, and unequivocal language can the Tribes' immunity from suit be waived. *Id.*

This Justice finds persuasive the 5th Circuit's statement that "any waiver of immunity is to be interpreted liberally in favor or the Tribe and restrictively against the claimant." *S. Unique Ltd. v. Gila R. Pima-Maricopa Indian Comm.*, 674 P.2d 1376, 1381 (Ariz. App. 1983); citing *Maryland Casualty Co. v. Citizens Nat'l Bank*, 361 F.2d 517 (5th Cir. 1966). Applying this standard, the procedure for appeal of Council action defined in §12 of the Enrollment Ordinance cannot be read as a waiver of sovereign immunity. Consequently, this court lacks jurisdiction in this suit against the tribe and cannot afford the relief requested by Appellant.

C. Ex Parte Young

The *Young* doctrine is a narrow exception made available under specific circumstances to avoid sovereign immunity. *Ex Parte Young* requires a plaintiff to plead and prove the following: (1) that the Council acted palpably outside the scope of its authority; (2) that the Council violated a federal statute, treaty, tribal constitutional provision or some other law to which full faith and credit of the Tribe is required; (3) that the violation is ongoing. If plaintiff successfully demonstrates the preceding, he may only seek prospective injunctive relief.

---

[*]*Editor's note:* Earlier the opinion stated: "The doctrine requires an agency to comply with its own self-imposed rules but it only applies when the agency creating those rules intends itself to be bound by the rule it has created. *United State ex rel. Accardi v. Shaugnessy*, 347 U.S. 260 (1954)."

A suit of damages or retrospective relief is not available under the Young exception.

Appellant did not plead *Young*. Appellant did not plead the elements of *Young*. Accepting all of Appellant's allegations as true, Appellant has failed to state a claim under *Young*. Appellant is the master of his case. Appellant's case is justly dismissed.

For the aforementioned reasons, I dissent.

NOTES

1. Judicial review of tribal enrollment decisions comes in many forms. In *Ballina v. Confederated Tribes of Grand Ronde*, 2003.NAGR.0000008 (Confederated Tribes of the Grand Ronde Community Ct. App., Sept. 19, 2003), the court confronted the question of whether a tribal constitutional amendment increasing the blood quantum requirements from 1/16 to 1/8 was retroactive:

> Because neither the text nor the history of the enrollment amendment manifests the voters' intent concerning its temporal reach, we must proceed to the next level of retroactivity analysis set forth in *Landgraf* [*v. USI Film Products*, 511 U.S. 244 (1994)], which incorporates a number of central concepts and principles. First, it has long been recognized that "[r]etroactive legislation presents problems of unfairness that are more serious than those posed by prospective legislation, because it can deprive citizens of legitimate expectations and upset settled transactions." . . . Thus, in American jurisprudence, there is a deeply rooted presumption against retroactive legislation. "Elementary considerations of fairness dictate that individuals should have an opportunity to know what the law is and to conform their conduct accordingly; settled expectations should not be lightly disrupted." . . . For those reasons, we adopt the presumption against retroactive legislation as explained in *Landgraf*, understanding "legislation" to include not only the Tribal Council's enactments but also voter-approved constitutional amendments.
>
> Second, "[w]hile statutory retroactivity has long been disfavored, deciding when a statute [or constitutional amendment] operates 'retroactively' is not a simple or mechanical task." . . . There are, however, some functional conceptions of legislative "retroactivity" that provide guidance in performing that task. For instance, "[a] law is retrospective if it 'changes the legal consequences of acts completed before its effective date.'" . . . Further, a retroactive statute is one that "takes away or impairs vested rights acquired under existing laws, or creates a new obligation, imposes a new duty, or attaches a new disability." *Sturges v. Carter*, 114 U.S. 511, 519 (1885). . . .
>
> . . . Applying those standards to the instant case, we conclude that application of the new criteria contained in the enrollment amendment to the applicants did not have retroactive effect, because there was no impairment of a vested right, no increase in liability for the applicants, and no new duties imposed on the applicants.

   Id. at ¶¶55-59.

2. However, many tribal legislatures restrict tribal court review of membership decisions by placing a deferential standard of review on courts. *E.g., Kaufmann v. Little Traverse Bay Bands of Odawa Indians Enrollment Office*,

2004 WL 5760773 (Little Traverse Bay Bands of Odawa Indians Tribal Court 2004) (applying a "clear error" standard to tribal enrollment decisions).

2. LIMITED TRIBAL COURT SCOPE OF REVIEW

COOKE v. YUROK TRIBE

Yurok Court of Appeals, No. YTCV 04-12,
7 NICS App. 78 (September 29, 2005)

Before: DAVID L. HARDING, Chief Justice; RANDAL E. STECKEL, Justice; JERRIE M. SIMMONS, Justice. . . .

I. Facts and Procedural History

This matter comes before the Court of Appeals on an appeal of a grant of summary judgment for Appellee, the Yurok Tribe. [T]he Appellant, Bernard Cooke, is the biological child of Joseph Cooke, deceased, who was non-Indian, and Ivora Nelson Cooke, deceased, who was an enrolled member of the Hoopa Valley Tribe at the time of her death on February 27, 1990.

. . . On June 9, 2004, the Tribe's Enrollment Committee determined Mr. Cooke was not eligible for enrollment in the Yurok Tribe. . . . On September 9, 2004, contrary to the recommendation of the Enrollment Committee, the Tribal Council denied Mr. Cooke's application for enrollment. . . .

II. Jurisdiction and Scope of Review

Although jurisdiction was not addressed in the Ruling of the Tribal Court, the Tribal Court has jurisdiction "to hear all appeals of enrollment." Enrollment Ordinance of the Yurok Tribe, §10.4. . . .

The scope of review of the Court of Appeals is expressly limited to determining whether "mistakes of law were made by the lower court." Yurok Tribal Court Rules of Appellate Procedure (1997), Rule 1(A). "The appellate court shall have no jurisdiction to hear appeals based upon any other ground." *Id.*, Rule 1(B).

III. Standard of Review

The Yurok Tribal Code and Yurok Rules of Court do not specify the standard of review for an appeal of an enrollment decision. The Tribal Code does, however, establish that the Tribal Court is to apply federal law where an issue is not addressed by Tribal law, custom or usage. Yurok Tribal Court Interim Ordinance, Yurok Tribal Code 1-05, August 9, 1996. As the United States Supreme has stated, "decisions by judges are traditionally divided into three categories, denominated questions of law (reviewed *de novo*), questions of fact (reviewed for clear error) and matters of discretion (reviewed for 'abuse of discretion')." *Pierce v. Underwood*, 487 U.S. 552, 558, 108 S. Ct. 2541, 2546 (1988). Because our review of a Yurok Tribal enrollment decision is limited to mistakes (i.e., questions) of law, our review is *de novo*. *De novo* review of questions of law means that this Court shows no deference to the legal conclusions of the lower court or Tribal Council. *Sklar v. Commissioner*, 282 F.3d 610, 612 (9th Cir. 2002).

IV. Analysis

This case requires interpretation of the Yurok Tribal Constitution. Because he meets the blood quantum requirement (1/8 Yurok) and because his grandfather was a Yurok allottee, Mr. Cooke appears to qualify for enrollment under the "Extraordinary Circumstances" provision of the Yurok Constitution. Article II, §3. The Tribal Enrollment ordinance tracks the Constitution word for word concerning eligibility. However, the Yurok Constitution also includes a provision that "No person who is a lineal descendant of a *present or former* member of another Tribe and who is without a parent enrolled with the Yurok Tribe shall qualify for membership in the Yurok Tribe." Article II, §4(c) (emphasis added).

The Tribe argues that Article II, §4(c) of the Yurok Constitution is an absolute limitation on membership and therefore the controlling law in this case. Because Mr. Cooke's mother was a member of the Hoopa Tribe at the time of her death in 1990 and neither of Mr. Cooke's parents is or was enrolled at Yurok, the Tribe argues that §4(c) establishes a non-discretionary bar to Mr. Cooke's application for enrollment.

Mr. Cooke's basic argument is that Article II, §4(c) does not apply because his mother is a "deceased" member of the Hoopa Tribe, not a "former" member. Mr. Cooke argues that "former" and "deceased" are not legally equivalent terms. To support his argument, Mr. Cooke points out that in an unrelated section of the Yurok Enrollment Ordinance (which was adopted only a few months after adoption of the Constitution), the Ordinance itself makes an explicit distinction between "deceased" and "former" members of the Yurok Tribe. . . .

As a secondary argument, Mr. Cooke points out that Yurok Constitution Article II, §3(c) opens membership to "any adopted person whose biological parents would have qualified, or would have qualified if alive for the Yurok Membership Roll." Mr. Cooke does not claim this section is directly applicable to him because he is not adopted. However, Mr. Cooke's pleadings can be construed as arguing that, because his mother died before the Yurok Tribe was officially recognized, his biological mother "would have qualified if alive" and that he should not be afforded less rights under the Constitution than an adopted person in the same circumstances. . . .

While Mr. Cooke sets forth a cogent argument that there is a legal distinction between a "former" member and a "deceased" member of a tribe, we are not persuaded that the distinction applies to Article II of the Yurok Constitution. Mr. Cooke is correct that §8 of the Yurok Enrollment Ordinance make a distinction between "former" and "deceased" members of the Yurok Tribe. However, the provision for separate registers of "former" and "deceased" members is clearly intended to facilitate administration of the membership rolls, with "former" members being defined to include "individuals who selected the 'buy-out' option under the Hoopa-Yurok Settlement Act, and all individuals who have been disenrolled pursuant to this Ordinance and the Constitution of the Yurok Tribe." Enrollment Ordinance, §8.2. While there is a separate register for "deceased" members, Enrollment Ordinance §8.3, there is nothing in the Enrollment Ordinance that suggests that "deceased" members would not also be considered "former" members as those terms are commonly used, despite the provision for separate registers.

The dictionary defines "former" as "preceding in time; earlier; past [in former times]." Webster's New World Dictionary, Second College Edition, 1979. We hold that, for the purposes of Article II of the Yurok Constitution, a "deceased" member of another Tribe is a "former" member of that Tribe.[2]

Mr. Cooke also sets forth a cogent argument that Article II, §3(c) appears to establish more favorable treatment for an adoptee than a lineal descendant of a Yurok Reservation allottee. However, as Mr. Cooke acknowledges, he is not an adoptee. We also agree with the Tribe that Article II, §4(c) is nondiscretionary and therefore would "trump" §3(c), which is clearly discretionary (a person "may" be determined to be eligible for membership under §3 whereas "no" person "shall" qualify for membership where §4(c) applies.)

As the Tribe argues, it is well settled that one of the most fundamental rights of a sovereign nation is the right to determine qualifications for the enrollment of its members. *See Santa Clara Pueblo v. Martinez*, 436 U.S. 49, 98 S. Ct. 1670 (1978). Regardless of whatever sympathies the members of this Court may have for Mr. Cooke or any other person who meets the blood quantum requirement for membership in the Yurok Tribe but is deemed ineligible for membership because of the combined actions of their parents and the drafters of the Yurok Constitution, it is simply not within the power of this Court to rewrite or ignore that Constitution. . . .

NOTE

Often, there is not much for a tribal appellate court to consider in reviewing tribal citizenship decisions. Note the *Cooke* Court recognizing that its review of the facts is very limited—the "clear error" standard. Other tribal courts apply a standard incorporated from administrative law, the "arbitrary and capricious" standard. *E.g., Miller v. Confederated Tribes of Grand Ronde*, No. 00-07-013, 2001.NAGR.0000010 (Confederated Tribes of the Grand Ronde Community Tribal Court, July 27, 2001) ("In these proceedings, the Court's standard of review is limited. The Court can reverse or remand only if it finds that the Enrollment Committee's decision was "arbitrary and capricious or a violation of Tribal Constitutional rights." ENROLLMENT ORDINANCE §(d)(4)(H).").

3. BLOOD DEGREE CERTIFICATION

HOFFMAN V. COLVILLE CONFEDERATED TRIBES

Colville Confederated Tribes Court of Appeals, No. AP05-093,
24 Indian Law Reporter 6163, 1997.NACC.0000010 (May 5, 1997)

The opinion of the court was delivered by: LaFOUNTAINE, P. J.

---

2. Even if we were to accept Mr. Cooke's argument that a "deceased" member of another tribe is not a "former" member of that tribe, under Article II, §4(c), Mr. Cooke would still be "without a parent enrolled with the Yurok Tribe." Mr. Cooke's suggestion that his mother "could have" disenrolled herself from the Hoopa Tribe and then enrolled in the Yurok Tribe requires a level of speculation that this Court is not authorized to engage in.

This matter came before this Appellate panel of Presiding Justice Frank S. LaFountaine, Justice Elizabeth Fry, and Justice Dennis Nelson of the Colville Tribal Court of Appeals. . . . [T]his Appellate Panel of the Colville Court of Appeals has decided to Affirm the decision of the Trial Court as to the following findings and/or conclusions, that:

1. The appellant, Floyd L. Hoffman, has failed to introduce clear and convincing proof that he is entitled to an increase in blood quantum based upon factual proof of additional Indian blood;

2. The appellant, Floyd L. Hoffman, has neither argued nor presented any tribal, state or federal statute or case law which requires the Tribes in either 1907 or 1937 to afford due process of law to its members in exercising the Tribes' powers of self-government through adoption and reductions of blood quantum conferred through adoption;

3. Appellant, Floyd L. Hoffman, has not pled or raised any customs of the Colville Confederated Tribes related to rights conferred through adoption and blood quantum established through adoption as needed to warrant a hearing pursuant to CTC §3.4.04 to determine a custom followed by the Colville Confederated Tribes defining rights and status conferred through an adoption in 1907 and defining what rights, if any, are protected during a reduction in blood quantum taking place in 1937; and

4. Appellant's petition for blood degree correction is denied.

. . .

On January 12, 1995, the appellant, Floyd L. Hoffman, and other Petitioners filed a Petition for Blood Degree Correction with the Tribal Court, pursuant to Amendment IX of the Constitution and By-Laws of the Confederated Tribes of the Colville Reservation and pursuant to the Colville [Tribal] Membership Code, CTC §§36.7.01 through 36.7.09. Petitioners were Floyd L. Hoffman, a Colville Tribal member; and his children [and grand children.] . . .

On September 7, 1995, the Trial Court [denied] the appellant's blood correction. . . .

Constitutional Amendments Dealing with Tribal Membership

On May 20, 1949, the tribal members of the Confederated Tribes of the Colville Reservation approved Amendment III of the Colville Tribal Constitution by a referendum vote, and Amendment III was later approved by the Commissioner of Indian Affairs on April 14, 1950. Amendment III amended the Tribal Constitution to add Article VII, Membership of the Confederated Tribes of the Colville Reservation.

Article VII created a new provision governing membership in the Tribes. Article VII recognized as tribal members the following persons:

(a) All persons of Indian blood whose names appear as members of the Tribes on the official census of Indians of the Colville Reservation as of January 1, 1937;

(b) All children possessing one-fourth or more Indian blood, born after January 1, 1937, to any member of the Tribes maintaining a permanent residence on the Colville Indian Reservation; and

(c) All children possessing one-fourth or more Indian blood, born after January 1, 1937, to any member of the Tribes maintaining residence elsewhere in the continental United States provided that the parent or guardian of the child indicate a willingness to maintain tribal relations and to participate in tribal affairs.

Article VII (Amendment III) also provided that the Business Council of the Tribes has the power to prescribe rules and regulations governing future membership in the Tribes, including adoption of the members and loss of membership, provided:

(a) That such rules and regulations shall be subject to the approval of the Secretary of the Interior;

(b) That no person shall be adopted who possesses less than one-fourth degree Indian blood;

(c) That any member who takes up permanent residence or is enrolled with a tribe, band or community of foreign Indians shall lose his membership in the Colville Tribes.

On May 9, 1959, the tribal members of the Confederated Tribes of the Colville Reservation approved Amendment V of the Colville Tribal Constitution by a referendum vote, and Amendment V was later approved by the Acting Commissioner of Indian Affairs on July 2, 1959.

Amendment V amended Article VII, Membership of the Confederated Tribes of the Colville Reservation of the Tribal Constitution and By-Laws. Amendment V added to Article VII a new Section 3, which provided that after July 1, 1959, no person shall be admitted to tribal membership unless such person possessed at least one-fourth (1/4) degree blood of the tribes, constituting the Confederated Tribes of the Colville Reservation.

On March 22, 1988, the tribal members of the Confederated Tribes of the Colville Reservation approved Amendment IX of the Colville Tribal Constitution by a referendum vote, and Amendment IX was later approved by the Secretary of the Interior on May 19, 1988.

Amendment IX amended Article VII, Membership of the Confederated Tribes of the Colville Reservation of the Tribal Constitution and By-Laws. Amendment IX added to Article VII a new Section 4, which provided the following:

(1) that all Indian blood identified and stated as being possessed by all persons whose names appear as members of the Confederated Tribes of the Colville Reservation on the official census of the Indians of the Colville Reservation of January 1, 1937, shall be considered Indian blood of the Tribes, which constitute the Confederated Tribes of the Colville Reservation;

(2) that no tribal member's blood degree will be decreased as a result of Amendment IX;

(3) that pursuant to procedure which shall be adopted by the Colville Business Council, any

(a) Applicant for membership, or

(b) Tribal member who is listed on the official census of the Indians of the Colville Reservation of January 1, 1937, or

(c) Tribal member descended from a tribal member whose name appears on the official census of the Indians of the Colville Reservation of January 1, 1937, may petition the Tribes, to officially recognize for enrollment purposes that a tribal member whose name appears on the official census of the Indians of the Colville Reservation of January 1, 1937, possesses Indian blood that is not listed on the official census of the Indians of the Colville Reservation of January 1, 1937, and such Indian blood, when properly authenticated by clear and convincing proof, shall be recognized as blood of the Colville Tribes.

Standard of Review — Clearly Erroneous

Appellant asserts that de novo review is justified because this case involves "review of documents not witness credibility" as "in" *Kinslow v. Business Committee of the Citizen Band Potawatomi Indian Tribe of Oklahoma*, 15 Indian L. Rep. 6007, 6009-10 (CB. Pot. Sup. Ct., Feb. 17, 1988). . . . The Court is not rejecting the appellant's assertion of law, but the Court does not believe a de novo review is required in this appeal.

The Tribes argued in their Response Brief that "a panel of this Court of Appeals has expressly adopted a 'deferential, clearly erroneous standard of review for factual determinations made by the trial court, as articulated in *Pullman-Standard v. Swint*, 456 U.S. 273, 102 S. Ct. 1781 (1982).' *Colville Confederated Tribes v. Nadene Naff*, Case No. AP93-12001-03, at 2, [2 CTCR 08, 2 CCAR 50, 22 Indian L. Rep. 6032] (Colv. Ct. App., Decision of January 22, 1995)." . . .

[T]he Supreme Court has articulated the policy behind the broad deference to trial court factual findings:

> The trial judge's major role is the determination of fact, and with experience in fulfilling that role comes expertise. Duplication of the trial judge's efforts in the court of appeals would very likely contribute only negligibly to the accuracy of fact determination at a huge cost in diversion of judicial resources. In addition, the parties to a case on appeal have already been forced to concentrate their energies and resources on persuading the trial judge that their account of the facts is a correct one; requiring them to persuade three more judges at the appellate level is requiring too much. . . . [T]he trial on the merits should be the "main event" . . . , rather than a "tryout" on the road. [Citations omitted.]

. . .

[Discussion]

As the evidence record in this appeal shows, and as the Trial Court clearly found, all Tribal census rolls prior to and including the 1937 roll were riddled with inconsistencies regarding blood degree. . . . Amendment IX in effect resolved those inconsistencies by — (1) preserving the blood degrees of 1937 enrollees as minimum blood degrees (regardless of the actual blood degree) and (2) providing a way to prove with clear and convincing evidence that a person actually possessed a higher degree of Colville blood.

In the present case on appeal, it is undisputed that Appellant, Floyd L. Hoffman, is listed on the 1937 roll as a Colville Tribal member with a blood degree of 5/32. He claims to possess a higher blood degree, and Amendment IX provides that he must prove it with "clear and convincing proof." . . .

. . . The substantive law applicable to this cause of action is set forth in CTC §36.7.03 (newly codified at Colville Tribal Law and Order Code, Title 8, §8-1-242, Standard of Proof), which provides that:

> In all actions for blood degree corrections the plaintiff shall be required to prove by clear and convincing evidence, that a blood degree other than that which is listed on the Roll for the person whose blood degree is at issue, is the correct blood degree and what the precise blood degree to be listed on the roll should be. There shall be a presumption, rebuttable by the plaintiff, that the blood degree listed on the roll is correct.

. . . The Trial Court correctly noted that the clear and convincing standard is an "onerous burden because it requires that the petitioner produce evidence . . . so clear and convincing that the opposition's evidence is plainly outweighed." Mem. Op. at page 11, *citing Kinslow v. Business Committee of the Citizen Band Potawatomi Indian Tribe of Oklahoma*, 15 Indian L. Rep. 6007 (C.B. Pot. Sup. Ct., Feb. 17, 1988) and *General Motors Acceptance Corp. v. Bitah*, 16 Indian L. Rep. 6002 (Nav. Sup. Ct., August 11, 1988). The Trial Court also noted that federal case law formulations of the clear and convincing evidence standard are not binding on the Trial Court, but acknowledged that the federal cases state "essentially the same" standard as the "plainly outweigh" formulation in the tribal court decisions. . . .

After reviewing the evidence of the appellant presented to the Trial Court, it is clear to this Appellate Panel that the appellant has failed to prove by clear and convincing evidence that he is entitled to a blood degree correction based upon factual proof. . . .

The constitutionally mandated starting point of this appeal is the 1937 Census. The evidence showed and the parties admitted that the appellant, Floyd Hoffman, is listed on the 1937 Census as possessing 5/32 Indian blood; Floyd Hoffman's mother, Helen Ferguson, is listed on the 1937 Census as possessing 5/16 Indian blood; Floyd Hoffman's father, Clarence Hoffman, possesses no Indian blood on the 1937 Census; Floyd Hoffman's grandparents, Joseph and Annie Ferguson, are listed on the 1937 Census as: Joseph Ferguson 1/2 Indian blood and Annie Etue Ferguson 1/4 Indian blood.

At trial, Appellant argued that his blood degree should be increased because Annie Ferguson possessed at least 1/2 Indian blood. In support of this argument, the appellant introduced the following evidence:

First, Appellant introduced "Delayed Death Certificate" from the 1935 Census showing that Joseph and Annie Ferguson possessed 21/32 Indian blood when they died. Under the law as set forth above and adopted by this Appellate Panel, the death certificates, without more, received little weight by the Trial Court because no evidence was introduced to indicate that the information upon which the death certificates were based was given in a formal setting, subject to cross examination and impeachment, or was given by a person personally acquainted with the Hoffmans.

Second, the petitioner admitted into evidence four (4) fee patent applications, two applications were dated 1928 and two applications were undated, all of which listed Helen Ferguson and Esther Mason Ferguson as possessing 5/8 Indian blood. No evidence was introduced that these patent applications were sworn applications made in a formal setting or subject to cross examination and impeachment. Though the applications were personally made by Helen and Esther Ferguson, no evidence was introduced that information contained in the applications was verified by the BIA and that the information provided was accurate.

Third, evidence was admitted showing that Esther Ferguson McClung, natural and full sister of Helen Ferguson Hoffman, Appellant's mother, is an enrolled member of the Colville Confederated Tribes possessing 5/16 Indian blood, while Helen Ferguson Hoffman is listed as possessing only 3/8 Indian blood. In 1983, the children of Esther Ferguson Mason successfully changed Esther Mason's blood degree to 5/8 Indian blood. This allowed the children, first cousins to Floyd Hoffman, to enroll in the Colville Confederated Tribes as possessing 5/16 Indian blood. Applying the above legal framework, this inconsistent information provides little weight in light of the fact that Esther Ferguson McClung is the only child of Joseph and Annie Ferguson listed on the 1937 Census as possessing 5/8th Indian blood.

Fourth, Appellant admitted into evidence a 1981 BIA letter stating that if there are "conflicting degrees of Indian blood" between natural brothers and sisters then the record should be changed to reflect the same level for all brothers and sisters. This evidence neither weighs in favor nor against Appellant since policy does not indicate whether the blood degree should be increased or decreased or which blood degree should be preferred in a case, such as in this appeal, where multiple degrees are listed.

Fifth, the appellant relied on a BIA letter dated February 21, 1910, showing that Joseph and Annie Ferguson were adopted into the Colville Confederated Tribes as each possessing 1/2 degree Indian blood. Under the law as set forth above, the letter, without more, received little weight by the Trial Court because no evidence was introduced to indicate that the information upon which the letter was based was given in a formal setting, subject to cross examination and impeachment, or was by a person personally acquainted with the Hoffmans.

Sixth, Appellant submitted Census records from 1899, 1903, 1904, 1907, 1908, 1912-13, 1913, 1924, 1924, 1930, 1933, 1935, 1937, and 1939 that showed: (1) Floyd Hoffman's blood degree fluctuated from 3/16 to 5/32 to 1/8; (2) Helen Ferguson Hoffman's blood degree fluctuated from 1/2 to 3/8 to 5/16 to 5/32; (3) Esther Ferguson Mason's (natural sister of Helen Ferguson Hoffman) blood degree fluctuated from 5/8 to 1/2 to 5/16; (4) Mabel Ferguson McClung's (natural sister of Helen Ferguson Hoffman) blood degree fluctuated from 1/2 to 5/16; and (5) Annie Etue Ferguson's blood degree fluctuated from 21/32 to 1/2 to "less" than 1/2 to 1/4 to 1/8.

The Trial Court noted that these records are contradictory on their face. Under the law as set forth above, such contradictory evidence received little weight by the Trial Court because no evidence was introduced to indicate that the information contained in the census records were given in a formal setting, subject to cross examination and impeachment, or was given by a person personally acquainted with the Hoffmans.

Finally, Appellant submitted a school record indicating that Annie Etue Ferguson possessed 1/2 degree Indian blood. Again, Appellant has failed to provide supporting evidence to indicate that the information upon which the school records were based was given in a formal setting, subject to cross examination and impeachment, or was given by a person personally acquainted with the Hoffmans.

To summarize Appellant's evidence, it is inconsistent. It does not provide a record that supports a finding of any one specific blood quantum by clear and convincing evidence. This Appellate Panel affirms Court's finding that it "does not find a clear weight of this [Appellant's] evidence supporting any specific blood quantum."

The Tribes, on the other hand, argue that the appellant's evidence, listed above, fails to prove by clear and convincing evidence that the blood degree listed on the 1937 Census for Floyd Hoffman is incorrect. In support of this argument, the Tribes introduced the following evidence that consistently supports a finding that Annie Etue Ferguson's actual Indian blood degree, as established through heredity, was 1/8th:

> First of all, the Tribes admitted into evidence a marked sworn and witnessed affidavit dated March 27, 1905 made by Cora Desautel Etue, Annie Etue Ferguson's mother, and witnessed by the U.S. Indian Agent at the Colville Agency, Miles, Washington. Though the purpose of the affidavit when made is not clear from the evidence, the affidavit purports to show a historical and genealogical record of Cora Desautel Etue, her husband and children. The document indicates that Cora Ferguson herself only possessed 1/4 Indian blood and Annie Etue Ferguson only possessed 1/8 Indian blood. Applying the legal analysis set forth above, this affidavit received considerable weight by the Trial Court. It is obvious from the face of the document that the document was made in a formal setting because it was witnessed and sworn to. In addition, the statement contained first hand information from Cora Desautel Etue who was intimately familiar with the facts concerning her family.

In analyzing the Tribes' evidence, the Trial Court reviewed the appellant's exhibits of official Colville "Individual History Cards" for Annie Etue Ferguson, Helen Ferguson, Mabel McClung and Esther Ferguson which shows that their blood degree quantum was consistent with Cora Etue's 1905 statement. No evidence was introduced on the setting in which a[n] "Individual History Card" is compiled. However, the Trial Court was aware, from previous blood degree correction cases, that the "Individual History Card" is one of the main ways for the Enrollment Office and the BIA to accurately reflect biographical information for each member. For this reason these cards received considerable weight by the Trial Court.

Finally, the Tribes introduced into evidence a 1968 letter from the BIA approving Colville Business Council Resolution 1968-50 requesting a decrease of Annie Etue Fergusons blood degree from 1/4 to 1/8. From this investigation and recommendation by the BIA, the Enrollment Office did decrease Annie Etue Ferguson's Indian blood on the 1937 Census from 1/4 to 1/8. However, because of the Enrollment's Office interpretation of

Amendment IX as stipulated to by the parties, the Enrollment Office increased Annie Etue Ferguson's Indian blood on the 1937 Census to 1/4 after Amendment IX was passed. As testified to by Audrey Sellars's at the Trial Court Hearing, this letter represents official action taken by the Enrollment Office in investigating and correctly representing the blood degree of Annie Etue Ferguson. For this reason, this letter received considerable weight by the Court.

From the above, the appellant has failed to meet his burden of proving by clear and convincing evidence that Floyd Hoffman's Indian blood on the 1937 Census should be increased to a specific blood degree which has been established as factually correct by clear and convincing evidence. Though Appellant had several documents admitted into evidence, he relied on only a few of the documents. Appellant failed to show the Trial Court the importance of each document at the Trial Court hearing. Many of the documents used by the appellant to make his case were contradictory. Appellant failed to explain the contradictions. In short, Appellant failed to clearly convince the Trial Court that the 1937 Census reflects a lower blood degree than actually exists. Appellant's evidence was not so clear and convincing that the evidence supporting the 1937 Census was plainly outweighed. The above findings and conclusions are affirmed by this Appellate Panel. . . .

The Trial Court stated in its Memorandum Opinion that "[I]f there were no written laws pertaining to the tribal adoption in 1907, 'custom law' is the relevant inquiry. Unlike Anglo statutory laws on adoption, Indian law is deeply rooted in the customs and traditions of the Tribes, which is woven into one's lifestyle and beliefs." *In Re P.*, J82-3021, 5-6 (Colv. Tr. Ct. 1983); *In Re: J.J.S.*, 11 Indian L. Rep. at 6031-32. Traditionally, "custom" is unwritten law. *In Re P.*, J82-3021 at pages 5-6. The Trial Court could have requested a "custom hearing" when "any doubt arises as to the customs of the Tribes. . . ." CTC §3.4.04. Also, see §56.07 of Colville Tribal Civil Rights Act. However, the burden of proof is on the appellant in this blood degree correction action to invoke CTC §3.4.04. Since the appellant has the burden of proof, he must affirmatively plead that a custom of the Tribes controls the law on an issue pertinent to his blood degree correction action in order for the Trial Court to request a customs hearing. This has not been done in this action. In the appellant's petition and subsequent pleadings, no specific allegations have been made regarding the applicability of custom law pertaining to adoption or blood corrections. Therefore, this Appellate Panel will affirm the decision of the Trial Court for not ordering a customs hearing. . . .

The decision of the Trial Court is affirmed, and the appeal is denied and dismissed.

NOTES

1. The Colville appellate court establishes a very high burden of proof for persons wishing to challenge a denial of their membership — the clearly erroneous standard. It appears the petitioner in this case, who was not represented by counsel, made a few strategic mistakes in relying entirely on the documentary evidence. In this case, it appears the documentary evidence submitted likely was incorrect. But what about other instances where there

is little documentary evidence? Could a live witness provide sufficient evidence?

2. The *Hoffman* Court affirmed the trial court's decision not to call for a hearing on tribal customary law. Could oral testimony that contradicts the written documentation control? How would a trial judge weigh the credibility of oral testimony (or even oral tradition) against written, and presumably verified, documents?

3. The trial court in the *Hoffman* matter held that the court had no jurisdiction to issue one of the orders requested by the petitioners—to be included on a judgment distribution roll—on grounds that the Tribes had not consented to suit. *See Hoffman v. Colville Confederated Tribes*, 22 Indian L. Rep. 6127, 6127 (Colville Confederated Tribes Indian Reservation Tribal Court, Sept. 7, 1995). The Colville Confederated Tribes had waived immunity for the limited purpose of allowing the tribal court to issue "injunctive relief correcting blood degrees." *Id.* at 6128.

4. In a portion of the opinion not excerpted above, the *Hoffman* appellate court also affirmed the trial court's determination that only one petitioner, Floyd Hoffman, had standing to maintain a blood correction claim in tribal court. *See Hoffman*, 22 Indian L. Rep. at 6128. The Tribes' constitution had limited the class of persons eligible to bring blood degree correction claims to:

> (1) a member, whether a natural person himself/herself, guardian or a minor or incompetent, or an administrator or executor of an unprobated estate; (2) an applicant for membership into the Colville Confederated Tribes; (3) a tribal member whose name appears on the January 1, 1937 official census of the Colville Reservation; or (4) a member descended from a tribal member whose name appears on the January 1, 1937 official census . . . of the Colville Confederated Tribes.

Id. at 6129. The trial court linked the standing issue to the Tribes' limited waiver of sovereign immunity. *See id.* at 6128. Why? What effect does this have?

5. Shortly after the Colville appellate court issued the *Hoffman* opinion, it applied the *Hoffman* evidentiary standards in another membership matter, *Pouley v. Colville Confederated Tribes*, 25 Indian L. Rep. 6024 (Colville Confederated Tribes Court of Appeals 1997). There, the court confronted the question of how to weigh documentary evidence that was "unsworn":

> *Hoffman* set forth the standard that sworn statements are given more weight than unsworn statements and as a general rule this is correct. In other words, the standard of proof should remain as set forth in *Hoffman*, but the Trial Court is cautioned to review each document for "circumstantial guarantees of trustworthiness" and not necessarily take the contents of each document at face value.
>
> It is the opinion of this panel that where unsworn evidence shows unusual consistency, it should be given greater weight than inconsistent, unsworn evidence. As was pointed out at oral argument, Victor Frank Desautel was consistently shown, without deviation, to be 1/2 Indian on every census record admitted. While censuses are admittedly generally unreliable from

year to year, where there is a conclusive consistency regarding an individual, they should be entitled to greater weight.

The Panel also believes that the Tardy Book, which is unsworn, is a census document. The Tardy Book is unique to the Tribes and has been a preferred document for enrollment purposes. The Panel believes that the Tardy Book qualifies as a traditional Tribal document and should be accorded greater weight than a regular census role—which is in accord with the Tribal Court's position that census rolls, whether prepared in 1937 or earlier, are inherently unreliable as sources of factually accurate blood degrees.

25 Indian L. Rep. at 6026.

6. In *Loges v. Confederated Tribes of Grand Ronde*, 4 Am. Tribal Law 171, 2003.NAGR.0000007 (Confederated Tribes of the Grand Ronde Reservation Tribal Court 2003), the court rejected an argument favoring enrollment by a person who would have qualified for membership under an earlier version of the tribe's constitution:

Petitioner's first claim is that the Tribal Constitution that was in effect when her blood quantum was changed or corrected should have been applied in her case. Apparently, Petitioner seeks to have her application judged under the standards that were in effect before the 1999 constitutional amendment that changed the enrollment requirements. Previously, the Tribal Constitution, as it applies in Petitioner's case, would not have required that she have a parent who was a Tribal member at the time of her birth and it would instead have been sufficient if she was "descended from a member of the Confederated Tribes of the Grand Ronde Community of Oregon[.]" Tribal Constitution, former Art v. section 1(b).

Other than the fact that Petitioner might prevail, there is no apparent reason to apply the earlier version of the constitutional provision in her case. As the Tribe notes, it does not keep track of the blood quantum of non-members. The Tribe acknowledges that the blood quantum of several members of Petitioner's ancestral family was changed and increased in the Tribal records in 1999. But that change did not give Petitioner any vested right or entitle her forever to apply for Tribal membership under the version of the Tribal Constitution that was then in effect. At most, Petitioner had then—and she had before—the opportunity and ability to apply for membership in the Tribe. But she did not pursue that opportunity until she applied for membership in 2001, after the constitutional amendment was in effect. It is her application that is the pivotal event. . . . Thus, the Enrollment Committee did not err in applying the amended version of the Tribal Constitution in Petitioner's case.

Id., 2003.NAGR.0000007 at ¶¶19-20.

Similar cases have arisen at Grand Ronde, a tribal community terminated by Congress and then later restored, challenging the tribe's amendments to its constitution allowing membership where tribal members had enrolled before termination and limiting membership for those that did not. In *In re Young*, 3 Am. Tribal Law 233, 2003.NAGR.0000007 (Confederated Tribes of the Grand Ronde Reservation Tribal Court 2001), the court rejected equal protection claims by family members who were ineligible but were similarly situated to family members who were eligible:

The Tribe did not deprive Petitioner of due process by considering their applications under the new amendment. . . . Applying the new amendment also did not result in any equal protection violation. The Tribe has the right to define its own membership for tribal purposes," *Santa Clara Pueblo v. Martinez*, 46 U.S. 49, 72 n. 32 (1978), and the Tribe was simply exercising that right, and drawing reasonable distinctions, when its members voted to amend the Constitution.

Petitioner claims that the new requirements are impossible to meet — that no person born during Termination could have a parent on the rolls of membership, as required now, as there was no membership roll during Termination. In fact, it appears that many persons born during Termination have been deemed to have a parent on the rolls — the roll as it existed at the time of Termination, and which was then carried over to the time of Restoration. This Court cannot repair the oversights of eligible members who could have, but did not, enroll prior to Termination.

The facts of this case are extremely sympathetic, as Ms. Young's family on the mother's side has been involved in Tribal matters for generations, and several family members are enrolled Tribal members. However, she advances no successful legal challenge to the new amendment's application in his case.

Id., 2003.NAGR.0000007 at ¶¶23-25.

4. DUAL ENROLLMENT AND INDIAN BLOOD OF OTHER TRIBAL NATIONS

In re Menefee[*]

Grand Traverse Band of Ottawa and
Chippewa Indians Tribal Court,
No. 97-12-092-CV, 2004 WL 5714978 (May 5, 2004)

Wilson D. Brott, Associate Judge.

I. Facts and Procedural History

. . . In June 1997, Petitioners Robin and Eva Menefee attempted to enroll their son, Jacob Mitchell Menefee as a member of the Respondent Grand Traverse Band of Ottawa and Chippewa Indians. On August 8, 1997, the membership office of the Respondent denied the application on the basis that Jacob Menefee was less than one-quarter Indian blood, and on the basis that he was already enrolled as a member of the Oneida of Thames Indian tribe in Canada. It is undisputed that the Oneida Tribe is not recognized by the United States government as a "federally recognized Indian tribe" as defined by 25 C.F.R. §83.1. Petitioner filed a lawsuit with this Court in October 1997 seeking to overturn the decision of the membership office. . . .

---

[*] *Disclosure:* The author of this book participated in the case as counsel for the Grand Traverse Band of Ottawa and Chippewa Indians.

II. Issues

The issues as presented to the Court and clarified by the Court of Appeals are as follows:

A. What is the definition of "Indian blood" as it relates to whether Petitioner meets the eligibility requirement of Article II, Section 1(b)(2)(a) of the Constitution that he is "at least one-fourth (1/4) Indian blood, of which at least one-eighth (1/8) must be Michigan Ottawa and/or Chippewa blood."

B. What is the meaning of "federally-recognized Indian Tribe, Band or Group" as it relates to whether Petitioner is prevented from being enrolled as a member pursuant to Article II, Section 2 of the Constitution, which states that "No person shall be eligible to be a member of the Grand Traverse Band if that person is enrolled in another federally-recognized Indian Tribe, Band, or Group."

Petitioner's argument hinges largely on history: that "Indian blood" should be interpreted to include Canadian Indian blood based upon the historical location and migration of the Ottawa and Chippewa Indians throughout the Great Lakes region (including both the United States and Canada), that the Court should not necessarily draw a distinction between or recognize the political boundaries of the United States and Canada. Further Petitioner argues that at some level, the United States government does recognize Canadian Indian tribes and gives special rights to American Indians born in Canada to cross the border between the United States and Canada. See 8 U.S.C. §1359.

Respondent argues that the Court should uphold the decision of the membership office to reject Petitioners' application for membership and requests that the Court adopt the interpretations of the Constitution relied upon by the membership office. Respondent argues that the history of migration of the tribes is irrelevant to the issue of interpreting the Constitution adopted by the Grand Traverse Band adopted in 1988. Respondent argues that the United States government placed certain constraints upon the Grand Traverse Band's Constitution before it would recognize the tribe, and urges the Court to interpret "Indian blood" as meaning essentially "American Indian blood," and not including Canadian Indian blood. . . .

III. Decision

The Court is faced with issues that go to the very essence of who the Grand Traverse Band of Ottawa and Chippewa Indians includes, as the issues relate to the determination of eligibility for membership in the Tribe. A tribe's right to define its own membership for tribal purposes has long been recognized as central to its existence as an independent political community. *Santa Clara Pueblo v. Martinez*, 436 U.S. 49, 72, n. 32 (1978). . . .

A. Blood quantum

This Court must interpret the definition of "Indian blood" as stated in Article II, Section 1(b)(2)(a). There is no question that prior to the existence of the United States of America and Canada, that the boundaries that presently exist were not recognized by the Ottawa and Chippewa peoples, who freely migrated across what is now the Canadian-U.S. border. However, it is impossible to ignore that fact that the United States and Canada have an established border, which has now been in place for over 200 years. The Grand Traverse Band of Ottawa and Chippewa Indians is a people made up of Ottawa and Chippewa Indians, which were part of a larger nation of Native Americans indigenous to the Great Lakes region. However, the Grand Traverse Band of Ottawa and Chippewa Indians is an Indian tribe that in many respects has its physical boundaries and legal authority created and/or defined by the laws of the United States of America.

Although the Ottawa and Chippewa Indian nations have been in existence for centuries, the notion of a "federally-recognized" tribe is a relatively new one. The Grand Traverse Band of Ottawa and Chippewa Indians was organized under the Indian Reorganization Act, and was "federally recognized" as an Indian tribe by the United States government in 1980. A history of the Grand Traverse band in terms of federal recognition is summarized as follows:

> The Grand Traverse Band is a federally recognized Indian tribe presently maintaining a government-to-government relationship with the United States. . . . The Band previously maintained a government-to-government relationship with the United States from 1795 until 1872, and is a successor to a series of treaties with the United States in 1795, 1815, 1836 and 1855. . . .
>
> In 1872, then-Secretary of the Interior, Columbus Delano, improperly severed the government-to-government relationship between the Band and the United States, ceasing to treat the Band as a federally recognized tribe. . . . Following termination of the relationship, the Band experienced increasing poverty, loss of land base and depletion of the resources of its community. . . .
>
> Between 1872 and 1980, the Band continually sought to regain its status as a federally recognized tribe. The Band's efforts succeeded in 1980 when it became the first tribe acknowledged by the Secretary of the Interior pursuant to the federal acknowledgment process, 25 C.F.R. Part 54 (now 25 C.F.R. Part 83). . . . On January 17, 1984, the Department of the Interior declared a single 12.5 acre parcel as the initial reservation of the Band. 49 Fed. Reg. 2025 (Jan. 17, 1984).
>
> The Band has a six-county service area in the Western District of Michigan, encompassing Antrim, Benzie, Charlevoix, Grand Traverse, Leelanau and Manistee Counties. . . .
>
> The history of the Band's original recognition, executive termination and later re-recognition is essentially parallel to that of the Pokogon Band of Potawatomi Indians, the Little Traverse Bay Bands of Odawa Indians, and the Little River Band of Ottawa Indians. All three tribes were parties to the same series of treaties and the same termination by Secretary Delano in 1872. . . .
>
> Between 1980 and 1988, the Band engaged in a protracted dispute with the Department of the Interior over the terms of its constitution. During this period, the Secretary of the Interior refused to take further land into trust for the Band. . . . In March 1988, after the dispute was resolved, the Secretary ratified the Band's Constitution. . . .

Grand Traverse Band of Ottawa and Chippewa Indians v. United States Attorney for the Western District of Michigan, 198 F. Supp. 2d 920, 924-925 (W.D. Mich. 2002). The present Constitution of the Grand Traverse Band of Ottawa and Chippewa Indians was adopted on March 29, 1988, by its members, and was approved by the Secretary of Interior. It is undisputed that the Constitution was drafted and amended several times prior to adoption under strict guidelines imposed by the Bureau of Indian Affairs. The Secretary of Interior had authority to approve or disapprove the proposed Constitution under 25 U.S.C. §476(a)(2). Many provisions of the Constitution of the Grand Traverse Band of Ottawa and Chippewa Indians were modified prior to its adoption in order to gain the approval and recognition of the United States government, including the membership provisions of the Constitution. Although it is certainly true that the Tribe's Constitution was ultimately adopted and approved by the members of the Grand Traverse Band, this Court cannot ignore the circumstances under which the current Constitution was adopted and the influence the United States government also exerted on its creation.

The federal government has strongly urged against the acceptance of Canadian Indian blood for the purposes of determining a blood quantum related to the membership requirements of tribal constitutions. *See* Letter from Marsha Kimball, United States Dept. of Interior to Larry Morrin, Bureau of Indian Affairs, dated February 22, 2002 concerning Little Traverse Bay Band; *and* Letter from Mark Anderson, United States Dept. of Interior to Earl Barlow, Bureau of Indian Affairs, dated September 30, 1993, concerning St. Croix Band of Chippewa Indians. Their argument is based upon the definition of "Indian" in 25 U.S.C. §479, which does not include Canadian Indians, and further upon other difficulties of determining the authenticity of Canadian Indian heritage. As noted by Respondent, membership in American Indian tribes is determined by tribal law, whereas membership in Canada is derived by Canadian federal or provincial law. As noted in the Kimball letter cited above:

> The Department [of Interior]'s position in other contexts is that Canadian Indians are non-Indians. That is certainly the case in which Canadian nationals, possessed of Canadian Indian blood, are arrested and held by tribal law police and court systems. Canadian Indian blood does not factor into whether that individual is an "Indian for the purposes of tribal criminal jurisdiction". Further the BIA should not be placed in a position in which it is required to evaluate and determine the authenticity of documents created by Canadian tribal entities. . . .
>
> The reliance on documents other than those generated by the officials of the United States adds an element of uncertainty and the potential for abuse in the establishment of this crucial original membership list.

Kimball letter, *supra*, p. 3-4.

While the Court believes that the Petitioner's argument is well grounded in history, this Court cannot ignore the context in which the current Constitution was adopted. Nor can this Court ignore the significant threat to the Tribe's federal recognition by United States government that would be presented if this Court adopted Petitioner's interpretation of the Constitution. Therefore, this Court is persuaded that the term "Indian Blood" as used in Article II, Section 1(b)(2)(a) of the Constitution was intended by the drafters of the Constitution to be limited to Indian blood from tribes which are recognized by the United States government within the boundaries of the continental United States, and was not intended to include Canadian Indian blood.

B. Federally-recognized Indian Tribe

Article II, Section 2 of the Grand Traverse Band of Ottawa and Chippewa Indians Constitution states that "No person shall be eligible to be a member of the Grand Traverse Band if that person is enrolled in another federally-recognized Indian Tribe, Band, or Group." This Court must interpret the meaning of "federally-recognized Indian Tribe, Band or Group" as it relates to Petitioner's request to be enrolled as a member of the tribe. . . .

This Court is satisfied, that the Respondent has adequately shown that the circumstances under which the Grand Traverse Band adopted its Constitution intended that "federally-recognized Indian tribe" refer to those tribes which have been recognized by the United States government as an Indian tribe. Furthermore, it is clear to this Court that the plain meaning of "federal recognition" is recognition by the United States government as an Indian tribe within the boundaries of the continental United States, and does not include Indian tribes physically located in other countries such as Canada. To interpret otherwise would require the Court to ignore the plain meaning of the phrase as it is used under the laws of the United States, and to ignore the circumstances under which the members of the Grand Traverse Band drafted and adopted its Constitution in 1988.

IV. Conclusion

For the reasons stated above, this Court holds that the decision of the Membership office in rejecting the Petitioner's application for membership was Constitutionally sound. This Court holds that "Indian blood" as stated in Article II, Section 1(b)(2)(a) of the Constitution was intended by the drafters of the Constitution to be limited to Indian blood from tribes which are recognized by the United States government within the boundaries of the United States, and was not intended to include blood from Canadian Indian tribes. This Court further holds that "federally-recognized Indian Tribe, Band or Group" as stated in Article II, Section 2 of the Constitution, refers to those tribes, bands or groups, which have been recognized by the United States government as an Indian tribe within the boundaries of the continental United States. . . .

NOTES

1. On occasion, Indians that are residents of other nations may be eligible for American Indian tribal citizenship, or at least federal services. One example is the Garden River Ojibway community just north of Sault Ste. Marie, Michigan, in Ontario, Canada. The Garden River community is part of the groups now known as the Bay Mills Indian Community and the Sault Ste. Marie Tribe of Chippewa Indians. *See Bay Mills Indian Community Land Claims Settlement*, Hearing before the Senate Committee on Indian Affairs, S. Hrg. 107-925, at 34 (Oct. 10, 2002) (Prepared Statement of L. John Lukfins, President, Executive Council, Bay Mills Indian Community).

2. As a general rule, Indian people may not be citizens of more than one Indian nation. As such, some Indian people who may have citizenship in one

Indian nation relinquish their citizenship in order to petition for citizenship with another tribe. Occasionally, litigation arises out of this relinquishment process.

In *Loy v. Confederated Tribes of Grand Ronde*, 4 Am. Tribal Law 132, 2003.NAGR.0000010 (Confederated Tribes of the Grand Ronde Reservation Court of Appeals 2003), the court struck down a one-year waiting period on relinquishment imposed by the tribal council:

> The Enrollment Committee was required to wait at least one year after Loy relinquished her Siletz tribal membership before considering her Grand Ronde enrollment application. Tribal Code §4.10(b)(4). We must address whether the Tribal Council had the authority to legislatively adopt this one-year waiting period, given the absence of such a requirement in the 1984 Grand Ronde Constitution, which stated with respect to dual membership:
>
> > Section 1. Requirements. The membership of the Confederated Tribes of the Grand Ronde Community of Oregon shall consist of all persons who are not enrolled as members of another recognized tribe, band or community and . . . .
> >
> > Section 2. Dual Membership Prohibited. No person who is an enrolled member of any other organized tribe, band, or Indian community officially recognized by the Secretary of the Interior shall be qualified for membership in the Confederated Tribes of the Grand Ronde Community of Oregon, unless he or she has relinquished in writing his or her membership in such tribe, band or community.
>
> GRAND RONDE CONSTITUTION, Art. V, §§1, 2 (1984). . . .
>
> The Constitution required the Tribal Council to "enact an ordinance establishing procedures for processing membership matters, including but not limited to application procedures. . . ." GRAND RONDE CONSTITUTION, Art. V, §3. The Tribe argues that the one-year waiting period is only a procedural requirement authorized under the foregoing provision. We disagree.
>
> [W]e view the one-year waiting period as being substantive because it "creates, defines, and regulates" the eligibility requirements for tribal membership. That conclusion is supported by the voters' subsequent amendment of Article V in 1999, which, in addition to changing the enrollment criteria, added the one-year waiting period as a requirement for those applicants who have relinquished membership in other recognized tribes. *See* GRAND RONDE CONSTITUTION, Art. V, §§1, 2 (1999). In addition, the sample ballot distributed to tribal voters indicated that the Constitutional amendment was designed "to increase requirements for enrollment" in the Tribe. The Tribal Council did not, and does not, have the authority to create by ordinance membership requirements inconsistent with those expressly defined in the Constitution. The Tribal Council could no more add the one-year waiting period to the membership requirements than it could change the Indian blood quantum the Constitution requires.
>
> Consequently, we hold that the Tribal Council exceeded its constitutional authority and violated the 1984 Grand Ronde Constitution when it added as a membership requirement a one-year relinquishment waiting period that was not contained in the Constitution. . . .

Id., 2003.NAGR.0000010 at ¶¶25-32.

C. DISENROLLMENT

Snowden v. Saginaw Chippewa Indian Tribe of Michigan

Appellate Court of the Saginaw Chippewa Indian Tribe of Michigan,
No. 04-CA-1017, 32 Indian L. Rep. 6047 (January 7, 2005)

By Frank Pommersheim, Associate Justice, for a unanimous Court. . . .

I. Introduction and Background

For the past decade, if not longer, the Saginaw Chippewa Indian Tribe
has been embroiled in extensive political and legal conflict over issues of
membership. While the cause of these disputes is deeply rooted in various
federal moves relative to membership, it has been left to the Tribe to resolve
these often painful issues. This case is one example. It focuses on the issue of
disenrollment.

The consolidated cases in this appeal grow out of an attempt by the Tribe to
disenroll two deceased Tribal members, Malina Hinmon and Mary Lee (Tipkey)
Snowden and their descendants. The descendants include two members of a
prior Tribal Council, as well as a former Chief Judge of the Tribal Court. . . .

II. Issue

This appeal raises a single issue, namely, whether the Tribal Council's
power to disenroll currently enrolled members is limited to the narrow
grounds expressly identified in the Tribal Constitution and if not, what are
the Tribal constitutional boundaries in establishing (substantive) grounds for
disenrollment.

III. Discussion

This case is not just about the meaning of the Saginaw Chippewa Tribal
Constitution of 1986, but it is also a story about a People and a Tribe enmeshed
in the coils of an unknowing and meddlesome Bureau of Indian Affairs and
Federal Government. This destabilizing federal force is amply demonstrated in
the history leading up to the adoption of the first Saginaw Chippewa Tribal
Constitution in 1937. The Saginaw Chippewa Tribe of Michigan came into
specific legal existence as a result of the Indian Reorganization Act (IRA) of
1934 and the adoption of the first Tribal Constitution in 1937. As is well know,
the thrust of the IRA was to encourage tribes to formally adopt the Act through
a tribal referendum and then adopt a constitution as provided by Sec. 16 of the
Act as well as a business charter as provided in Sec. 17 of the Act.

Many local Tribal leaders and people were interested in the possibilities
offered by the IRA. In fact, even before the referendum on the IRA itself, a
Business Committee headed by Elijah Elk was established to meet with various
tribal communities and to begin drafting a tribal constitution. The work of this
committee resulted in a (draft) constitution that was sent to Secretary of
Interior Harold Ickes on Nov. 27, 1934 for his approval.

The draft constitution is noteworthy in several respects that are directly
pertinent to this litigation. The proposed constitution's preamble began,

"We, the members of the Saginaw, Swan Creek, and Black River Bands of Chippewa Indians. . . ." The proposed Tribal Council recognized four districts—three of which were outside the boundaries of the Isabella Reservation—three representatives from Mt. Pleasant (i.e. Isabella Reservation), three from Bay City, one from Caro, and three from Hubbard Lake.

Action on this proposed Constitution was slowed as a result of BIA Commissioner John Collier's direction to Elijah Elk that no action could be taken until the formal referendum to accept the IRA took place. As a result, energy shifted away from the draft constitution toward developing a list of eligible voters to vote in the IRA referendum. The list that was compiled by tribal individuals and BIA special agent George Blakeslee contained the names of many tribal people living outside the boundaries of the Isabella Reservation. The referendum was held on June 17, 1935 and included at least two off reservation voting places. The referendum passed.

With the successful referendum accomplished, attention returned to the Constitution itself. The Tribe's desire to include all of its communities within its constitution—even those communities outside the Isabella Reservation—met strong resistance from Assistant Commissioner of Indian Affairs, William Zimmerman. Commissioner Zimmerman took the position that a tribe could only organize under the IRA if it had a reservation and its only members could be tribal people residing on the Reservation.

With this dubious interpretation at the forefront of his review of the proposed Constitution, he changed the preamble to read "We, the Indians residing on the Isabella Reservation it the State of Michigan. . . ." In addition, he changed the proposed Tribal Council representation to require all council members be elected from within the Reservation, and required that all Tribal members reside on the Reservation. Commissioner Zimmerman further advised the Tribe that subsequent to the referendum to accept the constitution the Tribe could "adopt" those individuals living off the reservation. In fact, this "adoption" language appears in Sec. 2 of Art. III—Membership of the 1937 Constitution.

All these "recommendations" were accepted by the Business Committee and incorporated in the proposed Tribal Constitution that was voted on and accepted by tribal members on March 27, 1937. Unfortunately, the 1937 Constitution—whatever its intent—sowed the seeds of membership confusion and discontent that yielded the bitter harvest at the core of this most challenging, even heartwrenching, litigation about the cultural and legal aspects of tribal belonging.

The shortcomings of the membership provisions of the 1937 Constitution were apparent from the beginning. The problems caused by severe land loss, conflicting allotment procedures, and artificial residency requirements virtually insured a confusing, inconsistent approach to enrollment. This flawed and inadequate patchwork approach was capped by Congress' insistence that as part of the settlement of the Saginaw Chippewa Tribe's successful land claim against the United States that a new Tribal Constitution—approved by Congress—be adopted by a vote of the members of the Saginaw Chippewa Tribe. The Constitution so adopted by majority vote was the Saginaw Chippewa

Tribal Constitution of 1986 which contains the membership and other relevant sections at issue in this case.

The most essential ingredient of tribal sovereignty is the ability of tribes "to maintain or establish [their] own form of government." FELIX S. COHEN, HANDBOOK OF FEDERAL INDIAN LAW 247 (1982). Indeed, "[t]his power is the first element of sovereignty." *Id.* Tribes accordingly allocate authority to their elected officials in the manner that they view as most conducive to the effective functioning of their political communities. "Tribal government . . . may reflect the tribe's determination as to what form best fits its needs based on practical, cultural, historical, or religious considerations." *Id.; see also Holmes v. St. Croix Casino*, 26 Indian L. Rep. 6089, 6092 (St. Croix App. Ct. 1999) ("The first element of sovereignty . . . is the power of the tribe to determine and define its own form of government. *Such powers include the right to define the power and duties of its officials. . . .*") (emphasis added); *Coin v. Mowa*, 25 Indian L. Rep. 6208, 6210 (Hopi App. Ct. 1997) ("In the federal scheme, the Tribe retains any power not abrogated by the federal government. *The Tribe exercises its retained sovereignty by allocating this power as it sees fit.*") (citation omitted and emphasis added).

Tribal constitutions frequently serve as the vehicle that Tribes use to define the allocation of power to their governing institutions, *see Terry-Carpenter v. Las Vegas Paiute Tribal Council*, 29 Indian L. Rep. 6041, 6043 (Las Vegas Paiute Ct. App. 2002), and, as this Court stressed in *Chamberlain [v. Peters*, 27 Indian L. Rep. 6085 (Saginaw Chippewa Indian Tribe Appellate Court 2000)], in constitutional systems it is often the solemn responsibility of the tribal courts to ensure that the Tribe's governing bodies do not exceed the bounds thereby placed on their authority. *Chamberlain*, 27 Indian L. Rep. at 6089 ("Among the most important functions of courts are constitutional interpretation and the closely connected power of determining whether law and acts of the legislature comport with the provisions of the Constitution. Courts were created to serve these purposes.") (quoting *Moran v. Council of the Confederated Salish & Kootenai Tribes*, 22 Indian L. Rep. 6149, 6155 (C.S. & K.T. Ct. App. 1995).

A. Structure of the Saginaw Chippewa Tribal Constitution of 1986

A central element in this process of establishing a constitutional government is the allocation of power between the Tribal Government and the "people." In determining what is the constitutional range of the Tribe's power to disenroll individuals who currently are legally recognized as Tribal members, it is helpful to review the overall structural design of the 1986 Constitution. The essential historical types of constitutions in Indian country are the "plenary" model in which all power is expressly granted to the Tribal Council or the enumerated or "limited" powers model in which the Tribal Council is provided a limited set of enumerated powers with a reservation of all such non-enumerated powers to "the people." An example of the former is the Grand Traverse Band of Ottawa and Chippewa Indians Constitution at Art. IV:

> The Tribal Council . . . shall be vested with all of the sovereign governmental executive and legislative powers of the Tribe not inconsistent with any

provision(s) of the Constitution or federal law. *Such powers shall include, but not be limited to, the following.* . . . (emphasis added).

An example of the latter is the Turtle Mt. Band of Chippewa Indians Constitution at Art. X:

Any right [or] power heretofore vested in the [Band], but not expressly referred to in the Constitution, shall remain in the Band, and may be exercised by the [Band] or by the Tribal Council · through the adoption of appropriate constitutional amendment if that be the wishes of the people.

Needless to say the Constitution of the United States is also an enumerated powers constitution.

The 1986 Saginaw Chippewa Constitution is clearly an enumerated powers Constitution at Art. VI (Powers of the Tribal Council) Sec. 2:

The Trial Council may exercise such further powers as may in the future be *delegated to it by members of the Tribe* (emphasis added).

Since Sec. 1 of Art. VI enumerated the powers of the Tribal Council, there is no doubt that Sec. 2 is in direct limitation of Tribal Council authority to those powers specifically identified in Sec. 1.

B. Express Constitutional Power to Disenroll

Sec. 1(m) of Art. VI of the Constitution expressly addresses issues of membership by recognizing Tribal Council authority:

To enact resolutions or ordinances not inconsistent with Art. III of this Constitution governing adoptions and abandonment of membership.

This language does not reflect any extensive or generalized power to disenroll. At best, it is reasonable to interpret the language as including Tribal Council authority to enact ordinances relevant to disenrollment in the context of "adoption" or "abandonment of membership." Apparently no such ordinances have ever been adopted and therefore Art. VI Sec. 1(m) is not relevant to the case at hand.

Art. III of the Constitution deals directly with membership. Sec. 1 deals with the qualifications for enrollment. (In fact, Sec. 1, and more particularly Sec. 1(c), is the Constitutional core of the Bryant case.) Sec. 1 provides no authority to the Tribal Council to legislate in the area of enrollment except as to "adoption." Sec. 1 contains no express powers of disenrollment.

Secs. 2 and 3 deal expressly with disenrollment and basically track the language of Art. VI(1)(m) about "abandonment" and "adoption." Sec. 2 mandates disenrollment if a tribal member becomes "an enrolled member of any other federally recognized tribe." Sec. 3 involves the potential disenrollment of an "adopted member" of the Tribe "by reason of marriage" wherein said marriage is dissolved by either annulment or divorce and said individual neither maintains Reservation residence nor remarries another tribal member within twelve months. An "adopted" tribal member is also subject to potential disenrollment by "re-establishing tribal relations with the tribe from which they are descendants by blood." Disenrollment under Sec. 2 is mandatory (i.e. "shall"). Disenrollment under Sec. 3 is discretionary (i.e. "may").

In sum, the only express constitutional authority to disenroll is limited to certain situations involving "adopted" tribal members and tribal members who "abandon" Saginaw Chippewa Tribal membership by enrolling in another federal[ly] recognized tribe.

C. Implied Constitutional Power to Disenroll

Both sides presumably do not dispute any of the above, which merely establishes the background and context for examining the pivotal issue whether there are any implied powers of disenrollment and if so, what they are. The fact that the Constitution is an enumerated powers constitution with limited express powers of disenrollment does *not* automatically foreclose the possibility of some limited — presumably very limited — implied powers of disenrollment.

Before examining such possibilities, it is necessary to address the Tribe's observation that this Court has made an "unwarranted assumption . . . that all persons listed on the tribal rolls had, in fact, been admitted to membership after first proving that they in fact and in law actually met the Tribe's constitutional membership criteria." (Appellee's Brief at 15.) This Court's "assumption" is indeed warranted and required by both legal and cultural norms of integrity. If someone has achieved a legal status (even if erroneously), they are entitled to that status until the government *proves* adequately to the contrary. The Tribe would have us *assume* the "guilt" rather than the "innocence" of Appellants. Such an approach would necessarily taint and even erode this Court's bedrock commitment to due process and cultural respect.

No constitutional text is completely transparent or self-disclosing and no constitution is beyond the necessity of interpretation. In fact, that is the request of the parties in this litigation, that the Court engage in constitutional adjudication. In this regard, the Tribe makes rather extensive claims that it has wide-ranging implied powers to disenroll that flow from Art. VI Secs. e, j, n and o.

The core of the Tribe's argument is that the interplay of Art. VI Secs. e, j, n, and o particularly the "general welfare" clauses of Secs (j) and (o) along with the "economic affairs" clause of Sec. (e) provide the Tribal Council with authority "essentially unrestricted as to *subject matter* so long as the Council's legislation can be fairly said to promote the Tribe's 'general welfare' or 'economic affairs' . . . so long as that legislation does not contravene any other explicit limitation on the Council's powers." (Appellee's Brief at 19.) This claim is rather bold, if not extravagant, in that it seeks to convert an enumerated powers Constitution into a plenary powers Constitution with an overwhelming presumption in favor of *any and all* Tribal Council action that would put the burden on the non-Tribal Council party to show "explicit limitation on the Council's power." This goes too far and would necessarily unhinge Tribal Council authority from the history and text of the Constitution.

The "general welfare" clauses at Secs. (j) and (o) are primarily related to matters of "tribal property . . . natural resources . . . to cultivate Indian arts, crafts" (sec. o). Neither of these enumerations, whether using the statutory interpretation maxims of *ejusdem generis* or *noscitur a sociis*[19] or ordinary common sense, appear related to issues of membership and more particularly to issues of disenrollment, and therefore they do not support any wide-ranging Tribal Council power to disenroll.

The Appellants' argument goes too far in the other direction. They claim that a limited powers Constitution—such as the one at bar—contains no implied powers whatsoever and the power to disenroll is limited to the express power to disenroll relative to "adoption" and "abandonment" as set out at Art. III Secs. 2 and 3 and Art. IV Sec. 1(m). For the Appellants, those limited express grounds for disenrollment negate any implied grounds for disenrollment.

The logic of this assertion is that the overall structure of the Constitution constrains any attempt to go beyond the express language of disenrollment. This argument is credible, but it is not compelling. The express grounds for disenrollment are really designed to cover a specific kind of disenrollment— disenrollment that comes into play *after* legitimate enrollment through the occurrence of a *condition subsequent* such as the divorce of an "adopted" trial member or "abandonment" of membership by obtaining membership in another federally recognized tribe.

The Constitution is silent on the ability of the Tribal Council to disenroll someone who did not meet—at the front end—the basic conditions for enrollment set out in Art. III, Sec. I. To interpret this constitutional silence as an absolute bar to *potential* disenrollment of such individuals would create a constitutional anomaly that would, for example, put "fraud" in the membership context beyond the pale of the constitutional text. Such a reading would seem a clear failure of constitutional justice.

A survey of other tribal constitutions is informative and consistent in this regard. No tribal constitution cited by the parties or otherwise known by the Court contains any express provision to disenroll on such basic grounds like "fraud" and "mistake." This does *not* lead to the conclusion that such power does *not* exist in any Tribe, but rather that it is so basic and ingrained in the understanding of what is necessary to become a (legitimate) tribal member that there is a very, very limited *implied* power to disenroll on grounds of fraud and mistake that inheres in the right to enroll itself. To put it another way, there is a very, very limited, but necessary, constitutional corollary relative to disenrollment that is an ineluctable part of the constitutional mandate of enrollment itself. Without such implied constitutional power, the Tribe would be powerless to deal with fraud and mistake in the enrollment

---

19. These Latin phrases, staples of statutory interpretation, may be translated as follows: *ejusdem generis* means of the same kind or class and refers to the textual principle that "[w]here general words follow specific words in [textual] enumeration, the general words are construed to embrace only objects similar in nature to those objects enumerated by the preceding specific words." 2A Sutherland, Statutes and Statutory Construction §47.17 (6th ed., Norman Singer, ed.). *Noscitur a sociis* literally means that something is known from its associates or more colloquially a word is known by the company it keeps. . . . These principles of statutory construction add up to the commonsensical notion that where the framers of a document group together a number of items in a particular textual enumeration, they do not do so randomly, but because they think of the items as related to one another and intend them to be read as such. . . .

process. Such an interpretation of the constitutional text would improperly exalt form over substance.

No, the Tribe may not disenroll people for whatever "good" reasons it might identify. No, the Constitution does not (and cannot) condone any constitutional failure of justice that would potentially endorse (constitutional) fraud and mistake in obtaining membership. Beyond such quite limited constitutional authority to disenroll on grounds of fraud or mistake, there are *no* other *implied* grounds for disenrollment.[20]

This Court has an unflagging duty to interpret the Constitution. That is, in fact, its highest calling. This duty and calling are never taken lightly and never confused with a mere review of policy. Tribal membership involves not only constitutional status, but also serves as the ultimate indication of cultural belonging. With this in mind, we urge the parties, as we did in the *Chamberlain* case, to place themselves in the heart of Native American jurisprudence by "healing, restoring balance and harmony, accomplishing reconciliation, and making social relations whole again." 27 Indian L. Rep. 6085, 6097 (2000).

IV. Conclusion

For all of the above stated reasons, the decision of Community Court is reversed. The implied Constitutional power to disenroll is limited to matters of fraud and mistake. Further, the guarantee of due process requires that exercise of such implied power must be set out in an appropriate ordinance that defines these substantive grounds for disenrollment and further complies with the procedural guarantees set out in Ordinance 14.

IT IS SO ORDERED.

NOTES

1. The Saginaw Chippewa Indian Tribe's citizenship conflicts continue to this day. In a pair of recent decisions, the tribal appellate court rejected the decision of the tribal administrative citizenship office that declined to give weight to a blood quantum determination made by the Tribe and memorialized in a Certificate of Degree of Indian Blood. *See Graverette v. Saginaw Chippewa Tribe of Michigan*, Nos. 09-CA-1040, 09-CA-1041 (Saginaw Chippewa Tribe of Michigan Court of Appeals, Aug. 16, 2010). *See also Tappen v. Tribal Certifiers*, No. 10-CA-0264 (Saginaw Chippewa Tribe of Michigan Court of Appeals, Aug. 16, 2010). The court wrote:

> The [Office of Administrative Hearings] and the Tribal Certifier also apparently read [the tribal statute] to deny consideration of federally or tribally issued Certificates of Degree of Indian Blood. . . . We do not believe that [the tribal statute] supports such an approach on the basis that tribal certificates of degree of Indian blood are unreliable. This is akin to accusing the Saginaw Chippewa Indian tribe of lying in official documents; we cannot

---

20. It is critical to remember that this case does *not* involve the review of any specific lower court decision to disenroll. The precise grounds for such potential disenrollment have *never* been established, much less applied. Identifying that relevant standard is what this case is about. Any actual case of disenrollment will be subject to the stringent due process and burden of proof standards of Ordinance 14 and subject to (potential) review by this Court.

countenance such an unsubstantiated conclusion without more explanation or an affirmative finding by the legislative body.

Graverette, at 3.

2. Angela Riley notes that tribal disenrollment cases often arise out of disputes over gaming wealth, as does the outsider scrutiny of such cases:

> News reports of banishment and disenrollment of individual Indians by wealthy tribes, in particular, are fueling deeply embedded misconceptions about tribal governments. Though it's not clear that there are more membership disputes today than in the past, they are certainly more widely reported than before. Tribes concede that they are carefully scrutinizing tribal membership decisions. One reason is that casino wealth has attracted masses of people who wouldn't have bothered to claim tribal membership before. Thus, tribes are faced with the unenviable task of verifying the membership of new and existing members.
>
> News reports of tribal members suffering disenrollment or banishment after, for example, contesting the scope of tribal leaders' powers, alleging civil rights violations, or opposing major economic development projects have added to negative public sentiments about tribal governments. Many tribes believe this is due much more to a backlash over gaming than anger over civil rights violations of individual tribal members. But, in any case, civil rights lawyers (including Indian attorneys themselves) are aggressively representing individual Indians and pressing for federal court review of tribal court decisions. These cases appear to inspire a level of opposition to tribal governments — coming especially from tribal members themselves — that was not seen immediately following *Santa Clara Pueblo*.

Angela R. Riley, *Tribal Sovereignty in a Post-9/11 World*, 82 N.D. L. Rev. 953, 959-60 (2006).

3. Tribal disenrollment decisions are often accompanied by the banishment of the disenrolled individuals. Professor Riley writes:

> [R]ecent stories of banishment in the news raise the inference that, at least in some instances, tribal members are being permanently exiled from their tribal communities in the absence of the other requisite governance factors. Allegations that tribal members have been banished for voicing dissent against tribal leadership are particularly troubling. In the case of one California rancheria, for example, the *Los Angeles Times* reported that 174 members — fifteen percent of the tribe's total enrollment — were banished because their common relative vocally opposed a proposed casino development deal. Another California tribe purportedly disenrolled seventy tribal members, including the vice chair of the tribal council, for signing a petition to recall other elected officials. Subsequently, two tribal members who expressed vocal opposition to the previous banishments were also disenrolled. In that instance, the tribal chairwoman, Glenda Nelson, reportedly said that the tribal members were disenrolled for the sake of tribal unity, because the dissidents' actions were destroying the tribe. Just recently, five tribal members were allegedly "shunned" by their tribe for several years for filing a lawsuit to demand review of tribal finances. They were not informed of their banishment — which will preclude them from accessing their tribal membership benefits for seven years — until almost a month after the tribal council's decision. And there are other cases that raise questions about the

rights of minority factions who claim they are being punished for speaking out against powerful elites. Such stories are troubling from an indigenous perspective, not only because injustice may be perpetrated on individual Indians, but because such stories raise the ire of the non-Indian community and further instigate misconceptions and animosity toward tribes, even when such incidences are extremely isolated.

Angela R. Riley, *Good (Native) Governance*, 107 Colum. L. Rev. 1049, 113-14 (2007).

4. Tribal courts confronted with the question of the revocation of tribal citizenship by tribal officials after the discovery of an error are split on whether the disenrolled member is entitled to keep per capita payments.

In *Kennard v. Dore*, No. 93-C-02, 1994.NAPA.0000001 (Passamaquoddy Tribe Appellate Division, July 14, 1994), the court wrote the following:

> For the Court below to agree that the Pleasant Point Tribal Council had the right to remove Brad Jr. from the membership rolls on December 15, 1993 but to somehow maintain that Brad Jr., clearly never entitled to Tribal membership, yet possessed some type of "entitlement" to per capita monies, which "entitlement" only Tribal members would have, is a veritable conundrum. If he is not a member he has no "entitlement" to per capita. If he is not a member the question may also be raised whether he ever had entitlement to I.C.R.A. protections. The decision of the Court below that — the part of the Court's decision conferring the "entitlement" and the finding of the I.CR.A. violation will stand — cannot stand. The record below shows due process disallowance of Kayla's application for membership and due process disenrollment of Brad Jr. When these things occurred any "entitlement" ceased *ab initio*. Any other result would result in an absurdity whereby a non-member would possess a continuing right to per capita income from a Tribe to which he did not belong. So much of the lower Court's decision finding a continuing "entitlement" in Brad Jr. to allocated per capita income being error, that decision is hereby reversed and it is ordered that all monies paid by the Nation to the Clerk of Tribal Court to be kept in escrow in this case, representing unpaid allocated per capita on behalf of Brad Jr., be immediately returned to the Nation.

Id. at ¶29.

5. Somewhat conversely, the court in *Deverney v. Grand Traverse Band of Ottawa and Chippewa Indians*, 2000 WL 35749822 (Grand Traverse Band Court of Appeals, Nov. 15, 2000), held that the revocation of tribal membership is not void ab initio until the disenrolled citizen has exhausted tribal remedies:

> [O]nce membership is granted, the court must give due process except where the Tribal Constitution expressly removes the court discretion or jurisdiction. This was clearly done in the second part of Article II, Section 2 of the Tribal Constitution for members who become members of another tribe after becoming members of this tribe. The Constitution sets out the remedy in that situation, but does not set out a remedy in the first part of that section. Since the parties framing the Constitution set out the remedy in one situation and knew how to apply it, the court cannot add it to another situation. This is particularly strong policy in this case where the tribe passed Ordinance 7 GTBC 202(b) six weeks after the Constitution was ratified. The argument

that it only applies to people enrolled under Article II, Section 1, is rejected as part (b) is unambiguous and does not speak to any such limitation on its face. This general reference is continued in 7 GTBC Sections 203 and 204 as to "any" person disenrolled.

The Tribe must be given the power to exercise its discretion in making a membership decision. A later-discovered error by the Certifier must be corrected as the particular case requires. It cannot be automatic and remove the Certifier's discretion or judgment. This court denies the argument that both parts of Section 2 are automatic and self-executing. This also is a rejection that both parts of Article II, Section 2 makes membership errors void *ab initio*.

Id. at *3-4.

6. In *Muscogee (Creek) Nation Citizenship Board v. Todd*, 7 Okla. Tribal Court Rep. 9 (Muscogee (Creek) Nation Supreme Court 2000), the court reversed a disenrollment order by the Nation's Citizenship Board:

The authority of the Board to revoke citizenship is based upon NCA 81-06, Section 4006: REMOVAL OF NAMES FROM THE CITIZENSHIP ROLL:

The Citizenship Board shall have the power to remove the names of persons from the Citizenship Roll of the Muscogee (Creek) Nation, by:

A. Designating a cause to remove from the roll, said cause hereby limited to:

1. Proof that the person is not Muscogee (Creek) Indian by blood,

2. Proof that the person is an enrolled member of another Indian tribe, nation, band or pueblo,

3. Proof that fraud, bribery, or misrepresentation were utilized at any stage in securing enrollment,

4. Voluntary resignation from citizenship by an enrolled citizen,

5. Order by a tribal court to remove a name from the Citizenship Roll.

B. Notification of the otherwise enrolled citizen that the cause for their name to be removed has been designated and that they have thirty days to request a hearing if any cause other than resignation or court order is involved.

C. Holding a hearing if requested by the person against whom cause has been designated. The hearing shall be an evidentiary proceeding where *the burden of proof shall be upon the Citizenship Board* to establish [by] a preponderance of the evidence that the designated cause is true and sufficient to remove the person from the Citizenship Roll. All certified copies of records in the citizen's file shall automatically be introduced by the Chairman. The citizen and any member of the Citizenship Board may subpoena witnesses. The decision of the Citizenship Board may be reviewed by the tribal courts as provided by this Ordinance.

NCA 81-06 §4006 (emphasis added).

This Court finds that the District Court did not err in remanding this case to the Muscogee (Creek) Nation Citizenship Board for the Board to comply with the mandated procedures for removal of a person from the Citizenship Rolls as set forth in NCA 81-06. . . .

The Citizenship Board is to follow the language of NCA 81-06 and shall not place the burden of proof upon the citizen to fight against a petition for removal.

Id. at 11-13.

The tribal court in *Todd* had applied by analogy the burden of proof adopted by the United States Supreme Court in denaturalization cases:

> The United States Supreme Court, in *Schneiderman v. United States*, 320 U.S. 118, 63 S. Ct. 1333 (1943), has addressed the burden of proof placed upon the government in de-naturalization cases. The United States Supreme Court requires the government to establish its allegations by clear, unequivocal and convincing evidence. Further, in *Fedorenko v. United States*, 449 U.S. 490, 101 S. Ct. 737 (1981), the Court said that American citizenship is a precious one, and that once citizenship has been acquired, its loss can have severe and unsettling consequences. For these reasons, we have held that the government "carries a heavy burden of proof in a proceeding to divest a naturalized citizen of his citizenship." The evidence justifying revocation of citizenship must be "clear, unequivocal, and convincing" and not leave "the issue in doubt."

Todd v. Muscogee (Creek) Nation Citizenship Board, 6 Okla. Tribal Court Rep. 170, 175 (Muscogee (Creek) District Court, Oct. 16, 1999). Are the due process concerns in American denaturalization proceedings the same as in a tribal disenrollment case? Did the Muscogee (Creek) Nation Supreme Court implicitly revoke this standard by not mentioning it in its opinion?

7. In disenrollment cases, tribal courts tend to give the benefit of the doubt to the potential disenrollee for due process purposes. For example, in *Delgado v. Puyallup Tribal Council*, No. 95-3604, 1996.NAPU.0000007 (Puyallup Tribal Court, April 3, 1996), the court faced an appeal of a disenrollment by a tribal administrative board involving the proper notice to be provided to the disenrollee:

> The Tribe contends that Ms. Delgado intentionally placed herself where she could not receive mail and thus it was of her own making that she was unable to be notified. This argument is disingenuous for two reason: 1) the Tribe's Enrollment Director distributed a memorandum on April 17, 1991, to all concerned parties that Ms. Delgado was able to receive only personal and emergency mail and that all mail for Ms. Delgado should be directed to the Enrollment Office and 2) there is no evidence before the court that shows any attempt was made to notify her of the disenrollment proceedings. There are no letters returned (regular or otherwise), no return receipt proving she was notified by certified mail, and no affidavits attesting to service of the notice.
>
> The evidence is clear that Ms. Delgado was not in the United States during the time in question. It is also clear that Ms. Delgado could receive mail that was either of a personal or an emergent nature.
>
> The court finds from the evidence presented that Ms. Delgado did not receive notice she was being considered for disenrollment from the Puyallup Tribe of Indians
>
> The court concludes as a matter of law that Ms. Delgado was denied due process of law in violation of the Tribal and United States Constitutions.

Id. at ¶¶52-55. The court reversed the disenrollment on that ground.

8. In rural tribal communities, it is a unique and difficult question for tribal courts and tribal governments to provide adequate notice to tribal citizens. Americans Indians often do not have addresses, and must rely upon post office boxes, but proper notice often requires more than mailing an official document to a post office box. Tribal courts often rely upon publication in tribal or local newspapers, but even that kind of notice may be insufficient in a case where the tribal government is moving toward disenrolling a citizen.

In one unusual case, Hoopa Valley Tribe citizens who wanted to challenge the enrollment of another citizen complained to the Tribe's appellate court that they did not receive adequate notice of the enrollment. *See Baldy v. Hoopa Valley Tribal Council*, 3 NICS App. 286, 288 (Hoopa Valley Tribe Court of Appeals, March 16, 1994). The appellants argued that the publication of the enrollment notice in the local newspaper, *The Kourier*, was insufficient:

> While the Appellants acknowledged that *The Kourier* regularly published legal notices of the Hoopa Valley Tribal Court, they also argued that other methods were more likely to inform tribal members of the hearing. When asked what other methods were available, Appellants suggested the tribal newsletter. However, the tribal newsletter is a monthly publication, sporadically published and did not customarily provide legal notice.

Id. at 289. The court dismissed the argument, noting:

> Assuming, *arguendo*, that every member of the Hoopa Valley Tribe has standing to contest enrollment matters, does this entitle every member to personal notice? Immediate family members are not affected by an enrollment decision any more than other tribal members. Even so, Julie McKinnon, one of the Appellants, was served by mail, as were other family members. Regardless, the method of notice advocated by the Appellants would require notice by mail to approximately 2,000 tribal members.
>
> To adopt such notice requirement would not only unduly burden the court clerk's office consisting of one employee, it is also unnecessary in light of the additional custom of posting legal notices in the Neighborhood Facilities Building. The Neighborhood Facilities Building is a community center of the Hoopa Valley Tribe, located on the reservation and frequented by a large majority of tribal members. Appellee noted that one of the appellants works at the building. Appellees also argued that Hoopa Valley is a small community and as such, news travels fast.

Id. at 289-90.

9. In *In re the Membership Revocation of Meza*, 7 NICS App. 111 (Sauk-Siuattle Tribal Court of Appeals 2006), the court upheld a tribal statute disenrolling several tribal citizens:

> On March 25, 2005, the Sauk-Suiattle Tribal Council (hereinafter "Tribal Council") enacted Sauk-Suiattle Resolution No. 03/27b/05, which rescinded Sauk-Suiattle Resolution No. 19/88, and Sauk-Suiattle Resolution Nos. 03/28b/05 thru 03/34b/05, which disenrolled Warren Bill, Janice Enick Bill, Julie Bill Meza, John Bill, Miriam Bill, Melton Bill and Gloria Bill (hereinafter "Appellants"). Sauk-Suiattle Resolution No. 19/88 amended the Skagit-Suiattle (Public Domain) census roll dated January 1, 1942, by adding the

name of Emily (Joe) Bill. After the passage of Sauk-Suiattle Resolution No. 19/88, Appellants had filed for and were granted membership into the Sauk-Suiattle Tribe on the basis that they were each a direct descendant of Emily Joe Bill. . . .

The Tribal Council convened special meetings on October 3, 2005, and November 1, 2005 to consider the proposed revocation of Appellant's Tribal membership based on the lack of evidence that the Appellants had direct descendancy from anyone listed on the Skagit-Suiattle (Public Domain) census roll dated January 1, 1942.[1] The Council revoked the Appellants' membership, concluding that the Appellants did not meet the qualifications for enrollment in the Sauk-Suiattle Indian Tribe because the Appellants had no direct descendancy from anyone listed on the Skagit-Suiattle (Public Domain) census roll dated January 1, 1942. . . .

The Appellants argue that the Tribal Council's decision to revoke their Tribal memberships was clearly unsupported by the record of decision. This Court disagrees.

The governing authority outlining the enrollability of an individual into the Sauk-Suiattle Indian Tribe is contained in the Sauk-Suiattle Indian Tribal Community Constitution and Bylaws, Article II, Membership, Section 1, which states:

> The membership in the Sauk-Suiattle Indian Tribe shall extend to the following persons provided they do not hold membership in another tribe except as provided for under the provisions of honorary membership.
>
> (A) All persons of Sauk-Suiattle Indian blood whose names appear on the Skagit-Suiattle (Public Domain) census roll dated January 1, 1942.
>
> (B) All persons who possess at least one-fourth (1/4) Indian blood born since the date of said roll who are direct descendants of persons named on the base roll.
>
> (C) Corrections may be made in kthe [sic] tribal membership roll at any time by the tribal council, subject to the approval of the secretary of the interior or his authorized representative.

Turning to the facts at bar, the Tribal Council's record of decision makes clear that the Appellants do not qualify for enrollment pursuant to the Sauk-Suiattle Indian Tribal Community Constitution and Bylaws, Article II, Membership, Section 1: (1) none of the Appellants appear on the Skagit-Suiattle (Public Domain) census roll dated January 1, 1942; (2) none of the Appellants, all of whom were born since the date of the Skagit-Suiattle (Public Domain) census roll dated January 1, 1942, are direct descendants of persons named in the Skagit-Suiattle (Public Domain) census roll dated January 1, 1942; and (3) the Tribal Council has not corrected the Tribal membership roll to add any of the Appellants. The record of decision does not contain any credible evidence showing that Emily Joe Bill should be properly listed on the Skagit-Suiattle (Public Domain) census roll dated January 1, 1942. Therefore, this Court holds that the decision of the Tribal Council revoking the Appellants' membership based on the evidence that the Appellants did not meet

---

1. At the time of these special meetings, the membership of the Tribal Enrollment Committee was the same as the membership of the Tribal Council and the Council appears to have been acting in the capacity of both Enrollment Committee and Council.

the qualifications for enrollment in the Sauk-Suiattle Indian Tribe because the Appellants had no direct descendancy from anyone listed on the Skagit-Suiattle (Public Domain) census roll dated January 1, 1942, was not clearly unsupported by the record of decision.

Id. at 112, 115-16.

This case demonstrates the *possibility* of political tides turning against individuals, resulting in the disenrollment of those individuals. Consider first the fact that the tribal council sat as the tribe's enrollment board, not an unusual occurrence in Indian country. Couple that fact with the standard of review, which limited the reviewing court to the record developed by the enrollment board (that is, the tribal governing body). Other tribal courts in other contexts have expressed concern about the potential for abuse in developing a factual record in this manner. That is not to say this case is an example of abuse. There is no reason to think that anything like that occurred here, but these facts suggest the possibility.

D. FEDERAL GOVERNMENT INTERVENTION

THE SCOPE OF FEDERAL GOVERNMENT AUTHORITY OVER TRIBAL MEMBERSHIP DISPUTES AND THE PROBLEM OF DISENROLLMENT

Brendan Ludwick, 51 Fed. Law. 37, 40-42 (October 2004)

"Secretarial Elections" Involving Tribal Constitutional Amendments

The Bureau of Indian Affairs has authority over tribal elections that involve amendments to a tribe's constitution. Under the Indian Reorganization Act, special statutory rules and regulations govern the procedure of these elections; they are referred to in the statute as "secretarial elections." . . .

[T]he BIA continues to hold considerable authority over secretarial elections, including the power to nullify the results of elections in some circumstances. In *Shakopee Mdewakanton Sioux v. Babbitt*, [107 F.3d 667 (8th Cir. 1997,] the tribe sought to amend the portion of its constitution that set out qualifications for membership in the tribe. Pursuant to 25 U.S.C. §476(c)(1), the tribe requested the secretary of the interior to call the election and conduct it, and an election board consisting of one BIA officer and two members of the tribal government posted a list of registered voters. In response to objections to the board's initial determinations with respect to eligibility, the board concluded that certain people were ineligible to vote and removed them from the list. The election proceeded, and, based upon the board's revised eligibility determinations, the amendment passed. However, after the election, some tribal members objected to the revised eligibility standards that the board had relied on in the election. Ultimately, the BIA was unable to determine whether the board's eligibility determinations were correct and decided to nullify the electoral results.

. . . The Eighth Circuit held that the secretary's interpretation of the statute—allowing the rejection of election results when the interior secretary is unable to determine whether the election has resulted in ratification by a majority of tribal members — was reasonable for the purposes of APA review. . . .

Perhaps a greater limitation on tribal sovereignty under the IRA may derive from the fact that secretarial elections are federal elections and, therefore, have implications for federal rights. As Professor Carole Goldberg explains, "If the Department of the Interior has review power over a tribal constitution based on the Indian Reorganization Act or some other federal law, the tribe may need to attend to possible violations of the Indian Civil Rights Act." . . . If a membership policy requires a constitutional amendment, then the BIA must review for compliance with the ICRA; but, in most other contexts, determination of tribal membership is outside the purview of federal jurisdiction.

Enrollment Appeals under 25 C.F.R. §62.4(a)

Enrollment determinations that do not involve a constitutional amendment are generally not subject to BIA review, unless the tribe explicitly consents to one by law. Section 62.4(a) of 25 C.F.R. authorizes BIA review of tribal enrollment determinations with tribal consent, providing, "A person who is subject of an adverse enrollment action may file or have filed on his/her behalf an appeal. An adverse enrollment action is . . . [t]he rejection of an application for enrollment or the disenrollment of a tribal member by a tribal committee *when the tribal governing document provides for an appeal of the action to the Secretary.*" (Emphasis added.)

In [*Cahto Tribe of the Laytonville Rancheria v. Pacific Regional Director, Bureau of Indian Affairs*, 38 IBIA 244 (2002),] the Indian Board of Appeals considered the scope of BIA review under §62.4(a) in a disenrollment action by the Cahto Tribe of the Laytonville Rancheria. In that case, the tribe's General Council elected to remove a group of members on the grounds that they were also members of other tribes and/or had received property under another tribe's reservation distribution plan. Through its attorney, the tribe sought BIA recognition of the disenrollment action. The BIA superintendent issued a decision stating that the BIA did not recognize the tribe's disenrollment action, and the BIA's regional director affirmed the superintendent's decision, stating, "Under ordinary circumstances, this office would agree that the Cahto Tribe has a right to interpret its own laws and to determine its own membership, and that the BIA has no right to interfere in this situation; however, after reviewing the case and the gravity of injustice inflicted [on the disenrolled family], I fully support the decision of the Superintendent not to recognize the Tribe's decision."

The tribe appealed to the Board of Indian Appeals, which held that BIA officials lacked jurisdiction over the enrollment dispute. . . .

. . . *Cahto* demonstrates the narrow scope of the BIA's authority under 25 C.F.R. §62.(a)(3). For BIA officials to intervene in an enrollment dispute pursuant to consent by tribal law, the BIA must explicitly act in direct response to an appeal by an aggrieved tribal member. Although the board is prevented from adjudicating enrollment disputes under federal law, the board may invalidate a BIA official's decision that exceeds this limited grant of authority. Such reasoning reflects a policy that respects tribal sovereignty in enrollment matters and limits federal interference.

In dictum that was arguably in conflict with this policy, however, the board in *Cahto* made two additional points worthy of mention. First, the board stated that, under exceptional circumstances, the BIA may have jurisdiction over an internal membership dispute even if the tribe has not consented by law. According to the board, this authority derives from the BIA's responsibility to carry out the government-to-government relationship and may be exercised when, as a result of the dispute, it is not possible to ascertain who is qualified to represent the tribe in dealings with the BIA. Second, the board noted that, when the BIA does have jurisdiction, it has "authority and responsibility" to review the decision for violations of the ICRA. Because the board found no basis for jurisdiction in *Cahto*, it declined to entertain the appellants' ICRA-based claims. The board stated, "ICRA is not an independent grant of authority and does not authorize BIA to scrutinize tribal actions not otherwise within its jurisdiction." . . .

NOTES

1. Tribal attorneys Timothy Joranko and Mark Van Norman predicted, ten years earlier than the Ludwick excerpt above did, that the Secretary of Interior would retain enormous authority over tribal membership criteria:

   > *Santa Clara Pueblo* has endured for fourteen years. During that time, Congress has rejected repeated attempts to create federal court remedies for alleged ICRA violations. By so doing, Congress has made clear its intention that tribal decisions are not to be subject to oversight in federal fora. Surely, Congress did not intend to single out tribal constitutional amendments as the only tribal action subject to federal court review under the ICRA. The adoption of constitutional amendments is a far greater exercise of tribal members' self-determination than ordinances and actions by tribal officials. Yet a comparison of *Santa Clara Pueblo* with §476(a) (1988) yields the result that tribal ordinances and official acts are not subject to federal review, but manifestations of the whole tribe's vision of their government, as embodied in their constitution-making, are. This result could not have been intended by Congress and it cannot be reconciled with Congress' commitment to Indian self-determination. . . .

   Timothy W. Joranko & Mark C. Van Norman, *Indian Self-Determination at Bay: Secretarial Authority to Disapprove Tribal Constitutional Amendments*, 29 GONZAGA L. REV. 81, 104 (1993-1994).

2. Federal courts recognize conclusively that they have no jurisdiction to decide internal tribal matters such as citizenship, but the suits keep coming. In *Smith v. Babbitt*, 100 F.3d 556 (8th Cir. 1996), the court rejected a series of claims by non-citizens of the Shakopee Mdewakanton Sioux (Dakota) Community, writing:

   > Careful examination of the complaints and the record reveals that this action is an attempt by the plaintiffs to appeal the Tribe's membership determinations. It is true that appellants allege violations of [various federal statutes], and the Tribe's Constitution. However, upon closer examination, we find that these allegations are merely attempts to move this dispute, over which this court would not otherwise have jurisdiction, into federal court.

In this regard, an excerpt from the plaintiffs' amended complaint is particularly telling. In attempting to establish the Secretary of the Interior's liability, the plaintiffs alleged that the "scheme" in which the Secretary participated involved[]

> several willful elements, including: (1) the improper inclusion of nonmembers on the Tribe's membership rolls; (2) the improper removal and exclusion of constitutionally qualified members from those rolls; (3) the improper exclusion from such rolls of constitutionally qualified members whose membership applications have been indefinitely postponed in their consideration; and (4) improper payments of gaming revenues to nonmembers who have been removed temporarily from the Tribe's membership rolls.

Amended Complaint at 4. As plaintiffs' own words illustrate, this conflict concerns nothing more than the Tribe's membership determinations.

The facts of this case further show that this dispute needs to be resolved at the tribal level. We note that the Mdewakanton Tribe has expressly waived sovereign immunity from suit in tribal court for actions disputing an individual's qualified status to receive per capita payments. Revenue Allocation Amendments at §14.5(B). Several of the appellants involved in this action have previously brought similar actions in tribal court. In fact, at different stages of this action, suits of this very nature were pending in tribal court. . . .

Id. at 559.

5
TRIBAL ELECTIONS

Most modern Indian nations utilize a republican form of government and engage in periodic elections to select governmental leaders, although there are numerous exceptions in the form of theocracies and other government structures. An enormous amount of litigation over the election of tribal officials arises in tribal courts, and even occasionally in federal courts, despite the fact that federal courts almost never have jurisdiction over those suits. A subset of these disputes are cases involving the removal of tribal officials from office via a public petition and referendum process.

In some unusual circumstances, tribal elections have generated incredibly difficult and heartbreaking intratribal conflicts. Tribal court judges have been asked to perform the difficult task of choosing between competing families, clans, and political factions — sometimes when an Indian community is on the verge of violence. The United States Supreme Court's hotly debated and controversial decision in *Bush v. Gore*, 531 U.S. 98 (2000), is a frequent occurrence in tribal communities.

As with any federal or state election, judicial review of tribal elections poses very special problems. Tribal courts face intense scrutiny when issuing an order preventing an election from going forward, or when disqualifying political candidates. Questions of judicial independence and judicial authority arise out of these controversies. Moreover, some tribal judges are themselves elected officials.

A. JUDICIAL REVIEW OF TRIBAL ELECTIONS

1. STANDARDS OF REVIEW

DARDEN V. CHITIMACHA ELECTION BOARD

Chitimacha Tribal Court of Appeals, No. CV-00-0075, 2001.NACH.0000001
(February 2, 2001)

Before, DELAHOUSSAYE, Chief Judge, and BIENVENUE and LABORDE, Associate Judges

The opinion of the court was delivered by: LABORDE, Associate Judge

Decision

This case involves a dispute over a Tribal election that was held on July 8, 2000. The winning candidate, Toby Darden[,] has been certified and seated, and has been holding office and serving the Tribe as a member of the Tribal Council since August 3, 2000.

Under Chitimacha law, Tribal elections are administered by the Tribal Election Board. One of the candidates in the July 8 election, John Paul Darden (Appellant), sought to challenge the determination of the Election Board that two absentee ballots were spoiled. . . . In the end, after following the appropriate procedures under Tribal law, and providing John Paul Darden with a full and fair opportunity to be heard, the Election Board reaffirmed its holding that the two absentee ballots were spoiled. . . .

In short, both the Election Board and the Tribal Court properly rejected John Paul Darden's efforts to change the result of the July 8 election. The ruling of the Tribal Court is correct because Tribal law expressly provides that the decision of the Election Board is final.

Facts and Procedural Background

On July 8, 2000, the Chitimacha Tribe held a duly called runoff election for a Tribal Council seat between John Paul Darden and Toby C. Darden. Two hundred and Forty-five (245) votes were cast in the election, including forty-four (44) by absentee ballot. Also on July 8, 2000, the Chitimacha Election Board, in tallying the ballots, determined that two of the 44 absentee ballots were spoiled. Following the canvassing of the ballots, the Chitimacha Election Board declared Toby Darden the winner by a vote of 123 to 122 and certified this outcome to the Tribal Council. . . .

Application of Law

The Election Board is authorized under Chitimacha law to administer all aspects of the Tribe's elections.[1] This includes contests of elections—challenges to the results of an election that has already been held. Indeed, the Code specifically provides that the decision of the Election Board on a contest of election is "final." Code, Title X, section 519. That article specifically provides as follows:

> The election Board will hear the dispute and render a decision, and notify the Tribal Council. The Election Board is the final Decision on appeals.

Moreover, the Tribal Council specifically amended this provision in 1990—changing the provision from one which specifically provided for Tribal Court review of Election Board decisions, to the current provision which does

---

1. Title IV, Section 501 (a) of the Code, governs the conduct of Tribal elections. There is no federal law that preempts or conflicts with Tribal law in this regard. Thus, the Tribal Election Code, coupled with the construction of that Code provided through the custom and usage of the Tribal Election Board in administering that Code, is controlling.

not.[2] Both the language and history of the provision make it clear that Chitimacha law provides that the Election Board decision on a contest of election is not subject to review in the Tribal Court.

Relying on Section 519, the Tribal Court held that "the Court lacks jurisdiction to overturn the decision of the Election Board." . . . The Tribal Court subsequently reaffirmed this determination, citing section 519 in holding that with regard to "the rights of Mr. [John Paul] Darden as a candidate to contest the election . . . the decision of the board is the final decision on appeal, concerning the challenge of the candidate." . . . These rulings are clearly correct and are affirmed by this Court.

In short, the Tribe's law is clear. The decision of the Election Board is "final." The Tribal Court had no jurisdiction to review the action of the Election Board, and properly dismissed the case. This Court finds this issue dispositive and therefore declines to address the remaining issues herein.

For the reasons set forth above, the decision of the Tribal Court, dismissing this action, is AFFIRMED at Appellant's costs. . . .

NOTES

1. Many tribes choose to limit or even eliminate judicial review of administrative election disputes. The *Darden* Court held that it had no subject matter jurisdiction to review any election dispute. Other tribes place significant limits on judicial review by establishing a standard of review that grants enormous deference to the administrative entity, often an election board, or by adopting a rule that election results are presumed valid. For example, in *Hornbuckle v. Cherokee Board of Elections*, No. CV-07-6790B (Eastern Band of Cherokee Indians Supreme Court, Sept. 30, 2007), the Eastern Band of Cherokee Indians had adopted a statute providing that

   [a]ny person filing a protest for election irregularities under Section 161-16(c) above, must establish during a hearing in front of the Board of Elections that the alleged irregularities unfairly and improperly or illegally affected the actual outcome of the election or that but for the alleged irregularities, the outcome of the election would have been different.

   Id. at ¶18 (quoting Cherokee Code §161-16(d)). As a practical matter, it is extremely difficult for a petitioner to demonstrate that election irregularities have affected the outcome of the election. In *Hornbuckle*, the court found the following:

   The Elections Board concedes that two (2) voters, Appellant Paul Hornbuckle and Kimmy Jackson were erroneously precluded from voting in Wolfetown. Assuming that these two voters would have voted for DeWayne "Tuff" Jackson, this would reduce the margin of victory to ten (10). . . .

---

2. On February 23, 1990, the Election Code was amended to provide that a decision of the Election Board "may be brought before the Chitimacha Tribal Court." On May 16, 1990, the Election Code was amended to alter this provision, specifically to provide that "the Election Board is the final decision on appeals."

Appellant claims thirteen (13) registered voters were not allowed to vote. The record before the Court, and approved by counsel for all parties, discloses that five (5) were, in fact allowed to vote. One (1) attempted to register too late. If the remaining seven (7) are assumed *arguendo* to have voted for DeWayne "Tuff" Jackson the final margin of victory is three (3).

Therefore, the Court is left with the inescapable conclusion that the Appellant has not shown that but for the irregularities, the actual outcome of the election has either been affected or that the outcome would have been different.

Id. at ¶¶25-28.

2. Other tribes have adopted an even stricter standard—that the election challengers bear the burden of establishing *beyond a reasonable doubt* that the alleged violations had a strong likelihood of affecting the outcome. *See Byrd v. Cherokee Nation Election Commission*, Nos. JAT-03-08 & JAT-03-09, 8 Okla. Tribal Court Rep. 172, 178 (Judicial Appeals Tribunal of the Cherokee Nation of Oklahoma 2003).

3. Often, the tribal court will apply a common law standard of review in which the court will not disturb findings of fact by the fact finder unless they are "clearly erroneous," but will review conclusions of law de novo. *E.g., Yellow Bird v. Three Affiliated Tribes Tribal Election Board*, 29 Indian L. Rep. 6018, 6019 (Three Affiliated Tribes of the Fort Berthold Reservation Dist. Ct., Sept. 27, 2001). This standard effectively grants enormous deference to the fact-finding capacities of election boards.

2. DE NOVO REVIEW

BAILEY v. GRAND TRAVERSE BAND ELECTION BOARD

Tribal Judiciary for the Grand Traverse Band of Ottawa and Chippewa Indians (en banc), No. 2008-1031-CV-CV, 2008 WL 6196206 (August 5, 2008)

PER CURIAM

Findings of Fact

In this case, Plaintiff Derek Joseph Bailey (hereinafter "Bailey") filed a complaint against the Grand Traverse Band Election Board (hereinafter "Election Board"). . . .

Bailey was a candidate for the Tribal Council Chairman position, running against the incumbent Tribal Council Chairman Robert Kewaygoshkum. On May 16, 2008, five business days prior to the general election scheduled for May 21, 2008, the Election Board received a written complaint from tribal member and Tribal Councilor Sandra Witherspoon, as well as a complaint from tribal member Ruth Anderson, both regarding alleged violations of the 2008 Election Regulations by candidate Derek Bailey. . . .

The complaints alleged that Bailey violated the 2008 Election Regulations by accessing a campaign website concerning his candidacy for Tribal Chairman from a Grand Traverse Band workplace computer. Both complaints also implied that the Election Board failed to investigate the circumstances surrounding Bailey's use of his computer when the issue of access to campaign websites was first brought to the Election Board's attention in March 2008, and that the Board should have addressed the issue at that point.

The Election Board scheduled an emergency meeting for 6:45 a.m. on May 19, 2008 to consider the substance of the allegations. . . . No notice or opportunity to appear at the meeting was provided to the complaining parties, nor to Bailey who was the subject of the complaints. After the Board met to discuss the complaints, . . . [it] approved the written Election Dispute Determination at a later meeting in the early evening of May 19, 2008. On the morning of May 20, 2008, roughly 22-23 hours before the polls were to open for the May 21, 2008 general election, the Election Board Chairman Samuel Evans sent the Election Dispute Determination via global e-mail to all gaming and government employees of the Grand Traverse Band of Ottawa and Chippewa Indians, as has been the Election Board's past practice. Receipt of this global e-mail by Bailey on the day before the election was the first notice that Bailey received that indicated that the Election Board had not only received complaints against him, but also had acted on the complaints.

The general election was held on May 21, 2008. Bailey was defeated in the general election by Kewaygoshkum by a vote of 233 to 210 votes. Bailey timely filed his complaint against the Grand Traverse Band Election Board (hereinafter "Election Board") challenging the actions of the Election Board in the days just prior to the May 21, 2008 general election. Bailey has alleged improprieties by the Election Board both as to the procedure used by the Election Board, as well as statements made within the written Election Dispute Determination. . . .

From the outset, Bailey has admitted that he used his work computer to access his campaign website (www.votederekbailey.com), but disputes the characterizations of the frequency and dates of his use as stated in the Election Dispute Determination. The evidence showed that all of Bailey's access to the website occurred prior to his formal filing for candidacy (with the last access being February 27, 2008). Bailey testified that he filed the paperwork to formally declare his candidacy on March 3, 2008. There is no evidence to suggest that Bailey accessed the website in question after he had declared himself to be a candidate for the Tribal Council Chairman position.

Pursuant to Article VII, Section 5(e) of the Constitution above, the Election Board adopted regulations governing the conduct of the 2008 primary and general elections. The Election Board has admitted that it failed to follow the Election Regulations in issuing the Election Dispute Determination concerning Bailey on May 20, 2008, the day before the general election. The Election Board has attempted to justify its failure to follow its own regulations based upon concerns about "rampant rumors" that were circulating relating to the Election Board not taking action as to Bailey's use of his work computer and "covering up" his alleged violations of election regulations, the "new evidence" of the IT Department report received by the Board, and the lack of time to effectively deal with the situation. The Election Board has argued that it felt it had no alternative but to issue its determination without input from the complaining parties or the candidate Derek Bailey who was accused of wrongdoing for these reasons. . . .

GTB Election Law

This Court's authority in election cases is limited by the Grand Traverse Band of Ottawa and Chippewa Indians Constitution. Article VII, Section 5 states:

> Section 5. Election Board
>
> (a) The Tribal Council shall appoint an Election Board, composed of five (5) registered voters of the Grand Traverse Band, to hold elections, certify election results, and settle election disputes other than allegations of impropriety by the Election Board. The decisions of the Election Board shall be final and conclusive on the Grand Traverse Band. . . .
>
> (c) **Allegations of impropriety by the Election Board shall be settled by the Tribal Judiciary.** . . . (Emphasis added.)

Article VII, Section 5(a) of the Constitution gives sole authority to resolve "election disputes" to the Defendant Election Board, except for allegations of impropriety by the Election Board. The Tribal Judiciary only has jurisdiction to resolve allegations of impropriety by the Election Board under the provisions of Article VII, Section 5(c). The Constitution does not define "allegations of impropriety" as stated in Article VII, Section 5. However, in order for both Section 5(a) and 5(c) to make sense and be in harmony with each other, "allegations of impropriety" must mean more than just disagreement with a decision made by the Election Board. To find otherwise would make the last sentence of Section 5(a) meaningless. *TwoCrow v. GTB Election Bd.*, Case No. 2008-998-CV-CV, Order Concerning Jurisdiction and Dismissing Complaint (2008); *Yannett v. GTB Election Bd.*, Case No. 2008-1003-CV-CV, Order Concerning Jurisdiction and Dismissing Complaint, (2008). If the drafters of the Constitution had wanted the Tribal Court to hear all appeals from decisions of the Election Board, they could have easily drafted the Constitution to provide that remedy. *Id.* Instead, it is the opinion of this Court that the intent behind Section 5(a) was to make the Election Board the final arbiter of election disputes in most circumstances, not the Tribal Judiciary. *Id.* Further, it is the opinion of this Court that the intent of Section 5(c) was to give the Tribal Court jurisdiction to provide an avenue of redress *only* under limited circumstances where the Election Board itself acted improperly, such as where the Election Board acted in violation of the law or the Board's own election rules, regulations and procedures; or where the Election Board's conduct showed bias or prejudice such that its ability to render a fair decision was compromised or impaired; or where the Election Board failed to carry out its responsibilities with integrity, impartiality and competence. *Id.*

Election results are "presumptively valid." *Barrientoz v. GTB Election Bd.*, Case No. 2006-316-CV-CV, Opinion and Order: Petitioner's Motion to Stay the GTB General Election, p. 4-5 (2006). This Court held in *Barrientoz* that: "Petitioners must demonstrate by clear and convincing evidence that: 1) the [Election] Board failed to comply with its own mandated policies and procedures in conducting and certifying the election; or 2) the Board followed its mandated policies and procedures, but that these policies and procedures are unconstitutional; or 3) the [Election] Board certified the election despite improper, or fraudulent practices which it had a duty to monitor and prevent. . . . [The Petitioners] would be required to demonstrate by clear and convincing evidence that the [Election] Board impropriety affected the outcome of the election." *Id.*, p. 6. While the Election Board has in essence conceded that they did not follow the 2008 Election Regulations in issuing its Election Dispute Determination as to Plaintiff Bailey, it argues that Bailey has not proven by clear and convincing evidence that the Election Board's failure to follow the Election Regulations affected the outcome of the election.

In the instant case, we find that Plaintiff has established by clear and convincing evidence that the Election Board failed to comply with its own duly adopted 2008 Election Regulations in several respects when it met on May 19, 2008, and when it issued its Election Dispute Determination on May 20, 2008. The Election Board has admitted that it failed to follow the 2008 Election Regulations in issuing its determination against Derek Bailey. For reasons explained more fully below, the Court finds that the Board acted improperly such as would give this Court jurisdiction under Article VII, Section 5(c) of the Constitution of the Grand Traverse Band of Ottawa and Chippewa Indians. . . .

Due Process

. . . The Constitution of the Grand Traverse Band of Ottawa and Chippewa Indians (hereinafter "GTB Constitution") guarantees tribal members the right to due process, and is very similar to the Fifth Amendment of the United States Constitution. Article X, Section 1 of the GTB Constitution provides in pertinent part:

> The Grand Traverse Band in exercising the powers of self-government shall not: . . .
>> (h) Deny to any person within its jurisdiction the equal protection of its laws or deprive any person of liberty or property without due process of law;

This provision is essentially the same as the due process rights guaranteed to tribal members under the Indian Civil Rights Act of 1968, 25 U.S.C. §1302(8). . . .

Other tribal jurisdictions have held that the Indian Civil Rights Act of 1968 guarantees procedural due process in hearings before tribal administrative agencies. *Mustach v. Navajo Board of Election Supervisors*, 1987.NANN.0000016, ¶31, Jan. 22, 1987. Procedural due process, under the Indian Civil Rights Act, relates to the requisite characteristics of proceedings seeking to effect a deprivation of liberty or property. *Id.* In the *Mustach* case, the Supreme Court of the Navajo Nation considered a case similar to this one where the Navajo Board of Election Supervisors failed to follow election law and regulations concerning a grievance filed by a candidate, citing concerns of inadequate notice and lack of a meaningful opportunity to be heard. The Court held that the failure of the Board of Election Supervisors to follow the election law was highly prejudicial to the plaintiff Mustach, and that he was denied procedural due process.

Id., ¶32-33. As a result of these and other procedural errors, the Navajo Supreme Court ordered that a special election take place. *Id.*, ¶40. . . .

. . . Given the significant and material failure of the Election Board to follow its own adopted 2008 Election Regulations, and the denial of any opportunity to provide any meaningful response prior to the election, we conclude that Plaintiff Derek Bailey's constitutional right to due process was violated by the Election Board in this matter. The procedural deficiencies and the action taken by the Election Board immediately before the election to comment upon Plaintiff's use of his work computer as outlined above, without any opportunity for Bailey to respond or challenge the action of the Election Board prior to the election, amounted to a deprivation of Bailey's liberty and/or property interests. In this case, Bailey was denied notice of the nature of the proceedings, and was denied an opportunity to be heard in a meaningful time and manner. . . . In short, Bailey has established that there has been a "patent and fundamental unfairness" in the election process, and a "purposeful deprivation of clear rights." . . .

The Election Board has argued that it took action essentially on an *ex parte* basis because there was not enough time to address the issues in the complaints. While the time frames would have undoubtedly been short, we specifically reject the notion put forth by the Election Board that it has the inherent authority to make election determinations on an *ex parte* basis. *Ex parte* is a Latin legal term meaning "from (by or for) one party." Typically, courts only grant *ex parte* relief under exigent circumstances or on an emergency basis, or where notice to the opposing party may precipitate adverse action, such as in a child custody or personal protection matter. A court order issued on the basis of an *ex parte* proceeding, therefore, will typically be temporary and interim in nature, and the person(s) affected by the order must be given an opportunity to contest the appropriateness of the order before it can be made permanent. There is no procedural due process defect in obtaining an emergency order of protection without notice to a respondent when the petition for the emergency protection order is supported by affidavits that demonstrate exigent circumstances justifying entry of an emergency order without prior notice, . . . and where there are appropriate provisions for notice and an opportunity to be heard after the order is issued. . . . However, in the instant case, there was no meaningful opportunity for Bailey to be heard prior to the election, as the Election Dispute Determination was circulated to the public via the global e-mail less than 24 hours before the polls opened. There is no provision in the 2008 Election Regulations authorizing the Election Board to make election determinations on an "ex parte" basis, nor was such relief sought by the complainant.

As stated above, the testimony and affidavits presented at the trial indicated that the Election Board acted without following its own regulations because it sought to "clear the air" and address the rumors and innuendo that were circulating throughout the community as to what Mr. Bailey had done (as well as that the Election Board had not done anything about it), and because the Election Board felt there was not enough time to deal with the complaints fully without delaying the election. We perceive that the Election Board found itself in what it thought was an untenable situation. Namely, the Election Board could not act until there was a complaint before it, but Election

Board members were aware of community rumors of their prior inaction and possible bias. Then the Election Board was presented with a last-minute complaint regarding the substance of the rumors circulating in the community. While we certainly have the benefit of hindsight, we find that the circumstances did not justify the Election Board's failure to follow the duly adopted regulations which were sufficient to address the complaints. To make a determination under these circumstances without affording the interested parties notice or an opportunity to be heard, and issue that determination less than 24 hours before the start of the election violated Bailey's fundamental right to due process.

Conclusion

In conclusion, we hold that the actions of the Election Board in failing to follow the provisions of the 2008 Election Regulations as outlined above, coupled with the time frame in which such action was taken that provided Bailey with no meaningful opportunity to respond or challenge the Election Board's actions, were so egregious that it resulted in a violation of Derek Bailey's right to due process. The only remedy which we find would adequately redress the Plaintiff in this situation is to order that a special election be held for the Tribal Council Chairman position. The Court does not make this decision lightly. We are very cautious about overturning a validly held election. The standards for overturning an election are strict, as they should be in the absence of a clear showing of unfairness. *Johnson v. June*, No. A-CV-31-82, 4 Nav. R. 79, 1983.NANN.0000050, ¶30, September 30, 1983. As stated by the Fort Peck Court of Appeals, Assiniboine and Sioux Tribes in *Reddoor v. Wetsit*, Appeal No. 95, 1990.NAFP.0000009, ¶130, January 18, 1990:

> As a general rule, a court of equity will not enjoin the canvass of votes or declaration of the result of an election, although there is considerable conflict in the decisions as to the underlying theory in support of denying injunctive relief in such a case. Some courts refuse the injunction on the theory that a court of equity either has no jurisdiction over questions purely political in character or that it will not interfere in political matters or protect purely political rights. Others have predicated their decision on the theory that the courts will not prevent the performance of a legal duty, and since the statute imposes on designated officers the duty to canvass the votes and declare the result, their acts in so doing are not subject to judicial control and supervision. The existence of an exclusive statutory remedy or the existence of an otherwise adequate remedy at law has also been held to preclude injunctive relief. Failure to show irreparable injury will also preclude enjoining the canvass of votes and the declaration of the result of an election, the theory generally being that until enforcement of the result of an election, as distinguished from its declaration, is attempted or threatened, there is no invasion of the complainant's personal or property rights. However, equity will act to enjoin the canvass of votes and the declaration of the result of an election where the existence of particular factors justifies or calls for equitable intervention to protect personal or property rights. 26 AM. JUR. 2d Elections Section 308 (1966).

In the final analysis, we must consider whether the election was honestly and fairly conducted. Slight irregularities are more than apt to creep into the procedure. To hold that slight irregularities, for which the voters were not to blame, should invalidate the election, is contrary to public policy. . . . If there has been an opportunity to correct irregularities in the election process prior to the election, the challenger should not, in the absence of fraud, irregularity or misconduct that affects or impeaches the election process or results, be heard to complain of them afterward. *Jones v. Election Board of the Fort McDowell Yavapi Nation*, Case No. CV-2000-005, 2000.NAFM.0000001, ¶46, February 1, 2000. In this case, the irregularities involved were far more than slight, Bailey had no opportunity to correct or even address them, and under these unique circumstances they in fact rose to the level of depriving Bailey of his constitutional rights.

We are also mindful that this decision will affect not only the Plaintiff Derek Bailey, but his campaign opponent, Robert Kewaygoshkum, who has not been a party to these proceedings. We would note that **absolutely no evidence** has been presented to indicate that the Election Board, nor any of its members individually, were influenced by or acted at the behest of Mr. Kewaygoshkum (or any other members of the Tribal Council or Tribal Administration). The evidence presented leads us to the conclusion that the Election Board acted out of concern for how the Board was being perceived in the community for its failure [to] deal with the rumors of Derek Bailey's computer use. As stated above, we do not find this to be an emergency or exigent circumstance to justify the failure to provide a candidate with his or her due process rights.

We are also mindful of the potential for "opening of the floodgates" to future election cases with arguments being made of additional Constitutional rights violations. However, we would point out that the circumstances of this case are unique. If the election disputes had been filed in early March, rather than just days before the election, chances are the Election Board would have followed the procedure set forth in the 2008 Election Regulations and would have given Mr. Bailey an opportunity to be heard. It is the failure to follow those Election Regulations which resulted in no meaningful opportunity for Bailey to be heard which cause us to conclude that Bailey's due process rights were violated and that a special election should result.

NOTES

1. The Grand Traverse Band Tribal Court had previously held in *Barrientoz v. GTB Election Board*, No. 2006-316-CV-CV (May 12, 2006), that the tribal court had jurisdiction to review "improprieties" in the actions of the election board:

   > The Judiciary has ruled that the Petitioners must demonstrate by clear and convincing evidence that: 1) the Board failed to comply with its own mandated policies and procedures in conducting and certifying the election; or 2) the Board followed its mandated policies and procedures but these policies and procedures are unconstitutional; or 3) the Board certified the election despite improper, or fraudulent practices which it had a duty to monitor and prevent. Further, if the court finds that the election was invalid due to fraud or impropriety that the Board had a duty to monitor and prevent, the election

certification would be deemed invalid per se. If the court finds the Petitioners have met the burden of tier one or two of the standard of proof, they would be required to demonstrate by clear and convincing evidence that the Board impropriety affected the outcome of the election.

Id. at 6.

The *Bailey* Court relied upon this standard to assert judicial review over the 2008 election. Note one provision of the Grand Traverse Band Constitution quoted above: "The decisions of the Election Board shall be final and conclusive on the Grand Traverse Band." Article V, Section 5(a). How is the *Barrientoz* standard consistent with this provision, which seems to provide for the finality of Election Board decisions? Why would a tribe choose to create an election board, and then grant it significant power to resolve election disputes without court review, as in the *Darden* case above? Does "impropriety" include any allegation of a violation of due process, according to the *Bailey* Court? Could the court's decision be read to include virtually all election challenges, or is there a firm limitation on the tribal court's jurisdiction?

2. What remedies are available to an election challenger? The *Bailey* Court threw out the results of the first election and ordered a new election. The *Barrientoz* Court ordered a stay of a general tribal council election of 45 days to allow the challenges to the primary tribal council election to be adjudicated. *See Barrientoz, supra,* at 9. These court orders are incredibly disruptive, creating the possibility that elected officials remain in office beyond the end of their term, or creating vacancies in the elected leadership of a tribe. Would it be more disruptive if a tribal court or election board order allowed a newly elected candidate to assume the duties of office while preserving the possibility that the adjudicating body might later determine that the election was invalid, forcing the recently installed official out of office?

Bailey was victorious over the incumbent chairman in the repeat election. *See Kewaygoshkum v. Grand Traverse Band Election Board,* 2008 WL 6196207 (Grand Traverse Band of Ottawa and Chippewa Indians Tribal Judiciary 2008) (en banc).

3. The Cheyenne River Sioux Tribal Court of Appeals dealt with the disruptive character of potential remedies in an election challenge in which the petitioner moved the trial court to enjoin the swearing in of the purported election winner in *Ducheneaux v. Cheyenne River Sioux Tribe Election Board,* 26 Indian L. Rep. 6155 (Cheyenne River Sioux Tribal Court of Appeals, June 2, 1999).

4. Election challenges, however, may be barred by the doctrine of laches, as the court in *Kewaygoshkum v. Grand Traverse Band Election Board,* 2008 WL 6196207 (Grand Traverse Band of Ottawa and Chippewa Indians Tribal Judiciary 2008) (en banc), noted:

There is a strong public interest in having election matters filed quickly because of potential prejudice and damage to the election process. . . . For these reasons, several courts, including this Court, have applied the doctrine of laches to late filed claims. *See Russell v. Grand Traverse Band of Ottawa and Chippewa Indians Election Board,* Case No. 00-03-108, (May 8, 2000). The doctrine of laches refers to circumstances where there is an unreasonable delay or negligence in pursuing a right or claim in a way that prejudices the party against whom relief is sought. . . .

Kewaygoshkum, 2008 WL 6196207 at *7.

B. QUALIFICATIONS OF TRIBAL GOVERNMENT ELECTORAL CANDIDATES

Begay v. Navajo Nation Election Administration

Navajo Nation Supreme Court, No. SC-CV-27-02 (July 31, 2002), 8 Navajo Rep. 241; 30 Indian L. Rep. 6035

The opinion of the court was delivered by: Chief Justice Robert Yazzie.

I. Procedural History

On May 3, 2002, the Appellant filed with the Navajo Nation Election Administration ("NNEA") an application for candidacy for the position of President of the Navajo Nation. On June 3, 2002, the NNEA informed the Appellant that he did not meet the residency requirements and was therefore disqualified as a candidate for President. . . .

The sole question here is whether the Appellant was disqualified as a candidate for the office of Navajo Nation President as a result of the unequal application of the requirements of permanent residency and continual presence. More broadly understood, the basic issue is one of fairness. Did the NNEA and the OHA [Office of Hearings & Appeals] apply the Navajo Election Code to Edward T. Begay as a presidential candidate in a fair way? The Navajo Nation Bill of Rights recognizes liberty as a fundamental right. (1 N.N.C. §3 (1995).) Liberty cannot be taken away unless it is done using a fair process ("due process") and the law must be evenly applied ("equal protection of the law"). *Id.* For purposes of due process of law under Navajo common law, the right to participate in the political process is considered a protected liberty right.[2] We announce the rule adopted in other jurisdictions that if any ambiguities exist in an election statute, the presumption lies in favor of the candidate. *See, e.g., Arnold v. Hughes*, 621 So.2d 1139, 1140 (La. 1993), *Romero v. Sandoval*, 685 P.2d 772, 775 (Co. 1984). Although we have never explicitly adopted this rule, it is clearly consistent with the approach taken in our past election decisions. . . .

---

2. We indicated in *Bennett v. Navajo Board of Election Supervisors*, 6 Navajo. R. 319, 325 (1990), that "the right or privilege of placing one's name in nomination for public elective office is a part of political liberty. . . ." We recognize that this use of the term "liberty" may seem odd to those not trained in the legal tradition. The common understanding of liberty is that it means freedom from restraint. However, the legal definition of "liberty" includes rights that are considered to be fundamental, such as the right to participate in the political process. This use of the word may be more clearly understood if one considers what is meant when we claim that this is a "free country." One of the main meanings of that phrase is that we are a democracy and that our rights to participate in the political process may not be unnecessarily infringed.

III. Standard of Review

Before we address the substantive issues of this case, we must determine what standard of review is appropriate to apply to a decision of the OHA. Where there are allegations of violations of due process, this Court "is not limited by . . . the scope of review set forth in Section [341]" of the Navajo Election Code. *Morris v. Navajo Board of Election Supervisors*, Nav. R. 75, 78 (1993). Rather, where we are addressing the legal interpretations of lower courts and administrative bodies, we apply a de novo standard of review.

IV. Analysis of the Statute

The Navajo Election Code lists the qualifications for candidacy for President. 11 N.N.C. §8(A). Among those qualifications are that the candidate:

> Must have permanent residence and have been continually physically present within the Navajo Nation as defined in 7 N.N.C. §254 for at least three (3) years prior to the time of elections.

11 N.N.C. §8(A)(1).

. . .

"Permanent Residence" is defined as:

> The place where a person physically lives with the intent to remain for an indefinite period of time. The permanent residence is a person's fixed and permanent home. Permanent means lasting, fixed, stable and not temporary, part-time, or transient. A person cannot have more than one permanent residence at the same time.

11 N.N.C. §2(Z).

Continually present is defined as:

> Being actually physically present within the Navajo Nation or living on Navajo Country in a fixed and permanent home without any significant interruption. An extended absence from Navajo Country in the course of employment or pursuit of a trade or business or for purposes as attending school and serving in the military service, is not significant interruption.

11 N.N.C. §2(G).

At first glance the statute seems clear. However, a close reading of the statute shows that its proper interpretation is difficult to ascertain. There are several difficulties with the statutory language that we could not conclusively resolve. Do the definitions of permanent residency and continual presence mirror the legal definitions of domicile and residency, respectively? The definition of the continual presence requirement in particular is difficult to interpret. That definition provides that a candidate must be "actually physically present within the Navajo Nation or living on Navajo Country in *a fixed and permanent home*." 11 N.N.C. §2(G) (1995) (emphasis added). Does this mean that a candidate must have "a fixed and permanent home" in the Navajo Nation, or does it mean that a candidate may be physically present in another way while not having a permanent home in the Navajo Nation? Do the exceptions apply to both prongs of the test or only to the continual presence requirement? Does the continual presence requirement merely add a durational requirement to the permanent residency requirement? Although Justice King-Ben's concurring opinion provides one possible interpretation, the Court, as a whole, could not agree on the proper answer to these questions.

These questions leave room for an unequal application of the general rule. Unequal application of a general rule can deny a liberty interest. *See Bennett v. Navajo Board of Election Supervisors*, 6 Nav. R. 319, 325 (1990). "This court has repeatedly dealt with situations where loose interpretations or applications of election laws create a potential for abuse or selective enforcement." *See Howard v. Navajo Board of Election Supervisors*, 6 Nav. R. 380, 382 (1991) (citations omitted).

V. Application of the Statute

The statute as written is confusing. However, if a confusing statute is applied in a fair and consistent manner, it may not deny liberty interests. Therefore, we must determine whether the statute was applied fairly and evenly.

The Appellant initially listed his Gallup, New Mexico home as his address. He received a letter on May 28, 2002, requesting that he clarify his residence. He explained, in a written response to the NNEA's letter, that he had a traditional or customary residence in the Churchrock Chapter. Ms. Antoinette Yellowhorse, another candidate for President, also received a letter requesting that she clarify her residence. The content of these letters was not the same. In the letter mailed to Ms. Yellowhorse, the explanation of the residency requirement indicated that there were some exceptions to the residency requirement. The Appellant's letter contained no such language. After a conversation with Ms. Yellowhorse, the director of the NNEA determined that, "she fell within the exception if you're going to school then you can be allowed to live off the reservation." . . .

The application for candidacy for President of Mr. Larry Curley was handled by Mr. Robert Black of the Tuba City office. Despite the fact that Mr. Curley listed an Albuquerque, New Mexico address, he was never sent a letter requesting clarification. . . . Rather, because he stated in his voter registration verification form that he worked in Albuquerque but owned some land 4 miles east of Birdsprings Chapter, he was certified as eligible under the "work" exception to the requirements.

There were also questions raised about the residence of Dahaani Baadaani. His application stated a Durango, Colorado address. Mr. Baadaani had submitted his application for candidacy on April 4, 2002, well in advance of the May 3 deadline. The NNEA was forced to qualify him because they neglected to examine his application until after the 30 day deadline had passed. . . .

Because OHA did not examine the Appellant's application in light of the continual presence requirement, OHA denied the Appellant the opportunity to demonstrate that he, too, qualified for the exceptions to that requirement. Indeed, they did not even inform him of the possibility that he might be covered by an exception. Edward T. Begay could have stated that he was absent from Navajo Country due to employment, trade, business, education, or military service. He initially moved to Gallup due to his wife's employment and children's education. The statute does not explicitly limit the employment or the education exceptions to the candidate himself. He purchased a house for investment and tax purposes. This seems to be a business purpose. Finally, his residence in Gallup is closer to his work in Window Rock than is his traditional home in Churchrock. He might therefore qualify for the employment exception.

Navajo common law strongly supports the role of families in meeting the needs of family members. This is very relevant. Navajo common law highly values respect. NNEA showed respect for one presidential applicant's desire for an education in Gallup and another's professional career in Albuquerque. It appears that the third was approved because of NNEA's own neglect. What about the Appellant? Did he have a right arising from Navajo practice of respect for his family's needs?

We do not know whether such arguments would have succeeded before NNEA or OHA. The point is that the failure to determine whether Appellant satisfied the "continually present" requirement denied him the opportunity to make these arguments or any others. The other applicants, in contrast, were allowed this opportunity.

The policy for examining candidate qualifications was applied unevenly. . . .

Vagueness of the election law and its loose and unequal application led to a denial of the Appellant's right to participate. In *Howard v. Navajo Nation Board of Election Supervisors*, 6 Nav. R. 380 (1991), the Court remedied a similar loose application of an Election Code provision. Chief Justice Tso and Associate Justice Bluehouse, in their majority opinion, decided not to strike down the statute as void on its face. Rather, they preserved the statute by finding that the statute was vague as applied. *Howard*, 6 Nav. R. 380-383. When a statute is vague or confusing, this Court can save the statute by interpreting it so as to avoid unfairness. *Howard*, 6 Nav. R. at 382. This Court can also direct the relevant authority to develop, for future cases, a consistent and fair interpretation and procedure. In the present case we decline to find the statute itself void for vagueness. Rather, we follow the approach of the majority in *Howard* and find it vague as applied because the statute could be read in several ways. It was read one way for two candidates, read differently for Appellant, and not read at all for a third candidate. If law is to mean anything, it must be consistent in the way people are treated. In this case, the candidacy definitions were unequally applied. We recommend that the NNEA develop a consistent and fair procedure for enforcing these provisions of the Election Code. We emphasize the importance of developing such a procedure well in advance of the next election.

VI. The Remedy

The appropriate remedy, when candidacy requirements have been unequally applied, is to order the candidate placed on the ballot. This does not mean that the Court finds that the candidate meets the candidacy requirements. Rather, it amounts to a conclusion that because the process was so badly flawed, it is unfair to exclude a candidate regardless of whether he would qualify or not.

For example, in *Deswood v. Navajo Board of Election Supervisors*, 1 Nav. R. 306 (1978), this Court was faced with a claim that candidacy requirements had been selectively applied. In that case, Peter Deswood had been disqualified from running for Navajo Tribal Council because he did not meet the age requirements. We found that the Navajo Board of Election Supervisors ("NBOES") had only examined the qualifications of four of 161 candidates. We therefore found that NBOES had "selectively applied its powers to decide candidates' qualifications." *Id.* at 311. Because NBOES had not consistently applied the law, this Court declined to address the actual question of Mr. Deswood's age. Rather, we ordered Mr. Deswood placed on the ballot, regardless of his age, because "the selective application of the power to disqualify candidates in the Navajo election requires this Court to void any use of the power by the Board of Election Supervisors." *Id.* at 311.

Therefore, and in accord with our precedent, we find that the appropriate remedy for the unequal application of the candidacy requirements is to order the Appellant placed on the ballot for the primary election for Navajo Nation President. We do so without addressing whether the Appellant would have qualified under the statutory requirements had they been fairly enforced. Rather, we find the unequal application of the laws was so unfair that the Appellant must be placed on the ballot regardless of whether he met the requirements or not. . . .

KING-BEN, Associate Justice, concurring opinion.

I concur with the holding of the majority. I agree that the statute was unevenly enforced. I write separately to express my belief that the requirements of 11 N.N.C. §8(A)(l) are clear on its face. . . .

As discussed in the majority opinion, it is not exactly clear what process the Navajo Election Administration applied in determining candidacy. However, if the election laws were applied equally as set out in 11 N.N.C. §8(A), the NNEA should have disqualified all the candidates who do not reside within the Navajo Nation as defined by 7 N.N.C. §254. In essence, this would mean that candidates Curley, Badaanii, and Begay would not qualify under the first prong of 11 N.N.C. §8(A) as they are not residents of the Navajo Nation as defined by 7 N.N.C. §254. If the election laws were applied strictly and equally, of the candidates in issue, the only candidate who would have qualified as a presidential candidate is Yellowhorse[. T]he NNEA, upon determining that she met the first prong of the test for determining residency would then determine why she has not been continually present within the Navajo Nation for the last three years. Yellowhorse met the "continually present" exception as her extended absence from Navajo Country is due to purposes of attending school at the University of New Mexico-Gallup Branch.

NOTES

1. The *Begay* Court addresses two difficult questions for Indian nations: who should represent Indian people in tribal government as elected officials, and where they should reside. On-reservation residents reasonably feel underrepresented when off-reservation residents are elected to tribal legislatures, especially when those legislatures are enacting criminal and regulatory laws that apply only to on-reservation residents.

However, modern tribal governments must contend with the fact that many of the best young and future leaders have left Indian country to earn an education at off-reservation colleges, universities, and professional schools. As the *Begay* Court notes, residency requirements can be used in an abusive fashion to exclude these Indians from leadership positions upon their return.

2. The Navajo Nation Supreme Court also confronted the interesting question whether candidates for elected office can also serve as elected officials in state government in *In the Matter of the Grievance of Wagner*, 7 Navajo Rep. 528 (Navajo Nation Supreme Court 2007). There, the Court held that tribal candidates cannot simultaneously serve in both governments:

> Tsosie also contends that [the Office of Hearings and Appeals] erred when it upheld the Navajo Nation Code's prohibition on serving simultaneously as a council delegate and a member of a state legislature. . . . Tsosie's primary contention is that the prohibition is in irreconcilable conflict with the Fundamental Law statute's provision that voters may choose leaders of their choice, 1 N.N.C. §203(A) (2005). He also argues that the exemption for school boards and county commissions violates the Equal Protection Clause of the Navajo Bill of Rights. See 1 N.N.C. §3 (2005). . . .
>
> It is true that under Fundamental Law, voters have the right to choose leaders of their choice. 1 N.N.C. §203(A) (2005). Candidates also have a Fundamental Law right to participate in the political system by running for office. *Begay v. Navajo Nation Election Administration*, No. SC-CV-27-02, slip op. at 3 (Nav. Sup. Ct. July 31, 2002). Tsosie points to this Court's recent opinion, *In re Appeal of Vern Lee*, No. SC-CV-32-06 (Nav. Sup. Ct. August 11, 2006), as precedent for striking down the simultaneous service prohibition under these fundamental rights. In *Lee*, this Court ruled that the residency requirement in the Election Code, which required presidential candidates to reside within the modem boundaries of the Navajo Nation as defined by the Navajo Nation Code, violated the rights of voters and candidates. *Id.*, slip op. at 7-8. Tsosie states the bar on simultaneous service similarly violates those rights.
>
> Tsosie misreads *Lee*, as the prohibition is consistent with Dine bi beenahaz'aanii. . . . In Navajo thinking, the selection of a person by voters is one of two requirements for a candidate to become a naat'aanii. That person must also accept the position, and, to accept, must take an oath to serve the laws of the sovereign government within whose system he or she will serve the people — "naat'aanii adee hadidziih." Only when a person accepts through an oath will all of the Navajo people say that a person has been properly installed as a naat'aanii — "naat'aanii idli bee bitooszii." In other words, "Dine binant'a'i bee bi'doosztiid" or "Dine binaat'aanii bee bi'doosziid." The oath for council delegates explicitly requires an incoming delegate to swear that "I will support, obey, and defend the Navajo Nation and all the laws of the Navajo Nation." . . . In Navajo the delegate swears "Dine hi naat'a do bibee nahaz'aanii bee seziidoo, bik'eh anisht'ee doo, bich'aah sezii dooleel." The Dine people will keep that delegate to his or her words. *See Kesoli v. Anderson Security Agency*, No. SC-CV-01-05, slip op. at 5-6 (Nav. Sup. Ct. October 12, 2005) ("Words are sacred and never frivolous in Navajo thinking."); *Office of Navajo Labor Relations v. Central Consolidated School District No. 22*, No. SC-CV37-00, slip op. at 5 (Nav. Sup. Ct. June 23,

2004) (same). The oath is absolute, and allows no conflict in loyalty. This requirement of absolute loyalty is reiterated in the Election Code itself, as one of the qualifications for a council delegate is that he or she must "maintain unswerving loyalty to the Navajo Nation." 11 N.N.C. §8(B)(5) (2005). Under these principles, a person may not swear allegiance to obey and serve simultaneously the laws of the Nation and the State of New Mexico. The prohibition is then consistent with our Fundamental Law, and it is not improper for the Election Code to require Tsosie to serve only one government.

Id.; slip op. at 7-8.

C. QUALIFICATIONS OF VOTERS

1. RESIDENCY

CROWE V. TRIBAL BOARD OF ELECTIONS

The Cherokee Supreme Court — Eastern Band of Cherokee Indians, No. 04-CV-530 (September 1, 2004), 2004.NACE.0000005

The opinion of the court was delivered by: MARTIN, Chief Justice . . .

In reviewing a final determination of the Board of Elections, this Court can only review alleged errors of law. We have no authority to make findings of fact. Chapter 7-5 (a) Cherokee Code. Our duty is to determine whether the findings of fact support the conclusion of law and decisions of the Board. . . .

The protest of Carroll Crowe states:

The Cherokee Code at section 161-10 (C) states, "Tribal members not living on Cherokee trust lands shall register in the Township in which they or their enrolled parents last resided."

The right to vote in our Tribal elections is restricted to registered voters. Each person's registration has residency requirements, and if those residency requirements are not met then you cannot register to vote. If someone votes who is not legally registered, then that vote is illegal and should not be counted.

For those persons who do not live on Cherokee trust lands, I challenge the election to show that those persons either used to live in the community for which they registered and cast an absentee ballot or their parents lived in that community. If this cannot be verified then that person was not entitled to register, and if not registered, then they could not vote. The election laws DO NOT make exceptions for grandparents or other extended family. It says, "in which they or their enrolled parents last resided". If someone cannot prove that either themselves or their enrolled parents resided in that particular community, then they cannot be legally registered to vote. . . . The law further places the restriction that both the parents must be or have been enrolled AND previously resided in the community for which the person wants to register in. Therefore, if both parents were not enrolled members then that person can only register under the single criteria that is based upon their own previous residency in that community. The law does not make allowances for a person's ancestry. It specifically restricts persons not living on Cherokee trust lands to their former residency or that of their enrolled parents. . . .

Appellant contends that, "Many of the absentee voters were not qualified (to vote) under Section 161-10." However, the evidence at this hearing shows that only two persons may have voted illegally in the election for Principal Chief. The appellant's evidence is unclear whether these two voted by absentee ballot, but does show that they voted for appellant. Although appellant argues that illegal absentee ballots were cast by voters, the transcript in this hearing contains no evidence to sustain this contention. Yet appellant urges the Board to review the entire voter registration list to determine whether anyone voted who was improperly registered. This overlooks that the burden of proof is upon the person protesting the election results. Appellant has the burden to show that illegal ballots were cast and that they affected the results of the election, that is, that without the challenged ballots the result of the election would have been different, in this case, that appellant would have been elected. This, appellant has failed to do. . . .

[B]efore an absentee ballot can be issued a Board member must certify that the voter is a registered and qualified voter of a Cherokee township. This certification raises a presumption of regularity as to the issuance of the absentee ballot. A protester of an election based on irregular absentee ballots has the burden to produce evidence before the Board to overcome this presumption and support the protest. This, appellant has failed to do. . . .

Mr. Crowe, a candidate for Chief, filed a timely protest of Chief's race in the 2003 general election. His protest is based on a literal interpretation of §161-10 (C), Cherokee Code, which states that "Tribal members not living on Cherokee trust lands shall register in the Township in which they or their enrolled parents last resided." He alleges that many absentee voters registered in the wrong township, so were improperly registered, and their vote cannot be counted. . . .

Our records indicate that a large number of absentee voters improperly registered in the wrong township. However, we are faced with an impossible task. All votes are cast anonymously. We can determine if an absentee voter voted. But we cannot determine who they voted for, unless further evidence is provided. Mr. Crowe has not met his burden in this regard.

A literal interpretation of §161-10 (C) would void the votes cast by improperly registered absentee voters. However, we must not read the election ordinance in isolation, but in the context of §2 of the Tribal Charter, which says:

> The Principal Chief or Vice-Chief and members of Council shall be elected to their respective offices by the enrolled members of the Eastern Band of Cherokee Indians, who have attained the age of eighteen (18) years.

If we read §161-10 (C) literally, we allow it to impose a restriction that is greater than that allowed in the Charter. The Charter imposes only two restrictions: that a person be a tribal member, and that they be at least 18 years of age. Any further restriction — such as that suggested by the protesters — would violate Tribal law.

We must recognize the role township registration plays in an at-large election. At-large candidates are elected by all of the voters, regardless of township.

A vote cast in one township carries the same weight as a vote cast in another township. All absentee votes are mailed to the same place — the Election Board office in Cherokee. Changing registration from one township to another would make no difference in where the votes are cast in an at-large election. . . .

Also, interpreting the township registration requirement as eligibility standard instead of a rule for registration seems contrary to Tribal history and custom.

The Election Board relies on personal representations of voters on their registration card, and information provided by the Enrollment Office. The Enrollment Office also relies on personal representations of members. That office does not have comprehensive residency lists for enrolled members. A person could live on the Qualla Boundary and then move away, and the Enrollment Office may or may not have a record of their residence here. A member's representation to the Election Board is the best information we have, and we must rely on it.

For the foregoing reasons, we deny Mr. Crowe's protest. . . .

Associate Justice TOINEETA and Chief Judge PHILO, sitting by designation, Concur.

NOTES

1. What is the purpose of a residency requirement in a tribal election? Would the reasons for a residency requirement in a tribal election be different from those in a non-tribal election?
2. Note the court stating that the election board's certification of the tribal election depended on the "personal representations of voters," and that it may in fact have serious errors. Does the petitioner's claim have additional merit, given this factual possibility?
3. The court asserts that tribal "history and custom" supports the outcome. How might this be so, especially since the court does not elaborate on Cherokee history and custom that might be relevant?
4. The Grand Traverse Band of Ottawa and Chippewa Indians prohibits tribal citizens residing outside of a six-county area within the Grand Traverse Band's traditional territories from voting in tribal elections. *See Russell v. Grand Traverse Band of Ottawa and Chippewa Indians Election Board*, 2000 WL 3579799, at *1 (Grand Traverse Band Tribal Court 2000) (discussing the six-county area residency requirement for eligibility to run for tribal office).

   The Grand Traverse Band constitution provides that

   [a]ny member duly enrolled in the Grand Traverse Band who is at least eighteen (18) years old, has been a resident for a period of at least six (6) months in the six-county area of Antrim, Benzie, Charlevoix, Grand Traverse, Leelanau, and Manistee, and is registered to vote on the date of any given tribal election shall be eligible to vote in that tribal election.

   GRAND TRAVERSE BAND OF OTTAWA AND CHIPPEWA INDIANS CONST. art. VII, §3(a) (1988).

Conversely, the Little Traverse Bay Bands of Odawa Indians allows any tribal citizen to run for office and to vote, regardless of residency. *See* LITTLE TRAVERSE BAY BANDS OF ODAWA INDIANS CONST. art. XII(A) ("The members of the Tribal Council, Chairperson and Vice-Chairperson shall be elected at large by popular vote.").

5. In *Jacobson v. Eastern Band of Cherokee Indians*, 2005.NACE.0000010 (Eastern Band of Cherokee Indians Supreme Court 2005), the court rejected an equal protection challenge to the Band's absentee ballot rules:

> The Plaintiff contends the Tribe has infringed on her fundamental right to vote by eliminating her ability to vote by absentee ballot. However, there is no fundamental right to vote by absentee ballot. . . . Noting that the framework of an absentee voting plan does not deny the right to vote itself, one Federal Court held as follows:
>
> > The right to vote is unquestionably basic to a democracy, but the right to an absentee ballot is not. Historically, the absentee ballot has always been viewed as a privilege, not an absolute right. It is a purely remedial measure designed to afford absentee voters the privilege as a matter of convenience, not of right.
>
> *Prigmore v. Renfro*, 356 F. Supp. 427, 432 (N.D. Ala. 1972).
>
> Since voting by absentee ballot is not a fundamental right, the Court does not review a challenge to C.C. §161.14(b)(6) under the "strict scrutiny" standard, but rather under the "rational basis" test. . . . Under this test, C.C. §161.14(b)(6) "must bear some rational relationship to a legitimate [Tribal] end and will be set aside as violative of the Equal Protection Clause only if based on reasons totally unrelated to the pursuit of that goal." . . .
>
> Having determined the appropriate standard of review for Plaintiff's claim, the Court now analyzes whether there are any genuine issues of material fact with regard to the relationship between this legislation and the legitimate ends of the Tribe. There are none. Clearly, a majority of the enrolled members voted in a plebiscite to return to the six criteria for absentee voting which originally comprised the absentee ballot procedures. Enacting an ordinance to comport with the expressed will of the people alone is a rational relationship to a legitimate Tribal end. However, the Council did more than just rubber stamp a referendum: additional debate and comment preceded and followed the vote.
>
> From this debate it is plain that the enrolled members wished their fellows who lived off of the Reservation to return to it to vote. Multiple reasons were advanced for this, but in general they amounted to a desire on the part of the enrolled members that non-residents return to Cherokee at least once during an election cycle to experience in person the flavor of what was happening politically on the Reservation. While there is an undercurrent in the record and arguments before the Court that the residents of the Reservation may have been dissatisfied with the increased political power wielded by non-residents by way of open absentee balloting, it remains, at most, a mere suggestion, unsupported by evidence or any material fact, and the Court cannot say that these rumblings represent the basis for the change in the law.
>
> Another rumbling in this record involves the tension between members who leave the Reservation to pursue a better life and those who stay.

Plaintiff is emphatic about it and alleges that the residency component amounts to discrimination against her because she has left the reservation and made her life elsewhere. Who could argue with the Plaintiff that enrolled members who leave the Reservation to pursue careers in law, medicine or business, or, like Plaintiff, to raise and care for her children, are not serving the ultimate interests of the Cherokee people and rising up the Nation?

No one. But again, this is a political decision, not a legal one, and thus, while this may feel to the Plaintiff like discrimination, legally, it is not.

Id. at ¶¶40-48.

2. AGE

WOUNDED HEAD v. TRIBAL COUNCIL OF THE OGLALA SIOUX TRIBE OF THE PINE RIDGE RESERVATION

United States Eighth Circuit Court of Appeals, 507 F.2d 1079 (January 3, 1975)

MATTHES, Senior Circuit Judge.

Pursuant to a provision of the Indian Reorganization Act of 1934, 48 Stat. 984, specifically 25 U.S.C. §476, the Oglala Sioux Tribe of the Pine Ridge Reservation of South Dakota adopted a constitution and bylaws. Pertinent to this litigation is Article 7 of the Tribe's constitution, which provides:

> Section 1. All members of the Tribe, 21 years or older who have resided on the reservation for a period of one year immediately prior to any election shall have the right to vote.
>
> Section 2. The time, place and manner, and nomination of councilmen and any other elective officers of the Council shall be determined by the Tribal Council by an appropriate ordinance.

On October 15, 1973, a tribal election official denied Garrett Wounded Head and Bernadine Nichols, Sioux tribal members 18 and 19 years of age respectively, the right to register and vote in a tribal election because they were not yet 21 years of age.[1] . . .

Acceptance of plaintiffs' trial theory necessarily requires equating tribal council action with action "by the United States, or by any state." It is authoritatively settled, however, that Indian tribes are uniquely situated within the

---

1. Apparently, the Solicitor was joined as a defendant because he had published an opinion which modified the Sioux tribal constitutional election provision in Secretarial elections, but not in tribal elections. Solicitor's opinion No. 36840 (November 9, 1971). In the memorandum the Solicitor concluded that the twenty-sixth amendment applies only to federal and state governments. The Solicitor resolved that Secretarial elections, those called by the Secretary of the Interior under 25 U.S.C. §476 to allow an Indian tribe to amend its constitution and bylaws, are a form of federal election subject to the twenty-sixth amendment, but purely internal elections of an Indian tribe, not covered by federal laws, are not subject to the limitations of that amendment. . . .

federal system. . . . In *Ex Parte Crow Dog*, 109 U.S. 556, 568 (1883), the Supreme Court stated:

> The pledge to secure to these people, with whom the United States was contracting as a distinct political body, an orderly government . . . that of self-government, the regulation by themselves of their own domestic affairs, the maintenance of order and peace among their own members by the administration of their own laws and customs.

. . . We hold that the twenty-sixth amendment does not apply to internal tribal elections. Plaintiffs appear reconciled to this conclusion. . . .

We turn now to the contentions of plaintiffs presented on appeal. In 1968, the Indian Civil Rights Act (ICRA), also known as the Indian Bill of Rights, was enacted by Congress in language taken nearly verbatim from the United States Constitution. 82 Stat. 77, 25 U.S.C. §§1302, 1303. The effect of the Act was to impose upon Indian tribal governments restrictions applicable to federal and state governments, with specific exceptions: the fifteenth amendment, portions of the fifth, sixth, and seventh amendments, and in some respects the equal protection clause of the fourteenth amendment. The legislative history of the Act reflects an intent to protect the individual rights of Indians, while fostering tribal self-government and cultural identity. . . . In thus creating a statute with twin, and possibly conflicting, goals, the form of government and the qualifications for voting and holding office were left to the individual tribes.

Plaintiffs advance several grounds to support their argument in favor of enfranchising all adults 18 years of age or older. The most important is that the equal protection clause of the ICRA requires the tribal council to set the minimum voting age at 18. The equal protection clause of the Act, 25 U.S.C. §1302(8) provides:

> No Indian Tribes in exercising powers of self-government shall—
> (8) deny to any person within its jurisdiction the equal protection of its laws or deprive any person of liberty or property without due process of law.

In approaching the equal protection question under the ICRA, two separate questions are presented: 1) whether the substantive meaning of the equal protection clause of the fourteenth amendment should be utilized to determine the scope of the equal protection clause of the ICRA in matters of internal tribal government; and 2) if so utilized, whether the age qualification is in fact violative of the equal protection clause of the ICRA. . . .

In any case, we regard *Oregon v. Mitchell*, 400 U.S. 112, 91 S. Ct. 260, 27 L. Ed. 2d 272 (1970), as dispositive of the equal protection issue. In *Oregon*, the majority, writing in five separate opinions, upheld the power of the federal government to set the age for voting in national elections, but concluded that the equal protection clause of the fourteenth amendment did not limit the power otherwise inherent in the states to fix the voting age at twenty-one for state and local elections. As a direct result of this decision, the twenty-sixth amendment, which we have held above does not apply to Indian tribal elections, was adopted to remedy the obvious logistical problems that would accompany concurrent federal, state, and local elections at the same voting place with electorates of different ages able to vote in some elections but not in others. The Solicitor and the Tribe properly conclude that, in light of *Oregon*, to apply the equal protection clause in the instant case would restrict the tribes to an even greater extent than the states and the federal government are restricted by the fourteenth amendment. Such an incongruous result is untenable in the absence of an express congressional intent to so intervene in Indian tribal affairs. But even if the full scope of the equal protection clause of the fourteenth amendment were applied to the facts of this case, it is questionable if that constitutional provision would mandate that 18 to 21 year-old Indians be allowed to vote. . . .

In summary, we hold in line with established authority that Congress has exclusive and plenary power to enact legislation with respect to the Indian tribes. In the absence of a constitutional mandate or express legislation by Congress to the contrary, a tribe has complete authority to determine questions such as the one here under consideration. Congress has failed to enact legislation authorizing members of the Sioux Tribe between the ages of eighteen and twenty-one to vote, and the ICRA does not expressly or impliedly require the Tribal Council to permit plaintiffs to vote at a tribal election. Finally, we note that the constitution of the Sioux Tribe is subject to amendment and plaintiffs have the right to participate in seeking to change the tribal constitution provision under attack. . . .

The judgment is affirmed.

NOTES

1. Tribal constitutions may set a minimum age limit for eligible voters different than that required under the United States Constitution for American elections, but not without difficulty in some instances. The Twenty-sixth Amendment to the United States Constitution, ratified in 1971, set the age limit at 18 as a result of the realization that a large percentage of Americans fighting in the Vietnam War were under the age of 21 and therefore ineligible to vote under the law at that time. *See* WILLIAM FUNK, INTRODUCTION TO AMERICAN CONSTITUTIONAL STRUCTURE 23 (2008); *cf. Oregon v. Mitchell*, 400 U.S. 112 (1970) (striking down the 1970 Voting Rights Act Amendments in which Congress attempted to reduce the voting age to 18).
2. Cases such as *Wounded Head* are historical footnotes now, since the United States Supreme Court held in *Santa Clara Pueblo v. Martinez*, 436 U.S. 49 (1978), that federal courts do not have subject matter jurisdiction over civil suits brought under the Indian Civil Rights Act.
3. Modern tribal courts rarely have addressed the question left open in *Wounded Head*; namely, whether the voting age requirement would violate a tribal equal protection clause or the Indian Civil Rights Act's equal protection clause. At least one tribal court held without discussion, and relying upon *Wounded Head*, that it would not. *See Jones v. Election Board of the Fort McDowell Yavapai Nation*, No. CV-2000-005, 2000.NAFM.0000001, at ¶¶40-42 (Trial Court of the Fort McDowell Yavapai Nation, Feb. 1, 2000).

D. TRIBAL CONSTITUTIONAL AMENDMENT ELECTIONS

1. ELECTION PROCEDURES

KAVENA V. HOPI INDIAN TRIBAL COURT

Hopi Tribal Appellate Court, 1989.NAHT.0000002 (March 21, 1989)

Before SEKAQUAPTEWA, Chief Judge, and ABBEY and BENDER, Judges
Per Curiam.

1. Factual and Procedural Background

This case arises out of the effort of a group of residents of First Mesa Village, a part of the Hopi Tribal Reservation, to change the traditional form of government of that village through a village referendum election pursuant to procedures established by the Hopi Constitution.

The Hopi Tribe is "a union of self-governing villages" (Hopi Const. Art. III, Sec. 1). There are nine such villages, of which First Mesa (the consolidated villages of Walpi, Sitchomovi and Tewa (sometimes also known as Hano)) is one. With respect to the form of government of the villages, the Hopi constitution provides (Hopi Const., Art. III, Sec. 3):

> Each village shall decide for itself how it shall be organized. Until a village shall decide to organize in another manner, it shall be considered as being under the traditional Hopi organization, and the Kikmongwi of such village shall be recognized as its leader." (Hopi Const., Art. III, Sec. 3)

The Hopi constitutional provisions for changing the form of village government are as follows (Hopi Const., Art. IV, Sec. 4):

> Any village which . . . wishes to make a change in [the traditional Hopi organization] . . . may adopt a village Constitution in the following manner: A Constitution, consistent with this Constitution and By-Laws, shall be drawn up, and made known to all the voting members of such village, and a copy shall be given to the Superintendent of the Hopi jurisdiction. Upon the request of the Kikmongwi of such village, or of 25% of the voting members thereof, for an election on such Constitution, the Superintendent shall make sure that all members have had ample opportunity to study the proposed Constitution. He shall then call a special meeting of the voting members of such village for the purpose of voting on the adoption of the proposed Constitution and shall see that there is a fair vote. If at such referendum not less than half of the voting members of the village cast their votes, and if a majority of those voting accept the proposed Constitution, it shall then become the Constitution of that village. . . .

First Mesa Village has, since its settlement, been governed according to the traditional form of Hopi village government, with a Kikmongwi as its leader. In October, 1987, a group of First Mesa residents called the People's Rights Committee (PRC) initiated an effort to change the traditional form of village government by filing a petition with the Superintendent of the Hopi jurisdiction, [an official of the Bureau of Indian Affairs]. The petition requested that an election be called for the purpose of voting on a proposed new constitution for the Village.

The petition filed by the PRC contained 297 signatures, 269 of which were subsequently determined by the Superintendent to be valid signatures. In ascertaining the number of voting members of the village, the Superintendent used a list of residents of the village who had registered to vote in the last previous election for Hopi tribal Chairman. This list contained 705 names. The Superintendent thereupon determined that the PRC's Petition represented a request by more than 25% of the voting members of the village for a referendum election as required by the Hopi Constitution. The Superintendent ultimately set such an election for June 7, 1988.

A second group of First Mesa residents, calling themselves the Walpi Hopi Sovereign Rights Committee (SRC) and seeking to retain the traditional form of village government, opposed the Superintendent's decision to call an election. . . .

[SRC sought federal court relief, but that case was dismissed on July 27, 1988.]

The Superintendent then re-scheduled the election for August 16, 1988. In response, the SRC filed an action in the Tribal Court of the Hopi Tribe, seeking once again to prevent the election from taking place. This Tribal Court action, *Kavena v. Hamilton*, was heard by Chief Judge Ames of the Tribal Court. In an opinion dated August 15, 1988, Chief Judge Ames agreed with the SRC's primary contention that the Superintendent had not used a correct list of the voting members of the village. . . .

Chief Judge Ames concluded that the referendum election should be stayed for an additional 90 days, until November 14, 1988: "[I]t is apparent more time and patience should be extended before a traditional form of government, which has existed for centuries, is placed in jeopardy. . . . Once eliminated, traditional organization most probably can never be recovered. That is irreparable harm and damage in its truest sense. More time should be allowed to make certain that a way of life does not fade into the past while making certain that the standards of the [Indian Civil Rights Act] are observed." . . .

2. Proceedings in this Court

This Court heard argument on the Petition for Extraordinary Relief via a telephone conference call held on November 11, 1988. At the conclusion of this telephone argument we issued an order staying the November 14 election.

Despite our stay order, a majority of the Election Board apparently decided to proceed with the November 14 election as scheduled. . . .

At the hearing before this Court on January 27, 1989, all counsel agreed that the November 14 election should not be treated as a valid village referendum election. We accept this agreement for the following two reasons:

First, the Hopi Constitution provides that a village referendum election can change the form of village government only if "not less than half of the voting members of the village cast their votes." We have been informed by the General Counsel of the Hopi Tribe that 389 ballots were cast on November 14. We are further informed that the final eligible voters list, as determined by the

Election Board appointed by the Tribal Court, consisted of 998 eligible voters and 319 challenged voters. Even if we were to assume that all voter challenges would be successful, the votes cast would not total the constitutionally required half of the eligible voters.

Second, this Court clearly had jurisdiction to issue its November 11, 1988, Order staying the November 14 election.

A valid election cannot be held in the face of such a stay. Thus, the November 14 election could not have effected a change in the form of village government no matter how many votes had been cast in it. . . .

The Constitution of the Hopi Tribe provides the only method by which a village which is under the traditional Hopi organization may adopt a different form of village government. A decision by a village to adopt a new form of government is a decision with extremely important potential consequences for the village, its members and residents, and the entire Hopi Tribe. It is essential, therefore, that the procedures provided by the Hopi Constitution be strictly followed.

Those procedures, however, were not adequately followed in this case. The most fundamental defect in the procedures that were used here concerns the BIA Superintendent's determination of whether enough voting members of the village had petitioned to ask for a village referendum election.

The method prescribed by the Hopi Constitution for changing the form of village government is the adoption, through such an election, of a village constitution. Such an election is to be held only if either the Kikmongwi of the village or "25% of the voting members thereof" request that an election be conducted. In this case the PRC submitted a petition to the Superintendent of the Hopi jurisdiction asking that a referendum election by held. That petition contained 269 valid signatures.

The Superintendent correctly decided that, in determining whether this petition was sufficient, it would be necessary to ascertain the total number of voting members of First Mesa village. The Superintendent sought to find this number, however, by asking the Hopi Tribal Council for a list of the First Mesa residents who were registered to vote in the last election for Tribal Chairman and Vice Chairman. Despite explicit contrary advice given by the Tribal Chairman, the Superintendent used this list as the basic list of First Mesa village voting members.

The Superintendent's use of this list was an incorrect implementation of the procedures provided by the Hopi Constitution. Hopi Village membership for purposes of ascertaining those eligible to vote in a referendum on a proposed village constitution is a special concept that is not equivalent to residence in the village at the time of a Tribal election. Village membership in a village, such as First Mesa, with the traditional Hopi organization, is a concept with much deeper meaning than mere physical presence or residence. Such membership involves the maintenance of religious and cultural ties and relationships with the village and its ceremonies. Many village members, for example, do not reside in the village of their membership. This can occur for a number of reasons, including the Hopi matrilineal tradition pursuant to which a husband will reside in the village of his wife's membership while retaining membership in his mother's village. Hopis may also reside off the reservation at their place of employment, while retaining membership in the village of their birth. Conversely, some of those who do physically reside in a traditional Hopi village may not be village members, often because they are members of other villages.

The proper procedure for the Superintendent to use in determining who are the voting members of a village is for him to ask the Kikmongwi of that village to provide a list of the voting membership. The Kikmongwi is explicitly recognized in the Hopi Constitution as the leader of a village that is still under a traditional form of organization. The Kikmongwi, moreover, has an explicit constitutional role to play in admitting individuals to village and tribal membership.[6] . . .

In this case, Chief Judge Ames correctly held that the list of village members for referendum voting purposes should have been based on a list supplied by the Kikmongwi. We believe, however, that the decision of whether a sufficient percentage (25%) of the voting members of a village had signed the election petition should then have been made before the election was held.

An election on so fundamental a matter as whether the traditional form of Hopi village organization should be abandoned is a major event in the history of a Hopi village and in the lives of many village members. A matter of such importance and potential disruptive effect should not go forward unless it is clear that the preconditions required by the Hopi Constitution have been met. It would also be extremely unfortunate to hold an election on a matter of such importance to the daily lives of village residents and then to place the outcome in doubt for a protracted period while legal proceedings took place. This is especially true if the "results" of the challenged election were announced or became known.

In addition to the fact that the adequacy of the referendum petition was not properly determined prior to the election, there were other important defects in the procedures leading up to the scheduled November 14 election. We mention them briefly here in order to provide guidance should the referendum election procedure be invoked in the future. . . .

2. In this case it appears that the Superintendent may have set a date for the election solely upon his determination that a sufficient number of signatures was present on the petition submitted to him. There is, however, a second finding that the Hopi Constitution requires to be made prior to the setting of a referendum election. Upon the submission of an adequate petition "the Superintendent shall make sure that all members have had an ample opportunity to study the proposed Constitution. He shall then call a special meeting of the voting members of such village, for the purpose of voting on the adoption of the proposed Constitution . . ." (Art. IV, Sec.4) (emphasis added).

The determination that there has been ample opportunity to study the proposed constitution must thus be made before the election is called. This

---

6. Under Art. II, Section 2, of the Hopi Constitution certain persons may be adopted into the Hopi tribe "in the following manner: Such person may apply to the Kikmongwi of the village to which he is to belong, for acceptance. According to the way of doing established in that village, the Kikmongwi may accept him. . . ."

requirement is not merely a technicality. The words of the Hopi Constitution undoubtedly reflect an understanding of the importance to village life of the decision to change its form of government. The Constitution requires that there be ample opportunity for all members to study the proposed change even before an election date is set, in order to make sure that there has been adequate time to consider the proposed change. . . .

4. Finally, as we read the Hopi Constitution the process of making a proposed change in village government know[n] to village members must start even before a petition is circulated and signatures gathered. After a proposed constitution is drawn up, it must "be made known to all the voting members of such village" at the same time as a copy is submitted to the Superintendent. Only after that publicity, does the Hopi Constitution contemplate the submission of an election petition. The preferable procedure would clearly seem to be to make the proposed change known to all village members before signatures are gathered, so that village members can hear both sides of the matter before deciding whether to sign a petition. Once again, in a matter of this importance, it is best to give as much opportunity as possible for reflection, study and discussion before a decision is made.

[A]ny future referendum election to change the form of government of First Mesa Village should not be called unless the procedures provided by the Hopi Constitution are newly initiated and followed, starting with the first step of those procedures — the submission of the proposed village constitution to the Superintendent at the same time as it is made known to all voting members of the village. We note further that, for these purposes, it may be necessary for those proposing a village constitution to obtain a list of voting village members from the Kikmongwi at the outset of their efforts, so that those not residing in the village can be informed of the proposal from the beginning. . . .

NOTE

The election over whether the First Mesa would adopt a nontraditional form of village government was a secretarial election. Federal regulations promulgated under 25 U.S.C. §476(c) provide procedures for the holding of secretarial elections required under federal statute, *see* 25 CFR Part 81, and these procedures may also be used by tribes for other secretarial elections involving tribal constitutions, *see* 25 CFR §81.2(b).

2. AMENDMENT BY PETITION AND REFERENDUM PROCESS

IN RE PROTEST AGAINST INITIATIVE PETITION

Cherokee Nation of Oklahoma Supreme Court, No. SC-06-12, 6 Am. Tribal Law 39, 9 Okla. Tribal Court Rep. 584 (December 19, 2006)

Chief Justice MATLOCK delivered the Opinion and Order of the Court, in which Justices HASKINS and WILCOXEN join.

[I.] Jurisdiction

This matter is properly before this Court pursuant to Article VIII of the Cherokee Constitution of 1999 and Legislative Act 15-04, Section XVII.

[II.] The Anatomy of the Litigation

1. This Court on October 5, 2006, [in *In re Numerical Sufficiency of Signatures*, 9 Okla. Trib. 507 (Cherokee 2006),] . . . approved the Election Commission's certification of the numerical sufficiency of signatures on the Initiative Petition which is the subject of these proceedings, and ordered the Election Commission to cause the publication of the filing of the Initiative Petition and determination of the apparent sufficiency of the required number of signatures and to further notice the citizens of their rights to protest the Initiative Petition.

2. In response to the Publication of Notice, the Petitioner/Protestant, Vicki Dee Baker, timely filed her protest . . . on November 1, 2006, setting forth her elements of protest against the Initiative Petition. The four (4) elements of protest were:

(1) Fraud,
(2) Insufficiency of Signatures,
(3) Petition Wording is Vague and Misleading, and
(4) Petition Violates the Constitution. . . .
(5) The Court, after examining the Volumes of the Initiative Petition and the language of the Initiative Petition, made a summary finding as a matter of law that the language of the Initiative Petition was constitutionally sufficient.
(6) The Court also found as a matter of law that there is a presumption that the signers read the Petition, and that this Court will not interfere with the action of electors under the theory that some may have been verbally deceived.
(7) The Cherokee Nation Election Commission, by their attorney James Cosby, on November 22, 2006 filed a Motion for Declaratory Judgment to determine whether or not the Principal Chief has the authority to call a Special Election concerning Initiative Petitions. . . .

[III.] Findings

. . .

B.

The Court further finds that the Principal Chief of the Cherokee Nation has the authority to call a "Special Election" concerning Initiative Petitions pursuant to Article XV, Section 4 of the Cherokee Nation Constitution of 1999 and Legislative Act 15-04, Section VII.

C.

The Court further finds that the evidence presented by the Petitioner/Protestant, considered in the most favorable light to the Petitioner, fails to overcome the burden of proof required to prove the Initiative Petition insufficient, and the Petition of Protest is therefore DENIED.

[IV.] Discussion

. . .

B.

Article XV, Section 4 of the Cherokee Nation Constitution of 1999 sets forth the following language concerning the calling of a Special Election:

> All elections on measures referred to the People of the Cherokee Nation shall be had at the next regular general election *except when the Council or the Principal Chief shall order a special election for the express purpose of making such reference.* Any measure referred to the People by the initiative. . . .

([E]mphasis added.) Legislative Act 15-04, Section VII sets forth:

> Whenever any *measure* shall be initiated by the People in the manner provided by law . . . , same shall be submitted to the People for their approval or rejection at the next regular *or special election as provided at Article XV, Section 4* of the Cherokee Nation Constitution.

([E]mphasis added.)

The word "measure" is defined by BLACK'S LAW DICTIONARY (4th ed. 1951), at page 1132, as "[t]he Rule by which anything is adjusted or proportioned." It is obvious that the word "measure," as used in Article XV, Section 4 of the Cherokee Nation Constitution of 1999 and Legislative Act 15-04, Section VII, is referring to proposed amendments to the Cherokee Nation Constitution by the Initiative.

C.

This Supreme Court in formulating the rules to govern proceedings to apply to this challenge of an Initiative Petition gave great deference to the strength of the direction of the Cherokee People in Article XV, Section 1 of the Cherokee Nation Constitution of 1999:

> [T]he People of Cherokee Nation reserve to themselves the power to propose laws and amendments to this Constitution and to enact or reject the same at the polls independent of Council.

([E]mphasis added.) . . .

The Court made rulings of law that the form of the Initiative Petition met the constitutional requirements, and that there must be a presumption that the signers of the Initiative Petition read the Initiative Petition and that an action for verbal fraud would not defeat an Initiative Petition.

This Court has considered the "rule of substantial compliance" formulated by the Oklahoma courts in the proceedings, *see In Re Referendum Petition for a Referendum Vote on Legislative Act 28-99,* No. JAT 01-06, [7 Okla. Trib. 382, 388 (Cherokee 2001)] and while not necessarily adopting the rule in total, it would appear that part of the rule which forgives technical and clerical defects as long as the critical requirement of notice to the electorate is accomplished should be adopted by this Court. . . .

In order to protect each qualified elector's right to participate in the Initiative, the Court applied the following presumptions and burdens of proof which must be overcome by the Petitioner/Protestant:

1. The certificate of each packet which composed a part of the total Initiative Petition is *prima facie* correct and imports a verity and presumption that must be rebutted by competent evidence.

2. If a certificate of a circulator is impeached, the probative value of that certificate is destroyed, and none of the signatures appearing on that page of the Petition will be counted unless affirmatively proven to be genuine.

3. The constitutional rights of qualified electors who sign the Initiative Petition must be protected by this Court, tempered only by the safeguard of the integrity of the process. Therefore, the Petitioner/Protestant must present sufficient evidence as to each certificate to overcome the presumptions set forth hereinbefore even though one or more certificates of a circulator has been impeached. The Court is charged with determining the validity of the process in these proceedings, and not to punish a circulator's indiscretions by disqualifying all his packets. If the Court were to invalidate signatures on certificates that the Petitioner/Protestant fails to impeach with competent sufficient evidence, then the Court would be violating the constitutional guarantees of those qualified electors who happen to be on such certificates. The proper conduct of the Court is to refer the persons suspected of violating Legislative Act 15-04, Section VI to the Department of Justice for investigation and possible prosecution, and such referrals will be made.

The Petitioner/Protestant presented John Summerfield as a witness, who along with his wife signed a signature page of a packet (identified as Petitioner's Exhibit 2) circulated by a person who was different than the named circulator, Darren Buzzard, on the packet, and the named circulator was the person who executed the verification certificate. There were nineteen (19) qualified signatures on this particular packet and the only signatures affirmatively proven were the signatures of John Summerfield and his wife Josephine Summerfield. Therefore, eighteen (18) signatures of the packet must be disqualified. The Petitioner then presented testimony from Carol Wyatt, who testified that she took a packet (identified as Petitioner's Exhibit 3) being circulated by Dwayne A. Barrett to her parents to obtain their signatures, and they did sign the signature page. Dwayne A. Barrett executed the verification certificate. There were nine (9) qualified signatures on this signature page, and the only signatures affirmatively proven were the signatures of Carol Wyatt's parents. Therefore, nine (9) signatures of this packet must be disqualified.

The Petitioner then presented sufficient evidence to disqualify the two (2) qualified signatures on the packet identified as Petitioner's Exhibit 4.

The Petitioner presented Marilyn Vann's testimony, wherein she testified that she discovered thirteen (13) signatures that were not on the voters list received by her from the Election Commission. The Court feels that her testimony was less than convincing, but will disqualify the thirteen (13) signatures on Petitioner's Exhibit 5 for purposes of considering a demurrer to the Petitioner/Protestant's evidence. The total number of signatures disqualified by the Petitioner/Protestant's witnesses and exhibits was forty-two (42). The Cherokee Nation Election Commission verified that there were three thousand and twenty-nine (3,029) signatures collected, and certified two thousand two hundred seventeen (2,217) of the signatures. The Cherokee Nation further certified that there were thirteen thousand nine hundred fourteen (13,914) votes cast in the last general election.

In order for the proposed amendment to the Constitution to be presented to the Cherokee People for approval or disapproval, the valid signatures must total at least fifteen percent (15%) of the total number of votes cast in the last general election. CHEROKEE CONST. [1999] art. XV, §3; LA 15-04, §XV.

The Court determines that fifteen percent (15%) of thirteen thousand nine hundred seventeen (13,917) is two thousand eighty-seven (2,087). The figure of two thousand eighty-seven (2,087) valid signatures is the number required to send the proposed constitutional amendment to a vote of the Cherokee People.

The Court subtracted the forty-two signatures from the number of two thousand two hundred seventeen (2,217) signatures verified by the Cherokee Nation Election Commission for a balance of two thousand one hundred seventy-five (2,175) qualifying signatures, which are more than the necessary figure of two thousand eighty-seven (2,087) signatures necessary to submit the proposed constitutional amendment to the Cherokee People for consideration.

IT IS THEREFORE ORDERED by the Court that the Petition of Protest is DENIED.

Justice DOWTY, dissenting in part and concurring in part. . . .

2. We have heard the testimony and received into evidence the Petitions from the Cherokee Nation Election Commission. We have also heard from the Protestants and the Proponents of the Petition and received their documentary evidence. It falls on us to conduct a *de novo* review and determine the sufficiency of the signatures on the Petitions. Since we have not adopted a specific procedure with regard to this review, we have differing opinions as well regarding the extent to which we should examine the Petitions. In my opinion, we should be thorough in our review, both as to signatures which may have been either excluded or included in error, as shown by the face of the documents, giving due consideration to the procedural law enacted by the Council in LA 15-04.

3. Having heard the testimony and evidence, having reviewed the Petitions and considered the debate and opinions of my colleagues, I have reached the conclusion that the process evidenced by these Petitions is so flawed that the sufficiency of signatures cannot be certified by this Court. Accordingly, I must respectfully dissent to the majority opinion. . . .

11. Hundreds of signature pages properly completed shows that the process is not burdensome and can be easily done right. However, the actions of a few have placed the process in jeopardy. Bringing to a vote a change in the organic document governing a sovereign Nation should require effort, and should be subject to safeguards that assure that the election is the will of the people in the exercise of the initiative. The requirements of LA 15-04 are not difficult if undertaken and carried out by competent, honest and conscientious

citizens, especially in the circulation of the Petitions. The conduct shown by the evidence and cited by my colleagues shows how the conduct of a few can undermine the hard work and good faith of others. Accordingly, given the totality of error shown by the evidence, and giving due regard to the doctrine of substantial compliance, I must decline to vote to certify the Initiative Petition of the Proponents and would find that the proposition should not go before the Citizens of the Cherokee Nation at the Special Election now scheduled. . . .

Justice LEEDS, dissenting.

This case involves a challenge to the sufficiency of an initiative petition. The proposed initiative seeks to place a constitutional amendment on the ballot at a special election. The amendment, if passed, will exclude a class of Cherokee citizens known as the Freedmen and invalidate the effect of this Court's decision in *Allen v. Cherokee Nation,* No. JAT 04-09[, 9 Okla. Trib. 255 (Cherokee] 2006). There is no doubt that the Cherokee people have the legal right to amend the Constitution to redefine citizenship. The Cherokee people must, however, abide by Cherokee law in exercising that right.

In this initiative petition process, there are numerous irregularities, clear violations of Cherokee law, and it has been shown that some of the circulators perjured their sworn affidavits. I cannot, in good conscience, join in the majority opinion.

We must be concerned for the rights of two groups of Cherokee citizens. We must preserve the right of Cherokee citizens to propose constitutional amendments through the lawful initiative process. In doing so, we must also be cognizant of the rights of Cherokee citizens who stand to be excluded. The integrity of our democratic process is at stake.

[I.] The Challenges to the Petition

This Court is asked to invalidate the initiative petition on the following grounds:

(1) some individuals who circulated the petitions violated Cherokee law in their attempts to collect the required number of signatures; . . .

[III.] The Election Commission's Report

. . . The Election Commission is charged with counting the petitions and reporting the number of valid signatures to this Court. The Election Commission certified that 3,029 signatures appeared and that 2,217 signatures were valid. The Election Commission invalidated 812 signatures. . . .

The Election Commission's report reveals that there are 131 signatures in excess of what is required to place the initiative on the February ballot. Therefore, if more than 131 signatures should be excluded on the basis of this Court's review, the initiative petition fails. . . .

[V.] Falsification of Affidavits

The challenger introduced evidence that some individuals who circulated the petitions violated Cherokee law by falsifying affidavits. The proponents offered no evidence to rebut this testimony.

It was shown that two of the circulators, Darren Buzzard and Dwayne Barrett, falsified petition affidavits. They violated the requirement that each circulator must swear before a notary that they personally witnessed all the signatures on a given petition. They swore before a notary that they personally circulated petitions that they did not in fact circulate. In doing so, they perjured themselves and their credibility as truthful circulators is impeached. This is particularly bothersome given the fact that Darren Buzzard attested to over 520 signatures.

Darrell Buzzard and Dwayne Barrett falsified affidavits as follows:

1. John Summerfield testified that Harley Buzzard actually circulated the petition that he and his wife signed, yet Darren Buzzard signed the affidavit that he personally witnessed each of the signatures. Darren Buzzard was not present when the signatures were collected. The petition was therefore falsely attested and must be discounted in its entirety.

2. Carol Wyatt, an employee of Cherokee Nation Enterprises, testified that she is actually the person who carried a petition to her parents' home to obtain their signatures. Dwayne Barrett signed the affidavit swearing that he was the person who witnessed all the signatures on that page. Dwayne Barrett was not present when the signatures were collected. The petition was therefore falsely attested and must be discounted in its entirety.

3. Melvin Garner, who is not a Cherokee citizen, testified that he nonetheless signed the petition and that he also signed his wife's name to the petition. Darren Buzzard was the circulator of this petition, and once again he swore that he witnessed each person sign the petition when in fact he did not. The petition was therefore falsely attested and must be discounted in its entirety.

What is equally troubling, with respect to the integrity of the process, is that neither Carol Wyatt, John Summerfield, or Melvin Garner recalled seeing the required warning page on the external petition pamphlets that were presented to them. Melvin Garner did not know that as a non-citizen, he was not allowed to sign the petition. He also was unaware that it was crime to sign someone else's name to the petition. Viewed in the very best light, these testimonies suggest that the circulators did not assemble and circulate the petitions in the manner required by law. The testimony also shows that these two circulators were dishonest about their collection efforts. These are not inadvertent mistakes or mere technicalities this Court can overlook. These actions are conscious and deliberate and show a disregard for following the law. . . .

The majority acknowledges that these individuals should be referred to the Attorney General for possible criminal prosecution for their fraudulent conduct. The majority is nonetheless willing to presume that these individuals were truthful in gathering the remaining signatures and attesting to the rest of the affidavits.

[VI.] Presumptions of Signature Validity

In giving the full effect to the initiative power of the Cherokee people, I agree that we must first presume that the signatures verified by the Election Commission are valid. The party that challenges the initiative process has the burden to show that the initiative petition should be invalidated. Once it is proven that either fraud or irregularities have occurred, the burden must then shift to the proponents of the petition to revive the signatures as valid and to rehabilitate the credibility of certain circulators.

In the present case, it has been proven that two of the circulators have filed false affidavits. It has been shown that Darren Buzzard falsified an affidavit on more than one occasion. This type of misconduct calls into question the verity of all the petitions that were carried by Darren Buzzard. The burden must shift to the proponents to show why the remaining signatures he allegedly collected should be counted.

A sworn statement before a notary is an oath that carries considerable weight. It is akin to the oath taken by witnesses who testify before this Court. If a witness is proven to have lied to this Court, the credibility of that particular[] witness is impeached. This is magnified when it is shown that the witness has lied to this Court more than once. We would no longer presume the witness to be trustworthy. The credibility of the circulators of a petition should be equally judged.

There is no Cherokee precedent for what a Court should do in this situation. Should the Court only disallow the signatures on the actual petitions that were specifically referenced at trial? Should the repeated falsification of circulator's affidavits lead to the disallowance of all the signatures gathered by that circulator on the grounds that he cannot be trusted? . . .

[Parts VII and VIII of Justice Leeds' dissenting opinion concludes that . . . "[e]ven if we adopt Oklahoma law as persuasive authority, as the majority urges, this Court [must still disallow 137 signatures], a number that would require us to invalidate the initiative petition."] . . .

[X.] Remedies

Although not alone in his failure to abide by the law, it is clear that Darren Buzzard, the most prolific circulator in the process, disregarded the rules and falsified affidavits. In the interest of justice, this Court has three viable options: (1) Disallow all signatures carried by Darren Buzzard because he cannot be trusted; (2) Disallow no less than 137 signatures that are specifically referenced in this opinion; or (3) Conduct a more thorough review to give the proponents a chance to rehabilitate the impeached circulators and give the challenger the opportunity to present the testimony of witnesses that were disallowed by this Court.

Options one and two would result in the invalidation of the petition and the cancellation of the February election. Option three would provide an adequate opportunity for both sides to address the problems raised in this petition. There are ten weeks before the special election and ample time to exercise this option. It is not reasonable to turn a blind eye and let the special election go forward under this cloud.

[XI.] Due Process

I am concerned about one of the majority's summary rulings in this case. During this expedited trial, the Court refused to allow the challenger to call certain witnesses. There was no pretrial conference or opportunity for the parties to challenge or defend a witness list. Instead, the challenger found out on the morning of the hearing that the Court would exclude certain witnesses.

The majority ruled that the challenger would not be permitted to proffer testimony to support her allegations of fraud and misrepresentations by the circulators of the petitions. The majority ruled that it is absolutely irrelevant what the circulators might have said to induce signatures. While I agree that we must presume that Cherokee voters can read a petition and decide for themselves whether they want to sign the petition, this rule is not without limitation. Other jurisdictions have invalidated entire initiative petitions based on the fact that some circulators misrepresented the legal effect of initiative petitions.[20]

I would certainly limit testimony to the sole issue of whether the effect of the petition was misrepresented. I would honor the right of the Cherokee voters to voice their opinions about the initiative. I would always honor the right of the Cherokee voters to strongly advocate for their position. However, if there was testimony that the circulators misrepresented the ultimate effect of the petition as a means to induce more signatures, the Court should have allowed that testimony. As it stands, we will never know what occurred because the majority refused to allow any testimony on this issue. . . .

[XIII.] Conclusion

The power to propose constitutional amendments is an awesome power. If we are going to amend our fundamental laws, we must ensure that the proper procedures are followed and that the integrity of the process is safeguarded.

This Court is the final gatekeeper of the integrity of the initiative process. In the interest of justice, this Court should have invalidated the initiative or, at the very least, conducted a more thorough review. To allow the initiative to move forward under this cloud of inequity is unconscionable. The majority has sent a clear message to the Cherokee people that our laws can be disregarded.

My decision does not preclude a future vote on this issue. The voters are already properly scheduled to vote on this constitutional amendment in the upcoming general election in June 2006. In the future, it may be very welcome to pass that the Freedmen or other classes of Cherokee citizens are excluded by majority vote. If this occurs, let it happen only after full compliance with, and respect for, our own laws.

I respectfully dissent.

NOTE

The Cherokee Nation electorate voted overwhelmingly to approve the amendment at issue in this case in 2007. *See* S. Alan Ray, *A Race or a Nation?*

---

20. In *Citizens Committee for D. C. Lottery Terminal Petition v. District of Columbia Board of Elections and Ethics*, 860 A.2d 813 (D.C. App. 2004), all signatures gathered by a citizens' group were stricken based on fraud where some of the circulators falsified affidavits and made false statements to voters about the ultimate effect of the petition. In *Operation King's Dream v. Connerly*, No. 06-12773, 2006 WL 2514115 (E.D. Mich. 2006), a federal district court in Michigan found that voter fraud existed where petition circulators told the voters they were signing a petition supporting affirmative action, when in fact the petition was to do away with affirmative action.

Cherokee National Identity and the Status of Freedmen's Descendants, 12 MICH. J. RACE & L. 387, 389 (2007).

E. THE PROBLEM OF HOLDOVER COUNCILS

CHAMBERLAIN V. PETERS

Saginaw Chippewa Tribe of Michigan Appellate Court, No. 99-CI-771, 27 Indian L. Rep. 6085 (January 5, 2000)

. . .

I. Factual Summary

. . .

A. Historical Background

. . . In November of 1995 Kevin Chamberlain and nine others (the Chamberlain Council), some of whom are signatory to the present petition, were elected to represent District 1 by the base voter rolls represented in the 1986 Constitution which included those persons also named in the TM Resolutions. Part of the platform of this Council included a promise to reform membership problems and a commitment to effectuate constitutional reforms. During these years, though, scant progress was made toward these intended reforms. Instead, the Council proved itself more successful in constructing the expanded Soaring Eagle Casino, the economic cornerstone of the Tribe. After two years had passed, it was time for new elections to take place, as required by the Saginaw Chippewa Tribal Constitution.

B. The Elections

On October 16, 1997, a primary election was held for District 1. The field of candidates was reduced to twenty as the law required. The following month, on November 4, the General Election was held. Only four of the sitting members of the Chamberlin Council were re-elected. The election results were challenged, and, as was the procedure of the time, the Council examined the results. The Council ruled the election was invalid. This declaration led next to a curative General Election. This election, held on January 27, 1998, had virtually the same results. The Chamberlain Council, again, declared the election to be invalid. This occurred as their terms of office expired and their mandate of reform came to an end.

From this point, and precisely beginning on February 18, 1998, a series of tribal court challenges advanced toward what appeared to be a cure to the problem of membership and the proper legal succession to office. In fulfillment of the court's directions to complete both its membership examination and the election process, the Chamberlain Council tried unsuccessfully to secure the services of genealogist Betty Bell. It then successfully secured the services of James Mills. Mr. Mills produced his recommendations citing what he perceived to be shortcomings in various categories of documents that should be produced in order to bring finality to questions of membership in the Tribe. Acting upon these recommendations, the Chamberlain Council issued notices in October of 1998 to more than 140 persons who previously had been considered members of the Tribe telling them that they had been "temporarily suspended" from membership unless they could produce documentation which would satisfy Mr. Mills and the Enrollment Advisory Board (EAB). The subsequent cascade of documentation, involving some 500 files, led Mr. Mills and the EAB to conclude that only six individuals truly appeared to have been questionably enrolled. After notification, two of these voluntarily relinquished membership in the Tribe. This, arguably, set the stage for a valid election.

On November 24, 1998, a second primary election was held for District 1. Surprisingly, the persons who had been temporarily suspended from membership were disallowed from either voting or running for office in this election. The election took place leading to the selection of 20 finalists. Of these 20, only one person was a member of the Chamberlain Council. The suspended members, all except for the questionable remaining four, were then inexplicably restored to membership. Before a general election cold be held, acting upon protests submitted by several members of the Tribe, the Chamberlain Council acted on December 15, 1998 to again nullify the election process. But, also in that month the Council enacted law that established an appellate court to hear appeals from the Community Court. It is this resolution that created this Court and the original jurisdiction contemplated in this case.

The day following the Council's nullification, the Community Court issued notices that hearing would be convened to determine whether the Chamberlain Council should be held in contempt of court for its apparent failure to hold a curative election. On December 29, 1998, Judge Bruce Havens convened the Community Court. After a disruptive proceeding the Chief Judge prepared his ruling. He determined that "the Tribal Council Defendants have shown a consistent pattern of disregard for the Constitutional and Ordinance mandates [of the Tribe] and they are acting outside of the scope of employment with the Tribe thereby subjecting themselves to individual liability for their conduct." Members of the Chamberlain Council found themselves under prosecution for criminal contempt before Associate Judge Ronald Douglas, after Judge Havens summarily recused himself, and subsequently resigned.

The second year of the Chamberlain Council's "holdover" term began with a dismissal of the contempt charges. The Tribe proceeded to its third round of elections. The third primary election was held on January 19, 1999. This time the Chamberlain Council again invalidated the election in a ruling entered on February 25, 1999, stating that the TM Resolutions unconstitutionally increased the membership rolls. These two events are the most significant developments relevant to this case: first, it is from the January 19, 1999 primary election that the Peters Council comes; and second, it is the unconstitutionality of the TM Resolutions that the Chamberlain Council relies upon for its continued maintenance of control beyond the end of its term of office.

Obviously incensed by this last turn of events, a group of members of the Tribe began to organize an alternative election outside of any existing governmental backing and purportedly authorized by Ordinance 4. They announced their intentions. The Chamberlain Council countered this initiative by enacting a law of sedition making the "simulation of governmental processes" a crime and punishable by imprisonment. On March 9, 1999, the alternative election proceeded, nonetheless, and resulted in a voter participation of approximately 37% of the voters in District 1. Several persons were then issued criminal citations, subsequently dismissed, pursuant to the sedition law.

It is important to note that the elections and court cases were not the only tracks of activity. From late in 1998 until the March 1999 alternative election both the supporters of the alternative election — which included the current Peters Council — and the Chamberlain Council were actively engaged in the pursuit of the political backing of the Assistant Secretary of the Interior Kevin B. Gover. As part of this strategy, while Assistant Secretary Gover postponed official action in this controversy, the Chamberlain Council initiated an alleged media critique of Gover's B.I.A. Administration.

On March 11, 1999, the Chamberlain Council passed a law redistricting District 1, the Isabella District, such that the District expanded beyond the boundaries of the reservation to include lands which had previously encompassed Saginaw lands as they appeared before those lands were ceded to the federal government.

On March 16, 1999, the visitors in the March 9 alternative election took the oath of office but there was no officially recognized transfer of government power. In the Community Court, on the same day, Judge Bruce S. Hinmon dismissed challenges to the Chamberlain Council's rulings that invalidated the November 1998 Primary and the December 1999 General Elections. Judge Hinmon based his decision on the sovereign immunity and political question doctrines.

Meanwhile, Assistant Secretary Gover finally weighed in on the controversy. By a letter dated June 9, 1999, he urged the Chamberlain Council to hold an election within the next 45 days. The letter implied that his office considered the January 19, 1999 primary election to have been valid — in spite of the Chamberlain Council's and the Court's rulings to the contrary. He further challenged that his Administration would be forced in the absence of such election, to "deal with the representatives of the two off-reservation districts and the ten persons from the Isabella District who received the highest number of votes in January 1999 as representatives of the Tribe."

The Chamberlain Council, aware of Gover's threatened course, nonetheless, scheduled a fourth round of elections beginning with a primary set for some time in September 1999, outside of the 45-day window established by Assistant Secretary Gover in his letter of June 9, 1999. As a result, on August 10, 1999, Assistant Secretary Gover adhered to his word and issued a letter stating:

> I am instructing the Area Director to proceed with the instructions I gave him on June 9. He is to deal with the representatives of the two off-reservation districts and the eleven persons from the Isabella District who received the highest votes in January 1999 as representatives of the Tribe on an interim basis.

Assistant Secretary Gover, letter of August 10, 1999.

It is not entirely clear what had happened at this juncture. Copies of the Assistant Secretary's letter were provided to tribal and BIA law enforcement, as well as the Federal Bureau of Investigation and the United States Marshall Service. Many of the tribal law enforcement personnel were employed directly by the BIA and also held supervisory positions. There is some suggestion in the record that Attorney Michael Phelan, who served in the capacity of legal counsel to the Tribe during the Chamberlain Administration had advised the police that they should give effect to the Secretary's letter. The Peters Council was sworn into office by a notary public. Conflict and confrontation ensued in the following month. It is from these series of events that this petition emerged.

The Peters Council then went directly to produce its version of curative elections. In order to accomplish this, the Peters Council enacted laws that restored the electorate — the body of eligible voters — to the *status quo* as it existed before the Chamberlain Council took office. In addition, it set up an election challenge process which involved neither the Council nor the Courts. Primary elections were held on October 2, 1999, by which 24 finalist candidates were selected. Immediately following this election, a petition was submitted to this Court in an attempt to receive a ruling of invalidation. This Court denied the request. A general election took place on November 2, 1999, in which twelve persons were selected to take office. Five minutes before the close of business on December 6, 1999, another petition was submitted, this time by Kevin Chamberlain and Benedict Hinmon, asking this Court to issue a temporary restraining order calling for a halt to the administration of the oaths of office on December 7, 1999, to the prevailing candidates in the November election. This Court has stayed its hand pending its ruling in this case, fully aware that the two are inextricably intertwined.

A final note to this factual summary is in order regarding the participation of the federal government, or lack thereof, in these proceedings. This Court convened two sessions, the first, as a pre-trial conference, and the second, as oral argument regarding the issues presented here. In anticipation of these hearings, and, at least, in the latter hearing, at the urging of both parties, we *sua sponte* invited the participation of the federal government in these proceedings and have received a mere letter of declination. . . .

III. Discussion

A. Validity of the Actions of the "Holdover" Chamberlain Council

We begin our discussion on the question of whether the Chamberlain Council possessed an unfettered right to continue to hold over in office despite the expiration of its constitutionally defined term of office. The answer to that question lies in its constituent elements. What authority did the Chamberlain Council have to continue in office beyond the end of its term? Did the Constitution mention the prospects of a holdover? If not, is there something within the theory and structure of the Constitution that provides for such a "holdover"? What, therefore, were the limits of its authority, if any? And if there were, how do we treat such unconstitutional actions?

It takes only a minimal review to recognize that the Constitution, adopted in 1986, and the laws of the Tribe, have not a single provision regarding the transition of power from one Council to the next. It does not follow that the Council in office at the time that a transition should occur is, therefore, left with open authority to reshape the government of the Tribe. Various other provisions of the Constitution provide either direct or implied limitations against Tribal Council action, irrespective of whether it is legally or illegally constituted. The most notable of such provisions, in this case, concern Article III, regarding membership, Article VI, Section 1(m), and Article VII. In addition, the Tribe is presumptively bound by the mandates of the Indian Civil Rights Act of 1968, 25 U.S.C. §1302(8), in particular, its references to "due process of law" and "equal protection of the laws."

We recognize that at the heart of the Chamberlain Council's justification for its continued validity beyond the end of the term of office is its assertion that the membership mandate had to be fulfilled *before* any valid elections could take place. In its estimation, it was, thus, essential to change the membership of the Tribe. This was effectuated by the dual initiatives to investigate the validity of membership claims, and, to amend the Constitution to reflect its vision of an ideal profile for membership. Both are problematic on legal and theoretical grounds.

Read together Article III — which sets a base membership roll based upon the particular rolls taken on November 10, 1883, November 13, 1885, November 7, 1891, and December 10, 1982 — and Article VI, Section 1(m) — which denies the Council any authority to pass laws affecting membership — signal a clear barrier to such Council actions that would affect the status of membership. Even the attempt to force individuals by law *ex post facto* to produce proof of membership, therefore, is highly suspect. . . . From a practical perspective, however, we concede that some laws that touch upon the issue of membership are allowable, though, tempered by the "due process" and "equal protection" clauses of the ICRA. Due process and notions of fundamental fairness suggest that the status of membership cannot be assailed without ample procedures, and especially so after a person has been admitted to membership in the Tribe.

The status of nominal membership is not the sole concern raised by the Chamberlain Council's actions. Membership consists of a bundle of rights and privileges, including, but not limited to, the right to be secure in one's identity as a member, the right to receive tribal benefits on an equal footing with other members, and the right to participate in the political process. The fact that over 140 persons were denied that right strips the Chamberlain Council of any cover of innocence and righteousness.

The theory and structure of the Constitution also serve to erode the Chamberlain Council's dual initiatives and its continued occupancy of office. Article IV, Section 8 provides that the Council "*shall* be elected every two years." (Emphasis added.) This modest statement forms the foundation for the government of the Tribe. It is mandatory and not discretionary. The election *must* take place. The performance of the election is a duty incumbent upon the Council, and the failure to hold an election can be deemed a neglect of that duty thus serving as a basis for removal from office. *See* Article IV, Section 14(a).

The "two year" limitation, moreover, places a very finite limitation upon the elected Council. A candidate knows before running for office that his or her term may last only two years and not beyond. And, in order to gain the public trust, a candidate voices certain public concerns that either do or do not succeed in gaining the public validation through the voting process. *See generally* Article IV. In this case, the Chamberlain Council ran on a particular platform that did indeed gain the public trust. But there is a clear constitutional implication that such platform must be fulfilled or completed within the given two years.

The holdover actions of the Chamberlain Council were clearly in violation of the Saginaw Chippewa Indian Tribal Constitution. The Tribal Constitution makes no provisions for a holdover tribal council and implicitly rejects such a possibility. Article IV, Section 8 of the Constitution states: "The Tribal Council shall be elected every two years in the month of November." This constitutional provision clearly does not envision any holdover possibility. In fact, it constitutionally guarantees members the right to elect a tribal council every two years.

The Chamberlain Council argument that its holdover actions were constitutionally authorized rests more directly, as counsel conceded at the hearing on October 16, 1999, on language in Election Ordinance No. 4 (at that time) that stated:

> Any voter may protest an election for the district in which he/she voted. The written notice of protest must be made to the Tribal Council within seven (7) days after the election. The notice must set out the grounds of the protest. The Tribal Council shall schedule a hearing on the protest within ten days. The Tribal Council decision will be *final*. (Emphasis added.)

While this election ordinance did grant substantial authority to the Tribal Council to decide election protests, it cannot be said that it granted authority in excess of constitutional limits. To do so would render the constitutional requirement of tribal elections every two years in November as guaranteed in Art. IV, Sec. 8, a mere nullity. To state the obvious, no tribal ordinance may render constitutional provisions inoperative.

The "logic" of the Chamberlain Council argument is fatally flawed at its core. It presumes an ongoing right to set aside tribal elections without reference to the tribal constitution or potential review by a tribal court. This is profoundly undemocratic and contrary to any notion of the balance of governmental powers. The mandate for reform that originally carried the Chamberlain Council to elected office eventually became a justification for what looked more and more like despotism. Lofty motives do not excuse unconstitutional and illegal issues.

The jurisprudential implications of such matters have been noted by other tribal courts. For example, the Confederated Salish and Kootenai Tribal Court of Appeals observed:

> Interpretation and application of the law to determine the legality of a particular act is the "heart of the judicial function." [Citing *Menominee Indian Tribe ex rel. The Menominee Indian Tribal Legislature v. Menominee Indian Tribal Court*, 20 Indian L. Rep. 6066, 6068 (Men. Tr. S. Ct. 1993)]. Among the most

important functions of courts are constitutional interpretation and the closely connected power of determining whether law and acts of the legislature comport with the provisions of the Constitution. Courts were created to serve these purposes.

Moran v. Council of the Confederated Salish and Kootenai Tribes, 22 Indian L. Rep. 6149, 6155 (C.S. & K.T. Ct. App. 1995). *See also* the classic federal precedent of *Marbury v. Madison,* 5 U.S. (1 Cranch.) 137 (1803).

The Chamberlain Council had two years to complete its pledge of resolving membership election and constitutional issues before its term of office expired in November 1997. *See* Saginaw Chippewa Indian Tribe of Michigan Constitution and Bylaws, as amended, Article IV, Sec. 8. During its tenure, it should be noted that its primary focus was on economic development and it did achieve major success in establishing a sound economic base for the Tribe. However, the alleged necessary governmental reforms were not extensively dealt with until late in its term or until its official term of office had expired. At the end of those first two years the Chamberlain Council could only be considered a "holdover" Council.

Arguably, the political mandate that elected it to office had to be accounted for *at that time* to the voting public, leaving the question to the existing membership whether membership and constitutional reforms should be continued under the same government. The Chamberlain Council's political platform *at that time* could have been the very same assertions made before Assistant Secretary Glover and before this Court throughout these proceedings, that it had identified issues of membership which required a curative constitutional amendment, and, that it would be its electoral platform to so amend the Constitution.

Nonetheless, continuing its quest to fulfill its expired political mandate, this "holdover" Council finally began to act on the political reforms it had promised, which involved a series of meetings with the federal government. Nearly one year after its term expired, on December 23, 1998, Chief Chamberlain and several representatives of the Tribe met with the BIA requesting Assistant Secretary Gover's assistance in expediting an election on a proposed Constitution that would address the Tribe's enrollment and membership problems.

As a "holdover" body, the Chamberlain Council did have a duty at the expiration of its term to ensure a constitutionally elected government and a proper and orderly transition of that body. This "holdover" Chamberlain Council failed in its efforts to conduct a valid election and consequently has not been able, since, to effectuate an orderly transfer of government within the internal mechanisms of the Tribe's government. Both the Chamberlain Council and the Peters Council thereafter sought to rely on a political resolution of the Chamberlain-created problem from the BIA's Assistant Secretary of Interior, Kevin Gover. Both of these requests to the Assistant Secretary totally ignored the internal tribal law and institutions of the Saginaw Chippewa Indian Tribe. In sum, both the "holdover" and "interim" councils were in error. *See* discussion *infra* at pp. 19-33. Moreover, this appeal to the United States government exemplifies both the negative impact that historical federal policy has had upon Indian tribes, and, the all-too-often tribal populist reliance on the well-established paternalistic posture of the BIA. This reliance on the federal government rather than upon the basic right and responsibility of self-government is counter to the established principles of tribal sovereignty and, as we shall see below, yielded a major intrusion into the internal governmental functions of this Tribe.

The previous discussion brings into question though, the validity of the actions of the Chamberlain Council taken from the end of its two-year term to the installation of the Peters Council — the "holdover" period. As stated above, the Tribal Constitution does not have any provision for an interim governing body or a "holdover" Council. Thus, the Chamberlain Council after its term expired apparently acted outside the scope of tribal constitutional authority. Such actions outside the scope of constitutional authority place the overall tribal government in a very tenuous position. There are a myriad of potential circumstances where a Council may be legally required to hold over. If, for instance, a major snowstorm had caused power shortages, road closures and a resultant failure of the election process, a Council may be required to hold over to endure that such elections eventually take place. Such events may require the expenditure of funds and, perhaps, an adjustment of the internal laws. But, it is clear than such "holdover" authority converts the mandate of such leadership away from initial platform concerns toward the primary duty to hold such elections. One cannot, in retrospect, say that any holdover or interim actions during such an emergency are manifestly illegal — *that* would require a case-by-case analysis. And under such analysis, the most suspect of actions must be those which accrue to the benefit of those holding office, or are contrary to the Constitution, the laws of the Tribe and applicable federal law.

Clearly, to provide the necessary continued stability and regularity in government, the actions of the "holdover" council must be deemed presumptively valid unless it can be established by clear and convincing evidence that those actions were contrary to the Tribal Constitution or applicable federal law, or, provided an undue benefit to those persons holding such "holdover" office. The most relevant areas that have surfaced as issues of concern include the adoption of an amended election code. *See* Saginaw Chippewa Indian Tribe of Michigan, Tribal Council Resolutions #99-101 & #99-104.

Even though the Chamberlain Council, in good faith, began these broad constitutional reforms, the timing for these actions was constitutionally erroneous. Its term had expired. In addition, to begin constitutional reforms during the "holdover" period is questionable as it is well-settled law that tribal officials are limited to the authority conferred upon them by their tribal constitutions or statutes. Thus the timing of the Chamberlain Council's actions is not only contestable, but the adoption of such ordinances containing provisions relating to a currently contested election is questionable.

Finally, according to the Constitution, the Tribal Council is vested with the authority to make provisions for all elections, "by *proper* ordinance." *See* SCITM Constitution, Article IV, Section 7. (Emphasis added.) Where a "holdover" or "interim" government attempts to change the constitutional democratic processes from those that existed at the time of its own election, we can only conclude that such changes are *improper* and violative of Article IV, Section 7.

These changes occurred on July 15 and 16, 1999. *See* SCITM Tribal Council Resolutions #99-101 & 104.

The timing of these actions brings to question the intent of the Chamberlain Council to cure any defect in the election process and conduct a legitimate tribal election. Once its terms had expired it was foreclosed from changing the laws of the Tribe that pertain to political succession. The Chamberlain Council was bound by the laws that installed it into office. Its primary duty was to ensure compliance with the pre-existing tribal law and to effect an orderly transition of government. To initiate any laws outside their constitutional authority, exceeded their legal and political mandate. . . .

NOTES

1. Notwithstanding the apparent illegality and impropriety of the Chamberlain Council's self-serving decisions to stay on as a "holdover" council, can you think of a time when a tribal council, or any individual tribal elected official, could legitimately remain in office beyond his or her term of office?

   Consider *Bullcoming v. Cheyenne and Arapaho Tribes*, 9 Okla. Trib. 528 (Cheyenne-Arapaho Supreme Court 2006), in which the court wrote:

   > When several former Business Committees failed to fill Supreme Court vacancies that would have resulted from the expiration of the then-normal eight-year Supreme Court terms of office, this Court both applied the "hold-over-in-office" provisions of CHEY.-ARAP. COURTS CODE §§103(f) and 205, and appointed Special Justices under Section 214 of that Code (and its own inherent power) in order to preserve its own jurisdiction and permit the maintenance of Supreme Court quorums. *See In re Appointment of Special Justices*, 8 Okla. Trib. 342, 368 & 485 (Cheyenne-Arapaho 2004); *In re Term of Office of the Justices*, 8 Okla. Trib. 164 (Cheyenne-Arapaho 2003). In so doing, we noted that Associate Justice Connie Hart Yellowman (appointed in 1991) and Associate Justice Dennis Belindo (re-appointed in 1997) were no longer meeting with the Court, *see id.* at 168-69, and we herein note further that Associate Justice Amos Black III (also re-appointed in 1997) has not met with the Court since May 19, 2004. Thus, the only regularly-appointed Supreme Court Justices now regularly convening as a part of this Court are Chief Justice Ryland Rivas and Associate Justice Dennis Arrow, who were appointed on the same day in 1995. Chief Justice Rivas and Associate Justice Arrow have "held over" in office under CHEY.-ARAP. COURTS CODE §§103(f) and 205.

   Id. As the previous excerpt suggests, some tribal governments anticipate situations in which tribal officials may validly remain in office beyond their term of office.

2. Perhaps judges occupy a special place in governance where a judicial holdover is more necessary than the holdover of most other offices. Consider *In re Service of Office of Justices*, 6 Okla. Trib. 573 (Cherokee Judicial Appeals Tribunal 1998):

   > In the time-tested, landmark case of *State ex rel. Eberle v. Clark*, 87 Conn. 537, 89 A. 172 (1913), the Connecticut Supreme Court found that a judge has a right and duty to hold over and exercise the duties and functions of the office until his successor is duly selected and qualified, even where there is no

explicit constitutional nor statutory provision regarding holdover. The Connecticut Supreme Court explained this rule of law as follows:

> The public interest requires that such officers shall hold over when no successor is ready and qualified to fill the office, otherwise important public offices might remain vacant to the public detriment in the absence of statutes providing for the filling of vacancies or through the neglect of appointing authorities to fill them. The rule has grown out of necessities of the case, so that there may be no time when such offices shall be without an incumbent.

The common law right and duty to hold over, as described by the Connecticut Supreme Court, is applicable to Justices of the Tribunal, and other appointed Cherokee Nation officials. In addition, and more importantly, under Cherokee law, the duty of a Justice to hold over is constitutionally mandated through Article XII, Section 1 of the Cherokee Constitution.

Id. at 577-78.

6

CIVIL RIGHTS

Like state and federal courts, tribal courts are a significant forum in which individuals under the jurisdiction of tribal government seek a remedy for civil rights violations. Congress's enactment of the Indian Civil Rights Act (ICRA) in 1968, along with the United States Supreme Court's decision in *Santa Clara Pueblo v. Martinez*, 436 U.S. 49 (1978), cemented the importance of tribal courts in vindicating civil rights.

Congress enacted ICRA as Title II of the 1968 Civil Rights Act. See 25 U.S.C. §1301 et seq. Portions of the ICRA that substantially mirror the Bill of Rights are popularly called the Indian Bill of Rights. The statute extends most of the constitutional protections of the American Constitution to individuals under the jurisdiction of Indian tribal governments. In order to preserve certain aspects of tribal government and sovereignty, Congress modified or left out some provisions of the Bill of Rights. The individual rights protections include the rights to free exercise of religion, free speech, press, assembly, and to petition for a redress of grievances; the right to be free of unreasonable searches and seizures without a search warrant to be issued only upon a showing of probable cause; the right to be free from being placed in double jeopardy and from self-incrimination; the right to due process and equal protection; the right to be free from taking of property without just compensation; the rights to a speedy trial, confront witnesses, and the assistance of counsel; the freedom from excessive bail and cruel and unusual punishment; the freedom from bills of attainder and ex post facto laws; and the right to a jury of at least six persons in all criminal cases carrying the possibility of imprisonment. Key differences between ICRA and the Bill of Rights include the absence of an establishment clause and a right to counsel at the government's expense. Also, the ICRA prohibited Indian tribes from sentencing convicted criminals to more than six months in prison and more than $500 in fines (later amended to one year and $5,000).

The Supreme Court had originally decided in *Talton v. Mayes*, 163 U.S. 376 (1896), that, since tribal sovereignty flowed from a time immemorial and tribes had not participated in the drafting of or consented to the United States Constitution, the individual rights protections that limited federal (and later, state) governments did not apply to tribal governments.

In the 1950s, non-Indians had brought several cases to the federal courts seeking a civil rights remedy for actions taken against them by tribal governments. In *Martinez v. Southern Ute Tribe*, 249 F.2d 915 (10th Cir. 1957), *cert. denied*, 356 U.S. 960 (1958), for example, the Tenth Circuit rejected a due process challenge to a tribal decision to deny membership rights to an individual Indian. In *Native American Church v. Navajo Tribal Council*, 272 F.2d 131 (10th Cir. 1959), the Tenth Circuit ruled that the Navajo Nation was not bound by the First Amendment and could prohibit the ritual use of peyote. And in *Barta v. Oglala Sioux Tribe*, 259 F.2d 553 (8th Cir. 1958), *cert. denied*, 358 U.S. 932 (1959), the Eighth Circuit ruled that the Fifth Amendment's due process clause and the Fourteenth Amendment's equal protection clause did not prohibit a tribe from taxing nonmembers more than members.

Judicial concern over civil rights violations by tribal courts in criminal cases came to a head in 1965, when the Ninth Circuit decided *Colliflower v. Garland*, 342 F.3d 369 (9th Cir. 1965). There, the Gros Ventre tribal court sentenced a woman to five days in jail for failure to remove her cattle from land leased to another person. The Ninth Circuit took jurisdiction over the case, even though the events took place on the reservation and the parties were all tribal members, on the theory that the federal government had funded the tribal jail. Likely, the court took the case because the tribal court had allowed Ms. Colliflower neither to have an attorney nor to confront witnesses against her, restrictions that would have been serious civil rights violations in state or federal courts.

Many senators and advocates were concerned that there were enclaves in the United States in which civil rights protections from governmental activity did not exist. The Senate took testimony from numerous individuals who claimed to have been treated unfairly by tribal governments. Others were concerned that many Indian tribes did not have an independent adjudicative body separate from the tribal council.

Specific provisions in the final version of the ICRA strongly imply that Congress intended to preserve as much of tribal culture as possible. Congress left out a provision equivalent to the Establishment Clause in order to preserve the rights of tribes to form and maintain theocratic government structures if they wished, and some tribes did.

After the enactment of ICRA, numerous individuals brought civil rights claims to federal courts that attempted to enforce the rights protected in the ICRA. In *Santa Clara Pueblo v. Martinez*, Julia Martinez brought a claim under the ICRA against her tribe seeking membership for her children. The Pueblo had enacted an enrollment ordinance that discriminated on the basis of sex against her and her children. The Supreme Court held that Congress, in enacting the ICRA, did not confer upon federal courts jurisdiction to resolve civil rights complaints against tribal governments and, in any event, tribal sovereign immunity barred her claim. The Court, per Justice Marshall, stated that complainants against tribal government actions must pursue a tribal forum.

Following *Martinez*, many Indian tribes began to more intensely develop their tribal courts. Tribes began to incorporate their own version of the Bill of Rights into new or amended tribal constitutions. As a result, tribal courts apply their own tribal customs and traditions to civil rights cases. Moreover, many Indian tribes have adopted constitutional protections to individual rights in either legislative or constitutional formats. While many of these statutes are based on ICRA, many are either more or less extensive than ICRA.

This chapter surveys the cases that modern tribal courts decide based on ICRA, but also civil rights cases arising out of tribal constitutional provisions that may or may not incorporate the Indian Bill of Rights.

A. DUE PROCESS

Civil rights cases against Indian tribes arise out of the American legal notion that individuals should have certain rights and privileges against the actions of government. These cases are brought under the Indian Civil Rights Act, or tribal statutory or common law recognizing individual rights. The Anglo-American conception of due process is at the heart of these claims. The government structures and relationships to individuals at issue—often administrative and business entities making decisions about employment and other economic interests of individuals—derive from American models. The entire background of these cases derives from Anglo-American law and relationships. Often tribes did not choose these models; tribes exist in a world where these models constitute the entire range of choice, forcing tribes to enter these arenas. And many tribes have done so in a manner consistent with their own traditions and culture. However, tribal courts' interpretation is well within the parameters of due process that state and federal courts apply. Due process is one of the most subjective legal doctrines in constitutional law. State and federal courts tend to apply a balancing test, reaching results that differ from those of other courts in often dramatic ways. While the Oglala Sioux tribal court might not apply due process the same way as the Little Traverse Bay Bands of Odawa Indians tribal court, they might apply the doctrine the same manner as the Idaho, South Dakota, or Michigan courts.

HIGH ELK v. VEIT

Cheyenne River Sioux Tribal Court of Appeals,
No. 05-008-A, 6 Am. Tribal Law 73, 2006 WL 5940784 (February 10, 2006)

Before Chief Justice FRANK POMMERSHEIM and Associate Justices, JAMES CHASING HAWK and ROBERT N. CLINTON

This matter involves litigation occasioned by frustration of the expectations of Plaintiffs, Jim Veit and Fred Kost, that their grazing authorization for Tribal Range Unit Number 162, which is assigned to Appellants Paul and Clara High Elk and Codi American Horse (the High Elk Defendants), would be renewed for the 2005 grazing year. Expecting such renewal, the Plaintiffs allegedly prepaid the initial payments for the anticipated rental for the 2005 grazing year so that proper payments could be made to the Bureau of Indian Affairs in a timely fashion. They did so without any written sublease or other pasturing agreement for the range unit in question for the 2005 grazing year based on their personal anticipation of renewal for the 2005 grazing year due to the alleged long standing relationship between the parties. Unfortunately for the Plaintiffs, the High Elk Defendants did not renew their previous authorization with the Plaintiffs for the 2005 grazing year. Instead, they entered into a pasturing authorization agreement with Duane and Sharon Keller (the Kellers), which was approved by the Bureau of Indian Affairs, and which resulted in the Kellers placing cattle on Range Unit Number 162 commencing some time in May, 2005.

. . . The present appeal purports to be an interlocutory appeal, although for reasons stated below [it] actually involves an appeal of a final collateral order entered at a time when the original Defendants, Paul and Clara High Elk and Codi American Horse, were no longer parties to any proceeding, that purported to attach or garnish rent payments due to the High Elk Defendants from the Kellers and directed such payments to be held in escrow, pending the outcome of the litigation. . . .

Appellants raise a series of objections to the attachment/garnishment order including lack of effective notice, lack of any bond or other security, lack of hearing as to hardship, and deprivation of due process of law in violation of the federal Indian Civil Rights Act of 1968, 25 U.S.C §1302(8). While some are phrased as procedural irregularities, most of these claims (other than the lack of property bond or other security) implicate the due process requirements of notice and hearing. In *Cheyenne River Sioux Tribe Housing Authority v. Howard*, No. 04-008A (Ch. Riv. Sioux Ct. App., Sept. 23, 2005) this Court recently reaffirmed the traditional Lakota values embodied in the term due process of law. Just as Lakota tradition requires the respectful listening to the position of all interested persons on any important issue, the legal requirement of due process of law requires that all persons interested in a matter receive adequate written notice of any proceeding that would implicate their personal interests, including their property or, as here, rent payments contractually owed to them, that they be made parties to any case or judgment that would affect those interests, and that they have a full and fair opportunity to participate as a party in any hearing on such issues. These requirements are further supplemented by the indispensable party provisions of Rule 19 of the Cheyenne River Sioux Tribal Rules of Civil Procedure. In the *Howard* case, this Court recently summarized the requirements of due process in a civil context as follows:

> This Court has long recognized that basic Lakota concepts of fairness and respect as well as the federal Indian Civil Rights Act, 25 U.S.C §1302(8), clearly guarantee all parties who appear before the courts of the Cheyenne River Sioux Tribe due process of law. *E.g. Dupree v. Cheyenne River Housing Authority*, 16 Indian L. Rep. 6106 (Chy. R. Sx. Ct. App. 1988). Basic to any concept of due process of law in a civil proceeding, such as this eviction case, is receipt of timely notice and the opportunity to be heard and present evidence at a hearing in support of one's case. *Mullane v. Central Hanover Bank*, 339 U.S. 306 (1950). The basic requirements of notice and hearing, which lie at the core of civil due process of law, do not constitute mere formal requirements or hoops that must be surmounted before judgment. Rather, due process involves functional procedural prerequisites designed to assure that every party has a

realistic opportunity to be heard in any case affecting their legal rights. Here, Mr. Howard was fighting to remain in the only home he lawfully occupied, a precious and important right, indeed, particularly for a person in Mr. Howard's fragile medical condition, even if he did own the home in question.

Every court of the Cheyenne River Sioux Tribe is bound both by customary Lakota concepts of respect and by the requirements of due process of law protected by the federal Indian Civil Rights Act, 25 U.S.C. §1302(8), to assure that the parties before them are all afforded due process of law. . . . Where the trial court finds any of these elements lacking or, as here, fails by its own omission to establish their presence, it proceeds at its peril since the judgment it enters may turn out to be defective, as here, for want of basic procedural fairness that denies due process of law. Furthermore, where an appeal is brought to this Court demonstrates the denial of the fundamental procedural elements of fairness, it is the duty of this Court to reverse the judgment or order before for want of due process of law, irrespective of whether that argument was directly raised by the party. Such serious procedural errors constitute plain error that must be noted by and acted upon by the Court.

Unfortunately, precisely the same language could be applied to the procedure in this case that led to the garnishment/attachment order at issue here. First, until receipt of the Complaint in the new action, first served on counsel at the September 15, 2005 hearing, Paul and Clara High Elk and Codi American Horse had never received any written notice of any demand for attachment or garnishment of rent payments unquestionably due to them from the Kellers pursuant to their pasturing agreement. Clearly, receipt of such written notice after the August 23, 2005 hearing had already ordered garnishment and on the same day and at the start of the September 15, 2005 hearing where the attachment/garnishment order was reiterated does not constitute adequate or effective notice permitting a party to appear and defend. Indeed, when counsel appeared at the September 15, 2005 hearing Paul and Clara High Elk and Codi American Horse were not parties to any pending action and were not thereafter served with summons and complaint in any effective manner that would provide adequate notice for attachment of their property on the same day. Second, counsel for the High Elks appeared at the September 15, 2005 [hearing] as an interested observer, not representing any remaining party to the proceeding. No reasonable attorney would think counsel in such a situation would be adequately prepared for and might reasonably expect to defend his clients' interests in an action to attach rent payments due his clients. Third, the hearing took place the same day counsel for the High Elk Defendants first received notice of the demand. Clearly, in the absence of some life or death emergency, not obvious on the face of this record, such short notice does not constitute adequate notice to comply with due process of law under the principles set forth above. Fourth, at the time the second garnishment/attachment order was issued the High Elk Defendants had not even been served with a summons and Complaint in this new action and it is, at best dubious, that the action was effectively pending on September 15, 2005 both for lack of effective service of process and for lack of filing of the Complaint with the trial court, which under the applicable rules commences the action. Thus, precisely why the trial court thought it had before it any pending action involving the High Elk Defendants remains a mystery to this Court based on the record before it.

The only major response to these problems offered by Appellees, James Veit and Fred Kost, is that the High Elks through their attorney, Curtis L. Carroll, waived all due process and other objections since he allegedly agreed to the attachment/garnishment order at the September 15, 2005 hearing. Curtis L. Carroll, attorney for the High Elk Defendant, flatly denies making any such agreement. . . . This Court can find on it no such agreement to the garnishment/attachment order by the attorney for the High Elk Defendants Curtis L. Carroll. . . .

For the reasons stated in this Opinion entry of the attachment/garnishment order at issue here constituted a departure from Lakota traditions of respect and honor, was contrary to law, and violated the guarantees of due process of law found in the federal Indian Civil Rights Act of 1968. 25 U.S.C. §1302(8). For these reasons the order must be and has already been vacated by this Court's Order of January 5, 2006.

Ho hecetu yelo.

It is so ordered.

NOTES

1. The *High Elk* court applies tribal customary law to reach a working definition of due process that is not dissimilar from how state and federal courts might define due process. But in Indian country, due process has more import to the courts than it might in federal or state courts. Consider the classic federal case *Mathews v. Eldridge*, 424 U.S. 319 (1976), from which the United States Supreme Court defined procedural due process for federal courts. That case involved a challenge to the statute enacted by Congress to determine whether and how Social Security benefits might be cut off in certain circumstances. A similar kind of government action by an Indian tribe would be subject to far more scrutiny on a political level than in the *Mathews* context, if for no other reason than the fact that tribal elected officials are far more likely to be answerable to adverse governmental decisions to individual citizens than is Congress or federal agencies.

   How does that factor impact due process? What about in the context of an adverse governmental decision by a tribal government against a non-tribal citizen?

2. In *In re D.H.*, 2009 WL 1619635 (Grand Traverse Band of Ottawa and Chippewa Indians Tribal Court 2009), the court concluded that the due process protections of the tribal constitution do not require that a parent be entitled to a jury trial in an Indian child welfare proceeding, even though state law required a jury trial:

   > Respondent further argues that fundamental due process rights guaranteed by the Constitution of the Grand Traverse Band of Ottawa and Chippewa Indians, and the United States Constitution dictate that Respondent should be entitled to a jury trial in this matter. While the Court agrees that Respondent is entitled to fundamental due process in this proceeding, the

Court is not persuaded that a jury trial is a component of that due process requirement in this type of proceeding. Nor is the Court persuaded that a judge cannot adequately protect Respondent's due process rights or reach a determination while also recognizing and acknowledging tribal customs and traditions of the Grand Traverse Band regarding child rearing as required under the Children's Code.

The Court agrees with Respondent that Tribal Council could adopt a provision in the Children's Code providing for a right to a jury trial, and that the Tribal Court could adopt a court rule providing for the right to a jury trial in this type of proceeding. However, neither has done so to date. . . . Again, the Court is not persuaded that a jury trial was intended by the Tribal Council in adopting the Children's Code, nor that the Tribal Judiciary has intended to provide for a jury trial in Children's Code proceedings.

2009 WL 1619635 at *2.

3. In the context of a tribal election dispute, in *Jacobs v. Zimmer*, 9 Okla. Trib. 410 (Cheyenne-Arapaho Tribal Court 2006), the court read the tribal constitution to protect the individual right to challenge an election:

What process must the election take? Plaintiff says that Article IX, §15(c) is confusing. It states that the election article of the new Constitution does not apply to this special election. Plaintiff says that in effect that could also be read to say that even Section 15(c) does not apply.

In constitutional construction a constitution is to be read where it has meaning and is not absurd. Therefore, to read it that way would make no sense. Thus, that section sets up the rules for the election. This was done to ensure that the election could occur within 30 days. However, you cannot just throw due process out the window. A key component of the elections that deals with due process are the challenges to candidates and to the election results. At the primary election there was no opportunity to challenge either. This is a due process violation.

Id. at 410.

B. EQUAL PROTECTION

While the interpretation by tribal courts of what constitutes due process may be equivalent to or even exceed the protections offered by state and federal courts, the same is not necessarily true in the equal protection context. In fact, the most famous case in this area is *Santa Clara Pueblo v. Martinez*, 436 U.S. 49 (1978), in which the United States Supreme Court upheld a tribal membership ordinance that discriminated against a woman and her family on the basis of gender. That case is not an aberration, as many tribal laws involve perfectly valid racial, gender, and religious classifications that might otherwise be found to violate the United States Constitution. *See generally Morton v. Mancari*, 417 U.S. 535 (1974).

Federal Indian law creates a great deal of room for Indian tribes to adopt blood quantum—and ancestry-based membership criteria, employment preferences, and voting requirements. Tribes that continue to respect traditional and customary law may apply hereditary and gender based rules in multiple contexts, from domestic relations to electoral candidates. However, outside of the context of tribal membership criteria, tribal employment preferences, and other legal classifications that go to the heart of who is an Indian and what is a tribe, tribal courts generally do conform to state and federal constitutional norms in relation to equal protection of the laws.

1. DISCRIMINATION ON THE BASIS OF IMMUTABLE CHARACTERISTICS

MOHEGAN TRIBAL GAMING AUTHORITY v. MOHEGAN TRIBAL EMPLOYMENT RIGHTS COMMISSION

Mohegan Gaming Disputes Court of Appeals, No. GDCA-AD-03-501, 4 Am. Tribal Law 482, 2003.NAMG.0000007 (November 20, 2003)

The opinion of the court was delivered by: GUERNSEY, C.J.

This case presents an issue central to the implementation of the Mohegan Tribal Employment Rights Ordinance, MTO 99-2 ("TERO"); namely, whether there exists a disproportionate impact threshold that must be met before the provisions of the Ordinance barring job qualifications that serve as a barrier to the employment of Native Americans are invoked. [W]e hold that a finding of disproportionate impact on Native Americans as a group is not required before the Mohegan Tribal Employment Rights Commission (hereafter the "Commission") may examine whether job qualification criteria serve as a barrier to the employment of any Native American.

Procedural Background

In January 2002, the Mohegan Tribal Gaming Authority (MTGA) posted a job opening for the position of "Sports and Entertainment Support Services Manager." The "Minimum Qualifications" for this position were described as follows:

> Three years of progressive experience in the area of sports, entertainment and facility management. Have a working knowledge of Word, Excel and database spreadsheets for the preparation, formatting and editing of routine to complex documents. Must have an understanding of budgets and be able to track expenditures; including internal and client-related expenditures. Must be proficient in Stratton Warren and Infinium software. Must be able to perform multi-task projects in a diverse and busy environment. Excellent communication and organization skills required.

Record on Appeal at 21. A Mohegan Tribal member, Ms. Kim Baker, along with a number of non-Native Americans, applied for this position. Ms. Baker met all qualifications except for "three years progressive experience in the area of sports, entertainment and facility management." The position was offered to a non–Native American, Robin Pelletier, already employed as an Administrator in the Sports and Entertainment Department at Mohegan Sun, who apparently met this qualification.

... Ms. Baker filed a complaint with the Department of Tribal Employment Rights, which resulted in an investigation by Ken Janus, the TERO Director. . . . Director Janus found that the failure to hire Ms. Baker constituted a violation of §VI(A) of MTO 99-2 and Mohegan Sun Hiring Policy #3 for "failure to hire tribal/native for position".

A Mohegan Tribal Employment Rights Commission hearing in this matter (Kim Baker v. Mohegan Sun) was conducted on March 20, 2002, focusing on the position requirement of "three years of progressive experience in the area of sports, entertainment and facility management." . . .

. . . After reviewing the particular job duties as listed for a successful applicant for the position, the Commission found them to be of a "clerical, administrative or customer service nature," and held that the Mohegan Sun had failed to demonstrate that the disputed job qualification was required by a business necessity. As such, the criteria were found to serve as a barrier to the employment of a Native American. . . .

The trial court [Manfredi, J.] held that a finding by the Commission that the job qualification at issue "serve[s] as a barrier to the employment of Native Americans" was a condition precedent to Commission action under Section VII(E). Absent such a finding, which was not made by the Commission in this case, the trial court held that Section VII(E) had no application, and the Commission was not empowered to look to whether or not a particular qualification was required by business necessity. Nevertheless the trial court examined United States Supreme Court precedent under Title VII of the Civil Rights Act of 1964 in seeking to define "business necessity," and utilizing the rationale of *Griggs v. Duke Power Company*, 401 U.S. 424 (1971), held that a job qualification was a business necessity if it was "reasonably related to job performance." The trial court further held that, on the record, the challenged job qualification was required by business necessity. . . .

Although the trial court's analysis of Section VII(E) is supported by the reference therein to "barriers to employment of Native Americans," suggestive of a *Griggs* analysis of disproportionate group impact, we hold that the fundamentally different (in fact, almost diametrically opposed) purposes of the Civil Rights Act of 1964 and TERO (MTO 99-2), coupled with the carefully designed procedures in TERO to protect the individual preference rights of Native Americans, requires the rejection of such an analysis.

Discussion

A. Disparate Impact and TERO

"The federal policy of according some hiring preference to Indians in the Indian service dates at least as far back as 1834." *Morton v. Mancari*, 417 U.S. 535, 541 . . . (1974). The "first major piece of federal legislation prohibiting discrimination in private employment," Title VII of the Civil Rights Act of 1964, "explicitly exempted from its coverage the preferential employment of Indians by Indian tribes or by industries located on or near Indian reservations." *Morton v. Mancari, supra*, 417 U.S. at 544. "This exemption is consistent with the Federal Government's policy of encouraging Indian employment and with the special legal position of Indians." *Morton v. Mancari, supra*, 417 U.S. at 544, quoting 110 Cong. Rec. 12723 (1964).

Against this background the Mohegan Tribe, like many other Indian tribes, adopted an ordinance declaring Native American preference as its public policy for employers and contractors operating on Mohegan land:

The public policy of the Mohegan Tribe of Indians of Connecticut (Mohegan Tribe) is to create employment and training opportunities for its Members and for other Native Americans. The purpose of this ordinance is to assist and require fair employment of Native Americans, prevent discrimination, and set forth the Native American preference requirements for employers and contractors operating on Mohegan land.

MTO 99-2, Section II. The basic policy of Native American Preference is set forth in Section VII(A):

Irrespective of the qualification of any non-Native American applicant or employee, any Native American applicant or Native American employee who meets the minimum qualifications required by the employment position at issue whether it concerns the hiring, promotion, training, retention, recall or any other element of said employment position, shall be selected by all covered employers before any non–Native American applicant or non–Native American employee. All covered employers shall be required to comply with all job posting requirements promulgated and issued by the Human Resources Department.

MTO 99-2 Section VII(A)(1). . . .

The term "minimum qualifications" is given a highly restrictive definition:

Minimum Qualifications means those job-related qualifications which are essential to the performance of the basic responsibilities for each employment position or contract, including any essential qualifications concerning education, training, and job-related experience but excluding any qualifications relating to ability or aptitude to perform responsibilities in other employment positions or other contracts. Demonstrated ability to perform essential and basic responsibilities shall be deemed satisfaction of necessary qualifications.

MTO 99-2 Section III. This is illustrative of a fundamental difference between Native American preference under TERO and the purpose of the disparate impact analysis of *Griggs v. Duke Power Company*. Under TERO, the preference exists irrespective of whether or not Native Americans as a group are at a disadvantage, whereas the *Griggs* analysis of disparate or disproportionate impact is used to determine whether or not to allow what might reasonably be termed a form of preference based on a prohibited basis. As such, the invocation of Native American preference as set forth in MTO 99-2 is in no way dependent on the factors enumerated in *Griggs*.

. . . Section VII(E) deals with job qualifications criteria and/or personnel requirements, and Appellee asserts that the trial court was correct in holding that a finding of disproportionate impact on Native Americans as a group was a condition precedent to a TERO challenge to any job qualifications or criteria. We do not agree, and hold that MTO 99-2 Section VII(E) was intended to reinforce, rather than dilute, the Native American preference policy of Section VII(A).

In construing a statute, a court is "called upon to look beyond the literal meaning of the words to the history of the law, its language, considered in all its parts, the mischief the law was designed to remedy, and the policy underlying it." . . . As we have discussed, the policy behind TERO is the enforcement of Native American preference, not the prevention of discrimination as set forth in Title VII of the Civil Rights Act of 1964. To impose on Native American preference a barrier to discriminatory practices, created in the context of Title VII of the Civil Rights Act of 1964, is illogical in that this preference was designed, for reasons of well-established and historically justified public policy, to promote a narrowly tailored policy of discrimination. . . .

We therefore hold that the trial court erred in requiring a finding by the Commission of disproportionate or disparate impact on Native Americans as a group as a condition precedent to Commission review of an alleged failure to comply with MTO 99-2. . . .

Standard of "Business Necessity"

The trial court [also] held that in proceedings before the Commission the challenged requirement of "three years progressive experience in the area of sports, entertainment, and facility management" had been shown to be a "business necessity." [T]he trial court held that a job qualification is a business necessity "if it is reasonably related to job performance and measures 'the person for the job and not the person in the abstract.'" . . .

The term "business necessity" is not defined in the Ordinance. Its interpretation, as the term is employed by the United States Supreme Court in *Griggs, supra,* ranges from "a manifest relationship to the employment in question," 401 U.S. at 432, to "a reasonable measure of job performance," 401 U.S. at 436, to "related to job performance," 401 U.S. at 432. The Supreme Court's conclusion as to the intent of Congress, however, provides further evidence of the opposing purposes of Title VII and TERO:

> Far from disparaging job qualifications as such, Congress has made such qualifications the controlling factor, so that race, religion, nationality, and sex become irrelevant.

Griggs v. Duke Power Co., supra, 401 U.S. at 436. As has already been shown, the purpose of MTO 99-2 is to provide for Native American preference and to curtail job qualifications that impede such preference. . . .

In the case of MTO 99-2, however, the policy of Native American preference is to be applied to any Native American job applicant who meets the "minimum qualifications" for the position. MTO 99-2, Section VII(A)(1). Inasmuch as we hold that the policies behind MTO 99-2 Section VII(A) and (E) are consistent, and that the standard of "required by business necessity" to be applied under Section VII(E) is intended to promote, not dilute, the policy Native American preference under Section VII(A), it necessarily follows that for a covered employer to establish that a job qualification is "required by business necessity" it must establish that the qualification is not a subterfuge for exceeding the "minimum qualifications" for that position. Given that the "minimum qualifications" for a position are those "essential to the performance of the basic responsibilities for each employment position or contract, including any essential qualifications concerning education, training, and job-related experience . . . ," a standard of "reasonably related to job performance" is insufficient to protect the policy behind MTO 99-2.

In view of our holding that the Mohegan Tribal Council has enacted a comprehensive, consistent procedure for the implementation and protection of the policy of Native American preference, to require a covered employer under Section VII(E) to show anything less than a compelling business necessity for job qualification criteria that serve as a barrier to the employment of a Native American applicant would be to undermine the purpose and functioning of the entire Ordinance. . . .

Accordingly, the judgment of the trial court is reversed and the case remanded to the Mohegan Tribal Employment Rights Commission for further proceedings consistent with this opinion. In this opinion the other judges concurred.

GUERNSEY, C.J.
EAGAN, J.
WILSON, J.

NOTES

1. Congress has created multiple Indian-preference-in-employment provisions. *E.g.*, 25 U.S.C. §450e(b)(1) (authorizing American Indian preference in employment for recipients of federal funds under the Indian Self-Determination and Education Assistance Act); 25 U.S.C. §§472, 472a (authorizing American Indian preference in employment in the Bureau of Indian Affairs and Indian Health Service). *See* Kaighn Smith, Jr., *Civil Rights and Tribal Employment*, 47 FED. LAW., March/April 2000, at 34, 39.

   Where Indian tribes might have a problem in equal protection terms is in the granting of a tribal preference — for example, in the Navajo Nation's rule ordering all employers on the Navajo Reservation to give preference in employment to all Navajos over members of other tribes. *E.g.*, *Cedar Unified School Dist. v. Navajo Nation Labor Commission*, 2007.NANN.0000018, at ¶31 n. 12 (Navajo Nation Supreme Court 2007) (leaving open the question whether tribal preference violates a bar on national origin discrimination); *Dawavendewa v. Salt River Project Agr. Improvement and Power Dist.*, 154 F.3d 1117 (9th Cir. 1998) (holding that the Navajo tribal preference provision violated federal law), *cert. denied*, 528 U.S. 1098 (2000).

2. Suits against tribal businesses that allege race discrimination in employment decisions must navigate the fields of sovereign immunity and employment discrimination doctrine. In *Bethel v. Mohegan Tribal Gaming Authority*, 2 Am. Tribal Law 273 (Mohegan Gaming Disputes Court of Appeals 2000), the court dismissed all but one count against the tribe, but remanded on the claim of race discrimination due to the employer's failure to provide a hearing in accordance with its own procedures:

   > Reading Count 8 most favorably to the plaintiff, the court holds that the allegations suffice to state a cause of action under the Discriminatory Employment Practices Ordinance. The date of the termination/transfer triggers time for hearings under the employee grievance policy. The employee incident report filed by plaintiff on June 11, 1999 describes a number of situations that occurred during the term of employment that he was unhappy with. . . . The court deems this a request for a hearing under step four of the grievance process. . . .

Because there was no "final written notice" or "final written warning," the time period for requesting consideration by a board of review panel has not begun to run. The plaintiff is entitled under the due process clause of the ICRA, and the Employee Handbook, to a hearing by a board of review panel. Therefore, the court concludes that this matter must be reversed as to Count 8 only and remanded to the trial court with directions that the plaintiff's request to be reinstated to the slot technician position be considered by the board of review panel. . . .

Bethel, 2 Am. Tribal Law at 381-82. The court did dismiss a claim under 42 U.S.C. §§1981 and 1983, noting:

In Count 9 plaintiff claims that the defendants violated his rights that are protected by 42 U.S.C. §1983. He alleges that the MTGA and the MTGE were acting "under color of law . . . as the employer, sovereign legislative body, and executive enforcement division for the Mohegan Tribal Nation." . . .

Generally, courts have held that an action by an Indian tribe is not the equivalent of the state action required to sustain an action under a 42 U.S.C. §1983 action. In *R.J. Williams Company v. Fort Belknap Housing Authority*, 719 F.2d 979 (9th Cir. 1983), . . . [t]he court held [that]

no action under 42 U.S.C. 1983 can be maintained in federal court for persons alleging deprivation of constitutional rights under color of tribal law. Indian tribes are separate and distinct sovereignties (citations omitted), and are not constrained by the fourteenth amendment." *R.J. Williams Company, supra* at 982. . . .

In the present appeal the complaint is devoid of any allegations that the MTGE, the MTGA, or the individual defendant Keane were acting under any authority other than that of the Mohegan tribe. The trial court properly dismissed Count 9 of plaintiff's complaint for failure to allege an essential element of a claim under 42 U.S.C. §1983.

In Count 11 plaintiff claims that the defendants discriminated against him based upon his race, in violation of 42 U.S.C. §1981. . . .

. . . Title VII of the Civil Rights Act of 1964, as amended, specifically excluded Indian tribes, such as the Mohegan tribe and the MTGE, MTGA, from the definition of an "employer" for the purpose of that Act. *See* 42 U.S.C. §2000e(b)(1). Further, 42 U.S.C. §2000e-2(i) specifically exempts from the protections of Title VII businesses on or near an Indian reservation and allows those employers to have employment preferences for Indians living on or near a reservation.

Bethel, at 382-83.

3. In *Riggs v. Estate of Attakai*, 7 Am. Tribal Law 534 (Navajo Nation Supreme Court 2007), the court applied principles of the Navajo Nation's Fundamental Law to hold that a grazing permit should be devised to a female member of the family, rather than the male. One Justice objected to the majority's reasoning, and wrote:

While I concur in the result reached in the majority opinion, I object to the majority's use of Navajo Fundamental Law to create a preference based on gender in grazing cases. The majority has used language within its opinion that has elevated consideration of a person's gender to a degree to make the factors used in *Begay v. Keedah* [to decide the award of a grazing permit] to be irrelevant. 6 Nav. R. 416, 421 (Nav. Sup. Ct. 1991). . . . However, the majority's focus on gender conflicts with the Navajo Bill of Rights prohibition against denying rights based on the account of sex. 1 N.N.C. §3 (2005). Under 7 N.N.C. §204 (2005), Navajo Fundamental Law is to be is used to interpret statutory law not to evade the operation of the law. Certainly, the Navajo Nation Bill of Rights must be considered prior to elevating gender to be the dispositive factor in awarding a grazing permit. Moreover, I find that nothing in the record supports the decision that experts in Navajo Fundamental Law would require the decision by the majority to use gender as the dispositive factor. . . .

For the majority's opinion to be consistent with *Begay v. Keedah*, one has to assume that a woman is automatically going to use the grazing permit "wisely and well." *See id.* at 421. Under the gender preference of the majority's opinion a male that had extensive grazing experience would lose to a female that may not have any experience with managing grazing. Neither a female nor male gender assures the beneficial use of land. Thus, I cannot support the majority's altering of the delicate balance of factors so wisely developed in *Begay v. Keedah*.

Riggs, 7 Am. Tribal Law at 538-39 (Benally, J., concurring in the judgment). The majority responded:

Contrary to the characterization in the dissenting opinion, this opinion does not mean that the gender of the claimant is dispositive. The dissent states that this opinion makes the *Keedah* factors "irrelevant." . . . In fact, the rule set out in this opinion is that the Keedah factors and traditional law on women's role in Navajo society should be considered together to decide the most logical trustee, not that if a female and a male both claim the permit, regardless of their connections to the land, the permit automatically must go to the female. Indeed, this opinion concludes that the Family Court erred in not applying the Keedah facts, and applies them directly to the facts, along with traditional law principles, to decide the case. . . . Further, the dissent's primary concern appears to be that the Court allegedly applies Fundamental Law where there are statutes covering a situation to improperly "evade" existing law. . . . However, this Court applies *Diné bi beenahaz'áanii* alongside statutory law as the law of the Navajo Nation, as mandated by the Navajo Nation Council. See 1 N.N.C. §203(E) ("The leader(s) of the Judicial Branch (*Alaaji' Hashkééjí Naat'ááh*) shall uphold the values and principles of *Diné bi beenahaz'áanii* in the practice of peace making, obedience, discipline, punishment, interpreting laws and rendering decisions and judgments.").

Riggs, 7 Am. Tribal Law at 537 n. 5.

4. Tribal employers may offer specific causes of action for employees who allege discrimination in employment decisions. In *Hoopa Valley Tribal Plant Management Dept. v. Smith*, 5 NICS App. 132 (Hoopa Valley Tribal Court of Appeals, Oct. 8, 1999), the court interpreted such a provision to grant broad deference to a terminated employee alleging discrimination, even though she was an introductory or probationary employee employed at will. The relevant procedure read:

If at any time during the introductory period it is determined that an employee's performance is unsatisfactory, the employee may be terminated without the right of appeal or hearing, *except in cases of alleged discrimination.*

Smith, at 5 NICS App. at 134 (quoting Personnel Policies and Procedures of the Hoopa Valley Tribal Council §6.1.3) (emphasis in original). The court concluded:

> The Personnel Policies do not address the effect of the tribe's failure to conduct the written evaluation thirty days prior to the conclusion of the introductory period. . . . [I]n the light most favorable to the non-moving party, Ms. Smith's written complaint can be construed as claiming that she was fired for reasons other than her job performance.
>
> It is possible that some form of discrimination occurred, based on the allegations of the employee's complaint. We therefore cannot say that it is ". . . beyond doubt that the Plaintiff can prove no set of facts in support of [her] claim which would entitle [her] to relief." . . . If it is possible that some form of prohibited discrimination occurred, we have no choice but to allow the employee to present her evidence. Any ambiguities are to be resolved in favor of a right of an employee to file a grievance and obtain judicial review. Hoopa Valley Tribal Code, §13.12.1; *Hoopa Valley Indian Housing Authority v. Gerstner*, 3 NICS App. 250, 256; 22 Ind. L. Rptr. 6002 (Hoopa 1993).

Smith, at 5 NICS App. at 136.

2. DISCRIMINATION ON THE BASIS OF MARITAL STATUS

Arizona Public Service Co. v. Office of Navajo Labor Relations

Navajo Nation Supreme Court, No. A-CV-08-87, 6 Nav. Rep. 246, 17 Indian L. Rep. 6105, 1990.NANN.0000003 (October 8, 1990)

Before Tso, Chief Justice, Bluehouse and Austin, Associate Justices.
The opinion of the court was delivered by: Tso, Chief Justice. . . .

Case Before the Court

The Arizona Public Service Company (APS) is an Arizona corporation engaged in the business of electric power generation. . . .

On December 1, 1960, APS obtained a lease from the Navajo Nation to "construct and operate . . . a large thermal electric power plant," [the so-called Four Corners Plant]. . . .

This dispute arises from a hiring policy adopted by APS on July 15, 1983. It was a company-wide policy which sought to deal with problems of nepotism, and it addressed two categories of employees. It dealt with blood relations of current employees by providing that such relatives could be only hired for positions which were two or more supervisory levels removed from relative employees. It prohibited the hiring of applicants related by marriage to current employees, namely spouses, fathers-in-law, mothers-in-law, daughters-in-law, sons-in-law, brothers-in-law, and sisters-in-law. APS also developed an employment application form to apply the policy. It contained the question, "Do you have any relatives working for APS? Name (if yes)." If the applicant named a relative by marriage in one of the prohibited degrees, the application was rejected. . . .

The policy had a significant impact on employees and job applicants at the Four Corners Plant. For the period between November, 1983 and September,

1986, a total of 18 employees lost their jobs or were denied employment because of the policy. One employee's application was rejected because he was determined to be an in-law to an employee when the relation was in fact that of two men married to sisters, so the applicant was in fact the brother-in-law of the employee's wife and not the employee. While the mistake was corrected within ten days, the applicant had to wait two and one-half months for another opening. One employee, who was told he was ineligible for rehire because his wife was employed, obtained a divorce in order to qualify for employment. Fourteen lost their jobs or were denied employment because of a brother-in-law employee, two because of a husband, one because of a wife, and one because of a sister-in-law. One employee resigned rather than accept a reprimand for failing to disclose a relationship, her brother-in-law was fired for nondisclosure, and another was refused rehire. Fifteen of the affected positions were those of laborers, and the remaining three positions were clerical, mechanic, and management jobs. In all, thirteen men and five women were affected.

The enforcement agency which addressed this problem was the Office of Navajo Labor Relations (ONLR). . . . It has broad powers to regulate, enforce, and determine violations of Navajo Nation labor law, and it has the authority to file complaints of violations of the Navajo Preference in Employment Act with the Navajo Labor Relations Board. . . .

The Navajo Labor Relations Board is the board of directors of ONLR. . . . It has broad enumerated powers and duties to enforce Navajo Nation labor and employment law, and it has the specific power to hear complaints brought by ONLR and issue determinations and enforcement orders for violations of Navajo Nation labor laws. . . .

The law at issue here is the Navajo Preference in Employment Act (NPEA). . . . The NPEA contains requirements that employers exercise preferential hiring practices in favor of Navajos, employment procedures, just cause employment tenure, health and safety guarantees, and training requirements. 15 N.T.C. §604(b).

The two employer obligations of that section which are most applicable to this case are: "All employers shall use nondiscriminatory job qualifications and selection criteria in employment"; and "[a]ll employers shall maintain a safe and clean working environment and provide employment conditions which are free of prejudice, intimidation and harassment." 15 N.T.C. §604(b)(7), (9). . . .

The actual case or controversy before the Court is whether the Board correctly found that APS' nepotism policy violated 15 N.T.C. §604(b). . . .

II. Application of the Act

The inquiry here is whether the Board correctly applied 15 N.T.C. §204(b)(7) and (9) to APS' nepotism policy, and whether Navajo statutory law prohibits such a policy. Section 204(b)(7) provides: "All employers shall use nondiscriminatory job qualifications and selection criteria in employment." Title 15, N.T.C. §605(b)(9) provides: "All employers shall maintain a safe and clean working environment and provide employment conditions which are free from prejudice, intimidation and harassment."

Stated negatively, section 204(b)(7) prohibits discrimination in adopting or applying job qualification standards and selection criteria. "Discrimination" is a word of art used in both labor and civil rights law. . . .

. . . The Board and the courts are instructed that "the provisions of this chapter [i.e. the Act] be construed and applied to accomplish the purposes set forth above." 15 N.T.C. §602(b). That is a command to apply the rule of liberal construction. . . .

Here, there are two things which are prohibited: Discrimination and prejudice. Prejudice, is "[a] forejudgment; bias; preconceived opinion." BLACK'S LAW DICTIONARY 1061 (5th ed. 1979).

There is both statutory discrimination and prejudice here. The Board correctly found that there was no demonstrated business justification for the nepotism policy, other than a general conclusion that the public "felt" APS favored relatives. APS did make a distinction, and actually made two. The policy established a general category of "nepotism," which is:

> Bestowal of patronage by public officers in appointing others to positions by reason of blood or marital relationship to appointing authority. BLACK'S LAW DICTIONARY 937 (5th ed. 1979).

The policy then went on to subdivide that classification into two separate ones, with different consequences for each. That is to say, those who belonged to the classification "blood relatives" could apply for and receive employment with APS so long as they were removed from the blood relation by two supervisory levels. Those who belonged to the classification "relatives by marriage" could not be employed, and where APS discovered two such relatives having a job, they were given the choice of who could quit or be fired. That was a severe Hobson's choice, given the strain between family loyalty and one's own job.

The "prejudice" of the situation arises out of a policy choice, the reasons for which are absent from the record, of why an employer would distinguish between the two groups. There was a preconceived opinion that somehow it is permissible to hire blood relatives, removing them from supervisory favors, yet not hire relatives by marriage. We hold that the prohibition on hiring and retaining relatives by marriage was a violation of the Act and that the Board correctly decided the application of the law. . . .

We are also dealing with civil rights statutes here. A civil rights statute need not spell out classifications, as we will demonstrate.

The term "civil rights" is elusive because it "implies a selective reference to interests which are deemed to be of superior quality in our scheme of legal values." 3 SUTHERLAND STAT. CONST. §74.01. The classes of rights which can fall under that category are open-ended in character, but they are most often concerned with personal liberty and, more recently, with the right to equal treatment. *Id.* We are dealing with equal treatment here.

State civil rights legislation is fairly recent, and prior to 1883, only three states had any. *Id.* §74.03. Following an 1883 Supreme Court decision that the Civil Rights Act of 1875 was unconstitutional, several states enacted statutes forbidding discrimination in public accommodations. *Id.* In modern times the states have enacted comprehensive legislation to regulate the denial of equal treatment in areas such as employment, and some deal with discrimination in utility services or public services. *Id*. The laws are wide and varied, but the important point is "states are allowed to extend civil rights protection beyond that provided by Congress." *Id*. Finally, one of the common prohibited classifications is the prohibition of discrimination on the basis of one's marital status. *Id*.

Civil rights laws are also given liberal construction, meaning that they are liberally construed, "in order that their beneficent objectives may be realized to the fullest extent possible. To this end, courts favor broad and inclusive application of statutory language by which the coverage of legislation to protect and implement civil rights is defined." *Id*. §74.05. "Correlatively, exceptions and limitations which restrict the operation of such laws are strictly construed." *Id*.

"Remedial policies expressed in civil rights laws may be judicially extended through the influence they have in the interpretation of legislation." *Id*.

Having reviewed the ground rules for the application of civil rights legislation, do we have a prohibition of marital status discrimination here? We begin with the rule that the right to marry is a fundamental right. It is an important and fundamental right as a matter of Navajo common law as well.

> Traditional Navajo society places great importance upon the institution of marriage. A traditional Navajo marriage, when consummated according to a prescribed elaborate ritual, is believed to be blessed by the "Holy People." This blessing ensures that the marriage will be stable, in harmony, and perpetual. Under traditional Navajo thought, unmarried couples who live together act immorally because they are said to steal each other. Thus, in traditional Navajo society the Navajo people did not approve of or recognize common-law marriages.

Validation of Marriage of Francisco, 6 Nav. R. 134, 135-136 (1989) (quoting *Navajo Nation v. Murphy*, 6 Nav. R. 10, 13 (1988)). Navajos scorn those who have relationships out of marriage, and the man in such a relationship is called a "stay-until-dawn man." The woman shares the scorn because the term implies her need to sneak the man out before neighbors arise and go out.

Not only is marriage important in Navajo common law, but relatives and relationships are as well. "Navajos think of such relationships [kinship] in a much broader and different sense than does the general American population." B. JOHNSON ED., NAVAJO STORIES OF THE LONG WALK PERIOD xix (1973) (Preface explaining relationships used in the stories). There is the biological family, with husband, wife and unmarried children; the extended family, which adds married daughters and their husbands as well as unmarried children; the outfit, with mixes of extended or biological families; the clan, with relationships which are not restricted to biological connections; and linked clans, with relationships among clans. *Id*. xix-xxi.

The APS nepotism policy as applied to married relations is ridiculous in the Navajo context because of the strong ties and obligations to relations outside the scope of the policy. The reciprocal obligation required of Navajos is summed up in the saying used to describe someone who has misbehaved: "He acts as if he had no relatives." . . .

The Board made a finding of fact which shows a proper application of the law and the serious violation of the public policy favoring the sanctity of marriage. The Board's finding shows that the Minnesota court was correct in its prediction of how a marital status employment policy can discourage marriage. One of APS' employees had been a power plant mechanic for about two months, and when he updated his employment application, APS agents informed him he was ineligible for rehire because his wife was a permanent employee. The couple obtained a divorce from the Shiprock District Court so he could qualify for rehire. He could not work for APS for three months because of his marriage, and when he requalified for employment by obtaining a divorce, it took him another year to get a job. APS forced this couple to divorce, given economic conditions.

In these decisions we have a governmental employer's marital status policy prohibited on the grounds of public policy, and a marital status discrimination statute applied in light of that policy. Are there any other policy factors which support the interpretation of our law in a similar fashion against this private employer?

In their work, Fairness and Justice (1986), Charles M. Haar and Daniel W. Fessler trace the history of the common law rule that those who provide a public service, including municipalities and corporations such as the one before the Court, must give equal treatment. They base their arguments upon the common law and show that equal access to basic services should be grounded in the common law and not constitutional law, which is defective in many respects. . . .

. . . Within the Navajo Nation all employers are in the nature of a public service enterprise, given high unemployment rates. We take judicial notice of the fact that when the Navajo Tribal Council enacted NPEA it did so to deal with unemployment rates much higher than the general population. There was sufficient governmental interest to enact statutes which prohibit discrimination, prejudice, intimidation, and harassment. . . .

. . . To recapitulate, one Navajo statutory provision requires that all employers use nondiscriminatory job qualifications and selection criteria, and another prohibits prejudice, intimidation and harassment in the workplace. The rights involved here are the fundamental ones of the right to marry (and have that relationship honored) and the right to a fair opportunity for employment. There are fundamental Navajo common law rights in the form of marriage, free association with relatives, and the preservation of traditions of working together. Public policy, including the ability of the state to place limitations upon arbitrary standards for employment, supports the ruling of the Board, and such underlies the Navajo Nation Preference Law.

At this point it is quite important that everyone understand what this opinion does not hold. We do not address the nepotism policy as far as it affects blood relations. We simply hold that the Board correctly interpreted and applied the law to prohibit marital status discrimination, and that our law is fully backed by principles of public policy and common law. We do not rule that APS must favor relatives in any manner, but only that employees should be chosen on the basis of their merit and qualifications and not some broadly preconceived notion of what may be proper employment limitations, when that notion has no demonstrated relation to work performance. There are other proper means of achieving the goal of eliminating favoritism, and we leave what they are to APS and the Board. . . .

V. Conclusion

. . . Ultimately what we have is a Navajo law which regulates employment. It prohibits arbitrary discrimination, and that is what the Board found in a well-stated and well-reasoned opinion. Upon a close examination of Navajo law we found that it reasonably addressed the employment policy in question—marital status discrimination—and prohibited it. The Board's reasoning was appropriate. While that reasoning may not be the same as that used by the Court, it is sufficient that it appropriately applied the law.

The February 9, 1987 administrative decision of the Navajo Labor Relations Board is affirmed.

NOTES

1. Does the borrowing of non-tribal statutory and common law by the *Arizona Public Service* Court render the decision more or less persuasive? Does it matter to whom—the Diné (Navajo) or outsiders—the Court may have been writing? Consider that the portion of the opinion not excerpted here involved the authority of the Navajo Nation to assert regulatory jurisdiction over the public utility, a question later resolved against the Nation by the Ninth Circuit. *See Arizona Public Service Co. v. Aspaas*, 77 F.3d 1128 (9th Cir. 1996).

2. A general ban on nepotism is almost impossible in most parts of Indian country, given the related facts that tribal membership is usually conditioned on family and ancestry and that there are relatively few tribal members to choose from in selecting employees. How does that fact play out in this decision?

3. Tribal courts and tribal legislatures have borrowed much equal protection doctrine from American courts, especially the levels of review of government action that implicated protected classes. For example, in *Delgado v. Wilson*, 2004.NAOW.0000019 (Oneida Appeals Commission Appellate Court 2004), the court reviewed the tribal legislature's decision to prohibit tribal employment if the employee holds a position with the Oneida Appeals Commission. The court wrote:

> Next, the statute must be analyzed under strict scrutiny, intermediate scrutiny or rational basis. The standard that applies to Mr. Delgado is rational basis. This standard applies to all classifications that are not based on a "suspect" or "semi-suspect" classification (i.e. that do not involve race, national origin, alienage, gender or legitimacy) and do not impair a fundamental right (i.e., do not impair the right to vote, access the courts or migrate interstate). Under this standard, the classification will be upheld so long as it is conceivable that the classification bears a rational relationship to a legitimate government objective.

According to Oneida Resolution #8-19-91-A, there is clearly a rational relationship to a legitimate government objective; that the Oneida Appeals Commission and the Oneida Tribal Administrative Procedures Act enhance a separation of powers between the legislative, executive and judicial responsibilities of the tribe. While the Legislative Analyst position was not stated in Oneida Resolution #3-20-92-A, it is clear that the intent is to enhance the separation of powers. To have a Legislative Analyst also be an Oneida Appeals Commissioner clearly violates the separation of powers.

Delgado, at ¶¶29-30.

3. RELIGIOUS FREEDOM

Considering Individual Religious Freedoms under Tribal Constitutional Law

Kristen A. Carpenter, 14 Kan. J.L. & Pub. Pol'y 561, 564-66, 569-75 (2005)

. . .

I. Some Hypothetical Religious Freedoms Cases

To suggest the type of cases where individual religious freedoms issues might manifest in tribal settings, this section presents a series of hypothetical stories having to do with a hypothetical tribe, the Winomee Indian Nation.

Hypothetical A

A ceremonial rattle is about to be repatriated to the Winomee Indian Nation from a federally funded museum. The tribal Cultural Resources Commission draws up a repatriation plan, intending to restore the rattle to the traditional medicine society that historically . . . cared for and used the rattle in ceremonies. But right before the rattle is to come home to the reservation, a leader in the local Native American Church ("NAC"), which has had a presence on the reservation for about fifty years now, petitions the Commission for shared custody of the rattle. The NAC leaders believe that the holy rattle has a place in their religion too. The Commission denies the request. Can the NAC leader sue the tribe for violating its religious freedom?

Hypothetical B

Amelia Sandstone is a member of the Winomee Indian Nation. In 2004, the Nation proposes to store nuclear waste on land within the reservation boundaries. The proposed storage location adjoins land on the reservation that was historically considered sacred and where a small number of tribal members still go for private retreat, prayer, and ceremony. Amelia has brought her concerns to the tribal council. The council members reject her concern, saying the land in question has not been an important ceremonial site in generations and, in any event, the tribe desperately needs the fees the federal government will pay for storage. Amelia believes that the waste will nevertheless contaminate and desecrate a sacred site. Can Amelia sue for violation of her religious freedoms?

Hypothetical C

Frankie Bear is a member of the Winomee Indian Nation. He grew up on the reservation, and then earned a B.A. and M.B.A. from top universities. He worked for a long time in corporate America, but moved back to the reservation several years ago and has enjoyed two successful terms on the tribal council. When the tribal chief decides not to seek re-election, Frankie wants to run for the position. But traditionally, only members of a certain Winomee religious society could serve as chief. Frankie's family is not in that particular religious society. Even though he has complied with all other requirements, the Tribal Registrar of Elections refuses to put Frankie on the ballot, because he is not a member of the society. Can Frankie sue the tribe for violating his individual religious freedom?

Hypothetical D

Anna Belmer is a member of the Winomee Indian nation. She is a devout Christian who believes very sincerely that traditional Winomee ceremonies are, at best, superstitious. Anna's daughter Sarah attends a tribally-run elementary school on the reservation. In the spirit of cultural self-determination, the school starts to offer a "tribal language and culture class." In it, the teacher shares information about traditional tribal ceremonies, stories, songs, and their meanings. Sarah comes home brimming with these lessons — to the secret delight of her grandmother. But Sarah's mother is furious and believes that the tribe, through the school, is forcing traditional Winomee religion on her daughter. Can Anna sue the tribal council for violating her individual religious freedom? . . .

III. The Law

The question is whether these individuals would have viable legal claims for violations of their religious freedoms. The minds of most Americans probably jump immediately to the deeply ingrained text and principles of the First Amendment of the United States Constitution: "Congress shall make no law respecting an establishment of religion, or prohibiting the free exercise thereof." Indeed, if the federal government or a state government committed the above-described acts, the individuals would probably have First Amendment claims.

In the first two hypotheticals, the individuals might sue under the Free Exercise Clause, arguing that the government, by denying access to the rattle or desecrating the sacred site[,] substantially infringed on their ability to practice their religion. In the last two hypotheticals, involving religion as an eligibility requirement for tribal officials and the teaching of tribal religion in the schools, the individuals might have a claim under the First Amendment's Establishment Clause, an argument that the state imposed religious belief on them.

None of the hypothetical plaintiffs would necessarily win their cases. Indeed, the Supreme Court has narrowly interpreted the Free Exercise Clause often denying religious freedoms protections for American Indian religious practitioners. . . .

C. Religious Freedoms under Tribal Constitutions

Indian tribes may provide for religious freedoms in their statutory, decisional, regulatory, or customary law. This section focuses individual religious freedoms appearing in tribal constitutions. This article . . . discusses several examples of tribal constitutional approaches to religious freedoms. It groups these into four categories: (1) constitutions with religious freedoms language that references, incorporates, or tracks the ICRA, (2) constitutions that do not use ICRA but echo U.S. principles of individual religious freedom, (3) constitutions with unique language on religion, clearly expressing distinct tribal values and norms, and (4) constitutions that do not reference religion or related concepts at all.

In the first group are tribal constitutions with religious freedoms provisions that reference, incorporate, or track the language of the ICRA. Several of these explicitly incorporate and set forth the ICRA. For example, the Crow Tribe's constitution provides: "In accordance with Title II of the Indian Civil Rights Act of 1968 (82 Stat. 77), the Crow Tribe of Indians in exercising its powers of self-government shall not: (a) make or enforce any law prohibiting the full exercise of religion." . . . The Miami Tribe's constitution sets forth:

> The Miami Tribe, in exercising its powers of self-government, shall not take any action which is in violations of the laws of the United States as the same shall exist from time to time respecting civil rights and civil liberties of persons. This article shall not abridge the concept of self-government or the obligations of the members of the Miami Tribe to abide by this Constitution and the ordinances, resolutions, and other legally instituted actions of the Miami Tribe. The protections guaranteed by the Indian Civil Rights Act of 1968 (82 Stat. 78) shall apply to all members of the Miami Tribe. [Constitution of the Miami Tribe of Oklahoma, art. VII (1995).]

Interestingly, while this constitution broadly protects individual civil rights, perhaps even those above and beyond ICRA's guarantees, it seems to balance these against tribal "self-government" and tribal members' "obligations."

In the second group are tribal constitutions with religious freedoms provisions that do not reference, incorporate, or track the ICRA, but still seem to echo the familiar language and principles of the federal First Amendment. For example, the Big Lagoon Rancheria Constitution provides: "[N]o member shall be denied freedom of . . . religion . . . or other rights guaranteed by applicable federal law." The Ute Indian Tribe of the Uintah and Ouray Reservation provides: "All members of the . . . Tribe . . . may enjoy, without hindrance, freedom of . . . worship." One special provision that recurs in a number of constitutions, such as the Choctaw Nation of Oklahoma, is that "no religious test shall ever be required as a qualification to any office of public trust in this Nation." Others such as the Muscogee Creek Tribe of Oklahoma, have a similar statement declaring all citizens have the right to vote in tribal elections "regardless of religion, creed, or sex."

In the third group are tribal constitutions with unique language on religion, clearly expressing distinct tribal values and norms. . . . The Yup'ik People of Bill Moore's Slough, in the "Land Policy and Constitution of the People of

Bill Moore's Slough," are very clear in their "Statement of Intent" about the collective nature of tribal rights and the relationship between land, tradition, and culture.

> We the Yup'ik people of Bill Moore's Slough being the original inhabitants of our land, having been placed here by our creator, to be the keepers of our land and having maintained this land as our creator intended us to keep it since the beginning, hereby declare our intent to continue managing it as we have always managed it in the past.
>
> In the past as well as the present our land and the culture of our people have been intertwined to the point where it would not be possible to maintain our traditional values and lifestyle should our land be alienated, altered or otherwise changed from its traditional relationship with our people.
>
> Therefore, it is our intent and the intent of this policy to maintain our land for all time forever for traditional uses.
>
> Furthermore, while others may attempt to change or eliminate our culture by methods of separating our people from our land, let it be known that we will resist such attempts.
>
> Let there be no misinterpretation nor ambiguities in this policy, it is a policy dedicated to the preservation of our traditional values, culture and lifestyle that we have maintained since the beginning.
>
> As a further point of clarification it is the position of Bill Moore's Slough that our people would not have survived as a people without maintaining our traditional relationship with the land. Therefore let this written land policy be considered by all parties concerned to be not only an integral part of the constitution of the people of Bill Moore's Slough but to be the primary law of our people and the basis for our cultural survival. [Land Policy and Constitution of the People of Bill Moore's Slough (1988).]

Having articulated the relationship between land, tradition, and survival, the Bill Moore's Slough Constitution then sets forth specific limitations on government and rights of individuals:

Article I
    A) The Bill Moore's Slough Elders Council shall pass all resolutions and laws dealing with land issues in conformity with the Bill Moore's Slough Land Policy.

    B) The Bill Moore's Slough Elders Council shall protect, preserve and defend the Bill Moore's Slough land, land policy and its people's traditional relationship with the land to the best of its ability.

Article II
    A) The Bill Moore's Slough Elders Council shall pass no laws jeopardizing certain freedoms and rights deemed to be given our people by our people's creator. Amongst these freedoms and rights are: the freedom to government by and for the people; the right to speak ones Conscience; the right to an education relevant to ones way of life; freedom from want, hunger, pain and fear; the right to liberty; the right to be Yupik; all rights guaranteed by Federal law including but not limited to Title II of the Indian Civil Rights Act of 1968.

The Poarch Creek Constitution speaks in terms of tribal interest, connecting religion and community survival, explaining that the purpose of the tribal government is to:

(1) Continue forever, with the help of God our Creator, our unique identity as members of the Poarch Band of Creek Indians, and to Poarch identity from forces that threaten to diminish it;

(2) Protect our inherent rights as members of a sovereign American Indian tribe;

(3) Promote our cultural and religious beliefs and to pass them in our own way to our children, grandchildren, and grandchildren's children forever; . . .

(8) Insure that our people shall live in peace and harmony among ourselves and with all other people.

[Constitution of the Poarch Band of Creek Indians, Preamble (Adopted June 1, 1985).]

It is in this context that the Poarch Creek Constitution then affords its members "the right to exercise the tribal rights and privileges of members of the Poarch Band of Creek Indians where not in conflict with other provisions of this Constitution, tribal laws and ordinances, or the laws of the United States."

Of particular interest is the "Constitution of the Iroquois Nations or The Great Binding Law, Gayanashagowa." The Iroquois Constitution is notable in that the Constitutional protections seem to be for the religion itself, and the people have responsibilities. In a section called "Religious Ceremonies Protected," the Iroquois Constitution provides:

99. The rites and festivals of each nation shall remain undisturbed and shall continue as before because they were given by the people of old times as useful and necessary for the good of men.

100. It shall be the duty of the Lords of each brotherhood to confer at the approach of the time of the Midwinter Thanksgiving and to notify their people of the approaching festival. They shall hold a council over the matter and arrange its details and begin the Thanksgiving five days after the moon of Dis-ko-nah is new. The people shall assemble at the appointed place and the nephews shall notify the people of the time and place. From the beginning to the end the Lords shall preside over the Thanksgiving and address the people from time to time.

101. It shall be the duty of the appointed managers of the Thanksgiving festivals to do all that is needed for carrying out the duties of the occasions.

The recognized festivals of Thanksgiving shall be the Midwinter Thanksgiving, the Maple or Sugar-making Thanksgiving, the Raspberry Thanksgiving, the Strawberry Thanksgiving, the Cornplanting Thanksgiving, the Corn Hoeing Thanksgiving, the Little Festival of Green Corn, the Great Festival of Ripe Corn and the complete Thanksgiving for the Harvest.

Each nation's festivals shall be held in their Long Houses.

102. When the Thanksgiving for the Green Corn comes the special managers, both the men and women, shall give it careful attention and do their duties properly.

103. When the Ripe Corn Thanksgiving is celebrated the Lords of the Nation must give it the same attention as they give to the Midwinter Thanksgiving.

104. Whenever any man proves himself by his good life and his knowledge of good things, naturally fitted as a teacher of good things, he shall be recognized by the Lords as a teacher of peace and religion and the people shall hear him.

[Constitution of the Iroquois Nations.]

The Iroquois Constitution, given to the people by Dekanawidah, makes clear that the people must fulfill duties to ensure the perpetuation of the ceremonies. Indirectly, of course, the duty of the people to protect the ceremonies ensures there will be ceremonies in which individuals can participate. Viewed in this light, the constitution could be read to provide an individual right to religious practice, but the more obvious focus of the provisions on festivals and ceremonial events seems to be on responsibilities. And while various other sections of the constitution outline rights of the people, including "lords," "war chiefs," and people from "foreign nations," these are similarly framed in terms of collective duties and welfare, and in the context of the Great Law. To understand this constitution more fully, we would need to see it in practice and consult with tribal leaders and members about its meaning. But, on its face, this constitution expresses the interconnected nature of people's rights and duties. . . .

NOTE

In *Townsend v. Port Gamble S'Klallam Housing Authority*, 6 NICS App. 179 (Port Gamble S'Klallam Tribal Court of Appeals 2004), the appellate court rejected a claim by a tribal citizen evicted from her tribal housing rental on grounds that she used her property for religious drumming amounting to a nuisance:

> Although not specifically stated as a ground for appeal, a reading of the record indicates that Appellant stated a defense of religious freedom, in that her exercise of the drumming and singing as a part of her worship in her church was protected by the Indian Civil Rights Act guarantee of freedom to practice her religion. . . . "Freedom of religion does not provide anyone with the right to conduct a true nuisance." . . . In interpreting the U.S. Constitution, which contains a freedom of religion clause, the U.S. Supreme Court held in *Braunfeld v. Brown*, 366 U.S. 599, 605 (1961), that the state may impose regulations that may have an indirect burden on practicing religion, in that case prohibiting retail stores from selling items on Sunday, even though it may affect persons practicing the Jewish religion, because they have as their Sabbath Saturday, and thus they wind up with two days they cannot run their stores, one prohibited by their religion, and one prohibited by the state. While the U.S. Constitution is not binding on Indian Nations, its guarantee of religious freedom may be looked to for guidance in Indian Civil Rights cases. No cases were found in Indian Nation decisions regarding freedom of religion under the Indian Civil Rights Act, so reference is made to the cases cited above. Therefore the court holds that the Port Gamble S'Klallam Tribe may enforce their nuisance ordinance, even though it may have an indirect effect on the practice of her religion by Appellant.
>
> Similarly, Appellant claims that the activities which were found to constitute a nuisance are religious activities protected by the American Indian Religious Freedom Act (AIRFA), Pub. L. 95-341, 92 Stat. 469, 42 U.S.C.

§1996. However, this Act concerns and is directed toward actions of the federal government, not actions by a tribal government or one of its entities. . . . It does not provide a private cause of action or procedures for enforcement.

Finally, when ICRA protections are raised in a sensitive context, such as protection of tribal religious practices against unwarranted intrusions, the Court is compelled to examine whether the Tribe's Constitution affords similar or greater protections. Article V — Bill of Rights, §3, Civil Liberties, states, in relevant part, that "members of the Community shall enjoy without hindrance, freedom of worship, . . . speech, . . . assembly, and association." This guarantee, however, does not mean that protection of religious activities is absolute. . . . [W]here the object of a law or regulation is not to prohibit or burden religious practices, or to coerce individuals into violating their beliefs, then a balancing of interests is not appropriate and individuals are not excused from complying with such law or regulation. Here, the purpose of the applicable law and regulation is to protect the health, safety and welfare of the community and its members, and the Appellant was given opportunity to comply or face the possibility of eviction.

Townsend, 6 NICS App. at 185-86.

C. FREEDOM OF SPEECH

Navajo Nation v. Crockett

Navajo Nation Supreme Court, No. SC-CV-14-94, 7 Navajo Rep. 237, 1995.NANN.0000006 (November 26, 1996)

Before Yazzie, Chief Justice, Cadman and Morris sitting by designation, Associate Justices.

The opinion of the court was delivered by: Cadman, Associate Justice.

This is an appeal of a jury verdict in favor of Navajo Nation entity employees and an order denying the Navajo Nation's motion for directed verdict.

I. Facts

Elvira Crockett, Lalora Charles Roy, and Charmaine Tso ("employees"), were employed by Navajo Agricultural Products Industry ("NAPI"), a Navajo Nation farming enterprise. The Economic Development Committee ("EDC") of the Navajo Nation Council is the oversight committee for NAPI. The NAPI Board of Directors reports management activity to the EDC. On November 17, 1992, the EDC held a meeting concerning NAPI. NAPI management was not informed of the meeting; however, the plaintiff employees attended.

The employees told of possible NAPI mismanagement and misconduct at the meeting. They also presented business documents to the EDC that were taken without NAPI management authorization. The EDC directed NAPI not to take retaliatory action against the employees for these actions.

Nevertheless, the employees were implicated, placed on indefinite administrative leave, and then terminated on December 23, 1992. . . . At trial, NAPI moved for a directed verdict which the district court denied. The jury returned a general verdict in favor of the employees, awarding them monetary damages. . . .

The issues on appeal are the following: . . .

3. Whether the district court correctly denied NAPI's motion for directed verdict on the employees' freedom of speech and due process claims. . . .

III. Directed Verdict

A. Free Speech

NAPI argues that the district court erred in denying its motion for a directed verdict on the issue of free speech. Navajo common law is the law of preference in the courts of the Navajo Nation. *Navajo Nation v. Platero*, No. A-CR-01-91, slip op. at 6 (decided December 5, 1991). This Court applies Navajo common law to determine whether an individual's right to free speech has been violated. It provides that an individual has a fundamental right to express his or her mind by way of the spoken word and/or actions. As a matter of Navajo tradition and custom, people speak with caution and respect, choosing their words carefully to avoid harm to others. This is nothing more than freedom with responsibility, a fundamental Navajo traditional principle.

The speech in this case involved 1) attending and speaking at the EDC meeting; 2) copying confidential documents; and 3) bringing the documents to the meeting. The parties debate whether the employees were fired for copying and removing the documents, a NAPI policy violation, or for attending and speaking at the meeting. The district court's determination of protected speech focused on the statements made and documents presented at the meeting. Thus, for purposes of review by this Court, the speech in question is statements made and documents presented by the employees at the EDC meeting.

Similar to the American system, however, there are Navajo traditional limitations on the content of speech. For example, on some occasions, a person is prohibited from making certain statements, and some statements of reciting oral traditions are prohibited during specific times of the year.

Furthermore, speech should be delivered with respect and honesty. This requirement arises from the concept of k e', which is the "glue" that creates and binds relationships between people. To avoid disruptions of relationships, Navajo common law mandates that controversies and arguments be resolved by "talking things out." This process of "talking things out," called hoozhoo-jigo, allows each member of the group to cooperate and talk about how to resolve a problem. This requirement places another limitation on speech, which is that a disgruntled person must speak directly with the person's relative about his or her concerns before seeking other avenues of redress with strangers.

In the employment context, relationships are established according to the personnel policies, and other instruments. When an employee has a complaint about a supervisor, according to Navajo custom and tradition, he or she should first approach the supervisor and discuss the problem in a respectful manner. Moreover, under the Navajo common law concept of nalyeeh, the employee should not seek to correct the person by summoning the coercive powers of a powerful person or entity, but should seek to correct the wrongful action by "talking things out." The employee should not seek a remedy from a stranger, but should rather explain the problem to the person or one of his or her relatives and ask that "things be put right." If this method proves unsuccessful, then the employee also has access to an internal employment grievance process. Even in this formal, modern process for addressing grievances, the traditional rules of respect, honesty, and kinship apply.

In situations where the complaint alleges employer mismanagement, distinct from internal personnel matters, an employee is entitled to consult others vested with the authority to hear such complaints, such as the organization's own committee, or an oversight of the Navajo Nation Council. An oversight committee is limited by 2 N.N.C. §191, "to legislation and policy decisions and shall not involve program administration. . . ." This removes most personnel complaints from the committees, and limits their review of director conduct to overall competence in management.

When discussing management concerns with the appropriate oversight committee, an employee must follow certain limitations. The employee must be respectful in his or her approach, and an initial inquiry with management to "talk things out" is encouraged. Second, the speech must involve matters of public concern and fall within the oversight authority of the committee. When an employee gives a statement before an official government committee, he or she speaks in a context that is inherently public in nature. This also includes any documents which the employee may distribute. Documents must be of a public nature and if they are confidential or restricted, then proper authorization for their distribution must be obtained.

An oversight committee often has to rely on information from sources other than those in positions of authority to ascertain the full picture. However, an employee is prohibited from raising internal personnel matters or other personal problems before a committee. The court should also consider whether the business is a government enterprise or private entity.

An employee must comply with these limitations when alleging that he or she was terminated or otherwise mistreated as a result of his or her speech. The employee must also show some nexus between the termination or other adverse employment action and the speech. One method for proving this element is in terms of time — whether the adverse employment action occurred shortly after the occurrence of the speech. That is, the employee must show his or her speech was a significant factor or motivation in the adverse employment action.

This Court finds the speech in question was "a matter of public concern." At the meeting, the employees expressed safety and environmental concerns, undue interference by the Bureau of Indian Affairs in P.L. 93-638 contracts, and allegations of misconduct and misfeasance on the part of NAPI management. The disclosure of misconduct or misfeasance by a government entity is a matter of public concern, as are questions of effectiveness and composition of the NAPI management board. Likewise, safety and environmental concerns have the potential to directly impact the general public, and therefore, are a matter of public interest. Members of the EDC had previously visited NAPI and invited the employees to contact them about their concerns with management, in particular Appellee Crockett. The chairman of the EDC also advised Crockett to bring supporting documentation to the meeting.

Moreover, the employees were speaking before an official body of the Navajo Nation Council. When an employee gives a statement before an official government committee, he or she speaks in a context that is inherently public in nature.

The second point of inquiry is whether NAPI's interest in promoting the efficiency of the public services it performs through its employees outweighs the employees' right to free speech. Indeed, NAPI has an interest in ensuring compliance with office policies and to maintain order and control over its employees. The jury concluded, however, that the employees were not terminated for violations of NAPI policy, and NAPI does not contest this finding on appeal. Furthermore, the employees' attendance at the meeting did not result in any significant harm to NAPI. The documents distributed at the meeting were never made public or put in the "wrong hands," nor was there evidence of disruption or disharmony in the office as a result. NAPI's interest to not disclose demoralizing or disruptive information is not an adequate interest to outweigh an individual's right to free speech.

Based on the foregoing, this Court finds that the district court did not err in its decision that the speech was a matter of public concern. The decision of the district court that the employees' speech was protected is affirmed. . . .

NOTES*

1. Many tribal constitutions guarantee free speech rights in varying forms. Some tribes guarantee free speech even without the "state action" requirement imposed by the First Amendment's language, "Congress shall make no law. . . ." The constitution of the Confederated Tribes of Warm Springs Reservation of Oregon provides, "[a]ll members of the Confederated Tribes may enjoy without hindrance, freedom of worship, speech, press and assembly." CONFEDERATED TRIBES OF WARM SPRINGS RESERVATION OF OREGON CONST. art. VII, §2. The Comanche Indian Tribe's constitution has nearly identical language: "All members of the Comanche Indian Tribe shall enjoy without hindrance freedom of worship, conscience, speech, press, assembly and association." COMANCHE INDIAN TRIBE OF OKLAHOMA CONST. art. X, §1. The Sisseton-Wahpeton Sioux Tribe's constitution similarly states, "[N]o person shall be denied freedom of conscience, speech, association, or assembly. . . ." SISSETON-WAHPETON SIOUX TRIBE, SOUTH DAKOTA CONST. AND BYLAWS art. IX, §1. Some tribes limit this protection to tribal members. The Blackfeet Constitution states, "All members of the tribe may enjoy without hindrance freedom of worship, conscience, speech, press, assembly, and association." BLACKFEET TRIBE OF THE BLACKFEET INDIAN RESERVATION OF MONTANA CONST. AND BYLAWS art. VIII, §3.

---

*Much of the material in the notes first appeared in Matthew L. M. Fletcher, *Theoretical Restrictions on the Sharing of Indigenous Biological Knowledge: Implications for Freedom of Speech in Tribal Law*, 14 KAN. J.L. & PUB. POL'Y 525, 536-44 (2005).

Other tribal constitutions regulate only governmental conduct that would otherwise restrict speech. The Chickasaw Constitution provides, "Every citizen shall be at liberty to speak, write, or publish his opinions on any subject, being responsible for the abuse of that privilege, and no law shall ever be passed curtailing the liberty of speech, or of the press." CHICKASAW NATION CONST. art. IV, §4. Others substantially mirror the provisions contained in the Indian Civil Rights Act, while other tribes adopt ICRA's provisions. Many tribal constitutions do not have constitutional protections relating to freedom of speech at all.

2. Tribal courts have generally interpreted the provisions of the Indian Civil Rights Act in accordance with the method recommended in 1969 by the leading commentary on the Act: "Unless the record shows a willingness to modify tribal life wherever necessary to impose ordinary constitutional standards, courts should take this legislation as a mandate to interpret statutory standards within the framework of tribal life." Note, *The Indian Bill of Rights and the Constitutional Status of Tribal Governments*, 82 HARV. L. REV. 1343, 1355 (1969). One tribal court follows a principle that, where no tribal "custom or tradition has been argued to be implicated . . . , [tribal courts] will look to general U.S. constitutional principles, as articulated by federal and [state] courts, for guidance. . . ." *Louchart v. Mashantucket Pequot Gaming Enter.*, 27 Indian L. Rep. 6176, 6179 (Mashantucket Pequot Tribal Ct. 1999).

   The most critical element that tends to guide tribal court analysis of fundamental individual rights is whether the activity at issue is a distinctly Anglo-American construct versus a traditional or cultural construct. For example, tribal courts are likely to apply federal constitutional law to decide a wrongful discharge claim or an unlawful search and seizure claim as opposed to a tribal membership claim.

3. Since most free speech claims heard in tribal courts arise during the course of employment or in the exercise of political rights, tribal courts most often apply federal law as persuasive authority to decide these cases. In *LaPorte v. Fletcher*, 2004 WL 5748553 (Little River Band of Ottawa Indians Tribal Ct. 2004), *aff'd*, 2005 WL 6344557 (Little River Band of Ottawa Indians Court of Appeals 2005), the tribal court rejected a freedom of speech challenge to an employee's demotion from chief of police and his challenge to a tribal statute that prohibited employees from making statements to the media regarding issues under negotiation. The employee as chief of police had allegedly stated to a local newspaper that the tribe had entered into an agreement with a local sheriff's department when in fact the tribe had not. Relying on several federal cases, the court upheld the tribal statute and the demotion.

4. In instances in which an individual's speech rights as a candidate for tribal election are implicated, at least one court applied a sliding-scale standard of review, choosing to apply intermediate scrutiny where the tribe imposed nondiscriminatory restrictions on candidate eligibility to avoid a chaotic tribal caucus process. *See Rave v. Reynolds*, 23 Indian L. Rep. 6021 (Winnebago Tribal Ct. 1995) ("*Rave I*"), *aff'd in part and rev'd in part*, 23 Indian L. Rep. 6150 (Winnebago Sup. Ct. 1996) ("*Rave II*").

5. Tribal courts apply a reduced standard of review on restrictions on the behavior of elected tribal leaders. In *Brandon v. Tribal Council for the*

Confederated Tribes of the Grand Ronde Community of Oregon, 18 Indian L. Rep. 6139 (Confederated Tribes of the Grand Ronde Community Tribal Ct. 1991), the tribal council suspended for three months one tribal council member who had made a "vulgar" statement during a public meeting, in accordance with a tribal statute that prohibited tribal council members from behaving in a manner that would bring discredit or disrespect to the tribe. The court then found a "compelling" reason for the statute, based in part on tribal traditions:

> The Grand Ronde Tribe has compelling reasons to have interpreted the ordinance so as to limit the vulgar language that may be uttered by councilmembers [sic] in public. . . . [T]he Tribe has the right to expect its councilmembers to conduct themselves in public with dignity and respect, and refrain from using words or phrases that a normal tribal member is privileged to use. Secondly, the type of language used by Mr. Brandon was arguably "fighting words" that were likely to create a violent or hostile situation, as indeed was created here. The tribe has a right to expect its tribal councilmembers to refrain from using such language so as to avoid fights or other altercations. Finally, the Grand Ronde Tribe has a vested interest in protecting its reputation throughout the community.

Id. at 6141.

The *Brandon* court created a doctrine of free speech that applied only to the tribe's elected officials. A tribe's reputation in business and intergovernmental negotiation is directly related to the quality and behavior of its elected leaders. As Professor Mark Rosen noted, the court appeared to be adopting an analogue of the federal doctrine that validly restricts the expression of federal employees. Mark D. Rosen, *Multiple Authoritative Interpreters of Quasi-Constitutional Federal Law: Of Tribal Courts and the Indian Civil Rights Act*, 69 FORDHAM L. REV. 479, 554 (2000). But the tribal court issued a decision that appeared to strongly imply the critical role that tribal leaders play in representing the tribe in tribal meetings, in government-to-government negotiations, and in business relationships.

6. The factual converse of the *Brandon* decision is likely *Flute v. Labelle* (Sisseton-Wahpeton Oyate Court, May 14, 2004). There, an elected tribal leader who was the subject of an unflattering letter to the editor of the local newspaper sued the author of the letter for defamation. The tribal court applied federal and South Dakota constitutional law in analogue and found that the plaintiff's petition met the requirements of libel per quod. Since the plaintiff could not show actual damages, the court awarded only nominal damages and ordered the defendant to "write a retraction letter to the Tribal newspaper correcting the false impression she left with readers. . . ." The court noted the political history of the defendant in particular, stating that she had been "one of many persons who several years ago engaged in a protest of tribal council action by occupying the Tribal Council chambers after a Council meeting ended." In short, the court applied federal and state common law in analogue that established the defendant's culpability, but applied that law to fashion a tribe-specific remedy that severely limited the defendant's liability.

7. Some tribal courts provide additional tribe-specific reasons for restricting or otherwise rewarding speech. In *Garcia v. Greendeer-Lee*, 30 Indian L. Rep. 6097 (Ho-Chunk Supreme Court 2003), the Ho-Chunk Supreme Court rejected a claim by a nonmember employee of the Ho-Chunk Nation that the tribe's personnel policies violated her right to choose her own religion. The employee, a Jehovah's Witness, sought paid leave for the time she attended a religious event. The tribe's Waksig Wogsa Leave Policy allowed for paid leave for attendance of certain tribe-specific religious events, but only unpaid leave for other events. The court majority found that the employee was not prohibited from participating in her religion and rejected the claim.

D. SPECIAL PROBLEMS OF CIVIL RIGHTS IN INDIAN COUNTRY

1. BANISHMENT/EXCLUSION

BANISHMENT AS CULTURAL JUSTICE IN CONTEMPORARY TRIBAL LEGAL SYSTEMS

Patrice H. Kunesh, 37 N.M. L. Rev. 85, 91-100 (2007)

. . .

II. Cultural and Legal Underpinnings of Banishment

A. Illuminating the Modern with the Primitive: The Cultural Backdrop

. . . Historically, Indian tribes have used banishment sparingly and as a last resort after exhausting customary and traditional methods of social discipline and sanction. In the past, most Indian cultures did not have the formal penal systems that exist in many tribal legal systems today. Rather, tribal communities typically addressed disputes, social transgressions, and serious offenses according to a complex system of social, cultural, and political relationships. . . .

Tribes also tend to engage respected community members, such as elders, to peacefully resolve intra-tribal disputes. . . . Some tribal peacemaking customs and traditions involve a "talking to" where a tribal elder or council member speaks to the individual about the tribe's values and beliefs and the consequences of misbehavior or misconduct. The Elder or Councilor would admonish the person against harboring vengeful feelings and encourage the restoration of harmonious relationships within the community.

Banishment was used as a last resort if all other efforts of the family and community failed. A decision to banish a tribal member was arrived at through extensive discussions and testimony about the individual's conduct and character. These discussions usually involved the governing council, the elders' council, or the entire community. In due course, a consensus was arrived at addressing the particular circumstances, the gravity of the offense, and the terms of the banishment. Banishment has had two main focal points—the community and the individual. Serious transgressions have the potential to threaten the cohesiveness of the community, weaken the tribe's authority and political structure, and encourage other deviant or harmful behavior. Through banishment, the tribe fulfills its duty to act justly on behalf of the people as a whole. The banishment order is directed to the individual, addresses the particular conduct that has compromised the community's safety and welfare, and encourages conformity with the tribe's social and cultural standards. . . .

Like historical banishment decisions, modern banishment orders often impose conditions on the individual's exclusion from the tribe. An order may, for example, set a definite time period for the banishment sentence, require restitution for the wrongdoing, or even mandate mental health assistance. If an individual has vandalized or stolen property, an order may require the individual to repair or replace the property or compensate the owner. In the event of a personal injury or insult, an order may restrict the person's presence in the community, similar to a restraining order. If, however, an individual has committed a grievous offense against another individual or the tribe, something completely beyond the norms and standards of the tribe (such as dealing drugs, sexual assault, or murder), an order may require his or her complete expulsion from tribal lands as well as prohibit the community from having any contact with the banished person. With the gradual imposition of more severe sanctions, the individual comes to understand that his or her conduct is offensive and adherence to the tribe's social norms is expected. Failing this inducement, the individual faces the dire consequences of living outside of the community.

The histories of three tribes—the Cheyenne, the Navajo, and the Seneca—exemplify this cultural practice of conformity through social pressure and banishment. Under the laws and customs of each of these tribes, banishment is rarely used and is imposed only when all other customary measures fail to protect the community or reform the individual.

1. The Cheyenne Way: Law-Ways

. . . Governed primarily by the Great Council with significant collaboration from the military societies, the Cheyenne resolved most of their disputes amenably through consensus. This practice had several remarkable qualities: it promoted "deference to another's judgment," concluded the dispute with firm finality, and established a harmonious relationship among the disputants.

. . .

The Cheyenne did not distinguish between a civil or private wrong and a criminal or public wrong; any wrongdoing concerned the whole community. A distinction was made, however, in determining the sanction for the particular offense in question. For example, an incorrigible tribal member was severely punished by the soldier society and then rehabilitated back into the tribe by another family or tribal member. In addition, violations of hunting rules were punished by chastisement and ostracism and then resolved through rehabilitation . . . , whereas murder was punished through banishment. . . . Other offenses, such as disobedience of the society's orders, abortion, theft, rape, incest, or abuse of power warranted reprimand, restitution, ostracism, banishment, or corporal punishment.

In addition to conventional punitive measures, "positive sanctions were also lavishly used" in shaping the character of tribal members. Successful acts of individual accomplishment and virtue were praised and publicly acclaimed. . . . Sharing and cooperation engendered harmonious relationships and spiritual and cultural beliefs were reinforced.

> [W]ealth was distributed and parents basked in the pleasures of largess and altruism, as well as of publicity. Reciprocity balanced the relationships. So, too, when young men followed the advice of their fathers in offering a good buffalo-kill to an old shaman, the shaman went to the carcass, and in accepting it performed a short sanctifying ritual in which he blessed the boy and his family. Returning through camp, he called aloud that he had received a buffalo gift and had performed the ceremony. Here too, the youth received public credit. [K.N. Llewellyn & E. Adamson Hoebel, The Cheyenne Way: Conflict and Case Law in Primitive Jurisprudence 247 (1941).]

These positive sanctions reinforced community values among their youth.

The Cheyenne, a nation united around the family, guided in all aspects of tribal life by their traditions and ceremonies, have struggled against powerful forces that would corrode, if not destroy, their identity and cultural practices. Recently, the Dog Soldiers of the Crazy Dog Society and the Kit Fox Society convened a council and decided to banish an Indian Health Services doctor for performing religious ceremonies on tribal lands, actions that the societies considered to be "a sacrilege and desecration to [their] culture." The doctor, a non-Indian, "was driven to the reservation line by the societies and informed he was banished from the reservation." When the banishment was later ruled illegal by the Northern Cheyenne Tribal Court, the doctor returned to work on the reservation. The Tribe's modern formal judicial proceedings prevailed over the old Cheyenne way.

2. The Navajo Way: beehaz'aanii

The Navajo, like many other tribes, have been culturally averse to formal systems of punishment. Indeed, "[t]he Navajo Nation Supreme Court has acknowledged that 'actual coercion or punishment were actions of last resort in Navajo common law.'" Traditional Navajo law made no distinction between civil and criminal acts; both "were usually dealt with in the same fashion, by requiring restitution to the victim by the offender." In either case, the main goals of punishment "were to put the victim in the position he or she was [in] before the offense by a money payment, punish in a visible way [by] requiring extra payments to the victim or the victim's family, and give a visible sign to the community that [the] wrong was punished."

Social order within the Navajo Nation is maintained by time-honored traditions and customs and also by tribal customary law, which have all been incorporated into the Navajo Tribal Code. . . . [The] traditional way of resolving disputes within the Navajo community and conciliating problems among members of the community, "a form of local mediation," was formally institutionalized into the Navajo Peacemakers Court. Peacemakers, or naat'aanii, are selected by parties attempting to resolve their disputes through the Peace-maker Court, and are often "community or religious leader[s] or respected elder[s]." The Peacemaker's role is to elicit discussion among all interested parties, including family members, apply Navajo customs and values, and attempt to reach a settlement agreeable to the parties involved in the dispute.

While restitution was the traditional Navajo remedy for almost all offenses, banishment, also referred to as shunning, was an acceptable sanction under Navajo customary law. " 'Shunning,' or the deliberate ostracizing of an offen-der by the community, was a traditional Navajo method of dealing with 'those who repeatedly offended or flaunted the will of the community.' " "Banish-ment, therefore, was essentially an extension of a time-honored Navajo practice" reserved for "a repeat offender, or one who committed a particularly heinous crime." Once banished, the individual was culturally excluded from the tribal community. Without significant social and financial support from family and relatives, it would be difficult, if not impossible, to continue living on the reservation.

3. The Seneca Way: Gayanashagowa

Peacemaking traditions were also vital to the Seneca Nation of Indians, one of the Six Nations of the Iroquois Confederacy, or Haudenosaunee, of New York. . . .

The Haudenosaunee peacemaking law and tradition was so integrated into the community that the "Seneca society was afflicted with little interpersonal conflict and transgressions of community norms. Individual behavior was governed by a strong unwritten social code that relied upon social and psy-chological sanctions, such as ridicule and embarrassment, as the primary methods of enforcement." The Seneca social structure and behavioral norms were maintained "by oral tradition supported by a sense of duty, a fear of gossip, and a dread fear of retaliatory witchcraft."

As in the Navajo culture, formal punishment was disfavored in Seneca society; social pressure and mutual consent corrected nearly all deviant behav-ior and resolved most disputes. However, "extreme violence, such as murder or the practice of witchcraft, were punishable by death or by restitution to the victim's family. If the wrongdoer repented, he could offer goods and services, and the matter would be resolved." Traditionally, banishment (*i.e.*, "complete ostracism") from the Seneca society was rarely needed because public indigna-tion was considered to be a sufficiently severe punishment. . . .

4. Common Themes across Tribal Boundaries

The historical traditions and customs of the Cheyenne, the Navajo, and the Seneca share several common themes. These tribes were markedly cohe-sive societies, unified around their families and dependent on one another for their sustenance and survival. Families and relatives shared mutual responsibility for instructing their youth, observing ceremonies, and incul-cating respect for the tribe's culture and values. Deviant or defiant behavior within their communities, outside the bounds of customarily accepted con-duct, could potentially threaten the tribe's unity and ultimately its ability to survive. . . .

a. Due Process Challenges

MONESTERSKY V. HOPI TRIBE

Hopi Tribal Appellate Court, Case No. 01AP000015, 2002.NAHT.0000003
(June 27, 2002)

Before, SEKAQUAPTEWA, Chief Justice, and ABBEY and HUMETEWA, Justices

Brief Statement of Facts

This matter came before the Hopi trial court as an appeal from an order of exclusion issued by the Chairman of the Hopi Tribe (Appellee) pursuant to Hopi Tribal Ordinance 46. The trial court affirmed the Appellee's administrative decision to exclude Appellant from the Hopi Reservation.

Appellant asserts that Ordinance 46 is unconstitutional. Appellant argues that the decision-making process of her exclusion denied her due process and therefore violated her civil rights.

Discussion

. . .

III. The Hopi Tribe Has an Inherent Power to Exclude Nonmembers

It is well settled that the Hopi Tribe, and all Indian tribal governments, have the inherent power to exclude nonmembers as an exercise of their sovereign power in order to protect the health and safety of tribal members. . . . Therefore, by enacting Ordinance 46, the Hopi Tribal Council has acted to prescribe its authority to "provide by ordinance for removal or exclusion from the jurisdiction of any nonmembers whose presence may be harmful to the members of the Hopi Tribe." CONSTITUTION AND BY-LAWS OF THE HOPI TRIBE, Article VI, section 1 (i).

. . . Ordinance 46 first explains that the Hopi Reservation is closed and shall be for the exclusive use and benefit of members of the Hopi Indian Tribe. Closure "means that entry into and use of the Hopi Indian Reservation is restricted to members of the Hopi Indian Tribe and those persons authorized to be upon the Hopi Reservation in accordance with Hopi and federal laws and regulations." 46.01.06(a).

In addition, Ordinance 46 provides the process for the exclusion and removal of nonmembers in order to protect the health, safety, economic security and general welfare of the Hopi people. The ordinance allows the Chairman to initiate the exclusion process for any nonmember for certain enumerated reasons.

Persons subject to exclusion are any nonmember:

(a) who enters or remains upon a closed portion of the Hopi Indian Reservation in violation of this Ordinance; or
(b) who violates any other Ordinance or law of the Hopi Indian Tribe or any Hopi Village; or

    (c) who violates any law of the United States; or

    (d) who engages in conduct that would be a violation of the criminal laws of the Hopi Indian Tribe if that nonmember were subject to the criminal laws of the Hopi Indian Tribe.

(46.02.01.) Nonmembers falling into one of the above categories "shall be deemed a person whose presence on the Hopi Indian Reservation may be harmful to members of the Hopi Indian Tribe. All such persons may be excluded and removed from the Hopi Indian Reservation." *Id.* . . .

IV. Excluded Nonmembers Must Demonstrate a Protected Liberty or Property Interest in Order to Be Entitled to Due Process

Appellant asserts that she was denied her due process rights in the exclusion proceedings against her. . . . Under the Indian Civil Rights Act's (ICRA) due process clause, the tribal government may not "deny to any person within its jurisdiction the equal protection of its laws or deprive any person of liberty or property without due process." In exclusion cases, the excluded would have to demonstrate either liberty or property interests that were significantly restricted by exclusion before due process would be required.

A. Appellant Has Not Demonstrated a Restriction of Her Liberty Interests

Federal courts' reviews of tribal decisions resulting in the exclusion of nonmembers have consistently held that nonmembers do not suffer a severe restriction on liberty by being excluded from tribal lands. . . . The remedy for any alleged ICRA violation or allegation of a restriction on personal liberty is limited to review under a writ of habeas corpus. Habeas corpus review is available to a person who is subject to detention. A potential issue, therefore, is whether "exclusion" constitutes detention.

In *Poodry v. Tonawanda Band of Seneca Indians*, tribal members were banished, stripped of their lands, their names, their enrollment status, and their Indian citizenship after being charged with treason. 85 F.3d 874 (2d Cir. 1996). The court found that his was a restriction on their liberty interests. While *Poodry* implied that exclusion in this case was analogous to detention, the facts of the present case are significantly different. Here, the Appellate is a non-Indian. Therefore, she can have no claim, legal or otherwise, to land within the Hopi Reservation.

In addition, those members excluded in *Poodry* were able to demonstrate that they had liberty interests on the reservation. *Poodry* implies that the exclusion as detention argument is limited to tribal members, or nonmembers who can demonstrate a significant liberty or property interest on the reservation. Appellant's argument that she has befriended many members of the Hopi Tribe and would suffer if not permitted to continue her association with those tribal members does not support a finding of restraint on personal liberty. Moreover, Appellant has no standing to assert the perceived third-party rights of any tribal member whom she claims would be detrimentally affected were she not permitted to remain on the Hopi Reservation.

B. Appellant Has Not Demonstrated a Restraint of Her Property Interests

Due process requirements are also triggered when a person's property interests are at stake. . . . However, these due process requirements are different from those required in cases where liberty is at stake. When personal liberty is threatened, and a person is being detained, they are entitled to a jury trial, representation by competent counsel, and other due process requirements. With property interests, the due process requirements are less stringent. Basic due process rights such as proper notice and an opportunity to defend oneself are included, but there is no fundamental right to a jury trial, for example.

When a party is the subject of a non-criminal investigation, where liberty is not at stake, but the party's property is at stake, that party is entitled to due process, albeit less restrictive than when liberty is at issue. . . . Appellant argues that she has personal property interests that will be jeopardized if she is required to leave the Hopi Reservation. She asserts that she owns several head of sheep, and that that ownership alone constitutes a property interest. This Court disagrees.

If Appellant's property were real property—land, in other words—she may have been able to show that she had property interests that would be threatened were she required to leave the Reservation. However, Appellant owns no land, and no property affixed to any land. This point is critical because, as a non-member, she can never qualify for land ownership or use within the Hopi Reservation. Thus, although her alleged sheep require grazing, they are tangible objects which may be removed from the land they now occupy.

Appellant's property interest in her sheep is in no way detrimentally harmed. She may either take them with her when she leaves the Hopi Reservation, or she may sell them at fair market value. It is the opinion of this Court that owning sheep does not bestow upon Appellant the type of property interests protected by the due process requirements set forth in the Indian Civil Rights Act and the Constitution of the United States. . . .

C. Ordinance 46 Satisfies Minimum Due Process Requirements

Pursuant to Ordinance 46, Appellant was given adequate notice of the proposal to exclude. She was also given the opportunity to respond in writing, and to have an administrative hearing. The process was civil in nature, and the inapplicability of Hopi criminal law to the Appellant was acknowledged. Appellant was not tried for criminal offenses, nor was she subjected to potential detention.

Ordinance 46 provides that a person subject to exclusion will have notice, a hearing, the right to present and examine witnesses, the right to be represented by counsel, and the right to present evidence as to why exclusion should not be ordered. These elements of due process satisfy what would be required in a civil administrative hearing where a party's property interests are at stake.

Due process requirements are triggered when a person's liberty or property interests are at stake. When a person's liberty is restricted, he or she is entitled to high standards. At no point was Appellant's liberty in jeopardy. . . .

Conclusion

The Hopi Tribal Court had jurisdiction to review the order of exclusion at issue on this case. The lower court found that there were no due process violations during Appellant's exclusion process. Therefore, it is hereby ordered that the judgment of the trial court, affirming Appellee's order excluding Appellant from the Hopi Reservation, is affirmed.

NOTES

1. In *Poodry v. Tonawanda Band of Seneca Indians*, 85 F.3d 874 (2d Cir.), *cert. denied*, 519 U.S. 1041 (1996), the court held that banished members of the Tonawanda Band could utilize the federal writ of habeas corpus to challenge their banishment. The petitioners in that case alleged they had received this notice:

> It is with a great deal of sorrow that we inform you that you are now banished from the territories of the Tonawanda Band of the Seneca Nation. You are to leave now and never return.
>
> According to the customs and usage of the Tonawanda Band of the Seneca Nation and the HAUDENOSAUNEE, no warnings are required before banishment for acts of murder, rape, or treason.
>
> Your actions to overthrow, or otherwise bring about the removal of, the traditional government at the Tonawanda Band of Seneca Nation, and further by becoming a member of the Interim General Council, are considered treason. Therefore, banishment is required.
>
> According to the customs and usage of the Tonawanda Band of Seneca Nation and the HAUDENOSAUNEE, your name is removed from the Tribal rolls, your Indian name is taken away, and your lands will become the responsibility of the Council of Chiefs. You are now stripped of your Indian citizenship and permanently lose any and all rights afforded our members.
>
> YOU MUST LEAVE IMMEDIATELY AND WE WILL WALK WITH YOU TO THE OUTER BORDERS OF OUR TERRITORY.

Poodry, 85 F.3d at 878.

According to Jill Tompkins, professor and tribal judge,

> *Poodry* involved a dispute on the Tonawanda Reservation concerning alleged misconduct by certain members of the Tonawanda Council of Chiefs. The alleged misconduct included misusing tribal funds, suspending tribal elections, excluding members of the Council of Chiefs from tribal business affairs and burning tribal records. The plaintiffs formed an Interim General Council of the Tonawanda Band. The plaintiffs were subsequently confronted by a large group of tribal members and presented with a document notifying them that they had committed treason and were banished from the reservation. The individuals serving the notice attempted without success "to take petitioners . . . into custody and eject them from the reservation."
>
> It was undisputed that there was not tribal forum available for review of the actions of the members of the Council of Chiefs. . . .

Jill E. Tompkins, *Traditional Tribal Justice Practices and the Indian Civil Rights Act: The Tension between Tribal Autonomy and Individual Rights* 18-19,

Materials published as part of the 16th Annual University of Washington Indian Law Symposium (Sept. 18-19, 2003).

Tompkins argued:

> If the view of the *Poodry* majority is adopted by other federal courts, arguments that tribal tradition and custom should inform the decision-making process will fall on deaf ears. In essence, tribes may again confront the attitude that ICRA is a federal statute, therefore federal precedents and standards should apply. . . .
>
> Tribes also need to consider whether traditional punishments are being decided upon for traditional reasons and in the most traditional manner. Historically, banishments were rare and done only in the more dire of circumstances. Present day political conflict fuels many of the exclusion and banishment decisions. . . .

Id. at 23.

2. Some tribes have outlawed banishment. In *Passamaquoddy Tribe v. Francis*, 2000.NAPA.0000001 (Passamaquoddy Tribal Appellate Court 2000), the court rejected the merits of an appeal by a tribal member sentenced to probation and who was required to seek permission before entering the reservation, despite a provision in the tribal constitution prohibiting the use of banishment. "Article IX, Section 3. Article IV, Section 2 of the Constitution provides that, 'Notwithstanding any provision of this Constitution, the government of the Pleasant Point Reservation shall have no power of banishment over tribal members.'" *Francis*, at ¶17. The court further wrote:

> Clearly, the permission requirement contained in the Tribal Court's conditions of probation does not come anywhere close to [the] severity and breadth of the banishment order at issue in *Poodry*. The burden was on Francis to demonstrate that the condition of probation requiring him to receive permission from the probation officer before coming onto the Pleasant Point constituted a "banishment"; the Court finds that he failed to meet his burden.
>
> Even if the condition of probation did constitute banishment, Francis voluntarily and knowingly accepted the condition as a means of avoiding prolonged incarceration for his multiple convictions. . . .

Id. at ¶¶26-27.

b. Equal Protection Challenges

BURNS PAIUTE INDIAN TRIBE v. DICK

Burns Paiute Tribal Court of Appeals, Nos. CV-15-93, CV-16-93, CV-17-93, 3 NICS App. 281 (February 14, 1994)

ROE, Chief Justice: . . .

Appellants were excluded from the Burns Paiute Indian Reservation following a joint hearing before the Burns Paiute Tribal Court. The trial court ordered the Appellants excluded from the Burns Paiute Indian

Reservation finding each Appellant violated the following sections of the tribe's Exclusion Ordinance which provides that;

> Any person, except a tribal member, may be excluded from the Burns Paiute Indian Reservation for committing any of the following acts:
>> a. the violation of any tribal law or ordinance;
>> b. the violation of any federal or state law; . . .
>> e. any other act that harms the health, welfare, safety, morals, image, cultural traditions, or spirit of the Burns Paiute Tribe.

The trial court found that Appellants, who were members of the Burns Paiute Tribe, had violated tribal laws or ordinances, both traffic and criminal. . . . The Appellants had excessively used alcohol although they were not arrested and their conduct after drinking alcohol was judged harmful to the health, welfare, safety and image of the Burns Paiute Tribe. The trial judge ordered them excluded from the reservation. The judge . . . directed [tribal] officers to take the Appellants to their homes to allow the Appellants fifteen minutes to gather what personal effects they could take and then escort them off the reservation.

The Appellants are Indian men who have lived on the Burns Paiute Reservation between two and seven years. They each live with a woman who is an enrolled member of the tribe. Two of the Appellants are married and one lives as man and wife. One of the Appellants has fathered a child who is an enrolled member of the tribe. Another Appellant is the stepfather of his wife's three children, and considered to be the children's psychological father. The children are enrolled members of the tribe, whom he supports and treats as his own. All of the Appellants have also established close ties with other members of the Burns Paiute Indian community. They are helpful to and voluntarily perform various chores for others in the community. They drive their neighbors to town, take them shopping, cut wood, cut and trim their lawns and perform other chores as needed. They are all employed doing seasonal work for the Forest Service. . . .

Appellants claim that they are arbitrarily singled out for exclusion, that other nonenrolled persons who have criminal convictions, frequent the reservation and no effort has been made to exclude them. They claim this is selective enforcement of the law in violation of their right to equal protection as provided by 25 USCA Section 1302 (8) and Article 8, Section (h) of the Burns Paiute Constitution.

This Court finds that in order for Appellants to show selective or discriminatory enforcement of the exclusion ordinance they must establish (1) that the respondent has not excluded others similarly situated for similar conduct and (2) the decision to exclude was based upon bad faith, or on impermissible grounds as, for example race, religion or the exercise of other constitutional rights.

The Appellants provided criminal records of non-members who frequent the reservation against whom petitions for exclusion have not been filed. They offered no evidence that the decision to exclude them was based on impermissible grounds or bad faith in violation of their rights under the Indian Civil Rights Act of 1968, 25 USCA 1302 (hereinafter ICRA).

The due process clause of the Indian Civil Rights Act of 1968 protects individual rights including "liberty." One aspect of liberty is the right to associate with persons of one's choice. . . . The Court of Appeals finds that the relationship between the Appellants and their wives and children are highly personal relationships and protected under the liberty provision of the due process clause of the ICRA. The trial court committed reversible error by ordering Appellants excluded from the reservation without considering these relationships and the serious, resulting breakup of the Appellants families and the effect on the tribal community.

This Court finds that the Tribe's exclusion ordinance was not sufficiently explicit to inform those who are subject to it what conduct will render them liable to its penalties. The unfairness of failure to notify potential defendants of the law's scope and reach can constitute a denial of due process. . . .

The Court of Appeals also finds that the exclusion ordinance is too broadly written. Under its provisions a non-tribal member could be excluded for committing a parking violation on the reservation or having committed an infraction in Florida. Sections (a) and (b). There is no rational basis for these sections to be so broadly written. A law is void for vagueness if it is framed in terms so vague that persons of common intelligence must necessarily guess at its meaning and differ as to its applicability. . . .

The Appellees argue that the ordinance could be interpreted in that manner but it was not the tribe's policy to do so. Counsel for Appellee was unable to answer the Court's query regarding what notice to a non-member would advise him/her or what conduct would make him/her a candidate for exclusion. . . .

The Burns Paiute Exclusion Ordinance as applied to Appellants is unconstitutionally overbroad [and] in violation of the equal protection and due process clauses of the ICRA.

NOTE

The fact pattern in *Penn v. United States*, 335 F.3d 786 (8th Cir. 2003), a federal court challenge to a tribal court exclusion order, is as compelling as it is troubling:

> Margaret Penn is one-eighth Turtle Mountain Chippewa Indian but is not enrolled in any Indian tribe, thus her status is that of a non-Indian. At all times relevant to this action Penn lived on land that was within the Standing Rock Sioux Indian Reservation but owned in fee by a non-Indian rancher. Penn is a lawyer who was chief prosecutor on the reservation until she was fired by tribal officials in August 1996. After her termination, Penn began working for Tender Hearts Against Family Violence, a nonprofit corporation serving the reservation. While employed at Tender Hearts, Penn filed a wrongful termination suit in tribal court against the tribe, the tribal chairman, the tribal council members, the chief judge, and others. In July 1998, recently terminated employees and members of the board of directors coordinated to oust Tender Hearts Director Kathy Smith. Penn was appointed by and a supporter of Smith. On July 24, 1998, Faith Taken Alive, the co-director of Tender Hearts, petitioned the Standing Rock Tribal Court for a "Traditional Custom Restraining Order." The petition alleged that Penn had a gun, had made threats against

tribal officials, and had filed a multimillion dollar lawsuit against the tribe. Without holding a hearing and relying solely on the uncorroborated, unsworn petition, Judge Isaac Dog Eagle issued a temporary restraining order excluding Penn from the reservation for thirty days. The July 24, 1998, order directed "any Police Officer" to "execute the Order of this Court and escort Margaret Penn from the Standing Rock Sioux Indian reservation boundaries." Although the order stated that a hearing would be scheduled at the conclusion of the thirty days, no hearing was ever held.

Bureau of Indian Affairs (BIA) Captain John Vettleson received the order from the tribal court on July 24. . . . Captain Vettleson consulted with BIA Standing Rock Superintendent Larry Bodin and BIA District Commander Richard Armstrong regarding the legality of the order. Each advised him to serve the order. . . . Captain Vettleson . . . then followed Penn as she drove her vehicle to the reservation boundary.

Id. at 787-88. Penn's federal claims failed. But what about an equal protection claim in tribal court? Or a due process claim? Would Ms. Penn have a valid claim under these facts if she sued under the Indian Civil Rights Act?

2. THE FREEDMEN

ALLEN v. CHEROKEE NATION TRIBAL COUNCIL

Cherokee Nation Judicial Appeals Tribunal, No. JAT-04-09, 6 Am. Tribal Law 18
(March 7, 2006)

STACY L. LEEDS, Justice.

Petitioner Lucy Allen is a descendant of individuals listed on the Dawes Commission Rolls as "Cherokee Freedmen." To become a tribal member under the current legislation, she must prove she is "Cherokee by blood." She asks this Court to declare 11 C.N.C.A. §12 unconstitutional because it is more restrictive than the membership criteria set forth in Article III of the 1975 Constitution. . . .

The Power of the Cherokee People

The Cherokee citizenry has the ultimate authority to define tribal citizenship. When they adopted the 1975 Constitution, they did not limit membership to people who possess Cherokee blood. Instead, they extended membership to all the people who were "citizens" of the Cherokee Nation as listed on the Dawes Commission Rolls.

The Constitution could be amended to require that all tribal members possess Cherokee blood. The people could also choose to set a minimum Cherokee blood quantum. However, if the Cherokee people wish to limit tribal citizenship, and such limitation would terminate the preexisting citizenship of even one Cherokee citizen, then it must be done in the open. It cannot be accomplished through silence.

The Council lacks the power to redefine tribal membership absent a constitutional amendment. The Council is empowered to enact enrollment procedures, but those laws must be consistent with the 1975 Constitution. The current legislation is contrary to the plain language of the 1975 Constitution.

The 1975 Cherokee Constitution

Article III of the 1975 Constitution defines eligibility for tribal membership very broadly:

> All members of the Cherokee Nation must be *citizens* as proven by reference to the Dawes Commission Rolls, including the Delaware Cherokees of Article II of the Delaware Agreement dated the 8th day of May 1867, and the Shawnee Cherokees as of Article III of the Shawnee Agreement dated the 9th day of June, 1869, and/or their descendants. ([E]mphasis added.)

There is simply no "by blood" requirement in Article III. There is no ambiguity to resolve. The words "by blood" or "Cherokee by blood" do not appear.

Article III only requires proof of citizenship by referencing the "Dawes Commission Rolls." Article III does not exclude anyone who is listed on the Dawes Commission Rolls.

It is important to note that the phrase "Dawes Commission Rolls" is plural. While the overwhelming majority of people on the Dawes rolls are Cherokee by blood, the rolls also include other people who the Cherokee Nation recognized as citizens at the time the Dawes rolls were compiled. Membership is not limited, in Article III, to those individuals only appearing on the "Cherokee by blood" pages of the Dawes rolls. . . .

If the Freedmen's citizenship rights existed on the very night before the 1975 Constitution was approved, then they must necessarily survive today. These rights were not terminated by the adoption of the 1975 Constitution. In fact, the 1975 Constitution affirms these rights by linking citizenship to one single document: the Dawes Commission Rolls.

The Disputed Legislation

The disputed legislation sets forth "membership requirements" in 11 C.N.C.A. §12. These "membership requirements" are more restrictive than the "membership" provision of Article III. 11 C.N.C.A. §12 states:

> A. Tribal membership is derived only through proof of Cherokee blood based on the Final Rolls.
> B. The Registrar will issue tribal membership to a person who can prove that he or she is an original enrollee listed on the Final Rolls by blood or who can prove . . . at least one direct ancestor listed by blood on the Final Rolls.

This legislation adds new and more restrictive membership requirements than those found in the Constitution. The legislation in subsection (A) states that "tribal membership is derived only through proof of Cherokee blood." This is contrary to the plain language of the Constitution.

In subsection (B), the legislation requires proof of lineage "by blood." This too is contrary to the plain language of Article III, which lacks any "blood" requirement whatsoever. The Constitution only requires proof of lineage from a "citizen." It does not require proof of Cherokee or Indian blood.

Providing proof of Cherokee blood is clearly one way to become a member. It is not the only way to prove membership. In fact, Article III expressly mentions the Shawnee and Delaware, who possess some Indian blood, but not

Cherokee blood. The Shawnee and Delaware are not citizens "by blood" of the Cherokee Nation.

Article III expressly includes all people[] who can prove that they were "citizens" on the Dawes Commission Rolls with no mention (one way or the other) about Cherokee or Indian blood quantum. The Cherokee Freedmen, the Shawnee and Delaware were all citizens at the time the Dawes rolls were finalized and they all continue as citizens to this day. . . .

The Dawes Commission Rolls

The Dawes Commission Rolls were not created by the federal government from scratch. When the Dawes Commission compiled the rolls, they referred to previous Cherokee Nation census records which also included a broad citizenry. Most of the people listed on the Dawes Rolls will also appear on the Cherokee Nation's own tribally controlled censuses that pre-date the Dawes rolls. The Cherokee Nation's own censuses included Freedmen in addition to "native Cherokees," intermarried whites, and Indians of other tribes, all of whom were recognized by the Cherokee Nation as citizens. The 1975 Constitution makes no reference to these tribal rolls, but instead, relies on the Dawes Rolls for inclusion and exclusion.

The Dawes Commission Rolls are the final citizenship rolls of the Cherokee Nation. On the basis of their Cherokee citizenship, the people who were listed on these rolls were entitled to allotments from the Cherokee Nation, including the Cherokee Freedmen. The Dawes Rolls include several groups of people and are not limited to Cherokees by blood. . . .

The Cherokee Nation is a Sovereign. The Cherokee Nation is much more than just a group of families with a common ancestry. For almost 150 years, the Cherokee Nation has included not only citizens that are Cherokee by blood, but also citizens who have origins in other Indian nations and/or African and/or European ancestry. Many of these citizens are mixed race and a small minority of these citizens possess no Cherokee blood at all.

People will always disagree on who is culturally Cherokee and who possesses enough Cherokee blood to be "racially" Indian. It is not the role of this Court to engage in these political or social debates. This Court must interpret the law as it is plainly written in our Constitution. . . .

The laws of the other four tribes that appeared on the Dawes Commission Rolls are not, of course, binding on the Cherokee Nation. The constitutions of the other tribes are instructive, however, in terms of the type of language that would be required to clearly terminate Freedmen citizenship rights.

In 1979, the Muscogee (Creek) Nation adopted a new Constitution that provided: "Each Muscogee (Creek) Indian by blood shall have the opportunity for citizenship in the Muscogee (Creek) Nation." [Constitution of the Muscogee (Creek) Nation, Art. II, Section 1 (1979).] In doing so, the Muscogee (Creek) Nation excluded Freedmen unless that individual can also prove Creek Indian blood pursuant to Muscogee (Creek) law.

In 1983, the Choctaw Nation of Oklahoma adopted a new constitution that limited membership to "all Choctaw Indians by blood whose names appear on the final rolls of the Choctaw Nation." [Constitution of the Choctaw Nation of Oklahoma, Article II, Section 1 (1983).] In doing so, the Choctaws decided to reference the Dawes Commission Rolls for membership, but they were very clear that they were only using those pages that list "Choctaws by blood." This clearly excluded the Choctaw Freedmen.

The Chickasaw Nation Constitution restricts citizenship to "Chickasaw Indians by blood" who are listed on the Dawes Commission final rolls. [Constitution of the Chickasaw Nation, Article II, Section 1 (1990).] They clarified exactly which portion of the Dawes Commission Rolls that could be referenced.

The language in the Choctaw, Chickasaw and Muscogee (Creek) Nation constitutions makes it unmistakably clear that membership is limited to their citizens "by blood" only. The Cherokee Constitution is a completely different matter. It lacks the type of clear language to terminate the pre-existing citizenship rights of the Freedmen. . . .

Drafting the 1975 Constitution

The dissenting opinion spends significant time discussing the "intent of the framers." The dissent improperly focuses on the Preamble of the Constitution rather than on the membership provisions of Article III. The dissent suggests that the individuals who drafted the 1975 Constitution intended to exclude the Cherokee Freedmen as a means of preserving tribal culture. The dissent then speaks in terms of "Cherokee Indian identity" and of "common character and ancestry." . . .

A truly "Cherokee" Nation, in a strictly cultural sense, might have limited citizenship to Cherokee ancestry and/or required a cultural tie to clan, religion or language. The 1975 Constitution does none of these things. . . .

The dissent's discussion of the intent of the framers lacks historical context. If this Court is to engage in a retrospective review of what the framer's thought, it should also focus on what those people knew, or must have known, about the citizenship status of the Cherokee Freedmen. The individuals who drafted the 1975 Constitution were well-educated and some were attorneys. They were familiar with Cherokee Nation legal history. When they included a direct reference to the Dawes Commission Rolls in the 1975 Constitution, they knew the Cherokee Freedmen were included in that document.

These individuals were also familiar with Cherokee history under the 1839 Constitution, the Cherokee Nation's treaties and agreements, and the allotment process. The authors could not have been unaware of the citizenship status of Cherokee Freedmen. At that point in time, the Cherokee Freedmen had been legal citizens of the Cherokee Nation for 110 years.

On the eve of the new 1975 constitution, the Cherokee Nation would have been very mindful of the citizenship rights of Cherokee Freedmen. Those rights had just been the subject of two federal court cases in which the Cherokee Nation participated. Both of these cases were concluded just a few years before the 1975 Constitution was drafted.

(1) In 1967, the United States Court of Claims ruled that the Cherokee Freedmen were entitled to receive payments from the Cherokee Nation judgment fund like any other Cherokee citizen listed on the Dawes Commission Rolls. [*Cherokee Nation v. US*, 180 Ct. Cl. 181 (1967), *affirming*, 12 Ind. Cl. Comm. 570 (1963).]

(2) In 1971, a small group of individuals who were not listed on the Dawes Commission Rolls tried to be included in these payments. This group argued that they were Freedmen who were inadvertently left off the Dawes Rolls. The federal court rejected their claims. [*Cherokee Freedmen & Cherokee Freedmen's Association v. the United States and the Cherokee Nation*, 195 Ct. Cl. 39, 1971 WL 17825 (1971).] Only those Freedmen that are actually listed on the Dawes Rolls were entitled to share in Cherokee Nation funds. This case reaffirms the notion that the Dawes Rolls (in their entirety) are the final citizenship rolls of the Cherokee Nation. . . .

In light of this long and consistent history, the 1975 Constitution was adopted with a membership provision which includes "citizens" and descendants of the Dawes Commission Rolls. If the Cherokee Freedmen are to be treated differently than all the other people on the rolls, then specific language should demonstrate that the Freedmen were being excluded. There is no such language.

Further Discussion of the 1866 Treaty

It has been argued that the Cherokee Freedmen were forced on the Cherokee Nation by the federal government and that the Cherokee Nation never voluntarily accepted the Freedmen as citizens. This is simply not the case.

In the Treaty of 1866, the Cherokee Nation agreed to extend citizenship to Freedmen and agreed to give them the same rights as "native" Cherokees. Although this treaty was signed at the end of the Civil War, when the Cherokee Nation was in a weaker bargaining position, it is nonetheless an agreement between two sovereign nations.

When the Cherokee Nation enters into treaties with other nations, we expect the other sovereign to live up to the promises they make. It is rightly expected that we will also keep the promises we make.

It cannot be overstated that the 1866 Treaty, in which the Cherokee Nation agreed to extend citizenship to the Freedmen[,] is the exact same treaty where the Cherokee Nation agreed to have other Indian tribes (ultimately the Shawnee and Delaware) relocated inside the Cherokee Nation. After the 1866 Treaty, the Cherokee Nation amended the 1839 Constitution to extend citizenship to the Freedmen as a matter of tribal law. After the 1866 Treaty, the Cherokee Nation also entered into individual treaties with both the Delaware and the Shawnee Indian tribes. Both of these actions show that the Cherokee Nation complied with the terms of 1866 Treaty. . . .

However, if the Cherokee Nation is going to make a decision not to abide by a previous treaty provision, it must do so by clear actions which are consistent with the Cherokee Nation Constitution. A treaty provision cannot be set aside by mere implication. This treaty discussion leads to the same conclusion as the constitutional discussion. If the Cherokee people want to change the legal definition of Cherokee citizenship, they must do so expressly. . . .

The *Riggs* Decision

In *Riggs v. Ummerteskee*, JAT 97-03, 3 Am. Tribal Law 10, 2001 WL 36155524 (2001), this Court ruled that 11 C.N.C.A. §12 was constitutional. At the time Riggs was decided it was a case of first impression under the 1975 Constitution.

The *Riggs* Court was presented with federal court decisions that had repeatedly upheld the citizenship rights of Cherokee Freedmen class. Those federal decisions were based on the federal treaty interpretation, federal interpretation of the 1839 Cherokee Constitution, and the federal documents from the Dawes Commission.

I agree with the *Riggs* Court on one point: citizenship is an internal matter for the Cherokee citizenry to ultimately decide. I do not fault the *Riggs* Court for basing their decision solely on the 1975 Constitution. I must, however, respectfully disagree with the *Riggs* Court's interpretation of the Constitution. The conclusion of *Riggs* Court is contrary to the plain language of Article III of the 1975 Constitution. If Article III was intended to limit membership to citizens "by blood," it should have said so.

[A] legislative act [must] be held unconstitutional if it adds new requirements to a constitutional provision. 11 C.N.C.A. §12 adds a "by blood" requirement that simply does not exist in Article III.

11 C.N.C.A. §12 is hereby deemed unconstitutional. This Court's decision in *Riggs v. Ummerteskee* is hereby reversed.

IT IS SO ORDERED.

[Special concurring opinion by Justice Dowty and dissenting opinion by Chief Justice Matlock omitted.]

NOTES

1. Shortly after the Cherokee high court issued the *Allen* decision, the Cherokee voters voted to amend the Cherokee Constitution to disqualify many of the Cherokee Freedmen from citizenship. *See In re Written Protest against the Initiative Petition "Proposing an Amendment to Article IV, Section 1 of the Cherokee Constitution of 1999 and Article III, Section 1 of the Cherokee Constitution of 1975,"* 6 Am. Tribal Law 39 (Cherokee Nation Judicial Appeals Tribunal 2006); *In re: Status and Implementation of the 1999 Constitution of the Cherokee Nation*, 9 Okla. Trib. 394, 6 Am. Tribal Law 63 (Cherokee 2006).

2. In *Graham v. Muscogee (Creek) Nation Citizenship Board*, No. CV 2003-53 (Muscogee (Creek) Nation District Court 2006), the court vacated a tribal citizenship board decision to deny citizenship to a Freedmen applicant and ordered the board to reconsider the application, but the Muscogee (Creek) Supreme Court summarily reversed the district court. *See Muscogee (Creek) Nation Citizenship Board v. Graham*, No. SC-2006-03 (Muscogee (Creek) Nation Supreme Court 2006).

3. DRUG TESTING

LOUCHART v. MASHANTUCKET PEQUOT GAMING COMMISSION

Mashantucket Pequot Tribal Court, No. MPTC-EA-99-105, 27 Indian L. Rep. 6176
(June 17, 1999)

The opinion of the court was delivered by: [Jill Tompkins], C.J.

[T]he plaintiff, Matthew Louchart, challenges the decision of the President/CEO of the Mashantucket Pequot Gaming Enterprise (hereinafter

"Gaming Enterprise") to suspend him from his employment as a Blackjack Floor Supervisor in the defendant's Gaming Department.

I. Factual Background

. . . Sometime prior to March 1998, the Mashantucket Pequot Tribal Gaming Commission and the Connecticut State Police commenced an investigation of two Foxwoods Resort Casino employees, Tracey Macri and Miguel Rivera, for illegal drug activities. . . . Macri was described to investigators as "having a severe addiction to cocaine" . . . and was thought to possibly be assisting Rivera in the distribution of drugs on Gaming Enterprise property. . . . A composite videotape showed Macri and Louchart walking together around a corner and into view. . . . After a few steps down the hallway toward the camera, Louchart reached into an inside breast pocket and withdrew a small package which he then placed into Macri's hand. . . . The contents of the package were not identified by the Gaming Enterprise. . . .

Sometime between March 1, 1998 and August 25, 1998, Rivera was arrested by the Connecticut State Police and Macri was terminated from employment for "drug-related activities." . . . The plaintiff was interviewed by Robert M. Hargraves, Sr., Special Investigator for the Compliance Department of Foxwoods Resort Casino, on August 25, 1998, "regarding his association and/or relationship with Tracey Macri." . . .

Louchart was advised that he would be given a drug test on Wednesday morning, August 26, 1998. . . . The plaintiff, upon hearing this, notified Hargraves that he would fail the test as he had smoked marijuana on August 9, 1998 during his vacation in Aruba which took place from July 29th to August 10th. . . . On August 26th at 9:00 a.m., Louchart appeared at the Compliance Office and met Allen Longendyke of the Gaming Enterprise's Employee Relations Office at the Nurse's Station to take his drug test. . . . The Employee Health Services "Drug Free Workplace Compliance and Duty Assessment Form" contains a section in which to indicate Drug Free Workplace compliance. The option "Does Not Comply" is marked on the form for Matthew Louchart's August 26, 1998 urine screen. . . .

On September 9, 1998, the plaintiff was suspended pending further investigation for misconduct, namely "failure to comply with the Drug Free Workplace Policy." . . .

The President/CEO issued written findings of fact and conclusions of law by memorandum dated January 6, 1999. . . . He found that:

> I . . . believe that the employee did fail the drug test in violation of the Standards of Conduct for the following reasons: . . .

. . . The President/CEO . . . recommended that the termination be reduced to a suspension with no back pay. He further stated that, "Compliance with EAP and continued drug testing should be a condition of continued employment." . . .

II. Conclusions of Law

This Court's role in reviewing an appeal by a Gaming Enterprise employee brought under the Law's provisions is to determine whether the President/CEO acted arbitrarily, capriciously or in abuse of his discretion. VIII M.P.T.L. ch. 1, §8(d), *Chickering v. Mashantucket Pequot Gaming Enterprise*, 1 MPR 41 (1998). . . .

This Court "may not retry the case or 'second guess' the decision of management . . . [; however, it is the law] that a court has the duty to decide whether, 'in its mind,' there is sufficient evidence in the record to support management's decision." *Flint v. Mashantucket Pequot Gaming Enterprise*, 1 MPR 43, 44 (1998). The Mashantucket Pequot Court of Appeals held in *Healy v. Mashantucket Pequot Gaming Enterprise*, 1 MPR 63, 66 (1999) that the Mashantucket Pequot judiciary possesses "authority to review under the [Indian Civil Rights Act, 25 U.S.C. §1302] the Gaming Enterprise's actions in the application and implementation of the Tribal Council's enactments relating to employer-employee relationships." A challenge to an employment disciplinary action involving a claim of a violation of the rights secured by the Indian Civil Rights Act is subject to the general test of whether the error is "more probably than not harmless," unless "there has been a significant deviation from a constitutional rule or a specific statutory requirement, [where] plain error exists and reversal is automatic." *Grossi v. Mashantucket Pequot Gaming Enterprise*, 1 MPR 55, 56 (1998).

The plaintiff raises three grounds for his appeal: first, that the Gaming Enterprise did not possess reasonable cause to believe that he was under the influence of drugs or in possession of the same, and that requiring him to undergo a drug test was a violation of its own policy; second, that the Gaming Enterprise's conduct in requiring him to undergo a drug test, without reasonable cause to believe that he was under the influence of, or in possession of, drugs violated his rights under Sections 1302(2) and (8) of the Indian Civil Rights Act; third, even if the drug test was appropriate, there was still no reasonable basis to conclude that he violated the "Substance and Alcohol Abuse and Drug Testing" policy or other Gaming Enterprise work rules, standards of conduct, or conditions of employment. The Court agrees with the plaintiff that the Gaming Enterprise did not have a reasonable suspicion that he was under the influence of drugs or alcohol which adversely affected or could have adversely affected his job performance and, thus, the requirement that he undergo a drug test was in violation of its own drug testing policy. Without the drug test, there is no reasonable basis for the President/CEO's decision to suspend the employee.

The Indian Civil Rights Act provides that: "No Indian tribe in exercising powers of self-government shall— . . . (2) violate the right of the people to be secure in their persons, houses, papers and effects against unreasonable search and seizures[;] . . . (8) . . . deprive any person of liberty or property without due process of law. 25 U.S.C. §1302 (2) and (8). The Mashantucket Pequot Tribal Council adopted the provisions of the Indian Civil Rights Act in 1993 as "tribal law" which "shall apply in the Tribal Court." *Healy* at 66, I M.P.T.L. ch. 3 §10(a). "To help ensure a safe and healthful working environment . . . ," the Mashantucket Pequot Tribal Nation has adopted for Gaming Enterprise employees a "Substance and Alcohol Abuse and Drug Testing" Policy (hereinafter "Drug Testing Policy"). . . . The Drug Testing Policy states that the Gaming Enterprise "prohibits any employee from having, selling, making or using any illegal drugs on Foxwoods Resort Casino premises or while conducting business off the premises." *Id.* There is no allegation that the plaintiff engaged in any of the enumerated prohibited acts. Further, the Drug Testing Policy provides, in pertinent part, that: "If Foxwoods Resort Casino has a reasonable suspicion that an employee is under the influence of drugs or alcohol which adversely affects or could adversely affect such employee's job performance, Foxwoods Resort Casino may require such employee to submit to a drug test. Refusal to submit to a drug test may result in disciplinary action, up to and including termination of employment." *Id.* . . .

The Drug Testing Policy does not define the term "reasonable cause." Section XI provides that employee appeals must be decided in accordance with tribal law; however, where no tribal law exists with respect to a particular issue, the Court "may be guided but shall not be bound by the principles of law applicable to similar claims arising under the laws of the State of Connecticut or of the United States." VIII M.P.T.L. ch. 1. This Court is mindful that: "The guarantees afforded to individuals under the ICRA, such as the right to due process, are similar but not identical to those provided for under the United States Constitution. Both federal and tribal courts have acknowledged that Congress did not intend the due process principles of the Constitution to disrupt settled tribal customs and traditions." *Johnson*, 1 Mash. at 118. In this appeal, no Mashantucket Pequot custom or tradition has been argued to be implicated. Thus, the Court will look to general U.S. constitutional principles, as articulated by federal and Connecticut courts, for guidance in this matter. . . .

The term "reasonable suspicion" is defined by Black's Law Dictionary (6th ed. 1990) as a suspicion of illegal activity which "must be based on specific and articulable facts, which taken together with rational inferences from those facts, reasonably warrant intrusion." . . . Tribal courts have also relied upon Fourth Amendment standards in determining the propriety of searches under tribal law and the Indian Civil Rights Act. *Duckwater Shoshone Tribe v. Thompson*, 25 ILR 6131, 6132 (Duckwater Shoshone Tr. Ct., 1998) ("Federal Indian Law experts agree that 25 U.S.C. §1302(2), which nearly mirrors the Fourth Amendment, is derived from the U.S. Constitution. . . ."); *Southern Ute Tribe v. Scott*, 18 ILR 6105 (S. Ute Tr. Ct., 1991) (utilizes U.S. Supreme Court rulings to determine voluntariness of consent to search).

In this appeal, the only basis for subjecting the plaintiff to the drug test was his association with a suspected drug user, Macri, and the passing of an unidentified item to her in a hallway. . . . There is no evidence that the item was drugs. There is no allegation that the plaintiff exhibited any physical or behavioral symptoms indicative of drug or alcohol consumption. There is no evidence that his job performance or judgment was affected in any way. The record does not support a finding of "reasonable suspicion" that the plaintiff was under the influence of drugs or alcohol. Moreover, assuming arguendo the alleged "suspicious behavior" occurring on March 1, 1998 constituted reasonable suspicion that the plaintiff was under the influence of drugs, the drug test was not ordered until five and a half months later. The event allegedly giving rise to the suspicion of drug use was too far removed in time to provide a basis for a test over five months later. Fourth Amendment case law in the criminal context has established:

> Generally, the greater the interval between an observation of criminality and an application for a warrant, the more likely it is that circumstances will have changed so that probable cause no longer exists. . . . When the affidavit recites an isolated violation, probable cause dwindles in direct proportion to the passage of time.

American Bar Association Criminal Justice Section, Guidelines for the Issuance of Search Warrants, (1990) p. 26. . . . Likewise, in the drug testing situation there must be some freshness to the information giving rise to the suspicion that the employee is under the influence of drugs or alcohol. In this case, the delay of over five months renders the information regarding the plaintiff's suspicious behavior too stale to constitute reasonable suspicion to require a drug test.

The plaintiff's confession of arguably legal marijuana use in Aruba came only after the Gaming Enterprise ordered the plaintiff to undergo the drug test. The results of the drug test were obtained in violation of the Gaming Enterprise's Drug Testing Policy as there was no reasonable suspicion to support the testing in the first instance. The Court finds that, without the illegal drug test, the President/CEO had no reasonable basis for concluding that the plaintiff violated the applicable work rules, standards or other conditions of employment established by the Enterprise for the position held by the plaintiff. VIII M.P.T.L. ch. 1, §8(d)(1). Having found that a review of the record establishes that it is devoid of rational evidence to support the ordering of the drug test, this Court "has a responsibility in the interest of justice to set aside management's action [in suspending the plaintiff] as arbitrary and capricious." . . .

Accordingly, the plaintiff's appeal is sustained and the decision of the President/CEO is reversed.

NOTES

1. The Mashantucket appellate court affirmed the trial court on the narrow grounds that "without the drug test, the record is devoid of any rational evidence to affirm the decision to discipline the appellee." *Louchart v. Mashantucket Pequot Gaming Enterprise*, 4 Mash. Pequot Rep. 10, 11, 2000 WL 35571834 (Mashantucket Pequot Court of Appeals 2000).

2. In *Gourd v. Robertson*, 28 Indian L. Rep. 6047 (Spirit Lake Sioux Tribal Court 2001), the court reviewed the positive drug test of a tribal gaming management employee. The tribe had declared that all gaming manager positions were " 'sensitive' positions at the Casino" and, for that reason, gaming managers could be subjected to random drug tests. The tribal court concluded:

   > Casino managers are in sensitive positions where they frequently have access to casino revenues and are charged with supervising other staff. Failing to properly monitor these employees may endanger the tribe's gaming enterprise and violate the tribe's Class III Gaming Compact with the State of North Dakota. These concerns undoubt[ed]ly explain why the Casino had made them "subject to greater sampling" under the random testing policy.

Gourd, 28 Indian L. Rep. at 6048.

The tribal court nevertheless overturned the Plaintiff's discharge on the basis that he had not been subject to a "truly random" drug testing process as mandated by the personnel policy.

The tribal court discussed the validity of random drug testing of government employees in safety-sensitive positions in dicta. Emulating the federal courts' "safety-sensitive"–type analysis, the tribal court wrote:

> Courts have recognized that employment-related drug testing by a governmental entity is a search as defined under the Fourth Amendment and incorporated into the Indian Civil Rights Act. . . . In general, the Indian Civil Rights Act prevents searches without warrants unless they meet the reasonableness requirement of the Fourth Amendment. Warrantless drug urinalysis testing of employees in safety-sensitive jobs may be consonant with the Fourth Amendment where part of a systematic, uniformly applied testing program (such as random testing), . . . or where based on the employer's individualized "reasonable suspicion" of drug use by the employee.

Id. (citing *Nat'l Treasury Employees Union v. Von Raab*, 489 U.S. 656, 665 (1989); *Skinner v. Ry. Labor Executives' Ass'n*, 489 U.S. 602, 624 (1989)) (other citations omitted).

3. In *Puyallup Tribe v. VanEvery*, 8 NICS App. 85 (Puyallup Tribal Court of Appeals 2008), the court offered "guidance" on the question of the tribal constitutional right to privacy in the context of the drug testing of a tribal shellfish diver:

> [T]he United State Congress enacted the Indian Civil Rights Act of 1968. This Act grants Indians federal statutory rights against a tribal government that are similar to the federal constitutional rights that they have against the federal and state governments under the Bill of Rights and the Fourteenth Amendment. Among the various statutory rights granted by the Indian Civil Rights Act, two are particularly relevant to the present case. The Indian Civil Rights Act states, in relevant part, that "[n]o Indian tribe in exercising powers of self-government shall . . . (2) violate the right of the people to be secure in their persons, houses, papers, and effects against unreasonable search and seizures, . . . ; [or] (8) . . . deprive any person of liberty or property without due process of law." The language of these statutory rights parallel the constitutional language in which the United States Supreme Court has anchored the constitutional right of privacy against the federal and state governments. Presumably, it is to these statutory rights conferred by the Indian Civil Rights Act that the Tribal Court and the Appellee intended to refer when they opined that the Port Clinic procedure for collecting urine violated the Tribal shellfish diver's constitutional right of privacy.
>
> To examine this issue, we look to federal court interpretation of constitutional rights. We are not bound by these decisions, however[,] as the Navajo Supreme Court noted: U.S. Constitutional "protections are a product of moral principles, and our own morality and tribal customs frame such principles in the Navajo way." [*Plummer v. Plummer*, 17 Indian L. Rep. 6151 (Navajo 1990).] Assuming, *for the sake of argument*, that the statutory rights conferred by the Indian Civil Rights Act are equivalent in all respects to the constitutional rights that their language tracks, it is

reasonable to further assume that the legal analysis developed by the United States Supreme Court for determining whether a particular federal or state government test procedure violates a person's constitutional right to privacy can also be used to determine whether a particular tribal government test procedure violates a tribal member's statutory right to privacy under the Indian Civil Rights Act. Thus, to evaluate the claim that the Port Clinic's procedure for collecting urine violates a Tribal member's statutory right to privacy, we may be guided by a decision of the United States Supreme Court, *Skinner v. Railway Labor Executives' Association*, in which it considered whether a similar procedure violated the test subject's constitutional right to privacy. . . .

In our opinion, an analogous argument that the Port Clinic procedure does not violate a Tribal Shellfish diver's statutory right to privacy can be made on the facts of the present case. Shellfishing is an industry regulated by the Tribe. The Tribal government has an interest in regulating the conduct of shellfishing to ensure safety. The Tribal government's interest in safe shellfishing includes the safety of the Tribal shellfish divers. The Tribal government's interest in ensuring the safety of the shellfish divers themselves plainly justifies prohibiting Tribal shellfish divers from using alcohol or drugs, and this interest also requires and justifies the exercise of supervision to assure that the restrictions are in fact observed. Moreover, the urine samples are collected in a medical environment, by personnel unrelated to the diver's employer, and is thus not unlike similar procedures encountered often in the context of a regular physical examination. Finally, the expectations of privacy of Tribal shellfish divers are diminished by reason of their participation in an industry that is regulated to ensure safety. While the procedures for collecting urine samples in *Skinner* did not involve direct observation of the employee urinating, we do not believe that this difference would alter the result of the Supreme Court's analysis. The Supreme Court specifically noted *"the desirability of such a procedure to ensure the integrity of the sample."* Accordingly, we believe that Port Clinic procedure for collecting urine does not constitute an undue infringement on the justifiable expectations of privacy of the Tribal shellfish divers, and that the Tribal government's interest in reliable and accurate urine tests for Tribal shellfish divers outweighs their privacy concerns in this context.

VanEvery, 8 NICS App. at 89-90, 92.

Compare a shellfish diver to an office-bound tribal government employee. Should tribal courts apply different constitutional analyses depending on the job in question in the context of drug testing?

4. SAME-SEX MARRIAGE

The Coquille Indian Tribe, Same-Sex Marriage, and Spousal Benefits: A Practical Guide

Julie Bushyhead, 26 Ariz. J. Int'l & Comp. L. 509, 525-35 (2009)

Traditionally, many Indian tribes were not concerned with a member's sexual orientation. Instead, those Tribes focused on a person's contribution to the community, which was a product of his/her gender. For some Tribes, gender identity encompassed more than merely biological sex, but a person's spiritual gender identity. Approximately 155 Indian Tribes recognized a group of people anthropologists refer to as "two-spirit" people. These people could be modernly described as people who were neither male nor female but a third gender because they spiritually embodied both male and female genders. [T]his historic native tradition embraces the biological reality that not everyone fits into the inflexible gender categories of male and female. If society holds marriage superior on the basis that marriage is reserved for people of opposite sex, then the goal of "opposites" is thwarted by the biological reality that some people may be neither male nor female. Societal education about gender marks the beginning of change in societal views encompassing gender, sexual orientation, and discrimination. Tribes have the opportunity to illustrate flaws in restricting marriage to opposite sex couples by connecting with a historical native tradition of recognizing two-spirit people. Finally, this section discusses the Tribes' inherent authority to promulgate laws regulating domestic relations.

A. Traditional Tribal View on Same-Sex Marriage

Coquille Chief Ken Tanner stated that the Coquille Cultural Committee performed thorough research in response to several members' request to address the issue of same-sex marriage and spousal benefits. The Committee found that oral history concerning "lifestyle and tribal methods of relating" revealed "no exclusions for people, in any way, [who engaged] in same sex marriages." Brian Gilley, a respected anthropologist who has conducted extensive research concerning "gay identity and social acceptance in Indian country" stated that[] "sexuality really wasn't turning the social organization on its head like it was in Euro-American society." Gilley attributes this to the fact that for many native tribes, "who an individual had sex with was not necessarily the primary concern, [tribes] were more concerned about a person's potential contribution to the community." Moreover, a person's role in the community was determined by gender identity, not necessarily biological sex. One native tradition of recognizing "two-spirit" people, historically practiced in approximately 155 tribes, illustrates the idea that gender identity is wholly separate from sexual orientation.

The name "two-spirit" is an attempt to explain this tribal tradition in the English language. In fact, most tribes had different names for people who possessed both a male and a female spirit. These individuals "were seen as being able to bridge the personal and spiritual gap between men and women." This unique gender identity was viewed as a gift from the Great Spirit, which was also named differently depending on each tribe's religious practices. The Navajo Tribe valued two-spirit people because they were "gifted with a more complex and nuanced understanding of both the masculine and feminine." They were "seen as making a valuable contribution to the whole," and as such were "treated with respect, even reverence." Two-spirit people are most clearly described as people falling into a third gender. Gilley explains that "this third gender often embodied a mixture of the social, ceremonial, and economic roles of men and women." Two-spirit people were identified through a variety of methods. Generally, two-spirit people exercised a plethora of "spiritual roles in the community including serving as healers, ambassadors, teachers, matchmakers, parents to orphaned children, and mediators of disputes." Many two-spirit individuals would "adopt orphans . . . and raise them as their own." Gilley points out that "the structure that we would think of as a family [was] being replicated without regard to a person's sexual organs or sexuality." These two-spirit individuals were "members of [the] community and [were] showing their usefulness to society and their behavior [reflected] values of [the] community." As illustrated, gender was a product of a person's role in the community, and "who you had sex with was really more up to your preference." In other words, sexual orientation was a non-issue. . . .

B. Tribal Sovereignty

Tribal sovereignty represents a tribe's inherent authority to govern its people and territories using the "governmental and legal systems" each tribe creates or adopts for its own. While the federal government has continually narrowed tribal sovereignty, tribal governments retain their sovereignty and authority to self-govern to the extent not limited by Congress. Congress limits tribal sovereignty by imposing federal laws that divest tribes of "plenary and exclusive power over their members and their territory." In spite of federal limitations, Tribes retain the power to form their own government, determine tribal membership requirements, legislate, and levy taxes. Among these, tribes have the "undisturbed" power to regulate domestic relations affecting tribal members.

Inherent tribal authority over domestic relations permits tribes to "decide matters of domestic and family law within Indian Country. For example, tribes may make laws regarding the testate or intestate succession of a deceased tribal member's property. The American Indian Probate Reform Act (AIPRA) restricts this power only to the extent that the succession laws concern "trust and restricted lands." In addition, the United States Supreme Court recognizes tribal authority to grant valid marriage licenses and similarly dissolve tribal marriages. Given this broad authority, tribes have the power to define marriage as they choose. As such, even where a tribe adopts a definition of marriage contrary to the federal or state definitions, the tribe will prevail in defining marriage as it pertains to the tribe's members. In other words, "some Indian tribes could become islands of nonconforming law in an area where the American people appear to have spoken with finality."

Of the 562 federally recognized tribes, only a few tribal legislatures have attempted to more narrowly define marriage and consider the possibility of legalizing or banning same-sex marriage. Among these, the Cherokee and Navajo tribes have amended their marriage laws to explicitly define marriage as a union available only to persons of the opposite sex (i.e. marriage between one man and one woman). The Coquille Tribe is the only tribe to take legislative action to allow same-sex marriage. On May 8, 2008, the Coquille Indian Tribe adopted a Marriage and Domestic Partnership ordinance. . . .

The Coquille Tribe's marriage ordinance recognizes that the right to marry is a fundamental right regardless of biological sex. In approving and adopting this ordinance, the Coquille Tribe stated that recognizing "certain" domestic relationships regardless of biological sex is "essential" to preserve the "political integrity, economic security, and the health and welfare" of the Coquille community and its recognized members. The Tribe exemplifies the meaning of "political integrity" by adopting a definition of marriage that intelligently recognizes the wholly arbitrary requirement that the parties be of opposite sex — most assuredly in the face of national, Native and non-Native, opposition to same-sex marriage.

While the Tribe broadly defines domestic relationships, it does place a few eligibility requirements on the fundamental right to marry. The Tribe permits marriage where the couple meets three requirements. First, at least one partner must be a member of the Coquille Indian Tribe at the time the marriage license is issued and at the time the marriage is solemnized. Second, both partners must be at least eighteen years of age at the time of marriage. Third, the partners must not be related by blood, "whether of the whole or half blood." Specifically, the couple must not be "first cousins or any nearer of kin," unless they are cousins by adoption only. In the situation where the partners are cousins by adoption only, the Tribe does not prohibit their marriage provided the other two requirements are met. The Tribe specifies that even where a couple meets the above three requirements, the marriage may be void or voidable in some situations.

The Tribe prohibits marriages where either party to the marriage has a current spouse or domestic partner living at the time of the marriage. This would potentially exclude those instances where a couple dissolved their previous marriage or domestic partnership prior to the marriage in question. The Tribe also has the power to annul marriages where one of the partners is incapable of making a marriage contract because of insufficient capacity due to minority or insufficient ability to understand the nature of the contract. Further, the Tribe may annul marriages where either party procured consent of the other by "fraud or force." In these instances where a marriage contract is voidable, any action by the Tribe to annul a marriage does not relieve the partners of a "married" status for purposes of spousal support and property settlement as required by Tribal law.

The Tribe also provides that it will recognize some marriages and domestic partnerships from other jurisdictions for the purpose of providing Tribal benefits. The Tribe limits this recognition to marriages and domestic partnerships where one of the parties is a member of the Coquille Tribe, both parties are eighteen (18) or older, the parties are not related by blood (excluding first cousins by adoption), providing benefits is not prohibited by federal law, and the parties present "adequate" proof of their marriage or domestic partnership. While the purpose of recognizing marriages and domestic partnerships involving a Coquille Tribal member is to provide spousal benefits, this ordinance does not limit the Tribal Council's authority to alter or eliminate the benefits available to spouses or domestic partners of Coquille members.

Just as the Coquille Tribe is making an effort to resist discrimination against same-sex couples in the community, Oregon is taking steps to recognize the "lasting, committed, caring and faithful relationships" formed by many "Gay and Lesbian Oregonians." . . .

What does it mean for same-sex couples that obtain a marriage license from the Coquille Tribe? These couples are in a unique position because of their ability to obtain benefits under the Coquille Indian Tribe, and in addition, obtain benefits as Oregon residents. Same-sex couples that obtain a marriage license from the Coquille Indian Tribe assume the respected status of "married." In addition, if these couples apply for domestic partnership status under Oregon law, they are eligible for spousal benefits under Tribal law and Oregon law. In contrast, other Oregonian same-sex couples that apply for domestic partnership status under the Oregon Family Fairness Act will not be considered "married" but domestic partners. While these couples will enjoy all the benefits afforded to married spouses under state law, they are denied the equal recognition of being married. Though the inequality suffered by couples married by the Coquille Tribe is arguably less than those united by a domestic partnership status under Oregon law, neither the Coquille couple nor the Oregon couple will be eligible for federal benefits such as Social Security. If and when other Tribes decide to enact laws making marriage available to couples regardless of biological sex, the result may differ depending on the state marriage/domestic partnership laws where the Tribe is located. Oregon, like California, enacted a domestic partnership law extending all statutorily created spousal rights afforded to married spouses to domestic partners. Whereas, same-sex couples married by a Tribe in Oklahoma would not enjoy any state or federal benefits; these couples would be reliant on the Tribe's extension of benefits alone. . . .

NOTES

1. The relevant Coquille Tribe laws are as follows:

> **Marriages and Domestic Partners (or "Marriage" or "Domestic Partnership")** means a formal and express civil contract entered into between two persons, regardless of their sex, who are at least 18 years of age, who are otherwise capable of entering a Marriage or a Domestic Partnership (as provided below), and at least one of whom is a member of the Coquille Indian Tribe. For the purposes of this definition, "Domestic Partners" includes without limitation, persons engaged in domestic partnerships or civil unions.

COQUILLE TRIBAL REGULATION §7410.010(3)(b) (2008) (emphasis in original). And:

> Any person seeking to have their Marriage or Domestic Partnership recognized by the Tribe must apply to the Tribal Member Services Program, and provide a certified copy of their marriage or domestic partnership license from a recognized jurisdiction. In the event of a question as to whether the license meets the requirements set forth in CITC 740.030, the decision of the Tribal Member Services Program is final.

COQUILLE TRIBAL REGULATION §7410.050 (2008).

2. Conversely, the Navajo Nation and the Cherokee Nation of Oklahoma each enacted bans on same-sex marriage. *See* Matthew L. M. Fletcher, *Same-Sex Marriage, Indian Tribes, and the Constitution*, 61 U. MIAMI L. REV. 53, 55 (2006). The Cherokee legislature enacted its statute *after* Kathy Reynolds and Dawn McKinley applied for a marriage license. *See* Christopher L. Kannady, *The State, Cherokee Nation, and Same-Sex Unions:* In re: Marriage License of

McKinley & Reynolds, 29 AM. INDIAN L. REV. 363, 368 (2004-2005). Litigation over the validity of the McKinley and Reynolds marriage ended on procedural grounds in favor of the marriage in 2006. *See In re: Marriage License of McKinley and Reynolds*, No. JAT-06-01 (Cherokee 2006); *Anglen v. McKinley*, No. JAT-05-11 (Cherokee 2005).

3. Navajo people continue to be split over the so-called Anderson legislation, enacted by the Navajo Nation tribal council over a veto by Chairman Joe Shirley. One commentator wrote:

> More recently, in the fall of 2007, one of the topics presented at the Diné Policy Institute was "family, marriage, and the Diné Marriage Act." The day-long session, which was conducted primarily in the Navajo language, resulted in an almost unified agreement among the participants that Navajos had traditionally recognized more than two genders. They also agreed that a third gender, the "nádleehí," was a person who had been valued in Navajo society. There were sharp disagreements on whether the "nádleehí" had engaged in same-sex sexual activity. Moreover, at least two Navajos questioned the link being made between the "nádleehí" and modern-day gay and lesbian. Traditional Navajos involved in the discussion readily cited creation narratives to make their points about traditional Navajo practices around marriage, sexuality, family, and homosexuality.

Jennifer Nez Denetdale, *Securing Navajo National Boundaries: War, Patriotism, Tradition, and the Diné Marriage Act of 2005*, 24:2 WICASO SA REV. 131, 142 (2009).

E. CIVIL RIGHTS AND SOVEREIGN IMMUNITY

MCCORMICK V. ELECTION COMMITTEE OF SAC AND FOX TRIBE OF INDIANS OF OKLAHOMA

Court of Indian Offenses for the Sac and Fox Tribe, 1 Oklahoma Tribal Court Rep. 8, 1980 WL 128844 (February 1, 1980)

PIPESTEM, Chief Magistrate.

Plaintiff brought this action in the Court of Indian Offenses of the Anadarko Area Office sitting at the Shawnee Indian Agency for the Sac and Fox Tribe of Oklahoma on October 9, 1979. The Plaintiff alleges that she is the duly elected Principal Chief of the Sac and Fox Tribe of Indians of Oklahoma, and that the Sac and Fox Election Committee and its members, individually and in their official capacities, have violated the rights guaranteed to the Plaintiff by the Tribal Constitution and Election Ordinance, the Oklahoma Constitution and laws as made applicable by the Tribal Constitution and Election Ordinance, and the Constitution of the United States when the Election Committee declared the election in controversy void due to alleged voter irregularities and called for a new election.

Defendant Gwendolynn McCormick filed an answer to Plaintiff's Complaint pro se in which she admits the facts as alleged in the Complaint. Defendant Cecilia Littlehead answered and generally denied the substance of the Complaint. Defendant Wanda Brown answered and interposed the defenses of sovereign immunity, the intra-tribal dispute doctrine, legislative and judicial privilege doctrine, exhaustion of administrative remedies doctrine, and entered a demurrer for failure to state a claim. Defendants Election Committee, Emery Foster, Pearl Rolette, Henrietta Massey, Rose Allen, Irene Allen Whitlow, Jane Hope Stevens, Etheline Dooley, Virginia I. York, and Geraldine Franklin entered their special appearance and moved to quash Plaintiff's Complaint relying on the intra-tribal dispute doctrine, the political question doctrine, and sovereign immunity. . . .

IV. Sovereign Immunity

Having determined that the Election Committee functions as an authorized arm of the Tribal government and that this Court exercises the inherent judicial powers of the Sac and Fox Tribe as a part of the tribal government, the issue of sovereign immunity may now be more adroitly addressed. This Court has no doubt that Congress has plenary authority to waive the Tribe's sovereign immunity, *Lone Wolf v. Hitchcock*, 187 U.S. 552 (1903); *Santa Clara Pueblo v. Martinez*, 436 U.S. 49 (1978), or that the appropriate Tribal legislative body could waive that immunity to the extent of allowing the Tribe to be sued in the Tribal Court. The question, then, is whether Congress or the Tribal legislature have waived that immunity to the extent that this suit may be maintained in this Court.

The Sac and Fox Tribe of Indians of Oklahoma is a federally recognized Indian tribe organized and functioning through a constitutional framework adopted by the tribe pursuant to the Oklahoma Indian Welfare Act, 25 U.S.C. §501 et seq. It is beyond cavil, and undisputed by any of the parties to this action, that the Sac and Fox Tribe of Indians is an Indian tribe possessed of the ordinary attributes of tribal sovereignty. Among the attributes of tribal sovereignty of Indian tribes like the Sac and Fox is the doctrine of sovereign immunity. *United States v. United States Fidelity & Guaranty Co.*, 309 U.S. 506, 512-13 (1940). In *Santa Clara Pueblo v. Martinez*, 436 U.S. 49, 58 (1978), the Supreme Court reiterated this now familiar principle that "Indian tribes have long been recognized as possessing the common-law immunity from suit traditionally enjoyed by sovereign powers." In invoking the doctrine of sovereign immunity, the tribes do so as an expression of the tribes' inherent legal status derived from tribal law and not as a delegation of authority from any other source.

In is settled law that an Indian tribe is protected by the doctrine of sovereign immunity unless Congress has unequivocally consented to a waiver of that immunity. . . . It is also settled law that an initial lawsuit may not be brought indirectly against a tribe by suing tribal officers or the United States as trustee for the tribe. *Seneca Constitutional Organization v. George*, 348 F. Supp. 48 (W.D. N.Y. 1972); *Barnes v. United States*, 205 F. Supp. 97 (D. Mont. 1962); *Adams v. Murphy*, 165 F. 304 (C.C.A. 1908); *Santa Clara Pueblo v. Martinez, supra.*

Plaintiff argues that the Supreme Court in *Santa Clara Pueblo v. Martinez, supra*, construed the Indian Civil Rights Act as an express waiver of tribal immunity in tribal courts. Plaintiff's Response Brief, pp. 2-3. Santa Clara held that a waiver of sovereign immunity cannot be implied but must be unequivocally expressed. It would be contradiction of Santa Clara to hold on the one hand that the Indian Civil Rights Act is ineffective to waive tribal sovereign immunity by implication in federal courts and on the other hand to hold that the same legislative enactment is effective to waive tribal sovereign immunity by implication in tribal courts. Therefore, the court rejects this argument.

Plaintiff cites no other federal or tribal enactments relating to the creation of this court by the tribe as expressly waiving sovereign immunity. Defendant Gwendolyn McCormick cites a letter from the Acting Secretary of the Interior (attached to Defendant's Brief) wherein the Acting Secretary concludes that the Courts of Indian Offenses under 25 C.F.R. 11.22 have authority of the kind necessary to hear and decide the issues in this case. Neither the Defendant nor the Acting Secretary of the Interior indicates the specifics of the source of that power in the absence of express Congressional or tribal consent to suit in tribal courts. *Parker v. Saupitty*, [CIV-79-A2, 1 Okla. Trib. 1 (Comanche CIO 1979)], by this Court expressly rejects that contention.

As immunity from suit is an inherent ingredient of the Tribal legal status as a dependent domestic nation, . . . and there has been no effective waiver of that immunity by Congress or the Tribe, I am, therefore, constrained to hold that the Sac and Fox Election Committee and the individual members thereof are immune from suit in this Court and that this action must be dismissed. It is therefore, unnecessary to address the balance of defendants' arguments.

In the evolution of tribal governments as governments, the tribal judicial forums, as the Supreme Court so adroitly pointed out in *Santa Clara*, must be the paramount mechanism for the enforcement of the substantive provisions of the Indian Civil Rights Act if tribal sovereignty is to be enhanced. Tribal constitutions and governing documents are becoming of increasing importance as tribal forums take on unprecedented responsibilities. Within the evolution of tribal government, the protection by the tribe of individual liberties and rights that may be violated by the tribe itself must be assigned a high priority.

However, the law is clear that, in the absence of an express and unequivocal waiver of sovereign immunity by the Sac and Fox Tribe, the unfinished business of providing a judicial forum for the resolution of the instant dispute remains exclusively within the province of the Sac and Fox Tribe. In the absence of that authorization, the tribal judiciary should not presume to fashion a remedy which ignores sovereign immunity, one of the inherent attributes of tribal sovereignty. . . .

NOTES

1. Other courts followed the *McCormick* Court's reasoning. For example, in *Sliger v. Stalmack*, 2000 WL 35750181 (Grand Traverse Band of Ottawa and Chippewa Indians Tribal Court 2000), the court reversed itself on whether ICRA constitutes a waiver of immunity:

   While Defendants concede that the Indian Civil Rights Act of 1968 (ICRA) granted certain rights, they argue that it did not necessarily grant corresponding remedies. Defendants argue that the United States Supreme

Court has already agreed with their argument. *See Santa Clara Pueblo v. Martinez*, 436 U.S. 49, 98 S. Ct. 1670, 56 L. Ed. 2d 106 (1978). The Supreme Court in *Santa Clara* decided that Congress only intended habeas corpus relief because that was the only relief expressly created. Like the federal courts, it is argued by Defendants, tribal courts should provide a consistent interpretation of that federal statute. "It would be [a] contradiction of *Santa Clara* to hold on the one hand that the Indian Civil Rights Act is ineffective to waive tribal sovereign immunity by implication in the federal courts and on the other hand to hold that the same legislative enactment is effective to waive the sovereign immunity by implication in tribal courts." *McCormick v. Election Committee of the Sac & Fox Tribe*, 1 Okla. Trib. 8, 20; 1980 WL 128844 (Sac & Fox CIO 1980). In reconsideration, this Court is convinced that the ICRA, while purporting to create certain rights, should be construed by this Court in a matter consistent with *Santa Clara* and *McCormick*. Therefore, the ICRA does not waive tribal sovereign immunity.

Id. at *1.

The same court had previously kept open the question in an earlier order:

This Court cannot say that Defendants are entitled to judgment as a matter of law. The Tribal Constitution provides a limited waiver of sovereign immunity for suits by tribal members for ". . . the purpose of enforcing rights and duties . . ." established by tribal law. *See* ARTICLE XIII, Section 2(a). However, the Indian Civil Rights Act of 1968, which applies to governmental action/inaction of all federally-recognized Indian tribes, mandates equal protection of the laws to any person within its jurisdiction. *See* 25 U.S.C., Sections 1301-1303. Furthermore, the Tribal Constitution itself provides a listing of constitutional rights in ARTICLE X. Although, the content title of Section 1 refers to members only, the specific text of subsection (h) says ". . . *any person* . . ." (emphasis [added]). Thus, the language in the federal mandate and the Tribal Constitution is exactly the same in regard to equal protection. The interplay, or apparent inconsistency, between these provisions of the law is not settled. This Court is not inclined to decide the matter in the absence of full briefing and argument so that it can make a fully-informed decision. However, it does appear that tribal members waived the sovereign immunity of their government to the extent that they could petition their courts for enforcement of "rights and duties" established by tribal law. Having done so, clearly it can be argued that the Indian Civil Rights Act of 1968 and, probably the Tribal Constitution, itself, extends the waiver to all other persons as well. Given the uncertainty of the law, this Court cannot say that Defendants are entitled to judgment as a matter of law.

Sliger v. Stalmack, 1999 WL 34986345, at *2 (Grand Traverse Band of Ottawa and Chippewa Indians Tribal Court 1999), *rev'd upon reconsideration*, 2000 WL 35750181 (Grand Traverse Band of Ottawa and Chippewa Indians Tribal Court 2000).

2. In *Davis v. Keplin*, 18 Indian L. Rep. 6148 (Turtle Mountain Band of Chippewa Indians Tribal Court 1991), the court held that ICRA did operate to abrogate tribal immunity, holding that "[t]he doctrine of tribal sovereign immunity is no longer absolute and has been effectively abrogated by this express, unequivocal expression of congressional intent to provide [ICRA] jurisdiction to the tribal court. . . ." *Id.* at 6149. *See also* Robert J. McCarthy,

Civil Rights in Tribal Courts: The Indian Bill of Rights at Thirty Years, 34 IDAHO L. REV. 465, 481 (1998) (discussing *Davis*).

Which line of cases has the better of the argument whether ICRA abrogates tribal immunity in tribal court?

3. Frank Pommersheim notes that Indian tribes have a difficult path to traverse in relation to the question of individual rights in Indian Country:

> Tribal councils and other decision makers are increasingly faced with the dilemma of individual rights. There is a need to fashion remedies in tribal court that allow for some resolution of individual claims against the tribe, but there is also a need to balance bona fide tribal concern that such relief might grind tribal activity to a halt or impoverish a tribal treasury.

FRANK POMMERSHEIM, BRAID OF FEATHERS: AMERICAN INDIAN LAW AND CONTEMPORARY TRIBAL LIFE 73 (1995).

7

CRIMINAL LAW AND PROCEDURE

Fundamental to tribal governance is the authority and capacity to exercise criminal jurisdiction over individuals within Indian country. Many of the richest and most colorful cases involving tribal law are criminal cases.

Traditionally, most American Indian nations did not prosecute crimes in the same manner as European and American nations. Instead of focusing entirely on retribution against the perpetrator or even on deterrence of other potential perpetrators, many Indian nations focused on the needs of the family of the victim or victims, as well as the overall needs of the community. *See generally* CARRIE E. GARROW & SARAH DEER, TRIBAL CRIMINAL LAW AND PROCEDURE 9-36 (2004). In a small tribal community, the murder of one person by another was the worst possible event that could happen, but the execution or banishment of the perpetrator was not the only possible outcome, as that might mean the loss of *two* persons who contributed to the welfare of the community, as opposed to only one. But that does not mean that Indian communities never punished criminals. Executions, physical incapacitations, and banishments were common, but perhaps not nearly as much as in European and American jurisdictions.

Consider the political murder of Spotted Tail by Crow Dog, two Lakota leaders, in the 1880s, resulting in the United States Supreme Court's decision in *Ex parte Crow Dog*, 109 U.S. 556 (1883). The families settled the dispute "for $600 in cash, eight horses, and one blanket." SIDNEY L. HARRING, CROW DOG'S CASE: AMERICAN INDIAN SOVEREIGNTY, TRIBAL LAW, AND UNITED STATES LAW IN THE NINETEENTH CENTURY 1 (1994). Federal officers, deeply dissatisfied with the tribe's version of justice, brought a federal prosecution, and the Dakota territorial court sentenced Crow Dog to hanging, but the Supreme Court reversed. Congress enacted the Major Crimes Act in 1885 in an effort to overturn the Court's decision. *See United States v. Kagama*, 118 U.S. 375 (1886).

Additionally, whether the alleged perpetrator was guilty likely was not in doubt. Given the closed and insular character of most Indian communities, the perpetrator probably would openly and voluntarily admit that he or she had committed the crime. Part of the process of healing the community, even for the perpetrator, was to talk it out. Denial of guilt injured the community and the perpetrator. Even to this day, some commentators have argued that the prosecution rates of American Indians in federal and state courts are higher because of the tendency of American Indians to confess guilt at a higher rate.

Through the nineteenth century, most Indian nations continued to handle criminal offenses in the traditional manner, even as their social and political structures were falling apart. Some tribes, most notably the Cherokee Nation, created a sophisticated law enforcement structure early in the nineteenth century based on tribal enforcers known as the Lighthorsemen and the Nation's well-known tribal court system. But relatively few Indian nations followed suit, and by the 1970s only a few dozen Indian nations were in the business of prosecuting crimes.

Instead, the federal government took control of law enforcement in most Indian communities, creating the notorious tribal police and Courts of Indian Offenses, enforcing the Law and Order Code promulgated in the Code of Federal Regulations. By the 1950s, Congress had authorized several states to take the lead in enforcing criminal laws in Indian country in statutes such as Public Law 280. These states included New York, Kansas, California, Wisconsin, Minnesota, Nebraska, Alaska, and Oregon. Other states also took criminal jurisdiction over some crimes.

The United States Supreme Court had long held that the United States Constitution and all its criminal procedure rights did not apply to Indian prosecutions. *See Talton v. Mayes*, 163 U.S. 376 (1896). As a result, in 1968 Congress enacted the Indian Civil Rights Act, 25 U.S.C. §§1301 et seq., with the intent of bringing most of the criminal procedure rights available to American citizens to Indian country. However, Congress did not require Indian tribes to provide paid counsel to indigent defendants, at the request of the United States Department of Justice.

In 1978, the United States Supreme Court held that Indian nations do not have inherent authority to exercise criminal jurisdiction over non-Indians. *See Oliphant v. Suquamish Indian Tribe*, 435 U.S. 191 (1978). In 1990, the Court extended that holding to nonmember Indians. *See Duro v. Reina*, 495 U.S. 676 (1990). Congress reaffirmed tribal jurisdiction over nonmember Indians in 1991. *See United States v. Lara*, 541 U.S. 193 (2004).

In the modern era, Indian nations continue to exercise criminal jurisdiction over tribal citizens and nonmember Indians within their territories. In 2010, Congress enacted the Tribal Law and Order Act, a statute that strongly supports tribal efforts to combat crime. Most significantly, Congress authorized tribal courts to sentence convicted criminals to up to three years in jail, assuming the conviction met basic American constitutional rules.

A. THE ORIGINS AND DEVELOPMENT OF TRIBAL LAW ENFORCEMENT

THE HISTORY OF TRIBAL POLICE

Barbara Luna-Firebaugh, Tribal Policing: Asserting Sovereignty,
Seeking Justice 17-23 (2007)

. . .

Traditional Policing, before 1860

Originally, prior to colonization, the keeping of law and order was the duty of clans or specially designated societies. Often clans were responsible for the conduct of their members. In other instances, military or warrior societies were entrusted with this responsibility for the good of the whole tribe. The clan or society was responsible not only for law enforcement but also the form that such law enforcement would take.

During early colonial times, tribal law enforcement responsibility was recognized in many treaties with the English Crown. Colonia treaties with the tribes, and later the treaties negotiated by the U.S. government, generally required that the tribes turn over non-Indian miscreants to national authorities for punishment. However, internal law enforcement issues were to be handled by the tribe itself.

Civilized Tribes

The Five Civilized Tribes illuminate an early example of traditional clan-based tribal police control in the late 1700s. In 1797, for example, the Cherokees created a mounted tribal police force with authority to deal with horse theft and other property crimes. The force became known in the early 1800s as the regulating companies and later, during the 1820s, as the Lighthorsemen. The jurisdiction of the Lighthorsemen was expanded to the apprehension of criminals, who were then turned over to tribal courts for trial and punishment. The crimes within the Lighthorsemen's purview extended to major crimes such as murder, rape, and robbery, as well as crimes against public order, such as intoxication.

. . . The creation and empowerment of the Lighthorsemen brought about the demise of clan revenge as the model for law enforcement. In 1810 the Cherokee adopted the Law of Abrogation of Clan Revenge. . . .

Lakota Law Enforcers

The same pattern of traditional clan or society leadership becoming the backbone of tribal law enforcement was evident later at Pine Ridge, where traditional Lakota law enforcers (*akicitas*) became the first members of the Pine Ridge police force. Here the large numbers of akicitas who moved into law enforcement established the connection between traditional Lakota law enforcement and the federal police agencies.

Akicitas had always policed Lakota society. They were appointed by the band's *wakiconze*, or camp administrator, from the membership of certain men's societies, and served terms of one year. They were empowered to police camp moves, regulate buffalo hunts, and enforce tribal laws and customs. They served as both judge and jury. . . .

Reservation Police, 1860-1880

Self-policing on a traditional level held throughout the postrevolutionary period; however, with the opening of the western frontier and the reservation period (1860-1880), the federal government moved to assert law enforcement jurisdiction over Indian Country.

The centralization of most Indian peoples on reservations and the proximity of non-Indian settlers led Indian agents in the 1860s and 1870s to organize reservation police forces, which led to the establishment of the Indian Police under the Bureau of Indian Affairs and brought the demise of clan and society-based authority. The BIA recruited, employed, and outfitted tribal members and standardized law-enforcement procedures. A bureaucratic, one-size-fits-all approach to tribal law enforcement became the norm throughout Indian Country.

The Rise of Reservation Police Forces

On many reservations, Indian people were from mixed bands or tribes, resulting in a breakdown in traditional lines of authority. In 1862, Indian agent Benjamin F. Lushbaugh unofficially established the Pawnee Indian police force. Lushbaugh selected six influential leaders from the various tribes or bands and formed them into a police agency with authority to stop certain kinds of problematic behavior. Band members were used to police the members of other bands. Other agents approached the problem of lawlessness by developing a legal code of conduct that would be enforced by tribal leaders selected by the agent. . . .

It is unclear precisely when the federal government officially established reservation law enforcement. However, during the 1870s Indian agents for the Pawnee, Klamath, Modoc, Navajo, Apache, Blackfeet, Chippewa, and Sioux established reservation-based Indian police agencies.

The Navajo Experiment

An early federal experiment in policing by Indian people on Indian reservations was conducted on the Navajo reservation in 1872. . . . After their return to the homeland [following the Long Walk] in 1870, complaints from surrounding settlements about cattle rustling and stock losses began to reemerge. A special council of Navajo leaders and the federal representative was held at Fort Wingate in July 1872. As with the Cherokee and the Lakota, a traditional war chief, Manuelito, took the lead. Manuelito proposed that he would "regulate this thieving himself." Special Indian Commissioner General O. O. Howard recruited a force of 100 young Navajos representing each of the thirteen bands and placed it under the command of Chief Manuelito. That force was charged with the responsibility of apprehending livestock thieves and was highly successful. . . .

The San Carlos Apache Police

Yet another of the earliest and most successful Indian police departments was established when John P. Clum was appointed as Indian agent on the San Carlos Agency in Arizona Territory in 1874. The San Carlos Agency was a classic example of a reservation where the traditional lines of authority had broken down. San Carlos was composed of members of various Apache bands, many of which had been in conflict with each other for generations. Thrust together on one reservation, the various bands remained at odds, causing an unsettled situation.

Two days after his arrival at the San Carlos agency, Clum appointed four leading Apaches as a police force. Their duties included arresting insubordinate Indians, indicting alcohol on the reservation, guarding prisoners, and other duties as assigned by the agent. As the reservation population increased with the addition of additional bands, within six months the police force was increased to sixty members. This force was highly successful in pacifying the various bands of Apache now resident at San Carlos. . . .

. . . [T]he idea of Indian policing became the official policy of the federal government.

The federal government found that the use of one tribe to police another was a useful tool, one that was to continue throughout the history of the Bureau of Indian Affairs Law Enforcement Services. "The Army's success in pacifying most of [the Apaches] depended on enlisting warriors from one band to track and fight against those of another." In fact, as Wilcomb E. Washburn has stated, "Indian police and courts were created in large measure for the purpose of controlling the Indian and breaking up tribal leadership and tribal government. Thus the federal government used tribal police against their own people and other Indians to control tribal leaders and to ensure the demise of representative tribal governments. . . .

The Formal Establishment of Federal Indian Police

In 1878 the Commissioner of Indian Affairs Report . . . included the following provision and language:

Indian Police
By act of May 27, at the last session of congress, provision was made for the organization at the various agencies of a system of Indian police. . . .

Too short a time has elapsed to perfect and thoroughly test the workings of this system, but the results of the . . . experiment at the thirty agencies in which it has been tried are entirely satisfactory, and commend it as an effective instrument of civilization. A simple code of rules for the guidance of the service has been prepared, and a plain, inexpensive uniform has been adopted.

Federal Control of Indian Police, 1880-1920

While funding problems remained, by 1880 two-thirds of the reservations in the United States had Indian police forces, and by 1890 police forces were to be found at virtually all agencies. These police forces varied in size from two to forty-three.

In a fundamental change from the earlier, agent-created reservation police forces, which greatly relied on the support of traditional authority within the tribes, the members of the new federal Indian police forces were generally identified as progressives rather than traditional, and they had usually received allotments of land for themselves and their families. . . . Thus insured a degree of civilization as perceived by the federal government and created the idea of the Indian police force as an agent of civilization. It also set up an adversarial dynamic between tribal citizens and Indian police.

. . . The police were charged with the curtailment of tribal chiefs' prerogatives and the advancement of the concept of the primacy of non-Indian law as the mode of operation, a function that provoked violent opposition from traditional Indian leaders. . . .

NOTE

The Cherokee Lighthorsemen, at least until 1825, utilized law enforcement tools that would be considered barbaric by modern standards:

> The lighthorse corps . . . served with extensive powers, fulfilling the combined roles of sheriff, judge, jury, and executioner. The number of laws they enforced increased yearly as mixed-blood leaders and missionary advisors moved the tribal government closer to Anglo-American institutions. Most of the laws dealt with protection of property, such as the one invoking a penalty of fifty lashes for cattle theft. Such laws also became more refined, the penalty for horse theft being amended to 100 lashes for the first offense, 200 for the second, and death for the third. Because there were no jails among the Indians, corporal punishment was invoked for all crimes, but with variations. For rape a first offender received fifty lashes on the back and had his left ear chopped off close to the head. If the rapist committed a second crime, the lighthorsemen administered 100 lashes and cut off the other ear. For the third offense, death was the punishment. . . .
>
> Lighthorsemen also used violence when suspects attempted escape. In one instance a prisoner who reached for a captain's gun was shot four times. There was no investigation of the incident. Such violence apparently was foreseen and expected, for the law of 1808 creating the lighthorse corps exempted officers for retaliation when they were forced to kill suspected criminals.
>
> Every lighthorseman was expected to serve as executioner when needed. Condemned criminals had their choice of how they were to be killed, which oftentimes led to gruesome executions. One condemned man, who had killed a friend with a Bowie knife, wished to die by the same weapon; the lighthorsemen granted his request by stabbing him to death. Most Cherokees requested death by rifle, while hanging was shunned for fear that the rope would damage the spirit.

Bob L. Blackburn, *From Blood Revenge to the Lighthorsemen: Evolution of Law Enforcement Institutions among the Five Civilized Tribes to 1861*, 8 AM. INDIAN L. REV. 49, 53-54 (1988).

B. JURISDICTION

1. NONMEMBER INDIANS

MEANS V. DISTRICT COURT OF THE CHINLE JUDICIAL DISTRICT

Navajo Nation Supreme Court, No. CS-CV-61-98, 7 Navajo Rep. 382; 26 Indian L. Rep. 6083 (May 11, 1999)

Before YAZZIE, Chief Justice, AUSTIN, Associate Justice, and TOLEDO, Associate Justice (sitting by designation).

The opinion of the court was delivered by: YAZZIE, Chief Justice. . . .

The petition alleges that the Navajo Nation lacks criminal jurisdiction over the petitioner, who is a member of the Oglala Sioux Nation. . . .

[W]e will decide the following questions:

1. Does the June 1, 1868 Treaty between the United States of America and the Navajo Nation recognize Navajo Nation criminal jurisdiction over individuals who are not members of the Navajo Nation or Tribe of Indians?

2. Has the petitioner consented to the criminal jurisdiction of the Navajo Nation by virtue of his assumption of tribal relations with Navajos?

3. Does the assertion of criminal jurisdiction over the petitioner violate equal protection of the law, and is the assertion of such jurisdiction a "political" or a "racial" classification?

I.

On December 28, 1997, the Navajo Nation charged the petitioner with three offenses: threatening Leon Grant in violation of 17 N.N.C. §310 (1995); committing a battery upon Mr. Grant in violation of 17 N.N.C. §316; and committing a battery upon Jeremiah Bitsui, also in violation of 17 N.N.C. §316. . . . The petitioner faces a maximum exposure of 450 days incarceration, a fine of $1,250, or both, along with the payment of restitution to the victims of the alleged offenses. 17 N.N.C. §220(C). . . .

A.

The Navajo Nation is the largest Indian nation in the United States in terms of geographic size. It has 17,213,941.90 acres of land (approximately 25,000 square miles) as of 1988, including Navajo tribal trust land, land owned in fee, individual Navajo allotments, and various leases. . . . The Navajo Nation membership is the second largest of all Indian nations within the United States, with a total estimated membership of 225,298 persons as of 1990. . . . The 1990 population of the Navajo Nation was 145,853 persons of "all races," with 140,749 American Indians, Eskimos and Aleuts, and 5,104 individuals of "other races. . . . Of that population, 96.62% was Indian and 3.38% was "non-American Indian." . . . Of the American Indian population, 131,422 individuals were Navajos and 9,327 were "other Indians." . . . Therefore, the percentage of nonmember Indians in the Navajo Nation population was 6.39%. . . .

The Navajo Nation courts had 27,602 criminal cases during Navajo Nation Fiscal Year 1998. . . . The largest single category of civil cases was petitions for domestic abuse protection orders, and there were 3,435 such cases during the fiscal year.

. . . In sum, the Navajo Nation courts are addressing the serious criminal and social problems of drunk driving, assaults and batteries (including aggravated assault and battery with deadly weapons), sex offenses against children, disorderly conduct, and public intoxication. Many of the crimes against persons are acts of in-family violence, and the civil domestic abuse restraining order numbers show that family violence may be the most serious social problem in the Navajo Nation.

Given the United States Indian education policy of sending Indian children to boarding schools, Indians in the armed services, modern population mobility, and other factors, there are high rates of intertribal intermarriage among American Indians. As noted, at least 9,327 "other" or nonmember Indians resided within the Navajo Nation in 1990. They are involved in some of the 27,000 plus criminal charges in our system and in the 3,435 plus domestic violence cases. The questions are whether nonmember Indians should have de facto immunity from criminal prosecution, given the failure of federal officials to effectively address crime in the Navajo Nation, and whether this Court should rule that thousands of innocent victims, Navajo and non-Navajo, should be permitted to suffer. We must sadly take judicial notice of the fact that, with a few exceptions, non-Indians and nonmember Indians who commit crimes within the Navajo Nation escape punishment for the crimes they commit. The social health of the Navajo Nation is at risk in addressing the petitioner's personal issues, as is the actual health and well-being of thousands of people. . . .

. . . Indian nation courts are at the front line of attempts to control crime and social disruption. They share a common responsibility with police, prosecutors, defenders, and social service programs to address crime and violence for the welfare of not only the Navajo People, but all those who live within the Navajo Nation or reside in areas adjacent to the Navajo Nation. Indian nations cannot rely upon others to address the problems. . . . The Navajo Nation courts have primary jurisdiction to deal with criminal offenses and they must be free to exercise that jurisdiction.

B.

The petitioner is a member of the Oglala Sioux Nation. . . . He was 58 years of age as of the date of the hearing, . . . and he resided for ten years within the Navajo Nation from 1987 through 1997. . . . He was married to Gloria Grant, an enrolled Navajo woman. . . . Leon Grant, whom the petitioner is charged with threatening and battering, is a member of the Omaha Tribe, and Jeremiah Bitsui, whom the petitioner is charged with battering, is Navajo. . . . Mr. Grant was the petitioner's father-in-law at the time of the incident. The petitioner moved from the Navajo Nation to Porcupine, South Dakota within the Pine Ridge Reservation, in December of 1997. . . .

The petitioner complained of a lack of hospitality toward him when he resided within the Navajo Nation. He said he could not vote, run for Navajo Nation office (including judicial office), become a Navajo Nation Council delegate, the president, vice-president, or be a member of a farm board. In sum, he could not attain any Navajo Nation political position. . . . He said he could not sit on a jury and received no notice to appear for jury duty. . . . That may be because the petitioner was not on any Navajo Nation registration or voter list and he was not on the voter registration list for Apache County, Arizona. . . . He complained at length about his inability to get a job or start a business because of Navajo Nation employment and contracting preference laws.

The petitioner's national reputation as an activist is well-known. On cross-examination, the prosecution attempted to develop the petitioner's active participation in the public and political life of the Navajo Nation. The prosecution highlighted the petitioner's attendance at chapter meetings and elicited the fact that subsequent to a 1989 incident when Navajos were shot by Navajos, he led a march to the court house for a demonstration to make a "broad statement" about political activities of the Navajo Nation. . . .

The "facts" the petitioner related during his testimony are only partially correct. While it is true that there are preference laws for employment and contracting in the Navajo Nation, they are not an absolute barrier to either employment or the ability to do business. There are many non-Navajo employees of the Navajo Nation (some of whom hold high positions in Navajo Nation government), and non-Navajo businesses operate within the Navajo Nation. The ability to work or do business within the Navajo Nation has a great deal more to do with individual initiative and talent than preference laws. The petitioner was most likely not called for jury duty because he did not register to vote in Arizona. Non-Navajos have been called for jury duty since at least 1979. *George v. Navajo Tribe*, 2 Nav. R. 1 (1979); *Navajo Nation v. MacDonald*, 6 Nav. R. [432, (1991)]. The 126 Sioux Indians listed in the 1990 Census can be called for jury duty if they are on a voter list and are called. If the petitioner was an indigent at the time of his arraignment, he would have been eligible for the appointment of an attorney.

II.

The first issue is whether the June 1, 1868 Treaty between the United States of America and the Navajo Nation gives the Navajo Nation courts criminal jurisdiction over individuals who are not members of the Navajo Nation or Tribe of Indians. We will first discuss the 1868 Treaty as a source of criminal jurisdiction and then apply it.

A.

There is a general and false assumption that Indian nations have no criminal jurisdiction over non-Indians and nonmember Indians. While the United States Supreme Court ruled that Indian nations have no inherent criminal jurisdiction over non-Indians in *Oliphant v. Suquamish Indian Tribe*, 435 U.S. 191 (1978), and that there is no inherent criminal jurisdiction over nonmember Indians in *Duro v. Reina*, 495 U.S. 676 (1990), criminal jurisdiction over nonmembers can rest upon a treaty or federal statute. The Supreme Court reserved the issues of affirmative congressional authorization or treaty provisions in both cases. *Oliphant*, 435 U.S. at 195-197; *Duro*, 495 U.S. at 684. Therefore, we will examine whether the Navajo Nation Treaty of 1868 is a source of Navajo Nation criminal jurisdiction over nonmember Indians. . . .

B.

The Treaty between the Navajo Nation or Tribe of Indians and the United States was negotiated at Fort Sumner, New Mexico Territory, on May 28, 29, and 30, 1868, and it was executed there on June 1, 1868. . . . We are primarily interested in language found in Article II of the Treaty, which we will call the "set apart for the use and occupation" clause, and that in Article I, which we will call the "bad men" clause.

Article II of the Treaty . . . begins with a boundary description and then says that "this reservation" is "set apart for the use and occupation of the Navajo tribe of Indians, and for such other friendly tribes or individual Indians as from time to time they may be willing, with the consent of the United States, to admit among them. . . ." Federal courts use this language as the basis for Navajo Nation civil jurisdiction. *Williams v. Lee*, 358 U.S. 217, 221-223 (1959); *Littell v. Nakai*, 344 F.2d 486, 488 (9th Cir. 1965); *UNC Resources, Inc. v. Benally*, 518 F. Supp. 1046, 1050 (D. Ariz. 1981). The Supreme Court held that the Navajo Nation retained its inherent criminal jurisdiction over members in *United States v. Wheeler*, 435 U.S. 313, 323 (1978).

The plain language of Article II indicates that the Navajo Reservation exists for the exclusive use of not only Navajos, but other Indians, either as tribes or as individuals, where both the Navajo Nation and the United States agree to their admission. Given that the jurisdiction of our courts is recognized in the Article II language, Indians such as the petitioner who are permitted to reside within the Navajo Nation fall within the same grouping as Navajo Indians in terms of the Treaty's coverage.

We see this provision applied in the historical record. On September 27, 1881, Agent Galen Eastman wrote to the Commissioner of Indian Affairs to inform him that about forty Pah-Utes (Paiutes) had arrived in a starving condition and were begging for food. They said "they were going to cease their predatory life and use the hoe thereafter." The Navajo reply was that "if the Great Father is willing, we will try you again and be responsible for your good behavior for we used to be friends and have intermarried with your people and yours with ours . . . but if you return to your bad life, thieving and murdering we (the Navajos) will hang you." Obviously, thinking of the language in Article II of the Treaty, Eastman asked for instructions.

The "bad men" among either "the Indians" or "Whites" language has been litigated in various contexts, but the closest interpretation on the issue of criminal jurisdiction was in the case of *State ex rel. Merrill v. Turtle*, 413 F.2d 683 (9th Cir. 1969). There, the State of Arizona arrested a Cheyenne Indian within the Navajo Nation using the "bad men among the Indians" Treaty language as its justification, and the court ruled that the arrest of an Indian had to follow the extradition provision in the "bad men" clause. 413 F.2d at 686. The "bad men" clause has been used as the basis for concurrent civil jurisdiction in the Navajo Nation courts. *Babbitt Ford, Inc. v. Navajo Indian Tribe*, 710 F.2d 587, 595 (9th Cir. 1983).

Using surrounding circumstances, history, and the "as the Indians understood it" canon of treaty construction, the issue of how to deal with "bad" Indians was the subject of specific discussions at Fort Summer. Barboncito,

the primary Navajo treaty negotiator, gave an opening speech where he outlined the hardships suffered by Navajos at the adjoining Bosque Redondo "reservation." He complained: "I think that all nations around here are against us
(I mean Mexicans and Indians) the reason is that we are a working tribe of
Indians, and if we had the means we could support ourselves far better than
either Mexican or Indian. The Comanches are against us I know it for they
came here and killed a good many of our men. In our own country we knew
nothing about the Comanches." . . . General William T. Sherman said this in
reply: "The Army will do the fighting, you must live at peace, if you go to your
own country the Utes will be the nearest Indians to you, you must not trouble
the Utes and the Utes must not trouble you. If, however, the Utes or Apaches
come into your country with bows and arrows and guns you of course can drive
them out but must not follow beyond the boundary line." . . .

Therefore, we conclude that the Chinle District Court has criminal jurisdiction over the petitioner by virtue of the 1868 Treaty. The petitioner entered
the Navajo Nation, married a Navajo woman, conducted business activities,
engaged in political activities by expressing his right to free speech, and
otherwise satisfied the Article II conditions for entry and residence and
Article I and II court jurisdiction.

III.

It is clear that the Navajo Nation has jurisdiction over its own "members."
Wheeler, 435 U.S. at 323. The United States Supreme Court addressed the issue
of membership and consent in the *Duro* decision and went on to say: "We held
in *United States v. Rogers*, 4 How. 567 (1846), that . . . a non-Indian could, by
adoption, 'become entitled to certain privileges in the tribe, and make himself
amenable to their laws and usages.' *Id.*, at 573; *see Nofire v. United States*, 164
U.S. 657 (1897)." . . .

We previously held, in *Navajo Nation v. Hunter*, [7 Nav. R. 194,] No. SC-CR-
07-95 (decided March 8, 1996), that the Navajo Nation has criminal jurisdiction over individuals who "assume tribal relations." . . .

We have previously ruled that our 1997 Navajo Nation Criminal Code will
be construed in light of Navajo common law, *Navajo Nation v. Platero*, 6 Nav. R.
[422 (1991)], and the Supreme Court–approved Navajo common law in the
Wheeler decision, 435 U.S. at 312-313. While there is a formal process to obtain
membership as a Navajo, *see* 1 N.N.C. §§751-759 (1995), that is not the only
kind of "membership" under Navajo Nation law. An individual who marries or
has an intimate relationship with a Navajo is a hadane (in-law). The Navajo
People have adoone'e or clans, and many of them are based upon the intermarriage of original Navajo clan members with people of other nations. The
primary clan relation is traced through the mother, and some of the "foreign
nation" clans include the "Flat Foot-Pima clan," the "Ute people clan," the
"Zuni clan," the "Mexican clan," and the "Mescalero Apache clan." *See* SAAD
AHAAH SINIL: DUAL LANGUAGE NAVAJO-ENGLISH DICTIONARY, 3-4 (1986). The list of
clans based upon other peoples is not exhaustive. A hadane or in-law assumes
a clan relation to a Navajo when an intimate relationship forms, and when that
relationship is conducted within the Navajo Nation, there are reciprocal obligations to and from family and clan members under Navajo common law.

Among those obligations is the duty to avoid threatening or assaulting a relative by marriage (or any other person).

We find that the petitioner, by reason of his marriage to a Navajo, longtime residence within the Navajo Nation, his activities here, and his status as a hadane, consented to Navajo Nation criminal jurisdiction. This is not done by "adoption" in any formal or customary sense, but by assuming tribal relations and establishing familial and community relationships under Navajo common law.

There is another aspect to consent by conduct. In *Tsosie v. United States*, 825 F.2d 393 (Fed. Cir. 1987), the Federal Circuit Court of Appeals discussed the "bad men among the Indians" language, saying that "[i]t is evident from the negotiations that the Navajos were not to be permanently disarmed, and could defend their reservation. They feared attacks by other Indian tribes, which they could repel, but pursuit and retaliation it was hoped they would refrain from, leaving that to the United States Army. The 'bad men' clause is not confined to United States Government employees, but extends 'to people subject to the authority of the United States.' This vague phrase, to effectuate the purpose of the treaty, could possibly include Indians hostile to the Navajos whose wrongs to the Navajos the United States will punish and pay for: thus the need for Indian retaliation would be eliminated." *Id.*, at 396.

Avoidance of retaliation and revenge is clear in the Treaty of 1868. General Sherman urged Navajos to leave the neighboring Mexicans to the Army, but he told Navajos they could pursue Utes and Apaches who entered the Navajo homeland. The Treaty speaks to the admission of Indians from other Indian nations. The thrust of the "bad men" clause was to avoid conflict. We use a rule of necessity to interpret consent under our Treaty. It would be absurd to conclude that our hadane relatives can enter the Navajo Nation, offend, and remain among us, and we can do nothing to protect Navajos and others from them. To so conclude would be to open the door for revenge and retaliation. While there are those who may think that the remedies offered by the United States Government are adequate, it is plain and clear to us that federal enforcement of criminal law is deficient. Potential state remedies are impractical, because law enforcement personnel in nearby areas have their own law enforcement problems. We must have the rule of peaceful law rather than the law of the talon, so we conclude that the petitioner has assumed tribal relations with Navajos and he is thus subject to the jurisdiction of our courts.

IV.

Now we reach the issue of whether the petitioner is denied equal protection of the law because he, as a nonmember Indian, is placed in the classification "Indian" for criminal prosecution, along with Navajos, when non-Indians are not. The petitioner is mistaken as to the classification into which he falls. In *Navajo Nation v. Hunter*, we held that any person who assumes tribal relations is fully subject to our law, and that a person who assumes tribal relations is considered to be an "Indian" and thus a "person" for purposes of 17 N.N.C. §208(17) (1995). The petitioner belongs to the classification hadane and not that of nonmember Indian. One can be of any race or ethnicity to assume tribal relations with Navajos. . . .

We stress that the petitioner is treated no differently than he would be treated in a state or federal court in a criminal case. At oral argument, the petitioner's attorney was asked what sixth amendment rights his client is denied in our judicial system. He could not answer, because there is no difference. The ability to run for public office or to be a judge has utterly nothing to do with a fair criminal trial. Our rules of criminal procedure and our Navajo Nation Bill of Rights make no distinction as to race, ethnicity or membership in the Navajo Nation. The Navajo Nation courts keep no records on the race or ethnicity of any litigant and the justices and judges of our courts understand what equality before the law means. The Navajo Nation has a substantial interest in the welfare and safety of all within its boundaries and the Nation has an obligation to protect all from crime insofar as it can.

V.

... This Court finds that the Chinle District Court has jurisdiction under the Treaty of 1868, the petitioner has consented to criminal jurisdiction over him, and that he is not denied the equal protection of the law. Accordingly, a final writ is denied, and this cause is remanded to the Chinle District Court for a prompt trial.

NOTES

1. In the *"Duro* fix" statute, Congress reversed the Supreme Court's holding in *Duro v. Reina*, 495 U.S. 676 (1990), that Indian tribes do not have inherent authority to prosecute Indians who are not members of the prosecuting tribe. *United States v. Lara*, 541 U.S. 193 (2004). Note that the Navajo Supreme Court does not rely upon the *Duro* fix as authority for its decision upholding tribal jurisdiction over Russell Means.

   Means took his case to the federal courts relying on the *Duro* decision, but was turned back on grounds that the United States Supreme Court had upheld the *"Duro* fix," the congressional statute recognizing tribal authority to prosecute nonmember Indians. *See Means v. Navajo Nation*, 432 F.3d 924 (9th Cir. 2005), *cert. denied*, 549 U.S. 952 (2006).

2. Other tribal courts engage in a different type of analysis in order to determine whether a criminal defendant is an "Indian person" over which an Indian tribe has jurisdiction. In *McIntosh v. Muscogee (Creek) Nation*, 7 Okla. Trib. 290, 295-97 (Muscogee (Creek) Nation Supreme Court 2001), the court reversed a conviction on grounds that the tribal prosecutor cannot seek to prove the Indian status of the defendant through cross-examination.

3. Nonmember Indians are a significant percentage of the persons living in tribal jurisdictions. Indian people frequently intermarry with Indians of other communities. Due to a series of federal court cases culminating in *Duro v. Reina*, 495 U.S. 676 (1990), the term "nonmember Indian" became an important legal term of art. A "nonmember Indian" is an Indian person (usually a member of a federally recognized tribe) who is residing in the territory of another Indian nation. Many, if not most, nonmember Indians are interwoven into tribal communities in ways far deeper than non-Indians who reside in the same communities. *See generally* Bethany R. Berger, *Justice*

and the Outsider: Jurisdiction over Nonmembers in Tribal Legal Systems, 37 Ariz. St. L.J. 1047, 1062-63 (2005); Philip S. Deloria & Nell J. Newton, *The Criminal Jurisdiction of Tribal Courts over Non-Member Indians*, 38 Fed. B. News & J., March 1991, at 70, 71-72.

2. NON–AMERICAN CITIZENS

Eastern Band of Cherokee Indians v. Torres

Cherokee Supreme Court of North Carolina, No. CR 03-1443; CR 03-1529; CR 03-1530; CR 03-1531; CR 03-1819, 2005 N.C. Cherokee Sup. Ct. LEXIS 6, 2005 WL 6437828 (April 15, 2005)

Before Harry C. Martin, Chief Justice, Brenda Toineeta, and Steven E. Philo, Chief Judge, Cherokee Court, sitting by designation. Philo, J, concurring.

Martin, C.J.

All parties stipulated that defendant Torres is a citizen of the republic of Mexico (United Mexican States).

Defendant Torres was charged with driving while impaired and failure to stop for a stop sign on September 10, 2003. While released on bond for these charges, defendant on September 21, 2003 was charged with driving while impaired and driving [with a revoked license]. Again, on pre-trial release, defendant was charged with second-degree child abuse of an enrolled member on November 13, 2003. During this time period, defendant was living . . . in Indian Country within the Qualla Boundary (the reservation of the Eastern Band of Cherokee Indians in North Carolina).

[The alleged crimes also occurred within the Qualla Boundary.]

The population of the Qualla Boundary, both permanent and temporary, is becoming larger and more diverse. Approximately 8,500 enrolled members live on the Qualla Boundary. More people visit Cherokee than any place in North Carolina, some three (3) million visitors a year. This case is not a unique, stand-alone case. It is not unusual for foreigners to appear in the Cherokee Court, in civil, criminal and infraction cases.

We now turn to the issue of jurisdiction.

This is a case of first impression. The issue for decision is: Does the Cherokee Court, an independent tribal court of the Eastern Band of Cherokee Indians, a federally recognized Indian tribe, have jurisdiction to try and to punish the defendant Torres, a citizen of Mexico who is not an Indian, for violating the criminal laws of the Eastern Band of Cherokee Indians? We answer the issue, yes.

Our research does not disclose any authority directly addressing this issue. We consider that the better reasoned analysis requires and supports the conclusion that the Cherokee Court does have criminal jurisdiction over non-Indians who are not citizens of the United States, *i.e.* aliens.

In reviewing issues of jurisdiction the Court is guided by Chapter 7, Section 2 (2000) of the Cherokee Code. Section 2(c) states: "The Judicial Branch shall not have jurisdiction over matters in which the exercise of jurisdiction has been specifically prohibited by a binding decision of the United States Supreme Court, the United States Court of Appeals for the Fourth Circuit or by an Act of Congress."

Our research does not disclose any Act of Congress specifically prohibiting the exercise of criminal jurisdiction by Indian tribal Courts over non-Indians who are not citizens of the United States. Nor do we find any such decision of the United States Court of Appeals for the Fourth Circuit.

. . . Throughout its extensive history of jurisprudence regarding Indian tribal sovereignty, the Supreme Court has never considered the powers and status of the Tribes with regard to non-citizens of the United States. The Cherokee Court, drawing upon history and references from precedent concluded that the Eastern Band of Cherokee Indians maintained the "inherent authority" to prosecute non-citizens of the United States.

The appellant relies entirely on *Oliphant*. He only cites two additional authorities, *Duro* and Chapter 14, Section 1.5 of the Cherokee Code. Appellant argues that *Oliphant* holds that Indian tribal courts do not have jurisdiction to try any non-Indians on criminal charges. . . .

. . . This Court agrees that Indian tribes are prohibited from exercising those powers of autonomous states that have been expressly terminated by the United States Congress and those powers inconsistent with their status, as dependent sovereign nations. *Oliphant*. Congress has not expressly limited the jurisdiction of Indian tribal courts over non-Indians in criminal cases.

This Court holds that neither Congress nor the United States Supreme Court nor the Fourth Circuit Court of Appeals has specifically prohibited the jurisdiction of Indian Tribal courts over non-Indian aliens of the United States on criminal charges.

A careful reading of *Oliphant* supports this conclusion. The Court in *Oliphant* does not address this issue directly. Oliphant and Belgarde were not aliens, but were citizens of the United States. Historically, the United States in its treaties and agreements with Indian tribes from the earliest days had two basic goals: to gain land from the Indians, and to protect citizens of the U.S. . . . Surely, the United States did not intend to protect English, Spanish, Dutch and other aliens, from the Indians.

The Court's restriction of its holding in *Oliphant* to "non-Indian citizens of the United States" has a significant historical basis, and is consistent with the Court's concerns of liberty, justice and fairness justifying the Court's ruling prohibiting the exercise of criminal jurisdiction over non-Indian citizens of the United States. The Court has traditionally recognized this distinction between citizens and non-citizens. Over a century ago, the Court indicated that the general "object" of Congressional statutes regarding Indian country was "to reserve to the courts of the United States [criminal] jurisdiction of all actions to which its own citizens are parties on either side." *In re Mayfield*, 141 U.S. 107, 115-116, 11 S. Ct. 939, 35 L. Ed. 635 (1891). . . .

A brief review of the history of the Cherokees reveals that in negotiating with the Cherokees the primary intent of the United States was the protection of the liberties of citizens of the United States. Six of the first nine treaties executed by the Cherokees and the United States contained special provisions applicable only to United States citizens. The first article of the Hopewell Treaty includes: "... the Cherokees shall restore all ... citizens of the United States ... to their entire liberty." 7 STAT. 18, Article 8. Article X holds that "all travelers, citizens of the United States, shall have liberty to go to any of the tribes or towns of the Cherokee to trade with them." No right of trade was granted for non-citizens. In the TREATY OF THE HOLSTON RIVER, 7 Stat. 39 (1791), the activity of citizens of the United States is restricted without reference to those not citizens, thus leaving non-citizens who venture into Indian Country to their own devices for protection. *See also* SECOND TREATY OF THE HOLSTON RIVER (1798), Article VII, 7 STAT. 62 (freedom of travel); FOURTH TREATY OF TELLICO (1805), Article II, 7 STAT. 95 (travel); SECOND TREATY OF WASHINGTON (1816), Article II, 7 STAT. 139 (freedom of navigation of rivers and waters within the Cherokee Nation [and of] use of ferries and public houses). *Id.*

When considering the inherent powers of tribes, the United States Supreme Court has held that tribes retain all powers of autonomous states except those which have been expressly terminated by Treaty or Act of Congress, or which are inconsistent with their status as domestic dependent nations. ... Over a century ago, the courts of the United States recognized that the Cherokees "have and exhibit the same interest in the enforcement of the law and in the protection of personal and property rights as the United States citizen resident therein. In some sense they have the higher interest, because they are owners of the soil, and constitute the more fixed and permanent population." *Carter v. United States*, 1 Indian Terr. 342, 37 S.W. 204 (Ct. App. Ind. Terr., 1896). ...

The law of *Oliphant* can be summarized in the following: "Such an exercise of jurisdiction over non-Indian citizens of the United States would belie the tribes' forfeiture of full sovereignty in return for the protection of the United States." ... By accepting the protection of the United States, Indian tribes did not relinquish their inherent sovereign powers of criminal jurisdiction over non-Indians who were not citizens of the United States, such as Torres. ...

Therefore, we hold that *Oliphant* does not control the Torres appeal. *Oliphant* concerns Indian tribal court jurisdiction of criminal cases against non-Indian citizens of the United States. Torres concerns Indian tribal court jurisdiction of criminal cases against non-Indian aliens of the United States.

We hold that the sovereign power of inherent jurisdiction of the Eastern Band of Cherokee Indians to try and punish non-Indian aliens of the United States has not been expressly terminated by Treaty, Act of Congress, or specifically prohibited by a binding decision of the Supreme Court of the United States or the United States Court of Appeals for the Fourth Circuit. ...

After the arrival of non-Indians to what is now the United States of America and before the existence of the United States of America, the Cherokee Indians exercised inherent jurisdiction over all non-Indians found within Cherokee Country. Following the formation of the United States of America, the Cherokee Nation entered into treaties with the United States over the years recognizing its relation with the United States as a "dependant sovereign nation," and the federal government assumed its fiduciary obligations for the Cherokees. As demonstrated previously in this opinion, this relationship resulted in the Cherokees giving up criminal jurisdiction over non-Indian citizens of the United States as being inconsistent with the status of the Cherokees as a dependant sovereign nation.

Not so, as to non-Indian aliens of the United States. In order to govern itself, manage its own affairs and safeguard its people as well as visitors (including citizens of the United States and aliens) to Cherokee Country, criminal jurisdiction over non-Indians aliens is an exercise of the inherent power of the Cherokee Nation, and is essential.

Torres, and all aliens who violate criminal laws within the United States[,] will be subjected to a strange court, under strange laws, in a strange land, whether the court is federal, state or tribal. The Cherokee Court provided Torres with all the protection and assistance that he would have received in federal or state court, including appointment of counsel, due process, speedy trial, bond and right of appeal. In addition, after defendant exhausts all of his remedies in the Cherokee Court, he may petition the United States District Court for a writ of habeas corpus and federal appellate review. So, Torres, or any alien, is not prejudiced by receiving a trial in tribal court. *See* 25 U.S.C. 1301 *et seq.* (1968). . . .

The facts of this case demonstrate the necessity of preserving the criminal jurisdiction of the Eastern Band of Cherokee Indians over non-Indian aliens of the United States in order to protect the safety, health, economic development, liberty and the general welfare of the Eastern Band of Cherokee Indians and all other people who live, work or visit on Tribal lands. The records of the Cherokee Court disclose that aliens of the United States are seeking and receiving the protection of the Cherokee Court in criminal cases arising on the Qualla Boundary against enrolled members of the Eastern Band of Cherokee Indians. To allow criminal jurisdiction when an alien is the victim and deny jurisdiction when an alien is the perpetrator, would indeed be inconsistent with the status of the Eastern Band of Cherokee Indians as a dependant sovereign nation. . . .

Further, the Court's holding, and the federal policy of self-determination of Indian tribes, is consistent with and supported by established norms of customary international law. *See* . . . International Convention on the Elimination of All Forms of Racial Discrimination (ICERD); . . . [Note,] *International Law as an Interpretive Force in Federal Indian Law*, 116 HARVARD LAW REV. 1751, 1762 (2003); [Curtis G. Berkey,] *International Law and Domestic Courts: Enhancing Self-Determination for Indigenous People*, 5 HARVARD HUMAN RIGHTS J. 65, 68 (1992).

This ruling is also supported by the traditions, customs and culture of the Eastern Band of Cherokee Indians.

The order of the Cherokee Court denying defendant/appellant's motion to dismiss is affirmed, and this case is remanded to the Cherokee Court.

[Concurring opinion of PHILO, C.J., omitted.]

NOTE

As is well known to students of federal Indian law, the United States Supreme Court held in *Oliphant v. Suquamish Indian Tribe*, 435 U.S. 191

(1978), that Indian tribes do not have inherent authority to prosecute "non-Indians." *Torres* would seem to run counter to that holding, but the reasoning in *Oliphant,* for a variety of reasons, may be suspect.

One of the key findings of the *Oliphant* Court was that Indian tribes had never exercised criminal jurisdiction over non-Indians. *Cf. id.* at 197 ("From the earliest treaties with these tribes, it was apparently assumed that the tribes did not have criminal jurisdiction over non-Indians absent a congressional statute or treaty provision to that effect."). Recent scholarship by an Eastern Band Cherokee judge and scholar belies that assumption:

> While Georgia sought to exercise jurisdiction over Cherokees, one case documents the Cherokee Nation's judicial branch of government exercising criminal jurisdiction over a white citizen of Georgia.
>
> On September 19, 1829, Jesse Stancell, a "white man," was arrested within the Cherokee Nation at Elejay and charged with horse stealing. Stancell was detained "in close custody for the space of thirty hours" during which time he was tried by a jury. George Saunders, who the Court Minute Book reveals had previously served as Foreman of Cherokee Supreme Court juries, served in the same capacity on Stancell's jury. Stancell was sentenced "to receive fifty stripes on the bare back, which was fifty less than what [was] common . . . for such offence." His captors "stripped [him], tied [him] up to a tree" and executed the sentence upon him. Saunders averred that "[w]e acted agreeably to the laws of our country in punishing the man."
>
> Crossing back into Georgia following this indignity, Stancell immediately made his way to the chambers of the Honorable Augustin S. Clayton, "Judge of the Supreme Courts of the western Circuit of" the State of Georgia and judicial nemesis of the Cherokees. Stancell's affidavit before Judge Clayton omitted the stolen horse and his jury trial. The affidavit characterized him not as a thief, but as a victim "to the great effusion of his blood, the laceration of his back and sides, leaving deep wounds, gashes and bruises on the same. . . ."
>
> Judge Clayton issued criminal process for the arrest of Saunders, who reported to the Phoenix as follows:
>
>> [T]he officers of that state sent armed men to take all the Indians that were concerned in whipping him. I understood that they were on their way, and went to the Long Swamp to meet them. They met me there. I there gave them my bond and security for my appearance at court at Gainsville in Hall County.
>
> The case continued to simmer for the next year. In his Annual Message to the people on October 16, 1830, Principal Chief John Ross commented on "the case of Judge Sanders for punishing a whiteman under the laws of the nation, for the crime of horse stealing"; as part of a litany of complaints against the Georgia Judiciary in general and Judge Clayton in particular, Georgia responded in part by passing a statute in 1830 which provided in part:
>
>> Sec. 3. And be it further enacted by the authority aforesaid. That after the time aforesaid, it shall not be lawful for any person or persons, under colour, or by authority, of the Cherokee tribe, or any of its laws or regulations, to hold any court or tribunal whatever, for the purpose of hearing and determining causes, civil or criminal; or to give any judgment in such causes, or to issue, or cause to issue any process against the person or property of any of said tribe. And all persons offending against the provisions of this section, shall be guilty of a high misdemeanor, and

subject to indictment, and on conviction thereof shall be imprisoned in the penitentiary at hard labour for the space of four years. . . . [Monroe E. Price, *Law and the American Indian*, Bobbs-Merrill Co., 39 (1973).]

This example exposes the exercise of criminal jurisdiction over a citizen of the United States by the Tribal Court. Such action is seen to be in the continuum of push and pull on the frontier between the States and the Cherokee Nation, with the Nation seeking a successful mechanism of enforcement of law in order to maintain stability. In this context, the Nation's exercise of enforcement machinery is both understandable and legitimate. It also reflected the actual state of affairs.

J. Matthew Martin, *The Nature and Extent of the Exercise of Criminal Jurisdiction by the Cherokee Supreme Court: 1823-1835*, 32 N.C. Cent. L. Rev. 27, 48-50 (2009).

Moreover:

As early as June of 1824, Agent McMinn advised the Secretary of War that he had turned a white man over to the Cherokee Light Horse for criminal punishment. McMinn did not possess sufficient evidence to bind the defendant, Daniel Rash, over for trial in Knoxville on charges of accessory to robbery because two witnesses would not leave the Cherokee Nation and be subjected to Court order to attend in Knoxville. Stymied, McMinn "replied that Rash was a proper subject of their laws, and had a right to receive the same penalties that would be inflicted on one of their own proper for a similar offence. . . ." "The Marshal then observed that by the laws of the Cherokee Nation he would at least be whipped, and asked if I would make any objection." Upon being told that the Agent "would not, the light horse then agreed, and gave him so well as I recollect about 39 lashes laid on with a very tender hand as, I understood."

The significance of this incident should not be underestimated. The Agent of the Secretary of War of the United States of America specifically transferred custody of a citizen of the United States to the Cherokee Nation for punishment for a crime committed within the jurisdiction of the Cherokees. The Supreme Court of the United States has yet to analyze Tribal Court criminal jurisdiction in conjunction with this evidence from the historical record.

Id. at 47-48.

3. NON-INDIANS — CIVIL OFFENSES

Muscogee (Creek) Nation v. One Thousand Four Hundred Sixty-three and 14/100 Dollars ($1,463.14)

Muscogee (Creek) Nation Supreme Court, No. SC 2005-01, 9 Oklahoma Tribal Court Rep. 83 (April 29, 2005)

Chief Justice Shirley, Vice Chief Justice Oliver, and Justices McNac and Wiley.

Per Curiam.

. . .

[I.] Facts

On June 15, 2004, Russell "Rusty" Miner and his brother Ricky Miner, both non-Indians, arrived at a gaming facility owned and operated by the Nation on a parcel of treaty land known as the Mackey site. . . . Russell Miner parked the vehicle in a designated handicapped parking space in front of the gaming facility. Neither of the Miner brothers are handicapped, nor did the vehicle have a handicap permit. After parking the vehicle, the Miner brothers patronized the casino. Testimony revealed that during their stay Ricky Miner went to the vehicle, took illegal drugs, and then returned to the inside of the casino. . . . While on routine patrol, Security Officer Thomas McMillen, an employee of the Creek Nation Casino, observed the vehicle parked in a handicapped space. Noticing that no handicap decal or sticker was prominently displayed, the officer looked through the window of the vehicle for a decal or sticker and observed a white powdery substance lying on the center console. . . .

. . . The officers obtained a white powdery substance on the console and an unzipped leather Day Planner containing $1,463.14 in cash. Russell Miner then told the officers that more drugs were located inside the console and possibly a firearm. The officers also recovered two white pill bottles containing a white crystallized substance.

Laboratory tests confirmed that the white powdery substance from the console and the crystallized substance from the pill bottles [was] 6.8 grams of methamphetamine[,] an illegal drug. 14 MUSCOGEE (CREEK) NAT. CODE ANN. §2-101(1). Russell Miner was issued a civil citation for disorderly conduct pursuant to 22 MUSCOGEE (CREEK) NAT. CODE ANN. §2-101(9) for the possession, use, distribution or intent to distribute a controlled dangerous substance [CDS].

Russell Miner was never arrested or issued any criminal citation. He knew at the time the citation was presented that it was a civil citation. On June 30, 2004, Russell Miner voluntarily appeared before the Muscogee (Creek) Nation District Court for the civil citation of disorderly conduct. He admitted to the violation and voluntarily paid a civil fine of $250.00 and court costs of $84.00.

Civil forfeiture proceedings were initiated pursuant to 22 MUSCOGEE (CREEK) NAT. CODE ANN. §2-102 for the forfeiture of the cash, the vehicle and the drugs found in the vehicle.

[II.] Jurisdiction

1. Regulatory Authority over Tribal Treaty Land

The conduct giving rise to this cause of action occurred on a parcel of tribal treaty land known as the Mackey Site. The Nation is the sole owner of the land and therefore possesses the right to exclude any and all individuals.

As a matter of tribal law, all conduct occurring on the Mackey site is subject to the laws of the Nation regardless of the status of the parties. The Mackey site is under the jurisdiction of the Nation because: (1) the land is located within the political and territorial boundaries of the Nation; and (2) the land is owned by the Nation. 27 MUSCOGEE (CREEK) NAT. CODE ANN. §1-102(A) (territorial jurisdiction).

The Courts of this Nation exercise general civil jurisdiction over all civil actions arising under the Constitution, laws or treaties which arise within the Nations' Indian country, regardless of the Indian or non-Indian status of the parties. 27 MUSCOGEE (CREEK) NAT. CODE ANN. §1-102(B) (civil jurisdiction). . . .

We hold that as a matter of tribal law and consistent with federal law, the Nation has exclusive regulatory jurisdiction over the land where Appellant's conduct occurred.

2. Regulatory and Adjudicatory Authority over All Persons

The Appellant argues that the Nation lacks jurisdiction over his conduct, regardless of the status of land, because he is a non-Indian. . . .

Appellant was issued a civil citation pursuant under Title 22 of the Muscogee (Creek) Nation Code, which applies to all persons, regardless of status. Title 22 governs Health and Safety, and includes civil infractions such as traffic violations and public safety concerns such as possession of illegal drugs. Civil fines are limited under Title 22 to $250.00. . . .

In addition, we find the United States' Supreme Court decision in *Washington v. Confederated Tribes of the Colville Indian Reservation*, 447 U.S. 134 (1980), as most analogous to this case. Although that case dealt with tribal powers of taxation, the Supreme Court noted that tribes may exercise a broad range of civil jurisdiction over non-Indians on reservations, particularly when the tribe has a significant interest in the non-Indians activities. *Id.* at 152. In *Colville*, the fact that the non-Indians were coming onto the reservation to purchase cigarettes was an important factor. Non-Indians will be subject to tribal regulatory authority when they voluntarily choose to go onto tribal land and do business with the tribe. Non-Indians who choose to purchase products, engage in commercial activities, or pay for entertainment inside Indian country place themselves within the regulatory reach of the Nation.

The Nation has a significant interest in the activities by any and all persons who enter the Nation's Indian country. The presence of illegal drugs and the need to rid the community of the drugs is of the utmost significance to the Nation, just as it is to all communities and all sovereigns.

We hold that as a matter of tribal law[,] jurisdiction was proper in this case based on the laws of the Muscogee (Creek) Nation alone. The Nation has exclusive jurisdiction to regulate the conduct of all persons on tribal land, particularly those that voluntarily come on to tribal land for the purpose of patronizing tribal businesses. . . .

. . . There should be no question that the presence of illegal drugs on a tribe's reservation is a threat to the health and welfare of the tribe. Illegal drugs are a threat to the health and welfare of all persons. Russell Miner possessed 6.8 grams of methamphetamine, an amount well beyond that considered for personal consumption. Also, the record reflects that Ricky Miner entered the vehicle and actually used the drugs on tribal property. . . . Most importantly, the Appellant's attorney, during oral argument, conceded that drug possession and/or drug use would directly affect the health and welfare of the Muscogee (Creek) Nation. . . .

The state also lacks jurisdiction [over] the criminal conduct inside the Nation's Indian country. Because the Nation does not have a cross-deputization agreement with Tulsa County, Oklahoma, the Nation would have no means of addressing Appellant's conduct through the assistance of another jurisdiction.

It is not clear whether the federal government would have criminal jurisdiction over this activity. This is not federal land and it is not land held in trust by the federal government. The General Crimes Act, which provides federal jurisdiction in criminal prosecutions over inter-racial crimes in Indian country, may not apply because possession of drugs would be considered a victimless crime.

There is simply no jurisdiction besides the Nation's that can adequately deal with drug traffic on tribal lands. The only means in which the Nation may reduce the amount of drugs brought onto tribal lands by non-Indians is through the limited provisions of the Nation's civil code. It is imperative that the Nation possess certain regulatory authority over all persons entering the Nation's land and business enterprises, as this case reflects.

3. Civil Forfeiture Proceedings

Although the civil citation for disorderly conduct and the forfeiture proceedings in this action are governed by the same chapter of Title 22, Public Safety, Appellant challenges the right of Nation to forfeit his vehicle, the cash found inside, and the illegal drugs. . . .

As noted above, there are criminal sanctions in the Nation's code for the same conduct, but Appellant is exempt from the criminal sanctions because the Criminal Code only applies to Indians. An Indian committing the same infraction could be tried criminally and also subjected to civil forfeiture proceedings. The forfeiture taking place is an *in rem* civil action against property used to transport or store drugs on tribal property. The forfeiture proceedings are not individual criminal penalties. . . .

We therefore hold, based on the foregoing reasons, that the Nation possesses the authority to regulate public safety through civil laws that restrict the possession, use or distribution of illegal drugs. We further hold that the Nation's courts possess civil adjudicatory jurisdiction over forfeiture proceedings including the forfeiture of (1) controlled dangerous substances; (2) vehicles used to transport or conceal controlled dangerous substances; and (3) monies and currency found in close proximity of a forfeitable substance.

NOTES

1. The Tenth Circuit affirmed, in a roundabout way, the decision of the Muscogee (Creek) Nation Supreme Court. Russell Miner sued in federal court seeking the return of his Hummer, but the court held that the Muscogee (Creek) Nation was immune from suit. *See Miner Elec., Inc. v. Muscogee (Creek) Nation*, 505 F.3d 1007 (10th Cir. 2007).
2. Several other tribes have begun to enforce tribal laws against non-Indians, using civil penalties such as fines and forfeiture, and judicial tools, such as civil contempt. *See generally* Carrie E. Garrow & Sarah Deer, Tribal Criminal Law and Procedure 97-103 (2004).

4. TERRITORIAL JURISDICTION

Navajo Nation v. Milosevich

District Court of the Navajo Nation Judicial District of Crownpoint, New Mexico, No. CP-TCV-154-90, 6 Navajo Rep. 542 (August 21, 1990)

The opinion of the court was delivered by: Judge Loretta Morris presiding.

This matter having come before the court on a civil traffic complaint and the court being notified that it may not have jurisdiction; this court now addresses this matter and enters its findings and orders as follows:

1. Defendant was cited by a police officer of the Navajo Nation on January 2, 1990, for exceeding posted speed restriction and going 67 miles per hour in a 55 miles per hour speeding zone;
2. Defendant was driving south of Gallup, New Mexico, on New Mexico State Road 602;
3. Defendant signed the traffic complaint stating that he acknowledges the receipt of the traffic citation and that he will appear in court on or before January 22, 1990. Defendant never appeared in court; . . .

Conclusions of Law

1. This court has jurisdiction pursuant to the Navajo Nation Motor Vehicle Code, amended in 1988, which states at section 100 that this court shall have exclusive original jurisdiction over all civil traffic infractions under Title 14 committed within the territorial jurisdiction. The jurisdiction conferred upon this court with respect to traffic infractions is civil jurisdiction. Civil jurisdiction is also conferred upon this court by 7 N.T.C. section 253(2) (1985 Supp.).

2. The territorial jurisdiction of this court extends to Navajo Indian Country and includes all lands within the exterior boundary of the Navajo Indian Reservation, Eastern Navajo Agency, and all lands within the limits of dependent Navajo communities, Navajo Indian allotments, and all other lands held in trust for, owned by, or leased by the United States to the Navajo Tribe or any Band of Navajo Indians. 7 N.T.C. section 254 (1985 Supp.). . . .

4. By bifurcating the code on traffic violations into criminal and civil categories, the Navajo Tribal Council, as the legislative body of the Navajo Nation, intended to protect all highway travellers and the public within its jurisdiction by incarcerating some traffic violators and by causing some to pay fines only, without any incarceration.

5. This court takes notice that many highway travellers, Indians and non-Indians, share and use the major highways within the Navajo Nation. . . .

Order

THEREFORE, IT IS HEREBY ORDERED, ADJUDGED, AND DECREED that this court has jurisdiction over a person, whether Indian or non-Indian, in traffic civil infraction cases. If the defendant wishes to further contest the jurisdiction of this court, he shall do so by filing the appropriate motions and appear in court.

IT IS FURTHER ORDERED, ADJUDGED, AND DECREED that the default of the defendant is hereby entered in the amount of $61.50 and the clerk shall register said default.

NOTES

1. In *People of the Little River Band of Ottawa Indians v. Champagne*, 35 Indian L. Rep. 6004 (Little River Band of Ottawa Indians Court of Appeals 2007),[*] the

---

Disclosure: The author participated in this matter as an appellate justice and wrote the opinion.

court accepted jurisdiction over a criminal act that has seemingly occurred off-reservation — attempted embezzlement — by a sitting tribal justice:

> The Constitution of the Little River Band of Ottawa Indians provides that "[t]he territory of the Little River Band of Ottawa Indians shall encompass all lands which are now or hereinafter owned or reserved for the Tribe . . . and all lands which are now or at a later date owned by the Tribe or held in trust for the Tribe or any member of the Tribe by the United States of America." CONST. art. I, §1. . . . In other words, this Court has jurisdiction over all crimes committed on both reservation lands and trust lands of the Little River Band. Such lands include the lands upon which the Little River Band's governmental and commercial entities rest.
>
> The Constitution provides that the Band must exercise jurisdiction over the Band's territory, subject to three limitations. Specifically, the Constitution provides that "[t]he Tribe's jurisdiction over its members and territory shall be exercised to the fullest extent consistent with this Constitution, the sovereign powers of the Tribe, and federal law." CONST. art. I, §2. As to the first limitation, the Constitution mandates that this Court take jurisdiction over criminal matters arising within the territory of the Band that involve tribal members. The Constitution provides that this Court must "adjudicate all . . . criminal matters arising within the jurisdiction of the Tribe or to which the Tribe or an enrolled member of the Tribe is a party." CONST. art. VI, §8(a)(1). *See also* Tribal Court Ordinance §4.01, Ordinance #97-300-01 (Aug. 4, 1997). [T]he locus of the crime was the territory of the Little River Band, not the accident location or Justice Champagne's residence. . . .
>
> As to the third limitation, federal law, nothing in federal law prohibits the prosecution of Justice Champagne for this crime. . . . Federal law has long recognized the rights and authority of federally recognized Indian tribes to exercise criminal jurisdiction over American Indians for crimes committed within Indian Country. . . .
>
> In his pre-trial motion, Justice Champagne argued that the State of Michigan should have exclusive jurisdiction in this matter. At oral argument, Justice Champagne asserted that the federal government should have exclusive jurisdiction. Justice Champagne is incorrect on both counts. As Judge Quick pointed out:

> Defendant is a member of the Tribe. The allegation against Defendant is that he engaged in criminal conduct against the Tribe. To assume a sovereign other than the Little River Band of Ottawa Indians has jurisdiction over this matter would be tantamount to determining that the Tribe has no power to govern its own affairs. Certainly, the Tribe's right of governance is unquestionable. The Little River Band of Ottawa Indians, through its inherent power to rule itself, does have jurisdiction over this matter.

> *Champagne I, supra,* at 6. Regardless of whether either the State of Michigan or the United States has jurisdiction over this matter,[1] this Court is

---

1. It is unlikely either the State of Michigan or the United States would exercise jurisdiction over this matter. Judge Quick noted that Michigan state law requires "that a criminal matter that involves fraudulent misrepresentations must be tried where the victim of the crime resides, and not where the defendant made the misrepresentations." *Champagne I, supra,* at 6 (citing *Schiff Co. v. Perk Drug Stores,* 270 N.W. 738 (Mich. 1936)). *See also* MICH. COMP. L. ANN. §§762.2-762.3 (noting

obligated by the Constitution of the Little River Band and by the ordinances of the Tribal Council to assert jurisdiction.

Id. at 6005-06.

2. In *People of the Little River Band of Ottawa Indians v. Kelsey*, 2009 WL 3262773 (Little River Band of Ottawa Indians Court of Appeals 2009), the court affirmed the conviction of a tribal member for sexual assault at the tribal community center, located on fee lands owned by the tribe. The court reasoned:

> It is common knowledge that the Tribal Community Center has been the center of Tribal community activities ever since it was purchased by the Tribe many years ago. In fact, this very Court conducted several hearings in those facilities when the Tribal courts were first established and it is where the Tribal court offices were located for many years. Thus, it is imperative that judicial notice be taken of the **tribal nature** of all the activities that have occurred at the Community Center over many years now. In addition, the Center is a community gathering point to host varied and numerous tribal meetings, to serve community meals and to provide tribal office space for the conduct of the business of a tribal sovereign.
>
> Criminal law simply put is the mere imposition of standards of behavior by defining that behavior which is unacceptable to the society, *i.e.* community, of people. It is clear to this Court that the Tribe's standards of behavior **ought** to apply to the behavior of Tribal members and other Indians in the Tribal Community Center. The general welfare of the Tribe depends upon individuals deferring from behavior that offends community standards. The interests of the Tribe are very strong here. This case involves a tribal member in an elected position acting as an agent of the Tribe at a Tribal activity who committed a crime against a Tribal employee in a public setting openly visible to other employees and Tribal members who were present. It also involves a Tribal Court finding that Defendant exercised political influence affecting the victim and the Tribe's welfare. . . .
>
> Nonetheless, the Court must consider whether the Tribe itself has imposed a limitation on the exercise of its inherent authority. Thus, we begin an examination of tribal law. Article I of the Tribal Constitution defines the "territory" of the Little River Band of Ottawa Indians as ". . . *all lands which are now or hereinafter* **owned by** *or reserved for the Tribe* . . ." (bold added for emphasis by this Court). *See* The Constitution of the Little River Band of Ottawa Indians, Article I, Sec. 1. In fact, the provision includes a **mandate** that such lands "**shall**" be included in the definition. A constitutional mandate is a mandate of the people of the Band because the Tribal Constitution, as the organic governing document of the Tribe, is their collective consent to be governed and it provides their framework for government. The design is mandated.
>
> Section 2 of that same Article requires that "[t]he *jurisdiction over its members and territory shall be exercised to the fullest extent consistent with this Constitution, the sovereign powers of the Tribe, and federal law.*"

---

jurisdiction and venue in criminal cases based on where the criminal act(s) occurred, not the residence of the defendant). Moreover, it is unlikely that the federal government would have jurisdiction in this matter as the amount of money involved is insufficient (or barely sufficient) to reach federal requirements — $5,000. *See* 18 U.S.C. §666(a)(1). *E.g., United States v. Heddon,* 2001 WL 406430 (6th Cir., April 3, 2001).

([B]old added again for emphasis by this Court.) [T]his Court recognizes that tribal jurisdiction is **larger** than territory because some tribal authority extends beyond its land, *e.g.* tribal membership and self-regulation of tribal treaty rights within treaty[-]ceded areas. The drafters of the Tribal Constitution wisely recognized such.

Kelsey, 2009 WL 3262773, at *1-2.

The court then held that tribal ordinances failing to recognize the tribal constitution's broad assertion of territorial authority were themselves unconstitutional. *See id.* at *2-3.

C. SUBSTANTIVE CRIMINAL LAW

Many Indian nations do not create their own criminal codes from scratch. Many tribes have adapted law and order codes imposed on them by the Bureau of Indian Affairs, and many others have adopted the criminal codes of the state in which the tribe is located. These codes often are called "borrowed" or "transplanted" law. Still other Indian nations have adopted indigenous criminal codes based on specific criminal activities unique to Indian country. Often, these criminal codes involve treaty hunting or fishing rights, or another activity solely related to on-reservation activity.

1. BORROWED CRIMINAL CODES

PEOPLE OF THE LITTLE RIVER BAND OF OTTAWA INDIANS v. CHAMPAGNE[*]

Little River Band of Ottawa Indians Court of Appeals, No. 06-178-AP,
35 Indian L. Rep. 6004 (2007)

Before EDMONDSON, FLETCHER, and KRAUS, Justices
FLETCHER, J.

I. Introduction

There are many trickster tales told by the Anishinaabek involving the godlike character Nanabozho. One story relevant to the present matter is a story that is sometimes referred to as "The Duck Dinner." *See, e.g.,* JOHN BORROWS, RECOVERING CANADA: THE RESURGENCE OF INDIGENOUS LAW 47-49 (2002); Charles Kawbawgam, *Nanabozho in a Time of Famine, in* OJIBWA NARRATIVES OF CHARLES AND CHARLOTTE KAWBAWGAM AND JACQUES LEPIQUE, 1893-1895, at 33 (Arthur P. Bourgeios ed., 1994); Beatrice Blackwood, *Tales of the Chippewa Indians*, 40 FOLKLORE 315, 337-38 (1929). There are many, many versions of this story, but in most versions, Nanabozho is hungry, as usual. After a series of failures in convincing (tricking) the woodpecker and muskrat spirits into being meals, Nanabozho convinces (tricks) several ducks and kills them by decapitating them. He eats his fill, saves the rest for later, and takes a nap. He orders his

---

Disclosure: The author participated in this matter as an appellate justice and wrote the opinion.

buttocks to wake him if anyone comes along threatening to steal the rest of his duck dinner. During the night, men approach. Nanabozho's buttocks warn him twice: "Wake up, Nanabozho. Men are coming." Kawbawgam, *supra*, at 35. Nanabozho ignores his buttocks and continues to sleep. When he awakens to find the remainder of his food stolen, he is angry. But he does not blame himself. Instead, he builds up his fire and burns his buttocks as punishment for their failure to warn him. To some extent, the trick has come back to haunt Nanabozho — and in the end, with his short-sightedness, he burns his own body.

The relevance of this timeless story to the present matter is apparent. The trial court, per Judge Brenda Jones Quick, tried and convicted the defendant and appellant, Hon. Ryan L. Champagne, a tribal member, an appellate justice, and a member of this Court, of the crime of attempted fraud. Justice Champagne's primary job during the relevant period in this case was with the Little River Band of Ottawa Indians. Part of his job responsibilities included leaving the tribal place of business in his personal vehicle to visit clients. While on one of these trips, Justice Champagne took a personal detour and was involved in an accident. The Band and later the trial judge concluded that his claim for reimbursement from the Band was fraudulent. Judge Quick found that Justice Champagne "attempted to obtain money by seeking reimbursement from the Tribe for the loss of his vehicle by intentionally making a false assertion that he was on his way to a client's home at the time of the accident." *People v. Champagne*, Opinion and Judgment at 6, No. 06-131-TM (Little River Band Tribal Court, Dec. 1, 2006) (*Champagne III*). Justice Champagne was neither heading toward the tribal offices nor toward a client's home.

Like Nanabozho, Justice Champagne perpetrated a trick upon the Little River Ottawa community — a trick that has come back to haunt him. It would seem to be a small thing involving a relatively small sum of money, but because the Little River Ottawa people have designated this particular "trick" a criminal act, Justice Champagne has burned himself.

Among the many legal arguments made before this Court at oral argument that will be addressed later in this Opinion and Order, Justice Champagne argues that the tribal customs and traditions of the Ottawa people do not recognize the crime of "attempt." Justice Champagne further appears to argue more generally that the Little River Band statute adopting relevant Michigan state criminal [laws] is inconsistent with Anishinaabek traditional tribal law and therefore this Court should not apply it to him. *Cf. LaPorte v. Fletcher*, No. 04142AP, at 9-10 (Little River Band Tribal Court of Appeals 2006) (Champagne, J.) ("It is the custom of the Little River Band of Ottawa Indians to believe that society must be mended to make whole again."). These are laudable and compelling arguments relating to the seeming contradiction between tribal goals to develop a modern and sophisticated legal system based on Anglo-American legal models while attempting to preserve the cultural distinctiveness of Ottawa culture through the development of tribal law and the preservation of tribal customs and traditions. *See generally* Michael D. Petoskey, *Tribal Courts*, 67 Michigan Bar Journal, May 1988, at 366, 366-69; Frank Pommersheim, Braid of Feathers: American Indian Law and Contemporary Tribal Life 66-67 (1995). As such, we take these arguments seriously. In other factual and legal circumstances, we might be compelled to consider such an argument as dispositive, but this matter does not oblige us to question current tribal law. As Justice Champagne all but admitted at trial and at oral argument, he attempted to procure money that was not owed him by the Little River Band for his own purposes. It is not obvious to this Court that Justice Champagne's failure in his attempt should excuse him from liability. More importantly, Justice Champagne does not and cannot identify an Ottawa custom or tradition that would excuse him for his actions. In fact, it would be a sad day for this community to acknowledge that an action reflecting an intention of an individual to fraudulently procure money from the Band is excused because the word "attempt" does not exist in Anishinaabemowin, as Justice Champagne alleged at oral argument.

As the remainder of this Opinion and Order shows, we have no choice but to AFFIRM the judgment below. . . .

III. Discussion

. . .

C. Lack of a Criminal Statute

The Little River Band's Tribal Council has both adopted an indigenous criminal code and incorporated provisions of the Michigan state criminal law statutes as a means of exercising its constitutional authority "to govern the conduct of members of the Little River Band. . . ." CONST. art. IV, §7(a)(1). The Band charged Justice Champagne with attempted fraud in accordance with the Law and Order — Criminal Offenses — Ordinance §11.02, Ordinance #03-400-03 (last amended July 19, 2006) (criminalizing and defining "fraud") and the Tribal Court Ordinance §8.02, Ordinance #97-300-01 (Aug. 4, 1997) ("Any matters not covered by the laws or regulations of the Little River Band of Ottawa . . . may be decided by the Courts according to the laws of the State of Michigan."). Through the state law incorporation statute, Section 8.02, the Band asserted that Michigan Compiled Laws Section 750.92 also applies to Justice Champagne. Section 750.92 is the State's "attempt" statute and provides, "Any person who shall attempt to commit an offense prohibited by law, and in such attempt shall do any act towards the commission of such offense, but shall fail in the perpetration, or shall be intercepted or prevented in the execution of the same, when no express provision is made by law for the punishment of such attempt, shall be punished. . . ." The Little River Band's criminal law statute has no parallel provision criminalizing "attempt." Justice Champagne, who attempted to defraud the Band but failed, was charged under this collection of statutes.

Justice Champagne forcefully argues that the lack of an indigenous "attempt" statute excuses his actions. His argument rests on the basis that the Little River Band's choice to incorporate elements of Michigan's criminal code is an abrogation of tribal sovereignty and a violation of tribal customs and traditions. This appears to be a facial attack on the validity of Section 8.02. As Judge Quick noted, however, "It does not diminish a sovereign's power to enact, by incorporation, laws as set forth by another jurisdiction, particularly when it is a matter of convenience. . . . Certainly, when the Tribal Council enacted specific laws, it could have done away with Ordinance #97-300-01, Section 8.02. This, it did not do. There, the Ordinance is binding on Defendant." *Champagne I, supra*, at 2. Regardless, whether or not the Tribal Council's decision to adopt state law was wise is irrelevant[,] the statutes apply to Justice Champagne as a member of the Band. We are bound to apply the law of the Little River Band. *See* Tribal Court Ordinance §8.01, Ordinance #97-300-01 (Aug. 4, 1997).

At oral argument, Justice Champagne referred this Court to his separate opinion in our 2006 decision in *LaPorte v. Fletcher*, No. 04-142-AP (Little River Band Tribal Court of Appeals 2006) (Champagne, J.). Justice Champagne represented the opinion to mean that the tribal courts should refrain from applying state law, especially where it is inconsistent with tribal customs and traditions. That opinion, the reasoning of which both of the other justices deciding that matter explicitly rejected, has no precedential value to this Court. Moreover, the subject of the separate opinion—whether the losing party to a closely contested civil suit should receive an award of attorney fees—is all but irrelevant to this matter. Finally, the separate opinion—arguing on a general level that tribal law should be used to bring the parties together to make the parties whole—tends to support a view that does not favor Justice Champagne's position in this matter. As noted in the introduction to this opinion, it does no justice to the tribal community to excuse the actions of a presiding appellate justice in attempting (and failing) to defraud the Little River Band. . . .

F. Challenges to the Trial Court's Findings of Fact

Justice Champagne offers no argument in any briefs filed before this Court that the findings of fact made by Judge Quick at trial were clearly erroneous. At oral argument, however, Justice Champagne argues that the Little River Band made an admission on an insurance form that he was, in fact, on company time when he was involved in the accident. Justice Champagne further asserts that his accident was caused by his sleepiness, which in turn derived from his "sleep apnea" condition. We are reluctant to address these arguments, given that the tribal prosecutor could not have prepared a response to these arguments in anticipation of oral argument as they were not briefed. But given that these arguments amount to an attempt to offer additional or supplementary testimony to that which was given at trial, we can dispose of these arguments easily.

In short, Justice Champagne's attempt to reargue the question of fault and causation is fundamentally irrelevant. The trial court did not rely upon the pretrial statements or the trial testimony about who was at fault in the accident. Judge Quick wrote, "I believe the prosecution proved Defendant lied about his responsibility for causing the accident; however, *I gave this fact no weight in determining whether or not Defendant was guilty of the charges against him*." *Champagne III, supra*, at 3 (emphasis added). Instead, the trial court relied upon the fact that Justice Champagne misrepresented to his employer about his destination to hold that he was guilty of attempted fraud. *See id.* at 3-6. Judge Quick concluded:

> Cumulatively, I found the testimony of these three witnesses and the accompanying exhibits to overwhelmingly prove, beyond any reasonable doubt, that

> Defendant was traveling west through the intersection at the time he broad-sided Ms. Joseph's vehicle, and was *not* making a wide right turn onto Maple as he claimed. . . .
>
> Since I was convinced, beyond a reasonable doubt, that Defendant was heading due west at the time of the accident rather than attempting to turn north as he claimed, and that traveling in that direction actually took him away from the home where he claimed he was headed, I found that he was not being truthful when he made the assertion that he was going to a client's home at the time of the accident.

Id. at 5-6 (emphasis in original). As noted by the tribal prosecutor at oral argument and by Judge Quick at trial, Justice Champagne's claims about "sleep apnea" do not support his defense to the claim that he attempted to deceive his employer about his destination at the time of the accident. *See id.* at 6. In short, nothing compels this Court to find that Judge Quick's findings of fact were clearly erroneous.

Conclusion

This Court is aware of the gravity of a criminal case involving a sitting appellate justice as a defendant. It is a sad day for the Little River Band Ottawa community and to this Court to be forced to sit in judgment of one of its own, but we are obligated to do so. At oral argument, Justice Champagne raised the possibility that his prosecution was "political." We have no doubt that Justice Champagne's assertion is true, but not in the way he means it. As one of the leaders of the community—*ogemuk*—Justice Champagne was held—and should be held—to a higher standard of conduct. *See generally* Const. art. VI, §2(a); art. VI, §§6(b)(1)-(2). As to Justice Champagne's claim that he was singled out by other leaders of this community, we have no competence or authority to make judgments as to the sound discretion of the tribal prosecutor to initiate a criminal proceeding.

For the above reasons, we AFFIRM the judgment of the trial court.

NOTES

1. Tribal courts routinely borrow federal and state common law to fill in gaps in tribal criminal law, especially in the context of the rights contained in the Indian Civil Rights Act. In *Teeman v. Burns Paiute Indian Tribe*, 4 NICS App. 185 (Burns Paiute Tribal Court of Appeals 1997), the court borrowed state and federal law to articulate the burden of proof in a case in which the defendant asserted self-defense as a defense to the prosecution:

   > Most Indian courts recognize a common law right to assert self-defense. Most states recognize self-defense in specific statutory provisions. But in federal law, the basis for an affirmative defense argument by a defendant is found in the proof issue of the "guilty state of mind" (*mens rea*) and in the due process provision of the Fifth Amendment to the United States Constitution. *Patterson v. U.S.*, 432 U.S. 197 (1977). . . . The majority of states, including Oregon, have opted for a requirement that the burden of production by the defendant must meet the "preponderance of the evidence" test.

It is now well settled, however, that the government may shift to the defendant the burden of going forward with evidence of self-defense. That is not a due process violation. . . .

The question of a deprivation of due process arises when a court, as here, places upon an accused the burden of proving that the law will permit the introduction of evidence of an exculpatory nature. The Burns Paiute Tribal Laws are specific in placing responsibility on the trial court judge to rule upon the questions of law presented at the trial (Chapter II, Section L. [1]). The tribal court has responsibility under tribal law to have legal resource materials available for that purpose. . . . It is the responsibility of the prosecution to prove the crime beyond a reasonable doubt as a due process right. . . .

It is not the responsibility of the defendant, however, to prove that she did not commit the crime.

Id. at 189-91.

2. In *Stepetin v. Nisqually Indian Community*, 2 NICS App. 224 (Nisqually Tribal Court of Appeals 1993), a deeply divided appellate court reversed a conviction for reckless driving on grounds that the tribal code adopting state law was void for vagueness:

The Nisqually Indian Community has enacted a provision which states as follows:

Where state law . . . does not conflict with the Tribal Code, the Tribal Court may resort to and enforce any state statute within tribal jurisdiction.

. . . Therefore, the ultimate issue addressed by the vagueness argument is whether this provision of Nisqually law was adequate to give fair notice to Mr. Stepetin that his conduct was prohibited by the Nisqually Tribal Code. Mr. Stepetin was alleged to have driven a truck at a high rate of speed along a gravel road on the Nisqually Reservation. Tribal members were in the vicinity and though no one was injured, a dog was struck and killed.

Any reasonable person should know that this type of conduct is prohibited in any community. However, we agree with defendant's counsel when he stated the issue as not whether Mr. Stepetin knew this conduct was wrong, but whether he knew it was a crime. The Nisqually incorporation statute does not advise Mr. Stepetin, or any other Nisqually Tribal member, that driving a motor vehicle in this manner was a crime. Therefore, we find that the statute is impermissibly vague.

We are aware that on the Nisqually Reservation word may travel quickly throughout the Reservation. However, we do not believe that this is, or should be, a substitute for proper enactment, enforcement, and notice of ordinances by the Community. . . .

Id. at 228-29.

In dissent, Chief Justice Rosemary Irvin wrote:

The majority, paraphrasing the defendant's attorney, states the issue of adequate notice as "not whether Mr. Stepetin knew this conduct was wrong, but whether he knew it was a crime." Majority Opinion at 8 [2 NICS App. at 229]. But traditionally, for a member of what is now the Nisqually Indian Community, there was no difference between wrongful conduct and that which was societally sanctioned. Interview with Barbara Lane, Ph.D., anthropologist specializing in Northwest Native American customs and traditions (Jan. 7, 1993). To say that the defendant knew that he had violated a community standard but that he did not know there was a written statute making this violation illegal is to make a distinction without a difference. . . .

In conclusion, Mr. Stepetin's knowledge of those common social duties imposed by traditional tribal mores constituted adequate notice that his conduct could trigger tribal sanctions.

Id. at 234-35 (IRVIN, C.J., concurring and dissenting).

2. INDIGENOUS CRIMINAL LAW

HOH INDIAN TRIBE v. HUDSON

Hoh River Court of Appeals, No. HOH-CrF-1/93-007,
3 NICS App. 304 (March 25, 1994)

Before: Chief Justice ELBRIDGE COOCHISE, Associate Justice CHARLES HOSTNIK, and Associate Justice JOHN L. ROE.

COOCHISE, Chief Justice: . . .

Facts

The Tribe alleged that on January 18, 1993, Mr. Hudson physically interfered with Steven E. Penn, Jr., who was actively engaged in legal fishing activity when he was hit by Mr. Hudson.

[S]ection 7.6 of the Hoh Indian Tribe Fishing Ordinance . . . states:

It is unlawful to physically interfer, [sic] disturb, or harass a fishermen actively engaged in legal fishing activity on waters within the usual and accustomed fishing areas of the Tribe.

On September 21, 1993, the Defendant was found guilty of Interference With Fishermen in a bench trial. . . .

Discussion

Interference With Fishermen requires the Hoh Tribe to prove beyond a reasonable doubt that (1) the Defendant physically interfered, disturbed, or harassed a fisherman, (2) who was actively engaged in legal fishing activity and, (3) was on waters within the usual and accustomed fishing areas of the Hoh Tribe. . . .

It is a general principle in non-tribal systems of justice that in reviewing the sufficiency of the evidence, "the question is whether, after viewing the evidence in the light most favorable to the State, any rational trier of fact could have found the essential elements of the crime beyond a reasonable doubt." . . .

There is no doubt that the Defendant assaulted Steven Penn. Steven Penn's testimony, as well as other circumstantial evidence, all pointed to the fact that an assault occurred. However, an essential element of Interference With Fishermen is whether Penn was actively engaged in fishing activity at the time the unlawful interference occurred.

This Court did not find a definition of the phrase "actively engaged" in the Hoh Fishing Ordinance. No evidence was introduced regarding the Hoh Business Committee's enactment of this section of the ordinance that would explain the intended meaning or goal of the ordinance or what activity would fall within the active engagement of fishing.

A general principle of statutory construction is that effect is to be given to every word. In construing the word "actively" against the background of the facts in this case, the Hoh Tribe argued that Steven and Essau Penn (the other person at the scene of the assault) were at the river and Steven Penn was holding an anchor when he was assaulted. The Hoh Tribe also argued that Penn did not need to be engaged in fishing at the moment he was assaulted. However, this would not give any effect to the word "actively" as an element of the offense charged.

The language of the ordinance indicates that actual fishing activity must be taking place in order to interfere, disturb or harass a fisherman. The Hoh Tribe argued that the ordinance intended to address fights occurring at the river while people were traveling to and from the fishing areas. That intent is not clearly expressed in the language used in the ordinance. Instead, the ordinance contains definite language of "actively engaged in legal fishing activity."

The trial court's findings of fact that Steven Penn had a net set in the river, capable of catching fish at the time of the alleged incident[,] was not supported by the evidence. There was no testimony that Steven Penn had a net set in the river or where the net was located. The drawing submitted into evidence was not introduced to determine Steven Penn's fishing location but rather the general area where the assault took place. There was no evidence concerning what type of "fishing activity" Penn was actively engaged in at the time of the assault or that he was even engaged in fishing activity.

According to testimony, Mr. Penn was picking up his anchor. His boat was not in the water at the time, but was on the beach. In response to the question "were you fishing on the river . . . when this incident happened?" the victim responded, "Yes." This is the only evidence that the victim was fishing at the time of the assault. There is no corroborating evidence of the type of fishing activity that Penn was engaged in other than Mr. Penn's conclusory statement that he was "fishing." . . .

In addition to proving the fisherman was actively engaged in fishing activity, the Defendant argued that it must also be proven that the fisherman was actively engaged in legal fishing activity at the time of the alleged violation. The Defendant argued that Mr. Penn was with Essau Penn, a non-member, and therefore could not have been legally fishing. Non-tribal members are not authorized fishermen under Section 4.2 of the Hoh Indian Tribe's General Fishing Ordinance No. 78-9-01.

The Court finds it is unnecessary to address the other elements of Interference With Fisherman. The Hoh Tribe has failed to meet the burden of proving beyond a reasonable doubt that the appellant interfered with Steven Penn while actively engaged in fishing, which is an essential element of the offense charged; therefore, based upon the foregoing discussion,

Order

IT IS HEREBY ORDERED that the trial court is reversed.

NOTE

In *Tulalip Tribes v. Joseph*, 8 NICS App. 47 (Tulalip Tribal Court of Appeals 2008), the court reversed the trial court's decision to dismiss two counts where the court had already made a determination that sufficient probable cause existed to bring the charges in a tribal fishing case:

> While due process and equal protection clauses are usually recognized as applying to individuals' rights before the court, it is imperative that courts recognize that the Tribe has those same rights to be heard and to present evidence. The prosecutor of the Tribe is representing the membership of the Tribe and the community. That representation is intended [to] reflect the moral compass of the Tribal community by charging those individuals who fail to abide by the laws of the Tribe with criminal sanctions. Once the Tribe has established probable cause to proceed, the court should allow the case to proceed to its conclusion.
>
> In the instant case, the court found probable cause in June to proceed with the case. Absent any motion by the parties, the judge should have allowed the Tribe to present its case against Mr. Joseph. We understand that one directive of §2.1.1 is to eliminate unjustifiable expense and delay, but dismissing cases *sua sponte* is not a practice that should be encouraged in our courts.
>
> On a second review immediately before the trial, the judge asked the prosecutor if the gear was properly registered to James Anderson. When the prosecutor acknowledged that it was properly registered to Mr. Anderson, the judge made a determination that if gear was properly registered to the owner, there could be no violation of this section. At first glance, this appears to be a valid assumption, but a closer reading of the Code section brings the issue into a clearer picture.
>
>> Ordinance 51, 7.1, Registration of Gear. All boats and gear used in exercising tribal fishing rights shall be registered in the name of the tribal member actually owning or having an interest in that boat or gear and marked in accordance with the procedures established by this Ordinance and **Tribal fishing regulations promulgated hereunder**. No gear shall be authorized under this Ordinance for use in exercising tribal fishing unless it is so registered and marked. (Emphasis added.)
>>
>> Regulation 2007-013, Other Restrictions. (9) It will be unlawful for a crab fisher to **remove or pull a crab pot from the water that is not registered by that fisher**, without prior permission from their enforcement program. [. . .] (11) All commercial pots must be marked with a valid crab pot tag issued by the Tulalip Tribes Enforcement Office. **Pot tag numbers are assigned to a given boat**. Pots will be transferred and harvested by that boat with the corresponding pot tag number. . . . (14) All subsistence harvesters must possess a subsistence crab fishing permit obtained from the Tulalip Fisheries Office. **Subsistence harvesters are allowed 2 pots per permit per boat** and a daily limit of 12 crab. (Emphasis added.)
>
> The trial judge looked at only one section of [the] Law and Order Code and then made a decision to dismiss. The prosecutor could look to at least one other resolution to determine if a violation had occurred. It doesn't appear that the

judge considered this resolution in his decision to dismiss. At trial, the prosecutor may have had evidence that showed the appellant violated these sections. At the very least, he should have had the opportunity to present his evidence to the Court. If the Court then determined that the sections didn't apply or that the prosecutor hadn't met his burden of proving all the elements of the crime, a dismissal would have been in order. We find that the judge erred in not allowing the case to go to trial.

Id. at 48-50.

D. CRIMINAL PROCEDURE

Much of the criminal procedure jurisprudence in American law is based on the reality that law enforcement officers, prosecutors, and even courts ran roughshod over the rights of criminal defendants throughout American history. For example, the critically important criminal procedure case *Miranda v. Arizona*, 384 U.S. 436 (1966), derived from a recognition that state and federal law enforcement officers had been trained to coerce confessions from criminal defendants using a plethora of physical and psychological tactics so abusive as to render the reliability of the confession highly questionable. *See generally* Livingston Hall & Yale Kamisar, Modern Criminal Procedure 101-8 (1965); Charles E. O'Hara, Fundamentals of Criminal Investigation 104-44 (3d ed. 1973).

As some have recognized, Indian nations traditionally did not coerce or elicit confessions using abusive or threatening tactics. There is no such tradition. However, being part of an Indian community alone would often compel Indian persons who had committed acts against the community to confess those acts before any form of healing could begin. Even today, Indian criminal suspects confess to their crimes at higher rates than other people, even presupposing that "there is no such thing as the right to be silent." Carrie E. Garrow & Sarah Deer, Tribal Criminal Law and Procedure 243 (2004).

In general, tribal courts apply a higher standard of care to tribal law enforcement officials, often requiring greater criminal procedure guarantees to tribal criminal defendants than those they would otherwise receive in state or federal courts.

1. DUE PROCESS

Nelson v. Yurok Tribe

Yurok Tribal Court of Appeals, No. 96-006, 5 NICS App. 119 (May 7, 1999)

Before: Fred Gabourie, Sr., Chief Justice; Douglas W. Luna, Justice; Michelle Demmert, Justice.

I. Introduction

. . . The tribal court, after a trial *de novo*, found the Appellant had violated the Yurok Tribal Fishing Rights Ordinance (YTFRO) and imposed the maximum fine of $200, which was suspended on condition that Appellant comply with tribal law for the following year. . . .

III. Factual Background

On Wednesday, September 25, 1996, . . . BIA officer, Tami Fletcher . . . found Appellant in possession of several salmon and cited Appellant pursuant to YTFRO §8(a) for fishing during closure hours pursuant to the Yurok Tribe's 1996 Harvest Management Plan (Plan). The BIA seized Appellant's dip-net and salmon, as provided for in the YTFRO. . . .

V. Issues on Appeal

In his Notice of Appeal, Appellant lists several grounds for his appeal from the *de novo* trial decision. Since the Appellant failed to submit a written brief and failed to appear for the scheduled oral arguments, the grounds for his appeal are based upon his Notice of Appeal and consolidated into two issues:

1) Was the Appellant denied procedural or substantive due process in the *de novo* trial?
2) Did the Appellant's conviction violate Article IX of the Yurok Constitution which protects "traditional practices" from infringement by acts of the Yurok Tribal Council?

VI. Discussion

Even though the Appellant failed to do more than file a notice of appeal, he raises an issue worth addressing. That is, in the exercise of its authority, may a tribe regulate tribal members' exercise of traditional practices regarding their right to fish? . . .

A. Applicable Tribal Law

The laws applicable to Appellant's appeal are the Yurok Constitution, the YTFRO, the Yurok Tribe's 1996 Harvest Management Plan, and the tribe's September 11, 1996, "Advance Notice of In-Season Adjustment."

The Yurok are a fishing people and the tribe's Constitution and fishing laws are expressly designed to conserve and restore the severely depleted Klamath River anadromous fishery for current members and future generations. The first paragraph of the Preamble to the Yurok Constitution states:

> Our people have always lived on this sacred and wondrous land along the Pacific Coast and inland on the Klamath River, since the Spirit People, *Wo-ge'*, made things ready for us and the Creator, *Ko-won-no-ekc-on Ne-ka-nup-ceo*, placed us here. From the beginning, we have followed all the laws of the Creator, which became the whole fabric of our tribal sovereignty. In times past and now Yurok people bless the deep river, the tall redwood trees, the rocks, the mounds, and the trails. We pray for the health of all the animals, and prudently harvest and manage the great salmon runs and herds of deer and elk. We never waste and use every bit of the salmon, deer, elk, sturgeon, eels, seaweed, mussels, candlefish, otters, sea lions, seals, whales, and other ocean and river animals. We also have practiced our stewardship of the land in the prairies and

forests through controlled burns that improve wildlife habitat and enhance the health and growth of the tan oak acorns, hazelnuts, pepperwood nuts, berries, grasses, and bushes, all of which are used and provide materials for baskets, fabrics, and utensils.

The last paragraph of the Preamble expressly provides:

Therefore, in order to exercise the inherent sovereignty of the Yurok Tribe, we adopt this Constitution in order to:

1) Preserve forever the survival of our tribe and protect it from forces which may threaten its existence;

2) Uphold and protect our tribal sovereignty which has existed from time immemorial and which remains undiminished;

3) Reclaim the tribal land base within the Yurok Reservation and enlarge the reservation boundaries to the maximum extent possible within the ancestral lands of our tribe and/or within any compensatory land area;

4) Preserve and promote our culture, language, and religious beliefs and practices, and pass them on to our children, our grandchildren, and to their children and grandchildren, on and on, forever;

5) Provide for the health, education, economy, and social wellbeing of our members and future members;

6) Restore, enhance, and manage the tribal fishery, tribal water rights, tribal forests, and all other natural resources; and

7) Insure peace, harmony, and protection of individual human rights among our members and among others who may come within the jurisdiction of our tribal government.

Article IV, §5 of the Yurok Constitution vests the Yurok Tribal Council with "the legislative power of the Yurok Tribe," including:

[T]he authority to enact legislation, rules and regulations not inconsistent with this Constitution; to further the objectives of the Yurok Tribe as reflected in the Preamble to this Constitution; administer and regulate affairs, persons and transactions within Tribal Territory; enact civil and criminal laws . . . manage tribal lands and assets.

. . . The YTFRO, as amended June 6, 1996, "was issued by the authority of the Yurok Tribal Council as provided by the Constitution of the Yurok Tribe." YTFRO §1(a) provides:

The purpose of this ordinance is to protect the fishery resources and therefore, tribal fishing rights by establishing procedures for the conservation of fish stock and exercise of federally reserved fishing rights. This YTFRO is intended to allow fishing opportunity to Yurok tribal members, while at the same time assuring adequate spawning escapement and the attainment of conservation objectives.

. . . In short, on the day in question, Wednesday, September 25, 1996, Appellant was entitled to fish at the mouth of the Klamath with his dip-net before 6:00 a.m. and after 6:00 p.m. Instead the Appellant chose to fish for an unknown number of hours before the 6:00 p.m opening. Appellant was first observed fishing at 4:30 p.m. and was cited at 5:30 p.m.

B. Procedural Due Process and Equal Protection

... In the case before us, the Yurok Tribe is a domestic dependent nation within the United States. ... The Yurok Tribe is entitled to legislate and enforce its own laws.[9] ...

In his Notice of Appeal, Appellant argues that the *de novo* trial judge was "not a licensed attorney and therefore, not qualified to adjudicate a criminal proceeding as a matter of federal and tribal due process." Appellant cites no authority for this proposition.

The tribe argues that: (1) it is neither tribal law nor practice to require a tribal judge to be a licensed attorney; (2) federal law has no such requirement; and (3) there is no evidence in the record as to whether the trial judge is or is not a licensed attorney. We agree.

Appellant further argues that the Special Judge was biased due to purported contractual relationships with the tribe. We agree with the tribe that this is a factual, not a legal issue and therefore, is not subject to appeal. Further, there is no evidence in the record to support this accusation and we therefore find the Appellant's accusation baseless. Even if it were true, it is legally irrelevant given Appellant's admission of fishing during closure. Finally, we note that the Special Judge gave Appellant the opportunity to make a motion to remove the judge, an opportunity that Appellant declined.

Ironically, the Appellant appeals the use of the Special Judge that was appointed *at his request* to avoid any appearance of bias. This is the same judge who restored Appellant's fishing rights and suspended the fine for Appellant's admitted violation of tribal law. Still not satisfied, Appellant has the temerity to now disavow his prior demands and contend that he should have been tried by the *original* tribal prosecutor and the *original* tribal judge, who convicted him in the first trial. His contentions are simply vexatious.

Appellant complains that the tribe "unfairly hired a law firm" to prosecute him. The law firm is the tribe's general counsel and was appointed to prosecute this case only because Appellant requested a new prosecutor. There is no impropriety, much less a due process violation.

In his Notice of Appeal, Appellant further claims that the "trial judge illegally and arbitrarily increased the fine imposed in the first trial." It was Appellant who demanded a trial *de novo*, which by definition erases the prior proceeding and begins a new proceeding from scratch. No tribal law or procedural rule precludes imposition of a higher or lower penalty in the second trial. On retrial the Special Judge suspended the fine, and Appellant will pay nothing if he complies with tribal law for one year. In the meantime, his fishing rights are restored.

Appellant has repeatedly and freely admitted that he was fishing at the time and place he was cited. He has further admitted that he had prior notice and warning that he was fishing in violation of tribal law. On appeal he implies for the first time, but does not directly state, that he may not have had adequate notice of the fishing restrictions due to insufficient publication by the tribe.

---

9. *Hoopa Yurok Settlement Act*, P.L. 100-580, 25 U.S.C. §§1300i-l(e) (October 31, 1988).

To accept Appellant's notice argument is to ignore his repeated admissions that he had prior notice and had been warned that he was illegally fishing. It is also to ignore his testimony that he knew at least two locations where the notices were posted. At the *de novo* trial, Appellant complained that where the notices are posted in Klamath, the glass cover sometimes fogs over, or the notice may be torn down. The tribe correctly argues that the Appellant certainly knows how to contact the tribal officer or fisheries department in order to confirm current restrictions. Instead, Appellant admits that he takes no interest in, or responsibility for, tribal law: "When I go fishing, I just go fishing." It is this contention that is at the heart of this case.

Based upon the entire record, we conclude that the Appellant failed to establish a *prima facie* case for a procedural due process violation. Having failed to establish a procedural due process violation, we will nevertheless examine his due process violation claims to determine if there were any substantive due process violations.

C. Substantive Due Process

The Appellant raises a number of claims regarding the application of the United States Constitution to these tribal court proceedings. The Indian Civil Rights Act (ICRA), 25 U.S.C. §1302(8) applies some but not all of the U.S. Constitution's Bill of Rights to all persons, including tribal members. The Yurok Constitution specifically incorporates the Indian Civil Rights in its Bill of Rights. [Yurok Const. Art. IX.]

Appellant argues that the tribe was required to appoint him legal counsel at the tribe's expense. The Indian Civil Rights Act expressly disavows any right to paid counsel; it requires only that the tribe allow the Appellant, at his own expense, to have the assistance of counsel for his defense. [25 U.S.C. §1302(6).] He is not entitled to a defense paid by the tribe. The fact that BIA officials acting on behalf of the tribe issued the citation does not change the fact that this is a tribal court proceeding in which the tribe is acting as an independent sovereign to prosecute a tribal member who violated tribal law. The tribe is not acting as an arm or agency of the United States, and the United States has no jurisdiction over this case. Under these circumstances, the Sixth Amendment of the Constitution simply does not apply. The Yurok Tribe does not have to provide paid legal counsel in a tribal court proceeding involving a tribal member and a fishing ordinance violation within the exterior boundaries of the reservation.

Appellant inexplicably states that the Special Judge prohibited him from "making an oral defense in [his] own behalf at trial." To the contrary, the transcript shows that Appellant made a spirited defense, and that two witnesses spoke on his behalf. The Special Judge did prevent Appellant from reading verbatim a long, prepared speech about his rights under the U.S. Constitution. The Special Judge properly told him that Indian tribal governments were accountable through the Indian Civil Rights Act of 1968, and that the Constitution did not apply pursuant to *Talton v. Mayes*, [163 U.S. 376 (1896),] but that his written speech, nevertheless, would be included in the record for the trial judge's review in preparing his decision and order. There is no tribal or federal due process rule that a defendant must be allowed to recite at trial an irrelevant text. In reaching this conclusion we also note that Yurok Tribal Code, 1-05, Title 5 §5.2 sets forth the obligations as to how the trial is to be conducted. The Special Judge conducted the *de novo* trial pursuant to this ordinance and also correctly protected the inherent rights of all trial judges to control the proceedings.

Despite his contention to the contrary, Appellant was not compelled to be a witness against himself. He never stated that he declined to testify, and he never asserted any right against self-incrimination. The Special Judge asked Appellant if he was representing himself, and Appellant voluntarily testified on his own behalf. Indeed, he wanted to read a lengthy statement. He cannot now complain that he was compelled to testify, or that once he voluntarily did so, that the Special Judge could not ask him questions.

Appellant complains that he did not have notice of the witnesses against him. The tribe argues that there were no witnesses against him at the trial *de novo* because he freely admitted that he was fishing during closure hours. There was no need to call the citing officers. Moreover, Appellant had actual and constructive notice of the witnesses against him. Before his first trial, he was given written notice of the three citing officers who would testify against him. He cannot genuinely claim that he did not know who would testify against him at the trial *de novo*. Even were he entitled to a formal re-notice of the witnesses against him, any lack of such notice is harmless error, as no witness testified against him. Indeed, the trial judge gave Appellant an opportunity to question the citing officer, which Appellant declined to do. We also note that prior to the *de novo* trial, the Appellant failed to exercise his right to subpoena witnesses.

During the *de novo* trial the Special Judge correctly noted that the entire United States Constitution does not apply to this proceeding. The Indian Civil Rights Act requires the tribe to apply due process under its tribal laws (25 U.S.C. §1302 (8)), and here the tribe has done so in excess: not only did the tribe order a second trial *de novo*, despite Appellant's repeated admissions of fishing during closure and repeated failure to appear, but the tribe granted Appellant's request for a different prosecutor and a different judge when there was no reason to do so. The only "overt intervention of the Yurok Tribal Executive Branch" was the tribal council's decision to bend over backwards to accommodate Appellant's demands.

Finally, Appellant argues that he was "singled out for selective enforcement of the tribal fishing law." The only evidence on this point is Appellant's repeated statements at his various court appearances that he is not the only one who violates the tribe's fishing ordinances. Even if this is true, a claim of selective enforcement requires far more than a showing that others break the law and do not get caught. There was neither selective enforcement nor a substantive due process violation in this case.

D. Constitutional Issue

The second major issue in this case is the Appellant's claim that the fishing restrictions of the YTFRO and Plan violate the Yurok Constitution's Article IX protection of "traditional practices," specifically his supposed right to dip-net at any time and place he wants. He bases this argument on the ground that the tribal resource conservation laws are irrational and tribal members have an absolute right to those resources. At the *de novo* trial, Appellant offered his opinion, but no factual or scientific evidence, that the tribe's resource conservation laws are irrational.

The tribe responded with several arguments. First, it is common knowledge that the salmon fishery of the Klamath River is in severe decline and requires careful management to restore and maintain the fishery for present and future generations. The tribe's fishing YTFRO and Plan, on their face, demonstrate the tribe's careful efforts to do so.

Second, the tribe's efforts are mandated by the Yurok Constitution itself, which dictates that the tribe "restore, enhance, and manage the tribal fishery." Appellant ignores this mandate, relying instead on Article IX and its protection of traditional practices.

Third, the tribe's Fishing YTFRO and Plan do not deny Appellant his traditional practices. Appellant is free to dip-net on the days and times prescribed, which are ample to provide him and all tribal fishers food and livelihood. Had he simply waited a couple of hours on the day he was cited, Appellant could have fished lawfully and unhindered for twelve straight hours.

Fourth, it is frivolous to suggest that the constitutional protection of traditional practices strips the tribe of any authority to regulate such practices to preserve a critical resource for generations to come, particularly when such conservation is expressly mandated by the same Constitution. In effect, the conservation regulations assure that tribal fishers will be able to continue their traditional practices for years to come.

Fifth, it is a commonplace of statutory construction that the more specific provision of law controls the less specific. Here, the constitutional fisheries conservation mandate is more specific than the broad protection of traditional practices. Even if some conflict were implied between these two constitutional provisions, they can be harmonized by acknowledging that the specific conservation mandate is regulatory, not prohibitory of traditional practices, and is in fact necessary to assure the health of the fishery so that tribal fishers will have traditional practices to carry on.

Sixth, it is for the tribe, not Appellant as an individual, to determine what is a rational and appropriate fisheries policy. If tribal members disagree with the policies of their elected tribal council and the tribe's technical fisheries staff, they are but one election away from changing those policies.

Based upon the entire record including the tribe's Preamble provisions cited earlier, we find the tribe's argument compelling. The tribe's exercise of its governmental powers was based upon a legitimate, rational, constitutionally provided mechanism to protect its tribal resources. There was no constitutional violation when the Yurok Tribe exercised its governmental authority to protect its resources by limiting a tribal member's right to fish in accordance with its ordinance and Harvest Management Plan.

E. Indian Rights

We note the Appellant's basic argument centers on the concept that his definition of a "traditional practice" for exercising his fishing rights is flawed for a number of reasons. First, as noted above, the Yurok tribal government has exercised its rights in accordance with federal and tribal law to define the areas and times for fishing, as correctly noted by the Special Judge. YTFRO §8(p), concerning dip-net fishing, provides that "eligible Indians may engage in dip-net fishing or angling at all times on the reservation *except when expressly prohibited.*"

We also note that the Appellant's claim of a right to exercise of "traditional practice" to fish any time he wishes violates the notion of rights and obligations between any government and its governed. That is, government relies upon the fundamental foundation that there is no such thing as individual sovereignty. Tribal governments are sovereign domestic dependent nations within the United States; individual tribal members are not. More importantly, tribal governments, in the exercise of power, also rely upon two fundamental rules of traditional Indian law. . . .

In this case, if the Appellant abided by the *de novo* court's decision and complied with tribal law for one year, he would restore his honor and bring respect back to his family, clan, and tribe, and he would be living in harmony with nature. In this case, we note that the Yurok Tribe has placed greater emphasis in its Constitution regarding the Second Rule, to live in harmony with nature, over that of traditionally exercising a fishing right.

Finally, we note, even if the Appellant's claim of a "traditional practice" is wrongly analyzed as a property right, he would still be subject to the tribal government's restrictions. The great scholar, Felix S. Cohen, noted that when looking at the dependancy of individual rights upon the extent of tribal property:

> The individual Indian, claiming a share in tribal assets, is subject to the general rule that he can obtain no greater interest than that possessed by the tribe in whose assets he participates. [Citations omitted.]

Handbook of Federal Indian Law, p. 185 (1942).

In the case at hand, the Appellant has no greater rights than the tribe. The tribe has placed upon itself and its members a traditional obligation of living in harmony with nature.

The judgment of the *de novo* trial court is hereby **affirmed**.

Chief Justice GABOURIE and Justice DEMMERT concur.

NOTES

1. Many tribal courts and tribal governments follow a general rule that if the prosecution chooses to pursue incarceration as a possible sentence for a given crime, the defendant is entitled to paid counsel. But if not, then the government is not required to provide paid counsel to indigent defendants. In *People v. Champagne*, 35 Indian L. Rep. 6004 (Little River Band of Ottawa Indians Court of Appeals 2007),[*] the court rejected a claim by a tribal member (and appellate justice) that he should be entitled to a jury trial for the crime of attempted embezzlement:

---

[*]*Disclosure:* The author participated in this matter as an appellate justice and wrote the opinion.

[T]he tribal prosecutor declined to seek jail time in this matter. . . .

Persons subject to the criminal jurisdiction of the Band and charged with "an offense punishable by imprisonment" have the right to a six-person jury trial in accordance with tribal law. CONST. art. III, §1(j). . . . Assuming without deciding that ICRA applies to the Little River Band, the Constitutional provision here mirrors the provision contained in the Act. *See* 25 U.S.C. §1302(10). . . . The Tribal Council has determined that where the tribal prosecutor informs the Court and criminal defendants before trial that the People will not seek jail time, no right to a jury trial attaches. *See* Criminal Procedures Ordinance §8.02, Ordinance #03-300-03 (effective Oct. 10, 2003). We concur in this assessment about the right to a jury trial. *See* CONST. art. VI, §8(a)(2). As such, no right to a jury trial ever attached in this matter.

Id. at 6006.

2. Many tribal communities have few lawyers available for hire or appointment, due to the demographics, geography, and other factors of Indian country. As such, many non-lawyers participate as "lay advocates" for tribal criminal defendants. In *Bullcoming v. Cheyenne and Arapaho Tribes*, 9 Okla. Trib. 528 (Cheyenne and Arapaho Tribes Supreme Court 2006), the court held that access to lay advocates is not a fundamental right, but is instead discretionary:

Second, Appellant argues that his due process rights were violated by the denial of his right to counsel and/or a "lay advocate." Appellant urges that those denials "put [him] at a disadvantage due to his unfamiliarity with the law, procedural requirements and the entire legal process"; that "he did not know how to object to evidence, . . . admit evidence or examine witnesses"; and that he did not know how "to provide an adequate defense for himself." . . .

In our recitation of the relevant facts above, we noted that the record did not indicate any factual claim of indigency by Appellant, . . . nor does it evidence any claim by him to appointed counsel, *cf.* CHEY.-ARAP. CRIM. PROC. CODE §102(a)(2). . . . Indeed, Appellant was represented by retained counsel at the early post-complaint stages of the proceedings, was represented by (different) retained counsel at the sentencing hearing, and is also represented by that counsel on appeal. . . . On that record, Appellant has failed to demonstrate any legally-cognizable right-to-counsel denial at all.

But in addition to generally providing criminal defendants with the right to defend either "in person or by counsel," *see* CHEY.-ARAP. CRIM. PROC. CODE §102(a), tribal law more specifically provides that

[t]he [d]efendant may represent himself or be represented by an adult enrolled Tribal member with leave of the Court, if such representation is without charge to the defendant, or by any attorney or advocate admitted to practice before the Tribal Court.

CHEY.-ARAP. CRIM. PROC. CODE §102(a)(2).

As noted above, early in the trial, Ida Hoffman (who this Court takes judicial notice is an adult enrolled tribal member) argued that Appellant could not afford legal counsel, and requested to "talk on his behalf." . . . Neither Ms. Hoffman nor Appellant Bullcoming had any right for that to occur under Subsection 102(a)(2)'s plain meaning, which conditions such representation on "leave of the Court." But the Court's refusal of

Ms. Hoffman's request (which could certainly be construed as a right to "represent" him within the meaning of Subsection 102(a)(2)) was based on her lack of "admission to practice" as an attorney before the Court, . . . and that reasoning was erroneous based on the disjunctive language ["or"] of Subsection 102(a)(2) quoted above.

The question that inevitably follows is whether that error was harmless, and we conclude that it was. First, because the requested "representation" was discretionary with the Court, Appellant was not deprived of any categorical legal right. Second, the Court did allow Ms. Hoffman to advise (if not speak for) Appellant during the course of the trial . . . in which capacity she could have (and may have) written advice or proposed questions to him, whispered potential follow-up questions, suggested strategies throughout the trial, and the like. . . . Third, this Court notes that Appellant chose not to testify (and thus remained immune from cross-examination), but because he personally cross-examined the Tribes' witnesses and was given some latitude to do so by the Court, as the trial actually "played out" he was in effect able to present the core of his defense without testifying (and thereby without opening himself to cross-examination). . . . Fourth, Appellant was able to replicate that effect through the quasi-testimonial style of his closing argument (again given some latitude by the District Court), . . . with that Court (and any reader of the Transcript) being able to easily ascertain both Appellant's factual positions and his attendant characterizations of those facts. Fifth, on appeal (and while represented by counsel) Appellant proffered broad conclusions but no specific examples of any prejudice that resulted from Ms. Hoffman's inability to speak on his behalf, more specifically neither arguing nor providing examples as to how Ms. Hoffman (or for that matter, an attorney) would have caused him to prevail (or for that matter, would have done better than he did) at trial.

Under the totality of the circumstances herein, and having already concluded that Appellant suffered no "right-to-counsel" deprivation, we further conclude that the District Court's denial of Ms. Hoffman's request to speak for Appellant for a legally-erroneous reason was harmless error.

Id.

3. In *Rosebud Sioux Tribe v. Luxon* (Rosebud Sioux Tribe Supreme Court, Oct. 30, 2009), the court adopted federal common law in determining whether a criminal defendant's conviction should be vacated on grounds of ineffective assistance of counsel:

The classic *federal constitutional* standard is articulated in *Strickland v. Washington*, 466 U.S. 668 (1984), but it does not automatically apply in this Tribal court context. That is so because the right to counsel in the tribal court context derives from the Tribal Constitution and federal statute, not the United States Constitution. The relevant Tribal constitutional provision is to be found at Art. X, Sec. 1(f), which guarantees the defendant the right "to have the assistance of counsel for his or her defense, including the right to have counsel subject to income guidelines." The analogous federal statutory provision is contained in the Indian Civil Rights Act, 25 U.S.C. §1302(6), and provides a defendant with the right "at his own expense to have the assistance of counsel for his defense."

In light of the strong affirmative language in the Tribe's Constitution and the Tribe's concomitant commitment to enhanced constitutional governance,

> this Court adopts the standard articulated in *Strickland v. Washington* as the proper measure to determine whether there has been ineffective assistance by counsel in a criminal case tried before the Rosebud Sioux Tribal Court. This well-known test consists of two parts: "First the defendant must show that counsel's performance was deficient. This requires showing that counsel made errors so serious that counsel was not functioning as the "counsel" guaranteed by the Sixth Amendment. Second, the defendant must show that the deficient performance prejudiced the defendant. This requires showing that counsel's errors were so serious as to deprive the defendant of a fair trial, a trial whose result is reliable." . . . A defendant's conviction may be set aside only if both parts of the test are satisfied.

Id. The court declined to vacate the conviction. The defendant first argued that defense counsel failed to file a motion to suppress certain evidence until the day of trial, and the court agreed that waiting until trial to file motions that are required to be filed before trial under tribal law was a violation of tribal appellate procedure rules. However, applying *Strickland*, the court noted that a timely suppression motion would not have been granted, rendering the attorney error nonprejudicial to the defendant.

2. SEARCH WARRANTS AND PROBABLE CAUSE

METLAKATLA INDIAN COMMUNITY V. WILLIAMS

Metlakatla Tribal Court of Appeals, No. 95-18, 4 NICS App. 91 (July 25, 1996)

Before: ELBRIDGE COOCHISE, Chief Justice; DENNIS L. NELSON, Justice; JOHN L. ROE, Justice. . . .

Metlakatla Police officers obtained a warrant to search Appellant's residence for alcoholic beverages, drugs, and contraband allegedly concealed in her house. Appellant alleges that the search warrant was invalid. Appellant further alleges that her arrest and subsequent conviction for resisting lawful arrest, threat, and indecent exposure were also improper.

The search warrant which Appellant challenges did not contain a specific address of the residence, not did it specify what part of the house was to be searched. The warrant authorizes a search of the "blue house" on Haines Street. The warrant does not identify with any further particularity the property to be searched except to state that it is "Gloria William's residence." The parties admit that there is more than one blue house on Haines Street. Respondent's assertion that "everyone knows where everyone else lives" in the community does not justify the failure of the warrant to "particularly describe" the property and the portion of the property to be searched.

The search warrant also failed to specify a time period within which it was to be executed. Further, there is no indication on the warrant regarding the date and time the warrant was issued. The warrant contains blank spaces specifically for such information, yet those blank spaces remain empty.

The Metlakatla Code of Criminal Offenses specifically addresses the parameters within which the Magistrate's Court may issue a search warrant. Title I, §8(b) of that Code provides that any Magistrate of the Magistrate's Court may issue[]

> a Search Warrant for the search and seizure of property in the ownership,
> custody or possession of any person subject to the jurisdiction of the Magis-
> trate's Court, which shall be signed by the Magistrate and issued only upon
> probable cause, supported by oath or affirmation, that an offense subject to the
> jurisdiction of the Magistrate's Court has been committed and which *shall
> name or describe the person or place to be searched and describe particularly any
> articles of property to be seized.*

Ordinance 653, Title I, §8(b) (emphasis added). The search warrant at issue in
this case does not comply with the requirements of the Code of Criminal
Offenses.

The right of individuals to be secure from unreasonable searches and seizures is guaranteed by the Indian Civil Rights Act (ICRA) of 1968. . . .

Even had the search warrant contained sufficient information, this Court
notes that the supporting affidavit contains no facts which would lead a reasonable person to believe that any crime had been or was being committed on
the property in question. The affidavit states only that the police officers could
"hear loud music and people talking loud from inside the residence" and that
Appellant slammed the door in the officer's face; neither of these facts would
lead to a reasonable belief that Appellant was committing a crime.

Conclusion

The search warrant at issue does not contain sufficient information to
satisfy the Code's due process requirements. This Court finds that the search
warrant is invalid on its face.

The judgment of the Magistrate's Court is hereby *reversed*. Appellant's conviction on charges of resisting lawful arrest, threat, and indecent exposure,
subsequent to the issuance and execution of the invalid search warrant, are
reversed.

NOTES

1. In *Skokomish Indian Tribe v. Cultee*, 8 NICS App. 68 (Skokomish Tribal Court
   of Appeals 2008), the court affirmed the issuance of an arrest warrant (and
   the introduction of the evidence seized upon the execution of the arrest) for
   failure to appear at a hearing despite the existence of a specific court rule
   covering the situation:

   > The primary mechanism for enforcing jurisdiction over a person is the court's
   > ability to compel the person to appear. . . . Based on the plain language in
   > STC 3.01.012(a), we hold it was the intent of the Tribe's legislative body to
   > grant the tribal judge the authority to order an arrest and compel future
   > attendance if a person fails to appear at a hearing to review or monitor com-
   > pliance with a postconviction order because such power is a "reasonable
   > means to protect and carry out" the court's jurisdiction. . . .
   >   . . . [O]rdering a person's arrest under STC 3.01.012(a) is only justified if
   > the order is appropriate and fair given the circumstances of the case.
   >   To determine whether an arrest order is appropriate and fair given the
   > spirit of the tribal law being applied depends on the totality of the
   > circumstances. . . . Where, however, a person fails to appear at a hearing to

review or monitor compliance with valid post-conviction orders, at a minimum consideration should be given to whether the person has failed to appear at previous scheduled hearings, the reason for the hearing, whether the person signed a promise to appear at the hearing, and whether the person was put on notice the failure to appear could result in the issuance of an arrest warrant. Because a totality of the circumstances analysis involves factual findings, a tribal judge's decision to order an arrest pursuant to a warrant under STC 3.01.012(a) is reviewed under the abuse of discretion standard. . . .

Here, the record shows the purpose of the hearing was to review Mr. Cultee's compliance with the tribal judge's post-conviction orders. Mr. Cultee signed a promise to appear at the November 9, 2007 hearing and was told his failure to appear could result in his arrest. . . . Given the record on appeal, under these circumstances the judge did not abuse her discretion when she ordered Mr. Cultee's arrest for failing to appear at the November 9, 2007 hearing.

We hold STC 3.01.012(a) grants the tribal court the authority to order an arrest through warrant as a reasonable means to protect and carry out its jurisdiction but only where under the totality of the circumstances the order is appropriate and fair under the spirit of tribal law. We affirm the tribal judge's ruling denying Appellant's suppression motion.

Id. at 71-73.

2. In *Rosebud Sioux Tribe v. Luxon* (Rosebud Sioux Tribe Supreme Court, Oct. 30, 2009), the court decided that an amendment to the tribal constitution was not intended to require more stringent protections for accused tribal court defendants. The court wrote:

> The place to begin is with the text of the new amendment to the Tribal Constitution. It reads in full that the Tribe shall not:
>
>> Search or arrest any person without informing them of their right to remain silent, to have access to an attorney, to be informed that anything they say can be held against them in a court of law, to have their rights explained at the time of the search and arrest, and to ask them if they understand these rights. Art. X, Sec. 1(d).
>
> This provision, while not identical, is very similar to the classic language that constitutes the Miranda warning established in the case with the same name:
>
>> Prior to any questioning, the person must be warned that he has the right to remain silent, that any statement he does make may be used as evidence against him, and that he has the right to the presence of an attorney, either retained or appointed. [*Miranda v. Arizona*, 384 U.S. 436, 444 (1966).]
>
> . . . The basic question before this Court, as indicated, is therefore whether the Tribal constitutional amendment reflects a basic Tribal intent to adopt *Miranda in toto* or to add additional requirements, or perhaps even subtract requirements. Despite the slight variation in text between the *Miranda* opinion and the Tribal constitutional amendment, no evidence was presented to suggest that there was any Tribal constitutional intent to have its amendment extend beyond *Miranda*. In the absence of such evidence, it is reasonable to conclude that Tribal intent was to adopt *Miranda* as its constitutional standard.

There are several other reasons that support such a reading. Given the sanction limitation of one year in jail or a $5000 fine or both in the Indian Civil Rights Act of 1968, 25 U.S.C. §1302(1) and the Rosebud Sioux Law and Order Code, it would appear unlikely (especially with no evidence to the contrary) that the intent of the amendment was to exceed the federal contours of *Miranda*, where there is no sanction limitation whatsoever.

Id.

E. SENTENCING

St. Peter v. Colville Confederated Tribes

Colville Confederated Tribes Court of Appeals, Nos. AP93-15400, AP93-15507, AP93-15508, AP93-15509 and AP93-15510, 20 Indian L. Rep. 6108, 1993.NACC.0000013 (September 28, 1993)

Before Chief Judge Collins, Judge Baker and Judge Bonga
The opinion of the court was delivered by: Collins, C.J.
This matter was brought before the Appellate Panel seeking review of five maximum sentences imposed by the Trial Court in the above cases. In her Memorandum Opinion; Judgment And Sentence, dated February 2, 1993, Judge Elizabeth Fry imposed maximum jail sentences for two counts of Disorderly Conduct, Assault, Trespass To Buildings, and Resisting Arrest, and specified that each sentence would run consecutively to any other incarceration. . . .

III.

The Indian Civil Rights Act, Act of April 11, 1968, P. L. 90-284, Sections 201-203, 82 Stat. 77-78, codified at 25 U.S.C. Sec. 1301-1303, places limitations on the exercise of tribal criminal jurisdiction. Those parts of ICRA which concern the instant appeal state:

"No Indian tribe in exercising powers of self-government shall —

(7) require excessive bail, impose excessive fines, inflict cruel and unusual punishments, and in no event impose for conviction of any one offense any penalty or punishment greater than imprisonment for a term of one year or a fine of $5,000, or both;

(8) deny to any person within its jurisdiction the equal protection of its laws or deprive any person of liberty or property without due process of law;" . . .

We note that the Colville Tribal Civil Rights Act, CTC 56.02(g), closely parallels the operative language in 25 U.S.C. Sec. 1302(7) with regard to prohibitions against imposing excessive bail, excessive fines, or infliction of cruel and unusual punishment. CTC 56.02(h) appears to contain identical language to that found in 25 U.S.C. Sec. 1302(8).

The Indian Civil Rights Act contains similar but not identical provisions as found in the Bill of Rights. *See generally, Comment, The Indian Bill of Rights and the Constitutional Status of Tribal Governments*, 82 Harv. L. Rev. 1343 (1969). The legislative history of the ICRA indicates congressional intent that the Act should be read consistent[ly] with the principles of tribal self-government and cultural autonomy. . . . *Santa Clara Pueblo v. Martinez*, 436 U.S. 49, 62-64 and n. 11-15 (examining ICRA legislative history).

Although the due process and equal protection provisions under ICRA, 25 U.S.C. Sec. 1302(8) are similar to corresponding constitutional principles under the Bill of Rights, they differ both in substance and origin. The Panel reads ICRA to mean that equal protection and due process guarantees refer to constitutional protections provided under tribal law and not federal law. . . . This interpretation is consistent with view that Congress, with modification, selectively incorporated certain provisions of the Bill of Rights into a substitute bill which was enacted to protect the individual rights of Indians while fostering tribal self government and cultural identity. Moreover, Congress did so recognizing that coextensive provisions of tribal constitutions and the Bill of Rights would not be identically aligned. . . . Thus, we interpret ICRA in light of the inherent power of tribes to create and administer a criminal justice system, . . . and a well established federal policy of preserving the integrity of tribal governmental structure, including the authority of tribal courts. . . . We also note that federal courts have been careful to construe notions of due process and equal protection under ICRA with due regard for historical, governmental and cultural values of Indian tribes. . . .

. . . In addition, the legislative history of ICRA clearly indicates that Congress did not intend to impose full constitutional guarantees under the Bill of Rights on litigants coming before the tribal court or to restrict the tribes beyond what was necessary to give the Act the effect Congress intended. . . . Among the goals intended by Congress in enacting ICRA were affording constitutional protections to litigants on one hand, and supporting tribal self government and cultural autonomy on the other. We therefore apply due process principles under ICRA with flexibility and in a manner contextually adapted by the Colville Confederated Tribes.

IV.

We also note that neither the Federal Rules of Criminal Procedure nor the Federal Rules of Evidence have been adopted for use in the Colville Tribal Court. Therefore, the Panel will consider case law construing F.R. Cr. P. 32 as advisory and will not apply the Federal Rules of Evidence as controlling what evidence is admissible in the Tribal Court for sentencing purposes. . . .

The Tribal Code expressly rejects use of common law rules of evidence, and directs the Court to "[u]se its own discretion as to what evidence it deems necessary and relevant to the charge and the defense." CTC 2.6.02. Further, prior to imposing sentencing, the judge is directed to allow a spokesman or the defendant to speak on behalf of the defendant and to present any information which would help the judge in setting punishment. 2.6.07. A literal reading of 2.6.07 shows that the only restriction on what information a spokesman or the defendant may present to the Court to consider in sentencing is that the information be of a type which will "help the judge in setting punishment." *Id.* Clearly, such information is strictly within the discretion of the sentencing judge. . . .

V.

The appellant alleges that the Trial Court erred by considering and relying upon misinformation as to his criminal history at sentencing. The appellant further contends that he has a due process right to be sentenced on the basis of accurate information. The source of the allegedly erroneous information referred to by Appellant is a computer printout from the Federal Bureau of Investigation.

The record shows that the computer printout was used by the Colville Tribal Court Probation Department to establish at least part of St. Peter's criminal history for the Presentence Investigation Report (hereinafter "PSIR"). The record also shows that the trial judge at least referred to the printout during the sentencing hearing. However, our review of the record indicates that the trial judge, in response to objections by appellant's counsel, disregarded state convictions reflected in the printout. . . .

[F]ederal constitutional principles . . . cannot, without a review of Tribal standards, be said to represent an accurate reflection of Tribal law. . . . [W]e do hold that a criminal defendant in Tribal Court has a due process right under the Indian Civil Rights Act and the Colville Tribal Civil Rights Act not to be sentenced on the basis of prior criminal convictions where the defendant was not advised of his right to counsel or was improperly denied his right to counsel. We do not believe that the defendant is denied due process when the Trial Court considers or relies on criminal convictions in which the defendant was simply unrepresented. . . .

Appellant's counsel alleged that one or more of St. Peter's convictions reflected in the FBI computer printout were invalid, but he did not mention which convictions were misrepresented by the printout. . . .

. . . We have no difficulty applying those principles to reviewing sentencing procedure under CTC 2.6.02 and CTC 2.6.07, and we hold, that when a defendant's criminal history is considered and relied upon by the trial judge to impose an enhanced criminal sentence, that information must be accurate. However, in order to successfully challenge a sentence imposed by the trial court on due process grounds, the defendant must do more tha[n] make a mere allegation that information coming directly before the court or used in the presentence report is materially false. The defendant must ask the sentencing judge for an opportunity to rebut such information and carry the burden to show the information is both material and false. Whether the trial court provides the defendant with an opportunity to rebut such controverted information by continuing sentencing and holding a separate evidentiary hearing is within the discretion of the court. If the trial judge refuses the defendant's request to set an evidentiary hearing on the issue, that decision will be subject to appellate review as to whether the trial judge abused his or her discretion.

Applying the above standards to the cases at bar, we find that the appellant was not denied an opportunity to rebut controverted information about his criminal record. The appellant did not request an evidentiary hearing on the accuracy of information contained in the FBI computer printout and PSIR. Nor has the appellant shown that the trial judge relied on the allegedly false information in imposing the sentences. Thus, the Panel does not believe that the appellant has carried his burden in showing (1) the information coming before the Court was material and false; and (2) that the Court relied on that information in sentencing.

VI.

The appellant also challenges the Trial Court's refusal to follow the recommendations contained in the Presentence Investigation Report that St. Peter be placed on probation and undergo substance abuse treatment. The PSIR did not recommend that St. Peter be sentenced to imprisonment on any of the five charges. The issue before us then is whether the Trial Court abused its discretion in sentencing St. Peter to imprisonment rather than long-term substance abuse treatment, as recommended in the PSIR. . . .

Although there are many reasons for conducting a presentence investigation, the appellant has cited no authority in support of his argument that the Trial Court must comply with the sentencing recommendations contained in a presentence report. We are aware of no statutory requirement under Tribal law which says the trial judge must order a presentence investigation or requires the trial judge to follow the recommendations contained in a PSIR. Further, requiring the trial judge to follow sentencing recommendations of the Probation Department would, in effect, divest the Court of sentencing authority. The Panel believes this is contrary to the discretionary authority delegated to the trial judge in CTC 2.6.02 and 2.6.07.

Accordingly, we hold that the Trial Court did not err by refusing to follow the recommendations contained in the PSIR and, instead, imposing successive jail terms.

VII.

We next address whether the Trial Court abused its discretion by sentencing David St. Peter to five maximum consecutive jail terms. . . .

The appellant was convicted of Disorderly Conduct, CTC 5.5.04, Assault, CTC 5.1.03, and Trespass To Buildings, CTC 5.2.18 which are "Class C" offenses, and Resisting Arrest, CTC 5.4.17, a "Class B" offense. Thus, the maximum consecutive penalties for all offenses is 540 days in jail, $6,500 in fines, or both. The appellant, having received credit for 10 days of jail time served, was sentenced to a jail term of 530 days. Although the trial court imposed maximum jail sentences on the appellant, she did not impose the maximum penalty available for the offenses.

The language chosen by the Tribal Business Council in CTC 5.7.01 et seq. limits the Trial Court's discretion in sentencing. The various offenses enumerated in the Code have been graded into classes for purposes of sentencing. These statutes prohibit the trial judge from imposing a greater sentence for a crime than provided for the class within which the offense falls. Further, all criminal offenses set out in the Code are classified as misdemeanors, which, by definition cannot result in imprisonment for more than one year. In addition, the Congress has restricted sentencing authority of the Tribal Court by placing an upper sentencing limit of one year imprisonment and a fine of $5,000 on the court. 25 U.S.C. Sec. 1301 et seq.

We note that the sentences imposed upon St. Peter by the trial judge were within statutory limits. It is evident that the Tribal Council has delegated considerable latitude to the Trial Court in sentencing criminal offenders within the statutory limits set out in the Code. Because the sentences fall within statutory limits, the Appellate Panel will review only the process by which punishment is determined rather than make an unjustified incursion into the province of the sentencing judge.

VIII.

We now turn to the appellant's argument that the Tribal Court abused its sentencing discretion by arbitrarily and capriciously imposing punishment or violating the prohibition against cruel and unusual punishment. . . .

IX.

It is a well established principle under federal law that sentences imposed within statutory limits are generally not reviewable by the appellate court. . . . Subject only to the limitations imposed by the statute and Constitution, the punishment to be given a convicted offender is in the discretion of the court. . . .

Where it is shown that the trial court failed to exercise its discretion or, in exercising its discretion has manifestly or grossly abused that discretion, will the appellate court intervene. . . .

XI.

. . . The fact that the PSIR was before the court and contained a recommendation to place St. Peter on 18 months probation, with involvement in adult vocational rehabilitation and alcohol programs, indicates that the trial judge considered rehabilitation along with deterrence in sentencing. We believe the Court was not bound to follow the recommendations of the Probation Department in sentencing. We believe that a trial judge would fail to exercise discretion if she were required to impose sentencing consistent with such recommendations. In view of St. Peter's past criminal involvement, including alcohol-related offenses after undergoing alcohol treatment on four separate occasions, and the dismissed Battery and Resisting Arrest charges, we find the trial judge did not abuse her discretion by rejecting the Probation Department's recommendations for sentencing.

From the preceding discussion, it is clear that the trial judge balanced the value of deterrence in sentencing with St. Peter's likelihood of alcohol rehabilitation and adult educational training as part of probation. It is equally clear that the trial judge determined that rehabilitation was not an appropriate sentencing goal in this instance. In light of St. Peter's past alcohol treatment and continued criminal conduct, we believe the trial judge did not abuse her discretion in reaching that conclusion. From this and the information before the Court, we conclude that the trial judge did not mechanically sentence St. Peter. We hold that the trial judge had sufficient information to meaningfully exercise her sentencing discretion and that she exercised her discretion by sufficiently individualizing sentencing so that the punishment fit not only the offenses, but the individual.

XII.

We are not aware of any provision under Tribal law that requires a trial judge to make a finding that a defendant would derive no benefit from rehabilitation before imposing a maximum jail sentence. From our reading of the Code it is clear that the Tribal Business Council delegated broad sentencing discretion to the trial judge, and imposed no such restrictions on the Tribal Court. . . .

We believe that placing a "no benefit" requirement on the Trial Court before it can sentence offenders to a maximum jail term would amount to a legislative act by the Court and an impermissible incursion into the province of the trial judge. This practice . . . would seriously impair the meaningful exercise of the trial judge's sentencing discretion by, in effect, requiring exhaustion of rehabilitative measures before deterrent sentencing could be considered. . . .

XV.

Finally, the appellant contends that the Trial Court erred by imposing consecutive rather than concurrent jail sentences. . . .

The appellant has cited no authority under Tribal law which requires the Trial Court to impose concurrent sentences. However, Appellant advances the theory that consecutive sentencing in the instant cases has violated his right to due process and his right to be free from cruel and unusual punishment under the Colville Tribal Civil Rights Act, CTC 56.02(g), (h), and the Indian Civil Rights Act, 25 U.S.C. 1302(7), (8).

The Colville Tribal Code and the Tribal Constitution are silent with regard to whether the Trial Court should impose concurrent or consecutive sentences. In addition, the Panel is not aware of any action by Congress which has divested the Tribal Court of authority to impose consecutive sentences. Accordingly, the Panel concludes that the decision to impose concurrent or consecutive jail sentences is within the discretion of the trial judge. Our review will, therefore, be based on whether the trial judge abused her discretion. . . .

While there has been federal legislation enacted to limit sentencing authority of the federal courts, no similar federal sentencing restrictions have been placed on tribal courts. In that regard, the relevant limitations on tribal court sentencing appear in the Indian Civil Rights Act. The Act provides that no Indian tribe shall "subject any person for the same offense to be twice put in jeopardy." 25 U.S.C. 1302(3), or "impose for conviction of any one offense any penalty or punishments greater than imprisonment for a term of one year or a fine of $5,000 or both." 25 U.S.C. Sec. 1302(8).

The language in 25 U.S.C. Sec. 1302(8) does not contain any indication that Congress intended that tribes refrain from imposing concurrent sentences for multiple offenses. The Act only limits the sentence which may be imposed for any one offense. Further, no restrictions on the Court's authority to impose consecutive sentences have been enacted by the Tribal Business Council and none appear in the Tribal Constitution. . . .

The Panel also finds that the decision to impose concurrent or consecutive jail sentences on an offender convicted of multiple offenses is left to the discretion of the Trial Court. Further, we find that the Tribal Court did not abuse its discretion by imposing consecutive jail terms in the instant cases.

The judgments and sentences are Affirmed.

NOTES

1. As noted in the opinion, the Indian Civil Rights Act purports to limit the ability of Indian nations to sentence convicted criminals to more than one year in jail and a $5,000 fine. 25 U.S.C. §1302(7).
2. In certain cases, a tribal court may avoid the one-year sentencing limitation placed upon them by Congress by imposing consecutive sentences, as was done in *St. Peter. See, e.g., Ramos v. Pyramid Lake Tribal Court*, 621 F. Supp. 967, 970 (D. Nev. 1985); Casey Douma, *40th Anniversary of the Indian Civil Rights Act: Finding a Way Back to Indigenous Justice*, 55 FED. LAW., March/April 2008, at 34, 34. A challenge to this practice is pending in the Ninth Circuit. *See Miranda v. Nielson*, No. 10-15308 (9th Cir.). In 2010, Congress enacted a statute that would allow tribal courts to sentence individuals to a three-year sentence if the tribal court procedures comport with specific federal constitutional guarantees. *See* 25 U.S.C. §1302(b) (2010).

CHAPTER 8

DOMESTIC RELATIONS

Key to the preservation of American Indian cultures and traditions is the ability and authority of Indian nations to adopt laws consistent with Indian culture for the adjudication of domestic relations, which largely include marriage and divorce, child custody and welfare, adoptions, inheritance and devise, and other related subject areas. It is in this realm, more so than virtually all other areas of law, that Indian nations have complete discretion to adopt their own laws and be ruled by them.

In *Kobogum v. Jackson Iron Co.*, 43 N.W. 602, 605 (Mich. 1889), a nineteenth-century Michigan Supreme Court case immortalized by Robert Traver's novel *Laughing Whitefish* (1965), the court upheld the inheritance rights of the child of a technically polygamous marriage between two Chippewa Indians in the Upper Peninsula of Michigan. The court wrote that "we had no more right to control [tribal] domestic usages than those of Turkey or India." Taking judicial notice "that among these Indians polygamous marriages have always been recognized as valid," the court identified a conundrum: "We must either hold that there can be no valid Indian marriage, or we must hold that all marriages are valid which by Indian usages are so regarded. There is no middle ground which can be taken, so long as our own laws are not binding on the tribes."

Times have changed. Most, if not all, Indian tribes no longer recognize polygamous marriages and Indian people tend to utilize the divorce laws as much as non-Indian people. The Upper Peninsula is no longer on the fringes of the American frontier. Moreover, the laws of states often do apply to Indians and sometimes even Indian tribes. It remains settled black-letter law, however, that Indian tribes retain plenary and exclusive inherent authority over "domestic relations among tribal members." FELIX S. COHEN, COHEN'S HANDBOOK OF FEDERAL INDIAN LAW, §4.01[2][c], at 215 (Nell Jessup Newton ed., 2005) (citing *Fisher v. Dist. Ct.*, 424 U.S. 382 (1976); *United States v. Quiver*, 241 U.S. 602 (1916)). The fact that tribes control their own domestic relations well into the modern era of federal-state-tribal relations is a function of the sui generis character of federal Indian law.

A. MARRIAGE

IN RE VALIDATION OF MARRIAGE OF FRANCISCO

Navajo Nation Supreme Court, No. A-CV-15-88, 6 Navajo Rep. 134, 16 Indian L. Rep. 6113, 1989.NANN.0000013 (August 2, 1989)

Before Tso, Chief Justice, BLUEHOUSE and AUSTIN, Associate Justices.
The opinion of the court was delivered by: BLUEHOUSE, Associate Justice. . . .

I.

This is a marriage validation case in which the Appellant, Loretta Francisco, appealed the July 20, 1988 decision of the Window Rock District Court denying validation of her common-law marriage.

Oliver Chaca and Loretta Francisco cohabitated as man and wife between approximately October 1978 and August 7, 1987 in Window Rock, Arizona. Chaca worked in Peach Springs, Arizona. Francisco, an enrolled member of the Navajo Tribe, and Chaca, a Hopi, combined their earnings, acquired personal property in both of their names, and accumulated debts in both of their names. The public knew of the parties' relationship. Chaca often introduced himself and Francisco as husband and wife, and visited Francisco at her place of employment. No children were born to the couple. Sometime in June 1987, they talked about marrying each other, but they did not obtain a marriage license, marry according to Arizona state law, or participate in a traditional Navajo wedding ceremony.

On August 7, 1987, Chaca died as the result of an automobile accident. . . . Francisco cannot collect any portion of the life insurance proceeds unless her common-law marriage is validated.

The Window Rock District Court applied 9 N.T.C. §2 to the parties' relationship and ruled that the statute means that Navajos can validly contract marriage with non-Navajos only in compliance with applicable state or foreign law. . . . The district court refused to validate the parties' marriage because they failed to contract it according to Arizona law.

II.

The subject of marriage within the Navajo Nation is perplexing because of the outdated and confusing laws found in Title 9 of the Navajo Tribal Code. Consequently, the Navajo courts are faced with the difficult task of reconciling the Navajo Tribal Council's intent with the parties' expectations in recovering veterans' and other benefits. *See, e.g., In re Marriage of Daw*, 1 Nav. R. 1 (1969). The lack of a coherent Navajo domestic relations code has caused Navajo courts to mingle common-law marriage with traditional Navajo marriage. . . . However, these two kinds of marriages differ substantially. A common-law marriage is "not solemnized in the ordinary way (*i.e.* non-ceremonial) but created by an agreement to marry followed by cohabitation. . . . Such marriage requires a positive mutual agreement, permanent and exclusive of all others, to enter into a marriage relationship, cohabitation sufficient to warrant a fulfillment of necessary relationship of man and wife, and an assumption of marital duties and obligations. . . . Such marriages are invalid in many states." . . . This type of marriage is a product of Anglo practice that is unknown and unrecognized in traditional Navajo society.

By contrast, contracting a traditional Navajo marriage has been described as follows:

1) The parties to the proposed marriage shall have met and agreed to marry.
2) The parents of the man shall ask the parents of the women for her hand in marriage.
3) The bride and bridegroom then eat cornmeal mush out of the sacred basket.
4) Those assembled in the hogan then give advice for a happy marriage to the bride and groom.
5) Gifts may or may not be exchanged.

Navajo Tribal Council Resolution CJ-2-40 (June 3, 1940).

"Traditional Navajo society places great importance upon the institution of marriage. A traditional Navajo marriage, when consummated according to a prescribed elaborate ritual, is believed to be blessed by the 'Holy People.' This blessing ensures that the marriage will be stable, in harmony, and perpetual." *Navajo Nation v. Murphy*, 6 Nav. R. 10, 13 (1988). Under traditional Navajo thought, unmarried couples who live together act immorally because they are said to steal each other. Thus, in traditional Navajo society the Navajo people did not approve of or recognize common-law marriages. . . .

After partaking in the traditional Navajo wedding ceremony, some couples do not obtain marriage licenses because, traditionally, the performance of the ceremony completely validates the union. Unfortunately, Navajos without marriage licenses often face problems, such as difficulty in acquiring Social Security and military benefits for their dependents. *See, e.g., Daw*, 1 Nav. R. at 1. . . .

A common-law marriage is invalid for reasons other than a defect in the ceremony because Title 9 states that Navajos can marry only in three ways: state, church, and tribal custom. 9 N.T.C. §§4(a)-4(b), 61. A common-law marriage is not recognized by Title 9. . . .

. . . Judicial recognition of common-law marriage is not necessary to protect those who participate in Navajo tribal custom marriages now that the cut-off date has been abolished. . . .

. . . The Navajo Tribal Council legislated this requirement: "In all cases the Courts of the Navajo Nation shall apply any laws of the United States that may be applicable and any laws or customs of the Navajo Nation not prohibited by applicable federal laws." 7 N.T.C. §204(a) (1985). For this reason, and because domestic relations is at the core of Navajo sovereignty, this Court is obligated to apply Navajo custom. "Navajo customs and traditions have the force of law." *In re Estate of Belone*, 5 Nav. R. 161, 165 (1987).

Navajo custom does not recognize common-law marriages, regardless of whether one or both spouses are Navajos. *See* R. Locke, The Book of the Navajo 20-23 (1976). Navajo tradition and custom do not recognize common-law marriage; therefore, this Court overrules all prior rulings that Navajo courts can validate unlicensed marriages in which no Navajo traditional ceremony occurred. For the same reason, this Court will not construe any section of Title 9 of the Navajo Tribal Code as authorizing judicial validation of common-law marriages. To enhance Navajo sovereignty, preserve Navajo marriage tradition, and protect those who adhere to it, Navajo courts will validate unlicensed Navajo traditional marriages between Navajos. For these reasons, the district court's refusal to validate the alleged common-law marriage between Chaca and Francisco is affirmed.

III.

As a sovereign Indian nation that is constantly developing, the Navajo Nation must be forever cautious about state or foreign law infringing on Navajo Nation sovereignty. The Navajo Nation must control and develop its own legal system because "the concept of justice has its source in the fabric of each individual society. The concept of justice, what it means for any group of people, cannot be separated from the total beliefs, ideas, and customs of that group of people." T. Tso, Chief Justice's Annual Report, Judicial Branch of the Navajo Nation Annual Rep. 1 (1988). Navajo life centers around the home, traditionally a hogan. *Id.* The Navajo Nation, within the four sacred mountains, is the Tribe's hogan and source of strength and wisdom. *Id.* Navajo "oral history contains no stories of leaders or assistance coming from outside." *Id.* Instead, Navajo tribal history reveals "that Navajos know best how to provide for Navajos." *Id.*

"Implicit in the Treaty of 1868 is the understanding that the internal affairs of the Navajo people are within the exclusive jurisdiction of the Navajo Nation government." *Billie v. Abbott*, 6 Nav. R. 66, 68-69 (1988) (citing *Williams v. Lee*, 358 U.S. 217, 221-22 (1959)). "The sovereignty retained by an Indian tribe includes 'the power of regulating [its] internal and social relations.'" *Id.* at 69 (quoting *United States v. Kagama*, 118 U.S. 375, 381-382 (1886)). "Navajo domestic relations is the core of the tribe's 'internal and social relations.'" *Id.* (quoting *Fisher v. District Court*, 424 U.S. 382 (1976)). Thus, "Navajo code law and Navajo common law regulate the domestic relations . . . of Navajos living in Navajo Indian Country." *Id.* at 67.

By saying that "[m]arriages between Navajos and non-Navajos may be validly contracted only by the parties' complying with applicable state or foreign law," 9 N.T.C. §2 allows outside law to govern domestic relations within Navajo jurisdiction. Such needless relinquishment of sovereignty hurts the Navajo Nation. The Navajo people have always governed their marriage practices, whether the marriage is mixed or not, and must continue to do so to preserve sovereignty. Regulation of marriages, an integral part of the Navajo Nation's right to govern its territory and protect its citizens, should be free from the reach of state and foreign law. The Navajo Nation must regulate all domestic relations within its jurisdiction if sovereignty has any meaning. Even the United States government found that local laws best govern domestic relations in most instances. . . . Enacted in 1957, 9 N.T.C. §2 has outlived its usefulness.

This Court recommends that the Navajo Tribal Council amend Title 9 of the Navajo Tribal Code so that it reflects Navajo regulation and control of domestic relations within Navajo territorial jurisdiction.

Affirmed.

NOTES

1. In *Naize v. Naize*, 24 Indian L. Rep. 6152 (Navajo Nation 1997), the court reaffirmed prior holdings authorizing the Navajo judiciary to award spousal maintenance payments in divorce cases even without an authorizing statute from the tribal legislature:

> At the outset, we establish that the Navajo Nation courts, serving as courts of equity, have the general authority to award alimony, particularly in cases where a divorced spouse is "not able to provide for her [or his] own maintenance and that of her [or his] remaining minor children without some sort of financial aid from" the former spouse. . . . This power exists independent of any Navajo Nation statute on the subject and is justified by the Navajo People's traditional teachings admonishing not to "throw one's family away." Public policy also supports the courts' exercise of this power. The general lack of economic and employment opportunities on the Navajo Nation, the Nation's lack of a well educated and skilled labor force, and the Nation's high divorce rate, which leaves children dependent on one spouse or relatives, all underlie the many requests to the courts for spousal maintenance. . . .
>
> The Navajo People's segmentary lineage system (clanship system) is the foundation of Navajo Nation domestic relations law. The system itself is law. Traditional Navajo society is matrilineal and matrilocal, which obligates a man upon marriage to move to his wife's residence. The property the couple bring to the marriage mingle and through their joint labors create a stable and permanent home for themselves and their children. The wife's immediate and extended family benefit directly and indirectly, in numerous ways, from the marriage.
>
> If the marriage does not survive, customary law directs the man to leave with his personal possessions (including his horse and riding gear, clothes, and religious items) and the rest of the marital property stays with the wife and children at their residence for their support and maintenance. Whatever gains the marital property generate goes to support the wife and children and to a lesser extent the wife's close relatives. This longstanding customary law is akin to modern spousal maintenance. Therefore, we conclude that Navajo common law gives the Navajo Nation courts' authority to award spousal maintenance in appropriate cases even in the absence of statutory law on the subject. Our laws require our courts to apply Navajo common law equally to both spouses when addressing spousal maintenance issues.

Naize, 24 Indian L. Rep. at 6152. The court then affirmed portions of the spousal maintenance awarded by the trial court:

> The Appellant argues that the Chinle Family Court abused its discretion when it awarded to the Appellee spousal maintenance. . . . We disagree. The Appellee's evidence in support of her request is not controverted . . . and strongly shows a need for an award of spousal maintenance.

The Appellee is a 58 year old elderly Navajo lady who was married to the Appellant for 22 years. She is uneducated and unemployable. Poor health and illiteracy makes her a poor prospect for vocational training or other training to acquire meaningful employment skills. Her poor health prevents her from weaving rugs or raising livestock to support herself and her son. She earns no wages and chances she will acquire capital assets are nonexistent. She is in constant need of medical attention. She had two operations, cannot move freely without pain, has tuberculosis related health problems, has a foot disorder which requires special needs, and needs funds for traditional ceremonies. She contributed to the marriage, as wife, mother, and homemaker, while the Appellant worked outside the home. The parties' only child lives with her and needs her support. She needs transportation to get medical care. Under these facts, we cannot find a better applicant for an award of spousal maintenance.

. . . Just enough evidence to tip the scale in favor of an award of spousal maintenance is all we require. The trial court has discretion to decide on sufficient evidence and we find no abuse of discretion here. We affirm the family court's award of spousal maintenance to the Appellee.

The Appellant does not dispute the amount of the spousal maintenance award and we do not address it. The time period that the Appellant is obligated to make monetary payments is also not an issue. The only other matter is the family court's order that the Appellant must supply the Appellee with wood and coal for an indefinite time period. We reverse this part of the spousal maintenance award because it violates that Navajo common law rule which requires finality in Navajo divorces. Harmony in the community and in the lives of the divorced spouses should be restored quickly following a divorce. *Apache v. Republic National Life Insurance Co.*, 3 Nav. R. 250, 254 (Window Rock D. Ct. 1982). We rely on the teachings of Apache:

> There was a principle of finality in Navajo customary divorce, and the principle of restoring harmony in the community by quickly and finally breaking ties so the community can soon return to normal is one which is common-sense. To permit a former spouse to keep such ties that she or he may be said to be lurking behind the hogan waiting to take a portion of the corn harvest is unthinkable, since each spouse returns to his or her own family after the divorce. Each former spouse should return home after making the break and disturb others no more. *Id.* at 254.

> Also, it is not fair to require the Appellant to supply wood and coal for life, while he is obligated to pay spousal maintenance for only three years.

Naize, 24 Indian L. Rep. at 6153.

2. Other courts also have refused to recognize "common-law marriages" under tribal law. *E.g.*, *In re Estate of Abeyta*, 2 SWITCA 4 (Pueblo of San Juan 1991).
3. In *Husband v. Wife*, 2003.NAMP.0000002 (Mashantucket Pequot Court of Appeals 2003), the court was confronted with whether to enforce a Connecticut state court divorce decree between two tribal members. The court chose to apply the doctrine of comity as its analysis:

> In stark contrast to the Full Faith and Credit Clause as revealed in case law, VI M.P.T.L. ch. 8, §2(b) requires the tribal court, prior to enforcement of a foreign judgment, to determine whether "such judgment . . . contravene[s] the public policy of the Mashantucket Pequot Tribe." It therefore would be

wholly at odds with the language of ch. 8, §2(b) to conclude that it intends to require application of "full faith and credit"—as that term is understood under settled constitutional law—to foreign marriage dissolution judgments.

Instead, we believe, Mashantucket Law requires that foreign judgments be evaluated, and where appropriate, recognized through the far more flexible construct of "comity," where consideration of public policy considerations is permissible.

Id. at ¶¶31-32.

The court then engaged in the analysis of whether the state court divorce decree violated tribal public policy:

On the issue of public policy, we agree with the Tribe that, as a general matter, enforcement of lawful dissolution of marriage judgment from the State of Connecticut does not contravene Mashantucket public policy. (Mashantucket Pequot Tribal Nation's Br. of Amicus Curiae at 5-6) ("Tribal Court recognition of state court orders that provide for the custody, care, education, visitation and support of [Wife's] child does not, in general, contravene the public policy of the Tribe."). Our independent review of Mashantucket law confirms this understanding. Initially, we recognize, as noted supra, that the use of the term "full faith and credit" in VI M.P.T.L. ch. 1, §2(c) is strong evidence that such recognition is consistent with Mashantucket policy. *See also* V M.P.T.L. ch. 1, §3(d). . . . Furthermore, the "Purpose" section of the Family Relations Law, which is perhaps the clearest indication of Mashantucket policy on this issue, recognizes that:

[F]amilies thrive when they receive appropriate emotional and financial support, and that the lives of children and families improve by strengthening parental responsibility for family and child support. The Tribe encourages the development of Tribal law and policies and procedures that protect and preserve the continuity of family and promote a uniform, efficient and equitable recognition and implementation of these responsibilities. VI M.P.T.L. ch. 1, §1(a).

Plainly, this provision accords substantial weight to judgments which adjudicate dissolution claims and properly and fairly place "financial support" on parents of children. This view of Mashantucket policy is confirmed by the Child Welfare Law as well, codified in Title V of the M.P.T.L. Chapter 1, §1 of that Title states in pertinent part:

The Mashantucket Pequot Tribe finds that there is no resource more vital to its continued existence and integrity than its children. . . . The Tribe hereby declares that it is the policy of this Nation to protect the health and welfare of children and families within the Mashantucket Pequot community, to promote the security of community, and to preserve the unity of the family by enhancing the parental capacity for good child care and development and providing a continuum of services for children and families with an emphasis, whenever possible, on prevention, early intervention, and community-based solutions.

Here, tribal children are among the main beneficiaries of the judgment under consideration, which requires the payment of child support. Their welfare—obviously a paramount consideration of the Tribe—militates strongly for adoption of the judgment. Moreover, in this case, there is no indication — and Husband does not contend — that the division of parental financial responsibility is inequitable. Under these circumstances, we have no trouble concluding that Mashantucket policy, in general, supports recognition of a lawful Connecticut dissolution judgment, particularly since child support is involved.

Id. at ¶¶39-43.

4. The author of *Anatomy of a Murder*, Robert Traver (the pen name of former Michigan Supreme Court Justice John Voelker), also wrote a novel called *Laughing Whitefish,* based on a series of nineteenth-century Michigan Supreme Court cases culminating in *Kobogum v. Jackson Iron Co.*, 43 N.W. 602 (Mich. 1889). *See also Compo v. Jackson Iron Co.*, 12 N.W. 901 (Mich. 1882); *Compo v. Jackson Iron Co.*, 16 N.W. 295 (Mich. 1883). The *Kobogum* decision established in Michigan the general rule that state courts must defer to tribal law in cases involving the internal, domestic relations of American Indians residing within their own territory.

The underlying dispute involved an almost fantastic and contrived story. An Upper Peninsula Ojibwe man — Marji Gesick, who likely would now be a member of the Keewenaw Bay Indian Community — led a group of mining company explorers in 1845 to an area that would later be known as the Jackson Mine, the site of one of the richest veins of iron ore in the nation. Upon the "discovery," the company people in 1846 offered Mr. Gesick "twelve undivided thirty-one one hundredths parts of the interest" of the mining company that would be set up on that land. Of course, after the mining company became hugely profitable it never paid Mr. Gesick his share. After Mr. Gesick walked on in 1861 or 1862, his daughter Charlotte Kobogum brought suit to recover the amount owed in the 1880s.

The critical questions involved the defenses presented by the company. First, the company argued that Charlotte had waited too long to bring the suit, decades after the mining company had become wealthy and valuable. Second, the company argued that Mr. Gesick was a polygamist, with marriages to as many as three wives without divorcing any of them, and that Charlotte, as the issue of the second marriage, could not inure to the benefit of Mr. Gesick's bargain under the settled public policy of the State of Michigan. In 1889, the Michigan Supreme Court finally vindicated the interests of Charlotte Kobogum and her family:

> The only question remaining is whether Marji Gesick's interests passed to his descendants recognized by the Indian laws and usages. If they did, there is no doubt of the rights of these complainants. . . . The United States supreme court and the state courts have recognized as law that no state laws have any force over Indians in their tribal relations. . . . There was not, during any of the period involved in these inheritances, any law or treaty of the United States on the subject of Indian marriages, or in any way interfering with Indian usages on the subject. The testimony now in this case shows what, as matter of history, we are probably bound to know judicially, that among these Indians polygamous marriages have always been recognized as valid, and have never been confounded with such promiscuous or informal temporary intercourse as is not reckoned as marriage. While most civilized

nations in our day very wisely discard polygamy, and it is not probably lawful anywhere among English speaking nations, yet it is a recognized and valid institution among many nations, and in no way universally unlawful. We must either hold that there can be no valid Indian marriage, or we must hold that all marriages are valid which by Indian usage are so regarded. There is no middle ground which can be taken, so long as our own laws are not binding on the tribes. They did not occupy their territory by our grace and permission, but by a right beyond our control. They were placed by the constitution of the United States beyond our jurisdiction, and *we had no more right to control their domestic usages than those of Turkey or India.* The treaties made between the United States and this very tribe, which are quite numerous, all recognize heritable relations among them, and in many instances, familiar to all old residents of the country, provided for the Indian families of persons who had other families; recognizing the Indian nation as entitled to say who should share in tribal benefits. As white men cannot withdraw themselves from state law, we should have no great difficulty in determining their personal status; but Indians who were members of their tribes were not obliged or authorized to look to state laws in governing their own affairs.

Kobogum, 43 N.W. at 507-08 (emphasis added; other emphases omitted).

B. PROBATE

IN RE: ESTATE OF SAMPSON

Mashantucket Pequot Probate Court,
No. PB 2000-100, 2002.NAMP.0000003 (January 18, 2002)

The opinion of the court was delivered by: EDWARD B. O'CONNELL, Judge

By application dated July 6, 2000, Margery M. Pinson (the "petitioner") represents that Constance L. Sampson (sometimes called the "decedent" or "testatrix") was a member of the Mashantucket Pequot Tribe who died in Mashantucket on July 1, 2000, leaving a last will and testament dated October 28, 1996. The petitioner requests that the will be admitted to probate and that letters testamentary be granted to her as the executrix of the will. Leslie Champlain and Yvette Champlain (the "respondents" or "contestants"), are grand-nieces and blood relatives of the decedent. They oppose the admission of the will on the ground that the decedent lacked testamentary capacity to make a will.

The will bequeaths specific legacies of $5,000.00 each to Evelyn Pinson, a niece of the decedent, and Virginia Diaz McConneghey, who had resided with the decedent for a number of years as a foster child. The residuary estate is devised and bequeathed to Margery M. Pinson, the decedent's sister, who survived the decedent.

The decedent was one of thirteen brothers and sisters, three of whom had predeceased her. The respondents are granddaughters of Mason Champlain, a deceased brother of the decedent. With the exception of Margery M. Pinson and Evelyn Pinson, none of the decedent's brothers and sisters are named as beneficiaries of the will, and none of their offspring are named as beneficiaries.

Asserting that the testatrix was "a greatly disturbed decedent who suffered from a constellation of psychotic problems, physical and mental limitations," to the degree that a conservator of her estate and person had to be appointed by the Groton Probate Court, the respondents contend that the testatrix lacked the testamentary capacity to make a will. The petitioner responds that the mere existence of a conservatorship does not compel the conclusion that the will is invalid, and that the testatrix was possessed of sufficient mental capacity to comprehend the effect of what she was doing when she signed the will.

Section 1 of Chapter 5 of the Mashantucket Pequot Probate Code provides:

> Any person eighteen years of age or older or an emancipated minor, and of sound mind, may dispose of his estate by will.

The corresponding Connecticut statute, Section 45a-250 of the Connecticut General Statutes similarly provides:

> Any person eighteen years of age of older, and of sound mind, may dispose of his estate by will.

Because the provisions of the Mashantucket Pequot Probate Code are similar, and in many cases identical, to the Connecticut General Statutes relating to probate matters, decisions of the Connecticut courts are a "useful source of guidance" when discussing testamentary capacity. *See Schock v. Mashantucket Pequot Gaming Enterprise*, 3 Mash. 258 (1999) (federal court interpretations of Federal Rules of Civil Procedure are helpful in interpreting an identical provision in the Mashantucket Rules of Civil Procedure), citing *Mamiye v. Mashantucket Pequot Gaming Enterprise*, 2 Mash. 141,142 (1997). . . . Here, the provisions of the Mashantucket Pequot Probate Code and the Connecticut General Statutes as to who may make a will are substantially similar, and Connecticut cases on testamentary capacity are particularly useful.

The parties do not dispute the principles of law and the tests that the court must apply in determining whether the testatrix possessed sufficient testamentary capacity, summarized as follows: The burden of proving testamentary capacity is on the party claiming under the will. . . . Accordingly, "[t]he burden of proof in the instant case to establish the capacity of the testatrix to make a will rested upon the [proponent]." . . . The proponent of the will must prove the fact of testamentary capacity by a preponderance of the evidence. . . . The presumption of capacity permits the proponent to rest upon proof of some evidence of testamentary capacity, shifting to the contestants the burden of going forward with the evidence upon the issue, . . . but the ultimate burden of proving testamentary capacity remains with the proponent. . . .

There is a "well established test for testamentary capacity, i.e. that the testator have mind and memory sound enough to know and understand the business upon which he was engaged at the time of execution [of the will]." . . . Stated another way, "[t]he test which we apply is the ability of the testator at the time of the execution of the will to understand the nature and elements of the particular transaction of making a will in which he is engaged." . . .

A testatrix "may be competent to make a will though she has not mental capacity sufficient for the management or transaction of business generally[;] . . . some mental impairment could occur and still leave the testatrix with a sound mind within the definition of testamentary capacity." . . . The fact that a conservator has been appointed for the testator is among the relevant evidence that may be considered, but is not dispositive. In *Reid v. Lord*, 102 Conn. 365 (1925), "the testator had been adjudged insane and a conservator set over him, still, as the contestants of the will concede, this is not conclusive [on the question of testamentary capacity]." *Id.* at 368. "A person may harbor insane delusions and yet have testamentary capacity. A delusion can affect testamentary capacity only when it enters into and controls to some degree the making of a will." . . .

The parties do not disagree on the applicability of the above principles. They are in vigorous disagreement, however, on the issue of whether the decedent was possessed of sufficient mind and memory to know and understand what she was doing at the time she executed her will.

Mrs. Sampson died on July 1, 2000. Three years and nine months earlier, on October 28, 1996, she signed her last will and testament while a resident of Mashantucket. Attorney John Duggan, licensed to practice law and experienced in the preparation of wills and administration of estates, prepared the will and supervised its execution. He first met Ms. Sampson in 1994, when he assisted her in preparing her tax return. On this occasion, and on several other occasions in subsequent years when he helped her prepare her tax returns, he would get from her the necessary information, prepare the return, and bring it back to her for her signature. He did not recall any unusual behavior during these meetings, and found her to be a "delightful" person.

In the fall of 1994, Ms. Sampson was residing in Groton, Connecticut. Although she received considerable income as a member of the Mashantucket Pequot Tribe, it was disappearing and not accumulating. Ms. Sampson was a generous person; some recipients of her generosity may have been taking advantage of this trait. Margery Pinson, the decedent's sister, sought the assistance of Attorney Duggan in establishing a conservatorship in the Groton Probate Court. With Attorney Duggan's assistance and participation, Ms. Pinson was appointed as the decedent's conservator.

Ms. Sampson moved to the Mashantucket Pequot reservation in 1995. Physical ailments common to people of her age began to develop; she was scheduled to undergo colon surgery on October 29, 1996.

Four days earlier, on October 25, 1996, Attorney Duggan met with Ms. Sampson at Mashantucket to discuss changes to her existing will. He testified that they met for about half an hour, and discussed her then-existing will and what changes were to be made and why. He was aware that Ms. Sampson was under a conservatorship. Mr. Duggan recalled that Ms. Sampson was understandably concerned about the upcoming surgery, but did not act or speak inappropriately. Although she did not know the balance of her accounts "to the last dime," she was aware of the nature and general amount of her assets. She knew who her relatives were, and had cogent reasons for making changes in her will. Attorney Duggan also discussed with her the possibility of a living will. She did not want one, however, as she was a practicing Jehovah's

Witness, and considered that a living will would be inconsistent with her religious tenets.

After preparing the revised will, Attorney Duggan again met with Ms. Sampson on October 28, 1996 at the house of Margery Pinson, on the Mashantucket reservation. As before, he discussed with her the changes from the previous will. He recalls that she expressed no doubt or hesitation, and did not appear to be confused or uncertain about the nature of her assets, the relationships with her family members, or how she wanted her estate to be distributed. Attorney Duggan was satisfied that Ms. Sampson possessed the requisite testamentary capacity; he watched her sign the will in the presence of two witnesses, including himself, and administered the oath on the self-proving affidavit signed by the other witness.

Ms. Sampson survived her surgery, and died about three and one-half years after she executed the will, at the age of sixty-nine. Attorney Duggan met with her on several occasions after she signed the will, usually regarding her tax returns, and observed nothing that would cause him to change his opinion that she had testamentary capacity at the time she signed the will.

As in many will contests, the respondents did not have first-hand, personal knowledge of the events surrounding the preparation and execution of the will, and are not in a position to directly contradict Attorney Duggan's recollections and impressions. They did, however, submit a considerable array of circumstantial evidence, which is appropriate: "The testator's mental condition is not capable of demonstration by direct evidence. It can only be shown by proof of circumstances from which the inference of mental condition may be drawn. The circumstances pointing to mental condition usually consist of miscellaneous acts o[r] expressions which taken singly are of little value but which in the aggregate portray a pattern of behavior from which the trier (sometimes with the assistance of opinions by experts) may reach a conclusion". FOLSOM, CONNECTICUT ESTATES, PRACTICE, PROBATE LITIGATION, (1992) §1.5, p. 11. Evidence of the testator's acts and condition during periods of time both prior and subsequent to the date of execution of the will may be admitted "solely for such light as it may afford as to his capacity at that point of time [of execution] and diminishes in weight as time lengthens in each direction from that point." . . .

The parties submitted evidence of circumstances relating to the decedent's physical and mental condition in the form of testimony by Mr. Duggan; testimony and medical records of physicians; the record and findings of the Groton Probate Court conservatorship proceedings; testimony of Attorney Eric Janney, appointed as Ms. Sampson's attorney by the Groton Probate Court, testimony of some of Ms. Sampson's family members, including the petitioner and the respondents; and testimony of Eleanor Sudol, a home health aide employed by Interim Healthcare.

Eleanor Sudol was employed by Interim Healthcare as a home health aide and daytime companion for Ms. Sampson from 1995 until her death in July 2000. She was with Ms. Sampson several times a week during the month of October, 1996, when the will at issue was executed. She often drove Ms. Sampson to visit her sister, Margery Pinson, who Ms. Sudol described as Ms. Sampson's "favorite." Ms. Sudol testified that Ms. Sampson decided where she wanted to go, what she wanted to eat, formed opinions of her own and could hold a coherent conversation. Ms. Sampson was aware that Ms. Pinson looked after her finances, telling Ms. Sudol that "I'm rich. Margery takes care of me." Ms. Sudol was aware that the decedent was on medications, but could recall no instances when the decedent was delusional or irrational.

Dr. Amarillys Rodriguez, employed by the Mashantucket Pequot Tribe to provide and supervise health care for tribal members, is a board certified family physician. She first met the decedent in 1992, through the decedent's sister Margery Pinson, who worked at the Mashantucket health center. At that time Ms. Sampson was living in Rhode Island. Dr. Rodriguez saw the decedent for specific medical conditions, and eventually began meeting with her about once a month for checkups. In the beginning Ms. Sampson was shy and reserved, but over the course of time began to trust and accept Dr. Rodriguez. Ms. Sampson had a number of physical problems, including diabetes, arthritis and coronary diseases. She was opinionated about her case, asking about procedures and consequences.

Dr. Rodriguez was also aware that the decedent had a history of psychiatric illnesses, including chronic depression and panic disorders. She knew about this through her review of the decedent's medical records and her own observations. Dr. Rodriguez prescribed an array of medications for the decedent's physical and mental conditions.

In October of 1993, Dr. Rodriguez admitted Ms. Sampson to Backus Hospital for heart problems. During the hospitalization, Dr. Rodriguez referred Ms. Sampson to Dr. Max Okasha, a psychiatrist, inasmuch as she was exhibiting signs of depression. He concluded that the decedent was suffering from an episode of major depression and panic disorder, and suggested a change in medication.

About a year after the Backus heart admission, in several reports to the Groton Probate Court in support of the conservatorship application, Dr. Rodriguez stated that the decedent was giving her money away, had short term memory problems and was "forgetful, redundant and sometimes doesn't understand simple instructions," particularly when she did not take her medications. Dr. Rodriguez felt that the decedent needed help in keeping track of and taking her large array of medications, and that it would assist Ms. Sampson if her sister Margery Pinson was in a position to actively monitor her finances and her care.

In August of 1995, Dr. Okasha again saw the decedent and decided to change her medication. That new medication provoked drastic changes; a few days later the decedent turned up at the emergency room in a panic and a week later was admitted to the Backus psychiatric ward in a confused, depressed, delusional and panicky state. After her medications were changed again, the decedent felt less depressed, her anxiety decreased, her panic attacks ceased, her delusions abated, and she was discharged from the hospital. Two months later, in October of 1995, Dr. Okasha noticed that the decedent was restless, pacing and rocking. He again changed her medication, and this was resolved.

After the October 1995 episode Ms. Sampson's psychiatric treatment was taken over by Dr. Alnoor Ramji, also a Norwich psychiatrist. Dr. Rodriguez felt that Dr. Okasha was certainly competent, but that Dr. Ramji might be more understanding of issues such as Ms. Sampson's lateness for appointments. She felt that Dr. Ramji might connect better with Ms. Sampson. The contestants attribute darker motives to this change in psychiatrists, but the court accepts Dr. Rodriguez' explanation.

Dr. Ramji treated Ms. Sampson from late 1995 until her death on July 1, 2000. In 1996, he saw her in his office on ten occasions, including October 18, 1996, ten days before the execution of her will. As did Dr. Okasha, Dr. Ramji found that the decedent suffered from organic brain disorder and schizophrenia, and that she needed to be on a number of psychiatric medications to control episodes of depression and panic disorder. He also considered that she suffered from short term memory problems, and that a home health aide service was of assistance in assuring compliance with her schedule of medications.

On October 29, 1996, the day after she executed her will, Ms. Sampson was hospitalized for colon surgery. Dr. Rodriguez testified that while hospitalized during the surgery and its aftermath, Ms. Sampson had to stop taking her medications and, as a result, "decompensated." When her medications were restored, however, Ms. Sampson resumed her former mental state.

Thereafter, Ms. Sampson physically declined in health over the years until her death on July 1, 2000. During this time, Dr. Rodriguez dealt with Margery Pinson regarding Ms. Sampson's health, and occasionally talked with Virginia Diaz McConneghy. She did not speak with any other family members.

Ms. Margery Pinson is the sister of the decedent and the major beneficiary of her estate and the named executrix. She testified that until the last years of her life, the decedent was poor and had few material possessions. She worked hard, often as a cleaning person in the homes of the well to do. While in Rhode Island, the decedent raised a foster child, Virginia Diaz McConneghey, under the auspices of the Rhode Island child welfare authorities. Ms. Pinson testified that she and her sister were a part of a large family, consisting of thirteen siblings, and that she and her sister were especially close: "Since we were children, Constance and I took care of each other." When living in Rhode Island, the decedent would stay with Ms. Pinson when Ms. Pinson's husband worked the night shift.

Ms. Pinson testified that the decedent, who was childless, was fearful that she would be put in a nursing home in her old age. Ms. Pinson promised her that this would not happen. Eventually, the decedent was the only one of her generation of siblings remaining in Rhode Island. She wanted to come and live on the Mashantucket reservation, but there were no openings at the time. The next best housing alternative at that time was the apartment in Groton, and the decedent lived there until she moved to the reservation.

Ms. Pinson recalled that the decedent knew she had money from the Tribe, but was good-hearted and prone to give it away, prompting Ms. Pinson to request the Groton conservatorship. The decedent knew she was getting money from the Tribe, and occasionally asked Ms. Pinson if she could see her checkbook and bankbook.

Ms. Pinson recalled that the decedent talked to her and her sister Mertice on the phone, and occasionally received visitors, but most of her other brothers and sisters and relatives did not pay much attention to her. Ms. Pinson would visit the decedent, or the decedent would visit her, every day when they were on the reservation. Before that, she would visit the decedent once a week when she was in Groton. They took trips together to vacation and tourist spots, such as Amish country and Bar Harbor. Ms. Pinson, who was present when the decedent signed her will, considered that Ms. Sampson was of sound mind at that time.

Renee Everett, a niece of the decedent, testified that she knew the decedent all her life, and that Ms. Sampson lived with her parents when Ms. Everett was younger. She also visited Ms. Sampson when she lived in Groton. She knew her aunt had psychological problems, often acting in a "childish" or temperamental manner, but did not consider that her aunt was "nuts."

Diedre Champlain, another niece of the decedent and a sister of Ms. Everett, also testified. She recalled visiting with her aunt in Rhode Island during her youth, and visiting with her once while the decedent lived in Groton. On one occasion she observed the decedent at the Mashantucket pharmacy acting inappropriately, on her hands and knees and rocking profusely. She reported this behavior to another niece at the pharmacy, Evelyn Pinson. This incident took place in 1993 or 1994, about two years before the execution of the will. Like Ms. Everett, Diedre Champlain saw the decedent out at tribal functions, but did not converse with her on those occasions other than say "hello," as an aide would do most of the talking. On cross-examination she agreed that Margery Pinson and Evelyn Pinson had a closer relationship with the decedent than did other members of the family.

Attorney Eric Janney was Ms. Sampson's court-appointed attorney during the Groton Probate Court conservatorship proceeding. He recalled that he was concerned with the decedent's ability to handle her financial affairs, and recommended that a conservator be appointed. Although she would get confused from time to time, she was clear about her illnesses in her one conversation with him. Attorney Janney considered that Ms. Sampson comprehended the effect of the conservatorship proceedings, and understood that her finances would be handled by her sister Margery.

Three expert witnesses, Dr. Rodriguez, Dr. Okasha and Dr. Ramji testified regarding the decedent's testamentary capacity.

Dr. Rodriguez, whose practice included geriatrics, considered that the decedent's short-term memory "wasn't perfect." The decedent did, however, remember the names of her brothers and sisters, and could recollect events in her childhood and adulthood. She had psychological problems, as evidenced by her records from Rhode Island mental health professionals and Dr. Rodriguez' own observations. She was afflicted with organic brain syndrome, schizophrenia and depression, but Dr. Rodriguez felt that the effects of these illnesses could be alleviated by medications, to the extent that Ms. Sampson was aware of her assets, her family and what she wanted to do with her money. Dr. Rodriguez acknowledged that Ms. Sampson took a large number of prescriptions, up to fourteen in a day, but felt that the drugs did not result in an unsound mind. Rather, it was when the decedent did not take her medications, or when the medications were changed, that resulted in disruptions and inappropriate behavior. She felt that, inasmuch as Ms. Sampson had sufficient funds to afford it, home health aides were useful in assuring that she kept to her schedule of medications.

Dr. Rodriguez saw the decedent on October 29, 1996, one day after she executed the will, when she met with the decedent at Lawrence & Memorial Hospital on the day of her colon surgery. Dr. Rodriguez testified that Ms. Sampson was alert, cooperative and understood what was happening. She was nervous, as are most people who face major surgery, but was not sad or crying or depressed. She understood and was aware of her assets in a general sense; she knew who were the members of her family; she remembered who did things for her over the years. In the view of Dr. Rodriguez, Ms. Sampson was of sound mind, capable of understanding what she was doing when she signed a document, such as her will on October 28, 1996, and the consent for surgery on the next day. Dr. Rodriguez based this conclusion on her medical training, her treatment of Ms. Sampson since 1993 and her conversation with Ms. Sampson on October 29, 1996, the day after she signed the will.

Dr. Ramji began treating the decedent in November of 1995, when he took over her psychiatric care from Dr. Okasha. He reported that despite having a "long and significant psychiatric history," she was "quite capable of distinguishing between right and wrong and to make appropriate decisions regarding her medical care" as evidenced by her discussing with him the pros and cons of moving from Groton to the reservation to be near Margery Pinson, "who she was very close to and in whom she had a lot of confidence and trust." Dr. Ramji was aware that the decedent was receiving assistance from home health care aides, but in his opinion that did not mean she was of unsound mind; it was more a matter of her being able to afford and take advantage of this type of service.

Dr. Ramji found the decedent to be "quite alert, verbal" over the course of his treatment. He considered that "her depression and psychosis were very well controlled by her medications," and that in 1996 her condition was "stable" except when her medications were stopped because of the colon surgery. After that surgery she "was stabilized quickly and returned to her former self."

Dr. Ramji saw the decedent in October 1996, the month that the will was executed. Based on his training, experience and treatment of the decedent, he was of the opinion that at the time she signed her will she was of sound mind, alert, oriented as to time and place and able to exercise good judgment. In his opinion, her medications worked well for her, and her depression was not so severe that it interfered with her soundness of mind.

Dr. Okasha first treated the decedent in October of 1993 upon a referral from Dr. Rodriguez. He also saw the decedent on several occasions during the next two years when she was in crisis, resulting in hospitalizations until her mental condition could be stabilized. He described the symptoms and behavior of the decedent during these crises, such as short term memory loss and disorientation as to time and place. He concluded that the decedent suffered from organic brain syndrome and schizophrenia. Although there were periods of time that the decedent's condition was acute, Dr. Okasha did not consider that she needed to be institutionalized. In his report and testimony, Dr. Okasha described generally the various and typical aspects and effects of these illnesses. He also observed that with medication the decedent could function on a day-to-day basis with assistance, but if she stopped taking medication her mental condition would deteriorate, and she would become confused and destabilized.

Dr. Okasha stopped treating the decedent in November of 1995. He did not opine regarding her soundness of mind on October 28, 1996, the date of the execution of her will.

Conclusion

Constance Sampson had a hard and difficult life. For most of it, she was poor; she did not have many material possessions. She had to work for what she had, often as a housecleaner for those who were better off than her. In her earlier years she was exposed to some of the harsh and unpleasant aspects of life in our society, but also participated in beneficial and joyful activities, to the point where she raised a foster child for the better part of a decade. She was not without the skills necessary to navigate through the vicissitudes of daily life.

Mentally, Ms. Sampson had her ups and downs, beginning when she was younger and lived in Rhode Island. All the physicians who testified agreed that she suffered from chronic brain syndrome, schizophrenia and depression. These physicians also agreed, however, that the effects of these illnesses can be ameliorated and controlled by medications. The task of this court is to determine whether these illnesses, when combined with the physical problems which began to beset her during her later years, created such a deficient state of mind and memory that she did not know and understand what she was doing when she signed her will.

The will itself provides no evidence of a mind that has lost its moorings. The primary beneficiary is Margery Pinson, the decedent's sister and lifelong friend. She frequently visited Ms. Pinson when they were both living in Rhode Island. Ms. Pinson was the conservator of her estate, an appointment endorsed by Attorney Janney. Ms. Pinson spoke or visited with the decedent every day when the decedent moved to Mashantucket. She would take the decedent on trips that were both special (e.g. vacations) and mundane (e.g. visits to doctors' offices). The close relationship between them was apparent to Elenor Sudol, who described Ms. Pinson as the decedent's "favorite." None of the decedent's other surviving siblings (all of whom were omitted from her will) objected to the admission of the will. In these circumstances Ms. Pinson can be fairly regarded as the natural object of the decedent's bounty. The dispositive terms of Ms. Sampson's will, which leaves the bulk of her estate to her close sister, are not evidence of a deranged mind.

Evidence of the testatrix' acts and condition at periods of time near the date of execution of the will is particularly useful when compared to evidence in points of time further removed from the date of execution, which "diminishes in weight as time lengthens [from the date of execution]." . . . Attorney Duggan discussed the terms of the will with the decedent several days before the execution of the will, when she gave him cogent reasons for her testamentary scheme. Her mind was capable of grasping the distinction between a testamentary will and a living will; she objected to the latter because of her religious beliefs. This is not evidence of a wandering mind; rather, it is evidence of a mind that can understand the concepts behind a living will. At the will execution itself, Mr. Duggan, who was aware of and had participated in the Groton conservatorship proceedings and as a result was alert to the issue of testamentary capacity, discerned no confusion or uncertainty on the part of the decedent, and was satisfied that she possessed the requisite testamentary capacity.

Dr. Rodriguez, who had cared for the decedent since 1992 and was aware of both the physical and mental aspects of her condition, saw the decedent the day after she signed the will. Dr. Rodriguez, who was aware [of] the necessity of discerning the decedent's mental condition because of the requirement that she sign a consent to surgery on that day, found that she was alert and comprehending of what was going on. Dr. Rodriguez, who had opportunities to observe the decedent on occasions both good and bad, saw that the decedent was not depressed or sad on that day. She was confident that the decedent was aware of the general nature of her assets, and that she knew who were the members of the family. Dr. Rodriguez knew that the decedent's mental state could deteriorate when she did not take her medications, but she saw no evidence of mental impairment on the day after the decedent signed her will.

Dr. Ramji saw the decedent a few weeks before she signed the will. He knew that she had a "long and significant" psychiatric history, but in his opinion that was not in itself evidence of an unsound mind. He considered that her mental illnesses "were very well controlled by her medications." These prescriptions did not dull her mind or reduce her to a catatonic state. Dr. Ramji felt that the decedent, when medicated, was "quite capable" of distinguishing right from wrong and making appropriate decisions. Dr. Ramji, who treated the decedent before, during and after the period of time when the will was executed, was of the opinion that at the time she signed the will the decedent was alert, oriented as to time and place, and able to exercise good judgment.

Dr. Okasha, who had treated the decedent earlier than Dr. Ramji, last saw the decedent almost a year before the will was signed. He saw her on occasions when her mental problems were acute. Even then, he did not find that she needed to be institutionalized. He did not opine regarding the decedent's soundness of mind on the date her will was signed. He did agree, however, that with medication she could function on a day-to-day basis.

For the reasons set forth above, and taking into account the testimony of all the witnesses, including family members, attorneys and medical experts, and exhibits submitted into evidence, the court finds that at the time the testatrix executed her will, she had mind and memory sound enough to know and understand the business upon which she was engaged. She may not have possessed the mental capacity to manage all aspects of her affairs, but her mind and memory were not so impaired that she did not know what she was doing when she executed her will. On that day, she knew who were the members of her family; she knew the general nature of her assets; she was capable of making appropriate decisions; she did not have any insane delusions that entered into and controlled the making of her will.

The proponent has met her burden of proving that the testatrix had testamentary capacity on October 28, 1996. Her will executed on that date is hereby admitted to probate. Upon the submission and approval of a final accounting, distribution will be made in accordance with the terms of the will.

NOTES

1. In an older work, one scholar described the Hopi rules of inheritance in relation to personal property:

> On a woman's death all her property is customarily inherited by her daughters. If the latter are still young at her death, the property will be held in trust for them by the husband or maternal relatives (usually the latter) until they grow older. The trustees may use this property, cultivate the land, use the peach crop, or live in the house, if they so desire, during their period of trusteeship. In regard to the man, his personal goods, stock and sheep are customarily inherited by his sisters, brothers, and clanspeople generally, the widow, sons and daughters ordinarily inheriting none at all. A conflicting, or possibly a newer, pattern allows the man, but not the woman, some testamentary choice and it is clear that today children inherit as well as the close clan connections; that is, there is a tendency to allow members of the bilateral kin group to share in the disposal of the goods. In this way a man may bequeath personally owned peach orchards to his children. I was informed also that not unusually a man leaves his property to the child of the person who took care of him in his old age, clan affiliation, seniority and sex of the beneficiary giving away before the principle that reward should go to the individual who looks after the aged. I do not know whether this custom applies also to women, but it may be noted that Dr. Parsons reports the same custom applying at Laguna for both parents and is inclined to think that "the principle of inheritance in return for service may be, if not applied to houses, then to other property, an underlying and ancient Pueblo principle."

Ernest Beaglehole, *Ownership and Inheritance in an American Indian Tribe*, 20 IOWA L. REV. 304, 307 (1935). Beaglehole also described the Hopi customs for inheritance of real property:

> The general rule governing the inheritance of land is that it descends within the lineage in the female line. Fields are inherited, that is, by the family connection within the clan. If a man is working in addition to his wife's clan lands, land belonging to his own clan, this land returns at death to his maternal family; his children may arrange to work this land in turn but it is clearly understood that the title to the land remains with the father's clan. The custom in regard to individually owned waste land is given above. The inheritance of this land by the deceased's own children probably represents a newer pattern and is not characteristic of older Hopi practice.
>
> With the extinction of a clan, the rule seems to be for a linked clan to take over the lands of the deceased clan and for originally separated lands to be merged together. One informant insisted, however, that the children of the clan and not a linked clan would inherit the land. At Mishongnovi the Kachina clan is represented by several surviving men. When they die the linked Parrot clan will take over Kachina land. Parrot clan is represented by four or five men and two women past child-bearing age, and will likewise soon die out. A Parrot woman remarked that since there is no pre-existing linkage to dictate which of the other Mishongnovi clans should absorb Parrot Kachina land, this land will ultimately go out of cultivation. It would not be right for an unrelated clan to use the land, nor could an individual cultivate it in his own right. In this case however it is likely that children of Parrot clan

will cultivate if they need land or else one of two patterns reported on First Mesa may be followed. A survivor may choose an unrelated girl to live in the maternal house and inherit the clan fields or else the family which by chance ceremonial tie or by fictitious or remote relationship takes up residence in the house of the extinct clan will inherit also the clan fields. A final method suggested by an informant was that the family which takes care of the clan survivor in his old age and in whose house he dies has the right to inherit house and land in return for services rendered.

Id. at 324-15.

2. The lack of wills that would allow for the orderly devise of federal trust land holdings by American Indian people in the last century and longer has contributed to the extraordinary problem of fractionated heirships. Douglas Nash and Cecelia Burke described the history of this issue:

> The General Allotment Act, also known as the Dawes Act, was passed by Congress in 1887. The Act had two primary goals: to eliminate tribal culture by assimilation of Indians into the expanding European-American culture and to open reservation lands to non-Indian ownership. . . .
>
> Between 1770 and 1890, treaties between Indian tribes and the United States were a key tool in securing vast territories of land from tribes — lands to be settled by non-Indians. Through treaties, tribes typically ceded significant portions of their lands, and the federal government agreed that the retained lands would serve as a reservation and homeland for the tribes forever. For example, a treaty with the Cherokee stated:
>
>> [T]he purpose of the treaty is to secure the Cherokee] a permanent home . . . which shall, under the most solemn guarantee of the United States, be, and remain, theirs forever — a home that shall never, in all future time, be embarrassed by having extended around it the lines, or placed over it the jurisdiction of a Territory or State, nor be pressed upon by the extension, in any way, of any of the limits of any existing Territory or State. [Treaty with the Western Cherokee, May 6, 1828, 7 Stat. 311.]
>
> These reserved lands (reservations), like aboriginal lands, were held by Indian title, meaning Indians had the right to use and occupy the lands subject to the sovereign's plenary power to extinguish Indian title at will. By the time of the General Allotment Act, reservation lands comprised only remnants of the original tribal land bases.
>
> The Allotment Act authorized the president to arbitrarily select those reservations to be allotted. Once a reservation was selected, a census was taken of its tribal inhabitants; the land was surveyed and partitioned into "allotments" — parcels of land between eighty and one hundred sixty acres. Beneficial title to these allotments were then assigned to individual Indians, with legal title held in trust by the United States for a period of twenty-five years. After that time, it was expected that the Indian owner would be "civilized" and "competent enough" to manage his own affairs and the government would issue a fee patent for his allotment. Upon receipt of the fee patent, the allottee would become subject to the laws of the state where his property was situated. . . .
>
> For those individual Indians retaining ownership, the General Allotment Act failed them in two ways. First, the Act failed to recognize the cultural resistance to individual land ownership. The concept of individual ownership

of land was foreign to many Indian people, making the allotment process meaningless, and the legislators viewed tribal communal living as needy since the indigenous ideas of wealth contrasted and disagreed with Western ideas of wealth. Furthermore, farming was considered "women's work" among many tribes. Most were not inclined to abandon established tribal values and structures in favor of new and foreign concepts of individual ownership.

Second, the Act ultimately contained a device that would render Indian allotments fractionated beyond any practical use or economic value. Section five of the General Allotment Act provides that the law of descent and partition in force in the state or territory where such lands are situated shall apply thereto after patents have been executed and delivered. This means that state laws of intestate succession would apply to the allotments held in trust, regardless of testacy — Indian people could not pass title to their trust allotments by a will. The typical result of applying state laws of intestate succession to an ownership interest in an allotment is that the decedent's heirs inherit undivided interests in the original allotment. When they die, their heirs inherit the interests and the process continues over generations until the original allotment has many, sometimes hundreds and even thousands, of owners of undivided interests.

The result is what has been come to be described as the "fractionation of Indian lands," and examples of it abound. By 1985, one 160-acre allotment made in 1887 had 312 heirs each holding a fractional interest. The largest interest held was 2.5 percent and the smallest interest was 0.00005625 percent, producing a yearly income of less than a penny. Another allotment was valued at $22,000 in 2003 but only produced $2,000 in annual income. Although it had 505 co-owners of undivided interests, the common denominator required to calculate fractional interests had grown to 220,670,049,600,000. If the tract could have been sold for its estimated value, the smallest interest would have been entitled to $0.00001824. One owner in this fractionated tract would earn $1.00 — every 32,880 years. The Bureau of Indian Affairs estimated the administrative cost to manage this tract to be $42,800.

In response to the negative effects of the General Allotment and Burke Acts, John Collier, then Commissioner of Indian Affairs, developed a proposal that would change United States Indian policy and declare the Dawes Act a catastrophe. Instead of granting Indians the "dignity of private property," Collier reported that allotment "has cut down Indian land holdings from 138,000,000 [the acres Indians owned when the Dawes Act was passed in 1887] to 47,000,000 [the acres they had left in 1934]." Two-thirds of the tribal reservation land base had been lost. Furthermore, allotment had "rendered whole tribes landless. It ha[d] thrown more than a hundred thousand Indians virtually into the breadline . . . [and] put the Indian allotted lands into a hopelessly checkerboarded condition.

Douglas R. Nash & Cecelia E. Burke, *The Changing Landscape of Indian Estate Planning and Probate: The American Indian Probate Reform Act*, 5 Seattle J. Soc. Just. 121, 124-28 (2006).

Indian tribes have been adopting tribal probate codes to help alleviate this problem:

> Tribal probate codes may include rules of intestate succession, other provisions that are consistent with federal law and policies set forth in section 102 of the Indian Land Consolidation Act ("ILCA") Amendments of 2000. . . .

A definition of spouse could recognize marriages by custom or tradition of a tribe. The inheritance rights of children adopted out might be provided for. Special provisions might also be made to protect family heirlooms and arti-facts. Careful consideration should be given to a tribe's customs, interests and desires and steps taken to insure those are addressed to the fullest extent possible in its probate code.

A tribal probate code may not prohibit the testamentary devise of an interest in trust or restricted land to a lineal descendent of the original allot-tee or to an Indian who is not a member of the Indian tribe with jurisdiction over such interest unless the code allows eligible devisees to renounce their interests, the opportunity for a devisee who is the spouse or lineal descendent of a testator to reserve a life estate without regard to waste and payment of fair market value to the devisee.

A tribe may adopt rules of intestate succession that differ from the federal rules and which will govern the descent and distribution of trust land subject to its jurisdiction. Tribal probate codes that are intended to govern the descent and distribution of trust or restricted land must be approved by the Secretary of the Interior before they become effective. Tribes do not have the authority to probate trust property interests, even with an approved code, but their tribal code will be applied in the federal probate process.

Douglas Nash & Cecelia Burke, *Passing Title to Tribal Lands: Existing Federal and Emerging Tribal Probate Codes*, 50 ADVOCATE, May 2007, at 26, 27.

3. As the history of Indian lands explains, the modern probate of trust land rights usually serves to exclude non-Indians from inheritance. The Oneida Nation of Wisconsin, for example, has adopted a statute allowing for the inheritance of trust land rights only by tribal members:

> Non-members of the Oneida Tribe and non-citizens of the United States cannot acquire Trust Land through inheritance. Where interests are specifically devised to individuals ineligible to inherit, the following options are provided: (A) Sale of interest to the Oneida Tribe or an eligible heir for its fair market value. (B) Acquire a life estate in the property if an eligible spouse.

In re Estate of Summers, 2002.NAOW.0000095, at ¶15 (Oneida Appeals Com-mission 2002) (quoting Article 9-2 of Real Property Law). In *Summers*, a child who otherwise would have inherited trust lands was excluded on the basis that he was a Lakota Indian, not Oneida. *See id.* at ¶14 ("Article 9-9 of Real Property Law disposes of real property assets entirely to the surviving spouse Rebecca M. Browneyes-Summers. The surviving spouse of Anderson R. Sum-mers Jr., is a Lakota Sioux Indian and therefore her inheritance is restricted by Article 9-2 of Real Property Law.").

4. In *In re Estate of Komaquaptewa*, 4 Am. Tribal Law 432 (Hopi Tribe Appellate Court 2002), the court held that the tribal courts had jurisdiction to hear probate and inheritance matters where the village government, which nor-mally had jurisdiction, refused to decide the matter:

> It is well settled that probate matters are left to the individual Villages pur-suant to the Hopi Constitution. Article III, Section 2 of the Constitution and By-Laws of the Hopi Tribe reserves to the separate villages jurisdiction to

regulate village members' inheritance of property. The Hopi Constitution, tribal ordinances and resolutions are devoid of procedure when a village declines or refuses to exert this authority. Therefore, this Court must examine the sources of power enabling the Tribal Court to address inheritance matters when a village refuses to do so.

The Tribal Court has jurisdiction over "[t]he ownership, use or possession of any real or personal property within the Reservation." Hopi Ordinance 21, §1.7.1(d)(3). Moreover, subsection (a) of Tribal Ordinance 21 states that [T]he Hopi Tribal Court shall have jurisdiction over all civil actions where there are sufficient contacts with the Hopi Indian Reservation upon which to base the exercise of jurisdiction, consistent with the constitution and laws of the Hopi Tribe and the United States. This section authorizes the broadest exercise of jurisdiction consistent with these limitations. Hopi Ordinance 21, §1.7.1(a). This section of Ordinance 21 expresses the Tribal Council's intent to authorize the Hopi Tribal Court to exercise the broadest jurisdiction consistent with the constitution and laws of the Hopi Tribe and the United States. *Village of Mishongnovi v. Humevestewa*, 11, No. 96AP000008 (Hopi 11/20/1998). Read in its entirety, Ordinance 21 grants the Tribal Court broad jurisdiction over property located on the Hopi reservation, its use and ownership.

If the Tribal Court did not exercise jurisdiction after a village declined its right to decide a member's probate claim, village members would be left without a tribal forum in which to assert their property rights. Hopi tribal members would be unable to raise factual and legal matters affecting their cultural and legal interests in property, leading to a violation of substantial rights and leaving aggrieved parties to contest probate matters in non-tribal judicial forums. Moreover, Hopi tribal and village customs and traditions would not receive the same consideration in a non-tribal forum and the results could be devastating to Hopi parties, the Tribe and the Villages. Therefore, this Court finds as a matter of law and public policy that the tribal court has jurisdiction to decide inheritance matters when a village declines to or avoids its responsibility to do so.

Estate of Komaquaptewa, 4 Am. Tribal Law at 441-43.

C. CHILDREN

1. CHILD CUSTODY

POLINGYOUMA v. LABAN

Hopi Tribe Appellate Court, No. AP-006-95, 1997.NAHT.0000018
(March 28, 1997)

Before SEKAQUAPTEWA, Chief Justice, and ABBEY, Justice.

Factual and Procedural Background

Appellant Barbara Polingyouma and Appellee Vernon Laban are both members of the Hopi Tribe. They were married in Flagstaff in 1988, shortly after the birth of their daughter, Chelsey. They returned to Hopi in late 1991 or early 1992 and lived in Kykotsmovi in a residence belonging to Appellee's parents. Chelsey began attending Hopi Day School. She was six years old when this action commenced.

In May 1994, Appellee filed for divorce and requested sole custody of Chelsey. . . .

After three days of testimony concluding on June 29, the trial court found both parents fit and ordered joint custody of Chelsey with alternating six month periods of physical custody during which the non-custodial parent would have visitation rights every other weekend. Appellee was given the first period of physical custody of Chelsey, from July 1, 1995 through January 1, 1996.

Appellant filed a motion for Stay of Execution of the custody order and Notice of Appeal on July 18, 1995. Appellee responded to the motion and Appellant moved to strike the response.

Oral arguments were held March 28, 1995 before Chief Justice Sekaquaptewa and Justice Abbey.

Issues Presented on Appeal

Essentially, appellant argues that the trial court erred in not giving sufficient consideration to custom in rendering the child custody order. Specifically, she claims that the trial court failed to consider customs at all and therefore erred as a matter of law. In addition, she pleads customary law directly to the Appellate court. Under Appellant's view of custom this Court should recognize a presumption of physical custody with the mother because a Hopi child belongs to the mother's clan and the mother's family has special customary duties relating to the child's religious and ceremonial upbringing.

Finally, she argues that the trial court applied Arizona law incorrectly by devising a joint physical custody arrangement that is not in the best interests of the child.

Standard of Review

Errors of law as well as any decisions made by the trial court as to definition or use of custom, culture or tradition are reviewed de novo. *Hopi Indian Credit Association v. Thomas*, CIV-020-84, AP-001-84.

Discussion

I. The Trial Court Considered Custom

Appellant's first claim, that the trial court failed to consider custom, must fail. The trial court's custody order, D-013-94, states explicitly that it considered custom. In the very first sentence the trial court acknowledges "having taken into consideration Hopi tradition and custom." Thus Appellant's claim that the trial court failed to consider custom altogether is refuted by the record.

II. Pleading Custom

Even though the Appellant cannot show here that the trial court failed to consider custom, she pleads custom directly to this court. Appellant's implicit claim is that the trial court applied customary law improperly if it applied it at all. We would require a trial transcript in order to determine whether custom was propounded at trial and whether it was properly considered. However, Appellant has not supplied a transcript with this appeal. Consequently, the record here is devoid of evidence of custom, except for appellant's assertions on appeal.

While this Court may take judicial notice of custom, the legal interpretation of custom should be resolved at the trial court level. *Id. Hopi Indian Credit Association* explains the process for introducing custom at trial. A party who intends to raise an issue of unwritten custom, tradition or culture must give notice to the trial court and to the other party. *Id.* In addition, the party seeking to introduce custom into the legal resolution[m]ust plead custom with sufficient evidence so as to establish the existence of the custom and show how it is relevant to the issue before the court. *Id.*

Lacking a trial transcript, we proceed cautiously here. While we cannot analyze the introduction of custom at the trial level under the Hopi Indian Credit Association standards, we may still take judicial notice of custom.

III. Hopi Custom and Childbearing

This Court is prepared to take judicial notice of three aspects of Hopi custom concerning children. Under traditional Hopi practice, a child is born into her mother's clan, lives with the mother's household and receives ceremonial training from the mother's household.

IV. Consistency of the Custody Order with Custom

The existence of custom relating to a child's involvement with the mother's household does not end the inquiry here. The traditional practice needs to be tested for relevancy to this particular dispute over physical custody in the context of modern Hopi life. Here we hold that the customs we judicially notice today are relevant to child custody arrangements because they impose specific requirements for the child's presence in the mother's household.

However, the relevancy of custom does not necessarily invalidate the custody arrangements ordered by the trial court. Appellant's entire argument is based on the presumption that Chelsey would reside in Flagstaff during the period of her father's physical custody. The trial court order clearly requires that both parents assure that Chelsey remain enrolled at Hopi Day School, requiring her physical presence at Hopi for the entire academic year and minimizing the type of disruption to Chelsey's life that Appellant purportedly seeks to avoid with this appeal. Furthermore, the oral arguments and Appellee's answering brief confirm Appellee's willingness to relocate to Hopi if the Court finds that to be in Chelsey's best interests. No evidence in the record suggests that the trial court order conflicts with the custom as we have recognized it above.

V. State Law Claims Need not be Considered

We need not reach Appellant's remaining claim that the trial court misinterpreted Arizona law by allowing "divided" physical custody, because state law does not control here. Under *Tribe v. Mahkewa*, AP-003-93 (1996), "[t]he Trial Court [has] discretion to apply federal law, state law, a combination of both, or neither. . . . Under Resolution H-12-76, federal and state laws are persuasive, not mandatory, authorities."

Order of the Court

The trial court order with respect to its award of joint custody to Appellant and Appellee is AFFIRMED. The question of whether the alternating six-month periods of physical custody violates custom is REMANDED to the trial court for proceedings consistent with this opinion.

The trial court may consider evidence of custom such as a ceremonial calendar submitted by the mother or mother's clan designee in order to determine if the physical custody arrangement is consistent with customary duties. The trial court, in its discretion, may modify the order with respect to the physical custody arrangements to accommodate legitimate customary obligations sufficiently substantiated.

NOTES

1. In *Goldtooth v. Goldtooth*, 3 Navajo Rep. 223 (Window Rock D. Ct. 1982), the court searched in many different legal authorities for a viable rule to apply in a child custody case in which one parent was Navajo and one parent was Hopi:

> The court, being confronted with a situation where both parents are fit and proper custodians, must wrestle with a way of reaching a decision. In the past two of the children have been with their mother and three of the children, ranging in age from one to five, have been with the father. This would seem to provide the court with a means of deciding the matter through split child custody. Apparently the court can do this, but there are dangers in such a plan.
>
>> Although authority can be found for the proposition that divided custody is generally to be avoided, it seems preferable to decide the question by reference to the consequences for the child in each case. The danger for the child is that shuttling between parents and divided control will cause him to feel insecure or confused. There is also the risk that each parent will use his own period of custody to destroy the child's affection for the other parent. On the other hand it is highly desirable for the child to know and have affection for both parents. And the natural desire of the parents to have more than momentary contact with his child must not be overlooked. Homer H. Clark, Jr., *The Law of Domestic Relations in the United States*, 590 (1968 Ed.).
>
>> There is a general caution against split or divided child custody. "Another issue that sometimes arises is whether siblings should be placed in the custody of one parent or should be separated. Courts usually say that the children should not be separated unless their welfare very clearly requires such a course, and this seems the best solution." *Id.*, at 586-587.
>
> It is obvious this court may have to consider either an all-or-nothing alternative of giving custody to one parent or take a look to see whether

split custody is justified. In any event the court must seek to serve the interests of the children as being above the interests of the adults here, and given the finding of this court that the plaintiff and the defendant are professional people with the interests of their children at heart, perhaps joint custody would be an approach in this case. . . .

Since the plaintiff frequently went to the Tuba City area for family purposes while following his profession in Phoenix, it appears that the logistics for joint custody may be present. The court finds the parents here to be loving and just nice people, and hopefully the necessary attitudes are there as well.

There is another aspect which this court considers in seeking a basis for its decision. We must not overlook the advantages of referring to Navajo culture and tradition, as is mandated by 7 NTC Sec. 204. One precedent for the use of custom and tradition is that found in *Deer v. Okpik*, a child custody decision of the Family Division of the Superior Court of Quebec. (1980) 4 Canadian Native Law Reporter 93 (Cour Supérieure de Québec, division de la famille, 1980). In that case a Caugnawaga Mohawk father sought the custody of his three-year-old son as against his Koactac Inuit (Eskimo) wife. After the child was born the couple lived together for eleven months, and then the mother returned to her home with the child. The mother was then employed as a translator, working various places, and the child was left to live with his maternal grandparents. That arrangement gave the child Inuit cultural surroundings. While the father was separated from the child and the mother was working in various places, the little boy—Sunchild—lived with his grandparents, who considered him as their own child. *Id.*, 94. The mother, without legal formalities, gave Sunchild to his grandparents in adoption in accordance with the tradition, custom and ways of the Inuit. *Id.* Under that custom, the court found there was no abandonment of the child by the mother. *Id.* The court also found Sunchild had been totally integrated into his grandparents' Inuit culture *Id.*, 95. While recognizing the natural law rights of the parents, the court held, in reasoning adopted by this court, that the dominant principle to guide the court is always that the interests of the child are the principal factor to be considered. *Id.*, 96. The court saw that there had been an adoption in accordance with Inuit custom and that the child was integrated into the Inuit community. To look to an award to either natural parent would be to disrupt the child's integration into the Inuit culture. While the court concluded that the parents could not be blamed for their conduct, it found that the best interests of the child required that he remain with his Inuit grandparents. The court also found that ancestral customs and traditions must be preserved under the law and that the decision of the court was in harmony with the Inuit customs and traditions presented to it. *Id.*, 97. Based on those findings the court granted the mother the legal custody of the child, gave his physical custody to the grandparents and gave the father visitation rights for three months during the summer. *Id.*

Deer v. Okpik, a case from the French civil law jurisdiction of Quebec, is cited for its excellent reasoning and its recognition of the fact you cannot separate native peoples from their culture and tradition. This court takes judicial notice of the fact that in Navajo culture and tradition children are not just the children of the parents but they are children of the clan. In particular, children are considered members of the mother's clan. While that fact could be used as an element of preference in a child custody case, the court wants to point out that the primary consideration is the child's strong relationship to members of an extended family. Because of those strong ties, children frequently live with various members of the family without injury. This is the condition throughout Indian Country (as Indian reservations as a whole are called). Therefore the court looks to that tradition and holds that it must consider the children's place in the entire extended family in order to make a judgment based upon Navajo traditional law.

This approach is in harmony with modern trends in child psychology as well. It is interesting to note that the Anglo-European society is increasingly discovering ways which we have known for centuries. . . .

[I]n a divorce the children must be given continuing and full contact not only with their parents but with their extended families, because every member of the family depends upon the others. The court must consider the "family perspective" and look [to]providing "continuity and mutuality of family relationships" in spite of a divorce. . . . The reality is that a divorce changes the form of relationship of family members but it does not end the family. . . . Therefore there are two recommendations of the Committee on the Family, Group for the Advancement of Psychiatry which this court will adopt:

1. The court's determination should aim at providing the child with an ongoing relationship with as many members of his or her family of origin as possible.
2. In determining parental competence, the court should seriously consider the comparative willingness of the two contestants to provide the child with access to the other parent, to siblings, grandparents, and other relatives.

The court has sought a basis for its decision and finds it in Navajo custom and tradition, reinforced by modern principles of child psychology. This family is in an excellent position to be maintained in harmony, notwithstanding the sorrow of divorce, and I hold that the best interests of these children require an award of joint custody to their parents.

Since we have here a Navajo father and a Hopi mother, a little should be said about the concept of joint custody as it appears to the court. The court will not follow the tragic precedent of the Navajo-Hopi Joint Use Area by failing to set guidelines for joint custody or arbitrarily dividing the children among the parents with no concern for those children. This court will enforce the children's rights in custody and it will only incidentally provide for the rights of the parents, where they are in harmony with those of the children. This court feels family ties and strengths should be enforced.

One problem in defining the conditions of joint custody is that the "law is incapable of effectively managing, except in a very gross sense, as delicate a relationship as that between parent and child." Goldstein, Freud, Solnit, *Beyond the Best Interests of the Child*, 8 (1973). . . .

Therefore the thrust of the court's order will be [to] require the parents here to devise a plan for submission to the court which will maintain strong family ties and full access to the children and among the children.

Goldtooth, 3 Navajo Rep. at 224-27.

2. In *Eberhard v. Eberhard*, 24 Indian L. Rep. 6059 (Cheyenne River Sioux Tribal Court of Appeals 1997), the court held in an opinion by Justice Robert Clinton that the federal Parental Kidnapping Prevention Act (PKPA), 28 U.S.C. §1738A applies to tribal courts, concluding that "Indian tribes are states or territories within the meaning of the 28 U.S.C. §1738A(b)(8) and

therefore constitute a 'State' as defined in that Act." In *Eberhard*, the appellate panel affirmed a trial court order deferring to an earlier-in-time divorce filing and order between tribal members in the courts of the State of California, holding that the PKPA required the tribal courts to find that California courts were the "home court" for purposes of adjudicating the divorce and child custody issues. *See id.* at 6059. Chief Justice Frank Pommersheim concurred, but added that other courts were likely to find that Congress did not intend for Indian tribes to be considered "states" under the Act, as one court already had by the time of the decision. *See id.* at 6068 (Pommersheim, C.J., concurring) (citing *Desjarlait v. Desjarlait*, 379 N.W.2d 139 (Minn. App. 1985).

That statute requires that "[t]he appropriate authorities of every State shall enforce according to its terms, and shall not modify . . . any [child] custody determination made consistently with the provisions of the section by a court of another State." 28 U.S.C. §1738A(a). "State" is defined to include "a State of the United States, the District of Columbia, the Commonwealth of Puerto Rico, or a territory or possession of the United States. . . ." 28 U.S.C. §1738A(b)(8).

Professor Robert Laurence criticized the *Eberhard* panel's decision first as not including a due respect for the application of relevant tribal law:

> Having found that the court below had jurisdiction over Shawn Eberhard, and therefore over his divorce, and over Shawn's daughter, and therefore over her custody, the court turned its attention to the reception that the tribal trial court should give to the California custody decree. The court wrote:
>
>> The preliminary question[] for this court, therefore, is whether Indian tribes and their reservations are within the phrase "State" or "a territory or possession of the United States," as used in the statutory definition of State found in the PKPA.
>
> I would have thought that the preliminary question for the court would have been whether the California decree was entitled to respect and enforcement under Cheyenne River Sioux tribal law. However, and surprisingly, the Cheyenne River Sioux Court of Appeals saw the issues before it as almost entirely involving federal and state, not tribal, law.
>
> There is, in fact, relatively little tribal law in *Eberhard*. The court closed its opinion with a few words in the Lakota language, and early on announced a Cheyenne River Sioux rule regarding the residency of children whose parents are married but have different residences, but the great bulk of the case concerned federal and state law, to wit, the Parental Kidnapping Prevention Act, the more general full faith and credit statute found in 28 U.S.C. §1738, and California's version of the Uniform Child Custody Jurisdiction Act. The court constructed its opinion around these off-reservation rules, notwithstanding the fact that the application of the first to tribes is problematic at best, the second is not directly relevant to the case at hand, and the third is definitely not the law of the Cheyenne River Sioux tribe.

Robert Laurence, *Full Faith and Credit in Tribal Courts: An Essay on Tribal Sovereignty, Cross-Boundary Reciprocity and the Unlikely Case of* Eberhard v.

Eberhard, 28 N.M. L. REV. 19, 29-30 (1998). Laurence secondly criticized the court for not recognizing that the federal statute was an infringement of tribal sovereignty:

> There are about a dozen ways in which the Cheyenne River Sioux Court of Appeals could have avoided the conclusion that the PKPA applies to Indian tribes. These avoidance devices . . . range from the straightforward ("[t]he statute does not mention Indian tribes") to the subtle ("[t]he legislative history shows that Congress intended one part of the original bill to apply to Indians and another part not to") to the majestic ("Congress does not have the power to require an Indian tribe to recognize the judgments of states").
>
> The court's rejection of all of these federal-law avoidance devices was shaped by one consideration: the court's insistence, in the face of the Tribe's opposition, that the PKPA, in particular, and federal "full faith and credit" legislation in general, are not infringements on tribal sovereignty. . . .
>
> [W]e see the non-disingenuous part of the court of appeals' argument: It does enhance tribal sovereignty for California and the other states to recognize Cheyenne River Sioux decrees and, even if done non-consensually, for Congress to require states to do so could be viewed as an enhancement of tribal sovereignty. Of course, by the nature of the judicial process, the Cheyenne River Sioux Court of Appeals can never technically "hold" that California has a federal obligation to enforce its tribal judgments, but it can say so strongly in dicta, as it did in *Eberhard*.
>
> *Eberhard*, then, is the court's attempt at a quid pro quo "bargain" with the state of California, and by implication with the rest of the states. . . .
>
> . . . I think the court needs to give careful consideration to the question of whether full faith and credit is the quid pro quo deal for which the Tribe should aim. The upside of reciprocity . . . is that tribal judgments and decrees will be recognized off-reservation. The downside is that off-reservation judgments and decrees must be recognized on-reservation.

Id. at 32-33, 35-37.

2. CHILD SUPPORT

IN THE INTEREST OF A.A.M.B.

Southwest Intertribal Court of Appeals for the Southern Ute Indian Tribe, No. 92-005-SUTC, 4 SWITCA 1 (January 7, 1993)

LUI-FRANK, Judge

This case has been appealed on the question of whether a father whose relationship to a child is established by court order can be held liable for past support of the child. . . . The state has filed suit under an assignment of rights executed by the child's guardian, who receives Aid to Families with Dependent Children (AFDC). . . .

We hold that the . . . parents remain responsible for support of their children under . . . the Southern Ute Indian Tribal Code, even when they no longer have custody of the children, and the legal custodian/guardian also has a duty of support.

The trial court ruled that past decisions of the court established that child support cannot be imposed retroactively after determination of paternity in the absence of legislative authority. *L.K. v. M.E.T.*, 17 ILR 6005, 6007 (S. Ute Tr. Ct. 1989); *R.L.W. v. G.N.B.*, 18 ILR 6048, 6049 (S. Ute Tr. Ct. 1991). . . .

L.K. v. M.E.T., 17 ILR 6005, 6006-7 (S. Ute Tr. Ct. 1989), was a paternity action brought by the La Plata County Child Support Enforcement Unit in a Uniform Reciprocal Enforcement of Support Act case for the State of California. The father in that case was a member of a federally recognized Indian tribe, residing on the Southern Ute Indian Reservation. He stipulated to paternity of the child, who resided in California. The trial court established paternity and awarded child support, but denied past child support. The court interpreted the relevant code provisions as establishing that because a father whose paternity has not been established has no rights to a child, he has no duty of support. . . .

R.L.W. v. G.N.B., 18 ILR 6048 (S. Ute Tr. Ct. 1991), involved contested paternity claims on two children and admissions to paternity on two other children. The question of past child support was decided in the same way as *L.K. v. M.E.T.*, *supra*. The facts of the case were illustrative of instances where ". . . an individual may in fact not know with any degree of certainty that he is the parent of the child, up until the point paternity is medically established. . . ." *Id.*, 6049. Therefore, the court held requiring a father in that instance to reimburse AFDC payments would be unjust. . . .

We hold that nothing in the Southern Ute Indian Tribal Code prevents the suit by any party supporting a child to obtain retroactive child support from a parent. Indeed, the code allows suits for child support. . . .

We reverse the order regarding retroactive child support and remand to the trial court to determine the amount of money expended by the state and what Mr. Williams must pay, in addition to current support. . . .

NOTES

1. In *Watson v. Watson*, 2010 WL 363057 (Navajo Nation Supreme Court 2010), the court reversed its own precedent, *Yazzie v. Yazzie*, 7 Navajo Rep. 203 (Navajo Nation Supreme Court 1996), in holding that the Navajo courts have discretion to award reasonable interest on child support arrearages.

2. Indian nations with successful and lucrative gaming operations often pay individual tribal members a periodic per capita revenue distribution, rendering some tribal members wealthy. In *Cypress v. Jumper*, 990 So. 2d 576 (Fla. App. 2008), the court held that some Florida Seminole members were so wealthy so as to obviate the need for child support. For criticism of that decision. *See* Marcia A. Zug, *Dangerous Gamble: Child Support, Casino Dividends, and the Fate of the Indian Family*, 36 WM. MITCHELL L. REV. 738 (2010).

   Most Indian nations will garnish per capita payments to cover child support costs. *E.g.*, *Fort McDowell Yavapai Nation v. Haynes*, 4 Am. Tribal Law 217 (Fort McDowell Yavapai Nation Supreme Court 2003); *Bradley v. Bradley*, 2001 WL 36239694 (Eastern Band Cherokee Supreme Court 2001); *In re Raphael*, 1998 WL 35289050 (Grand Traverse Band of Ottawa and Chippewa Indians Tribal Court 1998).

3. Indian nations also struggle with the federal mandate requiring cross-border recognition of child support judgments; largely, the struggle is with enforcing the mandate against state courts. *See generally* Danelle J. Daugherty, *Children Are Sacred: Looking beyond Best Interests of the Child to Establish Effective Tribal-State Cooperative Child Support Advocacy Agreements in South Dakota*, 47 S.D. L. REV. 282 (2002).

4. Tribal courts will reject efforts to force compliance with state law if tribal law on the question is applicable. *E.g.*, *Vigil v. Vigil*, 6 SWITCA 3 (Southwest Intertribal Court of Appeals for the Southern Ute Tribe 1995).

3. CHILD WELFARE

IN THE MATTER OF A MINOR CHILD (L.J.Y. v. T.T.)

Southwest Intertribal Court of Appeals for the Fort Mojave Tribe, No. 97-002-FMTC, 8 SWITCA 4 (March 3, 1997)

Appellate Panel: RODGERS, M. JUAN, FLORES

This is an appeal from a final judgment of the trial court removing the minor child from the custody of its mother, appellant L.Y.J., and granting custody of the child to his paternal grandparents, Mr. and Mrs. A.T. This Court concludes . . . that the procedures used by the trial court removed the child from his mother's custody without due process of law, violating the Indian Civil Rights Act. The court below erroneously applied tribal law. . . . However, because the facts in the record below do suggest that the Fort Mojave Indian Tribe Social Services office may have information that would support a petition of child neglect by the mother, it is in the best interests of the minor child that the order in this case be stayed to allow for a petition to be filed and a new proceeding to be properly heard. . . .

Proceedings Below

L.J.Y. and T.T. are the natural parents of the minor child. T.T and the minor child are enrolled members of the Fort Mojave Tribe. L.Y.J. is a member of one of the Colorado River Indian Tribes and now resides on the Colorado River Indian Tribes Reservation. . . .

T.T. filed the petition for custody of his son on November 17, 1995. The grounds given in the petition for removing the child from the custody of its mother were "[w]elfare and safety of my child. I feel that she has caused undue hardship on myself, family, and son." What the petition did not allege, in any manner, was that the minor child was neglected, abused in any way, or otherwise in any danger of harm. . . .

This action was a dispute solely between the two parents. However, during the hearing, the trial court clearly treated the matter as if a charge of negligence had been made against L.Y.J. by the Fort Mojave Tribe. T.T. and his mother were permitted to present allegations of negligence. However, the trial court, based solely on these unsupported allegations, made a determination that there would be a child custody placement pursuant to the Indian Child Welfare Act before L.Y.J. had any opportunity to make any statement to refute the allegations. . . .

. . . An employee of the Fort Mojave Social Services Department appeared at the hearing, and made an on-the-spot recommendation for placement of the minor child with his paternal grandparents. This recommendation was followed by the court in a temporary custody order entered on that same day, although no motion for a temporary custody placement was made and no evidence was presented to support such a placement. . . .

[The trial court granted permanent custody to the grandparents on February 8, 1996. On October 3, 1996, the trial court concluded that its prior order violated tribal law, and vacated the order, only to reverse itself on October 31, 1996.]

Legal Analysis

[A.] Tribal Law Violations

To this day, the minor child remains with his paternal grandparents. It was not until L.Y.J. was in court, with no notice sufficient to allow her any opportunity to prepare a response to a petition for custody filed by the natural father of the child, that she learned, for all practical purposes, that the Fort Mojave Tribe was charging her with negligence and removing her son from her custody. . . . Those orders do not comply with the minimum requirements of due process as required by the Indian Civil Rights Act, apply the Indian Child Welfare act erroneously, and do not comply with the law of the Fort Mojave Indian Tribe. . . . Therefore, we must reverse. . . .

When a parent seeks custody of a child under the Fort Mojave Indian Tribe law and order code, the parent must file a petition. Upon a showing of good cause, the court can permit other interested parties to intervene. . . . However, in the absence of a finding of good cause, the matter is one that is strictly between the parents. . . . [A] party can seek a temporary custody order. However, the motion for a temporary custody order must be supported by "an affidavit or verified petition setting forth detailed facts supporting the requested order." . . . The affidavit or verified petition must be given to all other parties so they can file opposing affidavits. . . . The trial court "shall deny the motion unless it finds that adequate cause for hearing the motion is established in the pleadings, in which case is shall [hold a hearing]." . . . Tribal law also mandates that notice of any child custody proceedings must be given to a child's parent "who may appear, be heard, and file a responsive pleading." . . .

In this case, T.T. did not make any motion for the court for a temporary custody order. . . . Furthermore, even if the initial petition is treated as such a motion, it did not set forth any detailed facts that would support the removal of a child from the custody of the parent. . . . Even if the petition had set forth adequate facts, Fort Mojave law requires the court to look to the best interests of the child in deciding whether to enter a temporary custody order. All relevant factors may be considered, including (1) the wishes of the child's parents as to his custody; (2) the wishes of the child as to his custodian; (3) the interaction and inter-relationship of the child with his parents, his siblings, and any other person who may significantly affect the child's best interest; (4) the child's adjustment to his home, school and community; (5) the mental and physical health of all individuals involved. . . . [A]ppellant was denied any notice as to the actual allegations made against her, and she was denied any meaningful opportunity to respond to the unsubstantiated allegations. Therefore, the issuance of the temporary custody order did not comply with tribal law concerning custody disputes between parents of a child. . . .

Invalid Application of the Indian Child Welfare Act

The Indian Child Welfare Act is a federal law that governs child custody proceedings [under] federal law [in state courts]. . . . 25 U.S.C. §1903. It has been held not to apply to custodial actions between parents. . . . Thus, it was legally erroneous for the trial court to treat this court action as one arising under the Indian Child Welfare Act. . . . In some instances tribes have voluntarily adopted the placement preferences in the Act as their own. Here, however, the written law of the tribe has its own preferences for child custody placements pending a hearing on a petition of neglect. . . . In a proceeding between two parents, if one parent is successful in challenging the custody of the other, the successful parent is awarded custody, not the grandparents. . . .

The Indian Civil Rights Act

This federal statute prohibits an Indian tribe, when exercising the powers of self-government, from denying "to any person within its jurisdiction the equal protection of its laws or deprive any person of liberty or property without due process of law." 25 U.S.C. §1302(8). The first step in a due process analysis is to establish whether a liberty or property interest is at issue. . . . While the concepts of liberty and due process do not always have the same definition in tribal law, this liberty interest is recognized and protected in the Fort Mojave Indian Tribe Law and Order Code. [Section] 434 states:

> Before depriving any parent of the custody of his child, the court shall give due consideration to the preferred right of the parents to the custody of their children, and it shall not transfer custody to another person, unless the court finds from all the circumstances in the case that the welfare of the child or the public interest requires it.

Therefore, appellant's rights to custody of her child are recognized as fundamental liberties under the law of the Tribe, and as such appellant cannot be denied her custodial rights without due process of law.

Due process is a fancy term for fair play. . . . While this term must also be defined in light of tribal custom and law, at a minimum, due process requires notice and an opportunity to be heard. . . . [T]he question is whether, given notice, the party had a chance to understand the claims against them and present a defense to them. . . .

Appellant was denied both of these minimal requirements of due process. The petition that was served on her was a petition for custody of a child by the child's other parent. There was no motion for a temporary custody order presented to her. Thus, she was not given any notice of the nature of the action filed against her. Similarly, the court hearing held on the same day that the petition was filed did not give appellant any meaningful opportunity to be heard. . . .

Conclusion

This Court must conclude that appellant's custodial rights to her minor son, as recognized and protected by the law and order code of the Fort Mojave Indian Tribe, were grievously violated by the trial court. However, as this is a matter that also involves a minor child, and because documentation in the record suggests that the trial court or the tribal social services department may have documentation that would support at least an inquiry as to whether appellant has neglected her minor child, the court must also conclude that it is in the best interests of the minor child that the Tribe, through the tribal court or tribal social services, be given the opportunity to act to protect the child from neglect, and that the minor child not be subject to a change in custody . . . [until] the Tribe can determine whether to bring an action alleging neglect. . . .

NOTES

1. In parental termination cases, tribal courts will apply tribal law in determining the burden of proof and the findings necessary to effectuate termination. *E.g.*, *In re the K. Children*, 7 SWITCA 6 (Southwest Intertribal Court of Appeals for the Fort Mojave Indian Tribe 1996).
2. In a soon-to-be-published manuscript, Cami Fraser of Michigan Indian Legal Services, surveyed the various Michigan tribal codes on termination of parental rights, finding fairly significant differences between tribes. She notes:

> [T]he tribal codes . . . vary as to the specific grounds listed and accompanying defining language. For example, the Grand Traverse Band sets out this list as grounds for termination of parental rights: abandonment, physical injury or sexual abuse, un-rectified conditions and circumstances, failure to provide proper care, conviction of violent or sexual crime, conviction of a felony, imprisonment for more than 2 years, parental rights to a sibling terminated, or parental kidnapping. Grand Traverse Code §10.125(b); *see also In re KMC*, 1999 WL 34986349 (Grand Traverse 1999); *In re SRS*, 8 Am. Tribal Law 172 (Grand Traverse Tribal Ct. 2009); *In re AS*, 1999 WL 34986338 (Grand Traverse Tribal Ct. 1999). At the other extreme, Bay Mills [Indian Community] only permits termination of parental rights on the following grounds: abandonment, physical injury or physical or sexual abuse, 12 months in care plus non-compliance of the parent, prior termination of parental rights. Bay Mills Code §724(B).
>
> The manner in which the tribal codes define the listed grounds also varies substantially. For example, the Saginaw Chippewa code defines abandonment as "when a parent leaves a child without communication or fails to support a child and there is no indication of the parent(s) willingness to assume the parental role(s) for a period exceeding six months." Saginaw Chippewa Code §2.201. Whereas the Sault Ste. Marie code defines it as "the failure of the parent to provide reasonable support and to maintain regular contact with his or her child when such failure resulted in destruction of the parental role with the child" and provides that abandonment "shall be judged according to customary practices in the Indian community." Sault Ste. Marie Code §30.302.

Cami Fraser, *Should This ICWA Case Be Transferred to Tribal Court? Issues for Parents' Attorneys to Consider and Discuss with Their Clients*, unpublished manuscript at 14-15 (Sept. 2010).

3. One commenter surveyed several tribal codes that demonstrate tribal reluctance to permanently terminate parental rights as well as tribal support for traditional adoptions:

> Some tribes have drafted creative code provisions to define children's interests that are helpful in illuminating tribal perspectives. The Zuni Code, for example, sets out standards or controlling principles that articulate children's "needs." The code recognizes "[a] child's need for love, nurturing, protection, and stability"; "[a] child's need for family"; "[a] child's need for identity and development"; and "[a] child's need for happiness." . . .
>
> . . . Maternal grandparents and aunts, in particular, often have discrete parenting functions and traditionally assumed responsibility for children when parents were unavailable. . . . [A] formal judicial decree to terminate parental rights is foreign to the culture of many tribes. In earlier times, informal arrangements took the place of formal child protection proceedings, with children in need being raised by extended family, clan members, or other persons sharing a communal bond with the children's family. . . .
>
> . . . The codes of several tribes now express a clear preference for open adoption. In some codes, that goal is accomplished by providing that some portion of parental rights will survive the adoption, and in other codes, the result is achieved by "suspending" rather than terminating parental rights. . . . Some tribes . . . view the status of parenthood more fluidly and permit adoption to rest on a suspension of parental rights. . . .
>
> Other tribal codes similarly evince a policy against the complete severance of parent-child relations. In the Sisseton-Wahpeton Sioux Tribe in South Dakota, open adoptions are described as "adoptive placements made through the Court when most, but not all parental rights have been terminated."

Barbara Ann Atwood, *Achieving Permanency for American Indian and Alaskan Native Children: Lessons from Tribal Traditions*, 37 Cap. U. L. Rev. 239, 279-82, 284-86 (2008). *See also* Barbara Ann Atwood, Children, Tribes, and States: Adoption and Custody Conflicts over American Indian Children 144-50 (2010).

4. The Pascua Yaqui Tribal Code provides for open adoptions, and is representative of many tribal codes that do the same:

> Adoptions under this Code shall be in the nature of "open adoptions." The purpose of such open adoptions is not to permanently deprive the child of connections to, or knowledge of, the child's natural family. The purpose of adoptions shall be to give the adoptive child a permanent home. To this end, the following shall apply and be contained in all adoptive orders and decrees.
>
> A. The adoptive parents and adoptive child shall be treated under the law as if the relationship was that of a natural child and parent, except as forth herein.
>
> B. The adoptive child shall have an absolute right, absence a convincing and compelling reason to the contrary, to information and knowledge about his natural family and his tribal heritage.
>
> C. The adoptive child and members of the child's natural extended family (including parents) may have the right to reasonable visitation,

subject to reasonable controls of the adoptive parents, unless otherwise restricted by the Court for a compelling reason.

D. Adoption shall not serve to prevent an adoptive child from inheriting from a natural parent in the same manner as any other natural child. The natural parents shall not be entitled to inherit from an adoptive child in the same manner as parents would otherwise be entitled to inherit. An adoptive child shall be entitled to inherit from adoptive parents and vice versa in the same manner as if natural parents and child.

2 Pasqua Yaqui Tribal Code §15.2. For more discussion of Pascua Yaqui law, *see* Lorinda Mall, *Keeping It in the Family: The Legal and Social Evolution of ICWA in State and Tribal Jurisprudence*, in Facing the Future: The Indian Child Welfare Act at 30, at 164 (Matthew L. M. Fletcher, Wenona T. Singel, and Kathryn E. Fort eds., 2009).

CHAPTER 9

PROPERTY

American Indian property rights jurisprudence, despite much rhetoric that Indian people often did not recognize individual ownership and other foundations of Anglo-American property rights, is largely consistent with Anglo-American property common law. The main differences involve the subject matters and fact patterns that arise, deriving from the unique relationship that Indian nations and people have with the United States government, which has historically acted as either the literal or assumed "owner" of all Indian property. As such, there are numerous property regimes arising under federal law that apply exclusively to Indian nations and people.

That said, key concepts in traditional and customary law shine through the property regimes that permeate Indian country that differ remarkably from Anglo-American jurisprudence. *Cf.* Kristen A. Carpenter, Sonia K. Katyal & Angela R. Riley, *In Defense of Property*, 118 YALE L.J. 1022 (2009). This chapter highlights both the structural complexities of Indian property regimes and the areas where tribal common law impacts these regimes.

A. TRADITIONAL PROPERTY SYSTEMS

RETELLING ALLOTMENT: INDIAN PROPERTY RIGHTS AND THE MYTH OF COMMON OWNERSHIP

Kenneth H. Bobroff, 54 Vanderbilt L. Rev. 1559, 1571-99 (2001)

. . .

III. Indigenous Private Property Systems

. . . Indian societies have had myriad different property systems, varying widely by culture, resources, geography, and historical period. Many of them have recognized property rights in land and have done so in ways that provided for transfer of land, rational inheritance, and legal change. Many continue to do so today. Indian property systems did differ in important ways from the Anglo-American property regime. Given the central importance of the land to native societies—indeed to most native peoples' very identities—it is not surprising that almost all Indian property systems restricted the decision to transfer land rights outside the tribe to tribal leaders. This led many outsiders, including nineteenth- and twentieth-century reformers, to conclude that title to Indian lands was invariably held by the tribe in common. . . .

A. Indians' Historical Property Systems

. . .

1. Indian Property Systems in New England

In his study of the ecology of colonial New England, William Cronon writes, "[t]he difference between Indians and Europeans was not that one had property and the other had none; rather, it was that they loved property differently." Southern New England Indian families had exclusive use of their cultivated fields (usually planted in corn) and the land their homes occupied. Maintenance of these property rights depended upon continued use of the land and was subject to periodic abandonment as intensive cultivation exhausted old fields and families cleared new land. Any member of the village could generally use non-agricultural lands, such as clam banks, fishing ponds, berry-picking areas, and hunting territories. Any member could use a village's territory to collect wild plants, cut wood for canoes, or gather sedges for mats, but sites used for fishing nets and weirs or hunting snares and traps could be owned by an individual or family. Property rights in land could become quite complicated, since they might include an exclusive right to take certain scarce resources from a particular place at a particular time (e.g. to trap deer in the winter) but not the right to exclude other villagers from taking a plentiful resource from that same place at a different time (e.g. to hunt migratory birds in the spring or fall). "Property rights," Cronon notes, "shifted with ecological use." Although Cronon prefers the term "usufruct" in describing New England Indians' property rights, the important observation is that their systems recognized exclusive rights in land, even if those rights required continued use, were rarely traded in a market, and were more finely "sliced" than the typical bundle of European property rights.

2. Algonquian Property Systems

Less agricultural societies often provided for private hunting rights in land. Northern Algonquian tribes, which ranged west into the Great Lakes . . . , appear to have developed family territory systems to govern hunting rights in land. In the early twentieth century, Aleck Paul, of the Temagami band of Chippewa at Bear Lake, Ontario, told an anthropologist, "[t]his division of the land started in the beginning of time, and always remained unchanged." According to Paul, his grandfather had parceled out the family hunting ground between his two sons, Paul's father and uncle, before his grandfather died:

> We were to own the land so no other Indians could hunt on it. Other Indians could travel through it and go there, but could not go there to kill the beaver. Each family had its own district where they belonged and owned the game. That was each one's stock, for food and clothes. If another Indian hunted on our territory, we, the owners, could shoot him. . . . I remember about twenty years ago some Nipissing Indians came north to hunt on my father's land. He told them not to hunt beaver. "This is our land," he told them; "you can fish

but must not touch the fur, as that is all we have to live on." Sometimes an owner would give permission for strangers to hunt for a certain time or on a certain tract. This was often done for friends or when neighbors had had a poor season.

These systems recognized exclusive hunting rights on lands within each families' boundaries, usually marked by rivers, ridges, lakes, or other natural landmarks such as swamps and clumps of cedars or pines. The property systems governing these territories seemed to have included inheritance within families, rules and sanctions against trespass, and the right to recover furs taken by non-owners. . . .

Such claims about specific Indian property systems are open to dispute.

Modern Anishinaabe cultural critic Gerald Vizenor views characterizations by anthropologists as distorted and inaccurate. Instead, he points to evidence supplied by visual stories, totemic creations, and other "mappery" of the Ojibwa, to argue that the native sense of motion and use of the land in the northern woodlands did not embrace inheritance or tenure of territory. . . . But while the available data may be inadequate to conclude exactly what Anishinaabe property laws were at specific times, they do strongly suggest that Ojibwa communities developed systems recognizing property rights in land, perhaps before European contact and without doubt in the centuries after contact but before allotment. . . .

3. Iroquois Property Systems

In the fertile areas of upstate New York, extending into Canada, the nations of the Haudenosaunee, known as the Iroquois League, long recognized exclusive property rights in agricultural fields and homes. Ownership of cleared land was held by individual families and clans and was maintained by continued use. Ownership included rights to control the use of a particular field and the disposition of the crops grown, both of which were held by women "matrons" in each family. . . .

Scholars have argued over the character and importance of property rights in Iroquois cultures. . . . Elisabeth Tooker has emphasized that Iroquois property ownership rested on use, not on transferable legal title. This distinction is significant insofar as it emphasizes that a woman holding a family's exclusive right to use a particular plot of cleared land did not hold the right to transfer use of the land outside the village or, especially, outside the League to non-Iroquois. As George Snyderman, an early anthropologist, noted, "the land belonged to all the people who inhabited it. No individual could enforce a personal claim to a specific piece of land. Neither could any individual by his own right and desire legally 'sell' lands." . . .

4. Inuit Property Systems

Much further north, in present-day Canada and Alaska, Inuit peoples, hunting and fishing societies, had extensive and well-regulated systems of property rights in land. Bands, each commonly known by a geographical name followed by the [suffix] -miut meaning "the people of," held specific land areas. The band (and in some instances the larger "tribe" or regional grouping) maintained the right to use its territory through use and occupancy. At the band level, the Inuit system of property rights included the right for individual band members to use the land, the right for the band to exclude others from the land, and the right to allow others to use the land. An established system existed for determining which community members were entitled to use the land (including processes for incorporation of outsiders into the community). They even possessed means to alienate some uses to outsiders. Moreover, bands formally granted use rights to non-Inuit communities, including Moravian settlers and Newfoundland fishing families. Band members and their neighbors also recognized the particular landmarks and transition zones that separated one band's lands from the lands of neighboring groups. . . .

. . . Inuit lands were held communally, meaning they were subject to the community's governance, but not in common, which implied they were available without limit to the first appropriator. This system ensured that the individual members of the band used the land and its resources in harmony rather than in conflict and so as not to endanger the group's security. The system's longevity and stability over generations is evidence of the system's usefulness.

5. Property Systems in the Five "Civilized" Tribes

The heavily agricultural Five "Civilized" Tribes (as non-Indians named the Cherokees, Chickasaws, Choctaws, Creeks, and Seminoles) . . . recognized property rights in land—formally and informally—before and after they adopted written constitutions and statutes. Before the Chickasaws, Choctaws, and Creeks were forced from their lands in the southeast, they tended private gardens (Creek women, as with the Iroquois, controlled these plots) close to individual families' homes. While fields outside the village were often cleared and tended communally, each family's plot was divided from the others and crops were gathered and stored separately. Long before removal west, Cherokees recognized extensive and well-developed rights in personal property—including in slaves, black and Indian alike. As for property in land, legal scholar John Phillip Reid concluded that communal property had little importance for pre-constitutional Cherokees, except for hunting grounds. Agricultural fields, crops, and homes all were owned individually and, Reid believed, usually by women.

Even the United States acknowledged that the Tribes recognized private property rights in land. In the removal Treaty of May 6, 1828, the United States promised to compensate each head of a Cherokee family for "property that he may abandon" after agreeing to emigrate west. . . .

After the United States forced the Five Tribes across the Arkansas River to what is now Oklahoma, the tribes re-created property systems. Article I of the Cherokee Constitution of 1839 declared that "[t]he Lands of the Cherokee nation shall remain common property. . . ." Nonetheless, the statutes and practices established by the Five Tribes recognized and protected private property rights in land. The Cherokee and Choctaw nations both passed laws in 1839 prohibiting anyone from settling on public lands within a quarter mile of the "house, field, or other improvements" of another without the latter's consent. The Chickasaw Nation later passed a similar trespass statute. Citizens could "open a farm" in any part of the public domain, provided that it did not encroach upon the property of another citizen. Moreover, they could hold the land during its agricultural uses, but if abandoned, the land reverted to the Nation and it became available for new settlement. . . .

. . . An opinion by U. S. Judge Isaac Parker in an 1891 condemnation proceeding describes Cherokee property law:

> While citizens of the Cherokee Nation do not have a fee to the lands they occupy, they can hold them forever, and fully enjoy the profits arising from them, and this right may be granted to their heirs or may descend by inheritance. Practically they get all the productions of the land, the same as though they held it in fee. If there is any peculiar value to the land, it attaches to the right of possession, and the occupant gets the benefit of it. . . . [W]hile they do not hold the fee to the land, I think their interest is so great as to entitle them, as perpetual occupants, to compensation for the additional servitude case upon their lands. [*Payne v. Kansas & A.V.R. Co.*, 46 F. 546, 559 (W.D. Ark. 1891), *rev'd on other grounds*, 49 F. 114 (8th Cir. 1892).]

. . .

6. Indian Property Systems in the Southwest

Private property rights among other agricultural tribes further west were common and, in most instances, persist today. In the Southwest, the Akimel O'odham (Pimas) received farm plots assigned by the village headman and council in return for assisting in irrigation canal construction and maintenance. These plots could be passed to heirs and loaned to others, though they were not generally sold or traded. Families among the Tohono O'odham . . . held perpetual use rights to specific farm plots within the village field system. These rights rested on continuous farming, but were inheritable from generation to generation. The Mohave people, who presently live on the Colorado River Indian Reservation, divided their aboriginal lands by clan, with each clan having songs to identify clan territory. Clan lands were in turn staked out with markers into family farming areas. Arguments over boundaries between farms were settled by a contest call[ed] "Thopirk," literally "strength against strength," amounting to a pushing contest similar to a tug-of-war. Families left without farm areas when the river shifted or when a particular area could not be flooded would be lent space in another family's garden, marked off with posts, or, sometimes, two corn stalks, to designate that the land was being used by someone other than the family controlling the area. . . .

Almost all the Rio Grande Pueblo property systems provide for family ownership of homes and agricultural plots, with grazing lands available for common use. San Juan Pueblo anthropologist Alfonso Ortiz, writing in the 1970s about his own pueblo, described a property system in which individuals and families enjoyed "use rights" to particular plots of farmland, to house sites, and to the communal grazing area. He noted that most families had fruit trees on their land, but that any wild plants could be freely gathered, even if growing in an otherwise cultivated field. The Pueblo's governing council has the rarely exercised authority to confiscate a family's land for serious and sustained misconduct. Both men and women inherit land. By the time of Ortiz's writing, most agricultural lands lay fallow, with some rented by individual families to outside Hispanic farmers. . . .

At Hopi . . . , anthropologists have reported that each autonomous village has its own lands which are assigned to that village's matrilineal clans. Boundary stones, set at the corners of each field formerly marked each clan allotment. Within each clan, fields are assigned to women of the clan and are inherited matrilineally. Beyond the clan lands, any man may establish a field as long as he cultivates it and may assign his field to another. Grazing is done in common. . . .

7. Indian Property Rights in California and the Pacific Northwest

. . . In California, even tribes that were not primarily agricultural recognized some family property rights, including, for instance, a woman's right to devise a particular oak tree to her daughter. The value of the transfer lay in the gathering of acorns, a diet staple of many California Indians. Among tribes in what is now northern California, along the Klamath River and the nearby Pacific coast, property was held in individual private ownership and included ownership rights in other tribes' territories. For example, Hupas owned property inside Yurok territory. Ownership could be divided over time, with several individuals each having rights to the same fishing spot at different times of the year. As one scholar notes, "[i]ndividual Hupas held the rights to specific hunting, fishing, and gathering grounds as privately owned property. These rights gave them the privilege of controlling use, rental, alienation, and inheritance, as well as liability for damages incurred on the property. . . . Individuals without land rights rented their use from others."

In much drier areas further south, the native peoples recognized property rights of various kinds at the time of Spanish contact. According to anthropologist Florence Connelly Shipek, southern California Indians, including Luiseño and Kumeyaay bands, recognized family or individual ownership of "fields of grain-grass or other annuals, perennials, various shrubs, oak and other trees, cactus patches, cornfields and other resources such as clay beds, basket-grass clumps, quarries, and hot and cold springs." Individuals owned widely varying amounts of land and often maintained land in several different areas. Ownership normally meant that the individual's family had labored to develop and maintain the resource. . . .

Among salmon fishing tribes of the Northwest coast — Tlingit, Tsimsian, Haida, Nuxalk, Kwakiutl, Nootka, Coast Salish, and Chinook — property rights were well-defined long before Europeans arrived. Anthropologists have concluded that production rights to specific hunting, gathering, and, especially, fishing grounds on the Northwest coast belonged to clan-houses, with stewardship, namely the right and obligation to direct resource production resting in the house's leader. Northwest Indians told ethnologists in the nineteenth and twentieth centuries that specific people owned particular fishing-sites and had to give permission in order for extended family members to use the site. D. Bruce Johnsen has relied upon anthropological reports to hypothesize that the well-established security of the clan-houses' property rights and the house leader's stewardship right allowed the house leaders to manage the fishery over many years in order to maximize salmon production. The house leader's "executive right" descended according to local rules of inheritance, to the owner's eldest son in some areas, to his sister's eldest son in others. Franz Boas reported that among the Kwakiutl, primogeniture held regardless of whether the first born child was male or female. The house leader's rights generally descended to a single individual to avoid excessive division of the land among the leader's children. Indians' property rights to these salmon fishing spots were recognized in treaties signed with the Northwest tribes in the 1850s and are still exercised today.

In addition to real property rights, Northwest coast tribes have long recognized extensive ownership rights in personal property, both tangible and intangible. In particular, intellectual property has been extremely important in Pacific coast cultures, with families holding exclusive rights to the use of particular names, carvings, paintings, and crests connected with the family's history. Violation of these rights — apparently the equivalent of copyright — could result in violence and bloodshed. Personal property in tangible goods was extremely important as well and, according to anthropologists, the potlatch ceremony developed as an important means for establishing social rank, providing social insurance, and maintaining a level of distribution of wealth. The potlatch was even used as a means of resolving disputes over ownership of fishing sites, with the party giving away or destroying the most property obtaining good title to the spot.

8. Indian Property Rights on the Great Plains

. . . [N]either the Comanches nor the Cheyenne recognized property rights in land as they ranged widely across the plains, but both recognized extensive individual property rights in moveable goods. . . . Private property in horses became the primary source of wealth among tribes in the horse culture and buffalo-hunting economy. Horses were owned by men, women, and children and the number of horses owned varied widely by individual.

Generally, tribes dependent upon the buffalo for their economy recognized no more than temporary property rights in seasonally occupied villages. Yet even some of these tribes seem to have recognized private property rights in land cultivated as individual family garden plots. The Pawnees, who had a mixed horticultural and hunting economy, recognized property rights in garden plots assigned to women by the village chief. Rights to these tilled fields (and their produce) were respected — even when the village had decamped for the summer camp — as long as the tiller wished, but reverted to the village for reassignment at her death.

The agricultural tribes of the Upper Missouri-Hidatsa, Mandan, Arikara, and Omaha, among others, depended upon corn and, like other agricultural tribes, established property rights in cultivated lands. . . .

B. The Persistence of Indian Property Rights after Allotment

Even after resettlement or confinement to reservations, many Indians continued to create or modify private property systems to meet their new circumstances. Confinement led some tribes to develop private property rights to manage what little land they had left. At Yakima, whose members had been primarily hunters and fishers, the Indian Agent assigned individual family plots that supported farming without generating land use or inheritance problems. By 1894, twenty years before Congress allotted their reservation, the Indian Agents reported that almost all the Salish and Kootenai Indians who settled on the Flathead reservation lived in their own houses, occupied definite fenced holdings, and cultivated crops of grain, hay, and vegetables and orchards of apples and plums. Sufficient arable land existed to allow each family to fence and use as much as desired. . . .

Even among some of the tribes once in the buffalo economy, private property rights developed after confinement to the reservations. Santee Dakota Indians . . . began farming and by the mid-1880s were close to being self-supporting, with individual Indians farming for themselves, protected in the recognition of private property rights to the land they cultivated. . . .

C. Indian Property Rights Today

Tribal legal systems today continue to recognize property rights in land. A prime example is the Navajo Nation. Navajo private property rights in land are fiercely asserted and protected, consistent with a long history of property and individual ownership in Diné culture. One early outside observer noted that Navajo common law recognized ownership in five classes of property: hard and soft goods; ceremonial values such as songs, medicines, names, and formulae; wild and domesticated animals; and agricultural or rangeland. Farms were held by both men and women, were marked by posts or fences, and were subject to loss through non-use. Stock ranges, springs, and water holes likewise were subject to ownership claims, trespass was recognized as a compensable offense, and land rights were passed through inheritance.

. . . Navajo land law follows the principle that "one must use it or lose it," applying policies "designed to assure that Navajo Nation lands are used wisely and well, and that those who actually live on them and nurture them" have rights to their use. The courts use customary family trusts and the concept of a "most logical heir" to avoid the fragmentation of land use rights otherwise caused by intestate inheritance. . . .

The Ho-Chunk Nation, located in Wisconsin, is laying the foundation to recreate a system of private property. Its recently passed constitution includes provision for purchase of individual members' property through condemnation proceedings, for land use regulation and zoning, and the power "to create and regulate a system of property including but not limited to use, title, deed, estate inheritance, transfer, conveyance, and devise."

In 1999, the Pueblo of Isleta established the Isleta Appellate Court for Land and Property Disputes. The Tribal Council established the Court as a traditional appellate court and directed it to apply traditional law in its decisions. Specifically, the Court was given jurisdiction over some 40 disputes — some originating in disagreements dating back more than 75 years — which the Tribal Council had not decided in its role as the appellate court of general jurisdiction. The Council appointed seven members of the Pueblo to the Court, including three attorneys and four elders. They conduct their proceedings in the Tiwa language. The Court has dealt with both substantive property law issues and traditional procedures for resolving disputes. Among the former have been questions of inheritance of family homes, whether homes can be partitioned, proper ceremonial use of homes, set-back restrictions on property use, and mechanisms for transfer and sale of family property. In deciding both substance and procedure, the Court has heard cases, trusting that the application of traditional legal principles would enunciate a coherent body of property law, much as English common law judges developed property law in medieval England.

NOTES

1. As the United States government and individual Americans imposed themselves upon American Indian nations more and more, Indian nations' view of property changed in order to adapt to changing conditions. For example:

> [T]he Cherokees gradually became a people of property. The official census of the Cherokee Nation in 1824 and published in the *Cherokee Phoenix* in 1828 revealed that the Cherokee Indians possessed considerable wealth, including slaves, livestock, wheels, and looms, as well as 120 gins, 10 ferries, 9 stores, a turnpike, 6 public roads, and a threshing machine. Elias Boudinot, editor of the *Phoenix*, estimated the aggregate value of this property at $2,200,000.

> RENNARD STRICKLAND, FIRE AND THE SPIRITS: CHEROKEE LAWS FROM CLAN TO COURT 94 (1975).

2. Tribal customary law continues to be forceful in some cases. Consider *In re Howard*, 1 Am. Tribal Law 438, 7 Navajo Rep. 262 (Navajo Nation Supreme Court 1997), in which the court refused to consider evidence of an oral will introduced in the form of a clandestine tape recording:

> Generally, under Navajo common law, information is property. A person's words are property. Taping them in a clandestine manner and without the knowledge and consent of the speaker is a form of theft. It is deceit. Despite any other rule governing telephonic or other electronic communications where a sender does not know a recipient or third person is recording the communication, we hold that as a matter of policy, framed by Navajo common law, the Navajo Nation courts will not receive recordings of electronic communications if they are made without the knowledge and consent of a speaker or sender or other legal authorization. We conclude that the Window Rock Family Court erred in receiving the tape and its transcript into evidence and relying on it to rule in favor of an oral will.

> *In re Howard*, 1 Am. Tribal Law at 444.

B. TRIBAL PROPERTY

CHILKAT INDIAN VILLAGE, IRA v. JOHNSON

Chilkat Indian Village Tribal Court, No. 90-01, 20 Indian L. Rep. 6127
(November 3, 1993)

BOWEN, Tribal Court Judge

Background

This case involves the 1984 removal of four house posts and a rain screen, known as the "Whale House artifacts," from the Chilkat Indian Village in Klukwan, Alaska. The Chilkat Indian Village (village, tribe) filed this action in this court on January 8, 1990, against Michael R. Johnson, his corporation, and the individuals comprising the "Whale House Group."

The complaint sets forth two causes of action. First, the village alleges that defendants attempted to convert tribal trust property to their exclusive use and benefit. Second, the village alleges that defendants violated a tribal ordinance which prohibits removal of such property from the village without prior notification of and approval by the Chilkat Village Council, which is the tribe's governing body. The village seeks declaratory and injunctive relief. . . .

A four-week court trial was completed on February 12, 1993. . . .

Applicable Law

The law applicable in this tribal court action is tribal law, which is comprised of both written and unwritten, custom law of the village. The written manifestations of applicable tribal law include the Constitution and By-Laws of the Chilkat Indian Village, as amended, Ordinance 80-001, establishing a Chilkat Indian Village trial and appellate court system, and what is perhaps the most significant written expression of tribal law applicable to this case, the Ordinance of May 12, 1976 (Artifacts Ordinance) which reads as follows:

> No person shall enter onto the property of the Chilkat Indian Village for the purpose of buying, trading for, soliciting the purchase of, or otherwise seeking to arrange a removal of artifacts, clan crests, or other traditional Indian art work owned or held by members of the Chilkat Indian Village, without first requesting and obtaining permission to do so from the Chilkat Indian Village Council.
>
> No traditional Indian artifacts, clan crests, or other Indian art works of any kind may be removed from the Chilkat Indian village without the prior notification of and approval by, the Chilkat Indian Village Council.

[A]rticle IV ("Powers of the Village") of the tribe's federally approved constitution and bylaws provides that the seven-member village council has the power to "prevent the sale, disposition, lease, or encumbrance of any land or waters, or other assets of the Village without the consent of the Council." Art. IV, §1(1)(e). Under section 1(n) of the same article, the council has the power to "preserve and cultivate the arts, crafts and culture of the Indians of this community and their customs. . . ."

. . . As is common in many tribal courts, strict rules of evidence applicable in state and federal court trials were not imposed by this court. The only rule of evidence at trial was relevancy.

Issues

. . . [T]he village had the authority to enact the Ordinance of May 12, 1976, governing removal of artifacts, and . . . the "alleged acquisition by a non-Indian of the artifacts in question would constitute conduct that would have some direct effect on the welfare of the tribe. . . ."

There is no dispute about the basic facts surrounding the physical removal of the artifacts from the Whale House in Klukwan during April 1984.[12] Rather,

---

12. Defendants William Thomas and Clifford Thomas, together [with] their uncle, Clarence Hotch (since deceased), and Buzzie and Vincent Hotch performed the actual removal while non-Indian art deal[er] Michael Johnson (who had travelled several hundred miles from Seattle, Washington) waited 22 miles away in Haines, Alaska. The artifacts were taken to Haines, where the men picked up Michael Johnson, and temporarily stored the artifacts in defendant Evans Willard's garage. William Thomas and Michael Johnson then discussed arrangements to ship the artifacts to Seattle, where they have since remained in a warehouse pursuant to the federal court's injunction.

the issues to be decided are: (1) whether the Whale House rain screen and four house posts constitute "artifacts, clan crests, or other traditional Indian art work[s]" within the meaning of the relevant tribal ordinance; (2) whether the tribe has the power to enforce the ordinance against the defendants, including the non-Indian art dealer, Michael Johnson and his corporation; (3) whether any or all of the defendants violated the ordinance; [and] (4) whether defendants have presented any defenses which preclude judgment against any or all of them. . . . Finally, this court will determine the appropriate relief and other remedial orders which should issue. . . .

Conclusions

I. The Whale House Rain Screen and House Posts as Artifacts, Clan Crests, and Indian Art within the Meaning of the Ordinance

The artifacts consist of four elaborately carved wooden posts (made of spruce and over nine feet high) and a wooded partition (made of thin cedar boards) called a rain screen. George Emmons wrote that they are "unquestionably the finest example of native art, either Tlingit or Tsimshian, in Alaska, in boldness of conception — although highly conventionalized in form — in execution of detail, and in arrangement of detail. The record indicates that if the artifacts were sold on the open market they would likely reap a price of several million dollars.

The artifacts were created around 1830. A prominent leader in Klukwan, Xetsuwu, resolved to build a new house (Whale House) in order to unify certain existing house groups of the Ganexteidi Clan. He commissioned the house posts from a famous carver who resided in the Stikine River area, near what is currently referred to as Old Wrangell, Alaska. The name of that artist remained unknown until 1987, when a written account was discovered which identified his name as Kadjisdu.extc. The artist, who made detailed sketches while being told about the clan's stories during the canoe trip to Klukwan, is said to have resided in Klukwan for one year while carving the posts. By some accounts he was paid 10 slaves, 50 dressed moose skins, and several blankets.

The four posts represented the four groups that were brought together to form the new Whale House. The posts and rain screen tell stories of the clan, not just of the Whale House. The artifacts and the Whale House itself were created and dedicated in the traditional manner. The Ganexteidi hired Eagles [Eagle Clan members] to construct the original house. The Eagles were then repaid in a traditional "payback party," and the property was brought out in a potlatch and dedicated as clan property.

As Dr. Smythe noted, Xetsuwu's vision to unify the Ganexteidi under a new house with these clan crests was successfully implemented. The clan, as well as the Chilkat Indians generally, became a strong and powerful people. They maintained control of valuable trade routes to interior Alaska, and became quite prosperous.

The historical resistance by members of the clan to a series of efforts by outsiders to purchase these great works is testimony in itself of the clan crest nature of the artifacts, which are held in trust by the clan.

Around 1899, Yeilgooxu (whose English name was George Shotirdge), *hitsati* of the Whale House, organized the construction of a new Whale House because the original one was in disrepair. Although a mudslide destroyed it before completion, the artifacts were rescued. Yeilgooxu refused the offers of his friend George Emmons to acquire the artifacts. Following the death of Yeilgooxu, Yeilxaak, who was *hitsati* of the Raven House, was chosen to be *hitsati* of the Whale House, in part because of his close ties with the Whale House.

Louis Shotridge, the son of Yeilgooxu, caused a furor in the tribal community when he attempted to purchase the Whale House artifacts for the University of Pennsylvania's University Museum. In 1922 he arranged a meeting of Ganexteidi leaders, and offered $3,500 for the artifacts. Although that was a tremendous amount of money at that time and place, the clan turned him down.[32]

As a function of the matrilineal nature of Tlingit social structure, Louis Shotridge, like his mother, was a member of the Kaagwantan Clan of the Wolf moiety—the opposite side of his father's clan (Ganexteidi) and moiety (Raven) affiliations. His disingenuous claims to the property under Western inheritance law were rejected by the village. Shotridge became obsessed with acquiring the artifacts, continued his efforts during the 1920s and 1930s, but was never successful. While working for the territorial government in 1937 as a stream guard Louis Shotridge suffered a mysterious death. A schoolteacher found him near his cabin south of Sitka, Alaska. He had laid there several days with a broken neck, and died an agonizing death 10 days later.

Obsession with acquiring the Whale House artifacts did not end with Louis Shotridge. Defendant art dealer Michael Johnson has also been obsessed with the artifacts' acquisition, and his actions in this respect have caused tremendous conflicts and ill will at Klukwan. While the Tlingit defendants cooperated with him to remove the artifacts in 1984, the evidence brought out at trial leads this court to conclude that they seem to regret their 1984 actions in concert with Michael Johnson. Their spokesman Bill Thomas expressed such regret, and all of the Tlingit defendants now want the artifacts returned to Klukwan, and want nothing more to do with Michael Johnson and his attempts to sell the artifacts.

This court concludes that, inexorably, the Whale House property at issue constitutes "artifacts, clan crests, or other Indian art works" within the meaning of the tribe's 1976 Ordinance prohibiting removal of such property without first obtaining the consent of the council at Klukwan. . . .

III. Violation of the Ordinance by Defendants

There is abundant evidence in the trial record establishing that all of the defendants, including Michael Johnson, violated the 1976 Ordinance. The Tlingit defendants did not counter any of the evidence regarding their role with Michael Johnson, as well as the actual removal. Neither did Michael Johnson, who elected not to attend the trial, offer any such evidence. This court finds that the Tlingit defendants violated the tribe's 1976 Ordinance. . . .

Defendant Michael Johnson conducted an obsessive campaign to acquire the artifacts. He dealt with any and all people in the village who might assist

---

32. New York anthropologist Edmund Carpenter, who in 1975 published an essay about Louis Shotridge and the artifacts, is quoted as saying: "There wasn't 35 bucks in the whole of Klukwan at the time and they turned it down. That's style." . . .

him to remove the artifacts. Acting through his corporation, he played village members off against each other, while making inconsistent representations to them. The evidence at trial uniformly established that Michael Johnson conspired with the Tlingit defendants to remove the artifacts, and that he aided and abetted the actual physical removal of the artifacts. This court finds that Michael Johnson and his corporation violated the tribe's 1976 Ordinance.

IV. Defendant's Defenses

Even though Bill Thomas was the only defendant (called by the plaintiff) to testify at trial, it was apparent from the questions posed by various defendants, as well as the full record (including the closing remarks of the Tlingit defendants), that the defendants intend to rely primarily on two defenses: (1) that under Tlingit custom, they had no choice but to obey their uncle, Clarence Hotch, and (2) that traditional Tlingit culture is dead, and this tribal law is not valid. The incompatibility of these mutually exclusive assertions has not escaped notice by this court.

As to the first assertion, there was a wealth of testimony at trial that the Tlingit defendants, as adult members of their clan, certainly did have the right to question a directive by their uncle which contravened established customs of the village — in this case that the artifacts could not be sold by a caretaker of one house, but rather were subject to the control of the entire Ganexteidi Clan (and regulated by the tribal government).

Additionally, in order to obey their uncle Clarence Hotch, the Tlingit defendants necessarily had to disobey a contrary directive by their uncle Victor Hotch. The evidence at trial showed that while Victor may have waffled in some years during the 1970s, by 1980 he had clearly expressed his disapproval of Michael Johnson's efforts, and instructed that the artifacts were not to be sold. The family understood that Victor had willed his stock in Klukwan, Inc. to Clarence pursuant to their agreement that Clarence would use this asset to preserve the artifacts.

The defendants' argument that Tlingit culture is essentially dead was unsupported by the trial evidence. While the culture has been under assault from non-Indian outsiders and institutions, the lengthy testimony of many credible witnesses at trial confirmed the vitality of Tlingit culture at Klukwan, and the continuing, important role of traditional law. This court finds that the Chilkat Indian Village maintains and nourishes its culture — even though that culture, like any, is dynamic and ever-changing as a function of time and changed circumstances. . . .

Relief and Order

. . . This court is convinced that as a matter of tribal law the artifacts must be returned to Klukwan. Placing them in the Whale House will return the parties to the status that existed before the illegal 1984 removal.[44] In other words, it will reinstate the pre-litigation status quo. This court also recognizes that there may

---

44. This remedial action should also promote healing of the most recent wounds suffered by the tribal community (including the Tlingit defendants) by the continuing efforts by outsiders to use tribal members to purchase and remove the Whale House artifacts from Klukwan.

be a lack of custodial capacity of the Whale House, and possibly the Ganexteidi Clan as a whole in Klukwan. After all, the clan, through its leaders, requested that the village (which enacted the 1976 Ordinance) bring this action enforcing the ordinance, and seek the return of the artifacts to the village on its behalf. Accordingly, this court hereby makes it clear that the plaintiff Chilkat Indian Village, in consultation with the Ganexteidi Clan, has ultimate authority to enforce its ordinance, effect the return of the artifacts to Klukwan, and otherwise exercise all necessary custodial responsibility in overseeing the care and future custodial arrangements of the Whale House artifacts. . . .

NOTES

1. Angela Riley notes the importance of the Michael Johnson case to persuade the Chilkat Indian Village first to enact its Artifacts Ordinance in 1976, and then later to persuade federal courts to recognize the importance of tribal law in this context:

> Expecting the world to recognize and abide by tribal law may seem idealistic. . . . However, tribal law may, in fact, influence rule makers and judges outside of the tribal court system. [T]he mere acknowledgment of tribal law in federal and state courts lends increased legitimacy and respect to tribal law systems.
>
> [T]ribal law has found its way into relatively few Anglo-American court decisions, but there have been successes. One example is the case of *Chilkat Indian Village v. Johnson*. . . .
>
> [After the Village unsuccessfully sued Johnson in federal court], the . . . Ninth Circuit heard the case on appeal. [870 F.2d 1469, 1470 (9th Cir. 1989).] In addressing whether the tribe's conversion claims arose under federal law, the Ninth Circuit expressly acknowledged the legal underpinnings of the tribe's claim by stating that the Village's proprietary interest in the artifacts was a "creature of tribal law or tradition." As to the claims against the Indian defendants, the court dismissed them, stating that the case against them belonged in tribal court. However, in doing so, the court recognized the customary law of the Tlingit people, referencing the Artifacts Ordinance and stating that the enforcement of the Ordinance against tribal members was an issue for the tribal courts.
>
> Although the Ninth Circuit did not adjudicate matters of tribal law (nor, most would argue, should it have), the mere incorporation of the Artifacts Ordinance in its opinion validated tribal law. When federal courts acknowledge tribal law in a published opinion — whether or not it actually influences the outcome of the case — it gives tribal law an increased legitimacy in the eyes of tribal members and the dominant culture.

Angela R. Riley, *"Straight Stealing": Toward an Indigenous System of Cultural Property Protection*, 80 Wash. L. Rev. 69, 123-25 (2005).

2. Kristen A. Carpenter's scholarship demonstrates that American Indian people often view tribal property rights as surviving the loss — and even desecration — of the land:

> Tribes' own laws and customs provide another source of Indian interests in sacred sites on public lands. For several reasons it is appropriate to look to

tribal law and custom as a source of property law on sacred sites. First, if the aim is to facilitate legal solutions that ensure religious freedoms for American Indians, such solutions will only be meaningful if they incorporate tribal values. Tribally enacted legislation serves as a clear expression of those values. Second, courts and scholars have generally accepted the role of "custom" in supporting citizens' interests in public lands. Third, preexisting land and property rights of indigenous peoples often survive the colonial process. . . .

Tribal law and custom also help to expose the limits of the ownership model and suggest alternatives to notions of absolute rights. Irrespective of who owns a particular sacred place, indigenous peoples may have undeniable, ongoing relationships with it. As Rebecca Tsosie has explained: "The mere fact that the land is not held in Native title does not mean that the people do not hold these obligations, nor . . . that they no longer maintain the rights to these lands." Even if a place has been desecrated, "a people's custodial responsibilities remain. No matter how damaged, the land retains its power and significance." Indigenous customs and laws may challenge Anglo American property law to be more cognizant of the responsibilities and relationships that transcend ownership.

Kristen A. Carpenter, *A Property Rights Approach to Sacred Sites Cases: Asserting a Place for Indians as Nonowners*, 52 UCLA L. Rev. 1061, 1112-13 (2005).

C. TRIBAL PROPERTY CODES

1. GRAZING LEASES

Riggs v. Estate of Attakai

Navajo Nation Supreme Court, No. SC-CV-39-04, 7 Am. Tribal Law 534
(June 13, 2007)

Before Yazzie, Chief Justice, and Ferguson and J. Benally, Associate Justices.
Yazzie and Ferguson filed the opinion of the Court. J. Benally filed an opinion concurring in the judgment. . . .

I.

The Court applies the following facts in deciding the case. When Mary Lou Attakai was 15 years old, her maternal grandfather, Paddock, gave her Grazing Permit No. 7-58, for 66 sheep units within District 7. The grazing permit was actually used by Mary Lou's mother and sisters, including Sista Riggs when Mary Lou moved away to other areas.[2] Sista Riggs has a separate permit she received as a result of a peacemaking after her mother's death. . . . Seven years after [Mary Lou's] death, when no probate petition was filed, Riggs filed a quiet title action requesting that the grazing permit be transferred to her. Phillip Attakai, surviving spouse of Mary Lou, and Tom Attakai filed an answer

---

2. The maternal clan is Ta'neezahnii. Other family members also had grazing permits within the area, including Riggs. Riggs is sister to Mary Lou and a maternal aunt to Tom Attakai.

claiming title when the quiet title action was filed. Tom Attakai died before the Family Court issued its decision.

II.

The question before this court is whether the Family Court erred in its determination when it granted the grazing permit to Tom Attakai without applying Navajo customs and traditional practices, and without considering Navajo Nation policies as acknowledged by this Court in prior quiet title actions. The Family Court concluded that Tom Attakai, being the son of Mary Lou, was of the same clan as Mary Lou, and that granting the permit to him would satisfy the wishes of the maternal grandfather Paddock to keep the permit within the clan by indicating the grazing permit "be used for the family." The Family Court reasoned that the traditional practice of maintaining the permit within the clan would be satisfied and that although Tom did not live in the area covered by the grazing permit, by awarding him the permit would give him and his sisters a "sense of home."

In *Begay v. Keedah*, 6 Nav. R. 416, 421 (Nav. Sup. Ct. 1991), this Court acknowledged the following Navajo Nation policies gleaned from Navajo statutes to be considered when determining the award of a grazing permit: 1) animal units in grazing permits must be sufficiently large to be economically viable, 2) land must be put to its most beneficial use, 3) the most logical person should receive land use rights, 4) use rights must not be fragmented, and 5) only those who are personally involved in the beneficial use of land may be awarded it. *Id.* The Court now holds that these factors are to be considered and applied consistent with the Navajo Fundamental Law which defines the role and authority of Dine women in our society. Traditionally, women are central to the home and land base. They are the vein of the clan line. The clan line typically maintains a land base upon which the clan lives, uses the land for grazing and agricultural purposes and maintains the land for medicinal and ceremonial purposes. The crucial role of women is expressed in the principles established by White Shell Woman and are commonly referred to as *Yoolgaii Asdzáán Bi Beehazáanii*. These principles include *Iiná Yésdáhí* (a position generally encompassing life; heading the household and providing home care, food, clothing, as well as child bearing, raising, and teaching), *Yódí Yésdáhí* (a position encompassing and being a provider of, a caretaker of, and receiver of materials things such as jewelry and rugs), *Nitl'iz Yésdáhí* (a position encompassing and being a provider of and a caretaker of mineral goodness for protection), *Tsodizin Yésdáhí* (a position encompassing spirituality and prayer). This is why the women are attached to both the land base and the grazing permits. For the most part, Navajos maintain and carry on the custom that the maternal clan maintains traditional grazing and farming areas.

Because they are keepers of the clan line and land base, Navajo women are often the most logical persons to receive land use rights to hold in trust for the family. They are also the ones who are burdened with putting the land base to its most beneficial use by managing the herd and the land upon which the herd graze for the benefit of the clan group. This means that keepers have to balance the number of sheep units with the size of the land base, making sure the land base remains compatible, sustainable and feasible for sufficient continued beneficial use. Overgrazed land cannot be put to beneficial use. This practice is consistent with preserving a large area by discouraging the fragmentation of grazing permits and the land base.[4] The Navajo Nation policy is to discourage the breaking up of land. Progressive fragmentation of the land decreases usefulness of the land. *See In the matter of the Estate of Wauneka*, 5 Nav. R. 79, 83 (Nav. Sup. Ct. 1986).

. . . The issue of the ownership of the permit is therefore reviewed de novo in light of the tradition of female management of the land and livestock using the factors set out in *Keedah*.

For the foregoing reasons, this Court concludes Riggs is the appropriate person. When Riggs filed her action, Tom Attakai lived away from the Castle Butte area. He lived in Sanders and later in Fort Defiance, whereas Sista Riggs consistently lived in the family area. Riggs had already been managing not only her own herd, but the herd held in trust for the family.

By placing the grazing permit with Sista Riggs, there is assurance that the land and herd will remain with the family, and that the grazing permit will remain intact and not be fragmented. The record contains testimony that Tom Attakai and his father had attempted to either sell or rent the grazing permit to others outside the family and clan.

. . . The Court concludes that Sista Riggs should be the trustee of the permit.

III.

The Court affirms the Family Court's decision that Tom Attakai's sisters should be the beneficiaries of the permit. . . . It is reasonable for the Family Court to decide that Sista may hold the permit for use in the Castle Butte area and allow Tom's sisters to use the permit in the future if they decide to. The Court therefore affirms that part of the Family Court's decision. . . .

V.

The Window Rock Family Court judgment, granting Tom Attakai Grazing Permit No. 7-58 is REVERSED and VACATED. This matter is REMANDED to the Family Court to enter an order granting Grazing Permit No. 7-58 to Sista Riggs to hold as trustee for the sisters of Tom Attakai. . . .

[Concurring opinion of Justice BENALLY omitted.]

NOTES

1. In western U.S. Indian communities, grazing rights are a frequent source of litigation. For example, the Navajo Nation has extended to its Office of Hearing and Appeals the jurisdiction to decide many grazing lease disputes. *E.g., Begay v. King*, 8 Am. Tribal Law 148 (Navajo Nation 2009).

---

4. In some cases, the probate code might allow a husband to obtain the grazing permit although he is of a different clan. Most likely he is permitted to hold the permit in trust for his children who are of the same clan as the deceased mother. In other cases a male member of the clan may be granted a permit so long as he meets the criteria set out in *Keedah*. It is not known how Old Man Paddock obtained the grazing permit in this case, but he made it clear it was to stay within the family.

2. In many tribal communities, especially rural reservations, attorneys are few and far between. Tribal courts are routinely confronted with representations by parties that they were unable to obtain counsel to prosecute or defend a matter. Tribal courts handle these claims in different ways. In *Smith v. Eckhart*, 2000.NACT.000006 (Crow Court of Appeals 2000), the court gave the defendants in a property line dispute extra time to secure counsel:

> Appellants have requested another chance to present their defense, since they were unable to retain counsel to assist them throughout the proceedings in the Tribal Court. It is an unfortunate fact that it is very difficult for most people to afford legal representation, especially when they are defendants in a lawsuit of someone else's making. In these circumstances, the most the trial court can do is to give the defendants reasonable time to obtain an attorney or lay advocate, or to prepare to present their case pro se. This accommodation must be tempered, however, by the opposing party's interest in obtaining a prompt and efficient resolution of the matter. The Tribal Council sought to achieve this balance when it enacted the Crow Rules of Civil Procedure.

Smith, at ¶¶31.

2. ALLOTMENTS

SMITH V. ECKHART

Crow Court of Appeals, No. 99-116, 2000 CROW 6; 2000.NACT.0000006
(September 29, 2000)

Before STEWART, C.J., GROS-VENTRE, J., and WATT, J.

This is an appeal from the Judgment of the Tribal Court (Yellowtail, S.J.) entered on October 29, 1999, permanently enjoining the Defendants/Appellants from interfering with the Plaintiffs/Appellees' construction and maintenance of a fence between their two trust allotments on the property boundary line established by a U.S. Bureau of Land Management survey. . . .

A. Summary of Facts and Proceedings

. . . Plaintiffs Burton and Miriam Smith are the owners by heirship of Crow Allotment No. 1896 located on the Crow Reservation near Pryor, Montana. The Defendants are the heirs to Crow Allotment No. 1821, which is located adjacent to and immediately north of the west half of Smiths' allotment. Title to both allotments is held in trust by the United States of America. Defendant Addlee Plain Bull Eckhart currently lives in a home near the Smith property boundary.

There has been a dispute between the parties over the boundary between their two allotments since at least 1992. That spring, the Smiths tore down an old 3-wire fence on the northern portion of their property. They planned to build a new fence several feet north of the existing fence, along a property boundary line that had been marked by the local Bureau of Indian Affairs Realty Office in 1987. When the Smiths began laying out the new fence in the Spring of 1993, one or more of the Defendants objected. The fence was not built that year.

During the intervening years, the parties had several brief confrontations about the use of the property north of the old fence. Burton Smith testified that without the new fence, he could not make use of his allotment, because he couldn't keep livestock on his land or protect his crops from other people's livestock.

Eventually, at the Smiths' request, the BIA Agency Superintendent authorized a formal survey of the property line. . . . The . . . survey was performed during the summer of 1998 by Mr. R. Wayne Wilson. . . .

The property line established by Mr. Wilson's survey was apparently close to the line staked earlier by BIA Realty, being north of the old fenceline and closer to the house on Defendants' property. In fact, the line cut through a portion of the driveway to Ms. Eckhart's home.

During Memorial Day weekend of 1999, the Smiths rented equipment and started building a fence along the property line established by the BIA/BLM survey. There is no evidence that the Smiths notified any of the Defendants before beginning construction. After they had set a few posts, the BIA Police and a sheriff's deputy arrived, apparently summoned by one of the Defendants. The officers advised the Smiths that, in order to keep the peace, they should not do anything further until the dispute was resolved by the Crow Tribal Court. . . .

The Tribal Court held that the . . . survey performed by Mr. Wilson established the boundary between the parties' two allotments. . . . The court found no evidence that the old fence removed by the Smiths was ever intended as a boundary fence, and held that its location had no legal significance to the determination of the boundary between the two tracts. . . .

The Tribal Court interpreted a Tribal fencing ordinance as requiring that boundary fences be constructed on the property line. Therefore, the Tribal Court concluded, the Smiths were entitled to erect their fence, in compliance with the ordinance, on the line established by the BLM survey. . . .

Based on the foregoing, the Tribal Court entered judgment for the Plaintiffs/Appellees, permanently enjoining the Defendants "from doing any act, or in any way interfering with Plaintiffs' construction, maintenance or use of a boundary fence between their respective real estate on the boundary line established by the Bureau of Land Management Survey[.]" . . .

C. Discussion

With the preceding background, we turn to the arguments raised in the Appellants' brief. . . .

2. Failure to Join Other Owners

. . . As the Tribal Court recognized at the end of the June 25 hearing, its orders and judgment can only bind the four named Defendants (and anyone acting for them). Because this case was not brought as a quiet title action, and all the owners were not properly joined by the plaintiffs, it would not be appropriate for the doctrine of collateral estoppel to completely bar any further challenge to the boundary line by other heirs to the Plain Bull allotment. Rather, in any new case filed by those other heirs, they would have the burden of proving that the Tribal Court's judgment and the BLM survey were erroneous.

Therefore, since, the Tribal Court has not finally adjudicated the unnamed owners' interest in their trust allotment, their joinder was not necessary under Rule 25 of the Crow Rules of Civil Procedure.

3. Violations of Tribal Fencing Ordinance

Although not raised as an issue in their appellate brief, the issue of the Smiths' non-compliance with the Tribal fencing ordinance was raised by the Defendants/Appellants at the June 25th hearing, and was addressed in the Tribal Court's decision. Because it was the only substantive issue raised by the Defendants in this case, and because of its importance in future disputes such as this, we will review the Tribal fencing ordinance as it applies to the facts of this case.

At the June 25th hearing, the Defendants introduced as evidence Ordinance No. 1, "Fencing Ordinance for the Crow Reservation," and the Tribal Council resolutions adopting and ratifying it. The Tribal fencing ordinance was apparently enacted to avoid disputes just such as this. It sets up a comprehensive procedure for construction of boundary fences, and recognizes certain rights with respect to the costs and ownership of the new fences.

Section VI of the Ordinance requires that all boundary fences be built on the property line. Boundary fences built beyond the line onto Indian land must be removed upon demand by the Indian owner or lessee. If the fence is between two tracts of Indian-owned land, then the Indian owner of the other tract is responsible for construction, maintenance and the cost of half the fence (Section III). Regardless of who pays the cost of the fence, it is deemed to be jointly owned (Section V). The Ordinance also sets out specifications for boundary fences, including the number of wires and spacing, post and stay spacing, corners and cattle guards (Section VII).

Section I of the Ordinance specifically requires 10 days' written notice to the adjoining landowners before beginning construction, and gives those landowners 60 days to complete their half of the fence. According to Section IX, if the other landowners fail to construct their half of the fence within the 60 days allowed, they waive any claim for trespass by the requesting party's livestock grazing across the boundary.

Section VIII of the Ordinance also provides:

> No fences built or existing upon lands within the exterior boundaries of the Crow Indian Reservation shall be removed without the prior written consent of each adjoining landowner whose lands the fence serves as a boundary for.

In his cross-examination of Burton Smith at the June 25th hearing, Mr. Turns Plenty elicited Mr. Smith's admission that he was not aware of the fencing ordinance, and never notified the Defendants prior to tearing down the old fence.

With respect to this alleged violation, the Tribal Court found that the old fence was not a boundary fence covered by the Fencing Ordinance, because the property line had never been surveyed before, and there was no evidence that the parties (or their predecessors) ever intended the old fence to serve as the boundary between their properties. . . . The Tribal Court went on to hold that the Plaintiffs were entitled to construct a boundary fence on the line established by the BLM survey, because Section VI of the Ordinance requires that boundary fences be constructed on the property line. . . .

This court will not set aside the Tribal Court's findings of fact unless they are "clearly erroneous." *Lande v. Schwend*, 1999 CROW 1, ¶47; see also Fed. R. Civ. P. 52(a). This court may affirm on any ground supported by the evidence. *Id.* at ¶48, citing *Crow Tribe v. Gregori*, 1998 CROW 2, ¶97.

In this case, BLM surveyor Wilson testified that the boundary between these two allotments had never been officially surveyed; in such circumstances, it was his opinion that the old fence was not relevant to the true property boundary. Plaintiff Smith testified that the old fence did not necessarily follow a straight line like a property boundary, that it was in a bad state of disrepair, and that [it] had to be rebuilt anyway in order to hold cows and calves. There is no evidence in the record contradicting any of this testimony. Based [on] this record, we cannot say that the Tribal Court's findings on this subject were clearly erroneous.

Also, the Tribal Court's conclusion (implicit in its holding) that the Ordinance only applies to boundary fences was a fair reading of the language in Section VII, which requires the consent of the other landowner "whose lands the fence serves as a boundary for." If the fence did not serve as a boundary between the properties, there was no requirement under Section VIII to obtain the Defendants' consent before removing the fence.

In many cases, though, it will not be clear from the record whether or not a fence was intended to serve as the boundary fence, just because it was not located precisely on the property line. Section VI contemplates this situation, by providing that if a mislocated boundary fence is encroaching on Indian-owned land, the Indian owner has the right to have it removed to the property line.[3] This right to remove a mislocated boundary fence to the property line, and the further requirement in Section VI that boundary fences be built on the property line, would appear to override the requirement in Section VIII for obtaining the consent of the other property's owners before removing a mislocated fence. However, this court is not called upon to resolve this potential conflict in the Ordinance in the present case, because the old fence was not a boundary fence whose removal was subject to Section VIII.

This does not dispose of another violation of Ordinance as revealed in the record — the Smiths' failure to give 10 days' written notice before beginning construction of the fence. According to Section I.A, the notice must "set forth in detail the plans for construction and maintenance of said fence[.]" The fact that this provision is the first matter covered in the Ordinance indicates that the notice requirement fulfills another important purpose of the Ordinance — to keep the peace. We agree with the point made by Mr. Turns Plenty in the

---

3. If the mislocated boundary fence is encroaching on non-Indian land, Section VI purports to waive the non-Indian's trespass claims, and the mislocated fence remains jointly owned. Although Mr. Smith testified that he is not an enrolled member of the Crow Tribe, he also testified that he was a descendant of the original allottee and inherited the allotment. Therefore, it would appear that both properties involved in this case are clearly "Indian-owned" for purposes of the Ordinance.

hearing, that it is a very serious matter not to notify you neighbor in advance before you begin pounding fence posts a few feet away from her home.

In this case, though, the Smiths' failure to give written notice is not sufficient grounds to reverse the Tribal Court's judgment. Although Mr. Smith acknowledged that ignorance is no excuse for violating the law, it is true that Tribal ordinances are not always readily available to the public, or, for that matter, to this court.[4] More importantly, the record reflects that the Defendants were aware that the Smiths wanted to build a fence for several years, had verbally discussed the possibility of an electrified fence, and that various incidents over the years made it difficult for the parties to communicate. Finally, any surprise and distress suffered by the Defendants because of the lack of written notice would tend to be offset by the inconvenience and distress suffered by the Plaintiffs while the Defendants prevented them from using a portion of their land, especially after the BLM survey established the property line.

For the foregoing reasons, the judgment of the Tribal Court is AFFIRMED. No costs.

NOTES

1. Many western tribal communities have been *allotted* by the federal government. Prior to the allotment era, which became official congressional policy in 1887 (but had been official federal administrative policy since the 1850s), most Indian communities were reservation based, with relatively large (compared to now) land bases collectively owned by the Indian tribe. The federal government subdivided these reservations, allotting 80 or 160 acres (or some other number) to Indian heads of household, and selling the remainder of the reservation mostly to non-Indians as "surplus lands." The allotted land for Indians typically came with a 25-year "trust period" in which the land would be held in trust by the United States and after which time the land would be freely alienable and taxable by the state. After Congress eliminated the allotment policy officially in 1934, there remained two kinds of tribal allotment properties—trust allotments and fee allotments. Trust allotments retain the immunity from taxation, but fee allotments do not. The *Smith* case demonstrates how modern tribal law includes disputes over allotted lands.

2. In *Barber v. Simpson*, 2006 WL 6358373 (Nevada Intertribal Court of Appeals 2006), the court rejected a claim by occupants of a trust allotment who asserted an aboriginal Indian title claim to the trust allotment property owners who were also Indians:

   > The facts before the court are unique. No case could be found where one individual Indian has asserted an aboriginal title against patent holders who are also Indian. There are three basic standards which must be met

---

4. Resolution No. 96-20, which ratifies and reaffirms the Fencing Ordinance, directs the Chairman to mandate that a copy of the Fencing Ordinance be attached to all grazing and farming leases prior to signature. This court takes judicial notice that the Ordinance has not been publicized consistently in this manner.

for aboriginal title to exist: (1) Appellant's ancestors must have lived on land in question from time immemorial to the exclusion of all others; (2) They must also have enclosed, cultivated and improved the land; and (3) They must have lived on the precise land for which aboriginal title is claimed. . . .

Although certain areas of SAC-6 may have become occupied by individuals, the evidence does not support a finding that the particular five acres to which Mr. Barber is now asserting aboriginal title had belonged to his lineal ancestors from time immemorial. Mr. Barber testified that his relatives lived on the land from the issuance of the patent and that his grandfather had told him they lived on the land before the issuance of the patent, but he does not explicitly state which land. . . .

The evidence presents no information as to whether or not Mr. Barber's ancestors excluded others from the land. Even if the evidence had supported a finding that they had lived on the land from time immemorial, if they did not exclude all others, no right of occupancy can exist. To exclude someone from property would suggest some form of an affirmative action to make sure that others do not occupy it. None is mentioned here. . . .

As there is no proof that the ancestors of Mr. Barber lived on the property from time immemorial or that, if they did live there, it was to the exclusion of all others. . . .

While the land in question which Mr. Barber's family occupied may once have been enclosed, the testimony does not show that the property was completely enclosed. Mr. Barber testified that fire and flood have left only a partial fence. . . . Mr. Simpson testified that there were no fences to his knowledge. . . . The property is not now fully enclosed. . . . The lack of full enclosure suggests that currently there is no effort to exclude parties from the property.

The land may have at one time since the issuance of the patent been under cultivation, but there is no evidence in the record showing how the property is currently being used. There is also no testimony showing how it had been cultivated, except some references to livestock. The testimony does not sustain a finding that the property is currently cultivated.

Some improvements have been made to the property. There are some old structures on the land and the trailer in which Mr. Barber lives. Some buildings were moved there many years ago from another place. One house burned down. . . . The mere existence of the improvements is not sufficient without proper enclosure and cultivation. . . .

Although his ancestors may have been on some portion of what became the allotment, it is by no means clear from the record that Mr. Barber's family lived on the five acres he is claiming before the issuance of the patent. Jenny Johnson, Mr. Barber's grandmother, lived on the land, but Mr. Barber testified that he did not know where she was born. . . . He himself is not sure that the patent was issued for the same land that his ancestors occupied. . . .

[A]boriginal title is not to be liberally endorsed. Its original purpose was to follow the public policy of assisting in the settlement of Indians, an issue which no longer exists. [I]t should be found only in the rarest of circumstances. Those circumstances are not found in the record before the court. Accordingly, the Court finds that no aboriginal title exists.

Barber, 2006 WL 6358373, at *2-5.

D. TRIBAL HOUSING

COQUILLE INDIAN HOUSING AUTHORITY V. HARRISON

Coquille Indian Tribal Court, No. H 98-005, 1999.NACQ.0000001 (April 6, 1999)

The opinion of the court was delivered by: DON OWEN COSTELLO, Chief Judge, Coquille Indian Tribal Court . . .

. . . For the reasons set forth below, the Court is of the opinion that plaintiff be awarded Judgment against defendants, and each of them, in the sum of $2,244.45 and, further, that defendants' counterclaims be dismissed and that plaintiff have Judgment thereon.

The Parties' Claims

[The tribal housing authority brought suit to evict the defendants, and for money damages resulting from damage to the property. Defendants raised various state law defenses to the eviction.]

The Court has territorial jurisdiction to hear this case because the facts which give rise to this dispute arose on the reservation of the Coquille Indian Tribe. CITC 610.200.1(b). The Court has subject matter jurisdiction because the dispute is an action in law falling within the Court's broad judicial authority. CONSTITUTION OF THE COQUILLE INDIAN TRIBE, Article VII, Section 4; CITC 610.200.1(1), (2).

Facts.

Having considered all of the evidence, the Court finds the following facts to be proven by a preponderance of the evidence.

Defendants, and each of them, signed a Coquille Indian Housing Authority Rental Lease (Lease) on October 29, 1996, for the rental of the subject premises at 2609 Mexeye Loop, Coos Bay, Oregon. . . . The Lease term was for one month commencing October 24, 1996, with automatic continuation ". . . from month to month thereafter subject only to respective rights of the parties to terminate . . ." as provided therein. . . .

Paragraph IV A of the Lease provides in relevant part that the ". . . Resident shall refrain self, household members and guests from destroying, defacing, damaging or removing any part of the unit or community development. The Resident shall be charged for the cost of damage repair and restoration."

Paragraph IV C provides in relevant part that the ". . . Resident or any member of the Resident's household or a guest or other persons under the Resident's control shall not engage in violence or any criminal activity, including drug-related criminal activity, in the housing community or CIHA office area. Such activity is a serious Lease violation and is grounds for termination of the Lease and immediate eviction. The term 'drug-related criminal activity' means the illegal manufacture, sale, distribution, use, or possession with the intent to manufacture, sell, distribute, or use [] a controlled substance (as defined in Section 102 of the Controlled Substance Act (21 U.S.C. 802)." . . .

[Paragraph] IV C provides in relevant part that an "expedited grievance procedure will be available to tenants evicted under Section IV, paragraph C of the Lease . . . where the eviction is for violence or criminal activity or a drug-related criminal activity."

Paragraph IV D of the Lease states that resident ". . . agrees to pay reasonable charges for repair of damage to the dwelling unit caused by the Resident, his family or any persons in the dwelling unit or on the dwelling property with the permission of the Resident."

Paragraph V E of the Lease provides in relevant part that ". . . in the event the Resident or any member of his household or guest has committed, or attempted to commit or threatened to commit any acts that physically injure any person lawfully upon the premises or any other premises of the CIHA or substantially damage any property of the CIHA, another Resident, or any person lawfully upon premises or other premises of the CIHA including drug dealing, this Lease may be terminated on 24-hour written notice." Paragraph V F provides in relevant part that immediately upon termination of Lease becoming effective, "the Resident shall quietly and peaceably remove himself, his family and his property from the premises and surrender possession thereof and the equipment and furnishings therein, in the condition as leased, reasonable wear and tear excepted. All amounts owed by CIHA by the Resident shall immediately become due and payable."

The premises were new when defendants took possession on October 24, 1996. Although defendants took good care of the place initially, defendants had continuing problems in complying with the conditions of the Lease during their tenancy. Shawn F. Scott, Director of CIHA, and his employees tried to help defendants more than most residents and [testified] that extraordinary efforts were made to accommodate them. For example, in early 1998, CIHA served a notice of termination on the defendants. Defendants filed a formal grievance of the notice of termination. Defendants avoided eviction in that instance by entering into an agreement to take certain steps in their personal lives, including drug counseling for Mr. Harrison, as a condition of continued tenancy.

On October 30, 1998, defendant Hobart Harrison became involved in an altercation with Calvin Summers and Thad Duggan at the Calvin Summers' residence, which is located across the street from defendants' premises. The Summers home is premises of the CIHA. The altercation was instigated by defendant Hobart Harrison. During this altercation, Hobart Harrison intentionally physically injured Calvin Summers and Thad Duggan in the Summers home. After the physical altercation, defendant Hobart Harrison intentionally damaged the personal property of Calvin Summers by puncturing the tire of Mr. Summers' vehicle with a knife.

Later the same evening, shortly after 8:00 p.m., Tribal Police Officer Christopher Stayton found a syringe with the plunger sitting next to it, a green handled spoon with a melted handle and what appeared to be a small piece of cotton in the bowl of the spoon and a small plastic bindle with a white powdery residue inside in the bathroom of the Harrison residence. The residue was tested to be methamphetamine, but the results were not available to CIHA until November 20, 1998. . . .

On November 3, 1998, Shawn F. Scott, Executive Director of CIHA, issued and signed a NOTICE OF TERMINATION OF LEASE AND TERMINATION OF

TENANCY . . . , which was received by defendants on that date. The notice informed defendants that their Lease and tenancy were being terminated for ". . . violent, criminal, and drug-related activities." Pursuant to the notice, defendants were given 72 hours to vacate the premises, failing which CIHA would file a lawsuit in Tribal Court for eviction. . . .

Defendants voluntarily vacated the premises at the end of the 72-hour period, on the afternoon of November 6, 1998, when CIHA's agent, Robert D. Van Loo, came to inspect the premises. When they vacated, defendants left numerous items of personal property on the premises, as well as large quantities of household garbage and waste. There was extensive damage within the premises, including such things as damaged carpet, numerous holes in the walls, missing screens, damaged linoleum and other deterioration beyond normal wear and tear. . . .

Although there is some dispute as to when the damages were caused, defendants do not dispute that they caused them. The exact timing of the damages is not significant. The premises were new when defendants took occupancy and were damaged when they vacated. Pursuant to the Lease, defendants are responsible for paying for these damages.

I find that the reasonable value to repair the damage to the premises which existed as of the time defendants left the premises on November 6, 1998, and to place new locks on the premises, is $2,633.38. That sum is owed by defendants to plaintiff, plus $43.98 for prorated rent, $3.50 for prorated CSD and $38.59 for water, less $475.00 for deposit paid by defendants. The resulting balance due is $2,244.45. . . .

CIHA terminated the Lease and evicted the defendants in accordance with the provisions of the Lease and of Tribal Law.

By instigating and intentionally engaging in a physical altercation with Calvin Summers and Thad Duggan, and intentionally and violently damaging the tire of the vehicle owned by Mr. Summers, defendant Hobart Harrison engaged in conduct in violation of provisions in paragraphs IV C and IV E of the Lease prohibiting violence in the housing community. Pursuant to paragraph IV E of the Lease, CIHA was lawfully entitled to terminate the Lease and both defendants' tenancies upon 24-hour notice.

A more liberal 72 hours' notice was given. The notice complied with the Lease conditions and with Coquille Indian Tribal Evictions Procedures (Resolution CY9542, August 26, 1995) regarding advice of rights to tenants because the notice informed Harrisons of the reasons for termination of Lease, and informed them that they had the right to reply to the notice as they wish, the right to examine and receive copies of any CIHA documents relevant to the termination and eviction, the right to a hearing according to CIHA grievance procedures, and the right to be represented by a person of their choosing at their expense. Defendants were aware of the formal grievance procedures and chose not to exercise their rights pursuant to the procedures. The defendants voluntarily vacated the premises, in compliance with the terms of the notice. Their tenancies ended when they vacated. Pursuant to paragraphs IV and V of the Lease, defendants are responsible for paying plaintiff in the total sum of $2,244.45.

Defendants left personal items behind, and did not take reasonable steps to reclaim their possessions. I conclude that they abandoned those possessions.

Plaintiff is not indebted to defendants for defendants' abandoned personal possessions.

The Residential Landlord and Tenant Act of the State of Oregon and the eviction procedures of Chapter 105 of Oregon Revised Statutes do not apply to this case. Accordingly, defendants' affirmative defenses and counter-claims should be dismissed.

Because defendants have interposed claims based upon state law which, if applied, may serve as a partial or total bar to plaintiff's recovery and entitle defendants to recover against plaintiff, the Court addresses the issue of applicability of state law in this case.

Whether state law applies in this Tribal Court case is a matter to be determined by this Court. In analyzing this issue, the Court takes judicial notice of the laws of this Tribe and applicable Federal Laws and laws of the State of Oregon, pursuant to Coquille Evidence Code (CEC) 202(1). . . .

The Preamble of the Constitution of the Coquille Indian Tribe states: "The Coquille Indian Tribe is and always has been a sovereign self-governing power . . . [i]n recognition of this sacred responsibility . . . the members of the Coquille Indian Tribe, being a federally recognized Indian tribe pursuant to Coquille Indian Restoration Act of June 28, 1989, 103 STAT. 91, . . . adopt this constitution in order to reaffirm our tribal government and to secure the rights and powers inherent in our sovereign status guaranteed to us by federal and tribal laws." . . .

Article VII of the Constitution provides for a Tribal Court. Article VII, Sec. 4 provides that the Court shall have the following powers:

> The tribal court and such inferior courts as the tribal council may from time to time ordain and establish shall be empowered to exercise all judicial authority of the tribe.
>
> The judicial power of the tribal court shall extend to all cases and matters in law and equity arising under this constitution, the laws and ordinances of or applicable to the Coquille Indian Tribe and customs of the Coquille Indian Tribe.

. . . The Tribe's sovereignty is not inferior to that of the State of Oregon. That the Tribe has the sovereign authority to self-govern and to enact or not enact legislation cannot be questioned.

Although the Coquille Indian Tribal Code provides that the laws of the State of Oregon ". . . may be used for guidance . . . ," CITC 620.010.2(c), the decision of whether this Court will seek that guidance in a given case is one which requires careful thought. After considering the issue carefully, it is the opinion of this Court that the provisions of Chapter 90 of Oregon Revised Statutes cited by defendants should not be used to guide the Court in reaching its decision in this case.

The cited sections of Oregon Revised Statutes are legislative acts of the Oregon Legislature. The legislative body of the Coquille Indian Tribe, the Tribal Council, has itself legislated certain procedures regarding evictions. . . . The legislature of the Coquille Indian Tribe considered issues of landlord and tenant rights and chose not to include in its legislation provisions similar in substance to those enacted by the Oregon Legislature in the cited provisions, ORS 90.322(7), 90.435 and 90.425.

This Court interprets the Constitution and the Tribal Court Ordinance (CITC Chapter 610) as mandates which establish a separation of the Tribal Council and the Tribal Court. For this Court to incorporate ORS Chapter 90 into this case would be an improper usurpation of the Tribal Council's legislative authority. This Court should not impose its judgment over that of the Tribal Council in an area which is the Tribal Council's sole province.

Each of the cited sections of Oregon Revised Statutes has its genesis in Oregon Laws 1973, Chapter 559. The Oregon Legislature in that year legislated remedies not previously available in this state. The Legislature of the Coquille Indian Tribe has not yet enacted such legislation. Whether it will do so in the future is a matter to be determined only by the Tribal Council.

NOTES

1. In *Raphael v. Grand Traverse Band of Ottawa and Chippewa Indians*, 1999 WL 34986350 (Grand Traverse Band Court of Appeals 1999), the court held that the beneficiary of a tribal property lease assignment did not have a property interest in the land:

   > The Trial Court Judge ruled that the assignment had failed under its terms and that there was not a need for an eviction hearing or a trial on the matter. The exhibit showed that the lease required an improvement as a residence within one year of its taking effect. There was no dispute that there was no improvement except for the placement of a travel trailer or camping unit which was undisputed as not qualifying for the Appellant's residence. The issue remains whether there was an interest, or whether it ever vested before the date of the eviction.
   >
   > A leasehold interest would always have a value and be subject to some level of rights. The testimony and the exhibits show that the interest was not created by the Tribe and that there was a legal action between the Tribe and the Grantor of the interest. It was undisputed that the federal court decision voided the rights of the Leelanau Indians, Inc. (LLI) to create leases before this lease was created. Any lease had to be created by the Appellee. There is no record that the Tribal Council or the housing agency created or ratified a lease. There was some evidence that the Council intended to ratify some leases, but no record that the vote was ever officially taken. . . .
   >
   > . . . Simply put, there was no loss to the Appellant. The lease restricted the valuation of the property to the lessee's residential use only. All leases were for tribal members and were not assignable without Council discretionary approval. . . .
   >
   > There was no property interest by the Appellant on the date of the eviction. This issue is affirmed.

   Raphael, 1999 WL 34986350, at *1-2.

2. In *Honie v. Hopi Tribal Housing Authority*, 1 Am. Tribal Law 346 (Hopi Tribe Appellate Court 1998), the court vacated the trial court's decision to certify a decision by a Hopi village regarding the assignment of a property lease:

   > A trial court has the authority to certify village orders in matters reserved to the villages. *Gaseoma v. The Hopi Tribe*, 1 Am. Tribal Law 268 [1997] . . . , citing Article III, Section 2(c) of the Hopi Constitution. . . . Certification

allows the trial court a means by which to formally recognize a village decision and to proceed to the enforcement of such village decisions with injunctive relief or other remedies.

A trial court, however, must hold an evidentiary hearing to determine whether all interested parties have been provided with a fundamentally fair opportunity to participate in the village decision-making process before the court can recognize and certify the village decision. At a minimum, all interested parties should be provided with adequate notice and a meaningful opportunity to be heard in the village decision-making process. . . . Only after the petitioner has established, through an evidentiary hearing, that the village has properly ensured that all interested parties have been provided with a fundamentally fair process in the village's decision-making process may the court certify the village decision and proceed to consider any available remedies in the courts.

Honie, 1 Am. Tribal Law at 351-52.

E. JURISDICTION

1. JURISDICTION UNDER TRIBAL LAW

Ross v. Sulu

Hopi Tribe Appellate Court, No. 88-AP-010, 1991.NAHT.000002 (July 5, 1991)

Before Sekaquaptewa, Chief Justice, and Abbey and Bender, Judges.

Factual and Procedural Background

This case involves a complaint for trespass to land filed in the Hopi Tribal Court by Plaintiff Sulu on behalf of the Tewa Kachina Clan of First Mesa Village. It calls for a determination of the jurisdiction of the Tribal Court, under the Hopi Constitution, to resolve conflicting land claims by different clans within a Hopi village. The case grows out of the following circumstances:

On September 4, 1987, the Hopi Butterfly-Badger Clan of First Mesa assigned to defendant Patsy Ross, a member of that Clan, a half-acre of land within the Village of First Mesa to be used as a home. The assignment was made on a Tribal Housing Authority Land Assignment form, and was signed by the male and female Butterfly-Badger Clan leaders and Kikmongwi of the Village of First Mesa. On September 8, 1988, Ross moved a mobile home onto the assigned land.

On September 9, 1988, Plaintiff Tom Sulu, Tewa Kachina Clan leader, filed a complaint in the Hopi Tribal Court on behalf of the Tewa Kachina Clan. The complaint alleged that the land onto which Ross had moved her mobile homes "lies within the territorial possession of the Tewa Kachina Clan" and that because Ross did not have the consent or authority of the Tewa Kachina Clan to reside on the land, she was a trespasser. The complaint sought a temporary restraining order and permanent injunction prohibiting Ross from setting up her mobile home on Tewa Kachina Clan land, an order requiring Ross to move her home, and damages. . . .

At trial, the court sought to determine which of the two competing clans — the Tewa Kachina Clan or the Hopi Butterfly-Badger Clan — had the right to assign the land in question. The court found that at some time in Hopi history the Hopi leaders had assigned certain lands in the First Mesa area to the Tewa people. The court then found, on the basis of evidence of recent use, that the land in question was in a Tewa area. The court granted Plaintiff Sulu's motion for directed verdict, found defendant Ross to be committing trespass, and enjoined her from maintaining a home on the land in question.

Defendant Ross's appeal to this court, raises the following issues:

1. Defendant alleges that the issues raised by the property dispute between the Tewa and Hopi Clans concern religious and political matters that are non-justifiable. Defendant alleges that, in any event, Hopi custom and Hopi Constitution require such property disputes to be resolved by traditional Village procedures rather than the Tribal Court.

2. Alternatively, defendant requests that the court find for her on the basis of Article III, Section 2 of the Hopi Constitution, which reserves to the Villages the assignment of farming land. Because the assignment to defendant was approved by the Village Kikmongwi, the traditional head of the Village recognized by Article III, Section 3 of the Hopi Constitution, defendant requests a finding that the land was assigned to her in accordance with the Constitution and, therefore, that defendant is not a trespasser.

3. Defendant requests alternatively that the court find that the Village of Tewa is a separate village, and dismiss the case for lack of subject-matter jurisdiction because disputes between villages are committed to the jurisdiction of the Hopi Tribal Council under Article VI, Section 1(h) of the Hopi Constitution. . . .

Discussion

Article III, Section 1 of the Hopi Constitution recognizes the Village of First Mesa as a single, self-governing village, consisting of the consolidated villages of Shitchumovi, Tewa and Walpi.[3] Article III, Section 2 of the Constitution reserves certain powers to such villages, including the power to assign farming land.[4] The parties in this case agree that the land in question here is farming land within the meaning of this provision. Accordingly, the power to assign the land at issue in this case is reserved to the Village of First Mesa.

With regard to the procedures through which land is to be assigned by the villages, Article VII, Section 1 of the Hopi Constitution provides that assignment of the use of farming land "shall be made by each village according to its established custom."[5] Hopi villages are free to adopt modern constitutions and governmental organization but, unless they do, they are considered as being

---

3. Article III, Section 1, provides: "The Hopi Tribe is a union of self-governing villages sharing common interests and working for the common welfare of all. It consists of the following recognized villages: First Mesa (consolidated villages of Walpi, Shitchumovi and Tewa) Mishongnovi, Kyakotsmovi, Sipaulavi, Bakabi, Shunopavi, Hotevilla, Oraibi, Moenkopi."

4. Article III, Section 2 provides: "The following powers . . . are reserved to the individual villages: . . . (d) To assign farming land, subject to the provisions of Article VII. . . ."

5. Article VII, Section 1 provides: "Assignment of the use of farming land within the traditional clan holdings of the villages of First Mesa, Mishongnovi, Sipaulavi, and Shunopavi . . . shall be made by each village according to its established custom. . . ."

under the traditional Hopi organization. That traditional organization recognizes the Kikmongwi of each village as the leader of the village.[6] The Village of First Mesa has not adopted a village constitution. The village, therefore, remains under the traditional Hopi organization, with the Kikmongwi as village leader.

These provisions of the Hopi Constitution, reserving certain powers to the Hopi villages, determine the outcome of the present case. The underlying dispute here is between two clans of the same, traditionally organized village. Each clan claims the right to assign the land in question. The determination of which clan has that right is to be made, not by the tribal court system, but by the village according to its established custom. Therefore, when the Tribal Court became aware that the case turned on an intravillage dispute between clans over a matter reserved for village decision, it should have dismissed the case for lack of jurisdiction, requiring the parties to seek resolution of the dispute through established customary village procedures. The Tribal Court's attempt to decide this dispute pursuant to its own procedures and substantive standards violated the expressly reserved constitutional right of the village to resolve the matter pursuant to its established custom. The reservation of village powers over certain matters [i]s an essential aspect of the Hopi Constitution, which recites that the Hopi Tribe is "a union of self-governing villages." Reservations of village authority are not to be lightly disregarded.

It might be argued here that the Village of First Mesa had already made such a resolution. Defendant Ross introduced a 1987 judgment, signed by the First Mesa Village Kikmongwi, assigning the land in dispute to her. From the record before us, however, we cannot tell whether or not this document was intended to constitute a village resolution of the disagreement as to rights in the land between the Hopi Butterfly-Badger Clan and the Tewa Kachina Clan. It is entirely possible that the Kikmongwi signed the document without being aware of the Tewa Kachina Clan's conflicting clauses. This 1987 document, therefore, cannot be considered on this record to constitute a village resolution of the conflict that gives use to this case.

Prior to trial in this case, the Tribal Court "remanded the matter to members of First Mesa Village in an attempt to reach a negotiated solution. That effort failed. This attempted negotiation did not satisfy the Hopi constitutional requirement that the matter be resolved according to the villages traditional procedures. The Tribal Court selected the negotiating parties, retained jurisdiction in the case, and ordered the parties to give a status report within a specified period. What is required is a decision [resolving] the dispute by the village according to procedures that it determines. . . .

The village procedures should be conducted through the leadership of the Kikmongwi, as explicitly recognized by the Hopi Constitution. Our decision today that the Tribal Court did not have jurisdiction to decide this dispute is limited to those cases where a disagreement between clans over which has the right to assign land is at the core of the case. Such clan disagreements are to be

---

6. Each village shall decide for itself how it shall be organized. Until a Village shall decide to organize in another manner, it shall be considered as being under the traditional Hopi organization, and the Kikmongwi of such village shall be recognized as its leader." Hopi Constitution, Art. III, Sec. 2.

resolved through established village custom rather than through tribal court adjudication. Our decision, however, does not apply in situations where there is no similar intravillage dispute between clans, each of which asserts the right to assign the land. If the person accused of trespassing on another's land has no claim of right flowing from a clan assignment, or if the validity of plaintiff's assignment through customary village procedures is undisputed, the plaintiff may have recourse to the Tribal Court to resolve a trespass claim. Thus, the ordinary trespass case can be brought in Tribal Court. . . . Only after the village resolves the underlying dispute pursuant to established custom can the parties come to Tribal Court for enforcement of their rights, [as] determined by the village, through trespass or other actions. . . .

The decision of the Tribal Court is vacated and the case is remanded to that Court with directions to dismiss for lack of jurisdiction.

NOTES

1. In *Medel v. Granados*, 2006 WL 6358377 (Nevada Intertribal Court of Appeals 2006), the court held that it had jurisdiction over all tribal lands in accordance with the tribal jurisdictional statute even where some of the land at issue was federal trust property:

> This Court agrees that the Washoe Tribe asserts broad jurisdiction over actions occurring within the Tribe's territorial jurisdiction, specifically allotments. The Tribe's Constitution defines "territorial jurisdiction" by stating that it applies to all tribal lands:
>
>> The Washoe Tribe takes jurisdiction over all Washoe Indian country, which shall extend to all tribal lands, including . . . the Washoe Pine Nut Allotments, held in trust by the United States, but on the Pine Nut Allotments, for hunting and fishing regulation purposes only. Territorial jurisdiction shall also extend to all lands hereafter acquired by or for the Washoe Tribe. Constitution and Bylaws of the Washoe Tribe of Nevada and California, Art. I, Sect. 1.
>
>> . . . The provisions of Section 1 of Article I of the Washoe Constitution were intended to assert broad general jurisdiction over all Washoe Indian country which includes the Washoe Pine Nut allotments. The language concerning hunting and fishing is clearly intended to narrowly apply to regulation of that subject matter, not to limit the overall civil and or criminal jurisdiction of the Washoe Tribe. . . . It is well settled law, as to civil disputes arising in Indian Country that tribal courts play such a vital role in tribal self-government, that interfering with a Tribe's jurisdiction is to interfere with an inherent attribute of sovereignty. . . . Here, the Pine Nut allotments are Indian Country within the above definition and are subject to the authority of the governing sovereign, the Washoe Tribe. Subsequently, Washoe, as a federally recognized tribe with inherent sovereign authority over its members and its territory is subject only to limitations imposed by Federal law. . . . Since this litigation involves only Indians, at least the same standards should be considered in confirming tribal jurisdiction. It is well settled law that tribal jurisdiction over tribal members is first and foremost a matter of internal tribal law. . . .

Further, we find no limitations imposed by Federal law. There is no general Federal statute limiting tribal jurisdiction over tribal members. There is no treaty or statute conceding the Washoe Tribe's civil jurisdiction over the Pine Nut Allotments. . . . There cannot be cessation of tribal jurisdiction by implication. Here, the Tribe has never ceded its civil jurisdiction. Thus, the Tribe's Constitutional provision concerning regulation of hunting and fishing on the Pine Nut allotments cannot be read in isolation and cannot be construed as ceding all of the Tribe's authority and jurisdiction.

Medel, 2006 WL 6358377, at *3-4.

2. However, in *Monteau v. Monteau*, 5 Am. Tribal Law 26 (Confederated Salish and Kootenai Tribes Court of Appeals 2004), the court held: "When proceeding *in rem*, the trial court cannot determine rights in property not within the territorial jurisdiction of the Tribes. The trial court lacked jurisdiction over the real property it awarded to the husband and the bank accounts it awarded to the wife. The trial court properly dismissed the action to the extent it dealt with property division." *Monteau*, 5 Am. Tribal Law at 34.

2. JURISDICTION UNDER THE FEDERAL *MONTANA* TEST

HOOVER V. COLVILLE CONFEDERATED TRIBES

Colville Confederated Tribes Court of Appeals, No. AP99-001, 29 Indian Law Rep. 6035, 2002.NACC.0000004 (March 18, 2002)

En Banc Before: Chief Justice ANITA DUPRIS, Justice ELIZABETH FRY, Justice DENNIS NELSON, Justice HOWARD STEWART, Justice EARL MCGEOGHEGAN, Justice DAVID BONGA, Justice EDYTHE CHENOIS, Justice CONRAD PASCAL, and Justice WANDA MILES, who contributed greatly to this opinion. Justice MILES passed away on November 12, 2001.

The opinion of the court was delivered by: FRY, J. . . .

Procedural History

Non-Indian Daniel Hoover (Hoover) filed an action in federal district court alleging the Colville Confederated Tribes (Tribes) lacked jurisdiction to regulate fee lands owned by him and located within the Colville Confederated Tribes Reservation. The district court determined the Colville Tribal Court had authority to determine its jurisdiction regarding Mr. Hoover's claim and ordered him to exhaust those remedies available in Tribal Court before seeking relief in the federal system.

The Tribes subsequently filed an action in Tribal Court seeking an injunction to restrain Hoover from developing his real property without complying with the provisions of the Colville Land Use and Development Code. The Tribal Court granted an injunction and Hoover appealed to this court arguing that the Tribes are without legal authority to regulate non-Indian fee lands located within their reservation.

Daniel Hoover died in 2000. The personal representative of his estate, Jerry Thon, has substituted in as plaintiff. . . .

[I.] Statement of Relevant Facts

[A.] History

Prior to the presence of the white man, the ancestors of the tribes and bands of the Colville Confederated Tribes[5] occupied an area comprised of what is now Eastern Washington, Southern Central British Columbia, and portions of Idaho and Oregon.

In 1872, President Grant created the Colville Confederated Indian Reservation by Executive Order — without a treaty and without the consent of the tribes and bands of Indians residing in the area. The original reservation was over three million acres in size, but was reduced to its present size of approximately one million four hundred thousand acres under an agreement dated May 9, 1891, when gold was discovered in the northern half of the Reservation.

The Reservation is located within portions of Okanogan and Ferry Counties in north central Washington State. . . . Approximately seventy-nine percent (79%) of the reservation lands are now held in trust for the Tribes and its members. The remainder is held by federal agencies or is owned in fee by Indians and non-Indians.

[B.] The Hellsgate Reserve

In 1977, the Tribes designated the southeast corner of the Reservation as the Hellsgate Game Reserve. The area was chosen because of its remote character, limited access, limited development, small population, natural geographic boundaries and critical range habitat. It is critical winter range habitat for deer, elk, and other wildlife.

The Reserve . . . is situated entirely within the exterior boundaries of Ferry County and contains slightly more than one hundred thousand acres.

Approximately 87% of the land within the Reserve is in trust status, 11% of the land is in non-Indian and Indian fee ownership, and the remaining 2% is owned by the Federal Bureau of Reclamation.

The Reserve contains no cities, towns, or areas of concentrated development or settlement. At the time of hearing, there were fourteen permanent homes and five summer cabins within its boundaries. Almost all the buildings existed prior to the Tribes' designation of the areas as a reserve and enactment of its Land Use and Development Code.

The Reserve is managed specifically for conservation of wildlife and native plants. The area plays an integral role in preserving game populations and maintaining the hunting and gathering traditions of the Tribes. It consists of diverse topography and habitat with rugged hill country, dry land range, clear streams and coniferous forests. It contains abundant and diverse wildlife, including elk and deer. Tribal members, whose average annual income is approximately $7,000.00, depend significantly on wildlife and plant life within the Reserve for cultural needs and sustenance.

The Tribes have managed and regulated the Reserve to preserve its natural and cultural values. They have implemented strict wildlife management practices, including restriction of camping and off-road vehicle use. . . .

---

5. The Colville Tribes consist of twelve distinct Tribes or Bands: San Poil, Nespelem, Colville, Okanogan, Methow, Wenatchee, Chelan, Entiat, Moses, Palouse, Chief Joseph Band of Nez Perce, and the Lakes.

The Hellsgate Reserve plays a significant role in the continuation of the Tribes' culture. It is a place designated to preserve their hunting and gathering traditions and allow for extended family camps. The camps are a valued part of tribal life and cultural survival; traditions which have passed down through generations.

The Reserve contains a variety of plants[7] used by tribal members for food, as medicine, and in traditional ceremonies required for continued survival of the Tribes' culture.

The plants and animals protected and preserved through comprehensive management of the Reserve are not only a food source, but also play a vital and irreplaceable role in the cultural and religious life of tribal members. Annual medicine dances, root feasts and ceremonies incorporate animal and plant life found within the Reserve. These dances, feasts, and ceremonies play an integral role in the well being and survival of the Tribes and their members.

[C.] Management and Regulation of the Reserve

The Tribes have managed and regulated the Hellsgate Reserve to preserve its natural and cultural values. Wildlife and fish are important to the Tribes' culture and provide an important food source to its members. The Tribes expend about three million dollars per year managing game, fish, and other species found within the Reservation. A significant portion of this money is earmarked for management activities and land acquisition within the Reserve.

In 1977, the Tribes, in cooperation with the United States Department of the Interior, acquired fifty head of elk from the Wind Caves National Monument in South Dakota to re-establish an elk herd on the Reservation for supplementation of subsistence deer herds. The Tribes' Fish and Wildlife Department determined the Hellsgate area was best suited for the elk, based upon extensive winter range habitat of the area. Since then, the elk, subject to comprehensive tribal management, have flourished, greatly increasing in number within the Reserve and in other areas of the Reservation. Estimates place the size of the herd within the Reservation at over eight hundred animals.

Hunting and fishing in the Reserve are limited. There is, for instance, a six-month subsistence deer season in effect elsewhere on the Reservation, while deer hunting within the Reserve has been limited to an annual nine-day buck hunt. Elk hunting, at the time of hearing, was limited to a restrictive lottery system. The Tribes do not permit non-member hunting on trust and fee lands within the Reserve. The no-hunting restriction on fee lands is through implementation of an intergovernmental agreement with the State of Washington.

. . . Tribal resource and law enforcement personnel devote significant portions of their time to [conservation and resource] management activities in the Reserve. These activities are funded by trust funds derived primarily from sales of timber and from grants and contracts through the Indian Self-Determination Act.

The Tribes permit timber harvests within the Reserve, provided they are conducted in a manner consistent with tribal wildlife management practices. Timber resources represented the largest revenue source for the Tribes at the

---

7. Culturally important plants include black camas, wild carrots, Indian potatoes, willow, rose bush, pine nut, black moss, huckleberry, and chokecherry.

time of hearing. All timber sales go through the Integrated Resource Management Planning (IRMP) process designed to minimize harm to the environment and to ensure compatibility with the purposes of the Reserve. The Tribes review timber harvest sales on fee lands within the Reserve in accordance with an intergovernmental agreement with the Washington State Department of Natural Resources and the Washington State Department of Ecology.

In 1992, the Tribes, Ferry County and Okanogan County entered into an Intergovernmental Land Use Planning Agreement (ILUPA) which provided for resolution of land use conflicts for private lands and a joint permit process for lands within Reservation boundaries. As a result of the agreement, the Tribes and the counties agreed on permit conditions for over two hundred developments and land use changes within the Ferry County side of the Reservation. In 1997, Ferry County unilaterally withdrew from the agreement, which remains in effect between the Tribes and Okanogan County.

Ferry County does not fund, participate in, or assist in the management or development of natural resources or wildlife within the Reserve. Land use plans for Ferry County treat the Reserve no differently than other rural areas within the county. It provides no zoning controls comparable to those of the Tribes.

[D.] Land Use and Development Code

... Prior to the adoption of the Land Use and Development Code in 1992, the Tribes issued public notices and held public meetings to solicit comments from both Indian and non-Indian communities. Land planning efforts included participation by the Reservation community and county governments.

The Code established zoning within the Reservation, including commercial, industrial, residential, special requirement, rural, forestry, game reserve, and wilderness. The zones set forth different levels of development and regulation consistent with the community values established in the Comprehensive Plan.

The Code requires all persons proposing subdivision and development within the Reservation, including the Reserve, to apply for a permit through the land use review process. Proposed land use activities are reviewed and permits are issued by the Colville Planning Department to ensure compatibility with the Code. There is provision for review of adverse decisions by the Land Use Review Board. Individuals questioning an appeal by the Land Use Review Board decision may seek judicial review in Tribal Court, a constitutionally separate branch of tribal government.

The Tribes permit a wide variety of development in highly populated areas of the Reservation having an adequate infrastructure. Some uses in less populated areas are severely restricted. In order to protect and provide for the general welfare of Reservation residents and to preserve the continued existence of the Tribes, a balance was achieved between the interests expressed by the general public and the protection of important cultural values. As a result, the Tribes have restricted development in certain areas. The Reserve is one such area and remains largely uninhabited and undeveloped in conformity with the Code.

The Tribes incorporate a holistic objective to planning based on ecosystems, watersheds, and natural boundaries. In 1994, the Tribes adopted an

Integrated Resource Management Plan (IRMP) based on their community values. The IRMP is an interdisciplinary method of evaluating impact to ecosystems and watersheds as a whole. The Plan has three phases[:] 1) data collection and analysis of past and current natural resources, 2) drafting a management document based upon membership values and desires, and 3) implementation and monitoring. A basic premise of the IRMP is that tribal members are experts when it comes to the use of their land.

[E.] Hoover's Development

Daniel Hoover purchased 72.75 acres of land within the boundaries of the Reserve in 1987. The land had been an allotment of a tribal member and was converted to fee status in 1925 under the Bureau of Indian Affair's policy of forced fee patents.[*]

Hoover built a residence on the property without notifying tribal officials and subdivided the land through Ferry County, selling two 20-acre parcels to non-Indians. Each parcel was developed with a single recreational-use cabin. One owner obtained a tribal permit to build with conditions for mitigating the impact on wildlife. In 1991, tribal officials became aware of the non-permitted land use by Hoover and notified him in writing of tribal land use requirements.

Hoover's remaining property consists of 32.75 acres adjoining tribally managed shorelands on Lake Roosevelt.[10] In 1992, Hoover sought to develop his property further by constructing a second residence without obtaining tribal permits. The Tribes and Ferry County attempted to resolve the permitting issues through an intergovernmental agreement mediation process (ILUPA). The process was cut short when Hoover sued the Tribes and Ferry County in federal court.

In December 1995, the Tribes became aware that Hoover was again attempting to subdivide his property further, without going through the Tribes' permitting process. The proposed subdivision of four lots comprised a "major sub-division" under the Tribes' Land Use and Development Code and required a conditional use permit. Under the Ferry County Zoning Code, it was considered a "minor sub-division," requiring little review and no evaluation of how it would impact the Reserve.

---

[*] *Author's Note:* The D.C. Circuit in *Covelo Indian Community v. Watt*, 1982 U.S. App. LEXIS 23138 at *8 n. 8 (D.C. Cir., Dec. 21, 1982) (citations omitted), defined forced fee patent claims as such:

> Forced fee patent claims refer to attempts to revoke fee patents erroneously issued by the Secretary of the Interior for lands that the United States had previously held in trust for the Indians. Congress has in the past allotted certain lands to individual Indians in trust. The United States holds these lands for the use and benefit of the allottee. While these lands are in trust status they are exempt from state ad valorem taxes and are subject to various restrictions. In 1906, Congress provided that the Secretary of the Interior could issue fee simple patents to an Indian before the trust period expired if the Secretary were satisfied that the allottee was competent and capable of managing his affairs. The issuance of a fee simple patent removed all restrictions, including immunity from taxation. The Secretary could issue a fee patent.

10. Lake Roosevelt is a lengthy man-made lake created by the construction of Grand Coulee Dam during the 1930's. The dam, in combination with others further down the Columbia River, virtually eliminated the annual salmon runs which had been a substantial food source for the Tribes.

The Tribes . . . notified [Hoover] in February 1996 that acting to subdivide, sell, and develop lots within the Reserve without obtaining requisite tribal permits constituted a violation of tribal law.

Hoover ignored the notice from the Tribes and submitted a final subdivision plat to Ferry County for recording. He indicated he planned to sell lots in a shoreline housing development without applying for approval from the Tribes.

[F.] Impact of Uncontrolled Fee Land Development with the Reserve

The population of north central Washington, including that of the Reservation, is growing rapidly. Ferry County more than doubled its population between 1970 and 1997, according to census data. Planning and zoning regulations were enacted by the Tribes to help address the impact of growth within the Reservation while attempting to preserve traditional community values.

Uncontroverted credible expert testimony and scientific studies presented at the hearing strongly indicate that unchecked increases in housing development within the Reserve will significantly adversely impact wildlife species and native plants. Specifically, species such as deer, elk, bear, cougar, and bald eagle are sensitive to human habitation and will decline in numbers with increased and uncontrolled housing development. Wildlife studies show increased housing will result in fewer mule deer. Studies also show forest and songbird species will decrease in number and bald eagles will nest further from shorelines when nearby housing developments appear.

Uncontrolled development will increase the number of roads, traffic, and off-road activity — all of which impact native wildlife and plants. Roads cause increased runoff and dust, which impact streams and watersheds. Roads divide wildlife corridors and create barriers to migration routes. Roads kill natural plant life and spread non-native noxious weeds, which crowd out native plants.

Increasing housing without land use controls will result in more septic systems, noise, dust, artificial lighting, wood use, smoke, and pets in natural areas. These factors negatively impact wildlife habitation.

The impact resulting from lack of land use control on fee lands within the Reserve is magnified because the fee lands are disproportionately located in low-lying areas adjoining water. Low elevation riparian lands within the Reserve are important components of the arid ecosystems on which wildlife depend, and are the most important winter range for deer and elk.

Native plants and animals within the Reserve are essential to ceremonies and other traditions of the Tribes. Tribal cultural practices such as camping, hunting, vision quests, and gathering medicines are not compatible with uncontrolled development and increased housing density. Uncontrolled development places at risk important components of the Tribes' cultural and religious traditions.

Unregulated development of fee lands within the Reserve would significant impact adjoining tribal trust lands. Increased car exhaust, wood smoke, water use, waste discharge, human activity, traffic, dust, garbage, and erosion from grading and construction, do not stop at fee land boundaries. The inability of the Tribes to apply comprehensive planning regulations to fee lands within the Reserve will substantially impair the Tribes' ability to preserve the general character, cultural and religious values, and natural resources associated with the Reserve.

The inability of the Tribes to fairly and impartially enforce comprehensive planning regulations to all lands within the Reserve presents a clear danger to the continued cultural identity and existence of the Tribes, and threatens the health and welfare of their members.

[II.] Issue

The sole issue before this court is whether real property owned by a non-Indian in fee is subject to zoning regulations of the Tribes when the property is within a Game Reserve situated entirely within the exterior boundaries of the Colville Confederated Tribes Reservation.

[III.] Discussion of Issue

. . . Federal courts have found congressional delegation of authority for tribes. *See Bugenig v. Hoopa Valley Tribe*, 229 F.3d 1210, 229 F.3d 1210 (9th Cir. 10/03/2000), (hereinafter *Bugenig I*), and *Bugenig v. Hoopa Valley Tribe*, 266 F.3d 1201 (9th Cir. 09/11/2001), (hereinafter *Bugenig II*), *United States v. Mazurie*, 419 U.S. 544 (1975), *Rice v. Rehner*, 463 U.S. 713 (1983). The statutory language delegating the requisite authority was viewed by Justice White, writing in *Brendale v. Confederated Tribes and Bands of the Yakima Indian Nation*, 492 U.S. 408 (1989), wherein he cited two statutes where Congress expressly delegated authority to Indian Tribes. . . .

The second statute cited by Justice White is the Clean Water Act, 33 U.S.C. §1377 et seq. It authorizes Indian tribes to be treated as states in setting clean water standards for federal Indian reservations. The term "federal Indian reservation" is defined as "all land within the limits of any Indian reservation under the jurisdiction of the United States government, notwithstanding the issuance of any patent, and including rights-of-way running through the reservation." 33 U.S.C. §1377(h). . . .

Congress has clearly delegated its authority to regulate water quality on federal Indian reservations to tribes meeting certain requirements. Challenges to its authority to do so have been rebuffed. *See Montana v. United States Environmental Protection Agency*, 137 F.3d 1135 (9th Cir. 1998), and *City of Albuquerque v. Browner*, 97 F.3d 415 (10th Cir. 1996).

The Tribes received authority from the federal Environmental Protection Agency in 1991 to enact water quality regulations for the entire reservation in accordance with the provisions of the Tribes' Constitution and Codes. This included fee lands owned by non-Indians within the boundaries of the Reservation. The Tribes were delegated authority to zone for control of water quality standards over Indians and non-Indians on the Colville Indian Reservation. We would be well advised to allow the Tribes to exercise zoning controls over land use even as they are appropriately exercising authority over water quality on their Reservation. *Cavenham Forest Products, Inc. v. Colville Confederated Tribes*, 1 CCAR 39 (Colville Confederated 02/22/1991). (recognizing Tribes' authority to require compliance with the Tribes' Land Use Ordinance by a non-Indian business on the Reservation). The *Cavenham* decision was based upon general principles of tribal sovereignty and applicability of the tests in the [*Montana v. United States*, 450 U.S. 544 (1981)] case.

Yet, there is an additional consideration in determining whether the Tribes' jurisdiction to regulate non-member fee land within the Reserve goes beyond the Clean Water Act. For this, we look to the *Montana* exceptions, and actions of the United States government in determining the character of Reserve.

[A.] The *Montana* Exceptions

The first *Montana* exception (consensual relationships) is not applicable to this case.

The second exception authorizes tribal regulation of "the conduct of non-Indians on fee lands within its reservation when that conduct threatens or has some direct effect on the political integrity, the economic security, or the health or welfare of the tribe." *Montana* at 565. The findings of fact show clearly that the requirements of the second exception have been fulfilled inasmuch as Hoover's proposed conduct (that of developing land for construction of additional residences within the Reserve) would affect the health and welfare of the members of the Tribes.

[1.] Health and Welfare

The average annual income of tribal members is thousands of dollars below the national poverty level and their employment rate is near fifty percent. Reduced economic circumstances and cultural traditions cause many members to depend on subsistence hunting of large game animals, primarily deer and elk. The dependence upon subsistence hunting is greater now than before construction of Grand Coulee Dam that, together with the construction of other dams downstream on the Columbia River, destroyed the salmon runs which had previously provided a substantial subsistence food source.

Hoover's planned development would have an impact on the ecology and environment because any increase in the number of homes within the Reserve would directly affect the deer and elk population. Were he granted permission to construct his development, the Tribes would have no ground to prevent other non-member fee owners from developing their properties within the Reserve. It is clear from the evidence adduced at trial that the Tribes had little choice in preventing Hoover from proceeding. They either had to allow him and others to build in the Reserve, and thus destroy or greatly diminish an important, necessary food and culture source, or prevent him from building and thus preserve a valuable source of subsistence hunting and cultural participation.

In addition to game animals, tribal members use many varieties of plants within the Reserve as a food source. The importance of the plants lies in their use for maintaining and preserving cultural traditions

[2.] Health and Welfare — Spirituality and Cultural Preservation

The trial court found[:]

> Plants and animals preserved through comprehensive management in the reserve are not only a source of food, but also play a vital and irreplaceable role in the cultural and religious life of Colville people. Annual medicine dances, root feasts, and ceremonies of the Longhouse religion all incorporate natural foods such as deer and elk meat and the roots and berries found in the Hellsgate Reserve. The ceremonies play an integral role in the current well being and future survival of Colville people, both individually and as a tribal entity. Finding of Fact 36.

Bugenig II is the only federal court in our experience to refer to the spiritual health of a tribe. It is well known in Indian Country that spirituality is a constant presence within Indian tribes. Meetings and gatherings all begin with prayers of gratitude to the Creator. The culture, the religion, the ceremonies — all contribute to the spiritual health of a tribe. To approve a planned development detrimental to any of these things is to diminish the spiritual health of the Tribes and its members.

The spiritual health of the American Indian is bound with the earth. Their identity as a people becomes invisible in the city, away from nature. It is the land and the animals which renew and sustain their vigor and spiritual health. . . .

The evidence is highly persuasive that the encroachment of human habitation would have a detrimental effect on the animals, plants, and herbs used for sustenance, medicinal, and ceremonial purposes — the continued existence of which is vital to the spiritual health of the Tribes and their members.

[B.] Implicit Authority

The United States Supreme Court has clearly stated that, aside from the *Montana* exceptions, Indian tribes may regulate non-member activities on reservations only when Congress has explicitly granted the tribes explicit authority to do so. We believe this approach unduly restrictive because it ignores the clear reality of circumstantial evidence. In almost all matters, courts should look at the totality of circumstances rather than seeking a specific mantra . . . and we see no rational reason to do otherwise here.

The Tribes' action in denying Hoover permission to develop his properties can be affirmed, at least in part, because of its authority under the Clean Water Act. Further analysis is instructive.

[1.] The Pacific Northwest Electric Power Planning and Conservation Act

Particularly germane to this case are the millions of dollars the federal government has provided the Tribes to purchase 9,272 acres of fee lands within the Reserve for the purpose of wildlife habitat enhancement.

The money for repurchase of fee lands within the Reserve was appropriated by Congress and distributed through the Bonneville Power Administration, an agency of the federal government. Congressional funding and authorization of this program is through the Pacific Northwest Electric Power Planning and Conservation Act of 1984, 16 U.S.C. 839 et seq. (hereinafter PNEPPCA).

The Act authorizes development of "regional plans and programs related to energy conservation, renewable resources, other resources, and protecting, mitigating, and enhancing fish and wildlife resources. . . ." 16 U.S.C. §839(3)(A).

The Reserve has been an ideal candidate to satisfy one of the Act's intended goals — the enhancement of fish and wildlife habitat. Funds have been appropriated through PNEPPCA to the Tribes for the purpose of protecting "renewable resources . . . and . . . enhancing fish and wildlife resources" within the Reserve. In accordance with a five-party agreement[16] with federal agencies and the Spokane Tribe of Indians, the Tribes retain primary management

---

16. The Lake Roosevelt Cooperative Management Agreement['s] participating parties consist of the National Park Service, the Bureau of Reclamation, the Bureau of Indian Affairs, the Spokane Tribe of Indians, and the Confederated Tribes of the Colville Indian Reservation.

authority of the portions of Lake Roosevelt within the Colville Indian Reservation. This includes Hoover's shoreline property.

[2.] Zoning Conflicts

The Clean Water Act expressly authorizes the Tribes to regulate water quality and sewer systems on the reservation, including the Reserve. We have found no other express congressional authority for the Tribes to regulate non-member fee lands. Arguably, this means all other zoning authority to regulate non-member fee lands within the Reserve resides with Ferry County. We see this as unworkable. Ferry County unilaterally withdrew from participation in the successful Interim Land Use Planning Agreement when Hoover filed his complaint in federal court. Ferry County has since approved development within the Reserve that is incompatible with the goals of the Tribes and federal government in maintaining the area in its natural pristine condition. It is well known in Indian Country that county governments do not, as a general rule, cooperate with Indian Tribes and do not provide the same level of services within reservations as they do in other areas of a county. We do not believe it [is] realistic to expect Ferry County Commissioners to be sympathetic with the Tribes' goal to regulate development within the Reserve in accordance with its land use regulations.

What then is the role of Ferry County regarding its zoning regulations applicable within the Reserve as to lot size and other building regulations? What is its interest in regulating zoning within a hundred thousand-acre game reserve, and how can it effectively adhere to its comprehensive plan when it does not have the authority to issue water quality regulations?

Clearly, the interests of Ferry County within the Reserve are minimal and are insignificant compared to those of the Tribes. The Tribes have multiple interests in the Reserve, not the least of which is retaining its culture, physical and spiritual health and welfare.

Again, we are of the opinion we should look at the totality of circumstances. We see the circumstances as this — the Tribes have express delegated authority to regulate water quality within the Reservation. The Tribes have enacted a Comprehensive Land Use and Development Code that is neutral in its application to Indians and non-Indians. The Tribes have closed the Reserve to unrestricted development and actively work to enhance its wildlife. The Reserve has a "vital and irreplaceable role in the cultural and religious life of Colville people." The large game animals within the Reserve are an important food source for the Colville people. Finally, Congress has appropriated millions of dollars for purchase of fee lands within the Reserve in order to help maintain the area in a natural state.

What are the interests of Ferry County vis-à-vis the Tribe? The Reserve is comprised of over one hundred thousand acres with less than twenty-five residential structures within it. Access to these permanent and summer homes is by a single road that traverses the length of the reserve. The Colville Tribal Police Department provides police protection. Emergency medical services are provided by the Colville Tribal Emergency Services.

Most of the structures, including Hoover's proposed development, are at or near the end of the road. Other than occasional road maintenance and sporadic police protection, the County appears to have little presence or interest in the Reserve. It does not appear to have any interest in determining the character of the land and certainly none in preserving the pristine nature of the land.

[3.] Characterization of the Reserve

The Tribes' ancestors and members have sustained themselves from the land for thousands of years. They harvested the roots and the berries from the plants for food and medicine; they caught salmon from the Columbia River, and they killed deer for meat. In 1977, with the Columbia River dammed and the salmon long gone, the Tribes acquired fifty head of elk to establish a large game animal to supplement the deer herds.

The elk were released in the Hellsgate area (the Reserve) because it was best suited to survival of the herd. This is the first record of initial efforts to characterize the area as a game reserve. The herd had now grown to over eight hundred animals and is subject to a closely regulated annual hunt.

In addition to introducing the elk herd, the Tribes and the federal government, for over ten years, have participated in a land buy-back program within the Reserve. The purpose of the program is to purchase fee lands and return them to their natural state. Over nine thousand acres have been purchased for this purpose—primarily with federal funds. The Tribes and the federal government are in the midst of a long-range plan to define and characterize the area as a natural habitat for plants and animals.

The Tribes, in addition to the buy-back program, have developed land use regulations for the Reserve. Public notice and public hearings were held prior to the adoption of the regulations. An appeals process with access to the tribal court was allowed. The regulations apply equally to tribal members and non-members—there is no preferential treatment.

The record is devoid of Ferry County's long-range plans for fee lands within the Reserve. However, a letter from the Ferry County Prosecuting Attorney dated August 12, 1991 was written in response to the Tribes' request for comments on its proposed Land Use and Development Code[, urging] the Tribes not to adopt the proposed Code as "there may be areas where enactments by other entities afford better protection of the environment and more orderly growth management." We have seen no evidence that this has occurred in the ten years since the letter was written.

We deduce from the record that there will be no additional land becoming available for development within the Reserve and that more fee lands will be purchased from non-Indians to be returned to their natural state. The result of this is predictable—services provided by Ferry County to non-Indians owning property in the Reserve will be diminished, along with the County's interest in the property. This will have little impact on non-Indians in the area, as public services such as fire and ambulance are being provided by the Tribes.

[IV.] Conclusion

The trial court correctly entered its Order permanently enjoining Daniel Hoover and those acting in concert with him from developing, improving, or otherwise changing the land use of his property within the Hellsgate Reserve without first obtaining the necessary permits from the Colville Tribes in conformity with the provisions of the Colville Land Use and Development Code. The order is AFFIRMED.

NOTES

1. Aside from the *Hoover* court's application of the *Montana* Test, the court adopts a "totality of the circumstances" test. What are the contours of the test, given the facts in this matter? Are they useful for application to other land uses in the Hellsgate Reserve? Or anywhere else in Indian country?

2. The *Hoover* court's application of the second *Montana* exception would seem to be sharply undermined, or even in direct conflict, with the United States Supreme Court's decision in *Atkinson Trading Co., Inc. v. Shirley*, 532 U.S. 645 (2001), which rejected claims by the Navajo Nation that it had taxing authority over non-tribal citizens on non-Indian-owned lands within the Navajo reservation. There, the Court denied that the fact that the Nation provided most of the public safety protections to the non-citizens had any relevance. Should that matter here? As we frequently must ask, why is the tribal court engaging in the *Montana* analysis at all? Or in the congressional delegation analysis?

3. The *Montana* Test does not apply when all parties to the matter are tribal citizens. This is an important jurisdictional fact that the parties may not assume to be relevant. In *Atkinson v. Beveridge*, 2000.NAFP.0000007 (Fort Peck Court of Appeals 2000), the court noted an instance in which the parties failed to properly plead this key jurisdictional fact:

   > It should be noted at the outset that nowhere in the Tribal Court record does it disclose that Roberta, Roy Emerson and Rose are tribal members. Accordingly, we labored under the assumption that we were dealing with the issue of whether our Tribal Court had subject matter jurisdiction involving a dispute over fee patented land owned by non-members. In her initial brief, Roberta briefly mentioned *Montana v. U.S.*, 450 U.S. 544, as standing for the proposition that Indian tribes lack power to regulate non-Indian hunting and fishing on reservation land owned in fee patented status. Roberta goes on to state that similar to the holding in *Montana*, "the Fort Peck Tribal Court lacks power to regulate access and recreational activities on property owned in fee patented status on the Fort Peck Indian Reservation." Regrettably, this reference to Montana further bolstered our assumption. Following oral argument, we learn that Roberta, Roy, and Rose are all members of the Fort Peck Tribes. Had we known the membership status of these litigants from the outset, we would not have placed the emphasis on *Montana*. It should be obvious that *Montana* has no application involving disputes over fee patented land within the exterior boundaries of the reservation when such land is owned by, and all of the litigants are tribal members, or have consented to Tribal Court jurisdiction. Although we sincerely regret sending our litigants on the proverbial "wild goose chase," we note with some relief that, those who were invited to that hunt were also those who scattered the geese in the first instance.

   Atkinson, at ¶20.

4. In *Delorme v. Stearns Bank*, 2002.NATM.0000001 (Turtle Mountain Band of Chippewa Indians Court of Appeals 2002), the court adjudicated an

on-reservation personal property repossession dispute by a non-Indian business:

> It appears from the cases discussing the *Montana* consensual relationship standard that the cause of action being asserted against the non-Indian must be pertaining to the consensual relationship between the Tribe and the non-Indian in order to confer subject matter jurisdiction upon the Court. . . . [*E.g.,*] *FMC v. Shoshone-Bannock Tribe*, 905 F.2d 1311 (9th Cir. 1990) (tribal court had jurisdiction over non-Indian who failed to comply with Indian preference law because non-Indian was working on tribal contract at the time). . . .
>
> However, not only is there a consensual relationship between the instant parties to this dispute in the form of a lease agreement, there is action taken by the Defendant on the Turtle Mountain Indian reservation, related to that consensual relationship, that allegedly violated tribal law. The tribal court, therefore, appears to have jurisdiction over the instant dispute under the first prong of the *Montana* test.

Id. at ¶¶26, 28.

5. In *Hoopa Valley Tribe v. Bugenig*, 5 NICS App. 37 (Hoopa Valley Tribal Court of Appeals 1998), the court affirmed the authority of the tribe to prohibit logging in an area the tribal council labeled a "buffer zone" around a tribal sacred site:

> [T]ribal elder Byron Nelson, Jr., testified,
>
>> The White Deerskin Dance is a world renewal dance. And the intent of the dance . . . is to put everything back in balance that's gotten out of balance from dance to dance. And that's the main emphasis of the dance, it is not only for the good of the Hoopa Tribe, but for all people.
>
> Mr. Nelson further stated:
>
>> This dance is the most important dance site of . . . all dances that the tribe has, particularly the White Deerskin Dance. The site is very ancient. There's scientific evidence that indicates it could be one of the oldest dance sites, oldest ceremonies in the country. The White Deerskin Dance is called Along the River Dance. As you can clearly see, this particular site isn't really along the river.
>>
>> When I was doing research on the history book, I kept running across these legends that told when the river went out the other way, meaning going left as it left the valley instead of the right direction. It goes now easterly toward Weitchpec.
>>
>> And so I had these geologists go out and study the area, and they found that the river did in fact go out to the left up through where Beaver Creek is now and come out in Martins Ferry in the Klamath River. And they stated that it was at least fifty-thousand years ago that the river did go off this way.
>>
>> So this dance and the trail would very well have gone along the river a long time ago. And the dance site was along the river at one time. So this site is very old. . . . This points to indicating that this is a very ancient site and it's been going on for thousands of years and it should be protected.

The book referred to in Mr. Nelson's testimony, entitled *OUR HOME FOREVER: The Hupa Indians of Northern California* (Nelson, Byron; Hupa Tribe, copyright 1978) contains an extended reference to the significance of the White Deerskin Dance to the Hupa people:

Beyond the coastal mountains of northwestern California, the Trinity River runs through a rich valley which has always been the center of the Hupa world, the place where the trails return. There, the legends say, the people came into being, and there they have always lived. From this central valley, Hupa land spread out in every direction. Starting at the junction of the Klamath and Trinity rivers, the boundary of Hupa territory ran west through the Bald Hills. It turned south along the divide between Pine and Redwood creeks, following the divide to the Grouse Creek area. There it headed east, crossing the Trinity at Cedar Flat. It ran north through the Trinity Alps, around Trinity Summit, and back to the river junction following a line west of Red Cap Creek. Within this land were fields of grass; groves of pine, madrona, and oak; streams, which supported many fish, birds, and animals; and mountain forests of pine, yew, fir, and oak filled with wildlife. The Hupa used all of these resources, but they made their homes and villages beside the Trinity River, in the valley from which they took their name.

At the very heart of that valley was *Takimildin*. This village known as the "Place of the Acorn Feast" was the site of three Hupa ceremonies; the place from which the tribe's main spiritual leader was chosen, and the spiritual center for the people of the valley. For longer than any man could remember, the sacred house had stood there. For thousands of years, spiritual leaders and members of the tribe had come here to pray and meditate, and dancers had met outside the big house on the night before the most sacred White Deerskin Dance to practice. From time to time, fire or flood destroyed the wooden walls of the big house, but the Hupa people always rebuilt it on its original, sacred foundations.

Long before the White Deerskin Dance began in late August or early September, the people of *Takimildin* and *Medildin* began their preparations.

Throughout the years the men worked on the regalia the dancers would use. They stuffed the heads of unusually marked white deerskins which gave the dance its name. These carefully prepared, decorated deerskins were considered tribal property. The dancers held them in trust. Although a child could inherit dance regalia, no individual could buy or sell the skins. Because the White Deerskin Dance revolved around *Takimildin* and the sacred house, the spiritual leader of *Takimildin* began the preparations for the dance each year. Then each district set up three of the six camps which would be used during the ten-day dance. Women prepared baskets of salmon and acorn soup and venison for the feasts. Dancers checked their costumes and rehearsed their steps. Peacemakers worked to settle any unresolved feuds, since the dance could not begin as long as conflict, dissension, or bad feeling remained in the valley. Those who had called the dance had to make a payment to any family in which there had been a death during the year. Holding a dance without this settlement would have offered an insult to the family's grief. Only when all of these things had been done could the dance begin.

The dancers met at *Takimildin*, and all of the people went by canoes to *Xowunkut*, the first dance place. There the spiritual leaders prepared the dance grounds, the women organized the feast, and the dancers dressed and painted themselves. When all was ready, dancers from one of the two districts took their places. At the center of the line stood the singer. He wore a headband of painted buckskin decorated with strips of wolf hair, and an open twine net which reached to his shoulders. On either side of him, the dancers who carried the deerskins formed a line. They wore headbands, but no nets. When the singer began, the dancers moved back and forth. Two dancers, who wore headdresses of sea lion tusks with closely twined nets which hung to their waists, carried red or black obsidian blades. Starting at opposite ends, they danced back and forth in front of the line of men holding the deerskins. When the dancers from the first district had completed a set, dancers from the other district took their places. The dance went on in this way through the afternoon.

After an evening of feasting and celebration, the people moved downriver to *Tsemeta*, just below the mouth of Hostler Creek, for the next dance. They danced, feasted, and played games there. Then came the Boat Dance. Dancing in four large dugout canoes, the dancers drifted downriver toward Meskut. Near the village the four canoes came toward the bank together and then backed out into the river ten times, then paddled forward and back before they landed. Then the people went to the dance grounds for the Mock Dance. This dance received its name because the dancers performed it like the regular dance, but substituted funny or improper things for those usually done. They might, for example, carry ordinary rocks in place of the rare obsidian blades. After dancing at *Meskut*, the people moved to *Tceindeqotdin* and *Tselundin* to repeat the dances and feasts. At *Tceindeqotdin* they enjoyed a day of rest, gambled and played games. Then they walked to the next dance site at the end of the valley beneath Bald Hill. For the last dances of the ceremony, they moved to *Noltukalai*, the place "among the oak tops" on Bald Hill. There, the legends say, the immortals watched the people of the valley dance with the precious white deerskins and the sacred obsidian blades.

Bugenig, 5 NICS App. at 38-41.

The Hoopa Tribal Council, after a significant public comment and approval process, adopted laws designed to protect these sacred sites.

> In September 1994, the Hoopa Valley Tribe notified all land owners within that portion of the reservation known as Bald Hill of a proposal which would, among other things, establish a buffer zone of one-half mile around the tribe's sacred White Deerskin Dance area and trail. . . .
>
> The harvest management plan included as one of its goals, to "*protect cultural and religious resources within the proposed sale area.*" . . .
>
> Among the issues was listed the following:
>
> 5. Buffer for Deerskin Dance Trail:
>
>> —A one-half mile no-action buffer on either side of the trail and surrounding the site is proposed for any projects initiated by this process. Public input as to the adequacy of buffer is requested.
>>
>> —Timber harvest may be proposed on fee land within the trial buffer. Can the Council regulate harvest on fee land to protect

cultural sites? Forestry will consult with the BIA regarding this potentially precedence-setting action.

In addition to notifying all tribal allottees, the non-tribal owners of six parcels of fee land within the Bald Hill area, including the Gould Family Trust, were mailed a copy of the project proposal and request for public involvement, which was captioned as follows:

> BALD HILL LANDOWNERS: This letter outlines proposed timber harvest activities that could affect you or your property. Please review and contact Tribal Forestry or your Council Representative if you have any questions or comments.

. . . Coincident with the notice and public hearings being conducted, the Hoopa Valley Tribe prepared an archaeological evaluation of the proposed timber harvest area and enlisted the participation of the Bureau of Indian Affairs in initiating a consultation with the State of California under Section 106 of the National Historic Preservation Act. The BIA letter stated in part:

> The results of [the] studies documented the presence of two archaeological/cultural sites in the APE that are evaluated as potentially eligible for inclusion on the National Register of Historic Places. The site of the White Deerskin Dance Grounds and trail is considered very significant to the tribe.

The letter further stated:

> As you can see from the enclosed AE document, the Hoopa Valley Tribe has prepared a plan to restrict any logging activities in the vicinity to the White Deerskin Dance Ground and associated trail that should avoid all impacts to the area, with the exception of minor visual impacts to the surrounding setting. The tribe will provide a one-half mile buffer around the site for logging activity avoidance and will also restrict logging traffic in the area during the actual dance activities.

On January 28, 1995, following extensive consultations with tribal leaders involved in tribal ceremonial dances, two public hearings and other public discussions in open tribal council meetings, the Hoopa Valley Tribal Council adopted a modified timber harvest plan for FY-95 that included the following listed mitigation measures:

> CULTURAL 1) A ONE-HALF MILE BUFFER AROUND THE WHITE DANCE GROUND ON BALD HILL AND THE TRAIL LEADING TO IT WILL BE MAPPED AND ADHERED TO IN ALL ACTIVITIES ASSOCIATED WITH THE 1995 BALD HILL TIMBER SALE. NO TIMBER HARVEST UNITS OR OTHER TIMBER SALE-RELATED ACTIVITY (EXCEPT LOG TRUCKS AND OTHER VEHICLES PASSING THROUGH BUFFER ZONE ON MAIN ROADS) WILL BE LOCATED WITHIN THE BUFFER ZONE. THIS PROHIBITION OF ACTIVITIES WILL APPLY TO TRIBAL TRUST LAND, TRUST ALLOTMENTS, AND FEE LAND WITHIN THE ½ MILE BUFFER.
>
> CULTURAL 2) ON THE FRIDAY AND SATURDAY* WHEN THE WHITE DEERSKIN DANCE IS HELD ON BALD HILL, LOG HAULING FROM THE BALD HILL 1995 TIMBER SALE WILL CEASE, TO MINIMIZE DISTURBANCE TO THE DANCERS AND THOSE ATTENDING THE DANCE.
>
> *Actual dates will be determined by Dance Leaders.

The Hoopa Valley Tribal Council gave notice of this action to all Bald Hill land owners both by letter and by publication in a local newspaper on January 25 and February 1, 1995.

Bugenig, 5 NICS App. at 42-44.

The court applied federal law in finding tribal authority to create the buffer zones:

> Both Appellant Bugenig and Respondent Hoopa Valley Tribe correctly point to the United States Supreme Court decisions in *Montana v. United States*, 450 U.S. 544 (1981) and *Brendale v. Confederated Tribes and Bands of the Yakima Indian Nation*, 492 U.S. 408 (1989) as providing the legal standards by which the facts of this dispute must be measured. The court below relied upon the *Brendale* clarification of the so-called *Montana* exceptions in concluding that jurisdiction over the logging activities conducted on Appellant Bugenig's fee land was properly the subject of tribal jurisdiction. . . .
>
> In *Brendale*, the Court . . . held that the Yakima Tribe possessed zoning authority over the Brendale property. The similarities between the Brendale property, located in an area of the Yakima Indian Reservation that remains 97 percent tribally controlled, and where "the tribe has preserved the power to define the essential character of that area" (*Brendale* at 3013) and the Bugenig land, located on a reservation that remains nearly 99 percent tribal and within an area of paramount spiritual importance to the Hupa people draws our attention.
>
> In developing a standard of comparison for determining the right of a fee landholder to develop his parcel "without regard to an otherwise common scheme" (*Brendale* at 3014), Justice Stevens asked, "More simply, the question is whether the owners of the small part of fee land may bring a pig into the parlor." He went on to state:
>
>> [T]he fact that a very small proportion of the closed area is owned in fee does not deprive the tribe of the right to ensure that this area maintains its unadulterated character. This is particularly so in a case such as this in which the zoning rule at issue is neutrally applied, is necessary to protect the welfare of the tribe, and does not interfere with any significant state or county interest. (*Brendale* at 3015.)
>
> At trial, the court found that "[b]y conducting logging activities not in compliance with tribal law, the defendant acted in contravention of tribal law, threatening and physically disturbing the integrity and sacred status of the White Deerskin Dance area and Trial [sic]." The court also found that the activity "threatened the health and welfare of the tribe and the Hoopa Valley People's customs and traditions. (Decision and Order at page 10.)
>
> The court further stated, "The Hoopa Valley Tribe has the power and authority to define areas of sacred significance and through establishment of the buffer no-cut zone in the Bald Hill area, has exercised that power. . . ."
>
> Our attention is drawn to the footnote accompanying the case law cited by the Supreme Court in support of the second *Montana* exception, wherein the Court stated:
>
>> As a corollary, this Court has held that Indian tribes retain rights to river waters necessary to make their reservation livable. *Arizona v. California*, 373 U.S. 546, 599 (1963).

Given that logic, it would seem to follow that a timber harvest regulation, neutrally applied, the purpose and effect of which is to preserve the sanctity of the Hoopa Tribe's most sacred spiritual location for the present and future use of tribal members would be a right retained by the Hupa people to ensure that their reservation remained livable. Or as Justice White would have it, the Hoopa Valley Tribe has neither relinquished nor abrogated, in the fact of Appellant Bugenig's effort to "bring a pig into the parlor" to the White Deer-skin Dance Ground, its inherent sovereign authority "to ensure that this area maintains its unadulterated character." (*Brendale* at 3015.)

Bugenig, 5 NICS App. at 46, 48-49.

Roberta Bugenig challenged the jurisdiction of the Hoopa Valley Tribe in federal court, but the Tribe prevailed in an important *en banc* opinion by the Ninth Circuit Court of Appeals. *See Bugenig v. Hoopa Valley Tribe*, 266 F.3d 1201 (9th Cir. 2001) (en banc), *cert. denied*, 535 U.S. 927 (2002). The court's reasoning was not that the Tribe had satisfied the *Montana* Test, but that Congress in ratifying the Hoopa Valley Tribe's Constitution in the Hoopa-Yurok Settlement Act effectively delegated federal authority to the Tribe to regulate non-Indians within the Hoopa Square.

3. JURISDICTION OVER OFF-RESERVATION TRIBAL LANDS

Niagara Aerospace Museum v. Seneca Niagara Falls Gaming Corp.

Seneca Nation of Indians Court of Appeals, No. 0179-05-01 (April 13, 2007)

Before Irma L. Cooper, Presiding Judge; Luana Jimerson; and Irene Warrior[*]
Per Curiam

I. Procedural History and Relevant Facts

... On July 19, 2005, Appellee Seneca Niagara Falls Gaming Corporation (hereinafter "Seneca") brought suit in the Peacemakers' Court, Cattaraugus Reservation, against Appellant Niagara Aerospace Museum (hereinafter "Aerospace"), seeking to evict Aerospace from the Seneca Office Building located in Niagara Falls, New York.

It appears that Seneca owns the building in fee simple. Seneca had purchased the office building using funds appropriated for the reacquisition of lost Seneca lands in accordance with the Seneca Land Claims Settlement Act of 1990, 25 U.S.C. §1774f(c). Aerospace held a lease entitled it to occupy the first three floors of the office building. ...

On the merits, the Peacemakers' Court found that a valid lease agreement exists between Seneca and Aerospace, that Aerospace violated the lease agreement, and granted Seneca's petition to evict Aerospace from the premises. ...

II. Jurisdiction

As always, this Court must consider first whether the courts of the Seneca Nation have jurisdiction over this matter. *See* Const. of the Seneca Nation of

---

[*]*Disclosure:* The author of this book participated in the case as a consultant to the Seneca Court of Appeals.

INDIANS OF 1848 (hereinafter "Seneca Constitution") §IV, ¶6; JUDICIARY ACT §4.1; CIVIL PROCEDURE RULES §§2-101–2-108. We conclude for the reasons below that Seneca courts do have jurisdiction to resolve this dispute.

The Peacemakers' Court held that it had jurisdiction over the dispute because the land had been purchased using Seneca land claims settlement funds and, in addition, because:

> [T]his land was subsequently accorded restricted fee status by operation of law, which means that it is Indian country, held in the same legal manner as previously existing Nation lands, such as the Cattaraugus, Allegheny and Oil Springs Indian Reservations of the Seneca Nation of Indians, and thus is subject to the jurisdiction of the Seneca Nation.

[Lower court opinion] at 3 (citing February 5, 2004 Internal Memorandum of the United States Dept. of Interior and November 12, 2002 Letter from United States Secretary of Interior Gayle A. Norton to then–Seneca Nation [p]resident Cyrus Schindler).

Seneca Nation courts have expansive jurisdiction and must decide matters "arising under th[e] Constitution, the customs or laws of the Nation, and to any case in which the Nation, a member of the Nation or any person or corporate entity residing on, organized on, or doing business on any of the Reservations shall be a party." SENECA CONST. §4, ¶6. In promulgating the rules of civil procedure for Seneca courts, the Seneca Nation of Indians Tribal Council explained that Seneca courts are courts of "general jurisdiction." CIVIL PROCEDURE RULES §2-101. Seneca courts have jurisdiction over persons and property of Seneca members and Seneca corporations and the persons and property of those non-members and non-residents engaged in disputes with Seneca members and corporations. *See id.* ("The Peacemakers Courts of the Seneca Nation of Indians shall have . . . jurisdiction . . . over all persons including corporation(s) . . . over all property . . . of members and non-members in dispute, and causes of action arising between persons including corporations . . . , and disputes and causes of action between non-resident and Tribal members. . . .").

The territorial jurisdiction of Seneca courts includes the persons and property at issue in this dispute. Section 2-103(a) provides, "The jurisdiction of the Seneca [courts] as exercised in these rules of civil procedure shall extend to all lands now within the Seneca Nation of Indians Reservations or *which may hereinafter be added thereto* . . ." (emphasis added). Of critical import is the next subsection: "To the extent not prohibited by federal and state law the jurisdiction of the Seneca Nation of Indians and its Peacemaker[s] Courts shall extend beyond the territorial limitation set forth [in subsection (a)] to effectuate the jurisdictional provisions [of sections 2-104–2-108]" (emphasis added). Finally, section 2-104(b)(3) provides for personal jurisdiction in a case like this one:

> (b) . . . [T]he Peacemaker Courts shall have civil jurisdiction over the following persons . . . :
>
> . . .
>
> (3) Any person who owns, uses or possesses *any property* with the Nation for any civil cause of action . . . arising from such ownership, use or possession. ([E]mphasis added.)

What is clear from these provisions is that the Seneca Constitution and the Seneca Civil Procedure Rules authorize Seneca courts to take jurisdiction in these matters. For our purposes, the jurisdiction of the Seneca Nation's courts is limited only by express prohibitions of federal and state law. *See* CIVIL PROCEDURE RULES §2-103(b). Absent an express federal or state prohibition, this Court must hold that the jurisdiction of Seneca courts expands beyond the boundaries of Seneca Reservations and may include territories owned by the Nation in fee simple located outside of the federally-recognized boundaries of the Nation's Reservations.

Aerospace nonetheless argues that this Court has no *territorial* jurisdiction over this matter.[1] . . . Aerospace's arguments rest in large part on federal Indian law. In particular, Aerospace insists that only the Secretary of Interior can issue a finding or determination that off-reservation Seneca-owned fee lands are "reservation" lands for purposes of determining the jurisdiction of Seneca courts. . . .

Aerospace is mistaken about both the plain language of this Court's rules and about federal Indian law. In this instance, we must determine Seneca court jurisdiction not in accordance with federal Indian law, but in accordance with Seneca law. *See generally* SENECA CONST. §IV, ¶6. One oft-misunderstood tenet of federal Indian law is that federally-recognized limitations on tribal jurisdiction apply only in federal courts. *Cf. Johnson v. M'Intosh*, 21 U.S. 543, 593 (1823) (noting that a sale of land by an Indian to a non-Indian might not be enforceable in American courts, but it would be enforceable under tribal law). Aerospace insists that the Secretary of Interior has not declared that the Seneca Office Building property enjoys "Reservation" status, . . . but the question of whether the federal government recognizes "Reservation" status is fundamentally irrelevant to our query.

Seneca rules require this Court only to review federal and state law (and Seneca law) to determine if there is an express prohibition on the exercise of tribal court jurisdiction in this kind of matter. Aerospace proffers no such federal or state prohibition and we find none as well. Seneca court rules are clear that this Court must interpret the extent of Seneca court jurisdiction liberally in order to effectuate the purposes of the Constitution and the court rules. *See* CIVIL PROCEDURE RULES §2-103(b). To accept Aerospace's argument would be to accept a limitation on Seneca court jurisdiction that is not mandated by either Seneca or foreign law. We decline this day to accept Aerospace's invitation to recognize illusory limitations on Seneca court jurisdiction. . . .

NOTE

1. The *Niagara Aerospace Museum* court did not delve into the question of whether federal law foreclosed the tribal court's jurisdiction over the non-tribal citizen leaseholders. But other courts must engage in that analysis. In *Smith v. Eckhart*, 2000.NACT.000006 (Crow Court of Appeals 2000), the court examined its jurisdiction over a boundary dispute between two

---

1. A careful review of the arguments advanced by Aerospace indicates that Aerospace does not contest the personal or subject matter jurisdiction of Seneca courts. . . .

trust allotments and in which the United States technically owned the land in trust:

> Crow Tribal Code [s]ection 3-2-204 confers jurisdiction to determine owner-ship rights and other interests in real property "limited only by federal law."

In this case, the Tribal fencing ordinance provides another source of juris-diction under Tribal law. Section X of Ordinance No. 1, adopted by Tribal Resolution No. 75-22 (April 12, 1975), provides:

> Jurisdiction is hereby conferred upon the Crow Tribal court, also known as the Court of Indian Offenses, and with the assistance of the Department of Interior through the Federal Courts, to adjudicate all disputs [sic] arising hereunder with the authority to apply any applicable federal law or regulation, any Tribal custom or law, or any applicable law of the state.

. . . Thus, both specific grants of jurisdiction refer to limitations of federal law, or assistance by the Federal Courts. These references, and the federal courts' jurisdiction to adjudicate interests in Indian allotments under 25 U.S.C. §345 and 28 U.S.C. §1353, raise a question of whether Tribal Court jurisdiction is pre-empted by, or concurrent with, that of the Federal courts.

We first reviewed a similar question in *Warren v. Gardner*, Civ. App. Dkt. No. 95-095 (Aug. 21, 1997), 1997 CROW 1, which involved a dispute over payment for an appraisal of Crow trust land. In *Warren*, this court held that a contract to appraise trust land did not directly or indirectly affect title to the land, and therefore was not subject to any exclusive federal-court jurisdiction which may exist to adjudicate interests in Indian allotments. *Id.* at ¶¶17-18.

Later, in *Lande v. Schwend*, Civ. App. Dkt. No. 92-30 (Mar. 4, 1999), 1999 CROW 1, this court sustained the Tribal Court's jurisdiction of a dispute involving payment for and tortious interference with a competent lease on Crow trust land. We distinguished the cases barring Tribal courts from order-ing federal officials to take certain actions. We also reviewed conflicting authority from the Eighth Circuit on Tribal Courts' jurisdiction to divide trust land in a divorce, or to recognize an easement across trust lands. *Id.*, ¶¶37-38 and 41. Our holding in *Lande* was based on the lack of controlling federal statutory or decisional law to the contrary, the importance of trust land to Tribal sovereignty, *see United States v. Plainbull*, 957 F.2d 724 (9th Cir. 1992), and the special provisions of the Crow Allotment Act allowing Crows to lease their own trust land without BIA approval. *Id.* at ¶¶42-43.

Before determining jurisdiction in the present case, it is important to understand the scope of the Tribal Court's judgment. This case was not brought as a "quiet title action," *i.e.*, to forever establish the legal boundary between the two allotments against all claimants. Although the Crow Tribal Code does not prescribe a special form for quiet title actions, such a com-plaint filed under State law would need to name all known owners of the property as defendants, along with "all other persons, unknown, claiming or who might claim any right . . . adverse to Plaintiff's ownership[.]" *See* MONT. CODE ANN. §70-28-104.

In the present case, the Complaint only sought to enjoin the person who lived on Allotment 1821 from interfering with the fence construction, and the Plaintiffs never made any attempt to serve process on all the other own-ers. The judgment on its face only binds the four named Defendants. As further explained below, other persons who own an interest in Allotment 1821 could still bring a new case to challenge the location of the boundary line if they can show that the Tribal Court's judgment and the BLM survey were erroneous. Thus, the Tribal Court's judgment in this case came close, but did not permanently adjudicate title to trust land.

Smith, at ¶¶18-25.

4. JURISDICTION OVER FEE LAND WITHIN RESERVATION BORDERS

ATKINSON V. BEVERIDGE

Fort Peck Court of Appeals, No. 328, 2 Am. Tribal Law 197, 2000.NAFP.0000007
(May 16, 2000)

The opinion of the court was delivered by: GARY P. SULLIVAN, Chief Justice
[The lower court granted an order restraining Robera Boyd Beveridge from blocking Rose and Denver Atkinson from crossing the Beveridge parcels to reach the Atkinson parcel.]

Brief Factual History and Procedural Overview

Appellant Roberta Boyd Beveridge (Roberta), a Tribal member, owns parcels 9, 10, and 11, Township 27 North, Range 51 East, M.P.M., Roosevelt County, MT, all of which is fee patented land lying within the exterior boundaries of the Fort Peck Reservation. Adjacent to Roberta's land is several acres that have accreted over the years. On or about June 28, 1999, she requested that the Fort Peck Tribes Executive Board grant her an easement over Tribal Lands in order that she might care for her livestock and otherwise maintain her property. On June 28, 1999, the Fort Peck Tribes granted the appellant the easement requested, conditioned upon her agreement to allow public access over her fee patented land.

At some point following the issuance of the easement by the Fort Peck Tribes, Roberta constructed a fence across her property, effectively denying access to anyone attempting to use the access road by vehicle. Roberta states that by constructing this fence she was not denying public access over her land, but rather, she was simply restricting such access to pedestrian traffic. She contended that vehicles entering onto her property became a nuisance too great to bear and that such vehicular traffic disturbed her quiet enjoyment of the property.

Rose and Denver Atkinson own property adjacent to Roberta's parcels and the land which has accreted. Roberta's fence effectively blocks Rose and Denver's vehicular ingress and egress from their property. . . .

Discussion

. . . Roberta contends that, "although the Tribal Court has personal jurisdiction, it lacks subject matter jurisdiction regarding the resolution of the ownership right of land accreting to (Roberta's) fee patent property." She goes on to assert that Rose and Denver's claim "involves the use and ownership rights of land owned by (Roberta) in fee patent status as well as land accreting thereto."

To support her position, Roberta cites *Woodtick v. Crosby*, 544 P.2d 812, a 1976 Montana Supreme Court case, which in turn, cites two United States Supreme Court cases, *Dickson v. Luck Land Co.* (1917) 242 U.S. 371; 37 S. Ct. 167 and *Larkin v. Pough* (1928) 276 U.S. 431; 48 S. Ct. 366. None of these cases involved Tribal Court jurisdiction, nor do they purport to confer general jurisdiction to State Courts regarding fee patented land within Indian Country.

In *Woodtick*, the plaintiff, a member of the Crow Tribe, petitioned a Montana District Court to cancel a deed given to defendant, alleging that by this deed the defendant became the non-Indian owner of more acreage of land within the Crow Indian Reservation than permitted under the provisions of the Crow Allotment Act and, therefore, pursuant to the explicit language of that Act, the deed was void. The District Court dismissed plaintiff's case stating that it lacked subject matter jurisdiction. The Montana Supreme Court acknowledged that Montana state courts "have jurisdiction over (fee patented land lying within the boundaries of an Indian reservation) only to the extent granted by Congress." The Woodtick court, in reversing the dismissal, went on to hold that Montana law ruled in that case because Congress has explicitly said that it does, citing the language of 25 U.S.C. 349, ". . . when the lands have been conveyed to the Indians by patent in fee . . . then each and every allottee shall have the benefit of and be subject to the laws, both civil and criminal of the State. . . ."

The obvious import of §349, as stated by the Ninth Circuit[,]

> is to define the status of the individual Indians in their relation to the state. Having been released from tutelage, the Indians are thereafter to be regarded as members of the community with the privileges and duties incident to citizenship. *Montana Power Co. v. Rochester*, 127 F.2d 189, 192 [(1942).]

There is nothing in the language of §349 that would even remotely suggest that the U.S. Congress was granting exclusive jurisdiction to State courts over matters involving fee patented land lying within the exterior boundaries of an Indian reservation. If Congress had intended to grant exclusive jurisdiction in such matters, it could have easily done so. In fact, Congress has granted limited jurisdiction to the States regarding Indian country. [The court notes 25 U.S.C. §1322, a provision in which Congress did extend state court jurisdiction into Indian Country.]

. . . As shown by §1322, Congress' grant of jurisdiction to the States "over civil (matters) between Indians or to which Indians are parties" within the exterior boundaries of an Indian reservation, comes only with the consent of "the tribe occupying the particular Indian country. . . ." We have no knowledge of the Fort Peck Tribes giving their consent to the State of Montana pursuant to this statute. Additionally, the grant of jurisdiction pursuant to §1322 requires action on the part of the State and Montana has accepted very limited jurisdiction as evidenced by M.C.A. 2-1-301 *et seq.*

Roberta states that she plans on filing a quiet title action in the near future regarding her property and her rights thereto and the adjudication of those issues may necessarily involve trust restricted lands. She goes on to state that her quiet title action would lie only in federal court. This is true because "state court would lack jurisdiction to adjudicate the disposition of Indian trust lands and the Tribal court would lack jurisdiction to adjudicate issues involving the fee patent property." In view of §1322(b) we agree that jurisdiction could not lie in State court. . . .

CONCUR: Gary M. Beaudry Associate Justice, Carroll J. DeCoteau Associate Justice

NOTE

In *McLeod v. Dupuis*, 4 Am. Tribal Law 103 (Confederated Salish and Kootenai Tribes Court of Appeals 2003), the court held in accordance with tribal statute that it had jurisdiction over a landlord-tenant dispute on fee lands within the Flathead Indian Reservation:

> The Tribal Trial Court did not err in exercising jurisdiction over this proceeding. Article I, Territory, of the Confederated Salish and Kootenai Tribes Constitution provides that the Tribes' jurisdiction "shall extend to the territory within the original confines of the Flathead Reservation as defined in the Treaty of July 16, 1855" as well as to other lands not relevant to this proceeding. Section 2-1-104, Civil Jurisdiction, CSKT Laws Codified provides in relevant part: . . .
>
> > (2) To the fullest extent possible, not inconsistent with federal law, the Tribes may exercise their civil, regulatory, and adjudicatory powers. To the fullest extent possible, not inconsistent with federal law, the Tribal Court may exercise subject matter and personal jurisdiction. The jurisdiction over all persons of the Tribal Court may extend to and include, but not by way of limitation, the following:
> >
> > > (a) All persons found within the Reservation.
> > >
> > > (b) All persons subject to the jurisdiction of the Tribal Court and involved directly or indirectly in: . . .
> > >
> > > > (ii) The ownership, use or possession of any property, or interest therein, situated within the Reservation;
> > > >
> > > > (iii) The entering into of any type of contract within the Reservation or wherein any aspect of any contract is performed within the Reservation.
>
> Thus, under this governing law, the Tribal Trial Court had both personal and subject matter jurisdiction over this proceeding. At the time the lawsuit was filed, both parties resided on the reservation. As indicated above, the leased property is located within the exterior boundaries of the reservation. The dispute arises from the lease of that property and concerns the use of the property.

McLeod, 4 Am. Tribal Law at 105.

10
CONTRACTS

This chapter surveys several areas of contract law as interpreted and applied by Indian nations. In large measure, tribal courts tend to adapt and apply Anglo-American contract common law to contract disputes. Many Indian nations have not adopted comprehensive contract law codes, nor do many tribal courts have an extensive body of common law decisions upon which to rely. As a result, tribal courts resolve most contract disputes in accordance with the law of the state in which the tribe is located. More and more, however, parties to contracts under the jurisdiction of tribal courts have begun to agree on choice of law provisions that detail which law the tribal court should apply in adjudicating contract disputes.

This chapter also details a few areas in which tribal customary and traditional contract law peeks through the veneer of Anglo-American contract law. In some cases—almost always cases exclusively involving tribal member parties—customary contract law directly affects the outcomes. Usually, in such cases the contract in question arises from an agreement between Indians that involves a uniquely cultural agreement, such as a family agreement.

Moreover, this chapter details the kind of contract disputes that arise either exclusively or more often in Indian country than outside of it. Contracts involving Indian nations as sovereigns are also featured, with the complicated questions of sovereign immunity interwoven repeatedly into the cases.

A. CONTRACT DOCTRINES UNDER TRIBAL LAW

1. CONTRACT FORMATION

MALATERRE V. ST. CLAIRE

Turtle Mountain Band of Chippewa Indians Appellate Court, No. 05-007
(January 19, 2006)

Before: Acting Chief Justice MONIQUE VONDALL-RIEKE, and Justices JERILYN DECOTEAU and MATTHEW L.M. FLETCHER[*]

---
[*]*Disclosure:* The author of this book participated in the case as a sitting appellate judge and wrote the opinion.

By Justice FLETCHER for a unanimous Court.

I. Procedural History and Facts

On June 30, 2004, Appellant Cindy Malaterre sued Bermilia St. Claire and the Estate of Alex St. Claire, Bermilia's deceased husband. All parties are enrolled members of the Turtle Mountain Band of Chippewa Indians and resided within the exterior boundaries of the Turtle Mountain Band's reservation centered around Belcourt, North Dakota. Since the filing of this suit, Bermilia St. Claire has walked on and the Estate of Bermilia St. Claire is substituted in her place as the Appellee.

Cindy Malaterre and her husband at that time, Todd St. Claire, lived in a Mutual Help home beginning in 1996. . . . Alex and Bermilia St. Claire were Todd's parents and Cindy's in-laws. . . . Alex and Bermilia lived in an older home, purchased in 1993. . . . In 2000, Alex St. Claire was severely injured in an automobile accident and became disabled. . . . Alex and Bermilia's home was of insufficient size to accommodate Alex's disability. . . .

On April 2, 2001, Cindy and Todd executed a letter stating that they "would like to gift" their home to Alex and Bermilia. . . . Alex and Bermilia then moved into Cindy and Todd's home; Cindy and Todd moved into Alex and Bermilia's home. . . . Cindy alleged and the Estate's counsel conceded at oral argument that the arrangement amounted to a "trade." . . . This last fact is consistent with the lower court's findings as well. . . .

In 2003, Cindy and Todd divorced. *See* Tribal Court's Order, Findings of Fact and Conclusions of Law at ¶9; *St. Claire v. Malaterre St. Claire*, Order for Dissolution of Marriage, No. 03-5106 (Turtle Mountain Band Tribal Court, Oct. 9, 2003). In the hearing before the lower court in this matter, Cindy testified — and the Tribal Court found — that Todd St. Claire had used violence or the threat of violence to force Cindy to enter into the "trade." *See* Tribal Court's Order, Findings of Fact and Conclusions of Law at ¶14; Civil Court Hearing, Testimony of Cindy Malaterre (Nov. 12, 2004).

In her complaint, Cindy Mataterre sought to have the house in which she and Todd St. Claire lived returned to her possession. . . . The lower court, per Judge Shirley Cain, heard testimony on this matter on November 11, 2004. Judge Cain found that Cindy and Todd had "gifted" their home to Alex and Bermilia for the purpose of allowing Alex to reside in a home that was handicap-accessible. . . . Judge Cain further found that Alex and Bermilia "gifted" their home to Cindy and Todd "in return." . . .

II. Standard of Review

This Court reviews the findings of fact made by the trial court with a great deal of deference. As this Court stated long ago, "[D]etermination of fact issues is primarily the responsibility of the trial court, the appellate court being responsible only for ascertaining that a factual conclusion is reasonably supported by the evidence." *Laducer v. Laducer*, Memorandum Decision, at 3-4 (TMAC 1990). If "substantial evidence [exists] to support the trial court's finding," then this Court must uphold those findings of fact. *Id.* at 4. . . .

Conversely, this Court will review the conclusions of law made by the tribal court without similar deference but instead under a *de novo* standard.

See Turtle Mountain Judicial Board v. Turtle Mountain Band of Chippewa Indians, No. 04-007, at 10 (TMAC 2005) (citing *LaFountaine-Gladue v. Ojibwe Indian School*, No. 94-004, at 3 (TMAC 1996)); *General Motors Acceptance Corp. v. Mathiason*, No. 05-002, at 4-5 (TMAC 2005). We "gran[t] no special deference to the tribal court's conclusions of law." *Turtle Mountain Judicial Board, supra*, at 10.

III. Discussion

A. The "Trade" of Homes

Given the deferential standard of review that constrains this Court's review of the findings of fact by the tribal court, we affirm the tribal court's determination that a contract had been formed between the two families resulting in the "trade" of the two homes. As a general matter, whether a contract has been formed is a question of fact. *E.g., Colville Tribal Enterprise Corp. v. Orr*, No. 98-008, 1998.NACC.0000009, at ¶19 (Colville Confederated Tribes Court of Appeals 1998) (holding that whether an implied contract has been formed is a question of fact); *Hood v. Bordy*, No. 07-90, 1991.NANN.000005, at ¶28 (Navajo Nation Supreme Court 1991) (holding that the tribal court's findings that an oral contract had been formed were conclusive). Under tribal law, a contract may be written or oral. *See* Turtle Mountain Band Tribal Code §7.0602. The tribal court, after taking testimony from the parties and several others in this matter, found as a matter of fact that Todd and Cindy had "gifted" their home in 2001 to Alex and Bermilia. . . . Alex and Bermilia "gifted" their home "in return" to Todd and Cindy. . . . This mutual "gifting" of homes meets the requirement under tribal law that the consideration must "resul[t] in a benefit to the promisor or a detriment to the promisee," Turtle Mountain Band Tribal Code §7.0502, and that it "must be of some legal value," *id*. at §7.0503. Moreover, a written instrument signed by Todd and Cindy provided evidence of the mutual "gifting" sufficient to generate a presumption that a contract existed. *See id*. at §7.0505. As a result, a "trade" was consummated, a contract was formed, and this Court affirms the determination of the tribal court that ownership of the homes was transferred.

We are mindful that there is no writing that demonstrates the "gifting" of Alex and Bermilia's home to Cindy and Todd. We note that the Tribal Code adopts the Anglo-American notion of the Statute of Frauds for real estate transactions, but with the exception that the tribal court retains the power "to compel specific performance of any agreement for the sale of real estate in case of part performance thereof." Turtle Mountain Band Tribal Code §7.06.03(3) But we are influenced by the fact that, in many tribal cultures, "[n]either writing, nor consideration, nor witnesses is required." Robert D. Cooter & Wolfgang Fikentscher, *Indian Common Law: The Role of Custom in American Indian Tribal Courts (Part II of II)*, 46 Am. J. Comp. L. 509, 548 (1998). Moreover, "[i]n a culture in which so much rests on oral tradition, a given word weighs much more than in a culture that writes. Therefore, an oral pledge is valid, even without consideration." *Id*. at 548 n. 90. Here, we are comforted that the "trade" of these homes is consistent with the relationship of the parties at the time of the transaction. *See generally id*. at 547

("Tribal people tend to form long-run relationships. . . . Long-run relationships build trust and reliance among the parties."); *see also* Petition/Complaint at ¶9 (alleging that Cindy Malaterre agreed to transfer her home to the St. Claires "in good faith"). Moreover, we agree with the implicit finding of the tribal court that affirming the existence of a contract will work no fraud or deceit on either party. *See* TURTLE MOUNTAIN BAND TRIBAL CODE §7.0604 (implying that prevention of "fraud or deceit" were purposes of enacting a Statute of Frauds). As a result, as a matter of law, we hold that the fact that there is no complete writing proving the existence of a contract is not a bar to the finding of the formation of the contract by the tribal court.

The finding of fact by the tribal court that Cindy Malaterre "gifted" her marriage home to the St. Claires under duress gives this Court a great deal of consternation, but after a great deal of consideration, this finding does not alter our conclusion. Under tribal law, "duress" and "undue influence," which we hold includes without limitation physical violence or the threat of physical violence, are factors sufficient to render a contract voidable. *See* TURTLE MOUNTAIN BAND TRIBAL CODE §§7.0302(1), (3). *Cf. Lewis v. Mashantucket Pequot Gaming Commission*, No. 97-117, 1997.NAMP.0000016, at ¶42-43 (Mashantucket Pequot Tribal Court 1997) (holding that a resignation of employment may be found to be involuntary if made under duress). The tribal court found that Cindy "gifted" her home "under duress by her ex-husband, Todd St. Claire," . . . and that "during her marriage to Todd St. Claire, Cindy Malaterre was a victim of domestic violence." . . . We are not satisfied that the tribal court took this fact into consideration when making the finding of fact that a contract had been formed. However, we decline to reverse the tribal court's ruling and rely upon the failure of counsel to appeal the "duress" issue by raising it in the appellant's brief. As a corollary, we note that Cindy Malaterre never alleged duress in her original complaint. *See* Petition/Complaint at ¶9 (alleging that Cindy Malaterre agreed to transfer her home to the St. Claires "in good faith"). As we have held elsewhere, the failure to raise this issue in the appellate brief operates to waive the question. *See Turtle Mountain Judicial Board, supra*, at 16. . . .

C. Order for Cindy Malaterre's Payment of $1000 to the Estate

We vacate the tribal court's order for Cindy Malaterre to make $1000 in payments on the home in which she currently resides before ownership may be finally transferred to her name. Tribal Judge Carey Vicenti (Jicarilla Apache) has stated that, in the tribal common law of contracts, "[r]epairing the relationship between the parties is the primary legal goal." Cooter & Fikentscher, *supra*, at 549 (quoting Carey Vicenti). Money damages are not a favored remedy. *See id.* at 547-49 (noting that specific performance is a more appropriate remedy, where possible). We note here that the tribal court ordered that Cindy may stay in her current residence but that she must pay $1000 to the St. Claire Estate. . . .

The origin of the $1000 payment is unclear from the record. The November 11, 2004, hearing is silent as to the origin of this obligation. The only document in the record noting a $1000 obligation is a Warranty Deed purporting to convey Cindy Malaterre's current residence to Richard L. Gourneau. . . . It is not clear from the record why Cindy Malaterre should be obligated to pay $1000 to the Estate. As a result, we vacate this portion of the Order. . . .

NOTES

1. The Turtle Mountain Band of Chippewa Indians enacted a code explicitly circumventing the statute of frauds, a well-known common law rule codified by virtually all American jurisdictions that requires a contract relating to land to be in writing. What are the reasons for requiring contracts relating to land to be in writing? Are those reasons applicable to tribal communities? Why or why not?

2. In *Phillips v. Dusty's Auto Sales*, 1997 Mont. Salish & Kootenai Tribe LEXIS 1 (Confederated Salish & Kootenai Tribes Court of Appeals 1997), the court confronted a claim by the buyer of a used truck who attempted to return the truck to the dealership after 20 days, asserting various contract defenses, including that the dealership breached an oral contract. The court, per Judge Cynthia Ford, a University of Montana law professor, wrote:

> Oral contracts, like written contracts, are valid and enforceable if and only if there is consideration for them. In this case, there is conflicting evidence about whether Dusty in fact promised to refund plaintiff's money. Even if he had made this promise, and even if it had been in writing (which both parties agree is not the case), Dusty's statement does not rise to the level of an enforceable contract because there was no consideration for it. Dusty did not get anything from plaintiff, nor did plaintiff promise to do anything in the future in exchange for Dusty's statement. Further, nothing in the sales documents or the law required Dusty to refund plaintiff's money. Dusty's statement, if made, was nothing more than a gratuitous remark, which he was legally free to honor or not. Dusty made no contract at the time Phillips brought the Jeep back in. Thus, as Judge Lozar correctly observed, "Plaintiff's contention that Defendant breached an oral contract to satisfy Plaintiff is without merit."

Phillips, 1997 Mont. Salish & Kootenai Tribe LEXIS 1, at *8-9.

3. In *Ho-Chunk Nation v. B&K Builders, Inc.*, 3 Am. Tribal Law 381 (Ho-Chunk Tribal Court 2001), the court declined to apply customary law that would have required the court to find the existence of a contract even where the tribal signatory to the contract was not authorized to execute the contract:

> The plaintiff contended in its pleadings that "[t]he Ho-Chunk Nation Trial Court has subject matter jurisdiction to resolve contract disputes," citing the case of *Ho-Chunk Nation v. Ross Olsen*, [2 Am. Tribal Law 299 (2000)] for that proposition. . . . In *Olsen*, the Court consulted the Ho-Chunk Nation Traditional Court . . . to ascertain "whether Ho-Chunk Nation custom and tradition recognized agreements analogous to the modern day 'contract.'" *Olsen* [2 Am. Tribal Law at 307]. The Traditional Court responded by relating that "according to the Ho-Chunk Nation's traditions and customs, once an agreement for the performance of services or production of goods is made, the parties have a duty to fulfill their obligations," meaning "that it was wrong for one party to keep a benefit obtained from an agreement without providing the agreed upon compensation." . . . While the Traditional

Court has acknowledged this fundamental concept, it has not extended this pronouncement to include causes of action such as promissory estoppel. *See Maureen Arnett v. Ho-Chunk Nation Department of Administration*, CV 00-60 (HCN Tr. Ct., Jan. 8, 2001) at 16-18. . . .

Unlike the case at bar, the issue of whether the signatory to the contract had properly delegated authority was not before the Court in *Olsen*. This concern, also, did not arise in several contract disputes involving private parties wherein the Court based its relief upon the above traditional principle. . . .

The constitutional documents require proper delegations of authority for entering into contractual arrangements, and the Court cannot waive these requirements. The plaintiff, as a result of its potential errors, advocates setting aside the provisions agreed upon by the defendants through the contracting process in favor of the Court establishing the substantive rights of the parties under custom and tradition. The Court has never attempted to apply custom and tradition for purposes of interpreting an agreement when one of the parties lacked the authority to enter into the agreement in the first instance. Such a practice would prove fundamentally unfair to the party having no reason to doubt the authority of the signatory. Moreover, custom and tradition would not address the dispositive issues identified above. The relevant constitutional provisions provide authoritative guidance in rendering this decision.

B&K Builders, 3 Am. Tribal Law at 391-92.

2. PAROL EVIDENCE RULE

SOUTHERN PUGET SOUND INTERTRIBAL HOUSING AUTHORITY V. JOHNSON

Shoalwater Bay Appellate Court, No. SHO-CIV 6/80-434, 1 NICS App. 29
(September 24, 1988)

Before: Shoalwater Bay Appellate Court; Chief Justice ELBRIDGE COOCHISE, Justice EMMA DULIK and Justice ROSEMARY J. IRVIN. . . .

The appellant was sued by the appellee for unlawful tenancy under a Mutual Help and Occupancy Agreement[*] executed between the parties and dated June 12, 1985. . . .

I.

The Parol Evidence Rule Does Not Apply to Proceedings in Shoalwater Bay Tribal Court

During the course of the trial, Judge LaFountaine refused to hear the testimony of twelve witnesses whom the defendant proffered to establish the circumstances and intentions of the parties at the time of signing the Mutual Help and Occupancy Agreement. The witnesses were offered to establish circumstances and intentions surrounding the execution of similar

---

[*]. *Author's Note:* — A "mutual help and occupancy agreement" is a sort of rent-to-own lease agreement created by federal housing regulations decades ago in an effort to create generous terms that would increase the likelihood that impoverished American Indians on reservation lands could become homeowners. These agreements have largely fallen out of favor since the enactment of the Native American Housing Assistance and Self Determination Act of 1996.

contractual agreements with the appellee. The Court excluded the testimony of all witnesses except the defendants, basing its decision on the Parol Evidence Rule.

Paramount to other concerns in the conducting of any trial in tribal court is the concern that any party to a proceeding be given a hearing and a fair hearing. Traditionally, anyone who had something to say regarding a matter in controversy would have the opportunity to have their say prior to a decision being rendered by the tribal elders. It is fundamental to tribal culture that parties to a conflict be allowed to have their say without legal doctrines being unfairly imposed to limit this right. Tribal Courts do not exist to enforce the letter of the law as much as they do to serve tribal people with a forum for a fair hearing and a just adjudication, one in which they may run their own case, within reasonable limits, with or without an attorney.

The Parol Evidence Rule is not, and never has been a rule of the Shoalwater Bay Tribe. The Parol Evidence Rule is a rule of substantive law of the State of Washington. The Tribal Court erred in applying the Rule and applying it as a rule of evidence to exclude witnesses.

The Parol Evidence Rule, as traditionally stated in Washington, provides:

> [P]arol or extrinsic evidence is not admissible to add to, subtract from, vary, or contradict written instruments which are contractual in nature and which are valid, complete, unambiguous, and not affected by accident, fraud, or mistake. . . . It is not a rule of evidence but one of substantive law.

Enrich v. Connell, 105 Wn. 2d 551, 555, 556, 716 P.2d 863 (1986).

> However the parol evidence rule only applies to a writing intended by the parties as an "integration" of their agreement; *i.e.*, a writing intended as a final expression of the terms of the agreement. . . . In making this preliminary determination of whether the parties intended the written document to be an integration of their agreement, which is a question of fact, the trial court must hear all relevant, extrinsic evidence, oral or written.

Enrich v. Connell, supra.

First, there is no requirement that the parol evidence rule be given credence in the Shoalwater Bay Tribal Court. Insomuch as it is used, it is advisory only. Secondly, even if used as advisory and applied to a matter pending in tribal court, it is considered by the Washington state court to be a rule of substantive law and not of evidence. Applied according to the rule in Washington state court, it cannot be used to cut off testimony which is relevant to a preliminary determination as to whether the parties to an agreement intended the written document to be an integration of their agreement. . . .

III.

. . . The following findings of the Trial Court [are vacated.] . . .

2) After considerable discussion, the trial court ruled that only one of witnesses, Anita Blake, could testify for the defendant. . . .
3) The court ruled that it would allow testimony concerning the interpretation of Section 5.4 of the Agreement, but would not allow cumulative testimony. . . .

THEREFORE IT IS HEREBY ORDERED: This matter is remanded to the Trial Court for retrial on all issues with the following instructions:

There is to be no limit on the number of witnesses who testify for or against the appellant until it can be shown that their testimony is repetitive and cumulative.

Further, the trial judge is not to take a party's word, representing himself pro se, as to whether potential witnesses will testify to the same information. The Court is to make an independent determination from the witnesses as to whether the proffered testimony will be repetitive and cumulative.

NOTES

1. In *Fletcher v. Grand Traverse Band Tribal Council*, 2004 WL 5714967 (Grand Traverse Band of Ottawa and Chippewa Indians Tribal Court 2004),[*] the court applied state law in refusing to consider evidence relating to alleged promises made to an employee of the Band:

   > This Court holds that it cannot consider evidence relating to promises made to the Plaintiff prior to her entering into the [employment contract] as such evidence is inadmissible under the parol evidence rule. The parol evidence rule provides that, when two parties have made a contract and have expressed it in a writing which they both have agreed to as being a complete and accurate integration of that contract, extrinsic evidence of antecedent and contemporaneous understandings and negotiations is inadmissible for the purpose of varying or contradicting the writing. . . . Parol evidence of contract negotiations, or of prior or contemporaneous agreements that contradict or vary the written contract, is not admissible to vary the terms of a contract which is clear and unambiguous. . . .
   >
   > This Court holds that paragraph 5.F. of the [employment contract] controls and is applicable to the Plaintiff's employment relationship with the Tribe. Therefore, as there is no dispute that Plaintiff was given 30 days' notice of her termination pursuant to paragraph 5.F. of the MSA, Plaintiff's claims based on a just cause employment relationship must fail.

   Fletcher, 2004 WL 5714967, at *8.

2. In *Kirn v. Indian Credit Corp.*, 1989.NAFP.0000012 (Fort Peck Court of Appeals 1989), the appellate court reversed a trial court decision to apply the parol evidence rule to a tort claim, noting that the case had involved a switch in trial judges below:

   > The tribal court did not appear to understand the difference between contract remedies and tort remedies after the substitution of Judge Vance for Judge Boyd. As appellant advised the tribal court, contract actions arise simply out of contracts either oral or written between parties. Parties can sue under a contract when the other party breaches the agreement. Furthermore, the remedies are limited and as a rule emotional damages are not recoverable in a contract action and many types of evidentiary rules govern the evidence that is introduced which includes the parol evidence rule.

---

[*] *Disclosure:* The plaintiff in this matter is a close relative of the author.

Appellants further advised the tribal court the tort action allows plaintiff much broader relief. The plaintiff in a tort action needs only show the defendant owed a duty of care to the plaintiff and that plaintiff breached that duty. Tort actions are generally utilized to provide relief to plaintiffs who have suffered personal or economic injuries. In a tort action, a plaintiff may recover emotional damages and the evidentiary rules such as the parol evidence would not apply. Appellants have attempted to establish the ICC, as the Kirn's primary lender, owed a duty of care that would include not providing "bad checks" to its debtors and that it breached that duty.

Kirn, 1989.NAFP.0000012, at ¶¶75-76.

3. IMPLIED CONTRACTS

COLVILLE TRIBAL ENTERPRISE CORP. v. ORR

Colville Confederated Tribes Court of Appeals, No. AP98-008,
26 Indian L. Rep. 6005, 1998.NACC.0000009 (December 4, 1998)

Before Chief Justice DUPRIS, Justice STEWART and Justice BONGA
PER CURIAM. . . .

Standards of Review

There are two issues before this Court for review: (1) did the Trial Court err by failing to find that sovereign immunity barred the instant action?; and (2) did the Trial Court err by finding that an implied contract existed between the parties?

The implied contract issue necessitates a review of the factual findings of the Trial Court, *i.e.* do the facts support the legal conclusion that an implied contract existed between the parties[?] The accepted standard of review by this Court of findings of fact is the "clearly erroneous" standard. *See CCT v. Nadene Naff*, [APCvF93-12001 to 003], 2 CTCR 08, p. 2, [2 CCAR 50], 22 ILR 6032 (1995), *Wiley v. CCT et al.*, [AP93-16237], 2 CTCR 9, p. 6, [2 CCAR 60], 22 ILR 6059 (1995), and *Palmer v. Millard et al.*, [AP94-005], 2 CTCR 14, p. 5, [3 CCAR 27, 23 ILR 6094] (1996). The sovereign immunity issue is a question of law, which requires a de novo review. *Id.*

[The court concludes that the Tribes have not waived sovereign immunity for this claim, and that the petitioner has not demonstrated that any of the possible waivers of immunity apply.]

Implied Contract

Even though we have held that the doctrine of sovereign immunity bars Orr's action for damages, the issue of whether there existed an implied contract between the parties, which is enforceable under the Tribes' Civil Rights Statute, still must be addressed. Orr brought the action under, inter alia, the CTC Chapter 1-5. We must inquire whether the facts in the record support a conclusion that Orr had an implied clause in his employment contract with CTEC which provided for a 180-day notice of termination as the Trial Court found. Further, if there is a right to 180-day notice or hearing, what is it based on?

We review the Trial Court's findings under a clearly erroneous standard to determine if the findings support a legal conclusion that an implied contract existed between the parties that included a 180-day notice of termination term. *See Naff, supra* at 2; *Wiley, et al.,* at 6; and *Palmer v. Millard et al.,* at 5. "A finding is 'clearly erroneous' when, although there is evidence to support it, the reviewing court on the entire evidence is left with the definite and firm conviction that mistake has been committed." . . .

The first inquiry is: what are the relevant facts in this case? The Trial Court's Findings of Facts show the following:

1) Roy Orr, a member of the Colville Tribes, served on the Board of Directors for CTEC between 1993 and March of 1995, at which time he was hired by CTEC as General Manager for the CTEC Gaming Division. . . .
2) In August 1995, Orr was promoted to a vice president position for CTEC, and negotiated a proposed contract with the then–Chief Executive Officer (hereinafter CEO) Clay Antiquoia. . . .
3) The Board of CTEC, who had approval authority, would not give final approval to Orr's proposed contract because the Board did not approve the six-month termination compensation clause in the proposed contract. . . .
4) The termination clause in question was included in two (2) officer contracts, but not in three (3) others, including Orr's. . . .
5) Neither Orr, three (3) of the Board members, nor the current CEO, Wendell George, were aware of a Board resolution setting out a contract format to use in negotiating contracts with officers; the format included a six-month termination clause similar to the one at issue in this case. . . .
6) Orr continually worked as a vice president of CTEC until his termination in April of 1997. . . .
7) Orr did not receive termination compensation or a hearing before the Board of Directors regarding his termination. . . .

Neither party has assigned error to these findings, so they become the accepted facts on appeal. *Johnson v. Whitman,* 463 P.2d 207, 209 (1969).

The record shows the following relevant facts not included in the Findings, but not disputed by the parties:

1) Orr was on the CTEC Board of Directors when the Francis Somday case went to Court, after which time the CTEC Board rewrote its Policies and Procedures Manual (Manual) to foreclose any other at-will employee from arguing his contract was modified by the Manual. . . .
2) Orr was aware that the "changes in the [M]anual were to make it crystal clear that officer level employees were at-will employees of CTEC. . . ."
3) Orr understood that the CEO could not bind CTEC on an employment contract, and that the CTEC Board had the final approval authority. . . .

Two Types of Implied Contract

There are two kinds of implied contracts, implied in fact and implied in law (quasi-contract). "Contracts implied in fact arise from facts and circumstances showing a mutual consent and intention to contract. . . . Quasi-contracts arise from an implied legal duty or obligation, and are not based on a contract between the parties or any consent or agreement." . . .

The Trial Court's legal conclusions do not identify which type of implied contract it concluded existed in this case, so we have analyzed both types and, based on the following opinion, we hold neither type of implied contract existed.

I. Implied in Fact

Fundamental contract law makes no distinction between the essential elements of an implied contract and an express contract. The difference is in the "mode of proof." Both require an analysis of the intentions of the parties to the transaction, and a showing of a meeting of minds between the parties. . . . The Court must assess the parties' acts and conduct viewed in the light of surrounding circumstances in order to ascertain a mutual assent to terms of a implied contract. . . .

Orr, who is asserting the existence of an implied contract, has the burden of proving ". . . each fact essential thereto, including the existence of a mutual intention. Where circumstantial evidence is relied on, the circumstances must be such as to make it reasonably certain that the parties intended and did enter into the alleged contract." . . .

In the instant case Orr initially negotiated his employment contract as a Vice President of CTEC with Clay Antiquoia. He and Antiquoia had mutual expectations that the contract would be approved. Mutual expectations do not amount to mutual assent.

Proving that a term was being negotiated is not proof of the mutual assent to the terms by the contracting parties. It is just proof that the parties were negotiating terms. . . .

Orr knew the contract was not final until approved by the Board of Directors. Reluctance of the Board, the final decision maker, to agree to a clause for 180-day severance, plus the actions of the Board not to finalize the contract based on the clause, show lack of intent of one of the parties to the contract. Orr's reliance on the willingness of both CEOs, Antiquoia and George, is misplaced. He knew neither CEO had final authority to finalize and approve his proposed employment contract.

Orr accepted the position of Vice President for a set salary and benefits, and with a knowledge, as a past Board member, that officers were at-will unless their contracts specifically provided other terms.

The Board of Directors did not offer Orr the contract term of a 180-day termination clause. "An acceptance of an offer must always be identical with the terms of the offer or there is no meeting of the minds and no contract." . . . "If the person who is seeking assent to a term knows or has reason to know that the other party does not intend his actions as expressions of a fixed purpose until a further action is taken, he has not made an offer." . . .

In assessing what the intent of the parties is, we must look at what their outward expressions and acts were, not what the unexpressed intent may have been. . . . In this case, the record is very clear that the Board of Directors did not intend to give Orr a 180-day termination clause. This is supported by the Trial Court's Findings and the testimony of Orr himself.

Upon a review on the entire evidence we are left with the definite and firm conviction that mistake has been committed; there was no implied-in-fact contract between the parties regarding the 180-day termination clause.

II. Implied in Law, or Quasi-Contract

"[Q]uasi-contracts arise from an implied legal duty or obligation, and are not based on a contract between the parties or any consent or agreement." . . . In order to show a quasi-contract in this case, it must be shown that CTEC had a legal duty or obligation to provide Orr with a 180-day termination clause. Orr argues that he had a due process right to such notice, or at least a hearing before the Board of Directors; these are the only arguments made that could be germane to a quasi-contract theory.

Orr argues that CEO George and another officer (Knapton) each had a 180-day termination notice, and their contracts were approved after Orr's was submitted to the Board for approval. The Findings also indicate that the termination clause in question was not included in two (2) other officers' contracts besides Orr's. . . .

A showing that two (2) out of five (5) officer contracts had the sought-after termination clause does not prove that CTEC legally had to treat everyone equitably and put it in every contract of an officer. It supports CTEC's argument that it is discretionary with the Board of Directors whether to include such a clause in its contracts.

Orr has not met his burden of showing CTEC had a legal obligation or duty to him to give him a 180-day termination clause in his contract. There is no showing of a violation of due process by the Board. Orr knew what his status was when he accepted the Vice President position.

Upon a review on the entire evidence we are left with the definite and firm conviction that mistake has been committed; there was no implied-in-law contract between the parties regarding the 180-day termination clause.

The general law is when an employment contract is not definite as to duration it is considered terminable-at-will. . . . Cf. . . . *Office of Navajo Labor Relations v. West World*, 21 [Indian L. Rep.] 6070, 6071 (Nav. Sup. Ct. Apr. 18, 1994).

We are sure the parties in this case did not start out with the intent to sever relationships. Orr was receiving a good salary (about $90,000.00), so CTEC must have valued his services when he was hired. Where did the communications fail? Who can say. There was a change in the CEO; there was a change in the Board make-up. Becoming a successful business corporation for a tribe is a double-edged sword; how does the Tribe balance what is good in maintaining its tribal identity with competing in a non-Indian business world? This is also true for tribal members, like Orr, who ask for the respect as a tribal member and a high-level job as a businessman in CTEC. The one side gives way to the other in times like this.

Orr knew the rules of the game. He knew the Board of Directors intended to create an at-will status for officers when he became an officer. He knew the

Board had the final say in approving officer contracts, and they did not approve his with the 180-day notice termination clause. Nothing in the record supports any other theory. . . .

NOTES

1. Tribal government and enterprise employers draft employee manuals with an eye to preempting implied contract claims. In *Willis v. Mohegan Tribal Gaming Authority*, 7 Am. Tribal Law 492 (Mohegan Gaming Trial Court 2008), the court noted:

> On Count One, plaintiff alleges that the defendant's conduct in denying his request for a board of review is a violation of its Board of Review Policy. . . .
> . . . However, the Handbook expressly states that "It is not intended to, nor does it, constitute an expressed or implied contract or promise of continued employment or that any policy or benefit described in it will continue or will not be changed." *Employee Handbook*, p. 2.

Willis, 7 Am. Tribal Law at 493.

2. Concomitantly, tribal *contractual* waivers of sovereign immunity may not be invoked through the allegation of an implied contract. In *Wilson v. Mashantucket Pequot Gaming Enterprise*, 3 Mash. Rep. 440, 2002 WL 34243999 (Mashantucket Pequot Tribal Court 2002), the court noted:

> Tribal law requires the existence of a written contract for the Court's jurisdiction over a contract to be properly invoked. *See* XII M.P.T.L. ch. 1, §3. . . . Plaintiff claims that an implied contract was created when he and Defendant signed the Employee Handbook. In order to prevail in a breach of implied covenant of good faith and fair dealing, however, Plaintiff must be able to prove that a written contract exists between him and Defendant that expressly waives the sovereign immunity of the Tribe. *See* [*Sawyer v. Mashantucket Pequot Tribal Nation*, 3 Mash. Rep. 413, 417 (Mash. Pequot Tribal Court 1999)]; *see also*, I M.P.T.L. ch. 1, §2(b). Plaintiff does not allege the existence of a written contract with Defendant, nor does he point to a contractual provision upon which to base his claim. Accordingly, the Court lacks jurisdiction to hear this claim, and Count 1 is dismissed.

Wilson, 3 Mash. Rep. at 443-44.

4. CONTRACT BREACH

PABLO V. CONFEDERATED SALISH & KOOTENAI TRIBES

Confederated Salish and Kootenai Tribes Court of Appeals, No. 92-CV-170-AP, 1994 Mont. Salish & Kootenai Tribes LEXIS 7 (April 20, 1994)

PEREGOY, Chair, Civil Appellate Panel:

Introduction

This appeal arises out of a dispute over a contract for educational leave and future employment between Joseph Pablo and the Confederated Salish and Kootenai Tribes. . . .

I. Factual Background

Joseph Pablo is a member of the Confederated Salish and Kootenai Tribes of the Flathead Reservation. . . .

Pablo began working for the Tribes as director of the Family Counseling Unit of the Family Assistance Division. . . . Pablo was appointed program manager of [Tribal Social Services] in January of 1990.

[During Pablo's tenure as] program manager of TSS, . . . there was no indication of the existence of personnel problems, and employee turnover was low. While TSS was subject to a critical federal review during his employment as program manager, Pablo succeeded in rectifying the problems identified in the program review.

In May of 1991, Anna Whiting-Sorrell, acting on behalf of department head Swaney, rated Pablo's overall job performance as program manager of TSS as "outstanding." Whiting-Sorrell found that "Mr. Pablo has taken the Social Service Program and brought it through a very difficult time in both morale and funding. For that he needs to be commended."

Pablo believed that he and the Tribes would mutually benefit and provide better services to the TSS clientele if he held a master's degree. . . . During the summer of 1991, with the encouragement and support of department head Swaney, Pablo received approval from the Tribal Council for a leave of absence to begin studies for an MSW at Eastern Washington University (EWU). The MSW degree is a two-year program which includes one year of on-campus course work and a one-year "practicum" of supervised work experience.

Pablo and the Tribes entered into a "Contract for Leave of Absence, Future Employment and Repayment of Educational Loan." The terms of the contract provided Pablo would be given a nine-month leave of absence for the 1991-92 academic year to complete course work, with a minimum "B" average. The Tribes were to loan him $8,000 at the rate of 7% interest, secured by real property owned by Pablo in Arlee. Upon returning from the educational leave, Pablo was to have resumed his duties and responsibilities as program manager of TSS. The contract required him to complete the MSW program by June 1993, and essentially provided that if Pablo thereafter worked for the Tribes for two years, the loan would be forgiven at the rate of $4,000 plus interest per year. It further provided that if Pablo did not complete the degree, or if he left his employment before the expiration of the two-year loan forgiveness period, either by choice or by termination for specific cause, he would be required to repay the loan. If he would be terminated for other than cause, the Tribes were required to repay the loan. The contract also provided that the prevailing party in litigation would be entitled to reasonable attorney fees and court costs. Finally, the Tribal Court was mandated to be the forum for any cause of action arising under the contract. The document was signed by Michael T. Pablo, Chairman of the Tribal Council, Joseph E. Dupuis, Executive Secretary of the Tribal Council, and Pablo.

. . . [Alcohol and Substance Abuse Prevention] administrator Whiting-Sorrell was to oversee TSS, as well as her own program. . . . In September 1991, Pablo commenced graduate study at EWU, four months after Whiting-Sorrell rated his performance "outstanding" as program manager of TSS.

Whiting-Sorrell volunteered to serve as program director of Tribal Social Services during Pablo's educational leave, although she had no education or experience in social work. She testified that she "took a lackadaisical approach" to her responsibilities when Pablo left, and that she had an "unrealistic" idea of the time required to supervise TSS. It took five months for Whiting-Sorrell to fully implement Pablo's interim management plan. A tribal social worker testified that TSS operations were "chaotic" and "troublesome" during Whiting-Sorrell's tenure, largely as a result of high turnover and changes she made. The social worker also felt that Whiting-Sorrell's lack of background for social work supervision rendered the management of TSS "difficult" for her. Another TSS employee testified that the general working atmosphere at TSS was "out of control" during the period Pablo was on educational leave, including "supervisors not knowing who is supervising who," and directives to secretaries to "write-up" social workers for perceived work deficiencies. . . .

Based upon her involvement with TSS during January 1992, Whiting-Sorrell perceived TSS to be experiencing certain managerial problems. . . .

In response, Executive Secretary Dupuis and managers Swaney and Whiting-Sorrell decided to institute a "transition" period upon Pablo's return to TSS. During this period, Whiting-Sorrell was to function as program manager of TSS, rather than Pablo. . . .

While his rate of pay remained the same as that prior to the "transition" period, Pablo eventually realized he had been effectively stripped of his authority and responsibility as program manager of TSS. . . . Instead, his duties and responsibilities became limited to those of lead social worker, although he was never given an amended job description to reflect such. ·

On June 30, 1992, Whiting-Sorrell issued Pablo a written reprimand for being "unavailable" to staff on a day that he was home with the flu, notwithstanding that he had called the office early the same day and stated he would be out for at least half of the day. On July 9, 1992, Kimberly Swaney, TSS office manager, issued a memorandum reprimanding Pablo for allegedly creating "undue stress" and "low morale" among the TSS staff, although she had no authority over Pablo. On July 22, Kim Swaney issued a second memorandum reprimanding Pablo, this time for alleged improper management of client files. Ms. Swaney sent copies of both memos to Whiting-Sorrell.

On July 23, Pablo notified Bearhead Swaney in writing that he was not content with his position under the transition structure of TSS. . . . In two discussions, Pablo informed Swaney that he wanted his position as program manager restored. Mr. Swaney declined, verbally citing unspecified "shortcomings" in Pablo's ability to administer TSS.

On July 24, Kim Swaney issued a third memorandum of reprimand to Pablo, directing him to submit a report to her that was apparently due in Tribal Court a few days thereafter. However, the memo indicated Pablo had earlier informed Ms. Swaney that the report had not been completed because the court hearing had been rescheduled. Notwithstanding this explanation, Ms. Swaney demanded that Pablo submit the report in the time frame she imposed, claiming that unnamed support staff members were under "undue stress" because the report had not been completed.

On July 29, 1992, Whiting-Sorrell issued Pablo another disciplinary memorandum, including the threat of termination, for missing a court hearing. . . . The record indicates . . . that the judge ultimately excused Mr. Pablo for his absence.

Pablo believed these memos constituted attempts to provide documentation for his firing. He further believed he no longer had the support of his supervisors for completion of the MSW. . . .

With one month remaining to finalize and begin his practicum, Pablo felt compelled to resign and develop a new practicum with another agency. He submitted his resignation on July 30, 1992, and began anew his efforts to develop a practicum that would lead to the award of the MSW degree. He subsequently worked out a practicum with the Western Montana Regional Mental Health Center, which EWU approved. The court takes judicial notice that Pablo successfully completed his practicum and was awarded the MSW degree by Eastern Washington University in mid-June of 1993, according to schedule. . . .

The trial court awarded Pablo damages for breach of the educational leave and future employment contract. With regard to such damages, the court ruled:

> Damages in a breach of contract situation are limited to those contemplated by the parties at the time the contract was entered, including any amount which would place the injured party in the same position he would have been had the contract been performed.[4]

Under this ruling, the court ordered the Tribes to pay Pablo's $8,000 student loan, plus interest.

On appeal, Pablo seeks additional damages. . . . Pablo also asks us to overturn the trial court's ruling that he was not constructively discharged. He further asks this court to find that the contract at issue contained an implied covenant of good faith and fair dealing, and to rule that the Tribes breached the covenant.

In a cross-appeal, the Tribes . . . contend that they did not materially breach the contract with Pablo, and that Pablo consented to and accepted any modification to the contract that may have occurred.

II. Discussion

. . .

C. Material Breach of Contract

The educational and future employment contract at issue provided, in significant part, that Pablo would resume his position as the program manager of Tribal Social Services immediately upon return from his educational leave. The trial court found that Pablo[ ]

> did not return to the position of Director of Social Services for the Confederated Salish and Kootenai Tribes when his employment with Defendants was reinstated in June of 1992, but instead was placed in a position with duties and

---

4. *See Pablo v. Confederated Salish and Kootenai Tribes*, No. CV-170-92, Tribal Court of the Confederated Salish and Kootenai Tribes, Memorandum and Order, July 14, 1993 at 11.

responsibilities normally associated with a lead social worker and was under the supervision of Anna Whiting Sorrell. (Citations omitted.)

While the Tribes do not challenge this finding or the conclusion that they breached the contract, they claim on appeal that the trial court's findings do not support a "material breach." Without citing any legal authority, they argue that because they only intended to deprive Pablo of his contractually guaranteed position on a temporary basis, the deprivation was not material. This argument is frivolous.

In determining whether a breach of contract is material, the significant circumstances must be considered. These include the extent to which the injured party will be deprived of a reasonably expected benefit; the extent to which the injured party can be adequately compensated for the lost benefit; the extent to which the party in breach has already partly performed or made preparations for performance; the likelihood that the party in breach will "cure" its failure to perform; and the extent to which the behavior of the party in breach meets standards of good faith and fair dealing. RESTATEMENT (SECOND) OF CONTRACTS, §275, . . . at 188 (1982). . . .

Returning to the position of program manager of TSS after his educational leave comprised the core of the "future employment" contract between Pablo and the Tribes. The record indicates that Pablo would not have taken an educational leave in the absence of binding, enforceable assurances that he would be able to return to his job. The evidence further indicates it was necessary for Pablo to function as program manager of TSS in order to complete the requirements for the practicum he had negotiated with EWU, and that the practicum was a necessary prerequisite to obtaining the MSW degree — all conditions necessary for Pablo to meet his contractual obligations. Accordingly, Pablo reasonably expected to return to his former job, and the deprivation of this contractually promised benefit, even if "temporary," was of sufficient duration to effectively repudiate the agreement. In short, the provision guaranteeing Pablo his job could not have been of more central importance to the contract, or more material.

Further, the evidence shows that the Tribes declined to cure their breach after several opportunities to return Pablo to his job, and that there was a substantial likelihood that the breach would have continued for at least the remainder of Pablo's educational program — which was the motivating factor for the parties to enter into the contract in the first place. The likelihood that the Tribes would not perform their end of the bargain by returning Pablo to his job in time to complete his negotiated, planned practicum further supports a ruling that the Tribes' breach of contract was material. The trial court correctly held that deprivation of this core contractual benefit constituted a compensable and, therefore, material breach. The Tribes have cited no plausible reason to disturb this sound ruling and we discern none. It is therefore affirmed.

D. Waiver of Breach of Contract

In this appeal the Tribes do not contest the trial court's ruling that they breached their contract with Pablo by unilaterally modifying its terms when they refused to allow him to return to work as the director of TSS. However, the Tribes contend Pablo waived his right to damages for the breach on the basis that he had knowledge of the modification, and for 34 days continued to perform and receive benefits under the contract. We disagree.

While a material breach does not automatically end a contract, it gives the injured party a choice between canceling the contract and continuing it. . . . If the injured party elects to terminate the contract and acts accordingly, both parties are relieved of further obligations. If the injured party ends the contract "within a reasonable time after becoming aware of the facts," he will not be held to have waived the breach. Nor will a waiver be found where the injured party unsuccessfully attempts to persuade the breaching promisor to reject his repudiation and proceed honorably in the performance of his agreement. . . .

Here, Pablo returned from his educational leave with the intent of carrying out his obligations under the contract, *i.e.*, performing as program manager of TSS, completing his practicum and obtaining his advanced degree, and using his education and experience to further serve the Tribes. He learned of the so-called "transition" period a few days after he returned to work. Soon thereafter Pablo informed department head Swaney that he desired to return to his promised position, as specified in the contract. This was the first of several opportunities Pablo gave the Tribes to cure their breach.

Several weeks later, Pablo again notified Bearhead Swaney, this time in writing, that he was not content with his position under the transition structure of TSS; that he intended to discuss the matter with Executive Secretary Dupuis; and that he would resign if he was not restored to his position of program manager of TSS. Pablo's memo followed two contemporaneous discussions with Mr. Swaney where Pablo again told him he wanted his position as program manager restored. . . . Swaney refused to honor the Tribes' contractual promise. Pablo thus fully realized than he had been effectively stripped of his authority and responsibility as program manager of TSS, and that the tribal management structure had no intention of returning him to his position for the foreseeable future, if at all. One week after this final consultation with the supervisory triumvirate, Pablo resigned.

Under the circumstances, Pablo terminated the contract within a reasonable time after becoming aware of the relevant facts, *i.e.*, that the Tribes had breached the agreement, and that it was futile to attempt to continue to get them to make good on their promise. Accordingly, we hold that Pablo did not waive the Tribes' breach of contract. . . .

E. Constructive Discharge

On appeal, Pablo challenges the trial court's findings of fact and conclusion of law which form the basis of the ruling that he was not constructively discharged. . . .

We thus turn to the question whether, in light of the totality of the circumstances, a reasonable person in Joe Pablo's position would have found the working conditions at TSS so intolerable or discriminatory that he or she would have felt compelled to resign. In this inquiry we are guided by the general rule that a "single isolated instance" of employment discrimination is insufficient as a matter of law to support a finding of constructive discharge. . . . Instead, a plaintiff alleging constructive discharge must show some "aggravating factors," such as a continuous pattern of discriminatory treatment, or a series of other intolerable working conditions. . . .

The evidence in this case shows that when the proper legal standard is applied, the working conditions imposed on Pablo after he returned from educational leave meet the test for constructive discharge. . . .

In the six weeks between his return from his educational leave and his resignation, Pablo was confronted with numerous incidents, conditions and requirements which we conclude a reasonable employee in his shoes would have found "so difficult or unpleasant," or sufficiently intolerable, to compel resignation. Most significantly, the Tribes refused to return him to his former position of program manager of TSS, a violation of the express terms of the educational leave and future employment contract. He thus was unilaterally stripped of the supervisory and administrative authority he had previously held, and for which he was trained. This occurred in a context where his previous job performance as program manager of TSS was rated as "outstanding" by essentially the same people who denied him his contractually promised position. Against this backdrop, Pablo was, in effect, demoted to the position of lead social worker, although he was never given a job description notifying him what his actual new duties and responsibilities would be. The record indicates that the position of lead social worker lacked the authority and responsibility to undertake the tasks Pablo had negotiated with Eastern Washington University for completion of his work practicum with the Tribes—a requirement for the MSW degree, as discussed below. In short, Pablo reasonably believed that his demotion would effectively prevent him from completing his practicum, his degree, and his contractual obligations.

Upon reviewing the entire evidence, we are firmly convinced that it was necessary for Pablo to function as program manager of TSS in order to complete the requirements of his practicum. Pablo's uncontradicted testimony to this effect is corroborated by the documentary record. . . . Accordingly, finding of fact number 17 is clearly erroneous, and is therefore set aside in its entirety. . . .

In addition to breaching the employment contract, the Tribes violated Ordinance 69B, their own Personnel Rules, Regulations, and Procedures Manual, when they effectively demoted Pablo. [The Manual] requires Department Head Swaney, in relevant part, "to insure that the performance of each employee is evaluated":

> C. As the need arises, *i.e.*, when an employee changes positions or when performance problems are occurring and there is a need to document specific areas which need improvement. Ordinance 69B at 25.

If, in fact, department head Swaney believed there were serious administrative problems warranting a transition period before Pablo was returned to his full responsibilities as program manager at TSS, he was required by tribal law to conduct a written performance appraisal of Pablo. . . . At no time during his employment was Pablo given notice of the specific reasons for his demotion. . . . Pablo was thus denied the opportunity to respond to the alleged problems which led to his demotion, the transition period, and ultimately to his resignation.

In addition to the above, other aggravating factors contributed to the intolerable working conditions which the Tribes imposed on Pablo after he returned from educational leave. He was required to answer to an interim manager who had no training in social work, and who disciplined and threatened to suspend and/or terminate him for what the record indicates are ostensibly pretextual or picayune reasons. He was further reprimanded on two occasions by an employee who had no authority over him, and whom Pablo had previously supervised. He was excluded from program manager meetings, and found that other government officials external to TSS were equally confused about his role. Some fellow staff members felt the atmosphere at TSS to be uncertain, chaotic and fearful, and shared Pablo's belief that he would be fired or forced to quit. . . .

Considering the totality of circumstances, as we must, the number and nature of "aggravating factors" between the time of Pablo's return from educational leave and his resignation created a pattern of intolerable working conditions sufficient to establish constructive discharge. . . . Considering the totality of the circumstances, Pablo's resignation was reasonable and constitutes constructive discharge. We hold accordingly, . . . that Pablo's resignation was voluntary. . . .

G. Damages

. . . Pablo suffered a loss of $28,338 in salary and wages during the contract period as a result of the Tribes' actions. In addition to tendering this amount to Pablo, the Tribes shall pay the interest on the $9,300 personal loan Pablo was forced to take out to complete his second year MSW, for such would not have been necessary but for the Tribes' breach of contract and constructive discharge. Of course, since we awarded Pablo lost salary and wages for the Tribes' violations of the contract, he is liable for the princip[al] of the $9,300 personal loan. Pursuant to Rule 14 of the CS&KT Tribal Appellate Rules, Interest on Judgments, the Tribes shall pay Pablo interest on the judgment of $28,338, at the maximum rate allowed by law, commencing on July 14, 1993, the day the lower court entered its judgment in this case, and continuing to the day payment is tendered. Pursuant to Rule 15, Tribal Appellate Rules, Costs on Appeal, costs associated with this appeal are hereby awarded to Pablo. . . .

NOTES

1. In *HCN Treasury Dept. v. Corvettes on the Isthmus*, 7 Am. Tribal Law 78 (Ho-Chunk Nation Supreme Court 2007), the court affirmed a trial court ruling that there was no subject matter jurisdiction over a contract breach claim because the tribal agent had no authority to enter into a contract, there was no signed contract, and no positive law to apply:

> This case comes to the Court as a contract dispute but with an important twist. . . . Remarkably, the contract in dispute is a rather routine one between a Hotel and Convention Center to rent space in the appellant's place of business in the ordinary course of business.
>
> The problem with this simple recitation of the issue is that there is no signed contract. Both parties proceeded on the basis that they thought they had the authority to enter into contracts. . . .
>
> . . . [T]he appellant posits that this is not a case in law, *i.e.*, a suit for damages, but rather a suit in equity. It claims this is an oral contract yet

fails to cite the law, custom or tradition which gives the Court's of this Nation subject matter jurisdiction.

... The problem the Court notes is that this is a confusion of principles. The appellant has sued for breach of contract but desires a remedy in equity, quantum meruit, which is measured in monetary terms, damages. This is still fundamentally a legal remedy which requires the Court's to have substantive law to apply. It is said that equity does not assist a party with unclean hands. In other words, a party who creates the problem should not be able to claim foul for its own misdeeds.

... [The facts leave] the Court without a clear indication that there was a meeting of the minds as to the substance of the contract. Both sides claimed the other was in breach at least to some of the terms, none of which were memorialized in writing.

HCN Treasury Dept., 7 Am. Tribal Law at 79-80. The court added that the tribal legislature had an opportunity to correct this problem by adopting commercial codes:

This problem is of the Nation's own making and can be solved by having the HCN Legislature enact a commercial code that explicitly and not implicitly delegates authority to enter into contracts to sub-entities of the Nation. While the appellant cites a parade of horribles that any person can refuse to pay the Nation and get away with it, this is highly overblown given that the Nation has operated for nearly 13 years under the current Constitution with no such litany of broken contracts evident. It is not for the Court[]s to make positive law. It can recognize custom and tradition as a basis of law, but given the fact that Ho-Chunk people did not develop an advanced commercial system which gave clear rules on what to do in case of a breach leaves this Court with little recourse. The HCN Constitution is explicit in giving the authority to make laws to the HCN Legislature. The Courts cannot exceed the authority which created them.

HCN Treasury Dept., 7 Am. Tribal Law at 80.

2. In *Tribal Credit Program of Confederated Salish and Kootenai Tribes of the Flathead Reservation v. Bell*, 7 Am. Tribal Law 10 (Confederated Salish and Kootenai Tribes Court of Appeals 2007), the court held that the foreclosure action against a mortgagor who succeeded in the interest of her deceased parents was a breach of contract:

This issue arises from the modification freely entered into by Tribal Credit and [defendant], whereby $200 every two weeks was deducted from her pay as a Tribal employee and applied in equal measure to each of the four loans then outstanding. [Defendant] performed her part of the bargain for over four years until Tribal Credit unilaterally commenced foreclosure proceedings. We hold that the [defendant was] not in default, that Tribal Credit breached the agreement thereby excusing the further performance of the [defendant]. . . .

However, it would not be equitable to excuse the debt entirely. To do so would unjustly enrich the [defendant]. . . .

We must also consider the effect of plaintiff's failure to respond to Michel's reasonable efforts to determine the status of her father's loan accounts. . . . Upon written request for good cause by an interested party, including the holder of an interest in the mortgaged real estate, a mortgagee has a duty to disclose in writing within a reasonable time, the terms and status of the underlying obligation. Failure to respond gives rise to liability for damages. . . .

We hold that plaintiff failed to sustain its burden of proof for foreclosure. We further hold that credit should be given for the sum of $79,203.19, which the record shows without contradiction that [defendant] paid on the two notes still in contention. However, she must account for the value of the benefit conferred upon her[.] . . . [W]e do not consider it equitable to permit plaintiff to recover interest after plaintiff had a reasonable time to respond to Melissa's status request. Also, even though the maintenance of insurance was not plaintiff's obligation, we do not consider it equitable to permit plaintiff to be reimbursed for insurance premiums when they made no move to recover the benefit.

Tribal Credit Program, 7 Am. Tribal Law at 18-20.

3. In *Loyal Shawnee Cultural Center, Inc. v. Peace Pipe, Inc.*, 6 Am. Tribal Law 71 (Cherokee Nation Supreme Court 2006), the court applied the federal Rule 19 of the Federal Rules of Civil Procedure in holding that the Shawnee Tribe of Indians was merely a "necessary" party, and not an "indispensable" party that would require dismissal in a contract breach action:

> Rule 19 of the Federal Rules of Civil Procedure has a two tier test to determine whether the Trial Court has discretion in ordering the joinder of a third party. If the Trial Court finds that the Shawnee Tribe of Indians is an indispensable party for determination of the issues between the [parties], then the Court would be compelled to order the joinder of the Shawnee Tribe of Indians; or, if the Court finds that the joinder of the Shawnee Tribe of Indians may be necessary to avoid a second proceeding to determine issues between the Plaintiff/Appellant and Shawnee Tribe of Indians concerning the same subject matter, then the Trial Court has discretion in the orderly administration of his cases, to determine the joinder of third parties.

Loyal Shawnee Cultural Center, 6 Am. Tribal Law at 71.

4. Like federal and state courts, tribal courts typically do not find that a tribe waives its immunity from suit by filing counterclaims to a breach of contract action. In *Novak Construction Co., Inc. v. Grand Traverse Band of Ottawa and Chippewa Indians*, 2001 WL 36194389 (Grand Traverse Band of Ottawa and Chippewa Indians Court of Appeals 2001), the court wrote:

> A second, equitable, argument is that the Tribe's filing a Counter-Claim over the same contract is a waiver of the defense of sovereign immunity since the tribe has brought itself into the court by its own consent. A third argument is that the Tribal Constitution grants this court the authority to hear cases "arising under the Constitution" and that the Tribal Council's entering into a contract is granted under Article V, Section 2; therefore granting jurisdiction of the Appeals Court. However, there are no authorities cited for those novel interpretations. This action clearly refers to a contract action so that it cannot involve reviewing legislative acts. It "arises" under the contract, not under the Constitution.
>
> Finally, the argument is that the Tribe is equitably estopped from asserting sovereign immunity if it is allowed to bring claims against the Plaintiffs/Counter Defendant/Appellants. This while removing their right to defend

or pursue their own claims which involve breach of the same contract rights that the Tribe relies on. . . .

The other arguments of the fundamental unfairness to leave a party with no remedy while allowing a government the authority to counter sue are denied as without a basis in law. This is evident in most jurisdictions as an attribute of sovereignty. With very limited exceptions, the federal government may sue a citizen for violation of a contract while that government enjoys sovereign immunity except where it has agreed to waive it. The state of Michigan has enacted legislation with a similarly harsh result to bar a suit in its courts by an unregistered, out-of-state contractor doing business in Michigan (a non-citizen of the sovereign) or by a non-licensed residential contractor (a citizen), yet Michigan may bring suit, or allow, an action against either one in spite of their own lack of a forum for a remedy. Those contractors could avoid the harsh results by taking action to avoid these results before entering into their contracts, just as the Plaintiff/Appellant could have done here, but failed to do anything in advance.

State and federal Statutes of Limitation regularly time-bar all remedies by individuals, but not for the government. Governments must make decisions that leave persons without a remedy while they remain subject to counterclaims in many areas. Most seem unfair to the person affected. There are many wrongs that do not have a right to a remedy in areas beyond sovereign immunity. . . .

Novak Const., 2001 WL 36194389, at *1-3.

B. CONTRACT DISPUTE RESOLUTION

1. ARBITRATION

CONFEDERATED TRIBES OF GRAND RONDE V. STRATEGIC
WEALTH MANAGEMENT, INC.

Confederated Tribes of the Grand Ronde Community of Oregon Tribal Court, No. C-04-08-003, 6 Am. Tribal Law 126, 32 Indian Law Rep. 6148 (August 5, 2005)

The opinion of the court was delivered by: SUZANNE OJIBWAY TOWNSEND, Acting Tribal Court Judge . . .

I. Issue Presented

Petitioner, the Confederated Tribes of the Grand Ronde Community of Oregon ("the Tribe" or "Petitioner") asks the Court to vacate or modify the award of $1,723,191.10 it was ordered to pay to Respondents Strategic Wealth Management ("SWM"), Patrick Sizemore, Paradigm Financial Service, Inc. ("Paradigm") and Mark Sizemore. This award represents attorney fees and costs to be paid to Respondents as prevailing parties, and is part of the Final Award dated August 13, 2004, in American Arbitration Association (AAA) Case No. 75 Y 181 00066 03JRJ, Confederated Tribes of the Grand Ronde Community of Oregon, Claimant and Strategic Wealth Management, Inc.,

Patrick Sizemore, Paradigm Financial Services, Inc., and Mark Sizemore, Respondents. . . .

II. Background

The parties do not dispute the relevant facts concerning their history and prior relationship.

In 1992, the Tribe selected Respondent SWM to provide financial and investment advice and services to the Tribe. The decision to hire SWM was made by the Grand Ronde Tribal Council at a meeting on January 8, 1992. The minutes from that meeting provide in relevant part as follows:

> [The Tribal Controller] suggested the Council consider selecting a portfolio method of investing funds whereby the money would be invested in a number of different areas (i.e., stock market, C.D.'s). Resolution No. 002-92. Following further explanation, [Councilman Ray McKnight] moved to adopt a resolution to authorize moving the Tribal funds from the Bureau of Indian Affairs to private money managers to insure better earnings and more accountability of the funds. [Councilwoman Kathryn Harrison] seconded the motion. Motion carried by a vote of 7 yes, 0 no and 0 abstentions.

. . . Resolution No. 002-92, which was approved by Tribal Council at the January 8, 1992, meeting, provides as follows:

> NOW, THEREFORE BE IT RESOLVED, that the Tribal Council for the Confederated Tribes of the Grand Ronde Community of Oregon hereby adopts the Tribal Trust Fund Investment Policy and authorizes the Tribal Chairman, Executive Officer, Finance Officer and one other Tribal Council member designated by the Tribal Chairman to execute the investment policy agreement with Strategic Wealth Management and to make tactical allocations as necessary throughout the life of this agreement.

On January 9, 1992, the Tribe and Respondent SWM entered into an Investment Advisory Agreement ("1992 Agreement") the terms of which provides that SWM would provide financial advice, training, consulting and investment services to the Tribal Council and to other Tribal managers and executives. . . .

The 1992 Agreement did not contain an attorney fees clause authorizing an award of fees to a prevailing party in subsequent actions under the Agreement.

Section 11(i) of the 1992 Agreement is a "choice of laws" provision that provides as follows:

> The validity of this Agreement and of any of its terms or provisions, as well as the rights and duties of the parties hereunder shall be governed by the laws of the State of Washington.

Section 11(h) of the 1992 Agreement provides as follows:

> All controversies which may arise between Client and Advisor concerning any transaction or the construction, performance or breach of this or any other agreements (sic) between them whether entered into prior, on, or subsequent to the date hereof, shall be determined by arbitration. Arbitration is final and binding on the parties. The parties are waiving their right to seek remedies in

court, including the right to jury trial. Pre-arbitration discovery is generally more limited than and different from court proceedings. The arbitrator's award is not required to include factual findings or legal reasoning and any party's right to appeal or to seek modification of rulings by the arbitrators is strictly limited. The panel of arbitrators will typically include a minority of arbitrators who were or are affiliated with the securities industry. Any arbitration shall be in accordance with the rules then applying of the American Arbitration Association, New York Stock Exchange or the National Association of Securities Dealers, at Client's election. If Client fails to make this election within five days of receipt of a written request, then he authorized Advisor to make this election. The award of the arbitrators or of the majority of them, shall be final and judgment (sic) upon the reward (sic) rendered may be entered into any court State or Federal, having jurisdiction. Client specifically agrees that at least one of the arbitrators must be knowledgeable to (sic) the type of securities transactions in his account or knowledgeable as to any investment recommended or effected (sic) on his behalf.

Patrick Sizemore provided the bulk of the initial services under the 1992 Agreement. Significant services were provided by SWM (through its President, Patrick Sizemore) on the Reservation by way of meetings, conferences, training sessions, financial updates, accounting reports and communications, both in person and by letter. . . .

In 1998, SWM presented a group of loans to the Tribe that had been brokered by Respondent Paradigm. Mark Sizemore, a brother of Patrick Sizemore was the President of Paradigm. Thereafter, the Tribe invested in at least 27 loans that had been brokered by Paradigm. Paradigm received brokerage fees on each loan, paid by the Tribe.

Disputes arose between the Tribe and SWM, and between the Tribe and Patrick Sizemore, Mark Sizemore and Paradigm. The Tribe combined its claims against all Respondents and filed suit in Multnomah County Circuit Court in *Confederated Tribes of the Grand Ronde Community of Oregon v. Strategic Wealth Management Inc., et al.*, Case No. 01-00-11623. The Tribe alleged claims against all Respondents under the Oregon Securities Act and for common law breach of fiduciary duty, fraud, negligent misrepresentation and breach of contract. The Tribe's claims involved both the 1992 Agreement with SWM and certain later agreements and dealings involving investment advice and related activities provided by SWM and the other Respondents. . . .

On or about February 3, 2003, the Tribe filed a Demand for Arbitration with the American Arbitration Association ("AAA"). Three AAA arbitrators were assigned to hear the Tribe's claims. Over the Tribe's objections as to the location, the arbitration hearings were held in Seattle, Washington over several days in March and April, 2004. The Final Award was issued on August 13, 2004.

The Final Award denied all of the Tribe's claims against all Respondents. The Final Award further included an affirmative award of attorney fees and costs against the Tribe in the following amounts:

In favor of Respondents SWM and Patrick Sizemore:

$1,273,395.00 in attorney fees,
$158,007.00 in costs;
$39,621.79 in arbitrator compensation costs

In favor of Respondents Paradigm and Mark Sizemore:

$145,375.00 in attorney fees,
$6,485.00 in costs;
$1,250.00 in AAA expenses;
$99,057.41 in arbitrator compensation costs.

In their Final Award, the arbitrators noted that the 1992 Agreement did not contain an attorney fees provision. However, the arbitrators reasoned that because the AAA rules in effect at the time of the arbitration authorized the arbitrators to "grant any remedy or relief that the arbitrator deems just and equitable within the scope of the agreement of the parties," they were authorized to look beyond the agreement to the Oregon Securities Law. The arbitrators found authority for the award of attorney fees and costs in the prevailing party "fee shifting" provisions of Oregon Securities Law, general Oregon law concerning the award of attorney fees and costs, and AAA Rules. . . .

The Tribe objected to Respondents' applications for attorney fees and costs in the arbitration proceeding on the basis that the Tribe had not waived its sovereign immunity with respect to such an affirmative award. In response, the arbitrators determined that the Tribe had waived its immunity from suit generally with respect to SWM in the 1992 Agreement and that such a general waiver encompassed an award of attorney fees and costs. The arbitration panel determined that the Tribe had also waived its sovereign immunity with respect to Patrick Sizemore individually, even though he was not a signatory to the 1992 Agreement. The panel noted that the Multnomah County Circuit Court had compelled arbitration of the Tribe's claims against both SWM and Patrick Sizemore under the 1992 Agreement, and thus applied that decision as the "law of the case."

With respect to Respondents Paradigm and Mark Sizemore, the arbitrators acknowledged that these Respondents were not signatories of the 1992 Agreement, or to any other contract binding the Tribe to arbitration. However, the arbitrators determined that the Stipulation and later Multnomah County Circuit Court Order implementing that stipulation constituted a waiver of the Tribe's sovereign immunity. . . .

III. Analysis
A. Jurisdiction

. . .

1. Personal Jurisdiction
a. Tribal Code

Section 310(d)(1)(A) of the Tribal Court Ordinance describes this Court's jurisdiction in relevant part as follows:

[A]ll civil actions where there are sufficient contacts with the Grand Ronde Reservation upon which to base jurisdiction consistent with the Constitution and laws of the Tribe and the United States. It is the intent of this paragraph to authorize the broadest exercise of jurisdiction consistent with these limitations. Without limiting the foregoing, the Court shall have jurisdiction over the following matters: proceedings involving . . .

> contracts to which the Tribe is a party; . . .

We first note that nothing in the Tribal Court Ordinances limits this Court's jurisdiction to those contracts, such as the 1992 Agreement, that are in writing. And, the Tribal Court Ordinance does not limit the Court's jurisdiction to only those activities that involve a contract, formal or otherwise. Rather, the Ordinance sets out a very broad jurisdictional provision that encompasses "all civil actions where there are sufficient contacts with the Grand Ronde Reservation upon which to base jurisdiction consistent with the Constitution and laws of the Tribe and the United States."

We find nothing in the laws of the Tribe or the Tribal Constitution to prohibit this Court from taking personal jurisdiction over Respondents in this matter; indeed based on the facts described above, taking jurisdiction over Respondents is fully consistent with the provisions of the Tribal Court Ordinance. . . .

2. Subject Matter Jurisdiction

Subject matter jurisdiction is defined as a "court's power to hear and determine cases of the general class or category to which the proceedings in question belong; the power to deal with the general subject involved in the action." BLACK'S LAW DICTIONARY (6th Ed.)

The authority of the Grand Ronde Tribal Court is set forth in the Tribe's Tribal Code. Tribal Court Ordinance Section 310(d)(1)(A) gives this Court subject matter jurisdiction over:

> [A]ll civil actions where there are sufficient contacts with the Grand Ronde Reservation upon which to base jurisdiction consistent with the Constitution and laws of the Tribe and the United States. It is the intent of this paragraph to authorize the broadest exercise of jurisdiction consistent with these limitations. Without limiting the foregoing, the Court shall have jurisdiction over the following matters: proceedings involving . . .
>
> contracts to which the Tribe is a party; . . .

Despite Respondents' desire to characterize the parties' dispute as limited to the arbitration proceeding itself, the issues before this Court all revolve around the 1992 Agreement, the later contracts, written or oral, under which the various Respondents provided services to the Tribe, and the various consensual services the Respondents provided to the Tribe on the Tribe's reservation.

Respondent also raised an issue under the provision of the 1992 Agreement which provides that judgment on the arbitration award "may be entered into any court, State or Federal, having jurisdiction." Absent language that clearly designates a certain forum as the exclusive forum, such a clause is not mandatory, and does not exclude another court. . . .

As noted above, all Respondents had significant relations with the Tribe such that this Court may extend personal jurisdiction over them in this action. Nothing in the contracts between the parties provides for jurisdiction exclusively in another court. The Tribal Court ordinance thus provides this Court with subject matter jurisdiction in this matter.

B. Sovereign Immunity

The concept of sovereign immunity derives from the common-law concept that the sovereign cannot be sued without its consent. *Nevada v. Hall*, 440 U.S. 410, 414-415 (1979). Indian Tribes enjoy sovereign immunity from suit similar to that enjoyed by the United States. *Santa Clara Pueblo v. Martinez*, 436 U.S. 49, 58, 98 S. Ct. 1670, 56 L. Ed. 2d 106 (1978); *United States v. U.S. Fidelity & Guaranty Co.*, 309 U.S. 506, 512; 60 S. Ct. 653, 656, 84 L. Ed. 894 (1940). Sovereign immunity shields tribes from suits for monetary damages, and its purpose is to protect the Tribe's assets from loss through litigation. *Cogo v. Central Council of the Tlingit & Haida Indians*, 465 F. Supp. 1286, 1288 (D. Alaska 1979). Only Congress or the Tribe itself may waive the Tribe's immunity from suit. *Kiowa Tribe of Oklahoma v. Manufacturing Technologies, Inc.*, 523 U.S. 751, 754, 118 S. Ct. 1700, 140 L. Ed. 2d 981 (1998).

As this Court has previously opined, tribal sovereign immunity is "rooted in the unique historical relationship between Indian tribes and United States government: Indian tribes are immune from suit because they are sovereigns predating the United States Constitution and because such immunity is necessary to preserve their autonomous political existence." *Guardipee*, Case No. C-91-002-LJM at 2-4. . . .

An Indian Tribe is not subject to suit in state court for either on- or off-reservation commercial conduct unless Congress or the Tribe has expressly waived the Tribe's immunity from suit. *Kiowa*, 523 U.S. at 760. As Respondents point out, it is not necessary that specific words waiving the Tribe's immunity be included in a waiver. *See C&L Enterprises, Inc. v. Citizen Band of Potawatomi Indian Tribe of Oklahoma*, 532 U.S. 411, 121 S. Ct. 1589, 149 L. Ed. 2d 623 (2001). Still, such a waiver of sovereign immunity must be unequivocally expressed and it is to be narrowly construed. *Santa Clara Pueblo*, 436 U.S. at 58; *United States v. Testan*, 424 U.S. 392, 399, 96 S. Ct. 948, 37 L. Ed. 2d 114 (1976). . . .

Finally, a voluntary waiver of sovereign immunity by an Indian tribe does not waive the Tribe's immunity for cross-claims or counter-claims. *United States v. U.S. Fidelity & Guaranty Co.*, 309 U.S. at 511-12; *Oklahoma Tax Commission v. Citizen Band Potawatomi Indian Tribe*, 498 U.S. 505, 509 (1991). And, a general waiver of sovereign immunity may not be construed to extend to attorney fees unless the sovereign has clearly indicated that it does. *Fitzgerald v. United States Civil Service Commission*, 554 F.2d 1186, 1189 (D.C. Cir. 1977) (holding that a general provision in the Veteran's Preference Act allowing the Veterans Commission "to take corrective action" was not a sufficiently express waiver of sovereign immunity to allow for the award of prevailing party attorney fees). . . .

Based on the history described above, it is clear that absent either a general waiver of immunity with respect to prevailing party attorney fees and costs under an applicable Tribal code provision or a clear specific waiver by the Tribe in a specific contract, the Tribe may not be assessed attorney fees and costs in any contractual dispute. For purposes of a waiver of sovereign immunity, this

Court finds that if the Tribe did not specifically waive its immunity from an award of prevailing party attorney fees and costs, then there is no jurisdiction for a court to enforce such an award, either under the Oregon Securities Law or any other Oregon or federal law. This analysis is consistent both with the purposes of the sovereign immunity doctrine, with the long line of jurisprudence interpreting that doctrine and with the "American Rule" that recovery of prevailing party fees is not implicit, but must be found in either statute or contract. *See Alyeska Pipeline Co. v. Wilderness Society*, 421 U.S. 240, 247 (1975).

As discussed below, only Congress and the Tribe itself may waive the Tribe's immunity from suit. Respondents do not argue that Congress has waived the Tribe's immunity from suit. This Court, then, looks to the facts presented to determine whether the Grand Ronde Tribal Council expressed, clearly and unequivocally, its legislative intent to waive its sovereign immunity with respect to an affirmative award of prevailing party attorney fees and costs.

1. SWM and Patrick Sizemore

Respondents contend that, with respect to SWM and its President, Patrick Sizemore, the Tribe waived its sovereign immunity when it entered into the 1992 Agreement. The Court looks to both the specific provisions of that Agreement and the history surrounding its adoption to determine legislative intent.

As noted above, the arbitration clause contained in the 1992 Agreement does not contain an attorney fees provision. The arbitration clause provided only that

> [a]ny arbitration shall be in accordance with the rules then applying of the American Arbitration Association, New York Stock Exchange or the National Association of Securities Dealers, at Client's election.

At the time the 1992 Agreement was signed, the AAA rules did not provide for an affirmative award of attorney fees. Despite the fact that neither the underlying contract nor the AAA rules referred to in the contract contained a fee shifting provision with respect to prevailing party attorney fees and costs at the time the Grand Ronde Tribal Council issued its Resolution approving the 1992 Agreement, Respondents urge the Court to imply such a waiver from the language in the 1992 Agreement requiring "all controversies" to be submitted to arbitration. In the alternative, Respondents suggest that the Court look outside the 1992 Agreement to AAA rules put in place after the 1992 Agreement was signed, or to the Tribe's use of Oregon securities laws to find a basis for the waiver.

With respect to an implied waiver, Respondents suggest a very expansive interpretation, arguing that because the arbitration provision in the 1992 Agreement requires the parties to arbitrate "all controversies" that may arise between Client and Advisor concerning "any transaction or the construction, performance or breach of this or any other agreement between them," then any claim Respondents have with the Tribe necessarily provides Respondents with a potential recovery against the Tribe's treasury. This Court declines to interpret the arbitration provision in the 1992 Agreement so broadly. To do so would fly in the face of traditional rules of statutory construction, which require courts to strive above all else to interpret the intent of the legislature. . . .

As noted above, Respondent SWM drafted the 1992 Agreement and presented it to the Tribe. It is thus proper for this Court to construe the contract in the light most favorable to the Tribe. A more reasonable interpretation of the 1992 Agreement's arbitration clause would limit the scope of the waiver to any claims arising directly under the contract for its breach, and perhaps to any claims necessarily or closely related to a breach of the Agreement. This interpretation does not necessarily or even incidentally include prevailing party attorney fees. Indeed, absent an attorney fee recovery clause in a statute or contract, recovery of attorney fees is generally not available. . . .

Respondents also point to the holding in *C&L Enterprises, Inc. v. Citizen Band of Potawatomi Indian Tribe of Oklahoma*, 532 U.S. 411, 121 S. Ct. 1589, 149 L. Ed. 2d 623 (2001), arguing that it is controlling here. In that case, the Citizen Band Potawatomi Indian Tribe of Oklahoma signed a construction contract with C&L Enterprises that included an arbitration clause. After arbitration, an award was rendered in favor of C&L Enterprises in an amount that included damages and attorney fees. On appeal, the U.S. Supreme Court determined that the agreement the Potawatomi Indian Tribe had signed constituted a clear consent to arbitration and that such a consent constituted a clear waiver of the Tribe's sovereign immunity from suit by C&L Industries, and also, by way of the choice of laws provision in the contract, constituted a consent to the enforcement of arbitral awards in Oklahoma State Court. Because the underlying arbitration award in *C&L Enterprises* included an award of attorney fees and costs, Respondents urge the Court to conclude that the holding is dispositive here.

This Court finds no indication that the court in *C&L Enterprises* considered the scope of the Tribe's waiver of sovereign immunity, and in particular the issue of whether the Tribe's waiver was broad enough to include an affirmative award of attorney fees and costs against the Tribe. Neither does the Court find anything in the holding to indicate that the decision altered longstanding requirements that a waiver of sovereign immunity must be clear and unequivocally expressed.

Although the arbitral award reviewed by the Court in *C&L Enterprises* included an award of attorney fees and costs against the Tribe, the propriety of the attorney fee award was not explicitly addressed, nor does it appear that the Tribe specifically raised the issue of attorney fees and costs as a separate issue. Rather, the Court more generally concluded that under the specific circumstances and with respect to the specific language of the contract before the Court, the Tribe had "clearly consented to arbitration and to the enforcement of arbitral awards in Oklahoma State Court . . ." and the matter was remanded back to State court for further proceedings. *C&L Enterprises*, 532 U.S. at 423. The holding in *C&L Enterprises* is thus of little assistance regarding the question whether a Tribe waives immunity for an affirmative award of attorney fees merely by entering into a contract with an arbitration clause.

And, even if the holding in *C&L Enterprises* applies such that the underlying arbitration clause constitutes a clear waiver of the Tribe's immunity with respect to its agreement to arbitrate and to have the arbitration award enforced in any court having jurisdiction to do so (a determination this Court need not and does not make), it would not follow that the arbitration clause is also an express waiver of the Tribe's immunity with respect to prevailing party fees and costs (or pre-judgment interest).

With respect to Respondents' contention that the Tribe waived its immunity for an award of attorney fees because the AAA rules had changed by the time the Tribe filed its suit and was ordered to arbitration, this Court finds little merit in that argument. It might be reasonable to interpret the arbitration provision as evidence of the Tribe's intent to be bound by any procedural rules that the AAA had in place at the time a claim under the agreement was arbitrated. However, the interpretation Respondents urge goes well beyond that. To interpret the Tribal Council's legislative action as intending to allow the scope of its waiver of immunity (and thus the degree of risk at which the public treasury was placed) to be substantively altered at will by later actions of an outside party is an interpretation this Court finds untenable. Such a broad construction of the Tribal Council's intent would defeat the very protections intended by the doctrine of sovereign immunity.

And, even if Respondents are correct that the Tribe agreed to be bound by any future changes to the AAA rules, it would not necessarily follow that the Tribe's agreement would provide authority for an arbitral award of prevailing party fees. This is so because under AAA rules, arbitrators would still require a statutory or contractual basis upon which to base such an award. . . . This authority would be found only in the parties' underlying contract (which it is not in this instance) or, in this case, in Oregon Securities Law.

Thus, the question becomes whether the Tribe waived its sovereign immunity with respect to an affirmative award of prevailing party attorney fees, simply by bringing suit under Oregon Securities Law. In answer to this question, cases interpreting waivers of sovereign immunity in the context of counterclaims and cross claims are more on point.

As discussed above, the United States Supreme Court has held that the United States is immune from cross-claims, except where Congress has consented to their consideration. *United States v. U.S. Fidelity and Guaranty Co.*, 309 U.S. at 512. And, with respect to counterclaims against a sovereign where immunity has not been waived, a claimant is limited in his recovery to amounts in recoupment. *Bull v. U.S.*, 295 U.S. 247, 262, 55 S. Ct. 695, 79 L. Ed. 1421 (1935). A claim for attorney fees is not in the nature of a recoupment, but is rather affirmative relief. *See Woelffer v. Happy States of American, Inc.*, 626 F. Supp. 499, 503 (N.D. Ill. 1985); *U.S. ex rel. Dept. of Fish and Game v. Montrose*, 788 F. Supp. 1485, 1495 (C.D. Cal. 1992). Absent an express waiver of sovereign immunity with respect to attorney fees against the plaintiff sovereign, such an award would constitute an impermissible affirmative judgment against the sovereign. . . . And, as noted above, a general waiver of sovereign immunity does not extend to cover attorney fees unless the Tribe makes such a waiver express. . . .

To summarize: Nothing in the arbitration provision or any other contract between the Tribe and SWM demonstrated an unequivocal and express waiver of sovereign immunity with respect to an affirmative award of prevailing party attorney fees and costs against the Tribe. And, nothing in the evidence presented to this Court demonstrates that the Grand Ronde Tribal Council either discussed or anticipated that it was authorizing a contract that would place it at risk for attorney fees and costs should it arbitrate claims under the 1992 Agreement. Nothing the Tribe did by way of filing its suit in Multnomah County Circuit Court can be said to constitute a waiver with respect to an affirmative award of attorney fees and costs.

In the absence of any facts to demonstrate the intent of the Tribal Council to waive its immunity with respect to the recovery of prevailing party attorney fees and costs, it would be improper for this Court to imply a waiver that was nowhere expressed by the Tribal Council, either explicitly or implicitly.

2. Paradigm and Mark Sizemore

Respondents point to the 2002 Stipulation wherein the Tribe agreed to arbitrate its claims against these Respondents as providing the requisite wavier of sovereign immunity. This reliance is misplaced.

In order to decide this case, it is not necessary for this Court to determine whether or not the attorney for the Tribe had specific authority to enter into the stipulation and to arbitrate the Tribe's claims against Respondents Paradigm and Mark Sizemore. This is so because the issue here is not the waiver with respect to the agreement to arbitrate; rather, the issue is the scope of the waiver, if any. In this instance, the Court concludes, as above, that even assuming the Tribe waived its immunity with respect to the agreement to arbitrate, there is nothing in the record to demonstrate that the scope of such a waiver covered an affirmative award of prevailing party fees and costs. . . .

Since 1994, the Grand Ronde Tribal Code has provided as follows:

> The Tribal Council retains the exclusive authority to waive the sovereign immunity of the Tribe including the Tribal Council members, Tribal Officer, Tribal Attorney, Tribal staff and committee members from suit. Any such waiver must be expressly and specifically authorized by Tribal Council Resolution.

Tribal Government Organization and Procedures Ordinance, Tribal Code Section 210(c)(2).

No evidence has been provided to the Court that the Tribe's legislative body—i.e., the Tribal Council—clearly and expressly waived the Tribe's immunity from suit with respect to Paradigm and Mark Sizemore's affirmative recovery of prevailing party attorney fees. . . .

Respondents raise additional defense, including:

C. Waiver and Estoppel

A claim of sovereign immunity is a "jurisdictional prerequisite which may be asserted at any state of the proceedings." . . .

The Tribe is not subject to claims of waiver or estoppel when it raises the defense of sovereign immunity. . . .

IV. Summary

This Court need not look to the specific provisions of either the Federal Arbitration Act or the Oregon Arbitration Act ("Arbitration Acts") in order to make its determination. It is not the case, as Respondents contend, that if the arbitrators simply "got it wrong" on the legal issue of the waiver of sovereign immunity, then Petitioner is limited to the specific and limited review provisions of the Arbitration Acts for its remedy. Because sovereign immunity is jurisdictional it may be raised at any point in a proceeding. When reviewing an arbitration award in the context of a claim of sovereign immunity, the court is not limited in its review, but reviews the issue of jurisdiction issue de novo. *Missouri River Services, Inc. v. Omaha Tribe of Neb.*, 267 F.3d 801, 852 (8th Cir. 2001).

Upon its de novo review of the limited question of whether the Tribe waived its sovereign immunity with respect to the affirmative award of prevailing party attorney fees and costs, this Court finds that the Tribe did not waive its sovereign immunity in any of the agreements it entered into with Respondents, nor did the Tribe waive its immunity when it chose to file suit under the Oregon Securities Laws or when it stipulated to arbitrate its claims with Respondents Paradigm and Mark Sizemore.

Because the Tribe did not waive its sovereign immunity with respect to an award of prevailing party attorney fees and costs, the arbitrators had no authority to award prevailing party fees and costs. By doing so, the arbitrators went beyond the terms of the agreement under which the arbitration occurred. Absent a waiver of sovereign immunity, a court has no jurisdiction to enforce such an award.

While this result may strike some as unfair, the Court notes that the doctrine of sovereign immunity has been in existence since the inception of the United States. The Court further points out that all Respondents are savvy businessmen with long histories of business dealings in Indian Country. Even if equity were a defense to the exercise of a sovereign's immunity from suit, which it is not in this case, these Respondents were in a better position than most both to recognize and to take action to reduce the risks associated with doing business with a Tribal Sovereign.

V. Conclusion

The Court concludes that the arbitration panel did not have authority to award attorney fees and costs against the Tribe because the Tribe did not waive its sovereign immunity with respect to such an award. By awarding attorney fees and costs against the Tribe, the arbitration panel thus exceeded the scope of its authority. For that reason, there is no jurisdiction for the enforcement of that award. That portion of the Final Award in American Arbitration Association Case No. 75 Y 181 00066 03JRJ, Confederated Tribes of the Grand Ronde Community of Oregon, Claimant and Strategic Wealth Management, Inc., Patrick Sizemore, Paradigm Financial Services, Inc., and Mark Sizemore, Respondents assessing attorney fees and costs against the Tribe is void and is hereby vacated.

NOTES

1. When an Indian tribe engages in commercial business operations both on and off the reservation, the tribal courts resolving the disputes that arise out of these transactions employ intertribal common law to resolve them.

Confederated Tribes of Grand Ronde v. Strategic Wealth Management, Inc. is a good example of a circumstance where tribal law adopted Anglo-American legal constructs as a means of adaptation to modern transactional and business needs. The underlying contract (a contract relating to financial and investment services) and the arbitration clause, coupled with its incorporation of tribal sovereign immunity, were all Anglo-American legal constructs utilized by the Tribes. The tribal code provisions establishing subject matter jurisdiction mirrored federal rules in significant ways. The federal common law allowing for tribal court jurisdiction over the nonmembers and the defenses raised by SWM were all Anglo-American legal constructs. The tribal court relied upon its own authority for the background policy relating to tribal sovereign immunity and many federal court cases for much of the remainder of the issues. All of this was intertribal common law.

Patrick Sizemore, president of SWM, and Mark Sizemore, president of Paradigm, were brothers who worked for years in Indian country, tailoring their businesses to tribal clients. They represented themselves and their businesses as being able to bridge the gap between on-reservation tribal capital and off-reservation business investment opportunities—experts in both finance and investment, and in relevant federal Indian law. The question of tribal sovereign immunity should not have been a surprise when they negotiated their contract with the Tribes.

2. The tribal appellate court affirmed the tribal court's decision in *First Specialty Ins. Co. v. Confederated Tribes of the Grand Ronde Community of Ore.*, No. A-05-09-001 (Grand Ronde App., Oct. 31, 2006), available at http://turtletalk.files. wordpress.com/2007/11/exh-11-tct-coa-opinion.pdf. A federal court affirmed that the Grand Ronde tribal court could assert jurisdiction over the Sizemores' claims. *See First Specialty Ins. Co. v. Confederated Tribes of the Grand Ronde Community of Ore.*, No. 07-05-KI (D. Or., Nov. 2, 2007).

3. In *Grand Traverse Band of Ottawa and Chippewa Indians v. C.H. Smith Co., Inc.*, 2002 WL 34487861 (Grand Traverse Band of Ottawa and Chippewa Tribal Court 2002), the court rejected the efforts of the Band to avoid arbitration by unilaterally voiding a construction contract:

> It is clear that the contract entered into between the parties contains a provision to arbitrate *"all claims, disputes, and other matters in question between OWNER and CONTRACTOR arising out of or relating to the Contract Documents or the breach thereof. . . ."* . . . This provision clearly and expressly relates to **all claims, disputes and others matters in question which relate to the contract between the parties**. The Complaint and Counterclaim solely and only allege claims that relate to the contract between Plaintiff and Defendant. Both parties allege breach of contract. . . .
>
> The issue is whether Plaintiff can unilaterally void the contract and thus avoid the agreement to arbitrate. . . .
>
> Both the Complaint and Counterclaims allege breach of contract. It is clear that all of claims made by Plaintiff relate to the contract. Similarly, it is clear that all of the counterclaims made by Defendant relate to the contract. Furthermore, it is clear that the parties agreed to resolve all such claims by arbitration.

C.H. Smith Co., 2002 WL 34487861, at *2 (emphasis in original).

4. Arbitration clauses in contracts with Indian nations may operate to waive the immunity of the tribe in tribal court, similar to the United States Supreme Court's decision in *C&L Enterprises, Inc. v. Citizen Band Potawatomi Indian Tribe of Oklahoma*, 532 U.S. 411 (2001).

   In *Ho-Chunk Nation v. B&K Builders, Inc.*, 3 Am. Tribal Law 381 (Ho-Chunk Tribal Court 2001), the court found a waiver in a construction contract arbitration clause:

   > The similarities existing between the Architectural Agreement and contract documents analyzed in [*C&L Enterprises*] make such judgment controlling. . . . In *Potawatomi*, the U.S. Supreme Court found that an arbitration clause represented a "clear" waiver of tribal sovereign immunity from suit, . . . based upon the following factors: 1) the arbitration clause contained a general enforcement provision, . . . 2) an incorporated contract document contained an enforcement provision with a designation of judicial forum, . . . 3) a choice of law provision referenced the applicable law of the place of the construction site, . . . 4) the applicable law designated state courts for enforcement of arbitral awards, . . . and 5) the authority of the official(s) executing the contract was not an issue of concern. . . .
   >
   > Likewise, the Architectural Agreement includes an arbitration clause with a general enforcement provision, indicating that "judgment may be entered upon [the arbitral award] in accordance with applicable law in any court having jurisdiction thereof." . . . The Architectural Agreement then identifies the applicable law as "the law of the principal place of business of the Architect. . . ." . . . Wisconsin law provides that "any party to the arbitration may apply to the court in and for the county within which such award was made for an order confirming the award." WIS. STAT. §788.09. Therefore, the plaintiff would need to arbitrate the contractual dispute as the Architectural Agreement contains a clear waiver of sovereign immunity. . . .

   B&K Builders, 3 Am. Tribal Law at 390.

5. Some tribal courts might find that boilerplate arbitration clauses violate tribal common law and refuse to enforce them as "unconscionable." For example, in *Green Tree Servicing, Inc. v. Duncan*, 7 Am. Tribal Law 633 (Navajo Nation Supreme Court 2008), the court refused to enforce a binding arbitration clause involving the foreclosure of a tribal citizen's home:

   > The lengthy arbitration clause in the contract states "[a]ll claims and controversies arising from or relating to this [c]ontract . . . shall be resolved by binding arbitration by one arbitrator selected by Assignee [Green Tree] with consent of the Buyer(s) [Duncan]." It further states that "[t]he parties agree and understand that they choose arbitration instead of litigation to resolve disputes." In all capital letters, it further states that "THE PARTIES VOLUNTARILY AND KNOWINGLY WAIVE ANY RIGHT THEY HAVE TO A JURY TRIAL EITHER PURSUANT TO ARBITRATION UNDER THIS CLAUSE OR PURSUANT TO A COURT ACTION BY ASSIGNEE (AS PROVIDED HEREIN)." . . . In other words, Duncan agreed to waive her right to file any court action and to instead arbitrate any dispute with Green Tree, and waived her right to a jury completely, but agreed to allow Green Tree to file a court action to repossess the mobile home.
   >
   > The question is whether such an agreement is enforceable under Navajo law. Green Tree submits that under Navajo law words are sacred. This Court

has upheld contracts if the language is clear and the parties voluntarily entered into the agreement. *See, e.g., Smith v. Navajo Nation Dept. of Head Start*, No. SC-CV-50-04, 6 Am. Tribal Law 683, 686-87, 2005 WL 6235868 at *2-3 (Nav. Sup. Ct. 2005). However, despite the clarity of language, the Court has also stricken agreements if they violate Navajo public policy expressed in our statutory law or in *Diné bi beenahaz'áanii. See Allstate Indemnity Co. v. Blackgoat*, No. SC-CV-15-01, 6 Am. Tribal 637, 642, 2005 WL 6235869 at *3-4 (Nav. Sup. Ct. 2005) (striking liability cap in insurance contract for purposes of pre-judgment interest as violative of Navajo principle of nályééh); *see also Smith*, No. SC-CV-50-04, 6 Am. Tribal Law at 686-87, 2005 WL 6235868 at *2-3 (stating test).

To discern Navajo public policy, the Court turns first to several provisions of the Navajo Nation Code. . . . Section 2-302(A) of the Navajo Uniform Commercial Code . . . states that if a court determines whether a contract, or any part of it, is "unconscionable," it is empowered (1) to refuse enforcement of the entire contract, (2) to enforce the remainder of the contract without the unconscionable clause or clauses, or (3) [to] limit the application of any clause to avoid an unjust result. The basic test is whether, "in the light of the general commercial background and the commercial needs of the particular trade or case, the clauses involved are so one-sided as to be unconscionable under the circumstances existing at the time of the making of the contract." . . . The concept of unconscionability "recognizes that in some cases the lack of bargaining power of one party compared to that of the other party will result in an oppressive contract." . . . Similarly, the Navajo Nation Unfair Consumer Practices Act discusses the concept of "unconscionable trade practice," which also considers the difference in understanding and bargaining power, and prohibits acts that result in unfair transactions. . . .

The Navajo Nation Code also includes provisions encouraging arbitration. The recently enacted Navajo Nation Arbitration Act authorizes the use of arbitration clauses. . . . The Act then balances the value of arbitration agreements with the value of fairness, and states that not all agreements to arbitrate are enforceable in the Navajo Nation.

There are also Fundamental Law principles that inform Navajo public policy on arbitration agreements in mobile home contracts. The Navajo maxim of *házhó'ógó* mandates "more than the mere provision of an English form stating certain rights . . . and requires a patient, respectful discussion . . . before a waiver is effective." *Eriacho v. Ramah District Court*, No. SC-CV-61-04, 6 Am. Tribal Law 624, 629-30, 2005 WL 6235849 at *3-4 (Nav. Sup. Ct. 2005). *Házhó'ógó* requires a meaningful notice and explanation of a right before a waiver of that right is effective. *Id. Házhó'ógó* is not man-made law, but rather a fundamental tenet informing us how we must approach each other as individuals. *Navajo Nation v. Rodriguez*, No. SC-CR-03-04, 5 Am. Tribal Law 473, 478, 2004 WL 5658107 at *5 (Nav. Sup. Ct. 2004). It is "an underlying principle in everyday dealings with relatives and other individuals." *Id.* Though primarily discussed previously in the criminal context, *házhó'ógó* equally applies in civil situations. *See Kesoli v. Anderson Security Agency*, No. SC-CV-01-05, slip op. at 6 (Nav. Sup. Ct. October 12, 2005).

Several other principles are relevant. In a recent case, the Court discussed the Navajo concept of *nábináheezlágo be t'áá lahjį algha' deet'a*, which is, finality is established when all participants agree that all of the concerns or issues have been comprehensively resolved in the agreement. *Casaus v. Diné College*, No. SC-CV-48-05, 7 Am. Tribal Law 509, 512-13, 2007 WL 5917128 at *3-4 (Nav. Sup. Ct. 2007). It is also said that in the process of "talking things out," or meeting the Navajo common law procedural requirement that everything must be talked over, *see Navajo Nation v. Crockett*, 7 Nav. R. 237, 241 (Nav. Sup. Ct. 1996), there is a requirement of *ííshjání ádooniíł*, that is, making something clear or obvious. *See Phillips v. Navajo Housing Authority*, No. SC-CV-13-05, 6 Am. Tribal Law 708, 711-12, 2005 WL 6236356 at *3-4 (Nav. Sup. Ct. 2005) (applying Navajo concept *ofííshjání ádooniíł* to require clear intent to retroactively grant sovereign immunity to Navajo Housing Authority); *Yazzie v. Thompson*, No. SC-CV-69-04, 6 Am. Tribal Law 672, 674, 2005 WL 6235970 at *2 (Nav. Sup. Ct. 2005) (same for Court rules on fees in domestic violence cases); *Rough Rock Community School v. Navajo Nation*, 7 Nav. R. 168, 174 (Nav. Sup. Ct. 1995) (same for qualifications of school board candidates). Navajo decision-making is practical and pragmatic, and the result of "talking things out" is a clear plan. *Rough Rock Community School v. Navajo Nation*, 7 Nav. R. 168, 174 (Nav. Sup. Ct. 1995). When faced with important matters, it is inappropriate to rush to conclusion or to push a decision without explanation and consideration to those involved. *Áádóó na'nile'dii éí dooda*, that is, delicate matters and things of importance must not be approached recklessly, carelessly, or with indifference to consequences. *Rodriguez*, No. SC-CR-03-04, 5 Am. Tribal Law at 478, 2004 WL 5658107 at *5. This is *házhó'ógó*. *Id*. If things are not done *házhó'ógó*, it is said that it is done *t'aa bizaka*.

An arbitration clause must be set in the manner of *házhó'ógó* (standard of care), so as to make a clause *ííshjání ádooniíł* (clear and obvious), therefore it will [] be made *t'aa na'nile'dii* (not recklessly, carelessly or with indifference to consequences) resulting in making the arbitration clause *nábináheezlágo be t'áá lahjį algha' deet'a* ([a] comprehensive agreement). This was shown in *Eriacho*, wherein the Navajo Nation argued that the explanation of right to a jury trial was not necessary due to Ms. Eriacho's apparent education level. *See* No. SC-CV-61-04, 6 Am. Tribal Law at 630 n. 2, 2005 WL 6235849 at *3-4 n. 2. In response, this Court rejected "any rule that conditions the respectful explanation of rights under Navajo due process on subjective assumption concerning the defendant. This right exists for all defendants in our system." *Id*.

Finally, these principles must be applied in the context of the importance of a home in Navajo thought. This Court has noted that a home is not just a dwelling, but a place at the center of Navajo life. *Fort Defiance Housing Corp. v. Lowe*, No. SC-CV-32-03, 5 Am. Tribal Law 394, 398, 2004 WL 5658062 at *2 (Nav. Sup. Ct. 2004). Based on this principle, the Court scrutinizes procedures to make sure they protect a home owner's ability to maintain a healthy home and family. *See id*.; *Phillips*, No. SC-CV-13-05, 6 Am. Tribal Law at 711-12, 2005 WL 6236356 at *3-4.

Considering all of these principles together, the Court holds that the specific arbitration clause in the financing contract is unenforceable. . . . This case ultimately concerns the repossession of a mobile home, and the ability to keep the home may depend on the availability of a home owner's counterclaims against a finance company seeking to take the home. The requirement that Duncan engage in arbitration instead of filing counterclaims in an action brought by Green Tree in a Navajo district court greatly burdens her ability to defend herself. She must figure out the arbitration process, spend potentially significant amounts of money and travel off the

Nation to participate. Importantly, Green Tree is under no similar obligation; under the agreement it may file a Navajo court action to assert its rights, and is protected from defending counterclaims. The burden is then only one way. The effect of this grossly unequal position is not clearly explained in the clause. An arbitration clause in a mobile home finance contract cannot be enforced if the contract does not contain clear and specific language explaining that the Navajo consumer understands that he or she is surrendering his or her rights to bring claims in a Navajo court, but nonetheless is allowing claims against him or her to compel surrender of the home.

Green Tree Servicing, 7 Am. Tribal Law at 639-42.

2. SUITS AGAINST TRIBAL BUSINESSES—WAIVERS OF SOVEREIGN IMMUNITY

World Extreme Cage Fighting, LLC v. Mohegan Tribal Gaming Authority

Mohegan Gaming Disputes Tribal Court, No. GDTC-CV-03-133-TBW, 2004.NAMG.0000001 (January 20, 2004)

The opinion of the court was delivered by: Wilson, J.

Introduction.

This action is brought in Two Counts seeking damages for an alleged breach of contract. . . . [T]he Plaintiff alleges that it and the Defendant, doing business at The Mohegan Sun Casino, entered into an agreement wherein it was agreed that the Plaintiff would present a live cagefighting event at the Defendant's arena, and that the Defendant breached the contract to the damage of the Plaintiff. . . .

Discussion.

It is agreed that the Defendant is a legal entity of The Mohegan Tribe of Indians of Connecticut, a federally recognized Indian Tribe. As such, the Tribe and its operating entities such as the Defendant, Mohegan Tribal Gaming Authority, are not subject to suit (even in a State Court or in this Court)—even for breach of contract involving commercial conduct—unless Congress has authorized the suit or the Tribe has waived its immunity. *Kiowa Tribe of Oklahoma v. Manufacturing Technologies, Inc.*, 523 U.S. 750 . . . (1998). It is agreed that Congress has not authorized the suit. The issue is whether the Tribe has waived its immunity.

This case concerns a written agreement, prepared by the Defendant, and presented to and signed by both parties. The agreement concerns a commercial event. The contract was entered into, was to be performed in, and was to be governed by the laws of the Mohegan Reservation of Connecticut. . . . Paragraph 20 also provides that this court "shall have exclusive jurisdiction of any and all matters pertaining to the construction of this agreement, disputes under this agreement, and enforcement of this agreement. Mohegan Sun [The Defendant] and WEC [The Plaintiff] hereby consent to such exclusive jurisdiction."

Paragraph 17 provides: "Equity. Each party recognizes that the rights granted hereunder are personal, valuable and unique and that a breach of any of the material provisions hereof will cause the other irreparable harm which may not be adequately compensated at law and each shall be entitled to equitable relief, including, without limitation, a preliminary injunction, to prevent such breach in addition to whatever actual damages may be had at law."

The Plaintiff relies on the two quoted paragraphs in support of its argument that the Defendant has waived its immunity. The Defendant, *contra*, contends that a waiver of sovereign immunity must be express and that the quoted provisions are not express enough, *in haec verba*, to waive immunity. The Defendant contends that paragraph 17 authorizes only an action in equity, with damages incidental thereto. This court does not agree. Paragraph 17, to the contrary, expressly recognizes and assumes the existence of a remedy at law, *i.e.*, to recover damages, and provides for equitable relief incidental thereto, or "in addition to." This in itself is an express waiver.

In addition, paragraph 20 provides that this court shall have exclusive jurisdiction over all matters pertaining to the contract, and the Defendant expressly consents to such exclusive jurisdiction. To what end is such recognition and consent to be employed, but for suits such as this? By such "consent" the Defendant voluntarily yielded to such an end; it acquiesced thereto; it agreed to it; it submitted; in short, it waived its immunity, expressly. . . .

The Defendant apparently argues that there is not any waiver of sovereign immunity unless there is a statement such as: "The Tribe will not assert the defense of sovereign immunity if sued for breach of contract." The U.S. Supreme Court has unanimously rejected such an argument. In *C&L Enterprises, Inc. v. Citizen Band Potawatomi Indian Tribe of Oklahoma*, 532 U.S. 411, 121 S. Ct. 1589 (2001), the court held that an agreement to arbitrate constituted a "clear waiver" of sovereign immunity, and that by such agreement to arbitrate, the tribe "plainly" consented to suit. The court said that arbitration clause "has a real world objective." 121 S. Ct. at 1596. So, in this case, to the real world end, the contract specifically authorizes judicial enforcement of the Plaintiff's rights in this action, in this court.

Based on the foregoing, this court is not required to apply the common law rule of contract interpretation that a court should construe ambiguous language against the interest of the party that drafted it. The rule is inapposite because the contract is not ambiguous. "Nor did the Tribe find itself holding the short end of an adhesion contract stick: The Tribe proposed and prepared the contract; [W.E.C] . . . foisted no form on a quiescent Tribe." (*C&L Enterprises v. Potawatomi Tribe*, op. cit. at 1597).

For the reasons stated, it is concluded that under the agreement the Defendant proposed and signed, the Defendant clearly consented to suit in this court and thereby waived its sovereign immunity from this suit. As to Count One, therefore, the Defendant's Motion to Dismiss is denied. As to Count Two, based on an "implied" contract, by definition there is no "express" waiver of any immunity, and the Motion to Dismiss is therefore granted as to Count Two.

NOTES

1. The court here suggests that the holdings of the United States Supreme Court virtually control the outcome in this case; specifically, the court seems to hold that *C&L Enterprises, Inc. v. Citizen Band Potawatomi Indian Tribe of Oklahoma*, 532 U.S. 411 (2001), circumscribes its discretion on questions of tribal sovereign immunity. *C&L Enterprises* held that a boilerplate construction contract that included a provision allowing for disputes to be resolved in arbitration, and enforced in state court, constituted a waiver of sovereign immunity. Why does the tribal court adopt the views of that Court on the question of implied waivers of tribal sovereign immunity? Or does it?

2. Moreover, is this contract the kind of question that is susceptible to a holding that the terms of the contract amount to a waiver?

3. Some tribes have peremptorily waived sovereign immunity in so-called proprietary contracts, as in the case of the Grand Traverse Band of Ottawa and Chippewa Indians:

> (a) Notwithstanding any other provisions of the Chapter, 15 GTBC §218, the Tribe hereby waives its sovereign immunity, as well as the sovereign immunity of the Grand Traverse Band Economic Corporation, for any contract claim brought in accordance with this section, provided:
>
> > (1) The claim arises from an express, written contract signed by all parties to the contract;
> > (2) The claim is brought by a party to the contract or a party expressly made a third-party beneficiary under the terms of the contract;
> > (3) The contract was entered into by the Grand Traverse Band Economic Development Corporation or a Tribal Business Enterprise, as defined in 15 GTBC Chapter 2, Part 1, subordinate to the Grand Traverse Band Economic Development Corporation; and
> > (4) The contract was entered into in the performance of a proprietary function, which means any activity conducted primarily for the purpose of producing a pecuniary profit for the Tribe, the Grand Traverse Band Economic Development Corporation, or a Tribal Business Enterprise excluding, however, any activity normally supported by a government unit by taxes or fees.
>
> (b) Notwithstanding 15 GTBC §202, the Tribe may not be subjected to suit under this section for:
>
> . . .
>
> > (5) Any suit based upon a contract that contains provisions concerning sovereign immunity and consent to suit. For any such contract, the contractual provisions relating to sovereign immunity supersede the application of this section.
>
> (c) The waiver extends solely to funds contained in the Grand Traverse Band Economic Development Corporation accounts, as defined in 15 GTBC §266.
>
> (d) The waiver of sovereign immunity contained in this section does not apply to any claim unless notice of the claim has been presented to the Tribe in writing within 180 days after such claim accrues, or within 90 days after

the claim has been discovered or should have been discovered in the exercise of reasonable diligence, whichever is later. Notice must be served personally, by certified mail, return receipt requested, or by any other courier or delivery service for which a return receipt is obtained, upon the Tribal Council Secretary, Grand Traverse Band of Ottawa and Chippewa Indians, 2605 N. West Bayshore Drive, Peshawbestown, Michigan 49682. The notice must identify the contract upon which the complaint is based, the nature of the claim, and the relief requested. Service of a suit based upon the claim satisfies the notice requirement.

(e) The Tribe and the Grand Traverse Band Economic Development Corporation consent to suit in any court of competence jurisdiction for suits based upon contract claims arising under this section; provided, that this consent does not preclude objections to venue, *forum non conveniens*, or subject matter jurisdiction.

6 GRAND TRAVERSE BAND CODE §208 (2003). *See also* SAULT STE. MARIE TRIBE OF CHIPPEWA INDIANS TRIBAL CODE §44.108 (1995) (enacting virtually the same waiver).

11

TORTS

Like the previous chapter on contract law, this chapter surveys several areas of tort law as interpreted and applied by Indian nations. In large measure, tribal courts tend to adapt and apply Anglo-American tort common law to contract disputes. Most Indian nations have not adopted comprehensive tort statutes, nor have tribal courts an extensive body of common law decisions upon which to rely. As a result, tribal courts resolve most contract disputes in accordance with the law of the state in which the tribe is located. More and more, however, tribal legislatures have enacted statutes generating rules for the filing of tort claims against tribal enterprises and tribal governments, especially in relation to tribal sovereign immunity.

This chapter also details a few areas in which tribal customary and traditional tort law may apply. In some cases, almost always cases exclusively involving tribal member parties, customary contract law directly affects the outcomes.

Moreover, this chapter details the kind of tort actions that arise in Indian country, either exclusively or more often than elsewhere.

A. TORT DOCTRINES UNDER TRIBAL LAW

1. NEGLIGENCE

SMITH V. SALISH KOOTENAI COLLEGE

Confederated Salish and Kootenai Tribes of the Flathead Indian Reservation Court of Appeals, No. AP-99-227-CV, 5 Am. Tribal Law 34 (May 26, 2004)

Before: MORAN, Chief Justice, MATT, Associate Justice and DESMOND, Substitute Associate Justice.

DESMOND J.:

On May 12, 1997, as part of their coursework in heavy equipment operation, three Salish Kootenai College ("SKC") students, Appellant James Smith, Shad Burland and James Finley, were traveling in a dump truck owned by the college on U.S. Highway 93, a state highway within the exterior boundaries of the Flathead Indian Reservation. Appellant Smith was driving. Tragically, a single vehicle rollover occurred. Shad Burland was killed and both James Finley and Appellant Smith were injured.

Appellant Smith is a member of the Umatilla Tribe. Shad Burland was, and James Finley is, enrolled in the Confederated Salish and Kootenai Tribes ("Tribes"). Legal claims of Mr. Burland's estate and Mr. Finley were resolved short of a trial.

Mr. Smith's claims against SKC were tried to a jury that, on September 29, 2000, after a week-long trial, returned a verdict in favor of SKC.[2] . . .

Before addressing Appellant Smith's specific points of appeal, some general comments are in order. Appellant Smith raises seven issues on appeal and contends that he was also denied a fair trial as a result of each error. A careful review of the trial transcript reveals otherwise. Appellant Smith was afforded a lengthy, carefully-conducted trial. The Court took the case seriously, as shown by its management of the trial and thoughtful consideration of the parties' legal arguments prior to, during and following the trial. After hearing a great deal of evidence, some of it inconsistent and some of it complicated expert testimony, the jury found that SKC was not negligent. Under the Constitution and laws of the Confederated Salish and Kootenai Tribes and relevant provisions of the Indian Civil Rights Act, Appellant Smith is entitled to a fair trial. He is not entitled to a perfect trial or to prevail at trial. *See, e.g., United States v. Hastings*, 461 U.S. 499 (1983); *Bruton v. United States*, 391 U.S. 123 (1968) (criminal cases.) Appellant Smith was provided a fair trial. We affirm the Tribal Trial Court in accordance with the following.

Appellant Smith makes the following arguments in support of his appeal on the merits:

1. The Tribal Trial Court erred when it declined to issue a curative instruction regarding SKC's investigatory notes.
2. The Tribal Trial Court erred when it disallowed Smith's use of testimony regarding Gordon Bartell's statements.
3. The Tribal Trial Court erred when it refused Smith's jury instructions regarding violations of laws and regulations as negligence per se or evidence of negligence.
4. The Tribal Trial Court erred when it refused Smith's jury instructions regarding "unavoidable accidents."
5. The Tribal Trial Court erred when it prohibited questions to witnesses and potential jurors regarding insurance.
6. The Tribal Trial Court erred when it ruled that SKC was owned by the Tribes.
7. There was insufficient evidence to support the jury verdict.

---

2. Tribal Trial Judge Winona Tanner's final Pretrial Order described the issues of fact to be tried regarding liability as follows:

(1) Was Defendant Salish-Kootenai College negligent and, if so, was its negligence a cause of Plaintiff's damages, if any?
(2) Was Plaintiff [Smith] contributorily or comparatively negligent and if so, was his negligence a cause of his damages, if any?

1. SKC's Investigatory Notes

At trial, Appellant Smith called as a witness Robert VanGunten, SKC's Director of Adult and Continuing Education. Mr. VanGunten testified concerning SKC's investigation of the accident. He stated that he had interviewed students and that he had taken notes of the interviews. However, no notes were produced in the course of discovery even though Appellant Smith had served SKC with a subpoena duces tecum directing it to produce all documents concerning the investigation. Counsel pursued the issue outside of the presence of the jury. Mr. VanGunten testified that he had attempted to find the notes but was unable to do so. . . .

Understandably concerned about SKC's inability to produce the notes, and skeptical about possible motives, Appellant Smith's counsel requested that the jury be instructed, "if a party had better evidence of the events or the information that existed at the time and they failed to produce it, then that could be viewed with distrust." . . . The Court declined the instruction, stating that the question of the whereabouts of any notes had been "asked and answered by the witness." . . .

At the beginning of the trial, the Court had instructed the jury as follows:

> If weaker and less satisfactory evidence is offered and it appears that it is within the power of the party to offer stronger and more satisfactory evidence, the evidence offered should be viewed with distrust.

. . . Appellant Smith contends that this instruction was insufficient to address the issue because it was given before the jury heard that Mr. VanGunten had made notes he was no longer able to locate and also because the emphasis should be on SKC's failure to produce the evidence, rather than offering "less satisfactory evidence." Appellee SKC asserts that this pretrial instruction adequately covered the issue. We agree.

When a standard of review has not been established by tribal law or prior court decision, we may look to the standard of review adopted by other courts. *Bick v. Pierce*, 23 Ind. Law. Rep. 6175, 6176 (CS&K Court of Appeals 1996). The standard of review we will apply to a trial court's decision on a jury instruction is abuse of discretion. *See Finstad v. W.R. Grace*, 2000 MT 228, 8 P.3d 778 (2000).

Further, we will apply the reasoning of the Court in *Schuff v. A.T. Klemens & Son*, which stated, "In reviewing for abuse of discretion, the reviewing court does not determine whether it agrees with the trial court. Rather, it considers whether the trial court, in its exercise of discretion, acted arbitrarily without employment of conscientious judgment or exceeded the bounds of reason in view of all circumstances." *Schuff*, 2000 MT 357, 16 P.3d 1002 (2000). We find no abuse of discretion here. After hearing the evidence, the Trial Judge apparently concluded that the facts did not support one premise of the proposed instruction, *i.e.*, that it was "within the power of the party to offer stronger and more satisfactory evidence." The trial judge evidently believed Mr. VanGunten's testimony that he simply was unable to locate any notes as opposed to Appellant Smith's assumption that "SKC concealed or destroyed the notes because they supported his theory of how and why this rollover happened." Appellant's Brief, p 13. Appellant Smith's characterization of

Mr. VanGunten's actions as "deceptive behavior," "discovery abuse," and "a surprise revelation that it [SKC] concealed and destroyed evidence," are not supported. The Trial Judge's ruling did not deny Appellant Smith a fair trial.

2. Gordon Bartell's Statements

Prior to the trial, answering Appellant Smith's Motion, the Trial Judge ruled statements of the late Gordon Bartell were inadmissible. Mr. Bartell was an instructor in the commercial driving program who assigned the three students their duties the day of the accident. (Mr. Bartell died before the trial.) At trial, Appellant Smith attempted to present testimony that SKC, through Mr. Bartell, had expressly directed him to drive on the day of the accident. The Court then, again, ruled the evidence inadmissible. Appellee SKC contends that the Trial Court's ruling was correct.

The Trial Court did not abuse its discretion. Evidence on this contested issue was presented to the jury. The substance of Mr. Bartell's testimony was admitted into evidence in a statement made by Mr. Finley to a Montana Highway Patrol Office on the day of the accident. . . . Appellant Smith's counsel was aware that the jury had been given this information because he stated, in his closing argument,

> I think there's been some discussion about the report that was passed around for you to read, the voluntary statement taken [sic] by James Finley at the hospital by Gordon the instructor. [sic] We know that this truck was first driven, on the statement it was driven by Shad Burland. But on instructions at the beginning of the day, at the beginning of the workday when Gordon, the instructor, was assigning daily duties to all, he told Shad Burland and James Smith to alternate drivers throughout the day.

. . . Appellant Smith contends that the Court should have permitted Mr. Finley and Appellant Smith him to testify directly on this subject. Although we agree with Appellant Smith that this question is relevant to the negligence issue, not just the comparative negligence issue, we find no error. The jury was presented evidence from Mr. Finley through the Highway Patrol report that Mr. Bartell directed Appellant Smith to drive. Appellant Smith's counsel reminded the jury of this in his closing argument. The jury's conclusion that SKC was not negligent is not necessarily inconsistent with that evidence.

3. Smith's Proposed Jury Instructions Regarding Violations of Laws and Regulations as Negligence Per Se or Evidence of Negligence

Appellant Smith's proposed jury instructions numbers 4 and 5 stated that violation of selected Federal Motor Carrier Safety Regulations adopted in Montana under §44-1-1005(1)(b), MONT. CODE ANN., would be negligence per se. Appellant Smith's proposed instructions numbers 36 and 37 stated that violations of regulatory standards other than law is evidence of negligence.

The regulations in question require regular inspection and maintenance of commercial motor vehicles and prohibit the use of commercial motor vehicles with, among other things, a cracked or broken leaf spring or a steering wheel "free play" thirty degrees or higher. The Trial Court refused the instructions.

For several reasons the Trial Court's decision was not an abuse of discretion. First, the jury was instructed adequately as to the duty of a vehicle owner to inspect and maintain his or her vehicle. Jury Instruction No. 24 addressed a vehicle owner's duty to[]

> exercise reasonable care to see that his vehicle is in reasonably safe and proper condition and must exercise reasonable care in the inspection of his vehicle to discover any defects which may prevent proper operation, and he is chargeable with knowledge of any defects which such inspection would disclose. He is thus liable for injuries which are shown to have resulted from conditions which he knew or should have known were so unsafe as to endanger others using the highways even though the particular injury in question may not have been foreseen.

. . . Second, as is outlined in the RESTATEMENT OF THE LAW, SECOND, TORTS,[9] the general standard of conduct required in tort law is that of a "reasonable prudent person under like circumstances." §874A, Comment e. Adoption of a more specific standard, when found in statutory or regulatory law, does not change the law of negligence, rather, "the expression of the standard of care in certain fact situations is modified; it is changed from a general standard to a specific rule of conduct." *Id.* The Trial Court clearly explained to the jury the general standard of care, i.e., the duty of inspection and maintenance. It chose not to accept Appellant Smith's proposed statement of a more specific rule of conduct.

Third, the Trial Court could have reasonably concluded that, in any event, Appellant Smith's contention regarding the applicability of the federal law and regulations was not correct. The Federal Motor Carrier Safety Regulations apply to vehicles "used in commerce." MONT. CODE ANN. §44-1-1005(b). That section provides in relevant part:

> (1) The department of justice shall:
>
> . . .
>
> > (b) provide standards for the safe operation of all motor vehicles used in commerce that exceed 26,000 pounds gross vehicle weight,

The Montana Department of Justice implemented this statutory limitation in §23.5.102(1), A.R.M. which states in relevant part:

> Any commercial motor vehicle . . . subject to regulation by the department under 44-1-1005, MCA, shall comply with and the department does hereby adopt, by reference, the following portions of the federal motor carrier safety regulations of the department of transportation.

The federal regulations promulgated pursuant to the Federal Motor Carrier Safety Act similarly limit their coverage. Section 49 C.F.R. 390.5 defines "motor carrier" as, "a for hire motor carrier or a private motor carrier." The regulation defines a "for hire motor carrier" as "a person engaged in the transportation of goods or passengers for compensation." Private motor carrier is defined as, "a person who provides transportation of property or passengers by commercial

---

9. We apply this statement of the law under §4-1-104, CSKT Laws Codified.

motor vehicle." The vehicle involved in the accident here, as a vehicle used for educational purposes, does not fit within this definition.

Thus, the jury was instructed on SKC's duty to inspect and maintain its vehicles and the Trial Court's decision to refuse jury instructions 4, 5, 36 and 37 was not in error.

4. Smith's Proposed Jury Instructions Regarding "Unavoidable Accidents"

On at least four occasions, in voir dire, his opening statement and his closing statement, SKC's counsel stated that what happened on May 12, 1997 was "just an accident," or words to that effect. He also asked the Montana Highway Patrol Officer if he had seen "some accidents that are not anybody's fault." (The officer replied, only once when a rock fell on a vehicle.)

Appellant Smith did not object at trial to any of the statements or the question to the highway patrol officer. He did, however, request proposed Jury instruction No. 33, which provided:

> The law does not recognize an unavoidable accident. The question you must decide is whether the defendant was negligent, and if so, what damages were caused by defendant's negligence.

Appellant Smith contends this instruction should have been given to "neutralize SKC's improper statements that accidents sometimes just happen." Appellant's Brief, p. 24.

Again applying the standard of review of abuse of discretion, we find no such abuse in the trial court's refusal of this instruction. Appellant Smith's interpretation of the Montana case law he cites is incorrect in this circumstance. Unlike the cases Appellant Smith cites, in this proceeding SKC did not request an unavoidable accident instruction and the trial judge did not give one. In fact, the jury heard the highway patrol officer's testimony, which had the same meaning as Jury Instruction No. 33. Furthermore, SKC's counsel's statements and questions were not improper. We find no error.

5. The Trial Court's Prohibition of Questions to Witnesses and Potential Jurors regarding Insurance

Prior to trial, the Trial Court granted SKC's Motion in Limine prohibiting questions to witnesses and potential jurors regarding insurance, relying on Rule 411, FED. R. EVID. This Rule prohibits reference to liability insurance because of its irrelevance and the belief "that knowledge of the presence or absence of liability insurance would induce juries to decide cases on improper grounds." Notes of Advisory Committee on Rules, Rule 411. (Citations Omitted.)

Appellant Smith presents no argument or theory that supports questioning witnesses about insurance in this case in the face of the general evidentiary rule against it. He cites a Montana Supreme Court case, *Garza v. Pepard*, 222 Mont. 244, 722 P.2d 610 (1986), in support of questioning jurors about insurance. However, in that case, the Montana Supreme Court, on an abuse of discretion standard of review, merely upheld a trial court's permitting such questioning in the factual circumstances of that matter. The Montana Supreme Court did not change the general rule against prohibiting questions to witnesses and potential jurors regarding insurance in *Garza v. Pepard*. We will not disturb the longstanding reasoning applicable to following Rule 411 Fed. R. Evid.

6. SKC Was Owned by the Tribes

Prior to the trial the Trial Court ruled that §4-2-204(2)(b), CSK&T Laws Codified applies in this matter. That provision states, in relevant part:

> (2) Limitations on tort recovery. Except as may be otherwise provided by law . . . when a corporation in which the tribes are an owner is found liable under the terms of this ordinance, the damages available to a prevailing party are limited as follows:
>
> . . .
>
>> (b) For claims arising from a single transaction or occurrence, a plaintiff may not recover a total compensatory sum greater than Two Hundred and Fifty Thousand Dollars ($250,000) or the maximum sum payable by an insurer under any policy required by federal law, whichever is less.

Thus, under the Trial Court's ruling, had he prevailed at trial, Appellant Smith's recovery would have been limited to $250,000. However, Appellant Smith did not prevail at trial. The jury was not made informed of the Trial Court's ruling. Since it found no negligence on the part of SKC, the jury did not proceed further and thus did not determine damages.

No reversible error occurred. When the jury deliberated, it was unaware of the Court's ruling under 4-2-204(2)(b). CSKT Laws Codified. Thus Appellant Smith's efforts to connect the Court's ruling on this provision to concerns that certain jurors may have possibly tried to protect the Tribe, as opposed the SKC are not persuasive. As for the basis of the Court's ruling, we cannot find it incorrect as a matter of law. In our February 17, 2003 decision on jurisdiction, we found the legal status of SKC relevant for purposes of determining subject matter jurisdiction and further found that "SKC is a tribal entity closely associated with and controlled by the Tribes. For purposes of determining jurisdiction, it must be treated as a tribal entity."

7. Sufficiency of Evidence to Support the Jury Verdict

Appellant Smith asserts that the jury's verdict was not supported by sufficient evidence. To the contrary, a review of the transcript indicates that sufficient evidence supported the jury's verdict. Evidence in support of Appellant Smith's theory of negligence was countered or explained by evidence presented by SKC. Appellant Smith's principal contentions, *i.e.*, that SKC was negligent in its alleged failure to inspect and maintain the vehicle were countered by witnesses and credible expert testimony. Thus it would not be proper for this Court to substitute its judgment for that of the jury.

Conclusion

As we stated in *Bartell v. Kerr*,

> [t]he jury was properly instructed on the issues under review. It made its decision on evidence that may have supported a contrary finding, but arriving at a conclusion in the midst of conflicting evidence is a jury's prime task.

Bartell v. Kerr, CSKT Court of Appeals, AP-94-104-CV, July 29, 1996 slip op. at 11.

Appellant Smith is dissatisfied with the jury's verdict. However, Appellant Smith was afforded a fair trial and we find no error.

NOTES

1. The Confederated Salish and Kootenai Tribes Appellate Court had previously ruled that the tribal court possessed jurisdiction over the plaintiff, Smith. Smith, an Indian person but not a citizen of the Tribes, originated the various lawsuits arising out of the tragic accident at issue in this matter, but when other parties counterclaimed against Smith, he asserted that the tribal court did not possess jurisdiction over the counterclaims against him, because he was a non-tribal citizen. *Smith v. Salish Kootenai College*, 3 Am. Tribal Law 22 (Confederated Salish and Kootenai Tribes Court of Appeals 2001).

   Smith brought his objection to tribal court jurisdiction over him to federal court, seeking a federal court order declaring that the tribal court had no jurisdiction over him. The district court held that the tribal court did have jurisdiction, and the Ninth Circuit affirmed. *Smith v. Salish Kootenai College*, 434 F.3d 1127 (9th Cir.) (en banc), *cert. denied*, 547 U.S. 1209 (2006).

   Note that the *Smith* claims were heard before a jury. There are special problems with empanelling a jury in Indian country. First, many tribal communities have limited territorial jurisdiction and population upon which to draw for a jury pool. The court in *Smith*, based on the relatively large and populous Flathead Indian Reservation, might not have the same practical difficulty that other courts might face, because of a much smaller reservation land base and a much smaller tribal population.

   Second, many tribal communities that do routinely empanel juries exclude non-tribal citizens from the jury pool, leading to what former Georgetown Law Center Dean Alex Aleinikoff calls a "democratic deficit." T. ALEXANDER ALEINIKOFF, SEMBLANCES OF SOVEREIGNTY: THE CONSTITUTION, THE STATE, AND AMERICAN CITIZENSHIP 115 (2002).

2. The rise of Indian gaming operations in Indian country has led to a corresponding rise in the number of non-Indians entering reservation and trust lands for gaming purposes. The Mashantucket Pequot Nation designed the Mashantucket Pequot Tribal Court to handle the influx of non-Indians and non-tribal citizens within its justice system. The Nation attracted former state judges and prominent tribal lawyers to sit on the bench in the tribal court.

   In *Barbosa v. Mashantucket Pequot Gaming Enterprise*, 4 Mash. Rep. 269, 2005. NAMP.000005 (Mashantucket Pequot Tribal Court 2005), the court held that the gaming enterprise could not be held negligent for failing to respond to an attack on a patron by another patron where the attack occurred over the course of only a couple of minutes:

   > [T]he plaintiff alleges that the defendant negligently failed to provide an
   > adequate level of security to the plaintiff. He points out that a waitress in

the area of the casino where the assault occurred saw [the defendants] hovering near the plaintiff and had an uneasy feeling that something was about to happen, yet did nothing. He observes that the first security officer who arrived at the scene, wearing a green jacket, did not attempt to physically restrain [the defendants]; he simply radioed to other security officers for help and told [the defendants] to stop kicking the plaintiff while pointing to the security cameras. . . .

The Gaming Enterprise responds that when the plaintiff was accosted in the concourse by [the defendants], who announced their intention to "kick his ass," he did not report this to any security officers, nor did he request anyone to keep an eye on them. The Gaming Enterprise points out that there were thousands of patrons in the casino on that night, and it had no warning from the plaintiff, who was the only person aware of the threat, that [the defendants] had voiced an intention to beat him. The Gaming Enterprise insists that its security personnel acted responsibly when they became aware of the assault. It contends that when the waitress had an uneasy feeling that things "didn't look right" there was no intervening time during which she could have acted on her suspicions, because they very next thing she saw was the beginning of the assault, and she immediately called security. Similarly, the Gaming Enterprise notes that a dealer at an adjacent table game instantly hit a panic button, causing a bevy of suited security officers to converge on the scene, when the commotion in the aisle erupted. The green-jacketed security officer testified that he was trained not to physically touch patrons, but rather radio to suited security officers when patrons become violent or unruly. Upon arriving at the scene, he immediately got on the radio and also told the assailants they were "on camera," which prompted the assailants to cease kicking the plaintiff and flee. . . .

"It is . . . settled law that the defendant, as a casino owner, is not an insurer of its invitees. The mere fact in and of itself that the plaintiff was injured on the premises does not constitute a lack of due care—or negligence—on the part of the defendant." *Ruffo v. Mashantucket Pequot Gaming Enterprise*, 1 MPR 3, 4 (1994). The fact that the plaintiff suffered a serious injury "is not enough for the recovery of damages." *Martello v. Mashantucket Pequot Gaming Enterprise*, 1 MPR 28 (1996). . . .

. . . The Gaming Enterprise did not have actual or constructive notice of the violent tendencies of [the defendants], or that the plaintiff was about to be assaulted. . . .

The beating administered by [the defendants] surely felt like an eternity to the plaintiff, but in fact occurred in only a few minutes, and ended shortly after the first security officer arrived at the scene. There was no evidence that if a higher level of training had been provided to the security officers, or if a greater number of security officers had been on duty, the plaintiff would not have been assaulted by [the defendants]. No testimony was presented as to how the Gaming Enterprise's training of security officers was deficient, why the security procedures were inadequate or what should have been the proper number of security officers in the area.

Barbosa, 4 Mash. Rep. at 271-73. The court also held that the gaming enterprise was not liable for negligently serving alcohol to the defendants, writing:

The plaintiff testified that McLane and Papadakis smelled of alcohol and that their speech was slurred, but presented no evidence whatsoever regarding the source or amount of the alcohol that they may have consumed. He introduced no evidence to enable the court to conclude that the Gaming Enterprise served alcoholic beverages to McLane and Papadakis. "[T]he plaintiff must remove this issue from the realm of conjecture and speculation." *Cole v. Mashantucket Pequot Gaming Enterprise*, 2 Mash. 104, 105 (1997), affirmed 1 MPR 49 (1998).

Barbosa, 4 Mash. Rep. at 275. The court did find in favor of the plaintiff in his claims against the defendants, awarding a $33,070 judgment against them. *See id*. at 275-76.

5. The *Barbosa* Court notes that it asserts personal jurisdiction over the defendants, who are residents of the State of New Hampshire, through the service of process provided by a Massachusetts process server/constable. The Foxwoods Casino's main competition for the northeastern gaming market, other than the Mohegan Sun Casino, is Atlantic City. As such, Foxwoods draws customers from all over the northeast, and perhaps the entire nation. One can imagine that it would be difficult for a person residing several states away to imagine being haled into court in a small Indian reservation in Connecticut to defend a tort claim. A defendant in a state court claim could remove the case to federal court in either Connecticut or the state in which the defendant resides, pending the federal court's discretion to remand the case back to state law. *See* 25 U.S.C. §§1441-1447; George L. Lieberman, *A Guide to Removal Remand*, 56 FED. LAW., August 2009, at 47.

But removal is not available to a defendant in a tribal court action. *E.g., Geroux v. Assurant, Inc.*, No. 08-184 (W.D. Mich., Oct. 23, 2009), available at http://turtletalk.files.wordpress.com/2009/11/geroux-v-assurant-dct-remand-order.pdf.

Note that the defendants in *Barbosa* did not appear to defend themselves, leading the tribal court — after hearing the case on the merits — to issue a default judgment against them. It becomes the burden of the plaintiff to seek enforcement of the tribal court judgment in a jurisdiction that has personal jurisdiction over the defendants, not an easy task. *E.g., Mashantucket Pequot Gaming v. Yau*, No. 117849/2009 (N.Y. Sup. Ct., Feb. 17, 2010), available at http://turtletalk.files.wordpress.com/2010/02/mashantucket-pequot-v-yau.pdf.

2. WRONGFUL DISCHARGE

WHITE-EAGLE v. HO-CHUNK NATION GRIEVANCE REVIEW BOARD

Ho-Chunk Nation Trial Court, No. CV 08-17, 8 Am. Tribal Law 62 (April 22, 2009)

TODD R. MATHA, Chief Judge. . . .

In 2001, the Court adopted a test for tortious constructive discharge. If a plaintiff asserted such a defense, the Court would require that he or she adequately demonstrate:

(1) the actions and conditions that caused the employee to resign were violative of [fundamental] public policy;

(2) these actions and conditions were so intolerable or aggravated at the time of the employee's resignation that a reasonable person in the employee's position would have resigned; and

(3) facts and circumstances showing that the employer had actual . . . knowledge of the intolerable actions and conditions and of their impact on the employee and could have remedied the situation.

Maureen Arnett et al. v. HCN Dep't of Admin., CV 00-60, -65 (HCN Tr. Ct., Jan. 8, 2001) at 16. . . .

A "constructive discharge is not in itself a cause of action, although it is routinely alleged as a separate count in complaints for wrongful discharge. Rather, constructive discharge is a defense against the argument that no suit should lie in a specific case because the plaintiff left the job voluntarily." *Id.* at 13. . . . Consequently, the Court concluded that a tribal plaintiff could assert such a defense by reference to a former statutory definition of "discharge," which constituted an "involuntary separation or termination of employment." *Id.* at 14. . . .

. . . The Court shall begin by commenting upon the nature of at-will employment. The ERA explains that an at-will "employee . . . is subject to termination with or without cause or notice," and "include[s] Executive Managers of the Nation's Gaming Facilities." ERA, §5.7o(l). Expanding on this concept, the Court previously explained that " 'either the employer or the employee may terminate the relationship at any time for any reason, or even no reason[,] and that the position is held for an unspecified amount of time.' " *Dan M. Sine v. Jacob Lonetree, as Pres. of the Ho-Chunk Nation*, CV 97-143 (HCN Tr. Ct., Aug. 3, 1998) at 6. . . . Therefore, "[i]t follows that there is no right to grieve because a grievance is a procedure whereby a party can challenge the basis of the decision to terminate an employee as unsubstantiated in law or in fact. If no reason need be given, it seems illogical to give someone a right to challenge. . . ." *Id.* at 8.

As a result, while the Court acknowledges the GRB's concern that the petitioner's resignation "allow[ed] supervisory management the opportunity to 'negotiate' the terms of separation to circumvent the disciplinary process," it considers the concern as misplaced. . . . Quite simply, a supervisor has no obligation "to engage in the disciplinary process, which is set in place to ensure the rights of the employee" in relation to an at-will employee's separation from employment because the individual maintains no property interest in his or her continued employment. *Id.* at 2. The Court appropriately resolves this constitutional issue since the HCN Legislature lacks the ability to confer constitutional adjudication authority upon an executive administrative agency. *LoneTree*, SU 07-04 at 4-6.

Yet, this determination does not necessarily conclude the inquiry. As the petitioner somewhat correctly notes, "the concept of constructive discharge is recognized as an exception to the employment-at-will doctrine." . . . However, a distinction exists in constructive discharge jurisprudence: "an employee must independently prove a breach of contract or tort in connection with employment termination. . . ." . . . The present case must involve the latter identified species of constructive discharge earlier acknowledged by the

Court. An at-will employee, by definition, exercises his or her duties in the absence of a contractual arrangement. "The nature of the plaintiff's at-will employment, authorizing termination for any reason, is incompatible with plaintiff's claim that [her] employer could not discharge [her] by subjecting [her] to intolerable conditions" in the absence of establishing a violation of a fundamental public policy. . . .

The Supreme Court of California explained the justification underlying the public policy exception to at-will employment. Briefly, "an employer has no right to terminate employment for a reason that contravenes fundamental public policy as expressed in a constitutional or statutory provision. An actual or constructive discharge in violation of fundamental public policy gives rise to a tort action in favor of the terminated employee." . . . More comprehensively,

> at root, the public policy exception rests on the recognition that in a civilized society the rights of each person are necessarily limited by the rights of others and of the public at large; this is the delicate balance which holds such societies together. Accordingly, while an at-will employee may be terminated for no reason, or for an arbitrary or irrational reason, there can be no right to terminate for an unlawful reason or a purpose that contravenes fundamental public policy. Any other conclusion would sanction lawlessness, which courts by their very nature are bound to oppose. . . . Just as the individual employment agreement may not include terms which violate fundamental public policy, so the more general "compensation bargain" cannot encompass conduct, such as sexual or racial discrimination, "obnoxious to the interests of the state and contrary to public policy and sound morality."

Gantt v. Sentry Ins., [824 P.2d 680, 686-87 (Cal. 1992)].
. . . "[T]ort claims for wrongful discharge typically arise when an employer retaliates against an employee for '(1) refusing to violate a statute . . . , (2) performing a statutory obligation . . . , (3) exercising a statutory right or privilege . . . , or (4) reporting an alleged violation of a statute of public importance.'" . . .

. . . Essentially, "even if [the petitioner] could raise a triable issue of fact as to constructive discharge, h[er] case cannot reach the trier of fact unless [s]he can also show a wrongful discharge in violation of fundamental public policy." . . .

Quite clearly, the petitioner has not alleged a violation of fundamental public policy, but has rather attempted to avoid presenting such a showing. . . . The petitioner has nonetheless cited four (4) potential statutory provisions capable of evidencing policy violations. First, the petitioner apparently claims that Executive Director Decorah failed to adhere to the principles underlying the practice of affording performance evaluations. . . . Yet, this assertion seemingly ignores the fact that the petitioner was an at-will employee dischargeable for any reason or no reason at all. Second, the petitioner apparently claims that Executive Director Decorah engaged in harassment when he requested that the petitioner submit her resignation. . . . The ERA sanctions harassment since capable of "creating an unreasonably intimidating, hostile, and objectively offensive working environment." ERA, §5.6d(1). The petitioner, however, can hardly contend that her supervisor's actions constituted harassment when she states in her resignation letter that Executive Director Decorah "offer[ed] the following: Severance Pay for two weeks, Guaranteed Unemployment, Placement on a Recall List, and no notation of the discharge on my record." . . . The petitioner's supervisor was under no obligation to offer the petitioner anything, and could have instead chosen to immediately terminate her. . . . Finally, the petitioner apparently claims that she could not be subjected "to coercive tactics that constitute a deprivation of a legally protected right." . . . The petitioner does not identify the legally protected right in question, but, as explained above, the petitioner maintained no right to procedural due process or to grieve, with the possible exception of a wrongful discharge in violation of fundamental public policy.

"The tort of wrongful discharge is not a vehicle for enforcement of an employer's internal policies. . . ." . . . Unfortunately, the petitioner pleads nothing else. While one may empathize with the petitioner's plight, she voluntarily accepted this potentiality by accepting an at-will position. The Court accordingly must deny the petitioner's request for relief, and shall not remand the case to the GRB for further consideration with instructions. . . .

NOTES

1. In *McFall v. Victories Casino*, 2003 WL 25880490 (Little Traverse Bay Bands of Odawa Indians Tribal Court 2003), the court held that while a tribal employee grievance process had fallen apart, enough checks and balances remained to provide the employee with sufficient due process and to sustain the finding that the employee's firing was justified:

   > Defendant reserved the right to summarily discharge an employee based upon the severity of the infraction, Defendant argues that the intimidating behavior of the Plaintiff, along with the cumulative impact of numerous grievance filed against him justified his [being] terminated. In fact, that was the reason given for Plaintiff's discharge. The question for this Court is whether the alleged infractions by the Plaintiff were severe enough that he should be summarily discharged from employment.
   >
   > It is important that management have sufficient latitude to manage without outside interference. Managers must have sufficient discretion to make decisions. . . . However, there must be adequate checks and balances. . . .
   >
   > The evidence in matter was that there was one write-up in plaintiff's personnel file. It was for intimidating behavior. Plaintiff argues that the write-up should have been removed, but in fact it had not been removed. There was no other disciplinary action taken against Plaintiff. However, on the day that Plaintiff was terminated the grievance panel made recommendations regarding three (3) separate grievances filed against Plaintiff. There were about two hours between each of the recommendations, *i.e.* a span of six hours. The first of these three recommendations was that Plaintiff receive and undergo management training, the second found him intimidating and recommended a written warning, and the third recommended his termination. It was upon this recommendation and a consultation with the Tribal Human

Resources Director that Plaintiff was terminated by the interim casino manager.

In the instant matter, Plaintiff's situation was reviewed by the grievance panel, the interim casino manager, and the Tribal Human Resources Director, three separate entities in the management loop to provide checks and balances. All three concluded that Plaintiff should be terminated. The process certainly was not perfect, but it contained enough checks and balances to ensure fairness to Plaintiff.

McFall, 2003 WL 25880490, at 4-5.

2. In *Watkins v. Cherokee Nation*, 5 Am. Tribal Law 3 (Cherokee Nation Judicial Appeals Tribunal 2004), the court denied the award of back pay to an aggrieved employee, limiting relief to reinstatement and retroactive benefits:

Petitioner correctly notes that in previous cases this Court has awarded reinstatement along with back pay and loss of benefits. Likewise, this Court has awarded attorney fees in Article XII cases. *See Cantrell v. Cherokee Nation and Cherokee Nation Enterprises*, JAT 97-01 (1999). Although there was a time period when this Court permitted recovery of back wages in employee appeals cases, intervening legislative enactments have limited the available remedies.

This Court has consistently upheld the Council's power to limit damages and other remedies. For instance, in *Nix v. Cherokee Nation*, JAT 93-03, the Court permitted the recovery of attorney fees. The Council subsequently enacted legislation barring attorney fees. In *Mauldin v. Cherokee Nation*, JAT 95-01, the Court denied attorney fees based on the new legislative restriction on remedies.

On the issue of back wages, this Court permitted such a recovery in cases that arose before the effective date of 51 C.N.C.A. §1029 (1996). Section 1029 defines and limits the available remedies. . . .

Watkins, 5 Am. Tribal Law at 4-5.

However, in *Webb v. Cherokee Nation*, 9 Okla. Trib. 107 (Cherokee Nation Judicial Appeals Tribunal 2005), the court granted summary judgment to an employee seeking back pay, asserting that a Cherokee legislative act from 2005 did not apply retroactively to prohibit the award of back pay to the employee. On remand, the employee lost on the merits. *See Webb v. Cherokee Nation*, 9 Okla. Trib. 140 (Cherokee Nation Judicial Appeals Tribunal 2005).

3. Many wrongful discharge claims must be dismissed by tribal courts on sovereign immunity grounds, though when plaintiffs sue individual tribal officers, the question is closer. The classic case on this matter is *Sulcer v. Barrett*, 2 Okla. Tribal Court Rep. 76 (Citizen Potawatomi Nation Supreme Court 2000), according to which the tribal business committee fired a tribal employee, resulting in a tort claim against each of the officials involved in the decision. The court upheld official immunity over a stinging dissent on grounds that the plaintiff alleged that the tribal officials had failed to follow their own procedures in terminating the plaintiff's employment:

Sovereign immunity cannot, however, be used to defend violation of or continuing conflict with the Constitution and By-laws of the Tribe.

Cudmore v. Cheyenne River Sioux Tribal Council, No. 81-226 (Ch. R. Sx. Tr. Ct., Oct. 9, 1981), 10 I.L.R. 6004. Whether this challenge is raised in the face of the Tribe's official legislative action, which is itself the offending violation or conflict, or in the midst of administrative action which is the point of offense, this Court is entrusted with the responsibility of making such determination and curing those conflicts.

Sulcer, 2 Okla. Tribal Court Rep. at 96-97 (Pitchlynn, J., dissenting). Justice G. William Rice, in a separate concurrence, defended the application of immunity in the case, writing:

> Here, the Business Committee did not fire Appellant directly, but by motion expressed its desire that the Tribal Administrator (who was also a member of the Business Committee) do so. The Tribal Administrator thereafter terminated Appellant pursuant to that motion. Had this action been filed against a line officer of the Tribe who fired a tribal employee without (allegedly) complying with the Tribal personnel policies or a Business Committee member acting without the authority of the Business Committee as a whole, I would perhaps reach a different conclusion. Clearly the tribal personnel policies and the cited resolution are intended respectively to provide procedural protections for tribal employees subjected to disciplinary actions by executive line officers of the Tribe, and against Business Committee members who interfere in tribal employee situations individually and without the authority of formal action by the Business Committee as a whole. The suggestion that personal motives may have played a role in the actions taken by the Appellees is certainly troubling. Almost thou persuadest me.
>
> However, even after additional briefing, I can find no authority for the proposition that either the personnel policies or the cited resolution were specifically intended to apply to the Business Committee acting together in a proper meeting as the legislative/executive body of the Tribe. Therefore, even if the fact that Appellant was actually terminated from her employment by the Tribal Administrator, who is not a defendant here, is overlooked under the theory that the Business Committee motion "forced" the Tribal Administrator to terminate Appellant, the question simply becomes whether the Business Committee has retained the authority to terminate a tribal employee without cause.

Sulcer, 2 Okla. Tribal Court Rep. at 87-88 (Rice, J., concurring).

4. One tribal court affirmed that a tribal legislature can legislatively reaffirm tribal sovereign immunity from suit for back pay or wrongful discharge damages, even after the tribal courts have concluded that tribal constitutional common law authorizes suits:

> Although there was a time period when this Court permitted the recovery of back wages in cases brought pursuant to Article VII of the Cherokee Constitution, intervening legislative enactments have limited the available remedies. As noted in [*In re*] *Bush*, this Court has consistently upheld the power of the Council to limit damages under Article II of the Constitution. [*See* 7 Okla. Trib. 426, 432 (Cherokee 2002).] In *Nix v. Cherokee Nation*, Case No. JAT-93-03, [6 Okla. Trib. 220 (Cherokee 1994),] this Court permitted the remedy of attorneys fees. [*Id.* at 222.] The Council subsequently enacted legislation barring attorneys fees, and in *Mauldin v. Cherokee Nation*, Case

No. JAT-95-01, [4 Okla. Trib. 455 (Cherokee 1995),] the Court denied attorneys fees based on the new legislative restriction on remedies. [*Id.* at 458.]

In re Cain, 7 Oklahoma Tribal Rep. 500, 504 (Cherokee Nation Judicial Appeals Tribunal 2002).

3. DEFAMATION

Perron v. Mashantucket Pequot Tribe

Mashantucket Pequot Tribal Court, No. MPTC-CV-97-138, 3 Mash. Rep. 479, 2002
WL 34244445, 2002.NAMP.0000009 (July 11, 2002)

The opinion of the court was delivered by: Thomas J. Londregan, Judge

I. Introduction

A. Findings of Fact

In 1995, Plaintiff Richard A. Perron, a detective with the Connecticut State Police, was working in the casino unit out of Meriden, Connecticut. . . . In the course of Connecticut State Police investigations of various financial crimes at the casino, Mashantucket Pequot Gaming Enterprise security personnel alerted Det. Perron . . . and other state police officers about a possible double-billing scheme at Foxwoods. Det. Perron was assigned as the primary investigating officer. . . .

The security department of the Gaming Enterprise also knew about the double-billing scheme. Security supervisor Michael Wilson testified that [because he and his supervisor, Richard E. Sebastian, director of security at the Gaming Enterprise,] . . . believed senior management might be involved in the scheme, he tried to keep the investigation confidential. . . .

Det. Perron shared Mr. Sebastian's suspicion that members of Foxwoods management were possible suspects in the double-billing scheme. . . .

On Sunday, November 12, 1995, the double-billing investigation switched into high gear when Det. Perron received a phone call at home from Mr. Wilson, who told the Plaintiff he had information about where to find documents that could corroborate the confidential informant's claims. Det. Perron called the on-duty supervisor, Sgt. O'Hara, for authorization to work overtime on the case, and then he agreed to accompany Wilson on the mission to uncover evidence of the double-billing scheme. Det. Perron accompanied Wilson to a tribal building on Route 184 in North Stonington, Connecticut. During their ride over to the Route 184 Building, Wilson told Perron that Sebastian had authorized entry into the office where they believed the records were kept and that he had also authorized the use of a locksmith if necessary. A security guard was on duty that day, and the outside door to the building was open, but, as anticipated, Wilson needed to call a locksmith to gain entry into the office where he hoped to find the documents.

At trial, Wilson and Sebastian testified that to justify entry into the office without raising suspicion and without compromising the secrecy of the investigation, Wilson, with Sebastian's permission, told the locksmith he needed to get into the office to investigate a foul odor. It is uncontroverted that Perron had nothing to do with initiating or perpetuating the foul-odor story. Once inside the office, Wilson attempted to cover the window with cardboard to shield his actions from the security guard, but Perron told him such precaution was unnecessary. It is uncontroverted that Det. Perron touched nothing in the office and that Wilson alone searched the office for the relevant documents, finding none.

After coming up empty-handed, Wilson called Sebastian, who gave him permission to enter the Klewin trailers, located on the Tribe's Reservation, to search for the documents. At the trailer, Wilson and Perron met security personnel, who used the access code to deactivate the security system. Wilson then "defeated" the lock of the office where he believed the documents were located, and he searched the room without finding the records he sought. It is uncontroverted that Det. Perron touched nothing in the office. . . .

It was also on December 7, 1995, that upper management first learned of the entries into the Route 184 Building and the Klewin trailer. . . . After a preliminary investigation into the matter, then–Senior Vice President of Operations George Henningsen and Robert T. Winter, general counsel, sent a memorandum dated December 11, 1995, to Mickey Brown summarizing the results of their investigation into the "unauthorized searches." Mr. Brown, then CEO of the Gaming Enterprise, in turn sent a memorandum to Mr. Hayward, with the Henningsen memorandum attached. . . .

The media coverage continued in a series of articles, editorials and advertisements that ran in area newspapers from December 16, 1995, through March 30, 1996. Several of Defendants' statements published in the media and to Governor Rowland inspired Plaintiff[] to sue Defendants for libel. Plaintiff[] did not complain, however, about the *New London Day*'s January 13, 1996, front-page article with the headline "Lawyer claims Mashantuckets blocking investigation: State police assigned to casino hire counsel." . . . The article begins: "Noted civil rights lawyer John Williams has been retained by two state police officers assigned to Foxwoods Resort Casino, and he claims a police investigation into possible organized crime there has been blocked by conspiring casino executives." Halfway through the first page of the article, Plaintiff Perron's name appears. The pertinent portions of the article read:

> The attorney said he expects his client, state police detective Richard Perron, to be cleared of any wrongdoing in a pending state police investigation triggered by a tribal complaint about police breaking into casino offices in November.
>   Tribal officials claimed Perron and casino security officials broke into finance offices and a construction trailer in November as part of a state police corruption probe. . . .
>   Williams said Perron was allowed into the offices by the casino's security director and that state police are given access to casino records under the terms of the tribe's gaming compact with the state.

. . . Toward the end of the article, the *Day* quotes Williams as saying, "I think it is absolutely clear that Detective Perron's job is to make sure that organized crime does not get its nose under the tent at Ledyard, and there are some people employed by the tribe who have a vested interest in seeing that he does not do that job."

The Internal Affairs Division of the state police thoroughly investigated the matter, and it fully exonerated Perron of any wrongdoing. . . . In March of 1996, however, Lt. Colonel William T. McGuire, second in command of the state police at the time, transferred the Plaintiff[] out of the casino unit against their wishes. McGuire testified that the transfer was not disciplinary in nature, but rather that it served the needs of the department.

Det. Perron was upset by the publicity surrounding the alleged break-ins and his subsequent transfer out of the casino unit. He reported at trial that the false media reports caused him considerable pain and suffering. He testified that when he read the articles in the newspapers he got depressed. "I was sick over it. . . . I contemplated suicide." He testified that he was "consumed" by the publicity and that "there were ups and downs and emotional moments." . . . Perron also reported that he had trouble sleeping and that his relationships with family members suffered as a result of the publicity and the investigation. Perron also testified that his emotional distress prevented him from taking an examination necessary to advance to the rank of sergeant, and that his failure to take the exam deprived him of the opportunity to earn more income. . . .

Det. Perron also reported at trial that his reputation at work suffered as a result of the false reports in the press. He testified, "[Among t]he people that I work with I'm known as the guy that broke into the trailers." He said that on some occasions when he went to execute a search warrant, other troopers would ask him "to open the door because of the articles." It is undisputed that Plaintiff Perron was neither suspended nor demoted as a result of the articles or his actions that prompted them. He presented no evidence other than his testimony that his reputation within the police force suffered as a result of the articles or the investigation into his conduct. In fact, his former commanding officer, Lt. Colonel McGuire, testified that he had a favorable impression of Perron's abilities as a detective. . . .

II. Discussion and Analysis

. . .

B. Count 2: Libel/Defamation (Perron)

Count 2 charges:

> Defendants made or caused to be made statements that were defamatory and untrue about . . . Richard Perron. The defamatory statement identifies . . . Perron to a reasonable reader. The defamatory statements were published to a third party, namely the Governor of the State of Connecticut, the news media and Plaintiff's employer, the Connecticut State Police. . . . Perron's reputation suffered . . . injury as a result of the conduct of the Defendants. . . .

. . . Plaintiff Perron argues that the December 11, 1995 letter to the Governor from Hayward and statements to the media printed on December 16, 1995, defamed him. He also argues that the Defendants' publication of identical ads in the *Courant* and the *Day* on February 22, 1996 defamed him. Despite the fact that he is a state police officer, Perron argues that he is a private citizen for purposes of analysis of the libel count. Defendants counter that as a state police officer Perron is a public official and as such he must prove actual malice by Defendants to recover for libel. Defendants also argue that Perron has not proved Defendants' speech was unprivileged and unprotected. For the reasons set forth fully below, the Court finds that Plaintiff Perron failed to prove that Defendants libeled him, and the Court enters judgment for the Defendants. . . .

2. Defendants Tribe and Tribal Council

In *Fletcher*, the Court said a communication is defamatory if it "tends so to harm the reputation of another as to lower him in the estimation of the community or deter third persons from associating or dealing with him." *Fletcher v. Mashantucket Pequot Tribe*, 3 Mash. 265, 271 (1998). . . . The necessary elements of a defamation action are that the defendant, without privilege, published false statements and that the statements harmed the plaintiff. *See Fletcher* at 271. . . . "Publication" means making the statement known to a third party. *See Fletcher* at 271. . . .

In analyzing a claim for libel, the Court must first decide whether Plaintiff is a public official, a public figure, or a private individual. The determination is necessary so the Court can decide the level of proof required. The question is one of first impression at Mashantucket, so the Court looks to the courts of other jurisdictions for guidance. *See* XII M.P.T.L. ch. 1, §1(a); *see also DeLorge v. Mashantucket Pequot Gaming Enterprise*, 3 Mash. 1 (1997). Should the Plaintiff be a public official or a public figure, the Court will analyze his libel claim under the standard enunciated by the U.S. Supreme Court in the seminal *New York Times Co. v. Sullivan*, 376 U.S. 254 (1964), decision. In *New York Times*, the Court held that a public official cannot recover "damages for a defamatory falsehood relating to his official conduct unless he proves that the statement was made with 'actual malice' — that is, with knowledge that it was false or with reckless disregard of whether it was false or not." *New York Times* at 279-280. The Court hereby adopts the *New York Times* holding requiring that public officials prove actual malice to recover for libel. The Court also holds that public figures "may recover for injury to reputation only on clear and convincing proof that the defamatory falsehood was made with" actual malice. *Gertz v. Robert Welch, Inc.*, 418 U.S. 323, 342 (1974). . . .

In federal courts and in the state of Connecticut, it is well-settled that police officers are public officials. *See Coughlin v. Westinghouse Broadcasting and Cable, Inc.*, 780 F.2d 340 (2d Cir. 1985) (upholding the district court's determination that the plaintiff, a rookie police officer, was a public official); *see also Moriarty v. Lippe*, 162 Conn. 371, 378 (1972) (noting that a patrolman appears to have "substantial responsibility" over the conduct of government affairs "sufficient to be a public official"). . . . The Court adopts the findings of its sister jurisdictions that a police officer is a public official for purposes of analyzing a libel claim, and it finds that because Plaintiff Perron is a state police officer he is a public official. Consequently, the Court holds that in order for Perron to prevail on his claim for libel, he must prove by clear and convincing evidence that Defendants published false statements with actual malice.

a. The Letter to Governor Rowland

Plaintiff argues that Hayward's letter defamed him because it contained false statements and was published to the Governor, and Defendants counter that the letter contained no false statements. Defendants argue, however, that the letter requesting an investigation into potential police misconduct was absolutely privileged as a "report of a suspected crime," . . . and is thus not subject to an action for libel.

The Court in *Fletcher* concluded that "[a]n essential element of a defamation claim is that the defendant was not privileged to publish the false statement." *Fletcher* at 272. In *Petyan v. Ellis*, 200 Conn. 243 (1986), the Connecticut Supreme Court considered whether statements made in judicial and quasi-judicial proceedings were privileged. *See Fletcher* at 272. "There has long been established that there is an absolute privilege for statements made in judicial proceedings." *Id.* (quoting *Petyan* at 245-46 . . .). In *Petyan*, the court held, "[L]ike the privilege which is generally applied to pertinent statements made in formal judicial proceedings, an absolute privilege also attaches to relevant statements made during administrative proceedings which are 'quasi-judicial' in nature." *Id.* . . . The effect of an absolute privilege "is that damages cannot be recovered for a defamatory statement even if it is published falsely and maliciously." *Id.*

To decide the question of privilege, the Court must ask whether the internal affairs investigation of Plaintiff Perron was a quasi-judicial proceeding. The question has not been addressed in this Court or in the Connecticut appellate courts, but Connecticut superior courts have held that investigatory or disciplinary hearings before the Commissioner of Public Safety regarding state police officers constitute quasi-judicial proceedings. . . .

[T]his Court . . . finds that the internal affairs investigation into Plaintiff Perron was indeed a quasi-judicial proceeding and that the letter to the Governor, a citizen's complaint of potential police abuses, was absolutely privileged. Consequently, the Court holds that the Defendants, who wrote the letter, are not liable to the Plaintiff for any false statements the letter may contain.

Even if the Court were to find that the statements in the letter were not privileged, the Plaintiff failed to prove by clear and convincing evidence that anything in the letter was false and that any statement in the letter was made with actual malice. The letter did not accuse the Plaintiff by name, nor did it accuse any state police officer outright of wrongdoing. Instead, the letter sought Governor Rowland's immediate help in investigating whether "a member of the State Police" was "involved in two illegal break-ins involving Mashantucket Pequot Tribal property." The Court sees nothing false or sinister in Defendants' seeking the Governor's aid in uncovering the truth about a matter of such public importance as a possible abuse of police power. Even if the Court were to find that the letter contained false statements, the Plaintiff submitted no credible evidence that the Defendants either knew that such statements were false or that they recklessly disregarded whether the statements were false or not. Accordingly, the Court finds that Plaintiff Perron failed to prove by clear and convincing evidence that Defendants made false statements with actual malice.

b. The December 16, 1995, Newspaper Articles

Perron also claims that two newspaper articles contained false statements that defamed him. One of the articles appeared in the *Hartford Courant*, the other in the *New London Day*. The *Hartford Courant* reported that "Brown sharply criticized the few state police officers he believes are responsible and calls the office entries 'inexcuseable [sic] and potentially illegal.'" Perron claims the language "inexcusable and potentially illegal" is libelous. Perron further objects to the language: "Brown said that Peron [sic] had to have known in advance that his entry into the offices was improper. 'Any suggestion that the detective involved in these entries believed them to be proper or somehow authorized is ludicrous,' he said." . . .

Some of the allegedly defamatory language attributed to Brown in the *Hartford Courant* appears verbatim in the *Day* article, but the article also contains other language, not appearing in the *Courant*, that Perron calls defamatory. In the *Day*'s front-page article, the offensive language begins: "State police have lost sight of the rights of the Mashantucket Pequot Tribe and the legal limits or proper police conduct in . . . irresponsible, and presumably unsupervised, investigative excesses," Brown said. . . . The article continues further to include allegedly defamatory statements attributed to Bruce MacDonald. The article reads: "Tribal spokesman Bruce MacDonald said the break-ins at Foxwoods were reminiscent of Watergate and the so-called 'plumbers' operation to detect administration leaks in the Nixon era." "'We've got a plumber-type group here, a renegade group,' MacDonald said. 'These people don't have the right to invade people's homes or businesses on a whim.'" . . . On the article's second page, Perron found more defamatory language attributed to MacDonald and Brown. The article reads: "MacDonald said there can be no defense when police break the law. 'This is an apparent attempt to justify what we feel was a clearly illegal action,' he said. 'These people took the law into their own hands, in our view. The tribe feels very strongly that they were wronged.'" . . . Finally, Perron points to the following quotation, attributed to Brown, as defamatory. "But Brown noted that 'the fact that no evidence of wrongdoing was found in these "searches" cannot excuse the methods employed.'"

In *Fletcher*, the Court found that "expressions of opinion are constitutionally protected. . . ." *Fletcher* at 273. . . . As a matter of law, the Court must determine whether Defendants' statements are protected as opinion or subject to a claim for libel as factual assertions. *See Fletcher* at 273. . . . Although language used may be "vehement, caustic and unpleasant . . . that does not make it libelous under the law." *Dow v. New Haven Independent, Inc.*, 41 Conn. Sup. 31, 34 (1987). "A public official must expect, in a society that guarantees free speech, that at times he or she will be the subject of rhetorical hyperbole. Nevertheless, that alone cannot be the basis for an action for libel." [*Id.*] at 34. *See Fletcher* at 273 ("even the most careless reader must have perceived that the word ['blackmail'] was no more than rhetorical hyperbole, a vigorous epithet used by those who considered [plaintiff's] negotiating position extremely unreasonable"). . . . The Court in *Fletcher* adopted guidelines set out in *Ollman v. Evans*, 750 F.2d 970 (D.C. Cir. 1984), for determining whether a statement is protected opinion or unprotected fact:

> [W]e must examine both the context in which the statements are made and the circumstances surrounding the statements. We must also look at the language itself to determine if it is used in a precise, literal manner or in a loose, figurative or hyperbolic sense. . . . [W]e must examine the statements to determine if they are objectively capable of being proven true or false. Finally, if the above analysis indicates that the statement is opinion, we must determine if it implies the allegation of undisclosed defamatory facts as the basis for the opinion. *Fletcher* at 273.

The Court finds as a matter of law that the language in the articles is not subject to being judged for its truth or lack thereof and that it falls in the fair comment or opinion category. The Court further finds that the opinions expressed do not imply any allegation of undisclosed defamatory facts as their basis. The use of language such as "ludicrous" and "plumbers-style operation" suggests an over-the-top response characteristic of what the common law of libel has called "rhetorical hyperbole." If calling the dealings of a real-estate developer "blackmail" qualifies as rhetorical hyperbole in [*Greenbelt Cooperative Publishing Assn. v. Bresler*, 398 U.S. 6 (1970)], and the use of the word "traitor" in [*Letter Carriers v. Austin*, 418 U.S. 264, 284-286 (1974)] also escapes liability for defamation, then the much tamer "ludicrous" language and "Watergate" innuendo found in the December 16, 1995, articles must also enjoy protection as "vigorous epithets" employed in the course of public debate. As such, the language is protected as opinion and is not actionable as libel. The remaining objectionable statements in the articles use terminology that signals their status as opinion. In the quotations of MacDonald, the phrases "we feel," "in our view" and "the Tribe feels very strongly" are classic signals to the reader that the statements are expressions of opinion rather than assertions of fact. The Court therefore finds that the language in the articles is protected as opinion and fair comment, and that, as such, the statements are not subject to claims for libel.

Even if the language were not protected, Plaintiff has failed to prove that Defendants made the statements with actual malice. As a public official, Plaintiff must expect that some of his actions will invite scrutiny, lively debate and vigorous comment. Since he failed to prove actual malice, he cannot recover libel for any of the statements in the December 16, 1995, articles.

c. The February 22, 1996, Advertisements

Plaintiff Perron also claims that an advertisement paid for by the Defendants libeled him. Virtually identical full-page advertisements, with the headline "There's A Right Way And A Wrong Way," ran on February 22, 1996, in the *Norwich Bulletin* and the *Hartford Courant*. The names of all seven Tribal Council members appear at the bottom of the ads, and the *Courant* ad carries the phrase "Paid for by the Mashantucket Pequot Tribal Council." A line atop the ad in each newspaper clearly identifies the article as an advertisement.

In *DeLorge v. Mashantucket Pequot Gaming Enterprise*, 2 Mash. 170 (1997), the Court held that the "truth of the communication provides a complete defense to defamation actions." *DeLorge* at 172. . . .

To determine whether any of the statements in the ad defamed the Plaintiff, the Court adopts the guidelines set forth in *Fletcher* and examines the context and surrounding circumstances of the statements. The ad begins:

> Recent criticism in the *New London Day* by the attorney for a state police detective, under investigation for surreptiously [sic] entering tribal offices, is both unfair and grossly misleading. The sensationalist statements in *The Day* do a disservice to the Mashantucket Pequot Tribal Nation and its 11,600 employees, including the approximately 1,000 people in management positions.

The authors of the ad assert that, contrary to the reports in the *Day*, the Tribe cooperates fully with federal and state law enforcement agencies. The ad says, "It is one thing for a lawyer whose client is under investigation to defend that client vigorously, but it is quite another matter for that very same lawyer to lash out and question the integrity of those who called for the investigation in the first place." In conclusion, the ad reads, "Before the *New London Day* makes any judgments about Foxwoods or the Tribe, it should look at the record, and not the claims of a lawyer trying to defend his clients by throwing mud on innocent people." The overall tone of the ad is critical of the *Day* for reporting alleged corruption among Foxwoods management without first analyzing the record. While the ad does use strong language condemning "the attorney for a state police detective," it names neither the attorney, nor any specific member of the state police, and the Plaintiff['s] name[] appear[s] nowhere in the ad. . . .

The context of the ad leads the Court to conclude that the ad's primary purpose was to criticize the *Day*, as the ad states, and not to vilify Detective Perron, whose name appears nowhere in the ad. The Plaintiff, however, claims that a sentence in the third paragraph of the ad defames him. The allegedly libelous language reads: "Despite what this man's lawyer says, there is nothing in our gaming compact with the state that allows state troopers to break into tribal offices." . . . Perron argues that the statement is false and therefore libelous because he "did not break into tribal offices." In order to decide whether the sentence libeled Perron, the Court must consider it within the full context of paragraph No. 3. The full paragraph reads:

> There is such a thing as protocol, a right way to do things and a wrong way. Despite what this man's lawyer says, there is nothing in our gaming compact with the state that allows state troopers to break into tribal offices. There is nothing in the compact which allows any tribal employee to break into tribal offices. There is a clearly defined process under the compact in which the Mashantucket Pequot Gaming Commission has the authority to investigate any criminal wrongdoing in the gaming enterprise. The state police officer and certain members of the Tribe's employees acted improperly. . . .

The Court finds that the statements in paragraph No. 3 mix assertion of fact with expression of opinion. Despite Perron's sincere belief that the compact allowed his entry, which was in fact authorized by the security department, the statement that the gaming compact does not allow "state troopers to break into tribal offices" is undeniably true, and as a true statement, it is protected against any claim for libel.

Perron objects to the Defendant's characterization of the entries as "break[ing] into tribal offices." When one considers the full context of paragraph No. 3, however, the reasonable reader understands that the ad does not accuse the Plaintiff of breaking and entering, but rather it expresses the opinion that a "state police officer . . . acted improperly."

The Plaintiff vehemently disagrees that he broke into tribal offices and by extension that he acted improperly. In is undisputed that the investigations into his actions resulted in no charges against him. That does not mean, however, that the ad was false. In deciding whether the statement was actually false or a protected expression of opinion, the Court considers the fact that Lt. Colonel McGuire, Perron's commanding officer, questioned Perron's judgment in the matter. The Court finds instructive the opinion of McGuire, who was second in command of the state police at the time of the break-ins and the ensuing transfer of the officers. If McGuire and other state police officers can disagree on whether Perron "acted improperly" in some capacity, then the assertion is incapable of being proved either true or false. Consequently, the Court finds the statements in paragraph No. 3 to be opinions protected by law from libel claims.

Even if the Court were to conclude that the statements were assertions of fact and therefore subject to a libel claim, as a public figure the Plaintiff must prove that the statements were made with "actual malice." Plaintiff offered no such proof. Accordingly, the Court finds that the ad did not defame him, and it hereby finds for Defendants on Count 2. . . .

NOTES

1. As a result of attempted labor organizing in Indian country, some tribes have adopted codes authorizing suit for defamation, a common tactic by governments and management to respond to organizing efforts. The Little River Band of Ottawa Indians is one such tribe, as its Protection against Defamation Act of 2006 shows:

   4.01. *Libel and Slander.*

   > a. Both libel and slander must be published or made in the presence of third parties who have the ability to rely or act upon the information received and understand the information provided as diminishing the reputation of the person to whom they are referring. Both libel and slander can be addressed to private individuals and to public officials.
   > b. Libel and slander of a public official must be made with malice.

   4.02. *Damages Authorized.* Except as provided in this section, in actions based on libel or slander the plaintiff is entitled to recover only for the actual damages which he or she has suffered in respect to his or her property, business, trade, profession, occupation, or feelings.

   > a. Exemplary and punitive damages shall not be recovered in actions for libel unless the plaintiff, before instituting his or her action, gives notice to the defendant to publish a retraction and allows a reasonable time to do so, and proof of the publication or correction shall be

admissible in evidence under a denial on the question of the good faith of the defendant, and in mitigation and reduction of exemplary or punitive damages.

b. For libel based on a radio or television broadcast, the retraction shall be made in the same manner and at the same time of the day as the original libel; for libel based on a publication, the retraction shall be published in the same size type, in the same editions and as far as practicable, in substantially the same position as the original libel; and for other libel, the retraction shall be published or communicated in substantially the same manner as the original libel.

4.03. *Defense.* If the defendant in any action for defamation gives notice in a justification that the statements published were true, this notice will serve as proof of absence of malice. However, it may make the defendant liable for the common law tort of invasion of privacy. In an action for defamation, even though the defendant has pleaded or unsuccessfully attempted to prove a justification he or she may prove mitigating circumstances including the sources of his or her information and the ground for his or her belief was true. Damages shall not be awarded in a defamation action for the publication of a fair and true report of matters of public record, a public and official proceeding, or of a governmental notice, announcement, written or recorded report or record generally available to the public, or act or action of a public body, or for a heading of the report which is a fair and true head note of the report. This privilege shall not apply to a libel which is contained in a matter added by a person concerned in the publication or contained in the report of anything said or done at the time and place of the public and official proceeding or governmental notice, announcement, written or recorded report or record generally available to the public, or act or action of a public body, which was not a part of the public and official proceeding or governmental notice, announcement, written or recorded report or record generally available to the public, or act or action of a public body. . . .

4.08. *Truth as a Defense.* In all actions for defamatory statements the truth may be given in justification as evidence; and, if it appears that the matter charged as defamatory is true and was published with good motives and for justifiable ends, the civil complaint shall be dismissed.

Little River Band of Ottawa Indians, Protection against Defamation Act of 2006, Ordinance No. 06-400-08 (2006). However, the first case brought under the statute related to public allegations by some tribal members against others on the question of tribal citizenship. *See Sam v. Ossignac*, No. 08-195-GC (Little River Band of Ottawa Indians Tribal Court 2008).

2. In *Russell v. Grand Traverse Band of Ottawa and Chippewa Indians Election Board*, 2000 WL 35749801 (Grand Traverse Band Tribal Court 2000), the court applied Michigan state law in holding that the plaintiff's defamation claims failed to meet the elements of defamation:

> With respect to Count III of Plaintiffs' Complaint, which alleged defamation on the part of Defendant GTB Election Board, this Court agreed with Defendant Election Board's contention that the required legal elements of a defamation claim were not present in Plaintiffs' Complaint. Due to the lack of Grand Traverse Band tribal law, statutory or otherwise, regarding

defamation, Defendant Election Board properly looked to Michigan law for the required elements of such a claim. *See Rouch v. Enquirer and News of Battle Creek* (after remand), 440 Mich. 238, 251, 487 N.W.2d 205 (1992). . . .

Russell, 2000 WL 35749801, at *1.

B. TRIBAL COMMON LAW CAUSES OF ACTION

Kimsey v. Reibach

Confederated Tribes of the Grand Ronde Community of Oregon Tribal Court, No. C-05-02-002, 6 Am. Tribal Law 119 (June 30, 2005)

The opinion of the court was delivered by: Edmund Clay Goodman, Chief Tribal Court Judge

A. Background; Introduction

Plaintiff Marvin Kimsey filed this action alleging that the Defendant, Jan Reibach, slandered and defamed him by making public statements suggesting that Mr. Kimsey was a homosexual. Mr. Kimsey alleges that Mr. Reibach caused him "per se and actual damages under the custom and tradition of tribal law" and that Mr. Reibach has negligently and intentionally inflicted emotional distress upon him. . . .

Having considered the arguments made in the briefs and at the hearing, I have determined that the Court lacks subject matter jurisdiction to hear an action sounding in tort between two private individuals because the Tribe has not enacted an Ordinance specifically delegating jurisdiction over such actions to the Tribal Court. Moreover, in the alternative, I also hold that even if this Court had subject matter jurisdiction to hear such an action, this case is "of such a nature that the Court should not hear it." It would not be appropriate for this Court to adjudicate the complicated issues involved in such a case in the absence of Tribally-enacted standards for addressing such issues. . . .

C. Discussion

. . .

2. The Court Lacks Subject Matter Jurisdiction over Defamation Actions Arising in Tort between Two Private Parties

. . . To resolve questions regarding the jurisdiction of the Tribal Court, we must first look to the Tribal Constitution, which states, in relevant part, as follows:

> The Tribal Court *shall be empowered* to exercise all judicial authority of the Tribe. Said authority shall include but not be limited to enforcement of the Indian Child Welfare Act of 1978 and the American Indian Religious Freedom Act of 1978, as well as the power to review and overturn tribal legislative and executive actions for violation of this Constitution or the Indian Civil Rights Act of 1968.

Tribal Constitution, Art. IV, Sec. 3 (emphasis added). This provision of the Constitution provides that the Court is to be granted certain judicial authority by the Tribal Council, making clear that under the Constitution the Court is to be granted certain powers, and therefore is a court of limited jurisdiction. . . . The language prohibits the Council from granting judicial authority to any Tribal institution other than the Tribal Court, but it does not require that the Court be granted general jurisdictional authority.

Mr. Kimsey cites to §710(d)(1)(A) of the Tribal Court Ordinance as demonstrating that the Tribe has granted the Court such general jurisdictional authority. . . .

. . . [T]he Tribe's intent was to have the Court function as a court of limited jurisdiction, particularly in light of the highlighted clause, with any additional jurisdictional authority to be expressly delegated by Ordinance.

In the years prior to 1998, the Tribe treated the Court as a court of limited jurisdiction, enacting a series of Ordinances granting the Tribal Court jurisdiction over specific subject matters. *See, e.g.*, Divorce Ordinance (no Tribal Code Section assigned), part (a) ("The purpose of this Ordinance is to grant authority to the Tribal Court to dissolve marriages."); Enrollment Ordinance, Tribal Code §410(d)(4)(H) (granting limited authority to Tribal Court to hear appeals of adverse enrollment determinations); Indian Child Welfare Ordinance, §710(c) ("The jurisdiction of the Tribe shall extend to child welfare matters involving all Grand Ronde children, wherever located."); Liquor Ordinance, §760(g) (establishing civil penalties and specifically providing for their enforcement in Tribal Court for violation of the Ordinance); Small Claims Court Ordinance (no Tribal Code Section assigned), part (a) ("The purpose of this Ordinance is to grant authority to the Tribal Court to adjudicate over matters involving small claims.").

In 1998, however, the Tribal Council significantly amended this provision of the Tribal Court Ordinance. . . .

[T]he Tribe still intends that jurisdiction over specific subject matter areas be delegated ordinance by ordinance.

Further, since 1998 the Tribe's practice of expressly granting the Court jurisdiction over specific subject matter areas has not changed. In 2002, for example, the Tribe enacted the Public Safety Ordinance (no Tribal Code Section assigned). Subpart (j) of that Ordinance contains a specific and express grant of jurisdiction to the Tribal Court to hear cases arising under that Ordinance. . . .

I therefore determine that in order to have jurisdiction over a defamation action arising in tort between two private individuals, there must be an Ordinance or other statutory enactment of the Tribal Council granting the Court specific jurisdiction to hear such matters and setting out the standards by which such matters should be adjudicated. A review of the Tribal Code indicates that there is no such Ordinance or statutory enactment. In the absence of such an enactment, I determine that this Court lacks the subject matter jurisdiction necessary to hear this case.

3. The Case Is "of Such a Nature That the Court Should Not Hear It"

In the alternative, I find also that even if an express grant of subject matter jurisdiction is not required, this case is "of such a nature that the Court should not hear it." Exercising the discretion granted under Tribal Code §310(d)(1)(A)(3), I would dismiss this case on this alternate ground as well. The problem for the Court is again with the lack of a specific enactment to guide the Court as to the standards to be applied in adjudicating such matters.

The fact that the parties so radically disagree as to whether the alleged statements of Mr. Reibach violate Tribal law, whether Tribal law allows for actions of slander per se, and whether such torts may be brought against a "marital community" underscore the necessity of having a specific tribal enactment setting out the standards for adjudicating such actions. Because there is nowhere to look in Tribal law for such standards, we are left with arguments based on the laws of the State of Oregon, the common law, and even reference to the works of William Shakespeare.[2] To move forward in the absence of Tribal standards would be to construe such absence as leaving it to the Court's sole discretion to import the laws of foreign jurisdictions to govern the relations between individuals within the Tribe's jurisdiction. I believe it is inappropriate to do so, as it would place the Court in the role of legislating such standards. That legislative role belongs to the Tribal Council.

Compare this lack of standards to govern the kind of tort asserted in this case with what the Tribe has done with regard to tort claims against the Tribal government and its officers and officials. The Tribe's Tort Claims Ordinance specifically grants the Tribal Court subject matter jurisdiction over certain tort claims against the Tribe, its agents, officials, and officers. Tribal Code §255.6. Moreover, that Ordinance defines "injury" for the purposes of adjudicating a tort action by reference to not only Tribal law, but also to "applicable federal law, and, to the extent consistent with Tribal law, laws of the State of Oregon. . . ." Tribal Code §255.6(b)(3). Further, the Ordinance expressly excludes injuries alleged to have resulted from "[a]ny intentional tort, including but not limited to . . . libel, slander, defamation. . . ." Tribal Code §255.6(e)(4)(C). The Ordinance sets out a specific grant of jurisdiction as well as the standards under which such claims are to be adjudicated. The Tribe has not enacted a similar Ordinance for tort claims between private individuals, and the Tribal Tort Claims Ordinance does not apply to such claims.

Given the complexity of the issues raised by the present case, and the risk of importing inappropriate norms to govern the relations between individuals within the jurisdiction of the Tribe, the Court determines that it would be appropriate to refuse to exercise jurisdiction to hear this case. This exercise of discretion to dismiss does not deprive Mr. Kimsey of a remedy, if indeed he has been harmed by Mr. Reibach's alleged statements. As his counsel has argued, the laws of the State of Oregon appear to provide him with a cause of action. Because Oregon is a Public Law 280 state, and because Public Law 280

---

2. While the Court enjoyed Plaintiff's reference to the statement from *Othello* regarding the relative merits of reputation and riches, relying on the poets to address matters of the public good, as Plato repeatedly cautions in his *Republic*, is highly problematic. It is questionable, at best, to rely on a statement that a poet places in the mouth of one of his characters as an indication of a matter of broader social significance, even with a poet as highly regarded and widely quoted as Shakespeare. One would have to, at a minimum, undertake a detailed literary and critical analysis to determine whether the statement was intended ironically, or as representing a minority view, rather than as a statement of an important social norm. Consider, for example, that the statement quoted by Mr. Kimsey is, in fact, a statement made by the play's villain, Iago.

grants the state courts jurisdiction over civil causes of action that arise on tribal land, Mr. Kimsey would not appear to be precluded from bringing this action in State court. . . .

NOTES

1. In *Burnett v. Pioneer Chevy, Inc.*, 2000 Mont. Salish & Kootenai Tribe LEXIS 1 (Confederated Salish and Kootenai Tribes Court of Appeals 2000), the plaintiff alleging torts relating to the termination of employment asked the tribal court to adopt the common law tort of intentional infliction of emotional distress. The court, per Judge Cynthia Ford, a University of Montana law professor, wrote:

> Plaintiff argues that the Confederated Salish and Kootenai Court of Appeals should adopt, as tribal common law, the tort of intentional infliction of emotional distress, as the Montana Supreme Court has done. *See Sacco v. High Country Independent Press, Inc.*, 271 Mont. 209, 896 P.2d 411 (1995). (Both parties concede that there is no tribal statutory provision establishing such a cause of action.) Defendant argues that it may be appropriate in some case for this Court to recognize such a tort, but that this particular case does not present the necessary elements even if such a tort were to be adopted.
>
> This Court is part of a sovereign government, and only this government can establish a new tort cause of action. The fact that other jurisdictions, including Montana, have allowed this relatively new cause of action is worthy of our attention, but not ultimately binding precedent on the courts of the Confederated Salish and Kootenai Tribes. (Many other states have considered, and rejected, establishment of this tort or have allowed it, but with different standards.) To date, the Tribal Council has not acted via ordinance on this issue. Thus, the road is open for the Court, should it believe that this tort is consistent with tribal customary law and/or that the Tribes will be well-served by having such a tort available to plaintiffs, to decide to allow such a claim and to delineate its elements. However, this is a matter of important public policy and requires careful consideration of the arguments on both sides. See, e.g., the careful and extensive discussion of the history and policy behind the development of the tort of infliction of emotional distress in *Sacco v. High Country Independent Press, Inc.*, 271 Mont. 209, 896 P.2d 411 (1995). In this case, there is not enough information about the basis for the trial court's dismissal of this count for this court to act.

Burnett, 2000 Mont. Salish & Kootenai Tribe LEXIS 1, at *18-20.

2. In one of the most famous modern tribal court cases, the Rosebud Sioux Supreme Court held in *Estate of Tasunke Witko v. G. Heileman Brewing Co.*, 23 Indian L. Rep. 6104 (Rosebud Sioux Supreme Court 1996), that it had jurisdiction over the non-Indian, off-reservation brewers of Crazy Horse Malt Liquor, an odious concoction marketed to Indian people, in a case brought by the descendants of Crazy Horse for damages against the makers and to hopefully force the end of its manufacture.

The factual description of the case by the court is striking:

> Tasunke Witko, popularly known as Crazy Horse, is a revered nineteenth century (1842?-1877) Lakota political and spiritual leader who lived all of

his life within the bounds of the Great Sioux Nation Reservation which included the present-day Rosebud Sioux Reservation. Tasunke Witko was a person of great moral character who steadfastly opposed the use and abuse of alcohol products by his people.

Mr. Seth H. Big Crow Sr., a member of the Rosebud Sioux Tribe and a resident of the Rosebud Sioux Reservation, is a direct descendant of Tasunke Witko. . . .

The G. Heilman Brewing Company, Hornell Brewing Company, and John Ferolito and Don Vultaggio, the defendants/appellees herein, are the manufacturers, distributors, and marketers of various alcoholic (and non-alcoholic) drinking products including, but not limited to, the ornately packaged "The Original Crazy Horse Malt Liquor." This particular product has been promoted, distributed, displayed for sale and sold from on or about March 17, 1992. . . .

During the period of March-June 1993, there was written and oral communication between the parties and other concerned (non-party) Lakota individuals and groups about the alleged "insult and injury" of defendants' actions and the likelihood of legal action if such activities of the defendants/appellees were not halted.

No mutually agreed upon solution emerged from these various exchanges. As a result, the Estate of Tasunke Wtiko filed a lawsuit against the defendants/appellees in the Rosebud Sioux tribal Court. An amended complaint was filed on September 23, 1993. The complaint and amended complaint asserted five separate causes of action, namely, the knowing and willful tortious interference with customary rights of privacy and respect owed to a decedent and his family, the tortious interference with plaintiff's property right commonly known as the "right of publicity," the negligent and intentional infliction of emotional distress on the heirs of the estate through acts of exploitation and defamation, violation of the Indian Arts and Crafts Act, and violation of the Lanham Act. These claims were asserted—where applicable—under both tribal and federal law.

The estate seeks wide-ranging relief including declaratory and injunctive relief, money damages, a written public apology, and culturally appropriate compensation such as "presenting to the Estate one (1) braid of tobacco, one (1) four-point Pendleton blanket and one (1) racing horse for each State, Territory or Nation in which said products have been distributed and offered for sale. . . .

Estate of Tasunke Witko, 23 Indian L. Rep. at 6105-06.

The Rosebud Sioux Supreme Court held that the tribal court had jurisdiction over these claims. *See id.* But the defendants successfully persuaded the federal appeals court that the Rosebud Sioux tribal courts had no jurisdiction over them. *See Hornell Brewing Co. v. Rosebud Sioux Tribal Court*, 133 F.3d 1087 (8th Cir. 1998). The tort claims died on the vine.

In 2001, one of the corporate defendants settled the suit and agreed to pay to the Estate 32 Pendleton blankets, 32 braids of sweet grass, 32 twists of tobacco and seven thoroughbred race horses. *See* David Melmer, *Beer Company Apologizes to Warrior's Family amid Ceremony in South Dakota*, INDIAN COUNTRY TODAY, May 9, 2001, 2001 WLNR 7619786.

C. RESOLUTION OF TORT CLAIMS

1. SUITS AGAINST INDIAN TRIBES UNDER TORT CLAIMS ORDINANCES

Nguyen v. Spirit Mountain Casino

Confederated Tribes of the Grand Ronde Community Tribal Court, No. 04-06-002,
5 Am. Tribal Law 126, 2004.NAGR.0000013 (November 1, 2004)

Katharine English, Chief Tribal Court Judge . . .

A. Background; Introduction

On June 4, 2004, Plaintiff Nguyen filed a complaint against four Defendants—Spirit Mountain Casino (Casino), Spirit Mountain Gaming, Inc. (SMGII), the Grand Ronde Gaming Commission (Commission), and the Confederated Tribes of the Grand Ronde Community of Oregon (Tribe). The complaint, seeking damages for personal injury based on theories of common law negligence, alleged that Plaintiff slipped, fell, and was injured in a women's bathroom at the Casino on October 18, 2003. The complaint averred that the Defendants were negligent in not regularly monitoring, inspecting and cleaning the women's bathroom, and in failing to warn Plaintiff about the alleged hazard and danger. The complaint sought both economic and non-economic damages.

Plaintiff sought to serve the summons and complaint on the Casino and SMGII by serving the Secretary of the Tribal Council and the Tribal Attorney. Plaintiff also served the Council Secretary and the Tribal Attorney as representatives of the Commission, but Plaintiff also served the "Chief Executive Officer" of the Commission. The Tribe was served by again serving the Secretary of the Tribal Council and the Tribal Attorney.

In a motion filed on behalf of all four of the Defendants, Defendants moved for the dismissal of Plaintiff's complaint, "upon the grounds that the Tribal Court lacks jurisdiction over the subject matter, that there has been insufficiency of process, insufficiency of service of process, and that Plaintiff has failed to state ultimate facts sufficient to state a claim for relief." . . .

. . . Citing Oregon case law, Plaintiff argues that she substantially complied with the notice requirements of the Ordinance. She contends that giving notice to risk management, to SMGII's insurer, and to the Tribal Attorney should suffice because they are all agents of SMGII. She also notes that the attorney is the authorized representative for the Casino. Giving notice to the Tribe should be enough because it is the sole shareholder in SMGII, and notice to it, thus, should be imputed to SMGII. She asserts that the Commission is a proper Defendant because it regulates the Casino and SMGII. . . .

C. Discussion

. . .

1. No Timely Tort Claim Notice Was Given to the CEO of SMGII

The Tribal Tort Claims Ordinance makes the giving of timely and proper notice of the claim a prerequisite to the filing of any Court action. In addition, when a tort claim is based on the act or omission of any Tribal corporation, such as SMGII, written notice also must be given to the CEO of the corporation. Section 255.6(d)(1) of the Ordinance provides:

> No action may be brought in Tribal Court for monetary damages under this Ordinance and no claim shall be valid for monetary damages under this Ordinance unless the person who claims to have suffered an injury shall send a written notice of the claim for monetary damages as provided in Section (d)(2) below by certified mail return receipt requested to the Secretary of the Tribal Council and the Office of Tribal Attorney. In the case of any claim wherein it is alleged an injury was caused by the act or omission of any Tribal Commission, authority, corporation or enterprise or any agent, employee or officer of such Tribal Commission, authority, corporation or enterprise, the written notice required by this section also shall be given to the chief executive officer of such Tribal Commission, authority, corporation or enterprise.

. . . "To be valid under th[e] Ordinance," the written notice of claim "shall have been given no later than 180 days after the act or omission giving rise to the injury." §255.6(d)(3). . . .

Those provisions could not be much clearer or more emphatic. Giving timely written notice under the Ordinance is an absolute prerequisite to bringing a tort case in Tribal Court. Without such notice, "[n]o action may be brought" and "no claim shall be valid for monetary damages[.]" §255.6(d)(1). And, when any claim alleges that an injury was caused by the act or omission of any Tribal authority, "corporation," or enterprise, the written notice must be given, not only to the Secretary of the Tribal Council and the Tribal Attorney, but "also" to the CEO of the authority, corporation, or enterprise. *Id.* There is nothing ambiguous or uncertain about that requirement and, by the Ordinance's own terms, the Court has no authority or discretion to overlook a litigant's failure to comply with the notice requirements.

In addition, if there were any ambiguity about the notice provisions, the Ordinance also emphasizes that those provisions are part of a limited waiver of sovereign immunity that is to be strictly and narrowly construed. Section 255.6(e)(5) provides that:

> The procedures and standards for giving notice of claims and commencing actions in Tribal Court . . . are integral parts of the limited waiver of sovereign immunity provided by this Ordinance and shall be strictly and narrowly construed. A tort claim for monetary damages against the Tribe shall be forever barred unless written notice of the claim is presented to the Tribe and an action for monetary damages relating to any such claim is commenced in Tribal Court in compliance with Section (d) of this Ordinance.

Again, that provision could scarcely be more emphatic. Thus, when Plaintiff contends that she has "substantially complied" with the notice requirements — even though admittedly she did not give written notice to the CEO of SMGII — she in essence asks the Court to do what it cannot do here, that is, rewrite, loosen, or forgive non-compliance with the Ordinance's notice provisions. . . .

. . . Under the Ordinance, Plaintiff had to give timely, written notice to the CEO of SMGII. She did not. That is the end of the inquiry. . . .

3. Neither the Commission nor the Tribe Is a Proper Defendant

Defendants' Motion to Dismiss the Commission and the Tribe as Defendants amounts to a 12(b)(6) Motion to Dismiss for "failure to state a claim upon which relief can be granted." Fed. R. Civ. P. 12(b)(6). Because those Defendants have no responsibility for the day-to-day operation of the Casino, and because Plaintiff's claims allege negligence in the operation and maintenance of the Casino, Defendants reason that those two Defendants cannot be liable. The Court agrees.

The Commission is a purely regulatory body. It was established "to regulate Class II and Class III gaming on Grand Ronde Indian Land," and it is to "exercise all powers necessary to regulate" such gaming. Gaming Ordinance §(g)(1)(8). Its duties include processing all license applications, denying, limiting, revoking, rescinding or suspending any license, if necessary, causing background checks to be performed, printing and making available all license application forms and licenses, collecting license fees, inspecting and examining all premises, equipment and supplies where gaming is conducted, reviewing gaming contracts, promulgating regulations that are necessary to carry out the Ordinance, imposing civil penalties and sanctions, and excluding certain individuals from the gaming facility. Gaming Ordinance §(g)(9). Its duties do not include maintaining the restrooms at the Casino.

Plaintiff wonders "how the Gaming Commission can properly regulate games and gaming activities inside the Casino without being involved in the operation of the Casino premises." According to Plaintiff, "[r]egulatory Commissions and authorities charged with overseeing the legal requirements of gaming activity must necessarily have some involvement with the operation and supervision of patrons involved in those gaming activities inside a Casino." That argument conflates regulation with operation. Undoubtedly, a regulatory body is "involved" with the business it regulates in the sense that it is the regulator. But that is not to say that the regulator has any responsibility over or ability to control day-to-day operations. If the logic of Plaintiff's argument were accepted, then a regulator could be sued whenever the business or entity it regulated committed a tort.

The Tribe is the sole shareholder in SMGII, but it does not control the day-to-day operation of the Casino. Instead, under the Gaming Ordinance it is the "corporation," that is SMGII, that is "responsible for ensuring sound development and management of all Class II and Class III gaming activities carried out under th[e] Ordinance." Gaming Ordinance §(q). Plaintiff contends that because the Tribe is the sole shareholder it "apparently has controlling authority and/or at least significant influence over SMGI and it's [sic] decisions concerning liability claims and possible settlement of those claims." The issue, however, is whether the Tribe has any authority over the day-to-day operation of the Casino, and in particular, over the maintenance of the restrooms at the Casino, not whether it has any "influence" over how SMGII responds to tort claims. Plaintiff's allegations focus on the condition of the women's restroom, not on anyone's settlement policies. Therefore, the Tribe also is not a proper Defendant. . . .

IT IS HEREBY ORDERED that Plaintiff's complaint be and it hereby is DISMISSED.

NOTES

1. In *Jones v. Four Winds Casino Resort*, No. 08-343-CV (Pokagon Band of Potawatomi Indians Tribal Court 2009), the tribal court interpreted the Pokagon Band's Tort Claims Ordinance, which provides in relevant part:

   > No claim may be brought under this Ordinance unless written notice of the claim is served upon the Gaming Enterprise by certified mail, return receipt requested within 120 days after the claim accrues.

   Pokagon Band of Potawatomi Indians Tort Claims Ordinance §9(A) (2001); *see also id.* §10 ("All Claims shall be filed with the Tribal Court within 180 days of the date on which the Claim accrued."). The plaintiff had suffered a personal injury at the Four Winds Casino, but did not file the proper notice within the 120-day limitation period:

   > Plaintiff urges the Court to rule that the Complaint was timely filed by application of equitable/judicial tolling. Plaintiff cites *Ward v Rooney-Gandy*, 265 Mich. App. 515 (2005), which provides: "While equitable tolling applies principally to situations in which a defendant actively misleads a plaintiff about the cause of action or in which the plaintiff is prevented in some extraordinary way from asserting his rights, the doctrine does not require wrongful conduct by a defendant[] . . . an element of equitable tolling is that a plaintiff must exercise reasonable diligence in investigating and bringing his claim." . . .
   >
   > In this case, it does not appear that the Plaintiff actively pursued her judicial remedies by filing a defective notice pleading during the statutory period or that she was misled or in any way tricked by misconduct of the Defendants. The Plaintiff merely missed the deadline set by the Tort Claims Ordinance requiring the filing of her claim within 180 days of its accrual.

   Jones, No. 08-343-CV, at 6-7.

2. In *Lubrano v. Brennan Beer Gorman Architects, LLP*, 7 Am. Tribal Law 369 (Mohegan Gaming Disputes Court of Appeals 2008), the court refused to apply the Mohegan Torts Code statute of limitations to a non-tribal entity:

   > [W]e are unable to identify any intention on the part of Mohegan Tribal Ordinances or regulations to treat non-Tribal entities the same as Tribal entities cloaked with sovereign immunity. In litigation in the Gaming Disputes Court, for example, actions against the Mohegan Tribe or the Mohegan Tribal Gaming Authority are subject to very different rules than those against non-Tribal entities[.] . . .
   >
   > Furthermore, there is the overriding concern that the adoption of the Torts Code as controlling in tort actions against non-Tribal entities would result in the stripping away of rights that patrons and others have against other patrons and non-Tribal entities, without the Tribal Council having enacted legislation evidencing any intention to do so. For instance, a patron injured in an assault by another patron, under State law would have a three year statute of limitations for the bringing of an action for damages; a patron injured in the parking lot by the negligent driving of another patron would have two years. To reduce all such statutes of limitation to the period of time in which an action can be filed against the MTGA is not only inconsistent with the admittedly disparate treatment of Tribal and non-Tribal entities, but

also would intrude upon the legislative authority of the Tribal Council. This we decline to do.

We hold that the Mohegan Torts Code has been, and continues to be, a limited waiver of sovereign immunity allowing the advancing of tort claims against the MTGA (and, in current form, against the Mohegan Tribe in non-gaming situations) in accordance with the mandate of the Tribal-State Gaming Compact, and that it has no applicability to tort claims against non-Tribal entities. Accordingly, tort claims against the non-Tribal defendants in the instant case remain subject to State law statutes of limitations.

Lubrano, 7 Am. Tribal Law at 377-78.

3. Many tribes have adopted similar tort claims ordinances that tend to limit negligence actions against the tribe to "dangerous conditions." For example, in *Argyle v. Grand Traverse Band Gaming Commission*, 8 Am. Tribal Law 167 (Grand Traverse Band of Ottawa and Chippewa Indians Tribal Court 2009), the court interpreted this provision in the tribal code:

The Defendant argues that the Plaintiff's claim is barred under the Tribal Code, specifically 6 GTBC §104, which provides for a limited waiver of sovereign immunity, and states as follows:

(a) **The sovereign immunity of the Tribe shall continue except to the extent that it is expressly waived by this ordinance.** . . .

(b) The Gaming Commission may be sued solely in the Grand Traverse Band of Ottawa and Chippewa Indians Tribal Court. . . .

(c) **The sovereign immunity of the Gaming Commission is waived in the following instances:**

(1) Injuries proximately caused by the negligent acts or omissions of the Gaming Commission;

(2) **Injuries proximately caused by the condition of any property of the Gaming Commission provided the claimant establishes that the property was in a dangerous condition;**

(3) Injuries proximately caused by the negligent acts or omissions of Tribal security officers arising out of the performance of their duties during the course and within the scope of their employment.

(Emphasis added). Defendant essentially argues that the Plaintiff's injuries were not caused by a "dangerous condition" as provided in 6 GTBC §104(c)(3) above.

"Dangerous condition" as used in Title 6 of the GTB Code is defined in 6 GTBC §102(g) as follows:

(g) "Dangerous Condition" means a physical aspect of a facility or the use thereof which constitutes an unreasonable risk to human health or safety, which is known to exist or which in the exercise of reasonable care should have been known to exist and which condition is proximately caused by the negligent acts or omissions of the Gaming Enterprise in constructing or maintaining such facility.

(1) . . . [A] dangerous condition should have been known to exist if it is established that the condition had existed for such a period of time and was of such a nature that, in the exercise of

reasonable care, such condition and its dangerous character should have been discovered.

(2) A dangerous condition shall not exist solely because the design of any facility is inadequate nor due to the mere existence of wind, water, ice or temperature by itself, or by the mere existence of natural physical condition.

The issue of interpretation of the scope of the limited waiver of sovereign immunity as it relates to the "dangerous condition" exception to sovereign immunity appears to be an issue of first impression. . . .

In the present case, in order to qualify for the waiver of sovereign immunity, the Plaintiff must be able to establish that her injuries were proximately caused by the condition of any property of the Gaming Commission provided the claimant establishes that the property was in a dangerous condition. 6 GTBC §104(c)(2). The argument focuses on whether the swivel chair Plaintiff attempted to sit on equates to a "dangerous condition," and whether the statutory provision was intended to apply to fixtures such as chairs.

The Court does not need to reach the issue of whether a swivel chair or any other fixture can be construed as a "physical aspect of a facility or the use thereof," under 6 GTBC §102(g). Rather, this Court concludes that a swivel chair does not in and of itself constitute an "unreasonable risk to human health or safety" as contemplated under 6 GTBC §102(g). Nor has Plaintiff provided any evidence to show that her injuries were proximately caused by any negligence on the part of Defendant. There has been no evidence presented to suggest there was a defect in the chair, nor that the chair was not properly constructed or maintained by Defendant. . . .

Argyle, 8 Am. Tribal Law at 170-71.

2. SUITS AGAINST TRIBAL ENTITIES COVERED BY INSURANCE

AMERIND RISK MANAGEMENT CORP. v. MALATERRE

Turtle Mountain Band of Chippewa Indians Court of Appeals,
No. TMAC-06-003 (July 5, 2007)

Before: Chief Justice B.J. JONES, Justices KARRIE AZURE and MONIQUE VONDALL-RIEKE

CHIEF JUSTICE JONES FOR THE COURT:

Amerind Risk Management Corp. appeals from a decision of the lower court sustaining a direct action against it for the alleged negligence of the Turtle Mountain Housing Authority resulting in a house fire in Unit #1221 that killed two Turtle Mountain members and seriously injured another. The administrators of the estates of the decedents and the injured party then commenced this action against the Turtle Mountain Housing Authority and its "insurer," Amerind Risk Management Corp. The Housing Authority was voluntarily dismissed, but the Tribal Judge, the Honorable Beverly May, denied the motion of Amerind to dismiss the direct action against it finding that the cause of action is permitted under this Court's decision in *St. Claire v. Turtle Mountain Casino*, No. TMAC 97-013 (May 11, 1998). . . . For the reasons stated herein this Court affirms the ruling of the Court below that the Appellees may bring a direct action against Amerind because federal law mandates that Indian Housing Authorities procure insurance to indemnify them against their liabilities arising from acts of negligence. The Appellees should have the opportunity to demonstrate that the Housing Authority and its employees were negligent and that this negligence resulted in a liability subject to indemnification. . . .

The real crux of this appeal centers on the joinder of the Appellant as a party defendant in the lawsuit below. The Appellant contends that no direct cause of action lied against it both because the type of indemnification it provides the Housing Authority hinges on a finding of liability against the Authority, which no such finding was made below, and is not designed to protect the public against losses caused by the Housing Authority. Even if it does, according to the Appellant, Amerind is not a typical "insurance company," but instead is a type of "risk management" self-insurance pool that is not separate and distinct from the Housing Authorities themselves and therefore any suit against it is necessarily one against the sovereign that funds it.

Resolution of this issue necessarily involves a reexamination of this Court's ruling in *St. Claire* which is relied upon [by] both parties to this appeal. This Court's decision in *St. Claire v. Turtle Mountain Chippewa Casino* has been the subject of numerous appeals to this Court since its pronouncement in 1998. Many of those suits have addressed the issue of whether insurance is mandated under federal and tribal law, while others have addressed the issue of whether the Tribe has waived immunity from suit by procuring mandated insurance. The *St. Claire* decision recognized that lawsuits involving the allegedly negligent actions of a sovereign should not be dismissed on sovereign immunity grounds if the law underlying the Tribe's procurement of insurance reflects a legislative intent to provide a remedy to those injured by the sovereign, rather than to merely indemnify the sovereign for any losses it sustains in the operation of its lawful duties and responsibilities. This distinction is important because in many circumstances the Tribe is required to obtain indemnity insurance as a condition of receiving federal dollars, for example, and the clear intent of the insurance mandate is to protect the Tribe's assets instead of protecting the public against losses. That type of mandatory insurance is not a clear and unequivocal waiver of the immunity of the Tribe, whereas a congressional act or act of tribal government that clearly mandates that insurance be procured in order to protect third persons from losses is clearly a waiver of the immunity of the Tribe up to the limits of the mandated insurance. . . .

Therefore, in order for the Appellees to surmount the general obstacle to bringing a direct action against an insurer they must demonstrate: 1) that the insurer is providing coverage pursuant to a mandate of federal or tribal law; and 2) that the type of insurance mandated is specifically designed to protect the public against losses and not merely to indemnify the insured. The latter inquiry would be self-defeating, however, if the Court merely examined the insurance policy to determine if there is reference to indemnification of public at large because all insurance policies necessarily include coverage for the insured only. If the insurance policy is mandated under the law, and includes language mandating that the carrier indemnify the insured for losses to the public, *St. Claire* suggests that the immunity of the insured entity would be waived to the limits of any insurance coverage. Otherwise, the insurance policy covering indemnification of the insured for losses to third-parties would be rendered superfluous because the insured would never be liable to the public because of its sovereign status.

This case presents an even more difficult public policy issue than that presented by the *St. Claire* case due to the deaths of two tribal members and the serious injuries to another because of the allegedly negligent acts of the Turtle Mountain Housing Authority. The Appellees spend some time in their brief pointing out the amounts of money paid by the Turtle Mountain Housing Authority to Amerind for risk-coverage purposes. The Court finds this information irrelevant. It cannot base its decision in this case on the mere fact that the Housing Authority has contributed substantially to Amerind in its quest to insure various Housing Authorities nationwide. Nor can the Court base a legal determination on the potential impact of permitting direct actions against insurance carriers on the underwriting of insurance policies for tribal programs. The Court can only assume that if an insurance policy requires the carrier to indemnify an insured for losses sustained by third parties those potential liabilities are written into the underwriting decisions and the decisions made by Amerind regarding the contributions of each Indian Housing Authority to its risk pool.

The crux of the *St. Claire* ruling is that if the law mandates that a tribal entity possess liability insurance that mandates indemnification of losses to the public, merely permitting the tribal entity and its insurer to use the mantra of sovereign immunity to defeat all claims violates the clear intent of federal and/or tribal law that such claims should be covered under the policy of insurance provided.

Amerind also contends that it is not the typical insurance company, but instead is a type of inter-tribal housing risk pool that distinguishes it from general commercial liability insurance carriers and separates it from this Court's decision in *St. Claire* that clearly dealt with a commercial insurance carrier. This argument troubles the Court because this Court finds it laudable that Indian Housing Authorities have come together and pooled their resources in order to fulfill their obligations under NAHASDA to ensure that each individual Indian Housing Authority remains viable after losses are sustained. Federal regulations expressly countenance this type of self-insurance. *See* 24 CFR Part 1000. Those regulations, however, contemplate that this type of self-insurance would be conducted through "nonprofit insurance entities owned and controlled by Indian tribes and tribally-designated housing entities." As such, Amerind contends, it is no different than the Indian Housing Authorities it indemnifies and should therefore share in the immunity of those entities. . . .

. . . [T]he Plaintiff voluntarily dismissed the Housing Authority from this suit. Amerind . . . argues that it is no different than the Housing Authorities it insures and is therefore entitled to the sovereign immunity defense. Even assuming that the Turtle Mountain Housing Authority may be immune from suit, the Court finds that its decision in *St. Claire* as well as its recent decision in *Gorneau v. Turtle Mountain Band of Chippewa Indians*, No. TMAC-02-10247 clearly hold that federal or tribal law mandating insurance to protect the public constitutes a limited waiver of the sovereign immunity defense that may be available to the party responsible for indemnifying the immune entity. As this Court held in *Gorneau*:

> a congressional act or act of tribal government that clearly mandates that insurance be procured in order to protect third persons from losses is clearly a waiver of the immunity of the Tribe up to the limits of the mandated insurance.

It is therefore of no utility for Amerind to argue that it should share in the immunity of the Housing Authorities that it indemnifies. *See also Smith Plumbing v. Aetna Casualty Insurance Co.*, 720 P.2d 499 (Ariz. 1986) (surety of immune Tribe not entitled to defend against its liabilities based upon the Tribe's immunity). If Amerind has a duty to indemnify the losses sustained by the Appellees it cannot avail itself of immunity to avoid its obligations. The Northern Plains Inter-Tribal Court of Appeals decision in *Mountain v. Fort Berthold Housing Authority and Amerind Risk Management Corporation*, CV-18-18-01 (September 24, 2003), is not to the contrary. In *Mountain* the Court reversed a decision of the trial court permitting a direct suit against Amerind. In so doing, however, the Court noted that the reasoning of *St. Claire* did not apply to the case at bar because the Appellee had failed to point to any federal law mandating that the Housing Authority there have insurance to protect the public against losses. The Court did not repudiate the ruling in *St. Claire* but instead found insufficient briefing on the issue.

The Court now turns its attention to the real dispositive issue in this case — what is the nature of the legal obligation of the Turtle Mountain Housing Authority and its insurer to the Appellees in this case? Neither party seems to dispute the fact that federal law mandates that Indian Housing Authorities possess insurance; instead, they contest what type of coverage is mandated. Under the Native American Housing Assistance and Self-Determination Act of 1996 (hereinafter NAHASDA) Indian Housing Authorities receiving monies pursuant to that law from the federal government must abide by NAHASDA and the federal regulations implementing it. One requirement under NAHASDA is that each recipient of NAHASDA monies shall "maintain adequate insurance coverage for housing units that are owned or operated or assisted with grant amounts provided under this Act." 25 U.S.C. §4133. This language, in and of itself, does not meet the significant hurdles confronting a party seeking to mount a direct action against an insurance carrier. Further fleshed out, however, federal regulations implementing NAHASDA clearly dictate that recipients of NAHASDA monies must provide insurance to cover liability claims. 24 C.F.R. §1000.136 dictates that the mandated insurance must include adequate amounts to "indemnify the recipients against loss from fire, weather, **and liability claims** for all housing units owned or operated by the recipient" [(emphasis added)]. The actual certificate of coverage, attached to the Appellant's reply brief as Exhibit D, provides that Amerind will cover any liability claim for personal injury or property damage up to $1,000,000. The Court has reviewed the policy and finds nothing therein excluding liability claims arising from losses sustained by tenants or guests in Housing units.

Amerind quite naturally argues that these federal laws and regulations clearly reference the obligation of it to indemnify the Housing Authority for liability claims and not to its direct liability for losses sustained by others not affiliated with the IHA. Amerind is correct in its assertion that this language differs from the language of the mandatory insurance discussed in cases relied upon by this Court in *St. Claire* because the insurance policies therein, especially the policy involved in the *James* case from the North Dakota Supreme Court expressly referenced indemnification of third-party losses (taxi customers). However, some common sense has to be interjected into the analysis of what HUD intended when it mandated insurance coverage for liability claims. Who would the IHA be liable to if it is immune from suit? Liability implies a legal obligation to indemnify the insured for the obligations owed by the IHA to a third party not associated with it for a covered act of negligence. It could not mean the duty to indemnify the IHA against its own losses sustained by its negligent actions because such is already covered in the policy or would be covered by worker's compensation, which does not seem to be the thrust of this particular risk pool. HUD clearly contemplated that third parties would have potential claims against IHA recipients of NAHASDA monies when the IHA or its employees were negligent. The mandated insurance is therefore designed to cover the losses of tenants occasioned by the negligence of IHA employees.

The Court therefore concludes that the lower court did not err in finding that a direct action could lie against Amerind if the Appellees can demonstrate that the Turtle Mountain Housing Authority was negligent and that said negligence breached a duty of care owed to them. The Court understands the difficult implications raised by permitting a suit against an insurance company when the insured is not joined in the suit. However, the tribal court below has subpoena and other authority over entities that may possess immunity if necessary to resolve a cause of action pending before it. In addition the Housing Authority has a duty to assist its insurer in defending suits against it and Amerind would have the authority to seek the Court's intervention below to enforce that obligation should the Housing Authority not assist.

NOTES

1. Other tribal courts have held more broadly than the *Malaterre* court that the purchase of insurance constitutes a waiver of tribal sovereign immunity, allowing damages to be capped at the extent of the insurance coverage. The Absentee Shawnee Tribe Supreme Court appeared to assume without deciding that the purchase of insurance would amount to a waiver, relying on Oklahoma law:

   The appellant's third proposition is that the Tribe is estopped from claiming sovereign immunity because it accepted and paid various C.I.B. corporation claims. . . . The record on appeal contains no competent evidence as to the appellant's third proposition, it appearing that the case never reached that stage. As additional authority under appellant's third proposition, the case of *State Board of Public Affairs v. Principal Funding Corp.*, 542 P.2d 503 (Okla. 1975), is cited. The *State Board* case reaffirms the well-known position that the State of Oklahoma is immune from suit without its express consent to being sued. However, the general rule is modified where a state agency purchases liability insurance pursuant to legislative authority, thus consenting to being sued and waiving sovereign immunity to the extent of the insurance coverage. *Id*. at 505. In the instant case, no "agency" of the tribe was involved, and the record does not contain any evidence that the Tribe intended to consent to being sued. If insurance coverage existed below, such has not been made a part of the record.

Kotch v. Absentee Shawnee Tribe, 3 Oklahoma Tribal Rep. 184, 194 (Absentee Shawnee Tribe Supreme Court 1993).

2. One court relied upon an Indian gaming compact to hold that the potential damage claims against the tribal defendant may actually go beyond the tribal tort claims ordinance limitation. In *Kalantari v. Spirit Mountain Gaming, Inc.*, 5 Am. Tribal Law 94 (Confederated Tribes of the Grand Ronde Community Tribal Court 2004), the court first noted the gaming compact language:

> [S]ection 8(G) of the Compact . . . reads:
>
> > The Tribe shall indemnify, defend and hold harmless the State, its officers, directors, employees and agents from and against any claims, damages, losses or expenses asserted against or suffered or incurred by the State or its officers, directors, employees and agents (except as may be the result of their own negligence) based upon or arising out of any bodily injury or property damage resulting or claimed to result in whole or in part from any act or omission of the Tribe relating to the inspection of any gaming or gaming related facility pursuant to this Compact.

Kalatari, 5 Am. Tribal Law at 97-98. But the court rejected the defendant's claims:

> [S]ection 8(G) requires the Tribe to "maintain public liability insurance with limits of not less than $250,000 for one person and $2,000,000 for any one occurrence for any bodily injury or property damage." In conformance with this provision, the Tribe has obtained liability insurance providing coverage up to $1,000,000 per person. Section 8(G) then provides that "[t]he Tribe's insurance policy shall have an endorsement providing that the insurer may not invoke Tribal sovereign immunity up to the limits of the policy."
>
> There seems to be little dispute that if that last sentence included the term "the insured," either in addition to or in lieu of "the insurer," and if the next sentence of the provision were deleted, that the Tribe would have waived its sovereign immunity up to the policy limits. Plaintiff has cited a case to the Court holding as much. *Jones v. Chitimacha Tribe of Louisiana*, No. CV-94-0035 (Chitimacha Ct. App. 1996). . . .
>
> Defendant's reliance on the use of "the insurer" in section 8(G) has some textual appeal. After all, the provision presumably could have, but did not, include the term "the insured." But this Court rejects that reading of the

Compact provision because it would render it meaningless. The "insurer," of course, has no sovereign immunity to waive, so reading the provision as Defendant does would render it nugatory. And, even setting that problem aside, the provision would still remain meaningless and unenforceable. Because there is no privity between the insurer of an allegedly negligent Defendant and an injured tort victim, it appears unlikely that the victim could sue the insurer directly. *See Romero v. Pueblo of Sandia/Sandia Casino*, 134 N.M. 553, 80 P.3d 490, 492 (2003) (noting that is the general rule). Furthermore, even if a tort victim could sue the insurer directly, it appears likely that the tribe would be an indispensable party, which, if the tribe had not waived its sovereign immunity, could not be joined. *See [Gallegos v. Pueblo of Tesuque*, 46 P.3d 668, 681 (N.M. 2002)]* (tribe is indispensable party in action brought against insurer).

Thus, for a variety of reasons, placing too much emphasis on the term "the insurer," as used in section 8(G), renders the waiver provision meaningless and unenforceable. . . . Because "the insurer" has no sovereign immunity to waive, and because section 8(G) should not be read into oblivion, the obvious intent of section 8(G) had to be to waive the Tribe's sovereign immunity. The Red Queen might disagree, but this Court has no cause to chase the rabbit down his hole.

. . . Here, the waiver is express and clear. The insurer has no sovereign immunity to waive; the Tribe does: the only not-nonsensical reading of section 8(G) is that the Tribe has waived its sovereign immunity when sued under the insurance policy it is obliged by the Compact to obtain.

Kalantari, 5 Am. Tribal Law at 100-02.

3. Commentators note that Indian tribes simply cannot rest easy behind the wall of sovereign immunity, and that insurance is absolutely necessary:

Indian tribes can and should take advantage of liability insurance as a practical line of defense for those claims that (intentionally or unintentionally) circumvent their sovereign immunity protection. Indeed, many Indian tribes with gaming operations are now required to carry a certain amount of liability insurance for casino patron claims pursuant to their tribal-state gaming compacts. For example, a tribe in California must maintain public liability insurance in the amount of $5 million per occurrence. Even where such requirements are imposed, however, Indian tribes can control the amount of exposure by limiting the amount of damages per person, not allowing punitive damages to be claimed, and/or limiting liability to the damages covered by insurance.

In addition to liability insurance for patron claims, Indian tribes also may want to explore coverages that potentially protect against other types of exposure. Several insurance carriers have developed policies and coverages tailored to the gaming industry's needs, including those of Indian gaming tribes. These types of coverages include:

- Buildings and their contents
- Business interruption
- Automobile liability (including valet parking)
- Law enforcement liability (including security guards)
- Crime/Bonds (including embezzlement and employee theft)
- Umbrella liability (including liquor liability)
- Workers compensation

- Employee benefits liability
- Employment related practices liability
- Professional liability
  These various types of insurance coverages may offer significant, additional protection against the types of claims that have been and will be asserted against Indian tribes, particularly those who engage in gaming activities and are viewed as "deep pockets."

Venus McGhee Prince, *Making the Gaming Business a "Safe Bet" for Tribes*, 9 GAMING L. REV. 314, 316-17 (2005).

D. PERSONAL JURISDICTION

MAHLER V. HINSHAW

Confederated Salish and Kootenai Tribes Appellate Court,
No. CV-3595-88, 1 NICS App. 73 (February 2, 1990)

Before: Chief Justice ELBRIDGE COOCHISE, Associate Justice CHARLES HOSTNIK, and Associate Justice HOLLIS CHOUGH.

HOSTNIK, Associate Justice: . . .

I. Background

On June 29, 1988, Plaintiffs filed a Complaint in the trial court of the Confederated Salish and Kootenai Tribes of the Flathead Reservation for damages based upon a wrongful death claim and a survival claim. The Complaint alleged that . . . Christian Mahler, riding a motorcycle, was involved in an accident with an automobile driven by Defendant Lynette Hinshaw. Christian Mahler allegedly sustained injuries in that accident that led to his death.

The Plaintiffs (Respondents on appeal) are the parents of Christian Mahler. . . .

II. Issues on Appeal

. . . Appellant contends the Flathead Tribal Court does not have jurisdiction over her. . . .

V. Personal Jurisdiction over Appellant

. . .

Personal Jurisdiction over Respondents

The Respondents voluntarily subjected themselves to the personal jurisdiction of the Court by applying to the Tribal Court for the relief requested in their Complaint. This Court's personal jurisdiction over the Respondents is not an issue.

Appellant raises the argument that the Tribal Court does not have jurisdiction over the estate of the decedent, because the decedent was not a tribal member. This argument confuses the true nature of these proceedings. The Tribal Court is not being asked to exercise jurisdiction to administer the decedent's estate. The Tribal Court is requested to entertain a tort action for personal injuries suffered by the parents of the decedent, as well as for a claim which is a claim of the decedent's estate.

Whether the Tribal Court has subject matter jurisdiction over a probate action is simply irrelevant to this inquiry. The co-personal representatives of the estate stand in the shoes of the decedent for purposes of this action. The decedent, if he had survived, could have come into Tribal Court to institute and prosecute a tort action for personal injuries.

The fact that decedent did not survive does not divest the Tribal Court of personal or subject matter jurisdiction.

Personal Jurisdiction over Appellant

The fundamental requirement for evoking personal jurisdiction is the existence of some relationship between the Tribe and the parties to the action such that it is reasonable for the Tribal Court to exercise control over the parties. *Estate of Bighorse*, [18 Indian L. Rep. 6048, 6049 (Confederated Salish & Kootenai Tribal Court 1988).]

Personal jurisdiction over the Appellant in this case is governed by Tribal Ordinance 36B. Under that ordinance, personal jurisdiction extends to and includes all persons found within the reservation. Confederated Salish and Kootenai Tribal Ordinance 36B (codified as Law and Order Code) Ch. II, Sec. 1(2)(a)(1). The Defendant, being a resident of a town which is located within the exterior boundaries of the Reservation, is a person found within the Reservation.

Under Tribal Ordinance 36B, the Tribal Court also has jurisdiction over Appellant because she is a person "subject to the jurisdiction of the Tribal Court and involved directly or indirectly in . . . the ownership, use or possession of any property [her motor vehicle] . . . situated within the reservation . . ." Law and Order Code, Ch. II, Sec. 1(2)(a)(2)(ii).

This is not a situation where the Appellant is merely using the roadways on the Reservation to pass through the Reservation. Appellant in fact resides on the Reservation and presumably uses those roads every day. She also is benefiting from Tribal resources. She benefits from Tribal Police protection, Tribal utilities, and other resources. Therefore, there are much greater ties to Appellant than if she were merely traveling through the Reservation.

There exists a sufficient relationship between the Tribe and the Appellant such that it is reasonable for the Tribal Court in this case to exercise control over her. The Tribal Court has personal jurisdiction over the parties to this action. . . .

NOTES

1. Even assuming federal courts would not recognize the authority of tribal courts to assert jurisdiction over the parties in this kind of case, why should that stop tribal courts from doing so anyway? The Confederated Salish and Kootenai jurisdictional code, like many other tribal codes and constitutions,

incorporated elements of federal law into the tribal court's analysis, for one, forcing the tribal court to apply federal precedents. But not all tribal laws are so dependent on federal law. If a tribal jurisdictional statute requires a tribal court to take jurisdiction over cases in a manner like the code discussed in the *Mahler* case, but without the reference to compliance with federal law, isn't a tribal court *obligated* to assert jurisdiction and to *not* reference federal law?

2. In a few remarkable cases, tribal courts have at least considered the question of whether a tribal court can have jurisdiction over claims brought against the United States. In *Jackson v. Grainger*, 1999 Mont. Fort Peck Tribe LEXIS 7 (Fort Peck Court of Appeals 1999), the court was confronted with a lawsuit by a prison inmate against tribal officials and the United States as a third party defendant. The United States Attorney Office's for the District of Montana did not file a formal motion to dismiss, but instead delivered a letter to the tribal court demanding that the court dismiss the claim against the federal government. On appeal, after the tribal court dismissed the claim, the court noted the unusual posture of the appeal:

> On July 30, 1997, the United States Attorney for Montana, Sherry Scheel Matteucci, was served with the summons and complaint. On August 7, 1997, Ms. Matteucci wrote a letter to Judge Spotted Bird, citing several jurisdictional cases involving "Indian Country." She concluded her letter, stating:
>
>> The Fort Peck Tribal Court has no jurisdiction over the federal government, its agents or employees under these circumstances. I therefore ask you (sic) dismiss, on your own motion, the Third Party Complaint in Civil Cause No. 96-6-093. Should you choose not to dismiss the Third Party Complaint, we will have no alternative but to seek a federal court order declaring any orders or judgments void.

Jackson, 1999 Mont. Fort Peck Tribe LEXIS 7, at 4-6. The trial court dismissed the complaint, but the appellate court vacated the order, writing:

> It goes without saying that virtually all defendants would prefer to avoid the cost, effort and aggravation of being sued. Likewise, it is not too surprising that a defendant will make every attempt to avoid the time consuming and costly process of answering a complaint. We are convinced that if we polled lawyers regarding various methods that they have used to extricate their clients from such rigors, we would have a virtual panoply of masterful schemes. However, we find that a letter addressed directly to the Court demanding a dismissal is a curious approach indeed. It appears to us that a Motion filed in the subject Court, or a demand directed to the complaining parties, would have been the most appropriate approach. Further, to warn or threaten the Court that the defendant will not appear in that Court, but rather, will go to a Federal Court seeking to nullify "any orders or judgments" of the Court, stretches even the most vivid imagination. Such conduct could easily be interpreted as disrespectful, defiant, and arrogant. We are convinced that this would not be the "scheme" of choice of most attorneys. We trust that the United States Attorney for Montana, in employing such a tactic, did not intend to be disrespectful, nor did she intend to intimidate our Tribal

Court. Our hope is that she was guilty of no more than an ill advised exercise of poor judgment.

Nonetheless, such a shortcut to avoid litigation in the Tribal Court, while extremely convenient for the United States, was unwarranted and totally inappropriate under the attendant circumstances.

Neither do we excuse our Tribal Court for yielding to a powerful party, even the great sovereign nation of the United States. If the Tribal Court, upon researching the cases furnished by the U.S. Attorney and upon further reflection of its earlier order granting the defendants leave to join the United States as a third party defendant, decided that it had erred, the proper method to resolve the matter did not include denying the rights of the defendants in the process. Citing what they believe to be a better approach to resolving the question of jurisdiction, the defendants' argue:

> So as to have afforded all involved the opportunity to be heard, the proper procedure would have been for the United States of America to have filed a Motion With the Tribal Court pursuant to Rule 7-1 (Fort Peck Tribal Court Rules of Civil Procedure), wherein the Defendants could have responded."

Again, we agree with the defendants.

Accordingly, we find that the defendants' were deprived of their due process rights accorded them under the Fourteenth Amendment to the U.S. Constitution, as well as the Indian Civil Rights Act of 1968 (25 U.S.C.S. 1302[8]).

Burnett, 1999 Mont. Fort Peck Tribe LEXIS 7, at 7-9.

To be sure, the great of authority suggests that tribal courts do not have jurisdiction over claims brought against the federal government, as the trial court stated:

> This order is based upon the opinions rendered in *United States v. Yakima Tribal Court of the Yakima Nation*, 806 F.2d 853 (9th Cir. 1986); *United States v. White Mountain Apache Tribe*, 784 F.2d 917 (9th Cir. 1986); *United States v. Blackfeet Tribe*, 369 F. Supp. 562 (D. Mont. 1973). This order is also based upon this Court's ruling in *New Medical Associates, Inc. v. Clark and Dept. of Interior and BIA*, Case No. CV P1671-92.

Burnett, 1999 Mont. Fort Peck Tribe LEXIS 7, at 5 (quoting the trial court).

E. ADJUDICATORY JURISDICTION OVER NONMEMBERS

BANK OF HOVEN (PLAINS COMMERCE BANK) v.
LONG FAMILY LAND AND CATTLE, INC.

Cheyenne River Sioux Tribal Court of Appeals, No. 03-002-A,
32 Indian L. Rep. 6001 (November 22, 2004)

PER CURIAM (Chief Justice FRANK POMMERSHEIM and Associate Justices EVERETT DUPRIS and PATRICK LEE).

I. Introduction and Background

The facts in this case involve a series of complex commercial interactions between Ronnie and Lila Long, the Long Family Land and Cattle Company, Inc., . . . and Plains Commerce Bank (formerly Bank of Hoven), . . . dating back to 1989. Kenneth Long was a non–Tribal member whose first wife, Maxine Long, was a member of the Cheyenne River Sioux Tribe. Kenneth and Maxine owned approximately 2,230 acres of Dewey County real estate in fee simple as well as a house in Timber Lake. All of this real estate is located within the exterior boundaries of the Cheyenne River Sioux Reservation. All of this real estate was mortgaged to the Bank for loans to the Long Family Land and Cattle Company, Inc.

Upon the death of Maxine, Kenneth became the sole owner of the real estate in Dewey County. At the time of Kenneth's death on July 17, 1995, Mr. Long and the Long Family Land and Cattle Company owed the Bank approximately $750,000. Mr. Long's estate acting through Paulette Long, Kenneth's second wife and personal representative of the estate, conveyed the Dewey County real estate, as well as the house in Timber Lake, to the Bank in lieu of foreclosure. As a result of this conveyance on December 5, 1996, the Long Family Land and Cattle Company was given credit for $478,000 on its outstanding debt to the bank.

Ronnie Long is a member of the Cheyenne River Sioux Tribe and is the son of Kenneth Long. Upon his father's death, Ronnie inherited Kenneth's interest in the 2,250 acres of land in Dewey County on the Cheyenne River Sioux Reservation as well as his father's 49% interest in the Long Family Land and Cattle Company, Inc. The other 51% of the Company is owned by Ronnie and his wife Lila, who is also a member of the Cheyenne River Sioux Tribe. The Company has always been an Indian controlled company.

After Kenneth Long's death, employees of the Bank came to the Longs' land on the Cheyenne River Sioux Reservation to inspect it as well as the cattle, hay and machinery on the land. In addition, Bank officers met several times with the Longs, officials of the Cheyenne River Sioux Tribe, and Bureau of Indian Affairs employees. These meetings all took place on the Cheyenne River Sioux Reservation. All of these activities were directed to establishing a basis from which the Bank would provide new loans to Ronnie Long and the Long Family Land and Cattle Company, Inc. for their ranching operation on this land.

The Bank initially proposed that it would sell the land back to the Longs (which was conveyed to the Bank by the Long Estate) via a 20-year contract for deed. Upon the advice of counsel, in a letter to Ronnie Long dated April 20, 1996, the Bank withdrew this offer because of "possible jurisdictional problems." . . . The revised proposal of the Bank offered the Longs only a two-year lease and option within which to purchase and pay for the land in full.

The Lease with Option to Purchase included a purchase price of $478,000 for the land. The other features of the lease provided that annual Crop Reserve Program (CRP) payments to the Longs were assigned to the Bank and the right of the Longs to exercise their option to purchase for $478,000 at the conclusion of the lease period. Another document captioned "Loan Agreement" was signed by both the Bank and the Longs. It recited a series of debits and credits of the Longs to the Bank, and also stated that the Bank would request that the BIA increase the loan guarantee to 90% of note #98181, that the Bank would make an operating loan to the Longs in the amount of $70,000. The Bank also agreed to make another loan of $53,000 to pay off note #98809 of $17,000 with the balance of $37,000 to be used to purchase 110 cattle. Both the Lease with Option to Purchase and the Loan Agreement were signed by the Bank and the Longs on December 5, 1996.

Shortly thereafter, mother nature intervened with a vengeance during the horrific winter of 1996-97. As a result of the failure to provide the $70,000 loan and the implacable force of the brutal winter, the Longs lost 230 cows, 277 yearlings, and 8 horses. The Bank did provide some additional loans that were quite modest. The Longs never recovered from these financial and weather-related blows and were unable to meet their outstanding debt to the Bank and were not able to exercise their option to purchase.

The Longs did not remove from the property in question at the expiration of the lease. The Bank began (state) eviction proceedings by sending a notice to quit to the Cheyenne River Sioux Tribal Court for service on the Longs. Service was apparently never effectuated. There was never any hearing or ruling by the state court. Without any order of eviction and with the Longs remaining in possession of the land, the Bank nevertheless sold the land. On March 17, 1999, the Bank sold 320 acres to Ralph Pesicka for cash and on June 29, 1999, the Bank sold the remaining 1,905 acres to Edward and May Jo Mack-jewski on a contract for deed. None of these purchasers are members of the Cheyenne River Sioux Tribe.

The Longs then commenced an action in the Cheyenne River Sioux Tribal Court seeking a restraining order preventing the Bank from selling the real estate. The Bank's motion to dismiss for lack of subject matter jurisdiction was denied as was the Longs motion for a restraining order against the Bank. The Longs subsequently amended their complaint to include several causes of action against the Bank that sought damages and other relief. The Bank counterclaimed seeking eviction of the Longs and damages. The Longs requested a jury trial on their claims. The Bank did not seek a jury trial on its counterclaim.

A two day jury trial was held on December 6 and 11, 2002. At the close of the Plaintiffs' case, Special Judge B.J. Jones dismissed Plaintiffs' claims that sought to void the contract, alleged fraud, failure of consideration, and unconscionability. The jury returned a verdict in favor of the Longs on their claims that the Bank breached the loan agreement, discriminated against the Longs based on their status as Indians, and acted in bad faith with regard to its dealings with the Longs. The jury awarded the Longs $750,000 along with prejudgment interest. Special Judge B.J. Jones determined that interest to be $123,131. The jury also found that the Bank did not use self-help remedies in an attempt to remove Plaintiffs from the land. A supplemental judgment was later entered permitting the Plaintiffs to exercise the option to purchase the 960 acres of the land they continued to occupy.

Both sides filed timely notices of appeal with this Court. Oral argument was heard on October 6, 2004. . . .

III. Discussion

A. Defendant/Appellant/Respondent Bank

1. Jurisdiction

The Bank's jurisdictional claim is quite limited in scope and is best understood as involving two separate (but overlapping) legal contentions. As to scope, the Bank argues that the Cheyenne River Sioux Tribal court does not have jurisdiction over the Longs' discrimination claim. . . . This presumably forecloses any federal appeal under the *National Farmers Union* exhaustion doctrine of any other issue involved in this case save the jurisdiction claim relative to the discrimination cause of action. *See e.g., National Farmers Union Ins. Cos. v. Crow Tribe of Indians*, 471 U.S. 845 (1985). The Bank's two legal arguments, while not drawn as sharply as they might be, assert that the trial court did not have jurisdiction over the discrimination claim because it is a federal claim barred under *Nevada v. Hicks*, 533 U.S. 353 (2002), and because no discrimination cause of action exists as a matter of Cheyenne River Sioux Tribal law. Each of these will be discussed in turn concluding with the pertinent jurisdictional analysis under *Montana v. United States*, 450 U.S. 544 (1981).

a) *Nevada v. Hicks* and Federal Causes of Action

The Bank alleges that Cheyenne River Sioux Tribal Court did not have subject matter jurisdiction over Plaintiffs' discrimination claim against the Bank. It is critical to note that the Bank does not challenge (on appeal) the general jurisdiction of the Cheyenne River Sioux Tribal Court over the lawsuit brought by the Longs against the Bank, but only against a single cause of action. Appellant's argument centers its claim on its reading of *Nevada v. Hicks*, 533 U.S. 353 (2002). More precisely, the Bank relies on *Hicks* for the limited proposition that tribal courts do not have jurisdiction over federal causes of action. Appellant's interpretation of *Nevada v. Hicks* in this regard is not incorrect, but it is inapposite. The Court in *Hicks* did hold that tribal courts do not have jurisdiction over a federal cause of action alleged under 42 U.S.C. §1983. The Bank argues by extension that tribal courts would have no jurisdiction over a discrimination claim grounded in 42 U.S.C. §1981(c). This is likely true, but misses the point. The Plaintiffs discrimination claim is based on a cause of action grounded in tribal, not federal, law.

Plaintiffs' amended complaint did not invoke 42 U.S.C. §1981 or any federal statute as the source of the discrimination claim and the Bank did not seek to question the source of law for this claim through a motion to dismiss for failure to state a claim on which relief might be granted. In addition, there were no jury instructions provided to the jury on an alleged federal cause of action for discrimination. . . .

. . . The case at bar is not a criminal case, does not involve state officers, and did not take place off the Reservation. It is therefore totally inapplicable as to causes of action arising on the Reservation involving private individuals. The *Hicks* opinion limited its holding "to the question of tribal court jurisdiction over state officers" leaving "open the question of tribal court jurisdiction and non-member defendants in general." 533 U.S. 358 n. 2.

b) Discrimination Causes of Action under Tribal Law

Notwithstanding its citation to *Nevada v. Hicks*, the Bank's claim is not really that the Tribal Court does not have subject matter jurisdiction over the discrimination claim, but rather there is no such cause of action under tribal law. In essence, the Bank is claiming that the Longs' discrimination claim should have been dismissed not for lack of jurisdiction, but for a failure to state a claim upon which relief might be granted. This is especially evident in that the Bank's motion to dismiss was not directed to all of the Plaintiffs' claims, but was limited to the discrimination cause of action premised on the (erroneous) theory that it was being pursued as a federal cause of action under 42 U.S.C. §1981. This more precise claim is also insufficient as a matter of law.

Private claims of discrimination based on status are recognized under federal and state statutes. *See, e.g.* 42 U.S.C. 2000 (d), et seq. (2003), SDCL §20-13-21 (2003). They are also recognized under the traditional (or common) law of the Cheyenne River Sioux Tribe.[3] While there is no express tribal ordinance creating a civil cause of action based on discrimination, there are nevertheless at least two other sources of tribal law that do recognize such a cause of action. They are tribal common law and the Cheyenne River Sioux Law and Order Code §1-4-3 which confers jurisdiction on the trial court over claims arising out of "tortious conduct."

Since it is well understood that a claim based on discrimination essentially sounds in tort, jurisdiction over "tortious conduct" necessarily includes jurisdiction over Plaintiffs' discrimination claim. In addition, there is basis for a discrimination claim that arises directly from Lakota tradition as embedded in Cheyenne River Sioux tradition and custom. Such a potential claim arises from the existence of Lakota customs and norms such as the "traditional Lakota sense of justice, fair play and decency to others," *Miner v. Banley*, Chy. R. Sx. Tr. Ct. App., No. 94-003 A, Mem. Op. and Order at 6 (Feb. 3, 1995); and "the Lakota custom of fairness and respect for individual dignity." *Thompson v. Cheyenne River Sioux Tribal Board of Police Commissioners*, 23 ILR 6045, 6048

---

3. Discrimination is prohibited under tribal customary law in much the same way that other injurious or tortious conduct is prohibited under the common law. While it is true that discrimination is frequently the subject of legislation, it is also actionable under the common law. The Supreme Court has long recognized that "an action brought for compensation by a victim of . . . discrimination is, in effect, a tort action." *Meyer v. Holley*, 537 U.S. 280, 285, 123 S. Ct. 824, 828 (2003) (citing *Curtis v. Loether*, 415 U.S. 189, 94 S. Ct. 1005 (1974)). In *Curtis*, the Court held that a claim for damages under the Civil Rights Act of 1968 "sounds basically in tort" and "is analogous to a number of tort actions recognized at common law." 415 U.S. 189, 195-196, 94 S. Ct. 1005, 1008-1009. The Court noted that, "[a]n action to redress racial discrimination may . . . be likened to an action for defamation or intentional infliction of mental distress," and further that "under the logic of the common law development of a law of insult and indignity, racial discrimination might be treated as a dignitary tort." 415 U.S. at 195-196, n. 10, 94 S. Ct. at 1008-1009, n. 10. These are precisely the kinds of actions over which the tribal courts have jurisdiction. Under tribal law, the courts "have jurisdiction over claims and disputes arising on the reservation." CRST By-Laws, Art. V, §1(c), including claims arising out of "tortious conduct." Cheyenne River Sioux Tribal Code §1-4-3. Cheyenne River Sioux Tribe's Amicus Brief at 14, footnote 3.

Chey. R. Sx. Tr. Ct. App. (1996). Such notions of fair play are core ingredients in federal and state definitions of discrimination. Therefore a tribally based cause of action grounded in an assertion of discrimination may proceed as a "tort" claim as defined in the Cheyenne River Sioux Tribal Code, as derived from Tribal tradition and custom, or even from the federal ingredients defined at 42 U.S.C. §2000-2001.

The core of the Longs' discrimination claim was based on the Bank's letter to the Longs dated April 26, 1996, . . . in which the Bank withdrew its offer to sell the land back to Longs on a 20-year contract for deed because it involved an "Indian owned entity" and related (but unidentified) "jurisdictional problems." The Bank's subsequent offer as contained in the lease with option to purchase required full payment within 60 days of the expiration of the two-year lease. . . . It is also significant to recall that the land involved is fee land not trust land. While trust land does involve certain federal restrictions on alienability, fee land does not. The Longs contended that this adverse and differential treatment of them was based on their status as "Indians" and constituted discrimination, a question that was ultimately resolved in their favor by the jury verdict.

It is a testament to the vitality and dignity of American jurisprudence that it would most certainly shock the conscience if a claim of discrimination — especially one based on the disparity of treatment on account or race or status — would not be cognizable in state or federal court. In this vein, the Cheyenne River Sioux Tribal Court is no different from its federal and state brethren in its unwillingness to ignore claims of discrimination. In the area of discrimination, there is a direct and laudable convergence of federal, state, and tribal concern.

c) Jurisdiction under *Montana v. United States*

Since there is a discrimination cause of action under Tribal law involving fee land, the most relevant case for jurisdictional purposes therefore is not *Nevada v. Hicks* but *Montana v. United States*, 450 U.S. 544 (1981). In *Montana*, the Court held that tribal courts generally do not have jurisdiction over non-Indians involving matters that arise on fee land within the reservation. This presumption against tribal court jurisdiction is nevertheless subject to *Montana*'s well-known proviso which states: "[T]o be sure, Indian tribes retain sovereign power to exercise some forms of civil jurisdiction over non-Indians on their reservations, even on non-Indian fee lands. A tribe may regulate, through taxation, licensing or other means, the activities of members who enter consensual relationships with the tribe or its members, through commercial dealing, contracts, leases or other arrangements. . . . A tribe may also retain inherent power to exercise civil authority over non-Indians on fee lands within its reservation when that conduct threatens charities or has some effect on the political integrity, economic security, or the health or welfare of the tribe." 450 U.S. at 565-66 (citations omitted).

It is clear that the case at bar satisfies both prongs. This case is the prototype for a consensual agreement as it involves a signed contract between a tribal member and a non-Indian bank. The contract deals solely with fee land located wholly within the exterior boundaries of the reservation. Fee land that was originally owned by the Longs, but owned by the Bank during the controverted events in this lawsuit. All bank loans in this matter were provided solely for the ranching operation by the Longs taking place on the Bank's land within the reservation. Numerous meetings of the Bank with the Longs, with Cheyenne River Sioux Tribal Officials, and Bureau of Indian Affairs personnel took place on the reservation, both when the land was owned by the Longs and subsequently when it was owned by the Bank.

It is somewhat misleading for the Bank to identify itself as an off-reservation Bank, because it owned the land on the Reservation that is the subject of this lawsuit. As a result, the Bank is more accurately described as owning property and engaged in business activities both on and off the Reservation.

In addition, the case clearly involves the "economic security" of the Tribe in that the Cheyenne River Sioux Tribe (along with the Bureau of Indian Affairs) was a direct participant actively consulted by both the Longs and the Bank seeking economic data and support relevant to the cattle operation on the Longs' land. If the economic security of the Tribe was not involved, the Tribe would not have played such a large role in these events in seeking to support and advance the opportunity for Tribal members to succeed in their ranching operation on the Reservation.

2. Breach of Contract Cause of Action

Appellant Bank asserts that the Longs' breach of contract claim was improperly submitted to the jury or if properly submitted to the jury, improperly decided by it because no contract existed as a matter of law or fact. In particular, the Bank contends that the key document captioned "Loan Agreement" which was prepared by the Bank and signed by both the Bank and the Longs on December 5, 1996 and recites, among other things, the Bank's commitment to provide two loans to the Long Land and Cattle Company, Inc. was not a contract at all. It was merely some kind of balance sheet that mainly recited a list of debts and credits relative to the real estate conveyed by the Long Estate to the Bank. In essence, according to the Bank, there was no consideration and hence no contract.

In the Bank's motion for judgment N.O.V. on this issue, Judge B.J. Jones decided against the Bank finding there was sufficient consideration when the "Loan Agreement" is considered as part of the Lease with Option to Purchase under the integrated document doctrine. These documents were contemporaneous, applied to the same subject matter, and were interrelated as to terms. . . . Judge Jones had already adopted the integrated document doctrine in denying the Defendant's motion for summary judgment on its counterclaim for eviction and it appropriately became the law of the case. This Court now adopts the substance of this rule as appropriate law within this jurisdiction. In this view, it is reasonable to construe the Loan Agreement along with the Lease with Option to Purchase and find sufficient consideration provided by the Longs in their commitment to assign their CRP payments to the Bank and their commitment to continue the operation of their ranch in an attempt to pay off their debts to the Bank without the Bank having to resort to legal action and the less than complete loan guarantees provided by the BIA.

The analysis set out by Judge Jones in his well-reasoned opinion of June 7, 2003 is persuasive. As noted above, there certainly was enough evidence submitted to the jury for it to have found adequate consideration. In reviewing a jury's determination on a motion for a judgment N.O.V., the South Dakota Supreme Court has established a reasonable standard of review, which this Court adopts. This standard directs the reviewing court to review the testimony and evidence in a light most favorable to the verdict or nonmoving party and then to decide without weighing the evidence if there is evidence which did support the verdict. *Matter of Estate of Holan*, 621 N.W.2d 588, 591 (S.D. 2000).

In sum, the application of the integrated documents doctrine is an appropriate legal standard within this jurisdiction. In addition, its legal elements of contemporaneity, similar subject matter, and interrelatedness of terms were also satisfied as a matter of law and there was a sufficient factual basis for the jury to find there was adequate consideration for a contract, and the Bank's failure to perform breached this contract.

3. Bad Faith Cause of Action

In a similar vein to the breach of contract claim, the Bank makes two contentions. First, that such a cause of action does not exist as a matter of law because it is subsumed in the breach of contract claim and second, even if such an independent cause of action does exist, there was insufficient evidence submitted to the jury to sustain a verdict upholding such a bad faith claim.

The question of law concerning a bad faith cause of action involves an issue of first impression within this jurisdiction. The trial court ruled that such a cause of action does exist within this jurisdiction and that it is one that is independent of any breach of contract claim. More precisely, it might be stated that the trial court ruled that the bad faith claim derives from but is severable and hence independent of the breach of contract claim. As Judge Jones stated in his order of June 7, 2003 on the post-trial motions, the heart of the breach of contract claim was the failure to provide the $70,000 loan, while the heart of the bad faith claim was the Bank's failure to follow through with its promise to seek an increase in the level of the BIA guarantee for several outstanding loans.

This statement of the governing law is reasonable and appropriate. While it appears that no other tribal court has addressed this issue, it is true that the rule articulated by the trial court is within the ambit of both South Dakota Law, *see e.g. Garrett v. Bank West, Inc.*, 459 N.W.2d 833 (S.D. 1990) and the general rule as articulated in the Restatement 2nd of Contracts §204 (1990) that every contract includes an implied covenant of good faith and fair dealing which prohibits either contracting party from preventing or injuring the other party's right to receive the agreed upon benefits of the contract.

The Bank's challenge to the sufficiency of the evidence in this issue is likewise rejected. Given the standard of review articulated in Part IIIA2 . . . , clearly there was sufficient evidence in the record concerning the Bank's failure to respond to the BIA's request for a more detailed application relative to potential increased loan guarantees from which the jury might conclude that the Bank acted in bad faith.

4. Excessive Damages Controlled by Passion or Prejudice

The jury awarded damages to the plaintiffs in the amount of $750,000. The Bank claims this was "excessive and controlled by passion and prejudice." . . . This conclusion remains just that, a conclusion unsupported by reason or law. Plaintiffs sought damages in the amount of $1,236,792 . . . and thus the award of $750,000 represents an award of only 60% of the amount requested. The trial judge also sustained a number of objections made by the Bank to the Plaintiffs' claimed damages and Exhibit 23 was changed accordingly. The Bank did not object, stating, "I have no objections with these changes," . . . and therefore the Bank waived any subsequent right to appeal. The absence of "prejudice" is also further evidenced by the jury's rejection of the Longs' claim of improper self-help eviction by the Bank.

The Plaintiffs provided extensive evidentiary data and testimony relative to their damages. The Bank had the same opportunity. Given the appropriate standard of review in challenging a jury finding of fact as noted above, this Court cannot conclude that the jury award in this context lacked a sufficient factual predicate, even disregarding the Bank's waiver of this issue.

Ordinarily, this would conclude the Court's analysis of this otherwise legitimate issue, but for the Bank's decision to characterize the entire trial as "tainted":

> Once a claim for discrimination was allowed to be tried to the jury, where no one but tribal members could serve, the Bank could no longer obtain a fair trial. Allegations of racial discrimination by a nonmember Bank located off the reservation *completely enflamed the jury*. They became incapable of rendering a fair and impartial verdict. The *race card tainted* the entire trial process (emphasis added) (Bank's brief at 23).

This rhetoric is itself inflammatory. At oral argument, counsel for the Bank admitted that he did not challenge any juror for cause, did not challenge the jury panel as a whole because it did not contain any non-tribal members, and perhaps most importantly, he did not request that the trial court use its discretionary power under Sec. 1-6-1(2) of the Tribal Code to "adopt procedures whereby non-enrolled Indians and non-Indians may be summoned for jury duty in cases in which one or more non-Indian parties are involved."

The Bank, apparently excusing its own ("benign") neglect of the issue at the trial, then twists it (somehow) to contend that the very existence of a discrimination cause of action was playing the "race card." The Bank's apparent "solution" to this "problem" is that claims of discrimination against non-resident Banks should not exist as a matter of tribal law. This asserts a rather extravagant privilege for the Bank that is presumably not available to others, especially tribal members and the Tribe itself. Whether intended or not, this is the Bank playing its own "race card," which at a minimum is quite baffling and potentially quite disturbing in the context of seeking to maintain a fair and reasonable legal context for the necessary commercial transactions involving individual Tribal ranchers and business people and the banking establishment. Both Tribal members and the Bank need each other and it is quite disheartening to have the Bank interject the potentially destabilizing "race card" into these proceedings. . . .

Unfortunately, a final concern must be addressed. In his concluding summation to this Court, counsel for the Bank stated that a lot of banks and lenders were watching this case. While it seemed jarring and inappropriate at the time, it is even more so upon reflection. It is difficult to see the statement as merely some form of artless advocacy, but rather more as some kind of threat impugning the integrity of the Cheyenne River Sioux Tribe's judicial system, which this Court finds most offensive and unprofessional. Such statements must not be made again. Though it hardly needs repeating, the Court restates its commitment to fair play, the rule of law, and cultural respect for all parties who appear in the courts of the Cheyenne River Sioux Tribe. . . .

Ho Hecletu Ye Lo

IT IS SO ORDERED.

NOTES

1. The United States Supreme Court disagreed with the *Bank of Hoven* court in *Plains Commerce Bank v. Long Family Land and Cattle Co.*,* 128 S. Ct. 2709 (2008). However, Justice Stevens in dissent quoted a line from the Cheyenne River Sioux Tribal Court of Appeals, the first time in history that any Supreme Court opinion has quoted from a tribal court opinion. *See Plains Commerce Bank*, 128 S. Ct. at 2732 n. 3.

2. In *Wolf Point Organization v. Investment Centers of America, Inc.*, 3 Am. Tribal Law 290 (Fort Peck Court of Appeals 2001), the court addressed claims by non-Indians that a treaty, as well as the tribe's own written rules, precluded tribal jurisdiction over nonmembers:

> April 15, 1874 Act. After giving the Court an overview of the Congressional history of the Assiniboine and Sioux Tribes, [defendants argue that] if Indian tribes did not expressly provide for civil jurisdiction over non-Indians in their treaties with the United States government during the "treaty making period" of 1787 through 1871, and if Congress did not expressly provide for such jurisdiction in the subsequent Congressional Acts which ratified those treaties, then Tribal Courts today, operating in the 21st century, have no such jurisdiction. We must respectively disagree. . . .
>
> . . . One needs only to review those federal decisions within the one hundred thirty ensuing years to conclusively show that tribal courts do have jurisdiction over non-Indians for reservation based claims. The U.S. Supreme Court, in one such decision, summarily stayed a diversity action in federal district court to allow a tribal court to determine its own jurisdiction over parallel litigation[.] . . . *Iowa Mutual Ins. Co. v. LaPlante*, 480 U.S. 9 (1987).
>
> Fort Peck Tribes' Constitution and By-Laws. . . . Article VII §5 [of the Fort Peck Tribes Constitution] states:
>
>> Section 5. To provide, subject to the review of the Secretary of the Interior, or his authorized representatives, for the maintenance of law and order and the administration of justice by establishing tribal courts and police force, and defining the powers and duties of same, and to promulgate

---

*Plains Commerce Bank purchased the Bank of Hoven during the pendency of the tribal and federal court litigation.

criminal and civil codes or ordinances governing the conduct of the members of the Tribes and non-member Indians residing within the jurisdiction of the Tribes.

Defendants [argue that] §5 limits the Tribal Executive Board's authority to "promulgate criminal and civil codes or ordinances governing the conduct of *members* and *nonmember Indians residing with the jurisdiction of the Tribes* (*only*)."

In order to arrive at that limiting conclusion, ICA and Shae necessarily imply that the word "only" appears at the conclusion of the sentence. However, the word "only" does not appear and we find no such limitation was intended.

Wolf Point Organization, 3 Am. Tribal Law at 295-98 (emphasis in original).

3. The same court also confronted arguments from a non-Indian-owned professional organization that the state regulatory structure in the field preempted tribal jurisdiction over it. The court disagreed, writing:

First, [defendant] assumes that because it is a Montana professional corporation, only the State of Montana can "regulate" their professional activities. This presumption obviously fails when [defendant] seeks to do business in another state or nation. Surely [defendant] would not argue that the State of North Dakota would have no authority to regulate their accounting activities within the boundaries of that state. Why then would [defendant] argue that the Assiniboine and Sioux Nation could not regulate their accounting activities? When the [defendant] lawyers sought pleadings before the Tribal Courts, were they not required to appear before the Fort Peck bar and obtain either membership or admittance pro hoc vice? If the Tribes have the authority to regulate Montana lawyers that appear before their courts, if would necessarily follow that they would have the authority to regulate other professions as well. While we know of no licensure requirement imposed by Fort Peck on accounting firms operating within the exterior boundaries of the Fort Peck Reservation, it is enough that such authority is resident in the Tribes to impose such a requirement if they so choose.

Secondly, we see nothing in the [plaintiff's] complaint that would suggest that the Tribal Court would be interfering in any way with [defendant's] professional status in the State of Montana. . . . [Plaintiff] does not seek to terminate the license of [defendant] or to impede or impair [defendant's] ability to practice its stated profession in any way. Therefore, we hold that our Tribal Court does have jurisdiction to adjudicate reservation based malpractice claims against non-Indian professional corporations doing business within the exterior boundaries of the Fort Peck Indian Reservation

Wolf Point Organization, 3 Am. Tribal Law at 303-04.

12
PROCEDURE AND JURISDICTION

This chapter surveys the way that American Indian tribal courts deploy their procedural tools to guarantee due process to all litigants, as well as to define the contours of tribal court jurisdiction.

Most tribal courts liberally construe civil procedure rules toward providing sufficient access to the courts. Many tribal court dockets include cases prosecuted by non-lawyer advocates or persons representing themselves, and many of the cases involve the tribal government, represented by counsel, as an opposing party. As such, tribal courts routinely provide great leniency favoring the non-lawyer parties. While many tribal courts have adopted civil procedure rules borrowed from state or federal courts, these rules tend to apply best to complex litigation. Most tribal court civil disputes are equivalent to small claims cases, and these court rules are overly complicated. Some tribal courts have adopted simplified rules. The Pokagon Band of Potawatomi Indians tribal court's evidence rules are, for example, a mere four pages long. *See* POKAGON BAND COURT RULES ch. 3 (2009), available at http://www.pokagon.com/court/CHP3_RulesofEvidenceAdopted20090601.pdf.

The jurisdiction of tribal courts, as has been noted in prior chapters, is affected by how federal courts have applied federal Indian law, but tribal courts primarily must construe their own jurisdiction in accordance with tribal law first. As such, tribal courts often look first to tribal constitutions, jurisdictional codes adopted by tribal legislatures, and other important organic documents such as treaties.

This is not to say that federal Indian law is inapplicable, especially for tribes that have incorporated federal common law into their constitutions and statutes (often as a result of federal intervention in tribal law making). In general, tribal courts have exclusive jurisdiction over civil suits arising in Indian country brought against on-reservation Indians. *See Williams v. Lee*, 358 U.S. 217 (1959). However, the United States Supreme Court has limited tribal court civil jurisdiction over nonmember defendants in cases such as *Montana v. United States*, 450 U.S. 544 (1981), and *Strate v. A-1 Contractors*, 520 U.S. 438 (1997), but a nonmember defendant usually must first exhaust tribal court remedies, including appeals, before the defendant can petition a federal court for a declaratory judgment on the jurisdiction of the tribal court. *See National Farmers Union Insurance Cos. v. Crow Tribe of Indians*, 471 U.S. 845 (1985); *Iowa Mutual Insurance Co. v. LaPlante*, 480 U.S. 9 (1987).

The chapter also will touch upon the tribal constitutional law of tribal court authority and powers, such as questions of justiciability, and tribal court contempt power, as well as issues of ethics and professional responsibility.

As with the contracts and torts chapters, this chapter will not attempt to comprehensively cover the common law civil procedure guidelines, but will instead survey key cases.

A. JURISDICTION

1. TERRITORIAL AND PERSONAL JURISDICTION

PacifiCorp v. Mobil Oil Corp.

Navajo Nation Supreme Court, No. SC-CV-27-01, 4 Am. Tribal Law 694,
8 Navajo Rep. 378 (November 23, 2004)

Before Yazzie, Chief Justice and Ferguson, Associate Justice.
Ferguson, Associate Justice. . . .

I

Plaintiff-Appellee/Cross-Appellant PacifiCorp is an Oregon corporation with its principal place of business in Oregon. . . . PacifiCorp has distribution and transmission lines, substations, and a switching station located within the Navajo Nation.

PacifiCorp began delivering electricity to customers located within the Navajo Nation in 1959. PacifiCorp does not generate electricity within the Navajo Nation. It delivers electric power to . . . nonmember customers like Defendants-Appellants/Cross-Appellees (collectively "Mobil").

Mobil is licensed by the Navajo Nation to extract oil and gas from the Nation's mineral lands for sale and export. . . .

Between 1989 and 1998 the parties entered into four contracts for the provision of electricity to Mobil's facilities. . . .

The Navajo Nation first enacted the Business Activity Tax (BAT) in 1978. 24 N.N.C. §§401-445. The Navajo Tax Commission notified PacifiCorp in 1987 that its services were subject to the BAT. PacifiCorp paid the BAT assessments, which had accrued through September 30, 1987, and since that time Pacifi-Corp has fully paid the BAT assessments. PacifiCorp does not challenge the Navajo Nation's authority to impose the BAT.

The contracts at issue incorporate Utah Electric Service Regulations that allegedly authorize PacifiCorp to pass along the cost of the BAT on a pro rata basis to each customer in its service area. Mobil challenged PacifiCorp's inclusion of the pro rata amount of the BAT as a separately itemized charge in Mobil's electric service bill, and has refused to reimburse PacifiCorp for the

BAT. PacifiCorp continued to provide electrical service to Mobil pursuant to the contracts. The meters at which electric service is provided and therefore the locus of the BAT owed by PacifiCorp are within the Navajo Nation at Mobil's facilities.

PacifiCorp sued Mobil in the United States District Court for the District of Utah for $1.8 million in accrued BAT charges. . . . The federal court declined to dismiss, but in the interests of comity the court stayed its proceedings pending a determination from the Navajo Nation of its own jurisdiction.

PacifiCorp then filed a complaint in Shiprock District Court asking for a declaratory ruling that the courts of the Navajo Nation are without subject matter jurisdiction over PacifiCorp's contract claim. . . .

The court held that it has concurrent jurisdiction over the suit because both PacifiCorp and Mobil have extensive contacts with the Navajo Nation and because the Navajo Nation is "no stranger to the contracts that are in dispute." . . .

II

The issu[e] in this case [is] whether the courts of the Navajo Nation have jurisdiction when a non-Navajo public utility seeks to collect a pro rata charge for the Navajo Business Activity Tax from another non-Navajo corporation receiving electric service on trust land within the Nation. . . .

III

A

First we address whether the Navajo Nation courts have subject matter jurisdiction over this dispute. . . . PacifiCorp argues that the district court misapplied federal law on subject matter jurisdiction of tribal courts. We disagree.

In their briefs, the parties argue whether PacifiCorp's activities within the Navajo Nation allow jurisdiction under the rule in *Montana v. United States*, 450 U.S. 544, 101 S. Ct. 1245, 67 L. Ed. 2d 493 (1981). . . .

In a recent case before this Court we held that *Montana* does not apply to non-Indian activity on tribal land. *Nelson v. Pfizer*, No. SC-CV-01-02, 4 Am. Tribal Law 680, 2003 WL 25794136 (2003). In that case we . . . ruled that subject matter jurisdiction is proper whenever the cause of action arises on tribal land within the Navajo Nation. . . .

Pfizer controls this case if the cause of action arises on tribal land within the Navajo Nation. We then must decide whether that requirement is met in this case.

B

PacifiCorp argues that the parties' contracts are outside the jurisdiction of the district court. In this case, parts of the contracts are performed on trust land within the Nation and parts performed off the Navajo Nation. Mobil's performance, payment of the BAT charge and payment for electrical service, occurs off the Navajo Nation. PacifiCorp's performance, provision of the electricity, occurs at Mobil's facilities on trust land within the Navajo Nation. We hold that in situations where a contract has a sufficient nexus to activity on tribal land within the Navajo Nation, the cause of action arises there for purposes of the Navajo Nation's jurisdiction. Our courts will have subject matter jurisdiction, whether or not the contract itself was signed within the Navajo Nation.[2]

The district court correctly concluded it has jurisdiction over this dispute, because there is a sufficient nexus. A significant portion of the performance of the contracts, PacifiCorp's provision of electricity, happened on tribal land within the Navajo Nation. Further, the issue in the case is the BAT, which is charged for services provided at Mobil's facilities on trust land within the Navajo Nation. Under these facts, we conclude there is a sufficient nexus to activity on tribal land to allow jurisdiction. We therefore uphold the district court, though on different grounds. . . .

NOTES

1. The Navajo Nation Supreme Court had previously held that the Navajo judiciary would not apply the *Montana* Test to jurisdiction cases involving nonmembers. *See Nelson v. Pfizer*, 8 Nav. R. 369, 376, 4 Am. Tribal Law 680 (2003). That court reasoned:

   > The implications of *Montana* for the Navajo Nation's power over its territory are clear. A rule requiring the application of *Montana* to all land restricts judicial authority over non-Indian conduct. We take judicial notice of the fact that trust land and tribally-owned fee land comprise virtually all land within the Navajo Nation. There are many non-Indian actors who impact the Navajo Nation in various and significant ways that may escape the authority of the Navajo Nation if our courts are required to apply the *Montana* exceptions to every civil case involving non-Indians. Judicial resources would be stretched if every case brought against a non-Indian required a detailed analysis of the various consensual relationships or direct effects on the Navajo Nation merely to establish jurisdiction. Further, application of *Montana* to every civil case with a non-Indian defendant undermines the federal policy encouraging the development of tribal courts. *See Iowa Mutual Ins. Co. v. La Plante*, 480 U.S. 9, 15 . . . ("Tribal courts play a vital role in tribal self-government . . . and the federal government has consistently encouraged their development.") (internal citations omitted). Finally, our responsibility to protect the sovereignty of the Navajo Nation counsels that we not surrender authority unnecessarily.

   Id. The court added that Navajo lower courts could continue to apply the *Montana* analysis, but it was not required: "A conclusion that the exceptions are not met will not end the analysis, but fulfillment of either one will satisfy the lower threshold we hold applies today." *Id.* at 377.

2. In *Hexum v. Dakota Development, Inc.*, No. C-09-433-098 (Sisseton-Wahpeton Sioux Tribal Court, Aug. 13, 2009) (unreported), the plaintiff in a personal injury action against a tribal gaming operation on federal trust land sought to dismiss her tribal court claims in order to proceed in state court on the ground that the United States Supreme Court had held the Lake Traverse Reservation to be disestablished in *DeCoteau v. District Court*,

---

2. It is immaterial that both parties in this case are non-Indian corporations. Our courts are open to all litigants, *Sells v. Epsil*, 6 Nav. R. 195, 199 (1990). . . .

420 U.S. 425 (1975). The tribal court, per Judge B.J. Jones, disagreed, holding that the trust lands upon which the gaming property rested remained "Indian Country" under 18 U.S.C. §1151:

> The lands upon which the Dakota Magic Casino is situated appear to have been restored to trust status pursuant to 25 USC §§461, a special statute designed to permit the Department of Interior to restore lands within the original boundaries of the Lake Traverse reservation to trust status. Those lands, once restored, become Indian country subject to federal and tribal criminal jurisdiction and exclusive tribal court civil jurisdiction when the Tribe or its members are sued as Defendants. *See Solem v. Bartlett*, 465 U.S. 463, at 467 and n.8 (1984). It is this ruling in *Solem* that led former United States Attorney John Schneider to offer an official opinion on May 23, 1997 that the Dakota Magic Casino is situated in "Indian Country."
>
> Were the Court to accept the argument being proffered by the Plaintiff that only trust lands that were allotted and that remain in the majority ownership of individual Oyate members, rather than the Oyate itself, are Indian country it would lead to some rather startling results. The tribal administration building, as well as the tribal jail, the Tiospa Zina Tribal School, the Dakota Western bag plant and all other tribal governmental buildings would not be Indian country under the Plaintiff's analysis because those buildings sit on lands that are held by the United States on behalf of the Tribe and not for individual Indians. Indeed, it would be unlikely that this Court is even lawfully sitting because it presides over a Court situated in the Tribal jail complex that sits on lands held by the United States in trust for the Tribe and not for individual Indians. Therefore, does this Court lack the jurisdiction to even rule on this motion because it is purporting to preside in a state jurisdiction and not within Indian country? This Court thinks not.

Hexum, at 3-5.

3. In *In re J.H.A.*, 7 NICS App. 104 (Port Gamble S'Klallam Tribal Court of Appeals 2006), the court held that the trial court erred in taking jurisdiction over a nonmember Indian whose only appearance was in the form of a letter submitted in a parallel matter seeking a continuance:

> [Dawn] Deam is not a member of the Port Gamble S'Klallam Tribe and she does not reside on the Port Gamble S'Klallam Reservation. Under Chapter 21 of the Port Gamble S'Klallam Tribal Code, the court acquires personal jurisdiction over a nonmember who is not a resident of the Port Gamble S'Klallam Reservation only if the person: (1) is served with a summons on the Reservation; (2) resided on the Reservation with a child who is the subject of the proceeding; (3) engaged in sexual intercourse on the Reservation when the child may have been conceived; or (4) consents to the jurisdiction of the court by entering a general appearance, filing a responsive document, or participating in the proceeding unless participation is for the purpose of contesting jurisdiction. PGSTC 21.01.04(b-e). The only provision of the code that arguably applies is whether Deam consented to jurisdiction under PGSTC 21.01.04(c) by filing a general appearance or responsive document.
>
> At the request of the parties, . . . the trial court dismissed the original petition, albeit without prejudice. . . . [The plaintiff], however, never refiled the petition. . . .

Even if the initial suit had not been dismissed, Deam's October 13, 2004 letter does not constitute consent to jurisdiction under the Code. In her letter, Deam requested the court continue its scheduled hearing, in part, so she could retain counsel. . . .

. . . We only hold that a pro se letter requesting a continuance of a hearing for the purpose of retaining counsel, in the absence of any response to the allegations contained in a petition or motion on the merits of the case, is not a "responsive document" under PGSTC 21.01.04(c). The trial court erred in concluding the October 13, 2004 letter was a "responsive document" under PGSTC 21.01.04(c) for the purpose of consent to personal jurisdiction.

In re J.H.A., 7 NICS App. at 107-08.

4. In *Ho-Chunk Nation v. Olsen*, 2 Am. Tribal Law 299 (Ho-Chunk Nation Trial Court 2000), the court held that it possessed jurisdiction over a nonmember defendant whose underlying commercial transaction occurred on tribal trust lands:

The tribal standards that define this Court's jurisdiction are articulated in the CONSTITUTION OF THE HO-CHUNK NATION [hereinafter HCN CONSTITUTION] and the HO-CHUNK NATION JUDICIARY ACT OF 1995 [hereinafter JUDICIARY ACT]. Article I, Sec. 2 of the HCN CONSTITUTION states in relevant part that "[t]he jurisdiction of the Ho-Chunk Nation shall extend to all [of its] territory . . . and to any and all persons or activities therein." HCN CONST., Art. I, Sec. 2. The HCN CONSTITUTION further addresses "Jurisdiction of the Judiciary" in Art. VII, Sec 5. which states that:

(a) The Trial Court shall have original jurisdiction over all cases and controversies, both criminal and civil, in law or in equity, arising under the Constitution, laws, customs, and traditions of the Ho-Chunk Nation. . . . Any such case or controversy arising within the jurisdiction of the Ho-Chunk Nation shall be filed in the Trial Court before it is filed in any other court.

HCN CONST., art. VII, Sec. 5. These grants of jurisdiction are further elaborated upon in Sec. 2 of the Ho Chunk Nation Judiciary Act of 1995, which states that:

The Ho-Chunk Nation Judiciary shall exercise jurisdiction over all matters within the power and authority of the Ho-Chunk Nation including controversies arising out of the Constitution of the Ho-Chunk Nation; laws, statutes, ordinances, resolutions and codes enacted by the Legislature; and such other matters arising under enactments of the Legislature or the customs and traditions of the Ho-Chunk Nation. This jurisdiction extends over the Nation and its territory, persons who enter its territory, its members, and persons who interact with the Nation or its members wherever found.

JUDICIARY ACT, Sec. 2. This paragraph implicitly addresses both subject matter and personal jurisdiction. The first sentence addresses subject matter jurisdiction in that it speaks to the sources of law from which the Court's power of review derives. The second sentence addresses personal jurisdiction through its indication that the assertion of subject matter jurisdiction is premised on the relationship and/or interaction of the litigants, the Ho-Chunk Nation, or its members. Both prongs of this standard must be satisfied for this Court to properly exercise jurisdiction.

In examining questions of personal jurisdiction, this Court is guided by the persuasive reasoning of *International Shoe Co. v. Washington*, 326 U.S. 310 . . . (1945) and its progeny. *International Shoe* articulated the principle that a court may assert personal jurisdiction over a defendant not located within the territory of the forum so long as the defendant has "certain minimum contacts with [the forum] such that the maintenance of the suit does not offend 'traditional notions of fair play and substantial justice.' " The progeny of International Shoe focused on defining "fair play and substantial justice." One line of cases elucidating this phrase premised the finding of personal jurisdiction on whether a defendant had purposely availed themselves of the chance to do business in the forum state. *See McGee v. International Life Insurance Co.*, 355 U.S. 220, 78 S. Ct. 199, 2 L. Ed. 2d 223 (1957).

The reasoning contained in the *McGee* line of cases is particularly instructive with regards to the case at bar, where the conduct in question occurred within, or transpired from, tribal territory. Negotiations for the "Purchase Agreement" took place on tribal trust land, the down payment was received on tribal trust land, and the products were to be delivered to a business located on either tribal trust land or land owned by the tribe in fee. The defendant purposefully engaged in contact with the Ho-Chunk Nation for the purpose of doing business, and it is reasonable and fair for him to be haled into the Ho-Chunk Nation's courts to answer the plaintiff's claims.

Olsen, 2 Am. Tribal Law 306-07.

2. APPELLATE JURISDICTION

Kalantari v. Spirit Mountain Gaming, Inc.

Confederated Tribes of the Grand Ronde Community of
Oregon Court of Appeals, No. A-04-03-003,
6 Am. Tribal Law 94, 2005.NAGR.0000002 (May 16, 2005)

The opinion of the court was delivered by: Johnson, Associate Justice.
Before: Miller, Chief Justice; and Johnson and Thompson, Associate Justices
Mark Johnson, Associate Justice
Defendant appeals from an interlocutory order determining that the limitation on non-economic damages contained in Tribal Code Section 255.6(h) is inapplicable to this personal injury case. We determine that the order in question is not a "final order" subject to appellate review under Tribal Code Section 310(h)(2) and dismiss the appeal for lack of subject-matter jurisdiction.

Plaintiff alleges that she was injured at the Spirit Mountain Casino on February 13, 2002, as a result of defendant's negligence. . . . [S]he claimed, among other relief, non-economic damages of $800,000. Among other defenses, defendant interposed the following provision of the Tribal Tort Claims Ordinance (TTCO): "No award, judgment or order shall be made under this Ordinance for pain and suffering or mental anguish and suffering or like claims in an amount greater than $100,000 for each injury." Tribal Code §255.6(h).

The trial court issued an order on "pre-trial issues" on March 24, 2004. The court found that a provision in the Tribe's gaming compact with the State of

Oregon had waived the damages limitation contained in the TTCO as it might otherwise have applied to injuries sustained by patrons at the Spirit Mountain Casino. This appeal followed. . . .

An order denying a motion for a summary judgment is not a "final order" and is ordinarily not appealable. . . . Recognizing as much, defendant urges that we adopt the "collateral order doctrine" described by the United States Supreme Court in *Cohen v. Beneficial Indus. Loan Corp.*, 337 U.S. 541, 545-47 (1949).

"Under the 'collateral order' doctrine of [*Cohen*], a small class of interlocutory orders are [sic] immediately appealable. . . . As defined by *Cohen*, this class embraces orders that 'conclusively determine the disputed question, resolve an important issue completely separate from the merits of the action, and [are] effectively unreviewable on appeal from a final judgment.'" . . . The United States courts frequently have used the doctrine to review the sort of immunity defense that defendant raises here. *See, e.g.,* . . . *Osage Tribal Council ex rel. Osage Tribe of Indians v. U.S. Dep't of Labor*, 187 F.3d 1174 (10th Cir 1999), *cert. den. sub nom. Osage Tribal Council v. Dep't of Labor*, 530 U.S. 1229 (2000).

Although we share the federal courts' concern that our jurisdictional statute be given a "practical rather than a technical construction," *Cohen*, 337 U.S. at 546, we find the collateral order doctrine inapplicable here. "A major characteristic of the denial or granting of a claim appealable under *Cohen*'s 'collateral order' doctrine is that[,] unless it can be reviewed before the proceedings terminate, it can never be reviewed at all." [*Mitchell v. Forsyth*, 472 U.S. 511, 525 (1985)]. The case before us today fails to satisfy this key element of the collateral order doctrine.

We emphasize that our decision rests on jurisdictional rather than prudential grounds. The collateral order doctrine is a construction given to the term "final order" in the jurisdictional statute, not an exception to it. . . . Although we question the dissent's assumption that the parties' presentation of the case on remand would be assisted by an advisory resolution of the merits of this appeal, it matters not to our decision. Our jurisdictional statute might have given us authority over a wider variety of interlocutory appeals, or even to render advisory opinions, but it does neither.

Both parties agree that defendant has waived its sovereign immunity from suit, at least up to the limits set forth in the TTCO. Where they disagree is in whether defendant has further waived the limits of its liability by the terms of its gaming contract with the state. Whether we affirm or reverse, the parties agree that the case must be remanded for a trial on defendant's liability, if any, for plaintiff's claimed injuries. At that trial, the court might award non-economic damages greater than $100,000, less than $100,000, or not at all. This serves to distinguish the case from ones like *Osage Tribal Council*, where the Osage tribe obtained an interlocutory review of an order rejecting its defense of sovereign immunity from suit. In that case, the Tenth Circuit reviewed the collateral order because the tribe's defense implied "immunity from suit, and not merely a defense to liability." *See* 187 F.3d at 1179. . . .

[T]he purpose of the collateral order doctrine in the sovereign immunity context is to shield the sovereign from having to answer litigation in which it can never be held liable in any event. Once the sovereign concedes, as it has here, that the litigation is proper, it undermines any claim of entitlement to an interlocutory appeal. . . . The error, if any, in the trial court's award of damages to plaintiff can be, and should be, reviewed on appeal from the final judgment.

Appeal dismissed. . . .

MILLER, Chief Justice, dissenting.

I respectfully dissent.

I would hold that this court should adopt the federal collateral order doctrine as an acceptable interpretation of our "final order" rule, Tribal Code §310(h)(2), and that we have jurisdiction to hear interlocutory appeals in the appropriate settings. . . .

I.

. . .

A. Sovereign Immunity Questions Are Effectively Unreviewable upon Appeal from Final Judgments

. . . [S]overeign immunity is the right to be free of litigating an issue that is subject to immunity, that it is not just a right to be free of liability after litigation, and that this right is lost if the government is required to defend first because the issue cannot be "effectively reviewed" after trial. "The entitlement is an immunity from suit rather than a mere defense to liability; and like an absolute immunity, it is effectively lost if a case is erroneously permitted to go to trial." . . .

. . . Once we permit defendant to be forced to litigate this case under the gaming compact and in excess of the waiver of sovereign immunity in the TTOC, we cannot effectively review the issues on a later appeal. At that point, we will be unable to grant defendant any real or effective relief from the violation of its immunity right not to have to litigate these issues. . . .

II.

. . . In a few years, this case will probably return to us, after enormous amounts of work and resources have been expended by plaintiff, defendant, and the trial court. We will then have to decide whether sovereign immunity should have prevented the gaming compact and the $800,000 non-economic damage issue from having been litigated. That will be a lamentable waste of resources and time if I am correct that sovereign immunity tells us these claims should not have been litigated at all. In that case, defendant's right not to be required to face these issues will have been irrevocably violated. . . .

I respectfully dissent.

ROBERT J. MILLER Chief Justice

NOTES

1. Other tribal courts appear to have accepted the collateral order doctrine as applied when a tribal sovereign seeks an interlocutory appeal of a lower court's refusal to dismiss a claim on the basis of sovereign immunity. *E.g.,* *Amerind Risk Management Corp. v. Malaterre*, No. TMAC-06-003, at 1 n. 1 (Turtle Mountain Band of Chippewa Indians Court of Appeals 2007).

2. Some tribal codes are inartfully drafted, or include provisions that may have become archaic or unclear. One such code provision is that a tribal court of appeals will conduct a "new trial" on appeal. In *In re James*, 2 NICS App. 196 (Lummi Tribal Court of Appeals 1992), the one appellate judge noted in concurrence that the tribal court code required the appellate court to conduct a "new trial":

> This case concerns what appears, at first glance, to present a pure legal issue: Should foster parents be granted the status of a party in a dependency proceeding in Tribal Court? However, when this issue is presented to the appellate court for decision, the court is required to follow that provision of the Lummi Tribal Code which requires a "new trial" on appeal. Section 1.8.05 of the Tribal Code's General Rules states as follows:
>
>> Within 45 days from the date of written notice of appeal, the Appellate Court shall convene unless delay is warranted by good cause, to hear the case on appeal at such place as may be designated. *A new trial shall be held and court procedures shall be the same as in other cases before the Reservation Court except that there shall be no right to trial by jury* [emphasis added].
>
> This provision of the Lummi Code impacts this court's ability to expeditiously handle appeals. However, this is the procedure which the Lummi Business Council has elected to adopt concerning appeals, and therefore this court must follow that procedure.
>
> Exactly what constitutes a "new trial" for purposes of an appeal is not defined by the Lummi Tribal Code. Whether a particular appeal demands a full trial or some more limited right to present testimony must be determined on a case-by-case basis. This necessarily leads to ambiguity and uncertainty, both for the panel of appellate judges and for those persons practicing before the Lummi Tribal Court of Appeals. This requirement also leads to an inordinate delay in reaching a decision by the Court of Appeals.
>
> As applied to this case, this provision afforded the appellants a full opportunity to introduce testimony in support of their position. . . . The Lummi Nation may desire to reexamine and further define the procedures to be followed in an appeal from a trial court decision.

James, 2 NICS App. at 210-11 (Hostnik, A.J., concurring).

3. In *TBA Credit Union v. Giem*, 2009 WL 3377997 (Little Traverse Bay Bands of Odawa Indians Tribal Appellate Court 2009), the court held that a trial judge did not have standing to move for reconsideration of an appellate order reversing the judge's decision below:

> Although Appellate Procedures Rule 7.504 does not explicitly state that only parties in interest may file a request for reconsideration, the rule nevertheless clearly limits standing for such a request to the parties to the case for several reasons.
>
> First, the text of the rule limits the right to request reconsideration of an Appellate Court decision by stating that "[a] copy of the request must be served upon **all other parties** and on the Tribal Court." (Emphasis added.) The reference to "all other parties" indicates that Rule 7.504 presumes that the person exercising the right to request reconsideration is also a party. Second, Rule 7.504(B) expressly states that "[a]ny **other party** may file a response" to a request for reconsideration. (Emphasis added.) Again, the

reference to "any other party" evidences an intent to limit the ability to request reconsideration to an actual party to the case.

Our reading of Rule 7.504 is also consistent with the broader context of the Appellate Procedures. Near the beginning of the procedures, Rule 7.303 states that in civil cases, the right to appeal is held by "any **party** adversely affected by a decision of the Tribal Court." (Emphasis added.) Thus, from the very outset, the Appellate Procedures make clear that the right to appeal is possessed only by a party to a case who was adversely affected by a decision of the court. Since the right to request reconsideration is the final step available within the general right to appeal, it necessarily follows that the right to reconsideration is similarly limited to parties adversely affected by earlier proceedings in the case.

In addition, the underlying policy of judicial economy, which the doctrine of standing helps protect, supports our decision today. The right to request reconsideration of an Appellate Court decision must be limited to parties in interest in order to promote the effective and efficient functioning of the court system. Since requests for reconsideration automatically stay all court proceedings, the receipt of numerous requests for reconsideration would introduce delay and frequently prevent the parties from promptly experiencing the enforcement of the Appellate Court's decision in a particular case.

TBA Credit Union, 2009 WL 3377997, at *1-2 (emphasis in original).

B. JUSTICIABILITY

1. STANDING

Village of Mishongnovi (Cultural Preservation Board) v. Humeyestewa

Hopi Tribe Appellate Court, No. 96A000008, 1 Am. Tribal Law 295, 1998.NAHT.0000017 (March 20, 1998)

Before Sekaquaptewa, Chief Justice, and Lomayesva and Abbey, Justices.

Opinion and Order

This case presents the issue of whether federal standing doctrine applies in Hopi Tribal Court in a case involving a dispute over who should rightfully control a bank account held in the name of the Village of Mishongnovi. Appellant and Respondents each allege that they are the rightful governing body of the Village. The ultimate resolution of the case turns on the determination of who is the Village's legitimate governing authority. As such, this case also raises the issue of whether this central factual determination is a political question that may be resolved by the tribal court.

Statement of Facts

Appellants seek control over a bank account held by respondents in the name of the Village of Mishongnovi. Appellant is the Cultural Preservation Board (CPB), which claims to be the operating board of Mishongnovi. . . . Respondents are members of the Board of Directors of the Village of Mishongnovi. The Board of Directors also claims to be the only legitimate governing body of the Village. . . .

[In November 1992,] respondent Bernita Humeyestewa closed out a Bank of America account in the name of the Village of Mishongnovi containing $68,441.63. Humeyestewa then deposited $68,609.39 into a First Interstate Bank account in the name of the Village of Mishongnovi.

Respondents are the only authorized signatories on the bank account. On December 1, 1992, Humeyestewa and respondent Rolanda Morris signed checks from the Village bank account payable to Roland Morris in the amount of $2065.44. Morris alone signed a check for $2600.00 to Cake Chevrolet.

Procedural History

On April 6, 1994, the Appellants filed a complaint as Mishongnovi's governing body against Respondents for conversion of Village funds contained in the Bank of America account. The complaint alleged that Respondents negligently allowed the improper expenditure of funds from the account. The Appellants sought replevin to obtain the funds and all other Village property possessed by the Respondents. The Appellants also sought a declaratory judgment from the court recognizing themselves as the lawful owner of the funds contained in the disputed bank account. . . .

[T]he tribal court on September 3, 1996 . . . dismissed the entire case for lack of standing by the Appellant. The court held that the Appellant did not have standing because it sought to advance a general interest common to members of the Mishongnovi Village, rather than a particularized interest. . . .

Issues on Appeal

. . .

  II. Is federal standing doctrine consistent with Hopi custom and tradition?
  III. What is the appropriate standing test in Hopi Tribal Court?
  IV. Does the Cultural Preservation Board have standing to present its claims in Tribal Court? . . .

Decision of the Court

. . .

II. Federal Standing Doctrine May Not Be Applied in Hopi Tribal Court Because It Is Inconsistent with Hopi Custom and Tradition

A. The Tribal Court Erred by Not Fully Analyzing the Applicability of Federal Standing Doctrine to Determine Its Consistency with Hopi Custom and Tradition

The standing issue presented in this case is one of first impression for this court. The essence of any standing question "is whether the litigant is entitled to have the court decide the merits of the dispute or of particular issues." *Warth v. Seldin*, 422 U.S. 490, 498 . . . [(1975)]. Standing is a concept used to determine if a party is sufficiently affected by a controversy to be the proper party to bring a lawsuit. Standing is a jurisdictional issue; ideally it relates to the power of court to hear and decide cases and does not concern the ultimate merits of the substantive claims involved in an action.

The purpose of standing doctrine is to ensure that: (1) litigants are truly adverse and therefore likely to present the case effectively; (2) the people most directly concerned are able to litigate the questions at issue; and (3) a concrete case informs the court of the consequences of its decisions. Fletcher, *The Structure of Standing*, 98 YALE L.J. 221, 222 (1988).

The requirements of standing in Hopi Tribal Court are not specified by the Hopi Constitution, Hopi Ordinance 21 (establishing and defining the jurisdiction of tribal courts), nor any other ordinance or resolution approved by the Hopi Tribal Council. This case raises the important issue of how standing should be determined in the absence of any guidance from these sources of law. The trial court in *Shungopavi v. Quamahongnewa*, No. 95CV000097, Order and Decision (1997), grappled with this issue and its decision in that case provides the only substantive discussion of standing in any Hopi case. The trial court in the instant case dismissed the case for lack of standing based on the court's reasoning in *Shungopavi v. Quamahongnewa*.

The facts in *Shungopavi v. Quamahongnewa* are worth noting because they bear some resemblance to the situation presented in this case. In *Shungopavi v. Quamahongnewa*, the plaintiff was the Village's Interim Board of Directors. The Interim Board brought an action against certain named individuals, including some who had previously served as members of the Shungopavi Board of Directors. . . . The Interim Board alleged that the defendants conspired among themselves to convert and divert village funds to their own use. . . . The Interim Board sought an order directing the defendants to turn over to the plaintiff all financial books and records related to the funds; an accounting of all expenditures of funds; damages for funds converted to personal use; punitive damages; and the return of all village property held by the defendants. . . .

The trial court considered whether the Interim Board had standing to bring the claim as part of its analysis of whether the court had jurisdiction to hear the matter. Noting the absence of Hopi law and cases on point, the trial court turned to federal and state case law for guidance. . . .

Although the trial court's opinion in *Shungopavi v. Quamahongnewa* is a thoughtful application of federal standing principles to a Hopi village dispute, it inappropriately applies foreign law without analyzing that law to determine whether it is consistent with Hopi custom and tradition.

In *Hopi Indian Credit Assoc. v. Thomas*, AP-001-84, Opinion and Order (1996), this court clarified the analytical steps a tribal court must undertake before it may use foreign law. "[T]he customs, traditions and culture of the Hopi Tribe must take precedence in a court's decision of what law to apply before a court reaches the use of any foreign law, including federal or Arizona state law" (except in instances where the Supremacy Clause of the U.S. Constitution is involved). . . . Specifically, the tribal court may resort to federal and state law in the absence of Hopi jurisprudence in an area of law only when that law is not inconsistent with the spirit or letter of Hopi law, custom, traditions or culture. . . . Hopi Res. H-12-76, §2(b).

Thus, the trial court in the present case should have carefully analyzed whether the operational effect of federal standing doctrine was consistent with Hopi custom and tradition before it applied the doctrine in the case before it. This type of careful analysis would have revealed that narrow federal standing doctrine, developed to restrict litigants' access to federal courts of limited jurisdiction, is inconsistent with Hopi customs of open and consensual dispute resolution and inappropriate given the Hopi tribal court's general jurisdictional authority.

B. The Restrictive Nature of Federal Standing Doctrine Is Antithetical to Hopi Traditions of Open Dispute Resolution

Federal standing doctrine blends constitutional requirements and so-called "prudential" considerations. . . . A plaintiff has standing in federal court only if she satisfies the "case or controversy" requirement of Article III of the Constitution. To satisfy the demands of Article III, a plaintiff must meet three "irreducible minimum requirements" of standing. . . .

First, the plaintiff must have suffered an "injury in fact"—an invasion of a legally protected interest which is "concrete and particularized" and "actual or imminent." . . . The United States Supreme Court defines "particularized" to mean that the alleged injury must affect the plaintiff in a personal and individual way. . . . The Court has used this narrow definition to repeatedly reject standing claims premised on an alleged injury derived from a plaintiff's taxpayer or citizen status. . . . It is this prong of the standing test that the tribal court cited in dismissing the CPB's claim for lack of standing. The second constitutional standing requirement is that a casual connection must exist between the injury and the conduct of which the plaintiff complains. In other words, the injury must be fairly traceable to the challenged action. . . . The third requirement is that is must be likely that the injury can be redressed by a favorable court decision. . . .

Much of the complexity and narrowness of federal standing doctrine is designed to ensure that the federal courts are confined to the limited, enumerated jurisdiction granted to them by Article III of the U.S. Constitution. The prudential considerations in particular reflect the Supreme Court's preoccupation with restricting access to federal courts in order to screen out litigation aimed at articulating and enforcing broad public values, such as the separation of church and state[.] . . .

Given the institutional and philosophical foundations of federal standing doctrine, it is not surprising that transplanting its elements into the body of Hopi common law poses substantial risk of rejection.

The exclusionary and highly formalistic operation of federal standing doctrine is a poor fit in the Hopi tribal court system, which exists in a radically different cultural and institutional context.

First, the Hopi tribal court system operates squarely within a custom and tradition of open and consensual dispute resolution. Hopi traditions of discussion and consensus decision-making emphasize maximizing opportunities to air grievances and encouraging participation by clan and village members. Imposing a restrictive standing regime on Hopi tribal courts would deny tribal members access to an important neutral arena for adjudication of disputes.

In addition, unlike the federal judiciary, Hopi tribal courts are courts of general jurisdiction. Ordinance 21, section 1.7.1(a), expresses the Tribal Council's intent to authorize the Hopi Tribal Court to exercise "the broadest jurisdiction" consistent with the constitution and laws of the Hopi Tribe and the United States.

Therefore, it is inappropriate to apply federal standing doctrine to proceedings in Hopi Tribal Court.

Other tribal courts have analyzed the applicability of federal standing doctrine in light of their respective tribal customs and traditions in much the same manner. The Supreme Court of the Winnebago Tribe of Nebraska adopted a modified standing doctrine in *Rave v. Reynolds*, 23 Indian L. Rep. 6150 (Winn. Sup. Ct. 1996), in deference to traditional Indian dispute resolution customs. Similarly, in *Bordeaux v. Wilkinson*, 21 Indian L. Rep. 6131 (Ft. Bert. Tr. Ct. 1993), the Tribal Court of the Three Affiliated Tribes of the Fort Berthold Reservation adopted a relaxed injury in fact requirement consistent with tribal concepts of communal property. In *Bordeaux v. Wilkinson*, the court held that the plaintiff had standing to challenge the authority of tribal council officers to award themselves bonus or merit pay because tribal property was at issue and the Three Affiliated Tribes embraced the concept of communal ownership of property. Therefore, the plaintiff was not required to show that the defendants' actions deprived her of money that would otherwise have gone to her in order to assert standing.

III. The Proper Test of Standing in Hopi Tribal Court Is Whether The Plaintiff Asserts Some Actual or Threatened Injury That Is Logically Related to the Legal Claims It Seeks to Present to the Tribal Court

This court must now articulate a tribal common law rule that will be consistent with Hopi customs of open dispute resolution and will serve certain important functions of standing doctrine. A Hopi common law standing rule should ensure that litigants in Hopi Tribal Court are truly adverse, that those parties most directly concerned are able to litigate the questions at issue, and that issues are raised in concrete cases that inform judges of the consequences of their decisions. This court has looked to the proceedings of other tribal courts for assistance in formulating an appropriate standing doctrine. The decision of the Supreme Court of the Winnebago Tribe of Nebraska in *Rave v. Reynolds*, 23 Indian L. Rep. 6150 (Winn. Sup. Ct. 1996), is particularly helpful on this point. The Winnebago Supreme Court articulated a common law rule of standing after rejecting the use of rigid federal standing doctrine as inconsistent with the laws and public policy of the Winnebago Tribe of Nebraska. The Winnebago Supreme Court announced that as a matter of tribal law, standing questions must be resolved by inquiring whether the party at issue is asserting some actual or threatened injury that is logically related to the legal claims it seeks to present to the court. *Rave v. Reynolds*, 23 Indian L. Rep. at 6158.

The Winnebago Supreme Court specifically declined to include an additional rule precluding its tribal courts from entertaining generalized grievances or claims of injury, such as those sustained by all citizens, taxpayers or voters. *Id*. The Winnebago Supreme Court rejected this rule "in light of the traditions of openness to the healing of disputes which have long characterized traditional Indian dispute resolution." *Id*. The court also expressly rejected the causal relationship and redressability prongs of federal standing doctrine. It noted that these tests "confuse the merits of the case with the preliminary question of standing and preclude an open airing of the dispute on the merits." *Id*. The court held that these prongs conflicted with the "participatory traditions" of Indian dispute resolution. *Id*. This court finds the Winnebago Supreme Court's formulation of a standing test useful and consistent with Hopi customs and traditions. Standing doctrine should be simple and flexible and should not pose an impenetrable barrier for tribal members to challenge the actions of their village and tribal officials. This court therefore announces the rule that in order to have standing in Hopi Tribal Court, a party need only assert some actual or threatened injury that is logically related to the legal claims it seeks to present to the court.

IV. The Cultural Preservation Board Meets the Standing Test Announced Today

In this case, the CPB alleges on behalf of the Village that respondents are holding Village funds in a bank account without proper authority; that the respondents' status as the only signatories for the bank account is preventing the Village from accessing these funds; and that some or all of respondents converted specific funds in a specific amount in an unlawful manner.

The injuries alleged by the CPB are logically related to the replevin, conversion and negligence claims it seeks to present to the court. The central injury alleged by the CPB is that it cannot gain access to the bank account in which Village funds are deposited because respondents are the only signatories on the account. This injury is related to the replevin claim in that replevin is an action whereby the owner or person entitled to repossession of goods may recover those goods from one who has wrongfully taken or detained the goods. BLACK'S LAW DICTIONARY, 900-901 (6th ed. 1991). The injury is also logically related to the conversion claim. Conversion is an unauthorized assumption and exercise of the right of ownership over goods belonging to another, to the alteration of their condition or the exclusion of the owner's rights. BLACK'S LAW DICTIONARY, at 231. Finally, the injury is related to the negligence claim because respondents control over the bank account could make them liable for negligently allowing the improper expenditure of funds from the account.

Because the injury it alleges logically relates to the claims it seeks to have adjudicated, the CPB has standing to bring its claim to tribal court. . . .

VI. The CPB Is Entitled to Have the Trial Court Decide Its Claims on the Merits

On remand the trial court is faced with the daunting task of sorting through each party's claim to be the only legitimate governing body of the Village of Mishongnovi. No single factor is likely to be determinative in this case. The trial court should base its decision on the totality of the facts, taking into account, for example, whether the Village's traditional leadership is intact; whether the traditional leadership has been displaced; and who is in the best position to manage the Village's funds.

NOTES

1. In *Anglen v. McKinley*, 6 Am. Tribal Law 17 (Cherokee Nation Judicial Appeals Tribunal 2005), the court held that tribal council members did not have standing to challenge the marriage of two women:

> The Cherokee standing doctrine has been well developed through a number of cases over the years. One of the previous cases dealt with the ability of a tribal council member to bring a lawsuit in this Court. In *Philips v. Eagle*, JAT-98-09, this Court allowed an individual council member to bring a lawsuit, in his official capacity, to enforce the rights of the Council as against the Deputy Chief. In *Philips*, it was alleged that the Deputy Chief was suspending council meetings and otherwise interfering with the business of the Tribal Council. In *Philips*, it was appropriate for the council member to seek redress in this Court because the individual Council Member had demonstrated the requisite harm.
>
> In some lawsuits, we have allowed private citizens to bring lawsuits to enforce certain rights. In *Mayes v. Blackfox*, JAT-02-18, this Court held that a citizen has standing to challenge whether a council seat was properly filled. Likewise, in *Cornsilk v. Cherokee Nation Tribal Council*, JAT-96-15, we held that a private citizen has standing to challenge the manner in which a vacant council seat was filled. Each of these cases speak to the right of Cherokee citizens to have the proper representative government. Each of these litigants demonstrated an individualized harm. Most recently, this Court held that private citizens who voted in the previous election had standing to bring a lawsuit pertaining to whether the 1999 Constitution was in effect. *In re Constitution*, JAT-05-04. . . .
>
> In other lawsuits, this Court has dismissed cases brought by private citizens because they failed to demonstrate individualized harm required for standing. In *Cornsilk v. Frailey*, JAT-05-03, a private citizen, who is Cherokee by blood, challenged a legislative act which effectively authorized the Cherokee Nation to continue in a pending federal lawsuit. The private citizen was not a party to the federal lawsuit, nor did he fall within the class of people who would be affected by the federal lawsuit. In *Mayes v. Thompson*, JAT-95-15, this Court similarly dismissed a federal lawsuit brought by a private citizen to challenge legislative acts that did not result in actual harm to the petitioner.
>
> Previously this year, this Court issued a decision in *In re McKinley & Reynolds*, JAT-04-15, dismissing a cause of action brought by Todd Hembree on his own behalf as a private citizen of the Cherokee Nation. In that case, we held that Hembree lacked standing to challenge because he could not demonstrate an actual injury. Hembree argued that his reputation would be injured if Respondents were allowed to marry. The Petitioners in this case raise a similar argument for actual injury, that they are protecting the Cherokee Nation from damage to reputation and they are seeking to stop actions these Petitioners view as inconsistent with Cherokee culture.
>
> Petitioners, as members of the legislative branch, must demonstrate that they have standing before they can proceed in litigation. Members of the Tribal Council, like private Cherokee citizens, must demonstrate a specific particularized harm. In the present case, the Council members fail to demonstrate the requisite harm.

Id. at 17-18.

2. *Political Question Doctrine.* In *Village of Mishongnovi v. Humeyestewa*, 1 Am. Tribal Law 295 (Hopi Tribe Appellate Court 1998), the court wrote:

> Respondents argue in their answering brief that the tribal court is precluded from determining who is the legitimate governing body of Mishongnovi because the dispute involves a "political question" that the Hopi Constitution has reserved for resolution by the village of Mishongnovi itself. Respondents urge the court to apply federal political question doctrine as a check on the tribal court's jurisdiction.
>
> Like federal standing doctrine, political question doctrine is aimed at preserving the separation of powers that is one of the defining features of the United States Constitution. Federal courts regard "political question" as controversies that revolve around policy choices and value determinations that are constitutionally committed to Congress or the Executive branch, and are not subject to judicial review. . . .
>
> The conceptual foundation for political question doctrine is the importance of preserving the separation of powers. This principle is only imperfectly applied to the Hopi system of government. Unlike the U.S. Constitution, the Hopi constitution does not establish a tripartite system of government and depends on the separation of executive, legislative and judicial functions to provide checks and balances. The Hopi Constitution vests legislative and executive authority in one branch of government, the Tribal Council. The Hopi Constitution also empowers the Tribal Council to establish courts "for the settlement of claims and disputes, and for the trial and punishment of Indians within the jurisdiction charged with offense" against the Tribal Council's ordinances. Hopi Constitution, Article VI, Section 1(g). Through Hopi Ordinance 21, the Tribal Council has invested the Tribal Court system with the "broadest exercise of jurisdiction" consistent with the constitution and laws of the Hopi Tribe and the United States. Hopi Ordinance 21, Chapter 1.7.1.
>
> Although the concern for separation of powers may not have the same resonance in the Hopi Tribal Court system as in the federal judiciary, political question doctrine may nonetheless be useful in determining whether the Tribal Court should refrain from deciding certain disputes. However, the [federal law] factors . . . must be modified to reflect the distinct institutional framework of Hopi government. Federal political question doctrine very specifically evolved out of a constitutional scheme that granted the federal judiciary only limited jurisdiction. In contrast, Hopi courts are courts of general jurisdiction and have been empowered by the Tribal Council to exercise broad authority to resolve disputes. Section 1.2.8(a) of Hopi Ordinance 21 gives the Hopi Tribal and Appellate Courts broad jurisdiction to answer certified questions of tribal law. This grant of authority implies that the court has broad jurisdiction to resolve issues that may arise from the Hopi system of government. Within this distinct institutional context, political question doctrine may restrain the Tribal Court's authority to resolve disputes only when the "textually demonstrable constitutional commitment" of the issue to another branch in the Hopi Constitution.
>
> In essence, respondents argue that Article III, Section 3 of the Hopi Constitution[2] reserves "to the villagers themselves" the power to decide which

---

2. "Each village shall decide for itself how it shall be organized." Hopi Constitution, Article III, Section 3.

rival faction is the rightful village authority. . . . [W]e do not find that Article III, Section 3 is a "textually demonstrable constitutional commitment" of this issue to a "coordinate branch of government." It is not at all clear from this or any other provision of the Hopi Constitution that the village or the Tribal Council alone may hear a challenge to the legality of the actions of individuals claiming to be a village's governing body. Because the Hopi Constitution does not explicitly give another entity of the Hopi government exclusive jurisdiction over this type of dispute, we hold that the political question doctrine does not preclude the Tribal Court from resolving the issues raised in this case.

Village of Mishongnovi, 1 Am. Tribal Law at 303-05.

3. *Mootness.* The Turtle Mountain Band of Chippewa Indians Court of Appeals allowed a constitutional case involving the authority of a political body to suspend a tribal court judge to proceed despite the fact that the tribal judge's term expired and she no longer sat on the bench, adopting the federal court doctrine that moot cases that are capable of repetition yet evading review can be justiciable. *See Turtle Mountain Judicial Board v. Turtle Mountain Band of Chippewa Indians*, No. 04-004 (Turtle Mountain Band of Chippewa Indians Court of Appeals 2005).[*] The court wrote:

> Given that Judge Cain's employment has ended, this Court raises on its own motion whether this action is moot. . . . An action is moot where "a controversy no longer exists. . . ." BLACK'S LAW DICTIONARY 1029 (8th ed. 2004). No actual controversy exists if events have occurred that make it impossible for this Court to issue relief, or when the lapse of time has made the issue moot. *See Komalestewa v. Hopi Tribe*, No. AP-004-90, 1996.NAHT.0000008 (Hopi Ct. App., March 29, 1996); *see also Howard Dana and Associates v. Navajo Housing Authority*, No. A-CV-04-81, 1982.NANN.0000008, at ¶11 (Navajo Ct. App., April 22, 1982) (dismissing appeal as moot where lower court issued order giving plaintiff adequate remedy at law). It appears that the relief the Band requests . . . would not actually result in the restoration of Judge Cain to the bench because the Band did not renew her contract in February of this year. Despite this seeming mootness, our inquiry does not end there.
>
> There is a critical exception to the mootness doctrine. We have adopted a rule that a case otherwise moot, but is "capable of repetition yet evading review," remains a live controversy. *See Tribal Council Majority Membership v. Bennett*, . . . at 4 (Turtle Mountain Band Ct. App., July 1996); *see also Benally v. John*, No. A-CV-27-81, 1983.NANN.0000042, at ¶17 (Navajo Ct. App., May 5, 1983) (same). . . .
>
> [T]his Court holds that this matter should not be dismissed as moot. This matter, relating to the independence of the tribal judiciary and to the fundamental meaning of Article XIV of the Turtle Mountain Band Constitution, [is] a public matter of great importance. The . . . Judicial Board, the tribal court judges, and the other branches of the Turtle Mountain Band government require guidance as to how to proceed in cases where the Judicial Board begins an investigation of a tribal court judge. And, given that both the Judicial Board and the Tribal Council have alleged a history that both have acted several times to remove tribal judges without due process, . . . Oral

---

[*]*Disclosure:* The author of this book participated in the case as a sitting appellate judge, and wrote the opinion.

Argument of Donald G. Bruce, Counsel for Judicial Board (May 12, 2005) (asserting that the Tribal Chairman and Tribal Council had once removed the entire Turtle Mountain Band Appellate Court); Judicial Board's Brief on Appeal at 1 (asserting that a former Turtle Mountain Band chairman once removed the appellate court); Band's Complaint, at 2, ¶9 (alleging that the Judicial Board has also suspended Chief Judge MaDonna Marcellais), this Court finds that it is likely this situation will recur. Hence, this matter meets the third criterion.

In addition to the importance of these constitutional issues and the likelihood that they will recur, it also appears that the Tribal Court might never again have the opportunity to hear and decide a similar case. The record, as well as previous cases reported by this Court, indicates that when judges are removed by either the Judicial Board or the Band, they are unlikely to contest their removal. *See Parisien v. Turtle Mountain Judicial Board*, No. TMAC-96-025, at 1-2 (Turtle Mountain Band Ct. App., October 1996) (exemplifying a case where the Judicial Board had previously suspended a sitting tribal judge who subsequently did not challenge the suspension); Oral Argument of Donald G. Bruce, Counsel for Judicial Board (May 12, 2005) (alleging that when the Band removed former Chief Appellate Judge B.J. Jones, he would not contest the removal). The fact that Judge Cain is not a party to this action, apparently because she chose not to file suit, also supports this conclusion. Other tribal courts facing important constitutional cases capable of repetition but evading review have also declined to dismiss an apparently moot case. *E.g., Council of Elders of the Mohegan Tribe v. Mohegan Tribal Employment Rights Commission*, No. CV-01-0006, 2001.NAMT.0000001, at ¶16 (Mohegan Ct. App., Nov. 26, 2001) (declining to dismiss case where tribal administrative agency revoked its orders in order to avoid judicial review); *Burnette v. Rosebud Sioux Tribe*, 1 Tribal Court Rptr. A-51, A-54 (Rosebud Sioux Tribal Ct., April 22, 1978) (declining to dismiss election challenge merely because election victors had already been seated on tribal council). We also note, finally, "in view of th[is case's] impact on the Tribal Judiciary, vindication of the principles at stake in th[ese] proceedings should not depend on the Tribal Judges' ability to hire private lawyers to figure out how to proceed in these extraordinary circumstances." *In re Matter of CLB 0201*, No. CIV-APP 02-01, 2002. NACT.0000004, at ¶61 (Crow Ct. App., March 5, 2002). . . .

Turtle Mountain Judicial Board, at 5-7.

2. ADVISORY OPINIONS

In Re Little Traverse Bay Bands of Odawa Indians

Little Traverse Bay Bands of Odawa Indians Tribal Judiciary,
No. AO-001-0803 (January 6, 2006)

Justice Singel, with whom Justices Budnick and Shepard and Judge Petoskey join. . . .

The Tribal Council of the Little Traverse Bay Bands of Odawa Indians filed a petition on August 26, 2003 in Tribal Court requesting an advisory opinion to determine whether the Tribal Council has the retained authority to overturn an individual licensing decision by the Gaming Regulatory Commission. The Tribal Council's request was submitted in accordance with the Judiciary's

Appellate Procedure Rule 7.302, which provides for the issuance of advisory opinions. . . .

Analysis

We first look to whether the Judiciary has the authority to issue an advisory opinion in response to the Tribal Council's petition.[5] The Appellate Procedures of the Tribal Appellate Court presume that it does, since it provides a procedure for issuing such opinions. Rule 7.302 of the Appellate Procedures provides the following:

7.302 Advisory Opinions

(A) Limited Acceptance. Requests for Advisory Opinions will only be accepted by a unanimous decision of the Judiciary Judges of the Tribal Court. The request may not involve a case in controversy. The request must meet the Court's jurisdictional standards, including standing, ripeness, mootness, and injury in fact.

(B) Discretionary. The Tribal Appellate Court may decide at any time [to] decline acceptance. . . . The Tribal Appellate Court in making its decision will consider such facts and circumstances that will lead to a fair and equitable result based on justice and protection of the tribe's sovereignty and future.

. . . If the Judiciary as a whole accepted Rule 7.302 as a valid appellate procedure, the Court would immediately proceed to weigh the factors identified in the rule and vote to determine whether the issuance of an advisory opinion in this instance had unanimous Judiciary support. Here, however, the Tribal Judiciary is split and does not agree on whether Rule 7.302 can be accepted as a valid appellate procedure.

Justice SINGEL, with whom Judge PETOSKEY joins. . . .

I. Section 1.206 of the Tribal Code Requires Separation of Powers

Section 1.206 of the Tribal Code provided the following:

The Tribal Judiciary shall be *independent* from the legislative and executive functions of the Tribal government and no person exercising the powers of the legislative and executive functions of government shall exercise powers properly belonging to the judicial branch of government.[*]

The mandate that the Tribal Judiciary shall be independent from the other functions of Tribal government creates a separation of powers between the

---

5. In accordance with Rule 7.302, which requires that all members of the Tribal Judiciary receive notice of a request for an advisory opinion and vote to determine whether to issue one, this opinion is rendered by the Tribal Court as a whole, including the Court's three Appellate Justices and the Court's Trial Court Judge.

*Editor's Note: In a portion of the opinion not excerpted here, the court noted that this statute has been effectively superseded by the Constitution of the Little Traverse Bay Bands of Odawa Indians, adopted by tribal voters on January 26, 2007, which constitutionalized the separation of powers discussed in the opinion:

Independent Branch of Government. The Judicial Branch shall be independent from the Legislative and Executive branches of the Tribal government and no person exercising the powers of any of the other two (2) branches of government shall exercise powers properly belonging to the Judicial Branch of Tribal government.

CONSTITUTION OF THE LITTLE TRAVERSE BAY BANDS OF ODAWA INDIANS art. IX, Part H, Section 1 (2007).

Judiciary and the Tribal Council. This separation means that the courts and the legislative and executive branches of government should refrain from encroaching on the other's sphere of responsibility. . . .

Under Rule 7.302 of the Judiciary's Appellate Procedures, the Judiciary has the discretion to issue advisory opinions in certain limited instances. If the Court were to actively issue advisory opinions, it would abrogate the judicial independence and separation of powers mandated by the Tribal Code. Particularly if the Court were to issue advisory opinions for the Tribal Council, as the Tribal Council has requested in this matter, the Court would appear to act as a private legal advisor for the Tribal Council rather than as an independent branch of government. If the Judiciary made a regular practice of offering advisory opinions for the Council, its independence would slowly but surely erode since it would become deeply ingrained in the Tribal Council's political function. Such involvement would divert judicial resources from legitimate court business. It would also prejudice the Judiciary, since it would prematurely expose the Court to legal questions framed exclusively by the Tribal Council. Since requests for advisory opinions are typically posed by a single party, the Court would also receive the benefit of briefing on only one side of the issue. As a result, if the same or a similar issue arose later in litigation, the Court would be less likely to view the issue with fresh eyes and complete neutrality. Rather than place the Judiciary in this position, the Tribal Council should pose legal questions to its own legal staff, which is retained by the Tribal Council for the express purpose of advising it on such matters. . . .

II. Section 1.202 of the Tribal Code Also Limits Judicial Decision-making Authority to Cases

Section 1.202(B) of the Tribal Code provided the following:

> The judicial power shall extend to all *cases* arising under the Tribal Constitution, statutes, ordinances, regulations, or judicial decisions, and all *cases* for which the Tribal Court is the appropriate forum based on the Tribe's inherent sovereignty, traditional custom or Federal Law.[7]

. . . To give meaning to this provision, we must first determine the meaning of the term "cases." . . .

In this instance, the statute does not define the term "cases." . . . However, there is strong evidence that the term "case" has a generally accepted contemporary meaning. This evidence consists of the many opinions from tribal, federal, and international courts that have examined the meaning of similar delegations of judicial power that limit jurisdiction to "cases." Although these cases are not controlling in the Little Traverse Bay Bands' courts, they nevertheless provide useful examples of the meaning commonly ascribed to the term "cases."

The Tribal Court of the Grand Traverse Band of Ottawa and Chippewa Indians interpreted the meaning of "case" in *In re Russell* [No. 96-03-025-CV (1996)] as "a controversy between adverse parties which requires a declaration of the parties' rights." It further stated that this requirement is satisfied when "a suit is brought in pursuance of an honest and actual antagonistic assertion of

---

7. . . . The new Constitution has a nearly identical provision. . . .

rights by one party against another, and valuable legal rights will be directly affected to a specific and substantial degree by the Court's decision." The court concluded that advisory opinions did not constitute cases and therefore should not be issued.

The Confederated Tribes of the Grand Ronde Community of Oregon Tribal Court interpreted the meaning of "cases" and "controversies" in *Flood v. Ryan* as actual cases which were not abstract or hypothetical. [27 Indian L. Rep. 6119, 6119-20 (2000).] The court held that "[t]he exercise of this Court's jurisdiction . . . requires the existence of an actual case or controversy, as opposed to the presentation of an abstract or hypothetical question."

The International Court of Justice also appears to define cases as separate and apart from advisory opinions. Article 36 of the Statute of the International Court of Justice provides that "[t]he jurisdiction of the court comprises of all *cases* which the parties refer to it and all matters specifically provided for in the Charter of the United Nations or in treaties and conventions in force." Article 65 of the same statute provides that the ICJ can issue advisory opinions. This specific authorization for advisory opinions separate from the statute's authorization for review of cases shows an implied assumption [that] cases and questions requesting advisory opinions are separate concepts. . . .

The opinions cited above indicate that the term "case" is generally accepted to mean a controversy between adverse parties that is capable of resolution by a conclusive decree that touches the rights of the parties. They also indicate that the term "case" generally excludes requests for advisory opinions because such requests are generally hypothetical, abstract and non-binding rather than actual disputes between adverse parties that require a final resolution of the parties' legal rights. Since we are not aware of any evidence, textual or otherwise, that indicates that the Tribal Council intended an alternative meaning of the term "case" to apply when it drafted and enacted Section 1.202 of the Tribal Code, and we have received no evidence that the term "case" has a different meaning as a matter of tribal custom, we decline to construe the term differently. As a result, the term "case" as used in Section 1.202 of the Tribal Code means a controversy between adverse parties that is capable of resolution by a conclusive decree that touches the rights of the parties. Since a request for an advisory opinion does not involve a controversy that is capable of resolution by a conclusive decree that touches the rights of the parties because advisory opinions are merely advisory and not conclusive as to the parties' rights, we therefore find that a request for an advisory opinion cannot fairly be considered a "case" under the Tribal Code.

The following opinion submitted by Justices Budnick and Shepard concludes that the term "cases" has a broader meaning that permits the Judiciary to consider requests for advisory opinions. Justices Budnick and Shepard rely on the legislative intent of the Tribal Council and cultural differences between the Odawa and western court systems to support their conclusion. In addition, Justices Budnick and Shepard challenge the notion that the word "cases" has an ordinary, obvious or typical meaning, or generally accepted contemporary meaning.

First, we disagree that the term "cases" should be interpreted differently as a result of legislative intent. In this instance, the Judiciary has received no evidence, written or oral, indicating what the Tribal Council's intent was at the time Section 1.202 of the Tribal Code was enacted. In the absence of any such evidence regarding legislative intent, we decline to insert or impose our own personal suppositions.

Second, we also disagree that the term "cases" should be interpreted differently as a result of the cultural differences between Odawa and western court systems. In our review of the questions presented in this matter, the Judiciary has not received any evidence that Odawa traditional customs support a different result than the one we reach here. While there may be many other instances when the traditional customs and beliefs of the Odawa community require that we interpret the law differently than other courts in non-Odawa settings, we decline to do so where we have no support for a different interpretation and where a different interpretation would create an unnecessary conflict with express provisions in the Tribal Code.

Third, we disagree with Justices Budnick and Shepard's statement that a word such as "cases" can never have an ordinary, obvious or typical meaning, or a generally accepted contemporary meaning. Justices Budnick and Shepard state that "[p]lain meaning is never plain." On the contrary, we maintain that there are many instances where a term has an ordinary or typical meaning, and it is the court's responsibility and essential function to remain faithful and give meaning to such ordinary and typical meanings of words used in Tribal laws. If the Judiciary did not respect and honor a commitment to assigning words their ordinary and typical meaning in the absence of special statutory definitions, then the Tribal Council would lack any certainty that its enactments would be interpreted in a consistent and predictable fashion. This result would cripple the Tribal Council's ability to draft laws, since it would always remain uncertain what meaning the Judiciary would assign to its words.

Justices Budnick and Shepard also conclude that the meaning of the term "cases" in Section 1.202(B) of the Tribal Code is different than the meaning assigned to the term in other jurisdictions because this provision of the Code also permits judicial review of "all cases for which the Tribal Court is the appropriate forum based on the Tribe's inherent sovereignty, traditional custom or Federal law. We disagree with this interpretation. Instead, we find that this sentence and its reference to inherent sovereignty, traditional custom and federal law do not alter the definition of cases to remove the need for a concrete controversy between adverse parties that is capable of resolution by a conclusive decree that touches the rights of the parties. Rather, this sentence expands the types of cases that may be eligible for judicial review. Since the first sentence of Section 1.202(B) permits judicial review of cases arising under [the Constitution, statutes, ordinances, regulations or judicial decisions of the Tribe, a] person might question whether the Judiciary also has authority to review cases involving substantive rights not explicitly recognized in the Constitution, statutes, ordinances, regulations or judicial decisions of the Tribe. For example, a person might wonder whether the court has the power to review a case involving the impingement of a right recognized as a matter of traditional custom but not as a matter of written law. Section 1.202(B)'s second sentence would permit judicial review of this type of question, since it expands the classes of cases eligible for review to include cases involving matters of traditional custom, inherent sovereignty and federal law. . . .

III. Section 1.202(A) of the Tribal Code Requires That Decisions Be Final and Binding

Section 1.202(A) of the Tribal Code also requires that "[r]ulings of the Tribal Appellate Court are final and binding." This provision requires that rulings of the Tribal Appellate Court must offer conclusive resolution of legal issues, and they must touch the legal rights of the parties before it. An advisory opinion would not satisfy this requirement of the Tribal Code. A party who obtains an advisory opinion is free to comply with it or ignore it and risk further liability or prosecution. Since the opinion is merely "advisory," it is not binding and therefore in violation of this provision of the Tribal Code. In addition, a party who obtains an advisory opinion or a person who did not participate in a request for an advisory opinion is free to pursue further legal resolution of the issue by bringing a suit in court. As a result, advisory opinions also fail to satisfy the Tribal Code's requirement that they be final.

IV. Response to Additional Statements in the Opinion of Justices Budnick and Shepard

Finally, the opinion of our respected colleagues Justices Budnick and Shepard states that "we would not want to prevent future generations from having the ability to adapt to the growing needs of the community." They conclude that the Judiciary should issue advisory opinions because they may be beneficial to the community. Our esteemed colleagues also express concern that this opinion will preclude the Judiciary from performing marriages, voluntary adoptions, guardianships, and other matters, and will prevent the court from developing traditional court forums.

Contrary to the opinion of Justices Budnick and Shepard, limiting the Judiciary's authority to the unambiguous mandates provided by tribal law does not have a harmful effect on future generations of Tribal members. Instead, by paying close attention to the . . . Constitution and the statutes enacted by the Tribal Council, this Court builds a solid foundation of respect for the Tribe's Constitution and the lawmaking function of the Tribal legislative body. This foundation will create a solid footing for future Tribal legislation, ensuring the Tribal membership that the laws created by the Tribal Council will not be ignored or overturned by the Judiciary unless they are unconstitutional or otherwise unlawful. We believe that the creation of such a solid legal foundation is the best way for the Court to benefit future generations.

In addition, we also note that this opinion does not absolutely prevent the issuance of advisory opinions by the Judiciary. If the Tribal Council had enacted a constitutional statute that permitted advisory opinions under the Interim Constitution, the Judiciary would have been bound to give effect to such a law. Similarly, under the new Constitution, the Judiciary is bound to interpret its power to issue advisory opinions in light of the new Constitution's provisions.

In response to Justices Budnick and Shepard's statement that this opinion will prevent the Court from performing marriage ceremonies or voluntary adoptions and will prevent the Tribe from developing other traditional dispute resolution forums, we reply that this opinion will have no such effect. First, the performance of marriage ceremonies by members of the Judiciary is not an exercise of the court's judicial power, so such ceremonies are not limited by the constitutional provision that limits the exercise of the Judiciary's judicial power to "cases." Rather, the performance of a marriage ceremony by a judge is an extra-judicial function that can be called on outside of the courtroom and during times that fall outside the court's normal hours of operation. Even if marriage ceremonies are performed in the courtroom, such ceremonies must be scheduled to accommodate the judicial duties of the court, such as court hearings and conferences. Furthermore, marriage ceremonies do not require the exercise of the court's adjudicatory powers, since such ceremonies only require that the officiating judge ensure that the technical requirements of the preparation of a marriage license and the proper solemnization of a marriage take place. As a result, the fact that the Judiciary's judicial power is limited to "cases" does not prevent the Tribe from authorizing the Judiciary to perform marriage ceremonies.

Second, the Court's ability to perform voluntary adoptions is not necessarily impeded by the constitutional limitation of the Judiciary's judicial power to "cases." This issue is not squarely before the Court at this time, however, and is best addressed if and when a case presenting this issue is heard by the Court.

Third, the Tribe's ability to establish traditional dispute resolution forums is also not impeded by the constitutional limitation of the Judiciary's judicial power to "cases." Such traditional forums would not be operated by the Judiciary, so their functions would not be limited to the constitutional limitations that apply to the Judiciary.

Finally, this opinion does not leave an interested person or entity with standing without a remedy. Under existing law, other legal proceedings could be initiated instead of a request for an advisory opinion to accomplish the same result. For example, a person with standing could bring a lawsuit seeking a declaratory judgment declaring the rights of the parties. Such a lawsuit would satisfy the requirement of the Tribal Code, since it would establish an actual case between adversarial parties, it would allow the Judiciary to act in its ordinary adjudicative capacity and preserve its independence, and it would result in a holding which, if appealed, would be final and binding. Such a lawsuit would also allow the Judiciary to apply the tasks which it is uniquely competent to perform. It would allow the Court to hear arguments and accept evidence from two adverse parties, ensuring that it received all relevant facts from both sides of the issue. It would also allow the court to apply the law to a concrete factual situation. For this reason, we do not believe that the Court's opinion leaves the Tribal Council or other persons interested in advisory opinions without recourse or a remedy in the event they seek a clarification of their rights. . . .

Justice BUDNIK, with whom Justice SHEPARD joins.

Analysis

The main issue that splits the Judiciary on this decision is whether we should use a strict interpretation of wording of the Interim Constitution or whether we should look at the overall intent and the impact on public policy and the future of the tribe.

I. Ambiguity of the Word "Cases"

. . . The plain meaning rule is a legal concept that certain words have a face value and should be interpreted as such. One could look at the word "cases" and interpret it to imply that there must be an element of controversy or cases could also be interpreted to mean a more generic term and not a legal limitation on the jurisdiction of the Judiciary. We see the word as ambiguous because it has more than one meaning. The plain meaning rule dictates that when there are two meanings for a particular word, the intent of the law must decide the appropriate interpretation.

Contextually, the definition of a case as a broad issue or matter acknowledges the American Indian cultural framework and is consistent with the Tribal Constitution. Especially so, when read in its entirety: "The judicial power shall extend to all cases arising under the Tribal Constitution, statutes, ordinances, regulations, or judicial decisions, and all cases for which the Tribal Court is the appropriate forum based on the Tribe's inherent sovereignty, traditional custom or Federal law."

Our interpretation of the framers' intent was to be able to seek remedies through the Tribal Court unless the court would be inappropriate. We respectfully see the word "cases" as a generic term and not a legal limitation on the jurisdiction of the Judiciary.

The Appellate statute has criteria as to when advisory opinions could be issued; using this criteria would prevent the Judiciary from inappropriate interference or actions.

Further, the phrase "based on the Tribe's inherent sovereignty, traditional custom or Federal law" is very broad language. It appears that the Tribal Court has jurisdiction to provide remedies beyond what would normally be considered by a Western Court (traditional custom), thus allowing the Judiciary to grow and provide adequate services to the tribal community as new needs develop.

The "plain meaning rule" is a Western legal construction that attempts to get to the true meaning of a word. The legal rule states that a court must accept the commonly accepted meaning of a word or phrase. Even the Western legal tradition is divided about when to use the plain meaning rule. Plain meaning is never plain. American and English judges have clashed about when and how a term should be defined by its common usage.

There are also exceptions to the "plain meaning rule":

> [P]lain meaning of such words may be followed when they are sufficient in and of themselves to determine the purpose, but court may look beyond such words to the purpose when the plain meaning leads to absurd or futile results, or an unreasonable result.

. . . The "commonly-accepted rules of legal construction" also state that the plain meaning rule does not apply when the meaning of a word is ambiguous or there is an absurd or unworkable result. Here, both of those would occur. If we applied "cases" in its narrowest sense the results would go against public policy thus creating an absurd and unworkable result. Further, if the Judiciary determined that we could only hear cases in controversy, this could potentially limit the court from performing marriage ceremonies, voluntary adoptions, guardianship and many other matters. This line of thinking could also prevent the Judiciary from developing other traditional court forums where the parties are not involved with a controversy, *i.e.* Youth Wellness Court, Indigenous Peacemaking Practices, or other areas where a formal case is not filed with the court. Based on Justices Petoskey and Singel's reasoning, using the narrow construction of the word "cases" to mean "cases in controversy," any code or law that was passed, *i.e.* marriage statute, would be seen as unconstitutional, since it would be beyond the jurisdiction and powers of the court as set forth in the constitution. The Court cannot exercise powers that have not been given to it by the people through the constitution. We cannot agree with this line of reasoning, and believe that the intention, as outlined in the LTBB Constitution, is to have a full-service court that meets the needs of the tribal members and is not limited to an adversarial system of justice.

II. Impact on Public Policy and Future Generations

Within Odawa culture, it is important to recognize that our actions today may impact our children of tomorrow. We would not want to prevent future generations from having the ability to adapt to the growing needs of the community. Binding future generations to something that may not fit their needs or lives is precisely what we must seek to avoid.

Resorting to the objective legal rules of Western society is incompatible with the traditional values we have struggled to preserve. Injecting objectivity where it does not belong will ensure that future generations cannot distinguish between Western values and our own. Despite all of this, however, we believe that advisory opinions are acceptable even using Western legal thought.

Advisory opinions are well within the range of appropriate responsibilities for the judiciary and do not infringe on either separation of powers or independence. The controversy regarding advisory opinions cannot be evaluated without considering their particular purpose. We do not set forth that advisory opinions are binding. Instead, they are opinions issued by the Tribal Court for the benefit of the Tribal Council and Tribal members. Advisory opinions can be ignored. The Tribal Council has the ability to proceed with a particular action, or follow the advice of the opinion or some hybrid of the two. In some cases, an advisory opinion may provide the Tribal Council with insight as to how the judiciary views a particular social, economic or legislative matter. In other cases, advisory opinions may provide guidance as to how the judiciary will interpret certain laws. There are many possibilities.

By providing insight into the minds of the justices, advisory opinions have an enormous potential to improve the efficiency of tribal governance and create open communication between branches. As the tribal government grows and begins fulfilling more of the needs of the tribal members, such discourse may be a useful tool for both the Tribal Council and the Tribal Court. Such interactions will likely have positive effects in creating ties between the people and the judiciary as well as ensure vigilance in dividing responsibilities between branches.

The Tribal Court is not meant to be an apolitical body. Instead, the Tribal Court is meant to enforce the laws of the Tribal Council while respecting and upholding tribal culture, traditions and beliefs. Pretending that words, phrases or even entire laws have objective meanings will serve to alienate the public and create discontent in our governance. By acknowledging that laws are based on interpretation, advisory opinions may help to strengthen respect for law and government.

At the very least, there is no harm in reserving the option of advisory opinions. Even if they are infrequently issued and sometimes denied, advisory opinions may have unique value for future generations. Closing the door will make it difficult for our children to revisit an issue. The Tribal Court has a responsibility to allow our culture to evolve and flourish in the way future generations see fit.

Additionally, no vital resources will be lost. The only resource required to write an advisory opinion is time. While time is a precious commodity, in the case of many advisory opinions, the time to write the opinion is an investment in good governance. If there is a shortage of resources, the judiciary always has the option of turning down or delaying an advisory opinion. There is no reason to believe that we will be faced with a massive influx of requests for advisory opinions. On the contrary, justices may be unwilling to accept many requests for advisory opinions because they have not completely formed their opinions about certain laws or seen them in practice. Nonetheless, it is important to have the option of issuing the advisory opinion if the need should arise. Finally, advisory opinions do not impair the functioning of an independent judiciary for the reason stated above.

Justice BUDNIK, with whom Justices SINGEL and SHEPARD and Judge PETOSKEY join.

The Judiciary also finds that even if Appellate Procedure 7.302 were valid, it would still refuse to issue an advisory opinion on the basis that the Tribal Council's request fails to meet the Court's jurisdictional standard of mootness. . . .

NOTES

1. Under what circumstances can tribal customary law trump tribal constitutional language, if ever? What does Justice Budnik mean when she notes that the tribal court is not meant to be "apolitical"?

2. In *Flood v. Ryan*, 2 Am. Tribal Law 84, 27 Indian L. Rep. 6119 (Confederated Tribes of the Grand Ronde Community of Oregon Tribal Court 2000), one of the cases discussed in the *Little Traverse* opinion, the court declined to issue an opinion on whether the court would have jurisdiction over a tort claim involving a nonmember defendant:

   The exercise of judicial power generally requires the existence of a justiciable case or controversy between parties who are before the court. . . . Although those federal and state court decisions may ultimately be grounded in provisions of the United States and the Oregon constitutions that do not apply directly to this Court, the Court sees no reason (and none has been offered) to jettison sound legal principle. The exercise of this Court's jurisdiction also requires the existence of an actual case or controversy, as opposed to the presentation of an abstract or hypothetical question.

Plaintiff's complaint posits nothing more than the following abstract inquiry: if plaintiff were to file his tort claim in Tribal Court, would the Court have jurisdiction over it? The only declaration that plaintiff seeks from the Court is one stating that it lacks jurisdiction over his tort claim. That abstract question presents no justiciable controversy. The question of whether the Court would have jurisdiction if some litigant were to take some action in the future is a hypothetical one only.

Plaintiff argues that the inquiry raised by his complaint is not abstract or hypothetical because a declaration that this Court lacks subject matter jurisdiction over his tort claim would allow his state-court case to proceed. . . .

. . . [W]hat would happen if this Court were to decide, contrary to plaintiff's assumption, that it does have subject matter jurisdiction over the underlying tort claim[?] Under plaintiff's present pleading, the case would then be at an end, the Court having decided that it has jurisdiction over a case not yet brought before it. In sum, no justiciable controversy is presented here.

Flood, 2 Am. Tribal Law at 85.

3. Other courts, applying tribal common law, also refuse to issue advisory opinions. *E.g., In re Navajo Bd. of Election Supervisors*, 6 Navajo Rep. 302, 304 (Navajo Nation Supreme Court 1990).

4. Other courts, in accordance with tribal statute, do issue advisory opinions. *E.g., Murphy v. Mohegan Tribal Gaming Authority*, 7 Am. Tribal Law 442 (Mohegan Gaming Disputes Tribal Court 2007) (issuing opinion that Connecticut law applied to an appellate procedure question); *Hopi Tribe v. Sahmea*, 1 Am. Tribal Law 373 (Hopi Tribe Appellate Court 1998) (issuing opinion on whether certain criminal charges against a defendant violated his double jeopardy rights).

C. TRIBAL COURT CONTEMPT POWER

BEAR SOLDIER DISTRICT v. BEAR SOLDIER INDUSTRIES

Standing Rock Sioux Tribal Court (February 21, 2005)

Opinion of Judge B.J. JONES

Once again this matter is before the Court on the Plaintiff District's efforts to enforce a jury verdict finding that Bear Soldier Industries, now known as Pinto Spirit Inc., committed fraud on the District when it obtained a loan of $722,000 to renovate certain housing in Bear Soldier District and failed to renovate the housing to make it habitable. The Plaintiff now requests that this Court convert the money judgment entered against Bear Soldier Industries Inc. and Pinto Spirit Inc. into a money judgment against Gary Minard, a corporate officer of both Bear Soldier Industries Inc. and Pinto Spirit Inc. . . .

. . . On February 14, 2003 this Court entered an order to enforce a jury verdict entered on behalf of the Plaintiff against the Defendants. The jury found that Bear Soldier Industries committed fraud in obtaining a tribal guarantee on a loan to Bear Soldier Industries Inc. in the amount of $722,000. . . .

Gary Minard, a non-Indian . . . [persuaded the tribal council to pass] a resolution authorizing the Chairman of the Standing Rock Sioux Tribe and its Chief Finance Officer to execute a guarantee on a $722,000 loan from the Wells Fargo Bank to Bear Soldier Industries Inc. and to assume the mortgages on the units in Bear Soldier West from the Standing Rock Housing Authority.

The original idea to renovate the Bear Soldier West units appeared to be a fairly sound one. The entity that was to renovate the units was to renovate them sufficiently so that they could become eligible for Section 8 housing certificates that would then be used to pay both the mortgages on the units and the loan from Wells Fargo. . . .

The most critical deficiency, however, was that the units were never repaired to the extent that the South Dakota Housing Authority certified them for Section 8 housing certificates. . . .

The District officers then brought an action against Bear Soldier Industries Inc., its corporate directors, and its attorney seeking a court declaration that Bear Soldier Industries Inc. had committed a fraud upon it both by representing to the Tribal Council that it spoke for the District and by obtaining a substantial loan, guaranteed by the Tribe, to renovate housing to make it habitable and had failed to perform adequate work. . . .

The jury rendered a verdict finding fraud and a violation of several provisions of federal and tribal law. . . .

The Court held numerous post verdict hearings in an attempt to enforce its orders. They include a May 10, 2004 hearing on a motion to quash a subpoena issued to Linda Comeau, which counsel for the Defendants was notified of but did not appear, and a May 14, 2004 hearing on the Plaintiff's motion to reduce the jury verdict to a money judgment against Pinto Spirit Inc. and the individual District officers of Bear Soldier Industries Inc. Counsel for the Defendant appeared at hearing on May 14, 2004 and resisted the motion. The Court took limited testimony from Tribal Finance Officer Larry Luger and Avis Little Eagle, Bear Soldier District Councilwoman, to determine whether the Defendant Corporation had complied with the Court's judgment and order entered on February 14, 2003 and subsequently affirmed in all respects by the Standing Rock Supreme Court on February 2, 2004.

The Court finds that since the jury's verdict finding that the Defendant corporation committed fraud in obtaining $722,000 in guaranteed loans to renovate housing in the Bear Soldier District, Pinto Spirit has defaulted on those loans and the Standing Rock Sioux Tribe, the guarantor for the notes, is now paying approximately $40,000 per month on both the notes to secure renovation funding for the Bear Soldier District's housing units and the individual mortgages on the units. Larry Luger testified that the Tribe will be liable, in the end, for approximately 8.5 million dollars in defaulted notes and mortgages executed by Bear Soldier Industries Inc. before it changed its corporate name to Pinto Spirit Inc. The units themselves remain, with few exceptions, uninhabitable and Avis Little Eagle testified that it would cost the District approximately $450,000 to correct the problems in the units to even make them habitable. In sum, the Standing Rock Sioux Tribe and Bear Soldier District appear to have been hoodwinked and the Tribe is now paying substantial monies that will inure to the benefit of no one.

The Court granted the motion to convert the judgment entered against Bear Soldier Industries into a judgment against Pinto Spirit on June 14, 2004 in the amount of $722,000 plus interest in the amount of $86,640 plus costs and attorney's fees to be taxed. The Court also granted the Plaintiff's motion to amend the pleadings post-trial to add a claim of personal liability against Gary Minard. The Court did not enter a judgment, however, against him at that time because attorney Kent Morrow indicated that he did not represent Minard in his individual capacity. Instead the Court opted to issue an order to show cause against Minard to give him a chance to show cause why he should not have been held in contempt of Court and why he should not be held liable in his personal capacity for the judgment entered against Bear Soldier Industries.

Minard was served, through his wife—an adult resident of his household—with the show cause order and the hearing was held on July 23, 2004 at the Tribal Court. Minard failed to appear in person or through counsel. The Court took further evidence and found Minard in contempt of court and order[ed] him detained until he came into compliance with the orders of this Court. The Court also found that Bear Soldier Industries Inc. and Pinto Spirit Inc. were sham corporations and that Minard should be held individually liable for his actions since the jury verdict in failing to comply with any order of the Court and transferring assets from Bear Soldier Industries Inc. to Pinto Spirit Inc. and then on to IQ Fund.

That July 23, 2004 order of contempt somehow got into the hands of the Burleigh County Sheriff who then began an attempt to find Minard to enforce the order. Minard commenced an action in the North Dakota District Court in Bismark, North Dakota to collaterally challenge the order finding him in contempt. The District Court refused to vacate the order of this Court and Minard appealed to the North Dakota Supreme Court which held that the Burleigh County Sheriff should not have made efforts to enforce the detention order until such time as the Plaintiff filed its judgment and order with the District Court pursuant to Rule 7.2 of the North Dakota Supreme Court.

Meanwhile, the order of contempt also came to the attention of the Tribal Chairman of the Tribe who intervened in this matter by writing a letter to the Captain of the BIA law enforcement, Stand Rock agency, directing him not to comply with the order of this Court, and to direct adjoining jurisdictions to ignore the order. The Court finds that this action was void as the Tribal Chairman had no authority to interfere with an order of this Court. It should be noted that this Court asked the Standing Rock Sioux Tribe to participate in this proceeding, but the Tribe opted to get itself removed from the case in its early stages and never participated in the proceedings. Notwithstanding the lack of authority of the Tribal Chairman to intervene, both the BIA police and county and city law enforcement opted not to comply with this Court's orders in this case, leaving the Court in the unenviable position of being denied its jurisdiction to enforce the jury verdict through its civil contempt powers.

The Court concludes from the actions of Gary Minard since entry of the judgment rendered as a result of the jury verdict that Minard has no intentions to comply with the orders of this Court. The Court also finds that the actions of

Minard in transferring the assets obtained as the result of the Wells Fargo Loan from one corporation, Bear Soldier Industries Inc. to another, Pinto Spirit Inc., and yet to another, IQ Fund, demonstrates an attempt to avoid the judgment entered by this Court. . . .

Minard also argues that he is not subject to this Court's jurisdiction. The Court disagrees with this argument also. At no time before, during or after the proceedings in this case has the Defendant raised challenges to this Court's jurisdiction. Now, apparently after Minard has decided he no longer wishes to engage in business on the Standing Rock reservation, he questions this Court's authority over him.

[The court engaged in a lengthy discussion of federal law relating to tribal court jurisdiction over non-tribal citizens.]

In this case, it is clear that Minard, by engaging in business as a corporation, submitted himself to this Court's jurisdiction. The United States Supreme Court has recognized that an Indian tribe has the right to regulate non-Indians who engage in business with the Tribe or its members on the reservation. *See Merrion v. Jicarilla Apache Tribe*, 445 U.S. 130 (1982); *see also Kerr-McGee v. Navajo Tribe of Indians*, 471 U.S. 195 (1985). In *Merrion*, in response to the argument by the non-Indians being taxed that the Tribe had no inherent authority to regulate non-Indians on trust lands within reservation boundaries the Court strongly disagreed and stated that this authority "does not derive solely from the Indian tribe's power to exclude non-Indians from tribal lands. Instead, it derives from the Tribe's general authority, as sovereign, to **control economic activity within its jurisdiction**, and to defray the cost of providing governmental services by **requiring contributions from persons or enterprises engaged in economic activities** within that jurisdiction." *Merrion*, at 137 (emphasis added). . . .

The Court finds that Minard has utilized the corporate laws of North Dakota and Delaware in an effort to avoid this Court's judgment against Bear Soldier Industries Inc. and Pinto Spirit Inc. This Court can hold an individual officer liable in his individual capacity if he utilizes the corporate structure as a way of avoiding legal obligations. . . .

This Court, despite the numerous protestations by Minard's counsel to the media and others to the contrary, has no personal animus against Minard or any of the other corporate officers of the Defendants. It does have a legal duty to carry out the verdict of a tribal jury and will not shirk from that duty notwithstanding criticism from the Defendants and the Tribal executives.

NOTES

1. The Hopi Tribe's appellate court noted the importance of the contempt power:

   > A trial court judge has a great responsibility not only for the legal aspects of the trial, but also for the orderly conduct of legal proceedings. Every court has the duty to ensure that its authority and dignity are respected so that it can administer justice without hindrance or embarrassment. . . . When a person

"willfully disregards the authority of the court," he is said to be in contempt of court. . . . A trial judge has the responsibility to punish for contempt if necessary so that the judge may maintain control over the proceedings and to enforce orders and directives which the judge issues.

In the matter of Sekayumptewa, 1997.NAHT.0000015, at ¶42 (Hopi Tribe Appellate Court, August 29, 1997) (citations omitted).

There are two categories of civil contempt — "compensatory and coercive." The first category usually involves damage awards. Civil contempt often involves incarceration, although it can also include fines paid to the government:

> The second kind of civil contempt is coercive civil contempt. This form is a close cousin of criminal contempt because under coercive civil contempt judges impose fines paid to the state or order imprisonment. The distinction between criminal and coercive contempts lies in their different purposes. Whereas criminal contempt punishes defendants for past disobedience, coercive civil contempt seeks to compel present and future compliance with the court's order.

Elaine W. Shoben & William Murray Tabb, Remedies: Cases and Problems 225 (2d ed. 1995).

Like Anglo-American–style courts, the contempt power is not necessarily Indigenous — tribal courts have borrowed the contempt power along with other Anglo-American judicial powers. The Sac and Fox Nation Supreme Court described the law of contempt as coming

> [t]o the Sac and Fox through an English legal tradition modified by enactors of the United States Constitution. From a polyglot and class-divided culture, preyed upon historically by self-serving tyrants and standing armies, the rebellious Englishmen who subsequently framed the United States Constitution wanted to observe a strict separation of executive, legislative, and judicial powers to prevent the concentration of too much power in the hands of any one person or group.

Bolding v. Lujan, 4 Okla. Trib. 239, 244, 1995 WL 1073435 (Sac & Fox Supreme Court, April 26, 1995) (citing The Federalist No. 47 (Madison)).

Conversely, the Sac and Fox people did not need such limits on their governmental power structures:

> The historically more homogenous and democratic citizen-warriors of the Sac and Fox did not need strictly separated exercise of these powers to protect themselves from internal tyrants. However, while the creation of a strictly separate public authority for the exercise of judicial power is a recent adoption for Sac and Fox[,] the Tribe has always recognized punishment for disobeying the public authority or conscience. Simply put, "contempt" is intentional offense to or disobedience of the public authority.

Bolding, 4 Okla. Trib. at 244. However, "[a]n immediate example of Sac and Fox exercise of 'contempt' power is the confiscation and destruction of an individual's personal property by camp police for disobeying orders of the Tribal Council." *Id.* at 244 n. 3.

Tribal courts have inherent authority to enforce compliance of lawful orders. The Hopi Tribe's appellate court wrote:

> The power to punish for contempt is not dependent on statutory authority, but inheres in any court. This inherent power has been recognized since the early days of the American judiciary, and has its roots in the English system of law. As well as recognizing an inherent power, the Hopi Tribe, the federal government and every state have statutes authorizing punishment for contempt of court. Other tribal courts have also recognized their power to punish for contempt.

In the matter of Sekayumptewa, 1997.NAHT.0000015, at ¶43 (Hopi Tribe Appellate Court, August 29, 1997) (citing *Ex parte Robinson*, 86 U.S. 505, 510 (1873)) (footnotes omitted).

2. The Violence Against Women Act provides that "any protection order issued . . . by the court of . . . and Indian tribe . . . shall be accorded full faith and credit by the court of another State or Indian tribe . . . and enforced as if it were the order of the enforcing State of tribe." 18 U.S.C. §2265(a). *See* Melissa L. Tatum, *Establishing Penalties for Violations of Protection Orders: What Tribal Governments Need to Know*, 13 KAN. J.L. & PUB. POL'Y 125, 125 (2003/2004). In the arena of enforcing the protection orders of other jurisdictions, Congress provided that "tribal court[s] shall have full civil jurisdiction to enforce protection orders, including authority to enforce any orders through civil contempt proceedings." 18 U.S.C. §2265(e).

However, at best, this language was ambiguous as to whether Congress really intended to expand tribal civil jurisdiction over non-Indians. *See* Tatum, *Establishing Penalties*, *supra*, at 133. In 2005, Congress again amended VAWA, adding stronger language regarding tribal civil jurisdiction over non-Indians, but without explicitly affirming civil jurisdiction over non-Indians. *See* Public Law 109-162, Title IX §902(2).

In order to qualify as an enforceable foreign order under VAWA, the foreign court order must satisfy two requirements. First, "a protection order must be issued by a court that has jurisdiction over the parties and the matter under the law of the State or Indian tribe." *State v. Esquivel*, 132 P.3d 751, 754 (Wash. App. 2006) (citing 18 U.S.C. §2265(b)(1)). Second, "the person against whom the order is sought must have been given reasonable notice and opportunity to be heard sufficient to protect due process rights." *Esquivel*, 132 P.3d at 754 (citing 18 U.S.C §2265(b)(2)).

The Washington Court of Appeals issued an order requiring state trial courts to enforce an order issued by the Colville Confederated Tribes tribal court in *Esquivel*. In that case, the tribal court filed a parenting plan restricting the father's conduct that the father subsequently violated on six separate occasions. The State of Washington filed criminal charges against the father as a result of these violations. The defendant did not contest the tribal court's jurisdiction over him, nor did he contest the process offered him at the tribal court level. Since the tribal court order and the subsequent state court prosecution followed the mandates of VAWA, the Washington Court of Appeals recognized the tribal court order.

D. JUDICIAL RECUSAL

PRATT V. HOOPA VALLEY TRIBAL POLICE

Hoopa Valley Tribal Court of Appeals, No. C-96-048,
4 NICS App. 193 (April 30, 1997)

Before: ELBRIDGE COOCHISE, Chief Justice; DOUGLAS W. HUTCHINSON, Justice;
ROBERT J. MILLER, Justice. . . .

I. Background

This matter originated as an appeal filed with the [Tribal Employment Rights Ordinance, or TERO] Commission by Daniel Pratt challenging the termination of his employment by the Department of Public Safety. . . .

. . . The Commission, finding that the penalty imposed was too harsh, reinstated Mr. Pratt. The Hoopa Valley Tribal Police appealed the TERO decision on the grounds that it was arbitrary, capricious, and not in accordance with the law. This appeal has not yet proceeded to a hearing on the merits because in October of 1996, Mr. Pratt filed a Motion for Order Disqualifying Judge Mike Ross from adjudicating the issues. Mr. Pratt based his motion on allegations of prejudice due to Judge Ross's prior position as the tribal chief of police as well as his personal and professional relationship with Leonard E. Masten, the Director of the Hoopa Valley Department of Public Safety, who had terminated Mr. Pratt from employment with the tribal police department. . . .

III. Standard of Review

The standard of review over trial court decisions regarding recusal of a judge is for an abuse of discretion. . . . *DeCoteau v. Ives*, 2 NICS App. 170, 172, 174 (Port Gamble S'Klallam 1992) (trial court evidentiary rulings and final judgments are reviewed for manifest abuse of discretion).

IV. Discussion

Appellant urges this Court to reverse the trial court order and to order the removal of Judge Ross from hearing or deciding this matter. Section 1.3.04 outlines the procedure for disqualification of a judge:

> A defendant, or other party, to any proceedings may accomplish a change of assignment of his/her case from one judge to another upon filing an affidavit of prejudice with the Court, giving satisfactory reason for such change. . . . The initial judge shall pass on the adequacy of the affidavit of prejudice and enter the appropriate order, either hearing the case or reassigning it to another judge. Such an order may be appealed immediately under the appellate procedures set out in this Code, and all further actions in such a case will be stayed pending the outcome of that appeal. . . . In no event shall the trial judge allow any action as set out in this section to influence his/her impartiality in any case or to any person.

Along with his Motion to Disqualify Judge Ross, Mr. Pratt submitted a declaration of prejudice, wherein he stated his belief that he could not obtain a fair and impartial hearing before Judge Ross for the following reasons: (1) Judge Ross once served as the Tribal Chief of Police and, therefore, would be biased; (2) Judge Ross has a close personal friendship with the current Police Chief, Leonard Masten; (3) Judge Ross and Chief Masten traveled together as part of their work on a statewide Indian Drug Task Force; and (4) Mr. Pratt's case involves the interpretation of the Rules and Regulations Manual of the Hoopa Valley Department of Public Safety and Emergency Services, which was authored by Judge Ross in 1985.

The trial court, in denying the motion for removal, found that Mr. Pratt had failed to show that Judge Ross's personal or professional relationship with Mr. Masten, his status as former police chief, or his involvement in authoring the regulations in question established prejudice or bias.

Title I, §1.2.9 of the Hoopa Valley Tribal Code sets out the standard for removal of a judge:

> Any judge of the Tribal Court or Appellate Court shall be disqualified to act as such in any case in which he or she has any direct interest, and shall not take part in the deliberation or determination of any matter . . . where for any . . . reason the judge cannot be impartial [or] where the judge finds that a *reasonable person* would believe that the Judge could not be impartial. [Emphasis added.]

Recently, this Court in *Hoopa Valley Tribal Council v. Risling*, 4 NICS App. 66 (Hoopa 1996) established the standard to be used when the impartiality of a judge or arbiter is questioned:

> Any judge or arbiter shall disqualify himself or herself in any proceeding:
>
> (1) in which his or her impartiality might reasonably be questioned; or
> (2) where he or she has personal bias or prejudice concerning a party; or
> (3) where he or she has personal knowledge of disputed evidentiary facts concerning the proceeding; or
> (4) where he or she has served in governmental employment and in such capacity participated as counsel, adviser or material witness concerning the proceeding or expressed an opinion concerning the merits of the particular controversy.

Risling, 4 NICS App. at 7-8.

In *Risling*, the parties sought to recuse two TERO Commissioners from deciding a grievance before the Commission because both Commissioners were former Tribal Council members who, during their tenure as Council members, might have learned of certain facts regarding the issues they were asked to rule upon as TERO Commissioners. Relying on evidence showing that both Commissioners may have been privy to confidential information regarding evidentiary facts at issue before the TERO Commission, this Court found that the parties had established sufficient facts upon which the appearance of impartiality might reasonably be questioned, requiring recusal of the two Commissioners.

The facts in the case now before this Court may be distinguished from the *Risling* facts. Mr. Pratt seeks to remove Judge Ross because of the potential for bias or the appearance of prejudice stemming from Judge Ross's prior employment as Tribal Police chief, his personal and professional relationship with

Chief Masten, and his status as sole drafter of the rules and regulations which the trial court eventually might be called upon to interpret. Appellant, however, fails to allege or sufficiently establish that Judge Ross, in his prior work or relationships, may have obtained knowledge of evidentiary facts at issue.

The standard we apply is the reasonable person standard; i.e., whether a reasonable person would believe that Judge Ross cannot be impartial because of his previous work or his personal and professional relationship with Chief Masten. We address Mr. Pratt's allegations of bias individually.

A. Former Police Chief Ross

Mr. Pratt admits that he did not work for the Hoopa Valley Tribal Police during the time that Judge Ross served as its Chief. The fact that Judge Ross once served as police chief for the very same organization from which Mr. Pratt's employment was severed does not raise a specter of bias. Mr. Pratt's employment with and termination from the police department occurred after Judge Ross had left his position as police chief. Therefore, during Judge Ross's tenure as police chief, he could not have obtained any knowledge of the facts in Mr. Pratt's current appeal, nor could he have expressed any opinions concerning the merits of a case which did not at the time exist. Judge Ross's prior employment with the police department does not create a situation in which his impartiality might reasonable be questioned.

B. Judge Ross's Personal Friendship with Current Police Chief Masten

Mr. Pratt believes that he cannot receive a fair hearing before Judge Ross because of the Judge's personal friendship with Police Chief Masten, who terminated Appellant from employment. Mr. Pratt has not established that Judge Ross has obtained any knowledge regarding evidentiary facts about this case by virtue of his friendship with Chief Masten. The personal relationship between Judge Ross and Chief Masten (who, this Court notes, is not a party to this case) does not on its face establish an appearance of impropriety or impartiality. Judges are often called upon to separate personal opinions from their decisions. Requiring a judge to recuse himself from hearing a case based solely on the fact of his friendship with a non-party witness does not serve the ends of judicial efficiency or economy.

C. Judge Ross's Former Professional Relationship
with Police Chief Masten

Mr. Pratt has produced no evidence to this Court that any actual or apparent bias results from Judge Ross's former or current professional relationship with Chief Masten. The fact that Judge Ross and Chief Masten worked and traveled together on a matter unrelated to Mr. Pratt's case has no demonstrated bearing on Judge Ross's ability to hear and decide this matter impartially.

D. Judge Ross's Role as Sole Drafter of the
Rules and Regulations Manual

It is undisputed that in 1985 Judge Ross authored the Rules and Regulations Manual in use by the Department of Public Safety. It also is undisputed that the underlying action in this case may hinge upon the interpretation, by the trial court, of particular rules and regulations which Mr. Pratt allegedly violated.

In and of itself, however, the fact that Judge Ross drafted rules which, in the future, he might interpret does not rise to the level of real or apparent bias requiring recusal. Tribal, state, and federal judges come from diverse backgrounds and bring to the bench a plethora of experience and skills. Some are former legislators. It is not uncommon for judges who have had substantial roles in the legislative process to be called upon to interpret the resulting laws; they are not required to recuse themselves from hearing cases relating to that legislation once they become judges.

V. Conclusion

Appellant's objection to the trial court's reference to the Rule of Necessity is not well taken. The Hoopa Valley Tribe, like many Indian tribes, is not only small but isolated. It is improbable, if not impossible, to find a judge who will have absolutely no knowledge regarding every case and every individual that comes before him. It is an equally onerous burden, both economically and logistically, to require the Tribe to rely heavily on pro tem judges.

As the trial court discussed, Hoopa is a small community. Many of its members have lived in the community for their entire lives. In small communities such as the Hoopa Valley Indian Tribe, it is impractical to require a judge to recuse himself from every case in which he has some knowledge of or relationship to parties or witnesses appearing before the court. In such communities, a reasonable person would believe that a judge could know and have personal or professional relationships with individuals in the community who may come before him in a judicial proceedings and still not have that knowledge affect his impartiality.

This Court agrees with the trial court that Mr. Pratt has failed to show that Judge Ross cannot be impartial or that a reasonable person would believe that Judge Ross cannot be impartial. The trial court, in its order, painstakingly addressed each of Mr. Pratt's concerns regarding potential bias and specifically found that Mr. Pratt had failed to provide sufficient evidence of either actual bias or the appearance of partiality. We find the trial court did not abuse its discretion in denying Mr. Pratt's motion.

NOTES

1. In *Amerind Risk Management Corp. v. Malaterre*, No. TMAC-06-003 (Turtle Mountain Band of Chippewa Indians Court of Appeals 2007), a defendant in a claim related to a fire at a tribal housing development sought recusal of the trial judge on the grounds that the judge lived in a tribal housing development. The trial judge refused to excuse herself from the case, and the appellate court affirmed, writing per Chief Judge B.J. Jones:

> In order to warrant a reversal of the order below on the ground of judicial bias the Appellant must overcome the presumption that a sitting Judge is impartial and should entertain all suits that come before her. The Appellant's argument is that the presiding Judge resided in a Housing Authority unit and is

therefore unable to impartially resolve the issue of the direct suit against it because a ruling against the Appellant could possibly inure in some way to her benefit. . . . This is far too speculative to warrant recusal. In order to recuse for a personal proprietary or pecuniary interest, or one affecting the individual rights of the judge, the challenging party must demonstrate that the presiding Judge possesses an interest that will turn on the outcome of the individual suit before her. It is not sufficient to merely speculate that the Judge may benefit from the ruling in the future. If this were the case, Judges would have to be recused in cases involving taxpayer suits or other suits involving classes of persons to whom the Judge belongs. Before a Judge is disqualified it must be demonstrated that she possesses a unique quality that distinguishes her from any other citizen or taxpayer and she has a direct pecuniary interest in the case before her. . . . The Appellant cannot demonstrate that Judge May had a pending lawsuit against the Housing Authority or its insurer, nor does it proffer sufficient proof that the presiding Judge would benefit from a ruling either way in this case. . . .

Amerind Risk Management Corp., at 2-3.

2. In *Hendrix v. Yurok Tribe*, 6 NICS App. 4 (Yurok Tribal Court of Appeals 2000), the court reversed a criminal conviction, in part, on grounds that the trial judge had engaged in *ex parte* communications with the prosecution:

> During arraignment, Appellant orally moved to dismiss the charges against him, alleging that the trial judge had had ex parte communications with the opposing party. The trial court denied the motion. Appellant contends the judge's statement, "I think that there is enough evidence here," was uttered before any evidence was presented, thereby indicating the judge had ex parte communications regarding the case. . . .
>
> We consider a number of facts set forth in the transcript: (1) at Appellant's arraignment, the judge called the matter "Case of Mattz v. Hendrix" when the criminal complaint is entitled "Yurok Tribe v. Larry Z. Hendrix"; (2) at the time of trial, the judge again announced: "This morning we have the defendant, Randy Mattz v. Larry Hendrix . . ."; and (3) the judge's statement at the start of trial concerning sufficient evidence. These factors not only show judicial bias, but also strongly indicate the judge had ex parte, pre-trial discussions with some individual or individuals regarding the circumstances and facts of the case. The trial judge should have recused herself and assigned some other judge to preside over this case.

Hendrix, 6 NICS App. at 9-10.

3. In *Monteau v. Monteau*, 5 Am. Tribal Law 26 (Confederated Salish and Kootenai Tribes Court of Appeals 2004), the court affirmed portions of a marriage dissolution order in which the wife's counsel had a past attorney-client relationship with the trial judge, but remanded others that might have been affected by the relationship:

> With the express requirement of disclosure on the record for appellate justices, it is reasonable to assume the Council intended the same requirement for trial judges. As a matter of law, the trial judge should have disclosed any facts that might reasonably lead a litigant to question his impartiality. . . . The fact that counsel for the wife had been his personal lawyer, in an action which also involved child custody, is such a fact.

While a past relationship must be disclosed, it does not automatically require a judge to disqualify himself. As persuasively argued by the wife, and as we noted in this action when refusing to disqualify Justice Hall, in small communities attorneys will often have professional relationships with other community leaders. Those relationships do not automatically disqualify a judge or justice. *See Cheney v. United States District Court*, 541 U.S. 913, 124 S. Ct. 1391, 158 L. Ed. 2d 225 (2004, Memorandum of Justice Scalia). Whether a particular relationship will require disqualification will depend upon the extent of the relationship and how recent in time. A decision not to disqualify is reviewed for an abuse of discretion. . . .

While we place a burden on the court to inform litigants and counsel of facts that may lead to questions of partiality, the burden of disclosure does not fall upon the judge alone, but also lies with counsel who knows of those facts. Counsel has a professional obligation of fairness to the opposing party and counsel. This would include disclosure of representation of the trial judge, except to the extent that such representation is a client confidence, *e.g.* information privileged under Rule 1.6 of the Rules of Professional Conduct. Counsel is also required as an officer of the court to disclose prior representation of the trial judge. A judge will not always be able to remember every fact that should be disclosed. Judges, too, can be forgetful. . . .

While there is a certain simplicity to the remedy of reinstating the judgment in effect at the time the disclosure should have been made and allowing the wife's motion to dismiss to be heard anew, that remedy serves neither party well. That remedy would require further proceedings in the trial court. Such proceedings are pointless if the court lacks jurisdiction as a matter of law. An appropriate remedy would be to leave in place those portions of the judge's decree and subsequent order that should be the same even if disclosure had been made and to remand only those portions where there might be a difference in result.

Monteau, 5 Am. Tribal Law at 31-32.

4. In *Henry v. After-Buffalo*, 4 Am. Tribal Law 184 (Confederated Tribes of the Grand Ronde Community Tribal Court 2003), the trial judge applied a "Rule of Necessity" in refusing to excuse herself from a matter at the request of one of the parties:

Setting aside any questions about the timeliness of the Motion and the fact that it is even less persuasive here than was the Motion denied in Pearsall, the Court concludes that the Motion lacks merit and sweeps far too broadly. This Tribal government has decided to hire, rather than elect or appoint its judges. Any judge hearing a case in this Court, or in the Tribe's Appellate Court, will be hired by the Council and paid to hear the case. If this Court and this Judge cannot hear this case, then no judge hired by the Council can. The Rule of Necessity thus allows the Court to hear the case, even assuming that there would otherwise be a conflict — a premise which the Court does not grant, but merely assumes for the sake of discussion. Plaintiffs' premise — that a judge hired by the Council cannot hear any case involving the Council or the Tribe — if accepted, would hamstring the Tribal Courts, and their contention amounts to a not particularly indirect attack on the Council's chosen method for obtaining and retaining judges, *viz.*, by contract.

Henry, 4 Am. Tribal Law at 187.

E. PROFESSIONAL RESPONSIBILITY FOR ATTORNEYS AND LAY ADVOCATES

IDM FINANCIAL, LLC v. NAPEAHI

Tulalip Tribal Court of Appeals, No. TUL-Ci-7/97-862,
5 NICS App. 78 (July 28, 1998)

Before: LARRY KING, Chief Justice; ROSE E. PURSER, Justice; CHARLES R. HOSTNIK, Justice.

HOSTNIK, J.:

The basic issue before this Court on appeal concerns the responsibility of unrepresented parties in tribal court proceedings. Neither of the parties to this proceeding was represented by an attorney or a spokesperson. It is a general notion that when unrepresented persons appear in any court, they are held to the standards of an attorney. They are to be familiar with the rules of the court and the procedures to be followed in handling cases before that particular court. . . .

IDM contends that the trial judge should have made the record more clear and forced it to answer the point blank question, "Do you want a continuance?" The trial judge discharged this responsibility when he asked IDM whether they were prepared to proceed on the countersuit, which was admittedly served on them as they walked into the courtroom on October 21, 1997. As pointed out by the Appellees, when the IDM representatives responded, "We would like to continue with our suit **first** . . ." that implies not only were they willing to proceed on the counterclaim, but they wanted to proceed on the suit as a whole. IDM contends that this is not what they meant, but only IDM knew that. It is therefore appropriately IDM's responsibility to clarify its position.

IDM indicates it had never been countersued previously. They thought that the court would conduct proceedings on the suit first, and then grant a continuance to conduct separate proceedings on the countersuit. The parties admit that the evidence on the suit and countersuit was intertwined. IDM was simply unfamiliar with normal court procedures in such circumstances. IDM chose to file suit in this Court. It is the responsibility of IDM to know the procedures and rules of the court in which it chose to file suit.

IDM is a corporation. A corporation cannot be represented pro se, but must have someone else represent it. Mr. Marzolf, when he appeared before the Tulalip Tribal Court representing IDM, was acting as its spokesperson. Part of being a spokesperson is the responsibility to be familiar with tribal laws and the rules and procedures of court.

Mr. Marzolf stated at oral argument that at the conclusion of the October 21 proceeding he was thoroughly confused as to what had transpired during the course of that proceeding. However, he did not indicate to the trial judge that he was confused, nor did he request clarification of whether another court date would be scheduled for the counterclaim. He simply left the courtroom. The trial judge reasonably relied upon IDM's assertion that it wanted to proceed with its case despite the fact it had just received the counterclaim. At no time did IDM request a continuance or another court date for testimony concerning the counterclaim, nor did IDM at any time indicate that it was unprepared to answer the allegations in the counterclaim. If IDM had requested a continuance, good cause certainly existed to grant such a request.

In certain situations, requiring parties appearing before a court to be held to the standards of any attorney or spokesperson may lead to harsh results. However, any other standard would create chaos in the court system and would require a judge to assist a party in presenting its case. Although a judge should take reasonable steps to insure that fair proceedings occur and to ensure that all parties have an opportunity to present their evidence, a judge cannot assist a party in presenting his or her case. The trial judge acted reasonably under the circumstances of this case and therefore, did not commit error.

Any Error was Harmless

Even if we assume that error was committed by the trial judge, such error was harmless. After extensive questioning by the appellate panel, IDM representatives indicated that if they had been allowed an opportunity to present evidence on the counterclaim, the only evidence they would have presented was the testimony of Detective Lee, and that the purpose of such testimony would be to show that the Defendants did not suffer any damages in this case. . . .

IDM has raised the claim that the trial judge acted inappropriately in allegedly giving legal advice to the Defendants at trial after the court had gone off the record. This allegation is based upon the transcript of October 14, 1997. At the end of that transcript the Defendants asked, "What do we do now?" The court replied, "Let's go off the record." Mr. Marzolf indicates that he left the courtroom at that point. He therefore does not know what was said by the trial judge to the Defendants, if anything. The Defendants indicate that the trial judge told them to seek legal advice. This is an entirely appropriate comment by the trial judge. IDM has no evidence, and no offer of proof upon which to base its assertion. There is no support in the record for that assertion by IDM. The Court therefore cannot find that this is a basis of error by the trial judge.

We therefore affirm the trial judge in all respects.

Chief Justice KING and Justice PURSER concur.

NOTES

1. In *In re Seanez*, No. SC-CV-58-10, 2010 WL 4182751 (Navajo Nation Supreme Court, Oct. 18, 2010), the court disbarred the chief legislative counsel for the Navajo Nation Council for gross misconduct:

   In legal opinions and memoranda that he issued as Chief Legislative Counsel to the Council, Mr. Seanez intentionally and knowingly advised the Council to act contrary to what he, a government practitioner of his experience, knows or ought to know to be law. He informed the Council that our holdings should not be followed, and presented his own arguments as the law that the Council must follow. Specifically, he dismissed our unambiguous holding that the People have ultimate authority to determine their governmental structure and amend all provisions that concern doctrines of separation of powers, checks and balances, accountability to the people, and service of the anti-corruption principle. *Shirley v. Morgan,* No. SC.CV-02-10, p. 25 (Nav. Sup. Ct. May 28, 2010), clarified in *Shirley v. Morgan, supra,* at 7 (Nav. Sup. Ct. July 16, 2010). In the face of our unambiguous holding, he persisted in advising the Council that they have "unquestioned" authority to amend Titles 2, 7 and 11 without restriction. This legal opinion of Mr. Seanez alone constitutes gross misconduct of a Navajo Nation Bar member.

In addition, in a legal memorandum to the Council, Mr. Seanez advised that the Court had no authority to invalidate the Navajo Government Development Act of 2007 and call for the reestablishment and re-funding of the Government Reform Commission. . . .

People as individuals will always have differing opinions regarding the application of various court holdings, regulations, policies and statutes. Such differences are a matter of free speech that this Court fully supports. However, we cannot and will not condone a government lawyer intentionally using his position to undermine the very foundation of a stable Navajo Nation government by providing justifications for unlawful conduct. There can be no doubt that Mr. Seanez knew, or should have known, that through his denial of this Court's authority he was facilitating the breaking of Navajo Nation laws.

Id., 2010 WL 4182751, at *3-5.

2. In *Feltman v. Muckleshoot Tribe of Indians*, 5 NICS App. 101 (Muckleshoot Tribal Court of Appeals 1999), the court reversed a trial court order disqualifying appellant's attorney because the attorney was a contract judge for the Northwest Intertribal Court System:

For many years, NICS has been able to provide high quality judicial services to its member tribes precisely because attorneys in the private practice of law have been generous with their time and talent on an hourly basis. Mr. Hostnik is one of a number of such practitioners, most of whom provide their services to NICS at a rate far below their usual hourly rate charged for providing legal services in a non-tribal setting.

The practical implication of upholding the trial court's disqualification of Mr. Hostnik would be to disqualify each and every other attorney who provides occasional, part-time judicial services to NICS from appearing as an advocate in any tribal court system that contracts with NICS for trial or appellate services. (Washington State Bar Association Ethics Opinion 160). We find that such an extreme remedy for a perceived appearance of a conflict of interest to be both unwarranted and unwise. . . .

The impractical and excessive nature of the remedy fashioned in the court below can best be viewed through analogy to a situation that could easily arise in the state court system. Would an attorney from the firm of Garvey, Schubert & Barer who took a seat on the trial or appellate court bench of the state have an inherent or perceived conflict in later hearing a case in which that firm represented one of the litigants? We think not. To hold NICS to a higher and more onerous standard for the practicing attorneys who serve as part-time judges at NICS would be, in our view, both unjust and unwise. The proper course of conduct in each case is disclosure, not disqualification. . . .

With respect to the Appellee's concern that a previous decision authored by Mr. Hostnik in his capacity as a NICS judge in *Hoopa Valley Indian Housing*

Authority v. Gerstner could be a precedent in this case at hand, we find no conflict. The various judges who serve on appellate panels for NICS are an intellectually vigorous and independent-minded group of individuals. . . .

Feltman, 5 NICS App. at 103-04.

3. In *In the matter of Robertson*, 4 NICS App. 111 (Hoopa Valley Tribal Court of Appeals (1996), the court held that the tribal court has statutory authority to regulate the conduct of attorneys and non-attorneys within the reservation but outside of the tribal court:

> The Ethics Code is clearly intended to be broadly construed to regulate the conduct of those practicing law on the Hoopa Valley reservation or otherwise within the jurisdiction of the Hoopa Valley Tribal Court:
>
> > The purpose of this Ordinance is to exercise comprehensive Tribal regulatory authority over the ethical conduct of spokespersons and attorneys practicing within the jurisdiction of the Hoopa Valley Tribal Court, as set forth below.
>
> Ordinance No. 1-94, p. 2, §32.0.2. Dario Robertson is clearly an "attorney" as that word is defined by the Ethics Code. *See* Ordinance No. 1-94, p. 4, §32.4.1.
> . . . As soon as an attorney accepts a case on the reservation, and practices law in any capacity, he is subject to the Ethics Code. . . .

Robertson, 4 NICS App. at 115-16.

F. CERTAIN PROCEDURE DOCTRINES UNDER TRIBAL LAW

1. STATUTES OF LIMITATIONS

BUGENIG V. HOOPA VALLEY TRIBE

Hoopa Valley Tribal Court of Appeals, No. A-02-007, 7 NICS App. 72 (September 13, 2005)

Before: FRED GABOURIE, Chief Justice; ROBERT MILLER, Justice; and LAWRENCE WATTERS, Justice.

Per curiam. . . .

This matter came before the Hoopa Valley Tribal Court of Appeals pursuant to Appellant's November 6, 2002 Notice of Appeal from a Decision and Order of the Hoopa Valley Tribal Court entered on October 22, 2002. Appellant challenges the Hoopa Valley Tribal Court's dismissal of her claims based on the statute of limitations. Following a series of continuances requested by the parties to facilitate settlement negotiations, oral argument was heard on June 13, 2005. We affirm the judgment of the Hoopa Valley Tribal Court. . . .

We review the record before us and in doing so, note the prior decision involving the same parties in *Bugenig v. Hoopa Valley Tribe*, 266 F.3d 1201 (9th Cir. 2001) (en banc), *cert. denied*, 535 U.S. 927 (2002). Appellant contests a decision of the Hoopa Valley Tribal Court that dismissed her claims related to the use of her property. The Tribal Court determined the claims were barred by the statute of limitations and held they arose many years earlier when she attempted to harvest timber on the property. She argues in this Court that the claims did not originate until 2002 when she again sought to harvest timber on the same property and thus, the Tribal Court erred in dismissing her administrative appeal and complaint as time barred.

The starting point in the analysis of the issues is the Tribe's adoption of its timber harvesting plan on January 28, 1995 after providing for public notice and comment. The plan included measures to protect specific sites of cultural significance to the Tribe that were formulated in cooperation with the Bureau of Indian Affairs (BIA) and the State of California under Sec. 106 of the National Historic Preservation Act. The plan established a one-half mile buffer zone, where timber harvesting was not permitted, around the White Deerskin Dance Ground. The White Deerskin Dance Ground is part of a trail that winds through the Hoopa Valley Reservation and along a portion of it known as Bald Hill. The ban on harvesting timber applied to "tribal trust land, trust allotments, and fee land within the 1/2 mile buffer." Decision of Hoopa Valley Tribal Council: Alternative for FY 1995 Timber Sale Program (Jan. 28, 1995).

The White Deerskin Dance is of significant cultural and historical importance to the Tribe. Byron Nelson, Jr., *OUR HOME FOREVER: The Hupa Indians of Northern California* (1978). The Tribe describes the dance as part of its traditional ceremonies for "world renewal." The Tribe also considers the Bald Hill dance site the most important one it has: "[T]he site is very ancient. There's scientific evidence that indicates that it could be one of the oldest dance sites, oldest ceremonies in the country."

Appellant acquired her property, located on Bald Hill inside the buffer zone within the exterior boundaries of the Hoopa Valley Reservation, with a deed recorded on June 1, 1995. She then applied to the California Department of Forestry and the County of Humboldt for a "timberland conversion" to alter some 2.5 acres of the land from timber to pasture. The State granted the permit and she applied to the Tribe for approval to haul the logs over Reservation land. The Tribe denied the request but she nevertheless sent it a check to cover the hauling fee on July 24, 1995. The Tribe returned the check to her along with a letter on July 28, 1995 explaining that within the designated area, "ONLY the Hoopa Valley Tribal Council has the authority to make land use changes."

[The Tribe's authority to enjoin Bugenig's activities was affirmed by the Ninth Circuit in *Bugenig v. Hoopa Valley Tribe*, 266 F.3d 1201 (9th Cir. 2001) (en banc), *cert. denied*, 535 U.S. 927 (2002).]

Appellant again sought approval to harvest timber on the property in another application in 2002. The Tribe's Forestry Department denied it. She then filed an administrative appeal and complaint for damages in the Hoopa Valley Tribal Court on July 3, 2002. The Tribal Court determined the claims were barred by the statute of limitations that applies to civil actions. Decision and Order, at 6 (Oct. 22, 2002). The Court also stated that "the claim presented here was, or should have been, presented to the Tribal Court in the earlier action." *Id.* at 5. Appellant thereafter filed the instant appeal. . . .

The Hoopa Valley Tribal Code sec. 2.3.13 (Limitations) provides that "[N]o Complaint shall be filed in a civil action unless the events shall have occurred within a three year period prior to the date of the complaint." Appellant contends that she meets this standard because the Tribe's Forestry Department denied her application for timber harvest activities on June 4, 2002 and subsequently, her administrative appeal and complaint, alleging a taking, was filed on July 3, 2002. The Tribal Court, in rejecting this position, decided that "[t]he events giving rise to plaintiff's claim of taking occurred on January 28, 1995, when the buffer zone was adopted." Decision and Order, at 6 (Oct. 22, 2002).

In our review, we turn to the Tribe's timber harvest plan which specified the buffer zone and included as one of its goals "to protect cultural and religious resources within the proposed sale area." . . .

Accordingly, the plan prohibited timber harvesting in the area of the White Deerskin Dance Trail and the buffer zone surrounding it. The Tribe decided to protect the site and provided the public with notice and the opportunity to comment. Copies of the text were sent to the property owners in the Bald Hill area and this included Appellant's predecessors in interest.

In its order of dismissal, the Tribal Court also held that the "[p]laintiff knew that Tribal law prohibited cutting of trees on her property by July 11, 1996 [the date of the permanent injunction], if not earlier." Decision and Order, at 6 (Oct. 22, 2002).

The record before us underscores this conclusion. The chronology indicates as follows:

The Tribe's timber harvest plan was promulgated on January 28, 1995;

the Tribal Council denied Appellant's application for a permit to haul cut logs from her property on June 19, 1995;

the Tribe reiterated its position in a "Cease and Desist Notice" issued on July 28, 1995 stating that timber harvesting was not permitted ("YOU ARE HEREBY NOTIFIED not to proceed with your project . . .");

the Tribe filed a complaint on August 3, 1995 for "a permanent injunction . . . barring timber operations" on the property;

the Tribe obtained a temporary restraining order on August 10, 1995 and a preliminary injunction on August 15, 1995 to halt Appellant's activities;

the Tribe sent another letter to Appellant on August 21, 1995 stating that cutting timber was not allowed ("This prohibition of activity within the buffer zone remains in effect.");

the California Department of Forestry revoked its earlier administrative approval of the conversion exemption in letters to Appellant dated October 10, 1995 and October 15, 1995 and informed Appellant in the second one that the "Conversion Exemption is not in compliance with the [state] forest practice rules specifically 1104.1a(2)1. Under this subsection, no timber operations are allowed on significant historical or archaeological sites";

Appellant visited the Tribe's Forestry Office in 1995 and was specifically informed that no timber harvesting was permitted in the area;

the Tribal Court issued its permanent injunction on July 11, 1996 "barring logging activities in the buffer no-cut-zone"; and

the Tribe then initiated further proceedings in which Appellant was held in contempt for violating the protection measures on October 24, 1996.

Under these circumstances, it is clear that the gravamen of Appellant's claims arose from her attempt to harvest trees in the buffer zone in 1995 and 1996. The Hoopa Valley Tribal Court's application of the three year statute of limitations was therefore correct in holding "Plaintiff knew that tribal law prohibited cutting of trees on her property by July 11, 1996 [the date of the permanent injunction], if not earlier." Decision and Order, at 6 (Oct. 22, 2002). . . .

Appellant's argument that she did not have a claim until filing another application for timber harvest activities in 2002 is without merit. The statute of limitations is not evaded by simply filing a new application for the same activities, on the same property with the same restrictions that were in place seven years earlier.

Appellant's further suggestion that the Hoopa Valley Tribal Court's injunction in 1996 allowed for timber harvesting on the property also does not square with the plain language in the notice of the buffer zone and the vigorous efforts of the Tribe to protect the area in question in litigation over the past decade and in cooperation with other agencies. In quoting portions of the order, Appellant has mistakenly interpreted the Tribal Court's decision and erroneously emphasized both a section of the notice provided the property owners in the area at the time the timber harvest plan was formulated and the Court's mandate to the appellant requiring clean-up at the site under the supervision of the Tribe's Forestry Department. . . .

NOTE

In *Little Traverse Bay Bands of Odawa Indians v. Harrington*, 2009 WL 3378173 (Little Traverse Bay Bands of Odawa Indians Tribal Appellate Court 2009), the court concluded that the Bands' complaint for contract breach must be dismissed for failure to prosecute, reversing a trial court order granting the Bands an additional 30 days to file an amended complaint:

[T]he Appellate Court believes that the threshold issue before us is whether the case should be dismissed for failure to prosecute by LTBB. This case has languished for over six years in the Tribal Court with no resolution. . . .

In general, courts have the inherent power to dismiss an action with prejudice if there has been a failure to prosecute the case within a reasonable amount of time. . . . [R]ather than grant LTBB an additional 30 days in which to file an amended complaint, we believe that the entire case should be dismissed for failure to prosecute.

. . . There is no evidence in the record of any filing by LTBB between the Tribal Court hearing on March 7, 2003, and October 2, 2007, when Judge Sekaquaptewa issued her order.

Harrington, 2009 WL 3378173, at 2-3.

2. ATTORNEY FEES

Neff v. Port Susan Camping Club

Tulalip Tribal Court of Appeals, No. TUL-CV-GC-2005-0368,
9 NICS App. 55 (May 29, 2008)

Before: Jane Smith, Chief Justice; Robert Anderson, Justice; Douglas Nash, Justice.

Anderson, J.:

[In previous appeals, the court had held that the Port Susan Camping Club, a private association, had good cause to terminate the member of Paul and Joan Neff. *See Neff v. Port Susan Camping Club*, 7 NICS App. 138 (Tulalip Tribal Court of Appeals 2006); *Neff v. Port Susan Camping Club*, 8 NICS App. 32 (Tulalip Tribal Court of Appeals 2007). The third appeal involved whether the private association was entitled to attorney fees.]

Attorneys Fees

Under Washington law attorney's fees may be awarded only when authorized by private agreement, a statute, or a recognized ground of equity. . . . The relationship between Neff and Port Susan is contractual. . . . Port Susan's bylaws, a part of this contract, contained a provision requiring that "any member" reimburse Port Susan for all legal expenses including attorney fees if Port Susan was the successful party in a legal dispute with that member. Contractual agreements on costs and attorney's fees are governed by RCW 4.84.330, which provides in relevant part:

> In any action on a contract or lease entered into after September 21, 1977, where such contract or lease specifically provides that attorney's fees and costs, which are incurred to enforce the provisions of such contract or lease, shall be awarded to one of the parties, the prevailing party, whether he is the party specified in the contract or lease or not, shall be entitled to reasonable attorney's fees in addition to costs and necessary disbursements.

Here, the parties have raised two main issues regarding the interpretation of this statute. The first issue is whether the action brought by Neff constitutes "an[ ] action on a contract" under RCW 4.84.330. The second issue is whether the Court should apply the "affirmative judgment rule" or the "proportionality rule" to determine which party is the "prevailing party" for the purposes of awarding attorney's fees under RCW 4.84.330.

RCW 4.84.330 governs when "any action [is brought] on a contract" to enforce an attorney's fees provision of that contract. For the purposes of this statute, an action is brought "on a contract" "when the action ar[ises] out of the contract and the contract is central to the dispute." . . . Neff's claim in this case was that Port Susan wrongfully terminated his membership and sought reinstatement. The litigation was about the meaning and effect of the contractual relationship between Neff and Port Susan such that the litigation satisfies the statutory requirement that it be and action brought on a contract.

Neff argues, however, that the trial court erred in granting Port Susan attorney's fees because Port Susan's bylaws only allow for fees to be assessed against its members. Neff contends since he was no longer a member of Port Susan when he instituted this lawsuit he should not be subject to the attorney's fees provision. This argument fails on the merits. Under RCW 4.84.330 it is irrelevant whether Neff was or was not a member of Port Susan at the commencement of this action. To establish if this action was "an action under a contract" the Court need only establish that two criteria are satisfied. First that the action arose out of a contract between Neff and Port Susan and second that the given contract is central to this dispute. . . . Both of these requirements are satisfied here. Neff commenced this action to reverse the termination of his membership rights which were governed by Port Susan's Charter and Bylaws and the enforcement of Neff's membership was the central issue to this dispute.

Under RCW 4.84.330, when an action is brought on a contract, the attorney's fees incurred to enforce that contract "shall be awarded to . . . the prevailing party." RCW 4.84.330. The statute defines a "prevailing party" as "the party [in] whose favor final judgment is rendered." RCW 4.84.330. The Washington Supreme Court held "for purposes of attorney fee awards, 'prevailing party' is generally one who received affirmative judgment in his or her favor." *Riss v. Angel*, 131 Wash. 2d 612, 633, 934 P.2d 669 (1997). . . .

Here, Neff contends the affirmative judgment rule, which is generally applied by Washington courts, is inappropriate to determine the allocation of attorney's fees in this case. He argues the Court should instead apply the "proportionality rule" created in *Marassi v. Lau*, 71 Wn. App. 912, 859 P.2d 605 (1993). . . . Under this approach, the defendant is awarded attorney fees for those claims it successfully defends, and the plaintiff is awarded attorney fees for the claims it prevails upon and these awards are then offset.

The proportionality rule applied in *Marassi* is not appropriate here. Unlike *Marassi*, where the plaintiff brought 12 "distinct and severable claims," there was only one distinct issue in this case: whether Port Susan correctly followed its Charter and Bylaws when terminating Neff's membership. . . . "A party need not recover its entire claim in order to be considered the prevailing party," but must have "substantially prevailed" on that claim to be entitled to attorneys fees. . . . Given that there was only one distinct claim in this litigation, and Port Susan substantially prevailed on this claim, the affirmative judgment rule is appropriate. Therefore, Port Susan is the "prevailing party" for the purposes of RCW 4.84.330. . . .

NOTE

In *Laban v. Yu Weh Loo Pah Ki Community*, 4 Am. Tribal Law 449 (Hopi Tribe Appellate Court 2003), the court denied attorney fees to the prevailing party under tribal statute on grounds that the attorney for the prevailing party did not move for attorney fees in a timely fashion:

H.I.R.C.C.P. Rule 25(e) provides for attorneys fees as follows:

> The court shall not award attorneys fees unless such have been specifically provided for by a contract . . . or unless it reasonably appears that the case has been prosecuted for purposes of harassment only, or that there was no

reasonable expectation of success on the party of the affirmatively claiming party.

The factual basis for an award of attorney's fees is subject to the clearly erroneous standard of review. . . .

There was no contract for attorney's fees between the parties, therefore the first prong of Rule 25(e) is inapplicable. Whether the Appellants provided the Appellees with due process, specifically a hearing on their termination, was a genuine issue in dispute. Thus, it was not clearly erroneous for the trial court to find that the Appellees' suit was not brought for harassment purposes only.

While the Appellant enjoys sovereign immunity from suits for damages, it nonetheless is subject to suits for injunctive relief pursuant to Hopi Resolution H-62-90. The Appellees amended their complaint seeking injunctive relief only. Therefore, the trial court's determination that the Appellees had a reasonable expectation of success on their due process claim was not clearly erroneous.

Laban, 4 Am. Tribal Law at 454.

3. ENFORCEMENT OF FOREIGN JUDGMENTS AND ORDERS

CROSS-JURISDICTIONAL RECOGNITION AND ENFORCEMENT OF JUDGMENTS:
A TRIBAL COURT PERSPECTIVE

Stacy L. Leeds, 76 N.D. L. Rev. 311, 349-58 (2000)

[Professor and tribal judge Leeds conducted an empirical study of the recognition and enforcement of tribal court judgments and orders by state courts.]

. . . Fifty-six percent of the respondent judges report at least one occasion in which another jurisdiction refused to recognize their tribal court orders, often in direct violation of state policy or federal law. Of those tribes indicating non-recognition, eighty percent report that their difficulties arose in a state forum, and twenty percent report problems with other tribal courts.

But the most striking result of the study is the extent to which states fail to recognize tribal court judgments even when required by federal law to do so. Of the respondents indicating that a state court has failed to recognize an order of their tribal court, over forty percent involved subject matters covered by the federal full faith and credit mandates of Violence Against Women Act and the Child Support Orders Act. Roughly one-third of the total reported instances of non-recognition involved custody disputes between parents. Twenty-seven percent of the courts that reported instances of non-recognition involved domestic violence orders after the enactment of Violence Against Women Act. The remaining instances of non-recognition cover a broad range of subject matter from state agencies refusing to recognize tribal court orders for purposes of vital statistics records to money judgments in consumer debt cases.

The standardized survey was designed to gather general information about tribal courts and their experiences with cross-jurisdictional recognition and enforcement of judgments. From the responses, the subject matter areas of child support, domestic violence protection and child custody were specifically targeted for more thorough analysis. These subject areas are extended full faith and credit by federal law and therefore provide the backdrop for determining state compliance with federal mandates. Respondent tribal judges highlighted the specific cases I discuss below, most of which are unreported. These specific instances of non-recognition provide a glimpse of the practical realities faced by tribal courts.

1. Child Support Orders — The Duckwater Shoshone Courts and the States of Utah and Nevada

The federal full faith and credit mandate for child support orders unambiguously includes tribal court orders:

The appropriate authorities of each State shall enforce according to its terms a child support order made consistently with this section by a court of another State. . . . "State" means a State of the United Sates, the District of Columbia, the Commonwealth of Puerto Rico, the territories and possessions of the United States, and Indian country. [28 U.S.C. §1738B.]

Yet a policy directive prepared by the State of Utah Department of Human Services, and still in use, blatantly violates the federal mandate on child support orders by including in its regulations, the following instruction to case workers: "Do not enforce a tribal court order on or off the reservation."

In 1990, the Duckwater Shoshone Court of Indian Offenses issued an order requiring child support payments. The State of Nevada later became involved by assisting the mother in her child support collection efforts against the father, who is incarcerated by the State of Utah. Nevada asked for assistance from Utah's child support enforcement agencies, but failed. Utah's child support enforcement agency closed their collection case because a tribal court issued the original order.

Upon notification that Utah refused to enforce the order, the Chief Judge of the Duckwater Shoshone Tribal and Juvenile Courts contacted officials in Utah and Nevada, providing detailed information about the Duckwater Shoshone Judicial System and reminding Utah of the federal full faith and credit mandate requiring enforcement. He also informed the U.S. Attorney's office of the state of Utah's failure to enforce pursuant to federal law. To date, Utah officials have not re-opened the case and assisted Nevada with collections. The U.S. Attorney for the District of Utah has taken no action.

The policy that justified Utah's refusal to enforce the order has not been updated since October 1992. Congress enacted the Child Support Orders Act federal mandate for nation-wide child support enforcement, including tribal court orders, in 1994. Years later, Utah has not updated its agency procedures to reflect the change in federal law, and federal agencies will not force compliance.

Again, the practical effects of non-enforcement of tribal court child support orders frustrate many policy directives. In this case, there are parental assets in Utah owed to a child in Nevada that the child must do without because of state intransigence. Interestingly, this is not due to the mother relocating to another state. Even if she currently resided in Utah, she would not receive state enforcement assistance to recover the child's money against the father. The policy mandates of the Child Support Orders Act seek to eliminate collection problems by "facilitat[ing] enforcement of child support order[s]" in order to provide greater financial stability for children. The Child Support Orders Act's policy has been circumvented, quite simply, as the Chief Judge of the Duckwater Shoshone puts it, because "Utah state agencies . . . do not abide by federal law."

2. Domestic Violence Protection Orders — The Mashantucket Pequot Tribe and State of Connecticut.

The Mashantucket Pequot tribal court entered a domestic violence protective order instructing an individual I will call Jack, to refrain from threatening or causing bodily harm to an individual I will call Jane. Jane alleges that Jack violated the order by attacking her within the jurisdiction of the State of Connecticut.

In this situation, federal law requires Connecticut to accord the Mashantucket Pequot protection order full faith and credit and enforce the order as if it were an order issued by a Connecticut court. The Connecticut criminal statutes, however, do not clearly accommodate this federal mandate, and appear to prevent effective cross-jurisdictional enforcement of orders. Connecticut law defines the crime of violation of a protective order as violations of an order issued pursuant to Connecticut law. Connecticut's family law statutes reference the Violence Against Women Act and direct that Connecticut protective orders are to be enforced in all other jurisdictions, but include no procedures for Connecticut to provide the same treatment to orders of other jurisdictions. In this instance, the failure to recognize foreign judgments does not single out tribal court orders for special disregard, but treats all foreign judgments similarly.

This non-enforcement leading to failure to prosecute for criminal violation of a standing protective order is of particular importance in situations of violence against Indian women because of a reprehensible gap in criminal jurisdiction for these types of crimes. Federal law divests tribes of criminal jurisdiction over non-Indians and, at times, over non-member Indians even when the perpetrator is a resident of the reservation. Federal jurisdiction of crimes within Indian country is limited to specific enumerated crimes, and does not include misdemeanor violations of protective orders. The lack of comprehensive criminal jurisdiction in Indian country means the majority of batterers who violate protective orders are subject to no prosecution at all, particularly if state criminal statutes narrowly define violations of protective orders so as to preclude prosecution. Although Indian women are more likely to experience domestic violence than any other category of citizens, they are not receiving the protection envisioned in Violence Against Women Act.

The Violence Against Women Act presents other practical problems in terms of notice, often requiring an individual to obtain two protective orders, one from a tribal court and one from a state court. The Iowa Tribe of Oklahoma and the Kickapoo Tribe of Oklahoma experienced this problem when attempting to provide notice of protection orders to state law enforcement officials in Oklahoma, where no electronic database or other registration procedures are available to tribal courts. Judges from both tribes indicate that when domestic violence victims present tribal orders to state law enforcement officials, they are routinely told that they must also obtain a state order because the state officials can "do nothing" with the tribal order. Some tribal court judges counsel individuals who are granted a tribal court protective order to also seek a state order in order to minimize potential problems.

3. Child Custody and Placement

Custody proceedings involving Indian children fall into two distinct categories for purposes of recognition, depending on who is seeking custody. Custody battles between parents are outside the scope of the Indian Child Welfare Act, which carries a federal full faith and credit mandate. Custody battles between parents are governed by the Child Custody Agreement and the Parental Kidnapping Prevention Act, but neither expressly include tribal court proceedings within its scope.

a. Indian Child Welfare Proceedings: The Ho-Chunk Nation and State of Oklahoma

The Indian Child Welfare Act directs state, federal and tribal courts to recognize a tribal court order concerning custody of an Indian child[.]

The United States, every State, every territory or possession of the United States, and every Indian tribe shall give full faith and credit to the public acts, records, and judicial proceedings of any Indian tribe applicable to Indian child custody proceedings to the same extent that such entities give full faith and credit to the public acts, records, and judicial proceedings of any other entity. [25 U.S.C. §1911(d).]

This clear federal mandate applies particularly in instances where the child is a ward of the tribal court, as in the following pending Ho-Chunk proceeding.

In late summer, 1998, on a petition of the tribe's child and family service officials, the Ho-Chunk Nation Tribal Court made a family of Indian children wards of the court. The court then entered an order placing the children in foster care. At the time the children were removed from the physical custody of their natural mother, they were spending the summer in the Ho-Chunk Nation and planning a return to Oklahoma, where they would be in the custody of their natural father during the school year. This custody arrangement had been established in a previous custody order entered by an Oklahoma court.

At summer's end, the mother could not return the children to Oklahoma because they were in the legal custody of the Ho-Chunk Nation. Oklahoma issued a warrant for the mother's arrest under a state kidnapping statute for her failure to comply with the Oklahoma custody order, and she was subsequently arrested by Wisconsin state officials and extradited to Oklahoma. She spent approximately three months in jail prior to a pretrial release. Her felony jury trial was scheduled in Ottawa County, Oklahoma for the fall of 1999. On the day of the jury trial, the judge dismissed the case sua sponte as moot, because the children had then been returned to their father. The state court judge never addressed the existence of the Ho-Chunk order to the Ho-Chunk nation's assumption of jurisdiction over the children. In the year since the warrant was issued, neither the prosecutor nor the district court judge in Oklahoma had made any effort to communicate with the tribal court.

b. Divorce Proceedings: The Southern Ute Tribe and Washington State

The type of scenario described in the introduction, when an unsatisfied parent in a divorce proceedings physically removes a child from one jurisdiction to another to avoid further tribal court rulings, is perhaps the most complicated issue presented in the area of recognition and enforcement. The Southern Ute Tribe, along with four other respondents to this study, report similar experiences. In no other area of law is recognition of judgments across jurisdictions more unpredictable, or more dangerous to children.

The Parental Kidnapping Prevention Act [28 U.S.C. §1738B] was intended to reduce cross-jurisdictional conflict in parental custody disputes. Although the Parental Kidnapping Prevention Act was enacted two years after the Indian Child Welfare Act, which specifically mandated full faith and credit for tribal court orders, it is silent as to tribes. The Parental Kidnapping Prevention Act's definition of "State," makes no reference to "Indian country" as do later laws such as the Child Support Orders Act or the Violence Against Women Act. The Parental Kidnapping Prevention Act language mirrors the full faith and credit implementing statute (28 U.S.C. §1738) and raises the same question of whether tribes should be considered "territories or possessions." The Fourth Circuit has classified tribes as "territories" for Parental Kidnapping Prevention Act purposes in an opinion reminiscent of Mackey, although without reference thereto. [*In re Larch*, 872 F.2d 66 (4th Cir. 1989).] At least one reported tribal court decision agrees with the Fourth Circuit interpretation. [*Eberhard v. Eberhard*, 24 Indian L. Rep. 6059, 6063-6064 (Chy. R. Sx. Ct. App. Feb. 18, 1997).] This statutory silence creates two kinds of problems: (1) whether the states must recognize tribal child custody orders; and (2) whether the tribes must recognize the orders of state courts or other tribal courts as final.

In addition to uncertainty surrounding the Parental Kidnapping Prevention Act's scope of applicability, conflicting interpretations of tribal court jurisdiction over divorce proceedings involving non-Indians also create problems. Even if the Parental Kidnapping Prevention Act expressly included tribes within its definition of "States," the outcome of many of these divorce cases would not change.

Revisiting the Southern Ute–Washington scenario is illustrative. According to the tribal court record, Susan C. initiated the proceedings and the tribal court had personal and subject matter jurisdiction. This should have foreclosed collateral review. Instead, the state court framed the issue as follows: Will a tribe's exercise of jurisdiction in a divorce proceeding between a reservation Indian and a non-Indian residing off the reservation preclude collateral attack in state court? The answer is unclear. The only clear pronouncement regarding tribal court jurisdiction in divorce proceedings is that exclusive jurisdiction lies with the tribe only when both parties are tribal members and domiciled within Indian country. When non-Indians are involved, state courts have at least concurrent jurisdiction, and results could differ depending on jurisdiction. If states adopt narrow views of tribal jurisdiction over the divorce proceeding and ancillary custody determinations, as Washington did in the Susan C. scenario, even an amendment to the general full faith and credit statute unequivocally including tribes (an unlikely political development) will not put an end to the problem. The only solution is to include tribes within the parameter of the Parental Kidnapping Prevention Act and the Child Custody Act as equal partners with the states in terms of jurisdiction.

NOTES

1. The Michigan Supreme Court has adopted a reciprocal comity rule for the enforcement of tribal court judgments:

> (A) The judgments decrees, orders, warrants, subpoenas, records, and other judicial acts of a tribal court of a federally recognized Indian tribe are recognized, and have the same effect and are subject to the same procedures, defenses, and proceedings as judgments, decrees, orders, warrants, subpoenas, records, and other judicial acts of any court of record in this state, subject to the provisions of this rule.
>
> (B) The recognition described in subrule (A) applies only if the tribe or tribal court
>
>> (1) enacts an ordinance, court rule, or other binding measure that obligates the tribal court to enforce the judgments, decrees, orders, warrants, subpoenas, records, and judicial acts of the courts of this state, and
>> (2) transmits the ordinance, court rule or other measure to the State Court Administrative Office. The State Court Administrative Office shall make available to state courts the material received pursuant to paragraph (B)(1).
>
> (C) A judgment, decree, order, warrant, subpoena, record, or other judicial act of a tribal court of a federally recognized Indian tribe that has taken the actions described in subrule (B) is presumed to be valid. To overcome that presumption, an objecting party must demonstrate that
>
>> (1) the tribal court lacked personal or subject-matter jurisdiction, or
>> (2) the judgment, decree, order, warrant, subpoena, record, or other judicial act of the tribal court
>
>>> (a) was obtained by fraud, duress, or coercion,
>>> (b) was obtained without fair notice or a fair hearing,
>>> (c) is repugnant to the public policy of the State of Michigan, or
>>> (d) is not final under the laws and procedures of the tribal court.
>
> (D) This rule does not apply to judgments or orders that federal law requires be given full faith and credit.

MICH. CT. R. 2.615.

2. In *Broad v. Plagens*, 8 Am. Tribal Law 191 (Grand Traverse Band of Ottawa and Chippewa Indians Tribal Court 2009), the court held that a request to enforce a foreign money judgment under Rule 2.615 amounted to a request to garnish the judgment debtor's tribal per capita payments, adopting a rule recommended by the tribal government as amicus:

> The remaining issue is whether the Tribal Court has authority to order withholding from per capita as part of the procedure for recognition of a foreign judgment. Recognition of a foreign judgment means that this Court will give that judgment full faith and credit, and will issue orders to enforce it as

required under Chapter 10 of the GTB Court Rules [tribal equivalent to Michigan Court Rule 2.615]. Garnishment, on the other hand, is but one of many collection tools available to a judgment creditor (such as execution, repossession, etc.). A careful review of Chapter 10 provides no provision or authority for the automatic garnishment/withholding from per capita proceeds upon recognition. Rather, the stated goal of Chapter 10 is to recognize the foreign judgment and to give it full faith and credit under the laws of the Grand Traverse Band of Ottawa and Chippewa Indians. Garnishment or per capita withholding is not a necessary result following recognition of a foreign judgment. Other remedies are also available to a petitioner/judgment creditor once the judgment is recognized. A petitioner/judgment creditor may utilize any collection measures which would go along with that recognition that are authorized by law.

. . . As noted above, the Notice of Opportunity to Object generated by the Court puts the respondent/judgment debtor on notice that his/her per capita distribution will be forwarded to the judgment creditor in the amount of the judgment. This Court has often received objections to foreign judgments on the basis of the withholding, as opposed to challenging the validity of the foreign judgment, thus it appears clear that respondents/judgment debtors frequently understand the implications of the notice. When timely objections are received from judgment debtors, the matters are scheduled for a hearing, and the respondent/judgment debtor is given notice and an opportunity to be heard. Therefore, although the forms issued by the Tribal Court should be modified to make it more clear to the respondent/judgment debtor that his/her per capita distribution may be subject to withholding as part of the foreign judgment proceeding, this Court is satisfied that the public is aware of the potential for per capita withholding given how long the procedure has been in place, and the respondents/judgment debtors are put on notice in the paperwork they receive as well. Therefore, the Court finds no due process violations in the procedure used by the Court.

Broad, 8 Am. Tribal Law at 199.

4. DEFAULT JUDGMENTS

ARQUETTE V. PARK PLACE ENTERTAINMENT CORP.

St. Regis Mohawk Tribal Court, No. 00CI0133 (March 20, 2001)

. . .

Findings of Facts and Law

A. Standard for Default Judgment

The St. Regis Mohawk Tribe Rules of Civil Procedure are very clear about the standard to be used for default judgment. Rule 10 states:

If the defendant files an answer to the complaint at or before the time that the motion is to be argued to the Judge, no default judgment shall be granted, and the matter shall proceed as though answered on time. **If the defendant does not answer by that time, a default judgment *shall* be entered.**

In granting a default judgment, the Judge *may* refuse to grant relief requested by plaintiff if granting the relief would be contrary to tribal law or would be unjust. The judge may not grant plaintiff greater relief on default than was requested in the complaint. (Emphasis added. . . .)

A default judgment is a tool used by this Court to prevent parties from deliberately dragging out cases and clogging the courts calendar. Although there is an inherent tension between the ability of a Court to maintain control of its calendar and the right of a litigant to be heard, the default judgment is a necessary tool to prevent parties using a flagrant disregard for tribal justice and deliberately failing to appear in Court. In this suit, the Defendants never filed an answer or appeared before the Court and Rule 10 makes it very clear that the Court must grant a default judgment, unless one of the two exceptions are present.

The Court takes this opportunity to make a few points. Throughout this case, the Defendants have had numerous opportunities to file an answer or make an appearance before the Court. A perusal of the record illustrates that at least four pretrial conferences or hearings have been held and numerous motions and notices have been served upon each Defendant. Moreover, it is clear Defendants Park Place and Clive Cummins are very aware of this hearing as they are seeking an injunction in federal court to halt the Tribal Court proceedings. The Court has done everything within its power to protect and respect the Defendants' rights. Nonetheless, they have failed to present themselves before the Court, attack the complaint and prevent a default judgment. Clearly, their failure to appear and answer the claims within the complaint is willful and wanton disregard of this Court and its authority. Such disregard is not taken lightly, and their actions force the Court to consider a default judgment.

Critics of the Court may judge the Court harshly if the Court grants the Plaintiffs' motion for default judgment and awards the requested damages. Those critics need to realize that the Court is bound by the law not political rhetoric. And this Court will not succumb to the political pressure that has been present throughout this case. Any blaming or finger pointing should be directed at the Defendants who will have no one to blame for a default judgment but themselves. It was their choice to refuse to appear before the Court and as a result must risk the consequences. Accordingly, as the Court has previously granted an Entry of Default and it will now use the standard delineated by tribal law to assess the default judgment.

B. The Plaintiffs' Requested Relief

In the complaint and the default judgment hearing held on February 20, 2001, the Plaintiffs requested four forms of relief; equitable relief or a finding that the casino management contract between Defendants Park Place, Clive Cummins and Defendants Ransom, Smoke, and Thompson is null and void and unenforceable; actual damages in the amount $1.782 billion; attorney costs; and punitive damages as the Court sees fit.

1. The Park Place Management Contract

A default based upon well-pleaded allegations in a complaint establishes a defendant's liability. . . . If the Court is presented with a well-pleaded complaint, then the facts are deemed as true and the Defendants' liability is established. At this point, the Court can no longer question the Defendants' liability, as the Defendants have forfeited their right to attack the complaint and the facts contained within.

The facts within this complaint establish the following: . . .

5. On or about April 14, 2000, Defendants Park Place and Clive Cummins entered into a course of conduct that was intended to and did fraudulently induce Defendants Ransom, Smoke, and Thompson to enter into a management contract with Park Place. . . .

11. The actions by Defendants . . . amounted to an attempt by Defendants to prevent the Plaintiffs from proceeding with their existing application to the U.S. Department of Interior to receive lands in trust for the St. Regis Mohawk Tribe of New York for the purpose of conducting the only legal gaming casino in New York which is not located on ancestral reservation land.

12. Due to Defendants Park Place and Clive Cummins tortuous interference with the previous contract with Mohawk Management and Monticello Raceway Development the Plaintiffs are entitled to damages.

A reading of the complaint and the above facts establishes the complaint is well pleaded. The complaint lays out how the Defendants engaged in conduct that interfered with two existing contracts regarding a Monticello casino and establish the Defendants' liability. There is nothing within tribal law that would direct to the Court to deny these facts. Some may argue it is unjust for the Court to accept a one-side interpretation of the facts. But the Defendants have chosen to give the Court no other recourse. Moreover, it would be unjust to the Plaintiffs, who have faithfully attended every hearing and respectfully complied with the Court's every request. The Plaintiffs have asked for their day in Court and complied with every rule to ensure the Defendants' rights are protected. To then have the Court fail to follow the law and refuse to accept these facts and the Defendants' liability as true would be unjust.

Accordingly, the Court accepts the facts contained within the complaint as true and finds the following. . . . Defendants Park Place and Clive Cummins knew of the existing agreements between Mohawk Management and Monticello Raceway Development Company LLC. Clearly they had to know about the existing contracts to represent to Defendants Ransom, Smoke, and Thompson that the existing contracts were invalid. This conduct by Defendants Park Place and Clive Cummins constitutes willful and wrongful interference in the contracts the St. Regis Mohawk Tribe had with Mohawk Management and Monticello Raceway Development and the Tribe's application to the U.S. Department of Interior for the placement of land into trust. . . .

2. Actual Damages

In the hearing on February 20, 2001 Plaintiffs specifically stated they are only seeking damages from Defendants Park Place and Clive Cummins. . . . The Plaintiffs are requesting actual damages for the value of the seven-year contract with Mohawk Management and Monticello Raceway Development and the worth of the proposed casino at the end of the contracts had the contracts not been interfered with by Defendants.

During the default judgment hearing, Plaintiffs introduced a letter dated April 6, 2000 from Kevin Gover, Assistant Secretary of Indian Affairs, to

New York State Governor Pataki concerning the Tribe's application to acquire 29.31 acres in Monticello for the purpose of developing a Class III gaming establishment. . . .

. . . [T]he letter included factual findings from the Bureau of Indian Affairs regarding the development of the casino. According to the findings, the Bureau of Indian Affairs had engaged in numerous studies of the 29.31 acres and projections for the Monticello casino. The best case money projections found that the Net Tribal Share at the end of the seven-year contract between the Tribe, Mohawk Management, and Monticello Raceway Development, would be $582,812,000. Barbara Lazare testified that the 1999 tribal budget was approximately $17 million and this income would have immensely helped tribal programs. Barbara Lazore further testified that community members would have received per capita payments of around $20,000 a year.

The Plaintiffs also introduced a report by Salomon Smith Barney, which was part of the application to take land into trust submitted to the Bureau of Indian Affairs. . . . The projections by Salomon Smith Barney valued the actual enterprise, after the expiration of the seven-year contract, at $1.2 billion. Salomon Smith Barney also valued the seven-year contract and projected a lesser value of $465 million. However, Plaintiffs argued that the factual findings by the Bureau of Indian Affairs was much more accurate. A close reading of the factual findings supports this argument, as it is clear the Bureau of Indian Affairs did their homework in assembling the factual findings. Moreover, the Bureau of Indian Affairs has more expertise in the field of Indian gaming and it seems more than likely that a letter submitted to Governor Pataki would contain figures the Bureau of Indian Affairs felt were reliable.

The evidence is quite persuasive and none of it was countered at the hearing. If the contract with Mohawk Management and Monticello Raceway Development had been free from interference the Tribe and community members would have profited immensely. Therefore, the Court finds the net Tribe's value of the seven-year contract between the St. Regis Mohawk Tribe, Mohawk Management, and Monticello Raceway Development for the Monticello casino to be $582,812,000 and the value of the casino, which the Tribe would own, at the end of the seven-year contract to be $1.2 billion.

The remaining question is whether it would be contrary to tribal law or unjust to award the Plaintiffs this amount in damages. There is no tribal law governing contracts, thus the Court looks to the fairness of awarding the said amount of damages to the Plaintiffs. We have a situation in which individuals purposely interfered in a contract that would have resulted in enormous profit to the Tribe and its members. Traditionally, when a Mohawk committed a wrongful act against another, the offender's family would attempt to restore the victim to their original status, apologize, and request forgiveness of the offender. Many years later, justice still requires that a wrongdoer restore the victim to their original position. In the present case, the members of the class action are the victims. And based upon the facts, it is abundantly clear the Tribe and its members would be well on their way with a profitable venture. Moreover, the unenforceable agreement between Defendants Park Place, Clive Cummins and Defendants Ransom, Smoke, and Thompson stated a casino would be underway four months from April 2000 and the Court takes judicial notice that such a casino does not exist nearly one year later. The Court chooses not to speculate as to why this is the case. Regardless, the Tribe and its members have been deprived of a profitable gaming venture worth $1.782 billion. Furthermore, these damages only assess the net tribal profit, not the jobs or other benefits that would have accrued due to the Monticello casino. To allow individuals to interfere with a contract of this monumental importance and walk away without paying the beneficiaries of this contract would truly be an injustice. Thus, the Court awards the Plaintiffs actual damages in the amount of $1.782 billion to be paid by Defendants Park Place and Clive Cummins. . . .

4. Punitive Damages

Tribal law is silent on the subject of punitive damages. Traditionally when an individual committed a wrongful act, the family of the wrongdoer compensated the victim or made them whole. Punitive damages, which are damages construed to punish the wrongdoer, were more than likely not a normal part of life. However, it is doubtful that families ever had to even contemplate conduct that interfered with multi-million dollar gaming contracts.

The purpose of punitive damages is to punish the wrongdoer and deter him from similar acts in the future. In Anglo courts punitive damages are normally awarded when there is deliberate misconduct, including fraud, which has caused substantial damage to the plaintiffs. In New York, punitive damages are awarded in cases involving gross, wanton, or willful fraud. . . .

The facts contained in the complaint and presented at the default hearing demonstrate that Defendants Park Place and Clive Cummins purposely misrepresented to Defendants Ransom, Smoke, and Thompson that their development and management contracts were invalid. The Bureau of Indian Affairs, who was involved in the government dispute, approved of these contracts and held them out as valid. Yet, Defendants Park Place and Clive Cummins proceeded forward and made fraudulent representations that interfered with profitable contracts and the Tribe's application to the Department of Interior. Clearly the only purpose in making these representations was to induce Defendants Ransom, Smoke, and Thompson to break the previous contracts and sign a deal with Park Place. There is no doubt that this is deliberate misconduct and willful fraud that caused substantial damage. It is difficult to define the enormous damage done by the Defendants Park Place and Clive Cummins with a monetary amount. Defendants interfered with a very profitable gaming venture. These contracts were not part of [a] gaming venture that possessed a remote possibility to produce enormous gain for the Tribe. The Mohawk Management and Monticello Raceway Development contracts were part of a gaming venture that according to the facts presented to the Court, held vast potential for the Tribe and the Monticello casino was as close to a sure thing as one could get. At the time of the Park Place deal, the Tribe had nearly completed the arduous process to take land into trust for the purpose of gaming. This is not a process the Bureau of Indian Affairs takes lightly; it is time consuming and contains many obstacles that tribes must overcome. And from the facts presented to the Court, Defendants Park Place and Clive Cummins did not interfere in this process for the Tribe's benefit. Rather, the Tribe has suffered a loss of $1.782 billion due to their interference.

Accordingly, the Court finds that Defendants Park Place and Clive Cummins engaged in deliberate misconduct and willful fraud by interfering with the Mohawk Management and Monticello Raceway Development contracts and the Tribe's application to the Department of Interior and punitive damages are warranted. Thus, Defendants Park Place and Clive Cummins are ordered to pay $5 million in punitive damages to the Plaintiffs. . . .

NOTES

1. The *Arquette* judgment touched off a series of federal court cases seeking to enforce the judgment, as well as to establish similar liability under federal law. These cases failed. *See Catskill Development, L.L.C. v. Park Place Entertainment Corp.*, 547 F.3d 115 (2d Cir. 2008), *cert. denied*, 129 S. Ct. 1908 (2009); *Vacco v. Harrah's Operating Co., Inc.*, No. 07-CV-663, 2009 WL 3164732 (N.D.N.Y., Sept. 28, 2009).

2. Notice is an important issue in reservation communities when Indian people live in rural areas. Default judgments are frequent, but tribal judges are confronted with claims of lack of notice and must find a way to deal with fairness and justice. In *Atchico v. Deherrea*, 6 Am. Tribal Law 151 (Fort Peck Court of Appeals 2005), the court held:

   > In *Bighorn v. Daniels Spang*, Appeal No. 385, this Court recognized the importance of adequate service in order to insure that due process requirements are met. Although service on someone other than a party or their counsel is allowed under tribal law, due process requires that a party to an action receive actual notice of all hearings. Service on a person of suitable age at the defendant's residence or business can create a presumption that adequate service has been achieve, but as matter of law presumptions are rebuttable. When motioning to set aside the default judgment, Ms. Gourneau indicated that she didn't receive notice of the hearing. In light of the strong preference for deciding cases on the merits, any default judgment entered should be set aside if the request is made in a timely manner and there are any grounds which would demonstrate good cause to set aside the default.

   Atchico, 6 Am. Tribal Law at 152.

3. Many tribal courts apply state court rules in this context. In *Yannett v. Grand Traverse Band Economic Development Authority, Inc.*, 2005 WL 6300971 (Grand Traverse Band of Ottawa and Chippewa Indians Tribal Court 2005), the court applied Michigan law:

   > The first step in the process toward an entry of a default judgment is to obtain an entry of default. Obtaining a default is normally a prerequisite to the entry of a default judgment. In Michigan courts, a default is entered by the court clerk in compliance with the timing requirements of MCR 2.108. *Emmons v. Emmons*, 136 Mich. App. 157, 163, 355 N.W.2d 898 (1984). The court clerk enters a default after the time for an answer has expired but before a responsive pleading has been filed. In this case, Plaintiff did not file a default or raise the issue of Defendant's late filing until after the Defendant had filed its Motion to Dismiss. As a result, this Court will not enter a default judgment against the Defendant.

   Yannett, 2005 WL 6300971, at *3.

13

TRIBAL REGULATORY AND ADMINISTRATIVE LAW

Indian tribal governments have begun to develop complicated and intricate administrative and bureaucratic bodies. Before the 1970s, the federal government tended to govern Indian nations. But the Nixon administration helped to shepherd through the Indian Self-Determination and Education Assistance Act in 1975, Public Law 93-638, which codified what would become known as 638 contracts, or self-determination contracts. For the first time, Indian nations could *contract* with the Bureau of Indian Affairs the governance of Indian tribes. Previously, Congress appropriated a set amount of dollars to administer tribal governments. Some dollars went to tribal courts, some to tribal law enforcement, some to tribal land use, or economic development, and so on — all of it administered by the Bureau of Indian Affairs (or the Department of Housing and Urban Development for tribal housing, or the Department of Health and Human Services for Indian Health Service programs). As of 1975, qualified Indian tribes could take over tribal government functions from the federal government, a proposal first articulated in an original draft of the Indian Reorganization Act in the 1930s.

Once Indian nations began to develop their own governmental services, Indian governmental bureaucracy began to grow. As a result, the law of tribal government administration began. Instead of appealing to the federal government bureaucracy in adverse governmental decisions, Indian people resorted to fighting their own governments. The resulting growth in tribal administrations has been remarkable, with the establishment and development of tribal administrative law a necessary concomitant of tribal sovereignty.

This chapter covers a few areas of tribal administrative law, with an emphasis in tribal employment law, perhaps one of the greatest growth industries in American Indian law.

A. EMPLOYMENT LAW*

1. TRIBAL ENTERPRISE EMPLOYMENT

SHANANAQUET V. GRAND TRAVERSE BAND OF OTTAWA AND CHIPPEWA INDIANS
ECONOMIC DEVELOPMENT CORP.

Grand Traverse Band of Ottawa and Chippewa Indians Court of Appeals,
No. 00-05-299-APP, 8 Am. Tribal Law 160 (March 18, 2003)

PER CURIAM.

The Plaintiff-Appellant Michael Shananaquet filed a Complaint in the Tribal court of the Grand Traverse Band of Ottawa and Chippewa Indians ("Grand Traverse Band") alleging wrongful termination from his position as general manager of the Leelanau Sands Casino of the Grand Traverse Band of Ottawa and Chippewa Indians Economic Development Corporation ("EDC"). . . .

The Tribal court granted defendant EDC's Motion for Summary Disposition based upon that Court's interpretation of the Constitution of the Grand Traverse Band and the Grand Traverse Band Code. . . .

The standard of review applied in this matter shall be the same as that [which] would be applied by the courts of the State of Michigan. The decision to grant or deny summary disposition is a question of law that is reviewed de novo. . . . The interpretation and application of a statutory provision is a question of law that is reviewed de novo by this Court. . . . This Court, therefore, will render its decision as if the Tribal court had previously made no decision.

Summary disposition may be granted on the ground that the plaintiff's claim is barred because of immunity granted by law. . . . "Indian tribes have long been recognized as possessing the common-law immunity from suit traditionally enjoyed by sovereign powers." *Santa Clara Pueblo v. Martinez*, 436 U.S. 49, 58, 98 S. Ct. 1670, 56 L. Ed. 2d 106 (1978). . . . The Grand Traverse Band as a federally recognized Indian tribe enjoys the same immunity from suit as other sovereign powers. The Grand Traverse Band's sovereign immunity from suit in any state, federal or Tribal court has been extended to the EDC by its federal charter as codified in the Grand Traverse Band Code. 15 GTBC 216(a). Consequently, the EDC possesses immunity from suit granted by law. The Tribal court, therefore, may properly grant summary disposition to the EDC based upon the EDC's immunity from suit.

The EDC's immunity from suit is an absolute bar to the Plaintiff's lawsuit unless there is a waiver of the EDC's immunity from suit. This Court must determine whether or not a waiver of immunity exists. "It is well settled that a waiver of immunity 'cannot be implied but must be unequivocally expressed.'" . . .

Author's Note: Much of the material in this section appears in Matthew L. M. Fletcher, *Tribal Employment Separation: Tribal Law Enigma, Tribal Governance Paradox, and Tribal Court Conundrum,* 38 U. MICH. J.L. REFORM 273-343 (2005).

The Plaintiff argues that the EDC exists as an arm of the Tribe and the EDC's powers are coextensive with the Tribe. The Plaintiff is asserting that the EDC is not a separate and distinct entity from the Grand Traverse Band. As such, the Plaintiff is asking the Court to treat the EDC as synonymous with the Grand Traverse Band and apply Articles X and XIII of the Grand Traverse Band's Constitution or the Indian Civil Rights Act to effect a waiver of the EDC's immunity from suit.

The federal charter for the EDC as codified in 15 GTBC 101 *et seq.* goes to great lengths to make it perfectly clear that the EDC is a separate and distinct entity from the Grand Traverse Band.

"This (EDC) is a distinct legal entity . . . and its corporate activities, transactions, obligations, liabilities and property are not those of the Tribe." 15 GTBC 203.

The EDC is a federally chartered Indian business corporation and any powers and immunities it may have are granted by the laws of the United States. *See* 15 GTBC 202.

"The (EDC) is a legal entity . . . distinct and separate from the (Grand Traverse Band)." 15 GTBC 206(a).

"The activities, transactions, obligations, liabilities, and properties of the (EDC) are not those of the (Grand Traverse Band)." 15 GTBC 206(b).

The Grand Traverse Band is connected to the EDC by the fact that a federal charter was issued to the Grand Traverse Band for the EDC and the fact that the Grand Traverse Band is a shareholder of the corporation albeit the sole shareholder. We find that the mere fact that a federal charter is issued to the Grand Traverse Band for the EDC or the fact that the Grand Traverse Band is the sole shareholder of the EDC is an insufficient reason to in effect pierce the corporate veil and determine that the acts of the corporation are the acts of the Grand Traverse Band or in other words, that the corporation is the Grand Traverse Band. A finding to the contrary by this Court would effectively obliterate the distinction between what is tribal and what is corporate in character.

Plaintiff insists that the EDC is constrained by the application of Articles X and XIII of the Grand Traverse Band Constitution. Article X of the Grand Traverse Band Constitution provides that: "The Grand Traverse Band in exercising the powers of self government shall not: (h) . . . deprive any person of liberty or property without due process of law." The Plaintiff's employment was with the EDC. The EDC, a federally chartered corporation, terminated Plaintiff's employment. There was no exercise of the powers of self government of the Grand Traverse Band in Plaintiff's employment termination. Article XIII Section 1 of the Grand Traverse Band Constitution contains the authority for the Tribal Council to waive the Grand Traverse Band's sovereign immunity by a resolution approved by an affirmative vote of five of the seven members of the Tribal Council. There is no contention that such a waiver exists. Article XIII Section 2(a) of the Grand Traverse Band Constitution provides for a waiver of sovereign immunity from suit in Tribal court for the Grand Traverse Band and Tribal Council members in their official capacities. The present matter is a lawsuit filed by an employee of the EDC against the EDC. The Grand Traverse Band and the Tribal Council members are not parties to this lawsuit. The EDC is neither synonymous with nor an arm of the Grand

Traverse Band. Actions of the EDC, therefore, cannot be treated as actions of the Grand Traverse Band. Article XIII Sections 1, and 2(a), therefore, have no applicability to the matters in issue before this Court. . . .

The final argument Plaintiff makes is that the EDC is estopped from asserting immunity from suit. Plaintiff claims that the EDC Personnel Policies create a property right in his employment the termination of which in contravention of those policies would create a manifest injustice. The EDC Personnel Policy states that: "These policies and procedures are not contractual conditions of employment." See page 8. This contract disclaimer clearly communicates to employees that the EDC did not intend to enter into an employment contract with Plaintiff or any other employee as a result of its Personnel Policies. The Plaintiff could not have formed a legitimate expectation that the EDC had entered into a contract with him that would elevate his employment with the EDC to a protected property right. Any variance in following the procedures provided in the EDC Personnel Policy would not involve the deprivation of a property right since none was created by a contract embodied in the EDC Personnel Policy. No manifest injustice will result to Plaintiff in refusing to apply the doctrine of estoppel to prevent the EDC from asserting immunity from his lawsuit. . . .

NOTES

1. The Grand Traverse Band later reversed itself partially on the tribal constitutional sovereign immunity question as it relates to tribal members, holding that Article XIII allows tribal members to pursue injunctive relief against the Band's EDC. *See Wilson v. Grand Traverse Band of Ottawa and Chippewa Indians Economic Development Corp.*, 2006 WL 6295938 (Grand Traverse Band Court of Appeals 2006). However, the tribal rule that states that even tribal members may not pursue damages against the tribal corporation remains extant. *E.g., Yannett v. Grand Traverse Band Economic Development Authority, Inc.*, 2005 WL 6300971 (Grand Traverse Band Tribal Court 2005).

2. An exception to the general rule that Indian tribe employees may only be dismissed for just cause is employment with an Indian tribe's economic development arm. Because it needs to function effectively in the business world, the tribal economic development corporation "must be able to make sound business decisions based solely upon business considerations." *Adams v. Grand Traverse Band of Ottawa & Chippewa Indians Economic Development Authority*, No. 89-03-001-CV, slip op. at 1-2 (Grand Traverse Band Tribal Ct. June 18, 1992). Many tribal businesses will treaty employees as at-will employees, whereas most tribal governments treat employees as just-cause employees.

3. Many tribal enterprise employers have chosen to extend greater protection to tribal enterprise employees by incorporating principles of administrative law into adverse employment action procedures. For example, Mashantucket Pequot tribal courts will uphold the discharge of tribal enterprise employees whenever there is a rational basis for the discharge, a standard

adopted via legislation. *See Olderman v. Mashantuket Pequot Gaming Enter.*, 27 Indian L. Rep. 6266, 6269 (Mashantucket Pequot Tribal Ct. Apr. 30, 1999).

2. TRIBAL GOVERNMENT EMPLOYMENT

Hoopa Valley Indian Housing Authority v. Gerstner

Hoopa Valley Court of Appeals, No. C-92-035, 3 NICS App. 248, 22 Indian L. Rep. 6002 (September 27, 1993)

Before: Chief Justice Elbridge Coochise, Associate Justice Charles R. Hostnik and Associate Justice John L. Roe.

Hostnik, Associate Justice:

This case involves an appeal from an employment termination. Plaintiff/Respondent was the Director of the Hoopa Valley Indian Housing Authority. The appeal comes before this Court for clarification of the appropriate procedures to be used in employment termination proceedings.

I. Procedural History and Background

By letter dated May 27, 1992, the Appellant, Hoopa Valley Indian Housing Authority Board of Commissioners (HVIHA), suspended the Respondent, Lila Gerstner, Executive Director of HVIHA, for various alleged violations of HVIHA policy. On June 2, 1992, Appellant HVIHA rescinded the thirty (30) day suspension, and suspended Respondent with pay, but only until June 19, 1992.

On the following day, Appellant mailed a Notice of Termination to Respondent by certified mail. The Notice of Termination advised Respondent that she had

> the right to appeal this dismissal action by requesting a hearing before the Board of Commissioners pursuant to HVIHA Administrative Policy Section 11.0(G), and, to the extent it is determined applicable to this action and still valid policy and not in conflict with the Tribal Employment Rights Ordinance (TERO), the Tribal Personnel Policies and Procedures Manual, Chapter VIII, Section 8.2, and the TERO. . . . Note: If you elect to file a grievance on this action your formal notice of request for a hearing by the Board of Commissioners ["tribal agency"] must be received at the HVIHA Administrative Office within ten (10) work days of your receipt of this Notice of Termination.

June 3, 1992, Letter to Lila Gerstner from John E. Robbins, Jr., Chairman, HVIHA.

Respondent filed a timely notice of appeal. On June 8, 1992, Appellant HVIHA notified Respondent of the hearing date and time, and provided Respondent with an explanation of how the hearing would be conducted—a record would be made and Respondent had a right to make a separate record; strict rules of evidence would not apply; hearsay would be admissible under certain circumstances; Respondent could call witnesses and introduce documentary evidence. Prior to the hearing, Respondent submitted a discovery request to HVIHA. Almost all of the requested documents were provided.

Respondent's grievance hearing was held on July 9, 1992. Respondent did not learn until the beginning of the grievance hearing that Appellant would not call witnesses to support the charges against Respondent, but rather would rely on the statements contained in the June 3, 1992, Notice of Termination.

Documentary evidence supporting Appellant's decision to terminate Respondent was introduced at the hearing. Respondent was allowed to call witnesses, but did not do so. Respondent addressed the grounds for termination, offered her own testimony and questioned the Commissioners in attendance. The Commissioners and counsel questioned the Respondent. A record of the hearing was transcribed and became part of the [tribal agency's] record.

Closing argument was submitted in writing by Respondent after the hearing. The HVIHA issued its decision on August 7, 1992, upholding their original decision to suspend and terminate Respondent. . . .

IV. Hearing Rights

. . . The Indian Civil Rights Act prohibits Indian Tribes from depriving any person of property without due process of law. 26 U.S.C. section 1302(8). The meaning of "due process" under the Indian Civil Rights Act has been construed to be the same as the meaning of "due process" under the Federal Constitution of the United States. *Red Fox v. Red Fox*, 564 F.2d 361, 364 (9th Cir. 1977). The United States Supreme Court, in construing Federal constitutional rights, has held that due process applies to discharge from public employment. *Slochower v. Board of Higher Education*, 350 U.S. 551, 100 L. Ed. 692, 76 S. Ct. 637 (1956).

Even though the decisions of Federal, State or other Tribal courts are not controlling in this Court, such decisions can be used as guidance in helping us address these issues. *See Ames v. Hoopa Valley Tribal Council and Hoopa Valley Department of Public Safety*, Case No. C-90-026 (Nov. 14, 1992) (Chief Justice Irvin concurring). The analysis employed by the U.S. Supreme Court in *Goldberg v. Kelly*, 397 U.S. 254, 25 L. Ed. 2d 287, 90 S. Ct. 1011 (1970) is particularly helpful. . . .

In the context of this case, we agree that continued employment with the Hoopa Valley Tribe and/or Tribal entities is an important property interest to which due process rights attach. Therefore, before an employee can be terminated from employment, that employee must be granted minimal due process rights.

Although we decide that due process rights must be granted to employees, including the right to a hearing before an impartial arbiter, that does not necessarily mean that formal trial and court procedures should apply. However, there are certain minimal rights of employees that should be protected in order to have a meaningful opportunity to be heard. Those rights include: (1) adequate notice, (2) a hearing decision by independent arbiter, (3) an initial burden of proof imposed on the employer, and (4) the right to confront and cross-examine those witnesses used against the employee.

Notice

In order to constitute adequate notice, the notice must clearly advise the employee of his or her rights to appeal the employer's disciplinary decision.

It is questionable whether the notice provided to Ms. Gerstner met this standard. However, we need not address that issue because Ms. Gerstner did not object to the notice given and is deemed to have waived any defect as to notice when she proceeded to hearing before the HVIHA Board of Commissioners, and again before the TERO Commission. In addition, Ms. Gerstner has failed to show that she suffered any prejudice due to any inadequacies which might have existed in the initial notice provided to her.

Independent Arbiter

The importance of the independent arbiter is addressed above. The decision maker's conclusion must rest solely on the evidence produced at the due process hearing. This is why a board or commission, which is the direct supervisor of an executive director and which conducts an investigation into disciplinary action against that director, cannot be an impartial arbiter. The potential is too great that the board may base its decision in part upon investigative facts not produced at the due process hearing.

Even if such investigative facts do not form a portion of the decision maker's conclusion, the appearance of unfairness is too high to be permissible. As noted by the *Goldberg* Court, an impartial decision maker is essential to having a fair hearing. *Goldberg, supra*, 397 U.S. at 271. Without an impartial decision maker, the process is fatally flawed.

As part of this right, it is required that a record be made of the proceedings before the independent arbiter. Since this is the hearing level at which the evidence is produced, a record is essential for later review by the . . . Tribal court. This will help insure that the arbiter's decision is based on evidence produced at the hearing.

Burden of Proof

In most contexts, the burden of proving the initial allegations is upon the party who makes the allegations. In the context of a termination from employment, it is the employer who is alleging that the employee's conduct justifies termination. Therefore, the employer should have the initial burden of proving that termination is justified.

An initial showing must be made by the employer of the basis for and the facts supporting the disciplinary action. This, again, is an element of fundamental fairness that must be a part of the termination process. The employee is entitled to know the employer's basis for the termination decision. In part, this comes in the termination letter which precedes the hearing, but there are frequently additional facts that are made known at the hearing which an employer uses to justify the termination decisions.

In addition, it is important for the arbiter to understand the basis for the disciplinary action, in order to be able to support the agency's decision. The HVIHA's action in this case of merely submitting documents and attempting to shift the burden of proof to the employee, did not allow an independent arbiter to fully understand the basis for the employer's termination decision.

Once an initial showing is made by the employer of the basis for the termination decision, the burden of proof properly shifts to the employee to show that the facts supporting the decision are untrue, or that the decision is unjustified for other reasons. It is unfair for the employee to have the initial burden of disproving the allegations before the allegations themselves are proven by the employer.

Right to Confront and Cross-Examine Witnesses

Personnel decisions leading to termination of employment are primarily factual in nature. "In almost every setting where important decisions turn on questions of fact, due process requires an opportunity to confront and cross-examine adverse witnesses." *Goldberg, supra*, 397 U.S. 269.

In dealing with factual matters, the credibility and veracity of the witnesses and documents submitted into evidence must be determined by the decision maker. Simply because a document is submitted into evidence does not make all statements contained in that document 100 percent true. The basis for the statements may show that the statements were made under duress, or were based upon the inaccurate information. The same is true of the testimony of witnesses. Therefore, it is essential that the employee be afforded the opportunity to confront and cross-examine witnesses and evidence.

In this case, the Housing Authority elected to submit into evidence various documents which allegedly supported its decision to terminate Ms. Gerstner. No witnesses were called to authenticate those documents, nor were any witnesses called to provide a foundation for the documents, explain the circumstances under which they were created, or provide an explanation as to how the documents demonstrated conduct so grievous that termination of employment was justified. This denied Ms. Gerstner her right to confront and cross-examine adverse witnesses.

Compelling Appearance of Witnesses

An issue raised by both parties concerning due process hearings conducted before an agency board or commission is the inability of either party to subpoena witnesses or compel them to appear. This impacts the employer's ability to meet its initial burden of proof, and it also impacts the employee's ability to adequately present a defense. However, this is not as problematic as it may first appear.

These actions, being disciplinary in nature, will generally be based upon the employee's performance on the job. Therefore, the large majority of potential witnesses will be other employees of the agency.

An employer clearly has both the ability and the authority to force its own employees to appear at agency hearings, because the employer can discipline those employees for failure to follow a lawful directive of the employer. Therefore, certainly the employer can compel the attendance of witnesses it intends to present at the administrative due process hearing.

The employee, however, is not in a position to force agency employees to attend that hearing. In the interest of fairness, since the independent arbiter is the employer itself, the employee should have the ability to provide a list of agency employee-witnesses he or she requests be compelled to appear and testify. The employer can then use its authority to compel the attendance of those employee witnesses, even though they will be called as witnesses for the disciplined employee.

In certain cases, non-agency employees may become important potential witnesses. Nonemployee witnesses subject to Tribal jurisdiction can be compelled to appear by subpoena obtained . . . from the Hoopa Valley Tribal court. . . .

A problem potentially exists with respect to non-agency employee witnesses who are not subject to Tribal jurisdiction. Several solutions are possible. First, voluntary attendance could be requested. Second, testimony of such witnesses could be preserved by pre-hearing deposition or video deposition, or even an affidavit. Finally, if necessary, off-reservation legal action to compel attendance could be commenced, perhaps in conjunction with issuance of a Tribal court subpoena.

Post-hearing Procedures

Once the due process hearing has occurred, it is important that the independent arbiter produce a written opinion stating the reasons for the decision, and the evidence relied upon to support that decision. This is important for purposes of later review by . . . the Tribal court. This also insures that an impartial decision is rendered based solely on the evidence produced at the due process hearing. . . .

Standard of Review

Once the due process hearing occurs, what is the appropriate standard by which that decision is reviewed? Resolution No. 91-71A was adopted to establish clear and uniform procedures for handling matters before the [tribal agency]. A portion of that ordinance specifies the standard to be employed by the Tribal court in reviewing Commission decisions.

That standard is as follows:

> The Court shall uphold the decision of the [tribal agency] unless it is proven that the decision of the [tribal agency] is arbitrary, capricious, or not in accordance with law.

Resolution No 91-71A, Section VI(f). This is a limited scope of review, which does not permit a Tribal court to conduct an entirely new hearing.

This Court has had a prior opportunity to address this issue in *Ames v. Hoopa Valley Tribal Council and Hoopa Valley Department of Public Safety*, No. C-90-026 (Nov. 14, 1991). In that case, Chief Justice Irvin, in her concurring opinion, reviewed the standard by which United States Federal Courts hear appeals from agency hearings under the Federal Administrative Procedures Act.

The opinion of Chief Justice Irvin was a concurring opinion, was not specifically adopted by the majority and, therefore, is not controlling or binding upon this Court. However, the reasoning of that concurring opinion is sound, and this Court hereby adopts the substantial evidence test set forth by Chief Justice Irvin in *Ames* as the appropriate standard by which due process hearings are to be reviewed. This includes review not only by the [tribal agency] from an agency due process hearing, but review by the Tribal court form a due process hearing conducted by the [tribal agency].

This is the standard which was adopted by the trial court in this case. The trial court determined that substantial evidence existed to support the [tribal agency's] decision. That standard was appropriate. In reviewing the trial court's decision, this Court finds that substantial evidence exists to support the trial court, utilizing the test suggested by Chief Justice Irvin in *Ames*. Therefore, the trial court's decision is hereby affirmed. . . .

NOTES

1. This case proceeded through a convoluted and long process, including two agency reviews of the employment decision. The Hoopa Valley Tribal Council had made a decision prior to this case to route all employee grievances through their "TERO Commission." A TERO is either a "Tribal Employee Rights Ordinance" or "Tribal Employee Rights Office." Tribal councils once created numerous TEROs as a means to generate employment in Indian country. TEROs often were like state employment agencies, with elements of labor unions, and helped to enforce Indian preference in employment rules against both tribal and non-tribal firms doing business in Indian country. Hoopa's decision to route employee grievances through the TERO Commission created a sort of conflict of interest, in that the TERO often assisted on-reservation workers in applying for work, some of whom would later appear before the Commission in its capacity as a tribal agency. In other Indian communities, a TERO serves as more of a watchdog than a decision maker. *E.g.*, 17 SWINOMISH TRIBAL Code ch. 5 (Sept. 4, 1985); CONFEDERATED TRIBES OF THE UMATILLA INDIAN RESERVATION TRIBAL EMPLOYMENT RIGHTS OFFICE CODE (Aug. 7, 1978); WINNEBAGO TRIBAL EMPLOYMENT RIGHTS ORDINANCE (TERO) (Sept. 19, 2005).

2. Not only is it analogous in some ways to a corporate board of directors, but tribal government employment also has many of the same characteristics of employment in federal, state, or local government. The chief similarity is that all four are governments subject to limitations in their ability to deprive an individual of property without due process. At the constitutional level, the Fifth Amendment constrains the federal government's ability to terminate an individual's employment, *see Bolling v. Sharpe*, 347 U.S. 497 (1954), and the Fourteenth Amendment constrains states and localities, *see Cleveland Bd. of Educ. v. Loudermill*, 470 U.S. 532 (1985). The Indian Civil Rights Act and tribal constitutions constrain the Tribes. As such, tribal government employees typically can be discharged only for "just cause." *E.g., Koon v. Grand Traverse Band of Ottawa & Chippewa Indians*, 2001 WL 36194126, at *1 (Grand Traverse Band Tribal Ct. July 20, 2001); *White v. Ho-Chunk Nation*, 24 Indian L. Rep. 6182, 6185 (Ho-Chunk Nation Trial Ct. Oct. 14, 1996).

3. With few exceptions, Indian tribes experience excessive difficulty with employment separations. Most tribal governments are relatively new and inexperienced. In an early opinion of the fledgling Grand Traverse Band Tribal court, long-time Chief Judge Michael Petoskey described the growth of the Grand Traverse Band:

> It is particularly instructive at the beginning [of] this decision to reflect upon the general course of conduct by tribal government. . . . In fact, it is a product of the Tribal Constitution that was adopted by tribal membership early in

1988, which was only four years ago. The federal government ignored the sovereign status of the Tribe from the treaty days until federal recognition in May of 1980. After recognition in 1980 and prior to the 1988 Constitution, an interim Tribal Council carried out most governmental activity. Prior to May 1980 few community resources were available to fund governmental activity. These realities give substance to a backdrop that provides the appropriate context in which to view the facts that give rise to the matter in controversy here. That backdrop makes it clear that the government of the Grand Traverse Band is new and in the process of development. Our new government is much more reactive than proactive. It engages in activities that gain their primary priority because they are of immediate concern or consequence. Tribal government is in its earliest stages of development. It is incomplete and inexperienced. History has not yet provided many lessons. This is the context of the present case.

Adams v. Grand Traverse Band of Ottawa & Chippewa Indians Econ. Dev. Auth., No. 89-03-001-CV, slip op. at 2 (Grand Traverse Band Tribal Ct. June 18, 1992).

Judge Petoskey also had occasion to write about the even newer tribal government at the Little Traverse Bay Bands of Odawa Indians:

From the outset, it should be noted that the Little Traverse Bay Bands tribal government is in an early stage of development. During this early stage, there will be many challenges faced by the community and its government. Among such challenges are the following: the lack of a clear understanding and definition about the appropriate roles and authority of various governmental institutions; the lack of a fully-developed government and service infrastructure, including the express adoption of rules, policies and procedures; and the lack of experience and training of various officials and staff. These challenges, in particular, contribute to the community learning from its experiences, conflicts and mistakes. None of this should be unexpected. After all, this exercise of tribal self-government by the community is relatively new. It is said that "one who makes no mistakes is doing nothing" and that "the price of unwillingness to take any risk because there is fear of making a mistake is to do nothing." All of us must have empathy and patience for each other, as we engage in the development of tribal community and its government. We will make mistakes along the way. The important thing is that we strive to not make mistakes, and that we learn from them when they are made.

Naganashe v. Little Traverse Bay Bands of Odawa Indians Election Bd., 1999 WL 34999581, at *1 (Little Traverse Bay Bands Tribal Ct. June 18, 1999).

3. EMPLOYMENT-RELATED ADMINISTRATIVE HEARINGS

SYNOWSKI v. CONFEDERATED TRIBES OF GRAND RONDE

Confederated Tribes of the Grand Ronde Community Court of Appeals,
No. A-01-10-001, 4 Am. Tribal Law 122, 2003.NAGR.0000003
(January 22, 2003)

Before: COSTELLO, Chief Justice, and MILLER and THOMPSON, Associate Justices
The opinion of the court was delivered by: THOMPSON, Associate Justice

Respondent-Appellant Confederated Tribes of Grand Ronde appeals from the trial court's order reversing the decision of the Independent Review Board (IRB), which upheld the termination of Petitioner-Appellee Richard Synowski's employment with the Tribe. The trial court concluded that Synowski's right to due process was violated at his IRB hearing because he had received inadequate notice and been denied the right to assistance of counsel at his own expense. We exercise jurisdiction under Tribal Code §310(h)(2) and affirm.

I. Background

In April 1997, the Tribe hired Richard Synowski as a mental health counselor at the Tribe's Health and Wellness Center [later, the Health Authority]. He had prior experience as a mental health counselor and held a master's degree. He was not, however, licensed as a professional counselor by the State of Oregon.

. . . In April 2000, the Health Authority adopted a policy requiring that all health care professionals, including counselors, be licensed in the State of Oregon. Because Synowski was not licensed, the Tribe terminated his employment.

Synowski filed a grievance, claiming he was fired without proper notice or justification.

He received a hearing before the IRB, at which he represented himself. The Tribe's rules for IRB hearings prohibit attorney representation of any party or witness at the hearing. The IRB upheld Synowski's termination. He then petitioned the trial court for review of the IRB's decision under Tribal Code §255.5(d), which provides for limited judicial review of the Tribe's employment decisions by the Tribal court.

After a complete review of the IRB record, the trial court reversed the IRB and remanded Synowski's case for a new hearing. It concluded that Synowski was entitled to a new hearing because his right to due process had been violated. . . .

III. Discussion

The Tribe's Human Resources Guidebook details the grievance procedures for employees. Regarding the hearings conducted by the IRB, the Guidebook provides, in part:

> The grievant and the supervisor or manager whose action is grieved may be present throughout the hearing, may present his/her position and witnesses and may ask questions of the other party and the other party's witnesses.
>
> The IRB may question witnesses and may request additional information from any party or call other witnesses, at its discretion. . . . Attorneys may not participate in the hearing on behalf of any party or witness. Human Resources Guidebook 66 (2000).

The trial court, applying the familiar three-factor test for due process set forth in *Mathews v. Eldridge*, 424 U.S. 319 (1976), concluded that the blanket prohibition against attorneys participating in IRB hearings denied Synowski due process. For the following reasons, we agree.

A. Due Process Rights

As the Tribe correctly notes, the right to due process for persons within the jurisdiction of the Tribe derives not from the United States Constitution but rather from the Indian Civil Rights Act of 1968 (ICRA), 25 U.S.C. §1301 et seq. . . . Under the Tribe's constitution, the Tribal court has "the power to review and overturn tribal legislative and executive actions for violation of . . . the Indian Civil Rights Act of 1968." Tribal Const. art. IV, sec. 3.

The ICRA protects non-Indians as well as Indians. It provides that "[n]o Indian tribe in exercising powers of self-government shall . . . deprive any person of liberty or property without due process of law." 25 U.S.C. §1302(8). "In reviewing tribal . . . procedures to determine if they comport with this due process guarantee, 'courts . . . [have] correctly sensed that Congress did not intend that the . . . due process principles of the [United States] Constitution disrupt settled tribal customs and traditions.'" *Randall v. Yakima Nation Tribal court*, 841 F.2d 897, 900 (9th Cir. 1988). . . .[4]

Our analysis of the assistance-of-counsel/due process issue presented here proceeds with an awareness of that fact. Significantly, however, the Tribe does not argue that any tribal custom or tradition is at risk if the general principles of due process under the United States Constitution are applied in this case. Indeed, in its opening brief the Tribe states, "The Trial Court correctly identified the three-factor test laid out in *Mathews v. Eldridge*[] as the standard for determining whether due process required the right to have counsel present at the IRB." Br. of Aplt. 19. Synowski also cites *Mathews* as controlling. We agree that test is appropriate in the context of this case.

B. The *Mathews v. Eldridge* Test

In *Mathews v. Eldridge*, the United States Supreme Court held that a court should consider the following three factors in determining what procedural protections are required to satisfy due process in a particular situation:

> First, the private interest that will be affected by the official action; second, the risk of an erroneous deprivation of such interest through the procedures used, and the probable value, if any, of additional or substitute procedural safeguards; and finally, the Government's interest, including the function involved and the fiscal and administrative burdens that the additional or substitute procedural requirement would entail. 424 U.S. at 335.

We consider each of those factors in turn.

1. The Private Interest Affected

The private interest affected by official action in this case — an employee's interest in continued employment — is undeniably significant. The trial court

---

4. We recognize that other tribal courts have adopted varying positions on this issue. *Compare, e.g., In re Welfare of D.D.*, 3 [NICS App.] 269, 270 (Port Gamble S'Klallum Indian Res. Ct. App. 1994) ("While the meaning of due process under the Indian Civil Rights Act is similar to due process as defined under the United States Constitution, it is different. An Indian Tribal court's interpretation and application of due process represents the unique tribal sovereign, its distinctive tradition, culture and mores."), with *Hoopa Valley Indian Housing Authority v. Gerstner*, 3 [NICS App.] 250, 258 (Hoopa Valley Indian Res. Ct. App. 1993) ("The meaning of 'due process' under the Indian Civil Rights Act has been construed to be the same as the meaning of 'due process' under the Federal Constitution of the United States.").

so found, and the Tribe takes no issue with that finding on appeal. In short, "the interest of an employee . . . in retaining his employment has long been recognized as substantial." . . .

2. The Risk of Erroneous Deprivation of Affected Interest

The risk of erroneous deprivation of the interest in continued employment also is significant if the employee fails to create a favorable record before the IRB, which under the Tribe's employee-grievance procedures is the only forum where the employee is given an opportunity to create a full evidentiary record.[6]

"The creation of a favorable record would require [the employee] to be personally well spoken, to have had the presence of mind to arrange, in advance of the hearing, witnesses in his or her behalf, and to cross-examine the [Tribe's] representatives." *Johnson v. Mashantucket Pequot Gaming Enterprise*, No. 1 Mash. 115, ¶49 (Mashantucket Pequot Tr. Ct. 1995) (holding that Mashantucket Pequot Tribe's prohibition against attorney representation of employees before the tribal employment review board violated the ICRA's due process clause), *affirmed*, No. 1 MPR 15 (Mashantucket Pequot Ct. App. 1996).

Although presumably some employees will be able to handle those challenging tasks without legal assistance, we can safely assume that many will not. *See Johnson*, No. 1 Mash. 115 at ¶50 ("Many of the Gaming Enterprise's employees, particularly the hourly employees, have limited educational backgrounds and have demonstrated the inability to communicate effectively in writing."). "Counsel can help delineate the issues, present the factual contentions in an orderly manner, conduct cross-examination, and generally safeguard the interests of the [employees]." *Goldberg v. Kelly*, 397 U.S. 254, 270-71 (1970). That is so even though, as the Tribe notes, the IRB hearing is not governed by formal rules of procedure and evidence. In our view, "[t]he right to be heard would be, in many cases, of little avail if it did not comprehend the right to be heard by counsel." *Powell v. Alabama*, 287 U.S. 45, 68-69 (1932).

Having reviewed the record of the IRB hearing in this case, we are convinced that Synowski would have benefited from the assistance of counsel. Further, we agree with the trial court's observation that Synowski's IRB hearing and those of the other discharged employees simultaneously being reviewed by the trial court "were relatively lengthy, sometimes contentious, always adversarial, and far from simple." *Synowski et al. v. Confederated Tribes of Grand Ronde*, Case No. C-00-11-003, etc., Order Remanding Cases to Internal Review Board 11 (2001).

---

6. There are four steps in the Tribe's grievance procedure: (1) within 30 days of the event(s) giving rise to the grievance, the employee must file a written grievance with Human Resources, which then attempts to resolve the grievance without a hearing; (2) if the grievance is not resolved to the employee's satisfaction at the first level, the employee may request a hearing before the IRB, at which the grievant and the supervisor or manager may present witnesses, cross-examine the opposing party's witnesses, and present argument; (3) if the employee obtains an adverse ruling from the IRB, the employee may petition the trial court for judicial review, which is limited to an on-the-record review of whether the "Final Employment Decision . . . (A) [v]iolates applicable provisions of the [Tribal] Constitution . . . ; (B) [v]iolates provisions, substantive or procedural, of applicable Tribal law or federal law; (C) [i]s arbitrary, capricious, an abuse of discretion, or otherwise not in accordance with applicable law; . . . or (D) [i]s not supported by substantial evidence on the record taken as a whole," Tribal Code §255.5(8); and (4) either party may appeal the trial court's ruling to this Court. Human Resources Guidebook 65-67 (2000); Tribal Code §310(h).

Finally, we are not persuaded by the Tribe's argument that the risk of erroneous deprivation of an employee's interest in continued employment is low because "the IRB hearing is not the only check against a mistaken or arbitrary decision by the Tribe" — *i.e.*, the employee "may petition the Trial Court for review of the decision terminating his employment and, if not satisfied with the result there, may appeal the decision to the Court of Appeals." Br. of Aplt. 22.

That argument discounts the importance of creating a favorable record before the IRB, which is critical to meaningful judicial review of the Tribe's employment decision. For many employees, creating such a record simply will not be possible without the guiding hand of counsel.

Although the employee may retain an attorney once the matter goes to court, by that time the record has been made and there is little an attorney can do to change it. Given the limited scope of judicial review of the Tribe's employment decisions, the quality of the IRB record may in many instances determine the employee's success in the courts.

3. The Tribe's Interest

As for the third *Mathews* factor, the Tribe contends the trial court gave insufficient weight to the Tribe's interest in barring attorneys, including its own attorneys, from IRB hearings. According to the Tribe, that interest is two-fold: (1) a financial concern — if employees are permitted to have attorneys at IRB hearings, then the Tribe will be required to have its attorneys present at those hearings; and (2) most importantly, a desire to keep the procedures as non-adversarial as possible, so as to enhance the employer-employee relationship, and "to provide a more level playing field for [the Tribe's] employees — particularly those employees that cannot afford representation at the hearing." Br. of Aplt. 23.

The Tribe's concerns are legitimate, but as the trial court concluded, they are not sufficiently weighty to overcome the significant interests at stake for the employee. Regarding the Tribe's financial concern, we do not accept its assertion that if employees are represented by attorneys at IRB hearings, then the Tribe always will be required to have its attorneys present. Insofar as that view is based on a belief that an employee's attorney, without the Tribe's attorney there as a counterbalance, may mislead a board made up of lay persons, that concern does not carry considerable weight. "Juries, [for example,] generally are wholly comprised of lay persons, yet American society trusts the jury to make the correct decision based on the evidence before it — despite being buffeted by the arguments of lawyers." *Johnson*, No. 1 Mash. 115 at ¶52.

In short, although the Tribe may feel more comfortable with its attorneys present at IRB hearings involving a represented employee, it has not pointed to anything that convinces us it would be compelled to have legal representation in every such case to receive a fair hearing.

As for the Tribe's desire to "provide a more level playing field" for employees, we disagree with its contention that the IRB hearing process is made more fair by reducing every employee to the level of greatest disadvantage — *i.e.*, proceeding without the assistance of counsel. The Tribe asserts that attorneys were not excluded from IRB hearings prior to January 2000, and that the prohibition against attorney participation was implemented "because employees complained that they couldn't afford attorneys and the Tribe had an unfair advantage by having its attorneys present." Br. of Aplt. 23 n. 7. Assuming that was the case, the Tribe's response—exclusion of all attorneys from IRB hearings—hardly made it fairer for the employees as a whole; the new rule simply addressed the complaint of those employees who could not afford an attorney. It is easily argued that the better response to that complaint—in terms of overall fairness—would have been a rule prohibiting the participation of the Tribe's attorneys in cases where the employee is unrepresented. In sum, we give little weight to the Tribe's interest in leveling the playing field.

Further, although certainly a worthy objective, the Tribe's desire to keep IRB hearings as non-adversarial as possible is not, in our view, significantly advanced by prohibiting the participation of counsel where the employee is willing to pay for an attorney. A review of the IRB hearing in the instant case confirms what one would expect in a trial-type proceeding where the stakes are high for both parties—the process is inherently adversarial. Here, an employee was facing deprivation of his livelihood based on his not being a licensed mental health counselor and the Tribe was intent on implementing an important policy requiring licensure of its counselors. The obvious conflict between those positions would not be materially enhanced by the participation of attorneys at the hearing. . . .

Finally, the Tribe does not argue, and we do not believe, that the participation of attorneys before the IRB necessarily would lengthen the hearings or make them more complex.

In fact, attorneys may in many cases help to streamline the process by narrowing the issues and ensuring that only relevant evidence and argument are presented. Further, whether there would be a significant fiscal impact on the Tribe depends entirely on how it decides to deal with the possibility an employee will be represented by an attorney. For example, permitting an employee to have counsel at an IRB hearing would not prevent the Tribe from amending its rules to require the employee intending to use counsel to give the Tribe notice of that intent. Such a requirement would lessen the fiscal impact of permitting attorney representation of employees, in that the Tribe would know early in the process which cases may require the participation of its attorneys at an IRB hearing.

4. Assessment of the *Mathews* Factors

Having considered the foregoing factors, we conclude that to comport with due process the Tribe must allow attorney representation of an employee at an IRB hearing. The significant interest of an employee in continued employment, coupled with a substantial risk of erroneous deprivation of that interest if the assistance of counsel is prohibited, clearly outweighs the Tribe's fiscal and administrative concerns. Permitting legal representation of employees at IRB hearings is consistent with the widely held view that "due process requires that a discharged employee's post-termination hearing be substantially more 'meaningful' [than the relatively abbreviated pretermination process]." . . . "At a minimum, this requires that the discharged employee be permitted to attend the hearing, to have the assistance of counsel, to call witnesses and produce evidence on his own behalf, and to know and have an opportunity to challenge the evidence against him." . . . Accordingly, we hold that the Tribe's rule prohibiting an employee from having the assistance of counsel, at his or her own expense, in an IRB hearing violates the due process clause of the ICRA.

IV. Conclusion

. . . Synowski therefore is entitled to a new hearing at which he may exercise his right to the assistance of retained counsel. . . .

AFFIRMED.

NOTES

1. Typically, tribal courts require petitioners to exhaust any available administrative remedies. Tribal courts desire the benefit of an administrative record and expertise. Exhaustion ensures judicial efficiency by making sure that managers can attempt to use their specialized skills to resolve the problem before a court considers the controversy. Without a requirement of exhaustion, complainants would be encouraged "to concoct claims outside the [statute], in an attempt to circumvent the administrative process." *Charles v. Furniture Warehouse*, 21 Indian L. Rep. 6103, 6104 (Navajo Nation Supreme Court 1994).

2. The meaning of "notice" is well understood. "Due process only requires notice that gives sufficient detail to allow an opposing counsel to prepare a defense." In *Smith v. Red Mesa Unified School District No. 27*, 22 Indian L. Rep. 6104 (1995), the Navajo Nation Supreme Court expounded in great deal on the reasons for adequate notice:

> The purposes of notice as an element of due process are to inform the individual of the basis for adverse action and to allow that person to pursue legal remedies with an understanding of what facts the employee must address. If the employee does not know why adverse action is taken, both due process and the [Navajo Preference in Employment] Act are violated. If, however, the employee knows the reasons for the employer's action, in either the notice under the Act or contemporaneous documents, then due process and the Act are satisfied. The employee must, at minimum, be able to point to written declarations by the employer which explain the reasons for the adverse action taken.

Id. at 6105-06.

Some courts require a pre-termination hearing:

> The Court has noted a few of the factors underlying the necessity of a pre-termination hearing, namely immediate loss of income and the associated embarrassment and humiliation flowing from severe employment discipline. Other factors include: the greater potential for accuracy in the employment decision; the expected lapse of time before securing other employment possibilities; the effect a questionable work record has on future employment possibilities; the inability to fully commit to another employer during the pendency of the individual's grievance/case; the resulting disruption to an individual's personal and economic life; the time needed to ultimately

resolve a grievance/complaint; and the potential inability to collect unemployment compensation due to the type of employment separation. [Citations omitted.]

Rhode v. Garvin, No. 00-39, at 16 (Ho-Chunk Nation Trial Court 2001).

3. Other Tribal courts have had the opportunity to articulate views of due process with other characteristics. In an administrative review context, the Grand Traverse Band Tribal court stated:

> Fairness can be instilled in the process by requiring that: (1) judicial discovery tools be made available to grievants; (2) grievants be advised that they may be represented by counsel at their own expense; and (3) grievants be given a reasonable amount of time to secure the services of counsel if they wish to be represented.

Koon v. Grand Traverse Band of Ottawa and Chippewa Indians, 1998 WL 35289046, at *1 (Grand Traverse Band Tribal court 1998).

4. Since tribes make mistakes, often tribal courts are asked to answer the question of whether a mistake constitutes reversible error. The Mashantucket Pequot Court of Appeals described the circumstances when a mistake will constitute reversible error:

> Some errors, however, implicate "constitutional rights so basic to a fair trial that their infraction can never be treated as harmless error." . . . Where the most basic fairness and integrity of the proceedings are involved, or where there has been a significant deviation from constitutional rule or a specific statutory requirement, plain error exists and reversal is automatic.

Grossi v. Mashantucket Pequot Gaming Enterprise, 26 Indian L. Rep. 6112 (Mashantucket Pequot Court of Appeals 1998).

Tribal courts tend to follow a general rule in relation to prejudicial error: "[n]ot all procedural irregularities, however, require a reviewing court to set aside an administrative decision; material prejudice to the complaining party must first be shown." *Fickett v. Brown*, 23 Indian L. Rep. 6190, 6196 (Mashantucket Pequot Tribal court 21995). Generally, errors made at the administrative, or pre-termination, hearing level can be "cured" by the subsequent post-termination hearing.

5. In *Short v. Hoopa Health Association*, 6 NICS App. 67 (Hoopa Valley Tribal Supreme Court 2001),* the court held that the failure of the Tribe to provide a pre-termination written evaluation did not constitute a violation of due process sufficient to justify reversal of the decision to discharge because the employee had actual notice of the reasons why the tribe terminated his employment:

> In the instant case the Tribe's failure to provide a written pre-termination evaluation is not a sufficient basis for reversing the TERO Commission and reinstating Appellant. This Court holds that a failure to provide a written pre-termination evaluation is not, in and of itself, a due process violation sufficient to require reinstatement or to grant the relief requested by Appellant.

---

*Disclosure: The author participated as counsel for the Hoopa Health Association in this matter.

> The TERO ordinance provides substantial due process protections both pre- and post-termination. In the case before us, the Tribe failed to provide Appellant with a single written pre-termination evaluation. However, this failure was overcome by the post termination protection of a TERO Commission hearing. The post-termination hearing met the minimum due process requirements set forth in *Hoopa Valley Indian Housing Authority v. Gerstner*, 3 NICS App. 250 (Hoopa Valley 1993). At the hearing the Tribe bore the burden of proving that termination was the appropriate remedy. Appellant had an opportunity to present evidence and confront the witnesses against him. Appellant had an opportunity to argue issues of law. The hearing officer and, ultimately, the full TERO Commission found sufficient factual basis for termination.

Id. at 70.

6. In *Johnson v. Mashantucket Pequot Gaming Enterprise*, 1995.NAMP.0000026 (Mashantucket Pequot Tribal Court 1995), *aff'd*, 25 Indian L. Rep. 6011 (Mashantucket Pequot Court of Appeals 1996), the court noted that "[t]he creation of a favorable record would require a plaintiff to be personally well spoken, to have had the presence of mind to arrange, in advance of the hearing, witnesses in his or her behalf, and to cross-examine the [employer]'s representatives." The court doubted that many hourly employees could effectively communicate at such an advanced level.

7. Alternatively, tribes might allow for non-lawyer or lay advocates to represent employees at the administrative review stage. The reasoning behind this provision might be that non-lawyers are less likely to create the kind of adversarial exchanges that lawyers would while providing employees a voice for their position. Nevertheless, allowance for lay advocates in the rules for administrative hearings is not necessarily an improvement. One tribal court noted that a lay advocate's commentary on the record before an administrative hearing panel consisted of "repeated use of leading questions, testifying by the spokesperson instead of through witnesses, [and] 'editorializing' . . . throughout the Transcript of Proceedings." *Hoopa Forest Industries v. Jordan*, 25 Indian L. Rep. 6159, 6160 n. 4 (Hoopa Valley Tribal Court March 25, 1998).

8. Employment hearing panels often become painful marathons of emotional, political, and sociological torment. The trial court in the *Synowski* case described a particularly difficult hearing where the Tribal government representatives employed a shotgun approach to indicting the performance of the employee.

> The cases did not stay . . . simple. . . . Instead, the issues shifted and multiplied.
>
> The hearings were relatively lengthy, unstructured, and undisciplined. In each hearing, the case against the [employee] was presented almost in a stream-of-consciousness fashion, with one accusation and criticism followed more-or-less randomly by another. By the conclusion of each hearing, any sense of orderly presentation of the issues was lost amid the myriad of additional claims that had been raised. The [employees] were not given adequate notice of plethora of claims that they would have to face at these hearings, and even the [administrative] panel members sometimes appear to have been confused about which issues were before them.

Apparently, anything that came to mind was considered fair game. . . .

[T]he employer seized on any complaint available or imaginable, whether related to the licensing policy, the problems of running the center, the quality of patient care, the keeping of files, attendance at meetings, graduate school transcripts, the choice of graduate school course work, etc. The danger of such an unconstrained and wide-ranging presentation at an [administrative] hearing is that the issues raised are likely to stray beyond those of which the [employee] has had any adequate, advance notice.

Synowski v. Confederated Tribes of Grand Ronde, 3 Am. Tribal Law 276, 280-82 (Confederated Tribes of the Grand Ronde Community Tribal Court 2001).

B. HOUSING

Navajo Housing Authority v. Betsoi

Navajo Nation Court of Appeals, No. A-CV-37-83, 5 Navajo Rep. 55; 1985.NANN.0000011 (September 13, 1985)

Before Tso, Acting Chief Justice, Bradley and Hilt, Associate Justices.

This case comes before the Court upon certified questions from two District Courts. These questions arose during Forcible Entry and Detainer actions against Mutual Help Housing participants. The Court is asked to resolve two basic issues:

1. Whether Mutual Help Housing participants are tenants or equity owners;
2. If it is determined Mutual Help Housing participants are equity owners, whether Forcible Entry and Detainer may be used against them.

Mutual Help Housing is a program developed by the Department of Housing and Urban Development to assist members of Indian Tribes to become home owners. Under the program Indian Housing Authorities are authorized to borrow money to cover the costs of constructing housing in Mutual Help Housing projects. The Indian Housing Authorities are also authorized to enter into agreements with the Bureau of Indian Affairs and departments within the Department of Housing and Urban Development (HUD) for the provision of funds and services. The Indian Housing Authority (in the Navajo Nation, the Navajo Housing Authority) enters into agreements with individual participants with the goal being for the participant to become the owner of the home. The participants under the Mutual Help and Occupancy Agreement with the Navajo Housing Authority agrees to:

A. Maintain his house and grounds to the satisfaction of the Authority and pay for all utility charges.
B. Pay a monthly administration charge to the Authority for expenses

C. Make additional payments toward home ownership based on his income and assets. These payments, called "equity payments;" will shorten the period of time before he becomes the owner of his house.

The monthly payments are used to establish an operating reserve and to reduce the loan balance attributed to a particular participant's house. In addition, "annual contributions" from HUD are applied to reduce the loan balance. Initially, the participant may also be required to contribute labor and/or a lump sum payment. When the loan, which the Navajo Housing Authority incurred to construct the dwelling[,] has been paid off, the participant is given title to the property.

It has been the practice of the Navajo Housing Authority to institute Forcible Entry and Detainer Actions (Eviction Proceedings) against Mutual Help Housing participants who become delinquent in their monthly payments. It is from such Forcible Entry and Detainer Actions in the trial courts that the issues have been raised in this Court. Specifically, the Mutual Help Housing participants assert that the use of Forcible Entry and Detainer against Mutual Help Housing participants deprives them of their property without due process of law as guaranteed under the Indian Civil Rights Act.

In determining the status of the Mutual Help Housing participants, the Court has considered the "Mutual Help and Occupancy Agreement" between the Navajo Housing Authority and the participant, the "Annual Contributions Contract" between the Navajo Housing Authority and HUD, and 44 Fed. Reg. No. 216, November 6, 1979 ["Indian Housing; Final Rule"] . . .

The rights and duties set out in these documents [are] revealing. Mutual Help Housing participants may be required to furnish land, materials or equipment, labor and/or money as a down payment; they may make structural changes or additions to the house with the consent of the Navajo Housing Authority; in the event of destruction of the house, the proceeds from the insurance carried by the Navajo Housing Authority may be used to rebuild the house or to pay off the indebtedness on the house with the remainder to the participant; and in the event of abandonment by the participant or termination of the agreement, the participant must receive the balance in the voluntary equity payments account and his Mutual Help contribution after certain expenses are deducted.

From the foregoing it is clear that the Mutual Help Housing participant has a status different from that of an ordinary tenant. The participant enters the agreement with the expectation of becoming a home owner; he usually contributes something in the nature of a "down payment"; he has use and control of the property in that he may assign his rights in the property and he may make structural changes or additions; and he has an interest in and a right to certain portions of insurance proceeds and Mutual Help contributions. The Court must conclude that a Mutual Help Housing participant has a property interest.

The Court has considered comparing that interest to those property interests commonly recognized in other jurisdictions in the United States. The Court has decided, however, not to label the interest for two reasons. One, the trust relationship between Indian Tribes and the Federal Government creates property interests on reservations that are unique to tribes. Two, the involvement of the federal government in Mutual Help Housing creates rights and obligations that are not analogous to those involved in most property ownership situations.

The Court holds that Mutual Help Housing participants have a property interest entitled to the due process guarantees of the Indian Civil Rights Act.

Next, the Court turns to the question of what is the due process to which Mutual Help Housing participants are entitled.

The Court has reviewed the Rules and Regulations from 44 Fed. Reg. No. 216 which pertain to Mutual Help Housing. §805.424 provides procedures for termination of a Mutual Help Housing agreement. §805.424 (b) reads as follows:

> (b) Notice of Termination of MHO Agreement by the IHA; Right of Homebuyer to Respond. Termination of the MHO Agreement by the IHA for any reason shall be by written Notice of Termination. Such notice shall state (1) the reason for termination; (2) that the Homebuyer may respond to the IHA in writing or in person of time regarding the reason for termination; (3) that in such response he may be represented or accompanied by a person of his choice, including a representative of the tribal government; (4) that the IHA will advise the tribal government concerning the termination; (5) that if, within 30 days after the date of receipt of the Notice of Termination, the Homebuyer presents to the IHA evidence or assurances satisfactory to the IHA that he will cure the breach and continue to carry out his MHO obligations, the IHA may rescind or extend the Notice of Termination; and (6) that unless there is such decision or extension the lease term and MHO Agreement shall terminate on the 30th day after the date of receipt of the Notice of Termination. The IHA may, with HUD approval, modify the provisions of the Notice of Termination relation to procedures for presentation and consideration of the Homebuyer's response. In all cases the IHA's procedures for the termination of an MHO Agreement shall afford a fair and reasonable opportunity to have the Homebuyer's response heard and considered by the IHA. Such procedures shall comply with the Indian Civil Rights Act and shall incorporate all the steps and provisions needed to achieve compliance with state, local or tribal law with the least possible delay.

It is in the procedures set forth above that a Mutual Help Housing participant's property interest must be protected. The Navajo Housing Authority has the flexibility under these provisions to establish guidelines and procedures to comply with due process requirements. There is opportunity for the Navajo Housing Authority to provide adequate notice of termination and time for the participant to either covert the default or work out a plan with the Housing Authority for correcting the default. The procedures outlined in §805.424 set forth above appear to the Court to be minimum requirements and there is no impediment to the Housing Authority in amplifying and expanding these procedures.

Although the Court does not intend to establish such guidelines and procedures for the Navajo Housing Authority, if a due process question comes before it in regard to Mutual Help Housing, the Court will examine the procedures carefully. Notice, opportunity to be heard, adherence to guideline and procedures, and the fairness of such guidelines and procedures, and any other requirements of due process and fairness will be considered by the Court.

Due to the flexibility which the Rules and Regulations in the above cited section [has] given to the Indian Housing Authorities, to establish procedures to insure due process in terminations, and due to the provision for refund of the Mutual Help Housing contributions, the Court does not at this time hold the Forcible Entry and Detainer actions against Mutual Help Housing participants violate due process requirements.

In each such action the trial court has the duty to scrutinize the termination proceedings which were had prior to a Forcible Entry and Detainer action being filed. Further, if any issues regarding the termination guidelines and procedures are raised in the trial court in a Forcible Entry and Detainer action, such issues may also be raised on appeal. At that time this Court will consider whether a Mutual Help Housing Participant's property interest has received the due process protections and guarantees to which it is entitled.

It is therefore Ordered that the proceedings in the trial courts, which are the subject of this case, proceed in accordance with this Opinion and Order.

NOTES

1. In *Chitimacha Housing Authority v. Martin*, 1994.NACH.0000002 (Chitimacha Indian Tribal Court of Appeals 1994), the court held that the Chitimacha Housing Authority failed to properly terminate a Mutual Help Ownership agreement by providing inadequate notice:

   24 CFR 905.446 governs the law of the termination of the MHO agreement. 24 CFR 905.446 (b) provides that:

   > Termination of the MHO agreement by the IHA for any reason shall be by written notice of termination. Such notice shall be in compliance with the terms of the MHO agreement. . . .

   Thus, Federal law requires that: (1) before the CHA can terminate a MHO agreement, there shall be a valid written notice of termination; and (2) that "such notice shall be in compliance with the terms of the MHO agreement." . . .

   Article 9.2 of the MHO agreement requires that the CHA provide the homebuyer with a written Notice of Termination. The agreement is very specific in regards to what the Notice of Termination must contain.

   > Termination of this Agreement by the IHA for any reason shall be by written notice of Termination. Such notice shall state (a) the reason for termination; (b) that the Homebuyer may respond to the IHA in writing or in person within a specified reasonable period of time regarding the reason for termination; (c) that in such response he may be represented or accompanied by a person of his choice, including a representative of the tribal government; (d) that the IHA will advise the tribal government concerning the termination; (e) that if, within 30 days after the date of receipt of the Notice of Termination, the Homebuyer presents to the IHA evidence or assurances satisfactory to the IHA that he will cure the breach and continue to carry out his MHO obligations, the IHA may

rescind or extend the Notice of Termination; and (f) that unless there is such a rescission or extension, the lease term and this Agreement shall terminate on the 30th day after the date of receipt of the Notice of Termination. The IHA may, with HUD approval, modify the provisions of the Notice of Termination relating to the procedures for presentation and consideration of the Homebuyer's response. In all cases the IHA's procedures for termination of this Agreement shall afford a fair and reasonable opportunity to have the Homebuyer's response heard and considered by the IHA. Such procedures shall comply with the Indian Civil Rights Act.

. . . The "Notice of Termination" failed to adequately comply with at least three subsections of Article 9.2 of the MHO Agreement. These failures go to the heart of the adequate notice provisions required under the MHO Agreement.

Article 9.2(b) requires the CHA to inform the homebuyer that he may respond to the housing authority in writing or in person within a reasonable period of time regarding the reason for the termination. . . . The evidence is clear that the CHA's Notice of Termination did not inform Mr. Martin of this right.

Article 9.2(e) . . . [and] Article 9.2(f) . . . require the notice of termination to specifically and unambiguously inform the homebuyer that: (1) if he complies, the termination may be rescinded or extended; and (2) that if there is no such rescission or extension, the agreement shall terminate on the 30th day after receipt of the notice.

The purported notice fails on both counts. It makes only a general mention that the effects of the termination can be cured by compliance and no mention that the effects of termination can be rescinded or extended. It does not provide the homebuyer with an unambiguous notice that the MHO agreement shall be terminated on the 30th day if no rescission or extension occurs. In fact, in the last paragraph of the letter, the homebuyer is informed of a grievance procedure which could easily suggest to the homebuyer that he has other avenues available to him before the termination is final.

The CHA's failure to inform Mr. Martin of his right to be represented [or accompanied to a hearing] by a person of his choice, including a representative of the Tribal governmental, is fatal to the adequacy of the Notice of Termination. . . .

Id. at ¶¶77-88.

2. In *Grand Traverse Band of Ottawa and Chippewa Indians Housing Dept. v. Shomin*, 2008 WL 6191997 (Grand Traverse Band Tribal Court 2008), the court dismissed a tribal eviction action on grounds that the Band did not comply with the notice requirements:

The notice of termination only gave Defendants 14 days to vacate the premises as stated in paragraph 10.B. of the lease, however, there is conflicting provision in paragraph 44.2.C. of the Grand Traverse Band Housing Department Occupancy Policy (hereinafter "Occupancy Policy"). That provision requires that the notice of termination provide "ample time" to vacate the unit, defined as 30 calendar days from the notice of termination. Defendants argue that the conflicting provisions should be interpreted in Defendants' favor, and that the Notice of Termination which only provided 14 days to vacate the premises violates the 30-day requirement. Plaintiffs admit that the two provisions conflict, but argue that there is a distinction between "serious violations" as stated in paragraph 10.B. of the lease, and that "serious violations" only require 14 days' notice pursuant to paragraph 10.D. of the lease.

Presumably under Plaintiff's interpretation, other less serious violations of the lease as stated in paragraph 44.2.D. of the Occupancy Policy would require 30 days' notice.

While perhaps a shortened time frame was intended for "serious violations" of the lease, the lease does not clearly state that the "serious violations" listed would result in a shorter time frame that that required under paragraph 44.2.C. of the Occupancy Policy. Actually, neither the notice provision of paragraph 10.D. of the lease nor the notice provision of paragraph 44.2.C. of the Occupancy Policy make reference to "serious violations." Both provisions are in direct conflict with each other as to how many days' notice must be given prior to termination of the lease. There is also substantial overlap between what is deemed a "serious violation" in paragraph 10.B. of the lease and paragraph 44.D. of the Occupancy Policy, such that either provision could arguably apply under the facts of these cases. As the leases in these cases were drafted by the Plaintiff, any inconsistency must be interpreted in favor of the Defendants. . . . Therefore, this Court interprets the conflict between paragraph 10.D. of the lease and paragraph 44.2.C. of the Occupancy Policy in favor of the Defendants. This Court holds that each Defendant was entitled to 30 days' notice prior to the termination of tenancy and the filing of the complaint for eviction, pursuant to paragraph 44.2.C. of the Occupancy Policy which is incorporated by reference into the lease.

Shomin, 2008 WL 6191997, at *2.

3. The procedures for evicting tribal citizens from tribal housing typically are onerous, but while there are many defenses available to defendants, many housing eviction cases are default judgments favoring the tribal housing agency because defendants fail to appear. *HCN Dept. of Housing Property Management Div. v. Whiterabbit*, 2 Am. Tribal Law 265, 269-70 (Ho-Chunk Nation Trial Court 2000), is such a case.

Ho-Chunk law in relation to housing evictions included the following provisions, reprinted in the *Whiterabbit* opinion:

Section 1. Declaration of the Eviction Ordinance

Sec. 1.03 This Eviction Ordinance shall be utilized to enforce evictions on all property owned by the Ho-Chunk Nation pursuant to Ho-Chunk Nation Constitution, Article I, Section I.

Sec. 1.04 All tenants and lessors shall agree to the jurisdiction of the Ho-Chunk Nation Court as the primary forum to resolve any dispute or controversy. Under Wis. Stat. Sec. 806.245, Judicial Records, order and judgments of an Indian Tribal Court in Wisconsin shall have the same full faith and credit in the courts of this state as do the acts, records, orders and judgments of any other State Court.

Sec. 1.06 This policy shall be used to evict tenants and lessors for nonpayment and other violations.

Section 2. Complaint in eviction actions.

Sec. 2.01 The complaint in an eviction action must be in writing and in accordance with Rule 3, Ho-Chunk Nation Rules of Civil Procedure, subscribed by the plaintiff or attorney. The complaint must:

(a) identify the parties and the real property subject of the action,
(b) state the facts which authorize the removal of the defendant,

(c) contain a legal description of the real property so long as it reasonably identifies the property location,

(d) contain a physical address including a street name, street number, and/or unit,

(e) if a cause of action, in addition to the claim for restitution, is joined, the same shall be separately stated. The relief shall be for the removal of the defendant or the property, or both, and, if an additional cause of action is joined for the other, relief sought by the plaintiff.

Section 3. Service and filing in eviction actions.

Sec. 3.01 The complaint and summons shall be served pursuant to Rule 5, Ho-Chunk Nation Rules of Civil Procedure.

Section 5. Order for judgment; writ of restitution.

Sec. 5.01 Order for judgment.

In an eviction action, if the court finds that the plaintiff is entitled to possession, the decision order shall be for the restitution of the premises to Plaintiff, and for such other relief as the Ho-Chunk Nation (hereinafter HCN) Trial Court orders. The judgment shall be entered accordingly as provided in HCN Rules of Civil Procedure.

Sec. 5.02 Writ of restitution.

At the time of decision order publication for the restitution of the premises, the HCN Trial Court shall order that a writ of restitution be issued. The writ shall be delivered to the tribal law enforcement officer (hereinafter TLO) or sheriff for execution. If judgment is against a non-tribal member on the Nation's property that is not trust land, the writ shall be issued to the county sheriff in accordance with Wis. Stats. 799.45. No writ shall be executed if received by the sheriff more than thirty (30) days after its issuance.

Sec. 5.03 Stay of Writ of Restitution

At the time of the decision order, upon application of the defendant with notice to the plaintiff, the court may, in cases where it determines hardship to exist, stay the issuance of the writ by a period not to exceed thirty (30) days from the date for the decision order.

(a) Any such stay shall be conditioned upon the defendant paying all rent or other charges due including court, moving and storage costs upon such terms and at such times as the court directs.

(b) The court may further require the defendant, as a condition of such stay, to give a bond in such amount and with such sureties as the court directs, conditioned upon the defendant's faithful performance of the conditions of the stay. Upon the failure of the defendant to perform any of the conditions of the stay the plaintiff may file an affidavit executed by the plaintiff or his or her attorney, stating the facts for such default, and a writ of restitution may be ordered.

Ho-Chunk Nation Rules of Civil Procedure

Rule 5. Notice of Service of Process

(A) Introduction. Service of process is the manner in which the parties are informed of the Complaint and of the opportunity to answer. Personal service is preferred, however, service at the person's home or usual place of business or employment is a second option. Other methods may be employed when, in the Court's discretion, they are the most likely to result in the actual notice of parties. . . .

(C) Methods of Service of Process.

. . .

(4) Service by Mail. Service of process may be accomplished by sending the required papers to a party by registered mail with return receipt requested. . . .

Rule 44. Presence of Parties and Witnesses

. . .

(C) Failure to Appear. If any party fails to appear at a hearing or trial for which they received proper notice, the case may be postponed or dismissed, a judgment may be entered against the absent party, or the Court may proceed to hold the hearing or trial. . . .

Rule 58. Amendment to or Relief from Judgment or Order

(A) Relief from Judgment. A Motion to Amend or for relief from judgment, including a request for a new trial shall be made within ten (10) calendar days of the filing of judgment. The Motion must be based on an error or irregularity which prevented a party from receiving a fair trial or a substantial legal error which affected the outcome of the action.

(B) Motion for Reconsideration. Upon motion of the Court or by motion of a party made not later than ten (10) calendar days after entry of judgment, the Court may amend its findings or conclusions or make additional findings or conclusions, amending the judgment accordingly. The motion may be made with a motion for a new trial. If the Court amends the judgment, the time for initiating an appeal commences upon entry of the amended judgment. If the Court denies a motion filed under this rule, the time for initiating an appeal from the judgment commences when the Court denies the motion on the record or when an order denying the motion is entered, whichever occurs first. If within thirty (30) days after the entry of judgment, the Court does not decide a motion under this Rule or the judge does not sign an order denying the motion, the motion is considered denied. The time for initiating an appeal from judgment commences in accordance with the Rules of Appellate Procedure.

(C) Erratum Order or Reissuance of Judgment. The Court may correct clerical errors in a court record, including the Judgment or Order, at any time.

(D) Grounds for Relief. The Court may grant relief from judgments or orders on motion of a party made within a reasonable time for the following reasons: (1) newly discovered evidence which could not reasonably have been discovered in time to request a new trial; or (2) fraud, misrepresentation or serious misconduct of another party to the action; or (3) good cause if the requesting party was not personally served in accordance with Rule 5(c)(1)(a) or (b); did not have proper service and did not appear in the action; or (4) the judgment has been satisfied, released, discharged or is without effect due to a judgment earlier in time.

Whiterabbit, 2 Am. Tribal Law at 266-68.

4. Tribal housing agencies have assessed former tenants for damages relating to waste or other misuse of tribal property. In *Mohegan Tribal Housing Authority v. Greene*, 6 Am. Tribal Law 466 (Mohegan Tribal Court 2006), the court assessed damages in accordance with tribal statute:

This Court may assess damages for waste, in connection with an eviction, against a defendant who has leased property from the MTHA. MTC §1-401(c) provides as follows:

> The judge shall also assess damage caused to the plaintiff by the default under the lease agreement, including damage for waste by the defendant, and any sums due The Mohegan Tribal Housing Authority under the lease agreement.
>
> Any amount owing The Mohegan Tribe/Tribal Housing Authority (if the plaintiff), including rent and damages assessed and ordered, may in addition to ordinary collection procedures, upon motion of the plaintiff attach to and be withheld from the next available per capita distribution pursuant to Section 2-183c(1) and (2).
>
> . . . When the Defendants vacated the Premises: the rugs in the living room, dining room and hall were stained to such an extent that they could not be repaired, so that the MTHA was required to remove them; several rooms contained extensive debris and trash; the house was infested with fleas; the kitchen and bathrooms required extensive cleaning; and the yard contained debris which had to be removed;
>
> The Defendants committed waste at the Premises, beyond ordinary wear and tear;
>
> The MTHA has incurred $2,191.55 in cleaning costs for the Premises, for the following: removal of trash and carpet from the house; removal of accumulated debris from the yard; cleaning of walls, floors and windows; cleaning of the kitchen and bathroom; extermination services; and dumpster services;

Greene, 6 Am. Tribal Law at 467-68.

5. But in *Grand Traverse Band of Ottawa and Chippewa Indians Housing Dept. v. Crowley*, 2005 WL 6300968 (Grand Traverse Band of Ottawa and Chippewa Indians Tribal Court 2005), the court held that defects in the tribal housing property could not be used to offset rental payments in an eviction action:

> This Court finds that there were defects with the rented property. Some of those defects were repaired by Plaintiff over the term of occupancy by the Defendant; some were not. Some were repaired by Defendant of her own accord and at her own expense, some were not. It is undisputed that Defendant continued to reside in the premises, despite its defects until evicted by this Court's Eviction Order. It is further undisputed that Defendant did not pay rent while residing in the premises for a very significant period of time. Furthermore, although Defendant made repeated requests to the Tribe's maintenance department to fix the defects, no attempts were made to "repair and deduct" or otherwise notify Plaintiff that Defendant was refusing to pay rent due to the alleged defects until Plaintiff sought to evict the Defendant.
>
> As noted before, this Court has found and continues to find that the issues with respect to the defects in the rented premises to do not rise to the level of a breach of the rental contract by the Plaintiff, and that Defendant is therefore not entitled to a reduction in the amount owed due to a breach of the lease or its covenants. Implicit in the Court's original Eviction Order was the finding that there had not been a breach of the lease which would excuse the amount of rent owing to the Plaintiff. Therefore, Plaintiff is entitled to the rent due, which is $7,286.30, plus court costs in the amount of $200.00. However, the amount of rent which should be ordered paid in this case should be reduced by $2,900.00 already ordered to be paid for the same leased premises as noted in the small claims judgment in File No. 04-03-212-SC. Judgment is therefore issued in favor of Plaintiff and against Defendant in

this case in the amount of $4,386.30 for rent, plus $200.00 in court costs, for a total judgment of $4,586.30. The small claims judgment in File No. 04-03-2124-SC shall remain in full force and effect, subject of course to payment already made toward that judgment by Defendants as outlined above. The amount owed to Plaintiff in this case shall be deducted from Defendant's December 2005 per capita distribution, and each successive per capita distribution until paid in full. An administrative fee (presently set at $100) shall be deducted from the Defendant's per capita distribution each time the Defendant's per capita distribution is accessed.

Crowley, 2005 WL 6300968, at *3.

6. Tribal housing agencies have to comply with a complicated mixture of tribal and federal procedural requirements in prosecuting eviction actions against tenants. In *Fort Peck Housing Authority v. Iceman*, 1 Am. Tribal Law 125 (Fort Peck Court of Appeals 1997), the court reversed a trial court eviction on grounds that the housing authority had failed to comply with its own rules:

> In order to answer the question of law in this case, we must first examine the following rules of law and determine whether FPHA violated federal or FPHA regulations by not granting Ramona Iceman an opportunity to be heard at the January 28, 1994 meeting.
>
> 24 CFR §950.340(a)(1) provides that Indian Housing Authority is required to adopt and promulgate grievance procedures which are appropriate to local circumstances. The procedures must comply with the Indian Civil Rights Act and shall assure that the tenants will:
>
> (i) Be advised of the specific grounds of any proposed adverse action;
> (ii) Have an opportunity for a hearing before an impartial party upon timely request;
> (iii) Have an opportunity to examine any documents or records or regulations related to the proposed action;
> (iv) Be entitled to be represented by another person of their choice at any hearing;
> (v) Be entitled to ask questions of witnesses and have others make statements on their behalf; and
> (vi) Be entitled to receive a written decision on the proposed action.
>
> ... The Housing Authority argues that nothing in either the Federal Indian Housing Regulations or the Fort Peck Housing Authority Grievance Policy prohibits the Board of Commissioners from reconsidering and rescinding its initial decision if that decision is contrary to the Fort Peck Housing Authority's own policy or Federal Law. The Housing Authority further argues that its grievance policy requires the Board to base its decision on "applicable laws, regulations, and policy" and thus when and initial decision is contrary to such laws, regulations, and policy, the Board is duty-bound to take appropriate action to correct it. The Housing Authority's argument is defective for two reasons:
>
> 1. The Housing Authority must show that rescinding the November 12, 1993 decision was based on law contrary to their decision. Here, the argument could have been made at the January 28, 1994 meeting before the Housing Board of Commissioners that Ramona Iceman falls into the drug elimination policy exception based on the theory that marijuana is not a narcotic drug. Ramona Iceman could have also argued equitable estoppel.

Neither argument was ever presented before the Housing Board. This Court does not at this time make a determination on either theory, nonetheless, the Housing Authority had a duty to hear Ramona's arguments and then decide whether their decision of November 12, 1993 was contrary to the Housing Authorities policy, or Federal Law.

2. A full, complete and fair opportunity to be heard was not granted to Ramona Iceman. On November 12, 1993 Ramona argued before the Board that she should fall in the exception and that she should not be evicted because she was seeking treatment for drug abuse; apparently (at that point in time) the Board agreed. Further, at that time the Board was not aware of any legal theory which would preclude them from allowing her to take advantage of the drug elimination policy exception. Nonetheless, the Board granted her an extension on her hearing; which held in abeyance her opportunity to be heard.

[Though the housing authority board initially agreed to hold a second hearing on April 15, 1994, the board decided to hold the hearing on January 29, 1994 instead.]

Fort Peck Housing Authorities Grievance Policy provides:

[V.E.1] Upon timely receipt of a hearing request; a hearing shall be scheduled before the Board of Commissioner, and written notice of the date and time of the hearing shall be mailed to the aggrieved party at least five (5) business days before the date of the hearing.

It is clear here that the grievance policy requires that a hearing shall be scheduled. Initially, Ramona Iceman had a scheduled grievance hearing on November 12, 1993, that hearing was continued and re-scheduled for April 15, 1994. The Board cannot unilaterally change that schedule without granting Ramona Iceman notice and opportunity to be heard. The facts here indicate that Ramona Iceman's opportunity to complete her grievance hearing was "short circuited"; the denial of notice and opportunity to be heard is fundamentally unfair.

Iceman, 1 Am. Tribal Law at 129-30.

C. LAND USE

GOBIN v. TULALIP TRIBES OF WASHINGTON

Tulalip Tribal Court of Appeals, No. TUL-Ci-12/00-420, 6 NICS App. 120, 2003 WL 25859176 (April 3, 2003)

Before: LAWRENCE NUMKENA, Chief Justice; GREGORY M. SILVERMAN, Justice; RICHARD A. WOODROW, Justice.

The present case involves cross-appeals by both parties below. The Appellant (Cross-Appellee) appeals the trial court's order of March 7, 2002. The appellant appeals the trial court's conclusions (1) that the Planning Commission and the Board acted lawfully in allowing the Comprehensive Plan to trump the Zoning Ordinance; (2) that the Planning Commission and the Board acted lawfully in denying Appellant's proposed housing project on the basis that it is inconsistent with the Comprehensive Plan; and (3) that

Appellant's Tribal Economic and Indian Civil Rights did not serve as the basis for monetary damages. The appellant further argues that the "Board" acted in violation of Ordinance 92, Code of Ethics for the Tulalip Board of Directors, through the appearance of bias.

The Respondent's (Cross-Appellant's) appeal argues that: (1) the trial court erred by unlawfully assuming and enforcing a judicial power of disqualification of voting Board members in an action brought under TTT §80.39.3 of the Zoning Ordinance; (2) the trial court erred by unlawfully ordering individual members of the Board of Directors to abstain, taking no part in the discussion or voting on the action; (3) the trial court erred by admitting extra-record evidence; (4) the trial court erred by admitting inadmissible extra-record evidence; (5) the court erred by determining that meetings held pursuant to TTT §80.38.1 are "judicial in nature"; and (6) that the court committed an error of law by ruling that the Board Secretary must certify all administrative records in zoning appeals.

The Land Use and Zoning Issues

The Appellant argues that the trial court committed two errors below. First, Appellant argues that the lower court erred when it held that the Tulalip Planning Commission and the Tulalip Board of Directors ("Board") acted lawfully in allowing the Comprehensive Plan to trump the Zoning Ordinance. Second, Appellant argues that the Planning Commission and the Board acted lawfully in denying Appellant's proposed housing project on the basis that it is inconsistent with the Comprehensive Plan. The Appellant further argues that her proposed Planned Residential Development ("PRD") meets the requirement of the Tulalip Zoning Ordinance ("TZO") and should have been approved as a matter of right. For the reasons set forth below, we affirm the judgment of the lower court.

Appellant is correct that where inconsistencies exist between the applicable zoning ordinance and a comprehensive plan, the more specific requirements of the zoning ordinance control. . . . While no tribal authority exists on this point of law, state law is clear and may be relied upon pursuant to Tulalip Tribal Ordinance ("TTO") 49. If the Tribe desires to require conformance to the targets set forth in the Tribe's Comprehensive Plan, then it should amend the Tulalip Zoning Ordinance ("TZO") to include those targets as requirements for approval under the relevant provisions of the Zoning Ordinance.

The Comprehensive Plan itself expressly acknowledges that it is merely a planning and guidance document that "shall be used as the basic source of reference and *as a guide* in reporting upon or recommending any proposed project, public or private, as to its purpose, location, form, alignment and timing." Comprehensive Plan, Chapter 8, at 4 (emphasis added) quoted in Staff Recommendation, RZ/SD 99-006, at 2 (Staff Report on Kim Gobin 20-acre Rezone/Subdivision Application).

Nor does the language of TZO §34 make the targets, goals and policies of the Comprehensive Plan mandatory. Subsection 34.3 (Subdivision Review) states that "[t]he Planning Board shall review all proposed subdivisions and make recommendations to the Board thereon with reference to approving or recommending any modifications necessary to assure conformance with the comprehensive plan goals, policies and objectives. . . ." TZO §34.3. Under this subsection, the Planning Board shall recommend "modifications necessary to assure conformance with the comprehensive plan." Significantly, the scope of this subsection is limited to approving or recommending *modifications*: it does not state that the Planning Board shall, or even may, recommend the denial of an entire proposed subdivision on the sole grounds that it does not conform to the Comprehensive Plan. Accordingly, the relevant inquiry concerns whether Appellant's Planned Residential Development ("PRD") proposal satisfies the requirements of the Tulalip Zoning Ordinance, not the Comprehensive Plan.

Appellant argues that the decision of the Tulalip Board of Directors denying her proposed PRD was arbitrary and capricious and, therefore, unlawful. A proposed PRD is also referred to as a rezone in the Tulalip Zoning Ordinance. Paragraph 38.1(g) states that the Board's "[d]enials of rezones, and approvals or denials of subdivisions, shall be by resolution." TZO §38.1(g). By Resolution No. 2000-403, on December 6, 2000, the Board denied Appellant's proposed rezone and subdivision. Specifically, the Board resolved that "[a]fter discussing the proposed planning commission recommendations and reviewing correspondence and [sic], The Tulalip Board of Directors hereby approves, adopts and certifies Tulalip Planning Commission Recommendation 2000-08." The Tulalip Tribes Resolution No. 2000-403 (December 6, 2000). Thus, to determine whether the Board's action was arbitrary and capricious, we must consider the Planning Commission Recommendation approved, adopted and certified by the Board.

The Planning Commission set forth its recommendation for the Appellant's rezone/subdivision request in the Tulalip Tribes Planning Commission Resolution No. 2000-008. Therein, it resolved that "[t]he Tulalip Planning Commission hereby recommends the Tulalip Board of Directors deny the proposed rezone and subdivision application for a Planned Residential Development (PRD)." Tulalip Tribes Planning Commission Resolution No. 2000-008 (October 11, 2000). Moreover, it further resolved that "[t]he Tulalip Planning Commission hereby adopts the Findings of Fact and Conclusions as set forth in the Tulalip Community Development Staff Recommendations for the Kim Gobin [i.e., the Appellant] rezone and subdivision as the basis for the commission's decision." *Id.* Accordingly, to determine whether the Planning Commission's recommendation and, a fortiori, the Board's denial, was arbitrary and capricious, we must consider the Staff Recommendations of the Tulalip Department of Community Development.

When we turn to the Conclusions set forth in the Staff Report of the Tulalip Department of Community Development, we discover that there are two and that both concern the inconsistency of Appellant's proposed rezone and subdivision with the Comprehensive Plan. The first conclusion states in relevant part that "[t]he proposed development reflects a suburban development in character and is not consistent with the comprehensive plan text which explains that new development in this area should reflect a density of one dwelling unity per 5 acres." Staff Recommendation, RZ/SD 99-006, §12, at 8 (Staff Report on Kim Gobin 20-acre Rezone/Subdivision Application). Similarly, the second conclusion states, in relevant part, that "[t]he PRD as proposed by the applicant is inconsistent with the comprehensive plan language that specifically refers to the north central border area of the reservation." *Id.*

Significantly, neither conclusion refers to the Zoning Ordinance. In particular, the DCD fails to mention §21 of the Tulalip Zoning Ordinance. This provision states that "[w]here sewer is not available PRD densities shall not exceed 2 dwelling units per acre in any zone." TZO §21.5. This requirement specifically concerned with PRDs directly conflicts with the more general requirement of the Comprehensive Plan that targets a density of one dwelling unit per 5 acres for rural areas. As already noted, where the Zoning Ordinance and the Comprehensive Plan conflict, the Zoning Ordinance controls. As a basis for decision in this matter, it is the proposed rezone and subdivision's consistency with the Zoning Ordinance that is relevant, not the Comprehensive Plan.

Turning to the Findings of Fact contained in the Staff Report of the Tulalip Department of Community Development, we learn that there are eleven such findings. Finding No. 6 states that:

> The application is for a *rezone* to Planned Residential Development (PRD). The PRD is a technique that could provide for small lots while still preserving open space and the rural character of the area.

Id. Finding No. 1 states that:

> The proposed rezone and subdivision is located in a Rural Residential Zone. Base zoning (shown on the Tulalip zoning map) for this site requires 10-acre lots for new subdivisions.

Id. at 7. Finding No. 5 states that:

> The area to the west of the property is primarily made up of residential homes on 5-acre lots. To the south and east of the proposed development, the land is largely undeveloped, consisting of lots that are 20 acres in size.

Id. at 8. Finding No. 2 states that:

> Section 12.0 of the zoning code states that the purpose of the Rural Residential zone is "to preserve the rural character of the outlying and sparsely populated areas as a transition zone between undeveloped lands and already developed areas."

Id. at 7. The remaining Findings of Fact (Nos. 3, 4 and 7) all concern the Comprehensive Plan.

It is not obvious how, if at all, these Findings of Fact support a denial of the proposed rezone and subdivision. Subsection 21.3 of the Zoning Ordinance states that "PRDs may be approved in: . . . Rural Residential" areas. Accordingly, on their face, neither the Conclusions, nor the Findings of Fact indicates how the proposed PRD fails to meet the requirements of the Zoning Ordinance. Indeed, if we limited ourselves to a review of the Findings of Fact and Conclusions set forth in the DCD Staff Report, adopted first by the Planning Commission and then by the Tulalip Board of Directors, we would be forced to agree with the Appellant that the denial of this proposed rezone and subdivision is arbitrary and capricious.

In the present case, however, it would be an unjust myopia to limit our review to the Findings of Fact and the Conclusions expressly adopted by the Planning Commission and the Board of Directors. The Finding of Facts and

Conclusions were but two sections from a lengthy Staff Report by the Department of Community Development. Clearly, the Planning Commission and the Board of Directors had carefully reviewed the entire Staff Report in forming their recommendation and decision. In this Court's opinion, therefore, it is only an infelicity of drafting that suggests that the Planning Commission's recommendation and the Board's decision were based upon an inadequate portion of that report. If we look to the body of the Staff Report, we may discern the true and adequate ground of the Board's decision.

While some might argue that this court should vacate and remand with instructions to the lower court to vacate the Board's decision and remand thereto, it is equally clear that the Board would merely redraft its original resolution to incorporate by reference the entire Staff Report, add some clarifying commentary, and the problem with their decision would be resolved. Such formalistic exercises do not serve justice and squander limited tribal resources.

Nor do we believe that our decision to consider the body of the Staff Report is inconsistent with *Beno v. Shalala*, 30 F.3d 1057 (9th Cir. 1994). In *Beno*, the court held that "agency action must be upheld, if at all, on the basis articulated by the agency itself." *Beno v. Shalala*, 30 F.3d at 1073-74. The court recognized that it nonetheless could "uphold a decision of less than ideal clarity if the agency's path may reasonably be discerned." *Id.* at 1073. . . . In the present matter, the path of the Department of Community Development may be reasonably discerned in the body of its Staff Report. The fact that the Planning Commission and the Board of Directors inadvertently failed to formally note their reliance on the entire staff report does not alter the fact that the basis of the agency action may be reasonably discerned therein. Accordingly, it is to the body of this staff report that we now turn.

Although the DCD focused primarily on the Comprehensive Plan, its concerns and observations are equally apposite to the requirements of the Tulalip Zoning Ordinance. Paragraph 34.4(e) of the Tulalip Zoning Ordinance states that "[a]ll subdivisions impacting environmentally and culturally sensitive land shall include protection measures consistent with the standards and requirements of this ordinance." TZO §34.4(e). Moreover, subsection 23.3 of the Tulalip Zoning Ordinance states:

> Any proposed . . . subdivision approval for development which would impact environmentally sensitive lands *shall be permitted only after* the exact location of environmentally sensitive area(s) has been identified by the proponent of the development proposal, a review of impacts to the environmentally sensitive area(s) is completed and buffer requirements or other mitigation necessary for protection of the sensitive lands *have been established* by the Executive Director of the Department of Community Development consistent with this ordinance and the text, goals, objectives, and policies of the 1994 Tulalip Comprehensive Plan.

TZO §23.3 (emphasis added). The definition of environmentally sensitive area(s) includes, *inter alia*, lakes. TZO §23.2. Thus, before the proposed rezone and subdivision can be permitted, the DCD must determine the impacts to local lakes and establish buffer requirements or other mitigation necessary for their protection. According to the Staff Report, the DCD was unable to complete their review of the impacts of the proposed PRD to Lake Agnes or Mary Shelton Lake due to the failure of the Appellant to address these matters in its application. Staff Recommendation, RZ/SD 99-006, §9, at 5 (Staff Report on Kim Gobin 20-acre Rezone/Subdivision Application). Apparently, this omission resulted from Appellant's belief that the DCD would perform such an assessment. *Id.* The Staff Report notes, however, that[]

> [t]his is not the case. The burden of determining impacts to wildlife habitat and lake resources fall[s] on the applicant. The [Appellant's] environmental assessment does state that the development will have no significant impact on surface and ground water. However, there is no discussion about how the applicant arrived at this decision, so staff is unable to follow the reasons for this statement. Absent more information on this issue, staff is unable to conclude that the development will have no significant impact on lake resources.

Id. Since the DCD was unable to conclude that the proposed rezone and subdivision will have no significant impacts on lake resources, then pursuant to subsection 23.3 it had to recommend denial of the proposed rezone and subdivision.

The DCD's recommendation to deny the proposed rezone and subdivision in its Staff Report to the Planning Commission was not inevitable. DCD completed its Staff Report on August 21, 2000, but would not deliver it to the Planning Commission until the latter's hearing on the proposed rezone and subdivision scheduled for September 1, 2000. By letter dated August 21, 2000, the DCD informed the Appellant that it could not recommend approval of the proposed PRD on the present record and invited the Appellant to seek a postponement of the Planning Commission hearing so that Appellant could work with the DCD to address the issues that caused the DCD concern. In particular, the DCD desired that the Appellant submit additional information on the proposed rezone and subdivision's impact on environmentally sensitive area(s). The Appellant failed to seek a postponement of the Planning Commission hearing on the proposed PRD and only responded to the DCD's letter on August 31, 2000, the day before the hearing. Appellant's response was a letter from her attorney and did not provide any additional information or data concerning the environmental impacts of the project.

Given the Appellant's failure to submit sufficient data and information to permit the DCD to complete its review of the project's impacts to environmentally sensitive area(s), including various lake resources, and the requirements of subsection 23.3 of the Zoning Ordinance, the Planning Commission and the Board of Directors had no option but to follow the recommendation of the DCD and deny the proposed rezone and subdivision. One can also reasonably discern from the Staff Report a second reason why the DCD recommended denial of the rezone and subdivision. In Section 10 of the Staff Report, the DCD notes that "[p]er Section 21.5 [of the Zoning Ordinance], densities for the PRD shall be calculated as an average density over the development area." Staff Recommendation, RZ/SD 99-006, §10, at 6 (Staff Report on Kim Gobin 20-acre Rezone/Subdivision Application). The Staff Report then sets out the requirement under section 21.5 that "[w]here sewer is not available, PRD density shall not exceed two (2) dwelling units per acre in any zone." *Id*. While the DCD does not elaborate the significance of this provision on its decision not to recommend the proposed PRD, an issue does exist whether the proposed PRD does in fact meet this requirement.

The Appellant's proposed PRD involves 21.49 acres and 26 dwelling units in a Rural Residential zone. Consistent with the requirements of subsection 21.4 of the Zoning Ordinance, the Appellant's proposal would establish fifty percent of this acreage as open space under a restrictive covenant adopted as part of plat approval and filed with the Tulalip Tribes and recorded with the Snohomish County Auditor. Subsection 21.4 refers to the area subject to the restrictive covenant as the open space/recreation area and notes that the "*open space/recreation area* shall be established through a restrictive covenant that places the burden of protecting and maintaining open space areas on the homeowners within the subdivision." TZO §21.4 (emphasis added).

The next provision of the Zoning Ordinance is subsection 21.5 concerning the density requirements for PRDs. As already noted, it states that "[d]ensities for the PRD shall be calculated as an average density *over the development area*." TZO §21.5 (emphasis added). This occurrence of the phrase "the development area" is the first such occurrence of this phrase in section 21 of the Zoning Ordinance. The phrase is not defined in section 3, the definitions section, of the Zoning Ordinance; nonetheless, its use in subsection 21.5 strongly suggests that it is intended to exclude the open space/recreation area and refer to that part of the PRD land on which the dwelling units are actually constructed.

This interpretation of the phrase "development area" is suggested by the fact that the application of the different density requirements contained in this subsection turn on whether the PRD has sewer available. If no sewer is available, then the density shall not exceed two dwelling units per acre. Clearly, the concern here is how many septic systems can function in the area of land on which the dwelling units are proximately constructed. In this regard, the existence of additional acreage on a distant part of the PRD is irrelevant; it will not affect the operation of the septic systems in the area of the PRD actually developed.

Under this analysis of the subsection 21.5, the development area is approximately 10.75 acres (one half of 21.49 acres) and, *a fortiori*, the maximum number of dwelling units that can be constructed consistent with subsection 21.5 is 23 (twice 10.75). As these calculations demonstrate, therefore, the proposed rezone and subdivision also fails to meet the density requirements of subsection 21.5 of the Zoning Ordinance.

For the foregoing reasons, we hold that the decision of the Tulalip Board of Directors to deny the Appellant's rezone and subdivision was not arbitrary and capricious, or unlawful. . . .

NOTES

1. Kim Gobin had previously argued successfully that Snohomish County had no jurisdiction over her land in *Gobin v. Snohomish County*, 304 F.3d 909 (9th Cir. 2002), *cert. denied*, 538 U.S. 908 (2003).

2. Certain provisions of the Navajo Nation's land use code read:

A. This Act is an enabling legislation that authorizes the Economic Development Committee to promulgate the Navajo Business Site Leasing Regulations; provided, however, that the Business Site Leasing Regulations contain factors that:

    1. Protect and preserve Navajo trust assets from loss, damage, unlawful alienation, waste and depletion;

    2. Promote the Navajo Nation control, interest of the Navajo Nation and support the use of the trust assets;

    3. Provide asset management system that prudently oversees the management, tracking and inventory of tribal assets;

    4. Account for and timely identify, collect, deposit and distribute income from the trust assets or reinvest income or monies into economic development activities or projects;

    5. Provide for records and recording system for accounts and leases and other operational and information system; and

    6. Provide other provisions that promote modern and up-to-date leasing practices.

5 Navajo Nation Code §2302.

D. TRIBAL POLICE POWERS

Skokomish Tribe v. Mosbarger

Skokomish Tribal Court of Appeals, No. I 12774, 7 NICS App. 90 (June 26, 2006)

Miller, J.: . . .

I. Factual Background

The following facts are undisputed on appeal: on May 25, 2005, Mosbarger was driving on Washington State Highway 106, at a point within the external boundaries of the Skokomish Reservation. She was cited by a tribal police officer for violating the Tribal Code due to driving her vehicle 31 miles per hour in a zone with a posted 20 mile per hour speed limit. She was exceeding the 20 mph speed limit in a "posted school zone" and "an active school zone" in front of the Hood Canal School on the reservation. The school is located directly on Highway 106. The 20 mph speed limit and the existence of the school zone were posted. The infraction occurred at approximately 9:01 a.m. on a Wednesday.

We take judicial notice of the following facts: the Hood Canal School is a grade school (kindergarten through eighth grade) attended by 351 students in March 2004, of which, according to a federal report filed by the school, 125 students were in the category of "Federally recognized, including Alaska Natives"; the office hours of the Hood Canal School are 7:30-4:00 and students are scheduled to be at school from 8:45 a.m. to 3:00 p.m. each school day; the

Hood Canal School was in session on May 25, 2005; and the Skokomish Tribal Nation has approximately nine hundred enrolled members/citizens.

In its appellate brief, the Tribe alleges that school was in session on the date Mosbarger was speeding in the school zone and that children were present on the school ground immediately adjacent to the highway. The Tribe also asserts that most, if not all, Skokomish Tribal children residing on the reservation attend the Hood Canal School. Mosbarger did not dispute these allegations by the Tribe. Parsons was cited for speeding for traveling 57 miles per hour in a 45 miles per hour posted zone on U.S. Highway 101 within the exterior boundary of the Reservation. . . .

III. Discussion

The jurisdictional issue presented in this appeal is whether the Tribal Government and the Tribal Court have regulatory and adjudicatory jurisdiction to prosecute the civil traffic infractions issued to Mosbarger and Parsons for speeding on the Skokomish Reservation. . . .

The Constitution of the Skokomish Tribe provides: "Except as prohibited by the Treaty of Point No Point and Federal Law, the Skokomish Tribe shall have jurisdiction over all persons, property, lands . . . and all activities occurring within the exterior boundaries of the Skokomish Indian Reservation." Skokomish Const., art. I, sec. 1[.] We are directed by tribal law to review the tribal treaty and federal law to determine the issue before us. We have reviewed the 1855 Skokomish Treaty of Point No Point and find no relevant provisions to guide us. See www.skokomish.org/SkokConstitution&Codes/Constitution/Treaty.htm. Thus, we will turn to federal case law because we are unaware of any federal statutory provisions that apply to this situation, and the parties have cited none.

There is extensive federal case law on the subject of tribal civil jurisdiction over non-Indians and their activities on Indian reservations. The rule that we must apply is found in *Montana v. United States*, 450 U.S. 544 (1981). The Supreme Court has called *Montana* the "pathmarking case concerning tribal civil authority over nonmembers." *Strate v. A-1 Contractors*, 520 U.S. 438, 445 (1997). . . .

A. Mosbarger

In addressing Mosbarger's appeal, we focus on the second *Montana* exception because the Tribe did not allege that she had entered any kind of contract or "other arrangements" with the Tribe or its members that might recognize jurisdiction in the Tribe under the first exception. The Supreme Court test for the second exception is plainly a factual one: Does the "conduct of non-Indians on fee lands within [a] reservation . . . threaten[] or ha[ve] some direct effect on the political integrity, the economic security, or the health or welfare of the tribe"[?] *Montana*, 450 U.S. at 566. We will apply that test to the factual situation presented in this case.

On May 25, 2005, Mosbarger was driving on the Skokomish Reservation on Washington State Highway 106. In a nearly identical situation in *Strate*, the Supreme Court decided to "align the [state highway] . . . with land alienated to non-Indians." *Strate*, 520 U.S. at 456. Following that decision, we will do the same. Because Mosbarger was speeding on land considered the equivalent of land within a reservation owned in fee simple by non-Indians, we must apply the *Montana* test. Under that test and its second exception, the Skokomish Tribe could not have jurisdiction over Mosbarger unless her "conduct threaten[d] or ha[d] some direct effect on the political integrity, the economic security, or the health or welfare of the tribe." *Montana*, 450 U.S. at 566. We hold that the facts in this case meet that test and the Tribe has authority to regulate Mosbarger and the speed limit on state roads by the school on the reservation and that the Tribal Court has adjudicatory jurisdiction to decide this case.

Mosbarger exceeded the tribal 20 mph speed limit for school zones by 11 miles per hour. She was aware that she was speeding within a school zone because the existence of the school zone and the speed limit was posted on the highway. She was ticketed on Wednesday May 25, which was a school day, at 9:01 a.m. in the morning. Numerous Indian and Skokomish children attend the school.

These facts establish that Mosbarger's "conduct threaten[d] or ha[d] some direct effect on the political integrity, the economic security, or the health or welfare of the tribe." *Montana*, 450 U.S. at 566. By speeding in front of the grade school, Mosbarger endangered every student in the school. See Oregon Department of Transportation, A Guide to School Area Safety (February 2005) (school zones are particularly hazardous because of large numbers of motorists and pedestrians; most children do not perceive traffic dangers like "an adult would under the same circumstances"); Elizabeth J. Young & Karen K. Dixon, The Effects of School Zones on Driver Behavior (May 2003, Georgia Institute of Technology) (speeding in school zones is dangerous to children). . . .

Jurisdictions throughout the United States recognize this seemingly self-evident fact — speeding near schools is extremely dangerous to children. See, e.g., ORS 801.462 (school zones are 20 mph statutory speeds limits); Oregon Dept. of Transportation, Children in Traffic (videos presenting traffic situations from the child's point of view and developmental limitations); Oregon Dept of Education, The Oregon Pedestrian and School Bus Safety Book and the Oregon Traffic Patrol Manual; American Automobile Association, Traffic Safety Services Catalog (materials for adult crossing guards, school bus safety, traffic safety education for preschool children and student pedestrians); Federal Highway Admin. & National Highway Traffic Safety Comm., Pedestrian Safety Program Resource Kit; Harborview Injury Prevention and Research Center, Seattle, Washington (pedestrian safety research and program for child pedestrian safety).

The Oregon Court of Appeals recently noted that the very "purpose" of a "speed limit is . . . to protect the health, welfare, and safety of citizens," and that this is "one of the most fundamental of all public policies." *Machado-Miller v. Mercereau & Shannon, LLP*, 43 P.3d 1207, 180 Or. App. 586, 594 (2002). Thus, it is evident that the Skokomish laws controlling speeding in the school zone on the reservation serve the purpose of protecting the health and welfare of the Tribe's minor citizens and the other children attending the Hood Canal School.

Also important to our decision affirming jurisdiction in this case under *Montana* is the fact that simply posting 20 mph signs and designating school zones has been shown not to control dangerous speeding around children. Traffic signs alone do not address nor solve the public policy issue for the Skokomish Tribe of protecting the health and welfare of its youngest citizens. See, e.g., Young & Dixon, at 4, 7 & 9; Charlie Saibel et al., Driver Perception of School Traffic Control Devices, ITE Journal, Vol. 69, Issue 11, at 38-42 (1999 Institute of Transportation Engineers, Washington D.C.); Patrick McCoy et al., School Speed Limit and Speeds in School Zones, Transportation Research Record 1254, at 1-7 (1990 Transportation Research Board, Washington D.C.). These studies show that speed limit signs are not effective at controlling speeding in school zones. Young & Dixon, at 4, 7 & 9; Saibel et al., at 38-42; McCoy et al., at 1-7. They conclude that only a police presence and the actual enforcement of school zone speed limits is effective in achieving lower and safer speeds. Young & Dixon, at 4. Consequently, the only effective tool to protect the young tribal citizens enrolled at Hood Canal School is for the Skokomish Tribe to proactively control speeding near the reservation school. Tribal police enforcement of the school zone speed limit is crucial to protect all the children at the Hood Canal School, Indian and non-Indian, and directly affects the protection and the health and welfare of the Tribe and its citizens.

Governmental entities throughout the United States recognize these facts and strive to protect their youngest citizens and their families from traffic related threats to their health and welfare by enacting and enforcing low speed limits near schools. The Skokomish Tribe agrees with this policy and is attempting to protect the physical health and welfare of its school aged children so that these future leaders and citizens can grow up to help perpetuate and govern the Tribe. It is instructive to note that in *Montana* the Supreme Court cited as an example of the proper application and definition of the second exception one of its own cases about adoptions of Indian children. *Montana*, 450 U.S. at 566 (citing *Fisher v. District Court*, 424 U.S. 382 (1976)). This citation implies that the Supreme Court intended that issues regarding the protection of tribal children could fall within the second exception. We agree and find that this is one of those factual situations where protecting the health and welfare of tribal members requires tribal jurisdiction over non-Indians speeding in the reservation school zone.

The Skokomish Tribe also complies with another aspect of the *Montana* exception when it protects its young citizens who attend the reservation school because the Tribe is working to advance its own political integrity and economic security. Nearly every society and government throughout human history has recognized the paramount need to educate, protect, and nurture its younger citizens to perpetuate the future existence and economic success of the society and the government itself. Most societies and governments spend enormous amounts of time, money, and effort in educating, protecting and preserving these societal resources. It appears to us beyond question that the political integrity of the Skokomish Tribe, that is, the preservation of its future existence and operation is well served by protecting its future leaders and citizens. Furthermore, the economic success of the Tribe is guaranteed by educating and protecting tribal youth to become productive tribal citizens in the future and by avoiding catastrophic injuries and the economic costs which could devastate family and tribal resources. Lastly, it is evident that protecting the health and welfare of the Tribe as a unit and of the individual tribal families and citizens depends upon the physical protection of its youngest citizens. Nothing less than an all-out effort to serve these fundamental public policies can be expected of the Tribe. . . .

In our view, the United States and the states and Indian tribes are political groupings of people. What affects one citizen or many citizens ultimately affects the health and welfare of the government and society as a whole. The *Montana* Court illustrated this very point by focusing on individuals when it expressed the two exceptions that define the parameters of tribal governmental control over non-Indians. The Court created the exceptions in regards to fishing and hunting regulations that the Crow Tribe was trying to impose on non-Indian individuals on the Crow Reservation. The *Montana* test was devised to protect individual non-Indians from the possible overextension of tribal jurisdiction. The test was based on the actions and impacts on tribal individuals in either the first exception's requirement that the non-Indian individual have entered some kind of consensual relationship with a tribe or with an individual tribal member, or the second exception's analysis of the impact of the non-Indian individual's conduct on the health and welfare of individual tribal members. Accordingly, the Supreme Court created and applied the *Montana* exceptions to the situations of individual Indians and non-Indians. To the Court, the tribe is the political representative of a group of Indian people and it is made up of the individual citizens, and the effect on Indian individuals is how the impact of the actions of non-Indians on a reservation is to be measured. When *Montana* discussed "the political integrity, the economic security, or the health or welfare of the tribe" we understand that the Court was talking about the tribal group, the tribal citizens/members, the individual Indians who make up the tribe. *See McClanahan v. Arizona State Tax Comm.*, 411 U.S. 164, 181 (1973) ("[W]hen Congress has legislated on Indian matters, it has most often dealt with the tribes as collective entities. But those entities are, after all, composed of individual Indians, and the legislation confers individual rights."); *Babbitt Ford, Inc. v. Navajo Indian Tribe*, 710 F.2d 587, 593-94 (9th Cir. 1983) (Navajo laws against self-help repossessions on the reservation protected the health and welfare of tribal members), *cert. denied*, 466 U.S. 926 (1984). We follow that understanding here.

Consequently, the application of the second exception of *Montana* requires us to review whether Mosbarger's conduct "threaten[ed] or ha[d] some direct effect on the political integrity, the economic security, or the health or welfare of the tribe[,]" *Montana*, 450 U.S. at 566, which includes an examination of the impact of her actions on individual tribal citizens. After examining the undisputed facts set out above, we hold that Mosbarger's conduct of speeding through a school zone on the reservation in violation of tribal law and the posted 20 mph speed limit did pose a serious risk and threatened and endangered young tribal citizens which in turn threatened the political integrity (the continued and future existence and welfare of the

Tribe), the economic security of the Tribe and individual Indians and Indian families (since enormous medical bills could have been incurred and the Tribe's collective earning power and future economic prospects could have been seriously limited), and the health and welfare of the Tribe's youngest citizens (which impacts the health and welfare of the Tribe as a whole). Mosbarger's conduct thus meets the factual test of the second exception and the Skokomish Tribe has regulatory and adjudicatory jurisdiction over her actions in the school zone on the Reservation.

Would any court or government wait until there were dead or injured children before taking the kind of protective steps the Skokomish Tribe is undertaking? We think not. And the *Montana* second exception does not require the tribal government to wait until an actual catastrophic event occurs before taking jurisdiction. The threat of a direct effect on these tribal and individual Indian interests is sufficient to establish tribal jurisdiction over the conduct of non-Indians on non-Indian owned fee lands on a reservation. . . .

Indeed, we think that if the U.S. Supreme Court was faced with this exact question it would agree that the *Montana* test expressly authorizes in the right circumstances a tribe's exercise of jurisdiction over external relationships and jurisdictional authority over non-Indians and their conduct on non-Indian owned lands. *Montana* did not concern tribal control over internal issues, tribal citizens, or tribal self-government issues. That case and its progeny decided when tribal governments and courts could reach outside their internal affairs and have regulatory and adjudicatory jurisdiction over non-Indians. *Montana* by its own express terms is about the external relations and powers of a tribe.

Consequently, we have applied *Montana* and its second exception straight up, as the Court defined it, to the factual situation before us. We have applied the test of when a tribal government can exercise its jurisdiction over persons and activities external to the tribal government which occurred within the reservation but on lands the Supreme Court directs us to consider as not being owned by the Skokomish Tribe. We hold that the second *Montana* exception is met in the specific factual setting of this case and that the Skokomish Tribe possesses governmental regulatory and judicial adjudicatory power to regulate and adjudicate the conduct of Mosbarger when she violated the speed limit in the school zone on a state highway within the reservation borders. . . .

NOTE

1. More and more tribal governments are turning toward the imposition of civil penalties as a means of enforcing law and order against non-Indians in Indian country. *E.g.*, Pokagon Band of Potawatomi Indians Code of Offenses §1(B) (2008) (noting that tribal criminal code will apply to non-Indians through the enforcement of that code through the imposition of civil offenses); Matthew L. M. Fletcher, *Rebooting Indian Law in the Supreme Court*, 55 S.D. L. Rev. 510, 526 (2010).

E. TRIBAL TRUST FUNDS

Seidel v. Mohegan Tribe of Indians of Connecticut

Mohegan Tribal Court of Appeals, No. CV-05-1226, 6 Am. Tribal Law 449,
2005.NAMT.0000005 (October 26, 2005)

The opinion of the court was delivered by: Before Jane W. Freeman, Judge

The Petitioner, Bethany Seidel, has petitioned the Court to authorize the distribution of per capita funds, from trust, to pay educational expenses of her two minor children, [Names Redacted] for the school year 2005-2006. The Mohegan Tribe of Indians of Connecticut ("Tribe"), Respondent, has filed an Answer indicating that it takes no position regarding the Petition.

The Court has jurisdiction of the parties and the subject matter. The Petitioner and the two minor children are members of the Tribe and the Respondent is the Tribe. The Court has subject matter jurisdiction pursuant to the Amended and Restated Ordinance of the Mohegan Tribe of Indians of Connecticut Establishing The Gaming Revenue Allocation Plan, Ordinance No. 2001-08, Section III.H.5., to authorize the trustee or trustees of trusts established for minor children under M.T.O. 2001-08 to make distributions to the parents or guardians of the trust beneficiaries, for the purposes and subject to the limitations set forth therein.

For the reasons hereafter stated, the Court holds that the Petitioner has not sustained her burden of showing, by a preponderance of the evidence, that the requested distributions from trust are necessary.

I. The Amended and Restated Ordinance of the Mohegan Tribe of Indians of Connecticut Establishing the Gaming Revenue Allocation Plan, Ordinance No. 2001-08

An Indian Tribe which makes per capita payments to its members from class II net gaming revenues is required to have an approved tribal revenue allocation plan. 25 U.S.C. §2710(b)(3)(A). The Tribe has adopted M.T.O. 2001-08 to meet this statutory requirement. M.T.O. 2001-08 makes provisions for the future welfare of minor tribal members while encouraging tribal member parents to pay for the immediate living needs of their children.

> The tribe also retains the inherent sovereign right to determine the best interests of its minor tribal members by providing for their future welfare by contributing per capita benefits to grantor trusts owned by the Tribe to be invested, with income earned on trust principal to be accumulated, for future distribution to those minor tribal members. The Tribe shall provide for the future of minors while encouraging tribal member parents to provide for the immediate living needs of their children as is their responsibility. All assets accumulated in the grantor trusts for future distribution to a minor tribal member shall be distributed at such time as the minor reaches the age of eighteen (18) and not before, except in the limited extraordinary circumstances provided in Section III.F.5.

M.T.O. No. 2001-08, Section I.

The limited extraordinary circumstances under which distributions may be made from trusts for the benefit of minor tribal members are as follows:

> In order to provide for the future safety and well being of tribal children, per capita benefits intended for future distribution to qualified minor tribal members shall be contributed by the Tribal Council to one or more trusts which are grantor trusts owned by the Tribe for federal income tax purposes. . . .
>
> Prior to the time the beneficiary reaches the age of eighteen (18), the Tribal Court may, after careful consideration of the facts, authorize the trustee or trustees of the trust or trusts to make distributions from the trust or trusts to the parents or guardians of the beneficiary only to defray unreimbursed medical expenses or only as necessary to defray expenses for health, education, or welfare incurred by or on behalf of the beneficiary as established by such parents or guardians. Any request for such disbursements shall include a detailed budget of monies necessary for essential living expenses to include health, education, or welfare costs and only upon presentment of a detailed justification for such essential living needs. The petitioning parent or guardian must show, by a preponderance of the evidence, that the amount requested to defray unreimbursed medical expenses or expenses for health, education or welfare, are reasonable and necessary. The Tribal Court may also require that the petitioning parent or guardian submit receipts of expenditures made from funds disbursed hereunder before any future disbursements are made.

M.T.O. 2001-08, Section III.H.5.

The Tribal Council has expressed a clear intent in M.T.O. 2001-08 to limit distributions from grantor trusts to extraordinary circumstances, where the amounts requested are reasonable and necessary. Further, the Tribal Court is limited to authorizing distributions from trust only where it has made a factual determination that the distributions are "necessary to defray expenses for health, education or welfare incurred by or on behalf of the beneficiary. . . ." M.T.O. 2001-08, Section III.H.5. The phrase "extraordinary circumstances" and the terms "reasonable" and "necessary" are not defined in M.T.O. 2001-08. To discern the meaning of a phrase, a court may look to the word's ordinary meaning. . . . To ascertain the commonly approved usage of words, it is appropriate to look to the dictionary definition of the terms. . . .

"Extraordinary circumstances" are "[a] highly unusual set of facts that are not commonly associated with a particular thing or event." Black's Law Dictionary, 7th Ed. "Extraordinary" has been defined as "going beyond what is usual, regular, common or customary . . . exceptional to a very marked extent." Webster's Third New International Dictionary. "Reasonable" has been defined as "being or remaining within the bounds of reason: not extreme: not excessive". *Id.* "Necessary" has been defined as "that cannot be done without: that must be done or had: absolutely required". *Id.*

The petition must be considered in light of these definitions and the clear legislative intent to limit distributions to extraordinary circumstances where the amounts requested are reasonable and necessary.

II. The Petition and the Facts

The petitioning parent seeking a distribution from a grantor trust in order to defray educational expenses, must show, by a preponderance of the evidence, that the amount requested is reasonable and necessary. M.T.O. 2001-08, Section III.H.5. The standard of proof of a fact by a preponderance of the evidence has been met when all the evidence, considered fairly and impartially, evinces a reasonable belief that it is more probable than not that the fact is true. . . . A hearing has been held by this Court to consider and determine the facts. In addition to considering the hearing testimony, the Court required the Petitioner to file copies of federal income tax returns for the past three years and to complete a court form entitled "Financial Disclosure Form — Petition For Distribution From Minor Child's Trust," all of which have been filed with the Court.

The Petitioner has requested the Court to authorize the distribution of per capita funds, from trust, to defray the educational expenses of her two minor children for the school year 2005-2006 ("current year"). The petition indicates that the total tuition costs for the two minor children for the current year are $30,900.00. At the hearing before the Court, however, the Petitioner clarified that she was only seeking distributions in amounts sufficient to pay the unpaid balance of the school tuition costs for the current year. At the Court's request, the Petitioner has filed statements from the Pine Point School, now attended by both of the minor children, showing all tuition payments made for the Petitioner's two minor children and the balance due on each tuition account for the current year (Pleading #109). The Court finds that: (1) the tuition for each minor child for the current year is $15,450.00; (2) $11,885.00 has been paid towards the current year's tuition for [Name Redacted], leaving a balance due of $3,565.00; (3) $7,775.00 has been paid towards the current year's tuition for [Name Redacted], leaving a balance due of $7,675.00; (4) to date, the Petitioner and/or her spouse have paid a total sum of $9,660.00 towards the current year's tuitions; and (5) $11,240.00 is the total unpaid tuition balance due for both minor children for the current year.

[Name Redacted] has previously been tested at the University of Connecticut Neag School of Education which concluded that her IQ tests placed her in the superior range and that she would thrive in an enriched learning environment. Her parents have concluded that Pine Point School has the ability to offer this learning environment. [Name Redacted] has benefited from the smaller classrooms at Pine Point as evidenced by the growth in her self confidence. The Petitioner's father was a former assistant superintendent of schools and the Petitioner and her spouse place a high value on their daughters' educations. In addition, the Petitioner and her spouse have encouraged and supported extensive extra-curricular activities for their daughters including, competitive skating, music lessons, karate and gymnastics. Participation in the competitive skating has required travel out of state. It is evident that the Petitioner and her spouse are dedicated to providing a superior education for their daughters and to supporting their extra-curricular activities. They have already committed substantial financial resources to both.

Parents have a common law duty to support their minor children within the reasonable limits of their ability. . . . The Tribe has recognized this obligation and provided that "[t]he Tribe shall provide for the future of minors while encouraging tribal member parents to provide for the immediate living needs of their children as is their responsibility." M.T.O. 2001-08, Section I. Nothing herein is intended to suggest that the Petitioner and her spouse have not fulfilled their responsibility to provide for the support and immediate living needs of their children. The sole issue presented is whether the Petitioner has sustained her burden of proving, by a preponderance of the evidence, that the distributions requested are reasonable and necessary, and whether limited extraordinary circumstances exist to warrant such distributions.

The Court finds that no extraordinary circumstances exist to warrant the requested distributions from trust. The Petitioner and her spouse have made more than adequate provisions for the health, welfare and education of their daughters. They have provided for a well rounded environment and outstanding educational opportunities for their daughters. Although the two tuitions for the current year total $30,900.00, the existence of this expense, alone, does not constitute an extraordinary circumstance nor do any other extraordinary circumstances exist. The unpaid tuition balance due for the current year for both minor children is $11,240.00 and the Petitioner's request for distribution has been limited to this amount. The Petitioner has not, however, sustained her burden of showing that the requested distributions totaling this amount are necessary. The Financial Disclosure Form filed by the Petitioner indicates that she and her spouse have liquid assets of $55,682.00 (bank accounts totaling $36,405.00 and stocks and bonds valued at $19,277.00); real estate equity totaling $297,538.00; and retirement assets valued at $157,090.00. The liquid assets alone, are more than sufficient to pay the unpaid balance of the tuitions for the current year. In addition, the real estate equity and 401K savings could be pledged as collateral for loans to finance educational expenses. While the income and expense section of the Financial Disbursement Form does show a modest monthly shortfall, the Court notes that some of the expenses are discretionary and are not *monies necessary for essential living expenses* (emphasis added). M.T.O. 2001-08, Section III.H.5.

III. Conclusion

The grantor trusts established by the Tribe under M.T.O. 2001-08 are intended to provide for the future welfare of minor tribal members. M.T.O. 2001-08, Section I. The preservation of trust assets for the future of the two minor children is therefore paramount, and in the absence of exceptional circumstances, which do not exist in this case, no distributions from their trusts should be made. The current health, education and welfare expenses for the two minor children are well within the financial ability of their parents to meet, and therefore it is not necessary to distribute monies from their grantor trusts for the current year.

For the foregoing reasons, the Court denies the Petitioner's request for distribution of per capita funds from trust, to defray the 2005-2006 school year educational expenses for [Names Redacted].

NOTE

In *In re Wilson*, 2006 WL 6285477 (Grand Traverse Band of Ottawa and Chippewa Indians Tribal Court 2006), the court adopted the *Seidel* rule in rejecting a claim to use tribal trust funds for modeling and acting classes:

Loans to parents from the minor trust fund were intended to be limited to pay for those basic needs which would be unmet resulting in substantial risk of harm or severe detriment to the child and possible loss of parental rights if those needs went unfulfilled. GTB parents may not require a child to pay for their own basic needs unless such risk exists. The loans from the minor trust funds are to be a means by which parents may fulfill their parental obligations when extraordinary circumstances severely limit their ability to do so. Minor trust loans are a means for parents to minimize risk of harm to their children when no other means to do so is available to them. Thus the circumstances in which a parent applies for a loan from minor trust funds must be both "limited" and "extraordinary". 18 GTBC §1605.

To that end the Court adopts the definition of "limited extraordinary circumstances" articulated in *Seidel v. Mohegan Tribe of Indians of Connecticut*, . . . as "going beyond what is usual, regular, common or customary." Usual, regular, common or customary would be those circumstances which are ordinarily associated with parental responsibilities to meet a child's basic needs. . . .

An example of a limited extraordinary circumstance would be a minor's sudden illness or injury that confronts a parent with uncovered medical expenses. Such an event would be both unforeseeable and limited by the need to protect the child in light of a parent's limited resources. The context of such a request would arise from circumstances that are both extraordinary and limited. Parents in this situation who would fail to provide for the child because of their own limited finances would under section 10 of the GTB Code be considered negligent at the very least. It is not only the circumstance of the child's illness that would require consideration by the court, but the parents' financial status and access to other resources for fulfilling their parental obligations.

While a child is still a minor, it is the responsibility of parents to provide basic education as defined herein. So long as a child is obtaining the educational skills defined as necessary and basic, the parent fulfills their parental obligation. Providing a child with enhanced educational opportunities is not a parental obligation required to maintaining parental rights. Every parent would like to provide their child with the opportunity to go beyond basic skill levels to pursue special talents. However, an extraordinary educational circumstance would be one which unforeseeably denied the child access to school or to the basic required curriculum. What the parent is not obligated to provide as a matter of a minimum legal threshold of parental responsibility according to section 10 of the GTB Code, a child should not be expected to provide for himself from his own resources or a future interests. . . .

While it may be reasonable for parents to desire that a child pursue particular talents and skills such as acting or modeling, it has been established that such talents and skills are not necessary to the child's health, education or welfare. . . .

Pursuing potential is often important to a child's sense of well being[;] however, the Council's fiduciary responsibility to ensure that the minor trust remain secure for all tribal minors must be weighed against the proposed need. . . .

Many parents who seek to access a child's trust fund account for a loan, fail to recognize that they are not borrowing from an individual trust account set up specifically for their child, but rather they are borrowing from pool of money held in trust for the benefit all GTB tribal children. It is the Council's fiduciary responsibility to all of the children of the tribe, to ensure that the pool of money is accessed only when necessary, for reasonable amounts and under extraordinary circumstances. The court holds that while it may be very important to provide Jason an opportunity to pursue his undeveloped talents for acting or modeling such a pursuit is not necessary to his health, education or welfare as defined herein. If each parent with a child who has a special potential were to access the minor trust funds in order to pay to develop that potential, the minor trust fund and the future interest of all GTB children in that fund would soon be depleted.

Wilson, 2006 WL 6285477 at *2-4.

14

TRIBAL ECONOMIES

One of the more critical lessons learned by the Founders at the time of the American Constitutional Convention was that a government cannot function without revenue. As a result, the Constitution provides the federal government with the power to lay taxes. State constitutions provide state governments and local governments the power to lay taxes.

Indian tribes are not states, nor are they local governments. Tribal governments have extreme difficulty in raising revenue; they have virtually no tax base. As one federal court noted, "the Indians have no viable tax base and a weak economic infrastructure. Therefore, they, even more than the states, need to develop creative ways to generate revenue." *Pueblo of Santa Ana v. Hodel*, 663 F. Supp. 1300, 1315 n. 21 (D.D.C. 1987). Property tax revenue is generally unavailable to tribal governments, mostly because taxing tribal members would be pointless and counterproductive. Moreover, often tribes control or own a relatively small proportion of land within their reservations.

Congress's attempts to assist Indian tribes in statutes, such as the Tribal Tax Status Act, have amounted to an empty action in most instances. As Professor Robert A. Williams, Jr., wrote in 1985, "[t]he Tribal Tax Status Act does not provide a mechanism that would enable tribes to create a thriving economic environment within Indian Country. Instead, it offers tribes only the theoretical ability to exercise broadly based taxing authority over a nonexistent tax base." Robert A. Williams, Jr., *Small Steps on the Long Road to Self-Sufficiency for Indian Nations: The Indian Tribe Governmental Tax Status Act of 1982*, 22 Harv. J. on Legis. 335, 385 (1985). In response to the lack of a stable tax base, Indian tribes have little resort except to pursue an alternative method of raising revenue: economic development.

A. MODERN RESERVATION ECONOMIC DEVELOPMENT

1. TRIBAL ECONOMIC DEVELOPMENT STRATEGIES

Two Approaches to Economic Development on American Indian Reservations: One Works, the Other Doesn't

Stephen Cornell and Joseph P. Kalt, Rebuilding Native Nations: Strategies for Governance and Development, 7, 19-27 (Miriam Jorgenson ed., 2007)

. . . In the last quarter of the twentieth century, American Indian nations began to invent a very different approach to reservation economic development. Only a relatively few nations have been involved, but more and more appear to be recognizing the value of this approach. We have called this the "nation-building" approach, thanks to its dual focus — conscious or unconscious — on asserting tribal sovereignty and building the foundational, institutional capacity to exercise sovereignty effectively, thereby providing a positive environment for sustained economic development. Once again, we can generalize from a variety of cases and details to identify five primary characteristics of the nation-building approach: it involves comprehensive assertions of sovereignty or self-rule; it involves backing up sovereignty with effective governing institutions; it matches those institutions to indigenous political culture; it has a strategic orientation; and it involves a leadership dedicated to nation building. . . .

In the Nation-Building Approach, Indian Nations Are in the Driver's Seat

The nation-building approach begins with sovereignty or self-rule: practical decision-making power in the hands of Indian nations. Indian nations have not always had such power. We can identify three distinct stages in the evolution of tribal sovereignty: law, policy, and practice. As a matter of law, the United States has recognized a substantial degree of tribal sovereignty since at least the early part of the nineteenth century and the U.S. Supreme Court decisions commonly known as the Marshall trilogy. Subsequent treaties, legislation, and judicial decisions in various ways modified this recognition, and over time tribal sovereignty — as a legal matter — has been increasingly constrained, but a significant legal foundation has survived.

In practice, however, Indian nations were steadily losing control over their own affairs. Over the rest of the nineteenth century, and despite this legal recognition, the United States assumed ever greater power over Indian lands and communities. Sovereignty may have been recognized in law, but it had no place in federal Indian policy. The federal government rapidly displaced Indian nations as the effective ruler of Indian Country.

The Indian Reorganization Act (IRA) of 1934 began a gradual reversal of this trend. While the IRA brought little substantive increase in tribal authority, it at least provided mechanisms through which Indian nations could begin to assert some governing power. The reversal was fragile, as the antitribal "termination" policy of the 1950s showed, but it gained momentum in the 1960s and

1970s with the shift to a federal policy of tribal "self-determination," made most explicit in the Indian Self-Determination and Education Assistance Act of 1975. As the federal government grudgingly accepted the principle that Indian nations should have maximum control over their own affairs, tribal sovereignty became more than simply a matter of law. It became federal policy. On paper, at least, Indian nations would now determine what was best for them.

This was a crucial development. While there is ample evidence that the federal government's notion of self-determination was a limited one, and many federal bureaucrats, particularly in regional offices of the BIA, maintained a fierce grip on decision-making power, the door to practical sovereignty — self-rule — had been opened. Over the next two decades, a growing number of tribes began to force their way through that door, taking over the management of reservation affairs and resources and making major decisions about their own futures. Tribal sovereignty gradually moved beyond law and policy to practice: taking advantage of the federal self-determination policy, some Indian nations began exercising the sovereignty promised by law but denied by federal paternalism and control.

This development — the move to practical sovereignty or genuine self-rule — turns out to be a key to sustainable development. There are two primary reasons why.

- Self-governance puts the development agenda in Indian hands. When federal bureaucrats, funding agencies, or some other set of outsiders sets the reservation development agenda, that agenda inevitably reflects their interests, perceptions, or concerns, not those of Indian nation citizens. When decisions move into tribal hands, agendas begin to reflect tribal interests, perceptions, and concerns.
- Self-governance marries decisions and their consequences, leading to better decisions. In the standard approach to reservation development, outsiders make the major decisions about development strategy, resource use, allocation and expenditure of funds, and so forth. But if those outsiders make bad decisions, they seldom pay the price. Instead, the Indian community pays the price. This means that outside decisionmakers face little in the way of compelling discipline; the incentives to improve their decisions are modest. After all, it's not their community whose future is at stake. But once decisions move into Indian hands, then the decisionmakers themselves have to face the consequences of their decisions.

Once they're in the driver's seat, tribes bear the costs of their own mistakes, and they reap the benefits of their own successes. As a result, over time and allowing for a learning curve, the quality of their decisions improves. In general, Indian nations are better decisionmakers about their own affairs, resources, and futures because they have the largest stake in the outcomes.

There are concrete, bottom-line payoffs to tribal self-rule. For example, a Harvard Project study of 75 tribes with significant timber resources found that, for every timber-related job that moved from BIA forestry to tribal forestry — that is, for every job that moved from federal control to tribal control — prices received and productivity in the tribe's timber operations rose. On average, tribes do a better job of managing their forests because these are their forests.

But the evidence is even broader. After fifteen years of research and work in Indian Country, we cannot find a single case of sustained economic development in which an entity other than the Indian nation is making the major decisions about development strategy, resource use, or internal organization. In short, practical sovereignty appears to be a necessary (but not sufficient) condition for reservation economic development.

In the Nation-Building Approach, Indian Nations Back Up Sovereignty with Effective Governing Institutions

But sovereignty alone is not enough. If sovereignty is to lead to economic development, it has to be exercised effectively. This is a matter of governing institutions. Why should governing institutions be so important in economic development? Among other things, governments put in place the "rules of the game": the rules by which the members of a society make decisions, cooperate with each other, resolve disputes, and pursue their jointly held objectives.

These rules are captured in constitutions, by-laws, or shared understandings about appropriate distributions of authority and proper ways of doing things: they represent agreement among a society's members about how collective life should be organized.

These rules — these patterns of organization — make up the environment in which development has to take hold and flourish. Some rules discourage development. For example, a society whose rules allow politicians to treat development as a way to enrich themselves and their supporters will discourage development. A society in which court decisions are politicized will discourage development. A society in which day-to-day business decisions are made according to political criteria (for example, according to who voted for a particular official in the last election) instead of merit criteria (for example, according to who has the necessary skills to run a good business, regardless of who their friends or relatives are) will discourage development. And the reverse is true as well. Where societies prevent politicians from enriching themselves from the public purse, provide fair court decisions, reward ability instead of voting records, and support other such rules, sustainable development is much more likely.

In other words, having effective governing institutions means putting in place "rules of the game" that encourage economic activity that fits tribal objectives. Whatever those objectives might be, our research indicates that several features of institutional organization are key to successful development.

- Governing institutions have to be stable. That is, the rules don't change frequently or easily, and when they do change, they change according to prescribed and reliable procedures.
- Governing institutions have to separate politics from day-to-day business and program management, keeping strategic decisions in the hands of elected leadership but putting day-to-day management decisions in the hands of managers.
- Governing institutions have to take the politics out of court decisions or other methods of dispute resolution, sending a clear message to tribal

citizens and outsiders that their investments and their claims will be dealt with fairly.
- Governing institutions have to provide a bureaucracy that can get things done reliably and effectively.

Again, there is substantial evidence in support of these requirements. For example, Harvard Project studies of tribally owned and operated businesses on Indian reservations found that those enterprises in which day-to-day business management is insulated from tribal council or tribal presidential interference are far more likely to be profitable — and to last — than those without such insulation. In the long run, this means more jobs for reservation citizens.

Similarly, research shows that tribes whose court systems are insulated from political interference — in which the tribal council has no jurisdiction over appeals and in which judges are not council-controlled — have significantly lower levels of unemployment — other things equal — than tribes in which the courts are under the direct influence of elected officials. This is because an independent court sends a clear message to potential investors — whether outsiders or tribal citizens — that their investments will not be hostage to politics or corruption.

When tribes back up sovereignty with stable, fair, effective, and reliable governing institutions, they create an environment that is favorable to sustained economic development. In doing so, they increase their chances of improving tribal welfare.

In the Nation-Building Approach, Governing Institutions Match Indigenous Political Culture

To be effective, governing institutions have to be legitimate in the eyes of the people. One of the problems that Indian nations have had is their dependence on institutions that they did not design and that reflect another society's ideas about how authority ought to be organized and exercised.

The governments organized under the Indian Reorganization Act, for example, tend to follow a simple pattern: strong chief executive, relatively weak council, no independent judicial function, and political oversight of economic activity. This approach has been applied across tribes with very different political traditions, leading to a mismatch, in many cases, between formal governing institutions and indigenous beliefs about authority. Historically, some tribes had strong chief executive forms of government in which decision-making power was concentrated in one or a few individuals, while others dispersed power among many individuals or multiple institutions with sophisticated systems of checks and balances and separations of powers. Still others relied on spiritual leaders for political direction, while some relied on broad-based, consensus decision-making.

Indian political traditions were diverse. But tradition is not the issue here. In some cases, indigenous political traditions are long gone. But in many nations, distinctive ideas about the appropriate organization and exercise of authority still survive and often are starkly at odds with IRA structures or other structures imposed on Indian nations. The crucial issue is the degree of match or mismatch between formal governing institutions and contemporary indigenous ideas — whatever their source — about the appropriate form and organization of political power. Where cultural match is high, economic development tends to be more successful. Where cultural match is low, the legitimacy of tribal government also is low, the governing institutions consequently are less effective, and economic development falters.

This is not necessarily a prescription for a return to ancient political traditions. Governing institutions have to pass two tests. As we have just suggested, they have to be culturally appropriate. But they also have to be able to get the job done. The tribal governments of long ago were invented to solve the problems of the times. The times have changed. In some cases, traditional forms and practices may be inadequate to the demands of the modern world. If so, the challenge for Indian nations is to innovate: to develop governing institutions that still resonate with deeply held community beliefs about authority but that are flexible enough to adjust to the demands of contemporary times.

In the Nation-Building Approach, Decision-making Is Strategic

One of the primary characteristics of the standard approach to reservation economic development is its quick-fix orientation. Under enormous pressure from impoverished communities and with few resources to work with, tribal leaders and planners become opportunists, grasping at any available option regardless of its sustainability or its suitability to tribal circumstances or long-term goals.

The alternative to this quick-fix orientation is strategic thinking: an approach to development that starts not with "what can be funded?" but with "what kind of society are we trying to build?" and moves on from there. A strategic approach involves a shift:

- from reactive thinking to proactive thinking (not just responding to crisis but trying to gain some control over the future);
- from short-term thinking to long-term thinking (twenty-five years from now, what kind of society do you want?);
- from opportunistic thinking toward systemic thinking (focusing not on what can be funded but on whether various options fit the society you're trying to create);
- from a narrow problem focus to a broader societal focus (fixing not just problems but societies).

This sort of shift requires determining long-term objectives, identifying priorities and concerns, and taking a hard-nosed look at the assets the tribe has to work with and the constraints it has to deal with. The result is a set of criteria by which specific development options can be analyzed: does this option support the nation's priorities, fit with its assets and opportunities, and advance its long-term objectives? If not, what will?

In the Nation-Building Approach, Leadership Serves Primarily as Nation-Builder and Mobilizer

Leadership's primary concern in the standard approach is the distribution of resources. In the nation-building approach, leadership's primary concern is putting in place the institutional and strategic foundations for sustained development and enhanced community welfare.

This often means a loss of power for some people and institutions. The standard approach empowers selected individuals but fails to empower the nation. The chairman or president and the members of the tribal council get to make the decisions, hand out the goodies, and reward supporters, but the nation as a whole suffers as its power — its capacity to achieve its goals — is crippled by an environment that serves the individual interests of office-holders but not the interests of the community as a whole. Equally crippling is a community attitude, encouraged by the standard approach, that sees government not as a mechanism for rebuilding the future but simply as a set of resources that one faction or another can control.

In the nation-building approach, leadership focuses on developing effective governing institutions, transforming government from an arena in which different factions fight over resources into a mechanism for advancing national objectives. What's more, in the nation-building approach, leadership is not limited to elected officials. It can be found anywhere: in the schools, in local communities, in businesses and programs. Its distinctive features are its public-spiritedness and its determination that empowering the nation as a whole is more important than empowering individuals or factions.

Of course the kind of leadership a nation has is determined in part by its governing institutions. Institutions that allow politicians to serve themselves — to advance their own agendas or factions, for example, by interfering in court decisions — will encourage self-interested and counterproductive leadership. Institutions that discourage such behavior with rules that, for example, focus leadership's attention on strategic issues and prevent them from micromanaging businesses or programs, will encourage forms of leadership that better serve the nation. It may take assertive and visionary leadership to put in place good governing institutions, but once those institutions are in place, they will encourage better leadership. . . .

NOTES

1. Professors Robert Miller and David Haddock argue, somewhat contrarily to the views expounded by Professors Cornell and Kalt, that tribal sovereignty can be a barrier to tribal economic development:

   > In Indian country, new elections and shifts in public opinion occasionally cause extreme changes in tribal policies. Perhaps it is the nature of small populations and political entities to be more affected by turnover in the personalities operating the government and from the shifting opinions of the electorate. . . .
   >
   > . . . When tribal council changes result in alterations of contracts and business developments it chills the ardor of investors to work in Indian Country.
   >
   > . . . In the same vein, John Mohawk notes that some tribal councils have changed the rules on Indian investors and engaged in "opportunistic behavior" and that this "can go a long way toward discouraging Indians from investing their resources in their own businesses." . . .
   >
   > In spring 1998, the Rosebud Sioux Tribe in South Dakota and Sun Prairie, a Nebraska pork producer, negotiated a lease for the construction of production facilities on tribal lands. . . .

Later, after a tribal general election, the composition of the tribal council changed. In addition, the Tribe held a referendum on the project and 556 people voted against the hog facilities and 451 voted in favor. The new tribal council no longer favored the project and decided to support the BIA's decision to void the lease. . . .

. . . Furthermore, in March 2003, the new tribal council requested that the BIA shut down the 48 hog barns that Sun Prairie had already built and was operating, which mostly employed tribal members. By then, Sun Prairie had invested about $20 million in the project. . . .

. . . Plainly, instances of political instability and the occasional disregard of contractual rights can make investors very cautious about dealing with tribes.

David D. Haddock & Robert J. Miller, *Can a Sovereign Protect Investors from Itself? Tribal Institutions to Spur Reservation Investment*, 8 J. SMALL & EMERGING BUS. L. 173, 201-06 (2004).

In a later writing, Haddock and Miller argued:

Enhanced tribal sovereignty, however, is a two-edged sword because it gives tribes more power to act opportunistically. Because tribes compete against states for investment, investors can easily vote with their feet by moving if states comprise a more secure jurisdiction. An expectation that tribes act opportunistically imposes a price in the form of less investment on reservations and a higher risk premium demanded by those investors who remain.

David D. Haddock & Robert J. Miller, *Sovereignty Can Be a Liability: How Tribes Can Mitigate the Sovereign's Paradox*, in SELF-DETERMINATION: THE OTHER PATH FOR NATIVE AMERICANS 194, 210 (Terry L. Anderson, Bruce L. Benson & Thomas E. Flanagan eds., 2006).

2. Other scholars have challenged more directly the conclusions of Professors Cornell and Kalt, arguing that competent tribal courts do not in fact serve to promote tribal economic development:

After controlling for several other variables, per capita income for Indians on reservations subject to PL 280 jurisdiction [a "PL 280 jurisdiction" is one in which a state has some form of criminal and civil jurisdiction over Indian country] grew by 30 percentage points more than per capita income for Indians on non–PL 280 reservations between 1969 and 1999. . . . First, there is anecdotal evidence that non-Indian investors and contractors prefer the relative security of state jurisdiction. Second, there is no evidence that Congress's selection of PL 280 tribes was biased toward tribes that would have had faster growth in the absence of the law. Third, state jurisdiction had its largest impact on Indian incomes in the decade-long period most immediately following the uniform implementation of PL 280.

Terry L. Anderson & Dominic P. Parker, *Sovereignty, Credible Commitments, and Economic Prosperity on American Indian Reservations*, 51 J.L. & ECON. 641, 658-59 (2008).

3. In a partial, and largely indirect, response to these concerns, Professors Kalt and Joseph Singer highlighted areas in which exercises of tribal sovereignty serve to create a strong public infrastructure necessary for economic development in Indian country:

With their strong incentives to highlight the extreme, the negative, and the controversial, the media and political demagogues leave impressions of exceeding hostility between tribes and neighboring non-Indian governments. This tends to obscure the rapidity with which tribes are investing in the capacity to govern and to build productive intergovernmental relations. . . . [For example:]

- The Swinomish Cooperative Land Use Program is based on memoranda of agreement and understanding [with] Skagit County, Washington. [T]he program entails a jointly drafted and adopted county tribal land use plan that provides a framework for conducting permitting activities within the boundaries of the checkerboarded Swinomish reservation and establishes a regulatory forum for resolving conflicts that arise. . . .
- The Great Lakes Indian Fish and Wildlife Commission, a tribally chartered intertribal organization, negotiated a memorandum of understanding (MOU) with the U.S. Forest Service. The MOU and attendant process recognizes and implements treaty-guaranteed hunting, fishing and gathering rights under tribal regulations and establishes a consultation process for management decisions that affect treaty rights in four National Forests located within areas ceded by the Chippewa in the Treaties of 1836, 1837 and 1842. . . .
- The Pueblo of Sandia has utilized 1987 amendments to the federal Clean Water Act permitting "treatment as state" status for tribes as the basis for promulgating its own water quality standards. . . . In the process, Sandia-generated data regarding river pollution levels have given the Pueblo a voice at the table in discussions regarding local water matters and have served as a counterweight to pollution claims made by local dischargers. . . .

These cases share common themes: Notwithstanding a stated federal policy of government-to-government relations with tribes and similar commitments by numerous state governments, making such recognition of tribal sovereignty operationally real falls heavily to the tribes—but it can be done. . . .

Joseph P. Kalt & Joseph William Singer, *Myths and Realities of Tribal Sovereignty: The Law and Economics of Indian Self-Rule*, Harvard Project of American Indian Economic Development, Joint Occasional Papers on Native Affairs No. 2004-03, at 23-27 (2004).

2. INDIAN PREFERENCE IN CONTRACTING

ONEIDA SEVEN GENERATIONS CORP. V. QUALITY CONSTRUCTION MANAGEMENT, LLC

Oneida Appeals Commission, Nos. 05-AC-020, 05-AC-022,
2006.NAOW.0000004 (April 18, 2006)

This case has come before the Oneida Appeals Commission. Judicial Officers: ANITA F. BARBER, GERALD CORNELIUS, LOIS POWLESS, KIM VELE and JENNIFER WEBSTER presiding.

I. Background

This case involves the application of the Oneida Indian Preference Law, Chapter 57, to a tribally chartered, wholly-owned subordinate organization of the Oneida Tribe, the Oneida Seven Generations Corporation (OSG). In seeking bids for a $5 million construction project on the Oneida Reservation, OSG failed to seek a bid from Indian-owned Quality Construction Management, LLC (QCM). QCM and three of its owners filed suit alleging a violation of Chapter 57. . . .

OSG came into existence as a tribally chartered entity in 1996 by virtue of a Corporate Charter granted by the Oneida Business Committee through its powers under Article IV, Section 1(h) of the Constitution and By-Laws of the Oneida Nation. While OSG is a separate legal entity on paper, the sole share-holder of OSG is the Oneida Tribe and the Tribe has significant control over OSG through its Charter. OSG's property manager at all relevant times was John Kroner, who also had contract signing authority on behalf of OSG.

QCM is a limited liability company formed in November 2003 under the laws of the State of Wisconsin. It is majority owned by Oneida Tribal members, Kurt Jordan, Chris Fuss, and Lance Vanden Heuvel. QCM provides General Contractor services for residential and commercial construction projects.

. . . OSG and the Tribe had plans to build a travel mart at the intersection of Highways 29 and 32 on the Oneida Reservation. The travel mart was designed to be a gas station, convenience store and small casino. OSG sought pricing information from three contractors some time in summer 2002. It does not appear a formal bid process was used. . . .

In January 2004, the Tribe, as the shareholder, told OSG to go forward with the travel mart project. Mr. Kroner testified he updated the earlier prices from 2002 due to the passage of time and fluctuations in the price of steel. Around January 2004, OSG signed a design-build contract with Smet Construction. . . .

On December 12, 2003, QCM was certified as a business to be on the Indian preference list maintained by the Indian Preference Department. . . .

When QCM found out the project was going forward and that it had not been invited to bid, it filed suit on February 4, 2005. . . .

II. Issues

Appellant-RespondentCross, OSG, identified three issues for resolution in its appeal:

1. Did the Oneida Indian Preference Law (OIPL) apply to OSG under the facts and circumstances of this case?
2. Did OSG breach the OIPL?
3. Were Petitioners entitled to attorney fees as damages?

. . .

III. Analysis

We address OSG's issues first.

1. Did the Oneida Indian Preference Law (OIPL) Apply to OSG under the Facts and Circumstances of this Case?

The trial court found the OIPL did apply and we affirm. OSG asserts the preference requirements of the ordinance do not apply to it because the OIPL only applies to contracts with the Tribe. Section 57.9-1 states:

> All entities of the Oneida Tribe, which include but are not limited to programs, enterprises and other subdivisions of the Oneida Tribe awarding contracts or

subcontracts for goods or services with the Oneida Tribe where the majority of the work, service or goods are performed or provided on or near the Oneida Reservation, shall give preference in contracting and subcontracting to Indian-owned businesses. . . .

Chapter 57, Sec. 57.9-1.

OSG does not apparently deny that it is an entity of the Tribe, it is awarding a contract, and that the majority of the work for the travel mart was to be on or near the Reservation. It contends it escapes complying with this section because the contract to be awarded was not "with the Oneida Tribe." In other words, the contract was with OSG, not with the Oneida Tribe and therefore not subject to sec. 57.9-1. Such a construction is not supported by common sense or the facts and circumstances of this case.

For the purposes of Chapter 57 only, OSG is sufficiently controlled by and affiliated with the Tribe that a contract with it is a contract with the Tribe. The evidence supports this conclusion for several reasons: 1) [t]he Oneida Tribe is the sole shareholder and thereby exerts considerable, if not total, influence and control over OSG's activities[;] 2) OSG is chartered under the portion of the Tribe's constitution which permits "subordinate" organizations for economic purposes which may receive any delegated governmental powers of the Tribe. Art. IV, Sec. 1(h), Oneida Const.[;] 3) [t]he charter itself contains several provisions which suggest OSG is a governmental extension of the Tribe and expected to comply with its laws in fashion similar to the Tribe, namely:

> **Article IV.**
>
> The Corporation is created under, and is subject to the laws, ordinances and jurisdiction of the Oneida Nation and banking commitment letter. The General Tribal Council expressly reserves to the Oneida Nation all its inherent sovereign rights as an Indian nation with regard to the activities of the Corporation.

OSG is created by the Tribe, wholly owned by the Tribe, subject to the jurisdiction of the Tribe and is capable of exercising governmental functions of the Tribe if those functions are delegated to it. It is not plausible that OSG would therefore be exempt from Chapter 57. The charter makes it clear that OSG is expected to follow tribal laws and in essence, for the purposes of Chapter 57, a contract with OSG is the equivalent of a contract with the Tribe. If subordinate tribal organizations like OSG were exempt from tribal laws, the Tribe could simply avoid compliance with its own laws by establishing chartered entities and claiming they are exempt because they are "not the Tribe."

2. Did OSG Breach the OIPL?

The trial court found that OSG did breach the OIPL and we affirm. Section 57.9-1 requires entities such as OSG to "give preference in contracting and subcontracting to Indian-owned businesses." OSG did not give preference to QCM. QCM, despite its certification in December 2003, was not even considered for the travel mart project. It is true there is some ambiguity in the ordinance as to what exactly constitutes "giving preference." In this instance, OSG was aware of Chapter 57 and knew in general about the Indian Preference Department. Mr. Kroner testified he knew about the law. Whatever giving preference means, OSG did nothing to include QCM. It seems the minimum would be to contact the Indian Preference Department, get the list of certified contractors and actively seek a bid from them for the project.

3. Were Petitioners Entitled to Attorney Fees as Damages?

Even though OSG did not give preference when awarding the travel mart project, it is impossible to say if QCM would have gotten the job. Even if QCM had been considered for the travel mart, Mr. Kroner testified he would not have awarded the job to QCM because of the size of the job and questions about QCM's ability to handle the job. There is some support in the record for Mr. Kroner's conclusion. QCM was a newer company that had only participated in relatively small jobs up to the time of the travel mart project.

In light of the speculative nature of compensatory damages, the trial court declined to award any to QCM. However, the trial court awarded attorney fees to QCM noting that if OSG had complied with Chapter 57, QCM would not necessarily have been in court. We agree. In addition, QCM has established a valid claim on the merits, but there is no adequate remedy available at this point. We also construe section 57.14-5(f) to permit an award of attorney fees.

. . . QCM's claims:

QCM urges this Court to award it an estimate of lost profits due to OSG's failure to give QCM an opportunity to bid on the travel mart project. QCM spends much of its brief arguing that it established what its lost profits would have been had it received the travel mart job and that estimates are sufficient for an award of damages. QCM has missed the point. What OSG failed to do was provide QCM an opportunity to bid. Lost profits might have been appropriate if OSG had wrongfully rejected QCM's bid. It is extremely difficult to calculate how the lost opportunity to bid damaged QCM. While OSG's violation is troubling, QCM's argument about lost profits jumps too far ahead.

There are many factors that would have come into play once QCM had been given the opportunity to bid. It is unknown what price QCM would have submitted or what the quality of their bid would have been. Mr. Kurt Jordan testified that the largest job QCM had done up to that point was $564,000, only a fraction of the size of the travel mart. Mr. Jordan testified that QCM had not been selected for several other larger jobs. Even if QCM had submitted a price-competitive bid of reasonable quality, we cannot say whether OSG would have selected QCM. Section 57.11 suggests that Indian Preference is achieved by lowering an Indian-owned contractor's bid amount by the percentages listed. . . .

QCM requests the Appeals Commission to assess punitive damages against OSG. We do not agree that OSG's conduct here was of such a nature to justify an award of punitive damages. . . .

QCM made much in its brief that a measure of damages is required in order to prevent further violations. We disagree. Early in this case the Petitioner voluntarily gave up its attempt at equitable relief. There were many different paths this case could have taken had QCM continued to seek equitable relief. Given the nature of the construction industry and the difficulty of assessing damages, early equitable relief would have been far more preferable and will be preferable in future cases. We expect OSG and others in similar situations will follow Chapter 57 now that the law has been clarified. In addition, future trial courts will be more apt to apply equitable remedies in light of our opinion today. . . .

NOTES

1. Indian preference is protected by federal law. Recently, the Bureau of Indian Affairs issued a short opinion letter to a query regarding the legality of the Indian preference in employment and contracting laws of the Seneca Nation of Indians. The letter summarized the law in the field:

> Title VII of the Civil Rights Act [of 1964], prohibits preferential employment on the basis of race, color, sex, national origin, and religion. However, Title VII contains a special exemption that makes Indian Preference permissible. Section 703(i) of the 1964 Civil Rights Act states:
>
>> Nothing contained in this title shall apply to any business or enterprise on or near an Indian Reservation with regards to any publicly announced employment practice of such business or enterprise under which a preferential treatment is to any individual because he is Indian.
>
> The Office of Federal Contract Compliance Programs Executive Order issued in 1977 states:
>
>> Work on or near Indian Reservations. It shall not be a violation of the equal opportunity clause for construction or non-construction, to extend a publicly announced preference in employment to Indians living on or near an Indian Reservation. The use of the word "near" would include all that area where a person seeking employment could reasonably be expected to commute to and from in the course of a work day. Contractors or subcontractors extending such a preference shall not, however, discriminate among Indians on the basis of religion, sex, or tribal affiliation, and the use of such preference shall not excuse a contractor from employment with the other requirements contained in this chapter.
>
> The Indian Self-Determination and Education Assistance Act (ISDEAA), Public Law 93-638, 1975, Section 7(b), provides for Indian Preference in employment and training, and contracting and subcontracting on all contracts negotiated or let on behalf of an Indian Tribe pursuant to the Act.
>> The United States Congress justified that Indian Tribes' powers to impose preferential requirements on the grounds that, "This exemption is consistent with the Federal Government's policy of encouraging Indian employment and with the special legal position of Indians."

   Letter from Kevin Bearquiver, BIA Tribal Government Services to Mark J. Gabriele, at 1-2 (Nov. 25, 2009), available at http://turtletalk.files.wordpress.com/2009/12/indian-preference-seneca.pdf.

2. Some tribes, such as the Navajo Nation, go one step further and apply *tribal* preference, where the tribe and the employers and contractors under the jurisdiction of the tribe must grant preference to tribal members ahead of nonmember Indians. *See Dawavendewa v. Salt River Project Agr. Imp. and Power Dist.*, 276 F.3d 1150, 1153 (9th Cir.) ("[T]he Navajo Preference in Employment Act ("NPEA") . . . states: "[a]ll employers doing business . . . [on or near the reservation] of the Navajo Nation . . . shall . . . [g]ive preference in

employment to Navajos." Nation Code tit. 15, §604 (1995)."), *cert. denied*, 537 U.S. 820 (2002).

3. TRIBAL BUSINESS ENTERPRISES

Hawl'Bay Ba:J Enterprises Inc. v. Vaughn

Southwest Intertribal Court of Appeals for the Hualapai Tribal Court, No. 95-004-HTC, 6 SWITCA 21 (November 15, 1995)

Appellate Judge Ann Rodgers . . .

[From the syllabus: "Appellants, a tribally-created Enterprise, entered into a loan commitment agreement with a bank without approval of the membership through a special election."]

The Constitutionality of the Enterprise Agreeing to the Terms of the Loan Commitment Letter

The narrow issue on appeal is . . . the Enterprise, by agreeing to the terms of the loan commitment letter, violated certain provisions of the Hualapai Constitution. . . .

Pertinent Provisions of the Hualapai Constitution

Article XVI, section (2)(b) of the Hualapai Constitution states:

Section 1. Waivers of Sovereign Immunity.

(b) Express waivers of sovereign immunity shall require the approval of at least thirty (30) percent of the total number of eligible voters of the Tribe voting in a special election if the waiver may:

> (1) expose the Tribe to liability in excess of $250,000, or its equivalent, or
> (2) expose more than one-hundred (100) acres of land to possible foreclosure or encumbrance.

Article V(n) of the Hualapai Constitution states:

The Tribal Council shall . . . have the following powers:

> (n) to lease tribal lands, natural resources, or other tribal assets within the jurisdiction of the Tribe, Provided, That leases involving more than one thousand (1000) acres or fifty thousands ($50,000.00) dollars shall also need the approval of the eligible voters of the Tribe voting in a special election . . . [.]

[1.] No violation of Article XVI, section (2)(b) of the Hualapai Constitution exists by virtue of execution of the loan commitment letter because there is no waiver of the Tribe's sovereign immunity.

. . . Under the terms of the first portion of Article XVI, section (2)(b) of the Hualapai Constitution, an explicit waiver of sovereign immunity must be approved by thirty percent of the eligible tribal members in a special election only where the waiver could expose the Tribe to liability in excess of $250,000 dollars, or its equivalent. In the loan commitment letter, it is unambiguous that the Enterprise is only waiving sovereign immunity; not the Tribe. Thus, it is not possible that the Tribe would be exposed to liability in any amount, much less that in excess of $250,000.00.

The Court is further convinced that there is no waiver of the Tribe's sovereign immunity by its review of the other documents in the record, particularly, the Articles of Incorporation for the Enterprise, the tribal resolutions creating and empowering the Enterprise, and the document known as the Plan of Operation. These documents clearly support the trial court's finding that the Enterprise is a distinct entity from the Tribe, and as such, does not have the power to waive sovereign immunity except as to the potential liability of the Enterprise itself.

The resolutions establish that the primary purpose for the creation of the Enterprise was to avoid political influence in the active management of certain business ventures. . . . The Articles of Incorporation empower the Enterprise to sue and be sued, however, that power is limited in that the Enterprise cannot consent to the attachment of any interest except that owned by the corporation itself. . . . Control of the Enterprise is vested in the board of directors[.] Under Article VII, §E, the board cannot incur contractual obligations unless it first determines that the Enterprise (as distinct from the Tribe) "has the ability to make payments when done." The "Plan of Operation" establishes that except for minor control over the annual budgets for the Enterprise, the Tribal Council intended that control of the corporation be removed from the Tribal Council and vested in the Board of Directors for the Enterprise. Section C governs capitalization of the Enterprise. After an initial investment of tribal funds, anything subsequently acquired by the Enterprise would be the property of the Enterprise, not the Tribe. This initial investment of tribal funds is reflected as the operating account on the accounting records of the Enterprise. Any additional advances of tribal funds to the Enterprise must either be a loan that generates interest income to the Tribe or be on the basis of additional capital investment in the Enterprise.

These documents establish an intent on the part of the Tribe to create an entirely separate entity to operate businesses on behalf of the Tribe. It does not reflect an intent that the Tribe operate these businesses through a corporate shell. While the initial funding which created the operating account could conceivably be taken if the Enterprise defaulted on the loan, there is no evidence on the record to establish that this amounts to $250,000.00 or more. The Court cannot presume that the Tribal Council has acted in an illegal manner. Instead, the presumption is that it has acted in accordance with all laws. Appellee did not present any evidence to rebut this presumption except the amount of the loan that the bank was willing to make to the Enterprise. Based upon the amount of the loan, appellee would have the Court imply that the initial investment exceeded $250,000.00. Contrary to appellee's position, the Court cannot make the implication that the Council is violating tribal law. It is clear that the Enterprise is not empowered to waive sovereign immunity so as to expose the Tribe to liability in any amount, much less that in excess of $250,000.00. Therefore, the fact that the loan commitment letter shows that the Enterprise will be borrowing $5.5 million dollars does not establish a violation of Article XVI, §2(b). . . .

NOTES

1. Angelique EagleWoman offered a cogent description of federal and tribally chartered corporations:

> Tribal economic development activities exist in various environments and climates throughout the continent. The overarching structure to these enterprises is the tribal government corporate model. Tribally chartered and owned corporations are the engine driving contemporary tribal economic development at all levels. Through the corporate framework, Tribes are able to build branches of enterprises under an umbrella tribal corporation or to have a variety of tribal corporations working in tandem all under the ultimate supervision of the tribal governing body. Tribal corporations are, for all intents and purposes, government-run businesses with Tribal Councils ultimately overseeing business activities. Unlike state law corporations, tribal corporations have been formed by federal statute and are governed by tribal law, not the body of law that has arisen around state law corporations.

> In the case of tribal corporations, a government owns the business, and the citizens constituting that government vote for representatives to govern the tribal corporation. That is to say, Indians do not vote corporate policy in tribally owned business as "shareholders" in the typical sense, but rather express their opinions through the usual means of electing and influencing elected representatives, who in turn appoint officers of the corporation and set policy. With tribally elected officials at the helm of tribal corporations or overseeing the tribal board of directors appointed to oversee tribal businesses, careful strategies must be developed to obtain the desired results. "[S]ome tribes may form businesses that intend to maximize profit, money that is then returned to the tribal government or to tribal members through a per capita payment. Some tribes do a little of both: profit maximizing and job creation." It is through tribal government-owned businesses that Tribal Nations are rebuilding economies and providing necessary services in Indian country. . . .

> The Indian Reorganization Act purported to create business structures for tribal governments in Sections 16 and 17. Under Section 16, Tribes had the option of creating tribal governments characterized with a central governing body that had the power and authority to initiate business decisions over tribal resources, revenues, and ventures. . . .

> By seeking federal charters under Section 17, Tribes have another option to bypass state laws for corporate entity recognition. Tribally held federal charters allow Tribes to incorporate as a tribal entity. The federally incorporated tribal entity then may receive from the Tribe "the power to purchase, take by gift, or bequest, or otherwise, own, hold, manage, operate, and dispose of property of every description, real and personal, including the power to purchase restricted Indian lands and to issue in exchange therefor interests in corporate property, and such further powers as may be incidental to the conduct of corporate business. . . ." . . .

> The formation of a federally incorporated tribal entity requires persistence and meeting the various requirements throughout the cumbersome federal process. A tribal governing body authorizes the intent for a federal incorporation of a tribal charter through a tribal resolution and must draft its proposed charter. The approved tribal charter has to be submitted to the BIA with the tribal resolution for approval and, subsequently, the Tribe must ratify the BIA-approved tribal charter to begin business operations. In comparison

under Section 16, a Tribe has the ability to create its own process to establish corporate entities under tribal law without involving the federal government in the process.

While Section 16 tribal corporations are shielded by the Tribe's own sovereign immunity from suit, litigation has arisen where courts have held that Section 17 tribal charter corporations do not possess tribal sovereign immunity. . . .

Angelique A. EagleWoman (Wambdi A. Wastewin), *Tribal Nation Economics: Rebuilding Commercial Prosperity in Spite of U.S. Trade Restraints — Recommendations for Economic Revitalization in Indian Country*, 44 TULSA L. REV. 383, 397-400 (2008).

2. After the Northern Plains Intertribal Court of Appeals adopted an 11-part common law test to determine whether a tribally charted corporation was entitled to tribal sovereign immunity in *Estate of D.F. v. SWST Fuel Inc.*, No CV-18-18-07 (2009), the Sisseton-Wahpeton enacted a statute designed to overrule the court's decision (or, alternatively, to require the application of a much simpler four-part test). *See* Sisseton-Wahpeton Oyate Tribal Council Resolution No. SWO-10-023 ("The Sovereign Immunity of the Tribe and Its Entities under Tribal Law"), available at http://turtletalk.files.wordpress.com/2010/03/sisseton-resolution.pdf.

4. SECURED TRANSACTIONS IN INDIAN COUNTRY

CULTURAL SOVEREIGNTY AND TRANSPLANTED LAW: TENSIONS IN INDIGENOUS SELF-RULE

Wenona T. Singel, 15 Kan. J.L. & Pub. Pol'y, Winter 2006, at 357, 357-63

Two forces that have a tremendous impact on tribal legal systems are in direct conflict with each other. . . .

The first force is the concept of cultural sovereignty. This concept refers to an indigenous counterforce to the dominant society's narrative of the meaning of tribal people's collective existence. . . .

Cultural sovereignty refers to tribes' efforts to represent their histories and existence using their own terms, and it acknowledges that each Indian nation has its own vision of self-determination as shaped by each tribe's culture, history, territory, traditions, and practices.

. . . As a result of repeated attempts to eliminate or assimilate tribes through paternalistic policies intended to assist tribal governments, traditional forms of tribal political authority have been weakened, and many elements of tribal legal systems have been shaped to imitate Anglo, non-Indian norms. Thus, the structure of tribal courts, legislative bodies, tribal codes and tribal case law often have been molded to fit non-Indian models.

The project to promote cultural sovereignty includes efforts to develop tribal legal systems in a way that reflects tribal histories, cultures, and community norms. . . .

Meanwhile, in spite of the important and effective efforts of many to promote cultural sovereignty in tribal communities, Indian nations continue to incorporate non-Indian law at a dramatic and, in some cases, accelerating rate.

I refer to this incorporated non-Indian law in tribal legal systems as transplanted law. Today, tribes continue to adopt transplanted law through voluntary acts, although the degree of voluntariness can vary greatly from case to case.

There are many examples of transplanted law in tribal legal systems. . . . The commercial law that has been and is currently being adopted by Indian tribes provides an illustration. This commercial law is perhaps best exemplified by the secured transactions codes that many Indian nations are adopting as tribal law.

Generally, a secured transactions code is a statute that governs the creation, attachment and perfection of a security interest in goods. A security interest is an interest in goods that a creditor takes when a debtor pledges the goods as collateral. The Uniform Commercial Code's [UCC] Article 9 is a model secured transactions code, and all states have adopted some form of it, often with minor variations to suit each state's needs and concerns.

[M]any tribes have developed a growing interest in enacting a form of secured transactions code as tribal law. This is because tribes have developed a growing recognition of the fact that secured transactions codes are often critical tools for promoting economic growth in Indian country. Without a secured transactions code enacted as tribal law, lenders remain wary of extending credit in Indian country because they cannot predict whether or how any security interest they may take in goods will be recognized or enforced under tribal law. This problem is exacerbated because Article 9 includes a choice of law provision providing that that the secured transactions law that governs the perfection of any security interest is generally the law of the location of the debtor. Under this choice of law rule, if the debtor is an individual or entity or Indian nation located in Indian country, then the law that governs the making and enforcement of security interests is always the tribe with jurisdiction over the Indian country in question. The result is that under the law of nearly every state, whenever a debtor is located in an area of Indian country where the relevant tribe with jurisdiction lacks a secured transactions code on the books, there is no definite set of rules that will govern the making and enforcement of a security interest. The uncertainty that results from this phenomenon creates a disincentive for lender investment in Indian country generally, and the effects of this disincentive are felt by individuals, by small and large businesses, and by tribal governments.

In response to the threat to economic growth that the absence of tribal secured transactions codes presents, many Indian nations have responded by enacting tribal secured transactions codes as tribal law. In addition, a few law schools have devoted resources to helping tribes develop tribal secured transactions codes, and the National Conference of Commissioners on Uniform State Laws (NCCUSL) also became involved in the effort to develop and promote the tribal enactment of this code. NCCUSL is a national organization that develops a wide variety of uniform laws for state enactment. In particular, NCCUSL monitors state law UCC developments and considers whether developments merit revision of the model form of the UCC. When NCCUSL creates or revises a uniform law, it combines the expertise of academics and practitioners from each of the fifty states and ultimately issues an official form of the model law in question which it then endorses for state adoption. The American

Law Institute (ALI) also reviews and decides whether to endorse the model laws that NCCUSL develops. Once the model form is endorsed by NCCUSL and ALI, both organizations then encourage each state legislature to adopt the model law with as few changes as possible. A guiding principle that informs the NCCUSL's development of model codes generally is that uniformity of the law from state to state promotes greater certainty, predictability, and efficiency in the law. In the area of commercial law, this uniformity encourages efficient economic transactions because parties are able to contract with each other without a significant investment of time and resources each time a party engages in commerce in a new state law jurisdiction. . . .

As the interest in enacting secured transactions codes in Indian country grew, so too did the number and variety of problems associated with successful tribal incorporation of the code. The first problem occurred at the outset, with tribes' failure to properly integrate the code into tribal law. In many cases, tribes adopted secured transactions codes by simply cutting and pasting either the model Article 9 of the UCC or an enacted state version of Article 9 and incorporating the cut-and-pasted product as tribal law. This method of tribal incorporation was the least likely to be successful, since it often failed to take into account previously-enacted tribal laws to ensure that the incorporated code did not conflict with existing tribal law. This method also suffered because the model Article 9 of the UCC and the various state-enacted versions of Article 9 are each laden with cross-references to other bodies of law which the drafters of Article 9 presume to be enacted by each respective jurisdiction. For example, Article 9 refers to other portions of the UCC governing sales and leases, debtor-creditor law, and commercial paper. If none of these other portions of the UCC are enacted as tribal law, then a tribe that adopts a model secured transactions code with references to concepts embedded in these other codes will ultimately enact a law that cross-references itself to a series of dead-ends, or non-existent law.

A second problem that tribes have encountered with the enactment of secured transactions codes is their inability to provide the necessary administrative support for successful implementation and enforcement of the code. In some cases, a tribe commits the necessary resources for drafting, reviewing and enacting the code, but once the code is adopted as tribal law, the law languishes on the books without any additional work to ensure that the code is effectively implemented. In some cases, this is the result of inadequate planning. In others, it may be the result of insufficient financial resources for the development of the administrative processes and the training of support staff the code requires. Tribes also encounter a third problem, that of inexperience with secured transactions codes; consequently, the code is rarely applied or enforced because the community lacks experience with the code's meaning and application. In this case, the code may be regarded as tribal law, but, as members of the community disregard the law and adopt practices that conflict with it as they engage in commercial transactions, the validity of the code may be diminished. Finally, a fourth problem that the adoption of secured transactions codes may trigger is the introduction of new meanings, norms and values regarding relationships between individuals that may not comport with and may even directly conflict with the meanings, norms and values that are integral to the community's identity and the cohesiveness of its members' relationships.

Among the various difficulties associated with the enactment of secured transactions codes as tribal law, the potential for conflict with cultural sovereignty is especially worthy of attention. . . . In contrast to the goals of cultural sovereignty, transplanted law represents a further step toward modeling tribal legal systems after Anglo legal systems. Transplanted law also represents a failure to organically develop tribal legal systems to fit the unique cultures, communities, territories, and traditions of indigenous peoples. In the case of a secured transactions code modeled after Article 9 of the UCC, the code challenges the development of cultural sovereignty to the extent that it displaces or modifies tribal norms and values that relate to the ownership of property and the relationship between debtors and creditors.

Given the continued and growing practice of tribal incorporation of transplanted, non-Indian law, it seems appropriate that we monitor and evaluate this process to identify three things: tribal practices and methods of incorporating transplanted law, the effects of tribal incorporation of transplanted law, and the methods that are available for evaluating the process of the adoption, incorporation, and enforcement of transplanted law. By examining these processes and analytical tools, we can better predict the effects of transplanted law, we can identify the risks and potential dangers of transplanted law, and we can identify mechanisms that may help resolve problems that arise with the incorporation of transplanted law. . . .

NOTES

1. The Little River Band of Ottawa Indians (located in Manistee, Michigan) adopted the State of Michigan's Uniform Commercial Code Article 9 (Secured Transactions) subject to the following modifications:

   Section 5. Amendments for Tribal Uniform Commercial Code
   . . .

   5.02. Security Interest in Pledged Revenues. Notwithstanding any other provision of this Ordinance or, to the extent applicable, the State UCC, the security interest in Pledged Revenues created by the Depository Agreement shall attach and be perfected in the Pledged Revenues (including with respect to any proceeds thereof) without possession by or on behalf of the Servicer, any Servicer, any Secured Payee, the Tribe and the Depository (in each case as defined in the Financing Documents), or any agent of the above, upon the receipt thereof, whether directly or indirectly, by or on behalf of the Tribe, or any agency or instrumentality of the Tribe, and shall continue while in the possession or under the control of any of the foregoing, all without the filing of any financing statement or statements.

   5.03. Financing Statements. Notwithstanding any other provision of this Ordinance or, to the extent applicable, the State UCC, a security interest requiring the filing of a financing statement to become effective shall be sufficient, and shall remain in effect once filed without need for further renewal or extension, (a) if filed on a Form UCC-1 presently acceptable for such purposes under the State UCC and (b) if filed in the office of the Tribal Court. The Tribal Court shall cause to be maintained such records available to the public as are commercially reasonable to evidence the filing of any such financing statements (and the information therein contained) and provide notice to other creditors, and shall upon request provide copies of any financing statements filed with such court. The Tribal Court shall have no other obligation under this Ordinance.

5.04. Applicability to Tribe as Government. This Ordinance shall be applicable to the Tribe notwithstanding any other provisions of this Ordinance or, to the extent applicable, the State UCC.

5.05. Location of Tribe. Notwithstanding any other provisions of this Ordinance or, to the extent applicable, the State UCC, the Tribe and all Collateral, as defined in the Financing Documents, shall be deemed located on the Tribal reservation and on land held in trust for the Tribe by the United States.

5.06. Remedies. Notwithstanding any other provisions of this Ordinance or, to the extent applicable, the State UCC, prior to exercising any non-judicial remedy (other than as provided under Section 6.2 of the Springing Depository Agreement) any secured creditor shall first notify the Tribal Police and the Tribal Court in writing of its intent to exercise non-judicial remedies.

LITTLE RIVER BAND OF OTTAWA INDIANS TRIBAL UNIFORM COMMERCIAL CODE, Ordinance No. 01-800-01 (April 4, 2001).

In the same ordinance, the Little River Band tribal council made the following findings:

> 1.02. Findings. The Tribal Council, in adopting this Ordinance, makes the following findings —
>
> . . .
>
> d. the terms of the financing agreements for the Little River Casino Resort Expansion Project require the application of a Tribal Uniform Commercial Code ("Tribal UCC") which is substantially similar to that adopted by the State of Michigan; and
>
> e. the Tribal Council finds that the adoption of a Tribal UCC based substantially on the State of Michigan's UCC is a critical factor in the financing agreements such that failure to do so will result in an inability to complete the project as a result of being unable to secure financing; and
>
> f. the Tribal Council finds that adoption of a Tribal UCC derived substantially from the State of Michigan UCC, as amended by 2000 Public Act 348, for the specific and narrowly tailored purpose of the Little River Casino Resort Expansion Project financing, and no other purpose, is within its authority.

Does the adoption of this ordinance invoke any of the concerns raised by Professor Singel about transplanted law?

2. Tribal financing expert Rob Gips wrote in 2003 that Indian tribal businesses, until very recently, faced incredible barriers in acquiring capital:

> One reason for this lack of economic development was access to capital, which was a major problem. Each time tribes attempted to borrow money, they faced numerous problems, as multiple legal issues needed to be resolved. These legal issues included questions about the ability of tribes to waive sovereign immunity, the validity of tribal consent to state court jurisdiction,

questions about the exhaustion of tribal court remedies, and uncertainty concerning the enforceability of security agreements involving cash and personal property collateral. Further compounding these problems was a third-party lack of understanding of tribal governments, tribal decision-making, and tribal courts. In addition, a lack of tribal experience and sophistication in dealing with capital markets and businesses also impacted a tribe's ability to borrow the needed funds. As a result, almost no lending occurred in Indian country.

Loans, when they did occur, generally took one of two forms — they were either guaranteed by the federal government or fully cash collateralized by the tribe itself. A cash collateralized loan, however, was not really a loan. Rather, it was a mechanism whereby banks re-loaned to tribes the tribes' own money. . . .

[I]in the early 1990s, when we decided to create and open Foxwoods and Tribal Assets Management approached approximately thirty-five lenders in this country and around the world, not a single bank or institutional investor would finance the project. For that reason we ended up turning to private lenders from Malaysia, who believed in what we were trying to do and were willing to take risks that others perceived to be insurmountable. The initial Foxwoods financing was about $60 million. . . .

The Mashantucket Pequot Tribal Nation now issues investment-grade bonds and has raised over one billion dollars through multiple financings. . . .

Robert L. Gips, *Current Trends in Tribal Economic Development*, 37 New Eng. L. Rev. 517, 517-19 (2003).

3. The economic downturn of late 2008 affected Indian tribes dramatically. Three gaming tribes defaulted on loan payments in 2009 and the Mashantucket Pequot Nation announced that it would seek forbearance from its senior lenders for its multi-billion dollar debt load. *See* Fitch Ratings, *Native American Gaming Insights — Off-Reservation Gaming Approvals: How Will the Feds Play Their Hand?*, at 1 (November 11, 2009), available at http://turtletalk.files.wordpress.com/2009/11/nov-2009-fitch-report.pdf.

5. TRIBAL CORPORATE LAWS

CABINETS SOUTHWEST, INC. v. NAVAJO LABOR COMMISSION

Navajo Nation Supreme Court, No. SC-CV-46-03, 8 Navajo Rep. 435,
2004.NANN.0000001 (February 10, 2004)

Before Bates Arthur, Chief Justice, and Ferguson, Associate Justice.
The opinion of the court was delivered by: Ferguson, Associate Justice. . . .

I.

. . . Petitioner Cabinets Southwest, Inc. (Cabinets) is a subsidiary of Navajo Housing Authority (NHA) formed under the Navajo Nation Corporation Code. NHA approved Cabinets' articles of incorporation by resolution, under the authority granted to NHA by the Navajo Nation Code. The articles of incorporation state that Cabinets will abide by Navajo law.

NHA entered into a lease with the Navajo Nation for a parcel of land held in fee by the Navajo Nation near Church Rock, New Mexico for the purpose of manufacturing cabinets for NHA residential units. The lease indicates that NHA and its employees, agents and sublessees would follow Navajo law. Though no sublease is in the record, it appears that Cabinets operates the cabinet plant on the fee parcel under the authority of its articles of incorporation and the lease.

Real Parties in Interest, Randall and Deniece Haven, were employees of Cabinets and worked at the plant. In early 2002 Cabinets terminated the Havens. The Havens requested arbitration to challenge their terminations. The arbitrator upheld their terminations, and the Havens filed complaints with the Navajo Nation Labor Commission under the Navajo Preference in Employment Act (NPEA), 15 N.N.C. §§601 et seq.

In the Labor Commission proceeding Cabinets filed two separate motions to dismiss the complaint. In its first motion, Cabinets claimed the NPEA did not apply to it, and therefore the Labor Commission lacked jurisdiction over the Haven's claims, because the plant is outside the territorial jurisdiction of the Navajo Nation. The Labor Commission denied that motion. . . .

The Labor Commission planned to have two more days of hearings when Cabinets filed the petition for a writ of prohibition before this Court. . . .

II.

The issu[e] presented [is] (1) whether the Navajo Nation Labor Commission lacks subject matter jurisdiction over a subsidiary of NHA when the subsidiary operates on land owned in fee by the Navajo Nation under a lease that includes the explicit consent to be bound by Navajo law. . . .

III.

Petitioner seeks a writ of prohibition because it claims that the property on which it operates is outside the territorial jurisdiction of the Navajo Nation, and therefore outside the reach of the NPEA. Specifically, Petitioner argues that the NPEA only applies to employers within the territorial jurisdiction of the Navajo Nation, and that the fee parcel owned by the Navajo Nation and leased to NHA is outside the Nation's territorial jurisdiction. . . .

After reviewing the documents submitted by both sides in this case, we believe we do not have to reach the question of whether the parcel is within the territorial jurisdiction of the Navajo Nation. This is because Cabinets is bound by an explicit consent to Navajo jurisdiction in the lease between NHA and the Navajo Nation. . . .

A.

The record in this case includes a lease between the Navajo Nation and NHA for the fee parcel at issue that explicitly acknowledges the reach of the NPEA to Cabinets' activities. That lease, approved by the Economic Development Committee of the Navajo Nation Council and executed by the Navajo Nation President and the Executive Director of NHA, was made for the specific purposes of "the manufacturing and sale of residential cabinets and for all other purposes consistent with this purpose." . . . In the lease NHA agreed that it and its "employees, agents, and Sublessees and their employees and agents . . . [will] abide by all laws, regulations, and ordinances of the Navajo Nation[.]" . . . Further, NHA separately consented to "the legislative, executive and judicial jurisdiction of the Navajo Nation in connection with all activities conducted by [NHA]." . . . Under the clear language of these sections, the activities on the fee parcel, the manufacture and sale of cabinets, [are] subject to the NPEA regardless of the exact status of the parcel itself.

The only question is whether NBA's consent to jurisdiction is binding on Cabinets. Cabinets argues that holding it to the language in the NHA lease would create a "legal fiction," as it claims to be a separate legal entity. . . . That argument misses the point. As previously observed, NHA agreed that any of its "employees, agents, and Sublessees" would be equally bound by Navajo law. The issue is then whether Cabinets is an employee, agent or sublessee of NHA.

Documents in the record show Cabinets' origin and its relationship to NHA. NHA formed Cabinets as a subsidiary of NBA to operate the cabinet business referenced in the lease with the Navajo Nation. . . . Cabinets incorporated as a non-profit entity under the Navajo Nation Non-Profit Corporation Act, 5 N.N.C. §§3301 et seq. . . . NHA approved the articles of incorporation under the power granted by the Navajo Nation Code in 6 N.N.C. §§605, 616(b)(14). . . .

The fact that Cabinets is a subsidiary organized by NBA under the Navajo Nation Corporation Code for the very purposes of the lease leads to the conclusion that it is an "agent" of NBA bound by the consent to jurisdiction in the lease. Cabinets' claim that it has not consented to the NPEA therefore fails. Acceptance of Cabinets' argument that it is a separate entity not bound by NBA's consent would allow corporations with consent clauses in leases with the Navajo Nation to form subsidiaries for the sole purpose of avoiding application of Navajo law. We cannot endorse such an argument.

If the lease provisions were not enough, Cabinets' own articles of incorporation state that it "shall abide by all criminal, civil and regulatory laws of the Navajo Nation." Article XIII. The NPEA is a regulatory law of the Navajo Nation. Therefore Cabinets' own organic document, filed under the laws of the Navajo Nation, and necessary for its very existence, explicitly acknowledges the applicability of Navajo Nation laws. It is absurd that an entity organized under Navajo law that explicitly consents to Navajo law in its organic document and operates on a parcel leased from the Navajo Nation under a lease explicitly consenting to Navajo law would still insist it is not bound by Navajo law. . . .

C.

The Council clearly intended to apply the NPEA to Navajo corporations when they have contracts with the Nation, regardless of the status of the land where the contract is performed. 15 N.N.C. §604(A) extends the NPEA separately to (1) activities within the territorial jurisdiction of the Navajo Nation, and to (2) activities performed under contracts with the Navajo Nation. We hold that the Navajo Nation's NPEA subject matter jurisdiction extends to the activities of Navajo corporations under contracts with the Nation, whether or not the contract is to be performed within the territorial jurisdiction of the Nation. Cabinets is a Navajo corporation and is bound by NHA's lease with the Navajo Nation. The NPEA therefore extends to Cabinets.

Because of the lease, Cabinets specifically consented to the application of the NPEA, and whether or not the parcel is within the territorial jurisdiction of the Navajo Nation, it is bound by that consent. Further, the Navajo Nation has the authority to regulate Navajo corporations outside its territory. The Navajo Nation Council explicitly intended that the NPEA apply to Navajo corporations when they have contracts with the Nation, regardless of the status of the land where the contract is to be performed. We will not issue a permanent writ of prohibition for lack of jurisdiction of the NPEA over Cabinets' activities in this case. . . .

NOTES

1. The Little Traverse Bay Bands of Odawa Indians' corporations code includes the following provisions:

   ### 12.101 Preamble and General Definitions

   The purpose of the Little Traverse Bay Bands of Odawa Indians' Tribal Comprehensive Business Codes is to establish the policy which the Tribe, its entities, private businesses and individuals may use to conduct business activities within its territorial and governmental jurisdiction. The policies shall apply to each of the Codes contained in Statute, The LTBB Odawa Tribal Comprehensive Business Codes. The provisions of this Statute shall be applied to promote its underlying purposes and policies.

   The LTBB Tribal Court has jurisdiction to adjudicate matters arising from this Statute.

   The Tribe recognizes that a strong Reservation economy must include both tribal and private sector development. It is the policy of LTBB to promote both tribal and private sector development within the exterior boundaries of the Reservation and elsewhere within the jurisdiction of the Tribe for Indian and non-Indian businesses. It is the policy of the Tribe to facilitate and enhance job stability, career opportunities and use of inherent Tribal powers to create and maintain a sound business environment within the Tribe's jurisdiction. Consistent with these goals, it is the policy of the Tribe to promote the least restrictive and most cost effective business environment.

   It is the policy of the Tribe that, without waiving any authority over business activities, LTBB shall neither knowingly and unnecessarily obstruct or hinder, nor unreasonably interfere with private sector businesses that operate in accordance with the provisions of this Statute and any other LTBB or applicable law. . . .

   It is the policy of the Tribe to allow the use of tribal land, natural and financial resources and opportunities for the promotion of economic benefits to create jobs, expand business opportunities and secure business independence in order to achieve the goals prescribed in this Statute, consistent with applicable regulations and statutes, enacted now or hereafter.

   Under this Statute, the Tribe may entertain proposals from private sector business interests for privatizing Tribal Governmental activities. If approved, the Tribe will enter into a contractual agreement with such business interests for carrying out such contracted services.

The Tribe authorizes businesses operating pursuant to the Tribe's Comprehensive Business Codes to apply for grants and other programs for which the Tribe is eligible, and that the Tribe does not express an interest in applying for, and operate such programs within the Tribe's jurisdiction. . . .

12.103 Purpose and Construction

A. The purposes of this Chapter 1 are:

1. to encourage commerce by providing limitations on the liability of participants in incorporated enterprises;
2. to reform the laws of business corporations by allowing greater flexibility in the organization and operation of close corporations;
3. to ensure that corporate assets are available for the satisfaction of valid claims of corporate creditors; and
4. to simplify, clarify and modernize the laws applicable to businesses created under the sovereign powers of the Tribe. . . .

12.107 Status Of Corporations

A. For the sole purposes of LTBB and federal taxation, regulatory jurisdiction and civil jurisdiction, the following corporate entities shall be entitled to all of the privileges and immunities of members of federally-recognized Indian tribes:

1. All for-profit corporations formed under Tribal law that are at least 51% owned by Indians who are members of federally-recognized tribes.
2. All non-profit corporations formed under Tribal law that have as their primary purpose the benefit of Tribal members, individuals who reside within the Reservation or any group of people comprised primarily of members of federally-recognized Indian tribes.

B. If a corporation's principal place of business is located on the reservation and the corporation is incorporated both under Tribal law and the laws of any state, then Tribal law and the Tribal charter documents shall take precedence over any conflicting state laws and charter documents in any dispute concerning the status of the corporation or the rights and obligations of any persons with respect to the corporation.

C. The Tribal Court shall have jurisdiction to decide all questions with respect to the status of corporations formed under Tribal law. . . .

12.109 Jurisdiction of Tribal Court

A. To the maximum extent consistent with due process of law, all corporations formed under Tribal law and all directors, officers and shareholders of such corporations, regardless of citizenship or Tribal membership shall be subject to the jurisdiction of the Tribal Court in all actions which arise out of the acts, omissions or participation of such persons in connection with the affairs of such corporations in accordance with these Codes.

B. This section shall not be construed as a waiver of sovereign immunity. . . .

LITTLE TRAVERSE BAY BANDS OF ODAWA INDIANS CORPORATIONS, BUSINESSES AND COMMERCIAL TRANSACTIONS CODE (Waganakasing Odawak Statute 2003-07, 2003).

2. In *High Elk v. Iron Hawk*, 6 Am. Tribal Law 80 (Cheyenne River Sioux Tribal Court of Appeals), the court remanded a case back to the trial court for

determination of whether the Tribal Secretary was *mandated* to issue articles of incorporation in cases where the application form submitted was correct but there also allegedly was a tribal preference against the applicant:

> The Appellee Tribe does not directly reject the notion of mandamus relief in the abstract, but vigorously contests it in this concrete instance. Most telling in this regard is the fact that the Appellee Tribe does not cite a single case, federal, tribal, or state, that has held the issuance of a writ of mandamus to be barred by sovereign immunity. Faced with this absence of precedent, the Tribe makes a more novel argument. The basis of the Tribe's sovereign immunity argument in this case is that the recognition of a "livestock cooperative association" under Tribal Ordinance 39 creates a "preference" in the Cooperative with respect to the Tribal Council granting of grazing permits to range units. According to the Tribe, this "preference" creates a right in tribal property that in turn properly invokes the Tribe's sovereign immunity protection.
>
> While this argument is ingenious, it is legally defective for two reasons. First, the mere existence of a "preference" for the Cooperative in the granting of range unit permits by the Tribal Council does not create an actual property right of the Cooperative in Tribal land but only a potential or inchoate preference right to the use of tribal property. The Cooperative, of course, has not even been certified and it has not been awarded any grazing leases by the Tribal Council. This potential or inchoate preference right does not rise to the level to properly invoke a Tribal sovereign immunity defense. The existence of a sovereign immunity defense cannot be contingent on future events or transactions that are not before the Court. This Court does not, and cannot, engage in anticipatory adjudication or rest its decision on such speculation. Second, any concern the Tribe might have about the legal bona fides of a certified Indian Livestock Cooperative Association may be remedied by its express authority under the existing Tribal Ordinance to bring a "proceeding to cancel or revoke such certificate." Sec. II, Tribal Ordinance 39. . . .
>
> Finally, the Court must analyze what duties Tribal Ordinance 39 does impose on the Tribal Secretary. In this regard, the essence of what remains is determining whether the Secretary's responsibilities under Ordinance 39 are wholly ministerial (i.e. whether they impose a legal duty to act) and whether she therefore must issue the Certificate of Incorporation if the form of the submitted Articles is proper or whether there is some element of discretion, for example, in determining whether the Articles are "duly signed and acknowledged" and thus her actions are not subject to remedy through an extraordinary writ of mandamus. Given that the Court below did not reach this issue because it dismissed the action on sovereign immunity grounds, the case is remanded for both a legal and a factual determination, if necessary, as to the adequacy of the Articles submitted to the Secretary.

High Elk, 6 Am. Tribal Law at 83-85.

3. In *Colorado River Indian Tribes v. Water Wheel Camp Recreation Area, Inc.*, No. 08-0003 (Colorado River Indian Tribes Court of Appeals, March 20, 2009), the court affirmed a trial court opinion piercing the corporate veil in a case in which the tribe sued for trespass against a non–Indian-owned corporation and its purported owner. The court wrote, noting unusual factual circumstances:

> Despite repeated discovery requests and enforcement orders, Appellants/ Defendants had refused to supply the basic corporate and financial records

required for the Tribe to ascertain the financial relationship between Defendants Water Wheel and Johnson and to ascertain whether and to what extent the corporate separation had been maintained. CRIT clearly was entitled to such records to determine whether it should amend its Complaint to add claim of piercing the corporate veil if such records disclosed that Defendant Robert Johnson was employing Defendant Water Wheel as a shell corporation to funnel the proceeds of the Water Wheel resort into his own personal accounts. CRIT was also entitled to discover whether it appeared that Defendant Johnson had adopted a strategy of overstaying the term of the Lease, continuing to collect rents from resort patrons during that period and potentially funneling those proceeds without any payments to the Tribe through Water Wheel into his own personal accounts so that in the event damages were awarded against Water Wheel, it could declare bankruptcy and Johnson could retain the potentially illegally secured proceeds. The persistence of Water Wheel and Johnson in refusing to supply requested corporate and financial records must have given the Tribal Court some suspicion that the Appellants/Defendants had adopted precisely such financial strategy.

Id. at 40. On appeal, the non-Indian defendants claimed their refusal to provide basic financial documents was "litigation strategy." *Id.* at 41. But the appellate court rejected that claim, noting:

Despite the informal claim of willingness to scan some of the requested financial records, the record suggests that Defendants never provided the requested records and never responded to the requests for admissions. Thus, the record simply does not support Appellants/Defendants "litigation theory" argument. The Tribal Court did not find any fraudulent act during discovery (as Appellants/Defendants maintain), just a dogged and persistent refusal to comply with reasonable discovery requests and orders for financial and corporate records. It may well be that this refusal concealed a fraud on the Tribe but neither the Tribal Court nor this Court will ever know whether that is true since the Appellants/Defendants persistently refused to disclose the records that would reveal the truth.

Since the findings of fact of the Tribal Court related to piercing the corporate veil were adopted as a preclusive sanction for noncompliance with discovery orders (not for fraudulent conduct), the protests of the Appellants/Defendants that they are not supported by evidence in the record entirely misses the point of such a sanction. Appellants/Defendants cannot simultaneously violate pretrial discovery requests and related court enforcement orders by withholding critical corporate and financial records and then protest that such evidence was not introduced by the Tribe at trial. The inability of the Tribe to present such evidence falls squarely on their dogged and persistent refusal to produce it in response to reasonable discovery requests and orders. Since the findings of fact of the Tribal Court relative to piercing the corporate veil were not based primarily on evidence presented during the trial on the merits, but, instead, adopted by the Tribal Court (as it expressly warned the Defendants it might do if they did not produce the necessary evidence) as a preclusive sanction for noncompliance with discovery requests and orders, the protests of Appellants/Defendants that the Tribe failed to prove the necessary elements of piercing the corporate veil under federal common law are entirely misplaced.

Id. at 43-44.

B. GAMING

UNITED STATES EX REL. AUGINAUSH V. MEDURE

White Earth Band of Chippewa Tribal Court, No. C-00-354, 8 Am.
Tribal Law 304 (August 27, 2009)

ANITA FINEDAY, J.

Statement of Facts as to Which No Dispute Exists

A. Parties

1. Gaming World International, Ltd. (GWI) at all times relevant herein was a corporation organized under the laws of the State of Delaware, on June 25, 1991, as a closely held entity, owned entirely by Angelo Medure. . . .

2. White Earth Reservation Business Committee (WERBC) is a federally recognized Indian Tribe which operates the Shooting Star Casino (SSC) pursuant to the provisions of the 1988 Indian Gaming Regulatory Act (IGRA), 25 U.S.C. §2701 et seq. . . .

3. Intervenor Plaintiff Raymond Auginaush is a resident and a member of the White Earth Band of Chippewa and represents all tribal members similarly situated.

4. The Bureau of Indian Affairs (BIA) is the party whose consent was required for a valid gaming management contract. By law, a casino management agreement is required to have the approval of the National Indian Gaming Commission (NIGC), whose designee through February 23, 1993, was Earl Barlow, Area Director, Bureau of Indian Affairs (BIA). Without the appropriate approval, a management contract is null and void. 25 C.F.R. §533.7. . . .

5. WERBC obtained financing for the construction of the SSC from the White Earth Land Settlement Act (WELSA), 25 U.S.C. §331, economic development fund, as well as commercial financing from the First National Bank Aitkin, Aitkin, Minnesota. Before the WELSA monies could be used, WERBC, by law, was required to have an approved financial ordinance and investment plan in place for the safeguarding of the WELSA funds. P.L. 99-264, §12, 25 U.S.C. §331, March 24, 1986.

B. July 1991 Letter of Intent

. . .

7. GWI was incorporated on June 25, 1991. Between June 25, 1991, and July 3, 1991, Angelo Medure purchased a trip for Darrell "Chip" Wadena, Chairman of the WERBC, and his wife and family to visit Florida and Disney World to make a favorable impression on them.

8. After the Florida trip, Angelo Medure directed his attorney to draw up a letter of intent which was dated July 3, 1991. . . .

9. On July 12, 1991, Angelo Medure, President, GWI, signed a letter of intent with Darrell Wadena, Chairperson, WERBC, for the exclusive right to improve, develop, manage, maintain and operate all tribal gaming activities at the Shooting Star Casino. . . .

12. The letter of intent . . . signed by GWI and WERBC gave GWI a right to obtain 40% of the net profits in exchange for an exclusive right to "improve,

develop, manage, maintain and operate all tribal gaming activities at the Shooting Star Casino." All undertakings of GWI and Angelo Medure or his agents after July 12, 1991, were to fulfill their obligation and commitment [to] "improve, develop, manage, maintain and operate all tribal gaming activities on the Shooting Star Casino." . . .

C. July 31, 1991 Management Contract — Unapproved

13. On July 31, 1991, a management contract was signed by GWI and WERBC. . . .

14. The July 31, 1991 contract required GWI to "operate, improve, develop, manage and maintain the property known as Shooting Star Casino." . . .

16. In July of 1991, Angelo Medure had no idea what the finances were for the WERBC, and assumed that WERBC had sufficient assets to construct the facility, which the July 31, 1991 agreement contemplated. . . .

17. The July 31, 1991 agreement contemplated the WERBC to construct, at its own cost, the casino facility, and GWI would put in all of the gaming equipment necessary for operating the business. . . .

18. The July 31, 1991 contract obligated GWI to provide the following:

  (a) personnel to conduct a program of instruction for applicants; . . .
  (b) be responsible for hiring and firing decisions at the casino; . . .
  (c) be responsible for security personnel which would include surveillance; . . .
  (d) be responsible for pre-development and development expenses and financing of the expenses; . . .

19. Although GWI was responsible for managing the facility, Angelo Medure testified that GWI had no employees at the casino at any time of the relationship. . . .

20. In exchange for all of the obligations undertaken by GWI, GWI was to receive 40% of the net profits after deducting development costs, which, in the 1991 agreement, excluded the cost of construction of the facility which was to be paid for by WERBC. . . .

21. Under the terms of the July 1991 contract . . . , GWI was responsible for obtaining financing for the improvement, development and management of the casino. . . .

22. As required by law, the July 31, 1991 contract was sent to Earl Barlow, BIA Area Office, Minneapolis, Minnesota, for approval. . . .

23. The WERBC used WELSA funds to finance construction of the casino making the first withdrawal on May 21, 1991, in a sum of $4 million. . . .

24. In August 1991, Erma Vizenor met with Earl Barlow, Area Director of the BIA, to inquire about the WELSA funds and how those funds would be protected. The meeting lasted into the late evening, after which Earl Barlow assured the representatives from White Earth that he would see to it that the WELSA funds were protected as a separate economic development fund. In order to solidify the understanding, Earl Barlow smoked a peace pipe with the tribal representatives creating a spiritual covenant to protect the WELSA money for future generations. . . .

26. The July 31, 1991 contract was never approved. . . .

D. November 1, 1991 Revised Management Agreement

27. In response to the comments raised by Marsha Kimball, GWI and WERBC submitted a revised contract dated November 1, 1991. . . .

30. The November 1, 1991 redrafted agreement obligated GWI to provide personnel to conduct a program of training, personnel to supervise and instruct job applicants, and continued the obligation of the manager to make all hiring and firing decisions. . . .

33. The November 1, 1991 contract was never approved by NIGC or MA. . . .

E. Temporary Casino Operation

34. The temporary SSC was opened on November 22, 1991. . . .

35. Medure was under the impression the temporary casino could be operated without an approved contract for a period of ninety (90) days. . . .

36. Medure presented, through his attorney and accountant, justification to convince the BIA to permit a 60/40 split contract instead of the 70/30 split, and allow for a 7 year contract instead of a 5 year contract, which were the upper limits allowed by law. 25 U.S.C. §2711. . . .

37. GWI attempted to convince BIA to approve the 60/40 split primarily because the BIA had approved a similar contract with Grand Casinos for management of the Mille Lacs facility. . . .

38. In a further effort to satisfy concerns raised by the BIA and the Office of Solicitor, GWI and WERBC submitted amendments to the management contract on February 11, 1992. . . .

39. In February 1992, when negotiating an amendment to the unapproved November 1, 1991 management contract, Medure had no idea what the tribal finances were or what WELSA referred to. . . .

40. Medure insists that in an effort to get the casino up and running, GWI finally relented to buying furniture and furnishings and the phone system. . . . The phone system, however, was leased from AT&T by WERBC. . . .

41. In order to obtain approval of the proposed 60/40 contract, GWI faxed to the Minnesota Chippewa Tribe a justification for the 40% distribution and a 7-year contract, which included such risks as providing housing, transportation, and living expenses for key employees; requiring engineering feasibility studies and marketing analysis to be completed; training school expenses and salaries; guaranteed employment contracts; furnishing the hotel at their own cost; all of the above expenses were argued to be expenses that would be incurred by GWI as their risk. . . .

42. Further justification was submitted by WERBC and GWI on January 13, 1992, which affirmatively alleged that GWI was required to make initial payments to the lender of up to 50% of the total costs and that Medure personally guaranteed notes and leases and that GWI would be risking up to $5 million in venture capital. . . . In the end, the only cash input by GWI was $41,881.00. . . .

F. February 23, 1992 Management Contract

43. On February 23, 1992, GWI and WERBC entered into another management agreement. . . .

45. The February 23, 1992 contract provided as follows:

(a) GWI would provide management personnel, training personnel, supervisory instruction personnel, and have complete control over employment decisions; . . .
(b) GWI had complete control over hiring and firing decisions to satisfy concerns raised by BIA; . . .
(c) GWI provided financing for the operation; . . .
(d) Obligated the Tribe at its own expense to provide for the construction of the casino; . . .
(e) Awarded to GWI 40% of the profits; . . .
(f) Continued the validity of the November 1, 1991 and July 31, 1991 agreements. . . .

G. Final Negotiations for Management Contract

49. Final negotiations between the BIA, GWI and WERBC took place on March 5 and 6, 1992, in Minneapolis, Minnesota. . . .

50. The resulting agreement dated March 6, 1992, is the only contract to have received even colorable approval by the BIA. . . .

51. On March 4, 1992, just two days before the March 6, 1992 contract was signed, Earl Barlow, Area Director, BIA, received a memorandum which provided guidance on minimum criteria to be used for considering anything more than a 70/30 split. The minimum criteria required (1) the management company to assume the majority of the risk; (2) the principal and interest on construction costs would be considered operating expenses; and (3) the term of the agreement would be equal to the term of the construction loans. . . . The BIA had concluded that GWI did not assume a majority of the risk and recommended the proposed contract be rejected. . . .

54. The contract provides GWI the exclusive right to hire and fire employees and provide security personnel. . . .

55. During final negotiations of the March 6, 1992 contract, Earl Barlow insisted on three changes to the contract, i.e. reducing the percentage split from 60/40 to 70/30; reducing the length of the contract from 7 years to 5 years, and a requirement that principal and interest payments of both the WELSA note and the Aitkin Bank note be taken out of operating expenses. . . .

60. When Earl Barlow approved the March 6, 1992 contract, Earl Barlow was told that all of the GWI employees would be paid out of the GWI 30% distribution. . . .

I. March 6, 1992 Management Agreement

68. The March 6, 1992 contract provided as follows:

(a) That all prior agreements, specifically the July 31, 1991 . . . , November 1, 1991 . . . , and February 23, 1992 . . . agreements, are rescinded and void and unenforceable; . . .
(b) GWI was to provide services to improve, develop, manage, and maintain the property known as Shooting Star, which is the same obligation they undertook in July of 1991; . . .

(c) GWI was responsible for all gaming and related activities, materials, equipment, furnishings, fixtures, for gaming and related activities, tools, maintenance and other support items necessary to operate the casino; . . .

(d) GWI was to select employees for management positions, including three appointed by the Band and to provide training aid and personnel to conduct programs of instruction. . . .

(e) GWI was to be responsible for all hiring and firing decisions, which provision was required by Earl Barlow but never abided by GWI. . . .

(f) GWI was charged with the responsibility of all business affairs, including the development, financing, improvement and management and maintenance of the enterprise. . . .

70. GWI and WERBC ignored the provisions of the March 6, 1992 contract. All employees who worked on site were SSC employees. GWI had no employees on the SSC properties. Even though the March 6, 1992 contract provided that the manager shall employ personnel, GWI did not do so. . . .

71. In spite of the contract provision indicating that GWI was to be managing the casino, Medure indicates that from day one he was subject to the control of the WERBC, Gaming Commission, his boss. . . .

72. Medure indicates he had to guarantee five years salary to all employees he recruited. He had no written agreement with any of the employees with the exception of Bob Colaluca and that contract did not contain any guarantee. . . .

73. Medure and GWI created a color brochure identifying the management team of GWI as including a number of individuals who were on the payroll of the SSC. . . . The 4-color brochure was put together to entice people to invest in his initial public offering. . . .

74. The 4-color brochure was created by Barb Leuben, who at the time was Marketing Director for SSC. Barb Leuben obtained all of the information from Medure and/or Ed Donafrio. . . . All of the individuals identified in [the brochure] are identified as being on the GWI Management Team. . . .

75. Barb Leuben lives with Medure, and was in an intimate relationship with Medure when WE Exhibit 42 was created. . . .

76. Ron Cook assisted Medure in setting up the management structure for the SSC, including recruitment of employees, ordering equipment, developing casino manuals, developing an employee handbook and a procedure and practice manual. . . .

77. Ron Cook developed an organizational chart to describe the structure of GWI, SSC which included all SSC department heads. Ron Cook, under the direction of Medure, created an organizational chart of GWI identifying himself as the Vice President. . . .

78. The only nonreimbursed cash investment made by GWI into the SSC was the cost of remodeling bathrooms in the temporary facility in a sum of $41,881.00. . . .

79. Ron Cook became a full-time SSC employee in December 1991, and has never held any position (director, officer or employee) with GWI. . . .

81. Ron Cook became General Manager of the SSC approximately in June of 1992. . . . As General Manager, he was directly responsible for twelve department heads, who comprised the management team. . . .

82. Ron Cook was never employed by GWI. . . .

85. GWI had no employees at the SSC. Even Medure was an employee of the SSC, and all of the employees at the SSC answered to the WERBC. . . .

88. The March 6, 1992 contract approved by Earl Barlow, BIA, obligates the manager to operate, improve, develop and manage the casino. . . .

89. Even though the March 6, 1992 contract required the manager to have full responsibility for hiring and firing employees, this provision was never carried out and no amendment of the agreement was obtained. The March 6, 1992 contract required GWI to have complete control of the gaming and related activities, including the cabaret. . . .

K. Application of 3-6-92 Management Contract

107. Reference to W-2 summary report for GWI for the years 1994 and 1995 . . . , reveal that GWI had no employees at the SSC. . . .

112. In June of 1994, Medure submitted an invoice for reimbursables, including $5,000.00 storage fees. Although no agreement was produced, he submitted the invoice for reimbursement believing he was entitled to an additional $5,000.00 per month. . . .

113. In August or September of 1992, Frank Johnson was approached by the Secretary-Treasurer of the WERBC inquiring how much money GWI was saving by not repaying WELSA, by paying GWI's top employees out of SSC operating expenses, and inquired how WERBC was making up the 10% to GWI. . . .

116. The definition of "operational expenses" which were to be taken off the top, before distribution of profits, was a key part of the formula. The more GWI could expense as "operational" meant more profits to GWI. Angelo Medure worked out the best deal he could by putting all GWI employees on the SSC payroll, which required the WERBC to pay 60% of GWI's employee costs. Medure Arbit. Tr. p. 740. . . .

N. Profit Split Methodology Remained Constant from November 1991 through August 1996

126. Over the course of the relationship between GWI and WERBC, GWI received $10,153,000.00 in profit distributions. Johnson Arbit. Tr. p. 1047; WE Ex. 48 (amount paid column). . . .

130. Following the BIA's rejection of the 60/40 split contract, Chairman Wadena asked Frank Johnson whether or not the SSC could pay some expenses for Gaming World to make up the additional 10%. . . .

131. Only after March 6, 1992, did the issue of reimbursables come to light. Reimbursables were a method of increasing the distributions to GWI to make up the 10%. . . .

132. GWI obtained $77,987.19 per month in excess distribution as a result of not paying back the WELSA note as specifically provided in the March 6, 1992 contract. . . .

O. Indictments of Wadena, Clark and Rawley

136. On August 29, 1995, Darrell "Chip" Wadena, Jerry Rawley and Rick Clark, Chairman, Secretary-Treasurer and District I Councilman, respectively, of the White Earth Band of Chippewa Indians, amongst others, were charged in a 43-count indictment for activities occurring from April 1991 through March 1994, for conspiracy, to defraud the White Earth Band in the construction of the casino which was financed in part by tapping the WELSA funds. . . .

137. In September 1995, the Tribal Council drew money on the SSC account to pay for attorneys' fees to defend the Tribal Council members, which attorneys' fees amounted to approximately $800,000.00. . . .

138. The indictments were based on the willful misapplication of tribal funds, theft, bribery, and misapplication concerning programs receiving federal funds. . . .

139. The methods used to misapply tribal funds were through bid rigging in December of 1993, at which time GWI was under contract to provide construction supervision. . . .

140. On June 24, 1996, Wadena, Clark and Rawley were convicted of 15, 23, and 17 felony counts, respectively, in Federal District Court. . . .

141. On August 12, 1996, Medure's employment with SSC was terminated. . . .

142. In November 1997, Medure settled a lawsuit against U.S. News and World Report. A sum of $3.712 million was deposited in the GWI bank account on November 25, 1997. On the same day, GWI and Angelo Medure made payments as consulting fees to companies that he controlled (RoMed Construction $510,000.00; Northern Paving $180,000.00; West Penn Asphalt $570,000.00) and individuals, including Ron Cook ($30,500.00), David Richards ($55,000.00), Ed Donafrio ($16,700.00), Barb Leuben ($7,500.00), Manny Marcos ($9,400.00), Ray Wirzman ($5,000.00), and Raymond Cook ($7,000.00). In addition, he made simultaneous payments to Angelo Medure ($613,000.00 and $9,000.00); Anthony Medure ($66,000.00); Charlotte Medure ($91,000.00). Medure indicated the payments were made for work they had done prior to the termination of the management agreement with WERBC in August 1996. . . .

143. Medure indicated in November of 1997, GWI had no employees, but yet he paid consultant fees to a number of former employees upon settlement of the libel case. . . .

145. On August 12, 1996, when GWI was terminated as manager of the SSC, the casino was in a state of disrepair. The hotel had not been maintained, machines were out of date, and carpeting was in need of repair. . . .

146. The arbitration panel consisting of Arbitrators Robert J. Sheran, Lawrence R. Yetka and Douglas K. Amdahl found that Darrell "Chip" Wadena and Angelo Medure were complicitous in unlawful acts committed by Darrell Wadena.

147. The Arbitrators further found that the piecemeal actions of the contracts leading principals, Chip Wadena and Angelo Medure established a conspiracy of unlawful means and unlawful goals.

148. The Arbitrators further found that the actions of Angelo Medure and Darrell "Chip" Wadena were piecemeal and contrary to lawful objectives and

demonstrated further evidence of an agreement to benefit Mr. Medure and Mr. Wadena at the expense of the White Earth Band of Chippewa's legitimate interests.

Conclusions of Law

149. That the March 6, 1992 contract is null, void, and unenforceable for the following legal reasons:

(a) The contract is null and void under the White Earth common law principles, contrary to public policy, and amounts to a sham contract;
(b) The contract is null and void under common law principles of unconscionability; and
(c) The contract is null and void because it did not receive the approval of NIGC or the BIA as required by federal law. 25 U.S.C. §2711; 25 U.S.C. §81; 25 C.F.R. §533.7. . . .

150. Gaming World International has received reasonable compensation for the services it provided in the management of the casino.

151. The corporate veil of Gaming World International, Ltd. is pierced on the basis that Gaming World International, Ltd. was the alter ego of Angelo Medure at the time of entering into the contract and that failing to pierce the corporate veil would be inequitable, result in injustice and be fundamentally unfair. . . .

153. The Intervenor Plaintiff and Plaintiff are entitled to the relief authorized under 25 U.S.C. §81 as it existed in 1992, when the contractual relationship was entered between GWI and Angelo Medure and the White Earth Band. . . .

Memorandum

The motion before the Court is a partial summary judgment motion brought by the Plaintiffs. The Plaintiffs are seeking the following:

1) A declaratory judgment ruling that the alleged management contract dated 3/6/1992 is null and void as a matter of law;
2) That the alleged management contract dated 3/6/92 is null and void on common law principles including contract formed under duress, a contract contrary to public policy and that the contract is a sham;
3) A ruling as a matter of law that the corporate veil of Gaming World Inc. (GWI) is pierced on the basis that GWI was an alter ego of Angelo Medure and that failing to pierce the corporate veil would be inequitable, result in injustice and be fundamentally unfair.

Motion for Summary Judgment

. . . Based on materials submitted and left undisputed by the Defendants, the Court has made the following conclusions of law as follows:

Validity of Qui Tam Provision

The 2000 Amendment to 25 U.S.C. §81 does not apply retroactively and is therefore an appropriate course of action by the White Earth Reservation

Business Council (WERBC). 25 U.S.C. §81, prior to the 2000 amendments, states that

> [n]o agreement shall be made by any person with any tribe of Indians for the payment or delivery of any money or other thing of value . . . unless such contract or agreement be executed and approved as follows: 1) Such agreement shall be in writing, and a duplicate of it delivered to each party. 2) It shall bear the approval or the Secretary of Interior and the Commissioner of Indian Affairs endorsed upon it. . . . All contracts or agreements made in violation of this action shall be null and void, and all money or other thing of value paid to any person by any Indian or Tribe, . . . on account of such services, . . . may be recovered by suit in the name of the United States in any Court of the United States.

25 U.S.C. §81 (1958). The requirement of approval of all contracts relating to Indian lands has been required since 1872.

. . . The contract at issue was signed on March 6, 1992. Both parties were fully aware of the qui tam provision when they entered into the contract. Accordingly, the provisions of 25 U.S.C. §81 which were in effect on March 6, 1992, govern this transaction.

Validity of the Contested Management Contract Dated March 6, 1992

A. The Contract Dated March 6, 1992 Is Unenforceable, Null and Void as a Matter of Law Because It Was Not Approved by the Secretary of Interior or the National Indian Gaming Commission (NIGC).

25 U.S.C. §81, as it read prior to the 2000 amendments, required approval by the Secretary of Interior and the Commissioner of Indian Affairs. This responsibility was vested by Congress under the Indian Gaming Regulatory Act (IGRA) . . . with NIGC which was established in 1993. . . .

. . . The NIGC was thus responsible for approving the contract. The NIGC did not review this contract until 1996, at which time it was rejected. . . .

C. The Contract Is Voidable under the Common Law Principle of Unconscionability and Fraud and as a Matter of Public Policy

a. Unconscionability

The primary reason behind the federal government's regulation of all contracts is because throughout history, the United States government considered itself the "great father" to Indian nations. *Cherokee Nation v. State of Georgia*, 30 U.S. 1, 5 Pet. 1, 8 L. Ed. 25, 1831 WL 3974 (1831). This protective attitude is reflected in a multitude of federal laws, including IGRA. The purpose of the limits on the net revenue split was to ensure that Indian tribes were not taken advantage of by management corporations and to shield tribes from organized crime or other corrupting influences while ensuring they benefit from gaming revenues. 25 U.S.C. §2702.

Neither party contests that Barlow refused to sign any contract prior to the negotiations on 3/2/92, which entitled GWI to a 60/40 split over 7 years because Barlow did not find that the contract met the minimum criteria for the split as required by IGRA. Under IGRA, the criteria for a 60/40 split over a 7 year term required the following:

1) The management company must have the majority of risk in the project.

2) The payback on the total capital investment (i.e. loans, notes, etc.) must be considered an operating expense prior to determining the distribution of net revenues.

3) The term of the agreement must be equal in length to the terms of any equipment leases or loan periods that are the responsibility of the management contract.

. . . Without these considerations, Congress believed there to be no reason for such contractual obligations. Barlow was protecting the Band from entering into a contract that was fundamentally unfair by its very terms. Unconscionability is defined as "extreme unfairness." BLACK'S LAW DICTIONARY 742 (3rd Pocket ed. 2001).

When the Court encounters a contract that is extremely unfair, it has the discretion to refuse to enforce a contract. RESTATEMENT (SECOND) OF CONTRACTS, §208 (1981). However, even with the terms of the contract as they were, it is clear that even prior to the 3/6/92 negotiations that GWI was not operating or planning to operate the Shooting Star Casino. It is difficult to ascertain what services GWI was providing to the Casino based on the plethora of evidence submitted by the Plaintiffs. GWI's performance in light of that which was required in the contract demonstrates a gross disparity in the values exchanged between the two parties. Furthermore, it would be poor precedent not to find the terms of the contract unconscionable given the extensive record provided by the Plaintiff. As a matter of public policy, it is important to the integrity of the tribe to ensure that all business dealings and contractual obligations are substantively fair for both parties.

b. Fraud

The Restatement (Second) of Contracts §164 (1981) states that

[i]f a party's manifestation of assent is induced by either a fraudulent or a material misrepresentation by one who is not a party to the transaction upon which the recipient is justified in relying, the contract is voidable by the recipient, unless the other party to the transaction in good faith and without reason to know of the misrepresentation either gives value or relies materially on the transaction.

The Plaintiff has stated and the Respondent's failed to contest that the representations made to Earl Barlow both prior to and during the negotiations of the 3/6/92 contract were false. During negotiations, GWI specifically agreed to the following:

1) Provide services to improve, develop, manage and maintain the property known as Shooting Star.

2) Be responsible for all gaming and related activities, materials, equipment, furnishings, fixtures, tools, maintenance and other support items necessary to operate the casino.

3) Select employees for management positions, including three appointed by the Band and to provide training aid and personnel to conduct programs of instruction.

4) Be responsible for all hiring and firing decisions.

5) Be responsible for all business affairs, including the development, financing, improvement, management and maintenance of the enterprise.

The record shows that both parties ignored these provisions. The Plaintiff's provided clear and convincing evidence, with no response from the Respondent's refuting this, that GWI did not employ personnel or guarantee the employee's salaries for five years. Furthermore, the total amount of work that was left uncompensated was GWI's $41,881.00 cash investment which went towards a bathroom remodel at the temporary casino facility. Erma Vizenor testified during the arbitration process in 2001 that after cancelling the contract with GWI, the Tribal Council stepped in and made over $3 million dollars in repairs and updates to machines required to be maintained by GWI under the 3/6/92 contract. . . . There is also sufficient and undisputed evidence that fraudulent activities including bid-rigging and the failure to repay WELSA funds occurred in order to benefit Rick Clark, Darrell "Chip" Wadena and GWI. . . . The representations made to Earl Barlow at the time he signed the provisional contract and rejected by the NIGC in 1996, meet the requirements of fraud. Therefore, this Court finds that the actions were fraudulent and the contract voidable.

Piercing of the Corporate Veil

A. The Corporate Veil of GWI Should Be Pierced to Allow the Recovery of Illegal Profits Taken by Angelo Medure

The concept of piercing the corporate veil is equitable in nature. As noted by the court in *Erickson-Hellekson-Vye Co. v. A. Wells Co.*, 217 Minn. 361, 15 N.W.2d 162 (1944)[,]

> [d]isregarding the legal concept that a corporation is a distinct entity, courts of equity have repeatedly held that where an individual owns all, or practically all, the stock of a corporation, the corporation and such individual will be regarded as one and the same if the equities of a case so require.

217 Minn. 381-82, 15 N.W.2d at 173. . . .

The practice of piercing the corporate veil is generally a creditor's remedy used to reach an individual who has used a corporation as an instrument to defraud creditors. . . . The standard of review of a District Court's exercise of equity is abuse of discretion; an abuse of discretion is shown if the Court disregarded the facts or applicable principles of equity. . . . Courts will pierce the corporate veil if an entity ignores corporate formalities and acts as the alter ego or instrumentality of a shareholder and the liability limitations of the corporate forum results in injustice or is fundamentally unfair. . . .

The Arbitrators found that Angelo Medure and GWI were complicitous in unlawful acts regarding contract performance. The Arbitrators found [that]

> [t]he piecemeal actions of the contract's leading principals, Chip Wadena and Angelo Medure, establish a conspiracy of unlawful means and unlawful goals. During the significant years covered by the March 6, 1992 contract, Mr. Wadena was in effective control of the White Earth Tribal Council and of the interests of the White Earth Indian Reservation. An appeal from the

contract approved by Mr. Barlow, a contract favoring the Tribe, was taken not by [GWI] but by the Wadena-controlled Tribal Council. Such actions, piecemeal and contrary to lawful objectives, are further evidence of an agreement to benefit Mr. Medure and Mr. Wadena at the expense of the [WERBC's] legitimate interest.

Award of Arbitrators, May 23, 2002. GWI was an instrumentality or "alter ego" of Angelo Medure and together they conspired to strip the profits of the casino and deprived the people of White Earth of repayment of the WELSA economic development fund. The first prong of the test has been met.

Although aware that any management contract required approval from NIGC and/or BIA, Angelo Medure and GWI continued to engage in withdrawing millions of dollars from the Shooting Star Casino in spite of an unapproved contract and in spite of having no employees at the casino. In spite of the contract provision indicating GWI managed the Casino, Medure abdicated that responsibility and became the employee of the Gaming Commission. Angelo Medure admits from day one he and GWI were subject to the control of WERBC, Gaming Commissions, who he referred to as his boss. . . .

In spite of having no employees on the Shooting Star Casino premises, Medure created a 4-color brochure identifying a management team of GWI to entice people to invest in his initial public offering. . . . According to the 3/6/92 contract, GWI was charged with the responsibility of development, financing, and improvement of the facility, the only out-of-pocket expense made by GWI was the cost of remodeling bathrooms in a temporary facility for a sum of $41,881.00.

After the BIA required a 70/30 split, GWI, Medure and Darrell Chip Wadena devised a scheme to increase distributions to GWI to make up the 10%. . . . Finally, to clearly demonstrate Medure's use of GWI as an instrument of fraud, after settling a lawsuit against U.S. News and World Report, a sum of $3.712 million was deposited in the GWI bank account on November 25, 1997. On the very same day, GWI and Angelo Medure made payments as "consulting fees" to construction, paving, and aggregate companies he controlled (RoMed Construction $510,000.00; Northern Paving $180,000.00; West Penn Asphalt $570,000.00) and individuals, including former SSC General Manager Ron Cook ($30,500.00), David Richards, GWI CFO ($55,000.00), Ed Donafrio, SSC Employee ($16,700.00), Barb Leuben, housemate and SSC Employee ($7,500.00), Manny Marcos, SSC Employee ($9,400.00), Ray Wirzman, SSC Employee ($5,000.00), and Raymond Cook, SSC Employee ($7,000.00). In addition, he made simultaneous payments to himself, Angelo Medure ($613,000.00 and $9,000.00); Anthony Medure (uncle) ($66,000.00); Charlotte Medure (wife) ($91,000.00). Medure indicated the payments were made for work they had done for GWI prior to the termination of the management agreement with WERBC in August 1996. . . .

These facts adequately and sufficiently show that GWI was the alter ego of Angelo Medure. After hearing five days of testimony, the Arbitrators said it most succinctly when they found a conspiracy of unlawful purposes and unlawful means between Medure and Darrell Chip Wadena to deprive WERBC of their rightful due under the casino management contract. GWI was insolvent and unable to make any payments on a judgment as of December 1997. . . .

Finally, the White Earth Nation has seen its White Earth Land Settlement Act economic trust fund funneled out of the reservation into the hands and pockets of Angelo Medure who created a corporate shell to give the appearance of legitimacy. Angelo Medure conspired with Gaming World International to deprive the People of White Earth the benefits of gaming. Implicit in the common law of White Earth is the concept of good faith and fair dealing, which is absent from the undisputed facts of this case. . . .

NOTES

1. In *Muscogee Nation ex rel. Foster v. Indian Country USA, Inc.*, 1 Okla. Tribal Court Rep. 109 (Muscogee (Creek) Nation Supreme Court 1987), the court interpreted a gaming management contract—likely one of the very first ever—to mean that the management company would receive only 40 percent of net profits:

    > It is the contention of Appellant [Muscogee Nation] that any salary and expenses incurred by Gordon Sjodin are to be paid out of Appellees' 40% split in accordance with said Management Agreement. That for said enterprise to pay the salary, travel and entertainment expenses incidental to Mr. Sjodin's employment is to perpetrate a fraud. That Mr. Sjodin is the President of Indian Country USA, Inc. That Appellant has no voice or authority whatsoever, except by a lawsuit, to question the monies paid to Mr. Sjodin. That if Appellees are not restrained and enjoined in this nefarious practice, net profits are subject to manipulation and Appellant will suffer irreparable damage.
    >
    > It is the contention of Appellees that Mr. Sjodin is an employee of said enterprise and as such, Appellees under said Management Agreement are legally entitled to deduct same as an operating expense.
    >
    > The Management Agreement is silent as to the paying of a general manager for said enterprise. The Appellees prepared and drafted said agreement. . . .
    >
    > The record is clear that Appellees were retained and engaged by Appellant to manage, administer and operate the Tribal Bingo Enterprise for the sole consideration of a 40% share of its net profits.

    Indian Country USA, 1 Okla. Tribal Court Rep. at 111-13.

2. As early as the 1960s and into the 1970s, a few Indian tribes in California, Florida, Maine, New York, and Wisconsin, desperate for tribal government revenue, opened high-stakes bingo parlors. The theory was straightforward. Federal jurisprudence has long held that state laws have no force in Indian country, and state criminal laws that might otherwise prohibit high-stakes bingo would likely not apply to tribally owned and operated bingo halls. Federal officials saw the potential for Indian tribes to make a significant amount of money in these endeavors. That money could be used to reduce Indian dependence on federal appropriations—a worthwhile political goal. Even local governments often cooperated with tribes to develop gaming operations. In the early 1980s, after a series of federal court decisions favoring this exercise of tribal sovereignty, tribes in other states followed the lead of the gaming tribes.

    The issue of whether states had jurisdiction to shut down or regulate Indian bingo halls and casinos reached the Supreme Court in *California v. Cabazon*

Band of Mission Indians, 480 U.S. 202 (1987). Frank Ducheneaux, former counsel on Indian Affairs to the House Committee on Interior and Insular Affairs from 1973 to 1990, stated the *Cabazon Band* decision "was a full vindication of the right of tribes to engage in gaming activity[.]" Franklin Ducheneaux, *The Indian Gaming Regulatory Act: Background and Legislative History*, 42 ARIZ. ST. L.J. 99, 154 (2010). Congress had been debating Indian gaming regulatory bills for several years, but *Cabazon Band* created the political impetus to finalize an Indian gaming act, and largely on the terms set by tribal interests.

On October 17, 1988, Congress enacted the Indian Gaming Regulatory Act. 25 U.S.C. §§2701 et seq. Congress first established three classes of Indian gaming. Class I gaming includes traditional tribal games, or gaming that would be regulated and authorized exclusively by Indian tribes. Congress defined class II gaming to mean high-stakes bingo, the type of games tribes first began in California, Florida, and New York, and the type at issue in the *Cabazon Band* litigation.

Congress defined class III games to include all other gaming. This broad definition includes casino-style gaming, such as slot machines, poker, blackjack, craps, and keno. Class III gaming is the kind of gaming that can be very lucrative for Indian tribes, although some forms of class II gaming can also generate enormous revenues. It is here that Congress's regulatory and authorization scheme became the most creative. Congress created a structure whereby Indian tribes could not conduct class III gaming without entering into a class III gaming compact with the governor of the state where the tribe wished to begin gaming.

Congress also created the National Indian Gaming Commission ("NIGC") to serve as the federal component of the regulatory scheme. Congress intended for federal and state regulation of Indian gaming to be light, unless the tribe consented to such regulation, and it did not intend the NIGC to act as a massive bureaucratic regulatory body. In fact, for several years, the NIGC's annual budget was limited to a mere $8 million, and Congress did not authorize the NIGC to promulgate substantive regulations. The tribes would be the primary regulator of class II gaming, while Congress left class III gaming to the tribes and the states. As a final and important policy, Congress prohibited states from collecting taxes on Indian gaming operations and revenues.

3. Gaming operations provide critical employment opportunities for tribal members and non-members alike, reducing the burden on state social services. A federal trial court noted the success of the Turtle Creek Casino, owned and operated by the Grand Traverse Band of Ottawa and Chippewa Indians, in its findings of fact after a trial in which the State of Michigan attempted to shut down the casino:

> In fiscal year 2001, Turtle Creek provided approximately 89% of the Band's gaming revenue. The casino now employs approximately 500 persons, approximately half of whom are tribal members. Revenues from the Turtle Creek Casino also fund approximately 270 additional tribal government positions, which administer a variety of governmental programs, including

health care, elder care, child care, youth services, education, housing, economic development and law enforcement. The casino also provides some of the best employment opportunities in the region, and all of its employees are eligible for health insurance benefits, disability benefits and 401(k) benefit plans. The casino also provides revenues to regional governmental entities and provides significant side benefits to the local tourist economy.

Grand Traverse Band of Ottawa & Chippewa Indians v. United States Attorney for the W. Dist. of Mich., 198 F. Supp. 2d 920, 926 (W.D. Mich. 2002), *aff'd*, 369 F.3d 960 (6th Cir. 2004).

C. TRIBAL TAXATION

ROSE v. ADAMS

Crow Court of Appeals, No. 95-27, 2000 CROW 1, 2000.NACT.0000005
(January 11, 2000)

Before, BIRDINGROUND, Chief Judge, STEWART, Associate Judge and DESMOND, Special Associate Judge.

The opinion of the court was delivered by: Special Judge DESMOND . . .

Parties

Appellants, five non-Indian owned businesses, are each involved in some type of recreation-oriented activity on the Crow Indian Reservation. Appellant Gordon Rose is the managing partner of Quill Gordon Fly Fishers, a business that sells fishing equipment, provides lodging and offers guiding services; its business offices are located on fee land, within the boundaries of the Crow Indian Reservation. Appellant Joe S. Bassett is the owner of the Schively Ranch, a guest ranch located on fee land but whose hunting preserve includes land leased from a tribal member and who conducts limited activities on trust land. Appellant Nick Forrester is the President of Recreation Development, Inc., a hunting and fishing lodge that sells fishing equipment and provides guiding services for fishing and bird hunting. He leases land from the 40 Mile Colony that is used as a bird hunting preserve. Some of that land is trust land, although he does not intentionally conduct activities on trust land. Appellant Dennis Whitledge is the Manager of the Little Big Horn Campground, which is located on fee land and contains a campground, motel, grocery store, gas station and laundromat. Appellant George Kelly is the President of Bighorn County Outfitters Inc. which sells products related to the fishing industry and provides lodging and fishing guiding services. . . .

Procedural Background

The Crow Tribal Council enacted the resort tax at issue on January 14, 1995. . . . The United States Bureau of Indian Affairs approved the tax on June 9, 1995, in accordance with Article VI, Section 10 of the Crow Tribal Constitution, which provides that tribal taxes are "subject to review by the

Secretary of Interior." The Bureau of Indian Affairs Area Director[approved the tax.]

. . . The resort tax is a "sales or transaction" tax that imposes a 4% tax on "the gross receipts from all goods and services sold or used on the Reservation in connection with a resort business." [Crow Tribal Tax Code, CTTC] §4.02. Section 4.01(a) CTTC, defines "resort businesses" as including but not limited to:

(1) Campgrounds, dude ranches, guest ranches, hunting and fishing lodges, bed and breakfast establishments, souvenir shops, hotels, motels and other lodging or camping facilities and

(2) Hunting and fishing guide services and recreation equipment rentals received or used on the Crow Reservation.

Section 4.04 CTTC provides that the tax "shall be imposed on the consumer" and shall be collected by the owner of a resort business from the consumer, and that the owner is entitled to keep 2% of the total tax due to cover administrative costs. The resort tax is similar to the Montana state lodging facility tax, which is a tax on users of lodgings for less than 30 days, collected by the businesses operating the lodging facility and to the Montana local option resort tax. See §15-65-101 et seq.; §7-6-1501 et seq. . . .

Appellants paid estimated taxes for the first quarter of 1995 under protest and filed this action on July 26, 1995. . . .

Decision

. . .

3. Analysis of the Power to Tax

We next describe the extent to which the power to tax remains an element of tribal inherent sovereignty, including the degree to which the power to tax is a component of self-government.

The power to raise revenue is an essential governmental power. Tribal authority to impose taxes on both Indians and non-Indians doing business on the reservation has long been recognized and protected. *See Morris v. Hitchcock*, 194 U.S. 384 (1904); *Buster v. Wright*, 135 F. 947 (8th Cir. 1905), *appeal dism'd*, 203 U.S. 599 (1906); [*Washington v. Colville Confederated Tribes*, 447 U.S. 134 (1980)]; *Kerr-McGee Corp. v. Navajo Tribe*, 471 U.S. 195 (1985); *Merrion v. Jicarilla Apache Tribe*, 455 U.S. 130 (1982).

In 1934, at the time of the enactment of the Indian Reorganization Act, when the Interior Department was asked to compile a list of remaining inherent Tribal powers supported by the Act, Solicitor Nathan Margold included the following summary of the tribal power to tax:

Chief among the powers of sovereignty recognized as pertaining to an Indian tribe is the power of taxation. Except where Congress has provided otherwise, this power may be exercised over members of the tribe and over nonmembers, so far as such nonmembers may accept privileges of trade, residence, etc., to which taxes may be attached as conditions. [Powers of Indian Tribes, 55 I.D. 14, 46 (1934).]

Later, in 1982, in *Merrion*, the United States Supreme Court reviewed the existence and source of tribal taxation authority in determining whether the Jicarilla Apache Tribe had the power to impose an oil and gas severance tax on non-Indian lessees. The Court stated that the power to tax is "an essential attribute of Indian sovereignty," because it is a "necessary instrument of self-government" and "territorial management." The Court explained that tribal taxation authority "enables a tribal government to raise revenue" for "essential services." As for the source of this tribal power, the Court stated that it "does not derive fully from the Indian tribe's power to exclude non-Indians from tribal lands." Rather,

> it derives from the tribe's general authority, as sovereign, to control economic activity within its jurisdiction, and to defray the cost of providing governmental services by requiring contributions from persons or enterprises engaged in economic activities within that jurisdiction. 455 U.S. at 137.

As stated above, in *Colville*, the United States Supreme Court upheld the tribe's power to impose a sales tax on transactions with non-Indians entering the reservation to purchase cigarettes. [T]he Court found a "widely held understanding within the Federal Government . . . that federal law . . . [had not brought about] a divestiture of Indian taxing power." The Court traced the historical viewpoints of the executive and judicial branches to nineteenth century opinions of the United States Attorney General and to federal court decisions from the early 1900s (noted above). Congressional endorsement of tribal tax powers was found in the IRA. For the Court, the section of the IRA confirming tribal powers under existing law constituted congressional recognition of a tribal government's "authority to tax the activities or property of non-Indians taking place or situated on Indian lands, in cases where the tribe has a significant interest in the subject matter." 447 U.S. at 152. The Court specifically found that the tribal power to tax had not been implicitly divested . . . , stating it "saw no overriding federal interest that would necessarily be frustrated by tribal taxation," and reiterating the rule made precise in the Marshall decisions that "tribal sovereignty is dependent on and subordinate to, only the Federal Government, not the State." Like the tourists who are subject to the Crow resort tax, the cigarette purchasers came voluntarily onto the reservation to transact their business.

. . . Additionally, the *Colville* Court cited with approval the cases of *Buster v. Wright* and *Morris v. Hitchcock*, each of which upheld tribal taxation of non-Indians on fee land. Perhaps more importantly for our purposes here, in *Montana* [*v. United States*, 450 U.S. 544 (1981)], the Court cited *Colville*, in support of its statement that in the proper circumstances, tribes retain the power to tax non-Indians, even for activities occurring on fee land. Further, according to an interpretation in Cohen, Handbook of Indian Law, (1982) the *Colville* Court's rationale requires a "tribal interest in the subject matter to justify a tribal tax," which in that case was supplied by use of trust land. On fee land, the interest can exist but must be based on some other situation. Cohen at 434 n. 27. Thus, while Appellants are correct that in *Colville* the Supreme Court stated its rule in the context of trust land, we do not agree that the *Colville* decision renders the Crow resort tax invalid.

Clearly, and justifiably so, the power to tax both Indians and non-Indians persists as an important element of tribal inherent sovereignty. As outlined above, currently the scope of tribal authority, while limited, remains meaningful. The Crow Tribe and other tribes are "a good deal more than 'private voluntary organizations.'" *United States v. Mazurie*, 419 U.S. 544 (1975). They are governments, and like governments everywhere must raise revenue to survive. . . .

In any event, the Tribal Court found "substantial evidence" showing that tourists receive benefits and accept privileges of trade provided by the Crow Tribe and its trustee agents, the Bureau of Indian Affairs and Indian Health Services ("IHS"), whose services the Tribal Court properly considered because the services are intended to benefit the Tribe and its members under a trust relationship. We see no reason to substitute our judgment for that of the Tribal Court on these findings. The Tribal Court made extensive findings on the governmental services available to tourists and on the link between tourist activity and increased demands for governmental services, some of which we have already referred to in our discussion of the second Montana exception.

The Tribal Court found Appellees' exhibits, "Report Concerning the Crow Tribe Resort Tax" and "Surrebuttal Report Concerning the Crow Tribal Resort Tax" of the Economics Resource Group (ERG) as well as the expert testimony of the reports' principal author, Professor Joseph Kalt, "clearly established that tourists receive tangible and intangible benefits from the Tribal government's expenditures." . . .

While the Tribe did not conduct its own formal study on tourism prior to enacting the tax, Appellee Tax Commissioner Adams testified that the Tribe had consulted several studies and other data that showed an increase in tourism. Commissioner Adams also testified that he was aware of the increase in tourism through newspaper articles, and attendance figures from the Little Big Horn Battlefield, Yellowtail Dam, Big Horn Canyon Recreational Area and an increase in the number of tourist businesses on the reservation. The Court found that the evidence at trial showed that on any day in July, the population on the Crow Reservation can rise by a factor of 30 to 40 percent as a result of the influx of tourists. The tax commission also relied on studies prepared for two proposed economic development projects and on traffic counts. The former chair of the Crow Tax Commission, Appellee Tyrone Ten Bear, testified that tribal members had noticed increases in law enforcement and traffic collection needs and he was aware of attendance figures from several tourist destinations, and information from the Montana Highway Department, the National Park Service and the HIS, which showed an increase in tourism on the reservation.

The Tribal Court found, on the basis of the ERG Reports that the Crow Tribe and its trustee agents, the BIA and HIS, "perform substantial governmental service and functions that tangibly benefit tourists on the Reservation." Specifically, the court found a "wide range of law enforcement, fire protection, road construction and maintenance, wildlife management, education, public utility services, health and welfare and other governmental services that make civil and economic commerce possible and fruitful." Slip op. at 18-19. Four of the five Appellants testified that they or their customers use BIA roads. Appellant Bassett testified that several years ago the tribal fire department put out a fire that threatened his property and that he keeps the department's telephone number near his telephone. Appellant Whitledge testified that he calls the tribal police when disturbances occur at his business.

[4]. Tribal Interests

Serious Tribal interests are implicated by the activities upon which the tax is imposed. . . . In this case, understandably, Appellants have tried to distance themselves, as a theoretical matter, from the legal authority of the Crow Tribe, emphasizing headquarter locations on fee lands, businesses' recreational activities on fee lands and that the main attraction for the majority of their customers is the Big Horn River, which is held and regulated by the State of Montana.

Yet, the evidence at trial indicated that the Tribal context has a great deal to do with Appellants' businesses, as their own testimony acknowledged. In its decision, the Tribal Court pointed out that Appellants Forrester, Bassett and Whitledge testified that to some extent, their business operations are enhanced by their location within an Indian reservation and that they use the "Indian mystique for marketing purposes." . . . Appellant Forrester testified that he employed guides trained in a program offered by Little Big Horn College, a Tribally-operated institution of higher education. Appellant Whitledge testified that the majority of his customers are members of the Crow Tribe. Further, some of the tourist opportunities are tribally-related or have tribal aspects, *e.g.*, the Auke Bay at the Big Horn Canyon Recreation area, the Little Big Horn Battlefield and the annual Crow Fair, one of the largest pow-wows in the country. . . .

Finally, the evidence presented at trial indicated that a great deal of the activity of Appellants' customers is conducted on trust land and illustrated the practical difficulty of using land status as a deciding factor. The Court found that Appellants' customers "routinely trespass on Indian trust property along the banks of the Big Horn River." Tribal Game Warden Arnold Costa testified that he observes 15 to 20 people per day trespassing from the Big Horn River onto trust property. Appellant Bassett testified that unintentional trespasses on tribal trust land are committed by himself and his customers at the Shively ranch, when they mend fences. Part of the hunting preserve leased by Appellant Forrester's business (Recreational Development, Inc.) includes tribal trust lands. Appellant Bassett leases 1400 acres from a tribal member for his dude ranch operation and grazes his cattle on this land.

[5]. The Tribal Court's Ruling That the Tribe Has Jurisdiction to Require Appellants to Collect the Tax Is Correct

As for the issue of whether or not the Tribe has the authority to require Appellants to collect the tax for them, the Tribal Court held that it was valid as a "minimal burden" on the businesses which is necessary to prevent tax avoidance, citing *Moe v. Confederated Salish and Kootenai Tribes*, 425 U.S. 463 (1976) and *Colville*. We agree.

The requirement that appellants collect the tax does not burden them impermissibly. As in Moe and Colville, the businesses are required to do little in the way of bookkeeping and in fact they are entitled to keep a portion of the collected tax to defray any administrative costs which may be incurred. The Tribal Court was correct in ruling that the administrative requirements are not regulation of Appellants within the meaning of Montana.

The Tribal Court's judgment is AFFIRMED in accordance with this Opinion.

NOTE

Professor Alexander Skibine argues that Indian tribes should begin taxing the income of tribal members who live off the reservation:

> My proposal is simple: persuade the tribes that they should tax not only their members living on the reservations, but also members living off the reservation. The tribes may also want to recruit the federal government in assisting them in collecting the tax. There are many ways this could be done. In conformity with my position that Indian tribes should be incorporated into the federal system under a third sphere of sovereignty, and therefore, whenever possible, be treated as states[,] the tribal income tax should be treated the same as state income taxes relative to the federal income tax and should be deducted from the amount of tax owed to the federal government. Because this integration of tribal tax systems into the federal system would be a major step, legislation should be enacted by Congress providing a mechanism for the United States to approve each tribal income tax scheme. Such approval could be made by either the Secretary of the Interior or the Internal Revenue Service. The United States should also be able to verify that the tribal taxes are in fact being assessed and collected.

Alex Tallchief Skibine, *Tribal Sovereign Interests beyond the Reservation Borders*, 12 Lewis & Clark L. Rev. 1003, 1042 (2008).

D. THE APPLICATION OF FEDERAL LAW
TO TRIBAL ENTERPRISES

Foxwoods Resort Casino and International Union, UAW, AFL-CIO

National Labor Relations Board, Region 34, No. 43-RC-2230 (October 24, 2007)

Peter B. Hoffman, Regional Director . . .

The Petitioner seeks to represent a unit of approximately 3,000 licensed poker, table game, and dual rate dealers employed at the Foxwoods Resort Casino in Mashantucket, Connecticut (herein called Foxwoods), which is owned by the Mashantucket (Western) Pequot Tribe (herein called the Tribe), and operated by a tribal venture, the Mashantucket Pequot Gaming Enterprise (herein called MPGE). Foxwoods is located on the Tribe's reservation, which consists of 1,600 acres of land held in trust by the United States Government, in perpetuity, for the benefit of the Tribe. Although otherwise in accord as to the scope and composition of the petitioned-for unit, the Employer, contrary to the Petitioner and Intervenor [the State of Connecticut], contends that the Board is precluded from asserting jurisdiction in this matter because doing so would constitute an impermissible infringement on the Tribe's federally recognized status as a sovereign nation, which it argues includes an inherent right to enact laws to regulate employment and labor relations for any of its ventures that function to benefit the Tribe. For the reasons set forth below, I find that the application of the Board's decision in *San Manuel Indian Bingo & Casino*, 341 NLRB 1055 (2004), *aff'd*, 475 F.3d 1306 (D.C. Cir. 2007) (herein called San Manuel), warrants the assertion of jurisdiction over the Employer in the instant case.

I. Facts

A. Foxwoods Operations

Foxwoods is the largest casino complex in the world, covering over one million square feet on the Tribe's reservation, with several hundred thousand square feet utilized solely for gaming purposes. Foxwoods is open to the public 24 hours a day, 365 days a year, attracting 12 million customers every year and generating annual Tribal income in excess of one billion dollars. Its gaming ventures include 7,000 slot machines, about 400 gaming tables, and the world's largest bingo hall. Its nongaming operations include three on-site hotels, about 30 eating and drinking establishments, three to four venues for live entertainment, and many retail shops. Many of the bars, restaurants and retail stores at Foxwoods are run by private enterprises that have a lease agreement with the Tribe; others are owned and operated by the Tribe, presumably through MPGE. The Tribe markets Foxwoods to diverse segments of the population throughout the Northeast. Less than one-tenth of one percent of Foxwoods' patrons are tribal members. Although Chairman Thomas testified that "there are traditional gaming aspects to our culture," he admitted that none of those "traditional games" are played at Foxwoods.

Foxwoods' day-to-day operations are managed by MPGE President John O'Brien, who is not a tribal member. O'Brien reports directly to Tribal Council Chairman Michael Thomas. Out of the approximately 9,000 employees employed at Foxwoods, only about 30 are tribal members, mostly occupying managerial positions. There is no evidence or claim that any of the petitioned-for employees are tribal members. Among the senior management, including Vice Presidents and Senior Vice Presidents, only one is a member of the Tribe. The senior members of management report directly to O'Brien. MPGE has no Board of Directors. The Tribal Council selects Foxwoods' top-level managers, establishes its budget and enacts its employment policies.

Foxwoods' gaming authority is derived from a "Compact" with the United States Secretary of the Interior, in accordance with the Indian Gaming Regulatory Act (IGRA). The Tribe's internal gaming regulating body is called the Mashantucket Pequot Proclamation Gaming Commission (herein called the Gaming Commission). The Gaming Commission consists of five members appointed by the Tribal Council Chairman, with the advice and consent of the Tribal Council. Three of the five Gaming Commission members must be tribal members. The Gaming Commission has primary responsibility for the oversight of tribal gaming operations, including licensing and inspection consistent with the terms of the Compact. In accordance with the Compact, the

State of Connecticut Division of Special Revenue issues Class III licenses to Foxwoods' gaming employees, including all of the employees in the petitioned-for unit. Although not entirely clear, it appears that the Tribe issues Class II gaming licenses to gaming employees who may not otherwise be licensed by the State, including bingo and similar operations.

According to Chairman Thomas, approximately 98% of the Tribe's revenues are derived from the operation of Foxwoods, which is used to fund various endeavors aimed toward promoting the Tribal community and Tribal self-government, including government, culture, health and welfare, housing, education, safety, repatriation and other business ventures, both on and off the reservation.

B. Tribal Operations

1. Tribal Governance

Although the Tribe does not have a treaty with the Federal government, it was officially recognized as a tribe by the Federal government in 1983. The Tribe's Constitution and By-Laws, originally enacted in 1970, establishes the tribal organization and sets forth its governance structure. It provides for the creation of a seven-member Tribal Council elected for staggered three-year terms at the annual meeting of the Tribe. The Chairman and Vice Chairman of the Tribal Council are selected by a vote of the tribal membership.

The Tribal Council is vested with the authority to create committees and appoint or employ officers to staff those committees as deemed necessary. These committees are subordinate to the Tribal Council, which delegates the committees' authority at its own discretion. Such committees may be standing, regular, or ad hoc. Standing and regular committees are comprised of Tribal members only, together with a Tribal Council member, the total number of committee members differing depending upon whether it is a standing or regular committee. The Tribal Council governs primarily through the passage of resolutions by majority vote. While a resolution may be passed by the committees, it is required to be ratified by the Tribal Council before it is enacted as tribal law. When tribal legislative matters have the potential to impact the Tribe as a whole, its passage may be subject to a ratification process.

There is also an Elders Council that comprises another aspect of the governmental structure. The Elders Council has two areas of authority: determining Tribal membership; and banishing non-Tribal members. Banishments are not reviewable by the Tribal Council.

The preamble to the Constitution and By-Laws states that the purpose for establishing the Tribe and its governmental authorities is "to conserve and develop our common resources and to promote the welfare of ourselves and our descendents. . . ." In apparent furtherance of these objectives, a host of committees have been authorized by the Tribal Council, including Natural Resource Protection; Economic Development; Community Planning; Education; Finance; Housing; Administrative Support; Parks & Recreation; Judicial; Public Safety; Health & Human Services; and Historical & Cultural Preservation. All funding for the committees comes through Tribal Council resolutions. As noted above, approximately 98% of the Tribe's revenues are derived from the operation of Foxwoods, which includes the rental fees from the various food, drink and retail vendors who operate independent businesses within the Foxwoods' complex. The remaining revenue comes from other tribal enterprise profits, Federal funding and taxes.

The Tribe also operates a variety of administrative departments for the advancement of Tribe members' health, safety, education and prosperity, and in furtherance of its interest in self-governance. These include the Career Development and Succession Planning Department; the Child Development Center; Child Protective Services; Cultural Resources Department; Department of Education; Department of Fire and Emergency Services; Department of Housing; Department of Interior; Tribal Procurement; Human Potential Development; Building Management Department; Office of Inspector General; Office of Land Use/TOSHA [Tribal Occupation Safety and Health Act] Commissioner; Office of Legal Counsel; Office of Natural Resource Protection; Parks and Recreation; Peacemakers Council; Police Department; Public Affairs Department; Public Relations Department; Records Management Department; National and State Governmental Affairs Offices (located in Hartford, Connecticut and Washington, D.C.); Tribal Clerk's Office; Tribal Health Services; Tribal Internal Audit; Tribal Manager's Office and Utilities Department. These administrative departments are funded through Tribal Council resolutions and are, for the most part, located on the reservation. Aside from the Tribe's internally-generated funding for many of these departmental activities, the Tribe's Annual Report reveals that the Bureau of Indian Affairs (BIA) provided the Tribe with $755,193.00 in fiscal year 2006.

The Department of Fire and Emergency Services is involved in off-reservation activities as well, as it has contracts with local non-tribal businesses to provide emergency medical services, and often provides fire safety assistance to surrounding non-tribal communities. Although the Tribe maintains its own Police Department, the record indicates that the Connecticut State Police also has some undefined jurisdictional role with regard to Foxwoods. All tribal police officers are also officers with the BIA and receive their training at the BIA academy.

The Tribe's non-gaming enterprises and commercial properties are governed by the Tribal Business Advisory Board. Such enterprises include the Hilton Mystic Hotel; the Spa at Norwich Inn; Lake of Isle Golf Course; and a resort in St. Croix. While these enterprises are located off tribal land and are profit generating, funds for such ventures are supplied through Tribal Council resolutions. The Tribe also operates two managed care pharmacies that are located on tribal land for the exclusive use of the Tribe and its employees. It also provides third-party claims administration services to Foxwoods, other Native American tribes, other employers and unions for medical, pharmacy, dental and vision benefit plans. These services include "provider network management, claims adjudication, utilization review and utilization management, as well as case management." According to the Tribe's Annual Report, Federal HIPAA regulations apply to the operation of these health benefit services.

2. Tribal Law and Judicial Procedures

The Employer relies upon its tribal laws and judicial procedures in support of its claim that the application of the National Labor Relations Act would interfere with its tribal sovereignty. In this regard, the Mashantucket Pequot Tribal Court (herein called the Tribal Court) was established in about 1992. It is located on the reservation and hears "civil disputes that arise within the Mashantucket community." The Tribal Court also hears criminal cases involving "Native Americans" who are accused of violating "the nation's laws while on the reservation." Criminal activity involving non–Native Americans are filed in the Connecticut Superior Court in New London, Connecticut. The Tribal Court's authority and processes are set forth in Title I of the Tribal Laws, which are in essence tribal statutes. The bound volume of Tribal Laws and the 2007 Supplement include substantive provisions dealing with such matters as tort claims, gaming, family relations, traffic safety, public safety, probate and land usage, as well as Tribal Court Rules, Rules of Evidence, Rules of Civil Procedure, Rules of Appellate Procedure and a Code of Professional Conduct. In criminal matters, jury trials are mandated, whereas in civil matters jury trials are at the discretion of the tribal judiciary. Juries are composed exclusively of tribal members. Many of these Tribal Laws draw heavily from established Federal and State law.

The Tribal Court Chief Judge is Thomas Weissmuller, who is not a tribal member. There are five other judges, with three judges on the trial side and three on the appellate side. The Tribal Court also employs a Bailiff, Administrative Assistant, Director of Probation and Pretrial & Family Investigative Services, and Judicial Clerk. All Tribal Court employees' salaries, as well as the operation of the Tribal Court itself, are financed through Tribal Council resolution.

The Tribal Court hears about 300 cases per year, primarily consisting of tort cases involving Foxwoods' patron "slip and fall" claims; construction contract litigation involving various non-tribal contractors working on the reservation; and domestic cases involving tribal divorces, child custody and support enforcement. About 30 cases on the Tribal Court's docket each year are appeals from tribal administrative bodies involving adverse employment actions filed by both tribal member and nontribal member employees.

3. Tribal Labor and Employment Laws and Policies

Tribal Laws provide a procedural review of disciplinary action (defined as termination or suspension of five days or more) issued against tribal and non-tribal member employees. More specifically, there is a "Board of Review" composed of a "randomly selected impartial panel of employees" that reviews the disciplinary action. For Foxwoods employees, an "advisory recommendation" is made to MPGE President O'Brien, who makes the final determination. An employee may then seek review of O'Brien's decision in the Tribal Court. However, the Tribal Court's scope of review is limited. In this regard, it may only consider "whether an Employee's procedural due process rights were violated". Chief Judge Weissmuller, who testified at the hearing, acknowledged that the Board of Review for Tribal employees is differently composed from that of the Board of Review for Foxwoods' employees.

The Tribal Council has enacted various other employment policies, many of which appear to apply only to MPGE. These policies include Sexual and Other Harassment, Family Medical Leave, Wages & Overtime, Equal

Employment Opportunity, Indian Preference, and ERISA. There is also a Workers' Compensation Code that was enacted in 1997. Employees covered under this code are defined as "any person who has entered into or works under any contract of service or apprenticeship with the employer. The "employer" is defined as "the Mashantucket Pequot Tribal Nation, its enterprises, governmental divisions or departments thereof. . . ." It is unclear whether this provision applies to employees in the petitioned-for unit, as there is no evidence that they have "entered into or work under any contract of service" with the Employer. There is also a Right to Work provision that was enacted in 2005, which prohibits the compulsory payment of dues to any labor organization. The Right to Work provision was amended on July 13, 2007 to, among other things, change the definition of employee to "any individual employed by an Employer," and to define the Employer as including the Tribe and its enterprises.

In July 2007, the Tribal Council enacted the Mashantucket Employment Rights Law (herein called MERL). MERL provides for the formation of the Mashantucket Employment Rights Office Commission (herein called MEROC), which is composed of five commissioners: one tribal member and two non-tribal members, and two alternates (one tribal member and one non-tribal member). Non-tribal members are appointed by majority vote of the Tribal Council. There is no dispute that MEROC is not yet operational since it has not been fully staffed. Other than procedural provisions regarding the establishment of MEROC and granting it the authority to issue decisions and remedies, there are no substantive provisions contained in MERL.

On August 16, 2007, the Tribe enacted the Mashantucket Pequot Labor Relations Law (herein called MPLRL). Chapter 1, Section 2 of MPLRL states that it was adopted "based on the recent reversal of 30 years of precedent by a federal agency and a federal court, [and because] the Tribe acknowledges that labor organizations may seek, and at least one is currently seeking, the right to represent tribal employees pursuant to federal law, commonly known as the National Labor Relations Act ("NLRA") 29 U.S.C. [Sections] 151-169." Chairman Thomas admitted that the labor organization referenced in this provision is the Petitioner herein. The MPLRL generally mirrors the representation and unfair labor practice provisions of the NLRA. Its stated purpose is to "provide tribal employees the right to organize and bargain collectively with their employers, to promote harmonious and cooperative relationships between the Tribe as an employer and tribal employees, and to promote the health, safety, political integrity and economic security of the Tribe." The MPLRL provides for union recognition through a secret ballot election as an exclusive collective bargaining representative, and enumerates a variety of "Prohibited Practices" that generally mirror the provisions of Sections 8(a) and 8(b) of the NLRA. It also provides for the following: direct dealing with union-represented employees to remedy grievances; restrictions on union picketing; withdrawal of recognition from unions that commit prohibited practices; awarding attorneys' fees and costs against employees for advancing frivolous claims; no bargaining obligation regarding union security clauses, the enforcement of tribal rules and regulations, and certain other terms and conditions of employment; no strikes or lockouts, with mandatory submission of contract disputes to binding arbitration; unit appropriateness determinations made in consideration of "[p]rinciples of efficient administration of the tribal government"; and the right to exclude union business agents from tribal land if he or she is deemed by MEROC to be of "questionable moral character." Since MEROC has not yet been established, the MPLRL provides for the Tribal Court to appoint a "Special Master" to "assume the responsibilities and duties of the MERO Commission" in processing petitions and resolving Prohibited Practices. If the union or Tribe is not satisfied with the impartiality of the appointed Special Master, they may appeal the appointment to the Tribal Court, which, after a hearing, will either let the appointment stand or appoint a replacement Special Master. All rulings of the Special Master or MEROC may be appealed to the Tribal Court.

After the filing of the instant petition, the Tribe's General Counsel sent the Petitioner a letter dated October 3, 2007, requesting that the petition be withdrawn and that the Petitioner comply with the processes as set forth in the MPLRL. The Petitioner has declined this request.

II. Analysis and Conclusion

In *San Manuel*, the Board adopted a new standard for determining whether it has jurisdiction over enterprises operated on tribal land by Native American Tribes. The Board initially noted that "statutes of 'general application' apply to the conduct and operation, not only of individual Indians, but also of Indian tribes." *Id.* at 1059, citing *Federal Power Commission v. Tuscarora Indian Nation*, 362 U.S. 99, 116 (1960) (assertion of eminent domain over tribal lands under same terms as non-Indian owned land appropriate where Congress has not expressly carved out an exemption for Indians). The Board then concluded that because "Congress intended the Act to have the broadest possible breadth permitted under the Constitution, the Act is a statute of general application." *Id.* . . .

The Board then adopted the three exceptions established in *Donovan v. Coeur d'Alene Tribal Farm*, 751 F.2d 1113, 1115 (9th Cir. 1985), for determining those circumstances under which the Act should not apply to operations on Native American tribal lands. Those exceptions are:

(1) the law "touches exclusive rights of self-government in purely intramural matters";
(2) the application of the law would abrogate treaty rights; or
(3) there is "proof" in the statutory language or legislative history that Congress did not intend for the law to apply to Indian tribes.

In the event that none of the exceptions apply, the Board decided that it must also examine "whether policy considerations militate in favor of or against the assertion of the Board's discretionary jurisdiction." *San Manuel, supra*, at 1062. The purpose of this final step, according to the Board, "is to balance the Board's interest in effectuating the policies of the Act with its desire to accommodate the unique status of Indians in our society and legal culture." *Id.*

In applying this new approach, the Board asserted jurisdiction over the San Manuel Indian Casino. It found that none of the *Coeur d'Alene* exceptions were applicable. With regard to the first exception, the Board found that the "operation of a casino is not an exercise in self-governance." *Id.* at 1063. Quoting *Coeur d'Alene*, the Board noted that "[i]ntramural matters generally involve topics such as 'tribal membership, inheritance rules, and domestic relations.'" *Id.* Even though the casino was owned by Native Americans and operated on tribal lands, it was nonetheless deemed "a typical commercial enterprise operating in, and substantially affecting, interstate commerce." *Id.* The Board expressly rejected the argument that because the profits derived from the operation of the casino funded the tribe's intramural needs, it should, by extension, constitute an intramural matter over which the Board would be prohibited from asserting jurisdiction. The Board reasoned that such a broad interpretation of "intramural" would have the anomalous result of the exception swallowing the rule that statutes of "general application" apply to Indian tribes. As to the second exception, the Board found that it did not apply because the San Manuel tribe was not a party to a treaty with the Federal Government. The third exception was also found inapplicable because "neither the language of the Act, nor its legislative history, provides any evidence that Congress intended to exclude Indians or their commercial enterprises from the Act's jurisdiction." *Id.*

In the final step of the analysis, the Board in *San Manuel* found that policy considerations favored the exercise of discretionary jurisdiction. In this regard, it noted that the casino was "a typical commercial enterprise," employing non-Indians and catering to non-Indian customers. The Board further found that the assertion of jurisdiction would not unduly interfere with the tribe's autonomy, as "the Act would not broadly or completely define the relationship between [the tribe] and its employees . . . [or] regulate intramural matters." *Id.* at 1063-64.

Based upon the foregoing and the record as a whole, I find that the Board's decision in San Manuel clearly requires the assertion of jurisdiction over the Employer in the instant case. . . .

In view of the foregoing, I find that the incidental affects on Tribal government that could potentially occur as a result of the application of the NLRA to Foxwoods' employees, which the Employer claims would directly threaten the Tribe's political or economic security, are insufficient to deny the exercise of the Board's jurisdiction herein. In this regard, the right to strike, the duty to bargain over mandatory subjects of bargaining, access by union agents, and the potential conflicts between collective bargaining and the Tribe's regulation of gaming activities, its Indian Preference Policy, and the tribal electoral process, are far too tenuous and speculative in nature to support the Employer's claims. Moreover, as noted by the Board in *San Manuel*, "[t]he Act does not dictate any terms of any agreement or even that an agreement be reached. The Board will treat the [tribe] just as it treats any other private sector employer." *San Manuel, supra* at 1064.

I find particularly unpersuasive the Employer's claim, unsupported by record evidence, that "a strike against the Tribal Gaming Enterprise would severely disrupt the Tribe's continuing ability to provide essential services" to its constituent members. As previously indicated, the Employer has annual gross revenues in excess of $1 billion, and approximately 98% of the Tribe's revenues are derived from the operation of Foxwoods. Thus, approximately 2 percent of the Tribe's annual income, at least $20,000,000, is derived from outside sources. The record does not indicate the Tribe's capital reserves, or the amounts needed to fund any of its essential services. Therefore, even if the Employer were to face a protracted strike, there is no evidence that it would have insufficient revenues and/or capital to provide the Tribe's 900 members with any essential public service. . . .

Accordingly, I find that the following employees of the Employer constitute a unit appropriate for the purpose of collective bargaining within the meaning of Section 9(b) of the Act.

NOTES

1. Less than a month after *Foxwoods Resort Casino*, the director for Region 7 of the National Labor Relations Board issued a strikingly similar opinion in *Soaring Eagle Casino and Resort and Local 486, International Brotherhood of Teamsters*, No. GR-7-RC-23147 (Nov. 20, 2007). The tribe in that case, the Saginaw Chippewa Indian Tribe, asserted its treaty rights to exclude non-Indians from tribal lands, something the Mashantucket Pequot Nation could not do directly. The result was the same, with little or no discussion from the regional director:

> [T]he mere existence of a treaty will not compel a conclusion that a statute of general application is not binding on an Indian tribe. The critical issue is whether the application of the statute would jeopardize a specific right that is secured by the treaty. . . . A treaty that confers only a general right of possession of, or exclusion of non-Indians from, tribal land will not be abrogated by Federal regulation because such a general right is analogous to the inherent right discussed and held insufficient to bar application of [the Occupational Health and Safety Act] in *Coeur d'Alene*.

Id. at 7-8.

2. As a result of the 2004 decision by the National Labor Relations Board to assert jurisdiction over tribal gaming operations in *San Manuel Indian Bingo & Casino*, 341 NLRB 1055 (2004), *aff'd*, 475 F.3d 1306 (D.C. Cir. 2007), many tribes enacted laws intending to encourage labor unions to take advantage of tribal regulation. *See, e.g.*, Little River Band of Ottawa Indians, Fair Employment Practices Code, Ordinance No. 05-600-03, codified at Little River Band of Ottawa Indians Tribal Code, Chapter 600, Title 3 (2005).

3. Professor Wenona T. Singel argues that Indian tribes should take every effort to persuade labor unions to utilize tribal labor laws, but that the road is a difficult one. *See* Wenona T. Singel, *The Institutional Economics of Tribal Labor Relations*, 2008 Mich. St. L. Rev. 487.

> Research has also shown that tribal communities are more likely to experience economic success if the political institutions and legal system operating with the community form a match with the tribe's culture, including its values, belief system, and traditions. This principle supports the notion that tribal protection of labor interests is more likely to be effective if the processes, remedies, and legal standards that apply to labor issues

possess a cultural match with the tribe. As a result, tribal labor policies and laws may be more likely to effectively address labor concerns than the laws and procedures set forth by the NLRA. . . .

In many cases, both native and non-native litigants prefer to resolve their disputes in tribal court rather than state court. This preference stems from a growing recognition that tribal courts are fair, efficient forums for conflict resolution. Greater reliance on tribal court adjudication of labor disputes would promote faster, less costly resolution of disputes. Furthermore, if parties rely upon the traditional forms of peacemaking that many tribal courts offer, they may find that the process of dispute resolution actually improves and strengthens relationships. Such effects would be a significant improvement over the adversarial method of dispute resolution, which often exacerbates the sense of alienation and oppositional entrenchment that the parties bring to a dispute. . . .

A substantial cost associated with reliance on tribal legal remedies for the resolution of employment concerns is the fact that many tribes do not have a large body of positive labor and employment law. Although the recent *San Manuel* decision has certainly triggered a rise in the number of tribal labor law enactments, many tribes still have no labor law enactments, little labor-related case law, and few fully implemented administrative bodies with the power to deal with employment issues. . . . With any emerging body of law, there is a degree of uncertainty associated with how the law will be interpreted, applied, and enforced. Also, as with any new legal regime, the persons affected by the law must invest in gaining the skills and knowledge necessary to effectively understand and apply the law. . . .

Another cost associated with reliance on tribal labor laws is the fact that many tribal employees are non-Indian. Non-Indians lack the right to vote in tribal elections, and they lack the right to hold office in tribal law-making bodies. Deprived of the right to vote, these non-Indian employees are deprived of a fundamental mechanism for influencing tribal policy-making.

On the other hand, non-Indians are not completely excluded from the opportunity to participate in tribal politics. Non-Indians can influence tribal policies that affect the rights and working conditions of employees by lobbying tribal leaders, providing information to tribal leaders in the form of testimony during legislative hearings, and even serving on tribal committees, boards, and other public entities that allow for non-Indian participation. Throughout Indian country, there are a large number of tribes that allow non-Indians to hold public office. For example, it is very common for non-Indians to serve as judges on tribal courts. Many non-Indians also are permitted to serve on tribal commissions, boards, and committees, including tribal gaming commissions and tribal economic development committees. Membership on these boards and committees allows non-Indian members of Indian communities to have an influence on tribal policy-making. For non-Indian employees of tribal enterprises, such membership can serve as a means of influencing tribal employment policies and practices. . . .

To encourage employees to use tribal labor law remedies, tribes can adopt a variety of strategies. One of the most important strategies should be the completion of steps designed to counteract the path dependent pattern of reflexive resort to federal labor law remedies over alternatives provided by tribal law. The prescriptions offered by Douglass North for defeating path dependent patterns in institutional development can be adapted for tribal use.

For example, North recommends the creation and support of organizations that have an interest in succeeding under a new legal system or institutional regime. A tribe hoping to encourage reliance on tribal labor law remedies could support the formation of employee organizations that have legally recognized rights under tribal law. To the extent that tribal law formally recognizes the status and rights of such labor organizations, these groups will have an interest in resorting to tribal remedies to vindicate their rights. . . .

In addition, employees will be more invested in a tribe's labor law regime if they can gain familiarity with the underlying values that inform tribal law and policy. . . . Although there is no silver bullet that can alter the deeply-held belief systems of tribal employees, tribal employers can at least take steps to actively teach employees about tribal culture and values and attempt, wherever appropriate, to include employees in the cultural life of the tribe.

North's third recommendation for promoting institutional change in the face of path dependent resistance is the encouragement of norms of behavior and codes of conduct that support the new institutional regime. One way that tribes could encourage such norms of behavior is to adopt methods of formally honoring and respecting tribal employees whose actions exemplify the norms of behavior that support tribal labor and employment institutions. For example, tribal employees who are actively involved in tribal civic life and tribal labor organizations recognized under tribal law could be publicly honored and rewarded. . . .

In addition to the suggestions above, some strategies are best avoided. These include failing to do anything at all and enacting labor laws that prohibit the election of a union. Failing to act can lead employees and outside labor interests to conclude that the only available remedies for the protection of labor are those derived from the NLRA. If tribes fail to adopt their own policies, they lose the opportunity to proactively exercise tribal sovereignty over promoting tribal welfare. Silence, therefore, can lead to greater dependence on federal policies and a weakened assertion of self-determination. Similarly, the enactment of a labor law regime that is more restrictive than the NLRA or other labor laws that apply to the public sector can be seriously damaging. Not only are such laws likely to lead to greater dissatisfaction and unrest among employees, but they could also potentially serve as national symbols of injustice in the news media and within the legal system.

Id. at 499-503.

TABLE OF CASES

INDEX